EPISTEMOLOGY: AN ANTHOLOGY

BLACKWELL PHILOSOPHY ANTHOLOGIES

Each volume in this outstanding series provides an authoritative and comprehensive collection of the essential primary readings from philosophy's main fields of study. Designed to complement the *Blackwell Companions to Philosophy* series, each volume represents an unparalleled resource in its own right, and will provide the ideal platform for course use.

EPISTEMOLOGY: AN ANTHOLOGY

Second Edition

Edited by Ernest Sosa, Jaegwon Kim,
Jeremy Fantl, and Matthew McGrath

Blackwell
Publishing

Editorial material and organization © 2000, 2008 by Blackwell Publishing Ltd

BLACKWELL PUBLISHING
350 Main Street, Malden, MA 02148-5020, USA
9600 Garsington Road, Oxford OX4 2DQ, UK
550 Swanston Street, Carlton, Victoria 3053, Australia

The right of Ernest Sosa, Jaegwon Kim, Jeremy Fantl, and Matthew McGrath to be identified as the Authors of the Editorial Material in this Work has been asserted in accordance with the UK Copyright, Designs, and Patents Act 1988.

First edition published 2000 by Blackwell Publishers Ltd
This edition published 2008 by Blackwell Publishing Ltd

9   2014

Library of Congress Cataloging-in-Publication Data

Epistemology : an anthology / edited by Ernest Sosa, Jaegwon Kim, Jeremy Fantl, and Matthew McGrath — 2nd ed.
    p. cm. — (Blackwell philosophy anthologies)
    Includes bibliographical references.
    ISBN 978-1-4051-6967-7 (hardcover : alk. paper) — ISBN 978-1-4051-6966-0 (pbk. : alk. paper)   1.
Knowledge, Theory of. I. Sosa, Ernest.

    BD161.E615 2008
    121—dc22

                                        2007042371

A catalogue record for this title is available from the British Library.

Set in 9.5/11.5pt Minion
by SPi Publisher Services, Pondicherry, India
Printed and bound in Singapore
by Markono Print Media Pte Ltd

The publisher's policy is to use permanent paper from mills that operate a sustainable forestry policy, and which has been manufactured from pulp processed using acid-free and elementary chlorine-free practices. Furthermore, the publisher ensures that the text paper and cover board used have met acceptable environmental accreditation standards.

For further information on
 ⁓ckwell Publishing, visit our website:
    blackwellpublishing.com

Contents

Preface to the Second Edition

Epistemology is a philosophical inquiry into the nature, conditions, and extent of human knowledge. It encompasses some of the most puzzling and persistent issues in all of philosophy, ones that extensively define its history. The problem of skepticism is one example, and the empiricism/rationalism controversy another, along with its Kantian and Hegelian aftermath. Such issues, although alien to common sense at first sight, in fact derive naturally from straightforward reflection on the most ordinary knowledge about the world around us, knowledge produced or sustained through perception, memory, or induction. Elementary reflection on such matters produces puzzles and paradoxes that have engaged philosophers from ancient times to the present.

This anthology is meant to supplement Blackwell's *Companion to Epistemology* and *Guide to Epistemology*. We made a conscious effort to include both selections that are representative of the best current discussion on the most central issues in the field, and selections which, though relevant to current debates, are somewhat older and appropriate for use in upper level undergraduate epistemology courses. Though the former selections are inevitably demanding, all readings, some of which are only excerpts, should all prove accessible in proper order to the attentive reader who approaches these issues for the first time.

The selections are collected in nine sections, each of which opens with an introduction that discusses the contained readings, and is followed by a list of further readings on the subject matter of that section. For further expert but introductory discussion of the issues, the reader is referred to the relevant Blackwell *Companion* and *Guide*.

The topics taken up in these nine sections by no means exhaust the field of epistemology. Space limits have made it impossible to include all topics in the field. We have consciously selected central issues but we have also drawn from contemporary work some of the most novel and radical responses to those issues. The resulting collection brings together a variety of approaches and solutions, still under vigorous debate. The current edition departs from the first in expanding the section on epistemological contextualism to take account of recent work on sensitive invariantism and relativism. We have also added a section devoted to perception, memory, and testimony, significantly restructured and reorganized other sections, and included some newer work. Space limitations have prevented us, once again, from including work on more specific issues – other minds and induction, for example. On these issues excellent work has been published and continues to appear.

Special thanks go to Sara Bagg and Justin McBrayer for their assistance, particularly in their contributions to the introductions to the various sections, as well as to Michael DiRamio, Brie Gertler, Joseph Shieber, and Baron Reed, for their work on the first edition. Also helpful were the comments and suggestions by anonymous referees.

Nick Bellorini, our editor, has been exceedingly patient and supportive.

Jeremy Fantl
Jaegwon Kim
Matthew McGrath
Ernest Sosa

Acknowledgments

The editors and publisher gratefully acknowledge the permission granted to reproduce the copyright material in this book:

1. Stroud, Barry, "The Problem of the External World," Chapter 1 in *The Significance of Philosophical Skepticism* (Oxford: Clarendon Press, 1984). © 1984 by Barry Stroud. Reprinted with permission from Oxford University Press.
2. Moore, G. E., "Proof of an External World," extracted from pp. 147–70 in Thomas Baldwin (ed.), *G. E. Moore: Selected Writings* (London & New York: Routledge, 1993). © 1993 by Thomas Baldwin. Reprinted with permission from Taylor & Francis Books (UK).
3. Moore, G. E., "Four Forms of Scepticism," pp. 220–2 in *Philosophical Papers* (New York: Collier Books, 1962). © 1962 by G. E. Moore.
4. Moore, G. E., "Certainty," extracted from pp. 171–96 in Thomas Baldwin (ed.), *G. E. Moore: Selected Writings*, (London & New York: Routledge, 1993). © 1993 by Thomas Baldwin. Reprinted with permission from Taylor & Francis Books (UK).
5. Klein, Peter, "How a Pyrrhonian Skeptic Might Respond to Academic Skepticism," pp. 75–94 in Steven Luper (ed.), *The Skeptics: Contemporary Essays* (Aldershot: Ashgate, 2003). © 2003 by Steven Luper. Reprinted with permission from Ashgate Publishing.
6. Williams, Michael, "Epistemological Realism," pp. 83–93, 101–19, 121–4, 129–39 in *Unnatural Doubts* (Oxford, Blackwell Publishers, 1991). © 1991 by Michael Williams. Reprinted with permission from the author.
7. Chisholm, Roderick, "The Myth of the Given," pp. 261–86 in R. Chisholm, *Philosophy* (Englewood Cliffs, NJ: Prentice-Hall, 1964). © 1964 by Roderick M. Chisholm.
8. Sellars, Wilfred, "Does Empirical Knowledge Have a Foundation?" pp. 293–300 in H. Feigel and M. Scriven (eds.), *The Foundations of Science and the Concepts of Psychology and Psychoanalysis, Minnesota Studies in the Philosophy of Science*, Vol. 1 (Minneapolis: University of Minnesota Press, 1956). © 1956. Reprinted with permission from University of Minnesota Press.
9. Sellars, Wilfred, "Epistemic Principles," pp. 332–49 in H. Casteneda (ed.), *Action, Knowledge, and Reality* (Indianapolis: Bobbs-Merrill, 1975). © 1975 by Wilfrid Sellars.
10. BonJour, Laurence, "Can Empirical Knowledge Have a Foundation?" pp. 1–13 in *American Philosophical Quarterly* 15, 1 (1978). © 1978 by *American Philosophical Quarterly*. Reprinted with permission from *American Philosophical Quarterly*.
11. Davidson, Donald, "A Coherence Theory of Truth and Knowledge," pp. 307–19 in Ernest Lepore (ed.), *Truth and Interpretation: Perspectives on the Philosophy of Donald Davidson* (New York: Blackwell, 1989). © 1989 by Ernest Lepore. Reprinted with permission from Blackwell Publishing.

12. Haack, Susan, "A Foundherentist Theory of Empirical Justification," pp. 283–93 in Louis Pojman (ed.), *The Theory of Knowledge: Classical and Contemporary Readings* (Belmont, CA: Wadsworth, 1999). © 1999 by Susan Haack. Reprinted by permission of Susan Haack, the copyright holder.

13. Sosa, Ernest, "The Raft and the Pyramid," pp. 3–25 in *Midwest Studies in Philosophy*, Vol. 5: Studies in Epistemology (Minneapolis: University of Minnesota Press, 1980); an appendix to this paper is drawn from Ernest Sosa, pp. 113–22 "How Do You Know?" *American Philosophical Quarterly* 11 (1974). © 1980 by Midwest Studies in Philosophy. Reprinted with permission from the author and University of Minnesota Press.

14. Klein, Peter, "Human Knowledge and the Infinite Regress of Reasons," pp. 297–325 in James Tomberlin (ed.), *Philosophical Perspectives*, 13 Epistemology, 1999. © 1999 by Philosophical Perspectives. Reprinted with permission from Blackwell Publishing.

15. Gettier, Edmund, "Is Justified True Belief Knowledge?" pp. 121–3 in *Analysis* (1963). © 1963 by Edmund Gettier. Reprinted with permission from the author.

16. Harman, Gilbert, Selections from *Thought* (Princeton: Princeton University Press, 1973). © 1973 by Princeton University Press, 2001 renewed PUP. Reprinted with permission from Princeton University Press.

17. Zagzebski, Linda, "The Inescapability of Gettier Problems," pp. 65–73 in *The Philosophical Quarterly* 44, 174 (Oxford: Blackwell Publishers, 1994). © 1994 by The Editors of *The Philosophical Quarterly*. Reprinted with permission from Blackwell Publishing.

18. Williamson, Timothy, "A State of Mind," pp. 21–48 in T. Williamson, *Knowledge and Its Limits* (Oxford: Oxford University Press, 2000). © 2000 by Timothy Williamson. Reprinted with permission from Blackwell Publishing.

19. Dretske, Fred, "Epistemic Operators," pp. 1007–23 in *The Journal of Philosophy* 67, 24 (Dec. 24, 1970). © 1970 by The Journal of Philosophy, Inc. Reprinted with permission from the author and *The Journal of Philosophy*.

20. Stine, Gail, "Skepticism, Relevant Alternatives and Deductive Closure," pp. 249–61 in *Philosophical Studies* 29 (Dordrecht, Netherlands: D. Reidel Publishing Co., 1976). © 1976 by *Philosophical Studies*. Reprinted with permission from Springer Science and Business Media.

21. Nozick, Robert, "Knowledge and Skepticism," pp. 172–85, 197–217 in *Philosophical Explanations* (Cambridge, MA: Harvard University Press, 1981). © 1981 by Robert Nozick. Reprinted with permission from Harvard University Press.

22. Sosa, Ernest, "How to Defeat Opposition to Moore," pp. 141–53 in *Philosophical Perspectives* 13, Epistemology (1999). © 1999 by *Philosophical Perspectives*. Reprinted with permission from Blackwell Publishing.

23. Vogel, Jonathan, "Are There Counterexamples to the Closure Principle?," pp. 13–27 in M. D. Roth and G. Ross (eds.), *Doubting*, (Kluwer Academic Publishers, 1990). © 1990 Kluwer Academic Publishers. Reprinted with permission from the author and Springer Science and Business Media.

24. Feldman, Richard and Earl Conee, "Evidentialism," pp. 15–34 in *Philosophical Studies* 48 (Kluwer Academic Publishers, 1985). © 1985 by *Philosophical Studies*. Reprinted with permission from the authors and Springer Science and Business Media.

25. Foley, Richard, "Skepticism and Rationality," pp. 69–81 in M. D. Roth and G. Ross (eds.), *Doubting* (Dordrecht, Netherlands: Kluwer Academic Publishers, 1990). © 1990 by Kluwer Academic Publishers. Reprinted with permission from the author and Springer Science and Business Media.

26. Goldman, Alvin, "What is Justified Belief?" pp. 1–23 in G. S. Pappas (ed.), *Justification and Knowledge* (Dordrecht, Netherlands: D. Reidel, 1976). © 1976 by D. Reidel Publishing Company. Reprinted with permission from the author and Springer Science and Business Media.

27. Vogel, Jonathan, "Reliabilism Leveled," pp. 602–23 in *The Journal of Philosophy* 97, 11 (Nov. 2000). © 2000 The Journal of Philosophy, Inc. Reprinted with permission from the author and *The Journal of Philosophy*.

28. BonJour, Laurence, "Externalist Theories of Empirical Knowledge," pp. 53–73 in P. French, T. Uehling, Jr., and H. Wettstein (eds.), *Midwest Studies in Philosophy*, Vol. 5 (Minneapolis: University of Minnesota Press,

1980). © 1980 by *Midwest Studies in Philosophy*. Reprinted with permission from the author and University of Minnesota Press.

29. Goldman, Alvin, "Internalism Exposed," pp. 271–93 in *The Journal of Philosophy* 96, 6 (Jun. 1999). © 1999 The Journal of Philosophy, Inc. Reprinted with permission from the author and *The Journal of Philosophy*.

30. Fumerton, Richard, "Externalism and Skepticism," pp. 159–81 in *Metaepistemology and Skepticism* (Lanham, MD: Rowman and Littlefield, 1995). © 1995 by Richard Fumerton. Reprinted with permission from Rowman & Littlefield Publishing Group.

31. Feldman, Richard and Earl Conee, "Internalism Defended," pp. 1–18 in *American Philosophical Quarterly* 38, 1 (January 2001). © 2001 by *American Philosophical Quarterly*. Reprinted with permission from *American Philosophical Quarterly*.

32. Plantinga, Alvin, "Warrant: A First Approximation," pp. 3–20 in *Warrant and Proper Function* (Oxford and New York: Oxford University Press, 1993). © 1993 by Alvin Plantinga. Reprinted with permission from Oxford University Press.

33. Zagzebski, Linda, Selections from *Virtues of the Mind*, pp. 134–7, 166–84 in L. Zagzebski, *Virtues of the Mind* (Cambridge: Cambridge University Press, 1996). © 1996 by Cambridge University Press. Reprinted with permission from the author and Cambridge University Press.

34. Greco, John, "Virtues and Vices of Virtue Epistemology," pp. 413–32 in *Canadian Journal of Philosophy* 23, 3 (1993). © 1993 by *Canadian Journal of Philosophy*. Reprinted by permission of University of Calgary Press.

35. Pritchard, Duncan, "Cognitive Responsibility and the Epistemic Virtues," pp. 181–201 in *Epistemic Luck* (Oxford: Oxford University Press, 2005). © 2005 by Duncan Pritchard. Reprinted with permission from Oxford University Press, Inc.

36. Sosa, Ernest, "The Place of Truth in Epistemology," pp. 155–79 in M. DePaul and L. Zagzebski (eds.), *Intellectual Virtue: Perspectives From Ethics and Epistemology* (Oxford and New York: Oxford University Press, 2003). © 2003 by Ernest Sosa. Reprinted with permission from the author.

37. Kvanvig, Jonathan L., "Why Should Enquiring Minds Want to Know?: *Meno* Problems and Epistemological Axiology," pp. 426–52 in *The Monist* 81, 3 (1998). © 1998, THE MONIST, La Salle, Illinois 61301, USA. Reprinted with permission from the author and publisher.

38. Elgin, Catherine Z., "True Enough," pp. 113–131 in *Philosophical Issues* 14, Epistemology (2004). © 2004 by *Philosophical Issues*. Reprinted with permission from Blackwell Publishing.

39. Quine, W. V., "Epistemology Naturalized," pp. 68–90 in *Ontological Relativity and Other Essays* (Columbia University Press, 1969). © 1969 by Columbia University Press. Reprinted with permission of the publisher.

40. Kim, Jaegwon, "What is 'Naturalized Epistemology'?" in J. Tomberlin (ed.), *Philosophical Perspectives* 2. Epistemology (Atascadero, CA: Ridgeview Publishing Co., 1988), pp. 381–405. © 1998 by *Philosophical Perspectives*. Reprinted with permission from Blackwell Publishing.

41. Antony, Louise M., "Quine as Feminist: the Radical Import of Naturalized Epistemology," pp. 185–225 in L. Antony and C. Witt (eds.), *A Mind of One's Own* (Boulder, CO: Westview, 1993). © 1993 by Westview Press, a member of the Perseus Books Group. Reprinted with permission from Westview Press, a member of the Perseus Books Group.

42. Putnam, Hilary, "There is a Least One A Priori Truth," pp. 153–170 in *Erkenntnis* 13 (Dordrecht, Netherlands: D. Reidel Publishing Co., 1978). © 1978 by D. Reidel Publishing Company. Reprinted with permission from the author and Springer Science and Business Media.

43. Casullo, Albert, "Revisability, Reliabilism, and A Priori Knowledge," pp. 187–213 in *Philosophy and Phenomenology Research* 49, 2 (Dec. 1988). © 1988 by *Philosophy and Phenomenology Research*. Reprinted with permission from Blackwell Publishing.

44. Bealer, George, "*A Priori* Knowledge and the Scope of Philosophy," pp. 121–42 in *Philosophical Studies* 81 (Kluwer Academic Publishers, 1996). © 1996 Kluwer Academic Publishers. Reprinted with permission from the author and Springer Science and Business Media.

45. Weinberg, Jonathan M., Shaun Nichols, and Stephen Stich, "Normativity and Epistemic Intuitions," pp. 429–60 in *Philosophical Topics* 29, 1 & 2 (2001). © 2001 by *Philosophical Topics*. Used with permission of the authors and University of Arkansas Press, www.uapress.com

46. Kornblith, Hilary, "Investigating Knowledge Itself," pp. 1–27 in H. Kornblith, *Knowledge and its Place in Nature* (Oxford: Clarendon, 2002). © 2002 by Hilary Kornblith. Reprinted with permission from Oxford University Press.

47. DeRose, Keith, "Solving the Skeptical Problem," pp. 1–7, 17–52 in *The Philosophical Review* 104, 1 (1995). © 1995 by *The Philosophical Review*. Reprinted with permission from *The Philosophical Review*.

48. Lewis, David, "Elusive Knowledge," pp. 549–67 in *Australasian Journal of Philosophy* 74, 4 (1996). © 1996 by *Australasian Journal of Philosophy*. Reprinted with permission from Taylor & Francis (UK).

49. Cohen, Stewart, "Contextualist Solutions to Epistemological Problems: Scepticism, Gettier, and the Lottery," pp. 289–306 in *Australasian Journal of Philosophy* 76, 2 (1998). © 1998 by *Australasian Journal of Philosophy*. Reprinted with permission from the author and Taylor & Francis (UK).

50. Stanley, Jason, "Introduction" and "Knowledge Ascriptions and Context-Sensitivity," pp. 1–15, 47–73 in *Knowledge and Practical Interest* (New York: Oxford University Press, 2005). © 2005 by Jason Stanley. Reprinted with permission from Oxford University Press, Inc.

51. Fantl, Jeremy and Matthew McGrath, "Evidence, Pragmatics, and Justification," pp. 67–94 in *The Philosophical Review* 111, 1 (Jan. 2002). © 2002 by Cornell University Press. All rights reserved. Used by permission of the publisher.

52. Hawthorne, John, "Sensitive Moderate Invariantism," pp. 157–91 in *Knowledge and Lotteries* (Oxford: Clarendon, 2004). © 2004 by John Hawthorne. Reprinted with permission from Oxford University Press.

53. MacFarlane, John, "The Assessment Sensitivity of Knowledge Attributions," pp. 197–233 in Tamar Szabó Gendler and John O'Leary Hawthorne (eds.), *Oxford Studies in Epistemology*, Vol. 1 (Oxford: Clarendon, 2005). © 2005 by Oxford University Press. Reprinted with permission from Oxford University Press, Inc.

54. Baker, Judith, "Trust and Rationality," pp. 1–13 in *Pacific Philosophical Quarterly* 68 (1987). © 1987 Pacific Philosophical Quarterly. Reprinted with permission from Blackwell Publishing.

55. Fricker, Elizabeth, "Against Gullibility," pp. 125–61 in B. K. Matilal and A. Chakrabarti (eds.) *Knowing from Words* (Dordrecht, Netherlands: Kluwer Academic Publishers, 1994). © 1994 Kluwer Academic Publishers. Reprinted with permission from the author and Springer Science and Business Media.

56. Burge, Tyler, "Content Preservation," pp. 457–88 in *The Philosophical Review*, 102, 4 (Oct. 1993). © 1993 by Cornell University Press. All rights reserved. Used by permission of the publisher.

57. Lackey, Jennifer, "Testimonial Knowledge and Transmission," pp. 471–90 in *The Philosophical Quarterly*, 49, 197 (Oct. 1999). © The Editors of *The Philosophical Quarterly*, 1999. Reprinted with permission from Blackwell Publishing.

58. Huemer, Michael, "The Problem of Memory Knowledge," pp. 346–57 in *The Philosophical Quarterly*, 80, 197 (1999). © 1999 University of Southern California and Blackwell Publishers Ltd. Reprinted with permission from Blackwell Publishing.

59. McDowell, John, "Criteria, Defeasibility, and Knowledge," pp. 455–79 in *Proceedings of the British Academy* 68 (1982). Annual Philosophical Lecture. © 1983 by The British Academy. Reprinted with permission from Proceedings of the British Academy LXVIII; 1982.

60. Reynolds, Steven L., "Knowing How to Believe with Justification," pp. 273–92 in *Philosophical Studies* 64, 3 (Dec. 1991). © 1991 by *Philosophical Studies*. Reprinted with permission from the author and Springer Science and Business Media.

Every effort has been made to trace copyright holders and to obtain their permission for the use of copyright material. The publisher apologizes for any errors or omissions in the above list and would be grateful if notified of any corrections that should be incorporated in future reprints or editions of this book.

PART I

Skepticism

Introduction

Like Rene Descartes, we have all asked ourselves at one time or another "Couldn't everything I seem to see, hear, etc. be illusory? Might I in fact be dreaming all this? If so, what do I really know of the outside world?" The skeptic's answers are pessimistic: yes, you could be dreaming, and so you know nothing of the outside world. The conclusion is outlandish, and yet the reasoning behind it hardly seems strained at all. We feel the pressure towards skepticism in the movement from the question about the trustworthiness of our senses to the question of our ability to know. Given that the bulk of our knowledge of the outside world derives from the senses, how can we know anything about the world unless we first show that our senses can be trusted? The core of the skeptical strategy is more general: how can one gain knowledge using a source of belief unless one first shows that the source is trustworthy?

In his selection, Barry Stroud presents the skeptic's argument in its most favorable light. The skeptic does not hold us up to an uncommonly high standard of knowledge only to make the obvious point that we fail to meet it. The skeptic invokes only the standards presupposed in everyday knowledge attributions. To use an example of Stroud's, if no goldfinch could possibly be a canary, then if one is to know that the bird one sees is a goldfinch, one must be able to rule out its being a canary. More generally, to know that p, one must be able to rule out every possibility one knows to be incompatible with one's knowing that p. The skeptic then has her wedge: to know that you're sitting beside a warm fire, you must be able to rule out any possibility which excludes this knowledge, including innumerable "skeptical possibilities," such as that you're dreaming, that you're being deceived by a malicious demon, and that you're a brain in a vat stimulated to have the experiences and apparent memories you now have. But it's hard to see how you can rule these out.

In each of the selections from the work of G. E. Moore, the tables are turned on the skeptic. Moore provides a counter-argument in "Proof of an External World." A good proof, he explains, proceeds from known premises to a distinct conclusion to which they can be seen to lead. He then produces an example: raising his hands, one after the other, he exclaims "Here is a hand. Here is another hand," and he concludes "There are hands." If asked to prove his premises, he would reject the demand, for not everything that is known can be proved.

Moore nevertheless takes the skeptic seriously. In "Certainty," he grants that if he doesn't know he is not dreaming, he doesn't know he is standing up giving a lecture. Still he asks why there is any more plausibility in using this premise as part of a *modus ponens* argument to conclude that he doesn't know he is standing up than in using it as a part of the corresponding *modus tollens* argument to conclude that he does know after all that he is not dreaming.

In "Four Forms of Scepticism," Moore fully admits that skeptical scenarios are logically possible, but he finds it more certain that something has gone afoul in the skeptical argument than that he lacks knowledge that he has hands (or is holding a pencil). Moreover, he concludes that since the only way he *could* know this is through some inductive or analogical argument from the character of his experience, such an argument *must* exist.

The selections from Stroud and Moore concern our knowledge of the external world. One might hope that, even if it is hard to answer the skeptical challenge for *knowledge*, at least it could be satisfactorily answered for *justification*. Peter Klein calls the view that we cannot be justified in our beliefs about how things *are* (as opposed to how they seem) "Academic skepticism" and contrasts it with an older form of skepticism: Pyrrhonism. Pyrrhonism, in Klein's view, is a more moderate skepticism than its Academic cousin, for Pyrrhonism allows that our beliefs can be conditionally or provisionally justified. But it is still a form of skepticism, because it denies that our beliefs can be completely justified. Only if reasoning could settle the matter of whether a belief is true could that belief be completely justified. But how can reasoning settle anything? If it were legitimate to end reasoning with a proposition for which we could not provide a further reason, then it seems reasoning could settle some matter. But this is not legitimate. Nor is it legitimate to reason in a circle. Therefore, the only way for reasoning to settle matters would be to complete an infinite regress of non-repeating reasons (a view Klein refers to as "infinitism," discussed in more detail in his contribution to Part II). While this would be a legitimate way to settle some matter, it cannot, in fact, be done.

The lesson for Academic skepticism is that the arguments invoked in favor of Academic skepticism are themselves fallacious in that they either rely on arbitrary premises or beg the question in favor of their conclusion. Thus, consider the Academic skeptic's claim that we cannot know whether we are dreaming or deceived by a malicious demon. This claim is central to the argument for Academic skepticism. If it is unsupported, it is arbitrary. To support the claim, the Academic skeptic must first demonstrate that we cannot know, say, that there is a table in front of us. But "I cannot know there is a table in front of me" is the ostensible conclusion of the skeptical argument. Therefore, Academic skepticism, like the inadequate models of reasoning, must either rely on arbitrary premises or beg the question.

Michael Williams argues that if there is such a thing as *knowledge of the external world*, the kind of knowledge the Cartesian skeptic questions, it seems impossible for us to see ourselves as having it. That is, the skeptic would carry the day. But he asks: *is* there such a thing as knowledge of the world? His answer is *no*. The concept of knowledge of the external world is a theoretical concept, and so, unlike practical concepts such as the concept of a chair, it lacks application entirely unless there is an appropriate unified domain of reality whose contours are there for it to match. But there is no such epistemic domain. There could be only if (empirical) beliefs divided into two classes: those that could only be known on the basis of beliefs about immediate experience, i.e., beliefs about the external world, and those that could be known directly from immediate experience. Yet an examination of our practices in attributing knowledge and justification suggests that beliefs do not divide into these epistemic categories nor into any objective epistemic categories.

Williams describes his view as a form of contextualism. But it is a version of contextualism quite different from those appearing in Part VIII of this volume. The contextualist theories of DeRose and Cohen, and to a lesser extent Lewis, presuppose the existence of a unified range of objective characteristics which, given a speech context, comprise the truth-conditions for knowledge attributions in that context. For DeRose, there are the objective (context-invariant) notions of sensitivity and strength of epistemic position, and for Cohen objective notions of strength of evidence or justification. For Lewis, there are the objective factors of one's evidence and which possibilities it rules out. For all three of these epistemologists, the function of context is to set the bar on which (or what degree) of a relatively unified range of objective factors count. Thus, for them, there is an independent place for epistemological inquiry into the nature of these objective factors as well as into how they feed into the semantics of knowledge attribution. According to Williams, by contrast, there is no range of objective factors, with the result that there is nothing at all to serve as an object of theoretical investigation for the epistemologist.

Part and parcel of repudiating skepticism, then, is repudiating traditional epistemology. Both rely for their livelihood on the assumption that Williams calls "epistemological realism," viz. that there are objective relations of epistemic priority waiting to be described.

Further Reading

Annas, Julia and Jonathan Barnes, *The Modes of Scepticism* (Cambridge: Cambridge University Press, 1985).

Burnyeat, M. F. (ed.), *The Skeptical Tradition* (Berkeley: University of California Press, 1983).

Clarke, Thompson, "The Legacy of Skepticism," *Journal of Philosophy* 69 (1972), pp. 754–69.

DeRose, K. and T. Warfield (eds), *Skepticism: A Contemporary Reader* (Oxford: Oxford University Press, 1999).

Fumerton, R., *Metaepistemology and Skepticism* (Langham, MD: Rowman and Littlefield, 1995).

Hadot, Pierre, *Philosophy as a Way of Life* (Oxford: Blackwell, 1995).

Hankinson, R. J., *The Sceptics* (London: Routledge, 1995).

Huemer, Michael, *Skepticism and the Veil of Perception* (Langham, MD: Rowman and Littlefield, 2001).

Landesman, Charles and Roblin Meeks (eds), *Philosophical Skepticism: From Plato to Rorty* (Oxford: Blackwell, 2002).

Klein, P., *Certainty: A Refutation of Scepticism* (Minneapolis: University of Minnesota Press, 1991).

Nozick, Robert, *Philosophical Explanations* (Oxford: Oxford University Press, 1981).

Popkin, Richard, *Scepticism from Erasmus to Spinoza* (Berkeley: University of California Press, 1979).

Roth, Michael D. and Glenn Ross (eds), *Doubting: Contemporary Perspectives on Skepticism* (Dordrecht: Kluwer Academic Publishers, 1990).

Sosa, Ernest, "The Skeptic's Appeal," in Marjorie Clay and Keith Lehrer (eds), *Knowledge and Skepticism* (Boulder, CO: Westview Press, 1989), pp. 51–68.

Strawson, P. F., *Skepticism and Naturalism: Some Varieties* (London: Methuen, 1985).

Stroud, Barry, "Understanding Human Knowledge in General," in Marjorie Clay and Keith Lehrer (eds), *Knowledge and Skepticism* (Boulder, CO: Westview Press, 1989), pp. 31–50.

——, *The Significance of Philosophical Scepticism* (Oxford: Oxford University Press, 1984).

Unger, Peter, *Ignorance: A Case for Scepticism* (Oxford: Clarendon Press, 1975).

Williams, Michael, *Unnatural Doubts* (Princeton: Princeton University Press, 1996).

CHAPTER 1

The Problem of the External World

Barry Stroud

Since at least the time of Descartes in the seventeenth century there has been a philosophical problem about our knowledge of the world around us.[1] Put most simply, the problem is to show how we can have any knowledge of the world at all. The conclusion that we cannot, that no one knows anything about the world around us, is what I call "scepticism about the external world", so we could also say that the problem is to show how or why scepticism about the external world is not correct. My aim is not to solve the problem but to understand it. I believe the problem has no solution; or rather that the only answer to the question as it is meant to be understood is that we can know nothing about the world around us. But how is the question meant to be understood? It can be expressed in a few English words familiar to all of us, but I hope to show that an understanding of the special philosophical character of the question, and of the inevitability of an unsatisfactory answer to it, cannot be guaranteed by our understanding of those words alone. To see how the problem is meant to be understood we must therefore examine what is perhaps best described as its source – how the problem arises and how it acquires that special character that makes an unsatisfactory negative answer inevitable. We must try to understand

the *philosophical* problem of our knowledge of the external world.

The problem arose for Descartes in the course of reflecting on everything he knows. He reached a point in his life at which he tried to sit back and reflect on everything he had ever been taught or told, everything he had learned or discovered or believed since he was old enough to know or believe anything.[2] We might say that he was reflecting on his knowledge, but putting it that way could suggest that what he was directing his attention to was indeed knowledge, and whether it was knowledge or not is precisely what he wanted to determine. "Among all the things I believe or take to be true, what amounts to knowledge and what does not?"; that is the question Descartes asks himself. It is obviously a very general question, since it asks about everything he believes or takes to be true, but in other respects it sounds just like the sort of question we are perfectly familiar with in everyday life and often know how to answer.

For example, I have come to accept over the years a great many things about the common cold. I have always been told that one can catch cold by getting wet feet, or from sitting in a draught, or from not drying one's hair before going outdoors in cold weather. I have also learned that the common cold is the effect of a virus transmitted by an already infected person. And I also believe that one is more vulnerable to colds when over-tired, under stress, or otherwise in less than the best of health. Some of these beliefs seem

Originally published in B. Stroud, The *Significance of Philosophical Skepticism* (Oxford: Clarendon Press, 1984), ch. 1.

to me on reflection to be inconsistent with some others; I see that it is very unlikely that all of them could be true. Perhaps they could be, but I acknowledge that there is much I do not understand. If I sit back and try to think about all my "knowledge" of the common cold, then, I might easily come to wonder how much of it really amounts to knowledge and how much does not. What do I really know about the common cold? If I were sufficiently interested in pursuing the matter it would be natural to look into the source of my beliefs. Has there ever been any good reason for thinking that colds are even correlated with wet hair in cold weather, for example, or with sitting in a draught? Are the people from whom I learned such things likely to have believed them for good reasons? Are those beliefs just old wives' tales, or are they really true, and perhaps even known to be true by some people? These are questions I might ask myself, and I have at least a general idea of how to go about answering them.

Apart from my impression of the implausibility of all my beliefs about the common cold being true together, I have not mentioned any other reason for being interested in investigating the state of my knowledge on that subject. But for the moment that does not seem to affect the intelligibility or the feasibility of the reflective project. There is nothing mysterious about it. It is the sort of task we can be led to undertake for a number of reasons, and often very good reasons, in so far as we have very good reasons for preferring knowledge and firm belief to guesswork or wishful thinking or simply taking things for granted.

Reflection on or investigation of our putative knowledge need not always extend to a wide area of interest. It might be important to ask whether some quite specific and particular thing I believe or have been taking for granted is really something I know. As a member of a jury I might find that I have been ruling out one suspect in my mind because he was a thousand miles away, in Cleveland, at the time of the crime. But I might then begin to ask myself whether that is really something that I know. I would reflect on the source of my belief, but reflection in this case need not involve a general scrutiny of everything I take myself to know about the case. Re-examining the man's alibi and the credentials of its supporting witnesses might be enough to satisfy me. Indeed I might find that its reliability on those counts is precisely what I had been going on all along.

In pointing out that we are perfectly familiar with the idea of investigating or reviewing our knowledge on some particular matter or in some general area I do not mean to suggest that it is always easy to settle the question. Depending on the nature of the case, it might be very difficult, perhaps even impossible at the time, to reach a firm conclusion. For example, it would probably be very difficult if not impossible for me to trace and assess the origins of many of those things I believe about the common cold. But it is equally true that sometimes it is not impossible or even especially difficult to answer the question. We do sometimes discover that we do not really know what we previously thought we knew. I might find that what I had previously believed is not even true – that sitting in draughts is not even correlated with catching a cold, for example. Or I might find that there is not or perhaps never was any good reason to believe what I believed – that the man's alibi was concocted and then falsely testified to by his friends. I could reasonably conclude in each case that I, and everyone else for that matter, never did know what I had previously thought I knew. We are all familiar with the ordinary activity of reviewing our knowledge, and with the experience of reaching a positive verdict in some cases and a negative verdict in others.

Descartes's own interest in what he knows and how he knows it is part of his search for what he calls a general method for "rightly conducting reason and seeking truth in the sciences".[3] He wants a method of inquiry that he can be assured in advance will lead only to the truth if properly followed. I think we do not need to endorse the wisdom of that search or the feasibility of that programme in order to try to go along with Descartes in his general assessment of the position he is in with respect to the things he believes. He comes to find his putative knowledge wanting in certain general respects, and it is in the course of that original negative assessment that the problem I am interested in arises. I call the assessment "negative" because by the end of his *First Meditation* Descartes finds that he has no good reason to believe anything about the world around him and therefore that he can know nothing of the external world.

How is that assessment conducted, and how closely does it parallel the familiar kind of review of our knowledge that we all know how to conduct in everyday life? The question in one form or another will be with us for the rest of this book. It is the question of what exactly the problem of our knowledge of the external world amounts to, and how it arises with its special philosophical character. The source of the problem is to be found somewhere within or behind the kind of thinking Descartes engages in.

One way Descartes's question about his knowledge differs from the everyday examples I considered is in being concerned with *everything* he believes or takes to be true. How does one go about assessing all of one's knowledge all at once? I was able to list a few of the things I believe about the common cold and then to ask about each of them whether I really know it, and if so how. But although I can certainly list a number of the things I believe, and I would assent to many more of them as soon as they were put to me, there obviously is no hope of assessing everything I believe in this piecemeal way. For one thing, it probably makes no sense, strictly speaking, to talk of the number of things one believes. If I am asked whether it is one of my beliefs that I went to see a film last night I can truly answer "Yes". If I were asked whether it is one of my beliefs that I went to the movies last night I would give the same answer. Have I thereby identified two, or only one, of my beliefs? How is that question ever to be settled? If we say that I identified only one of my beliefs, it would seem that I must also be said to hold the further belief that going to see a film and going to the movies are one and the same thing. So we would have more than one belief after all. The prospects of arriving even at a principle for counting beliefs, let alone at an actual number of them, seem dim.

Even if it did make sense to count the things we believe it is pretty clear that the number would be indefinitely large and so an assessment of our beliefs one by one could never be completed anyway. This is easily seen by considering only some of the simplest things one knows, for example in arithmetic. One thing I know is that one plus one equals two. Another thing I know is that one plus two is three, and another, that one plus three is four. Obviously there could be no end to the task of assessing my knowledge if I had to investigate separately the source of each one of my beliefs in that series. And even if I succeeded I would only have assessed the things I know about

the addition of the number one to a given number; I would still have to do the same for the addition of two, and then the addition of three, and so on. And even that would exhaust only my beliefs about addition; all my other mathematical beliefs, not to mention all the rest of my knowledge, would remain so far unexamined. Obviously the job cannot be done piecemeal, one by one. Some method must be found for assessing large classes of beliefs all at once.

One way to do this would be to look for common sources or channels or bases of our beliefs, and then to examine the reliability of those sources or bases, just as I examined the source or basis of my belief that the suspect was in Cleveland. Descartes describes such a search as a search for "principles" of human knowledge, "principles" whose general credentials he can then investigate (HR, 145). If some "principles" are found to be involved in all or even most of our knowledge, an assessment of the reliability of those "principles" could be an assessment of all or most of our knowledge. If I found good reason to doubt the reliability of the suspect's alibi, for example, and that was all I had to go on in my belief that he was in Cleveland, then what I earlier took to be my knowledge that he was in Cleveland would have been found wanting or called into question. Its source or basis would have been undermined. Similarly, if one of the "principles" or bases on which all my knowledge of the world depends were found to be unreliable, my knowledge of the world would to that extent have been found wanting or called into question as well.

Are there any important "principles" of human knowledge in Descartes's sense? It takes very little reflection on the human organism to convince us of the importance of the senses – sight, hearing, touch, taste, and smell. Descartes puts the point most strongly when he says that "all that up to the present time I have accepted as most true and certain I have learned either from the senses or through the senses" (HR, 145). Exactly what he would include under "the senses" here is perhaps somewhat indeterminate, but even if it is left vague many philosophers would deny what Descartes appears to be saying. They would hold that, for example, the mathematical knowledge I mentioned earlier is not and could not be acquired from the senses or through the senses, so not *everything* I know is known in that way. Whether

Descartes is really denying the views of those who believe in the non-sensory character of mathematical knowledge, and whether, if he were, he would be right, are issues we can set aside for the moment. It is clear that the senses are at least very important for human knowledge. Even restricting ourselves to the traditional five senses we can begin to appreciate their importance by reflecting on how little someone would ever come to know without them. A person blind and deaf from birth who also lacked taste buds and a sense of smell would know very little about anything, no matter how long he lived. To imagine him also anaesthetized or without a sense of touch is perhaps to stretch altogether too far one's conception of a human organism, or at least a human organism from whom we can hope to learn something about human knowledge. The importance of the senses as a source or channel of knowledge seems undeniable. It seems possible, then, to acknowledge their importance and to assess the reliability of that source, quite independently of the difficult question of whether *all* our knowledge comes to us in that way. We would then be assessing the credentials of what is often called our "sensory" or "experiential" or "expirical" knowledge, and that, as we shall see, is quite enough to be going on with.

Having found an extremely important "principle" or source of our knowledge, how can we investigate or assess *all* the knowledge we get from that source? As before, we are faced with the problem of the inexhaustibility of the things we believe on that basis, so no piecemeal, one-by-one procedure will do. But perhaps we can make a sweeping negative assessment. It might seem that as soon as we have found that the senses are one of the sources of our beliefs we are immediately in a position to condemn all putative knowledge derived from them. Some philosophers appear to have reasoned in this way, and many have even supposed that Descartes is among them. The idea is that if I am assessing the reliability of my beliefs and asking whether I really know what I take myself to know, and I come across a large class of beliefs which have come to me through the senses, I can immediately dismiss all those beliefs as unreliable or as not amounting to knowledge because of the obvious fact that I can sometimes be wrong in my beliefs based on the senses. Things are not always as they appear, so if on the basis of the way they appear to me I believe that they

really are a certain way, I might still be wrong. We have all found at one time or another that we have been misled by appearances; we know that the senses are not always reliable. Should we not conclude, then, that as a general source of knowledge the senses are not to be trusted? As Descartes puts it, is it not wiser never "to trust entirely to any thing by which we have once been deceived" (HR, 145)? Don't we have here a quite general way of condemning as not fully reliable *all* of our beliefs acquired by means of the senses?

I think the answer to that question is "No, we do not", and I think Descartes would agree with that answer. It is true that he does talk of the senses "deceiving" us on particular occasions, and he does ask whether that is not enough to condemn the senses in general as a source of knowledge, but he immediately reminds us of the obvious fact that the circumstances in which the senses "deceive" us might be special in certain ascertainable ways, and so their occasional failures would not support a blanket condemnation of their reliability.

Sometimes, to give an ancient example, a tower looks round from a distance when it is actually square. If we relied only on the appearances of the moment we might say that the distant tower is round, and we would be wrong. We also know that there are many small organisms invisible to the naked eye. If the table before me is covered with such organisms at the moment but I look at it and say there is nothing on the table at all, once again I will be wrong. But all that follows from these familiar facts, as Descartes points out, is that there are things about which we can be wrong, or there are situations in which we can get false beliefs, if we rely entirely on our senses at that moment. So sometimes we should be careful about what we believe on the basis of the senses, or sometimes perhaps we should withhold our assent from any statement about how things are – when things are too far away to be seen properly, for example, or too small to be seen at all. But that obviously is not enough to support the policy of never trusting one's senses, or never believing anything based on them. Nor does it show that I can never know anything by means of the senses. If my car starts promptly every morning for two years in temperate weather at sea level but then fails to start one morning in freezing weather at the top of a high mountain, that does not support the policy of never trusting my car to start again once I return to the temperate lower altitude from which I so foolishly took it. Nor does it show that I can never know whether my car will ever start again. It shows only that there are certain circumstances in which my otherwise fully reliable car might not start. So the fact that we are sometimes wrong or "deceived" in our judgements based on the senses is not enough in itself to show that the senses are never to be trusted and are therefore never reliable as a source of knowledge.

Descartes's negative assessment of all of his sensory knowledge does not depend on any such reasoning. He starts his investigation, rather, in what would seem to be the most favourable conditions for the reliable operation of the senses as a source of knowledge. While engaging in the very philosophical reflections he is writing about in his *First Meditation* Descartes is sitting in a warm room, by the fire, in a dressing gown, with a piece of paper in his hand. He finds that although he might be able to doubt that a distant tower that looks round really is round, it seems impossible to doubt that he really is sitting there by the fire in his dressing gown with a piece of paper in his hand. The fire and the piece of paper are not too small or too far away to be seen properly, they are right there before his eyes; it seems to be the best kind of position someone could be in for getting reliable beliefs or knowledge by means of the senses about what is going on around him. That is just how Descartes regards it. Its being a best-possible case of that kind is precisely what he thinks enables him to investigate or assess at one fell swoop all our sensory knowledge of the world around us. The verdict he arrives at about his putative knowledge that he is sitting by the fire with a piece of paper in his hand in that particular situation serves as the basis for a completely general assessment of the senses as a source of knowledge about the world around us.

How can that be so? How can he so easily reach a general verdict about all his sensory knowledge on the basis of a single example? Obviously not simply by generalizing from one particular example to all cases of sensory knowledge, as one might wildly leap to a conclusion about all red-haired men on the basis of one or two individuals. Rather, he takes the particular example of his conviction that he is sitting by the fire with a piece of paper in his hand as representative of the best position any of us can ever be in for knowing things about the world around us on the basis of the senses. What is true of a representative case, if it is truly representative and does not depend on special peculiarities of its own, can legitimately support a general conclusion. A demonstration that a particular isosceles triangle has a certain property, for example, can be taken as a demonstration that all isosceles triangles have that property, as long as the original instance was typical or representative of the whole class. Whether Descartes's investigation of the general reliability of the senses really does follow that familiar pattern is a difficult question. Whether, or in precisely what sense, the example he considers can be treated as representative of our relation to the world around us is, I believe, the key to understanding the problem of our knowledge of the external world. But if it turns out that there is nothing illegitimate about the way his negative conclusion is reached, the problem will be properly posed.

For the moment I think at least this much can be said about Descartes's reasoning. He chooses the situation in which he finds himself as representative of the best position we can be in for knowing things about the world in the sense that, if it is impossible for him in that position to know that he is sitting by the fire with a piece of paper in his hand then it is also impossible for him in other situations to know anything about the world around him on the basis of his senses. A negative verdict in the chosen case would support a negative verdict everywhere else. The example Descartes considers is in that sense meant to be the *best* kind of case there could be of sensory knowledge about the world around us. I think we must admit that it is very difficult to see how Descartes or anyone else could be any better off with respect to knowing something about the world around him on the basis of the senses than he is in the case he considers. But if no one could be in any better position for knowing, it seems natural to conclude that any negative verdict arrived at about this example, any discovery that Descartes's beliefs in this case are not reliable or do not amount to knowledge, could safely be generalized into a negative conclusion about all of our sensory "knowledge" of the world. If candidates with the best possible credentials are found wanting, all those with less impressive credentials must fall short as well.

It will seem at first sight that in conceding that the whole question turns on whether Descartes knows in this particular case we are conceding very little; it seems obvious that Descartes on that occasion does know what he thinks he knows about the world around him. But in fact Descartes finds that he cannot know in this case that he is sitting by the fire with a piece of paper in his hand. If the case is truly representative of our sensory knowledge in general, that will show that no one can know anything about the world around us. But how could he ever arrive at that negative verdict in the particular case he considers? How could anyone possibly doubt in such a case that the fire and the piece of paper are there? The paper is in Descartes's hand, the fire is right there before his open eyes, and he feels its warmth. Wouldn't anyone have to be mad to deny that he can know something about what is going on around him in those circumstances? Descartes first answers "Yes". He says that if he were to doubt or deny on that occasion that he is sitting by the fire with a piece of paper in his hand he would be no less mad than those paupers who say they are kings or those madmen who think they are pumpkins or are made of glass. But his reflections continue:

> At the same time I must remember that I am a man, and that consequently I am in the habit of sleeping, and in my dreams representing to myself the same things or sometimes even less probable things, than do those who are insane in their waking moments. How often has it happened to me that in the night I dreamt that I found myself in this particular place, that I was dressed and seated near the fire, whilst in reality I was lying undressed in bed! At this moment it does indeed seem to me that it is with eyes awake that I am looking at this paper; that this head which I move is not asleep, that it is deliberately and of set purpose that I extend my hand and perceive it; what happens in sleep does not appear so clear nor so distinct as does all this. But in thinking over this I remind myself that on many occasions I have in sleep been deceived by similar illusions, and in dwelling carefully on this reflection I see so manifestly that there are no certain indications by which we may clearly distinguish wakefulness from sleep that I am lost in astonishment. And my astonishment is such that it is almost capable of persuading me that I now dream. (HR, 145–6)

With this thought, if he is right, Descartes has lost the whole world. He knows what he is experiencing, he knows how things appear to him, but he does not know whether he is in fact sitting by the fire with a piece of paper in his hand. It is, for him, exactly as if he were sitting by the fire with a piece of paper in his hand, but he does not know whether there really is a fire or a piece of paper there or not; he does not know what is really happening in the world around him. He realizes that if everything he can ever learn about what is happening in the world around him comes to him through the senses, but he cannot tell by means of the senses whether or not he is dreaming, then all the sensory experiences he is having are compatible with his merely dreaming of a world around him while in fact that world is very different from the way he takes it to be. That is why he thinks he must find some way to tell that he is not dreaming. Far from its being mad to deny that he knows in this case, he thinks his recognition of the possibility that he might be dreaming gives him "very powerful and maturely considered" (HR, 148) reasons for withholding his judgement about how things are in the world around him. He thinks it is eminently reasonable to insist that if he is to know that he is sitting by the fire he must know that he is not dreaming that he is sitting by the fire. That is seen as a necessary condition of knowing something about the world around him. And he finds that that condition cannot be fulfilled. On careful reflection he discovers that "there are no certain indications by which we may clearly distinguish wakefulness from sleep". He concludes that he knows nothing about the world around him because he cannot tell that he is not dreaming; he cannot fulfil one of the conditions necessary for knowing something about the world.

The Cartesian problem of our knowledge of the external world therefore becomes: how can we know anything about the world around us on the basis of the senses if the senses give us only what Descartes says they give us? What we gain through the senses is on Descartes's view only information that is compatible with our dreaming things about the world around us and not knowing anything about the world. How then can we know anything about the world by means of the senses? The Cartesian argument presents a challenge to our knowledge, and the problem of our knowledge of the external world is to show how that challenge can be met.

When I speak here of the Cartesian argument or of Descartes's sceptical conclusion or of his negative verdict about his knowledge I refer of course only to the position he finds himself in by the end of his *First Meditation*. Having at that point discovered and stated the problem of the external world, Descartes goes on in the rest of his *Meditations* to try to solve it, and by the end of the *Sixth Meditation* he thinks he has explained how he knows almost all those familiar things he began by putting in question. So when I ascribe to Descartes the view that we can know nothing about the world around us I do not mean to suggest that that is his final and considered view; it is nothing more than a conclusion he feels almost inevitably driven to at the early stages of his reflections. But those are the only stages of his thinking I am interested in here. That is where the philosophical problem of our knowledge of the external world gets posed, and before we can consider possible solutions we must be sure we understand exactly what the problem is.

I have described it as that of showing or explaining how knowledge of the world around us is possible by means of the senses. It is important to keep in mind that that demand for an explanation arises in the face of a challenge or apparent obstacle to our knowledge of the world. The possibility that he is dreaming is seen as an obstacle to Descartes's knowing that he is sitting by the fire, and it must be explained how that obstacle can either be avoided or overcome. It must be shown or explained *how* it is possible for us to know things about the world, given that the sense-experiences we get are compatible with our merely dreaming. Explaining how something is nevertheless possible, despite what looks like an obstacle to it, requires more than showing merely that there is no impossibility involved in the thing – that it is consistent with the principles of logic and the laws of nature and so in that sense *could* exist. The mere possibility of the state of affairs is not enough to settle the question of how our knowledge of the world is possible; we must understand how the apparent obstacle is to be got round.

Descartes's reasoning can be examined and criticized at many different points, and has been closely scrutinized by many philosophers for centuries. It has also been accepted by many, perhaps by more than would admit or even realize that they accept it. There seems to me no doubt about the force and the fascination – I would say the almost overwhelming persuasiveness – of his reflections. That alone is something that needs accounting for. I cannot possibly do justice to all reasonable reactions to them here. In the rest of this chapter I want to concentrate on deepening and strengthening the problem and trying to locate more precisely the source of its power.

There are at least three distinct questions that could be pressed. Is the possibility that Descartes might be dreaming really a threat to his knowledge of the world around him? Is he right in thinking that he must know that he is not dreaming if he is to know something about the world around him? And is he right in his "discovery" that he can never know that he is not dreaming? If Descartes were wrong on any of these points it might be possible to avoid the problem and perhaps even to explain without difficulty how we know things about the world around us.

On the first question, it certainly seems right to say that if Descartes were dreaming that he is sitting by the fire with a piece of paper in his hand he would not then know that he is sitting by the fire with a piece of paper in his hand. When you dream that something is going on in the world around you you do not thereby know that it is. Most often, of course, what we dream is not even true; no one is actually chasing us when we are lying asleep in bed dreaming, nor are we actually climbing stairs. But although usually what we dream is not really so, that is not the real reason for our lack of knowledge. Even if Descartes were in fact sitting by the fire and actually had a piece of paper in his hand at the very time he was dreaming that he is sitting by the fire with a piece of paper in his hand, he would not thereby know he was sitting there with that paper. He would be like a certain Duke of Devonshire who, according to G. E. Moore, once dreamt he was speaking in the House of Lords and woke up to find that he *was* speaking in the House of Lords.[4] What he was dreaming was in fact so. But even if what you are dreaming is in fact so you do not thereby know that it is. Even if we allow that when you are dreaming that something is so you can be said, at least for the time being, to think or to believe that it is so, there is still no real connection between your thinking or believing what you do and its being so. At best you have a thought or a belief which just happens to be true, but that is no more than coincidence and not knowledge. So Descartes's first step relies on what seems to be an undeniable fact about dreams: if you are dreaming that something is so you do not thereby know that it is so.

This bald claim needs to be qualified and more carefully explained, but I do not think that will diminish the force of the point for Descartes's purposes. Sometimes what is going on in the world around us has an effect on what we dream; for example, a banging shutter might actually cause me to dream, among other things, that a shutter is banging. If my environment affects me in that way, and if in dreams I can be said to think or believe that something is so, would I not in that case know that a shutter is banging? It seems to me that I would not, but I confess it is difficult to say exactly why I think so. That is probably because it is difficult to say exactly what is required for knowledge. We use the term "know" confidently, we quite easily distinguish cases of knowledge from cases of its absence, but we are not always in a position to state what we are going on in applying or withholding the term in the ways we do. I think that in the case of the banging shutter it would not be knowledge because I would be *dreaming*, I would not even be awake. At least it can be said, I think, that even if Descartes's sitting by the fire with a piece of paper in his hand (like the banging shutter) is what in fact causes him to dream that he is sitting by the fire with a piece of paper in his hand, that is still no help to him in coming to know what is going on in the world around him. He realizes that he could be dreaming that he is sitting by the fire even if he is in fact sitting there, and that is the possibility he finds he has to rule out.

I have said that if you are dreaming that something is so you do not thereby know that it is so, and it might seem as if that is not always true. Suppose a man and a child are both sleeping. I say of the child that it is so young it does not know what seven times nine is, whereas the grown man does know that. If the man happens at that very moment to be dreaming that seven times nine is sixty-three (perhaps he is dreaming that he is computing his income tax), then he is a man who is dreaming that something is so and also knows that it is so. The same kind of thing is possible for knowledge about the world around him. He

might be a physicist who knows a great deal about the way things are which the child does not know. If the man also dreams that things are that way he can once again be said to be dreaming that something is so and also to know that it is so. There is therefore no incompatibility between dreaming and knowing. That is true, but I do not think it affects Descartes's argument. He is led to consider how he knows he is not dreaming at the moment by reflecting on how he knows at that moment that he is sitting by the fire with a piece of paper in his hand. If he knows that at all, he thinks, he knows it on the basis of the senses. But he realizes that his having the sensory experiences he is now having is compatible with his merely dreaming that he is sitting by the fire with a piece of paper in his hand. So he does not know on the basis of the sensory experiences he is having at the moment that he is sitting by the fire. Nor, of course, did the man in my examples know the things he was said to know on the basis of the sensory experiences he was having at that moment. He knew certain things to be so, and he was dreaming those things to be so, but in dreaming them he did not *thereby* know them to be so.

But as long as we allow that the sleeping man does know certain things about the world around him, even if he does not know them on the basis of the very dreams he is having at the moment, isn't that enough to show that Descartes must nevertheless be wrong in his conclusion that no one can know anything about the world around him? No. It shows at most that we were hasty or were ignoring Descartes's conclusion in conceding that someone could know something about the world around him. If Descartes's reasoning is correct the dreaming physicist, even when he is awake, does not really know any of the things we were uncritically crediting him with knowing about the way things are – or at least he does not know them on the basis of the senses. In order to know them on the basis of the senses there would have to have been at least some time at which he knew something about what was going on around him at that time. But if Descartes is right he could not have known any such thing unless he had established that he was not dreaming at that time; and according to Descartes he could never establish that. So the fact about dreams that Descartes relies on – that one who dreams that something is so does not thereby know that it is so – is enough to yield his conclusion if the other steps of his reasoning are correct.

When he first introduces the possibility that he might be dreaming Descartes seems to be relying on some knowledge about how things are or were in the world around him. He says "I remind myself that on many occasions I have in sleep been deceived by similar illusions", so he seems to be relying on some knowledge to the effect that he has actually dreamt in the past and that he remembers having been "deceived" by those dreams. That is more than he actually needs for his reflections about knowledge to have the force he thinks they have. He does not need to support his judgement that he has actually dreamt in the past. The only thought he needs is that it is now *possible* for him to be dreaming that he is sitting by the fire, and that if that possibility were realized he would not know that he is sitting by the fire. Of course it was no doubt true that Descartes had dreamt in the past and that his knowledge that he had done so was partly what he was going on in acknowledging the possibility of his dreaming on this particular occasion. But neither the fact of past dreams nor knowledge of their actual occurrence would seem to be strictly required in order to grant what Descartes relies on – the possibility of dreaming, and the absence of knowledge if that possibility were realized. The thought that he *might* be dreaming that he is sitting by the fire with a piece of paper in his hand, and the fact that if he were he wouldn't know he was sitting there, is what gives Descartes pause. That would worry him in the way it does even if he had never actually had any dreams exactly like it in the past – if he had never dreamt about fires and pieces of paper at all. In fact, I think he need never have actually dreamt of anything before, and certainly needn't know that he ever has, in order to be worried in the way he is by the thought that he might be dreaming now.

The fact that the possibility of dreaming is all Descartes needs to appeal to brings out another truth about dreams that his argument depends on – that anything that can be going on or that one can experience in one's waking life can also be dreamt about. This again is only a statement of possibility – no sensible person would suggest that we *do* at some time dream of everything that actually happens to us, or that everything we dream about does in fact happen sometime. But it is very plausible to say that there is nothing we *could* not dream about, nothing that could be the case that we *could* not dream to be the case. I say it is very plausible; of course I cannot prove it to be true. But even if it is not true with complete generality, we must surely grant that it is possible to dream that one is sitting by a fire with a piece of paper in one's hand, and possible to dream of countless other equally obvious and equally mundane states of affairs as well, and those possibilities are what Descartes sees as threatening to his knowledge of the world around him.

There seems little hope, then, of objecting that it is simply not possible for Descartes to dream that he is sitting by the fire with a piece of paper in his hand. Nor is it any more promising to say that even if he were dreaming it would not follow that he did not know that he was sitting there. I think both those steps or assumptions of Descartes's reasoning are perfectly correct, and further defence of them at this stage is unnecessary. If his argument and the problem to which it gives rise are to be avoided, it might seem that the best hope is therefore to accept his challenge and show that it can be met. That would be in effect to argue that Descartes's alleged "discovery" is no discovery at all: we *can* sometimes know that we are not dreaming.

This can easily seem to be the most straightforward and most promising strategy. It allows that Descartes is right in thinking that knowing that one is not dreaming is a condition of knowing something about the world around us, but wrong in thinking that that condition can never be met. And that certainly seems plausible. Surely it is not impossible for me to know that I am not dreaming? Isn't that something I often know, and isn't it something I can sometimes find out if the question arises? If it is, then the fact that I must know that I am not dreaming if I am to know anything about the world around me will be no threat to my knowledge of the world.

However obvious and undeniable it might be that we often do know that we are not dreaming, I think this straightforward response to Descartes's challenge is a total failure. In calling it straightforward I mean that it accepts Descartes's conditions for knowledge of the world and tries to show that they can be fulfilled. That is what I think cannot be done. To put the same point in another way: I think Descartes would be perfectly correct in saying "there are no certain indications by which we may clearly distinguish wakefulness from sleep", and so we could never tell we are not dreaming, *if* he were also right that knowing that one is not dreaming is a condition of knowing something about the world around us. That is why I think one cannot accept that condition and then go on to establish that one is not dreaming. I do not mean to be saying simply that Descartes is right – that we can never know that we are not dreaming. But I do want to argue that either we can never know that we are not dreaming or else what Descartes says is a condition of knowing things about the world is not really a condition in general of knowing things about the world. The straightforward strategy denies both alternatives. I will try to explain why I think we must accept one alternative or the other.

When Descartes asks himself how he knows that he is sitting by the fire with a piece of paper in his hand why does he immediately go on to ask himself how he knows he is not dreaming that he is sitting by the fire with a piece of paper in his hand? I have suggested that it is because he recognizes that if he were dreaming he would not know on the basis of his senses at the moment that he is sitting there, and so he thinks he must know that that possibility does not obtain if he is to know that he is in fact sitting there. But this particular example was chosen, not for any peculiarities it might be thought to possess, but because it could be taken as typical of the best position we can ever be in for coming to know things about the world around us on the basis of the senses. What is true of this case that is relevant to Descartes's investigation of knowledge is supposed to be true of all cases of knowledge of the world by means of the senses; that is why the verdict arrived at here can be taken to be true of our sensory knowledge generally. But what Descartes thinks is true of this particular case of sensory knowledge of the world is that he must know he is not dreaming if he is to know that he is sitting by the fire with a piece of paper in his hand. That is required, not because of any peculiarities of this particular case, but presumably because, according to Descartes, it is a necessary condition of any case – even a best possible case – of knowledge of the world by means of the senses. That is why I ascribed to Descartes the quite general thesis that knowing that one is not dreaming is a condition

of knowing something about the world around us on the basis of the senses. Since he thinks the possibility of his dreaming must be ruled out in the case he considers, and the case he considers is regarded as typical and without special characteristics of its own, he thinks that the possibility that he is dreaming must be ruled out in every case of knowing something about the world by means of the senses.

If that really is a condition of knowing something about the world, I think it can be shown that Descartes is right in holding that it can never be fulfilled. That is what the straightforward response denies, and that is why I think that response must be wrong. We cannot accept the terms of Descartes's challenge and then hope to meet it.

Suppose Descartes tries to determine that he is not dreaming in order to fulfil what he sees as a necessary condition of knowing that he is sitting by the fire with a piece of paper in his hand. How is he to proceed? He realizes that his seeing his hand and seeing and feeling a piece of paper before him and feeling the warmth of the fire – in fact his getting all the sensory experiences or all the sensory information he is then getting – is something that could be happening even if he were dreaming. To establish that he is not dreaming he would therefore need something more than just those experiences or that information alone. He would also need to know whether those experiences and that information are reliable, not merely dreamt. If he could find some operation or test, or if he could find some circumstance or state of affairs, that indicated to him that he was not dreaming, perhaps he could then fulfil the condition – he could know that he was not dreaming. But how could a test or a circumstance or a state of affairs indicate to him that he is not dreaming *if* a condition of knowing *anything* about the world is that he know he is not dreaming? It could not. He could never fulfil the condition.

Let us suppose that there is in fact some test which a person can perform successfully only if he is not dreaming, or some circumstance or state of affairs which obtains only if that person is not dreaming. Of course for that test or state of affairs to be of any use to him Descartes would have to know of it. He would have to know that there is such a test or that there is a state of affairs that shows that he is not dreaming; without such information he would be no better off for telling that he is not dreaming than he would be if there were no such test or state of affairs at all. To have acquired that information he would at some time have to have known more than just something about the course of his sensory experience, since the connection between the performance of a certain test, or between a certain state of affairs, and someone's not dreaming is not itself just a fact about the course of that person's sensory experience; it is a fact about the world beyond his sensory experiences. Now strictly speaking if it is a condition of knowing *anything* about the world beyond one's sensory experiences that one know that one is not dreaming, there is an obvious obstacle to Descartes's ever having got the information he needs about that test or state of affairs. He would have to have known at some time that he was not dreaming in order to get the information he needs to tell at *any* time that he is not dreaming – and that cannot be done.

But suppose we forget about this difficulty and concede that Descartes does indeed know (somehow) that there is a test or circumstance or state of affairs that unfailingly indicates that he is not dreaming. Still, there is an obstacle to his ever using that test or state of affairs to tell that he is not dreaming and thereby fulfilling the condition for knowledge of the world. The test would have to be something he could know he had performed successfully, the state of affairs would have to be something he could know obtains. If he completely unwittingly happened to perform the test, or if the state of affairs happened to obtain but he didn't know that it did, he would be in no better position for telling whether he was dreaming than he would be if he had done nothing or did not even know that there was such a test. But how is he to know that the test has been performed successfully or that the state of affairs in question does in fact obtain? Anything one can experience in one's walking life can also be dreamt about; it is possible to dream that one has performed a certain test or dream that one has established that a certain state of affairs obtains. And, as we have seen, to dream that something about the world around you is so is not thereby to know that it is so. In order to know that his test has been performed or that the state of affairs in question obtains Descartes would therefore have to establish that he is not merely dreaming that he performed the test

successfully or that he established that the state of affairs obtains. How could that in turn be known? Obviously the particular test or state of affairs already in question cannot serve as a guarantee of its own authenticity, since it might have been merely dreamt, so some further test or state of affairs would be needed to indicate that the original test was actually performed and not merely dreamt, or that the state of affairs in question was actually ascertained to obtain and not just dreamt to obtain. But this further test or state of affairs is subject to the same general condition in turn. *Every* piece of knowledge that goes beyond one's sensory experiences requires that one know one is not dreaming. This second test or state of affairs will therefore be of use only if Descartes knows that he is not merely dreaming that he is performing or ascertaining it, since merely to dream that he had established the authenticity of the first test is not to have established it. And so on. At no point can he find a test for not dreaming which he can know has been successfully performed or a state of affairs correlated with not dreaming which he can know obtains. He can therefore never fulfil what Descartes says is a necessary condition of knowing something about the world around him. He can never know that he is not dreaming.

I must emphasize that this conclusion is reached *only* on the assumption that it is a condition of knowing anything about the world around us on the basis of the senses that we know we are not dreaming that the thing is so. I think it is his acceptance of that condition that leads Descartes to "see so manifestly that there are no certain indications by which we may clearly distinguish wakefulness from sleep". And I think Descartes is absolutely right to draw that conclusion, *given* what he thinks is a condition of knowledge of the world. But all I have argued on Descartes's behalf (he never spells out his reasoning) is that we cannot both accept that condition of knowledge and hope to fulfil it, as the straightforward response hopes to do. And of course if one of the necessary conditions of knowledge of the world can never be fulfilled, knowledge of the world around us will be impossible.

I think we have now located Descartes's reason for his negative verdict about sensory knowledge in general. If we agree that he must know that he is not dreaming if he is to know in his particular case that he is sitting by the fire with a piece of paper in his hand, we must also agree that we can know nothing about the world around us.

Once we recognize that the condition Descartes takes as necessary can never be fulfilled if he is right in thinking it is indeed necessary, we are naturally led to the question whether Descartes is right. Is it really a condition of knowing something about the world that one know one is not dreaming? That is the second of the three questions I distinguished. It is the one that has received the least attention. In asking it now I do not mean to be going back on something I said earlier was undeniably true, viz., that if one is dreaming that something about the world is so one does not thereby know that it is so. That still seems to me undeniable, but it is not the same as Descartes's assumption that one must know that one is not dreaming if one is to know something about the world. The undeniable truth says only that you lack knowledge if you are dreaming; Descartes says that you lack knowledge if you don't know that you are not dreaming. Only with the stronger assumption can his sceptical conclusion be reached.

Is that assumption true? In so far as we find Descartes's reasoning convincing, or even plausible, I think it is because we too on reflection find that it is true. I said that not much attention had been paid to that particular part of Descartes's reasoning, and I think that too is because, as he presents it, the step seems perfectly convincing and so only other parts of the argument appear vulnerable. Why is that so? Is it because Descartes's assumption is indeed true? Is there anything we can do that would help us determine whether it is true or not? The question is important because I have argued so far that *if* it is true we can never know anything about the world around us on the basis of the senses, and philosophical scepticism about the external world is correct. We would have to find that conclusion as convincing or as plausible as we find the assumption from which it is derived.

Given our original favourable response to Descartes's reasoning, then, it can scarcely be denied that what I have called his assumption or condition *seems* perfectly natural to insist on. Perhaps it seems like nothing more than an instance of a familiar commonplace about knowledge. We are all aware that, even in the most ordinary circumstances when nothing very important turns on the outcome, we cannot know a particular thing unless we have ruled out certain possibilities that we recognize are incompatible with our knowing that thing.

Suppose that on looking out the window I announce casually that there is a goldfinch in the garden. If I am asked how I know it is a goldfinch and I reply that it is yellow, we all recognize that in the normal case that is not enough for knowledge. "For all you've said so far," it might be replied, "the thing could be a canary, so how do you know it's a goldfinch?" A certain possibility compatible with everything I have said so far has been raised, and if what I have said so far is all I have got to go on and I don't know that the thing in the garden is not a canary, then I do not know that there is a goldfinch in the garden. I must be able to rule out the possibility that it is a canary if I am to know that it is a goldfinch. Anyone who speaks about knowledge and understands what others say about it will recognize this fact or condition in particular cases.

In this example what is said to be possible is something incompatible with the truth of what I claim to know – if that bird were a canary it would not be a goldfinch in the garden, but a canary. What I believe in believing it is a goldfinch would be false. But that is not the only way a possibility can work against my knowledge. If I come to suspect that all the witnesses have conspired and made up a story about the man's being in Cleveland that night, for example, and their testimony is all I have got to go on in believing that he was in Cleveland, I might find that I no longer know whether he was there or not until I have some reason to rule out my suspicion. If their testimony were all invented I would not know that the man was in Cleveland. But strictly speaking his being in Cleveland is not incompatible with their making up a story saying he was. They might have invented a story to protect him, whereas in fact, unknown to them, he was there all the time. Such a complicated plot is not necessary to bring out the point; Moore's Duke of Devonshire is enough. From the fact that he was dreaming that he was speaking in the House of Lords it did not follow that he was not speaking in the House of Lords. In fact he was. The possibility of dreaming – which was actual in that case – did not imply the falsity of what was believed. A possible deficiency in the basis of my belief can interfere with my knowledge without itself rendering false the very thing I believe. A hallucinogenic drug might cause me to see my bed covered with a huge pile of leaves, for example.[5] Having taken that drug, I will know the actual state of my bed only if I know that what I see is not just the effect of the drug; I must be able to rule out the possibility that I am hallucinating the bed and the leaves. But however improbable it might be that my bed is actually covered with leaves, its not being covered with leaves does not follow from the fact that I am hallucinating that it is. What I am hallucinating could nevertheless be (unknown to me) true. But a goldfinch simply could not be a canary. So although there are two different ways in which a certain possibility can threaten my knowledge, it remains true that there are always certain possibilities which must be known not to obtain if I am to know what I claim to know.

I think these are just familiar facts about human knowledge, something we all recognize and abide by in our thought and talk about knowing things. We know what would be a valid challenge to a claim to know something, and we can recognize the relevance and force of objections made to our claims to know. The question before us is to what extent Descartes's investigation of his knowledge that he is sitting by the fire with a piece of paper in his hand follows these recognized everyday procedures for assessing claims to know. If it does follow them faithfully, and yet leads to the conclusion that he cannot know where he is or what is happening around him, we seem forced to accept his negative conclusion about knowledge in general just as we are forced to accept the conclusion that I do not know it is a goldfinch or do not know the witness was in Cleveland because I cannot rule out the possibilities which must be ruled out if I am to know such things. Is Descartes's introduction of the possibility that he might be dreaming just like the introduction of the possibility that it might be a canary in the garden or that the alibi might be contrived or that it might be a hallucination of my bed covered with leaves?

Those possibilities were all such that if they obtained I did not know what I claimed to know, and they had to be known not to obtain in order for the original knowledge-claim to be true. Does Descartes's dream-possibility fulfil both of those conditions? I have already said that it seems undeniable that it fulfils the first. If he *were* dreaming Descartes would not know what he claims to know. Someone who is dreaming does not thereby know anything about the world around him even if the world around him happens to be just the way he dreams or believes it to be. So his dreaming *is* incompatible with his knowing. But does it fulfil the second condition? Is it a possibility which must be known not to obtain if Descartes is to know that he is sitting by the fire with a piece of paper in his hand? I think it is difficult simply to deny that it is. The evident force of Descartes's reasoning when we first encounter it is enough to show that it certainly strikes us as a relevant possibility, as something that he should know not to obtain if he is to know where he is and what is happening around him.

When that possibility strikes us as obviously relevant in Descartes's investigation we might come to think that it is because of a simple and obvious fact about knowledge. In the case of the goldfinch we immediately recognize that I must know that it is not a canary if I am to know it is a goldfinch. And it is very natural to think that that is simply because its being a canary is incompatible with its being a goldfinch. If it were a canary it would not be a goldfinch, and I would therefore be wrong in saying that it is; so if I am to know it is a goldfinch I must rule out the possibility that it is a canary. The idea is that the two conditions I distinguished in the previous paragraph are not really separate after all. As soon as we see that a certain possibility is incompatible with our knowing such-and-such, it is suggested, we immediately recognize that it is a possibility that must be known not to obtain if we are to know the such-and-such in question. We see that the dream-possibility satisfies that first condition in Descartes's case (if he were dreaming, he wouldn't know), and that is why, according to this suggestion, we immediately see that it is relevant and must be ruled out. Something we all recognize about knowledge is what is said to make that obvious to us.

But is the "simple and obvious fact about knowledge" appealed to in this explanation really something that is true of human knowledge even in the most ordinary circumstances? What exactly is the "fact" in question supposed to be? I have described it so far, as applied to the case of the goldfinch, as the fact that if I know something p (it's a goldfinch) I must know the falsity of all those things incompatible with p (e.g., it's a canary). If there were one of those things that I did not know to be false, and it were in fact true, I would not know that p, since in that case something incompatible with p would be true and so p would not be true. But to say that I must know that all those things incompatible with p are false is the same as saying that I must know that truth of all those things that must be true if p is true. And it is extremely implausible to say that that is a "simple and obvious fact" we all recognize about human knowledge.

The difficulty is that there are no determinate limits to the number of things that follow from the things I already know. But it cannot be said that I now know all those indeterminately many things, although they all must be true if the things that I already know are true. Even granting that I now know a great deal about a lot of different things, my knowledge obviously does not extend to everything that follows from what I now know. If it did, mathematics, to take only one example, would be a great deal easier than it is – or else impossibly difficult. In knowing the truth of the simple axioms of number theory, for example, I would thereby know the truth of everything that follows from them; every theorem of number theory would already be known. Or, taking the pessimistic side, since obviously no one does know all the theorems of number theory, it would follow that no one even knows that those simple axioms are true.

It is absurd to say that we enjoy or require such virtual omniscience, so it is more plausible to hold that the "simple and obvious fact" we all recognize about knowledge is the weaker requirement that we must know the falsity of all those things that we *know* to be incompatible with the things we know. I know that a bird's being a canary is incompatible with its being a goldfinch; that is not some farflung, unknown consequence of its being a goldfinch, but something that anyone would know who knew anything about goldfinches at all. And the idea is that that is why I must know that it is not a canary if I am to know that it is a goldfinch. Perhaps, in order to know something, p, I do not need to know the falsity of all those things that are incompatible with p, but it can seem that at least I must know the falsity of

all those things that I *know* to be incompatible with p. Since I claim to know that the bird is a goldfinch, and I know that its being a goldfinch implies that it is not a canary, I must for that reason know that it is not a canary if my original claim is true. In claiming to know it is a goldfinch I was, so to speak, committing myself to knowing that it is not a canary, and I must honour my commitments.

This requirement as it stands, even if it does explain why I must know that the bird is not a canary, does not account for the relevance of the other sorts of possibilities I have mentioned. The reason in the goldfinch case was said to be that I know that its being a canary is incompatible with its being a goldfinch. But that will not explain why I must rule out the possibility that the witnesses have invented a story about the man's being in Cleveland, or the possibility that I am hallucinating my bed covered with a pile of leaves. Nor will it explain why Descartes must rule out the possibility that he is dreaming. What I claimed to know in the first case is that the man was in Cleveland that night. But, as we saw earlier, it is not a consequence of his being in Cleveland that no one will invent a story to the effect that he was in Cleveland; they might mistakenly believe he was not there and then tell what they think is a lie. Nor is it a consequence of my bed's being covered with leaves that I am not hallucinating that it is. But we recognize that in order to know in those cases I nevertheless had to rule out those possibilities. Similarly, as the Duke of Devonshire reminds us, it is not a consequence of Descartes's sitting by the fire with a piece of paper in his hand that he is not dreaming that he is. So if it is obvious to us that Descartes must know that he is not dreaming if he is to know that he is sitting by the fire, it cannot be simply because the possibility in question is known to be incompatible with what he claims to know. It is not.

If there is some "simple and obvious fact about knowledge" that we recognize and rely on in responding to Descartes's reasoning it must therefore be more complicated than what has been suggested so far. Reflecting even on the uncontroversial everyday examples alone can easily lead us to suppose that it is something like this: if somebody knows something, p, he must know the falsity of all those things incompatible with his knowing that p (or perhaps all those things he knows to be incompatible with his knowing that *p*). I will not speculate further on the qualifications or emendations needed to make the principle less implausible. The question now is whether it is our adherence to any such principle or requirement that is responsible for our recognition that the possibility that the bird is a canary or the possibility that the witnesses made up a story must be known not to obtain if I am to know the things I said I knew in those cases. What exactly are the procedures or standards we follow in the most ordinary, humdrum cases of putative knowledge? Reflection on the source of Descartes's sceptical reasoning has led to difficulties in describing and therefore in understanding even the most familiar procedures we follow in everyday life. That is one of the rewards of a study of philosophical scepticism.

The main difficulty in understanding our ordinary procedures is that no principle like those I have mentioned could possibly describe the way we proceed in everyday life. Or, to put it less dogmatically, if our adherence to some such requirement were responsible for our reactions in those ordinary cases, Descartes would be perfectly correct, and philosophical scepticism about the external world would be true. Nobody would know anything about the world around us. If, in order to know something, we must rule out a possibility which is known to be incompatible with our knowing it, Descartes is perfectly right to insist that he must know that he is not dreaming if he is to know that he is sitting by the fire with a piece of paper in his hand. He knows his dreaming is incompatible with his knowing. I have already argued that if he is right in insisting that that condition must be fulfilled for knowledge of the world around us he is also right in concluding that it can never be fulfilled; fulfilling it would require knowledge which itself would be possible only if the condition were fulfilled. So both steps of Descartes's reasoning would be valid and his conclusion would be true.

That conclusion can be avoided, it seems to me, only if we can find some way to avoid the requirement that we must know we are not dreaming if we are to know anything about the world around us. But that requirement cannot be avoided if it is nothing more than an instance of a general procedure we recognize and insist on in making and assessing knowledge-claims in every-

day and scientific life. We have no notion of knowledge other than what is embodied in those procedures and practices. So if that requirement is a "fact" of our ordinary conception of knowledge we will have to accept the conclusion that no one knows anything about the world around us.

I now want to say a few more words about the position we would all be in if Descartes's conclusion as he understands it were correct. I described him earlier as having lost the whole world, as knowing at most what he is experiencing or how things appear to him, but knowing nothing about how things really are in the world around him. To show how anyone in that position could come to know anything about the world around him is what I am calling the problem of our knowledge of the external world, and it is worth dwelling for a moment on just how difficult a problem that turns out to be if it has been properly raised.

If we are in the predicament Descartes finds himself in at the end of his *First Meditation* we cannot tell by means of the senses whether we are dreaming or not; all the sensory experiences we are having are compatible with our merely dreaming of a world around us while that world is in fact very different from the way we take it to be. Our knowledge is in that way confined to our sensory experiences. There seems to be no way of going beyond them to know that the world around us really is this way rather than that. Of course we might have very strongly held beliefs about the way things are. We might even be unable to get rid of the conviction that we are sitting by the fire holding a piece of paper, for example. But if we acknowledge that our sensory experiences are all we ever have to go on in gaining knowledge about the world, and we acknowledge, as we must, that given our experiences as they are we could nevertheless be simply dreaming of sitting by the fire, we must concede that we do not know that we are sitting by the fire. Of course, we are in no position to claim the opposite either. We cannot conclude that we are not sitting by the fire; we simply cannot tell which is the case. Our sensory experience gives us no basis for believing one thing about the world around us rather than its opposite, but our sensory experience is all we have got to go on. So whatever unshakeable conviction we might nevertheless retain, that conviction cannot be knowledge. Even if we are in fact holding a piece of paper by the fire, so that what we are convinced of is in fact true, that true conviction is still not knowledge. The world around us, whatever it might be like, is in that way beyond our grasp. We can know nothing of how it is, no matter what convictions, beliefs, or opinions we continue, perhaps inevitably, to hold about it.

What *can* we know in such a predicament? We can perhaps know what sensory experiences we are having, or how things seem to us to be. At least that much of our knowledge will not be threatened by the kind of attack Descartes makes on our knowledge of the world beyond our experiences. What we can know turns out to be a great deal less than we thought we knew before engaging in that assessment of our knowledge. Our position is much more restricted, much poorer, than we had originally supposed. We are confined at best to what Descartes calls "ideas" of things around us, representations of things or states of affairs which, for all we can know, might or might not have something corresponding to them in reality. We are in a sense imprisoned within those representations, at least with respect to our knowledge. Any attempt to go beyond them to try and tell whether the world really is as they represent it to be can yield only more representations, more deliverances of sense experience which themselves are compatible with reality's being very different from the way we take it to be on the basis of our sensory experiences. There is a gap, then, between the most that we can ever find out on the basis of our sensory experience and the way things really are. In knowing the one we do not thereby know the other.

This can seem to leave us in the position of finding a barrier between ourselves and the world around us. There would then be a veil of sensory experiences or sensory objects which we could not penetrate but which would be no reliable guide to the world beyond the veil. If we were in such a position, I think it is quite clear that we could not know what is going on beyond the veil. There would be no possibility of our getting reliable sensory information about the world beyond the veil; all such reports would simply be more representations, further ingredients of the evermore-complicated veil. We would know nothing but the veil itself. We would be in the position of someone waking up to find himself locked in a room full of television sets and trying to find out what is going on in the world outside. For all he can know, whatever is producing the patterns he can see on the screens in front of him might be something other than well-function cameras directed on to the passing show outside the room. The victim might switch on more of the sets in the room to try to get more information, and he might find that some of the sets show events exactly similar or coherently related to those already visible on the screens he can see. But all those pictures will be no help to him without some independent information, some knowledge which does not come to him from the pictures themselves, about how the pictures he does see before him are connected with what is going on outside the room. The problem of the external world is the problem of finding out, or knowing how we could find out, about the world around us if we were in that sort of predicament. It is perhaps enough simply to put the problem this way to convince us that it can never be given a satisfactory solution.

But putting the problem this way, or only this way, has its drawbacks. For one thing, it encourages a facile dismissive response; not a solution to the problem as posed, but a rejection of it. I do not mean that we should not find a way to reject the problem – I think that is our only hope – but this particular response, I believe, is wrong, or at the very least premature. It is derived almost entirely from the perhaps overly dramatic description of the predicament I have just given.

I have described Descartes's sceptical conclusion as implying that we are permanently sealed off from a world we can never reach. We are restricted to the passing show on the veil of perception, with no possibility of extending our knowledge to the world beyond. We are confined to appearances we can never know to match or to deviate from the imperceptible reality that is forever denied us. This way of putting it naturally encourages us to minimize the seriousness of the predicament, to try to settle for what is undeniably available to us, or perhaps even to argue that nothing that concerns us or makes human life worthwhile has been left out.

If an imperceptible "reality", as it is called on this picture, is forever inaccessible to us, what concern can it be of ours? How can something we can have no contact with, something from which we are permanently sealed off, even make sense to us at all? Why should we be distressed by an alleged limitation of our knowledge if it is not even possible for the "limitation" to be overcome? If it makes no sense to aspire to anything beyond what is possible for us, it will seem that we should give no further thought to this allegedly imperceptible "reality". Our sensory experiences, past, present, and future, will then be thought to be all we are or should be concerned with, and the idea of a "reality" lying beyond them necessarily out of our reach will seem like nothing more than a philosopher's invention. What a sceptical philosopher would be denying us would then be nothing we could have ordinary commerce with or interest in anyway. Nothing distressing about our ordinary position in the familiar world would have been revealed by a philosopher who simply invents or constructs something he calls "reality" or "the external world" and then demonstrates that we can have no access to it. That would show nothing wrong with the everyday sensory knowledge we seek and think we find in ordinary life and in scientific laboratories, nor would it show that our relation to the ordinary reality that concerns us is different from what we originally thought it to be.

I think this reaction to the picture of our being somehow imprisoned behind the veil of our own sensory experiences is very natural and immediately appealing. It is natural and perhaps always advisable for a prisoner to try to make the best of the restricted life behind bars. But however much more bearable it makes the prospect of life-imprisonment, it should not lead him to deny the greater desirability, let alone the existence, of life outside. In so far as the comfort of this response to philosophical scepticism depends on such a denial it is at the very least premature and is probably based on misunderstanding. It depends on a particular diagnosis or account of how and why the philosophical argument succeeds in reaching its conclusion. The idea is that the "conclusion" is reached only by contrivance. The inaccessible "reality" denied to us is said to be simply an artefact of the philosopher's investigation and not something that otherwise should concern us. That is partly a claim about how the philosophical investigation of knowledge works; as such, it needs to be explained and argued for. We can draw no consolation from it until we have some reason to think it might be an accurate account of what the philosopher does. So far we have no such

reason. On the contrary; so far we have every reason to think that Descartes has revealed the impossibility of the very knowledge of the world that we are most interested in and which we began by thinking we possess or can easily acquire. In any case, that would be the only conclusion to draw if Descartes's investigation does indeed parallel the ordinary kinds of assessments we make of our knowledge in everyday life.

We saw that I can ask what I really know about the common cold, or whether I really know that the witness was in Cleveland on the night in question, and that I can go on to discover that I do not really know what I thought I knew. In such ordinary cases there is no suggestion that what I have discovered is that I lack some special, esoteric thing called "real knowledge", or that I lack knowledge of some exotic, hitherto-unheard-of domain called "reality". If I ask what I know about the common cold, and I come to realize that I do not really know whether it can be caused by sitting in a draught or not, the kind of knowledge I discover I lack is precisely what I was asking about or taking it for granted I had at the outset. I do not conclude with a shrug that it no longer matters because what I now find I lack is only knowledge about a special domain called "reality" that was somehow invented only to serve as the inaccessible realm of something called "real knowledge". I simply conclude that I don't really know whether colds are caused by sitting in draughts or not. If I say in a jury-room on Monday that we can eliminate the suspect because we know he was in Cleveland that night, and I then discover by reflection on Tuesday that I don't really know he was in Cleveland that night, what I am denying I have on Tuesday is the very thing I said on Monday that I had.

There is no suggestion in these and countless similar everyday cases that somehow in the course of our reflections on whether and how we know something we are inevitably led to change or elevate our conception of knowledge into something else called "real knowledge" which we showed no signs of being interested in at the beginning. Nor is it plausible to suggest that our ordinary assessments of knowledge somehow lead us to postulate a "reality" that is simply an artefact of our inquiries about our knowledge. When we ask whether we really know something we are simply asking whether we know that thing. The "really" signifies that we have had second thoughts on the matter, or that we are subjecting it to more careful scrutiny, or that knowledge is being contrasted with something else, but not that we believe in something called "real knowledge" which is different from or more elevated than the ordinary knowledge we are interested in. Knowing something differs from merely believing it or assuming it or taking it for granted or simply being under the impression that it is true, and so forth, so asking whether we really know something is asking whether we know it as opposed to, for example, merely believing it or assuming it or taking it for granted or simply being under the impression that it is true.

If that is true of our ordinary assessments of knowledge, and if Descartes's investigation of his knowledge that he is sitting by the fire with a piece of paper in his hand is just like those ordinary cases, his discovery that he doesn't know in the case he considers will have the same significance as it has in those ordinary cases. And if that example is indeed representative of our knowledge of the world around us, the kind of knowledge we are shown to lack will be the very kind of knowledge we originally thought we had of things like our sitting by the fire holding a piece of paper. Without a demonstration that Descartes's philosophical investigation differs from our ordinary assessments in some way that prevents its negative conclusion from having the kind of significance similar conclusions are rightly taken to have in everyday life, we can derive no consolation from the ungrounded idea that the reality from which he shows our knowledge is excluded does not or should not concern us anyway. It is the investigation of his everyday knowledge, and not merely the fanciful picture of a veil of perception, that generates Descartes's negative verdict.

But even if we did try to console ourselves with the thought that we can settle for what we *can* know on Descartes's account, how much consolation could it give us? The position Descartes's argument says we are in is much worse than what is contemplated in the optimistic response of merely shrugging off any concern with an imperceptible "reality".

For one thing, we would not in fact be left with what we have always taken to be the familiar objects of our everyday experience – tables and chairs, trees and flowers, bread and wine. If Descartes is right, we know nothing of such things. What we perceive and are in direct sensory contact with is never a physical object or state of affairs, but only a representation – something that could be just the way it is even if there were no objects at all of the sort it represents. So if we were to settle for the realm of things we could have knowledge about even if Descartes's conclusion were correct, we would not be settling for the comfortable world with which we began. We would have lost all of that, at least as something we can know anything about, and we would be restricted to facts about how things seem to us at the moment rather than how they are.

It might still be felt that after all nothing is certain in this changing world, so we should not aspire to firm truths about how things are. As long as we know that all or most of us agree about how things seem to us, or have seemed to us up till now, we might feel we have enough to give our social, cultural, and intellectual life as much stability as we can reasonably expect or need. But again this reaction does not really acknowledge the poverty or restrictedness of the position Descartes's sceptical conclusion would leave each of us in. Strictly speaking, there is no community of acting, experiencing and thinking persons I can know anything about if Descartes is correct. Other people, as I understand them, are not simply sensory experiences of mine; they too, if they exist, will therefore inhabit the unreachable world beyond my sensory experiences, along with the tables and chairs and other things about which I can know nothing. So at least with respect to what I can know I could not console myself with thoughts of a like-minded community of perceivers all working together and cheerfully making do with what a communal veil of perception provides. I would have no more reason to believe that there are any other people than I have to believe that I am now sitting in a chair writing. The representations or sensory experiences to which Descartes's conclusion would restrict my knowledge could be no other than my own sensory experiences; there could be no communal knowledge even of the veil of perception itself. If my own sensory experiences do not make it possible for me to know things about the world around me they do not make it possible for me to know even whether there are any other sensory experiences or any other perceiving beings at all.

The consequences of accepting Descartes's conclusion as it is meant to be understood are truly disastrous. There is no easy way of accommodating oneself to its profound negative implications. But perhaps by now we have come far enough to feel that the whole idea is simply absurd, that ultimately it is not even intelligible, and that there can be no question of "accepting" Descartes's conclusion at all. I have no wish to discourage such a reaction. I would only insist that the alleged absurdity or unintelligibility must be identified and made out. I think that is the only way we can hope to learn whatever there is to be learned from Descartes's investigation.

Notes

1 It has been argued that the problem in the completely general form in which I discuss it here is in Descartes, and that nothing exactly similar appears in philosophy before that time. See M. F. Burnyeat, "Idealism and Greek Philosophy: What Descartes Saw and Berkely Missed", *The Philosophical Review* (1982).

2 See the beginning of the first of his *Meditations on First Philosophy* in *The Philosophical Works of Descartes*, edited and translated by E. S. Haldane and G. R. T. Ross (2 vols, New York, 1955), vol. I, p. 145. (Hereafter cited as HR.)

3 See his *Discourse on the Method of Rightly Conducting Reason and Seeking Truth in the Sciences* in HR, pp. 81 ff.

4 See G. E. Moore, "Certainty", this vol., ch. 4.

5 A memorable example H. H. Price gave in a lecture in 1962. It is my impression that Price was reporting on an actual hallucination of his.

CHAPTER 2

Proof of an External World

G. E. Moore

It seems to me that, so far from its being true, as Kant declares to be his opinion, that there is only one possible proof of the existence of things outside of us, namely the one which he has given, I can now give a large number of different proofs, each of which is a perfectly rigorous proof; and that at many other times I have been in a position to give many others. I can prove now, for instance, that two human hands exist. How? By holding up my two hands, and saying, as I make a certain gesture with the right hand, "Here is one hand", and adding, as I make a certain gesture with the left, "and here is another". And if, by doing this, I have proved *ipso facto* the existence of external things, you will all see that I can also do it now in numbers of other ways: there is no need to multiply examples.

But did I prove just now that two human hands were then in existence? I do want to insist that I did; that the proof which I gave was a perfectly rigorous one; and that it is perhaps impossible to give a better or more rigorous proof of anything whatever. Of course, it would not have been a proof unless three conditions were satisfied; namely (1) unless the premiss which I adduced as proof of the conclusion was different from the conclusion I adduced it to prove; (2) unless the premiss which I adduced was something which I *knew* to be the

From G. E. Moore, *Philosophical Papers* (New York: Collier Books, 1962), pp. 144–8.

case, and not merely something which I believed but which was by no means certain, or something which, though in fact true, I did not know to be so; and (3) unless the conclusion did really follow from the premiss. But all these three conditions were in fact satisfied by my proof. (1) The premiss which I adduced in proof was quite certainly different from the conclusion, for the conclusion was merely "Two human hands exist at this moment"; but the premiss was something far more specific than this – something which I expressed by showing you my hands, making certain gestures, and saying the words "Here is one hand, and here is another". It is quite obvious that the two were different, because it is quite obvious that the conclusion might have been true, even if the premiss had been false. In asserting the premiss I was asserting much more than I was asserting in asserting the conclusion. (2) I certainly did at the moment *know* that which I expressed by the combination of certain gestures with saying the words "Here is one hand and here is another". I *knew* that there was one hand in the place indicated by combining a certain gesture with my first utterance of "here" and that there was another in the different place indicated by combining a certain gesture with my second utterance of "here". How absurd it would be to suggest that I did not know it, but only believed it, and that perhaps it was not the case! You might as well suggest that I do not know that I am now standing up and talking – that perhaps after all I'm not, and that it's not quite certain that

I am! And finally (3) it is quite certain that the conclusion did follow from the premiss. This is as certain as it is that if there is one hand here and another here *now*, then it follows that there are two hands in existence *now*.

My proof, then, of the existence of things outside of us did satisfy three of the conditions necessary for a rigorous proof. Are there any other conditions necessary for a rigorous proof, such that perhaps it did not satisfy one of them? Perhaps there may be; I do not know; but I do want to emphasise that, so far as I can see, we all of us do constantly take proofs of this sort as absolutely conclusive proofs of certain conclusions – as finally settling certain questions, as to which we were previously in doubt. Suppose, for instance, it were a question whether there were as many as three misprints on a certain page in a certain book. A says there are, B is inclined to doubt it. How could A prove that he is right? Surely he *could* prove it by taking the book, turning to the page, and pointing to three separate places on it, saying "There's one misprint here, another here, and another here": surely that is a method by which it *might* be proved! Of course, A would not have proved, by doing this, that there were at least three misprints on the page in question, unless it was certain that there was a misprint in each of the places to which he pointed. But to say that he *might* prove it in this way, is to say that it *might* be certain that there was. And if such a thing as that could ever be certain, then assuredly it was certain just now that there was one hand in one of the two places I indicated and another in the other.

I did, then, just now, give a proof that there were *then* external objects; and obviously, if I did, I could *then* have given many other proofs of the same sort that there were external objects *then*, and could now give many proofs of the same sort that there are external objects *now*.

But, if what I am asked to do is to prove that external objects have existed *in the past*, then I can give many different proofs of this also, but proofs which are in important respects of a different *sort* from those just given. And I want to emphasise that, when Kant says it is a scandal not to be able to give a proof of the existence of external objects, a proof of their existence in the past would certainly *help* to remove the scandal of which he is speaking. He says that, if it occurs to anyone to question their existence, we ought to be able to

confront him with a satisfactory proof. But by a person who questions their existence, he certainly means not merely a person who questions whether any exist at the moment of speaking, but a person who questions whether any have *ever* existed; and a proof that some have existed in the past would certainly therefore be relevant to *part* of what such a person is questioning. How then can I prove that there have been external objects in the past? Here is one proof. I can say: "I held up two hands above this desk not very long ago; therefore two hands existed not very long ago; therefore at least two external objects have existed at some time in the past, QED". This is a perfectly good proof, provided I *know* what is asserted in the premiss. But I *do* know that I held up two hands above this desk not very long ago. As a matter of fact, in this case you all know it too. There's no doubt whatever that I did. Therefore I have given a perfectly conclusive proof that external objects have existed in the past; and you will all see at once that, if this is a conclusive proof, I could have given many others of the same sort, and could now give many others. But it is also quite obvious that this sort of proof differs in important respects from the sort of proof I gave just now that there were two hands existing *then*.

I have, then, given two conclusive proofs of the existence of external objects. The first was a proof that two human hands existed at the time when I gave the proof; the second was a proof that two human hands had existed at a time previous to that at which I gave the proof. These proofs were of a different sort in important respects. And I pointed out that I could have given, then, many other conclusive proofs of both sorts. It is also obvious that I could give many others of both sorts now. So that, if these are the sort of proof that is wanted, nothing is easier than to prove the existence of external objects.

But now I am perfectly well aware that, in spite of all that I have said, many philosophers will still feel that I have not given any satisfactory proof of the point in question. And I want briefly, in conclusion, to say something as to why this dissatisfaction with my proofs should be felt.

One reason why, is, I think, this. Some people understand "proof of an external world" as including a proof of things which I haven't attempted to prove and haven't proved. It is not quite easy to say *what* it is that they want proved – *what* it is that is such that unless they got a proof of it, they would not say that they had a proof of the existence of external things; but I can make an approach to explaining what they want by saying that if I had proved the propositions which I used as *premisses* in my two proofs, then they would perhaps admit that I had proved the existence of external things, but, in the absence of such a proof (which, of course, I have neither given nor attempted to give), they will say that I have not given what they mean by a proof of the existence of external things. In other words, they want a proof of what I assert *now* when I hold up my hands and say "Here's one hand and here's another"; and, in the other case, they want a proof of what I assert *now* when I say "I did hold up two hands above this desk just now". Of course, what they really want is not merely a proof of these two propositions, but something like a general statement as to how *any* propositions of this sort may be proved. This, of course, I haven't given; and I do not believe it can be given: if this is what is meant by proof of the existence of external things, I do not believe that any proof of the existence of external things is possible. Of course, in some cases what might be called a proof of propositions which seem like these can be got. If one of you suspected that one of my hands was artificial he might be said to get a proof of my proposition "Here's one hand, and here's another", by coming up and examining the suspected hand close up, perhaps touching and pressing it, and so establishing that it really was a human hand. But I do not believe that any proof is possible in nearly all cases. How am I to prove now that "Here's one hand, and here's another"? I do not believe I can do it. In order to do it, I should need to prove for one thing, as Descartes pointed out, that I am not now dreaming. But how can I prove that I am not? I have, no doubt, conclusive reasons for asserting that I am not now dreaming; I have conclusive evidence that I am awake: but that is a very different thing from being able to prove it. I could not tell you what all my evidence is; and I should require to do this at least, in order to give you a proof.

But another reason why some people would feel dissatisfied with my proofs is, I think, not merely that they want a proof of something which I haven't proved, but that they think that, if I cannot give such extra proofs, then the proofs that I have given are not conclusive proofs at all. And this, I think, is a definite mistake. They would say: "If you cannot prove your premiss that here is one hand and here is another, then you do not know it. But you yourself have admitted that, if you did not know it, then your proof was not conclusive. Therefore your proof was not, as you say it was, a conclusive proof." This view that, if I cannot prove such things as these, I do not know them, is, I think, the view that Kant was expressing in the sentence which I quoted at the beginning of this lecture, when he implies that so long as we have no proof of the existence of external things, their existence must be accepted merely on *faith*. He means to say, I think, that if I cannot prove that there is a hand here, I must accept it merely as a matter of faith – I cannot know it. Such a view, though it has been very common among philosophers, can, I think, be shown to be wrong – though shown only by the use of premisses which are not known to be true, unless we do know of the existence of external things. I can know things, which I cannot prove; and among things which I certainly did know, even if (as I think) I could not prove them, were the premisses of my two proofs. I should say, therefore, that those, if any, who are dissatisfied with these proofs merely on the ground that I did not know their premisses, have no good reason for their dissatisfaction.

CHAPTER 3

Four Forms of Scepticism

G. E. Moore

We pass next to the argument: "Descartes's malicious demon is a logical possibility." This is obviously quite different from both the two preceding. Russell does not say that any percepts *are* produced by Descartes's malicious demon; nor does he mean that it is practically or theoretically possible for Descartes's malicious demon to produce in me percepts like this, in the sense in which it is (perhaps) practically possible that a conjurer should, and theoretically possible that a physiologist should by stimulating the optic nerve. He only says it is a *logical possibility*. But what exactly does this mean? It is, I think, an argument which introduces quite new considerations, of which I have said nothing so far, and which lead us to the root of the difference between Russell and me. I take it that Russell is here asserting that it is *logically possible* that this particular percept of mine, which I think I know to be associated with a percept belonging to someone else, was in fact produced in me by a malicious demon when there was no such associated percept: and that, therefore, I cannot know for certain what I think I know. It is, of course, being assumed that, *if* it was produced by a malicious demon, then it follows that it is not associated with a percept belonging to someone else, in the way in which I think I know it is: that is how the phrase "was produced by a malicious demon" is being used. The questions we have to consider are, then, simply

these three: What is meant by saying that it is *logically possible* that this percept was produced by a malicious demon? Is it *true* that this is logically possible? And: If it is true, does it follow that I don't know for certain that it was *not* produced by a malicious demon?

Now there are three different things which might be meant by saying that this proposition is logically possible. The first is that it is not a self-contradictory proposition. This I readily grant. But from the mere fact that it is not self-contradictory, it certainly does not follow that I don't know for certain that it is false. This Russell grants. He holds that I do know for certain to be false, propositions about my percepts which are not self-contradictory. He holds, for instance, that I do know for certain that there is a white visual percept now; and yet the proposition that there isn't is certainly not self-contradictory.

He must, therefore, in his argument, be using "logically possible" in some other sense. And one sense in which it might naturally be used is this: Not logically incompatible with anything that I know. If, however, he were using it in this sense, he would be simply begging the question. For the very thing I am claiming to know is that this percept was *not* produced by a malicious demon: and of course the proposition that it was produced by a malicious demon *is* incompatible with the proposition that it was *not*.

There remains one sense, which is, I think, the sense in which he is actually using it. Namely he is

From G. E. Moore, *Philosophical Papers* (New York: Collier Books, 1962), pp. 220–2.

saying: The proposition "This percept was produced by a malicious demon" is *not* logically incompatible with anything you know *immediately*. And if this is what he means, I own that I think Russell is right. This is a matter about which I suppose many philosophers would disagree with us. There are people who suppose that I *do* know immediately, in certain cases, such things as: That person is conscious; at least, they use this language, though whether they mean exactly what I am here meaning by "know immediately" may be doubted. I can, however, not help agreeing with Russell that I never do know *immediately* that that person is conscious, nor anything else that is *logically incompatible* with "This percept was produced by a malicious demon." Where, therefore, I differ from him is in supposing that I do know for certain things which I do not know immediately and which also do *not* follow logically from anything which I do know immediately.

This seems to me to be the fundamental question at issue in considering my classes (3) and (4) and what distinguishes them from cases (1) and (2). I think I do know *immediately* things about myself and such things as "There was a sound like 'Russell' a little while ago" – that is, I think that memory is *immediate* knowledge and that much of my knowledge about myself is immediate. But I cannot help agreeing with Russell that I never know immediately such a thing as "That person is conscious" or "This is a pencil," and that also the truth of such propositions never follows logically from anything which I do know immediately, and yet I think that I do know such things for certain. Has he any argument for his view that if their falsehood is *logically possible* (i.e. if I do not know *immediately* anything logically incompatible with their falsehood) then I do *not* know them for certain? This is a thing which he certainly constantly assumes; but I cannot find that he anywhere gives any distinct arguments for it.

So far as I can gather, his reasons for holding it are the two assumptions which he expresses when he says: "If (I am to reject the view that my life is one long dream) I must do so on the basis of an analogical or inductive argument, which cannot give complete certainty."[1] That is to say he assumes: (1) My belief or knowledge that this is a pencil is, *if* I do not know it immediately, and if also the proposition does not follow logically from anything that I know immediately, in some sense "based on" an analogical or inductive argument; and (2) What is "based on" an analogical or inductive argument is never certain knowledge, but only more or less probable belief. And with regard to these assumptions, it seems to me that the first must be true in some sense or other, though it seems to me terribly difficult to say exactly what the sense is. What I am inclined to dispute, therefore, is the second: I am inclined to think that what is "based on" an analogical or inductive argument, in the sense in which my knowledge or belief that this is a pencil is so, may nevertheless be certain knowledge and *not* merely more or less probable belief.

What I want, however, finally to emphasize is this: Russell's view that I do not know for certain that this is a pencil or that you are conscious rests, if I am right, on no less than four distinct assumptions: (1) That I don't know these things immediately; (2) That they don't follow logically from any thing or things that I do know immediately; (3) That, *if* (1) and (2) are true, my belief in or knowledge of them must be "based on an analogical or inductive argument"; and (4) That what is so based cannot be *certain knowledge*. And what I can't help asking myself is this: Is it, in fact, as certain that all these four assumptions are true, as that I *do* know that this is a pencil and that you are conscious? I cannot help answering: It seems to me *more* certain that I *do* know that this is a pencil and that you are conscious, than that any single one of these four assumptions is true, let alone all four. That is to say, though, as I have said, I agree with Russell that (1), (2) and (3) *are* true; yet of no one even of these three do I feel *as* certain as that I do know for certain that this is a pencil. Nay more: I do not think it is *rational* to be as certain of any one of these four propositions, as of the proposition that I do know that this is a pencil. And how on earth is it to be decided which of the two things it is *rational* to be most certain of?

Note

1   Bertrand Russell, *An Outline of Philosophy*
    (Allen & Unwin: London, 1927), p. 218.

CHAPTER 4

Certainty

G. E. Moore

Suppose I say: "I know for certain that I am standing up; it is absolutely certain that I am; there is not the smallest chance that I am not." Many philosophers would say: "You are wrong: you do not know that you are standing up; it is *not* absolutely certain that you are; there is *some* chance, though perhaps only a very small one, that you are not." And one argument which has been used as an argument in favour of saying this, is an argument in the course of which the philosopher who used it would assert: "You do not know for certain that you are not dreaming; it is not absolutely certain that you are not; there is *some* chance, though perhaps only a very small one, that you are." And from this, that I do not know for certain that I am not dreaming, it is supposed to follow that I do not know for certain that I am standing up. It is argued: If it is not certain that you are not dreaming, then it is not certain that you are standing up. And that *if* I don't know that I'm not dreaming, I also don't know that I'm not sitting down, I don't feel at all inclined to dispute. From the hypothesis that I am dreaming, it would, I think, certainly follow that I don't *know* that I am standing up; though I have never seen the matter argued, and though it is not at all clear to me how it is to be proved that it would follow. But, on the other hand, from the hypothesis that I am dreaming,

it certainly would not follow that I am *not* standing up; for it is certainly logically possible that a man should be fast asleep and dreaming, while he is standing up and not lying down. It is therefore logically possible that I should both be standing up and also at the same time dreaming that I am; just as the story, about a well-known Duke of Devonshire, that he once dreamt that he was speaking in the House of Lords and, when he woke up, found that he *was* speaking in the House of Lords, is certainly logically possible. And if, as is commonly assumed, when I am dreaming that I am standing up it may also be correct to say that I am *thinking* that I am standing up, then it follows that the hypothesis that I am now dreaming is quite consistent with the hypothesis that I am both thinking that I am standing up and also actually standing up. And hence, if as seems to me to be certainly the case and as this argument assumes, from the hypothesis that I am now dreaming it *would* follow that I don't know that I am standing up, there follows a point which is of great importance with regard to our use of the word "knowledge" and therefore also of the word "certainly" – a point which has been made quite conclusively more than once by Russell, namely that from the conjunction of the two facts that a man thinks that a given proposition p is true, and that p is in fact true, it does *not* follow that the man in question *knows* that p is true: in order that I may be justified in saying that I know that I am standing up, something more is required than the

From G. E. Moore, *Philosophical Papers* (New York: Collier Books, 1962), pp. 240–6.

mere conjunction of the two facts that I both think I am and actually am – as Russell has expressed it, true belief is not identical with knowledge; and I think we may further add that even from the conjunction of the two facts that I feel certain that I am and that I actually am it would not follow that I know that I am, nor therefore that it *is* certain that I am. As regards the argument drawn from the fact that a man who dreams that he is standing up and happens at the moment actually to be standing up will nevertheless not *know* that he is standing up, it should indeed be noted that from the fact that a man is dreaming that he is standing up, it certainly does not *follow* that he *thinks* he is standing up; since it does sometimes happen in a dream that we *think* that it is a dream, and a man who thought this certainly might, although he was dreaming that he was standing up, yet *think* that he was not, although he could not *know* that he was not. It is not therefore the case, as might be hastily assumed, that, if I dream that I am standing up at a time when I am in fact lying down, I am necessarily *deceived*: I should be deceived only if I thought I was standing when I wasn't; and I may dream that I am, without thinking that I am. It certainly does, however, often happen that we do dream that so-and-so is the case, without at the time thinking that we are only dreaming; and in such cases, I think we may perhaps be said to *think* that what we dream is the case *is* the case, and to be deceived if it is not the case; and therefore also, in such cases, if what we dream to be the case happens also to *be* the case, we may be said to be thinking truly that it is the case, although we certainly do not *know* that it is.

I agree, therefore, with that part of this argument which asserts that if I don't know now that I'm not dreaming, it follows that I don't *know* that I am standing up, even if I both actually am and think that I am. But this first part of the argument is a consideration which cuts both ways. For, if it is true, it follows that it is also true that if I *do* know that I am standing up, then I do know that I am not dreaming. I can therefore just as well argue: since I do know that I'm standing up, it follows that I do know that I'm not dreaming; as my opponent can argue: since you don't know that you're not dreaming, it follows that you don't know that you're standing up. The one argument is just as good as the other, unless my opponent

can give better reasons for asserting that I don't know that I'm not dreaming, than I can give for asserting that I do know that I am standing up.

What reasons can be given for saying that I don't know for certain that I'm not at this moment dreaming?

I do not think that I have ever seen clearly stated any argument which is supposed to show this. But I am going to try to state, as clearly as I can, the premisses and the reasonings from them, which I think have led so many philosophers to suppose that I really cannot now know for certain that I am not dreaming.

I said, you may remember, in talking of the seven assertions with which I opened this lecture, that I had "the evidence of my senses" for them, though I also said that I didn't think this was the only evidence I had for them, nor that this by itself was necessarily conclusive evidence. Now if I had *then* "the evidence of my senses" in favour of the proposition that I was standing up, I certainly have *now* the evidence of my senses in favour of the proposition that I *am* standing up, even though this may not be all the evidence that I have, and may not be conclusive. But have I, in fact, the evidence of my senses *at all* in favour of this proposition? One thing seems to me to be quite clear about our use of this phrase, namely, that, if a man at a given time is only dreaming that he is standing up, then it follows that he has *not* at that time the evidence of his senses in favour of that proposition: to say "Jones last night was *only* dreaming that he was standing up, and yet all the time he had the evidence of his senses that he was" is to say something self-contradictory. But those philosophers who say it is possible that I am now dreaming, certainly mean to say also that it is possible that I am *only dreaming* that I am standing up; and this view, we now see, entails that it is possible that I have *not* the evidence of my senses that I am. If, therefore, they are right, it follows that it is not certain even that I have the evidence of my senses that I am; it follows that it is not certain that I have *the evidence of my senses* for anything at all. If, therefore, I were to say now, that I certainly have the evidence of my senses in favour of the proposition that I am standing up, even if it's not certain that I am standing up, I should be begging the very question now at issue. For if it is not certain that I am not dreaming, it is not certain that I even have the evidence of my senses that I am standing up.

But, now, even if it is not certain that I have at this moment the evidence of my senses for anything at all, it is quite certain that I *either* have the evidence of my senses that I am standing up *or* have an experience which is *very like* having the evidence of my senses that I am standing up. *If* I am dreaming, this experience consists in having dream-images which are at least very like the sensations I should be having if I were awake and had the sensations, the having of which would constitute "having the evidence of my senses" that I am standing up. Let us use the expression "sensory experience," in such a way that this experience which I certainly am having will be a "sensory experience," whether or not it merely consists in the having of dream-images. If we use the expression "sensory experience" in this way, we can say, I think, that, if it is not certain that I am not dreaming now, then it is not certain that *all* the sensory experiences I am now having are not mere dream-images.

What then are the premisses and the reasonings which would lead so many philosophers to think that all the sensory experiences I am having now *may* be mere dream-images – that I do not know for certain that they are not?

So far as I can see, one premiss which they would certainly use would be this: "Some at least of the sensory experiences which you are having now are similar in important respects to dream-images which actually have occurred in dreams." This seems a very harmless premiss, and I am quite willing to admit that it is true. But I think there is a very serious objection to the procedure of using it as a premiss in favour of the derived conclusion. For a philosopher who does use it as a premiss, is, I think, in fact *implying*, though he does not expressly say, that he himself knows it to be true. He is *implying* therefore that he himself knows that dreams have occurred. And, of course, I think he would be right. All the philosophers I have ever met or heard of certainly did know that dreams have occurred: we all know that dreams *have* occurred. But can he consistently combine this proposition that he knows that dreams have occurred, with his conclusion that he does not know that he is not dreaming? Can anybody possibly know that dreams have occurred, if, at the time, he does not himself know that he is not dreaming? If he *is* dreaming, it may be that he is only dreaming that dreams have occurred; and if

he does not know that he is not dreaming, can he possibly know that he is *not* only dreaming that dreams have occurred? Can he possibly know therefore that dreams *have* occurred? I do not think that he can; and therefore I think that anyone who uses this premiss and also asserts the conclusion that nobody ever knows that he is not dreaming, is guilty of an inconsistency. By using this premiss he implies that he himself knows that dreams have occurred; while, if his conclusion is true, it follows that he himself does not know that he is not dreaming, and therefore does not know that he is not only dreaming that dreams have occurred.

However, I admit that the premiss is true. Let us now try to see by what sort of reasoning it might be thought that we could get from it to the conclusion.

I do not see how we can get forward in that direction at all, unless we first take the following huge step, unless we say, namely: since there have been dream-images similar in important respects to some of the sensory experiences I am now having, it is logically possible that there should be dream-images *exactly like all* the sensory experiences I am now having, and logically possible, therefore, that all the sensory experiences I am now having *are* mere dream-images. And it might be thought that the validity of this step could be supported to some extent by appeal to matters of fact, though only, of course, at the cost of the same sort of inconsistency which I have just pointed out. It might be said, for instance, that some people have had dream-images which were *exactly like* sensory experiences which they had when they were awake, and that therefore it must be logically possible to have a dream-image exactly like a sensory experience which is *not* a dream-image. And then it may be said: If it is logically possible for some dream-images to be exactly like sensory experiences which are not dream-images, surely it must be logically possible for *all* the dream-images occurring in a dream at a given time to be exactly like sensory experiences which are not dream-images, and logically possible also for all the sensory experiences which a man has at a given time when he is awake to be exactly like all the dream-images which he himself or another man had in a dream at another time.

Now I cannot see my way to deny that it is logically possible that all the sensory experiences

I am having now should be mere dream-images. And if this is logically possible, and if further the sensory experiences I am having now were the only experiences I am having, I do not see how I could possibly know for certain that I am not dreaming.

But the conjunction of my memories of the immediate past with these sensory experiences *may* be sufficient to enable me to know that I am not dreaming. I say it *may* be. But what if our sceptical philosopher says: It is *not* sufficient; and offers as an argument to prove that it is not, this: It is logically possible *both* that you should be having all the sensory experiences you are having, and also that you should be remembering what you do remember, and *yet* should be dreaming. If this *is* logically possible, then I don't see how to deny that I cannot possibly know for certain that I am not dreaming: I do not see that I possibly could. But can any reason be given for saying that it *is* logically possible? So far as

I know nobody ever has, and I don't know how anybody ever could. And so long as this is not done my argument, "I know that I am standing up, and therefore I know that I am not dreaming," remains at least as good as his, "You don't know that you are not dreaming, and therefore don't know that you are standing up." And I don't think I've ever seen an argument expressly directed to show that it is not.

One final point should be made clear. It is certainly logically possible that I *should have* been dreaming now; I *might* have been dreaming now; and therefore the proposition that I *am* dreaming now is not self-contradictory. But what I am in doubt of is whether it is logically possible that I should *both* be having all the sensory experiences and the memories that I have and *yet* be dreaming. The conjunction of the proposition that I have these sense experiences and memories with the proposition that I am dreaming does seem to me to be very likely self-contradictory.

CHAPTER 5

How a Pyrrhonian Skeptic Might Respond to Academic Skepticism

Peter Klein

How much do we know? My answer is that we do not know what the extent of our knowledge is. But since that answer is not *immediately* evident it will require us to employ our reasoning. Thus, the question really becomes this: can our reasoning ever give a definitive reply to the question about the extent of our knowledge? And that is just a specific instance of the general question: is our reasoning able to settle anything, where some claim is *settled by reasoning* just in case no further reasons are required to make the proposition completely justified? It is crucial to note that in the way in which I will be using "completely justi-fied"; a proposition could be completely justified and false. Hence, I am not asking whether reason-ing is infallible. In addition, a proposition could be completely justified and defeasible. Hence, I am not asking whether reasoning can produce indefeasible justifications. The question is whether reasoning – the process of producing reasons for our beliefs – is ever such that further, as yet unused, reasons cannot be legitimately required.

Although I will be arguing that reasoning cannot settle anything, there is a rather quick and dirty argument to that same conclusion that might seem obviously correct which I wish to

reject at the outset. It is this: any argument for the claim that reasoning can settle matters will, of necessity, beg the question because one is employing the very capacity that is at issue in the argument.

Now, some might respond to that argument by saying that some circular reasoning is permissible – especially if it is logically impossible to avoid it.[1] But I believe all circular reasoning to a disputed conclusion that has no warrant aside from that provided by the argument is fallacious (more about this later). Thus, if "reasoning can settle matters" were undisputed and had some prima facie warrant not dependent upon an argu-ment (or arguments), then perhaps the fact that it cohered with other propositions could raise its warrant. But I take it that neither of those condi-tions obtains. Since the pre-Socratics, the ability of reasoning to settle matters has been contested, and whatever warrant a favourable assessment of reasoning has derives from an argument (or arguments). Thus, if the argument(s) for the claim that reasoning can settle matters employed that very proposition as a premise, that argument (or those arguments) could provide no basis for thinking that our methods of arriving at beliefs can settle matters.[2]

But why should one think that all arguments to the conclusion that good reasoning is reliable must employ that proposition as a premise? Here is an argument that does not do that:

Originally published in Steven Loper (ed.), *The Skeptics: Contemporary Essays* (Aldershot: Ashgate, 2003), pp. 75–94.

1   Good reasoning satisfies conditions C.
2   Anything satisfying conditions C can settle matters.
3   Therefore, good reasoning can settle matters.

Is that argument circular? No. No premise employs the conclusion. And I can see no reason why a sub-argument for either premise (1) or for premise (2) must employ (3) in one of its premises and so on. I think that there might be such an argument with true premises that can provide us with some reasons for thinking that reasoning can settle matters (but those reasons would not *settle* whether reasoning settles matters).

So, what would lead anyone to think that such arguments must be circular? The answer, I believe, is that any prudent person who believes (3) will employ what he/she takes to be good reasoning in fashioning the argument for (3). But doing so does not commit the fallacy of circular *reasoning*. Indeed, doing so makes one's practices consistent with one's beliefs. As we will see, satisfying the belief/practice consistency requirement is a problem for the foundationalist but not for a type of skeptic – the Pyrrhonian type. My point here is that were I not to use what I took to be good reasoning in arguing for (3), I would legitimately be accused of not practising what I preach.

Nevertheless, I do believe (but am not prepared to say that I know) that our reasoning cannot settle anything, including the question about the extent of our knowledge. Pessimism, however, is not the proper response to that assessment of the power of reasoning. I value reasoning, as I think we all do. (The "we" in the previous sentence means "adult human beings".) What we value is having good enough reasons for our (actual) beliefs so that it is (i) more reasonable to hold them than to withhold them and (ii) more reasonable to hold them than to hold any contrary propositions. We might not value having such good reasons above all other things – like faith, or the pursuit of evil, or the satisfaction of our appetites. But even the religious, the wicked or the hedonist value reasoning instrumentally because they want their beliefs to be efficacious and they believe that reasoning will assist them in achieving that goal.

Wanting good enough reasons is one thing, but if we begin inquiry with the hope or expectation that reasoning can settle matters, pessimism or dogmatism will be the *likely* result. Pessimism, if we believe that our goal hasn't yet been satisfied; dogmatism, if we believe that our goal has been reached because we might then refuse to inquire further thinking that only misleading new information could be uncovered.[3] But if we set what I think is the only realistic goal, namely *provisionally justified belief*, that is belief in a proposition that, *as far as we have reasoned* satisfies (i) and (ii) above, we can – and at least sometimes will – recognize that further inquiry is always appropriate.

Thus, this chapter can be seen as a defence of a form of Pyrrhonism (named after Pyrrho, *c.*300 BC) which endorses neither the claim that we have knowledge nor the claim that we do not have knowledge. This must be carefully distinguished from the more common form of skepticism that many, if not most, contemporary philosophers find interesting primarily because it seems to them to be *both* highly implausible and perniciously difficult to reject once the argument for it is investigated. That form of skepticism has been called "Academic skepticism" because it was endorsed by members of the Late Academy founded by Plato, "Cartesian skepticism" because of the arguments investigated by Descartes and his critics in the mid-seventeenth century, and "switched world" skepticism by contemporary philosophers because it involves imaging oneself to be in some possible world that is both vastly different from the actual world and at the same time absolutely indistinguishable (at least by us) from the actual world. I will most often use "Academic skepticism" but in order to avoid wearisome repetition, I will occasionally refer to the same view with one of the other labels. Its central claim is that we do not (in fact, cannot) have knowledge or *any* type of justified belief – even provisionally justified belief. I will examine the standard argument for Academic skepticism from the Pyrrhonian perspective in order to illustrate my general claim that reasoning cannot settle matters.

Academic Skepticism

Here is a way of stating the standard argument for Academic skepticism:[4]

1 If a person, say S, is justified (to some positive degree, *d*) in believing that there is a table before her, then S is justified (to degree *d*) in believing that she is not in one of the skeptical scenarios in which there is no table but it appears just as though there were one.

2 S is never justified (to degree *d*) in believing that she is not in one of the skeptical scenarios in which there is no table but it appears just as though there were one.

Therefore, S is never justified (to degree *d*) in believing that there is a table before her.

This is deeply puzzling because it appears that the premises are true, that the argument is valid (that is, it is not possible for the premises to be true and the conclusion false) but, at the same time, the conclusion appears false. Further, it *seems* that there are only *three* possible responses: (1) deny at least one premise of the argument; (2) deny that the argument is valid; (3) accept the conclusion.[5] None of those options seems initially promising.

The belief that we have no knowledge seems preposterous and the argument certainly seems valid. Thus, the strategy of choice for rejecting Academic skepticism has been to deny at least one of the premises. But the prospects of finding a basis for rejecting a premise are dim because, on close inspection, the arguments for doing so seem to rest on assumptions that are both unmotivated and ones which the Academic skeptic should reject. There are many types of those arguments, but I will consider only one type in order merely to illustrate my point (as opposed to demonstrating it). I chose this argument against Academic skepticism because it has struck many as the most plausible and also because investigating it will prove to be very useful later.

To unbag the cat now: I do not think that there is a good response available within the three alternatives just mentioned but I will propose a *fourth* alternative response to Academic skepticism that employs the general considerations about the limits of reasoning which I will be exploring. But, for now, let us focus on what I think is the most plausible argument against Cartesian skepticism that can be given within the three options listed above.

It is an argument based upon some supposed counter-examples to the general principle underlying premise 1. That principle, called the closure principle, goes like this:

Closure principle: if someone, say S, is justified (to any positive degree, *d*) in believing some proposition, say *p*, and if *p* strictly implies another proposition, say *q*, then S is justified in believing (to degree *d*) that *q*.

The issue is: does closure hold for justified belief? Closure certainly does hold for some properties, for example truth. If *p* is true and it strictly implies *q*, then *q* is true. It just as clearly does not hold for other properties. If *p* is a belief of mine, and *p* strictly implies *q*, it does not follow that *q* is a belief of mine. For I might fail to see the implication or I simply might be epistemically perverse or I might be "wired" incorrectly (from birth or as the result of an injury). I might, for example, believe all of the axioms of Euclidean plane geometry, but fail to believe (or perhaps even refuse to believe) that the exterior angle of a triangle is equivalent to the sum of the two opposite interior angles.

Since closure does not hold for belief, it probably doesn't hold for justified belief when that entails that S actually has the belief.[6] In addition, since a necessary truth is entailed by every proposition, if S were justified in believing any proposition, then S would be justified in believing every necessary truth. But these are matters of detail and the principle can be repaired to account for these minor problems. We could, for example, restrict the range of the propositions justifiably believed to contingent ones, and we could restrict the entailments to known ones, and we could stipulate that S could be justified in believing that *p* without actually believing that *p*. The real issue is this: does closure hold for what we are *entitled* to believe (even if we don't, in fact, believe it)?

It certainly seems that it does. For if I am entitled to believe *p* and *p* strictly implies *q*, then how could I fail to be entitled to believe *q*? If, for example, I am justified in believing that today is Wednesday, then I must be justified in believing that it is not Thursday. Nevertheless, the principle has been challenged. Consider this much discussed counter-example to the closure principle developed by Fred Dretske:

something's being a zebra implies that it is not a mule ... cleverly disguised by the zoo authorities to look like a zebra. Do you know that these animals are not mules cleverly disguised? If you are tempted to say "Yes" to this question, think a moment about what reasons you have, what evidence you can produce in favor of this claim. The evidence you *had* for thinking them zebras has been effectively neutralized, since it does not count toward their *not* being mules cleverly disguised to look like zebras. (1970, pp. 1015–16)

Dretske is speaking of "knowledge" rather than beliefs to which one is entitled, but that seems irrelevant since the issue concerns the supposed lack of sufficient evidence or reasons for the claim that the animal is not a cleverly disguised mule.[7] In other words, Dretske grants that there is an adequate source of justification for the claim that the animal is a zebra, but he claims that the adequate source of evidence that you have for identifying the animals as zebras is not an adequate source for determining that they are not cleverly disguised mules.

The crucial thing to note about this proposed counter-example is that it works only if the closure principle entails that the *very same* evidence that justifies S in believing that the animals are zebras *must* justify S in believing that they are not cleverly disguised mules because, it is presumed, that is the only evidence that we can be sure S has. To generalize, the purported counter-example depends upon the assumption that the closure of justified belief depends upon it being the case that the very same evidence, *e*, that justifies S in believing the entailing proposition, *p*, also justifies S in believing the entailed proposition *q*. Thus, letting "*x***R***y*" mean that *x* is an adequate reason for *y*, the counter-example depends upon assuming that if closure holds between *p* and *q*, then the evidence "path" must look like this:

Pattern 1

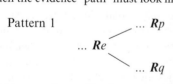

Evidence paths specify what propositions serve as good enough reasons, *ceteris paribus*, for believing other propositions. So, in Pattern 1 type cases, if S has good enough reasons for believing the proposition *e*, then S is entitled to "take" the evidence path to proposition *p*, and S is entitled to take the path to proposition *q*. So if S can get to point *e* on the path, S can get to points *p* and *q*.

This pattern illustrates the constraint on closure imposed by Dretske, namely that whenever *p* entails *q*, the adequate evidence, *e*, for *p* is the *very* same evidence that is adequate for *q*.

No doubt this constraint sometimes correctly portrays the relevant evidential relationships when some proposition, *p*, entails some other proposition, *q*. For example, suppose I have adequate evidence that Anne has two brothers, then it would seem that the very same evidence would be adequate for believing that Anne has at least one brother. But the Academic skeptic would (or at least should) point out that closure need not require that type of evidence path in all cases in which one proposition entails another.

There are two other possibilities for instantiating closure that can be depicted as follows:

Pattern 2 ... ***R****e***R***p*... ***R****q*
Pattern 3 ... ***R****e* (where *e* includes *q*) ***R****p*

In Pattern 2 cases there is some adequate evidence, *e*, for *p*; and *p*, itself, is the adequate evidence for *q*, since *p* strictly implies *q*. For example, if I have adequate evidence for believing that 2 is a prime number, I can use that proposition as an adequate reason for believing that there is at least one even prime. In Pattern 3 cases the order of the evidence is reversed because *q* serves as part of the evidence for *p*. For example, I am justified in believing that water is present if I am justified in believing that there is present a clear, odourless, watery-tasting and watery-looking fluid at STP. This pattern is typical of abductive inferences.

Thus, showing that there is no Pattern 1 type evidence path available to S in the zebra-in-the-zoo case is not sufficient to show that closure fails. Indeed, I would suggest that the animals looking like zebras in a pen marked "zebras" are, *ceteris paribus*, adequate evidence to provisionally justify the claim that they are zebras; and once S is entitled to believe that the animals are zebras, S can reasonably deduce from that proposition that they are not cleverly disguised mules. That is, S can employ an evidence path like that depicted in Pattern 2.[8] Or alternatively, if S had *some* reason to think that the animals were cleverly disguised mules, then S would have to eliminate that possibility before she could justifiably believe that they are zebras. In other words, in that case S would have to employ an evidence path like the one depicted in Pattern 3.

I think it is clear that this alleged refutation of Academic skepticism based upon the rejection of closure rests upon a premise that requires further reasons to support it, namely the premise that the appropriate evidential relationship between "the animals are zebras" and "the animals are not cleverly disguised mules" is that depicted in Pattern 1. There are other patterns of reasoning that instantiate closure and until some reason is given for thinking that the appropriate pattern in this case is Pattern 1, reasoning would have failed to settle whether closure should be rejected.

Thus, one of the purposes of exploring this argument against Academic skepticism has been fulfilled, namely to illustrate the general claim I will be defending shortly that our reasoning cannot settle matters. The other purpose was to gesture in the direction of a general claim that the prospects are dim for the success of any one of the three alternative responses to the argument for Academic skepticism mentioned above. I have certainly not demonstrated that there is no way to respond to the Academic skeptic within the three alternatives. But I have shown that one of the better known responses is not compelling.

So, here is what remains for me to do:

1 Argue that reasoning, in general, cannot settle matters, but that provisionally justified belief is still possible.
2 Apply that general conclusion to the arguments *for* academic skepticism in order to delineate the fourth alternative response mentioned earlier.

Pyrrhonian Skepticism

My belief that reasoning cannot settle matters can be traced to a famous passage in Sextus Empiricus's *Outlines of Pyrrhonism* in the chapter called "The Five Modes" in which he discusses the regress problem. Although the chapter title mentions five modes, two of them repeat those found elsewhere.[9] They are the modes of discrepancy and relativity and are important here because they provide the background for understanding the description of the three modes of reasoning. Specifically, it is presumed that the relevant object

of inquiry is subject to actual or potential dispute and that reasoning is employed to resolve the dispute. The issue before us then is whether there is a mode of reasoning that can settle matters about which there is some dispute. Of those modes, Sextus writes:

> The Mode based upon regress *ad infinitum* is that whereby we assert that the thing adduced as a proof of the matter proposed needs a further proof, and this again another, and so on *ad infinitum*, so that the consequence is suspension [of assent], as we possess no starting-point for our argument … We have the Mode based upon hypothesis when the Dogmatists, being forced to recede *ad infinitum*, take as their starting-point something which they do not establish but claim to assume as granted simply and without demonstration. The Mode of circular reasoning is the form used when the proof itself which ought to establish the matter of inquiry requires confirmation derived from the matter; in this case, being unable to assume either in order to establish the other, we suspend judgement about both. (1993, I, pp. 166–9)

I will call the first account of the normative conditions required for complete justification "infinitism".[10] Today we commonly refer to the second account as "foundationalism". Finally, I will refer to the third possibility as "coherentism" – but some important distinctions between forms of coherentism will be discussed below.

The regress problem, then, can be stated briefly in this way: there is a trilemma facing all who attempt to use reasoning to settle matters. Either foundationalism, coherentism or infinitism is the appropriate method of responding to the regress of reasons. Foundationalism appears to advocate a process of reasoning that relies upon arbitrary propositions at the base. (What makes a proposition arbitrary will be discussed later.) Coherentism is nothing but a thinly disguised form of circular reasoning. Finally, infinitism advocates a process of justification that could never be completed.

Put another way: there are only three normative constraints that could apply to any instance of reasoning. For either the process of producing reasons properly stops at foundational beliefs or it doesn't. If it does, then foundationalism is correct. If it doesn't, then either reasoning is properly circular, or it is properly infinite and non-repeating.[11]

There are no other possibilities.[12] Thus, if none of these forms of reasoning can settle matters, no form can.

My view of the matter is that (1) the hinted-at arguments of the Pyrrhonians against *foundationalism* and *coherentism*, when properly fleshed out, *do* render plausible the claim that those forms of reasoning are inherently unacceptable models of good reasoning because they cannot provide the basis for *any* type of rational practice leading to the acceptance of beliefs. But (2) infinitism, when properly understood, appears acceptable and can lead to *provisional justification*.

So, I want now to take up foundationalism and coherentism and provide some reasons for thinking that they cannot provide a good model for reasoning, where *reasoning* is understood simply to be the process of producing reasons for our beliefs. Then, we will turn to infinitism. Finally, I want to apply the lessons learned in the general discussion of reasoning to the problem with which we started, namely the standard argument for Academic skepticism, in order to explain the fourth alternative response, mentioned above, to that form of skepticism.

Foundationalism

Foundationalism comes in many forms. But all forms hold that all propositions are either basic propositions or non-basic propositions and no proposition is both. *Basic propositions* have some autonomous bit of warrant that does not depend (at all) upon the warrant of any other proposition.[13] *Non-basic* propositions depend (directly or indirectly) upon basic propositions for all of their warrant.

I do not believe that this account of the structure of reasons can provide a model of reasoning that can be rationally practised. My discussion of this issue will be reminiscent of Laurence BonJour's (1978) rejection of foundationalism but unlike his argument, I am *not* claiming (here) that this account of the structure of reasons is false.[14] My claim is that a foundationalist cannot rationally practise his foundationalism because it inevitably leads to arbitrariness, that is asserting a proposition for no reason at all.

To see that foundationalism cannot provide a rational model of reasoning consider a discussion between two people: the Foundationalist, Fred, and the Pyrrhonian Skeptic, Sally. Fred begins by saying that he believes that p. He might say something quite strong like "I know that p" or "p is certainly true" or "I have conclusive reasons for p", or he might just say "p is true" or even just "p" with the appropriate gusto. The Pyrrhonian Skeptic, Sally, asks Fred-the-foundationalist why he believes that p is true. Fred gives his reason for believing that p, say q. Again, Sally asks Fred why he believes that q is true. Fred replies. This goes on a while. Finally, Fred (being a foundationalist) replies by citing what he takes to be a basic proposition, b.

Sally then asks Fred, "Why do you think b is true?" Fred, being a self-conscious foundationalist, replies that b is properly basic and has some warrant that does not depend upon any further reason for thinking b is true.[15] To use our terminology, Fred is claiming that b has some autonomous bit of warrant. Sally replies as follows, "But Fred, what I asked you was 'What makes you think b is true?' and you replied, in part, by claiming that b is a basic proposition. So you must think that because a proposition is basic there is some positive likelihood, however small, that it is true. Right? That is, you must think that propositions possessing the autonomous bit of warrant are more likely to be true than they would be were they not to possess that autonomous bit of warrant. Why do you think that possession of autonomous warrant is linked in any way with truth?"

We have come to the crucial point in the discussion. For Fred faces a dilemma. Either Fred will give a reason for thinking that the possession of autonomous warrant is at least somewhat truth-conducive or he won't.

Consider the first alternative. If Fred has a reason for thinking that propositions possessing the autonomous bit of warrant are, in virtue of that fact, likely to be true (even to some small extent), then the regress has not actually stopped, for Fred has a reason for thinking that b is true. Fred has given up his foundationalism in order to satisfy a perfectly reasonable question, namely "Do you think the possession of autonomous warrant is linked to truth?"

Now, consider the second alternative and suppose that Fred does not have a reason for thinking that b's possession of the autonomous bit of warrant makes it at all likely that b, or any other basic proposition, is true. Then Fred ought (rationally) to give up assenting to all basic and non-basic propositions.[16] After all, Fred has no reason for thinking that the basic ones are (somewhat likely to be) true by virtue of whatever he thinks makes them basic and, being a foundationalist, he believes that without the warrant provided by the basic propositions, the non-basic ones are not warranted. He has been forced to admit that accepting basic propositions and everything that depends upon them is arbitrary – meaning by *arbitrary* that there are no better reasons for thinking that they are true than for thinking that they are false.[17]

Consider an example: suppose that it is argued, along contextualist lines, that some propositions just don't need to be justified – what makes a proposition *properly* basic is some fact about the context – perhaps that it is accepted by some specified group of people.[18]

First, I don't think that is a plausible characterization of the property that could possibly make a proposition basic.[19] I grant that on many occasions the foundationalist will not be challenged to provide a reason for the offered basic proposition – perhaps because everyone in the relevant context believes it and accepts it as a reason for further beliefs. But it is crucial to note that the unchallenged stopping points could include a wide variety of propositions. Suppose the issue at hand is whether there is an American football game on TV today. The response, "Today is New Year's Day" might stop the conversation. Similarly, "The newspaper said so" or "My mother told me" could all be conversation-stoppers. But are they basic in the sense required by the foundationalist? I doubt it. They do not have any autonomous warrant. For if I didn't believe that I was correctly reading the calendar, or that I am correctly remembering the newspaper story, or that I understood what my mother said, the conversation-stopping propositions would possess *no warrant at all*.

Second, and more to the point, even if contextualism correctly identified what makes a proposition basic, the crucial point here is that the contextualist response does not serve to stop the regress. For the foundationalistic contextualist will still be asked this: does the fact that a proposition is a conversation-stopper give anyone any reason for thinking that it is true? And Fred's dilemma returns.

Now consider a more traditional brand of foundationalism and suppose that Fred offers a first-person introspective report as the basic proposition, for example "I seem to remember that there is a football game on TV today". When asked why he thinks that it is true that he seems to remember that there is a game, Fred could say that he has no reasons for thinking it is true – he just does think it is true. Arbitrariness looms. What is much more likely is that Fred will come up with a story about how he acquires knowledge of his memories – a story told to get Sally to see why introspection delivers propositions that are (at least) likely to be true. It could be a relatively straightforward story about our privileged access to certain kinds of our states, for example certain kinds of mental states, as contrasted with our ability to gain knowledge of other of our states. Privileged access, it could be claimed, is just that sort of access such that the content of what is delivered is very likely to be true. Or the story that Fred could tell could be a relatively complex one – perhaps even one that Fred thinks contains a priori propositions – about the meaning of some "methodologically basic" words and the conditions for their application which guarantee that they are "true in the main".[20] The content of the story is not crucial here. What is crucial is that Fred is giving his reasons for thinking that propositions of a certain sort are likely to be true. Thus, in order to avoid arbitrariness, Fred has offered reasons for thinking that introspection reports or propositions about methodologically basic items are likely to be true. In other words, the regress continues.

It is crucial to recall that I am *not* claiming that foundationalism is false. Perhaps some propositions do have autonomous warrant which is truth-conducive and all other propositions depend for some of their warrant upon those basic propositions (although I doubt it). What I am claiming is that there is a deep irrationality in being a practising self-conscious foundationalist. If Fred remains true to his foundationalism, he will not provide a reason for thinking that the basic proposition, *b*, is true unless that reason ultimately depends upon other basic propositions. But basic propositions are supposed to have some warrant that does not depend upon another proposition being warranted. So, the question to Fred can be put this way: on the assumption that you cannot appeal to any other proposition, do you still think *b* is true? Fred not only won't have any such reason for thinking *b* is true, given that constraint, he *cannot* have one (if he remains true to his foundationalism). Arbitrariness is inevitable. Of course, foundationalists typically realize this and, in order to avoid arbitrariness, tell some story that, if true, would provide a reason for thinking basic propositions are at least somewhat likely to be true. But then the regress of reasons has continued. Foundationalism, then, cannot provide a good model for reasoning since, when practised, it endorses arbitrariness.

Coherentism

Let us now turn to coherentism. This section can be much shorter because we can apply some of the lessons learned in the discussion of foundationalism.

At its base, coherentism holds that there are no propositions with autonomous warrant. But it is important to note that coherentism comes in two forms. What I choose to call the "warrant-transfer form" responds to the regress problem by suggesting that the propositions are arranged in a circle and that warrant is transferred within the circle – just as basketball players standing in a circle pass the ball from one player to another.[21] I could, for example, reason that it rained last night by calling forth my belief that there is water on the grass and I could reason that there is water (as opposed to some other liquid, say glycerin, that looks like water) on the grass by calling forth my belief that it rained last night.

At the beginning of the chapter, I claimed that all circular reasoning in which the contested conclusion was employed as a premise and for which no warrant existed beyond what was available to be transferred via the argument was fallacious. That is the model of reasoning embedded in the warrant-transfer form of coherentism. It seems to me that Aristotle explained why it is fallacious. As he put it: this is a "simple way of proving anything" (1994: bk I, ch. 3, 73a5). The propositions in the circle might be mutually probability enhancing, but the point is that we could just as well have circular reasoning to the conclusion that it did not rain last night because the liquid is not water and the liquid is not water because it

did not rain last night. In this fashion anything could be justified – too simply! It is ultimately arbitrary which set of mutually probability enhancing propositions we believe because there is no basis for preferring one over the other.

The warrant-transfer coherentist could attempt to reply to this objection by claiming that there is some property in one of the two competing circles that is not present in the other and the presence of that property makes one and only one of the circles properly circular. For example, in one and only one of the circles are there propositions that we actually believe, or perhaps believe spontaneously (BonJour 1985). More generally, the coherentist could claim that all and only circles with some property, *P*, have some initial plausibility. But then it is clear that the warrant-transfer coherentist has adopted a form of foundationalism because she is now claiming that all and only the propositions in circles with *P* have the autonomous bit of warrant. And, all that we have said about the dilemma facing the foundationalist transfers immediately. Is the possession of *P* truth-conducive or not? If it is … well, you can see how that would go.

So much for the warrant-transfer version of coherentism. The second form of coherentism, what we can call the "warrant-emergent form", does not imagine the circle as consisting of propositions that transfer their warrant from one proposition to another. Rather warrant for each proposition in the circle depends upon the fact that they are mutually probability enhancing. Coherence itself is the property by virtue of which each member of the set of propositions has warrant. Warrant emerges all at once, so to speak, from the web-like structure of the propositions. The coherentist can then argue that the fact that the propositions cohere provides each of them with some prima facie credibility.

This might initially seem to be a more plausible view since it avoids the circularity charge. But, aside from the fact that there are, again, just too many competing circles that are coherent, there is one, by now very familiar, problem with this alternative. It is crucial to note that the coherentist is now explicitly assigning some initial positive warrant to all of the individual propositions in a set of coherent propositions that does not depend upon the warrant of any other proposition in the set. In other words, he is assigning to them what we have called the autonomous bit of warrant. Thus, this coherentist has, once again, endorsed a form of foundationalism and, once again, the dilemma facing the foundationalist returns.

Let me sum up where we are at this point. There seems no way for the foundationalist or the coherentist to avoid arbitrariness *and* at the same time stop the regress. It is now time to consider what happens if the regress is unavoidable.

Infinitism

Infinitism is the view that the answer to the regress problem is that the regress never properly ends. There is always another reason, one that has not already been employed, that can legitimately be required for each reason that is given for a belief. Only if there is an infinite set of non-repeating reasons available for a belief is it fully justifiable.

There is an obvious objection to this form of reasoning as a method for settling what we should believe. Here's a close paraphrase of the objection as put by Jonathan Dancy:

> Suppose that all justification is inferential. We justify belief A by appeal to belief B, and belief B by appeal to C. The result is that A is justified only if B and C are. Justification by inference is conditional justification only; A's justification is conditional upon the justification of B and C. But if all justification is conditional in this sense, then nothing is actually non-conditionally justified. (1985, p. 55)[22]

My response is that Dancy is absolutely right: infinitism does not sanction non-conditional justification. But that is quite different from the objections we discovered to foundationalism and coherentism. There we found that those models of reasoning were unacceptable because they endorsed arbitrariness or circularity. We have just seen that infinitism is not able to provide an account of a type of reasoning that would *settle* matters because each belief in the set of offered reasons is only provisionally justified. But that does *not* lead to the conclusion that infinitism is unable to be practised rationally.

So the question becomes this: can the practising infinitist be provisionally justified in believing

one proposition over its competitors and provisionally justified in believing it rather than withholding belief?

First, it is important to note that the infinitist can rationally practise what she thinks is the correct solution to the Pyrrhonian trilemma even though the process of justifying a proposition is never completed. When needed, the infinitist can always seek a further reason. Contrast this with, say, the foundationalist who must produce a reason for which no further reason *can* be given – even when sincerely requested.[23]

Second, infinitism provides a good model for provisionalism. Here's how it goes. The infinitist finds a reason, q, for her belief, p. She would not think that it is settled whether p is true because she knows that she will never complete the process of providing the infinite set of reasons for p (if there is such a set). However, if she does locate *a* reason for p and she doesn't have an equally good or better reason against it, it would be more reasonable to believe p than to deny p or withhold *p because she does have a reason for believing it.* Indeed, on many occasions perhaps we can't help but believe p – at least to some extent – if we have better reasons for it than against it. But we can assess the epistemic situation and, as infinitists, come to recognize that we ought not to think it is settled that p, even though it is more reasonable to believe p than to deny p or to withhold p.

A Clarification and Partial Defence of Infinitism

Nevertheless, it is one thing to claim that infinitism can provide an acceptable account of rational belief and another to claim that infinitism is true. This is not the place for a full-blown defence of infinitism.[24] But I would like to consider one reason that has been offered for rejecting it because doing so will help to clarify infinitism.

The worry is simply this: how could I have an infinite number of beliefs? I have a finite mind. Here is how John Williams puts this worry:

> The [proposed] regress of justification of S's belief that p would certainly require that he holds an infinite number of beliefs. This is psychologically, if not logically, impossible. If a man can

believe an infinite number of things, then there seems to be no reason why he cannot know an infinite number of things. Both possibilities contradict the common intuition that the human mind is finite. Only God could entertain an infinite number of beliefs. But surely God is not the only justified believer. (1978, pp. 311–12)

I think this worry (or perhaps set of worries) can be resolved by clarifying what infinitism claims. It is crucial to remember that infinitism is not a form of dogmatism. It acknowledges that we do not ever have fully justified beliefs – perhaps that epistemic state is available only to a being that could *consciously* and *simultaneously* entertain an infinite number of beliefs. But the issue here is not whether we can be fully justified, it is whether we can have provisionally justified beliefs.

Nevertheless, there is a deep worry here that does not depend essentially upon how many or how few conscious states, that is non-overlapping temporal states, humans can occupy during a finite time period. The worry is this: there is no reason to believe that there is an infinite number of propositions available to us that could serve as reasons for our beliefs.

The response to that worry is twofold. *First*, like foundationalism and coherentism, infinitism comes in two varieties – an optimistic and pessimistic form. What both varieties of infinitism have in common is the belief that the normative conditions for full or complete justification include the existence of an infinite series of non-repeating reasons available to us for our beliefs. The optimistic form goes on to claim that in the required sense there are such reasons available. The pessimistic variety says that there are no such reasons available.[25]

Consider the parallel with foundationalism. A foundationalist holds that the normative conditions of complete justification require that all of our non-foundational beliefs rest on some basic beliefs with autonomous warrant. An optimistic foundationalist – a Cartesian, for example – could claim that there are such foundational beliefs. A pessimistic foundationalist – a Humean, for example – could claim that (at least for many of our important beliefs) there is no such set of basic beliefs.

Infinitism is like foundationalism and coherentism because all three are theories about the normative conditions required for full justification. And each could have an optimistic or pessimistic form. Thus, it would not be an objection to infinitism to claim that there is no such infinite set of available propositions. Pessimistic infinitism is an available option.

Perhaps, though, the worry here is that infinitism comes in only the pessimistic form. If that were true, it would not constitute an *epistemic* reason for rejecting infinitism. For that which we have reason to believe true is sometimes quite discouraging. If pessimistic infinitism were the only reasonable alternative, we might strongly wish it to be otherwise and so, perhaps, it would be better, in some sense, were infinitism false.

But, *second*, I think the worry that infinitism comes in only the pessimistic form misconstrues what, in general, is required for a belief to be available and what, in particular, infinitism requires for beliefs to be available. Generally, beliefs are dispositions to sincerely assert something under the appropriate conditions. We can have those dispositions even if we have never consciously entertained the proposition. For example, I think that we all believe that pears don't normally grow on apple trees, that $61 + 346 = 407$, and that Chicago is east of every city in California, but most of us have never before considered those propositions. Thus, we might very well have an infinite number of beliefs even though we will never consciously entertain an infinite number of propositions.

Equally, if not more, important is the fact that we have the capacity to develop new reasons for our beliefs when we are called upon to do so. For example, at a certain point in human history we did not believe that diseases were caused by microscopic organisms. Nevertheless, we had the capacity to form that belief. Of course, we needed new experiences, insight and perhaps a certain amount of luck in order to form it. But the new belief was formed. Thus, beliefs might be *available* to us in the requisite sense even though we do not have them.

Infinitism requires only that there be an infinite set of distinct propositions each member of which we have the capacity to legitimately call forth as reasons for our beliefs.[26] It does not require that we have already formed the beliefs with those propositions as their contents. Optimistic infinitism says that there is such a set.

Pessimistic infinitism says that at some point we will run out of such available reasons. It predicts that we will hit a permanent brick wall of ultimate arbitrary beliefs or we will have to employ a reason that has already appeared in the path of reasons. History suggests to me – but of course it does not fully justify for me – that when we need new reasons for our beliefs we can find them.

No belief is ever fully justified for any person. The process of justifying a proposition is never completed. That is a consequence of infinitism. But that is not because there is no infinite set of propositions available that could serve as good reasons for our beliefs. Rather, no belief is fully justified because at no point in time will we have completed the process of justifying our beliefs. All justification is provisional. And as mentioned at the very beginning of this paper, that's a good thing to recognize since it provides a basis for avoiding pessimism and dogmatism.

Academic Skepticism Reconsidered

Now, before concluding, I want to return to the puzzle with which we began, namely the argument for Academic skepticism, and test what we have learned about reasoning. Does the standard argument beg the question or depend upon an arbitrary assumption for which there are no better reasons for believing than there are for denying? Recall where we left off. We saw that the argument for Academic skepticism looked pretty good: the premises seemed true and the argument seemed valid. Nevertheless, the conclusion seemed false. We also saw that one argument against premise 1 ended with an arbitrary assumption, namely that the closure of justified beliefs depended upon the claim that all reasoning sanctioned by closure was like that depicted in Pattern 1. Thus, we discovered one important instance of the general Pyrrhonian claim that arguments that end, end either arbitrarily or commit the fallacy of begging the question.

But there is another lesson here related to our discovery of the various patterns of reasoning that instantiate closure. For a careful examination of them reveals the fourth alternative, mentioned earlier, for appraising the standard argument *for* Academic skepticism, namely that it, too, either begs the question or is based upon an arbitrary

assumption. If that were true, the argument would give us no good reason for accepting that form of skepticism.

Recall the three patterns of reasoning exhibiting closure:

Pattern 1

Pattern 2   ... $Re Rp$... Rq
Pattern 3   ... Re (where e includes q) Rp

And recall the standard argument for Academic skepticism:

1. If a person, say S, is justified (to some positive degree, d) in believing that there is a table before her, then S is justified (to degree d) in believing that she is not in one of the skeptical scenarios in which there is no table but it appears just as though there were one.
2. S is never justified (to degree d) in believing that she is not in one of the skeptical scenarios in which there is no table but it appears just as though there were one.

Therefore, S is never justified (to degree d) in believing that there is a table before her.

Now, suppose that the Academic skeptic thinks that closure regarding justification holds between "there is a table before me" and "I am not in one of the skeptical scenarios in which there is no table but it appears just as though there were one" because the requisite evidential path exemplifies Pattern 1. That is, he holds that the *very same* evidence that is adequate for arriving at the proposition that there is a table is adequate for denying the skeptical hypothesis. Grant that premise 1 is true for that reason. But, now, when the Academic skeptic argues for premise 2 – as surely he must since it is not immediately evident – the sub-argument for premise 2 must be good enough to establish that there is no evidence adequate to justify the proposition that there is a table before him because the argument must be good enough to show that S cannot arrive at point e on the evidence path. For if S were able to do that, S would be able to arrive at the denial of the skeptical hypothesis. Hence, the argument for premise 2 would be sufficient to show that the conclusion is true and the argument employing premises 1 and 2 begs the question since the argument for premise 2 alone establishes the conclusion. The standard argument does not work.

The situation vis à vis this version of the argument for Academic skepticism is similar to this one for God's existence:

1   The Bible says "God exists".
2   Whatever the Bible says is true.

Therefore, God exists.

As stated, this argument doesn't beg the question. Similarly, as stated, the standard argument for Cartesian skepticism does not beg the question. But if the argument for premise 2 in the argument for God's existence were that the Bible was written by God and whatever God writes is true, then the argument would beg the question because the sub-premises employed in the argument for premise 2 imply the conclusion. My claim is that if the Cartesian skeptic thinks premise 1 in his argument is true because the appropriate evidential relationships are depicted by Pattern 1, he will be forced to beg the question when he gives his argument for premise 2.

I think this point becomes clearer when we look at Pattern 2. If the Cartesian skeptic thinks that closure holds in this case because one must arrive on the inference path at the proposition that there is a table before one arrives at the denial of the skeptical hypothesis, then in arguing for the second premise the skeptic must show that we cannot arrive at the proposition that there is a table, because if we did, we could get to the denial of the skeptical hypothesis (since that is what this instantiation of closure maintains). But if the sub-argument for premise 2 shows that we can't arrive at the proposition that there is a table, then that sub-argument already establishes the conclusion.

Finally, suppose the skeptic thinks that closure holds because the evidential relationship is depicted by Pattern 3. Here the skeptic is claiming that we must first eliminate the skeptical hypothesis in order to arrive at the proposition that there is a table before us.[27] That evidential prerequisite is not immediately evident and, hence, requires some reasons. Would we have to eliminate *every*

possible alternative before we arrive at the one that is acceptable? Return to the zebra-in-the-zoo case. Would we have to eliminate the hypothesis that the zebra-like looking things are cleverly disguised aliens or *very* cleverly disguised members of the long lost tribe of Israel before arriving at the proposition that they are zebras? I doubt it. So, why should we have to eliminate the skeptical hypothesis before arriving at the proposition that there is a table before us? Is the skeptical hypothesis prima facie plausible? No. Is there some evidence that it is true? No. In fact, the requirement that we eliminate every contrary hypothesis to p before we are entitled to believe p has the consequence that we must have entailing evidence for p – and surely that is too strong a requirement for being justified in believing a contingent, empirical claim such as "there are zebras in the pen".[28] So, this argument for Academic skepticism rests upon an arbitrary assumption that we must eliminate the skeptical hypothesis before we are justified in believing any contingent, empirical proposition.

Thus, on careful inspection, this finite argument – like all such arguments, if the Pyrrhonian is correct – either ends in an arbitrary assumption or begs the question. Thus, the fourth alternative for rejecting the argument for Academic skepticism involves conceding that even if all of the premises are true and even if it is valid, the argument, at least so far, gives us no good reason for accepting the conclusion.

Conclusion

We have come a long way and covered a lot of ground. To sum up, I have argued for the following two main points:

1   Reasoning cannot settle matters, but it can provide provisional justification. Further inquiry is always in order.
2   The standard argument for Academic skepticism with the conclusion that reasoning cannot produce any type of justified belief, including provisionally justified belief, has been shown to be an instance of the general constraints that Pyrrhonists believe apply to all finite arguments. They either rest on arbitrary assumptions or they beg the question.

One important caveat: I have argued that no belief is unconditionally justified. But even that conclusion has to be taken only provisionally – if I am right. My reasoning here has been finite in length. Maybe there aren't good reasons for some of the, as yet, unsupported suppositions in this chapter. And maybe I begged the question. Prudence requires that we view the two main points of the chapter as only provisionally justified.

Notes

I want to thank Anne Ashbaugh, Michael Bergmann, Claudio de Almeida, Mylan Engel, Michael Huemer, Michael Lynch, Steven Luper, Kenton Machina, Stephen Maitzen, Robert Martin, Brian McLaughlin, George Pappas, John Post, Bruce Russell and Thomas Vinci for their help with various aspects of this chapter. Earlier versions of some ancestor parts of it were presented in March 1999, at the Mississippi Philosophical Association and in June 1999, at the Bled Conference in Epistemology, and at the Rutgers Summer Institute for Minority Students in Philosophy, July 2000, at Acadia University, September 2000, and at the Illinois Philosophical Association, November 2000. The discussions that followed helped me in refashioning the arguments in this version. In addition various parts of this chapter draw on Klein (1999), (2000b) and (2000a).

1   This is the view developed in Lehrer (1997) and (2000, esp. pp. 142–4).

2   I think that the difficult task in providing an account of what makes circular reasoning fallacious is to spell out clearly what is meant by the conclusion being "employed in" a premise.

3   The only way out of this predicament is to withhold belief about whether we have been successful in settling an issue by the employment of reasoning. But note that I am not claiming that if we believe that we know something, we will, in fact, ignore contrary evidence if (or when) it appears. At that point we could both lose our belief that we know and acknowledge the contrary evidence. Thus, there is no real "Kripke problem" – the alleged consequence of believing that we know, namely that we become permanently (and perhaps even rationally) convinced of the truth of what we believe we know. I have discussed this elsewhere; see Klein (1984).

4   I chose to put the argument in terms of degrees of justified belief rather than knowledge for two reasons: 1) the argument for Academic skepticism about knowledge usually depends upon assuming that knowledge is at least adequately justified true belief and it is the supposed lack of fulfilment of the justification condition that leads to the denial of knowledge, and 2) it is the power of reasoning to justify beliefs that is the primary concern of this chapter and, consequently, even if knowledge did not entail adequately justified beliefs, if there were a good argument showing that our beliefs were never justified to any positive degree, my claim that reasoning can make a belief provisionally justified would have been undercut.

5   Hume claimed that the only way to deal with skepticism was simply not to think about it. That might work for some, but not for me – and it didn't work for Hume either!

6   Strictly speaking, it could be that beliefs which are justified are closed under entailment because justified beliefs are a subset of beliefs and the subset could be closed while beliefs are not. But the same objections to the closure of beliefs, *simpliciter*, seems to apply to justified beliefs as well.

7   Robert Audi gives some other examples in which it appears that one can have sufficient evidence for the entailing proposition but not for the entailed one (1988, esp. pp. 77 ff.). I discuss these examples in some detail in Klein (1995, pp. 213–36). Briefly, I think these counter-examples fail for the same reasons that Dretske's proposed counter-examples fail.

8   I have argued for that in Klein (1984), in Klein (1995) and in Klein (2000a).

9   The modes of relativity and discrepancy recapitulate passages in Sextus's chapter "Concerning the Ten Modes" in Sextus (1933). Sextus attributes this formulation of the modes to Aenesidemus.

10   The term "infinitism" is not original to me. To the best of my knowledge, the first use of a related term is in Moser (1984), in which he speaks of "epistemic infinitism". Also, Post (1987, p. 91) refers to a position similar to the one I am defending as the "infinitist's claim".

11   The reason for the "non-repeating" condition is that were the propositions to repeat, the result would be a form of coherentism – infinitely long circles.

12   Strictly speaking, there is a fourth possibility, namely that there are foundational propositions and that there are an infinite number of propositions between the foundational one and the one for which reasons are initially being sought. Interestingly, such a hybrid view might be indistinguishable in practice from infinitism and, hence, not subject to the "foundationalist's dilemma" to be discussed later. Thus, I think for our purposes we can treat this as a form of infinitism or an acceptable form of foundationalism because it is the ability of the three patterns of reasoning (foundationalism, coherentism and infinitism) to provide a basis for rational practice that is the criterion which will determine whether any of the patterns is acceptable. As far as I know this possibility has never been explored; it might be worthwhile to do so.

13   I put it that way in order to make clear that foundationalism can embrace some aspects of coherentism. Propositions with only minimal justification can mount up, so to speak, by gaining extra credibility. Thus, the definition of foundationalism includes both weak and strong foundationalism as characterized in BonJour (1978, pp. 1–13).

14   In other places I have argued that foundationalism is false; see Klein (1999).

15   That is, there is no reason that can be given that does not ultimately depend upon other basic propositions. There could be reasons for believing the basic ones for they could cohere with other propositions and coherence could add some degree of warrant. But Fred would see that Sally would then just ask about the set of basic propositions. In other words, she would ask, "What makes you think that every member of the set of basic propositions is true?"

16   There is one move Fred might make here. Steven Luper suggests that it is rational to accept foundational beliefs even though they cannot be supported by reasons. Here is a close paraphrase of his argument. The epistemic goal is to acquire a complete and accurate picture of the world. Granted, at base our reasons are arbitrary but "an injunction against believing anything… would obviously make it impossible for us to achieve the goal of arriving at a complete and accurate understanding of what is the case… Indeed, given that our ultimate beliefs are arbitrary, it is rational to adopt management principles that allow us to retain these foundational yet arbitrary views, since the alternative is to simply give up on the attempt to achieve the epistemic goal" (Luper-Foy 1990, p. 45). Briefly, the claim is that since the goal of an epistemic agent is to acquire a complete and accurate picture of the world, accepting a basic, though arbitrary, reason is rational since if one did not accept it, there would be no possibility of attaining the goal. It is "rational to do and believe things without reason" (p. 40) because if we did not, we could not attain our goal.

But I don't think Fred can employ this line of reasoning. For if Fred's basic beliefs are arbitrary, that is if there is no available reason for thinking that they are even somewhat likely to be true, then Fred, being a foundationalist, would have no reason for thinking that *any* of the *non-basic propositions* are true either. If, ultimately, it is rational to accept some "basic" proposition, *b*, for prudential considerations, then no epistemic warrant can be transferred to the non-basic ones from the basic ones. Thus, if the non-basic propositions have any epistemic warrant at all, it must arise completely from some source other than the basic beliefs. And that view isn't foundationalism. Coherence naturally suggests itself. But as we will see soon, that solution to the regress problem can't provide a model for rational practice.

17 I want to thank Steven Luper for his comments that forced me to be clearer about what counts as an arbitrarily adopted proposition. I take it that a proposition is arbitrarily accepted just in case there is no better reason for accepting it than denying it, but it is accepted anyway. Thus, in the argument considered earlier against closure (and hence against Academic skepticism) accepting the premise that closure entails Pattern 1 type evidential structures is arbitrary because there are better reasons for denying that than there are for accepting it (and hence there are no better reasons for accepting than denying it). Also, when the infinitist stops giving her reasons for beliefs (as she must), her last reason given need not be arbitrary because she might have better reasons for believing it than denying it – although she hasn't yet given them.

18 See, for example, Cohen (1987, 1988), Lewis (1979, 1996), Wittgenstein (1977) and DeRose (1995, 1992). There are also hints at such a view in Aristotle (*Metaphysics*, 1006a–1011b).

19 I have considered (and rejected) the contextualist response to Academic skepticism in Klein (2000a).

20 See Donald Davidson (1986) for this type of defence of the claim that certain methodologically basic propositions must be "true in the main". Davidson, of course, was defending what he took to be a brand of coherentism. But as we will soon see, some forms of coherentism are really nothing but foundationalism in disguise.

21 I do not think the expressions "warrant-transfer coherentism" or "warrant-emergent coherentism" are original to me. Nor is the distinction between the two types of coherentism. But I do not recall where I first ran across the use of those expressions or the discussion of these issues. Ernest Sosa does distinguish between various forms of coherentism. In addition, he argues that what I call the "warrant-emergent" form is actually a form of what he calls "formal foundationalism". Thus, the claim that some forms of coherentism are actually forms of foundationalism is not original to me; see Sosa (1980), reprinted in Sosa (1991, pp.

165–91). In addition, BonJour (1978) distinguishes between linear and non-linear coherentism. That distinction parallels the one here between warrant-transfer coherentism and warrant-emergent coherentism.

22 The original passage is as follows:

Suppose that all justification is inferential. When we justify belief A by appeal to belief B and C, we have not yet shown A to be justified. We have only shown that it is justified if B and C are. Justification by inference is conditional justification only; A's justification is conditional upon the justification of B and C. But if all justification is conditional in this sense, then nothing can be shown to be actually non-conditionally justified.

I modified the passage to avoid what seems to me to be an unfortunate level confusion that conflates one's being justified with showing that one is justified. I also changed the passage to make clear that the alleged problem is with the infinite chain, per se, as opposed to the chain diverging because more than one proposition is offered as a reason for a belief.

23 Once again, I am indebted to Steven Luper for this point.

24 See Klein (1999) for a fuller defence.

25 Of course there is a third option – neutrality, that is being neither optimistic nor pessimistic. The reasons presented here for thinking that infinitism is not inherently pessimistic can be applied to the neutral view as well.

26 I point to various alternative accounts of what would make a proposition one which is *correctly* called forth in Klein (1999). There I call such propositions "objectively available" as reasons.

27 Keith Lehrer makes that claim on behalf of the skeptic in Lehrer (1971, pp. 292–4). Lehrer no longer accepts this argument (I think); see Lehrer (1974, pp. 238–40) and Lehrer (2000, pp. 132–7).

28 Here is the argument: both ($\sim p$ & q) and ($\sim p$ & $\sim q$) are contraries of p. If the denials of both are required to be in the evidence for p, then that evidence entails p because $\{\sim(\sim p \& q), \sim(\sim p \& \sim q)\}$ entails p.

References

Aristotle. 1994. *Posterior Analytics*, trans. J. Barnes, 2nd edn (Oxford: Clarendon Press).

Audi, Robert. 1988. *Belief, Justification, and Knowledge* (Belmont: Wadsworth).

BonJour, Lawrence. 1978. "Can Empirical Knowledge Have a Foundation?," *American Philosophical Quarterly* 15, pp. 1–13.

——. 1985. *The Structure of Empirical Knowledge* (Cambridge, MA: Harvard University Press).

Cohen, Stewart. 1987. "Knowledge, Context, and Social Standards." *Synthese* 73, pp. 3–26.

——. 1988. "How to be a Fallibilist." *Philosophical Perspectives* 2, pp. 91–123.

Dancy, Jonathan. 1985. *Introduction to Contemporary Epistemology* (Oxford: Blackwell).

Davidson, Donald. 1986. "A Coherence Theory of Truth and Knowledge," in Henrich 1983.

DeRose, Keith. 1992. "Contextualism and Knowledge Attributions," *Philosophy and Phenomenological Research* 52, pp. 913–29.

——. 1995. "Solving the Skeptical Problem," *Philosophical Review* 104, pp. 1–52.

Dretske, Fred. 1970. "Epistemic Operators," *Journal of Philosophy* 67, pp. 1007–23.

Klein, Peter. 1995. "Skepticism and Closure: Why the Evil Genius Argument Fails," *Philosophical Topics* 23, pp. 213–36.

——. 1999. "Human Knowledge and the Infinite Regress of Reasons," *Philosophical Perspectives* 13, Epistemology, pp. 297–326.

——. 2000a. "Contextualism and the Real Nature of Academic Skepticism," *Philosophical Issues* 10, pp. 108–16.

——. 2000b. "The Failures of Dogmatism and a New Pyrrhonism," *Acta Analytica* 15, 24, pp. 7–24.

Lehrer, Keith. 1971. "Why Not Skepticism?," *Philosophical Forum*, pp. 206–98.

——. 1974. *Knowledge* (Oxford: Oxford University Press).

——. 1997. *Self Trust: A Study of Reason, Knowledge, and Autonomy* (Oxford: Clarendon Press).

——. 2000. *Theory of Knowledge*, 2nd edn (Boulder, CO: Westview Press).

Lewis, David. 1979. "Scorekeeping in a Language Game," *Journal of Philosophical Logic* 8, pp. 339–59.

——. 1996. "Elusive Knowledge," *Australasian Journal of Philosophy* 74, pp. 549–67.

Luper-Foy, Steven. 1990. "Arbitrary Reasons," in M. Roth and G. Ross (eds) *Doubting: Contemporary Perspectives on Skepticism* (Dordrecht: Kluwer), pp. 39–55.

Moser, Paul. 1984. "A Defense of Epistemic Intuitionism," *Metaphilosophy* 15, 3, pp. 196–204.

Post, John. 1987. *The Faces of Existence* (Ithaca, NY: Cornell University Press).

Sextus Empiricus. 1933. *Outlines of Pyrrhonism*, trans. R. G. Bury (London: W. Heinemann, Loeb Classical Library).

Sosa, Ernest. 1980. "The Raft and the Pyramid," *Midwest Studies in Philosophy* 5, pp. 3–25.

——. 1991. *Knowledge in Perspective* (Cambridge: Cambridge University Press).

Williams, John. 1978. "Justified Belief and the Infinite Regress Argument," *American Philosophical Quarterly* 15, 4, pp. 311–12.

Wittgenstein, Ludwig. 1977. *On Certainty* (Oxford: Blackwell).

CHAPTER 6

Epistemological Realism

Michael Williams

Generality and Epistemic Priority

Although a defender of the naturalness of sceptical doubts must hold that foundationalism is a by-product of scepticism, not a presupposition, so far we have seen nothing to suggest that the case for scepticism can be understood apart from the doctrine of the priority of experiential knowledge over knowledge of the world. This result would not be decisive if this essential doctrine could itself be derived from the truistic elements in the sceptic's arguments. But we have seen nothing to suggest this either. On the contrary, everything points the other way.

This leaves one option: to see how the truistic elements in the sceptic's arguments take on sceptical significance, we must look to the distinctive character of the traditional epistemological project. The sceptic (or traditional epistemologist) must argue that, in the context of a distinctively philosophical investigation of our knowledge of the world, the crucial ideas about epistemic priority are *forced* on us by our ordinary understanding of knowledge or justification. If he can do so, he will have rebutted the charge that he simply takes them for granted.

In trying to explain how what might otherwise seem to be truisms take on a surprising significance, it is natural to look first to the traditional epistemologist's aim of assessing the *totality* of our knowledge of the world. Because he wants to explain how we are able to know anything at all about the external world, his plan is to assess all such knowledge, all at once. But surely, the argument now goes, if we are to understand how it is possible for us to know *anything at all* about external reality, we must trace that knowledge to knowledge we should still have even if we knew nothing about the world. No explanation of how we come to have knowledge of the world that depended on our already having some would show the required generality: it would not be an explanation of how we have *any* such knowledge. But this is as good as to say that, once we accept the legitimacy of the epistemologist's question – and we have seen no reason to suppose that it is unintelligible – we must also accept the priority of experiential knowledge, since experiential knowledge is what remains when knowledge of the world is set aside.

This is Stroud's view, which explains why he thinks that the diagnosis of scepticism that traces it to foundationalism gets things upside down. According to Stroud:

> What we seek in the philosophical theory of knowledge is an account that is completely general in several respects. We want to understand

Originally published in M. Williams, *Unnatural Doubts* (Oxford: Blackwell Publishers, 1991), pp. 83–93, 101–19, 121–4, 129–39.

how any knowledge at all is possible – how anything we currently accept amounts to knowledge. Or less ambitiously, we want to understand with complete generality how we come to know anything in a certain specified domain.[1]

It is the distinctively philosophical goal of understanding certain kinds of knowledge with "complete generality" that leads to attempts to ground knowledge of a given kind on some "epistemologically prior" kind of knowledge, and the reason is that no other strategy will yield the right kind of generality. Unfortunately, the lesson of scepticism seems to be that such attempts are bound to fail, so that there is no hope of understanding human knowledge in general.

We can characterize the unusual generality of the traditional epistemological undertaking by saying that the traditional epistemologist imposes a *totality condition* on a properly philosophical understanding of our knowledge of the world. Acceptance of this condition, I believe, is what lies behind the feeling that arguments concerning conceptual points are unfair to the sceptic. Purely conceptual points – the neutrality of experience or the "non-dreaming" implication of ordinary perceptual knowledge – have no intrinsic epistemological significance. Moreover, since such sceptical significance as they possess depends entirely on a tacit commitment to the priority of experiential knowledge over knowledge of the world, they themselves give no grounds for accepting any such general relation of epistemological priority. But perhaps they do not have to. Perhaps the very nature of epistemological investigation forces us to recognize that relation; and once it is recognized, the sceptic's truistic conceptual points are all he needs to reach his conclusion.

For example, one might argue that the (truistic) claim that my knowing (perceptually) that P implies my knowing that I am not dreaming that P is not equivalent to the claim the sceptic must assimilate it to: that my knowing that P requires my being able to rule out the possibility that I am dreaming that P independently of my knowledge that P (or indeed anything like it). But the suggestion now is that the totality condition, rather than the non-dreaming condition alone, is what imposes the crucial restriction. So, in the context of the traditional attempt to understand our

knowledge of the world, an otherwise innocuous claim gives the sceptic what he needs.

Acceptance of the totality condition on a properly philosophical understanding of our knowledge of the world is also the deep source of the epistemologist's dilemma, for the dilemma springs from a fatal interaction of the totality condition with the objectivity requirement. This is the requirement that the knowledge we want to explain is knowledge of an objective world, a world that is the way it is independently of how it appears to us to be or what we are inclined to believe about it. Now, as we have seen, the totality condition requires us to try to trace our knowledge of the world to something more fundamental, which can only be experiential data. But, as a sceptical argument along Ayer's lines reveals, it is impossible to explain how such data could ever function as evidence. They cannot be linked empirically with any facts about the world for, in accepting such linkage, we would be crediting ourselves with knowledge of the world, in violation of the totality condition. On the other hand, conceptual connections between experiential data and worldly fact seem to be ruled out by the familiar thought-experiments that the sceptic appeals to to establish the neutrality and autonomy of experience. And if, in a desperate attempt to avoid scepticism, we insist on such connections, we make the way the world is depend on how it appears to us, in violation of the objectivity requirement. Accordingly, in the context of the attempt to assess the totality of our knowledge of the world, it seems impossible either to respect or violate the objectivity requirement: whatever we do looks like succumbing to the sceptic.

Nevertheless, although the epistemologist's dilemma arises from the interaction of the totality condition and the objectivity requirement, I take the totality condition to be fundamental. Many philosophers would disagree, for they see the objectivity requirement, with its commitment to a "realistic" view of truth, as the deep source of sceptical problems. But it is not clear, to me at least, that the objectivity requirement, any more than its relative the neutrality of experience, has any particular sceptical potential outside the context of an assessment of worldly knowledge governed by the totality condition.

I say that the totality condition is fundamental. More strictly, however, what is fundamental is the attempt to conduct an *assessment* of our knowledge of the world in the light of that condition. If the priority of experiential knowledge over knowledge of the world is implicit in the traditional epistemological project, this is not solely on account of that project's unusual generality. Also crucial is the kind of understanding it suggests we seek. As Quine has argued, if all we want is some kind of causal or developmental account of the emergence of our knowledge of the objective world, there is nothing viciously circular in our appealing to what we now know about the world in an explanation of how we came to be in our current position.[2] And where there is no threat of circularity, there is no pressure to accede to a general doctrine of epistemic priority.

As Quine is of course well aware, traditional epistemology is under pressure to accept such a doctrine because it seeks a different kind of understanding. Its aim is to explain how it is that our beliefs about the world amount to knowledge. Thus when Stroud says that what we want from a theory of knowledge is an account of how our knowledge of the world emerges out of something that is not our knowledge of the world,[3] he does not mean that we want an explanation of how our current way of looking at things developed out of some previous way: i.e. out of knowledge (or what our ancestors thought of as knowledge) that is not *ours*. This is a task for historians and anthropologists. Nor is he thinking of an account of how our knowledge emerges out of something that is not our *knowledge*. Quine's idea of a naturalized epistemology is a gesture in this direction, for it is supposed to issue in a causal explanation of how our interactions with the environment lead us to form certain beliefs; and if there is a worthwhile project here, it is presumably one for psychologists and neurophysiologists. What is missing from both these projects is the idea of an assessment. Each could as well, in fact more properly, be offered as an account of the emergence of our *beliefs*. But only a legitimating account of the basis or emergence of our beliefs will give an account of our *knowledge*. The sort of theory Stroud has in mind is therefore one that traces our knowledge of the world to something that is *ours*, and that is *knowledge*, but not knowledge *of the world*. What could this be except experiential knowledge? Even Quine is forced to something like this position

when he tries to connect his "naturalized" epistemology with traditional sceptical problems.

It seems, then, that something very like foundationalism falls out of a methodological constraint on a properly philosophical examination of knowledge of the world. So we have, apparently, found what we were looking for: a defence of the claim that foundationalism is a by-product of scepticism, not a presupposition. When this possibility was first mooted, I suggested that it would have to turn out that scepticism and foundationalism have a common root. We have now located that common root in the attempt to gain a certain kind of understanding of our knowledge of the world. In effect, we have glossed Hume's thought that we set foot on the road to scepticism as soon as we ask distinctively philosophical questions about knowledge. True, this will not yield a defence of the naturalness of sceptical doubts unless, as Hume thought, that form of questioning is itself fully natural. However, even on this point, the sceptic has strengthened his position. It is hard to see how there could be anything *unintelligible* in what seems only to be an attempt to understand knowledge in an unusually general way, so the prospects for a convincing therapeutic diagnosis of scepticism seem bleak. But it is not obvious offhand that the prospects for a satisfactory theoretical diagnosis are any brighter, for how can mere generality entail extensive theoretical commitments?

This is not all. Suppose that we agree that the traditional epistemological project leads inevitably to the conclusion either that we have no knowledge or that, if we do, we will never understand how we do; and suppose we insist that, since this is its outcome, it *must* involve some distortion of our epistemological position: can we say that identifying this distortion will let us see how knowledge is possible after all? Stroud suggests not. We should not think that:

> if we did come to see how and why the epistemological enterprise is not fully valid, or perhaps not even fully coherent, we would then possess a satisfactory explanation of how human knowledge in general is possible. We would have seen, at best, that we cannot have any such thing. And that too, I believe, would leave us dissatisfied.[4]

This is a powerful objection to any theoretical diagnosis of scepticism. Attempts to answer the sceptic directly run into the epistemologist's dilemma. But, if Stroud is right, attempts at diagnostic responses meet a similar fate. Suppose we find that we cannot hope to ground our knowledge of the world in the way that traditional epistemology has invited us to, because of some defect in the ideas about justification involved in the notion of even trying: we would still not have explained to ourselves how it is that we ever come to know anything about the world. Unless we show that the sceptic's question is actually unintelligible, it will remain dissatisfyingly unanswered. So this is our new dilemma: if the traditional epistemological project is coherent, it is doomed to fail; and if it isn't, we are still left in a position hard to distinguish from scepticism. It may be scepticism at second order, but it is scepticism for all that. We may *have* knowledge of the world, but we will never be able to explain to ourselves how we do. We may know things about the world, but we will never know that we know them.

Knowledge as an Object of Theory

In asking whether there is such a thing as knowledge of the world, I am not asking the very same question the sceptic asks but one that I think cuts deeper. I am asking how we have to think about "knowledge of the world" for that phrase to pick out a proper object of theory. So if it sounds too strange even to hint that there might not be anything for the theory of knowledge to be a theory of, my question can be rephrased. What matters is whether "our knowledge of the world" picks out the kind of thing that might be expected to be susceptible of uniform theoretical analysis, so that failure to yield to such analysis would reveal a serious gap in our understanding.

To raise these questions is to begin to examine a move that gets made before epistemological arguments, and particularly sceptical arguments, even get started. This is the introduction of the objects of epistemological inquiry. We shall be trying to isolate views that, for the most part, even the most determined anti-sceptics share with their adversaries. Philosophers who respond to scepticism do not doubt that there is something to defend against the sceptic's attacks. If they are dubious about our prospects for giving a

direct refutation of scepticism, they call for a diagnosis of the sceptic's questions which will reveal them, first impressions to the contrary, as less than fully coherent. Even Stroud, who thinks our most pressing need as epistemologists is to understand how traditional epistemological inquiry misrepresents our epistemic position, if it does, seems not to doubt the existence of its objects. For the idea that there is something called "our epistemic position" is just another aspect of the idea that there is such a thing as "human knowledge" or "our view of reality." But is there? Or are there fewer things in heaven and earth than are dreamt of in our epistemology?

Now, it is tempting to use "human knowledge" and "our knowledge of the external world" as though it were obvious that such phrases pick out reasonably definite objects of study. But it isn't obvious, or shouldn't be. We can talk of "our knowledge of the world," but do we have any reason to suppose that there is a genuine totality here and not just a loose aggregate of more or less unrelated cases? My sense is that the totality condition is far more problematic than it first seems.

Consider, for example, Nagel's characterization of the aim of epistemology as "to form a conception of reality which includes ourselves and our view of reality among its objects."[5] This offhand allusion to "our view of reality" takes a lot for granted. To suppose that there is such a thing as "our view of reality," which might then be the "object" of a single theoretical enterprise, is to assume that human knowledge constitutes some kind of surveyable whole, an idea that is not, on the surface, very promising. There are no clear criteria for individuating beliefs and, even if there were, it is far from clear that there would be any systematic way of enumerating all the things we believe. Phrases like "our system of beliefs" and "our view of reality" are so vague that we cannot be confident they refer to anything.

Nothing changes if we pull back to narrower categories such as knowledge of the external world. When it comes to such "specified domains," whether there is anything to understand will depend on how the domains are specified. To try to understand all knowledge in the standard epistemic domains is to suppose that the beliefs in those domains hang together in some important way. But how? "Knowledge of the external world" covers not only all the natural sciences and all of history, it covers all everyday, unsystematic factual claims belonging to no particular investigative discipline. Since, even within a single subject, theories, problems and methods tend to proliferate with the progress of inquiry, so that even the most systematic disciplines tend to become less rather than more unified, it is doubtful whether we can take a synoptic view of physics, never mind everything we believe about the external world. It is not obvious that it makes sense even to try.

Recall Stroud's claim that in the philosophical study of human knowledge we want "to understand how any knowledge at all is possible – how anything we currently accept amounts to knowledge." He finds that engaging in this project "feels like the pursuit of a perfectly comprehensible intellectual goal.[6] Perhaps it does once we have grown familiar with theoretical ideas that we shall be examining shortly. But we must try to recover some naivete here. Then I think we see that, when we first encounter the challenge to show how any knowledge of the world is possible, we cannot tell whether we have been given a perfectly comprehensible goal or not. In fact, the obvious difficulty in commanding a synoptic view of our worldly beliefs suggests that we haven't. We cannot, therefore, just *see* whether the epistemological challenge make sense. What we can do, however, is to ask how we might make sense of it.

I think that we can find a somewhat oblique recognition of this problem even in Descartes. Descartes admits that getting to a general doubt by questioning his beliefs one at a time would not be easy: perhaps the examination would never be completed. Hume too dismisses a piecemeal approach as a "tedious lingering method."[7] But these grudging concessions are misleading: for they imply that the main obstacles to going over our beliefs *seriatim* are time and energy, whereas the question is certainly not one of convenience. If we are to make sense of the project of explaining how anything we believe about the world amounts to knowledge, we need a way of reducing our beliefs to order. We have to bring them under principles or show them as resting on commitments that we *can* survey. We must reveal some kind of *theoretical integrity* in the class of beliefs we want to assess.[8] If we can do this, human knowledge is a possible object of theoretical investigation. But not otherwise.

The very nature of the traditional project demands that the principles in question be all-pervasive. For example, if we are to assess the totality of our beliefs about the world, there must be principles that inform all putative knowledge of the world *as such*. But what could they be? I take it to be obvious that, in one way, our beliefs do not show any kind of theoretical integrity. They do not, that is, add up to an ideally unified theory of everything. There is no way now, and none in prospect, of integrating all the sciences, much less all of anyone's everyday factual beliefs, into a single coherent system: for example, a finitely axiomatized theory with specified rules of inference. In this way, Nagel's phrase "our view of reality" borders on the absurd. We have not got *a* "view of reality" but indefinitely many. The idea, taken for granted by coherence theorists of justification, that we have a "system" of beliefs ought to be suspect.

"Our beliefs," then, do not amount to a single, integrated "view of reality." They are not *topically integrated*. But this need not be fatal to the project of understanding human knowledge in general. For even if our beliefs are not topically integrated, they might be *epistemologically* integrated. This is to say: they might be subject, in so far as they are meant to be justified or to amount to knowledge, to the same fundamental, epistemological constraints. This is what is usually suggested, or rather assumed. Thus Descartes ties his pre-critical beliefs together, thereby constituting their totality as an object of theoretical inquiry, by tracing them all to "the senses." No matter how topically heterogeneous, and no matter how unsystematic, his beliefs have this much in common: all owe their place to the authority of the senses. If this authority can be called in question, each loses its title to the rank of knowledge.

We have seen that this talk of "the senses" is poised between a causal truism and a contentious epistemological doctrine. Now we see more clearly why the epistemological doctrine is and must be what is intended. Only by tracing our beliefs about the world to a common "source," which is to say a common evidential ground, can we make "beliefs about the world" the name of a coherent kind. In the absence of topical integration, we must look to epistemological considerations for the theoretical integrity we require.

Hume may have seen, though perhaps dimly, that an epistemologically based form of theoretical integrity is a precondition for a properly general, hence "philosophical," understanding of human knowledge. He compares assessing particular beliefs and particular sciences one at a time to a strategy of "taking now and then a castle or village on the frontier"; and he contrasts this "tedious" method with marching up to "the capital or center of these sciences, to human nature itself." In explaining the principles of human nature, he tells us, "we in effect propose a compleat system of the sciences." But the completeness envisaged does not involve topical integration. It derives rather from the fact that all sciences, whatever their subject matter, "lie under the cognizance of men, and are judged of by their powers and faculties." Their subjection to the same underlying epistemological constraints, rooted in our "powers and faculties" is thus what makes possible a sweeping evaluation of "all the sciences."[9]

Hume sees the fact that all sciences lie "under the cognizance of men" as showing that all are "in some measure dependent on the science of MAN." But it seems clear that the science of man is not, or ought not to be, dependent on the other sciences. (Hume is apologetic about his occasional excursions into natural philosophy.) This asymmetry belongs to the logic of Hume's project, indeed to the logic of the traditional epistemological enterprise. Since he is attempting, with a view to its reform, a wholesale assessment of our knowledge of both the physical and the moral world, he cannot take any of that knowledge for granted. This means that it must be possible to investigate our "powers and faculties," the epistemological aspect of the human condition, without relying on any worldly knowledge. Our epistemological self-knowledge must be both autonomous and fundamental. Thus the project of assessing the totality of our knowledge of the world does more than presuppose that experiential knowledge is in some very deep way prior to knowledge of the world. It also assigns a definite privilege to knowledge of such epistemological facts. These features of the traditional project point to very extensive theoretical commitments.

The fact that the traditional epistemological enterprise is committed to the autonomy of epistemology sheds further light on the significance of externalism in the theory of knowledge. By suggesting that our capacity for knowledge depends on our situation in the world, and not just on our own "internal" capacities, externalism challenges the idea of our "epistemic position" as an autonomous object of theory. If our epistemic position is not something that can be investigated without knowing something about how we are placed in the world, there can be no question of our assessing the totality of our knowledge of the world on the basis of insights into our epistemic position. Perhaps we do not even have a fixed epistemic position. And if we find that we do not, it is doubtful whether we will be able to retain a clear conception of "our knowledge of the world" as an appropriate object of theory.

Unlike Hume, Descartes aspires to topical as well as epistemological integration: hence his metaphor of the tree of knowledge whose roots are metaphysics, trunk physics, and branches medicine, mechanics, and morals, a figure that contrasts interestingly with Hume's citadel of reason. But even for Descartes, topical integration is something to be achieved rather than assumed. His initial survey of his beliefs takes for granted only their epistemological integrity. As is familiar, he makes the point in terms of the metaphor of foundations: undermine the foundations and the whole edifice crumbles. The metaphor is a very natural one for, as we have seen, there is a clear sense in which epistemology, understood as the attempt to comprehend how any knowledge is possible, is intrinsically foundational. To see human knowledge as an object of theory, we *must* attribute to it some kind of systematic basis. This may involve inference from some class of fundamental evidence-conferring beliefs, as traditional foundationalists maintain; or it may involve governance by certain "global" criteria of explanatory integration, as coherence theorists think. But *something* must regulate our knowledge of the world: something that we can identify and examine independently of any such knowledge. We should therefore not be too eager to *oppose* the account of scepticism that traces it to the generality of the epistemological enterprise to that which traces it to foundationalism. (Nor, for that matter, should we be too eager to oppose foundationalism to the coherence theory.) If we give up the idea of pervasive, underlying epistemological constraints; if we start to see the plurality of constraints that inform the various special disciplines, never mind ordinary, unsystematic factual discourse, as genuinely irreducible; if we become suspicious of the idea that "our powers and faculties" can be evaluated independently of everything having to do with the world and our place in it: then we lose our grip on the idea of "human knowledge" as an object of theory. The clear contrast between castles on the frontier and the fortress at the centre dissolves. Perhaps there is no capital, each province, as Wittgenstein said of mathematics, having to take care of itself. The quest for an understanding of human knowledge as such, no longer feels like "the pursuit of a perfectly comprehensible intellectual goal."

The same is true of more modest aims, such as understanding how our beliefs about the external world amount to knowledge. As a way of classifying beliefs, "beliefs about the external world" is only quasi-topical, bringing together beliefs belonging to any and every subject, or no well-defined subject at all. They are united only by their supposed common epistemological status. The essential contrast to "beliefs about the external world" is "experiential beliefs" and the basis for the contrast is the general epistemic priority of beliefs falling under the latter heading over those falling under the former. "External" means "without the mind"; and it is taken for granted that we have a firmer grasp of what is "in" the mind than of what is outside it.

There is no doubt that this epistemological distinction is readily mastered: readily enough for arguments based on it to strike us as "immediately gripping." But a teachable distinction does not guarantee theoretical integrity in the kinds of things distinguished. There are various ways of failing. I discuss two examples in this section and one in the next.

My first example illustrates a relatively mild form of failure. In his natural history of heat, Bacon gives a long list of examples of heating. It includes examples of heating by radiation, friction, exothermic reactions, and by "hot" spices that "burn" the tongue.[10] Everything he mentions is ordinarily said to involve "heat," so we cannot deny that his list reflects ordinary usage. But what we have here is a clear case in which a nominal kind, comprising all the things commonly called "hot," has no automatic right to be considered a natural kind. It is no objection to the kinetic

theory that it doesn't cover the tremendous "heat" produced in my mouth by a chicken vindaloo, never mind the heat often generated by philosophical arguments. We don't complain that, since the theory doesn't apply to hot curries or heated arguments, it fails to explain heat in a satisfactorily general way.

Given that we want to know whether there is any such thing as, say, "our knowledge of the world," this kind of failure may seem too weak to be of interest. Failure to take in hot curries and heated arguments does not tempt us to say that there is no such thing as heat. But we could say that there is no such thing as *nominal* heat, the nominal kind being *merely* nominal. We can tie together some of the examples of heat and, having done so, treat them as the only genuine examples, discarding the others as resembling the genuine examples only superficially, hence as not really, but only metaphorically, hot. This is, indeed, what Bacon himself goes on to do when he argues that heat is a form of motion. Anyway, it is clear that there need be no theory of all the things commonly called "hot": a hot curry is hot even when it has gone cold. Nor need the lack of such a theory because for intellectual dissatisfaction. It is just another example of an ordinary principle of classification failing to cut nature at the joints. By the same token there does not *have* to be a theory of all the things normally called "examples of knowledge." And if there isn't, it has to be shown that this reveals a lack. It may be that there is no such thing as knowledge (or knowledge of the external world, etc.) in just the way that there is no such thing as Bacon's nominal heat.

All this notwithstanding, I agree that the example of heat doesn't get me very far. All that happens in this case is that a nominal kind fails to coincide exactly with a theoretically coherent kind. So I move to my second example: the supposed division of sentences into analytic, or true by virtue of meaning, and synthetic, or true by virtue of fact. Quine is famously sceptical about this distinction because he is dubious about the atomistic conception of meaning that he takes to lie behind it.[11] Quine's view of meaning is holistic – the meaning of a given sentence depends on its role in a wider theory – and this holistic conception of meaning suggests that there is no privileged way of distinguishing a theory's "meaning postulates" from its empirical assumptions, any more than there is a way of determining which out of alternative complete axiom sets is the right one.

Against Quine, Grice and Strawson argue that the analytic/synthetic distinction must be genuine and significant because it is teachable in such a way as to enable the student to apply it to new cases.[12] The reply, well known by now, is that all kinds of dubious distinctions have proved to be teachable in this way, for even terms belonging to a false theory can admit of consensual application on the part of those who accept it. If the fact that, at one time, everyone could agree on who was the village witch does not mean that there really were witches, the fact that appropriately trained students can pick out examples of analytic sentences does nothing to show that any sentences are genuinely analytic. But the point I want to make does not require agreement on this particular example. Whether or not we agree with Quine on the question of analyticity, the fact remains that distinctions can be teachable and projectible while failing to correspond to any theoretically coherent division of objects. When a classification rests on an implied background theory, there is no immediate inference from the existence of an easily mastered kind-term to the theoretical integrity of its associated kind.

The application to our current problem is obvious. In accordance with my project of theoretical diagnosis, I have been arguing that the kinds of knowledge investigated by the traditional epistemologist are theoretical kinds. So, just as the ability of believers in the analytic/synthetic distinction to agree on what to count as paradigm instances of analytic sentences does not mean that there are analytic sentences, the fact that we can agree on what to count as examples of knowledge of the external world does not mean that there is knowledge of the external world. The underlying principle of classification, whatever it is, might be bogus. As a result, we cannot simply help ourselves to classifications of this kind on the grounds that nothing else promises the right kind of generality. That such principles of classification pick out coherent objects of theoretical investigation needs to be shown.

In the case of heat, to sort out the genuine from the spurious examples we rely on a physical theory which identifies some underlying property, or structure of more elementary components, common to

hot things. Explaining theoretically significant kinds this way is typical of scientific realism. For the scientific realist, deep structural features of the elementary components of things determine the boundaries of natural, as opposed to merely nominal or conventional, kinds. This suggests an analogy. Since, if human knowledge is to constitute a genuine kind of thing – and the same goes for knowledge of the external world, knowledge of other minds, and so on – there must be underlying epistemological structures or principles, the traditional epistemologist is committed to *epistemological realism*. This is not realism as a position within epistemology – the thesis that we have knowledge of an objective, mind-independent reality – but something quite different: realism about the objects of epistemological inquiry.

The epistemological realist thinks of knowledge in very much the way the scientific realist thinks of heat: beneath the surface diversity there is structural unity. Not everything we call knowledge need be knowledge properly so called. But there is a way of bringing together the genuine cases into a coherent theoretical kind. By so doing – and only by so doing – we make such things as "knowledge of the external world" the objects of a distinctive form of theoretical investigation. We make it possible to investigate knowledge, or knowledge of the world, *as such*.

I expect that at first it seemed bizarre to question the existence of the objects of epistemological inquiry. Who can deny that we evaluate claims and beliefs epistemologically, sometimes deciding that they express or amount to knowledge, sometimes not? And who can deny that these claims or beliefs concern such things as objects in our surroundings, other people's thoughts and experiences, events in the past, and so on? No one. So it is easy to assume that, if our claims ever warrant positive assessment, there must be knowledge of the external world, knowledge of other minds, knowledge of the past, and so on. Even more obviously, there must be knowledge. But I hope the examples just considered make plausible the thought that there doesn't *have* to be. All we know for sure is that we have various practices of assessment, perhaps sharing certain formal features. It doesn't follow from this that the various items given a positive rating add up to anything like a natural kind. So it does not follow that they add up to a surveyable whole, to a genuine totality rather than a more or less loose aggregate. Accordingly, it does not follow that a failure to understand knowledge of the world with proper generality points automatically to an intellectual lack. To sum up, though I readily admit that we have teachable distinctions here, all this ensures is that there will be things that we can agree on as *examples* of, say, knowledge of the external world. It does not guarantee any theoretical integrity of the kind to which the examples are assigned. This is the sense in which there need be no such thing as knowledge of the world.

At this point, someone is likely to object that there is no immediate inference from the lack of a certain type of theoretical integrity in a given kind to its spuriousness. Still less is there an inference to the non-existence of things of that kind. Take the sort of loose, functional classification of things that is common in everyday life, such as the division of dining room furniture into table and chairs. We do not expect to be able to formulate a physical theory of what makes an object a chair. But we are not tempted to conclude that chairs do not exist.[13]

This objection assumes that "knowledge of the external world" is like "chair" rather than like "witch" (or "analytic"). But is it? The distinctive feature of terms like "witch" is that they are *essentially theoretical*. Essentially theoretical distinctions are distinctions that we see no point in continuing to make, or even no way of drawing, once the theory behind them has been rejected. If Quine is right, "analytic/synthetic" is like this, for he holds that giving up a certain conception of meaning involves losing all sense of how to make a fixed, objective division between a theory's meaning postulates and its empirical assumptions. Essentially theoretical classifications must therefore be distinguished from classifications that have been theoretically rationalized but which retain independent utility. Distinctions like this are apt to survive the rejection of theories with which they have become associated. Our first example, heat, is a case in point. Rejecting the caloric theory of heat, or the phlogiston theory of combustion, did not tempt us to conclude that there are no hot things or that nothing burns. Some philosophers would take this view of "analytic," for they think that there is a robust and useful pre-theoretical notion of synonymy that survives Quinean scepticism about meanings. If

they are right, the analytic/synthetic distinction is not essentially theoretical. But where a classification is essentially theoretical, we are happy to say that there are no things of that kind, if we once become convinced that the background theory is false. Thus there are no witches (or, if Quine is right, analytic sentences).

Though I do not claim that the concept of an essentially theoretical classification is knife-edged, I do want to say that "knowledge of the external world" is quite clearly essentially theoretical. There is no commonsense, pre-theoretical practice that this way of classifying beliefs rationalizes: its sole function is to make possible a certain form of theoretical inquiry, the assessment of knowledge of the world as such. As we have seen, this classification cuts across all familiar subject-matter divisions and, in addition, presupposes the autonomy of epistemology. Even the sense of "external" is unfamiliar from a commonsense standpoint. "External" does not mean "in one's surroundings," for even one's own body, with its "internal organs," is an "external" object. It was a radical innovation on Descartes's part to externalize his own body.[14] As I have already remarked, "external" in "external world" means "without the mind." And since being within the mind depends on being given to consciousness, the essential contrast to "knowledge of the external world" is "experiential knowledge": the classification is epistemological through and through.

But what if the proper analogy for "knowledge of the external world" were not "witch" but "heat"? I do not believe that it is because I do not see that there is any pre-theoretical utility to the concept, or any theory-independent way of drawing even approximately the right boundaries round it. But this is not all. In bringing to centre-stage the issue of epistemological realism, I am not questioning particular theories of the structure of empirical knowledge, as we might question particular theories of heat, but the very idea that knowledge has any fixed, context-independent structure. The analogy is therefore not with cases where one structural theory replaces another but with those where we abandon any idea of coming up with a theory of that kind. If there are no witches, we may debate witch-crazes and witchcraft beliefs, but not whether sympathetic magic is superior to contagious.

Suppose, however, that I am wrong about all this. Suppose, that is, that "knowledge of the external world" is like "chair": then what? So far as I can see, nothing to the purpose. In connection with such loose, functional classifications, we do not expect theoretical understanding, which is why such classifications survive the recognition that no such understanding will be forthcoming. We do not feel that there is an irremediable intellectual lack because there will never be a science of chairs. But that is exactly what we are supposed to feel in the absence of a suitably anti-sceptical theory of knowledge of the external world. This shows that, even by the traditional epistemologist's own standards, "knowledge of the external world" cannot be like "chair." It must pick out something in which theoretical integrity is to be expected, and this means that the existence of the objects of traditional epistemological inquiry is far less assured than that of furniture.

Explanation or Deflation?

Let me suggest one further case for comparison. It has to do with deflationary views of truth. Philosophers who take a deflationary approach want no more from a theory of truth than a description of the logical behaviour of "true" and some account of why it is useful to have such a device in our language. Quine is a good example of such a philosopher. According to Quine, if we consider a sentence like "'Snow is white' is true if and only if snow is white" we see that: "To ascribe truth to the sentence is to ascribe whiteness to snow. … Ascription of truth just cancels the quotation marks. Truth is disquotation."[15]

Applied to a given sentence, the truth-predicate is dispensable. It comes into its own, however, with respect to sentences that are not given, as when we say that all the consequences of a given theory are true. But even here, to say that certain sentences are true is just to say that the world is as *they* say it is. As Quine remarks, "one who puzzles over the adjective 'true' should puzzle rather over the sentences to which he ascribes it. 'True' is transparent."[16]

Though I am very sympathetic to this view, my interest here is less in its correctness than its character. This view of truth is striking on account of what it does *not* say. Compared with traditional theories of truth, it says nothing about what makes all true sentences true. On the contrary, a deflationist will hold that his remarks on the behaviour and utility of the truth-predicate say just about everything there is to say about truth. To approach truth in a deflationary spirit is emphatically not to think of "true" as denoting a theoretically significant property, explicating which will illuminate what is involved in any sentence's being true. What is involved in a given sentence's being true is exhaustively captured by the sentence itself. On a deflationary view, then, true sentences constitute a merely nominal kind. We could even say that, for a deflationist, though there are endlessly many truths, there is no such thing as truth.

The traditional theorist sees things quite differently. In his eyes, "truth" *is* the name of an important property shared by all true sentences, a property that can be expected to repay theoretical analysis. This property may be correspondence to fact, incorporability in some ideally coherent system of judgments, or goodness in the way of belief, depending on whether he favours a correspondence, coherence, or pragmatic theory. But whatever his theoretical preference, he will hold that, since true sentences constitute not just a nominal but a theoretical kind, no theory of truth is satisfactory which does not explain what makes true sentences true. We set our sights too low if we aim only to capture the use of a word or explain the point of a concept: there is more to understanding truth than appreciating the utility of the truth-predicate.[17]

We see, then, that traditional and deflationary theories are not theories of exactly the same kind. As Stephen Leeds puts it, the traditional theories are genuinely theories of truth whereas deflationary theories are theories of the concept of truth (or, we could say, accounts of the use of "true").[18] Leeds's illuminating distinction is readily applied to epistemological theories. We can distinguish theories of knowledge from theories of the concept of knowledge. I think that the debate sparked by Gettier's demonstration that the standard "justified true belief" analysis fails to state a sufficient condition for knowledge is best seen as concerning the concept of knowledge. The kind of extra constraint on justification that seems to be required – for example that an inference cannot yield knowledge if it involves a false lemma essentially – is rather formal, nothing being said about what beliefs can serve as justifying evidence for what. This is why it is possible to discuss issues raised by the Gettier problem without ever getting entangled in sceptical problems. Theories that say nothing about whether examples of justified beliefs about objective states of affairs reveal any essential similarities, beyond highly formal ones of the "no false lemmas" variety, are neutral with respect to whether we should think of our knowledge of the world as an appropriate object of theory. By contrast, traditional foundational and coherence theories, which are much more closely involved with scepticism, put forward general, substantive constraints on justification and so make room for a project of assessing our knowledge of the world as a whole. They are theories of knowledge and not just theories of the concept of knowledge.[19]

Of course, there is no obstacle in principle to supplementing one's views about the concept of knowledge with views about knowledge itself.[20] But one could also advance such views in a deflationary spirit. One philosopher who has done so, I believe, is Austin. Wittgenstein may be another.

The availability of deflationary accounts of a notion like truth changes the whole problem-situation. Naively, we might be inclined to suppose that just as in physics we study the nature of heat, so in philosophy we study the nature of truth. But once plausible deflationary views are on the table, the analogy between truth and things like heat can no longer be treated as unproblematic, for the question raised by such views is precisely whether there is any need to think of truth as having a "nature." We can conclude, *mutatis mutandis*, that if we have a plausible account of the concept of knowledge, it is a further step to insist on an account of knowledge as well. A deflationary account of "know" may show how the word is embedded in a teachable and useful linguistic practice, without supposing that "being known to be true" denotes a property that groups propositions into a theoretically significant kind. We can have an account of the use and utility of "know" without supposing that there is such a thing as human knowledge.

What makes this suggestion particularly pointed is that appearances certainly do not favour the view that a phrase like "knowledge of the world" picks out a theoretically coherent kind. For one thing, justification, like explanation, seems interest-relative, hence context-sensitive.

This is in part what Austin is driving at in insisting that demands for justification are raised and responded to against a background of specifically relevant error possibilities. What is relevant will depend on both the content of the claim in question and the context in which the claim is entered. If all evidence is relevant evidence, then, abstracting from such contextual details, there will be no fact of the matter as to what sort of evidence could or should be brought to bear on a given proposition.

If context-sensitivity goes all the way down, there is no reason to think that the mere fact that a proposition is "about the external world" establishes that it needs, or is even susceptible of, any particular kind of evidential support. No proposition, considered in abstraction, will have an epistemic status it can call its own. To suppose that it must is precisely to fall in with what I call "epistemological realism." To treat "our knowledge of the world" as designating a genuine totality, thus as a possible object of wholesale assessment, is to suppose that there are invariant epistemological constraints underlying the shifting standards of everyday justification, which it is the function of philosophical reflection to bring to light. Exposing this epistemological deep structure will be what allows us to determine, in some general way, whether we are entitled to claim knowledge of the world. But if this is so, foundationalist pre-suppositions are buried very deeply in the Cartesian project. They do not just fall out of the totality condition's exclusion of any appeal to knowledge of the world in the course of our attempt to gain a reflective understanding of that knowledge. They turn out to be involved in the very idea of there being something to assess.

These are my suspicions in outline. Now we must look at some details.

Foundationalism

My main concern is the relation between scepticism and foundationalism. So having distinguished between theories of knowledge and theories of the concept of knowledge, I must say what kind of a theory I take foundationalism to be.

One way to understand foundationalism is to see it as a doctrine about the formal character of justifying inferences. Formal foundationalism, as we may call it, is the view that justification depends on the availability of terminating beliefs or judgments, beliefs or judgments which amount to knowledge, or which are at least in some way reasonably held to, without needing support from further empirical beliefs. Formal foundationalism is sometimes thought to contrast with "coherentist" theories of knowledge or justification. According to theories of this type, a given belief becomes justified through incorporation in some suitably "coherent" system of beliefs or "total view." Empirical inference is thus a matter of moving from one total view to another. The terminating judgments, which the foundationalist sees as fixed points constraining the possibilities of inferential justification, are unnecessary. Some philosophers see the commitment to beliefs that function as fixed points as *the* essential feature of foundationalism, hence the complaint, prominent in a recent systematic defence of the coherence theory, that the key error in foundationalism is its "linear" conception of inference.[21]

I have my doubts about the contrast between foundationalism and the coherence theory, but they can wait. The point I want to make here is that anyone who traces scepticism about our knowledge of the external world to the foundationalist doctrine of epistemic priority must have more than formal foundationalism in mind. We can call this stronger doctrine "substantive" foundationalism. The distinction between formal and substantive foundationalism turns on the account given of terminating beliefs or judgments. Substantive foundationalism involves more than the formal doctrine that inference depends on letting certain beliefs function as fixed points: it adds a distinctive account of the kind of beliefs capable of performing that function. Since I think that a genuinely foundationalist view of knowledge and justification must be substantive, whenever I refer to foundationalism *simpliciter* I shall have substantive foundationalism in mind.[22]

Substantive foundationalism is a theory of knowledge, whereas formal foundationalism is only (a contribution to) a theory of the concept of knowledge. One way to see this is to recall that Wittgenstein's view of knowledge, which concedes that all justification takes place against a background of judgments affirmed without special testing, can be seen as *formally* foundationalist. But this point about our ordinary practices of

justification, while it might offer a way into the fully general problem of the regress of justification, gives no basis for supposing that there is a particular sceptical problem about our knowledge of objective reality. The transition to that problem depends on the tacit assumption that the fixed points recognized by commonsense justifications fall into some fairly obvious kind, so that once they have been questioned there must be some other, more primitive kind of judgment that we are forced to look to for their support. The thought that the functional role recognized by formal foundationalism corresponds to some kind of broad topical division of our beliefs is what I take to be the essential characteristic of substantive, as opposed to merely formal, foundationalism.

This is the way, then, in which there is more to what I am calling (and what has generally been called) "foundationalism" than the purely structural doctrine of formal foundationalism. What is missing from formal foundationalism is any hint as to the kinds of beliefs that function as fixed points or as to what qualifies a belief to play that role. But we have not yet got quite to the heart of why formal foundationalism is too weak a doctrine to capture all that is essential to a foundationalist conception of knowledge and justification. The key point is this: that not only does formal foundationalism give no account of what sorts of beliefs are epistemologically prior to what, and why, it does not even imply that any such account needs to be given. If foundationalism is a *purely* formal or structural doctrine, we have no reason to think that a given belief has *any* particular or permanent epistemological status. Perhaps the same belief can be a fixed point at one time, or in one particular context of inquiry or justification, but a candidate for justification at another time or in another context. Nothing in formal foundationalism excludes this.

By contrast, substantive foundationalism presupposes epistemological realism. I first introduced the idea of epistemological realism by way of analogy with scientific realism. We can now get a clearer sense of the appropriateness of the analogy. A micro-structural theory of a physical phenomenon is not purely structural. It will identify both certain structures and the types of entities fitted to occupy appropriate places in them. (Think of models of the atom.) Similarly with the foundationalist: he both attributes to justifying inferences a certain structural character *and* identifies the types of beliefs fitted to play the various structurally defined roles: basic, inferential, etc. Thus for the (substantive) foundationalist beliefs have an *intrinsic epistemological status* that accounts for their ability to play one or other of the formal roles the theory allows. Beliefs of one kind can be treated as epistemologically prior to beliefs of some other kind because they *are* epistemologically prior; some beliefs play the role of basic beliefs because they *are* basic; others receive inferential justification because they *require* it; and all because of the kinds of beliefs they are. According to foundationalists, our beliefs arrange themselves into broad, theoretically coherent classes according to certain *natural* relations of epistemological priority. Beliefs to which no beliefs are epistemologically prior are epistemologically basic. Their credibility is naturally intrinsic, as that of all other beliefs is naturally inferential. This is a much more peculiar doctrine than is generally recognized.[23]

On the foundationalist view, a belief's intrinsic epistemological status derives from the content of the proposition believed. The foundationalist's maxim is "Content determines status." Not, however, the details of content: what matter are certain rather abstract features, for example that a belief is about "external objects" or "experience." Thus it comes naturally to foundationalists to talk of basic propositions or basic statements, as well as of basic beliefs. Propositions recording the data of experience are held to be, by their very nature, epistemologically prior to propositions about external objects, which is why they are apt for the expression of basic beliefs. In light of this, we can characterize foundationalism as the view that our beliefs, simply in virtue of certain elements in their contents, stand in *natural epistemological relations* and thus fall into *natural epistemological kinds*. The broad, fundamental epistemological classes into which all propositions, hence derivatively all beliefs, naturally fall constitute an epistemic hierarchy which determines what, in the last analysis, can be called on to justify what. This means that, for a foundationalist, every belief has an inalienable epistemic character which it carries with it wherever it goes and which determines where its justification must finally be sought. The obvious illustration is the

thought that any belief whatever about "external objects" must in the end derive its credibility from the evidence of "the senses," knowledge of how things appear.

I call the foundationalist's supposed relations of epistemological priority "natural" to emphasize the fact that they are supposed to exist in virtue of the nature of certain kinds of beliefs and not to depend on the changing and contingent contexts in which beliefs become embedded. For the foundationalist, in virtue of his epistemological realism, there is a level of analysis at which epistemic status is not, as Quine once said of one important epistemic feature, conventionality, "a passing trait." Beliefs are more like the members of a highly class-conscious society in which a person, no matter what he does, always carries the stigma or cachet of his origins. The quest for epistemic respectability is thus never entirely *une carrière ouverte aux talents*. A given belief, though useful in all sorts of ways, generally and quite properly (in appropriate contexts) taken for granted, and beyond any specific reproach, can never be allowed quite to forget that it *presupposes the existence of the external world* and is therefore, by that fact alone, subject to some kind of residual doubt, unless it can trace its lineage to more respectable data.

The foundationalist conception of fundamental epistemological relations, cutting across ordinary subject divisions and operating independently of all contextual constraints, receives an early articulation in Descartes's notion of "the order of reasons." Descartes writes, "I do not follow the order of topics but the order of arguments. ... [In] orderly reasoning from easier matters to more difficult matters I make what deductions I can, first on one topic, then on another."[24] However, it is far from obvious that there is such an order of reasons, operating independently of the division of topics. It is not at all clear that some matters are intrinsically – that is to say independently of all circumstances and all collateral knowledge – "easier" than others. The way that justification and inquiry proceed in common life, or for the matter theoretical science, is far from evidently favourable to the foundationalist conception of epistemological relations. In both science and ordinary life, constraints on justification are many and various. Not merely that, they shift with context in ways that are probably impossible to reduce to rule. In part, they will have to do with the specific content of whatever claim is at issue. But they will also be decisively influenced by the subject of inquiry to which the claim in question belongs (history, physics, ornithology, etc.). We can call these *topical* or, where some definite subject or distinctive form of inquiry is involved, *disciplinary* constraints. Not entertaining radical doubts about the age of the Earth or the reliability of documentary evidence is a precondition of doing history *at all*. There are many things that, as historians, we might be dubious about, but not these.

Disciplinary constraints fix ranges of admissible questions. But what is and is not appropriate in the way of justification may also be strongly influenced by what specific objection has been entered to a given claim or belief. So to disciplinary we must add *dialectical* constraints: constraints reflecting the current state of a particular argument or problem-situation. In this respect justification is closely akin to explanation, which is also context-sensitive because question-relative.

I shall have more to say about disciplinary constraints and about the relation between justification and explanation. But for now let me note that, in ordinary examples of requiring and producing justifications, the epistemological status of a given claim can also depend on the particular situation in which the claim is entered, so that justification is also subject to a variety of *situational* constraints. Here I have in mind the wordly and not just the dialectical situation. Consider yet again Wittgenstein's remark that "My having two hands is, in normal circumstances, as certain as anything I could produce in evidence for it."[25] Entered in the right setting, a claim to have two hands might function like a foundationalist's basic statement, providing a stopping place for requests for evidence or justification: hence the element of formal foundationalism in Wittgenstein's view. But in other circumstances *the very same claim* might be contestable and so might stand in need of evidential support. The content of what is claimed does not guarantee a claim some particular epistemic standing. Not merely is status often dependent on the details of content, it is *never* determined by content alone. As Wittgenstein notes:

If a blind man were to ask me "Have you got two hands?" I should not make sure by looking. If I were to have any doubt of it, then I don't know why I should trust my eyes. For why shouldn't I test my *eyes* by looking to find out whether I see my two hands? *What* is to be tested by *what*? (Who decides *what* stands fast?)[26]

The point is that, in the absence of a detailed specification of a particular context of inquiry, the sort of specification that would fix the relevant contextual constraints on justification, the question "What is to be tested by what" has no answer. Questions about justification are essentially context-bound. This is something a foundationalist will deny. He must of course make allowances for the way that what tests what can shift with context. But – and this is the crucial point, he cannot allow that such contextual determination goes all the way down. At the fundamental level, what is to be tested by what is objectively fixed, which is why there is no question of anybody's *deciding* the matter. The answer is determined by the epistemological facts themselves: by fundamental, objective relations of epistemological priority. This is not exactly an "intuitive" view.

Continuing with the example of my knowing (in normal circumstances) that I have two hands, recall also that there is no obvious way to generalize from an example like this. In normal circumstances, the proposition that I have two hands is as certain as anything we could cite as evidence for it. But there is no obvious, non-trivial way of saying what other propositions are, in normal circumstances, as certain as anything we could cite as evidence for them. Normally, I am as certain as I could be of anything that my name is Michael Williams: but beyond this, what does the proposition that my name is Michael Williams have in common with the proposition that I have two hands? What feature of their content explains their belonging to the same epistemic kind? As far as I can see, there isn't one. So even if someone said that the claim to have two hands did have a kind of intrinsic status – that of being certain in normal circumstances – we would still not be able to treat the example as *paradigmatic* of propositions belonging to a definite epistemic kind, for which we could articulate some alternative, non-trivial criterion of membership.[27] Again, the foundationalist sees things quite differently. For him, highly abstract divisions of propositions according to content (propositions about external objects versus experiential propositions, propositions about the past versus propositions about the present, etc.) have to coincide with fixed differences in epistemological status. But what we should learn from the example under discussion is that no such coincidence can be simply assumed. To cite again another of Wittgenstein's reminders, "a proposition saying that here is a physical object may have the same logical status as one saying that here is a red patch."[28] Without natural epistemological kinds, the foundationalist's permanent underlying structure of epistemological relations goes by the board.

We see from this that the antidote to foundationalism, indeed to epistemological realism generally, is a *contextualist* view of justification.[29] To adopt contextualism, however, is not just to hold that the epistemic status of a given proposition is liable to shift with situational, disciplinary, and other contextually variable factors: it is to hold that, independently of all such influences, a proposition has no epistemic status whatsoever. There is *no fact of the matter* as to what kind of justification it either admits of or requires. Thus stated, contextualism implies a kind of externalism, for though appropriate contextual constraints will have to be met, if a given claim is to express knowledge, they will not always have to be known, or even believed, to be met.[30] But when we realize that the point of contextualism is to oppose the sceptic's or traditional epistemologist's epistemological realism, the externalist element in contextualism ought to be more palatable. The problem with externalism was that it seemed to deprive us of the possibility of answering a perfectly intelligible question: how do we come to know anything whatsoever about the external world? What we now see is that this question is not at all intuitive but reflects theoretical presuppositions that are not easy to defend. Contextualism, with its implied externalism, is not offered as a question-begging direct answer to an undeniably compelling request for understanding, but as a challenge to justify the presumption that there is something to understand.

Methodological Necessity

We have already seen that, to flesh out the idea of "human knowledge" as a possible object of theoretical investigation, we have to suppose that there are pervasive epistemological constraints or relations. That is to say, at least some constraints on what propositions demand evidential support and on what propositions can provide it must be *context-invariant*. If we do not always insist on respecting these constraints in a fully rigorous way, this need not mean that they do not apply. To admit that certain constraints are often waived is different from, indeed incompatible with, claiming that they are inapplicable.

This is a very substantial commitment and it is not clear why we should accept it. An examination of ordinary practices of justification strongly suggests that constraints, governing what sorts of evidence can properly be brought to bear on a disputed claim, what needs to be defended, and what can safely be taken for granted, though subject to other kinds of contextual determination as well, are at least *topic-relative*, which is to say determined in part by the subject under discussion.

We might criticize Hume's offhand suggestion that only carelessness and inattention save us from a permanent, debilitating awareness of the truth of scepticism, hence from lapsing into a state of chronic, paralysing doubt. In particular contexts, disciplines etc., exempting certain propositions from doubt is what determines the *direction* of inquiry. As Wittgenstein remarks: "It may be … that all enquiry on our part is set so as to exempt certain propositions from doubt, if they are ever formulated. They lie apart from the route travelled by enquiry."[31]

If some of these propositions cease to lie apart from the route travelled by inquiry, then inquiry travels by a different route. Or perhaps no clear route remains for it to travel by. This is obviously the case with investigations in particular scientific or scholarly disciplines. Disciplinary constraints have a great deal to do with the kinds of questions that can and cannot legitimately be raised without radically affecting the direction of inquiry. Thus, introducing sceptical doubts about whether the Earth really existed a hundred years (or five minutes) ago does not lead to a more careful way of doing history: it changes the subject, from history to epistemology. So when Wittgenstein asks: "am I to say that the experiment which perhaps I make to test the truth of a proposition presupposes the truth of the proposition that the apparatus

I believe I see is really there?"[32] he is clearly inviting the answer "No." And the reason for answering "No" is that the possibility mentioned, while relevant to certain general, epistemological problems, is completely beside the point in the context of a specific experiment in chemistry or physics. To bring it up is not to introduce greater rigour into the investigation in hand but to shift attention to another kind of investigation entirely.

"[T]hat something stands fast for me," Wittgenstein remarks, "is not grounded in my stupidity or credulity."[33] We now see that this is so, at least in part, because it is grounded in my *interests*. It is not that I think that no proposition that stands fast could ever be questioned, though in certain cases I should be likely to feel, as Wittgenstein says, "intellectually very distant" from someone inclined to raise questions. It is just that some doubts are logically excluded by forms of investigation that I find significant, important, or perhaps just interesting. This has nothing to do with dogmatism, credulity or carelessness. Wittgenstein sums up the key points in the following well-known passages:

> The questions that we raise and our doubts depend on the fact that some propositions are exempt from doubt, are as it were like hinges on which those turn.
>
> That is to say, it belongs to the logic of our scientific investigations that certain things are indeed not doubted.
>
> But it isn't that the situation is like this: We just can't investigate everything, and for that reason we are forced to rest content with assumption. If I want the door to turn, the hinges must stay put.[34]

Of course, if I do not want the door to turn I can nail it shut; or I might want it to open the other way, in which case I will move the hinges. But if I want the door to turn this way, it is not just more *convenient*, if a little slapdash, to place the hinges where they are: there is nowhere else to put them.

By fixing a range of admissible questions, we determine a form of inquiry. But this means that a form of inquiry is determined by more than purely formal constraints. As Wittgenstein puts it: "'The question doesn't arise at all.' Its answer would characterise a *method*. But there is no sharp boundary between methodological propositions and propositions within a method."[35] For a subject like history, there is more to method than abstract procedural rules. This is because the exclusion of certain questions (about the existence of the Earth, the complete and total unreliability of documentary evidence, etc.) amounts to the acceptance of substantial factual commitments. These commitments, which must be accepted, if what we understand by historical inquiry is to be conducted at all, have the status, relative to that form of inquiry, of *methodological necessities*.

I have introduced the idea of a proposition's being exempted from doubt as a matter of methodological necessity in connection with the disciplinary constraints that determine the general directions of highly organized forms of inquiry. But it is evident that something similar goes on in more informal, everyday settings. Asking some questions logically precludes asking others: all sorts of everyday certainties have to stand fast if we are to get on with life. Again, however, I want to emphasize that our situation is misread both by the Human naturalist and by the sceptic. The naturalist sees our everyday inability to entertain radical doubts as showing that nature has simply determined us to believe certain things, however groundless they seem to us in our more reflective moments. By contrast, I want to claim that exemption from doubt – epistemic privilege – is a matter of methodology, not psychology. In a specific context, certain exemptions will be *logically* required by the direction of inquiry. We are therefore determined by Nature to hold certain things fast only in so far as we are naturally inclined to interest ourselves in matters requiring us to exempt them from doubt.

This is far from the only point that we must emphasize. It is also crucial to note that, if epistemic status is determined by the direction of inquiry, the reason why, in a given inquiry, certain propositions have to stand fast has to be separated from the reason why that inquiry results in knowledge, if it does. Here we recur, from a slightly different angle, to the externalist element in contextualism. In particular contexts of inquiry, certain propositions stand fast as a matter of methodological necessity. But inquiries informed by them will yield knowledge only if those propositions are true, which they need not always be.

The general moral here is that questions about a proposition's epistemic status must always be separated from questions about its truth. If epistemic status is fixed by the direction of inquiry, epistemic status is context-sensitive. Truth however is not. A proposition is either true or not. But, according to the contextualist view I favour, we cannot say, in a similarly unqualified way, that a proposition is either open to doubt or not. Sometimes it will be and sometimes it won't. Generally speaking, a proposition is neither true because it stands fast nor stands fast because it is true.

We can also see why it was so important at the outset to distinguish between formal and substantive foundationalism. If foundationalism is equated with a certain view of the formal structure of justification – i.e. with the view that inferential justification always requires beliefs that function as "fixed points – a contextualist view of justification can be seen as (formally) foundationalist. But it certainly need not be substantively foundationalist. There are no limits as to what might or might not, in an appropriate context, be fixed.

In an earlier chapter, I tried to show that arguments for radical scepticism presuppose the priority of experiential knowledge over knowledge of the world. This enabled me to conclude that attempts to establish the intrinsic epistemological priority of experiential knowledge on the basis of the greater intrinsic dubitability of objective knowledge are question-begging. The only reason for thinking that such knowledge is intrinsically more dubitable is provided by the existence of sceptical arguments which, when unpacked, turn out to take the doctrine of the priority of experiential knowledge for granted.

This result did not allow us to conclude straight away that scepticism rests on a gratuitous epistemological assumption. What it did suggest, however, is that the source of the doctrine of the priority of experiential knowledge is not evidence from our ordinary justificational practices but rather the distinctively philosophical project of trying to understand how it is possible for us to know anything whatsoever about the external world. The totality condition that the sceptic (or the traditional philosopher) imposes on a philosophical understanding of our knowledge of the world is what forces us to see that knowledge as somehow derivative from experience. No other way of seeing it permits an assessment, hence a legitimating explanation, at the proper level of generality.

We are now in a position to see why this argument does not prove what it needs to prove. All it shows is that the doctrine of the priority of experiential knowledge over knowledge of the world is *a methodological necessity of the traditional epistemological project*. But since the sceptic himself is irrevocably committed to distinguishing between methodological necessity and truth, it does not show, nor by his own standards can the sceptic take it to show, that that doctrine is true.

The result is that the inference from the essential generality of the traditional epistemological project fails to establish the kind of relations of epistemological priority needed to threaten us with scepticism. To yield sceptical results, these relations must reflect more than *mere* methodological necessities: they must correspond to fully objective epistemological asymmetries. It is not enough to point out that if we are to attempt an assessment of our knowledge of the world as a whole we must *take* experiential knowledge to be epistemologically prior to the knowledge we want to assess. Success or failure in the enterprise will have the significance the sceptic and the traditional epistemologist mean it to have only if experiential knowledge really is, as a matter of objective epistemological fact, more basic than knowledge of the world. If it isn't, or more generally if no epistemological relations are in the sense I have indicated fully objective, no attempt to ground knowledge of some allegedly problematic kind on some appropriately prior kind of knowledge will amount to an attempt at assessment. Should the attempt fail, or even inevitably fail, the sceptic will be left with a harmless logico-conceptual point but with no way of advancing to his pessimistic epistemological conclusion.

I remarked that the argument from the totality condition to the absolute priority of experiential knowledge over knowledge of the world rests on two assumptions: that there is something to assess, and that charting its relation to experience amounts to assessing it. I have concentrated on the first, but by so doing have shown what to say about the second. As a pure methodological proposal, there is nothing wrong with setting propositions about the world against experiential propositions, for the purposes of exploring possible relations between them. Like Goodman, we could think of phenomenalism as an interesting constructive project. We could ask, "To what extent can a phenomenalist reconstruction of the world be carried through?" without thinking that we were even addressing any questions of epistemic legitimacy.[36] Think of the way we can model arithmetic in set theory: though this is an interesting piece of mathematics, we need ancillary epistemological assumptions to think of it as relevant to an "assessment" of arithmetic. But this is not the spirit in which the sceptic thinks of the relation between experiential knowledge and knowledge of the world. He needs a fully objective epistemological asymmetry, and this is what no argument from methodological necessity will ever yield.

Some philosophers, Carnap for example, hold that the sceptic fails to undermine ordinary knowledge of the world because his statements, as he intends them to be taken, mean nothing at all. As a statement "internal" to our everyday linguistic framework, "There are material objects" is a trivial consequence of any statement about the world. But as an "external" statement about that framework, an attempted statement, though made in the very same words, will lack "cognitive significance." However, the sceptic might be equally unsuccessful if his statements, as they must be understood in the unusual context of philosophical reflection, mean something different from what they ordinarily mean. Thus Thompson Clarke suggests that the very general common-sense propositions with which Moore confronts the sceptic can be taken two ways, the "plain" way and the "philosophical" way. For example:

Suppose a physiologist lecturing on mental abnormalities observes: *Each of us who is normal knows that he is now awake, not dreaming or hallucinating, that there is a real public world outside his mind which he is now perceiving, that in this world there are three-dimensional animate and inanimate bodies of many shapes and sizes. ...* In contrast, individuals suffering from certain mental abnormalities each believes that what we know to be the real public world is his imaginative creation.[37]

The italicized, plain propositions are "verbal twins" of propositions typically attacked and defended in discussions of philosophical scepticism. But in plain contexts, nobody doubts that they are true, even though plain common sense recognizes the very phenomena – dreaming, hallucinating, and so on – that the sceptic appeals to in his attempt to show that we can never know that we are in touch with "a real public world." Whether there is a clash between philosophy and common sense will depend, therefore, on the relation between philosophical and plain knowing.

Here Clarke is more subtle than Carnap, for he recognizes that the sceptic has an account of the relation between philosophy and common sense which both preserves the relevance of philosophical discoveries to ordinary plain knowing and makes it hard to think that sceptical claims are less than fully meaningful.[38] Ordinary, plain knowing is hemmed by practical considerations. By contrasts, to philosophize is "to step outside the nonsemantical practice" and, meaning simply what one's words mean, ask whether we really know what we (plainly) take ourselves to know. Compared with our philosophizing, ordinary thinking is "restricted." All the sceptic has to do is to get us to look beyond the restrictions. This is easy enough since there is a standing invitation to look "beyond the plain" in our conception of knowledge as knowledge of an objective world. We want to know what there is: not just relative to this and that particular restriction, imposed by this or that practical purpose or limitation, but *absolutely.*

Still, the final distance between Clarke and Carnap is not as great as their initial divergence might suggest. Clarke too holds that, in the end, both "philosophical common sense" *and* its sceptical denial "are a spurious fiction if our conceptual-human constitution is not standard." Amongst other things, a conceptual-human constitution of the standard type requires that "Each concept or the conceptual scheme must be divorceable intact from our practices, from whatever constitutes the essential character of the plain" and that we, as concept users, are "purely ascertaining observers who, usually by means of our senses, ascertain, when possible, whether items fulfill the conditions legislated by concepts."[39] But the sceptic himself shows that our conceptual-human constitution cannot be of the standard type. Our plain knowledge that we are not dreaming right now – the sort of knowledge expressed by the physiologist – cannot be undermined by the plain possibility that we might, in fact, be asleep. But it would be if our conceptual-human constitution were of the standard type. For on this point the sceptic is right: there are no marks or features that conclusively distinguish waking experience from dreaming. So the fact of plain knowing, combined with the sceptic's point about dreaming or hallucinating, shows that our conceptual-human constitution is not of the standard type. This insight is part of the legacy of scepticism.

In representing the sceptic as helping bring about his own undoing, Clarke prefigures the strategy followed by Wright. Wright, we may recall, argues that the sceptic does indeed show that his target-propositions – for example, that there is a real, public world – are beyond justification. They are beyond justification because the sole evidence we can bring to bear on them only functions as evidence if they are already known to be true. Thus sensory experience only counts in favour of any proposition about the public world on assumptions that already commit us to that world's existence. But the lesson to learn from this is that the propositions the sceptic represents as groundless, factual assumptions, are not really factual at all. If a proposition's factuality requires some account of the cognitive powers that would be required for knowing that proposition to be true, and if the sceptic shows that, in the case of some propositions, no such account can be given, scepticism is self-undermining. This argument shares with Clarke's more than just structural similarities.

None of these arguments appeals to me. I do not want to distinguish between internal and external questions or between plain and philosophical meanings of statements. Nor do I wish to claim that, for deep philosophical reasons, apparently factual statements are really not factual at all. The reason is that I think that all these reactions to scepticism reveal the deep and pervasive influence of epistemological realism. I suggested earlier that one of the epistemological realist's central commitments is to the doctrine that content determines status. Now I claim that the attempt to insulate common sense from sceptical undermining by finding a different meaning, or no factual meaning at all, in the apparently commonsensical propositions the sceptic examines is

driven by that same doctrine. If a statement is certain in one context but not in another, the argument assumes, this can only be because a change in context induces a change in meaning. So if, plainly speaking, we do know that we are awake at the moment, whereas, philosophically speaking, we don't, our plain and philosophical propositions can only be "verbal twins." But if, as I have argued, epistemological status is never determined by content alone, there is no such easy inference from a difference in status to a difference in content. We can explain the context-boundedness of sceptical doubts without getting entangled in this baroque apparatus of plain and philosophical meanings. As we shall see in a moment, this is all to the good.

Once again, I must emphasize that my argument on these matters will not be complete until I have examined the sceptic's own favoured account of the nature of philosophical reflection. Even so, however, I think it is fair to conclude that we are well on the way to accomplishing the primary goal of theoretical diagnosis, which is to get the sceptic to share the burden of theory. But there is a nagging question that is likely to surface again at this point. If we are left with one theory of knowledge confronting another, and we will never be able to determine conclusively which is correct, doesn't the sceptic win ties and so triumph at second order?

If we abandon epistemological realism, there is a clear sense in which we no longer see such things as "knowledge of the world" as appropriate objects of theory. At most, we will have a theory of the concept of knowledge. We will not have a theory of knowledge as well. A fortiori, we will not be left confronting the sceptic's theory with a theory of our own.

Perhaps this will look like a purely verbal manoeuvre, for we shall certainly be left with epistemological views, whether or not we want to think of them as a theory of knowledge. But the point isn't just verbal. For what we have seen is that the sceptic's theoretical commitments are in fact far more extensive than those of his contextualist opponent. Contextualism simply takes seriously and at face-value what seem to be evident facts of ordinary epistemic practices: that relevant evidence varies with context, that content alone never determines epistemological status, and so on. The theoretical resources required to explain these appearances away belong entirely to the sceptic. So it might be reasonable to object that the sceptic wins ties, if the outcome of my theoretical diagnosis were a tie. And if I had followed philosophers like Carnap, Clarke, or Wright and rested my diagnosis on difficult and controversial views about meaning, perhaps it would have been. But as things stand it isn't.

This is not all. It seems to me entirely reasonable to hold that extra theoretical commitments demand extra arguments. But where will the sceptic find them? Not in evidence from everyday practice, which fits in as well or better with contextualism. Presumably, then, in some kind of general, theoretical considerations. Here, however, we run into the fallaciousness of the argument from methodological necessity: by the sceptic's own standards, there is no inference from the fact that we must *take* experiential knowledge to be generally prior to knowledge of the world, if we are to make room for a project of assessing our knowledge of the world as a whole, to its really being so. But if the argument from methodological necessity does not show that the sceptic's principles are true, what would? It is hard to say: for although the argument from methodological necessity is fallacious, it is not as if there are other ways of arguing for the priority of experiential knowledge. On the contrary, as we

have seen repeatedly, attempts to argue for it directly beg the question. So the doctrine has to be true but unarguable.

I think that the sceptic's difficulties are compounded when we turn from this relatively particular doctrine to epistemological realism in general. It is not easy to imagine what a convincing argument for epistemological realism would even look like, or what evidence it could appeal to. This is where the clash between scepticism and our ordinary attitudes really does work to the sceptic's disadvantage. It does so because our ordinary practices of justification not only tolerate but invite a contexualist construction: and contextualism is the antidote to epistemological realism.

True, a contextual view of knowledge and justification will seem unsatisfactory to a philosopher who continues to feel the lack of an understanding of human knowledge in general. But if my argument to this point is correct, he will feel this lack only if he is already predisposed to epistemological realism. Once more, we are starting to run round a very small circle of ideas. The sceptic's foundationalism, together with the epistemological realism it embodies, is a brute metaphysical commitment. The theoretical diagnostician could hardly ask for more.

Notes

1 Barry Stroud, "Understanding Human Knowledge in General," in Marjorie Clay and Keith Lehrer (eds), *Knowledge and Skepticism* (Boulder, CO: Westview, 1989), p. 32.

2 W. V. Quine, "Epistemology Naturalized," this vol., ch. 39. On Quine's problematic attitude towards traditional epistemology, see Barry Stroud, *The Significance of Philosophical Scepticism* (Oxford: Oxford University Press, 1984), ch. VI.

3 Barry Stroud, "Skepticism and the Possibility of Knowledge," *Journal of Philosophy* 81, pp. 545–51. p. 551.

4 "Understanding Human Knowledge," p. 49.

5 Thomas Nagel, *The View from Nowhere* (Oxford: Oxford University Press, 1986), p. 68.

6 "Understanding Human Knowledge," p. 32.

7 René Descartes, "Meditations on First Philosophy: First Meditation," in *The Philosophical Works of Descartes,* vol. 1, trans. Elizabeth Haldane and G. R. T. Ross (Cambridge: Cambridge University Press, 1972), p. 145; David Hume, *A Treatise of Human Nature,* ed. L. A. Selby-Bigge, 2nd edn rev. P. H. Nidditch (Oxford: Oxford University Press, 1978), p. xx (hereafter, *THN*).

8 I am grateful to Simon Blackburn for this useful phrase.

9 These quotations and the next, *THN*, pp. xv–xvi.

10 *Novum Organum*, bk II in J. Spedding, R. Ellis, and D. Heath (eds), *The Works of Francis Bacon* (London: Longman, 1857–8), vol. IV. My example is slightly unfair to

Bacon in that he did not intend to give instances of everything that would, in common parlance, be said to involve "heating." His aim was to collect instances which "agree in the same nature, though in substance the most unlike": *Novum Organum*, II, aphorism xi.

11 W. V. Quine, "Two Dogmas of Empiricism," in W. V. Quine (ed.), *From a Logical Point of View* (New York: Harper, 1963).

12 H. P. Grice and P. F. Strawson, "In Defence of a Dogma," *Philosophical Review* (1956).

13 I must thank Alvin Goldman for pressing me on this point.

14 Myles Burnyeat ("Idealism and Greek Philosophy: What Descartes Saw and Berkeley Missed," *Philosophical Review* 90, pp. 3–40) thinks that Descartes's externalization of his own body is the key move in his invention of the problem of our knowledge of the external world. I see it as a consequence of his epistemological realism.

15 W. V. Quine, *Pursuit of Truth* (Cambridge MA: Harvard University Press, 1990), p. 80.

16 Ibid., p. 82.

17 However, it seems to me that the more a purely disquotational account of "true" can be shown to capture whatever we want out of the truth-predicate, the less reason there is for thinking that there must be some "truth-making" property that all true sentences share: the invitation to apply Occam's Razor ought to be, irresistible.

18 Stephen Leeds, "Theories of Reference and Truth," *Erkenntnis* (1978).

19 Attempts to discuss the Gettier problem and traditional sceptical questions in the same breath often seem rather contrived. The epistemological analogue of Leed's distinction explains why.

20 Keith Lehrer notes that the "definitional or formal" in his theory of knowledge, which "constitutes an analysis or explication of the concept of knowledge," "leaves open substantive issues." See Lehrer, "Knowledge Reconsidered" in Clay and Lehrer (eds), *Knowledge and Skepticism*, quotation p. 132.

21 Laurence BonJour, *The Structure of Empirical Knowledge* (Cambridge, MA: Harvard University Press, 1985), pp. 89 ff. Subsequent citations given by *Structure* and page numbers.

22 The terminology of formal versus substantive foundationalism is also employed by Ernest Sosa: see "The Raft and the Pyramid," this vol., ch. 13. However, I am uncertain whether my usage is the same as Sosa's. According to Sosa, "A type of *formal foundationalism* with respect to a normative or evaluative property ϕ is the view that the conditions (actual and possible) within which ϕ would apply can be specified in general, perhaps recursively. *Substantive foundationalism* is only a particular way of doing so" (p. 278, italics in original). From my point of view, everything depends on what is allowed to count as a "general" specification.

23 Though I have grave doubts about the notion of intrinsic credibility, having written about all this elsewhere (*Groundless Belief* (Oxford: Blackwell), chs 2, 3, and 5) I will not repeat myself. My interest here is in the foundationalist's conception of epistemological priority, which I see as his deepest theoretical commitment.

24 Letter to Mersenne (24 December, 1640), quoted from Anthony Kenny (ed.), *Descartes: Philosophical Letters* (Minneapolis: University of Minnesota Press, 1981), p. 87.

25 Ludwig Wittgenstein, *On Certainty* (Oxford: Blackwell, 1969), p. 250; hereafter *OC*.

26 Ibid., p. 125.

27 Failure to appreciate this point is what vitiates Marie McGinn's intuitive reconstruction of the case for scepticism.

28 *OC*, p. 53.

29 For a succinct defence of contextualism, see David B. Annis, "A Contextualist Theory of Epistemic Justification," *American Philosophical Quarterly* (1978), reprinted in Moser, *Empirical Knowledge* (Totowa, NJ: Rowman and Littlefield, 1986). Annis sees Pierce, Dewey, and Popper as having been, historically, the key contextualists. He may be right, though I have doubts about how far these philosophers saw into the implications of contextualism. For example, I doubt whether Popper would be as suspicious as he is about justification if he were really a thoroughgoing contextualist.

30 Obviously, this kind of externalism is not the same as pure reliabilism, except in so far as the apparent theoretical simplicity of some

forms of reliabilism is a sham. Consider, for example, Colin McGinn's suggestion (in "The Concept of Knowledge," in *Midwest Studies in Philosophy* IX (1984)) that knowing that *p* depends on the availability of a "way of telling" that *p*. This analysis does not guarantee any theoretical integrity in "ways of telling" and is therefore compatible with a contextual, hence anti-epistemological-realist, conception of knowledge.

31 *OC*, p. 88.
32 Ibid., p. 163.
33 Ibid., p. 235.
34 Ibid., pp. 341–3.
35 Ibid., p. 318, emphasis in original. Cf. the metaphor of the river bed at pp. 95–8.
36 Nelson Goodman, *Ways of Worldmaking* (Indianapolis: Hackett, 1978), ch. 1.
37 Thompson Clarke, "The Legacy of Skepticism," *Journal of Philosophy* 69, pp. 754–69; p. 756.
38 Ibid., pp. 758 ff.
39 Ibid., pp. 762, 761.

PART II

The Structure of Knowledge and Justification

Introduction

The Pyrrhonian problematic can be formulated as follows. One can be justified in believing that p only if one has a reason to believe that p. But if a proposition that q is one's reason to believe that p, it can provide justification only if it is a *good* reason – that is, only if it, too, is something one is justified in believing. This leaves three possibilities for any tree of justification: (1) all its branches terminate; (2) at least one of its branches contains a loop; (3) at least one of its branches is infinite. Thus, we have the three traditional theories of justification: foundationalism, coherentism, and the rather less popular infinitism. To be complete, there is a fourth option not mentioned, namely that skepticism is true, and there are no trees of justification, for no one is ever justified in believing anything.

This description of the Pyrrhonian problematic corresponds closely to the way Roderick Chisholm sees the epistemological terrain. Faced with these options, he chooses foundationalism. This means admitting that there are some propositions that we are justified in believing but for which we lack reasons in the form of further propositions we are justified in believing. Chisholm fully embraces this consequence. Having made the statement "There lies a key," if one is asked "What is your justification for thinking *that*?," one must provide an answer, but eventually, in the chain of questions, a claim about one's present experience will be challenged: "What is your justification for thinking you have such-and-such experience?" To this, Chisholm thinks one can do no better than to answer: "My justification is that I have such-and-such experience." Similarly, faced with a challenge to a claim regarding one's present belief that p, one must repeat oneself, saying "My justification for thinking I believe that p is that I believe that p."

Wilfrid Sellars attacks the doctrine of the given precisely on the issue of the epistemological status of these foundational beliefs. If there is knowledge that is unsupported by further knowledge, as Chisholm would have to acknowledge, then reports of this knowledge, like reports of any piece of knowledge, must have authority (Chisholm and Sellars seem to assume that the structure of justification is the same as the structure of knowledge). But a report can have authority only if the person making it recognizes its authority. Thus, even in the case of my knowledge that what I see before me is green, my report "This is green" must have authority that I recognize. Moreover, in this case, the authority can only lie in the reliable connection between the production of tokens of "This is green" and the presence of green objects. So if I am to know through observation that what I see is green, I must recognize the truth of this generalization. How, then, do I know the truth of the generalization? My present knowledge is based on memory knowledge of instances of it. What of my knowledge of these instances? Are we headed for a regress? No, answers Sellars, for although I have such memory knowledge, the experiential beliefs from which these memories are derived need not have been instances of knowledge. (Presumably, these instances of memory knowledge, too, have authority that is also recognized by the subject in the form of a belief that reports of "This was green, and I experienced it to be so" co-vary with actual past encounters with green objects.)

Sellars' account rules out Chisholm's given. Formulated in the language of beliefs rather than of reports: if all knowledge of particular matters of fact, including observational knowledge, depends on general knowledge, and if in turn this general knowledge itself depends on knowledge of particular matters of fact, then empirical knowledge has no foundation.

Laurence BonJour joins Sellars in arguing that foundationalism fails to solve the problem that it was designed to solve, viz. the Pyrrhonian problematic. He bases his argument on the very nature of epistemic justification as essentially connected to the cognitive goal of truth. What this connection amounts to, he claims, is that a belief is justified only if one has good reason to think it is true. Not only this: one must have good reason to think, regarding whatever feature that in fact makes the belief justified, that beliefs possessing that feature are likely to be true. The problem for foundationalists is that there is only one conceivable way foundational beliefs could count as justified: one would have to know, regarding whatever feature makes foundational beliefs foundational, that beliefs with that feature were likely to be true. Yet this is not knowable *a priori*, at least about any of the sources of empirical knowledge. Nor can it be known *a posteriori*, for it could only be established using circular reasoning, which is eschewed by foundationalists.

BonJour anticipates objections to his interpretation of the conditions required for having good reason to think a belief true. In favor of givenists, he acknowledges that the search for the given is a search for something that justifies foundational beliefs. Nonetheless, they seek the impossible. There cannot be a state of mind that is able to impart justification but needs no justification itself. To impart justification, a state must have assertive content, and having assertive content suffices for standing in need of justification.

If Sellars and BonJour are right that foundationalism is inadequate, then the door is open for alternatives. Donald Davidson proposes a coherentist theory based on conclusions about meaning and content. Meaning, coherence, and truth, he argues, are internally connected. The meaning of one's words and one's thoughts depends on one's being interpretable as a coherent (indeed a rational) believer, most of whose beliefs are true. Since a fully informed or omniscient interpreter would also interpret any believer as having mostly true beliefs, it follows that all believers, ourselves included, have mostly true beliefs. This would establish a further connection to justification, according to

Davidson, for in seeing that most of our beliefs are true, we gain a presumptive reason in favor of retaining any arbitrary one of them.

Susan Haack sees merit in both the coherentist and foundationalist approaches. Her aim is to connect epistemic justification essentially with truth-conduciveness. After examining varieties of foundationalist and coherentist theories, she claims that we remain in need of an account of how there could be both logical and causal relations between experience and beliefs. Only a logical relation can ensure the rational or justificatory connection between experience and belief. And only a causal connection can ensure the linking of empirical justification with truth. For an empirical worldly fact can enter our cognitive economy only through experience.

Haack proposes to provide both the logical and causal connection by employing a distinction between belief states (S-beliefs) and the contents of those states (C-beliefs). She begins by giving an evidentialist account of justification: agent A is more/less justified in believing that p depending upon how good A's evidence is for p. The distinction between S- and C-beliefs is then employed in characterizing A's evidence. A's evidence consists of three sorts of items: A's S-reasons, A's C-reasons, and A's experiential C-evidence for believing that p. The S-reasons are themselves S-beliefs sustained ultimately by A's experiential S-states. The role of experience in sustaining S-beliefs, Haack claims, identifies what was right about experientialist foundationalism. A's C-reasons for believing that p are the C-beliefs that serve as the contents of A's S-reasons for believing that p. Coherentists were right to emphasize the non-linear character of C-reasons in justification. No class of C-beliefs is basic in the nexus of C-reasons. Finally, A's experiential C-evidence consists of true propositions to the effect that A is in a certain state, viz. the state that constitutes A's experiential S-evidence for believing that p. It is the last element of A's evidence, Haack believes, that supplies the necessary connection between justification and truth. One might be tempted to doubt this: surely, a proposition to the effect that it seems visually as if there is something green before me provides no guaranteed link to truth. It could very well be that my experience is unveridical. How could the mere fact that I have an experience as of something green before me be evidence in favor of there being something green before me? Haack's answer is that the appropriate description of the experience characterizes it in a world-involving way. Thus, a visual experience as if there being something green before me is to be described as the kind of experience a normal subject would be in, in normal circumstances, when looking at a green thing. This would seem to provide the link between justification and truth. That I am in the kind of experiential state that is normally or typically caused by a green thing does seem to make it objectively more probable that there is a green thing before me.

Thus, we have foundherentism. Foundationalist elements survive in the claim that experiential S-reasons form the causal bedrock, coherentist elements in the claim that the structure of C-reasons do not have a linear structure. The connection with truth, missed by coherentism and by many forms of foundationalism, is secured through the claim that part of the C-evidence for a belief includes truths describing experiences in terms of their typical external causes.

Like Haack, Ernest Sosa attempts to reconcile coherentism and foundationalism – the raft and the pyramid. Traditional foundationalism and coherentism alike are committed to a kind of "formal" foundationalism, which holds that epistemic conditions supervene on non-epistemic conditions in a way that can be specified in general, perhaps recursively. Formal foundationalism, according to Sosa, derives its plausibility from the claims that epistemic conditions are normative and that all normative conditions are supervenient. If a state of affairs is good, it must be good because it is a state of pleasure or because it is a state of desire satisfaction, etc. It cannot be *barely* good or good ultimately owing merely to the goodness of some other state(s). So, too, if a belief is justified, some non-epistemic condition must account for its justification. Sosa goes on to argue that the thesis of formal foundationalism conflicts with internalist theories of justification (perhaps such as Sellars'). If one's justification for believing that *p* is fixed ultimately by non-epistemic facts, then such justification cannot in every case also require the possession of further justified beliefs.

In the final selection of this section, Peter Klein argues in favor of the often dismissed position of infinitism. Infinitism provides an account of justification according to which the structure of justificatory reasons is infinite and non-repeating. Klein argues that infinitism provides an acceptable account of rational beliefs, while other epistemic theories, such as foundationalism and coherentism, cannot. This is because infinitism is the only epistemic theory that can satisfy two plausible constraints upon reasoning – that reasoning neither be arbitrary nor beg the question. Infinitism is similar to foundationalism in holding that not every belief counts as a reason but differs to the extent that the infinitist also holds PAA (the principle of avoiding arbitrariness), which states that there are no foundational reasons and so every reason stands in need of another reason. Infinitism is similar to coherentism in holding that only reasons can justify a belief but differs to the extent that the infinitist also holds PAC (the principle of avoiding circularity), which states that justifying reasons cannot beg the question. For much of the paper Klein deals with the main objections to infinitism, including (1) the finite mind objection, (2) the objection that if some knowledge is inferential then some knowledge must not be, (3) a reductio argument against the possibility of an infinite regress providing a justification for beliefs, and (4) skeptical objections.

Further Reading

Alston, William, "Two Types of Foundationalism," in *Epistemic Justification* (Ithaca, NY: Cornell University Press, 1989), pp. 19–38.

Audi, Robert, *The Structure of Justification* (New York: Cambridge University Press, 1993).

Bender, J. (ed.), *The Current State of the Coherence Theory* (Dordrecht: Kluwer Academic Publishers, 1989).

BonJour, Laurence, *The Structure of Empirical Knowledge* (Cambridge, MA: Harvard University Press, 1985).

BonJour, Laurence and Ernest Sosa, *Epistemic Justification: Internalism vs. Externalism, Foundations vs. Virtues* (Oxford: Blackwell, 2003).

Chisholm, Roderick, *The Foundations of Knowing* (Minneapolis: University of Minnesota Press, 1982).

——, *Theory of Knowledge* (Englewood Cliffs: Prentice-Hall, 1966, 2nd edn 1977, 3rd edn 1989).

DePaul, Michael (ed.), *Resurrecting Old-Fashioned Foundationalism* (Langham, MD: Rowman and Littlefield, 2000).

Fantl, Jeremy, "Modest Infinitism," *Canadian Journal of Philosophy* 33 (2003), pp. 537–62.

Gillett, Carl, "*Infinitism* Redux? A Response to Klein," *Philosophy and Phenomenological Research* 66 (2003), pp. 709–17.

Haack, Susan, *Evidence and Inquiry: Towards Reconstruction in Epistemology* (Oxford: Blackwell, 1993).

Lehrer, Keith, *Theory of Knowledge* (Boulder, CO: Westview Press, 1990).

Lewis, C. I., *An Analysis of Knowledge and Valuation* (LaSalle, IL: Open Court Publishing Company, 1946).

Plantinga, Alvin, *Warrant: The Current Debate* (Oxford: Oxford University Press, 1993).

Rescher, Nicholas, *Methodological Pragmatism* (New York: New York University Press, 1977).

Sellars, Wilfrid, "Empiricism and the Philosophy of Mind," reprinted in Sellars, *Science, Perception and Reality* (London: Routledge and Kegan Paul, 1963).

——, "Givenness and Explanatory Coherence," *Journal of Philosophy* 70 (1973), pp. 612–24.

Sosa, Ernest, *Knowledge in Perspective: Selected Essays in Epistemology* (Cambridge: Cambridge University Press, 1991).

CHAPTER 7

The Myth of the Given

Roderick M. Chisholm

1. The doctrine of "the given" involved two theses about our knowledge. We may introduce them by means of a traditional metaphor:

(A) The knowledge which a person has at any time is a structure or edifice, many parts and stages of which help to support each other, but which as a whole is supported by its own foundation.

The second thesis is a specification of the first:

(B) The foundation of one's knowledge consists (at least in part) of the apprehension of what have been called, variously, "sensations," "sense-impressions," "appearances," "sensa," "sense-qualia," and "phenomena."

These phenomenal entities, said to be at the base of the structure of knowledge, are what was called "the given." A third thesis is sometimes associated with the doctrine of the given, but the first two theses do not imply it. We may formulate it in the terms of the same metaphor:

(C) The *only* apprehension which is thus basic to the structure of knowledge is our

apprehension of "appearances" (etc.) – our apprehension of the given.

Theses (A) and (B) constitute the "doctrine of the given"; thesis (C), if a label were necessary, might be called "the phenomenalistic version" of the doctrine. The first two theses are essential to the empirical tradition in Western philosophy. The third is problematic for traditional empiricism and depends in part, but only in part, upon the way in which the metaphor of the edifice and its foundation is spelled out.

I believe it is accurate to say that, at the time at which our study begins, most American epistemologists accepted the first two theses and thus accepted the doctrine of the given. The expression "the given" became a term of contemporary philosophical vocabulary partly because of its use by C. I. Lewis in his *Mind and the World-Order* (Scribner, 1929). Many of the philosophers who accepted the doctrine avoided the expression because of its association with other more controversial parts of Lewis's book – a book which might be taken (though mistakenly, I think) also to endorse thesis (C), the "phenomenalistic version" of the doctrine. The doctrine itself – theses (A) and (B) – became a matter of general controversy during the period of our survey.

Thesis (A) was criticized as being "absolute" and thesis (B) as being overly "subjective." Both criticisms may be found in some of the "instrumentalistic" writings of John Dewey and philosophers

Originally published in R. Chisholm, *Philosophy* (Englewood Cliffs, NJ: Prentice-Hall, 1964), pp. 261–86.

associated with him. They may also be found in the writings of those philosophers of science ("logical empiricists") writing in the tradition of the Vienna Circle. (At an early stage of this tradition, however, some of these same philosophers seem to have accepted all three theses.) Discussion became entangled in verbal confusions – especially in connection with the uses of such terms as "doubt," "certainty," "appearance," and "immediate experience." Philosophers, influenced by the work that Ludwig Wittgenstein had been doing in the 1930s, noted such confusions in detail, and some of them seem to have taken the existence of such confusions to indicate that (A) and (B) are false.[1] Many have rejected both theses as being inconsistent with a certain theory of thought and reference; among them, in addition to some of the critics just referred to, we find philosophers in the tradition of nineteenth-century "idealism."

Philosophers of widely diverging schools now believe that "the myth of the given" has finally been dispelled.[2] I suggest, however, that, although thesis (C), "the phenomenalistic version," is false, the two theses, (A) and (B), which constitute the doctrine of the given are true.

The doctrine is not merely the consequence of a metaphor. We are led to it when we attempt to answer certain questions about *justification* – our justification for supposing, in connection with any one of the things that we know to be true, that it is something that we know to be true.

2. To the question "What justification do I have for thinking I know that *a* is true?" one may reply: "I know that *b* is true, and if I know that *b* is true then I also know that *a* is true." And to the question "What justification do I have for thinking I know that *b* is true?" one may reply: "I know that *c* is true, and if I know that *c* is true then I also know that *b* is true." Are we thus led, sooner or later, to something *n* of which one may say: "What justifies me in thinking I know that *n* is true is simply the fact that *n* is true." If there is such an *n*, then the belief or statement that *n* is true may be thought of either as a belief or statement which "justifies itself" or as a belief or statement which is itself "neither justified nor unjustified." The distinction – unlike that between a Prime Mover which moves itself and a Prime Mover which is neither in motion nor at rest – is largely a verbal

one; the essential thing, if there is such an *n*, is that it provides a stopping place in the process, or dialectic, of justification.

We may now re-express, somewhat less metaphorically, the two theses which I have called the "doctrine of the given." The first thesis, that our knowledge is an edifice or structure having its own foundation, becomes (A) "every statement, which we are justified in thinking that we know, is justified in part by some statement which justifies itself." The second thesis, that there are appearances ("the given") at the foundation of our knowledge, becomes (B) "there are statements about appearances which thus justify themselves." (The third thesis – the "phenomenalistic version" of the doctrine of the given – becomes (C) "there are no self-justifying statements which are not statements about appearances.")

Let us now turn to the first of the two theses constituting the doctrine of the given.

3. "Every justified statement is justified in part by some statement which justifies itself." Could it be that the question which this thesis is supposed to answer is a question which arises only because of some mistaken assumption? If not, what are the alternative ways of answering it? And did any of the philosophers with whom we are concerned actually accept any of these alternatives? The first two questions are less difficult to answer than the third.

There are the following points of view to be considered, each of which *seems* to have been taken by some of the philosophers in the period of our survey.

(1) One may believe that the questions about justification which give rise to our problem are based upon false assumptions and hence that they *should not be asked* at all.

(2) One may believe that no statement or claim is justified unless it is justified, at least in part, by some other justified statement or claim which it does not justify; this belief may suggest that one should continue the process of justifying *ad indefinitum*, justifying each claim by reference to some additional claim.

(3) One may believe that no statement or claim *a* is justified unless it is justified by some other justified statement or claim *b*, and that

b is not justified unless it in turn is justified by *a*; this would suggest that the process of justifying is, or should be, *circular.*

(4) One may believe that there are some particular claims *n* at which the process of justifying should stop, and one may then hold of any such claim *n* either: (a) *n* is justified by something – viz., *experience* or *observation* – which is not itself a claim and which therefore cannot be said itself either to be justified or unjustified; (b) *n* is itself *unjustified;* (c) *n justifies itself;* or (d) *n* is *neither justified nor unjustified.*

These possibilities, I think, exhaust the significant points of view; let us now consider them in turn.

4. "The question about justification which give rise to the problem are based upon false assumptions and therefore should not be asked at all."

The questions are *not* based upon false assumptions; but most of the philosophers who discussed the questions put them in such a misleading way that one is very easily misled into supposing that they *are* based upon false assumptions.

Many philosophers, following Descartes, Russell, and Husserl, formulated the questions about justification by means of such terms as "doubt," "certainty," and "incorrigibility," and they used, or misused, these terms in such a way that, when their questions were taken in the way in which one would ordinarily take them, they could be shown to be based upon false assumptions. One may note, for example, that the statement "There is a clock on the mantelpiece" is not self-justifying – for to the question "What is your justification for thinking you know that there is a clock on the mantelpiece?" the proper reply would be to make some other statement (e.g., "I saw it there this morning and no one would have taken it away") – and one may then go on to ask "But are there any statements which can be said to justify themselves?" If we express these facts, as many philosophers did, by saying that the statement "There is a clock on the mantelpiece" is one which is not "certain," or one which may be "doubted," and if we then go on to ask "Does this doubtful statement rest upon other statements which are certain and incorrigible?" then we are using terms

in an extraordinarily misleading way. The question "Does this doubtful statement rest upon statements which are certain and incorrigible?" – if taken as one would ordinarily take it – does rest upon a false assumption, for (we may assume) the statement that there is a clock on the mantelpiece is one which is not doubtful at all.

John Dewey, and some of the philosophers whose views were very similar to his, tended to suppose, mistakenly, that the philosophers who asked themselves "What justification do I have for thinking I know this?" were asking the quite different question "What more can I do to verify or confirm that this is so?" and they rejected answers to the first question on the ground that they were unsatisfactory answers to the second.[3] Philosophers influenced by Wittgenstein tended to suppose, also mistakenly, but quite understandably, that the question "What justification do I have for thinking I know this?" contains an implicit challenge and presupposes that one does not have the knowledge concerned. They then pointed out, correctly, that in most of the cases where the question was raised (e.g., "What justifies me in thinking I know that this is a table?") there is no ground for challenging the claim to knowledge and that questions presupposing that the claim is false should not arise. But the question "What justifies me in thinking I know that this is a table?" does not challenge the claim to know that this is a table, much less presuppose that the claim is false.

The "critique of cogency," as Lewis described this concern of epistemology, presupposes that we *are* justified in thinking we know most of the things that we do think we know, and what it seeks to elicit is the nature of this justification. The enterprise is like that of ethics, logic, and aesthetics:

> The nature of the good can be learned from experience only if the content of experience be first classified into good and bad, or grades of better and worse. Such classification or grading already involves the legislative application of the same principle which is sought. In logic, principles can be elicited by generalization from examples only if cases of valid reasoning have first been segregated by some criterion. In esthetics, the laws of the beautiful may be derived from experience only if the criteria of beauty have first been correctly applied.[4]

When Aristotle considered an invalid mood of the syllogism and asked himself "What is wrong with this?" he was not suggesting to himself that perhaps nothing was wrong; he presupposed that the mood *was* invalid, just as he presupposed that others were not, and he attempted, successfully, to formulate criteria which would enable us to distinguish the two types of mood.

When we have answered the question "What justification do I have for thinking I know this?" what we learn, as Socrates taught, is something about ourselves. We learn, of course, what the justification happens to be for the particular claim with which the question is concerned. But we also learn, more generally, what the criteria are, if any, in terms of which we believe ourselves justified in counting one thing as an instance of knowing and another thing not. The truth which the philosopher seeks, when he asks about justification, is "already implicit in the mind which seeks it, and needs only to be elicited and brought to clear expression."[5]

Let us turn, then, to the other approaches to the problem of "the given."

5. "No statement or claim would be justified unless it were justified, at least in part, by some other justified claim or statement which it does not justify."

This regressive principle might be suggested by the figure of the building and its supports: no stage supports another unless it is itself supported by some other stage beneath it – a truth which holds not only of the upper portions of the building but also of what we call its foundation. And the principle follows if, as some of the philosophers in the tradition of logical empiricism seemed to believe, we should combine a frequency theory of probability with a probability theory of justification.

In *Experience and Prediction* (U. of Chicago, 1938) and in other writings, Hans Reichenbach defended a "probability theory of knowledge" which seemed to involve the following contentions:

(1) To justify accepting a statement, it is necessary to show that the statement is probable.
(2) To say of a statement that it is probable is to say something about statistical frequencies. Somewhat more accurately, a statement of the form "It is *probable* that any particular *a* is a *b*" may be explicated as saying "Most *a*'s are *b*'s." Or, still more accurately, to say "The probability is *n* that a particular *a* is a *b*" is to say "The limit of the relative frequency with which the property of being a *b* occurs in the class of things having the property *a* is *n*."
(3) Hence, by (2), to show that a proposition is probable it is necessary to show that a certain statistical frequency obtains; and, by (1), to show that a certain statistical frequency obtains it is necessary to show that it is probable that the statistical frequency obtains; and therefore, by (2), to show that it is probable that a certain statistical frequency obtains, it is necessary to show that a certain frequency of frequencies obtains. ...
(4) And therefore "there is no Archimedean point of absolute certainty left to which to attach our knowledge of the world; all we have is an elastic net of probability connections floating in open space" (p. 192).

This reasoning suggests that an infinite number of steps must be taken in order to justify acceptance of any statement. For, according to the reasoning, we cannot determine the probability of one statement until we have determined that of a second, and we cannot determine that of the second until we have determined that of a third, and so on. Reichenbach does not leave the matter here, however. He suggests that there is a way of "descending" from this "open space" of probability connections, but, if I am not mistaken, we can make the descent only by letting go of the concept of justification.

He says that, if we are to avoid the regress of probabilities of probabilities of probabilities ... we must be willing at some point merely to make a guess; "there will always be some blind posits on which the whole concatenation is based" (p. 367). The view that knowledge is to be identified with certainty and that probable knowledge must be "imbedded in a framework of certainty" is "a remnant of rationalism. An empiricist theory of probability can be constructed only if we are willing to regard knowledge as a system of posits."[6]

But if we begin by assuming, as we do, that there is a distinction between knowledge, on the one hand, and a lucky guess, on the other, then we must reject at least one of the premises of any argument purporting to demonstrate that knowledge is a system of "blind posits." The unacceptable conclusion of Reichenbach's argument may be so construed as to follow from premises (1) and (2); and premise (2) may be accepted as a kind of definition (though there are many who believe that this definition is not adequate to all of the uses of the term "probable" in science and everyday life). Premise (1), therefore, is the one we should reject, and there are good reasons, I think, for rejecting (1), the thesis that "to justify accepting a proposition it is necessary to show that the proposition is probable." In fairness to Reichenbach, it should be added that he never explicitly affirms premise (1); but some such premise is essential to his argument.

6. "No statement or claim *a* would be justified unless it were justified by some other justified statement or claim *b* which would not be justified unless it were justified in turn by *a*."

The "coherence theory of truth," to which some philosophers committed themselves, is sometimes taken to imply that justification may thus be circular; I believe, however, that the theory does not have this implication. It does define "truth" as a kind of systematic consistency of beliefs or propositions. The truth of a proposition is said to consist, not in the fact that the proposition "corresponds" with something which is not itself a proposition, but in the fact that it fits consistently into a certain more general system of propositions. This view may even be suggested by the figure of the building and its foundations. There is no difference in principle between the way in which the upper stories are supported by the lower, and that in which the cellar is supported by the earth just below it, or the way in which that stratum of earth is supported by various substrata farther below; a good building appears to be a part of the terrain on which it stands and a good system of propositions is a part of the wider system which gives it its truth. But these metaphors do not solve philosophical problems.

The coherence theory did in fact appeal to something other than logical consistency; its proponents conceded that a system of false propositions may be internally consistent and hence that logical consistency alone is no guarantee of truth.

Brand Blanshard, who defended the coherence theory in *The Nature of Thought*, said that a proposition is true provided it is a member of an internally consistent system of propositions and *provided further* this system is "the system in which everything real and possible is coherently included."[7] In one phase of the development of "logical empiricism" its proponents seem to have held a similar view: a proposition – or, in this case, a statement – is true provided it is a member of an internally consistent system of statements and *provided further* this system is "the system which is actually adopted by mankind, and especially by the scientists in our culture circle."[8]

A theory of truth is not, as such, a theory of justification. To say that a proposition is true is not to say that we are justified in accepting it as true, and to say that we are justified in accepting it as true is not to say that it is true. Whatever merits the coherence theory may have as an answer to certain questions about truth, it throws no light upon our present epistemological question. If we accept the coherence theory, we may still ask, concerning any proposition *a* which we think we know to be true, "What is my justification for thinking I know that *a* is a member of the system of propositions in which everything real and possible is coherently included, or that *a* is a member of the system of propositions which is actually adopted by mankind and by the scientists of our culture circle?" And when we ask such a question, we are confronted, once again, with our original alternatives.

7. If our questions about justification do have a proper stopping place, then, as I have said, there are still four significant possibilities to consider. We may stop with some particular claim and say of it that either.

(a) it is justified by something – by experience, or by observation – which is not itself a claim and which, therefore, cannot be said either to be justified or to be unjustified;

(b) it is justified by some claim which refers to our experience or observation, and the claim referring to our experience or observation has *no* justification;

(c) it justifies itself; or

(d) it is itself neither justified nor unjustified.

The first of these alternatives leads readily to the second, and the second to the third or to the fourth. The third and the fourth – which differ only verbally, I think – involve the doctrine of "the given."

Carnap wrote, in 1936, that the procedure of scientific testing involves two operations: the "confrontation of a statement with observation" and the "confrontation of a statement with previously accepted statements." He suggested that those logical empiricists who were attracted to the coherence theory of truth tended to lose sight of the first of these operations – the confrontation of a statement with observation. He proposed a way of formulating simple "acceptance rules" for such confrontation and he seemed to believe that, merely by applying such rules, we could avoid the epistemological questions with which the adherents of "the given" had become involved.

Carnap said this about his acceptance rules: "If no foreign language or introduction of new terms is involved, the rules are trivial. For example: 'If one is hungry, the statement "I am hungry" may be accepted'; or: 'If one sees a key one may accept the statement "there lies a key."'"[9] As we shall note later, the first of these rules differs in an important way from the second. Confining ourselves for the moment to rules of the second sort – "If one sees a key one may accept the statement 'there lies a key'" – let us ask ourselves whether the appeal to such rules enables us to solve our problem of the stopping place.

When we have made the statement "There lies a key," we can, of course, raise the question "What is my justification for thinking I know, or for believing, that there lies a key?" The answer would be "I see the key." We cannot ask "What is my justification for seeing a key?" But we *can* ask "What is my justification for thinking that it is a *key* that I see?" and, if we *do* see that the thing is a key, the question will have an answer. The answer might be "I see that it's shaped like a key and that it's in the lock, and I remember that a key is usually here." The possibility of this question, and its answer, indicates that we cannot stop our questions about justification merely by appealing to observation or experience. For, of the statement "I observe that that is an A," we can ask, and answer, the question "What is my justification for thinking that I observe that there is an A?"

It is relevant to note, moreover, that there may be conditions under which seeing a key does *not* justify one in accepting the statement "There is a key" or in believing that one sees a key. If the key were so disguised or concealed that the man who saw it did not recognize it to be a key, then he might not be justified in accepting the statement "There is a key." Just as, if Mr. Jones unknown to anyone but himself is a thief, then the people who see him may be said to see a thief – but none of those who thus sees a thief is justified in accepting the statement "There is a thief."[10]

Some of the writings of logical empiricists suggest that, although some statements may be justified by reference to other statements, those statements which involve "confrontation with observation" are not justified at all. C. G. Hempel, for example, wrote that "the acknowledgement of an experiential statements as true is psychologically motivated by certain experiences; but within the system of statements which express scientific knowledge or one's beliefs at a given time, they function in the manner of postulates for which no grounds are offered."[11] Hempel conceded, however, that this use of the term "postulate" is misleading and he added the following note of clarification: "When an experiential sentence is accepted 'on the basis of direct experiential evidence,' it is indeed not asserted arbitrarily; but to describe the evidence in question would simply mean to repeat the experiential statement itself. Hence, in the context of cognitive justification, the statement functions in the manner of a primitive sentence."[12]

When we reach a statement having the property just referred to – an experiential statement such that to describe its evidence "would simply mean to repeat the experiential statement itself" – we have reached a proper stopping place in the process of justification.

8. We are thus led to the concept of a belief, statement, claim, proposition, or hypothesis, which justifies itself. To be clear about the concept, let us note the way in which we would justify the statement that we have a certain belief. It is essential, of course, that we distinguish justifying the statement *that* we have a certain belief from justifying the belief itself.

Suppose, then, a man is led to say "I believe that Socrates is mortal" and we ask him "What is your justification for thinking that you believe, or for thinking that you know that you believe, that Socrates is mortal?" To this strange question, the only appropriate reply would be "My justification for thinking I believe, or for thinking that I know that I believe, that Socrates is mortal is simply the fact that I *do* believe that Socrates is mortal." One justifies the statement simply by reiterating it; the statement's justification is what the statement says. Here, then, we have a case which satisfies Hempel's remark quoted above; we describe the evidence for a statement merely by repeating the statement. We could say, as C. J. Ducasse did, that "the occurrence of belief is its own evidence."[13]

Normally, as I have suggested, one cannot justify a statement merely by reiterating it. To the question "What justification do you have for thinking you know that there can be no life on the moon?" it would be inappropriate, and impertinent, to reply by saying simply "There *can* be no life on the moon," thus reiterating the fact at issue. An appropriate answer would be one referring to certain *other* facts – for example, the fact that we know there is insufficient oxygen on the moon to support any kind of life. But to the question "What is your justification for thinking you know that you believe so and so?" there is nothing to say other than "I *do* believe so and so."

We may say, then, that there are some statements which are self-justifying, or which justify themselves. And we may say, analogously, that there are certain beliefs, claims, propositions, or hypotheses which are self-justifying, or which justify themselves. A statement, belief, claim, proposition, or hypothesis may be said to be self-justifying for a person, if the person's justification for thinking he knows it to be true is simply the fact that it *is* true.

Paradoxically, these things I have described by saying that they "justify themselves" may *also* be described by saying they are "neither justified nor unjustified." The two modes of description are two different ways of saying the same thing.

If we are sensitive to ordinary usage, we may note that the expression "I believe that I believe" is ordinarily used, not to refer to a second-order belief about the speaker's own beliefs, but to indicate that the speaker has not yet made up his mind. "I *believe that I believe* that Johnson is a

good president" might properly be taken to indicate that, if the speaker *does* believe that Johnson is a good president, he is not yet firm in that belief. Hence there is a temptation to infer that, if we say of a man who is firm in his belief that Socrates is mortal, that he is "justified in believing that he believes that Socrates is mortal," our statement "makes no sense." And there is also a temptation to go on and say that it "makes no sense" even to say of such a man, that his *statement* "I believe that Socrates is mortal" is one which is "justified" for him.[14] After all, what would it mean to say of a man's statement about his own belief, that he is *not* justified in accepting it?[15]

The questions about what does or does not "make any sense" need not, however, be argued. We *may* say, if we prefer, that the statements about the beliefs in question are "neither justified nor unjustified." Whatever mode of description we use, the essential points are two. First, we may appeal to such statements in the process of justifying some *other* statement or belief. If they *have* no justification they may yet *be* a justification – for something other than themselves. ("What justifies me in thinking that he and I are not likely to agree? The fact that I believe that Socrates is mortal and he does not.") Second, the making of such a statement does provide what I have been calling a "stopping place" in the dialectic of justification; but now, instead of signalizing the stopping place by reiterating the questioned statement, we do it by saying that the question of its justification is one which "should not arise."

It does not matter, then, whether we speak of certain statements which "justify themselves" or of certain statements which are "neither justified nor unjustified," for in either case we will be referring to the same set of statements. I shall continue to use the former phrase.

There are, then, statements about one's own beliefs ("I believe that Socrates is mortal") – and for statements about many other psychological attitudes – which are self-justifying. "What justifies me in believing, or in thinking I know, that I *hope* to come tomorrow? Simply the fact that I *do* hope to come tomorrow." Thinking, desiring, wondering, loving, hating, and other such attitudes are similar. Some, but by no means all, of the statements we can make about such attitudes, when the attitudes are our own, are self-justifying – as are statements containing such phrases as "I think

I remember" or "I seem to remember" (as distinguished from "I remember"), and "I think that I see" and "I think that I perceive" (as distinguished from "I see" and "I perceive"). Thus, of the two examples which Carnap introduced in connection with his "acceptance rules" discussed above, viz., "I am hungry" and "I see a key," we may say that the first is self-justifying and the second not.

The "doctrine of the given," it will be recalled, tells us (A) that every justified statement, about what we think we know, is justified in part by some statement which justifies itself and (B) that there are statements about appearances which thus justify themselves. The "phenomenalistic version" of the theory adds (C) that statements about appearances are the *only* statements which justify themselves. What we have been saying is that the first thesis, (A), of the doctrine of the given is true and that the "phenomenalistic version," (C), is false; let us turn now to thesis (B).

9. In addition to the self-justifying statements about psychological attitudes, are there self-justifying statements about "appearances"? Now we encounter difficulties involving the word "appearance" and its cognates.

Sometimes such words as "appears," "looks," and "seems" are used to convey what one might also convey by such terms as "believe." For example, if I say "It appears to me that General de Gaulle was successful," or "General de Gaulle seems to have been successful," I am likely to mean only that I believe, or incline to believe, that he has been successful; the words "appears" and "seems" serve as useful hedges, giving me an out, should I find out later that de Gaulle was not successful. When "appear"-words are used in this way, the statements in which they occur add nothing significant to the class of "self-justifying" statements we have just provided. Philosophers have traditionally assumed, however, that such terms as "appear" may also be used in a quite different way. If this assumption is correct, as I believe it is, then this additional use does lead us to another type of self-justifying statement.

The philosophers who exposed the confusions to which the substantival expression "appearance" gave rise were sometimes inclined to forget, I think, that things do appear to us in various ways.[16] We can alter the appearance of anything we like merely by doing something which will affect our sense organs or the conditions of observation. One of the important epistemological questions about appearances is "Are there self-justifying statements about the ways in which things appear?"

Augustine, refuting the skeptics of the late Platonic Academy, wrote:

> I do not see how the Academician can refute him who says: I know that this appears white to me, I know that my hearing is delighted with this, I know this has an agreeable odor, I know this tastes sweet to me, I know that this feels cold to me .... When a person tastes something, he can honestly swear that he knows it is sweet to his palate or the contrary, and that no trickery of the Greeks can dispossess him of that knowledge.[17]

Suppose, now, one were to ask "What justification do you have for believing, or thinking you know, that this appears white to you, or that tastes bitter to you?" Here, too, we can only reiterate the statement: "What justifies me in believing, or in thinking I know, that this appears white to me and that the tastes bitter to me is the fact that this *does* appear white to me and that *does* taste bitter."

An advantage of the misleading substantive "appearance," as distinguished from the verb "appears," is that the former may be applied to those sensuous experiences which, though capable of being appearances of things, are actually not appearances of anything. Feelings, imagery, and the sensuous content of dreams and hallucination are very much like the appearances of things and they are such that, under some circumstances, they could be appearances of things. But if we do not wish to say that they are experiences wherein some external physical things *appears* to us, we must use some expression other than "appear." For "appear," in its active voice, requires a grammatical subject and thus requires a term which refers, not merely to a way of appearing, but also to something *which* appears.

But we may avoid *both* the objective "*Something* appears blue to me," and the substantival "I sense a blue *appearance*." We may use another verb, say "sense," in a technical way, as many philosophers did, and equate it in meaning with the passive voice of "appear," thus saying simply "I *sense* blue," or the like. Or better still, it seems to me, and at the expense only of a little awkwardness, we can use "appear" in its passive voice and say "I am *appeared to* blue."

Summing up, in our new vocabulary, we may say that the philosophers who talked of the "empirically given" were referring, not to "self-justifying" statements and beliefs generally, but only to those pertaining to certain "ways of being appeared to." And the philosophers who objected to the doctrine of the given, or some of them, argued that no statement about "a way of being appeared to" can be "self-justifying."

10. Why would one suppose that "This appears white" (or, more exactly, "I am now appeared white to") is not self-justifying? The most convincing argument was this: If I say "This appears white," then, as Reichenbach put it, I am making a "comparison between a present object and a formerly seen object."[18] What I am saying *could* have been expressed by "The present way of appearing is the way in which white objects, or objects which I believe to be white, ordinarily appear." And this new statement, clearly, is not self-justifying; to justify it, as Reichenbach intimated, I must go on and say something further – something about the way in which I remember white objects to have appeared.

"Appears white" *may* thus be used to abbreviate "appears the way in which white things normally appear." Or "white thing," on the other hand, *may* be used to abbreviate "thing having the color of things which ordinarily appear white." The phrase "appear white" as it is used in the second quoted expression cannot be spelled out in the manner of the first; for the point of the second can hardly be put by saying that "white thing" may be used to abbreviate "thing having the color of things which ordinarily appear the way in which *white things* normally appear." In the second expression, the point of "appears white" is not to *compare* a way of appearing with something else; the point is to say something about the way of appearing itself. It is in terms of this second sense of "appears white" – that in which one may say significantly and without redundancy "Things that are white may normally be expected to appear white" – that we are to interpret the quotation from Augustine above. And, more generally, when it was said that "appear"-statements constitute the foundation of the edifice of knowledge, it was not intended that

the "appear"-statements be interpreted as statements asserting a comparison between a present object and any other object or set of objects.

The question now becomes "Can we formulate any significant 'appear'-statements *without* thus comparing the way in which some object appears with the way in which some other object appears, or with the way in which the object in question has appeared at some other time? Can we interpret 'This appears white' in such a way that it may be understood to refer to a present way of appearing *without* relating that way of appearing to any other object?" In *Experience and Prediction*, Reichenbach defended his own view (and that of a good many others) in this way:

> The objection may be raised that a comparison with formerly seen physical objects should be avoided, and that a basic statement is to concern the present fact only, as it is. But such a reduction would make the basic statement empty. Its content is just that there is a similarity between the present object and one formerly seen; it is by means of this relation that the present object is described. Otherwise the basic statement would consist in attaching an individual symbol, say a number, to the present object; but the introduction of such a symbol would help us in no way, since we could not make use of it to construct a comparison with other things. Only in attaching the same symbols to different objects, do we arrive at the possibility of constructing relations between the objects. (pp. 176–7)

It is true that, if an "appear"-statement is to be used successfully in communication, it must assert some comparison of objects. Clearly, if I wish *you* to know the way things are now appearing to me, I must relate these ways of appearing to something that is familiar to you. But our present question is not "Can you understand me if I predicate something of the way in which something now appears to me without relating that way of appearing to something that is familiar to you?" The question is, more simply, "Can I predicate anything of the way in which something now appears to me without thereby comparing that way of appearing with something else?" From the fact that the first of these two questions must be answered in the negative it does not follow that the second must also be answered in the negative.[19]

The issue is not one about communication, nor is it, strictly speaking, an issue about language; it concerns, rather, the nature of thought itself. Common to both "pragmatism" and "idealism," as traditions in American philosophy, is the view that to *think* about a thing, or to *interpret* or *conceptualize* it, and hence to have a *belief* about it, is essentially to relate the thing to *other* things, actual or possible, and therefore to "refer beyond it." It is this view – and not any view about language or communication – that we must oppose if we are to say of some statements about appearing, or of any other statements, that they "justify themselves."

To think about the way in which something is now appearing, according to the view in question, is to relate that way of appearing to something else, possibly to certain future experiences, possibly to the way in which things of a certain sort may be commonly expected to appear. According to the "conceptualistic pragmatism" of C. I. Lewis's *Mind and the World-Order* (1929), we grasp the present experience, any present way of appearing, only to the extent to which we relate it to some future experience.[20] According to one interpretation of John Dewey's "instrumentalistic" version of pragmatism, the present experience may be used to present or disclose something else but it does not present or disclose itself. And according to the idealistic view defended in Brand Blanshard's *The Nature of Thought*, we grasp our present experience only to the extent that we are able to include it in the one "intelligible system of universals" (vol. I, p. 632).

This theory of reference, it should be noted, applies not only to statements and beliefs about "ways of being appeared to" but also to those other statements and beliefs which I have called "self-justifying." If "This appears white," or "I am appeared white to," compares the present experience with something else, and thus depends for its justification upon what we are justified in believing about the something else, then so, too, does "I believe that Socrates is mortal" and "I hope that the peace will continue." This general conception of thought, therefore, would seem to imply that no belief or statement can be said to justify itself. But according to what we have been saying, if there is no belief or statement which justifies itself, then it is problematic whether any belief or statement is justified at all. And there-fore, as we might expect, this conception of thought and reference has been associated with skepticism.

Blanshard conceded that his theory of thought "does involve a degree of scepticism regarding our present knowledge and probably all future knowledge. In all likelihood there will never be a proposition of which we can say, 'This that I am asserting, with precisely the meaning I now attach to it, is absolutely true.'"[21] On Dewey's theory, or on one common interpretation of Dewey's theory, it is problematic whether anyone can now be said to *know* that Mr Jones is working in his garden. A. O. Lovejoy is reported to have said that, for Dewey, "I am about to have known" is as close as we ever get to "I know."[22] C. I. Lewis, in his *An Analysis of Knowledge and Valuation* (Open Court, 1946) conceded in effect that the conception of thought suggested by his earlier *Mind and the World-Order* does lead to a kind of skepticism; according to the later work there *are* "apprehensions of the given" (cf. *An Analysis*, pp. 182–3) – and thus beliefs which justify themselves.

What is the plausibility of a theory of thought and reference which seems to imply that no one knows anything?

Perhaps it is correct to say that when we think about a thing we think about it as having certain properties. But why should one go on to say that to think about a thing must always involve thinking about some *other* thing as well? Does thinking about the other thing then involve thinking about some third thing? Or can we think about one thing in relation to a second thing without thereby thinking of a third thing? And if we can, then why can we not think of one thing – of one thing as having certain properties – without thereby relating it to another thing?

The linguistic analogue of this view of thought is similar. Why should one suppose – as Reichenbach supposed in the passage cited above and as many others have also supposed – that to *refer* to a thing, in this instance to refer to a way of appearing, is necessarily to relate the thing to some *other* thing?

Some philosophers seem to have been led to such a view of reference as a result of such consid-erations as the following: We have imagined a man saying, in agreement with Augustine, "It just does appear white – and that is the end of the matter." Let us consider now the possible reply

"That it is not the end of the matter. You are making certain assumptions about the language you are using; you are assuming, for example, that you are using the word 'white,' or the phrase 'appears white,' in the way in which you have formerly used it, or in the way in which it is ordinarily used, or in the way in which it would ordinarily be understood. And if you state your justification for this assumption, you *will* refer to certain other things – to yourself and to other people, to the word 'white,' or to the phrase 'appears white,' and to what the word or phrase has referred to or might refer to on other occasions. And therefore, when you say 'This appears white' you are saying something, not only about your present experience, but also about all of these other things as well."

The conclusion of this argument – the part that follows the "therefore" – does not follow from the premises. In supposing that the argument is valid, one fails to distinguish between (1) *what* it is that a man means to say when he uses certain words and (2) his assumptions concerning the adequacy of these words for *expressing* what it is that he means to say; one supposes, mistakenly, that what justifies (2) must be included in what justifies (1). A Frenchman, not yet sure of his English, may utter the words "There are apples in the basket," intending thereby to express his belief that there are potatoes in the basket. If we show him that he has used the word "apples" incorrectly, and hence that he is mistaken in his assumptions about the ways in which English speaking people use and understand the word "apples," we have not shown him anything relevant to his *belief* that there are apples in the basket.

Logicians now take care to distinguish between the *use* and *mention* of language (e.g., the English word "Socrates" is mentioned in the sentence "'Socrates' has eight letters" and is used but not mentioned, in "Socrates is a Greek.")[23] As we shall have occasion to note further, the distinction has not always been observed in writings on epistemology.

11. If we decide, then, that there is a class of beliefs or statements which are "self-justifying," and that this class is limited to certain beliefs or statements about our own psychological states and about the ways in which we are "appeared to," we may be tempted to return to the figure of the edifice: our knowledge of the world is a structure supported entirely by a foundation of such self-justifying statements or beliefs. We should recall, however, that the answers to our original Socratic questions had *two* parts. When asked "What is your justification for thinking that you know *a*?" one may reply "I am justified in thinking I know *a*, because (1) I know *b* and (2) if I know *b* then I know *a*." We considered our justification for the *first* part of this answer, saying "I am justified in thinking I know *b*, because (1) I know *c* and (2) if I know *c* then I know *b*." And then we considered our justification for the first part of the second answer, and continued in this fashion until we reached the point of self-justification. In thus moving toward "the given," we accumulated, step by step, a backlog of claims that we did not attempt to justify – those claims constituting the *second* part of each of our answers. Hence our original claim – "I know that *a* is true" – does not rest upon "the given" alone; it also rests upon all of those other claims that we made *en route*. And it is not justified unless these other claims are justified.

A consideration of these other claims will lead us, I think, to at least three additional types of "stopping place," which are concerned, respectively, with memory, perception, and what Kant called the a priori. Here I shall comment briefly on the first two.

It is difficult to think of any claim to empirical knowledge, other than the self-justifying statements we have just considered, which does not to some extent rest upon an appeal to memory. But the appeal to memory – "I remember that A occured" – is not self-justifying. One may ask "And what is your justification for thinking that you remember that A occured?" and the question will have an answer – even if the answer is only the self-justifying "I think that I remember that A occurred." The statement "I remember that A occured" does, of course, imply "A occurred"; but "I think that I remember that A occurred" does not imply "A occurred" and hence does not imply "I remember that A occured." For we can remember occasions – at least we think we can remember them – when we learned, concerning some event we had thought we remembered, that the event had not occurred at all, and consequently that we had not really remembered it. When we thus find that one memory conflicts with another, or, more accurately, when we thus find that one thing that we think we remember conflicts with another thing that we think we remember, we may correct one or the other by making further inquiry; but the results of any such inquiry will always be justified in part by other memories, or by other things that we think that we remember. How then are we to choose between what seem to be conflicting memories? Under what conditions does "I think that I remember that A occurred" serve to justify "I remember that A occurred"?

The problem is one of formulating a rule of evidence – a rule specifying the conditions under which statements about what we think we remember can justify statements about what we do remember. A possible solution, in very general terms, is "When we think that we remember, then we are justified in believing that we do remember, provided that what we think we remember does not conflict with anything else that we think we remember; when what we think we remember does conflict with anything else we think we remember, then, of the two conflicting memories (more accurately, ostensible memories) the one that is justified is the one that fits in better with the other things that we think we remember." Ledger Wood made the latter point by saying that the justified memory is the one which "coheres with the system of related memories"; C. I. Lewis used "congruence" instead of "coherence."[24] But we cannot say precisely what is meant by "fitting in," "coherence," or "congruence" until certain controversial questions of confirmation theory and the logic of probability have been answered. And it may be that the rule of evidence is too liberal; perhaps we should say, for example, that when two ostensible memories conflict neither one of them is justified. But these are questions which have not yet been satisfactorily answered.

If we substitute "perceive" for "remember" in the foregoing, we can formulate a similar set of problems about perception; these problems, too, must await solution.[25]

The problems involved in formulating such rules of evidence, and in determining the validity of these rules, do not differ in any significant way from those which arise in connection with the formulation, and validity, of the rules of logic. Nor do they differ from the problems posed by the moral and religious "cognitivists" (the "non-intuitionistic cognitivists") that I have referred to elsewhere. The status of ostensible memories and perceptions, with respect to that experience which is their "source," is essentially like that which such "cognitivists" claim for judgments having an ethical or theological subject matter. Unfortunately, it is also like that which other "enthusiasts" claim for still other types of subject matter.

12. What, then, is the status of the doctrine of "the given" – of the "myth of the given"? In my opinion, the doctrine is correct in saying that there are some beliefs or statements which are "self-justifying" and that among such beliefs and statements are some which concern appearances or "ways of being appeared to;" but the "phenomenalistic version" of the doctrine is mistaken in implying that our knowledge may be thought of as an edifice which is supported by appearances alone.[26] The cognitive significance of "the empirically given" was correctly described – in a vocabulary rather different from that which I have been using – by John Dewey:

> The alleged primacy of sensory meanings is mythical. They are primary only in logical status; they are primary as tests and confirmation of inferences concerning matters of fact, not as historic originals. For, while it is not usually needful to carry the check or test of theoretical calculations to the point of irreducible sensa, colors, sounds, etc., these sensa form a limit approached in careful analytic certifications, and upon critical occasions it is necessary to touch the limit.... Sensa are the class of irreducible meanings which are employed in verifying and correcting other meanings. We actually set out with much coarser and more inclusive meanings and not till we have met with failure from their use do we even set out to discover those ultimate and harder meanings which are sensory in character.[27]

The Socratic questions leading to the concept of "the given" also lead to the concept of "rules of evidence." Unfortunately some of the philosophers who stressed the importance of the former concept tended to overlook that of the latter.

Notes

1   Philosophers in other traditions also noted these confusions. See, for example, John Wild, "The Concept of the Given in Contemporary Philosophy," *Philosophy and Phenomenological Research* I (1940), pp. 70–82.

2   The expression "myth of the given" was used by Wilfrid Sellars in "Empiricism and the Philosophy of Mind," in Herbert Feigl and Michael Scriven (eds), *Foundations of Science and the Concepts of Psychology and Psychoanalysis*, Minnesota Studies in the Philosophy of Science, vol. I (U. of Minn., 1956), pp. 253–329.

3   Dewey also said that, instead of trying to provide "Foundations for Knowledge," the philosopher should apply "what is known to intelligent conduct of the affairs of human life" to "the problems of men." John Dewey, *Problems of Men* (Philosophical, 1946), pp. 6–7.

4   C. I. Lewis, *Mind and the World-Order* (Scribner, 1929), p. 29.

5   Ibid., p. 19. Cf. Hans Reichenbach, *Experience and Prediction* (University of Chicago, 1938), p. 6; C. J. Ducasse, "Some Observations Concerning the Nature of Probability," *Journal of Philosophy* XXXVIII (1941), esp. pp. 400–1.

6   Hans Reichenbach, "Are Phenomenal Reports Absolutely Certain?" *Philosophical Review* LXI (1952), pp. 147–59; the quotation is from p. 150.

7   Brand Blanshard, *The Nature of Thought*, vol. II (Macmillan, 1940), p. 276.

8   C. G. Hempel, "On the Logical Positivists' Theory of Truth," *Analysis* II (1935), pp. 49–59; the quotation is from p. 57.

9   Rudolf Carnap, "Truth and Confirmation," in Herbert Feigl and W. S. Sellars (eds), *Readings in Philosophical Analysis* (Appleton, 1949), p. 125. The portions of the article quoted above first appeared in "Wahrheit und Bewährung," *Actes du congrès international de philosophie scientifique*, IV (Paris; 1936), pp. 18–23.

10 Cf. Nelson Goodman, *The Structure of Appearance* (Harvard, 1951), p. 104. If Goodman's book, incidentally, is not discussed in this collection of essays, the fault is with our conventional classification of philosophical disciplines. The book, which is concerned with an area falling between logic and metaphysics, is one of the most important philosophical works written by an American during the period being surveyed.

11 C. G. Hempel, "Some Theses on Empirical Certainty," *Review of Metaphysics* V (1952), pp. 621–9; the quotation is from p. 621.

12 Ibid., p. 628. Hempel's remarks were made in an "Exploration" in which he set forth several theses about "empirical certainty" and then replied to objections by Paul Weiss, Roderick Firth, Wilfrid Sellars, and myself.

13 C. J. Ducasse, "Propositions, Truth, and the Ultimate Criterion of Truth," *Philosophy and Phenomenological Research* IV (1939), pp. 317–40; the quotation is from p. 339.

14 Cf. Norman Malcolm, "Knowledge of Other Minds," *Journal of Philosophy* LV (1958), pp. 969–78. Reprinted in Malcolm, *Knowledge and Certainty: Essays and Lectures* (Prentice-Hall, 1963).

15 The principle behind this way of looking at the matter is defended in detail by Max Black in *Language and Philosophy* (Cornell, 1949), pp. 16 ff.

16 One of the best criticisms of the "appearance" (or "sense-datum") terminology was O. K. Bouwsma's "Moore's Theory of Sense-Data," in *The Philosophy of G. E. Moore*, ed. Schilpp, pp. 201–21. In *Perceiving: A Philosophical Study* (Cornell, 1957), I tried to call attention to certain facts about appearing which, I believe, Bouwsma may have overlooked.

17 Augustine, *Contra academicos*, xi, 26; translated by Sister Mary Patricia Garvey as *Saint Augustine Against the Academicians* (Marquette, 1942); the quotations are from pp. 68–9.

18 *Experience and Prediction*, p. 176.

19 It may follow, however, that "the vaunted incorrigibility of the sense-datum language can be achieved only at the cost of its perfect utility as a means of communication" (Max

Black, *Problems of Analysis* (Cornell, 1954), p. 66), and doubtless, as Black added, it would be "misleading, to say the least" to speak of a "language that cannot be communicated" – cf. Wilfrid Sellars, "Empiricism and the Philosophy of Mind" – but these points do affect the epistemological question at issue.

20 This doctrine was modified in Lewis's later *An Analysis of Knowledge and Valuation* (Open Court, 1946) in a way which enabled him to preserve the theory of the given.

21 *The Nature of Thought*, vol. II, pp. 269–70. Blanshard added, however, that "for all the ordinary purposes of life" we *can* justify some beliefs by showing that they cohere "with the system of present knowledge"; and therefore, he said, his theory should not be described as being "simply sceptical" (vol. II, p. 271). Cf. W. H. Werkmeister, *The Basis and Structure of Knowledge* (Harper, 1948), part II.

22 Quoted by A. E. Murphy in "Dewey's Epistemology and Metaphysics," in P. A. Schilpp (ed.), *The Philosophy of John Dewey*, (Northwestern, 1939), p. 203. Dewey's theory of inquiry, however, was not intended to be an epistemology and he did not directly address himself to the questions with which we are here concerned.

23 Cf. W. V. Quine, *Mathematical Logic* (Norton, 1940; rev. edn, Harvard, 1951), sec. 4.

24 Ledger Wood, *The Analysis of Knowledge* (Princeton, 1941), p. 81; C. I. Lewis, *An Analysis of Knowledge and Valuation*, p. 334.

25 Important steps toward solving them were taken by Nelson Goodman in "Sense and Certainty," *Philosophical Review* LXI (1952), pp. 160–7, and by Israel Scheffler in "On Justification and Commitment," *Journal of Philosophy*, LI (1954), pp. 180–90. The former paper is reprinted in *Philosophy of Knowledge*, ed. Roland Houde and J. P. Mullally (Lippincott, 1960), pp. 97–103.

26 Alternatives to the general metaphor of the edifice are proposed by W. V. Quine in the introduction to *Methods of Logic* (Holt, 1950; rev. edn, 1959), in *From a Logical Point of View* (Harvard, 1953), and in *Word and Object* (Wiley, 1960).

27 John Dewey, *Experience and Nature*, 2nd edn (Norton, 1929), p. 327.

CHAPTER 8

Does Empirical Knowledge Have a Foundation?

Wilfrid Sellars

I have arrived at a stage in my argument which is, at least prima facie, out of step with the basic presuppositions of logical atomism. Thus, as long as *looking green* is taken to be the notion to which *being green* is reducible, it could be claimed with considerable plausibility that fundamental concepts pertaining to observable fact have that logical independence of one another which is characteristic of the empiricist tradition. Indeed, at first sight the situation is *quite* disquieting, for if the ability to recognize that *x* looks green presupposes the concept of *being green*, and if this in turn involves knowing in what circumstances to view an object to ascertain its color, then, since one can scarcely determine what the circumstances are without noticing that certain objects have certain perceptible characteristics – including colors – it would seem that one couldn't form the concept of *being green*, and, by parity of reasoning, of the other colors, unless he already had them.

Now, it just won't do to reply that to have the concept of green, to know what it is for something to be green, it is sufficient to respond, when one is *in point of fact* in standard conditions, to green

Originally published in H. Feigl and M. Scriven (eds), *The Foundations of Science and the Concepts of Psychology and Psychoanalysis*, Minnesota Studies in the Philosophy of Science, vol. I (Minneapolis: University of Minnesota Press, 1956), pp. 293–300.

objects with the vocable "This is green." Not only must the conditions be of a sort that is appropriate for determining the color of an object by looking, the subject must *know* that conditions of this sort *are* appropriate. And while this does not imply that one must have concepts before one has them, it does imply that one can have the concept of green only by having a whole battery of concepts of which it is one element. It implies that while the process of acquiring the concept green may – indeed does – involve a long history of acquiring *piecemeal* habits of response to various objects in various circumstances, there is an important sense in which one has *no* concept pertaining to the observable properties of physical objects in Space and Time unless one has them all – and, indeed, as we shall see, a great deal more besides. [...]

One of the forms taken by the Myth of the Given is the idea that there is, indeed *must be*, a structure of particular matter of fact such that (a) each fact can not only be noninferentially known to be the case, but presupposes no other knowledge either of particular matter of fact, or of general truths; and (b) such that the noninferential knowledge of facts belonging to this structure constitutes the ultimate court of appeals for all factual claims – particular and general – about the world. It is important to note that I characterized the knowledge of fact belonging to this stratum as not only noninferential, but as presupposing no knowledge of other matter of fact, whether particular or general. It might be thought that this is a redundancy, that knowledge (not belief or conviction, but knowledge) which logically presupposes knowledge of other facts *must* be inferential. This, however, as I hope to show, is itself an episode in the Myth.

Now, the idea of such a privileged stratum of fact is a familiar one, though not without its difficulties. Knowledge pertaining to this level is *non-inferential*, yet it is, after all, *knowledge*. It is *ultimate*, yet it has *authority*. The attempt to make a consistent picture of these two requirements has traditionally taken the following form:

Statements pertaining to this level, in order to "express knowledge" must not only be made, but, so to speak, must be worthy of being made, *credible*, that is, in the sense of worthy of credence. Furthermore, and this is a crucial point, they must be made in a way which *involves* this credibility. For where there is no connection between the making of a statement and its authority, the assertion may express *conviction*, but it can scarcely be said to express knowledge.

The authority – the credibility – of statements pertaining to this level cannot exhaustively consist in the fact that they are supported by *other* statements, for in that case all *knowledge* pertaining to this level would have to be inferential, which not only contradicts the hypothesis, but flies in the face of good sense. The conclusion seems inevitable that if some statements pertaining to this level are to express *noninferential* knowledge, they must have a credibility which is not a matter of being supported by other statements. Now there does seem to be a class of statements which fill at least part of this bill, namely such statements as would be said to *report observations*, thus, "This is red." These statements, candidly made, have authority. Yet they are not expressions of inference. How, then, is this authority to be understood?

Clearly, the argument continues, it springs from the fact that they are made in just the circumstances in which they are made, as is indicated by the fact that they characteristically, though not necessarily or without exception, involve those so-called token-reflexive expressions which, in addition to the tenses of verbs, serve to connect the circumstances in which a statement is made with its sense. (At this point it will be helpful to begin putting the line of

thought I am developing in terms of the *fact-stating* and *observation-reporting* roles of certain sentences). Roughly, two verbal performances which are tokens of a non-token-reflexive sentence can occur in widely different circumstances and yet make the same statement; whereas two tokens of a token-reflexive sentence can make the same statement only if they are uttered in the same circumstances (according to a relevant criterion of sameness). And two tokens of a sentence, whether it contains a token-reflexive expression – over and above a tensed verb – or not, can make the same *report* only if, made in all candor, they express the *presence* – in *some* sense of "presence" – of the state of affairs that is being reported; if, that is, they stand in that relation to the state of affairs, whatever the relation may be, by virtue of which they can be said to formulate observations of it.

It would appear, then, that there are two ways in which a sentence token can have credibility: (1) The authority may accrue to it, so to speak, from above, that is, as being a token of a sentence type *all* the tokens of which, in a certain use, have credibility, e.g. "2 + 2 = 4." In this case, let us say that token credibility is inherited from type authority. (2) The credibility may accrue to it from the fact that it came to exist in a certain way in a certain set of circumstances, e.g. "This is red." Here token credibility is not derived from type credibility.

Now, the credibility of *some* sentence types appears to be *intrinsic* – at least in the limited sense that it is *not* derived from other sentences, type or token. This is, or seems to be, the case with certain sentences used to make analytic statements. The credibility of *some* sentence types accrues to them by virtue of their logical relations to other sentence types, thus by virtue of the fact that they are logical consequences of more basic sentences. It would seem obvious, however, that the credibility of empirical sentence types cannot be traced without remainder to the credibility of other sentence types. And since no empirical sentence type appears to have *intrinsic* credibility, this means that credibility must accrue to *some* empirical sentence types by virtue of their logical relations to certain sentence tokens, and, indeed, to sentence tokens the authority of which is not derived, in its turn, from the authority of sentence types.

The picture we get is that of there being two *ultimate* modes of credibility: (1) The intrinsic credibility of analytic sentences, which accrues to tokens as being tokens of such a type; (2) the credibility of such tokens as "express observations," a credibility which flows from tokens to types.

Let us explore this picture, which is common to all traditional empiricisms, a bit further. How is the authority of such sentence tokens as "express observational knowledge" to be understood? It has been tempting to suppose that in spite of the obvious differences which exist between "observation reports" and "analytic statements," there is an essential similarity between the ways in which they come by their authority. Thus, it has been claimed, not without plausibility, that whereas *ordinary* empirical statements can be *correctly* made without being *true*, observation reports resemble analytic statements in that being correctly made is a sufficient as well as necessary condition of their truth. And it has been inferred from this – somewhat hastily, I believe – that "correctly making" the report "This is green" is a matter of "following the rules for the use of 'this', 'is' and 'green.'"

Three comments are immediately necessary:

(1) First a brief remark about the term "report." In ordinary usage a report is a report made *by* someone *to* someone. To make a report is to *do* something. In the literature of epistemology, however, the word "report" or "*Konstatierung*" has acquired a technical use in which a sentence token can play a reporting role (a) without being an *overt* verbal performance, and (b) without having the character of being "by someone to someone" – even oneself. There is, of course, such a thing as "talking to oneself" – *in foro interno* – but, as I shall be emphasizing in the closing stages of my argument, it is important not to suppose that all "covert" verbal episodes are of this kind.

(2) My second comment is that while *we* shall not assume that because "reports" *in the ordinary sense* are *actions*, "reports" in the sense of *Konstatierungen* are also actions, the line of thought we are considering treats them as such. In other words, it interprets the correctness of *Konstatierungen* as analogous to the rightness of actions. Let me emphasize, however, that not all *ought* is *ought to do*, nor all correctness the correctness of *actions*.

(3) My third comment is that if the expression "following a rule" is taken seriously, and is not weakened beyond all recognition into the bare notion of exhibiting a uniformity – in which case the lightning, thunder sequence would "follow a rule" – then it is the knowledge or belief that the circumstances are of a certain kind, and not the mere fact that they *are* of this kind, which contributes to bringing about the action.

In the light of these remarks it is clear that *if* observation reports are construed as *actions*, *if* their correctness is interpreted as the correctness of an *action*, and *if* the authority of an observation report is construed as the fact that making it is "following a rule" in the proper sense of this phrase, *then* we are face to face with givenness in its most straightforward form. For these stipulations commit one to the idea that the authority of *Konstatierungen* rests on nonverbal episodes of awareness – awareness *that* something is the case, e.g. *that this is green* – which nonverbal episodes have an intrinsic authority (they are, so to speak, "self-authenticating") which the *verbal* performances (the *Konstatierungen*) properly performed "express." One is committed to a stratum of authoritative nonverbal episodes ("awareness") the authority of which accrues to a superstructure of *verbal actions*, provided that the expressions occurring in these actions are properly *used*. These self-authenticating episodes would constitute the tortoise on which stands the elephant on which rests the edifice of empirical knowledge. The essence of the view is the same whether these intrinsically authoritative episodes are such items as the awareness that a certain sense content is green or such items as the awareness that a certain physical object looks to someone to be green.

But what is the alternative? We might begin by trying something like the following: An overt or covert token of "This is green" in the presence of a green item is a *Konstatierung* and express observational knowledge if and only if it is a manifestation of a tendency to produce overt or covert tokens of "This is green" – given a certain set – if and only if a green object is being looked at in standard conditions. Clearly on this interpretation the occurrence of such tokens of "This is green" would be "following a rule" only in the sense that they are instances of a uniformity, a uniformity differing from the lightning–thunder case in that it is an acquired causal characteristic of the language user. Clearly the above suggestion, which corresponds to the "thermometer view" criticized by Professor Price, and which we have already rejected elsewhere, won't do as it stands. Let us see, however, if it can't be revised to fit the criteria I have been using for "expressing observational knowledge."

The first hurdle to be jumped concerns the *authority* which, as I have emphasized, a sentence token must have in order that it may be said to express knowledge. Clearly, on this account the only thing that can remotely be supposed to constitute such authority is the fact that one can infer the presence of a green object from the fact that someone makes this report. As we have already noticed, the correctness of a report does not have to be construed as the rightness of an *action*. A report can be correct as being an instance of a general mode of behavior which, in a given linguistic community, it is reasonable to sanction and support.

The second hurdle is, however, the decisive one. For we have seen that to be the expression of knowledge, a report must not only *have* authority, this authority must *in some sense* be recognized by the person whose report it is. And this is a steep hurdle indeed. For if the authority of the report "This is green" lies in the fact that the existence of green items appropriately related to the perceiver can be inferred from the occurrence of such reports, it follows that only a person who is able to draw this inference, and therefore who has not only the concept *green*, but also the concept of uttering "This is green" – indeed, the concept of certain conditions of perception, those which would correctly be called "standard conditions" – could be in a position to token "This is green" in recognition of its authority. In other words, for a *Konstatierung* "This is green" to "express observational knowledge," not only must it be a *symptom* or *sign* of the presence of a green object in standard conditions, but the perceiver must know that tokens of "This is green" *are* symptoms of the presence of green objects in conditions which are standard for visual perception.

Now it might be thought that there is something obviously absurd in the idea that before a token uttered by, say, Jones could be the expression of observational knowledge, Jones would have to know that overt verbal episodes of this kind are reliable indicators of the existence, suitably related to the speaker, of green objects. I do not think that it is. Indeed, I think that something

very like it is true. The point I wish to make now, however, is that if it *is* true, then it follows, as a matter of simple logic, that one couldn't have observational knowledge of *any* fact unless one knew many *other* things as well. And let me emphasize that the point is not taken care of by distinguishing between *knowing how* and *knowing that*, and admitting that observational knowledge requires a lot of "know how." For the point is specifically that observational knowledge of any particular fact, e.g. that this is green, presupposes that one knows general facts of the form *X is a reliable symptom of Y*. And to admit this requires an abandonment of the traditional empiricist idea that observational knowledge "stands on its own feet." Indeed, the suggestion would be anathema to traditional empiricists for the obvious reason that by making observational knowledge *presuppose* knowledge of general facts of the form *X is a reliable symptom of Y*, it runs counter to the idea that we come to know general facts of this form only *after* we have come to know by observation a number of particular facts which support the hypothesis that X is a symptom of Y.

And it might be thought that there is an obvious regress in the view we are examining. Does it not tell us that observational knowledge at time t presupposes knowledge of the form *X is a reliable symptom of Y*, which presupposes *prior* observational knowledge, which presupposes *other* knowledge of the form *X is a reliable symptom of Y*, which presupposes still other, and *prior* observational knowledge, and so on? This charge, however, rests on too simple, indeed a radically mistaken, conception of what one is saying of Jones when one says that he *knows* that p. It is not just that the objection supposes that knowing is an *episode*; for clearly there are episodes which we can correctly characterize as knowings, in particular, *observings*. The essential point is that in characterizing an episode or a state as that of *knowing*, we are not giving an empirical description of that episode or state; we are placing it in the logical space of reasons, of justifying and being able to justify what one says.

Thus, all that the view I am defending requires is that no tokening by S *now* of "This is green" is to count as "expressing observational knowledge" unless it is also correct to say of S that he *now* knows the appropriate fact of the form *X is a reliable symptom of Y*, namely that (and again I oversimplify) utterances of "This is green" are reliable indicators of the presence of green objects in standard conditions of perception. And while the correctness of this statement about Jones requires that Jones could *now* cite prior particular facts as evidence for the idea that these utterances *are* reliable indicators, it requires only that it is correct to say that Jones *now* knows, thus remembers, that these particular facts *did* obtain. It does not require that it be correct to say that at the time these facts did obtain he *then knew* them to obtain. And the regress disappears.

Thus, while Jones' ability to give inductive reasons *today* is built on a long history of acquiring and manifesting verbal habits in perceptual situations, and, in particular, the occurrence of verbal episodes, e.g. "This is green," which is superficially like those which are later properly said to express observational knowledge, it does not require that any episode in this prior time be characterizeable as expressing knowledge. (At this point, the reader should reread the opening section of this chapter.)

The idea that observation "strictly and properly so-called" is constituted by certain self-authenticating nonverbal episodes, the authority of which is transmitted to verbal and quasi-verbal performances when these performances are made "in conformity with the semantic rules of the language," is, of course, the heart of the Myth of the Given. For the *given*, in epistemological tradition, is what is *taken* by these self-authenticating episodes. These "takings" are, so to speak, the unmoved movers of empirical knowledge, the

"knowings in presence" which are presupposed by all other knowledge, both the knowledge of general truths and the knowledge "in absence" of other particular matters of fact. Such is the framework in which traditional empiricism makes its characteristic claim that the perceptually given is the foundation of empirical knowledge.

If I reject the framework of traditional empiricism, it is not because I want to say that empirical knowledge has *no* foundation. For to put it this way is to suggest that it is really "empirical knowledge so-called," and to put it in a box with rumors and hoaxes. There is clearly *some* point to the picture of human knowledge as resting on a level of propositions – observation reports – which do not rest on other propositions in the same way as other propositions rest on them. On the other hand, I do wish to insist that the metaphor of "foundation" is misleading in that it keeps us from seeing that if there is a logical dimension in which other empirical propositions rest on observation reports, there is another logical dimension in which the latter rest on the former.

Above all, the picture is misleading because of its static character. One seems forced to choose between the picture of an elephant which rests on a tortoise (What supports the tortoise?) and the picture of a great Hegelian serpent of knowledge with its tail in its mouth (Where does it begin?). Neither will do. For empirical knowledge, like its sophisticated extension, science, is rational, not because it has a *foundation* but because it is a self-correcting enterprise which can put *any* claim in jeopardy, though not *all* at once.

CHAPTER 9

Epistemic Principles

Wilfrid Sellars

I

The explication of knowledge as "justified true belief", though it involves many pitfalls to which attention has been called in recent years, remains the orthodox or classical account and is, I believe, essentially sound. Thus, in the present lecture I shall assume that it can be formulated in such a way as to be immune from the type of counter-examples with which it has been bombarded since Gettier's pioneering paper in *Analysis* and turn my attention to another problem which has dogged its footsteps since the very beginning. This problem can be put in the form of two questions: If knowledge is justified true belief, how can there be such a thing as self-evident knowledge? And if there is no such thing as self-evident knowledge, how can *any* true belief be, in the relevant sense, justified?

But first let us beat about in the neighboring fields, perhaps to scare up some game, but, in any case, to refamiliarize ourselves with the terrain. Thus, are there not occasions on which a person can be said to be justified in believing something which he would not appropriately be said to know? Presumably, to be justified in believing something is to have good reasons for believing it,

as contrasted with its contradictory. But *how* good? Adequate? Conclusive? If adequate, adequate for what? If conclusive, the conclusion of what is at stake?

We are all familiar with Austin's point concerning the performative character of "I know". We are also familiar with the fact that, whereas to say "I promise to do *A*" is, other things being equal, to promise to do *A*, to say "I know that-*p*" is not, other things being equal, to know that-*p*. Chisholm's distinction between the *strict* and the *extended* sense of "performative utterance" is helpful in this connection. According to Chisholm,

> An utterance beginning with "I want" is not performative in [the] strict sense, for it cannot be said to be an "act" of wanting. But "I want" is often used to accomplish what one might accomplish by means of the strict performative "I request". Let us say, then, that "I want" may be a "performative utterance" in an *extended sense* of the latter expression.[1]

He asks in which, if either, of these senses an utterance of "I know" may be performative. After reminding us that "I know" is not performative in the strict sense of the term, he allows that "[it] is often used to accomplish what one may accomplish by the strict performative 'I guarantee' or 'I give you my word'" and "hence may be performative in an extended sense of the term".[2]

Originally published in H. Castaneda (ed.), *Action, Knowledge, and Reality* (Indianapolis: Bobbs-Merrill, 1975), pp. 332–49.

He argues, however, that "I know" is not always a substitute for "I guarantee", pointing out that:

> Just as an utterance of "I want" may serve *both* to say something about me and to get you to do something, an utterance of "I know" may serve both to say something about me and to provide you with guarantees. To suppose that the performance of the nondescriptive function is inconsistent with the simultaneous performance of the descriptive function might be called, therefore, an example of the *performative fallacy*.[3]

I think that Chisholm is quite right about this. On the other hand, it seems to me that he overlooks the possibility of a connection between "I know" and "I guarantee" other than the one he considers. "I know that-*p*" might be related to "I guarantee that-*p*" not just as an autobiographical description which on occasion performs the same role as the latter but as one which contains a reference to guaranteeing in its very meaning. Is it not possible to construe "I know that-*p*" as essentially equivalent to "*p*, and I have reasons good enough to support a guarantee" (i.e., to say "I guarantee" or "You can rely on my statement")? Such an account would enable us to recognize a performative element in the very meaning of the verb "to know" without construing "I know" as a performative in the strict sense. It would also preserve the symmetry between first person and other person uses of the verb "to know" which seems to be a pre-analytic datum. Thus, "He knows that-*p*" would entail "He has reasons good enough to support a guarantee that-*p*".[4]

Furthermore, this account would enable us to appreciate the *context dependence* of the adequacy involved. Reasons which might be adequately good to justify a guarantee on one occasion might not be adequate to justify a guarantee on another. Again, the presence of such a performative element in the very meaning of the verb "to know" would account for the fact (if it is a fact) that we rarely think in terms of "I know" in purely self-directed thinkings; that we rarely have thoughts of the form "I know that-*p*" unless the question of a possible guarantee to someone other than ourselves has arisen. Of course, we *can* "tell ourselves" that we know something, but, then, so can we be said to make promises to ourselves.

II

Yet even after justice has been done, perhaps along the above lines, to the performative element in the meaning of the verb "to know", it seems to me that we must recognize a closely related use of this expression which, though it may have implications concerning action, is not in any of the above senses performative. For once the *ethical* issue of how good one's reasons for a belief must be in order to justify *giving a guarantee* is solved, there remains the problem of how good reasons must be to justify believing that-*p*, where to believe that-*p* is obviously not an *action*, let alone a performatory action in either the strict or the extended sense.

Confronted by this question, we are tempted to set apart a class of cases in which the reasons are not only good enough to justify believing that-*p* but good enough to make it absurd *not* to believe that-*p* (or, perhaps, to believe its contradictory). It is perhaps, some such concept as this which is (in addition to the truth condition) the non-performative core of the meaning of the verb "to know".

I think the above discussion has served its primary purpose by highlighting the concept of having good reasons for believing that-*p*. For the solution of the problem which was posed in my opening remarks hinges ultimately on a distinction between two ways in which there can be, and one can have, good reasons for believing that-*p*.[5]

Now one pattern for justifying a belief in terms of good reasons can be called *inferential*. Consider the schema:

> *p*;
> So, I have good reasons, all things considered, for believing *q*.

On reflection, this schema tends to expand into:

> I have good reasons, all things considered, for believing *p*;
> So, *p*;
> So, I have good reasons, all things considered, for believing *q*.

Further reflection suggests that arguments conforming to this schema have a suppressed premise. What might it be? Consider the following expanded schema:

I have, all things considered, good reasons for believing *p*;
So, *p*;
p logically implies *q*;
So, I have, all things considered, good reasons for believing *q*.

The line of thought thus schematically represented would seem to involve the principle,

Logical implication transmits reasonableness.

In cases of this type, we are tempted to say, we have *derivative* good reasons, all things considered, for believing *q*. We say, in other words, that the reasonableness of believing *q* is "inferential".

Notice that the above line of thought is obviously an oversimplification, undoubtedly in several respects. In particular, it is important to note that if I have independent grounds for believing *not-q*, I may decide that I do *not* have good reasons, all things considered, for believing that-*p*. After all, if *p* implies *q*, *not-q* equally implies *not-p*. Yet in spite of its oversimplifications, the above train of thought takes us nearer to the distinctions necessary to solve our problem.

I have been considering the case where one proposition, *p*, logically implies another, *q*, and have claimed, with the above qualifications, that logical implication transmits reasonableness. Perhaps we can also take into account, with trepidation, "probabilistic" implication, which would give us the following schema:

It is reasonable, all things considered, to believe *p*;
So, *p*;
p probabilistically implies *q* to a high degree;
So, all things considered, it is reasonable to believe *q*.

Probabilistic justification of beliefs in accordance with this pattern would, presumably, be illustrated by inductive arguments and theoretical explanations. In each case, we move from a premise of the form:

It is reasonable, all things considered, to believe *E*,

where "*E*" formulates the evidence, to a conclusion of the form:

It is reasonable, all things considered, to believe *H*,

where "*H*" formulates in the first case a law-like statement and in the second case a body of theoretical assumptions.

III

As has been pointed out since time immemorial, it is most implausible to suppose that all epistemic justification is inferential, at least in the sense of conforming to the patterns described above. Surely, it has been argued, there must be beliefs which we are justified in holding on grounds other than that they can be correctly inferred, inductively or deductively, from other beliefs which we are justified in holding. In traditional terms, if there is to be *inferential* knowledge, must there not be *non-inferential* knowledge – beliefs, that is, the reasonableness of which does not rest on the reasonableness of beliefs which logically or probabilistically imply them?

We are clearly in the neighborhood of what has been called the "self-evident", the "self-certifying", in short, of "intuitive knowledge". It is in this neighborhood that we find what has come to be called the *foundational* picture of human knowledge. According to this picture, beliefs which have inferential reasonableness ultimately rely for their authority on a stratum of beliefs which are, in some sense, self-certifying. The reasonableness of moves from the level of the self-evident to higher levels would involve the principles of logic (deductive and inductive) and, perhaps, certain additional principles which are *sui generis*. They would have in common the character of transmitting authoritativeness from lower-level beliefs to higher-level beliefs.

IV

Let us reflect on the concept of such a foundational level of knowledge. It involves the concept of beliefs which are *reasonable*, which have *epistemic authority* or *correctness*, but which are not reasonable or authoritative by virtue of the fact that they are beliefs in propositions which are implied by other propositions which it is reasonable to believe. Let us label them, for the moment, "non-inferentially reasonable beliefs".

How can there be such beliefs? For the concept of a *reason* seems so clearly tied to that of an *inference* or *argument* that the concept of non-inferential reasonableness seems to be a *contradictio in adjecto*. Surely, we are inclined to say, for a belief (or believing) to be reasonable, there must be a reason for the belief (or believing). And must not this reason be something other than the belief or believing for which it is the reason? And surely, we are inclined to say, to believe something *because* it is reasonable (to believe it) involves not only that there *be* a reason but that, in a relevant sense, one *has* or is in *possession of* the reason. Notice that I have deliberately formulated these expostulations in such a way as to highlight the ambiguities involved when one speaks of reasonable beliefs.

In attempting to cope with these challenges, I shall leave aside problems pertaining to inferential and non-inferential reasonableness in logic and mathematics and concentrate on the apparent need for "self evidence" in the sphere of empirical matters of fact.

How might a self-justifying belief be construed? One suggestion, modified from Chisholm's *Theory of Knowledge*,[6] is to the effect that the justification of such beliefs has the form,

> What justifies me in claiming that my belief that *a* is *F* is reasonable is simply the fact that *a* is *F*.

But this seems to point to the existence of inferences of the form,

> It is a fact that *a* is *F*;
> So, it is reasonable to believe that *a* is *F*,

and one might begin to wonder what principle authorizes this inference.

Something, clearly, has gone wrong. In order for any such argument to do the job, its premise would have to have authority; it would have to be something which it is reasonable to believe. But if we modify the schema to take this into account, it becomes:

> It is reasonable to believe it to be a fact that *a* is *F*;
> So, it is reasonable to believe that *a* is *F*,

which, in virtue of the equivalence of

> believing *a* to be *F*

with

> believing it to be a fact that *a* is *F*,

is obviously unilluminating.

V

Now many philosophers who have endorsed a concept of intuitive knowledge are clearly committed to the position that there is a level of *cognition* more basic than *believing*. This more basic level would consist of a sub-conceptual[7] awareness of certain facts. In terms of the framework that I have sketched elsewhere, there would be a level of cognition more basic than *thinkings* or tokenings of sentences in Mentalese – more basic, in fact, than symbolic activity, literal *or* analogical. It would be a level of cognition unmediated by concepts; indeed it would be the very *source of* concepts in some such way as described by traditional theories of abstraction. It would be "direct apprehension" of facts; their "direct presence" to the mind.[8]

Schematically we would have,

> It is a fact (which I directly apprehend) that *a* is *F*;
> So, it is reasonable to have the *conceptual belief* that *a* is *F*.

This multiplication of distinctions raises two serious problems: (1) What sort of entities are *facts*? Do they belong to the real (extra-conceptual) order? That "fact" is roughly a synonym for "truth", and "true" is appropriately predicated of conceptual items (in overt speech or Mentalese) should give pause for thought.

Then there is also the question: (2) How is "direct apprehension" to be understood? If the apprehend*ing* is distinguishable from the apprehend*ed*, is it not also "separable"? Might not apprehending occur without any *fact* being apprehended? If so, an "apprehending that-*p*" might not be an apprehending of the fact that-*p*. Hitting, in baseball, implies that something is hit. "Swinging" does not. To *hit* is to *swing successfully*. Of course, "apprehend", like "see", is, *in its ordinary sense*, an achievement word. But does this not mean that, as in the case of "see", there is a place for "*ostensibly* apprehending", i.e., *seeming to apprehend*, a concept which does not imply achievement?

Many who use the metaphor "to see" in intellectual contexts overlook the fact that in its literal sense "seeing" is a term for a *successful* conceptual activity which contrasts with "seeming to see". No piling on of additional metaphors (e.g., "grasping", which implies an object grasped) can blunt this fact. Now the distinction between *seeing* and merely *seeming to see* implies a criterion. To rely on the metaphors of "apprehending" or "presence of the object" is to obscure the need of criteria for distinguishing between "knowing" and "seeming to know", which ultimately define what it means to speak of knowledge as a *correct* or well-founded *thinking* that something is the case.

If so, to know that we have apprehended a fact, we would have to know that the criteria which distinguish *apprehending* from *seeming to apprehend* were satisfied. In short, I suspect that the notion of a non-conceptual "direct apprehension" of a "fact" provides a merely verbal solution to our problem. The regress is stopped by an *ad hoc* regress-stopper. Indeed, the very metaphors which promised the sought-for foundation contain within themselves a dialectical moment which takes us beyond them.

VI

What is the alternative? I suggest that the key to our problem is provided by the Verbal Behaviorist model, developed elsewhere. It is, we have seen, a simple, indeed radically over-simplified, model, but it will provide us, I believe, with the outline of a strategy for getting out of the classical labyrinth.

According to this model, it will be remembered, the primary sense of

The thought occurred to Jones that snow is white

is

Jones said "snow is white",

where the verb "to say" was stripped of some of its ordinary implications and roughly equated with "to utter words candidly as one who knows the language". In particular, it was purged of the illocutionary and perlocutionary forces which Austin and Grice find so central to their theory of meaning. "To say", in this sense, was also equated with "thinking-out-loud".

According to the *VB*, as I describe him, we must also introduce, in order to take account of those cases where one thinks silently, a *secondary* sense of

The thought occurred to Jones that snow is white,

in which it refers to a short-term proximate propensity to think-out-loud that snow is white. When this propensity is "uninhibited", *one thinks-out-loud*, i.e., thinks in the primary sense of this term (as construed by *VB*). There can be many reasons why, on a particular occasion, this propensity is inhibited. But, for our purposes, the most important is the general inhibition acquired in childhood when, after being taught to think-out-loud, one is trained not to be a "babbler". One might use the model of an on–off switch which gets into the wiring diagram when the child learns to keep his thoughts to himself.

I have argued elsewhere that yet another concept of "having the thought occur to one that-*p*" can be introduced which stands to the second as the theoretical concept of electronic processes stands to the acquisition (and loss) of the power to attract iron filings (or a bell clapper) by a piece of soft iron in a coil of wire attached to an electric circuit. I argued that the classical concept of thought-episodes can be construed as part of a theoretical framework designed to explain the acquisition and loss of verbal propensities to think-out-loud. In approaching the problem of the status of non-inferential knowledge, however, I shall return to the *VB* model and concentrate, indeed, on the primary sense of having the thought occur to one that-p, i.e., think-out-loud that-p.

I have argued elsewhere that perceptual experience involves a sensory element which is in no way a form of thinking, however intimately it may be connected with thinking. This element consists of what I have variously called "sense impressions", "sensations", or "sensa". I argued that these items, properly construed, belong in a theoretical framework designed to explain:

(a) the difference between merely thinking of (believing in the existence of) a perceptible state of affairs and *seeing* (or seeming to see) that such a state of affairs exists;

(b) how it can seem to a person that there is a pink ice cube in front of him when there isn't one – either because there is something there which is either not pink or not cubical, or because there is nothing there and he is having a realistic hallucination.

I've explored problems pertaining to the nature and status of this sensory element on many occasions,[9] but further exploration of this theme would leave no time for the problem at hand.

What is important for our purposes is that perceptual experience also involves a conceptual or propositional component – a "thinking" in a suitably broad sense of this accordion term. In perception, the thought is caused to occur to one that, for example, there is a pink ice cube in front of one. It is misleading to call such a thought a "perceptual judgment" – for this implies question-answering activity of estimating, for example, the size of an object. (I judge that the room is ten feet tall.) Perhaps the best term is "taking something to be the case". Thus, on the occasion of sensing a certain color configuration, one takes there to be an object or situation of a certain description in one's physical environment.

Let us consider the case where

Jones sees there to be a red apple in front of him.

Given that Jones has learned how to use the relevant words in perceptual situations, he is justified in reasoning as follows:

I just thought-out-loud "Lo! Here is a red apple" (no countervailing conditions obtain); So, there is good reason to believe that there is a red apple in front of me.

Of course, the conclusion of this reasoning is not the *thinking* involved in his original perceptual experience. Like all justification arguments, it is a higher-order thinking. He did not originally *infer* that there is a red apple in front of him. Now, however, he is inferring from the character and context of his experience that it is veridical and that there is good reason to believe that there is indeed a red apple in front of him.

Notice that although the justification of the belief that there is a red apple in front of (Jones) is an inferential justification, it has the peculiar character that its essential premise asserts the occurrence of the very same belief in a specific context.[10] It is this fact which gives the appearance that such beliefs are *self*-justifying and hence gives the justification the appearance of being *non-inferential*.

It is, as I see it, precisely this feature of the unique pattern of justification in question which, misinterpreted, leads Chisholm to formulate as his principle for the "directly evident",

What justifies me in counting it as evident that *a* is *F* is simply the fact that *a* is *F*.[11]

To be sure, Chisholm's examples of the "directly evident" are not taken from the domain of *perceptual* beliefs, but rather, in true Cartesian spirit, from one's knowledge about what is going on in one's mind at the present moment. Indeed, he rejects the idea that particular perceptual beliefs of the kind which I illustrated by my example of the red apple are ever directly evident.

On the other hand, though he does think that particular perceptual beliefs of this type can at best be *indirectly evident*, he does think that they can be *reasonable*. Should we say "*directly* reasonable"? I, of course, would answer in the affirmative. Yet it is not clear to me that Chisholm would be happy with this suggestion. If (as he should) he has at the back of his mind the reasoning;

There (visually) appears to me to be a red apple here;

So, it is reasonable for me (to believe) that there is a red apple here,

then he should not object to speaking of the reasonableness in question as "direct", for the premise does not contain a predicate of epistemic evaluation. If, on the other hand (as he should not), he has at the back of his mind the following reasoning,

It is *evident* to me that there (visually) appears to me to be a red apple here;
So, it is *reasonable* for me (to believe) that there is a red apple here,

we could expect him to object to speaking of his reasonableness as "direct".

This tension sets the stage for a corresponding comment on Chisholm's third epistemic principle, which concerns the case where what we visually take to be the case is the presence of something having a "sensible characteristic *F*" (where "*F*" ranges over the familiar Aristotelian list of proper and common sensibles). The principle reads as follows:

(C) If there is a certain sensible characteristic *F* such that *S* believes that he perceives something to be *F*, then it is *evident* to *S* that he is perceiving something to have that characteristic *F*, and also *evident* that there is something that is *F*.

I shall not pause to quibble over such matters as whether, in the light of Chisholm's definition of "evident", it can ever be evident to me that I am perceiving something to be pink or that something in front of me is pink – even if the claim is limited to the facing side. A high degree of reasonableness will do. The point which I wish to stress is that once again the question arises, does Chisholm think of the evidence involved in the principles as "direct" or "indirect"? This time it is clear that he thinks of it as *indirect*. As I see it, then, he has at the back of his mind the following reasoning:

It is *evident* to me that there appears to me to be a pink object here;
So, it is *evident* to me that I perceive a pink object to be here and *evident* to me that there is a pink object here.

The contrasting reasoning would be:

There appears to me to be a pink object here;
So, it is *evident* to me that I perceive a pink object to be here and *evident* to me that there is a pink object here.

Now I suspect that what has misled Chisholm is the fact that if I were to argue,

There appears to me to be a pink cube here;
So, it is highly reasonable for me (to believe) that there is a pink object here,

a skeptic could be expected to challenge me by asking "What right have you to accept your conclusion, unless you have a right to accept the premise? Are you not implying that *you know* that there appears to you to be a pink object here; and must not this claim be a tacit *premise* in your argument?" But, surely, the skeptic would just be mistaken – not, indeed, in asserting that in some sense I *imply* that I know that there appears to me to be a pink object here, but in asserting that this implication must be taken to be a premise in my reasoning, if it is to be *valid*, and, hence, if the corresponding epistemic principle is to be *true*. But in that case, the latter principle would be *not* Chisholm's (C), but rather:

(C') *If it is evident to S that there is a certain sensible characteristic F …*

The larger import of the above reply to the skeptic will be sketched in my concluding remarks. For the moment, let me say that from my point of view something very like Chisholm's principle (C) is sound but concerns the *direct* evidence (or, better, *direct* high degree of reasonableness) of certain perceptual beliefs. Let me formulate it as follows:

(S) If there is a certain sensible characteristic *F* such that *S* believes that he perceives something to be *F*, then it is *evident* to *S* that there is something that is *F* and, hence, that he is perceiving something to be *F*.

Notice that I have reversed the relative position of the two clauses in the consequent as they appear in Chisholm's principle. This is because, on my interpretation, the *core* of the principle is

(S1) If I ostensibly see there to be an *F* object here, then it is highly reasonable for me (to believe) that there is an *F* object here.

And the move to

(S2) If I ostensibly see there to be an *F* object here, then it is highly reasonable for me (to believe) *that I see* there to be an *F* object here

is justified by the conceptual tie between "ostensibly see", "see", and truth.

VII

Chisholm's principle (C) and his other epistemic principles pertaining to perception and memory are themselves justified, as he sees it, by the fact that unless they, or something like them, are true, then there could be no such thing as perceptual knowledge to the effect, to use his example, that there is a cat on the roof. We have here a justification of the "this or nothing" kind familiar to the Kantian tradition. The principles also seem, on occasion, to be treated as candidates for the status of synthetic *a priori* (and even, one suspects, self-evident) truth.

As I see it, on the other hand, these epistemic principles can be placed in a naturalistic setting and their authority construed in terms of the nature of concept formation and of the acquisition of relevant linguistic skills. The model which I have been using is, indeed, a very simple one, and I have largely limited my use of it to the epistemic authority of perceptual beliefs. But if the strategy which I have suggested is successful, it is a relatively simple matter to extend it to memory beliefs. I have discussed the case of non-inferential knowledge of our own mental states in some detail, using this same general strategy, on a number of occasions.[12]

But, surely, it will be urged, facts about learning languages and acquiring linguistic skills are themselves empirical *facts*; and to know these facts involves perception, memory, indeed, all the epistemic activities the justification of which

is at stake. Must we not conclude that any such account as I give of the principle that perceptual beliefs occurring in perceptual contexts are *likely to be true* is circular? It must, indeed, be granted that principles pertaining to the epistemic authority of perceptual and memory beliefs are not the sort of thing which *could* be arrived at by inductive reasoning from perceptual belief. But the best way to make this point is positive. *We have to be in this framework to be thinking and perceiving beings at all.* I suspect that it is this plain truth which is the real underpinning of the idea that the authority of epistemic principles rests on the fact that unless they were true we could not see that a cat is on the roof.

I pointed out a moment ago that we have to be in the framework of these (and other) principles to be thinking, perceiving, and, I now add, acting beings at all. But surely this makes it clear that the exploration of these principles is but part and parcel of the task of explicating the concept of a rational animal or, in *VB* terms, of a language-using organism whose language is *about* the world in which it is *used*. It is only in the light of this larger task that the problem of the status of epistemic principles reveals its true meaning.

From the perspective of this larger task, the metaphor of "foundation and superstructure" is seen to be a false extrapolation, to use a Deweyan turn of phrase, from specific "problematic situations" with respect to which it *is* appropriate. And when we concern ourselves, as Philosophy ultimately demands, with *how it is* with man and his world, as contrasted with the catch-as-catch-can procedures which generate man's awareness of himself and his world, surely we can say, as I wrote some fifteen years ago in an earlier essay on this topic,

There is clearly *some* point to the picture of human knowledge as resting on a level of propositions – observation reports – which do not rest on other propositions in the same way as other propositions rest on them. On the other hand, I do wish to insist that the metaphor of "foundation" is misleading in that it keeps us from seeing that if there is a logical dimension in which other empirical propositions rest on observation reports, there is another logical dimension in which the latter rest on the former.

Above all, the picture is misleading because of its static character. One seems forced to choose between the picture of an elephant which rests on a tortoise (What supports the tortoise?) and the picture of a great Hegelian serpent of knowledge with its tail in its mouth (Where did it begin?). Neither will do. For empirical knowledge, like its sophisticated extension, science, is rational, not because it has a *foundation* but because it is a self-correcting enterprise which can put *any* claim in jeopardy, though not *all* at once.[13]

Notes

1   R. M. Chisholm, *Theory of Knowledge* (Englewood Cliffs, NJ: Prentice-Hall, 1966), pp. 16–17.

2   Ibid.

3   Ibid., p. 17.

4   Notice that the above account of the relation of "I know" to a performative is not quite the same as Urmson's. According to the latter, as represented by Chisholm, to say that Mr Jones *knew* some proposition to be true is to say that Mr Jones was "in a position in which he was entitled to say 'I know'". This account, as Chisholm points out, brings us back to the original problem of how the first person use of the verb is to be construed.

5   I have called attention elsewhere to the importance of distinguishing between questions concerning the reasonableness of believing that-*p* from questions concerning the reasonableness of "acting on the proposition that-*p*", including guaranteeing that-*p*. The concept of acting on a proposition is clear only in simple cases, as when, for example, the proposition occurs as a premise in the agent's practical reasoning. When the agent takes probabilities into account, a far more complicated story is necessary to clarify the sense in which a person can be said to have acted on a given proposition. For a discussion of these problems, see my "Induction as Vindication", *Philosophy of Science* 31 (1964), pp. 197–232.

6   Chisholm, *Theory of Knowledge*, p. 28. Chisholm's principle concerns "what justifies us in counting it as evident that *a* is *F*". But the "evident" is defined on p. 22 as a special case of the "reasonable".

7   Where "sub-conceptual" is far from being used as a pejorative term.

8   It is clearly some such position which is envisaged by many who explicitly reject the equation of knowledge with justified true belief.

That it is *implicit* in Chisholm's position becomes clear not only when we reflect (as above) on what his principle concerning the directly evident might mean, but when we take into account his use of such phrases as "state of affairs" that "'presents itself to him'" or that "'is apprehended through itself'" (Chisholm, *Theory of Knowledge*, p. 28) and his general commitment to a fact ontology (ibid., chap. 7, *passim*), a "fact", in the relevant sense, being a "state of affairs which exists" (ibid., p. 104). "Exists" in this context should not be confused with the "existential quantifier" but should be considered as a synonym for "obtains". It is obviously not self-contradictory to say that some states of affairs do not obtain.

9   Most recently in my *Science and Metaphysics* (London: Routledge and Kegan Paul, 1967), ch. 1, and in "Science, Sense Impressions, and Sensa: A Reply to Cornman", *Review of Metaphysics* 25 (1971), which is a reply to Cornman's "Sellars, Scientific Realism, and Sensa", *Review of Metaphysics* 24 (1970).

10   I called attention to this feature of the justification involved in "non-inferential" knowledge in *Science, Perception and Reality* (London: Routledge and Kegan Paul, and New York: Humanities Press, 1963), chap. 3. Thus, I wrote "… one only knows what one has a right to think to be the case. Thus, to say that one directly knows that-*p* is to say that his right to the conviction that-*p* essentially involves the fact that the idea that-*p* occurred to the knower in a specific way" (ibid., p. 88). I suggested that this "kind of credibility" be called "trans-level credibility", and the pattern of inference involved in the reasoning which mobilizes this credibility, "trans-level inference". A similar point was less clearly made in Sections 32–9 of my "Empiricism and the Philosophy of Mind",

in Herbert Feigl and Michael Scriven (eds), *Minnesota Studies in the Philosophy of Science* vol. I (Minneapolis: University of Minnesota Press, 1956). Reprinted as chapter 5 of my *Science, Perception and Reality*.

11 Chisholm, *Theory of Knowledge*, p. 28.

12 Most recently in my *Science and Metaphysics*, esp. pp. 71 ff., 151 ff.

13 "Empiricism and the Philosophy of Mind", sec. 38; quoted from *Science, Perception and Reality*, p. 170.

CHAPTER 10

Can Empirical Knowledge Have a Foundation?

Laurence BonJour

The idea that empirical knowledge has, and must have, a *foundation* has been a common tenet of most major epistemologists, both past and present. There have been, as we shall see further below, many importantly different variants of this idea. But the common denominator among them, the central thesis of epistemological foundationism as I shall understand it here, is the claim that certain empirical beliefs possess a degree of epistemic justification or warrant which does not depend, inferentially or otherwise, on the justification of other empirical beliefs, but is instead somehow immediate or intrinsic. It is these non-inferentially justified beliefs, the unmoved (or self-moved) movers of the epistemic realm as Chisholm has called them,[1] that constitute the foundation upon which the rest of empirical knowledge is alleged to rest.

In recent years, the most familiar foundationist views have been subjected to severe and continuous attack. But this attack has rarely been aimed directly at the central foundationist thesis itself, and new versions of foundationism have been quick to emerge, often propounded by the erstwhile critics themselves. Thus foundationism has become a philosophical hydra, difficult to come to grips with and seemingly impossible to kill. The purposes of this paper are, first, to distinguish and clarify

the main dialectical variants of foundationism, by viewing them as responses to one fundamental problem which is both the main motivation and the primary obstacle for foundationism; and second, as a result of this discussion to offer schematic reasons for doubting whether any version of foundationism is finally acceptable.

The main reason for the impressive durability of foundationism is not any overwhelming plausibility attaching to the main foundationist thesis in itself, but rather the existence of one apparently decisive argument which seems to rule out all non-skeptical alternatives to foundationism, thereby showing that *some* version of foundationism must be true (on the assumption that skepticism is false). In a recent statement by Quinton, this argument runs as follows:

> If any beliefs are to be justified at all, ... there must be some terminal beliefs that do not owe their ... credibility to others. For a belief to be justified it is not enough for it to be accepted, let alone merely entertained: there must also be good reason for accepting it. Furthermore, for an inferential belief to be justified the beliefs that support it must be justified themselves. There must, therefore, be a kind of belief that does not owe its justification to the support provided by others. Unless this were so no belief would be justified at all, for to justify any belief would require the antecedent justification of an infinite series of beliefs. The terminal ... beliefs that are needed to bring the regress of justification to a

Originally published in *American Philosophical Quarterly* 15, 1 (1978), pp. 1–13.

stop need not be strictly self-evident in the sense that they somehow justify themselves. All that is required is that they should not owe their justification to any other beliefs.[2]

I shall call this argument *the epistemic regress argument*, and the problem which generates it, *the epistemic regress problem*. Since it is this argument which provides the primary rationale and argumentative support for foundationism, a careful examination of it will also constitute an exploration of the foundationist position itself. The main dialectical variants of foundationism can best be understood as differing attempts to solve the regress problem, and the most basic objection to the foundationist approach is that it is doubtful that any of these attempts can succeed. (In this paper, I shall be concerned with the epistemic regress argument and the epistemic regress problem only as they apply to empirical knowledge. It is obvious that an analogous problem arises also for *a priori* knowledge, but there it seems likely that the argument would take a different course. In particular, a foundationist approach might be inescapable in an account of *a priori* knowledge.)

I

The epistemic regress problem arises directly out of the traditional conception of knowledge as *adequately justified true belief*[3] – whether this be taken as a fully adequate definition of knowledge or, in light of the apparent counter-examples discovered by Gettier,[4] as merely a necessary but not sufficient condition. (I shall assume throughout that the elements of the traditional conception are at least necessary for knowledge.) Now the most natural way to justify a belief is by producing a justificatory argument: belief *A* is justified by citing some other (perhaps conjunctive) belief *B*, from which *A* is inferable in some acceptable way and which is thus offered as a reason for accepting *A*.[5] Call this *inferential justification*. It is clear, as Quinton points out in the passage quoted above, that for *A* to be genuinely justified by virtue of such a justificatory argument, *B* must itself be justified in some fashion; merely being inferable from an unsupported guess or hunch, e.g., would confer no genuine justification upon *A*.

Two further points about inferential justification, as understood here, must be briefly noted. First, the belief in question need not have been *arrived at* as the result of an inference in order to be inferentially justified. This is obvious, since a belief arrived at in some other way (e.g., as a result of wishful thinking) may later come to be maintained solely because it is now seen to be inferentially justifiable. Second, less obviously, a person for whom a belief is inferentially justified need not have explicitly rehearsed the justificatory argument in question to others or even to himself. It is enough that the inference be available to him if the belief is called into question by others or by himself (where such availability may itself be less than fully explicit) and that the availability of the inference be, in the final analysis, his reason for holding the belief.[6] It seems clear that many beliefs which are quite sufficiently justified to satisfy the justification criterion for knowledge depend for their justification on inferences which have not been explicitly formulated and indeed which could not be explicitly formulated without considerable reflective effort (e.g., my current belief that this is the same piece of paper upon which I was typing yesterday).[7]

Suppose then that belief *A* is (putatively) justified via inference, thus raising the question of how the justifying premise-belief *B* is justified. Here again the answer may be in inferential terms: *B* may be (putatively) justified in virtue of being inferable from some further belief *C*. But then the same question arises about the justification of *C*, and so on, threatening an infinite and apparently vicious regress of epistemic justification. Each belief is justified only if an epistemically prior belief is justified, and that epistemically prior belief is justified only if a still prior belief is justified, etc., with the apparent result that justification can never get started – and hence that there is no justification and no knowledge. The foundationist claim is that only through the adoption of some version of foundationism can this skeptical consequence be avoided.

Prima facie, there seem to be only four basic possibilities with regard to the eventual outcome of this potential regress of epistemic justification: (i) the regress might terminate with beliefs for which no justification of any kind is available, even though they were earlier offered as justifying premises; (ii) the regress might proceed infinitely backwards with ever more new premise beliefs being introduced and then themselves requiring justification; (iii) the regress might circle back upon itself, so that at some point beliefs which appeared earlier in the sequence of justifying arguments are appealed to again as premises; (iv) the regress might terminate because beliefs are reached which are justified – unlike those in alternative (i) – but whose justification does not depend inferentially on other empirical beliefs and thus does not raise any further issue of justification with respect to such beliefs.[8] The foundationist opts for the last alternative. His argument is that the other three lead inexorably to the skeptical result, and that the second and third have additional fatal defects as well, so that some version of the fourth, foundationist alternative must be correct (assuming that skepticism is false).

With respect to alternative (i), it seems apparent that the foundationist is correct. If this alternative were correct, empirical knowledge would rest ultimately on beliefs which were, from an epistemic standpoint at least, entirely arbitrary and hence incapable of conferring any genuine justification. What about the other two alternatives?

The argument that alternative (ii) leads to a skeptical outcome has in effect already been sketched in the original formulation of the problem. One who opted for this alternative could hope to avoid skepticism only by claiming that the regress, though infinite, is not vicious; but there seems to be no plausible way to defend such a claim. Moreover, a defense of an infinite regress view as an account of how empirical knowledge is actually justified – as opposed to how it might in principle be justified – would have to involve the seemingly dubious thesis that an ordinary knower holds a literally infinite number of distinct beliefs. Thus it is not surprising that no important philosopher, with the rather uncertain exception of Peirce,[9] seems to have advocated such a position.

Alternative (iii), the view that justification ultimately moves in a closed curve, has been historically more prominent, albeit often only as a dialectical foil for foundationism. At first glance, this alternative might seem even less attractive than the second. Although the problem of the knower having to have an infinite number of beliefs is no longer present, the regress itself, still infinite, now seems undeniably vicious. For the justification of each of the beliefs which figure

in the circle seems now to presuppose *its own* epistemically prior justification: such a belief must, paradoxically, be justified before it can be justified. Advocates of views resembling alternative (iii) have generally tended to respond to this sort of objection by adopting a holistic conception of justification in which the justification of individual beliefs is subordinated to that of the closed systems of beliefs which such a view implies; the property of such systems usually appealed to as a basis for justification is internal *coherence*. Such coherence theories attempt to evade the regress problem by abandoning the view of justification as essentially involving a linear order of dependence (though a non-linear view of justification has never been worked out in detail).[10] Moreover, such a coherence theory of empirical knowledge is subject to a number of other familiar and seemingly decisive objections.[11] Thus alternative (iii) seems unacceptable, leaving only alternative (iv), the foundationist alternative, as apparently viable.

As thus formulated, the epistemic regress argument makes an undeniably persuasive case for foundationism. Like any argument by elimination, however, it cannot be conclusive until the surviving alternative has itself been carefully examined. The foundationist position may turn out to be subject to equally serious objections, thus forcing a re-examination of the other alternatives, a search for a further non-skeptical alternative, or conceivably the reluctant acceptance of the skeptical conclusion.[12] In particular, it is not clear on the basis of the argument thus far whether and how foundationism can itself solve the regress problem; and thus the possibility exists that the epistemic regress argument will prove to be a two-edged sword, as lethal to the foundationist as it is to his opponents.

II

The most straightforward interpretation of alternative (iv) leads directly to a view which I will here call *strong foundationism*. According to strong foundationism, the foundational beliefs which terminate the regress of justification possess sufficient epistemic warrant, independently of any appeal to inference from (or coherence with) other empirical beliefs, to satisfy the justification condition of knowledge and qualify as acceptable justifying premises for further beliefs. Since the justification of these *basic beliefs*, as they have come to be called, is thus allegedly not dependent on that of any other empirical belief, they are uniquely able to provide secure starting-points for the justification of empirical knowledge and stopping-points for the regress of justification.

The position just outlined is in fact a fairly modest version of strong foundationism. Strong foundationists have typically made considerably stronger claims on behalf of basic beliefs. Basic beliefs have been claimed not only to have sufficient non-inferential justification to qualify as knowledge, but also to be *certain, infallible, indubitable*, or *incorrigible* (terms which are usually not very carefully distinguished).[13] And most of the major attacks on foundationism have focused on these stronger claims. Thus it is important to point out that nothing about the basic strong foundationist response to the regress problem demands that basic beliefs be more than adequately justified. There might of course be other reasons for requiring that basic beliefs have some more exalted epistemic status or for thinking that in fact they do. There might even be some sort of indirect argument to show that such a status is a consequence of the sorts of epistemic properties which are directly required to solve the regress problem. But until such an argument is given (and it is doubtful that it can be), the question of whether basic beliefs are or can be certain, infallible, etc., will remain a relatively unimportant side-issue.

Indeed, many recent foundationists have felt that even the relatively modest version of strong foundationism outlined above is still too strong. Their alternative, still within the general aegis of the foundationist position, is a view which may be called *weak foundationism*. Weak foundationism accepts the central idea of foundationism – viz. that certain empirical beliefs possess a degree of independent epistemic justification or warrant which does not derive from inference or coherence relations. But the weak foundationist holds that these foundational beliefs have only a quite low degree of warrant, much lower than that attributed to them by even modest strong foundationism and insufficient by itself to satisfy the justification condition for knowledge or to qualify them as acceptable justifying premises for other beliefs. Thus this independent warrant must somehow be argumented if knowledge is to be achieved, and the usual appeal here is to coherence with other such minimally warranted beliefs. By combining such beliefs into larger and larger coherent systems, it is held, their initial, minimal degree of warrant can gradually be enhanced until knowledge is finally achieved. Thus weak foundationism, like the pure coherence theories mentioned above, abandons the linear conception of justification.[14]

Weak foundationism thus represents a kind of hybrid between strong foundationism and the coherence views discussed earlier, and it is often thought to embody the virtues of both and the vices of neither. Whether or not this is so in other respects, however, relative to the regress problem weak foundationism is finally open to the very same basic objection as strong foundationism, with essentially the same options available for meeting it. As we shall see, the key problem for any version of foundationism is whether it can itself solve the regress problem which motivates its very existence, without resorting to essentially *ad hoc* stipulation. The distinction between the two main ways of meeting this challenge both cuts across and is more basic than that between strong and weak foundationism. This being so, it will suffice to concentrate here on strong foundationism, leaving the application of the discussion to weak foundationism largely implicit.

The fundamental concept of strong foundationism is obviously the concept of a basic belief. It is by appeal to this concept that the threat of an infinite regress is to be avoided and empirical knowledge given a secure foundation. But how can there be any empirical beliefs which are thus basic? In fact, though this has not always been noticed, the very idea of an epistemically basic empirical belief is extremely paradoxical. For on what basis is such a belief to be justified, once appeal to further empirical beliefs is ruled out? Chisholm's theological analogy, cited earlier, is most appropriate: a basic belief is in effect an epistemological unmoved (or self-moved) mover. It is able to confer justification on other beliefs, but apparently has no need to have justification conferred on it. But is such a status any easier to understand in epistemology than it is in theology? How can a belief impart epistemic "motion" to other beliefs unless it is itself in "motion"? And, even more paradoxically, how can a belief epistemically "move" itself?

This intuitive difficulty with the concept of a basic empirical belief may be elaborated and clarified by reflecting a bit on the concept of epistemic justification. The idea of justification is a generic one, admitting in principle of many specific varieties. Thus the acceptance of an empirical belief might be morally justified, i.e. justified as morally obligatory by reference to moral principles and standards; or pragmatically justified, i.e. justified by reference to the desirable practical consequences which will result from such acceptance; or religiously justified, i.e. justified by reference to specified religious texts or theological dogmas; etc. But none of these other varieties of justification can satisfy the justification condition for knowledge. Knowledge requires *epistemic* justification, and the distinguishing characteristic of this particular species of justification is, I submit, its essential or internal relationship to the cognitive goal of truth. Cognitive doings are epistemically justified, on this conception, only if and to the extent that they are aimed at this goal – which means roughly that one accepts all and only beliefs which one has good reason to think are true.[15] To accept a belief in the absence of such a reason, however appealing or even mandatory such acceptance might be from other standpoints, is to neglect the pursuit of truth; such acceptance is, one might say, *epistemically irresponsible*. My contention is that the idea of being epistemically responsible is the core of the concept of epistemic justification.[16]

A corollary of this conception of epistemic justification is that a satisfactory defense of a particular standard of epistemic justification must consist in showing it to be truth-conductive, i.e. in showing that accepting beliefs in accordance with its dictates is likely to lead to truth (and more likely than any proposed alternative). Without such a meta-justification, a proposed standard of epistemic justification lacks any underlying rationale. Why after all should an epistemically responsible inquirer prefer justified beliefs to unjustified ones, if not that the former are more likely to be true? To insist that a certain belief is epistemically justified, while confessing in the same breath that this fact about it provides no good reason to think that it is true, would be to render nugatory the whole concept of epistemic justification.

These general remarks about epistemic justification apply in full measure to any strong foundationist position and to its constituent account of basic beliefs. If basic beliefs are to provide a secure foundation for empirical knowledge, if inference from them is to be the sole basis for the justification of other empirical beliefs, then that feature, whatever it may be, in virtue of which a belief qualifies as basic must also constitute a good reason for thinking that the belief is true. If we let "ϕ" represent this feature, then for a belief B to qualify as basic in an acceptable foundationist account, the premises of the following justificatory argument must themselves be at least justified:[17]

(i) Belief B has feature ϕ.
(ii) Beliefs having feature ϕ are highly likely to be true.

Therefore, B is highly likely to be true.

Notice further that while either premise taken separately might turn out to be justifiable on an *a priori* basis (depending on the particular choice of ϕ), it seems clear that they could not both be thus justifiable. For B is *ex hypothesi* an empirical belief, and it is hard to see how a particular empirical belief could be justified on a purely *a priori* basis.[18] And if we now assume, reasonably enough, that for B to be justified for a particular person (at a particular time) it is necessary, not merely that a justification for B exist in the abstract, but that the person in question be in cognitive possession of that justification, we get the result that B is not basic after all since its justification depends on that of at least one other empirical belief. If this is correct, strong foundationism is untenable as a solution to the regress problem (and an analogous argument will show weak foundationism to be similarly untenable).

The foregoing argument is, no doubt, exceedingly obvious. But how is the strong foundationist to answer it? *Prima facie*, there seem to be only two general sorts of answer which are even remotely plausible, so long as the strong foundationist remains within the confines of the traditional conception of knowledge, avoids tacitly embracing skepticism, and does not attempt the heroic task of arguing that an empirical belief could be justified on a purely *a priori* basis. First, he might argue that although it is indeed necessary for a belief to be justified and *a fortiori* for it to be basic that a justifying argument of the sort schematized above be in principle available in the situation, it is *not* always necessary that the person for whom the belief is basic (or anyone else) know or even justifiably believe that it is available; instead, in the case of basic beliefs at least, it is sufficient that the premises for an argument of that general sort (or for some favored particular variety of such argument) merely be *true*, whether or not that person (or anyone else) justifiably believes that they are true. Second, he might grant that it is necessary both that such justification exist and that the person for whom the belief is basic be in cognitive possession of it, but insist that his cognitive grasp of the premises required for that justification does not involve further empirical beliefs which would then require justification, but instead involves cognitive states of a more rudimentary sort which do not themselves require justification: *intuitions* or *immediate apprehensions*. I will consider each of these alternatives in turn.

III

The philosopher who has come the closest to an explicit advocacy of the view that basic beliefs may be justified even though the person for whom they are basic is not in any way in cognitive possession of the appropriate justifying argument is D. M. Armstrong. In his recent book, *Belief, Truth and Knowledge*,[19] Armstrong presents a version of the epistemic regress problem (though one couched in terms of knowledge rather than justification) and defends what he calls an "Externalist" solution:

> According to "Externalist" accounts of non-inferential knowledge, what makes a true non-inferential belief a case of *knowledge* is some natural relation which holds between the belief-state ... and the situation which makes the belief true. It is a matter of a certain relation holding between the believer and the world. (p. 157)

Armstrong's own candidate for this "natural relation" is "that there must be a *law-like connection* between the state of affairs *Bap* [i.e. *a*'s believing that *p*] and the state of affairs that makes '*p*'

true such that, given *Bap*, it must be the case that *p*" (p. 166). A similar view seems to be implicit in Dretske's account of perceptual knowledge in *Seeing and Knowing*, with the variation that Dretske requires for knowledge not only that the relation in question obtain, but also that the putative knower *believe* that it obtains – though *not* that this belief be justified.[20] In addition, it seems likely that various views of an ordinary-language stripe which appeal to facts about how language is learned either to justify basic belief or to support the claim that no justification is required would, if pushed, turn out to be positions of this general sort. Here I shall mainly confine myself to Armstrong, who is the only one of these philosophers who is explicitly concerned with the regress problem.

There is, however, some uncertainty as to how views of this sort in general and Armstrong's view in particular are properly to be interpreted. On the one hand, Armstrong might be taken as offering an account of how basic beliefs (and perhaps others as well) satisfy the adequate-justification condition for knowledge; while on the other hand, he might be taken as simply repudiating the traditional conception of knowledge and the associated concept of epistemic justification, and offering a surrogate conception in its place – one which better accords with the "naturalistic" world-view which Armstrong prefers.[21] But it is only when understood in the former way that externalism (to adopt Armstrong's useful term) is of any immediate interest here, since it is only on that interpretation that it constitutes a version of foundationism and offers a direct response to the anti-foundationist argument set out above. Thus I shall mainly focus on this interpretation of externalism, remarking only briefly at the end of the present section on the alternative one.

Understood in this way, the externalist solution to the regress problem is quite simple: the person who has a basic belief need not be in possession of any justified reason for his belief and indeed, except in Dretske's version, need not even think that there is such a reason; the status of his belief as constituting knowledge (if true) depends solely on the external relation and not at all on his subjective view of the situation. Thus there are no further empirical beliefs in need of justification and no regress.

Now it is clear that such an externalist position succeeds in avoiding the regress problem and the anti-foundationist argument. What may well be doubted, however, is whether this avoidance deserves to be considered a *solution*, rather than an essentially *ad hoc* evasion, of the problem. Plainly the sort of "external" relation which Armstrong has in mind would, if known, provide a basis for a justifying argument along the lines sketched earlier, roughly as follows:

(i) Belief *B* is an instance of kind *K*.
(ii) Beliefs of kind *K* are connected in a law-like way with the sorts of states of affairs which would make them true, and therefore are highly likely to be true.

Therefore, *B* is highly likely to be true.

But precisely what generates the regress problem in the first place is the requirement that for a belief *B* to be epistemically justified for a given person *P*, it is necessary, not just that there be justifiable or even true premises available in the situation which could in principle provide a basis for a justification of *B*, but that *P* himself know or at least justifiably believe some such set of premises and thus be in a position to employ the corresponding argument. The externalist position seems to amount merely to waiving this general requirement in cases where the justification takes a certain form, and the question is why this should be acceptable in these cases when it is not acceptable generally. (If it were acceptable generally, then it would seem that any true belief would be justified for any person, and the distinction between knowledge and true belief would collapse.) Such a move seems rather analogous to solving a regress of causes by simply stipulating that although most events must have a cause, events of a certain kind need not.

Whatever plausibility attaches to externalism seems to derive from the fact that if the external relation in question genuinely obtains, then *P* will not go wrong in accepting the belief, and it is, in a sense, not an accident that this is so. But it remains unclear how these facts are supposed to justify *P*'s acceptance of *B*. It is clear, of course, that an external observer who knew both that *P* accepted *B* and that there was a law-like connection between such acceptance and the truth of *B* would be in a position to construct an argument to justify *his own* acceptance of *B*. *P* could thus serve as a useful epistemic instrument, a kind of

cognitive thermometer, for such an external observer (and in fact the example of a thermometer is exactly the analogy which Armstrong employs to illustrate the relationship which is supposed to obtain between the person who has the belief and the external state of affairs (p. 166 ff.)). But *P* himself has no reason at all for thinking that *B* is likely to be true. From his perspective, it *is* an accident that the belief is true.[22] And thus his acceptance of *B* is no more rational or responsible from an epistemic standpoint than would be the acceptance of a subjectively similar belief for which the external relation in question failed to obtain.[23]

Nor does it seem to help matters to move from Armstrong's version of externalism, which requires only that the requisite relationship between the believer and the world obtain, to the superficially less radical version apparently held by Dretske, which requires that *P* also believe that the external relation obtains, but does not require that this latter belief be justified. This view may seem slightly less implausible, since it at least requires that the person have some idea, albeit unjustified, of why *B* is likely to be true. But this change is not enough to save externalism. One way to see this is to suppose that the person believes the requisite relation to obtain on some totally irrational and irrelevant basis, e.g. as a result of reading tea leaves or studying astrological charts. If *B* were an ordinary, non-basic belief, such a situation would surely preclude its being justified, and it is hard to see why the result should be any different for an allegedly basic belief.

Thus it finally seems possible to make sense of externalism only by construing the externalist as simply abandoning the traditional notion of epistemic justification and along with it anything resembling the traditional conception of knowledge. (As already remarked, this may be precisely what the proponents of externalism intend to be doing, though most of them are not very clear on this point.) Thus consider Armstrong's final summation of his conception of knowledge:

> *Knowledge of the truth of particular matters of fact* is a belief which must be true, where the "must" is a matter of law-like necessity. Such knowledge is a reliable representation or "mapping" of reality. (p. 220)

Nothing is said here of reasons or justification or evidence or having the right to be sure. Indeed the whole idea, central to the western epistemological tradition, of knowledge as essentially the product of reflective, critical, and rational inquiry has seemingly vanished without a trace. It is possible of course that such an altered conception of knowledge may be inescapable or even in some way desirable, but it constitutes a solution to the regress problem or any problem arising out of the traditional conception of knowledge only in the radical and relatively uninteresting sense that to reject that conception is also to reject the problems arising out of it. In this paper, I shall confine myself to less radical solutions.

IV

The externalist solution just discussed represents a very recent approach to the justification of basic beliefs. The second view to be considered is, in contrast, so venerable that it deserves to be called the standard foundationist solution to the problem in question. I refer of course to the traditional doctrine of cognitive givenness, which has played a central role in epistemological discussions at least since Descartes. In recent years, however, the concept of the given, like foundationism itself, has come under serious attack. One upshot of the resulting discussion has been a realization that there are many different notions of givenness, related to each other in complicated ways, which almost certainly do not stand or fall together. Thus it will be well to begin by formulating the precise notion of givenness which is relevant in the present context and distinguishing it from some related conceptions.

In the context of the epistemic regress problem, givenness amounts to the idea that basic beliefs are justified by reference, not to further *beliefs*, but rather to states of affairs in the world which are "immediately apprehended" or "directly presented" or "intuited." This justification by reference to non-cognitive states of affairs thus allegedly avoids the need for any further justification and thereby stops the regress. In a way, the basic gambit of givenism (as I shall call positions of this sort) thus resembles that of the externalist positions considered above. In both cases the justificatory appeal to further beliefs which generates the

regress problem is avoided for basic beliefs by an appeal directly to the non-cognitive world; the crucial difference is that for the givenist, unlike the externalist, the justifying state of affairs in the world is allegedly apprehended *in some way* by the believer.

The givenist position to be considered here is significantly weaker than more familiar versions of the doctrine of givenness in at least two different respects. In the first place, the present version does not claim that the given (or, better, the apprehension thereof) is certain or even incorrigible. As discussed above, these stronger claims are inessential to the strong foundationist solution to the regress problem. If they have any importance at all in this context it is only because, as we shall see, they might be thought to be entailed by the only very obvious intuitive picture of how the view is supposed to work. In the second place, givenism as understood here does not involve the usual stipulation that only one's private mental and sensory states can be given. There may or may not be other reasons for thinking that this is in fact the case, but such a restriction is not part of the position itself. Thus both positions like that of C. I. Lewis, for whom the given is restricted to private states apprehended with certainty, and positions like that of Quinton, for whom ordinary physical states of affairs are given with no claim of certainty or incorrigibility being involved, will count as versions of givenism.

As already noted, the idea of givenness has been roundly criticized in recent philosophical discussion and widely dismissed as a piece of philosophical mythology. But much at least of this criticism has to do with the claim of certainty on behalf of the given or with the restriction to private, subjective states. And some of it at least has been mainly concerned with issues in the philosophy of mind which are only distantly related to our present epistemological concerns. Thus even if the objections offered are cogent against other and stronger versions of givenness, it remains unclear whether and how they apply to the more modest version at issue here. The possibility suggests itself that modest givenness may not be a myth, even if more ambitious varieties are, a result which would give the epistemological foundationist all he really needs, even though he has usually, in a spirit of philosophical greed, sought considerably more. In what follows, however, I shall sketch a line of argument which, if correct, will show that even modest givenism is an untenable position.[24]

The argument to be developed depends on a problem within the givenist position which is surprisingly easy to overlook. I shall therefore proceed in the following way. I shall first state the problem in an initial way, then illustrate it by showing how it arises in one recent version of givenism, and finally consider whether any plausible solution is possible. (It will be useful for the purposes of this discussion to make two simplifying assumptions, without which the argument would be more complicated, but not essentially altered. First, I shall assume that the basic belief which is to be justified by reference to the given or immediately apprehended state of affairs is just the belief that this same state of affairs obtains. Second, I shall assume that the given or immediately apprehended state of affairs is not itself a belief or other cognitive state.)

Consider then an allegedly basic belief that-p which is supposed to be justified by reference to a given or immediately apprehended state of affairs that-p. Clearly what justifies the belief is not the state of affairs simpliciter, for to say that would be to return to a form of externalism. For the givenist, what justifies the belief is the *immediate apprehension* or *intuition* of the state of affairs. Thus we seem to have three items present in the situation: the belief, the state of affairs which is the object of the belief, and the intuition or immediate apprehension of that state of affairs. The problem to be raised revolves around the nature of the last of these items, the intuition or immediate apprehension (hereafter I will use mainly the former term). It *seems* to be a cognitive state, perhaps somehow of a more rudimentary sort than a belief, which involves the thesis or assertion that-p. Now if this is correct, it is easy enough to understand in a rough sort of way how an intuition can serve to justify a belief with this same assertive content. The problem is to understand why the intuition, involving as it does the cognitive thesis that-p, does not *itself* require justification. And if the answer is offered that the intuition is justified by reference to the state of affairs that-p, then the question will be why this would not require a second intuition or other apprehension of the state of affairs to justify the original one. For otherwise one and the same cognitive state

must somehow constitute both an apprehension of the state of affairs and a justification of that very apprehension, thus pulling itself up by its own cognitive bootstraps. One is reminded here of Chisholm's claim that certain cognitive states justify themselves,[25] but that extremely paradoxical remark hardly constitutes an explanation of how this is possible.

If, on the other hand, an intuition is not a cognitive state and thus involves no cognitive grasp of the state of affairs in question, then the need for a justification for the intuition is obviated, but at the serious cost of making it difficult to see how the intuition is supposed to justify the belief. If the person in question has no cognitive grasp of that state of affairs (or of any other) by virtue of having such an intuition, then how does the intuition give him a *reason* for thinking that his belief is true or likely to be true? We seem again to be back to an externalist position, which it was the whole point of the category of intuition or givenness to avoid.

As an illustration of this problem, consider Quinton's version of givenism, as outlined in his book *The Nature of Things*.[26] As noted above, basic beliefs may, according to Quinton, concern ordinary perceptible states of affairs and need not be certain or incorrigible. (Quinton uses the phrase "intuitive belief" as I have been using "basic belief" and calls the linguistic expression of an intuitive belief a "basic statements"; he also seems to pay very little attention to the difference between beliefs and statements, shifting freely back and forth between them, and I will generally follow him in this.) Thus "this book is red" might, in an appropriate context, be a basic statement expressing a basic or intuitive belief. But how are such basic statements (or the correlative beliefs) supposed to be justified? Here Quinton's account, beyond the insistence that they are not justified by reference to further beliefs, is seriously unclear. He says rather vaguely that the person is "aware" (p. 129) or "directly aware" (p. 139) of the appropriate state of affairs, or that he has "direct knowledge" (p. 126) of it, but he gives no real account of the nature or epistemological status of this state of "direct awareness" or "direct knowledge," though it seems clear that it is supposed to be a cognitive state of some kind. (In particular, it is not clear what "direct" means, over and above "non-inferential.")[27]

The difficulty with Quinton's account comes out most clearly in his discussion of its relation to the correspondence theory of truth:

> The theory of basic statements is closely connected with the correspondence theory of truth. In its classical form that theory holds that to each true statement, whatever its form may be, a fact of the same form corresponds. The theory of basic statements indicates the point at which correspondence is established, at which the system of beliefs makes its justifying contact with the world. (p. 139)

And further on he remarks that the truth of basic statements "is directly determined by their correspondence with fact" (p. 143). (It is clear that "determined" here means "epistemically determined.") Now it is a familiar but still forceful idealist objection to the correspondence theory of truth that if the theory were correct we could never know whether any of our beliefs were true, since we have no perspective outside our system of beliefs from which to see that they do or do not correspond. Quinton, however, seems to suppose rather blithely that intuition or direct awareness provides just such a perspective, from which we can in some cases apprehend both beliefs and world and judge whether or not they correspond. And he further supposes that the issue of justification somehow does not arise for apprehensions made from this perspective, though without giving any account of how or why this is so.

My suggestion here is that no such account can be given. As indicated above, the givenist is caught in a fundamental dilemma: if his intuitions or immediate apprehensions are construed as cognitive, then they will be both capable of giving justification and in need of it themselves; if they are non-cognitive, then they do not need justification but are also apparently incapable of providing it. This, at bottom, is why epistemological givenness is a myth.[28]

Once the problem is clearly realized, the only possible solution seems to be to split the difference by claiming that an intuition is a semi-cognitive or quasi-cognitive state,[29] which resembles a belief in its capacity to confer justification, while differing from a belief in not requiring justification itself. In fact, some such conception seems to be implicit in most if not all givenist positions. But when stated thus baldly, this "solution" to the problem seems hopelessly contrived and *ad hoc*. If such a move is acceptable, one is inclined to expostulate, then once again any sort of regress could be solved in similar fashion. Simply postulate a final term in the regress which is sufficiently similar to the previous terms to satisfy, with respect to the penultimate term, the sort of need or impetus which originally generated the regress; but which is different enough from previous terms so as not itself to require satisfaction by a further term. Thus we would have semi-events, which could cause but need not be caused; semi-explanatia, which could explain but need not be explained; and semi-beliefs, which could justify but need not be justified. The point is not that such a move is always incorrect (though I suspect that it is), but simply that the nature and possibility of such a convenient regress-stopper needs at the very least to be clearly and convincingly established and explained before it can constitute a satisfactory solution to any regress problem.

The main account which has usually been offered by givenists of such semi-cognitive states is well suggested by the terms in which immediate or intuitive apprehensions are described: "immediate," "direct," "presentation," etc. The underlying idea here is that of *confrontation*: in intuition, mind or consciousness is directly confronted with its object, without the intervention of any sort of intermediary. It is in this sense that the object is *given* to the mind. The root metaphor underlying this whole picture is vision: mind or consciousness is likened to an immaterial eye, and the object of intuitive awareness is that which is directly before the mental eye and open to its gaze. If this metaphor were to be taken seriously, it would become relatively simple to explain how there can be a cognitive state which can justify but does not require justification. (If the metaphor is to be taken seriously enough to do the foundationist any real good, it becomes plausible to hold that the intuitive cognitive states which result would after all have to be infallible. For if all need for justification is to be precluded, the envisaged relation of confrontation seemingly must be conceived as too intimate to allow any possibility of error. To the extent that this is so, the various arguments which have been offered against the notion of infallible cognitive states count also against this version of givenism.)

Unfortunately, however, it seems clear that the mental eye metaphor will not stand serious scrutiny. The mind, whatever else it may be, is not an eye or, so far as we know, anything like an eye. Ultimately the metaphor is just far too simple to be even minimally adequate to the complexity of mental phenomena and to the variety of conditions upon which such phenomena depend. This is not to deny that there is considerable intuitive appeal to the confrontational model, especially as applied to perceptual consciousness, but only to insist that this appeal is far too vague in its import to adequately support the very specific sorts of epistemological results which the strong foundationist needs. In particular, even if empirical knowledge at some point involves some sort of confrontation or seeming confrontation, this by itself provides no clear reason for attributing epistemic justification or reliability, let alone certainty, to the cognitive states, whatever they may be called, which result.

Moreover, quite apart from the vicissitudes of the mental eye metaphor, there are powerful independent reasons for thinking that the attempt to defend givenism by appeal to the idea of a semi-cognitive or quasi-cognitive state is fundamentally misguided. The basic idea, after all, is to distinguish two aspects of a cognitive state, its capacity to justify other states and its own need for justification, and then try to find a state which possesses only the former aspect and not the latter. But it seems clear on reflection that these two aspects cannot be separated, that it is one and the same feature of a cognitive state, viz. its assertive content, which both enables it to confer justification on other states and also requires that it be justified itself. If this is right, then it does no good to introduce semi-cognitive states in an attempt to justify basic beliefs, since to whatever extent such a state is capable of conferring justification, it will to that very same extent require justification. Thus even if such states do exist, they are of no help to the givenist in attempting to answer the objection at issue here.[30]

Hence the givenist response to the antifoundationist argument seems to fail. There

seems to be no way to explain how a basic cognitive state, whether called a belief or an intuition, can be directly justified by the world without lapsing back into externalism – and from there into skepticism. I shall conclude with three further comments aimed at warding off certain likely sorts of misunderstanding. First. It is natural in this connection to attempt to justify basic beliefs by appealing to *experience*. But there is a familiar ambiguity in the term "experience," which in fact glosses over the crucial distinction upon which the foregoing argument rests. Thus "experience" may mean either an *experiencing* (i.e., a cognitive state) or something *experienced* (i.e., an object of cognition). And once this ambiguity is resolved, the concept of experience seems to be of no particular help to the givenist. Second. I have concentrated, for the sake of simplicity, on Quinton's version of givenism in which ordinary physical states of affairs are among the things which are given. But the logic of the argument would be essentially the same if it were applied to a more traditional version like Lewis's in which it is private experiences which are given, and I cannot see that the end result would be different – though it might be harder to discern, especially in cases where the allegedly basic belief is a belief about another cognitive state. Third. Notice carefully that the problem raised here with respect to givenism is a logical problem (in a broad sense of "logical"). Thus it would be a mistake to think that it can be solved simply by indicating some sort of state which seems intuitively to have the appropriate sorts of characteristics; the problem is to understand how it is *possible* for any state to have those characteristics. (The mistake would be analogous to one occasionally made in connection with the free-will problem: the mistake of attempting to solve the logical problem of how an action can be not determined but also not merely random by indicating a subjective act of effort or similar state, which seems intuitively to satisfy such a description.)

Thus foundationism appears to be doomed by its own internal momentum. No account seems to be available of how an empirical belief can be genuinely justified in an epistemic sense, while avoiding all reference to further empirical beliefs or cognitions which themselves would require justification. How then is the epistemic regress problem to be solved? The natural direction to look for an answer is to the coherence theory of empirical knowledge and the associated non-linear conception of justification which were briefly mentioned above.[31] But arguments by

elimination are dangerous at best: there may be further alternatives which have not yet been formulated; and the possibility still threatens that the epistemic regress problem may in the end be of aid and comfort only to the skeptic.

Notes

1   Roderick M. Chisholm, *Theory of Knowledge* (Englewood Cliffs, NJ: Prentice-Hall, 1966), p. 30.

2   Anthony Quinton, *The Nature of Things* (London: Routledge and Kegan Paul, 1973), p. 119. This is an extremely venerable argument, which has played a central role in epistemological discussion at least since Aristotle's statement of it in the *Posterior Analytics*, Book I, ch. 2–3. (Some have found an anticipation of the argument in the *Theaetetus* at 209E–210B, but Plato's worry in that passage appears to be that the proposed definition of knowledge is circular, not that it leads to an infinite regress of justification.)

3   "Adequately justified" because a belief could be justified to some degree without being sufficiently justified to qualify as knowledge (if true). But it is far from clear just how much justification is needed for adequacy. Virtually all recent epistemologists agree that certainty is not required. But the lottery paradox shows that adequacy cannot be understood merely in terms of some specified level of probability. (For a useful account of the lottery paradox, see Robert Ackermann, *Knowledge and Belief* (Garden City, NY: Doubleday, 1972), pp. 39–50.) Armstrong, in *Belief, Truth and Knowledge* (London: Cambridge University Press, 1973), argues that what is required is that one's reasons for the belief be "conclusive," but the precise meaning of this is less than clear. Ultimately, it may be that the concept of knowledge is simply too crude for refined epistemological discussion, so that it may be necessary to speak instead of degrees of belief and corresponding degrees of justification. I shall assume (perhaps controversially) that the proper solution to this problem will not affect the issues to be discussed here, and speak merely of the reasons or justification

making the belief *highly likely* to be true, without trying to say exactly what this means.

4   See Edmund Gettier, "Is Justified True Belief Knowledge?" this vol., ch. 15. Also Ackermann, *Knowledge and Belief*, ch. V, and the corresponding references.

5   For simplicity, I will speak of inference relations as obtaining between beliefs rather than, more accurately, between the propositions which are believed. "Inference" is to be understood here in a very broad sense; any relation between two beliefs which allows one, if accepted, to serve as a good reason for accepting the other will count as inferential.

6   It is difficult to give precise criteria for when a given reason is *the* reason for a person's holding a belief. G. Harman, in *Thought* (Princeton: Princeton University Press, 1973), argues that for a person to believe for a given reason is for that reason to *explain* why he holds that belief. But this suggestion, though heuristically useful, hardly yields a usable criterion.

7   Thus it is a mistake to conceive the regress as a *temporal* regress, as it would be if each justifying argument had to be explicitly given before the belief in question was justified.

8   Obviously these views could be combined, with different instances of the regress being handled in different ways. I will not consider such combined views here. In general, they would simply inherit all of the objections pertaining to the simpler views.

9   Peirce seems to suggest a virtuous regress view in "Questions concerning Certain Faculties Claimed for Man," *Collected Papers* V, pp. 135–55. But the view is presented metaphorically and it is hard to be sure exactly what it comes to or to what extent it bears on the present issue.

10 The original statement of the non-linear view was by Bernard Bosanquet in *Implication*

and Linear Inference (London, 1920). For more recent discussions, see Harman, *Thought*; and Nicholas Rescher, "Foundationalism, Coherentism, and the Idea of Cognitive Systematization," *The Journal of Philosophy* 71 (1974), pp. 695–708.

11 I have attempted to show how a coherence view might be defended against the most standard of these objections in "The Coherence Theory of Empirical Knowledge," *Philosophical Studies* 30 (1976), pp. 281–312.

12 The presumption against a skeptical outcome is strong, but I think it is a mistake to treat it as absolute. If no non-skeptical theory can be found which is at least reasonably plausible in its own right, skepticism might become the only rational alternative.

13 For some useful distinctions among these terms, see William Alston, "Varieties of Privileged Access," *American Philosophical Quarterly* 8 (1971), pp. 223–41.

14 For discussions of weak foundationism, see Bertrand Russell, *Human Knowledge* (New York: Simon and Schuster, 1949), part II, ch. II, and part V, chs. 6 and 7; Nelson Goodman, "Sense and Certainty," *Philosophical Review* 61 (1952), pp. 160–7; Israel Scheffler, *Science and Subjectivity* (New York, 1967), chapter V; and Roderick Firth, "Coherence, Certainty, and Epistemic Priority," *The Journal of Philosophy* 61 (1964), pp. 545–57.

15 How good a reason must one have? Presumably some justification accrues from any reason which makes the belief even minimally more likely to be true than not, but considerably more than this would be required to make the justification adequate for knowledge. (See note 3, above.) (The James–Clifford controversy concerning the "will to believe" is also relevant here. I am agreeing with Clifford to the extent of saying that epistemic justification requires some positive reason in favor of the belief and not just the absence of any reason against.)

16 For a similar use of the notion of epistemic irresponsibility, see Ernest Sosa, "How Do You Know?" *American Philosophical Quarterly* II (1974), p. 117.

17 In fact, the premises would probably have to be true as well, in order to avoid Gettier-type counterexamples. But I shall ignore this refinement here.

18 On a Carnap-style *a priori* theory of probability it could, of course, be the case that very general empirical propositions were more likely to be true than not, i.e. that the possible state-descriptions in which they are true outnumber those in which they are false. But clearly this would not make them likely to be true in a sense which would allow the detached assertion of the proposition in question (on pain of contradiction), and this fact seems to preclude such justification from being adequate for knowledge.

19 Chs 11–13. Bracketed page references in this section are to this book.

20 Fred I. Dretske, *Seeing and Knowing* (London: Routledge and Kegan Paul, 1969), ch. III, especially pp. 126–39. It is difficult to be quite sure of Dretske's view, however, since he is not concerned in this book to offer a general account of knowledge. Views which are in some ways similar to those of Armstrong and Dretske have been offered by Goldman and by Unger. See Alvin Goldman, "A Causal Theory of Knowing," *The Journal of Philosophy* 64 (1967), pp. 357–72; and Peter Unger, "An Analysis of Factual Knowledge," *The Journal of Philosophy* 65 (1968), pp. 157–70. But both Goldman and Unger are explicitly concerned with the Gettier problem and not at all with the regress problem, so it is hard to be sure how their views relate to the sort of externalist view which is at issue here.

21 On the one hand, Armstrong seems to argue that it is *not* a requirement for knowledge that the believer have "sufficient evidence" for his belief, which sounds like a rejection of the adequate-justification condition. On the other hand, he seems to want to say that the presence of the external relation makes it rational for a person to accept a belief, and he seems (though this is not clear) to have *epistemic* rationality in mind; and there appears to be no substantial difference between saying that a belief is epistemically rational and saying that it is epistemically justified.

22 One way to put this point is to say that whether a belief is likely to be true or whether

in contrast it is an accident that it is true depends significantly on how the belief is described. Thus it might be true of one and the same belief that it is "a belief connected in a law-like way with the state of affairs which it describes" and also that it is "a belief adopted on the basis of no apparent evidence"; and it might be likely to be true on the first description and unlikely to be true on the second. The claim here is that it is the believer's own conception which should be considered in deciding whether the belief is justified. (Something analogous seems to be true in ethics: the moral worth of a person's action is correctly to be judged only in terms of that person's subjective conception of what he is doing and not in light of what happens, willy-nilly, to result from it.)

23 Notice, however, that if beliefs standing in the proper external relation should happen to possess some subjectively distinctive feature (such as being spontaneous and highly compelling to the believer), and if the believer were to notice empirically, that beliefs having this feature were true a high proportion of the time, he would then be in a position to construct a justification for a new belief of that sort along the lines sketched at the end of section II. But of course a belief justified in that way would no longer be basic.

24 I suspect that something like the argument to be given here is lurking somewhere in Sellars' "Empiricism and the Philosophy of Mind" (reprinted in Sellars, *Science, Perception, and Reality* (London: Routledge and Kegan Paul, 1963), pp. 127–96), but it is difficult to be sure. A more recent argument by Sellars which is considerably closer on the surface to the argument offered here is contained in "The Structure of Knowledge," his Machette Foundation Lectures given at the University of Texas in 1971, in Hector-Nerl Casteneda (ed.), *Action, Knowledge, and Reality: Critical Studies in Honor of Wilfrid Sellars* (Indianapolis, 1975), Lecture III, sections III–IV. A similar line of argument was also offered by Neurath and Hempel. See Otto Neurath, "Protocol Sentences," tr. in A. J. Ayer (ed.), *Logical Positivism* (New York, 1959), pp. 199–208; and Carl G. Hempel,

"On the Logical Positivists' Theory of Truth," *Analysis*, 2 (1934–5), pp. 49–59. The Hempel paper is in part a reply to a foundationist critique of Neurath by Schlick in "The Foundation of Knowledge," also translated in Ayer, *Logical Positivism*, pp. 209–27. Schlick replied to Hempel in "Facts and Propositions," and Hempel responded in "Some Remarks on 'Facts' and Propositions," both in *Analysis* 2 (1934–5), pp. 65–70 and 93–6, respectively. Though the Neurath–Hempel argument conflates issues having to do with truth and issues having to do with justification in a confused and confusing way, it does bring out the basic objection to givenism.

25 Chisholm, "Theory of Knowledge," in Chisholm et al., *Philosophy* (Englewood Cliffs, NJ: Prentice-Hall, 1964), pp. 270 ff.

26 Bracketed page references in this section will be to this book.

27 Quinton does offer one small bit of clarification here, by appealing to the notion of ostensive definition and claiming in effect that the sort of awareness involved in the intuitive justification of a basic belief is the same as that involved in a situation of ostensive definition. But such a comparison is of little help, for at least two reasons. First, as Wittgenstein, Sellars, and others have argued, the notion of ostensive definition is itself seriously problematic. Indeed, an objection quite analogous to the present one against the notion of a basic belief could be raised against the notion of an ostensive definition; and this objection, if answerable at all, could only be answered by construing the awareness involved in ostension in such a way as to be of no help to the foundationist in the present discussion. Second, more straightforwardly, even if the notion of ostensive definition were entirely unobjectionable, there is no need for the sort of awareness involved to be *justified*. If all that is at issue is learning the meaning of a word (or acquiring a concept), then justification is irrelevant. Thus the existence of ostensive definitions would not show how there could be basic beliefs.

28 Notice, however, that to reject an epistemological given does not necessarily rule out

other varieties of givenness which may have importance for other philosophical issues. In particular, there may still be viable versions of givenness which pose an obstacle to materialist views in the philosophy of mind. For useful distinctions among various versions of givenness and a discussion of their relevance to the philosophy of mind, see James W. Cornman, "Materialism and Some Myths about Some Givens," *The Monist* 56 (1972), pp. 215–33.

29 Compare the Husserlian notion of a "prepredicative awareness."

30 It is interesting to note that Quinton seems to offer an analogous critique of givenness in an earlier paper, "The Problem of Perception," reprinted in Robert J. Swartz (ed.), *Perceiving, Sensing, and Knowing* (Garden City, NY: Doubleday, 1965), pp. 497–526; cf. especially p. 503.

31 For a discussion of such a coherence theory, see my paper cited in note 11, above.

CHAPTER 11

A Coherence Theory
of Truth and Knowledge

Donald Davidson

In this paper I defend what may as well be called a coherence theory of truth and knowledge. The theory I defend is not in competition with a correspondence theory, but depends for its defense on an argument that purports to show that coherence yields correspondence.

The importance of the theme is obvious. If coherence is a test of truth, there is a direct connection with epistemology, for we have reason to believe many of our beliefs cohere with many others, and in that case we have reason to believe many of our beliefs are true. When the beliefs are true, then the primary conditions for knowledge would seem to be satisfied.

Someone might try to defend a coherence theory of truth without defending a coherence theory of knowledge, perhaps on the ground that the holder of a coherent set of beliefs might lack a reason to believe his beliefs coherent. This is not likely, but it may be that someone, though he has true beliefs, and good reasons for holding them, does not appreciate the relevance of reason to belief. Such a one may best be viewed as having knowledge he does not know he has: he thinks he is a skeptic. In a word, he is a philosopher.

Setting aside aberrant cases, what brings truth and knowledge together is meaning. If meanings

Originally published in Ernest LePore (ed.), *Truth and Interpretation: Perspectives on the Philosophy of Donald Davidson* (New York: Blackwell, 1989), pp. 307–19.

are given by objective truth conditions there is a question how we can know that the conditions are satisfied, for this would appear to require a confrontation between what we believe and reality; and the idea of such a confrontation is absurd. But if coherence is a test of truth, then coherence is a test for judging that objective truth conditions are satisfied, and we no longer need to explain meaning on the basis of possible confrontation. My slogan is: correspondence without confrontation. Given a correct epistemology, we can be realists in all departments. We can accept objective truth conditions as the key to meaning, a realist view of truth, and we can insist that knowledge is of an objective world independent of our thought or language.

Since there is not, as far as I know, a theory that deserves to be called "the" coherence theory, let me characterize the sort of view I want to defend. It is obvious that not every consistent set of interpreted sentences contains only true sentences, since one such set might contain just the consistent sentence S and another just the negation of S. And adding more sentences, while maintaining consistency, will not help. We can imagine endless state-descriptions – maximal consistent descriptions – which do not describe our world.

My coherence theory concerns beliefs, or sentences held true by someone who understands them. I do not want to say, at this point, that every possible coherent set of beliefs is true (or contains mostly true beliefs). I shy away from this because it is so unclear what is possible. At one extreme, it might be held that the range of possible maximal sets of beliefs is as wide as the range of possible maximal sets of sentences, and then there would be no point to insisting that a defensible coherence theory concerns beliefs and not propositions or sentences. But there are other ways of conceiving what it is possible to believe which would justify saying not only that all actual coherent belief systems are largely correct but that all possible ones are also. The difference between the two notions of what it is possible to believe depends on what we suppose about the nature of belief, its interpretation, its causes, its holders, and its patterns. Beliefs for me are states of people with intentions, desires, sense organs; they are states that are caused by, and cause, events inside and outside the bodies of their entertainers. But even given all these constraints, there are many things people do believe, and many more that they could. For all such cases, the coherence theory applies.

Of course some beliefs are false. Much of the point of the concept of belief is the potential gap it introduces between what is held to be true and what is true. So mere coherence, no matter how strongly coherence is plausibly defined, can not guarantee that what is believed is so. All that a coherence theory can maintain is that most of the beliefs in a coherent total set of beliefs are true.

This way of stating the position can at best be taken as a hint, since there is probably no useful way to count beliefs, and so no clear meaning to the idea that most of a person's beliefs are true. A somewhat better way to put the point is to say there is a presumption in favor of the truth of a belief that coheres with a significant mass of belief. Every belief in a coherent total set of beliefs is justified in the light of this presumption, much as every intentional action taken by a rational agent (one whose choices, beliefs and desires cohere in the sense of Bayesian decision theory) is justified. So to repeat, if knowledge is justified true belief, then it would seem that all the true beliefs of a consistent believer constitute knowledge. This conclusion, though too vague and hasty to be right, contains an important core of truth, as I shall argue. Meanwhile I merely note the many problems asking for treatment: what exactly does coherence demand? How much of inductive practice should be included, how much

of the true theory (if there is one) of evidential support must be in there? Since no person has a completely consistent body of convictions, coherence with *which* beliefs creates a presumption of truth? Some of these problems will be put in better perspective as I go along.

It should be clear that I do not hope to define truth in terms of coherence and belief. Truth is beautifully transparent compared to belief and coherence, and I take it as primitive. Truth, as applied to utterances of sentences, shows the disquotational feature enshrined in Tarski's Convention T, and that is enough to fix its domain of application. Relative to a language or a speaker, of course, so there is more to truth than Convention T; there is whatever carries over from language to language or speaker to speaker. What Convention T, and the trite sentences it declares true, like "'Grass is green' spoken by an English speaker, is true if and only if grass is green", reveal is that the truth of an utterance depends on just two things: what the words as spoken mean, and how the world is arranged. There is no further relativism to a conceptual scheme, a way of viewing things, a perspective. Two interpreters, as unlike in culture, language and point of view as you please, can disagree over whether an utterance is true, but only if they differ on how things are in the world they share, or what the utterance means.

I think we can draw two conclusions from these simple reflections. First, truth is correspondence with the way things are. (There is no straightforward and non-misleading way to state this; to get things right, a detour is necessary through the concept of satisfaction in terms of which truth is characterized.[1]) So if a coherence theory of truth is acceptable, it must be consistent with a correspondence theory. Second, a theory of knowledge that allows that we can know the truth must be a non-relativized, non-internal form of realism. So if a coherence theory of knowledge is acceptable, it must be consistent with such a form of realism. My form of realism seems to be neither Hilary Putnam's internal realism nor his metaphysical realism.[2] It is not internal realism because internal realism makes truth relative to a scheme, and this is an idea I do not think is intelligible.[3] A major reason, in fact, for accepting a coherence theory is the unintelligibility of the dualism of a conceptual scheme and a "world" waiting to be coped with. But my realism is certainly not Putnam's metaphysical realism, for *it* is characterized by being "radically non-epistemic", which implies that all our best researched and established thoughts and theories may be false. I think the independence of belief and truth requires only that *each* of our beliefs may be false. But of course a coherence theory cannot allow that all of them can be wrong.

But why not? Perhaps it is obvious that the coherence of a belief with a substantial body of belief enhances its chance of being true, provided there is reason to suppose the body of belief is true, or largely so. But how can coherence alone supply grounds for belief? Mayhap the best we can do to justify one belief is to appeal to other beliefs. But then the outcome would seem to be that we must accept philosophical skepticism, no matter how unshaken in practice our beliefs remain.

This is skepticism in one of its traditional garbs. It asks: Why couldn't all my beliefs hang together and yet be comprehensively false about the actual world? Mere recognition of the fact that it is absurd or worse to try to *confront* our beliefs, one by one, or as a whole, with what they are about does not answer the question nor show the question unintelligible. In short, even a mild coherence theory like mine must provide a skeptic with a reason for supposing coherent beliefs are true. The partisan of a coherence theory can't allow assurance to come from outside the system of belief, while nothing inside can produce support except as it can be shown to rest, finally or at once, on something independently trustworthy.

It is natural to distinguish coherence theories from others by reference to the question whether or not justification can or must come to an end. But this does not define the positions, it merely suggests a form the argument may take. For there are coherence theorists who hold that some beliefs can serve as the basis for the rest, while it would be possible to maintain that coherence is not enough, although giving reasons never comes to an end. What distinguishes a coherence theory is simply the claim that nothing can count as a reason for holding a belief except another belief. Its partisan rejects as unintelligible the request for a ground or source of justification of another ilk. As Rorty has put it, "nothing counts as justification unless by reference to what we already accept,

and there is no way to get outside our beliefs and our language so as to find some test other than coherence."[4] About this I am, as you see, in agreement with Rorty. Where we differ, if we do, is on whether there remains a question how, given that we cannot "get outside our beliefs and our language so as to find some test other than coherence", we nevertheless can have knowledge of, and talk about, an objective public world which is not of our own making. I think this question does remain, while I suspect that Rorty doesn't think so. If this is his view, then he must think I am making a mistake in trying to answer the question. Nevertheless, here goes.

It will promote matters at this point to review very hastily some of the reasons for abandoning the search for a basis for knowledge outside the scope of our beliefs. By "basis" here I mean specifically an epistemological basis, a source of justification.

The attempts worth taking seriously attempt to ground belief in one way or another on the testimony of the senses: sensation, perception, the given, experience, sense data, the passing show. All such theories must explain at least these two things: what, exactly, is the relation between sensation and belief that allows the first to justify the second? and, why should we believe our sensations are reliable, that is, why should we trust our senses?

The simplest idea is to identify certain beliefs with sensations. Thus Hume seems not to have distinguished between perceiving a green spot and perceiving that a spot is green. (An ambiguity in the word "idea" was a great help here.) Other philosophers noted Hume's confusion, but tried to attain the same results by reducing the gap between perception and judgement to zero by attempting to formulate judgements that do not go beyond stating that the perception or sensation or presentation exists (whatever that may mean). Such theories do not justify beliefs on the basis of sensations, but try to justify certain beliefs by claiming that they have exactly the same epistemic content as a sensation. There are two difficulties with such a view: first, if the basic beliefs do not exceed in content the corresponding sensation they cannot support any inference to an objective world; and second, there are no such beliefs.

A more plausible line is to claim that we cannot be wrong about how things appear to us to be.

If we believe we have a sensation, we do; this is held to be an analytic truth, or a fact about how language is used.

It is difficult to explain this supposed connection between sensations and some beliefs in a way that does not invite skepticism about other minds, and in the absence of an adequate explanation, there should be a doubt about the implications of the connection for justification. But in any case, it is unclear how, on this line, sensations justify the belief in those sensations. The point is rather that such beliefs require no justification, for the existence of the belief entails the existence of the sensation, and so the existence of the belief entails its own truth. Unless something further is added, we are back to another form of coherence theory.

Emphasis on sensation or perception in matters epistemological springs from the obvious thought: sensations are what connect the world and our beliefs, and they are candidates for justifiers because we often are aware of them. The trouble we have been running into is that the justification seems to depend on the awareness, which is just another belief.

Let us try a bolder tack. Suppose we say that sensations themselves, verbalized or not, justify certain beliefs that go beyond what is given in sensation. So, under certain conditions, having the sensation of seeing a green light flashing may justify the belief that a green light is flashing. The problem is to see how the sensation justifies the belief. Of course if someone has the sensation of seeing a green light flashing, it is likely, under certain circumstances, that a green light is flashing. We can say this, since we know of his sensation, but he can't say it, since we are supposing he is justified without having to depend on believing he has the sensation. Suppose he believed he didn't have the sensation. Would the sensation still justify him in the belief in an objective flashing green light?

The relation between a sensation and a belief cannot be logical, since sensations are not beliefs or other propositional attitudes. What then is the relation? The answer is, I think, obvious: the relation is causal. Sensations cause some beliefs and in *this* sense are the basis or ground of those beliefs. But a causal explanation of a belief does not show how or why the belief is justified.

The difficulty of transmuting a cause into a reason plagues the anticoherentist again if he tries

to answer our second question: What justifies the belief that our senses do not systematically deceive us? For even if sensations justify belief in sensation, we do not yet see how they justify belief in external events and objects.

Quine tells us that science tells us that "our only source of information about the external world is through the impact of light rays and molecules upon our sensory surfaces".[5] What worries me is how to read the words "source" and "information". Certainly it is true that events and objects in the external world cause us to believe things about the external world, and much, if not all, of the causality takes a route through the sense organs. The notion of information, however, applies in a non-metaphorical way only to the engendered beliefs. So "source" has to be read simply as "cause" and "information" as "true belief" or "knowledge". Justification of beliefs caused by our senses is not yet in sight.[6]

The approach to the problem of justification we have been tracing must be wrong. We have been trying to see it this way: a person has all his beliefs about the world – that is, all his beliefs. How can he tell if they are true, or apt to be true? Only, we have been assuming, by connecting his beliefs to the world, confronting certain of his beliefs with the deliverances of the senses one by one, or perhaps confronting the totality of his beliefs with the tribunal of experience. No such confrontation makes sense, for of course we can't get outside our skins to find out what is causing the internal happenings of which we are aware. Introducing intermediate steps or entities into the causal chain, like sensations or observations, serves only to make the epistemological problem more obvious. For if the intermediaries are merely causes, they don't justify the beliefs they cause, while if they deliver information, they may be lying. The moral is obvious. Since we can't swear intermediaries to truthfulness, we should allow no intermediaries between our beliefs and their objects in the world. Of course there are causal intermediaries. What we must guard against are epistemic intermediaries.

There are common views of language that encourage bad epistemology. This is no accident, of course, since theories of meaning are connected with epistemology through attempts to answer the question how one determines that a sentence is true. If knowing the meaning of a sentence (knowing how to give a correct interpretation of it) involves, or is, knowing how it could be recognized to be true, then the theory of meaning raises the same question we have been struggling with, for giving the meaning of a sentence will demand that we specify what would justify asserting it. Here the coherentist will hold that there is no use looking for a source of justification outside of other sentences held true, while the foundationalist will seek to anchor at least some words or sentences to non-verbal rocks. This view is held, I think, both by Quine and by Michael Dummett.

Dummett and Quine differ, to be sure. In particular, they disagree about holism, the claim that the truth of our sentences must be tested together rather than one by one. And they disagree also, and consequently, about whether there is a useful distinction between analytic and synthetic sentences, and about whether a satisfactory theory of meaning can allow the sort of indeterminacy Quine argues for. (On all these points, I am Quine's faithful student.)

But what concerns me here is that Quine and Dummett agree on a basic principle, which is that whatever there is to meaning must be traced back somehow to experience, the given, or patterns of sensory stimulation, something intermediate between belief and the usual objects our beliefs are about. Once we take this step, we open the door to skepticism, for we must then allow that a very great many – perhaps most – of the sentences we hold to be true may in fact be false. It is ironical. Trying to make meaning accessible has made truth inaccessible. When meaning goes epistemological in this way, truth and meaning are necessarily divorced. One can, of course, arrange a shotgun wedding by redefining truth as what we are justified in asserting. But this does not marry the original mates.

Take Quine's proposal that whatever there is to the meaning (information value) of an observation sentence is determined by the patterns of sensory stimulation that would cause a speaker to assent to or dissent from the sentence. This is a marvellously ingenious way of capturing what is appealing about verificationist theories without having to talk of meanings, sense-data, or sensations; for the first time it made plausible the idea that one could, and should, do what I call the theory of meaning without need of what Quine calls meanings. But Quine's proposal, like other forms of verificationism, makes for skepticism. For clearly a person's sensory stimulations could be just as they are and yet the world outside very different. (Remember the brain in the vat.)

Quine's way of doing without meanings is subtle and complicated. He ties the meanings of some sentences directly to patterns of stimulation (which also constitute the evidence, Quine thinks, for assenting to the sentence), but the meanings of further sentences are determined by how they are conditioned to the original, or observation sentences. The facts of such conditioning do not permit a sharp division between sentences held true by virtue of meaning and sentences held true on the basis of observation. Quine made this point by showing that if one way of interpreting a speaker's utterances was satisfactory, so were many others. This doctrine of the indeterminacy of translation, as Quine called it, should be viewed as neither mysterious nor threatening. It is no more mysterious than the fact that temperature can be measured in Centigrade or Fahrenheit (or any linear transformation of those numbers). And it is not threatening because the very procedure that demonstrates the degree of indeterminacy at the same time demonstrates that what is determinate is all we need.

In my view, erasing the line between the analytic and synthetic saved philosophy of language as a serious subject by showing how it could be pursued without what there cannot be: determinate meanings. I now suggest also giving up the distinction between observation sentences and the rest. For the distinction between sentences belief in whose truth is justified by sensations and sentences belief in whose truth is justified only by appeal to other sentences held true is as anathema to the coherentist as the distinction between beliefs justified by sensations and beliefs justified only by appeal to further beliefs. Accordingly, I suggest we give up the idea that meaning or knowledge is grounded on something that counts as an ultimate source of evidence. No doubt meaning and knowledge depend on experience, and experience ultimately on sensation. But this is the "depend" of causality, not of evidence or justification.

I have now stated my problem as well as I can. The search for an empirical foundation for meaning or knowledge leads to skepticism, while a coherence theory seems at a loss to provide any reason for a believer to believe that his beliefs, if coherent, are true. We are caught between a false answer to the skeptic, and no answer.

The dilemma is not a true one. What is needed to answer the skeptic is to show that someone with a (more or less) coherent set of beliefs has a reason to suppose his beliefs are not mistaken in the main. What we have shown is that it is absurd to look for a justifying ground for the totality of beliefs, something outside this totality which we can use to test or compare with our beliefs. The answer to our problem must then be to find a *reason* for supposing most of our beliefs are true that is not a form of *evidence*.

My argument has two parts. First I urge that a correct understanding of the speech, beliefs, desires, intentions and other propositional attitudes of a person leads to the conclusion that most of a person's beliefs must be true, and so there is a legitimate presumption that any one of them, if it coheres with most of the rest, is true. Then I go on to claim that anyone with thoughts, and so in particular anyone who wonders whether he has any reason to suppose he is generally right about the nature of his environment, must know what a belief is, and how in general beliefs are to be detected and interpreted. These being perfectly general facts we cannot fail to use when we communicate with others, or when we try to communicate with others, or even when we merely think we are communicating with others, there is a pretty strong sense in which we can be said to know that there is a presumption in favor of the overall truthfulness of anyone's beliefs, including our own. So it is bootless for someone to ask for some *further* reassurance; that can only add to his stock of beliefs. All that is needed is that he recognize that belief is in its nature veridical.

Belief can be seen to be veridical by considering what determines the existence and contents of a belief. Belief, like the other so-called propositional attitudes, is supervenient on facts of various sorts, behavioral, neuro-physiological, biological and physical. The reason for pointing this out is not to encourage definitional or nomological reduction of psychological phenomena to something more basic, and certainly not to suggest epistemological priorities. The point is rather understanding. We gain one kind of insight into the nature of the propositional attitudes when we relate them systematically to one another and to phenomena on other levels. Since the propositional attitudes are deeply interlocked, we cannot learn the nature of one by first winning understanding of another. As interpreters, we work our way into the whole system, depending much on the pattern of interrelationships.

Take for example the interdependence of belief and meaning. What a sentence means depends partly on the external circumstances that cause it to win some degree of conviction; and partly on the relations, grammatical, logical or less, that the sentence has to other sentences held true with varying degrees of conviction. Since these relations are themselves translated directly into beliefs, it is easy to see how meaning depends on belief. Belief, however, depends equally on meaning, for the only access to the fine structure and individuation of beliefs is through the sentences speakers and interpreters of speakers use to express and describe beliefs. If we want to illuminate the nature of meaning and belief, therefore, we need to start with something that assumes neither. Quine's suggestion, which I shall essentially follow, is to take *prompted assent* as basic, the causal relation between assenting to a sentence and the cause of such assent. This is a fair place to start the project of identifying beliefs and meanings, since a speaker's assent to a sentence depends both on what he means by the sentence and on what he believes about the world. Yet it is possible to know that a speaker assents to a sentence without knowing either what the sentence, as spoken by him, means, or what belief is expressed by it. Equally obvious is the fact that once an interpretation has been given for a sentence assented to, a belief has been attributed. If correct theories of interpretation are not unique (do not lead to uniquely correct interpretations), the same will go for attributions of belief, of course, as tied to acquiescence in particular sentences.

A speaker who wishes his words to be understood cannot systematically deceive his would-be interpreters about when he assents to sentences – that is, holds them true. As a matter of principle, then, meaning, and by its connection with meaning, belief also, are open to public determination. I shall take advantage of this fact in what follows and adopt the stance of a radical interpreter when asking about the nature of belief. What a fully informed interpreter could learn about what a speaker means is all there is to learn; the same goes for what the speaker believes.[7]

The interpreter's problem is that what he is assumed to know – the causes of assents to sentences of a speaker – is, as we have seen, the product of two things he is assumed not to know, meaning and belief. If he knew the meanings he would know the beliefs, and if he knew the beliefs expressed by sentences assented to, he would know the meanings. But how can he learn both at once, since each depends on the other?

The general lines of the solution, like the problem itself, are owed to Quine. I will, however, introduce some changes into Quine's solution, as I have into the statement of the problem. The changes are directly relevant to the issue of epistemological skepticism.

I see the aim of radical interpretation (which is much, but not entirely, like Quine's radical translation) as being to produce a Tarski-style characterization of truth for the speaker's language, and a theory of his beliefs. (The second follows from the first plus the presupposed knowledge of sentences held true.) This adds little to Quine's program of translation, since translation of the speaker's language into one's own plus a theory of truth for one's own language add up to a theory of truth for the speaker. But the shift to the semantic notion of truth from the syntactic notion of translation puts the formal restrictions of a theory of truth in the foreground, and emphasizes one aspect of the close relation between truth and meaning.

The principle of charity plays a crucial role in Quine's method, and an even more crucial role in my variant. In either case, the principle directs the interpreter to translate or interpret so as to read some of his own standards of truth into the pattern of sentences held true by the speaker. The point of the principle is to make the speaker intelligible, since too great deviations from consistency and correctness leave no common ground on which to judge either conformity or difference. From a formal point of view, the principle of charity helps solve the problem of the interaction of meaning and belief by restraining the degrees of freedom allowed belief while determining how to interpret words.

We have no choice, Quine has urged, but to read our own logic into the thoughts of a speaker; Quine says this for the sentential calculus, and I would add the same for first-order quantification theory. This leads directly to the identification of the logical constants, as well as to assigning a logical form to all sentences.

Something like charity operates in the interpretation of those sentences whose causes of assent come and go with time and place: when the interpreter finds a sentence of the speaker the speaker assents to regularly under conditions he recognizes, he takes those conditions to be the truth conditions of the speaker's sentence. This is only roughly right, as we shall see in a moment. Sentences and predicates less directly geared to easily detected goings-on can, in Quine's canon, be interpreted at will, given only the constraints of interconnections with sentences conditioned directly to the world. Here I would extend the principle of charity to favor interpretations that as far as possible preserve truth: I think it makes for mutual understanding, and hence for better interpretation, to interpret what the speaker accepts as true when we can. In this matter, I have less choice than Quine, because I do not see how to draw the line between observation sentences and theoretical sentences at the start. There are several reasons for this, but the one most relevant to the present topic is that this distinction is ultimately based on an epistemological consideration of a sort I have renounced: observation sentences are directly based on something like sensation – patterns of sensory stimulation – and this is an idea I have been urging leads to skepticism. Without the direct tie to sensation or stimulation, the distinction between observation sentences and others can't be drawn on epistemologically significant grounds. The distinction between sentences whose causes to assent come and go with observable circumstances and those a speaker clings to through change remains however, and offers the possibility of interpreting the words and sentences beyond the logical.

The details are not here to the point. What should be clear is that if the account I have given of how belief and meaning are related and understood by an interpreter, then most of the sentences a speaker holds to be true – especially the ones he holds to most stubbornly, the ones most central to the system of his beliefs – most of these sentences *are* true, at least in the opinion of the interpreter. For the only, and therefore unimpeachable, method available to the interpreter automatically puts the speaker's beliefs in accord with the standards of logic of the interpreter, and hence credits the speaker with plain truths of logic. Needless to say there are degrees of logical and other consistency, and perfect consistency is not to be expected. What needs emphasis is only the methodological necessity for finding consistency enough.

Nor, from the interpreter's point of view, is there any way he can discover the speaker to be largely wrong about the world. For he interprets sentences held true (which is not to be distinguished from attributing beliefs) according to the events and objects in the outside world that cause the sentence to be held true.

What I take to be the important aspect of this approach is apt to be missed because the approach reverses our natural way of thinking of communication derived from situations in which understanding has already been secured. Once understanding has been secured we are able, often, to learn what a person believes quite independently of what caused him to believe it. This may lead us to the crucial, indeed fatal, conclusion that we can in general fix what someone means independently of what he believes and independently of what caused the belief. But if I am right, we can't in general first identify beliefs and meanings and then ask what caused them. The causality plays an indispensable role in determining the content of what we say and believe. This is a fact we can be led to recognize by taking up, as we have, the interpreter's point of view.

It is an artifact of the interpreter's correct interpretation of a person's speech and attitudes that there is a large degree of truth and consistency in the thought and speech of an agent. But this is truth and consistency by the interpreter's standards. Why couldn't it happen that speaker and interpreter understand one another on the basis of shared but erroneous beliefs? This can, and no doubt often does, happen. But it cannot be the rule. For imagine for a moment an interpreter who is omniscient about the world, and about what does and would cause a speaker to assent to any sentence in his (potentially unlimited) repertoire. The omniscient interpreter, using the same method as the fallible interpreter, finds the fallible speaker largely consistent and correct. By his own standards, of course, but since these are objectively correct, the fallible speaker is seen to be largely correct and consistent by objective standards. We may also, if we want, let the omniscient interpreter turn his attention to the fallible interpreter of the fallible speaker. It turns out that the fallible interpreter can be wrong about some things, but not in general; and so he cannot share universal error with the agent he is interpreting. Once we agree to the general method of interpretation I have sketched, it becomes impossible correctly to hold that anyone could be mostly wrong about how things are.

There is, as I noted above, a key difference between the method of radical interpretation I am now recommending, and Quine's method of radical translation. The difference lies in the nature of the choice of causes that govern interpretation. Quine makes interpretation depend on patterns of sensory stimulation, while I make it depend on the external events and objects the sentence is interpreted as being about. Thus Quine's notion of meaning is tied to sensory criteria, something he thinks that can be treated also as evidence. This leads Quine to give epistemic significance to the distinction between observation sentences and others, since observation sentences are supposed, by their direct conditioning to the senses, to have a kind of extralinguistic justification. This is the view against which I argued in the first part of my paper, urging that sensory stimulations are indeed part of the causal chain that leads to belief, but cannot, without confusion, be considered to be evidence, or a source of justification, for the stimulated beliefs.

What stands in the way of global skepticism of the senses is, in my view, the fact that we must, in the plainest and methodologically most basic cases, take the objects of a belief to be the causes of that belief. And what we, as interpreters, must take them to be is what they in fact are. Communication begins where causes converge: your utterance means what mine does if belief in its truth is systematically caused by the same events and objects.[8]

The difficulties in the way of this view are obvious, but I think they can be overcome. The method applies directly, at best, only to occasion sentences – the sentences assent to which is caused systematically by common changes in the world. Further sentences are interpreted by their conditioning to occasion sentences, and the appearance in them of words that appear also in occasion sentences. Among occasion sentences, some will vary in the credence they command not only in the face of environmental change, but also in the face of change of credence awarded related sentences. Criteria can be developed on this basis to distinguish degrees of observationality on internal grounds, without appeal to the concept of a basis for belief outside the circle of beliefs.

Related to these problems, and easier still to grasp, is the problem of error. For even in the simplest cases it is clear that the same cause (a rabbit scampers by) may engender different beliefs in speaker and observer, and so encourage assent to sentences which cannot bear the same interpretation. It is no doubt this fact that made Quine turn from rabbits to patterns of stimulation as the key to interpretation. Just as a matter of statistics, I'm not sure how much better one approach is than the other. Is the relative frequency with which identical patterns of stimulation will touch off assent to "Gavagai" and "Rabbit" greater than the relative frequency with which a rabbit touches off the same two responses in speaker and interpreter? Not an easy question to test in a convincing way. But let the imagined results speak for Quine's method. Then I must say, what I must say in any case, the problem of error cannot be met sentence by sentence, even at the simplest level. The best we can do is cope with error holistically, that is, we interpret so as to make an agent as intelligible as possible, given his actions, his utterances and his place in the world. About some things we will find him wrong, as the necessary cost of finding him elsewhere right. As a rough approximation, finding him right means identifying the causes with the objects of his beliefs, giving special weight to the simplest cases, and countenancing error where it can be best explained.

Suppose I am right that an interpreter must so interpret as to make a speaker or agent largely correct about the world. How does this help the person himself who wonders what reason he has to think his beliefs are mostly true? How can he learn about the causal relations between the real world and his beliefs that lead the interpreter to interpret him as being on the right track?

The answer is contained in the question. In order to doubt or wonder about the provenance of his beliefs an agent must know what belief is. This brings with it the concept of objective truth, for the notion of a belief is the notion of a state that may or may not jibe with reality. But beliefs are also identified, directly and indirectly, by their causes. What an omniscient interpreter knows a fallible interpreter gets right enough if he understands a speaker, and this is just the complicated causal truth that makes us the believers we are, and fixes the contents of our beliefs. The agent has only to reflect on what a belief is to appreciate that most of his basic beliefs are true, and among his beliefs, those most securely held and that cohere with the main body of his beliefs are the most apt to be true. The question, how do I know my beliefs are generally true? thus answers itself, simply because beliefs are by nature generally true. Rephrased or expanded, the question becomes, how can I tell whether my beliefs, which are by their nature generally true, are generally true?

All beliefs are justified in this sense: they are supported by numerous other beliefs (otherwise they wouldn't be the beliefs they are), and have a presumption in favor of their truth. The presumption increases the larger and more significant the body of beliefs with which a belief coheres, and there being no such thing as an isolated belief, there is no belief without a presumption in its favor. In this respect, interpreter and interpreted differ. From the interpreter's point of view, methodology enforces a general presumption of truth for the body of beliefs as a whole, but the interpreter does not need to presume each particular belief of someone else is true. The general presumption applied to others does not make them globally right, as I have emphasized, but provides the background against which to accuse them of error. But from each person's own vantage point, there must be a graded presumption in favor of each of his own beliefs.

We cannot, alas, draw the picturesque and pleasant conclusion that all true beliefs constitute knowledge. For though all of a believer's beliefs are to some extent justified to him, some may not be justified enough, or in the right way, to constitute knowledge. The general presumption in favor of the truth of belief serves to rescue us from a standard form of skepticism by showing why it is impossible for all our beliefs to be false together. This leaves almost untouched the task of specifying the conditions of knowledge. I have not been concerned with the canons of evidential support (if such there be), but to show that all that counts as evidence or justification for a belief must come from the same totality of belief to which it belongs.

Notes

1 See my "True to the Facts", *The Journal of Philosophy* (1960), pp. 216–34.

2 Hilary Putnam, *Meaning and the Moral Sciences* (London: Routledge and Kegan Paul, 1978), p. 125.

3 See my "On the Very Idea of a Conceptual Scheme", in *Proceedings and Addresses of the American Philosophical Association* (1974), pp. 5–20.

4 Richard Rorty, *Philosophy and the Mirror of Nature* (Princeton: Princeton University Press, 1979), p. 178.

5 W. V. Quine, "The Nature of Natural Knowledge", in S. Guttenplan (ed.), *Mind and Language* (Clarendon Press, Oxford, 1975), p. 68.

6 Many other passages in Quine suggest that Quine hopes to assimilate sensory causes to evidence. In *Word and Object* (Massachusetts: MIT Press, 1960), p. 22, he writes that "surface irritations … exhaust our clues to an external world". In *Ontological Relativity* (New York: Columbia University Press, 1969), p. 75, we find that "The stimulation of his sensory receptors is all the evidence anybody has had to go on, ultimately, in arriving at his picture of the world." On the same page: "Two cardinal tenets of empiricism remain unassailable …. One is that whatever evidence there *is* for science *is* sensory evidence. The other … is that all inculcation of meanings of words,

must rest ultimately on sensory evidence." In *The Roots of Reference* (Illinois: Open Court Publishing Company, 1974), pp. 37–8, Quine says "observations" are basic "both in the support of theory and in the learning of language", and then goes on, "What are observations? They are visual, auditory, tactual, olfactory. They are sensory, evidently, and thus subjective. … Should we say then that the observation is not the sensation …? No …" Quine goes on to abandon talk of observations for talk of observation sentences. But of course observation sentences, unlike observations, cannot play the role of evidence unless we have reason to believe they are true.

7 I now think it is essential, in doing radical interpretation, to include the desires of the speaker from the start, so that the springs of action and intention, namely both belief and desire, are related to meaning. But in the present talk it is not necessary to introduce this further factor.

8 It is clear that the causal theory of meaning has little in common with the causal theories of reference of Kripke and Putnam. Those theories look to causal relations between names and objects of which speakers may well be ignorant. The chance of systematic error is thus increased. My causal theory does the reverse by connecting the cause of a belief with its object.

CHAPTER 12

A Foundherentist Theory of Empirical Justification

Susan Haack

Let us remember how common the folly is, of going from one faulty extreme into the opposite.[1]

Does the evidence presented establish beyond a reasonable doubt that the defendant did it? Given the evidence recently discovered by space scientists, am I justified in believing there was once bacterial life on Mars? Is scientific evidence especially authoritative, and if so, why? Should we take those advertisements claiming that the Holocaust never happened seriously, and if not, why not?…Questions about what makes evidence better or worse, about what makes inquiry better or worse conducted, about disinterestedness and partiality, are of real, daily – and sometimes of life-and-death – consequence.

Of late, however, cynicism about the very legitimacy of such questions has become the familiar philosophical theme of a whole chorus of voices, from enthusiasts of the latest developments in neuroscience, to radical self-styled neo-pragmatists, radical feminists and multiculturalists, and followers of (by now somewhat dated) Paris fashions.

This cynicism is unwarranted; but dealing with it requires something a bit more radical than epistemological business-as-usual. Evidence is

often messy, ambiguous, misleading, inquiry is often untidy, inconclusive, biased by the inquirers' interests; but it doesn't follow, as the cynics apparently suppose, that standards of good evidence and well-conducted inquiry are local, conventional, or mythical. And an even half-way adequate understanding of the complexities of real-life evidence and the untidiness of real-life inquiry requires a re-examination of some of those comfortably familiar dichotomies on which recent epistemology has relied – the logical versus the causal, internalism versus externalism, apriorism versus naturalism, foundationalism versus coherentism.

Though the other dichotomies will also come under scrutiny, the main theme here will be that foundationalism and coherentism – the traditionally rival theories of justified belief – do not exhaust the options, and that an intermediate theory is more plausible than either. I call it "foundherentism."

I   The Case for Foundherentism

Foundationalist theories of empirical justification hold that an empirical belief is justified if and only if it is either a basic belief justified by the subject's experience,[2] or else a derived belief

Originally published in Louis Pojman (ed.), *The Theory of Knowledge: Classical and Contemporary Readings*, 2nd edn (Belmont, CA: Wadsworth, 1999), pp. 283–93.

justified, directly or indirectly, by the support of basic beliefs. Coherentist theories of empirical justification hold that a belief is justified if and only if it belongs to a coherent set of beliefs. In short, foundationalism requires a distinction of basic versus derived beliefs and an essentially one-directional notion of evidential support, while coherentism holds that beliefs can be justified only by mutual support among themselves.

The merit of foundationalism is that it acknowledges that a person's experience – what he sees, hears, etc. – is relevant to how justified he is in his beliefs about the world; its drawback is that it requires a privileged class of basic beliefs justified by experience alone but capable of supporting the rest of our justified beliefs, and ignores the pervasive interdependence among a person's beliefs. The merit of coherentism is that it acknowledges that pervasive interdependence, and requires no distinction of basic and derived beliefs; its drawback is that it allows no role for the subject's experience.

Foundationlists, naturally, are keenly aware of the problems with coherentism. How could one possibly be justified in believing there's a dog in the yard, they ask, if what one sees, hears, smells, etc., plays no role? And isn't the coherentist's talk of mutual support among beliefs just a euphemism for what is really a vicious circle in which what supposedly justifies the belief that p is the belief that q, and what justifies the belief that q the belief that r…and what justifies the belief that z is the belief that p?

Coherentists, naturally, are no less keenly aware of the problems with foundationalism. What sense does it make to suppose that someone could have a justified belief that there's a dog in the yard, they ask, except in the context of the rest of his beliefs about dogs, etc.? Besides, why should we suppose that there *are* any beliefs both justified by experience alone and capable of supporting the rest of our justified beliefs? After all, foundationalists can't even agree among themselves whether the basic beliefs are about observable physical objects, along the lines of "there's a dog," or are about the subject's experience, along the lines of "it now seems to me that I see what looks like a dog" or "I am appeared to brownly." And anyway, only propositions, not events, can stand in logical relations to other propositions; so how *could* a subject's experience justify those supposedly basic beliefs?

As the two styles of theory have evolved, with each party trying to overcome the difficulties the other thinks insuperable, they have come closer together.

Strong foundationalism requires that basic beliefs be fully justified by the subject's experience; pure foundationalism requires that derived beliefs be justified exclusively by the support, direct or indirect, of basic beliefs. But weak foundationalism requires only that basic beliefs be justified to some degree by experience; and impure foundationalism, though requiring all derived beliefs to get some support from basic beliefs, allows mutual support among derived beliefs to raise their degree of justification.

Uncompromisingly egalitarian forms of coherentism hold that only overall coherence matters, so that every belief in a coherent set is equally justified. But moderated, inegalitarian forms of coherentism give a subject's beliefs about his present experience a distinguished initial status, or give a special standing to beliefs which are spontaneous rather than inferential in origin.

In a way, these moderated forms of foundationalism and coherentism lean in the right direction. But the leaning destabilizes them.

Weak foundationalism concedes that basic beliefs need not be fully justified by experience alone; but then what reason remains to deny that they could get more (or less) justified by virtue of their relations to other beliefs? Impure foundationalism concedes that there can be mutual support among derived beliefs; but then what reason remains to insist that more pervasive mutual support is unacceptable? And weak, impure foundationalism allows both that basic beliefs are less than fully justified by experience, and that derived beliefs may be mutually supportive; but now the insistence that derived beliefs can give no support to basic beliefs looks arbitrary, and the distinction of basic and derived beliefs pointless.[3]

Moderated, inegalitarian coherentism concedes that some beliefs are distinguished by their perceptual content or "spontaneous" origin; but isn't this implicitly to concede that justification is not after all a relation exclusively among beliefs, that input from experience is essential?

Not surprisingly, these fancier forms of foundationalism and compromising kinds of coherentism, though more sophisticated than their simpler ancestors, tend to be ambiguous and unstable. On the foundationalist side, for example, under pressure of just the kinds of difficulty my analysis identifies, C. I. Lewis moves from a pure to an impure foundationalism and then, briefly, to a kind of proto-foundherentism.[4] And on the coherentist side, under pressure of just the kind of difficulty my analysis identifies, BonJour tries to guarantee experiential input by adding an "Observation Requirement" – which, however, is ambiguous; on one interpretation it is genuinely coherentist, but doesn't allow the relevance of experience, and on the other it allows the relevance of experience, but isn't genuinely coherentist.[5] (BonJour now acknowledges that, after all, coherentism won't do.)[6]

Neither of the traditionally rival theories can be made satisfactory without sacrificing its distinctive character. The obvious conclusion – though those still wedded to the old dichotomy will doubtless continue to resist it – is that we need a new approach which allows the relevance of experience to empirical justification, but without postulating any privileged class of basic beliefs or requiring that relations of support be essentially one-directional: in other words, a foundherentist theory.

II   Explication of Foundherentism

The details get complicated, but the main ideas are simple.

A foundherentist account will acknowledge (like foundationalism) that how justified a person is in an empirical belief must depend in part on his experience – my version will give a role both to sensory experience, and to introspective awareness of one's own mental states. As coherentists point out, though experience can stand in causal relations to beliefs, it can't stand in logical relations to propositions. But what this shows is not that experience is irrelevant to empirical justification, but that justification is a double-aspect concept, partly causal as well as partly logical in character.

A foundherentist account will acknowledge (like coherentism) that there is pervasive mutual support among a person's justified beliefs. As foundationalists point out, a belief can't be justified by a vicious circle of reasons. But what this shows is not that mutual support is illegitimate, but that we need a better understanding of the

difference between legitimate mutual support and vicious circularity – my version will rely on an analogy between the structure of evidence and a crossword puzzle.

Of course, the viability of the foundherentist approach doesn't depend on my being completely successful in articulating it. No doubt there could be other versions of foundherentism falling within these general contours but differing in their details.

I take as my starting point the following vague, but very plausible, formulation: "A is more/less justified, at t, in believing that p, depending on how good his evidence is."

By starting from here I take for granted, first, that justification comes in degrees: a person may be more or less justified in believing something. (I also assume that a person may be more justified in believing some things than he is in believing others.)

I also take for granted, second, that the concepts of evidence and justification are internally connected: how justified a person is in believing something depends on the quality of his evidence with respect to that belief.

I assume, third, that justification is personal: one person may be more justified in believing something than another is in believing the same thing – because one person's evidence may be better than another's. (But though justification is personal, it is not subjective. How justified A is in believing that p depends on how good *his*, A's, evidence is. But how justified A is in believing that p doesn't depend on how good A *thinks* his evidence is; and anyone who believed the same thing on the same evidence would be justified to the same degree.)

And I assume, fourth, that justification is relative to a time: a person may be more justified in believing something at one time than at another – because his evidence at one time may be better than his evidence at another.

"A is more/less justified, at t, in believing that p, depending on how good his evidence is." The main tasks, obviously, are to explain "his evidence" and "how good." The double-aspect character of the concept of justification is already in play; for "his," in "his evidence," is a causal notion, while "how good" is logical, or quasi-logical, in character.

The concept of justification is causal as well as logical across the board[7] – its causal aspect is not restricted to experiential evidence alone. Quite generally, how justified someone is in believing something depends not only on *what* he believes, but on *why* he believes it. For example: if two people both believe the accused is innocent, one because he has evidence that she was a hundred miles from the scene of the crime at the relevant time, the other because he thinks she has an honest face, the former is more justified than the latter. In short, degree of justification depends on the quality of the evidence that actually causes the belief in question.

The word "belief" is ambiguous: sometimes it refers to a mental state, someone's believing something [an S-belief];[8] sometimes it refers to the content of what is believed, a proposition [a C-belief]. "A's evidence" needs to be tied somehow to what causes A's S-belief, but must also be capable of standing in logical or quasi-logical relations to the C-belief, the proposition believed.

The idea is to begin by characterizing A's S-evidence with respect to p – this will be a set of states of A causally related to his S-belief that p; and then to use this as the starting point of a characterization of A's C-evidence with respect to p – this will be a set of propositions capable of standing in logical or quasi-logical relations to the C-belief that p.

If A initially came to believe that the rock-rabbit is the closest surviving relative of the elephant because a fellow-tourist told him he read this somewhere, and later still believes it, but now because he has learned all the relevant biological details, he is more justified at the later time than at the earlier. So, if they are different, "A's S-evidence with respect to p" should relate to the causes of A's S-belief that p at the time in question rather than to what prompted it in the first place.

What goes on in people's heads is very complicated. There will likely be some factors inclining A towards believing that p, and others pulling against it. Perhaps, e.g., A believes that Tom Grabit stole the book because his seeing Grabit leave the library with a shifty expression and a suspicious bulge under his sweater exerts a stronger positive pull than his belief that it is possible that Tom Grabit has a light-fingered identical twin exerts in the opposite direction. Both sustaining and inhibiting factors are relevant to degree of justification, so both will be included in A's S-evidence.

In this vector of forces [the causal nexus of A's S-belief that p], besides A's present experience and present memory traces of his past experience, and other S-beliefs of his, such factors as his wishes, hopes, and fears will often play a role. But A's desire not to believe ill of his students, say, or his being under the influence of alcohol, though they may affect whether or with what degree of confidence he believes that Grabit stole the book, aren't themselves part of his evidence with respect to that proposition.

So "A's S-evidence with respect to p" will refer to those experiential and belief-states of A's which belong, at the time in question, to the causal nexus of A's S-belief that p. The phrase "with respect to" signals the inclusion of both positive, sustaining, and negative, inhibiting, evidence [respectively, A's S-evidence for p, and A's S-evidence against p]. A's S-evidence with respect to p will include other beliefs of his [A's S-reasons with respect to p]; and his perceptions, his introspective awareness of his own mental goings-on, and memory traces of his earlier perceptual and introspective states [A's experiential S-evidence with respect to p].

The part about memory needs amplifying. A's experiential S-evidence may include present memory traces of past experience – such as his remembering seeing his car-keys on the dresser. This corresponds to the way we talk of A's remembering seeing, hearing, reading, etc. We also talk of A's remembering that p, meaning that he earlier came to believe that p and has not forgotten it. How justified A is in such persisting beliefs will depend on how good his evidence is – his evidence at the time in question, that is. A person's evidence for persisting beliefs will normally include memory traces of past perceptual experience; my belief that my high-school English teacher's name was "Miss Wright," for instance, is now sustained by my remembering hearing and seeing the name used by myself and others.

Testimonial evidence, in a broad sense – what a person reads, what others tell him – enters the picture by way of his hearing or seeing, or remembering hearing or seeing, what someone else says or writes. Of course, A's hearing B say that p won't contribute to his, A's, believing that p, unless A understands B's language. But if A believes that p in part because B told him that p, how justified A is in believing that p will depend in part on how justified A is in thinking B honest and reliable. But I anticipate.

A's S-evidence with respect to p is a set of states of A causally related to his S-belief that p. But in the part of the theory that explains what makes evidence better or worse, "evidence" will have to mean "C-evidence," and refer to a set of propositions. The two aspects interlock: A's C-evidence with respect to p will be a set of propositions, and how good it is will depend on those propositions' logical or quasi-logical relations to p; but *which* propositions A's C-evidence with respect to p consists of depends on which of A's S-beliefs and perceptual, etc., states belong to the causal nexus of the S-belief in question.

A's C-reasons with respect to p, obviously enough, should be the C-beliefs, i.e., the propositions, which are the contents of his S-reasons. For example, if one of A's S-reasons with respect to p is his S-belief that female cardinal birds are brown, the corresponding C-reason will be the proposition that female cardinal birds are brown.

But what about A's experiential C-evidence? My proposal is that "A's experiential C-evidence with respect to p" refers to propositions to the effect that A is in the perceptual/introspective/memory states which constitute his experiential S-evidence with respect to p. Since a perceptual, etc., state can't be part of the causal nexus of A's S-belief that p unless A is *in* that state, these propositions are all true. But they need not be propositions that A believes.[9]

So A's experiential C-evidence has a distinctive status. A's C-reasons may be true or may be false, and A may be more or less justified, or not justified at all, in believing them. But A's experiential C-evidence consists of propositions all of which are, *ex hypothesi*, true, and with respect to which the question of justification doesn't arise. (This is the foundherentist way of acknowledging that the ultimate evidence for empirical beliefs is experience – very different from the forced and unnatural way in which foundationalism tries to acknowledge it, by requiring basic *beliefs* justified by experience alone.)

In line with the way we ordinarily talk about the evidence of the senses – "Why do I think there's a cardinal in the oak tree? Well, I can see the thing; that distinctive profile is clear, though the light's not too good, and it's quite far away, so I can't really see the color" – I suggest a characterization of A's experiential C-evidence in terms of propositions to the effect that A is in the sort of perceptual state a normal subject would be in when seeing this or that in these or those circumstances. For example, if A's experiential S-evidence with respect to p is his perceptual state, its looking to him as it would to a normal observer seeing a female cardinal bird at a distance of forty feet in poor light, the corresponding experiential C-evidence will be a proposition to the effect that A is in the kind of perceptual state a normal observer would be in when looking at a female cardinal bird in those circumstances.

Built into my account of experiential evidence is a conception of perception as, in a certain sense, direct. This is not to deny that perception involves complicated neurophysiological goings-on. Nor is it to deny that the judgments causally sustained by the subject's experience are interpretative, that they depend on his background beliefs as well – which, on the contrary, is a key foundherentist thought. It is only to assert that in normal perception we interact with physical things and events around us, which look a certain way to all normal observers under the same circumstances.

You may be wondering why I include the subject's sensory and introspective experience as evidence, but not, say, his extra-sensory perceptual experience. Well, the task here is descriptive – to articulate explicitly what is implicit when we say that A has excellent reasons for believing that p, that B is guilty of wishful thinking, that C has jumped to an unjustified conclusion, and so on. As those phrases "excellent reasons" and "guilty of wishful thinking" indicate, his other beliefs should be included as part of a subject's evidence, but his wishes should not. Actually, I think it most unlikely there is such a thing as ESP; but it is excluded because – unlike sensory experience, for which we even have the phrase, "the evidence of the senses" – it has no role in the implicit conception of evidence I am trying to make explicit.

The concepts of better and worse evidence, of more and less justified belief, are evaluative; so, after the descriptive task of explication, there will be the ratificatory question, whether our standards of better and worse evidence really are, as we hope and believe they are, indicative of truth. But that comes later.

The present task is to explicate "how good" in "how good A's C-evidence is." What factors raise, and what lower, degree of justification?

Foundationalists often think of the structure of evidence on the model of a mathematical proof – a model which, understandably, makes them leery of the idea of mutual support. My approach will be informed by the analogy of a crossword puzzle – where, undeniably, there is pervasive mutual support among entries, but, equally undeniably, no vicious circle. The clues are the analogue of experiential evidence, already-completed intersecting entries the analogue of reasons. As how reasonable a crossword entry is depends both on the clues and on other intersecting entries, the idea is, so how justified an empirical belief is depends on experiential evidence and reasons working together.

Perhaps needless to say, an analogy is only an analogy, not an argument. Its role is only to suggest ideas, which then have to stand on their own feet. And there are always disanalogies; there will be nothing in my theory analogous to the solution to today's crossword which appears in tomorrow's newspaper, for instance, nor any analogue of the designer of a crossword.

But the analogy does suggest a very plausible multi-dimensional answer to the question, what makes a belief more or less justified? How reasonable a crossword entry is depends on how well it is supported by the clue and any already-completed intersecting entries; how reasonable those other entries are, independent of the entry in question; and how much of the crossword has been completed. How justified A is in believing that p, analogously, depends on how well the belief in question is supported by his experiential evidence and reasons [supportiveness]; how justified his reasons are, independent of the belief in question [independent security]; and how much of the relevant evidence his evidence includes [comprehensiveness].

On the first dimension, A's C-evidence may be conclusive for p, conclusive against p, supportive-but-not-conclusive of p, undermining-but-not-conclusive against p, or indifferent with respect to p/ with respect to not-p.

Foundationalists often take for granted that evidence is conclusive just in case it deductively implies the proposition in question; but this isn't quite right. Inconsistent premises deductively imply any proposition whatever; but inconsistent evidence isn't conclusive evidence for anything – let alone conclusive evidence for everything!

Think, for example, of a detective whose evidence is: the murder was committed by a left-handed person; either Smith or Brown did it; Smith is right-handed; Brown is right-handed. Though this deductively implies that Smith did it, it certainly isn't conclusive evidence for that belief (let alone conclusive evidence for the belief that Smith did it *and* conclusive evidence for the belief that Brown did it *and* conclusive evidence for the belief that extra-terrestrials did it!).

Deductive implication is necessary but not sufficient for conclusiveness. Evidence E is conclusive for p just in case the result of adding p to E [the p-extrapolation of E] is consistent, and the result of adding not-p to E [the not-p-extrapolation of E] is inconsistent. E is conclusive against p just in case its p-extrapolation is inconsistent and its not-p-extrapolation consistent. But if E itself is inconsistent, both its p-extrapolation and its not-p-extrapolation are also inconsistent, so E is indifferent with respect to p.

Often, though, evidence is not conclusive either way, nor yet inconsistent and hence indifferent, but supports the belief in question, or its negation, to some degree. Suppose the detective's evidence is: the murder was committed by a left-handed person; either Smith or Brown did it; Smith is left-handed; Brown is left-handed; Smith recently saw the victim, Mrs Smith, in a romantic restaurant holding hands with Brown. Though not conclusive, this evidence is supportive to some degree of the belief that Smith did it – for, if he did, we have some explanation of why.

The example suggests that supportiveness depends on whether and how much adding p to E makes a better explanatory story. But a better explanatory story than what? Conclusiveness is a matter of the superiority of p over its negation with respect to consistency. But if p is potentially explanatory of E or some component of E, it is not to be expected that not-p will be too. So I construe supportiveness as depending on the superiority of p over its rivals with respect to explanatory integration; where a rival of p is any proposition adding which to E improves its explanatory integration to some degree, and which, given E, is incompatible with p.

The word "integration" was chosen to indicate that E may support p either because p explains E or some component of E, or vice versa – that there is "mutual reinforcement between an explanation and what it explains."[10] (So the concept of explanatory integration is closer kin to the coherentist concept of explanatory coherence than to the foundationalist concept of inference to the best explanation.)

Usually, as conclusiveness of evidence is taken to be the province of deductive logic, supportiveness of evidence is taken to be the province of inductive logic. But at least if "logic" is taken in its now-usual narrow sense, as depending on form alone, this looks to be a mistake. Explanation requires generality, kinds, laws – a motive for the murder, a mechanism whereby smoking causes cancer, and so forth. If so, explanatoriness, and hence supportiveness, requires a vocabulary which classifies things into real kinds; and hence depends on content, not on form alone. (Hempel drew the moral, many years ago now, from the "grue" paradox.[11]) But there is supportive-but-not-conclusive evidence, even if there is no formal inductive logic.

Supportiveness alone does not determine degree of justification, which also depends on independent security and comprehensiveness. Suppose our detective's evidence is: the murder was committed by a left-handed person; either Smith or Brown did it; Smith is right-handed, but Brown left-handed. The detective's evidence is conclusive that Brown did it; nevertheless, he is not well-justified in believing this unless, among other things, he is justified in believing that the murder was committed by a left-handed person, that either Smith or Brown did it, etc.

The idea of independent security is easiest to grasp in the context of the crossword analogy. In a crossword, how reasonable an entry is depends in part on its fit with intersecting entries, and hence on how reasonable those entries are, independently of the entry in question. Similarly, how justified a person is in believing something depends in part on how well it is supported by his other beliefs, and hence on how justified he is in believing those reasons, independently of the belief in question.

It is that last phrase – in my theory as with a crossword puzzle – that averts the danger of a vicious circle. The reasonableness of the entry for 3 down may depend in part on the reasonableness of the intersecting entry for 5 across – independent of the support given to the entry for 5 across by the entry for 3 down. Similarly, how justified A is in believing that p may depend in part on how justified he is in believing that q – independent of the support given his belief that q by his belief that p.

And, though "justified" appears on the right-hand side of the independent security clause, there is no danger of an infinite regress – any more than with a crossword puzzle. As in the case of a crossword eventually we reach the clues, so with empirical justification eventually we reach experiential evidence. And experiential C-evidence does not consist of other C-beliefs of the subject, but of propositions all of which are, ex hypothesi, true, and with respect to which the question of justification doesn't arise. This is not to deny that, as crossword clues may be cryptic, experiential evidence may be ambiguous or misleading; on the contrary, my account of experiential C-evidence is intended to recognize that it often is. It is only to say that the question of justification arises with respect to a person's beliefs, but not with respect to his experiences.

As how reasonable a crossword entry is depends not only on how well it is supported by the clue and other intersecting entries, and on how reasonable those other entries are, but also on how much of the crossword has been completed, so degree of justification depends not only on supportiveness and independent security, but also on comprehensiveness – on how much of the relevant evidence the subject's evidence includes.

Comprehensiveness promises to be even tougher to spell out than supportiveness and independent security; the crossword analogy isn't much help here, and neither is the nearest analogue in the literature, the total evidence requirement on inductions, which refers, not to the totality of relevant evidence, but to the totality of relevant available evidence – and then there is the further problem that relevance itself comes in degrees.

I am assuming, however, that (degree of) relevance is an objective matter. Naturally, whether I think your handwriting is relevant to your trustworthiness depends on whether I believe in graphology; but whether it is relevant depends on whether graphology is true.

As this reveals, though relevance, and hence comprehensiveness, is objective, judgments of relevance, and hence judgments of comprehensiveness, are perspectival, i.e., they depend on the background beliefs of the person making them.

The same goes for judgments of supportiveness and independent security. How supportive you or I judge E to be with respect to p, for example, will depend on what rivals of p we happen to be able to think of; but how supportive E *is* of p does not. Quality of evidence is objective, but judgments of quality of evidence are perspectival.

Because quality of evidence is multi-dimensional, we should not necessarily expect a linear ordering of degrees of justification; e.g., A's evidence with respect to p might be strongly supportive but weak on comprehensiveness, while his evidence with respect to q might be strong on comprehensiveness but only weakly supportive. Nor, *a fortiori*, does it look realistic to aspire to anything as ambitious as a numerical scale of degrees of justification. But something can be said about what is required for A to be justified to *any* degree in believing that p.

One necessary condition is that there *be* such a thing as A's C-evidence with respect to p. If A's S-belief that p is caused simply by a blow to the head, or by one of those belief-inducing pills philosophers are fond of imagining, A isn't justified to any degree in believing that p. Since it is the justification of empirical beliefs that is at issue, another necessary condition is that A's C-evidence should include some experiential C-evidence – present experiential evidence, or memory traces of what he earlier saw, heard, read, etc. This is my analogue of BonJour's Observation Requirement, obviously much more at home in foundherentism than his requirement was in his coherentist theory. (It is not meant to rule out the possibility that some of a person's beliefs may not be sustained directly by experiential evidence, not even by memory traces, but rely on other beliefs and their experiential evidence – as in an unconventional crossword some entries might have no clues of their own but rely on other entries and their clues.[12]) A third necessary condition is that A's C-evidence with respect to p should meet minimal conditions of supportiveness, independent security, and comprehensiveness; e.g., it should be better than indifferent in terms of supportiveness. Jointly, these necessary conditions look to be sufficient.

What about the upper end of the scale? Our ordinary use of phrases like "A is completely justified in believing that p" is vague and context-dependent, depending *inter alia* on whether it is

A's particular business to know whether p, and how important it is to be right about whether p; perhaps it also runs together strictly epistemological with ethical concerns. This vague concept [*complete* justification] is useful for practical purposes – and for the statement of Gettier-type paradoxes. In other philosophical contexts, however, "A is completely justified in believing that p" is used in a context-neutralized, optimizing way, requiring conclusiveness, maximal independent security, and full comprehensiveness of evidence [COMPLETE justification].

The account sketched here has been personal, i.e., focussed firmly on our friend A. But this is not to deny that in even the most ordinary of our everyday beliefs we rely extensively on testimonial evidence. And where the sciences are concerned, reliance on others' evidence – and hence on the interpretation of others' words and judgments of others' reliability – is absolutely pervasive. (This reveals that not only the social sciences but also the natural sciences presuppose the possibility of interpreting others' utterances: think, e.g., of an astronomer's reliance on others' reports of observations.)

Anyhow, thinking about evidence in the sciences prompts me to ask whether it is possible to extrapolate from my account of "A is more/less justified in believing that p" to a concept of justification applicable to groups of people. It might be feasible to do this by starting with the degree of justification of a hypothetical subject whose evidence includes all the evidence of each member of the group, and then discount this by some measure of the degree to which each member of the group is justified in believing that other members are competent and honest.

III   The Ratification of Foundherentism

Thus far the task has been to articulate our standards of better and worse evidence, of more and less justified belief. But what do I mean by "our"? And what assurance can I give that a belief's being justified, by those standards, is any indication that it is true?

When I speak of "our" standards of better and worse evidence, I emphatically do not mean to suggest that these standards are local or parochial, accepted in "our," as opposed to "their," community. Rather, I see these standards – essentially, how well a belief is anchored in experience and how tightly it is woven into an explanatory mesh of beliefs – as rooted in human nature, in the cognitive capacities and limitations of all normal human beings.

It is sure to be objected that the evidential standards of different times, cultures, communities, or scientific paradigms differ radically. But I think this supposed variability is at least an exaggeration, and quite possibly altogether an illusion, the result of mistaking the perspectival character of judgments of evidential quality for radical divergence in standards of better and worse evidence.

Because judgments of the quality of evidence are perspectival, people with radically different background beliefs can be expected to differ significantly in their judgments of degree of justification. It doesn't follow that there are no shared standards of evidence. If we think of the constraints of experiential anchoring and explanatory integration rather than of specific judgments of the relevance, supportiveness, etc., of this or that evidence, I believe we will find commonality rather than divergence.

Again, the point is easier to see in the context of the crossword analogy. Suppose you and I are both doing the same crossword puzzle, and have filled in some long central entry differently. You think, given your solution to that long central entry, that the fact that 14 down ends in a "T" is evidence in its favor; I think, given my solution to that long central entry, that the fact that it ends in a "D" is evidence in its favor. Nevertheless, we are both trying to fit the entry to its clue and to other already-completed entries. Now suppose you and I are both on an appointments committee. You think the way this candidate writes his "g"s indicates that he is not to be trusted; I think graphology is bunk and scoff at your "evidence." Because of a disagreement in background beliefs, we disagree about what evidence is relevant. Nevertheless, we are both trying to assess the supportiveness, independent security, and comprehensiveness of the evidence with respect to the proposition that the candidate is trustworthy.

But even if I am wrong about this, even if there really are radically divergent standards of evidential quality, it wouldn't follow that there are no objective indications of truth; *variability* of standards does not, in and of itself, imply *relativity* of standards.[13] So those epistemic relativists who have inferred that, since judgments of justification vary from community to community, there can be no objectively correct standards of better and worse evidence, have committed a *non sequitur* as well as relying on a dubious premiss.

As for those who have succumbed to epistemic relativism because they have given up on the concept of truth, I have room here only to say that theirs seems to me an entirely factitious despair.[14] In any case, all that will be required of the concept of truth in what follows is that a proposition or statement is true just in case things are as it says.

Supposing – as I believe, and so do you – that we humans are fallible, limited but inquiring creatures who live in a world which is largely independent of us and what we believe about it, but in which there are kinds, laws, regularities; and supposing – as I believe, and so do you – that our senses are a source, though by no means an infallible source, of information about things and events in the world around us, and introspection a source, though by no means an infallible source, of information about our own mental goings-on; then, if any indication of how things are is possible for us, how well our beliefs are anchored in our experience and knit into an explanatory mesh is such an indication. (And supposing – as I believe, and so, probably, do you – we have no other sources of information about the world and ourselves, no ESP or clairvoyance or etc., then this is the only indication we can have of how things are.)

That last paragraph was nothing like an a priori ratification of foundherentism; for those "supposing" clauses are empirical in character. Assumptions about human cognitive capacities and limitations are *built into* our standards of evidential quality; so the truth-indicativeness of those standards depends on the truth of those empirical assumptions. But neither was that last paragraph much like the appeals to psychology or cognitive science on which some epistemological naturalists of a more extreme stripe than mine propose to rely; for the assumptions referred to in my "supposing" clauses, though empirical, are of such generality as to be rather philosophical than scientific in character.

Those assumptions would surely be presupposed by any conceivable scientific experiment.

But they are well integrated with what the sciences of cognition have to tell us about the mechanisms of perception and introspection, and of when and why they are more or less reliable, and with what the theory of evolution suggests about how we came to have the sort of information-detecting apparatus we do. As one would hope, the epistemological part of my crossword – the part where the entries are themselves about crosswords – interlocks snugly with other parts.

But what am I to say to those readers familiar with Descartes' failed attempt to prove "what I clearly and distinctly perceive is true," who are bound to suspect that I must be arguing in a circle? After pointing out that I have not offered a ratificatory argument in which some premiss turns out to be identical with the conclusion, nor an argument relying on a certain mode of inference to arrive at the conclusion that this very mode of inference is a good one – only that, to borrow Peirce's words, by now "the reader will, I trust, be too well-grounded in logic to mistake mutual support for a vicious circle of reasoning."[15]

And what am I to say to readers worried about the Evil Demon, who are bound to object that I have not ruled out the possibility that our senses are not a source of information about the external world at all? After pointing out that since, *ex hypothesi*, his machinations would be absolutely undetectable, if there were an Evil Demon *no* truth-indication would be possible for us – only that my claim is a conditional one: that, if any truth-indication is possible for us, the foundherentist criteria are truth-indicative. (I could discharge the antecedent, and arrive at a categorical conclusion, by adopting a definition of truth along Peircean lines, as the opinion that would survive all possible experiential evidence and the fullest logical scrutiny; but I prefer the more cautious, and more realist, strategy.)

Determined skeptics won't be persuaded; but determined skeptics never are! And the rest of you may notice that foundherentism enables us to sidestep another dichotomy which has – if you'll pardon the pun – bedeviled recent epistemology: *either* a hopeless obsession with hyperbolic skepticism, *or* a hopeless relativism or tribalism preoccupied with "our (local, parochial) epistemic practices." Foundherentism, I believe, provides a more realistic picture of our epistemic condition – a robustly fallibilist picture which, without sacrificing objectivity, acknowledges something of how complex and confusing evidence can be.

Notes

This brief statement of foundherentism is based primarily on my *Evidence and Inquiry: Towards Reconstruction in Epistemology* (Oxford: Blackwell, 1993), especially chapters 1, 4, and 10. I have also drawn on material from earlier articles of mine, especially "Theories of Knowledge: an Analytic Framework," *Proceedings of the Aristotelian Society* LXXXIII (1982–3), pp. 143–57 (where foundherentism was first introduced), "C. I. Lewis," in *American Philosophy*, ed. Marcus Singer, Royal Institute of Philosophy Lecture Series, 19 (Cambridge: Cambridge University Press, 1985), pp. 215–39, and "Rebuilding the Ship While Sailing on the Water," in R. Barrett and R. Gibson (eds), *Perspectives on Quine* (Oxford: Blackwell, 1990), pp. 111–27 (where some of the key ideas of foundherentism were developed). I have drawn as well on material from the symposium on *Evidence and Inquiry* published in *Philosophy and Phenomenological Research* LVI.

3 (1996), pp. 611–57, and from the debate with BonJour in *Synthese* 112.1 (July 1997), pp. 7–35.

1 Thomas Reid, *Essays on the Intellectual Powers* (1785), in R. E. Beanblossom and K. Lehrer (eds), *Thomas Reid: Inquiry and Essays*, (Indianapolis, IN: Hackett, 1983), vol. VI, p. 4.

2 I restrict my attention here to experientialist forms of foundationalism, ignoring, e.g., foundationalist theories of a priori knowledge.

3 My characterization of foundationalism is quite standard; cf. for example, Alston's in J. Dancy and E. Sosa (eds), *Companion to Epistemology* (Oxford: Blackwell, 1992), p. 144, or Sosa's in "The Raft and the Pyramid," this vol., ch. 13. But matters have been confused because, in "Can Empirical Knowledge Have a Foundation?", this vol., ch. 10, and *The Structure of Empirical Knowledge* (Cambridge, MA: Harvard University Press, 1986), p. 28, BonJour uses "weak foundationalism" to refer

a style of theory which is both weak *and* impure, in my sense, and in addition allows mutual support among basic beliefs and – apparently – allows "basic" beliefs to get support from "derived" beliefs. As my scare quotes indicate, once one-directionality has been so completely abandoned it is unclear that the theory really qualifies as foundationalist at all; certainly the basic/derived distinction has become purely *proforma*. See also Haack, "Reply to BonJour," *Synthese* 112.1 (July 1997), pp. 25–35.

4   See *Evidence and Inquiry*, ch. 2, for details.

5   See ibid., ch. 3, for details.

6   Laurence BonJour, "Haack on Justification and Experience," *Synthese* 112.1 (July 1997), pp. 13–15.

7   An idea I first began to work out in "Epistemology *With* a Knowing Subject," *Review of Metaphysics* XXXIII.2 (1979), pp. 309–36.

8   Expressions introduced in square brackets are my new, technical terms, or special, technical uses of familiar terms.

9   So my theory is not straightforwardly externalist, since A's S-evidence must consist of states of A – states, furthermore, of which A can be aware; but neither is it straightforwardly internalist, since A's experiential C-evidence consists of propositions A need not believe or even conceive.

10 W. V. Quine and J. Ullian, *The Web of Belief* (New York: Random House, 1970), p. 79.

11 N. Goodman, "The New Riddle of Induction" (1953), in *Fact, Fiction and Forecast* (Indianapolis, IN: Bobbs-Merrill, 2nd edn, 1965), pp. 59–83; C. G. Hempel, "Postscript on Confirmation" (1964), in *Aspects of Scientific Explanation* (New York: Free Press, 1965), pp. 47–52.

12 In case a desperate foundationalist is tempted to try seizing on this in hopes of salvaging the derived/basic distinction, let me point out that beliefs without direct experiential evidence could contribute to the support of beliefs with direct experiential evidence; and that this maneuver would identify no plausible *kind* of belief as basic/as derived – think, e.g., of a scientist whose belief that electrons are composed thus and so is sustained by what he sees in the bubble chamber.

13 See also Susan Haack, "Reflections on Relativism: From Momentous Tautology to Seductive Contradiction," *Noûs* Supplement (1996), pp. 297–315, and in James E. Tomberlin (ed.), *Philosophical Perspectives, 10: Metaphysics* (Oxford: Blackwell, 1996), pp. 297–315; reprinted in Haack, *Manifesto of a Passionate Moderate: Unfashionable Essays* (Chicago: University of Chicago Press, 1998), pp. 149–66.

14 I have more to say in "Confessions of an Old-Fashioned Prig," in *Manifesto of a Passionate Moderate*, pp. 7–30.

15 C. S. Peirce, *Collected Papers*, eds C. Hartshorne, P. Weiss, and A. Burks (Cambridge, MA: Harvard University Press, 1931–58), 6.315.

CHAPTER 13

The Raft and the Pyramid

Ernest Sosa

Contemporary epistemology must choose between the solid security of the ancient foundationalist pyramid and the risky adventure of the new coherentist raft. Our main objective will be to understand, as deeply as we can, the nature of the controversy and the reasons for and against each of the two options. But first of all we take note of two underlying assumptions.

1 Two Assumptions

(A1) Not everything believed is known, but nothing can be known without being at least believed (or accepted, presumed, taken for granted, or the like) in some broad sense. What additional requirements must a belief fill in order to be knowledge? There are surely at least the following two: (a) it must be true, and (b) it must be justified (or warranted, reasonable, correct, or the like).

(A2) Let us assume, moreover, with respect to the second condition A1(b): first, that it involves a normative or evaluative property;

Originally published in *Midwest Studies in Philosophy, Vol. 5: Studies in Epistemology* (Minneapolis: University of Minnesota Press, 1980), pp. 3–25; an appendix to this paper is drawn from Ernest Sosa, "How Do You Know?" *American Philosophical Quarterly* 11 (1974), pp. 113–22.

and, second, that the relevant sort of justification is that which pertains to knowledge: epistemic (or theoretical) justification. Someone seriously ill may have two sorts of justification for believing he will recover: the practical justification that derives from the contribution such belief will make to his recovery and the theoretical justification provided by the lab results, the doctor's diagnosis and prognosis, and so on. Only the latter is relevant to the question whether he knows.

2 Knowledge and Criteria

a. There are two key questions of the theory of knowledge:
   (i) What do we know?
   (ii) How do we know?
   The answer to the first would be a list of bits of knowledge or at least of types of knowledge: of the self, of the external world, of other minds, and so on. An answer to the second would give criteria (or canons, methods, principles, or the like) that would explain how we know whatever it is that we do know.

b. In developing a theory of knowledge, we can begin either with a(i) or with a(ii). Particularism would have us begin with an answer to a(i) and only then take up a(ii) on the basis of that answer. Quite to the contrary, methodism would reverse that order. The particularist thus tends to be antiskeptical on principle. But the methodist is as such equally receptive to skepticism and to the contrary. Hume, for example, was no less a methodist than Descartes. Each accepted, in effect, that only the obvious and what is proved deductively on its basis can possibly be known.

c. What, then, is the obvious? For Descartes it is what we know by intuition, what is clear and distinct, what is indubitable and credible with no fear of error. Thus for Descartes basic knowledge is always an infallible belief in an indubitable truth. All other knowledge must stand on that basis through deductive proof. Starting from such criteria (canons, methods, etc.), Descartes concluded that knowledge extended about as far as his contemporaries believed.[1] Starting from similar criteria, however, Hume concluded that both science and common sense made claims far beyond their rightful limits.

d. Philosophical posterity has rejected Descartes's theory for one main reason: that it admits too easily as obvious what is nothing of the sort. Descartes's reasoning is beautifully simple: God exists; no omnipotent perfectly good being would descend to deceit; but if our common sense beliefs were radically false, that would represent deceit on His part. Therefore, our common sense beliefs must be true or at least cannot be radically false. But in order to buttress this line of reasoning and fill in details, Descartes appeals to various principles that appear something less than indubitable.

e. For his part, Hume rejects all but a minuscule portion of our supposed common sense knowledge. He establishes first that there is no way to prove such supposed knowledge on the basis of what is obvious at any given moment through reason or experience. And he concludes, in keeping with this methodism, that in point of fact there really is no such knowledge.

3 Two Metaphors: The Raft and the Pyramid

Both metaphors concern the body or system of knowledge in a given mind. But the mind is of course a more complex marvel than is sometimes supposed. Here I do not allude to the depths plumbed by Freud, nor even to Chomsky's. Nor need we recall the labyrinths inhabited by statesmen and diplomats, nor the rich patterns of some novels or theories. We need look no further than the most common, everyday beliefs. Take, for instance, the belief that driving tonight will be dangerous. Brief reflection should reveal that any of us with that belief will join to it several other closely related beliefs on which the given belief depends for its existence or (at least) its justification. Among such beliefs we could presumably find some or all of the following: that the road will be icy or snowy; that driving on ice or snow is dangerous; that it will rain or snow tonight; that the temperature will be below freezing; appropriate beliefs about the forecast and its reliability; and so on.

How must such beliefs be interrelated in order to help justify my belief about the danger of driving tonight? Here foundationalism and coherentism disagree, each offering its own metaphor. Let us have a closer look at this dispute, starting with foundationalism.

Both Descartes and Hume attribute to human knowledge an architectonic structure. There is a nonsymmetric relation of physical support such that any two floors of a building are tied by that relation: one of the two supports (or at least helps support) the other. And there is, moreover, a part with a special status: the foundation, which is supported by none of the floors while supporting them all.

With respect to a body of knowledge K (in someone's possession), foundationalism implies that K can be divided into parts K_1, K_2…such that there is some nonsymmetric relation R (analogous to the relation of physical support) which orders those parts in such a way that there is one – call it F – that bears R to every other part while none of them bears R in turn to F.

According to foundationalism, each piece of knowledge lies on a pyramid such as that shown in Figure 13.1. The nodes of such a pyramid (for a proposition P relative to a subject S and a time t) must obey the following requirements:

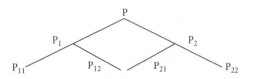

Figure 13.1

a. The set of all nodes that succeed (directly) any given node must serve jointly as a base that properly supports that node (for S at t).

b. Each node must be a proposition that S is justified in believing at t.

c. If a node is not self-evident (for S at t), it must have successors (that serve jointly as a base that properly supports that node).

d. Each branch of an epistemic pyramid must terminate.

For the foundationalist Descartes, for instance, each terminating node must be an indubitable proposition that S believes at t with no possibility of error. As for the nonterminal nodes, each of them represents inferential knowledge, derived by deduction from more basic beliefs.

Such radical foundationalism suffers from a fatal weakness that is twofold: (a) there are not so many perfectly obvious truths as Descartes thought; and (b) once we restrict ourselves to what is truly obvious in any given context, very little of one's supposed common sense knowledge can be proved on that basis. If we adhere to such radical foundationalism, therefore, we are just wrong in thinking we know so much.

Note that in citing such a "fatal weakness" of radical foundationalism, we favor particularism as against the methodism of Descartes and Hume. For we reject the methods or criteria of Descartes and Hume when we realize that they plunge us in a deep skepticism. If such criteria are incompatible with our enjoyment of the rich body of knowledge that we commonly take for granted, then as good particularists we hold on to the knowledge and reject the criteria.

If we reject radical foundationalism, however, what are we to put in its place? Here epistemology faces a dilemma that different epistemologists resolve differently. Some reject radical foundationalism but retain some more moderate form of foundationalism in favor of a radically different coherentism. Coherentism is associated with idealism – of both the German and the British variety – and has recently acquired new vigor and interest.

The coherentists reject the metaphor of the pyramid in favor of one that they owe to the positivist Neurath, according to whom our body of knowledge is a raft that floats free of any anchor or tie. Repairs must be made afloat, and though no part is untouchable, we must stand on some in order to replace or repair others. Not every part can go at once.

According to the new metaphor, what justifies a belief is not that it be an infallible belief with an indubitable object, nor that it have been proved deductively on such a basis, but that it cohere with a comprehensive system of beliefs.

4 A Coherentist Critique of Foundationalism

What reasons do coherentists offer for their total rejection of foundationalism? The argument that follows below summarizes much of what is alleged against foundationalism. But first we must distinguish between subjective states that incorporate a propositional attitude and those that do not. A propositional attitude is a mental state of someone with a proposition for its object: beliefs, hopes, and fears provide examples. By way of contrast, a headache does not incorporate any such attitude. One can of course be conscious of a headache, but the headache itself does not constitute or incorporate any attitude with a proposition for its object. With this distinction in the background, here is the antifoundationalist argument, which has two lemmas – a(iv) and b(iii) – and a principal conclusion.

a. (i) If a mental state incorporates a propositional attitude, then it does not give us direct contact with reality, e.g., with pure experience, unfiltered by concepts or beliefs.

(ii) If a mental state does not give us direct contact with reality, then it provides no guarantee against error.

(iii) If a mental state provides no guarantee against error, then it cannot serve as a foundation for knowledge.

(iv) Therefore, if a mental state incorporates a propositional attitude, then it cannot serve as a foundation for knowledge.

b. (i) If a mental state does not incorporate a propositional attitude, then it is an enigma how such a state can provide support for any hypothesis, raising its credibility selectively by contrast with its alternatives. (If the mental state has no conceptual or propositional content, then what logical relation can it possibly bear to any hypothesis? Belief in a hypothesis would be a propositional attitude with the hypothesis itself as object. How can one depend logically for such a belief on an experience with no propositional content?)

    (ii) If a mental state has no propositional content and cannot provide logical support for any hypothesis, then it cannot serve as a foundation for knowledge.

    (iii) Therefore, if a mental state does not incorporate a propositional attitude, then it cannot serve as a foundation for knowledge.

c. Every mental state either does or does not incorporate a propositional attitude.

d. Therefore, no mental state can serve as a foundation for knowledge. (From a(iv), b(iii), and c.)

According to the coherentist critic, foundationalism is run through by this dilemma. Let us take a closer look.[2]

In the first place, what reason is there to think, in accordance with premise b(i), that only propositional attitudes can give support to their own kind? Consider practices – e.g., broad policies or customs. Could not some person or group be justified in a practice because of its consequences: that is, could not the consequences of a practice make it a good practice? But among the consequences of a practice may surely be found, for example, a more just distribution of goods and less suffering than there would be under its alternatives. And neither the more just distribution nor the lower degree of suffering is a propositional attitude. This provides an example in which propositional attitudes (the intentions that sustain the practice) are justified by consequences that are not propositional attitudes. That being so, is it not conceivable that the justification of belief that matters for knowledge be analogous to the objective justification by consequences that we find in ethics?

Is it not possible, for instance, that a belief that there is something red before one be justified in part because it has its origins in one's visual experience of red when one looks at an apple in daylight?

If we accept such examples, they show us a source of justification that serves as such without incorporating a propositional attitude.

As for premise a(iii), it is already under suspicion from our earlier exploration of premise b(i). A mental state M can be nonpropositional and hence not a candidate for so much as truth, much less infallibility, while it serves, in spite of that, as a foundation of knowledge. Leaving that aside, let us suppose that the relevant mental state is indeed propositional. Must it then be infallible in order to serve as a foundation of justification and knowledge? That is so far from being obvious that it seems more likely false when compared with an analogue in ethics. With respect to beliefs, we may distinguish between their being true and their being justified. Analogously, with respect to actions, we may distinguish between their being optimal (best of all alternatives, all things considered) and their being (subjectively) justified. In practical deliberation on alternatives for action, is it inconceivable that the most *eligible* alternative *not* be objectively the best, all things considered? Can there not be another alternative – perhaps a most repugnant one worth little if any consideration – that in point of fact would have a much better total set of consequences and would thus be better, all things considered? Take the physician attending to Frau Hitler at the birth of little Adolf. Is it not possible that if he had acted less morally, that would have proved better in the fullness of time? And if that is so in ethics, may not its likeness hold good in epistemology? Might there not be justified (reasonable, warranted) beliefs that are not even true, much less infallible? That seems to me not just a conceivable possibility, but indeed a familiar fact of everyday life, where observational beliefs too often prove illusory but no less reasonable for being false.

If the foregoing is on the right track, then the antifoundationalist is far astray. What has led him there?

As a diagnosis of the antifoundationalist argument before us, and more particularly of its second lemma, I would suggest that it rests on an Intellectualist Model of Justification.

According to such a model, the justification of belief (and psychological states generally) is parasitical on certain logical relations among propositions. For example, my belief (i) that the streets are wet, is justified by my pair of beliefs (ii) that it is raining, and (iii) that if it is raining, the streets are wet. Thus we have a structure such as this:

B(Q) is justified by the fact that B(Q) is grounded on (B(P), B(P⊃Q)).

And according to an Intellectualist Model, this is parasitical on the fact that

P and (P⊃Q) together logically imply Q.

Concerning this attack on foundationalism I will argue (a) that it is useless to the coherentist, since if the antifoundationalist dilemma impales the foundationalist, a form of it can be turned against the coherentist to the same effect; (b) that the dilemma would be lethal not only to foundationalism and coherentism but also to the very possibility of substantive epistemology; and (c) that a form of it would have the same effect on normative ethics.

a. According to coherentism, what justifies a belief is its membership in a coherent and comprehensive set of beliefs. But whereas being grounded on B(P) and B(P⊂Q) is a property of a belief B(Q) that yields immediately the logical implication of Q and P and (P⊂Q) as the logical source of that property's justificatory power, the property of being a member of a coherent set is not one that immediately yields any such implication.

It may be argued, nevertheless, (i) that the property of being a member of a coherent set would supervene in any actual instance on the property of being a member of a particular set *a* that is in fact coherent, and (ii) that this would enable us to preserve our Intellectualist Model, since (iii) the justification of the member belief B(Q) by its membership in *a* would then be parasitical on the logical relations among the beliefs in *a* which constitute the coherence of that set of beliefs, and (iv) the justification of B(Q) by the fact that it is part of a coherent set would then be *indirectly* parasitical on logical relations among propositions after all.

But if such an indirect form of parasitism is allowed, then the experience of pain may perhaps be said to justify belief in its existence parasitically on the fact that P logically implies P! The Intellectualist Model seems either so trivial as to be dull, or else sharp enough to cut equally against both foundationalism and coherentism.

b. If (i) only propositional attitudes can justify such propositional attitudes as belief, and if (ii) to do so they must in turn be justified by yet other propositional attitudes, it seems clear that (iii) there is no hope of constructing a complete epistemology, one which would give us, in theory, an account of what the justification of any justified belief would supervene on. For (i) and (ii) would rule out the possibility of a finite regress of justification.

c. If only propositional attitudes can justify propositional attitudes, and if to do so they must in turn be justified by yet other propositional attitudes, it seems clear that there is no hope of constructing a complete normative ethics, one which would give us, in theory, an account of what the justification of any possible justified action would supervene upon. For the justification of an action presumably depends on the intentions it embodies and the justification of these, and here we are already within the net of propositional attitudes from which, for the Intellectualist, there is no escape.

It seems fair to conclude that our coherentist takes his antifoundationalist zeal too far. His antifoundationalist argument helps expose some valuable insights but falls short of its malicious intent. The foundationalist emerges showing no serious damage. Indeed, he now demands equal time for a positive brief in defense of his position.

5   The Regress Argument

a. The regress argument in epistemology concludes that we must countenance beliefs that are justified in the absence of justification by other beliefs. But it reaches that conclusion only by rejecting the possibility in principle of an infinite regress of justification. It thus opts for foundational beliefs justified in some non-inferential way by ruling out a chain or pyramid of justification that has justifiers, and justifiers of justifiers, and so on *without end*. One may well find this too short a route to foundationalism, however, and demand more compelling reasons for thus rejecting an infinite regress as vicious. We shall find indeed that it is not easy to meet this demand.

b. We have seen how even the most ordinary of everyday beliefs is the tip of an iceberg. A closer look below the surface reveals a complex structure that ramifies with no end in sight. Take again my belief that driving will be dangerous tonight, at the tip of an iceberg, (I), as presented in Figure 13.2. The immediate cause of my belief that driving will be hazardous tonight is the sound of raindrops on the windowpane. All but one or two members of the underlying iceberg are as far as they can be from my thoughts at the time. In what sense, then, do they form an iceberg whose tip breaks the calm surface of my consciousness?

Here I will assume that the members of (I) are beliefs of the subject, even if unconscious or subconscious, that causally buttress and thus justify his prediction about the driving conditions.

Can the iceberg extend without end? It may appear obvious that it cannot do so, and one may jump to the conclusion that any piece of knowledge must be ultimately founded on beliefs that are *not* (inferentially) justified or warranted by other beliefs. This is a doctrine of *epistemic foundationalism*.

Let us focus not so much on the *giving* of justification as on the *having* of it. *Can* there be a belief that is justified in part by other beliefs, some of which are in turn justified by yet other beliefs, and so on without end? Can there be an endless regress of justification?

c. There are several familiar objections to such a regress:

(i)   *Objection*: "It is incompatible with human limitations. No human subject could harbor the required infinity of beliefs."
      Reply: It is mere presumption to fathom with such assurance the depths of the mind, and especially its unconscious and dispositional depths. Besides, our object here is the nature of epistemic justification in itself and not only that of such justification as is accessible to humans. Our question is not whether humans could harbor an infinite iceberg of justification. Our question is rather whether *any* mind, no matter how deep, could do so. Or is it ruled out *in principle* by the very nature of justification?

(ii) *Objection*: "An infinite regress is indeed ruled out in principle, for if justification were thus infinite how could it possibly end?"
      Reply: (i) If the end mentioned is *temporal*, then why must there be such an end? In the first place, the subject may be eternal. Even if he is not eternal, moreover, why must belief acquisition and justification occur seriatim? What precludes an infinite body of beliefs

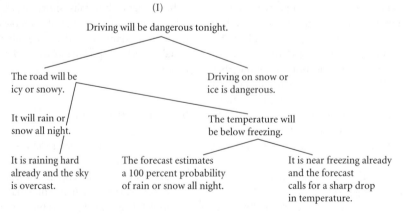

(I)

Driving will be dangerous tonight.

The road will be icy or snowy.

Driving on snow or ice is dangerous.

It will rain or snow all night.

The temperature will be below freezing.

It is raining hard already and the sky is overcast.

The forecast estimates a 100 percent probability of rain or snow all night.

It is near freezing already and the forecast calls for a sharp drop in temperature.

Figure 13.2

acquired at a single stroke? Human limitations may rule this out for humans, but we have yet to be shown that it is precluded in principle, by the very nature of justification. (ii) If the end mentioned is justificatory, on the other hand, then to ask how justification could possibly end is just to beg the question.

(iii) *Objection*: "Let us make two assumptions: first, that S's belief of q justifies his belief of p only if it works together with a justified belief on his part that q provides good evidence for p; and, second, that if S is to be justified in believing p on the basis of his belief of q and is to be justified in believing q on the basis of his belief of r, then S must be justified in believing that r provides good evidence for p via q. These assumptions imply that an actual regress of justification requires belief in an infinite proposition. Since no one (or at least no human) can believe an infinite proposition, no one (no human) can be a subject of such an actual regress."[3]

Reply: Neither of the two assumptions is beyond question, but even granting them both, it may still be doubted that the conclusion follows. It is true that each finitely complex belief of form "r provides good evidence for p via $q_1 \ldots q_n$" will *omit* how some members of the full infinite regress are epistemically tied to belief of p. But that seems irrelevant given the fact that for each member r of the regress, such that r is tied epistemically to belief of p, there *is* a finite belief of the required sort ("r provides good evidence for p via $q_1 \ldots q_n$") that ties the two together. Consequently there is no apparent reason to suppose – even granted the two assumptions – that an infinite regress will require a single belief in an infinite proposition, and not just an infinity of beliefs in increasingly complex finite propositions.

(iv) *Objection*: "But if it is allowed that justification extend infinitely, then it is too easy to justify any belief at all or too many beliefs altogether. Take, for instance, the belief that there are perfect numbers greater than 100. And suppose

a mind powerful enough to believe every member of the following sequence:

(σ1) There is at least one perfect number > 100
There are at least two perfect numbers > 100
There are at least three perfect numbers > 100

If such a believer has no other belief about perfect numbers save the belief that a perfect number is a whole number equal to the sum of its whole factors, then surely he is *not* justified in believing that there are perfect numbers greater than 100. He is quite unjustified in believing any of the members of sequence (σ1), in spite of the fact that a challenge to any can be met easily by appeal to its successor. Thus it cannot be allowed after all that justification extend infinitely, and an infinite regress is ruled out."

Reply: We must distinguish between regresses of justification that are actual and those that are merely potential. The difference is *not* simply that an actual regress is composed of actual beliefs. For even if all members of the regress are actual beliefs, the regress may still be *merely potential* in the following sense: while it is true that *if* any member *were* justified then its predecessors *would* be, still none is in fact justified. Anyone with our series of beliefs about perfect numbers in the absence of any further relevant information on such numbers would presumably be the subject of such a merely potential justificatory regress.

(v) *Objection*: "But defenders of infinite justificatory regresses cannot distinguish thus between actual regresses and those that are merely potential. There is no real distinction to be drawn between the two. For if any regress ever justifies the belief at its head, then every regress must always do so. But obviously not every regress does so (as we have seen by examples), and hence no regress can do so."[4]

Reply: One can in fact distinguish between actual justificatory regresses and merely potential ones, and one can do so both abstractly and by examples.

What an actual regress has that a merely potential regress lacks is the property of containing only justified beliefs as members. What they both share is the property of containing no member without successors that would jointly justify it.

Recall our regress about perfect numbers greater than 100; i.e., there is at least one; there are at least two; there are at least three; and so on. Each member has a successor that would justify it, but no member is justified (in the absence of further information external to the regress). That is therefore a merely potential infinite regress. As for an actual regress, I see no compelling reason why someone (if not a human, then some more powerful mind) could not hold an infinite series of actually justified beliefs as follows:

(σ2)   There is at least one even number
There are at least two even numbers
There are at least three even numbers

It may be that no one could be the subject of such a series of justified beliefs unless he had a proof that there is a denumerable infinity of even numbers. But even if that should be so, it would not take away the fact of the infinite regress of potential justifiers, each of which is actually justified, and hence it would not take away the fact of the actual endless regress of justification.

The objection under discussion is confused, moreover, on the nature of the issue before us. Our question is *not* whether there can be an infinite potential regress, each member of which would be justified by its successors, such that the belief at its head is justified in virtue of its position there, at the head of such a regress. The existence and even the possibility of a single such regress with a belief at its head that was *not* justified in virtue of its position there would of course settle that question in the negative. Our question is,

rather, whether there can be an actual infinite regress of justification, and the fact that a belief at the head of a potential regress might still fail to be justified despite its position does *not* settle this question. For even if there can be a merely potential regress with an unjustified belief at its head, that leaves open the possibility of an infinite regress, each member of which is justified by its immediate successors working jointly, where every member of the regress is in addition actually justified.

6   The Relation of Justification and Foundationalist Strategy

The foregoing discussion is predicated on a simple conception of justification such that a set of beliefs β conditionally justifies (*would* justify) a belief X iff, necessarily, if all members of β are justified then X is also justified (if it exists). The fact that on such a conception of justification actual endless regresses – such as (σ2) – seem quite possible blocks a straightforward regress argument in favor of foundations. For it shows that an actual infinite regress cannot be dismissed out of hand.

Perhaps the foundationalist could introduce some relation of justification – presumably more complex and yet to be explicated – with respect to which it could be argued more plausibly that an actual endless regress is out of the question.

There is, however, a more straightforward strategy open to the foundationalist. For he *need not* object to the possibility of an endless regress of justification. His essential creed is the more positive belief that every justified belief must be at the head of a terminating regress. Fortunately, to affirm the universal necessity of a terminating regress is *not* to deny the bare possibility of a nonterminating regress. For a single belief can trail at once regresses of both sorts: one terminating and one not. Thus the proof of the denumerably infinite cardinality of the set of evens may provide for a powerful enough intellect a *terminating* regress for each member of the *endless* series of justified beliefs:

(σ2)   There is at least one even number
There are at least two even numbers
There are at least three even numbers

At the same time, it is obvious that each member of ($\sigma2$) lies at the head of an actual endless regress of justification, on the assumption that each member is conditionally justified by its successor, which is in turn actually justified.

"Thank you so much," the foundationalist may sneer, "but I really do not need that kind of help. Nor do I need to be reminded of my essential creed, which I know as well as anyone. Indeed my rejection of endless regresses of justification is only a means of supporting my view that every justified belief must rest ultimately on foundations, on a terminating regress. You reject that strategy much too casually, in my view, but I will not object here. So we put that strategy aside. And now, my helpful friend, just what do we put in its place?"

Fair enough. How then could one show the need for foundations if an endless regress is not ruled out?

7 Two Levels of Foundationalism

a. We need to distinguish, first, between two forms of foundationalism: one *formal*, the other *substantive*. A type of *formal foundationalism* with respect to a normative or evaluative property ϕ is the view that the conditions (actual and possible) within which ϕ would apply can be specified in general, perhaps recursively. *Substantive foundationalism* is only a particular way of doing so, and coherentism is another.

Simpleminded hedonism is the view that:

(i)   every instance of pleasure is good,
(ii) everything that causes something good is itself good, and
(iii) everything that is good is so in virtue of (i) or (ii) above.

Simpleminded hedonism is a type of formal foundationalism with respect to the good.

Classical foundationalism in epistemology is the view that:

(i)   every infallible, indubitable belief is justified,
(ii) every belief deductively inferred from justified beliefs is itself justified, and

(iii) every belief that is justified is so in virtue of (i) or (ii) above.

Classical foundationalism is a type of formal foundationalism with respect to epistemic justification.

Both of the foregoing theories – simpleminded hedonism in ethics, and classical foundationalism in epistemology – are of course flawed. But they both remain examples of formal foundationalist theories.

b. One way of arguing in favor of formal foundationalism in epistemology is to formulate a convincing formal foundationalist theory of justification. But classical foundationalism in epistemology no longer has for many the attraction that it had for Descartes, nor has any other form of epistemic foundationalism won general acceptance. Indeed epistemic foundationalism has been generally abandoned, and its advocates have been put on the defensive by the writings of Wittgenstein, Quine, Sellars, Rescher, Aune, Harman, Lehrer, and others. It is lamentable that in our headlong rush away from foundationalism we have lost sight of the different types of foundationalism (formal vs. substantive) and of the different grades of each type. Too many of us now see it as a blur to be decried and avoided. Thus our present attempt to bring it all into better focus.

c. If we cannot argue from a generally accepted foundationalist theory, what reason is there to accept formal foundationalism? There is no reason to think that the conditions (actual and possible) within which an object is spherical are generally specifiable in nongeometric terms. Why should we think that the conditions (actual and possible) within which a belief is epistemically justified are generally specifiable in nonepistemic terms?

So far as I can see, the main reason for accepting formal foundationalism in the absence of an actual, convincing formal foundationalist theory is the very plausible idea that epistemic justification is subject to the supervenience that characterizes normative and evaluative properties generally. Thus, if a car is a good car, then any physical replica of that car must be just as good. If it is a good car in virtue of such properties as being economical, little prone to break down, etc., then surely any exact replica would share all such properties and would thus be equally good. Similarly, if a belief is epistemically justified, it is presumably so in virtue of its character and its basis in perception, memory, or inference (if any). Thus any belief exactly like it in its character and its basis must be equally well justified. Epistemic justification is supervenient. The justification of a belief supervenes on such properties of it as its content and its basis (if any) in perception, memory, or inference. Such a doctrine of supervenience may itself be considered, with considerable justice, a grade of foundationalism. For it entails that every instance of justified belief is founded on a number of its nonepistemic properties, such as its having a certain basis in perception, memory, and inference, or the like.

But there are higher grades of foundationalism as well. There is, for instance, the doctrine that the conditions (actual and possible) within which a belief would be epistemically justified *can be specified* in general, perhaps recursively (and by reference to such notions as perception, memory, and inference).

A higher grade yet of formal foundationalism requires not only that the conditions for justified belief be specifiable, in general, but that they be specifiable by a simple, comprehensive theory.

d. Simpleminded hedonism is a formal foundationalist theory of the highest grade. If it is true, then in every possible world goodness supervenes on pleasure and causation in a way that is recursively specifiable by means of a very simple theory.

Classical foundationalism in epistemology is also a formal foundationalist theory of the highest grade. If it is true, then in every possible world epistemic justification supervenes on infallibility cum indubitability and deductive inference in a way that is recursively specifiable by means of a very simple theory.

Surprisingly enough, coherentism may also turn out to be formal foundationalism of the highest grade, provided only that the concept of coherence is itself both simple enough and free of any normative or evaluative admixture. Given these provisos, coherentism explains how epistemic justification supervenes on the nonepistemic in a theory of remarkable simplicity: a belief is justified if it has a place within a system of beliefs that is coherent and comprehensive.

It is a goal of ethics to explain how the ethical rightness of an action supervenes on what is not ethically evaluative or normative. Similarly, it is a goal of epistemology to explain how the epistemic justification of a belief supervenes on what is not epistemically evaluative or normative. If coherentism aims at this goal, that imposes restrictions on the notion of coherence, which must now be conceived innocent of epistemically evaluative or normative admixture. Its substance must therefore consist of such concepts as explanation, probability, and logical implication – with these conceived, in turn, innocent of normative or evaluative content.

e. We have found a surprising kinship between coherentism and substantive foundationalism, both of which turn out to be varieties of a deeper foundationalism. This deeper foundationalism is applicable to any normative or evaluative property ϕ, and it comes in three grades. The *first* or lowest is simply the supervenience of ϕ: the idea that whenever something has ϕ its having it is founded on certain others of its properties which fall into certain restricted sorts. The *second* is the explicable supervenience of ϕ: the idea that there are formulable principles that explain in quite general terms the conditions (actual and possible) within which ϕ applies. The *third* and highest is the easily explicable supervenience of ϕ: the idea that there is a *simple* theory that explains the conditions within which ϕ applies. We have found the coherentist and the substantive foundationalist sharing a primary goal: the development of a formal foundationalist theory of the highest grade. For they both want a simple theory that explains precisely how epistemic justification supervenes, in general, on the nonepistemic. This insight gives us an unusual viewpoint on some recent attacks against foundationalism. Let us now consider as an example a certain simple form of argument distilled from the recent antifoundationalist literature.[5]

8 Doxastic Ascent Arguments

Several attacks on foundationalism turn on a sort of "doxastic ascent" argument that calls for closer scrutiny.[6] Here are two examples:

A. A belief B is foundationally justified for S in virtue of having property F only if S is justified in believing (1) that most at least of his beliefs with property F are true, and (2) that B has property F. But this means that belief B is not foundational after all, and indeed that the very notion of (empirical) foundational belief is incoherent.

It is sometimes held, for example, that perceptual or observational beliefs are often justified through their origin in the exercise of one or more of our five senses in standard conditions of perception. The advocate of doxastic ascent would raise a vigorous protest, however, for in his view the mere fact of such sensory prompting is impotent to justify the belief prompted. Such prompting must be coupled with the further belief that one's senses work well in the circumstances, or the like. For we are dealing here with *knowledge*, which requires not blind faith but *reasoned* trust. But now surely the further belief about the reliability of one's senses itself cannot rest on blind faith but requires its own backing of reasons, and we are off on the regress.

B. A belief B of proposition P is foundationally justified for S only if S is justified in believing that there are no factors present that would cause him to make mistakes on the matter of the proposition P. But, again, this means that belief B is not foundational after all and indeed that the notion of (empirical) foundational belief is incoherent.

From the vantage point of formal foundationalism, neither of these arguments seems persuasive. In the first place, as we have seen, what makes a belief foundational (formally) is its having a property that is nonepistemic (not evaluative in the epistemic or cognitive mode), and does not involve inference from other beliefs, but guarantees, via a necessary principle, that the belief in question is justified. A belief B is made foundational by having some such nonepistemic property that yields its justification. Take my belief that I am in pain in a context where it is caused by my being in pain. The property that my belief then has, of being a self-attribution of pain caused by one's own pain is, let us suppose, a nonepistemic property that yields the justification of any belief that has it. So my belief that I am in pain is in that context foundationally justified. Along with my belief that I am in pain, however, there come other beliefs that are equally well justified, such as my belief that someone is in pain. Thus I am foundationally justified in believing that I am in pain only if I am justified in believing that someone is in pain. Those who object to foundationalism as in A or B above are hence mistaken in thinking that their premises would refute foundationalism. The fact is that they would not touch it. For a belief is no less foundationally justified for having its justification yoked to that of another closely related belief.

The advocate of arguments like A and B must apparently strengthen his premises. He must apparently claim that the beliefs whose justification is entailed by the foundationally justified status of belief B must in some sense function as a *necessary source* of the justification of B. And this would of course preclude giving B foundationally justified status. For if the *being justified* of those beliefs is an *essential* part of the source of the justification of B, then it is ruled out that there be a wholly *non-epistemic* source of B's justification.

That brings us to a second point about A and B, for it should now be clear that these cannot be selectively aimed at foundationalism. In particular, they seem neither more nor less valid objections to coherentism than to foundationalism, or so I will now argue about each of them in turn.

A′. A belief X is justified for S in virtue of membership in a coherent set only if S is justified in believing (1) that most at least of his beliefs with the property of thus cohering are true, and (2) that X has that property.

Any coherentist who accepts A seems bound to accept A′. For what could he possibly appeal to as a relevant difference? But A′ is a quicksand of endless depth. (How is he justified in believing A′ (1)?

Partly through justified belief that *it* coheres? And what would justify *this*? And so on...)

B′. A belief X is justified for S only if S is justified in believing that there are no factors present that would cause him to make mistakes on the subject matter of that belief.

Again, any coherentist who accepts B seems bound to accept B′. But this is just another road to the quicksand. (For S is justified in believing that there are no such factors only if... and so on.)

Why are such regresses vicious? The key is again, to my mind, the doctrine of supervenience. Such regresses are vicious because they would be logically incompatible with the supervenience of epistemic justification on such nonepistemic facts as the totality of a subject's beliefs, his cognitive and experiential history, and as many other nonepistemic facts as may seem at all relevant. The idea is that there is a set of such nonepistemic facts surrounding a justified belief such that no belief could possibly have been surrounded by those very facts without being justified. Advocates of A or B run afoul of such supervenience, since they are surely committed to the more general views derivable from either A or B by deleting "foundationally" from its first sentence. In each case the more general view would then preclude the possibility of supervenience, since it would entail that the source of justification *always* includes an *epistemic* component.

9 Coherentism and Substantive Foundationalism

a. The notions of coherentism and substantive foundationalism remain unexplicated. We have relied so far on our intuitive grasp of them. In this section we shall consider reasons for the view that substantive foundationalism is superior to coherentism. To assess these reasons, we need some more explicit account of the difference between the two.

By coherentism we shall mean any view according to which the ultimate sources of justification for any belief lie in relations among that belief and other beliefs of the subject: explanatory relations, perhaps, or relations of probability or logic.

According to substantive foundationalism, as it is to be understood here, there are ultimate sources of justification other than relations among beliefs. Traditionally these additional sources have pertained to the special content of the belief or its special relations to the subjective experience of the believer.

b. The view that justification is a matter of relations among beliefs is open to an objection from alternative coherent systems or detachment from reality, depending on one's perspective. From the latter perspective the body of beliefs is held constant and the surrounding world is allowed to vary, whereas from the former perspective it is the surrounding world that is held constant while the body of beliefs is allowed to vary. In either case, according to the coherentist, there could be no effect on the justification for any belief.

Let us sharpen the question before us as follows. Is there reason to think that there is at least one system B′, alternative to our actual system of beliefs B, such that B′ contains a belief X with the following properties:

(i)   in our present nonbelief circumstances we would not be justified in having belief X even if we accepted along with that belief (as our total system of beliefs) the entire belief system B′ in which it is embedded (no matter how acceptance of B′ were brought about); and

(ii) that is so despite the fact that belief X coheres within B′ at least as fully as does some actual justified belief of ours within our actual belief system B (where the justification of that actual justified belief is alleged by the coherentist to derive solely from its coherence within our actual body of beliefs B).

The coherentist is vulnerable to counterexamples of this sort right at the surface of his body of beliefs, where we find beliefs with minimal coherence, whose detachment and replacement with contrary beliefs would have little effect on the coherence of the body. Thus take my belief that I have a headache when I do have a splitting headache, and let us suppose that this *does* cohere within my present body of beliefs. (Thus I have no reason to doubt my present introspective beliefs, and so on. And if my belief does *not* cohere, so much the worse for coherentism, since my belief is surely justified.) Here then we have a perfectly justified or warranted belief. And yet such a belief may well have relevant relations of explanation, logic, or probability with at most a small set of other beliefs of mine at the time: say, that I am not free of headache, that I am in pain, that someone is in pain, and the like. If so, then an equally coherent alternative is not far to seek. Let everything remain constant, *including* the splitting headache, except for the following: replace the belief that I have a headache with the belief that I do *not* have a headache, the belief that I am in pain with the belief that I am *not* in pain, the belief that someone is in pain with the belief that someone is *not* in pain, and so on. I contend that my resulting hypothetical system of beliefs would cohere as fully as does my actual system of beliefs, and yet my hypothetical belief that I do *not* have a headache would not therefore be justified. What makes this difference concerning justification between my actual belief that I have a headache and the hypothetical belief that I am free of headache, each as coherent as the other within its own system, if not the actual splitting headache? But the headache is *not* itself a belief nor a relation among beliefs and is thus in no way constitutive of the internal coherence of my body of beliefs.

Some might be tempted to respond by alleging that one's belief about whether or not one has a headache is always *infallible*. But since we could devise similar examples for the various sensory modalities and propositional attitudes, the response given for the case of headache would have to be generalized. In effect, it would have to cover "peripheral" beliefs generally – beliefs at the periphery of one's body of beliefs, minimally coherent with the rest. These peripheral beliefs would all be said to be infallible. That is, again, a possible response, but it leads to a capitulation by the coherentist to the radical foundationalist on a crucial issue that has traditionally divided them: the infallibility of beliefs about one's own subjective states.

What is more, not all peripheral beliefs are about one's own subjective states. The direct realist is probably right that some beliefs about our surroundings are uninferred and yet justified. Consider my present belief that the table before me is oblong. This presumably coheres with such

other beliefs of mine as that the table has the same shape as the piece of paper before me, which is oblong, and a different shape than the window frame here, which is square, and so on. So far as I can see, however, there is no insurmountable obstacle to replacing that whole set of coherent beliefs with an equally coherent set as follows: that the table before me is square, that the table has the same shape as the square window frame, and a different shape than the piece of paper, which is oblong, and so on. The important points are (a) that this replacement may be made without changing the rest of one's body of beliefs or any aspect of the world beyond, including one's present visual experience of something oblong, not square, as one looks at the table before one; and (b) that it is so, in part, because of the fact (c) that the subject need not have any beliefs about his present sensory experience.

Some might be tempted to respond by alleging that one's present experience is *self-intimating*, i.e., always necessarily taken note of and reflected in one's beliefs. Thus if anyone has visual experience of something oblong, then he believes that he has such experience. But this would involve a further important concession by the coherentist to the radical foundationalist, who would have been granted two of his most cherished doctrines: the infallibility of introspective belief and the self-intimation of experience.

10   The Foundationalist's Dilemma

The antifoundationalist zeal of recent years has left several forms of foundationalism standing. These all share the conviction that a belief can be justified not only by its coherence within a comprehensive system but also by an appropriate combination of observational content and origin in the use of the senses in standard conditions. What follows presents a dilemma for any foundationalism based on any such idea.

a.   We may surely suppose that beings with observational mechanisms radically unlike ours might also have knowledge of their environment. (That seems possible even if the radical difference in observational mechanisms precludes overlap in substantive concepts and beliefs.)

Table 13.1

Human	Extraterrestrial being
Visual experience	ϕ experience
Experience of something red	Experience of something F
Belief that there is something red before one	Belief that there is something F before one

b. Let us suppose that there is such a being, for whom experience of type ϕ (of which we have no notion) has a role with respect to his beliefs of type ϕ analogous to the role that our visual experience has with respect to our visual beliefs. Thus we might have a schema such as that in Table 13.1.

c. It is often recognized that our visual experience intervenes in two ways with respect to our visual beliefs: as cause and as justification. But these are not wholly independent. Presumably, the justification of the belief that something here is red derives at least in part from the fact that it originates in a visual experience of something red that takes place in normal circumstances.

d. Analogously, the extraterrestrial belief that something here has the property of being F might be justified partly by the fact that it originates in a ϕ experience of something F that takes place in normal circumstances.

e. A simple question presents the foundationalist's dilemma: regarding the epistemic principle that underlies our justification for believing that something here is red on the basis of our visual experience of something red, is it proposed as a fundamental principle or as a derived generalization? Let us compare the famous Principle of Utility of value theory, according to which it is best for that to happen which, of all the possible alternatives in the circumstances, would bring with it into the world the greatest balance of pleasure over pain, joy over sorrow, happiness over unhappiness, content over discontent, or the like. Upon this fundamental principle

one may then base various generalizations, rules of thumb, and maxims of public health, nutrition, legislation, etiquette, hygiene, and so on. But these are all then derived generalizations which rest for their validity on the fundamental principle. Similarly, one may also ask, with respect to the generalizations advanced by our foundationalist, whether these are proposed as fundamental principles or as derived maxims or the like. This sets him face to face with a dilemma, each of whose alternatives is problematic. If his proposals are meant to have the status of secondary or derived maxims, for instance, then it would be quite unphilosophical to stop there. Let us turn, therefore, to the other alternative.

f. On reflection it seems rather unlikely that epistemic principles for the justification of observational beliefs by their origin in sensory experience could have a status more fundamental than that of derived generalizations. For by granting such principles fundamental status we would open the door to a multitude of equally basic principles with no unifying factor. There would be some for vision, some for hearing, etc., without even mentioning the corresponding extraterrestrial principles.

g. It may appear that there is after all an idea, however, that unifies our multitude of principles. For they all involve sensory experience and sensible characteristics. But what is a sensible characteristic? Aristotle's answer appeals to examples: colors, shapes, sounds, and so on. Such a notion might enable us to unify perceptual epistemic principles under some more fundamental principle such as the following.

If σ is a sensible characteristic, then the belief that there is something with σ before one is (prima facie) justified if it is based on a visual experience of something with σ in conditions that are normal with respect to σ.

h. There are at least two difficulties with such a suggestion, however, and neither one can be brushed aside easily. First, it is not clear that we can have a viable notion of sensible characteristics on the basis of examples so diverse as colors, shapes, tones, odors, and so on. Second, the authority of such a principle apparently derives from contingent circumstances concerning the reliability of beliefs prompted by sensory experiences of certain sorts. According to the foundationalist, our visual beliefs are justified by their origin in our visual experience or the like. Would such beliefs be equally well justified in a world where beliefs with such an origin were nearly always false?

i. In addition, finally, even if we had a viable notion of such characteristics, it is not obvious that fundamental knowledge of reality would have to derive causally or otherwise from sensory experience of such characteristics. How could one impose reasonable limits on extraterrestrial mechanisms for noninferential acquisition of beliefs? Is it not possible that such mechanisms need not always function through sensory experience of any sort? Would such beings necessarily be denied any knowledge of the surroundings and indeed of any contingent spatiotemporal fact? Let us suppose them to possess a complex system of true beliefs concerning their surroundings, the structures below the surface of things, exact details of history and geography, all constituted by concepts none of which corresponds to any of our sensible characteristics. What then? Is it not possible that their basic beliefs should all concern fields of force, waves, mathematical structures, and numerical assignments to variables in several dimensions? This is no doubt an exotic notion, but even so it still seems conceivable. And if it is in fact possible, what then shall we say of the noninferential beliefs of such beings? Would we have to concede the existence of special epistemic principles that can validate their noninferential beliefs? Would it not be preferable to formulate more abstract principles that can cover both human and extraterrestrial foundations? If such more abstract principles are in fact accessible, then the less general principles that define the human foundations and those that define the extraterrestrial foundations are both derived principles whose validity depends on that of the more abstract principles. In this the human and extraterrestrial epistemic principles would resemble rules of good nutrition for an infant and an adult. The infant's rules would of course be quite unlike those valid for the adult. But both would still be based on a more fundamental principle that postulates the ends of well-being and good health. What more fundamental principles might support both human and extraterrestrial knowledge in the way that those concerning good health and well-being support rules of nutrition for both the infant and adult?

11 Reliabilism: An Ethics of Moral Virtues and an Epistemology of Intellectual Virtues

In what sense is the doctor attending Frau Hitler justified in performing an action that brings with it far less value than one of its accessible alternatives? According to one promising idea, the key is to be found in the rules that he embodies through stable dispositions. His action is the result of certain stable virtues, and there are no equally virtuous alternative *dispositions* that, given his cognitive limitations, he might have embodied with equal or better total consequences, and that would have led him to infanticide in the circumstances. The important move for our purpose is the stratification of justification. Primary justification attaches to virtues and other dispositions, to stable dispositions to act, through their greater contribution of value when compared with alternatives. Secondary justification attaches to particular acts in virtue of their source in virtues or other such justified dispositions.

The same strategy may also prove fruitful in epistemology. Here primary justification would apply to *intellectual* virtues, to stable dispositions for belief acquisition, through their greater contribution toward getting us to the truth. Secondary justification would then attach to particular beliefs in virtue of their source in intellectual virtues or other such justified dispositions.[7]

That raises parallel questions for ethics and epistemology. We need to consider more carefully the concept of a virtue and the distinction between moral and intellectual virtues. In epistemology, there is reason to think that the most useful and illuminating notion of intellectual virtue will prove broader than our tradition would suggest and must give due weight not only to the subject and his intrinsic nature but also to his environment and to his epistemic community. This is a large topic, however, to which I hope some of us will turn with more space, and insight, than I can now command.

Summary

1. *Two assumptions*: (A1) that for a belief to constitute knowledge it must be (a) true and (b) justified; and (A2) that the justification relevant to whether or not one knows is a sort of epistemic or theoretical justification to be distinguished from its practical counterpart.

2. *Knowledge and criteria.* Particularism is distinguished from methodism: the first gives priority to particular examples of knowledge over general methods or criteria, whereas the second reverses that order. The methodism of Descartes leads him to an elaborate dogmatism whereas that of Hume leads him to a very simple skepticism. The particularist is, of course, antiskeptical on principle.

3. *Two metaphors: the raft and the pyramid.* For the foundationalist every piece of knowledge stands at the apex of a pyramid that rests on stable and secure foundations whose stability and security do not derive from the upper stories or sections. For the coherentist a body of knowledge is a free-floating raft every plank of which helps directly or indirectly to keep all the others in place, and no plank of which would retain its status with no help from the others.

4. *A coherentist critique of foundationalism.* No mental state can provide a foundation for empirical knowledge. For if such a state is propositional, then it is fallible and hence no secure foundation. But if it is *not* propositional, then how can it possibly serve as a foundation for belief? How can one infer or justify anything on the basis of a state that, having no propositional content, must be logically dumb? An analogy with ethics suggests a reason to reject this dilemma. Other reasons are also advanced and discussed.

5. *The regress argument.* In defending his position, the foundationalist often attempts to rule out the very possibility of an infinite regress of justification (which leads him to the necessity for a foundation). Some of his arguments to that end are examined.

6. *The relation of justification and foundationalist strategy.* An alternative foundationalist strategy is exposed, one that does not require ruling out the possibility of an infinite regress of justification.

7. *Two levels of foundationalism.* Substantive foundationalism is distinguished from formal foundationalism, three grades of which are exposed: first, the supervenience of epistemic justification; second, its explicable supervenience; and, third, its supervenience explicable by means of a simple theory. There turns out to be a surprising kinship between coherentism and substantive foundationalism, both of which aim at a formal foundationalism of the highest grade, at a theory of the greatest simplicity that explains how epistemic justification supervenes on nonepistemic factors.

8. *Doxastic ascent arguments.* The distinction between formal and substantive foundationalism provides an unusual viewpoint on some recent attacks against foundationalism. We consider doxastic ascent arguments as an example.

9. *Coherentism and substantive foundationalism.* It is argued that substantive foundationalism is superior, since coherentism is unable to account adequately for the epistemic status of beliefs at the "periphery" of a body of beliefs.

10. *The foundationalist's dilemma.* All foundationalism based on sense experience is subject to a fatal dilemma.

11. *Reliabilism.* An alternative to foundationalism of sense experience is sketched.

Appendix[8]

What one is rationally justified in believing obviously depends on the data in one's possession. But what data one has can depend on how much and how well one investigates. Consider, therefore, the following possibility. What if A is rationally justified in believing x given his body of data D_1 whereas B is not rationally justified in believing x given his body of data D_2, where D_2 includes D_1 but is much more extensive as a result of A's irresponsible negligence and B's commendable thoroughness? The present account might unfortunately grant A knowledge while denying it to B, for A's neglect so far has no bearing on any epistemic pyramid.

We have considered a situation where someone lacks knowledge owing to his misuse of his cognitive equipment, either by letting it idle when it should be functioning or by busily employing it dysfunctionally. Another situation where someone lacks knowledge despite having rationally justified correct belief might be called the Magoo situation – where S lacks adequate equipment to begin with (relative to the question in hand: whether p).[9] It is because of this type of lack that despite his extensive experience with cable cars, Mr Magoo does not know that his cable car will arrive safely when, unknown to him, bombs are raining all around it. Of course, even if you have less than 20–20 vision you can still know that there is an elephant in front of you when you see one there. So not just any defect will make your equipment inadequate for a judgment on the question whether p. I would venture that it must be a defect that prevents you from acquiring information that (i) a normal inquirer in the epistemic community would acquire in that situation *and* (ii) makes a difference to what you can reasonably conclude on the question whether p (or at least to how reasonably you can draw the conclusion).

The possibility of inadequate cognitive equipment requires a further and more striking departure from the traditional conception of knowledge. Despite having warranted correct belief, someone may lack knowledge owing to his neglectful data-collection. There lack of knowledge could be traced back to epistemic irresponsibility, to substandard performance

blamed on the investigator. In the present example, blame is out of place. By hypothesis, Magoo conducts impeccable "inquiry" both in arriving at his data and on the basis of his data. But he still falls short of knowledge, despite his warranted, correct belief. His shortcoming is substandard equipment, for which we may suppose him to be blameless. Hence something other than epistemic justification or correct belief can help determine what one knows or does not know. Even if one correctly believes that p with full rational justification and free of irrational or neglectful unbelief, one may still be in no position to know, because of faulty cognitive equipment.

In all of the foregoing cases, someone misses or is liable to miss available information which may be highly relevant and important and may make a difference to what he can conclude on the question in hand. In each case, moreover, he seems culpable or discredited in some sense: he would seem less reliable than otherwise for his role in any such case. But there appear to be situations where again someone misses available information with no culpability *or* discredit. Harman gives an example where S reads in a newspaper that some famous person has been assassinated, but does not read the next edition, where all reports of the assassination are denied by highly authoritative and trustworthy people. If practically the whole country reads the next edition and people don't know what to believe, does S alone know of the assassination, provided the next edition is in fact a pack of lies?[10] I suppose we would be inclined to say that he does not know (especially if had he read the next edition, *he* would not have known what to believe). But what if only two or three people get a chance to read the next edition before it is recalled by the newspaper? Should we now say that out of millions who read the first story and mourn the loved leader not one knows of his death? I suppose we would be inclined to say that the fake edition and the few deceived by it make no difference concerning what everybody else knows. It seems plausible to conclude that knowledge has a further "social aspect," that it cannot depend on one's missing or blinking what is generally known.

Our departures from the traditional conception of knowledge put in relief the relativity of knowledge to an epistemic community. This is brought out most prominently by the requirement that inquirers have at least *normal* cognitive equipment (e.g., normal perceptual apparatus, where that is relevant). But our new requirement – that inquirers not lack or blink generally known relevant information – also brings out the relativity. A vacationer in the woods may know that *p* well enough for an average vacationer, but he won't have the kind of knowledge his guide has. A guide would scornfully deny that the tenderfoot really knows that *p*. Relative to the epistemic community of guides (for that area) the tenderfoot lacks relevant generally known information, and misses relevant data that the average guide would grasp in the circumstances.

These departures from the traditional account may make better sense if we reflect that the honorific term "knowledgeable" is to be applied only to those who are reliable sources of information, surely an important category for a language-using, social species.

We have now taken note of two types of situation where correct, fully warranted belief falls short of knowledge owing to no neglect or faulty reasoning or false belief. Despite commendable thoroughness and impeccable reasoning unspoiled by falsehood, one may still fail to be "in a position to know," owing either to faulty cognitive equipment or to missed generally known information. I am not suggesting that these are the only ways to be out of position to know. I have no complete list of epistemic principles describing ways of arriving at a position to know or of being blocked from such a position. My suggestion is only that there are such principles, and that in any case we must go beyond the traditional emphasis by epistemologists on warrant and reasoning as determinants of knowledge. Despite the importance of warranted correct belief in determining what we know, the Gettier examples show that it is not alone enough to guarantee knowledge. What is more, warranted correct belief supported by reasoning *unspoiled by falsehood* seems immune to Gettier examples, but it still falls short of knowledge, as we have seen.

My conclusion is that to understand knowledge we must enrich our traditional repertoire of epistemic concepts with the notion of *being in a position to know (from the point of view of a K, e.g., a human being)*. Thus a proposition is evident (from the point of view of a *K*) to a subject only if *both* he is rationally justified in believing it *and* he is in a position to know (from the *K* point of view) whether it is true. It may *be* (and not just appear) evident to Magoo from *his* point of view that he will reach the other side safely, but it seems wrong to say of Magoo as he steps into the cable car with bombs raining all around that it *is* quite evident to him that he will arrive safely. It seems wrong *for whom* to say this? For one of us, naturally; that is, for a normal human from *his* point of view. And since a normal human could not help seeing and hearing the bombs, from the human point of view Magoo is not in a position to know that he will arrive safely, inasmuch as he is missing relevant information that a normal human would gather in the circumstances. Hence Magoo does not have *human* knowledge that he will arrive safely, for it is not evident to him from the human point of view that he will so arrive.

Consider this account:
(A) S knows that *p* iff
    (a)   it is true that *p*;
    (b)   S believes that *p*; and
    (c)   there is a non-defective epistemic pyramid for S and the proposition that *p*.

Every node of such a pyramid must be true *and* evident. And for every node *n* that has successors, the successors must serve as grounds that give the subject S rational warrant for believing *n*. What now seems too narrow about this account emerges with the explanation of what a pyramid of knowledge is, and of what the evident is. For in this explanation what is evident to S is identified with what S is rationally justified in believing. But it now seems plain that for *x* to be evident to S, *two* conditions must be satisfied: (i) that S be rationally justified in believing *x*, and (ii) that S be in a position to know whether *x* is true. And we must also take note of the relativity of knowledge to an epistemic community. Let us therefore replace (A) with the following:

(B) S knows (from the *K* point of view) that *p* iff
    (a)   it is true that *p*;
    (b)   S believes that *p*; and
    (c)   there is a non-defective epistemic pyramid (from the *K* point of view) for S and the proposition that *p*.

Every node of such a pyramid must now be true and evident from the *K* point of view.

Normally when epistemologists discuss knowledge (of the colors and shapes of surrounding objects, of one's own or one's neighbor's mental states, and so on), they plainly do so from the *human* point of view. But other points of view are possible even in ordinary conversation. The expert/layman distinction is replicable in many different contexts, and with each replication we have a new epistemically relevant distinction in points of view, with expert knowledge on one side and layman knowledge on the other.

Neither Magoo nor the newspaper reader who alone has not seen the new edition is in a position to know (from the human point of view) about the relevant subject matter. Thus we can understand their ignorance and, by parity of reasoning, the ignorance of all those who are out of position to know that *p* because they lack either adequate cognitive equipment or relevant information that is generally known to those who have taken an epistemic stand on the question whether *p* (where to suspend judgment *is* to take an epistemic stand, whereas to be totally oblivious to the matter is not).

What it is for S's belief that *p* to be fully grounded has been explained by means of our epistemic pyramids. That answer points in the right direction, but it can be made more precise: e.g., by clarifying the grounding relation. Moreover, we have found that a fully grounded correct belief is not necessarily knowledge, and this for at least two reasons: (i) it may rest directly or indirectly on some false ground, and (ii) the believer may not be in a position to know.

We have tried to allow for these possibilities by broadening epistemic pyramids, by making room for our new epistemic notion of being-in-a-position-to-know, and by noting that to support knowledge epistemic pyramids must be non-defective, i.e., must contain no false nodes. But pyramids are objectionable for other reasons as well: (i) they may mislead by suggesting that terminal nodes provide a "foundation" in one or another undesirable sense, or by suggesting that terminal nodes must come first in time, so that one may later build on them; (ii) more seriously, there is an unacceptable vagueness in the very idea of such a pyramid, which derives mainly from the vagueness of the "grounding" relation in

terms of which pyramids were defined. What follows is an attempt to solve these problems by switching pyramids upside down into trees.

Let us emphasize, however, that this will not commit one to a picture of knowledge according to which there is a bedrock of self-evident propositions. It is perfectly consistent with the present theory that part of what makes *any* proposition evident is its coherence with a network of mutually supporting propositions. Since there is bound to be a multitude of such coherent networks, however, a non-arbitrary narrowing of the field must be supported by something other than coherence.

We turn finally to an account (C) according to which S knows that *p* provided that both (a) S correctly believes that *p*,[11] and (b) there is a set of propositions that fully and non-defectively renders it evident to S that *p* (where a set "non-defectively renders it evident to S that *p*" if and only if it does so without attributing to S any false belief).[12]

Supposing this account correct, every bit of knowledge has a tree like that shown in Figure 13.3. Note that each node of such a tree is a proposition. Thus the "root" node is the-proposition-that-p_1, and the first terminal node (from the left) the- proposition-that-p_{111}.[13]

There is an important difference between these trees and our earlier pyramids. Except for terminal nodes, every node of a tree is an epistemic proposition, whereas not a single node of a pyramid need be epistemic at all. Pyramids display propositions that are evident to A (*not* propositions that such and such other propositions are evident to S), and they also show which propositions ground (for S) any proposition for which S has grounds. Trees display true epistemic propositions concerning S and they also show what "makes these propositions true" *via* epistemic principles. A tree must do this for *every* epistemic proposition that constitutes one of its nodes. That is to say, trees contain no epistemic terminal nodes. It is in this sense that trees provide *complete* epistemic explanations of the truth of their root nodes.

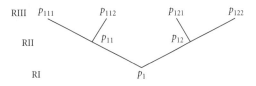

Figure 13.3

Notes

1 But Descartes's methodism was at most partial. James Van Cleve has supplied the materials for a convincing argument that the way
out of the Cartesian circle is through a particularism of basic knowledge. See James
Van Cleve, "Foundationalism, Epistemic
Principles, and the Cartesian Circle," *The
Philosophical Review* 88 (1979), pp. 55–91 and
E. Sosa and J. Kim (eds), *Epistemology: An
Anthology* (Malden, MA; Oxford: Blackwell,
2000), pp. 242–60. But this is, of course, compatible with methodism on inferred knowledge. Whether Descartes subscribed to such
methodism is hard (perhaps impossible) to
determine, since in the end he makes room
for all the kinds of knowledge required by
particularism. But his language when he
introduces the method of hyperbolic doubt,
and the order in which he proceeds, suggest
that he did subscribe to such methodism.

2 Cf. Laurence BonJour, "The Coherence Theory
of Empirical Knowledge," *Philosophical Studies*
30, pp. 281–312, and, especially, Michael
Williams, *Groundless Belief* (Oxford: Blackwell,
1977); and Bonjour, "Can Empirical Knowledge
Have a Foundation?," this vol., ch. 10.

3 Cf. Richard Foley, "Inferential Justification
and the Infinite Regress," *American
Philosophical Quarterly* 15 (1978), pp. 311–16.

4 Cf. John Post, "Infinite Regresses of
Justification and of Explanation," *Philosophical
Studies* 34 (1980).

5 The argument of this whole section is developed in greater detail in my paper "The
Foundations of Foundationalism," *Nous* 14,
pp. 547–65.

6 For some examples of the influence of doxastic ascent arguments, see Wilfrid Sellars's
writing in epistemology: "Empiricism and the
Philosophy of Mind," in *Science, Perception
and Reality* (London: Routledge and Kegan
Paul, 1963), esp. section VIII, and particularly
p. 168. Also I. T. Oakley, "An Argument for
Skepticism Concerning Justified Belief,"
American Philosophical Quarterly 13 (1976),
pp. 221–8; and BonJour, "Can Empirical
Knowledge Have a Foundation?."

7 This puts in a more traditional perspective
the contemporary effort to develop a "causal
theory of knowing." From our viewpoint,
this effort is better understood not as an
attempt to *define* propositional knowledge,
but as an attempt to formulate fundamental
principles of justification.

Cf. the work of D. Armstrong, *Belief, Truth
and Knowledge* (Cambridge: Cambridge
University Press, 1973), and that of F. Dretske,
A. Goldman, and M. Swain, whose relevant
already published work is included in
G. Pappas and M. Swain (eds), *Essays on
Knowledge and Justification* (Ithaca and
London, 1978). But the theory is still under
development by Goldman and by Swain,
who have reached general conclusions about
it similar to those suggested here, though not
necessarily – so far as I know – for the same
reasons or in the same overall context.

8 From "How Do You Know?" *American
Philosophical Quarterly* 11, 2 (1974),
pp. 113–22.

9 The Magoo situation is the situation of that
unfortunate nearsighted and hearing-
impaired cartoon character who fortunately
escapes disaster at every turn.

10 Gilbert Harman, "Induction," in Marshall
Swain (ed.), *Induction, Acceptance and
Rational Belief* (Dordrecht: Reidel, 1970),
esp. Sect. IV, pp. 95–7.

11 Whether knowledge entails belief at all is of
course a vexed question of long standing,
but there is no room for it here. A helpful
and interesting discussion is found in Keith
Lehrer's "Belief and Knowledge,"
Philosophical Review 77 (1968), pp. 491–9.

12 In what follows, the relativity of knowledge
to an epistemic community is left implicit, as
it normally is in ordinary thought and
speech.

13 Strictly speaking, what we have here is obviously a *partial tree schema*. For convenience,
however, I speak of trees even when I mean
partial tree schemata. Also, it should not be
thought that every tree must have exactly
three ranks (RI, RII, and RIII). On the contrary, a tree may have any number of ranks,
so long as it has more than one.

CHAPTER 14

Human Knowledge and the Infinite Regress of Reasons

Peter D. Klein

Introduction

The purpose of this paper is to ask you to consider an account of justification that has largely been ignored in epistemology. When it has been considered, it has usually been dismissed as so obviously wrong that arguments against it are not necessary. The view that I ask you to consider can be called "Infinitism."[1] Its central thesis is that the structure of justificatory reasons is infinite and non-repeating. My primary reason for recommending infinitism is that it can provide an acceptable account of *rational beliefs*, i.e., beliefs held on the basis of adequate reasons, while the two alternative views, foundationalism and coherentism, cannot provide such an account.

Typically, just the opposite viewpoint is expressed. Infinitism is usually mentioned as one of the logically possible forms that our reasoning can take; but it is dismissed without careful consideration because it appears initially to be so implausible.[2] Foundationalists often begin by somewhat cavalierly rejecting infinitism. Then they proceed by eliminating coherentism through a series of complex and carefully developed arguments. Coherentists often follow a similar general strategy by first rejecting infinitism without any careful examination of the view and then they

provide well considered reasons for rejecting foundationalism. Of course, if there are no convincing reasons for rejecting infinitism, then these typical defenses of foundationalism and of coherentism fail.

I will not rehearse the many arguments against foundationalism or coherentism in any detail here. But very briefly, foundationalism is unacceptable because it advocates accepting an arbitrary reason at the base, that is, a reason for which there are no further reasons making it even slightly better to accept than any of its contraries. Traditional coherentism is unacceptable because it advocates a not too thinly disguised form of begging the question; and seemingly more plausible forms of coherentism are just foundationalism in disguise.

Thus, if having rational beliefs is a necessary condition of some type of knowledge, both foundationalism and coherentism lead directly to the consequence that this type of knowledge is not possible because each view precludes the possibility of having beliefs based upon adequate reasons. On the other hand, infinitism makes such knowledge at least possible because it advocates a structure of justificatory reasons that satisfies the requirements of rational belief possession.

This paper has two main sections. In the first section I sketch infinitism in broad outline and argue that it is the only account of the structure of reasons that can satisfy two intuitively plausible

Originally published in *Philosophical Perspectives* 13, Epistemology (1999), pp. 297–325.

constraints on good reasoning. In the second section I defend infinitism against the best objections to it.

I. A Sketch of Infinitism

Let me begin by pointing out some important similarities and dissimilarities between infinitism and the two alternative accounts of justification. Infinitism is *like* most forms of *traditional coherentism* in holding that only reasons can justify a belief.[3] Infinitism is *unlike* traditional coherentism because infinitism does not endorse question begging reasoning.[4] Indeed, this can be captured in what can be called the "Principle of Avoiding Circularity" (PAC).

> PAC: For all x, if a person, S, has a justification for x, then for all y, if y is in the evidential ancestry of x for S, then x is not in the evidential ancestry of y for S.

By "evidential ancestry" I am referring to the links in the chains of reasons, sometimes branching, that support beliefs.[5] For example, if r is a reason for p, and q is a reason for r, then r is in the evidential ancestry of p, and q is in the evidential ancestry of both p and r.[6] I will not defend PAC in this paper because it strikes me as an obvious presupposition of good reasoning. It is intended merely to make explicit the intuition behind the prohibition of circular reasoning.

Not all so-called "coherentists" would deny PAC. These "coherentists" are really closet foundationalists because it is not the propositions within a set of coherent propositions that serve as reasons for other beliefs in the set; rather *the* reason for every belief in the set is simply that it is a member of such a set.[7] Thus, these non-traditional coherentists avoid question begging reasoning by a two stage procedure. First, they define what it means for a set of propositions to be coherent (perhaps mutual probability enhancements plus some other conditions) and, then, they claim that the reason for accepting each proposition in the set is that it is a member of such a set of beliefs. That is consistent with endorsing PAC. But as we will see, this type of coherentism, like foundationalism, can offer no hope of blocking the regress of reasons.

Infinitism is *like* foundationalism in holding that there are features of the world, perhaps nonnormative features, that make a belief a reason. Not just any old belief is a reason. Infinitism is *unlike* foundationalism because infinitism holds that there are no ultimate, foundational reasons. *Every* reason stands in need of another reason. This can be stated in a principle – the Principle of Avoiding Arbitrariness (PAA).

> PAA: For all x, if a person, S, has a justification for x, then there is some reason, r_1, available to S for x; and there is some reason, r_2, available to S for r_1; etc.

Note that there are two features of this principle. The first is that it is reasons (as opposed to something else like appropriate causal conditions responsible for a belief) that are required whenever there is a justification for a belief. The second is that the chain of reasons cannot end with an arbitrary reason – one for which there is no further reason. I conjoin these features in one principle because both are needed to capture the well-founded intuition that *arbitrary beliefs*, beliefs for which no reason is available, should be avoided. I will consider some objections to both aspects of PAA shortly.

Some foundationalists could accept PAA by claiming that the available reason, r, could just be x, itself. They could assert that some propositions are "self-justified." That is not ruled out by PAA; but coupled with PAC, that possibility is ruled out. Indeed, the combination of PAC and PAA entails that the evidential ancestry of a justified belief be infinite and non-repeating. Thus, someone wishing to avoid infinitism must reject either PAC or PAA (or both).[8] *It is the straight-forward intuitive appeal of these principles that is the best reason for thinking that if any beliefs are justified, the structure of reasons must be infinite and non-repeating.*

PAA requires that the reason for a belief must be *available* to S. "Availability" is a key notion in my account of infinitism for, among other things, it has the potential for anchoring justification, as understood by the infinitist, in non-normative properties.[9] So, it would be well for us to dwell a bit on that notion.

There are two conditions that must be satisfied in order for a reason to be available to S.

It must be both "objectively" and "subjectively" available. I will discuss each condition in turn.

There are many accounts of objective availability. Each specifies either some normative or non-normative property or, perhaps, a mixed property that is sufficient to convert a belief into a reason.[10] For example, one could say that a belief, r, is objectively available to S as a reason for p if (1) r has some sufficiently high probability and the conditional probability of p given r is sufficiently high; or (2) an impartial, informed observer would accept r as a reason for p; or (3) r would be accepted in the long run by an appropriately defined set of people; or (4) r is evident for S and r makes p evident for S[11]; or (5) r accords with S's deepest epistemic commitments[12]; or (6) r meets the appropriate conversational presuppositions[13]; or (7) an intellectually virtuous person would advance r as a reason for p.[14]

Infinitism, per se, is compatible with each of these depictions of objectively available reasons.[15] In addition, whether any of these mentioned accounts proves ultimately acceptable or whether another, unmentioned account is the best one is unimportant for the purposes of this paper. What is crucial to note at this point is that not just any proposition will function as a reason for other beliefs. If, for example, I offer as my reason for believing *that all fish have fins* my belief that *all fish wear army boots and anything wearing army boots has fins*, my offered-reason entails *that all fish have fins*, but on the accounts mentioned above it is not an objectively available reason. It has a low probability of being true; an impartial observer would not accept it; it would not be accepted in the long run by any appropriately defined set of people; there is no evident proposition that makes it evident; accepting it does not accord with my deepest epistemic commitments; there is no actual context in which appealing to that proposition will persuade anyone that all fish have fins; and an intellectually virtuous person would not offer it. Contrast this case with another. My belief *that dark clouds are gathering over the mountains and it is mid-winter in Montana* could satisfy the objective availability constraints contained in all of the accounts mentioned above for functioning as a reason for the proposition *that a snowstorm is likely*.

There is second feature of "availability" to S that is subjective. There might be a good reason, r,

that is *objectively* available for use by any person, but unless it is properly hooked up with S's own beliefs, r will not be *subjectively* available to S. In an appropriate sense to be discussed later, S must be able to call on r.

It is this subjective sense of "availability" that has provoked many of the objections to infinitism. For example: How can a "finite" human mind have an infinite number of beliefs?[16] I think that rhetorical question involves a deep misunderstanding of the infinitist's position that will be discussed in some detail when we consider the objections to infinitism, but let me now just state the obvious: Humans have many beliefs that are not occurrent. It is in the non-occurrent sense of "belief" that the members of an infinite series of reasons might be subjectively available to S. Roughly, but I hope good enough for the purposes of this paper, let us say that S believes p just in case S would affirm that p, or endorse p in another fashion – perhaps sotto voce – in some appropriately restricted circumstances. For example, S may not now be thinking that she is in Montana in mid-winter looking at dark clouds gathering, but if asked why she believes a snowstorm is imminent, she will consciously affirm that she is in Montana in mid-winter looking at dark clouds gathering. The point is that she has the belief even before she forms the conscious thought.[17]

Having briefly sketched the two ways in which a belief must be available, let me return to the central motivation for infinitism – the two intuitive principles. As mentioned above, I think the only way to avoid infinitism is to reject either PAC or PAA. PAC seems completely safe to me. The old rejoinder that a large enough circle of reasons is acceptable, strikes me as just plain wrong. That a circle is larger might make it more difficult to detect the flaw in the reasoning, but large circles, nevertheless, involve question begging reasoning. An error in reasoning is still an error no matter how difficult it is to detect.

What probably is meant by invoking the "large circle" is that it has seemed plausible to argue that one has a better reason for accepting a proposition if, *ceteris paribus*, it is a member of a larger set of coherent propositions. There is greater "mutual support" in larger sets. This feature of a non-traditional coherentist account is offered as a way of maintaining a coherentist position while still accepting PAC.[18] Indeed, I think PAC, once understood, will be accepted in any context of discussion that presupposes a distinction between good and bad reasoning. Circular reasoning is just not acceptable.

But PAA might not seem so secure. Can't something other than reasons make a belief justified? For example, couldn't a belief be justified just in case it arose in some reliable fashion? Or couldn't there be a "meta-justification" available that (i) shows that some propositions are justified but that (ii) is not, itself, directly involved in the justification of the proposition? And, finally, couldn't it be epistemically rational to accept some propositions even when there is no reason for believing them? Perhaps arbitrariness isn't such a bad thing after all!

There are, no doubt, other objections to PAA, but the three just mentioned seem the most serious. First, the intuitive appeal of reliabilism needs to be reckoned with. Second, the move to a "meta-justification" seems initially plausible. Finally, there is an ingenious argument developed by Stephen Luper-Foy to the effect that it is rational to accept basic beliefs even though they are not rational beliefs – that is, even though there is no reason that can be given to believe that they are true. Let us consider these objections in order.

(a) Reliabilism?

Reliabilism, or at least the relevant form, holds either that *reasons* are not always required to justify a belief or that knowledge does not require justification, if "justification" is used in such a way as to entail that only rational beliefs are justified. A reliabilist could accept the claim that the structure of reasons is infinite and simply deny that reasons are required either for knowledge or for justification. A "moderate" form of reliabilism maintains that not all forms of knowledge or justification require reasoned belief. A "radical" form of reliabilism maintains that no form of knowledge requires reasoned belief. What are we to make of these claims? Does knowledge or justification require having reasons?

I maintain that being able to produce reasons for beliefs is a distinctive characteristic of adult human knowledge. Apparently, nothing else knows in this way. Of course, many things have knowledge that is not *rational* belief. Dogs scratch at doors knowing, in *some* sense, that they will be opened; but dogs do not have reasons. Even adult humans know (in *that* sense) when they do not have reasons. As Fred Dretske says, when adult humans are in Minnesota in mid-winter, they know that it is cold without having reasons.[19]

Nevertheless, even some reliabilists employ intuitions involving the having of adequate reasons in order to distinguish cases of justified belief from cases of unjustified beliefs. Alvin Goldman, one of the architects of reliabilism, considers a case in which a subject, S, believes "I am in brain-state B" just in case S is in brain-state B. The belief acquisition method is perfectly reliable, but "we can imagine that a brain surgeon operating on S artificially induces brain-state B. This results, phenomenologically, in S's suddenly believing – out of the blue – that he is in brain-state B, without any relevant antecedent beliefs. We would hardly say, in such a case, that S's belief that he is in brain-state B is justified."[20]

I think the best explanation for Goldman's intuition about this case is that some reliabilists still feel the bite of the evidentialist requirement that in some cases we – adult humans – must have reasons for our beliefs in order for them to count as knowledge.

More directly, I am convinced by examples like Keith Lehrer's Truetemp Case that there is a sense of "know" such that belief, though completely reliable, is not knowledge in the relevant sense. Recall that Mr. Truetemp has a thermometer-cum-temperature-belief-generator implanted in his head so that within certain ranges of temperatures he has perfectly reliable temperature beliefs. As Lehrer puts it:

> He accepts [beliefs about the temperature] unreflectively ... Thus he thinks and accepts that the temperature is 104 degrees. It is. Does he know that it is? Surely not.[21]

Some reliabilists might maintain that Mr. Truetemp does, indeed, know. Now, as I see it, the issue is not whether Mr. Truetemp "knows" in *some* sense that the temperature is 104 degrees. He may very well have knowledge in some sense – the same sense in which a dog can "recognize" her owner's voice or in which a thermometer "knows" the room temperature. In the other sense of "know" – the sense that is only predicated of humans who have reached "the age of reason" – Mr. Truetemp lacks knowledge because he does not have a subjectively available reason for thinking that it is 104 degrees. There is nothing he could think of which is a reason for believing that it is 104 degrees. In other words, "knowledge" might not refer to a natural kind – there being only *one* fundamental type. Ernest Sosa makes this point persuasively when he writes:

> The challenge of doxastic assent might well be thought a pseudo-challenge, however, since it would deny knowledge to infants and animals. Admittedly, there is a sense in which even a supermarket door "knows" when someone approaches, and in which a heating system "knows" when the temperature in a room rises above a certain setting. Such is "servo-mechanic" knowledge. And there is an immense variety of animal knowledge, instinctive or learned, which facilitates survival and flourishing in an astonishingly rich diversity of modes and environments. Human knowledge is on a higher plane of sophistication, however, precisely because of its enhanced coherence and comprehensiveness and its capacity to satisfy self-reflective curiosity. Pure reliabilism is questionable as an adequate epistemology for such knowledge.[22]

Thus, I believe that radical reliabilism – the view that claims that having reasons is never necessary for knowledge – fails to capture what is distinctive about adult human knowledge.

On the other hand, the intuitive appeal of moderate reliabilism can be adequately recognized without giving up PAA. For one can grant that in some senses of "know," rational beliefs are not required for knowledge. Where "knows that p" means roughly "possess the information that p" we can say of "servo-mechanic" objects that they possess knowledge that p. They do not need reasons. Nevertheless, there is another sense of "know" such that the mere possession of information is not adequate. The information must be supported by appropriate reasons. Beliefs that come "out of the blue" do not qualify as knowledge in this sense.

There is one further, relevant move available to the infinitist. It could even be granted that *no* form of knowledge requires having rational beliefs. That is, radical reliabilism could be accepted. But even granting that, the infinitist's claim remains significant if only because, if correct, it would delineate an important condition of rational beliefs, even such beliefs were not required for knowledge. Foundationalism and coherentism would remain less attractive than infinitism as accounts of rational belief.

(b) Meta-justifications?

Let us now turn to what Laurence BonJour calls "meta-justifications" – justifications designed to show that certain types of beliefs are acceptable even in the absence of another belief that serves as a reason. Such beliefs are acceptable, it is claimed, because they have some property, call it P, and beliefs having P are likely to be true.[23] Both non-traditional coherentism and foundationalism are alike in that they hold that there is some such property, P.

Let us turn directly to foundationalism. Can it avoid advocating the acceptance of arbitrary reasons by moving to meta-justifications? Suppose it is claimed that a foundational proposition is justified because it has a certain causal history (e.g., involving the proper use of our senses or memory) or that it is justified in virtue of its content (e.g., it is about a current mental state or it is about some necessary truth). Pick your favorite accounts of the property, P. I think, as does BonJour, that the old Pyrrhonian question is reasonable: Why is having P truth-conducive?[24] Now, either there is an answer available to that question or there isn't. (BonJour thinks there is.) If there is an answer, then the regress continues – at least one more step, and that is all that is needed here, because that shows that the offered reason that some belief has P or some set of beliefs has P does not stop the regress. If there isn't an answer, the assertion is arbitrary.

Now, let me be clear here in order to anticipate a possible objection. I am not claiming that in order for a belief to be justified or known, either we must *believe* that it is justified or we must be *justified in believing* that it is justified. As many have pointed out, that confuses p's being justified with a belief about p's justificatory status.[25] I am not supposing that the foundationalist, or for that matter, the non-traditional coherentist thinks that what Alston has called "epistemic beliefs" (beliefs about the epistemic status of beliefs) must play a role in the justification of all beliefs.[26] Quite the contrary. I think the foundationalist typically advocates an explicit process of reasoning that ends with beliefs which have P rather than with epistemic beliefs about P. The meta-justification is invoked in order to avoid the appearance of arbitrariness for it is designed to show why the "final" beliefs are likely to be true. My point is merely that moving to the meta-level, that is, arguing that such beliefs are likely to be true because they possess a certain property, P, will not avoid the problem faced by foundationalism. Either the meta-justification provides a reason for thinking the base proposition is true (and hence, the regress does not end) or it does not (hence, accepting the base proposition is arbitrary). The Pyrrhonians were right.

The same is true of non-traditional coherentism. Claiming that a belief is justified because it is a member of a set of propositions that is coherent cannot stop the regress in any but an arbitrary way. The non-traditional coherentist must produce a meta-justification for the belief that propositions satisfying that requirement are likely to be true. As BonJour says:

> … one crucial part of the task of an adequate epistemological theory is to show that there is an appropriate connection between its proposed account of epistemic justification and the cognitive goal of *truth*. That is, it must somehow be shown that justification as conceived by the theory is *truth-conducive*, that one who seeks justified beliefs is at least likely to find true ones.[27]

So the non-traditional coherentist, like the foundationalist, will move to a meta-level in an attempt to show why a belief that coheres with others is likely to be true.[28] But the same question will arise: Why is coherence truth-conducive?[29]

To generalize: Foundationalism and non-traditional coherentism cannot avoid the regress by appealing to a meta-claim that a belief having some property, P, is likely to be true. That claim itself requires an argument that appeals to reasons. Indeed, the appeal to such a meta-claim invokes just the kind of dialectical context involving what is distinctive about adult human knowledge. For surely a reason is required to justify the belief that propositions with property, P, are likely to be true; and whatever justifies that claim will require a reason; and – well, you get the point.

Thus, the move to a meta-justification cannot stop the regress without violating either PAA or PAC.

(c) Harmless arbitrariness?

One objection to PAA remains to be considered: Perhaps it is rational to accept arbitrary, non-rational, beliefs even though there are no reasons for thinking that they are true. If that were the case, it would presumably dampen the enthusiasm some epistemologists have for foundationalism, for they think that the foundational propositions are not arbitrary (they appeal to meta-justifications to show that). In addition, it would call into question a primary motivation for traditional coherentism, namely that it is irrational to accept a belief without a reason. But it would also undermine my argument for infinitism based in part on PAA because that principle is designed to capture the widely endorsed intuition that it is rational to accept a belief only if there is some reason for thinking the belief is true.

Stephen Luper-Foy has argued that it is rational to accept foundational beliefs even though they cannot be supported by reasons. Here is his argument (some of what follows is close paraphrase, some is direct quotation as indicated):

> The epistemic goal is to acquire a complete and accurate picture of the world. Granted at base our reasons are arbitrary but "an injunction against believing anything … would obviously make it impossible for us to achieve the goal of arriving at a complete and accurate understanding of what is the case … Indeed, given that our ultimate beliefs are arbitrary, it is rational to adopt management principles that allow us to retain these foundational yet arbitrary views, since the alternative is to simply give up on the attempt to achieve the epistemic goal."[30]

His point, I take it, is that since the goal of an epistemic agent is to acquire a complete and accurate picture of the world, accepting a basic, though arbitrary, reason is rational since if one did not accept it, there would be no possibility of attaining the goal. It is "rational to do and believe things without reason"[31] because if we did not, we could not attain our goal.

There are two responses. First, if I am right, we need not worry about reasons being arbitrary, since the regress does not stop. There are no arbitrary, ultimate reasons because there are no ultimate reasons. But more to the point at hand, if the regress did end with an arbitrary reason (as Luper-Foy is assuming at this point in his argument), I think his argument for making it rational to accept arbitrary reasons does not succeed.

Luper-Foy is using a prudential account of rationality such that we are prudentially rational just in case our chosen means to a goal are efficient in achieving that goal. But such an instrumental conception of rationality is acceptable only if the definition of rationality is understood to imply that it is rational to adopt a means to a given goal only if the means are more likely to achieve *that* goal rather than some incompatible and highly undesirable goal. Suppose, as Luper-Foy claims, that the epistemic goal is to gain a complete and accurate picture of the world, then believing x would be rational only if believing x furthered that goal instead of the incompatible and highly undesirable goal, let us say, of obtaining a complete and inaccurate picture of the world. But if my basic beliefs are arbitrary, that is, if there is no available reason for thinking that accepting them is more likely to contribute to obtaining an accurate picture than an inaccurate picture, then, for all I know, accepting the basic beliefs could equally well lead to obtaining a complete and inaccurate picture of the world. So, if at the base, reasons are arbitrary, it is not even prudentially rational to accept them since doing so is no more likely to satisfy rather than frustrate my epistemic goals.

II.   Objections to Infinitism

We have completed the examination of what I take to be the best reasons for rejecting PAA and found that they are inadequate. As mentioned earlier, I take PAC to be the *sine qua non* of good reasoning. Nevertheless, in spite of the fact that there appear to be no good grounds for rejecting PAA or PAC taken individually, the view that results from accepting both of them, namely infinitism, has never been advocated by anyone with the possible exception of Peirce.[32] The remainder of this paper will focus on the reasons that have been advanced against infinitism. Of course, if only for the sake of consistency, I cannot take it that this matter is finally settled. But I do think the proposed objections to the position fail.

So, what are the arguments designed to show that the structure of reasons could not be infinite and non-repeating? They can be divided into four types presented in the order in which I think they present deep issues for the infinitist – beginning with the least troubling and moving to the most troubling: 1) Varieties of the Finite Human Mind Objection; 2) the Aristotelian Objection that If Some Knowledge Is Inferential, Some Is Not Inferential; 3) the *Reductio* Argument Against the Possibility of an Infinite Regress Providing a Justification for Beliefs (most clearly developed by John Post and I. T. Oakley); 4) the Specter of Skepticism Objection – namely that nothing is known unless reasoning somehow settles the matter.

Objection 1. The finite mind objection

Very roughly, the intuition behind this objection is that the human mind is finite and if such a mind is to have reasons for beliefs (a requirement for the distinctive adult human kind of knowledge), it cannot be the case that such beliefs are justified only if there is an infinite chain of reasons. Here, for example, is what John Williams says:

> The [proposed] regress of justification of S's belief that p would certainly require that he holds an infinite number of beliefs. This is psychologically, if not logically, impossible. If a man can believe an infinite number of things, then there seems to be no reason why he cannot know an infinite number of things. Both possibilities contradict the common intuition that the human mind is finite. Only God could entertain an infinite number of beliefs. But surely God is not the only justified believer.[33]

As stated, it is a bit difficult to get a purchase on this objection. It cannot mean simply that we are finite beings – occupying a finite amount of space and lasting a finite duration of time – and consequently, we cannot be in an infinite number of states (in particular, belief states). A "finite" thing, say a one foot cube existing for only ten minutes, has its center at an infinite number of positions during the ten minutes it moves, say, from point {0,0,0} in a three dimensional Cartesian coordinate system to, say, point {1,1,1}. So, a finitely extended thing can be in an infinite number of states in a finite amount of time.

But Williams does not leave matters at this fuzzy, intuitive level. What he means, I think, is that there is something about belief states or justified belief states in particular which is such that no finite human can be in an infinite number of them. The argument, as best as I can ferret it out, is this: It is impossible to consciously believe an infinite number of propositions (because to believe something takes some time) and it is impossible to "unconsciously believe" ("unconscious belief" is his term) an infinite number of propositions because the candidate beliefs are such that some of them "defeat human understanding."[34]

Granted, I cannot consciously assent to an infinite number of propositions in my lifetime. The infinitist is not claiming that in any finite period of time – the "threescore and ten" assigned to us, for example – we can consciously entertain an infinite number of thoughts. It is rather that there are an infinite number of propositions such that each one of them would be consciously thought were the appropriate circumstances to arise.

Williams is, indeed, right that the putative examples given thus far in the literature of infinite sets of propositions in which each member is subjectively available are not plausible because consciously thinking some of them is impossible. But, of course, it is a non-sequitur to claim that because some examples fail, they all will.

Richard Foley, for example, suggests that since I believe that I am within one hundred miles of Boston, I believe that I am within two hundred miles of Boston, and I believe that I am within 300 miles, etc.[35] Williams correctly points out that eventually a proposition in such a series will contain a "number so large that no one can consider it."[36] Robert Audi gives a similar argument against the possibility of a mind like ours having an infinite number of beliefs.[37]

It is easy to see the general reason why such examples fail.[38] They all presuppose a finite vocabulary for expressing beliefs. Hence, it would *seem* that any method of generating an infinite series of beliefs by some manipulation on the items in the vocabulary (e.g., conjoining them, disjoining them) will eventually produce a member in the set that is too "large" or too "long" for us to consider.

But even with a finite vocabulary, we do have another way of picking out objects and forming beliefs about them. We can use indexicals. We can point to an object and say "this." We can also say of an object that it has some shape, say α. Now, suppose that there were an infinite number of discernable objects with the shape α. I claim that there would be an infinite number of propositions each of the form "this is α-shaped" such that were we to discern the object referred to by "this" in each proposition, we would consciously think "this is α-shaped" under the appropriate circumstances. So, *if* there were an infinite number of α-shaped discernable objects, then there would be an infinite set of propositions such that each member would be consciously endorsed under the appropriate circumstances – i.e., when we discern the object and consider whether it is α-shaped. Of course, this is only a hypothetical claim. I do not know whether there is an infinite number of such discernable objects. But it does not matter for my point. My claim is merely that, in principle, nothing prevents so-called "finite minds" from being such that each proposition in an infinite set of propositions is subjectively available. There might not be an infinite number of such discernable objects, but we certainly have the capacity to think about each such object that we discern that it is α-shaped. Therefore, we have the capacity to believe each member of an infinite set of propositions. No member in the set gets too "large" or too "long" or too "complex" for us to grasp.

I mentioned earlier that I thought there was a deep misunderstanding of the infinitist's position underlying the infinite mind objection. Now is the time to consider it. I have already said that the infinitist is not claiming that during our lifetime we consciously entertain an infinite number of beliefs. But what might not be so obvious is that the infinitist is also not even claiming that we *have* an infinite number of what Williams calls "unconscious beliefs" if such beliefs are taken to be *already formed* dispositions. (We might, but that isn't necessary for infinitism.) Consider the following question: Do you believe that 366 + 71 is 437? I take it that for most of us answering that question brings into play some of our capacities in a way that answering the question "Do you believe that 2 + 2 = 4?" does not. For I simply remember that 2 + 2 = 4. I have already formed the belief that manifests itself when I consciously think that 2 + 2 = 4. By contrast, I had not already formed a similar disposition concerning the sum of 366 plus 71. We do not simply remember that 366 + 71 = 437. Rather, we do a bit of adding. We are *disposed to think* that 366 + 71 = 437 after a bit of adding given our belief that 6 + 1 = 7, that 7 + 6 = 13, etc. We have a second order disposition – a disposition to form the disposition to think something. Thus, there is clearly a sense in which we believe that 366 + 71 = 437. The proposition that 366 + 71 = 437 is subjectively available to me because it is correctly hooked up to already formed beliefs.

We have many second order dispositions that are counted as beliefs. For example, you believe that apples do not normally grow on pear trees even though you had never formed the disposition to consciously think that (at least up until just now!). Infinitism requires that there be an infinite set of propositions such that each member is subjectively available to us. That requires that we have the capacity to form beliefs about each member. It does not require that we have already formed those beliefs.

The distinction between already formed first-order beliefs and dispositions to form a first-order belief is important for another reason. Earlier I had argued that there was a way, in principle, to show that even with a finite vocabulary, we could have an infinite number of beliefs by employing indexicals. Nevertheless, that response will not be useful here since we cannot point to reasons (as we can point to objects) with "this" or "that" unless the reasons are already formed. The problem is to show that there can be an infinite number of reasons given a finite vocabulary each of which can be entertained by a human being.

The solution to this problem is ready-to-hand. Since we can appeal to second order dispositions, we can say that when our vocabulary and concepts fall short of being able to provide reasons, we can develop new concepts and ways of specifying them. That is, we can discover, develop or invent new concepts to provide a reason for our beliefs.

This seems to happen regularly. When we have no ready-to-hand explanation of events, we devise new concepts that can be employed in understanding those events. Consider the following: the development of the concept of unconscious mechanisms to account for our behavior, the development of the concept of quarks to provide for some unity in our understanding of subatomic particles and their interactions, and the development of evolutionary theory to account for the fossil record as well as the diversity and commonality among species. In each case there was a temporary stopping point reached in our ability to provide reasons for our beliefs. But we have the capacity to develop new concepts that can provide us with further reasons for our beliefs.

Let me sum up my response to this first reason for thinking that a finite mind cannot have an infinite number of justified beliefs. We have seen that the notion of "belief" is ambiguous. It can refer to already formed dispositions and it can refer to the disposition to form dispositions. It is in the second sense that the infinitist is committed to the claim that there is an infinite number of beliefs both subjectively and objectively available to us whenever (if ever) we have distinctively adult human knowledge.

There is a second argument that is sometimes given for supposing that the requirements of having an infinite number of *justified* beliefs cannot be satisfied. Both Richard Foley and Richard Fumerton suppose that in order for S to be justified in believing that p on the basis of e, S must (at least paradigmatically for Foley) *justifiably* believe that e justifies p. Fumerton puts it this way:

> To be justified in believing one proposition P on the basis of another E one must be 1) justified in believing E and 2) justified in believing that E makes probable P.[39]

It is easy to see that if this condition of inferential justification were coupled with infinitism, the consequence would be that any person having a justified belief must have a belief that gets "so complex" that no human could ever have it. Foley argues to the same conclusion by claiming that a condition like (2) is a feature of the "best justifications" and that any theory of justification will include a description of the best justifications.[40]

I agree that such a requirement would force the rejection of infinitism. But as I mentioned earlier, I can see no reason to agree to the premiss that in order for S to be justified in believing that p on the basis of e, S must be *justified* in believing that e is a good reason for p. I think this simply confuses having a justified belief that p with having justified beliefs about p's justificatory status. This amounts to requiring that S not only be an epistemologist, but also that S have a well reasoned epistemology in order to be justified in believing, for example, that a thunderstorm is likely. Epistemology is important, but having a justified epistemology is not required in order to have justified beliefs! Thus, this argument provides no grounds for thinking that the chain of good reasons, even if infinite, includes beliefs that are too complex for us to grasp.[41]

Objection 2. The Aristotelian objection that if some knowledge is inferential, some is not inferential.

In the *Posterior Analytics* Aristotle claims that if some knowledge is the result of inference, some knowledge must not be the result of inference. I think that is correct. And I grant that some knowledge is the result of inference. So, some knowledge is not the result of inference. But, somewhat surprisingly, it does not follow that the structure of justificatory reasons is finite.

Assume, as I think it is evident that Aristotle does, that at some early time in the development of a human being, the being is completely ignorant. At some later point, the being has knowledge. It would not be possible to account for all of the being's knowledge on the basis of previously obtained knowledge, for that *could not* give us an account of the original, first, change from ignorance to knowledge. So, all knowledge could not be *produced* by inference from previous knowledge – not because the structure of justificatory reasons could not be infinite but because all knowledge could not arise from previous knowledge if at one time we are ignorant and at a later time we are knowledgeable. But nothing in this argument prevents the chain of justificatory reasons from being infinite. We could acquire most of our beliefs in ways that do not involve reasons as causes. My claim is merely that in order to have the distinctively adult human type of knowledge,

there must be reasons of the appropriate sort available. Thus, it can be granted that we, humans, move from a state of complete ignorance to a state of having the distinctively adult human type of knowledge during our lifetimes and still maintain, as I do, that we make that transition only when there are reasons subjectively and objectively available for our beliefs.

Now, Aristotle may never have intended, at least in the *Posterior Analytics*, that the description of the role of experience in the acquisition of knowledge be used to show that there are beliefs for which there are no reasons.[42] Nevertheless, there is a passage in the *Metaphysics* that might be cited to show that Aristotle endorsed an argument against infinitism:

> There are, both among those who have these convictions [man is the measure of all things] and among those who merely profess these views, some who raise a difficulty by asking, who is to be the judge of the healthy man, and in general who is likely to judge rightly on each class of question. But such inquiries are like puzzling over the question whether we are now asleep or awake. And all such questions have the same meaning. These people demand that a reason shall be given for everything, for they seek a starting point and they seek to get this by demonstration, while it is obvious from their actions that they have no conviction. But their mistake is what we have stated it to be: they seek a reason for things for which no reason can be given; for the starting point of demonstration is not demonstration.[43]

Now, I grant that there are occasions when it is absurd to ask for reasons for a belief. Roughly, those are the occasions in which it is clear that the conversational presuppositions are not to be questioned. For example, when we are distinguishing features of waking states from features of dream states, it is absurd to ask whether we can tell the difference. But it does not follow that such questions are always inappropriate. Indeed, when the presuppositions of the conversational context are revealed, they can be questioned. Thus, one can grant what I think Aristotle is suggesting, namely that demonstration can take place only within a context of agreed upon presuppositions and that it is absurd to ask for reasons to justify those presuppositions within that kind of a context. He is right. But, of course, the contextual situation can change.

Objection 3. The reductio argument against the possibility of an infinite regress providing a justification for beliefs

The gist of the argument is this: If there were an infinite regress of reasons, any arbitrarily chosen contingent proposition would be justified. That is absurd. So there can't be an infinite regress of justification.

The argument has two forms. Let me deal with them in the order of their ascending plausibility. I. T. Oakley's argument is this (what follows is a close and, I hope, fair paraphrase):

> Let us suppose that S is justified in believing p in the way envisaged by the regress theorist. That is, there is a regress from p to r, to s to t, etc. Now, conjoin with every member of the series a further belief of S's, say q. If the first set of beliefs {p, r, s, t, etc.} is justified, so is the new set of conjunctive beliefs {(p&q), (r&q), (s&q), (t&q), etc.}. And if (p&q) is justified, then q is justified.[44]

I think this argument rests on an assumed principle of justification, namely this: If e justifies p, then (e & q) justifies (p & q). If that assumed principle were true, and if (p & q) justifies p and justifies q, then I think this argument does constitute a *reductio* of infinitism. But the assumed principle of justification is false – or better, it is clear that it and the principle endorsing justification over simplification cannot both be true. For, jointly, they lead to the unwelcome consequence that any arbitrary proposition, q, is justified given *any* theory of justification.

To see that, suppose, that there is some proposition, e, and any theory of justification such that e is justified and e justifies p. Then, by parallel reasoning, since e justifies p, then (e & q) justifies (p & q). And, by parallel reasoning, q is justified. So, there is a quick and dirty way of showing that every proposition would be justified given *any* theory of justification.

But surely what is wrong here is that the argument fails to note what is essential to infinitism. It is a consequence of the infinitist's constraints on constructing a non-question begging chain that the ancestors of x in the chain cannot "contain" x.[45]

The assumed principle violates that constraint and is a clear violation of PAC because the only reason offered for (p & q) is (e & q). Indeed, *every* link in the proposed infinite chain is question begging, for q is contained in each. Thus, this objection fails because the type of infinite chain presupposed in this objection does not have the appropriate *form*.[46]

There is another *reductio* argument that has been advanced against infinitism that does not violate the proposed constraints on the *form* of the chain of reasons. Here is a close paraphrase of the argument as given by John Post:

> Consider an example of an infinite regress that does not violate the appropriate constraints. Let p be contingent and use *modus ponens* as follows:
>   …, r &(r→(q &(q→p))), q & (q→p), p
> This sort of infinitely iterated application of *modus ponens* guarantees that for any contingent proposition, p, one can construct an instance of an infinite regress.[47]

Post takes that as a *reductio* of the infinitist's position. I agree that if on some view of justification every contingent proposition were justified, the view would be unacceptable.[48] But Post has assumed that the infinitist takes the mere existence of such a chain of propositions with the appropriate form (non-repeating and infinite) to be a sufficient condition for a belief's having a justification. However, as I emphasized at the outset, the existence of such a chain is necessary, but it is not sufficient. The beliefs in the chain must also be "available" to S as reasons. Thus, not all infinite chains having the required structural properties make beliefs justified.

In considering Post's objection, Ernest Sosa distinguishes between what he calls chains that provide potential justification and those that provide actual justification.[49] I think Sosa is right.[50] As I see it, there is a potential justification for every contingent proposition; that is, there is an infinite chain of propositions like the one Post describes for every proposition. But only some chains contain reasons. Hence, not every proposition will have a justification because a proposition has a justification only if each member of the chain is available as a reason in both the objective sense and subjective sense to serve as a reason.[51]

Objection 4. The specter of skepticism

This is the most difficult objection to answer because it is the most difficult to fully understand. It apparently goes to some deeply held intuitions that, perhaps, I do not fully appreciate. The objection rests upon a Cartesian-like view that the whole point of reasoning is to "settle" an issue. According to that view, ideally, reasoning should produce *a priori* demonstrations; but where that is not possible or feasible (for example with regard to empirical propositions), something approximating a demonstration is required in order for a proposition to be justified or known. Reasoning should settle what it is we are to believe. If it can't, then what's the point of employing it? Reasoning is valuable, at least in part, because it can produce a final guarantee that a proposition is more reasonable than its contraries. But if the reasoning process is infinite, there can be no such guarantee. Thus, one of the claimed virtues of infinitism, namely, that it makes the distinctively adult human type of knowledge possible, is an illusion because that type of knowledge obtains only if reasoning can settle matters.

Here is the way that Jonathan Dancy puts the objection:

> Suppose that all justification is inferential. When we justify belief A by appeal to belief B and C, we have not yet shown A to be justified. We have only shown that it is justified if B and C are. Justification by inference is conditional justification only; A's justification is conditional upon the justification of B and C. But if all justification is conditional in this sense, then nothing can be shown to be actually non-conditionally justified.[52]

Now, there is an unfortunate conflation in the passage that should be avoided – namely, failing to distinguish between *showing* that a belief is justified and a belief's being justified. Nevertheless, that equivocation could be removed and the objection remains: if all justification is provisional, no belief becomes unprovisionally justified.[53]

This is an old objection. It is, I think, what the Pyrrhonists thought made the infinite regress unacceptable as a theory of rational belief. Sextus wrote:

> The Mode [of reasoning] based upon the regress *ad infinitum* is that whereby we assert that the

thing adduced as a proof of the matter proposed needs a further proof, and this again another, and so on *ad infinitum*, so that the consequence is suspension, as we possess no starting-point for our argument.[54]

I have endorsed the Pyrrhonian objections to foundationalism and coherentism. Why not accept their argument against the infinite regress?

The answer is simply that although every proposition is only provisionally justified, that is good enough if one does not insist that reasoning settle matters once and for all. Once that is recognized, surprisingly enough, the Pyrrhonian goal of avoiding dogmatism while continuing to inquire is obtainable.

I readily grant that the kind of final guarantee that Descartes and others have sought is not available if infinitism is correct. In general, as we have seen, the foundationalist's reliance upon a meta-justification to locate a property shared by all "basic" propositions is not a viable strategy for avoiding the regress. In particular, why should Descartes' suggestion for a truth-conducive property, namely clarity-and-distinctness, be accepted without a reason being given? Indeed, Descartes, himself, thought that a reason was required for believing that clarity-and-distinctness is truth-conducive. He attempted to provide that reason by producing an argument demonstrating the existence of an epistemically benevolent god. But surely that is only a temporary stopping point in the regress of reasons because the premises in that argument need to be supported by further reasons in order to avoid arbitrariness.

But, let me take the objection more seriously. Is a proposition justified only when belief in it *results from a process of justification that has been concluded*? Richard Fumerton has argued against infinitism because "[f]inite minds cannot *complete* an infinitely long chain of reasoning, so, if all justification were inferential we would have no justification for believing anything. [emphasis added]"[55]

This objection to infinitism implicitly appeals to a principle that we can call the *Completion Requirement*: In order for a belief to be justified for someone, that person must have actually completed the chain of reasoning that terminates in the belief in question. The infinitist cannot accept the Completion Requirement because it is clearly incompatible with infinitism. Justifications are never finished. More to the point, however, the Completion Requirement demands more than what is required to have a justified belief even on non-infinitist accounts of justified beliefs.

To see that, apply the Completion Requirement to a foundationalist conception of justification coupled with the dispositional account of belief mentioned above that includes second order dispositions. The result would be that most, if not all, of our beliefs are not justified. I have thousands and thousands of beliefs – if not infinitely many. I have not carried out the process of reasoning to many (if any) of those beliefs from some foundational beliefs (even if there were foundational beliefs). In fact, I couldn't have explicitly entertained any significant number of the propositions I believe. There are just too many.

Nevertheless, Fumerton's claim that S's belief is not justified merely because there is a justification available to S seems correct. In discussing the requirements for a belief's being justified, he draws an important distinction between S's merely *having* a justification for P and S's belief that P being justified. He claims, correctly I believe, the former is necessary but not sufficient for the latter:

> The expression "S has a justification for believing P" will be used in such a way that it implies nothing about the causal role played by that justification in sustaining the belief. The expression "S's belief that P is justified" will be taken to imply both that S has justification and that S's justification is playing the appropriate causal role in sustaining the belief.[56]

I think that an infinitist must grant the distinction between S's merely *having* a justification for the belief P and the belief P *being* justified for S. PAC and PAA specified necessary conditions for S's having a justification; they did not specify what else is required in order for S's belief to be justified. The question, then, becomes this: Can the infinitist draw the distinction between S *having* a justification for P and S's belief P *being* justified?

Ernest Sosa and others have suggested that the infinitist will be hard pressed to distinguish between S's merely having available a justification for a proposition and the proposition's being justified for S. Return to the case discussed earlier in which S calculates the sum of two numbers by employing some "already formed" dispositions. Now suppose (Sosa would suggest) that S had, instead, merely guessed that the sum of the two numbers is 437, and, also, that when exploring whether the guessed sum is actually correct, S does a bit of adding and sees that the sum that he had guessed was, in fact, the right answer.[57] Presumably we want to say that although S had a justification available (if S can add) prior to calculating the sum, the belief that the numbers summed to 437 was not even provisionally justified until S does a bit of adding. So, merely *having* a justification available will not suffice for a belief's *being* provisionally justified.

Here is the way Sosa states the point:[58]

> Someone who guesses the answer to a complex addition problem does not already know the answer just because, given a little time, he could do the sum in his head. If he had not done the sum, if he had just been guessing, then he *acquires* his knowledge, he does not know beforehand … We are not just interested in the weaker position of someone who *would* be able to defend the belief, but only because its exposure to reflection would lead the subject to new arguments and reasonings that had never occurred to him, and that in any case had played no role in his acquisition or retention of the target belief.[59]

Now one might respond by saying that arriving at the sum of two numbers is not appropriately analogous to coming to believe, for example, that I hear my neighbor's dog, Fido, barking. Summing two large numbers requires (at least for most of us) some conscious process; whereas coming to believe that it is Fido barking does not require having gone through a process of conscious reasoning. To repeat, the Completion Requirement is just too strong in many cases. I can be justified in believing that it is Fido barking even if I have not arrived at that belief through some conscious process of reasoning.

Nevertheless, a question still remains even about my belief that it is Fido barking: How is the infinitist to distinguish between (1) the case of a lucky guess that it is Fido barking when a justification is available and (2) the case in which the belief is actually justified?[60]

The crucial point to recall is that for the infinitist *all* justification is provisional. S *has* a provisional justification for a proposition, p, only if there is a reason, r_1, both subjectively and objectively available to S for p; whereas S's belief p *is* provisionally justified only if S's belief r_1 "is playing the appropriate causal role in sustaining" (to use Fumerton's expression) S's belief p. But what about the belief r_1? Doesn't it have to be provisionally justified in order for the belief p to be provisionally justified? No. There does have to be a reason, r_2, for r_1 that is subjectively and objectively available if S is to *have* a justification for p, but the belief r_2 does not have to be provisionally justified in order for the belief p to be provisionally justified. It is sufficient that the belief p is causally sustained by the belief r_1 for the belief p to be provisionally justified. Beliefs originating from wild guesses would not be provisionally justified. Thus, the infinitist can make the requisite distinction between the case of a lucky guess when a justification is available and the case in which the belief is justified.

Still, I suspect that there is a deep skeptical worry lurking here. Infinitism envisions the possibility that if we begin to provide the reasons available for our beliefs, we might eventually arrive at a reason for which there is no further reason that is both subjectively and objectively available. Perhaps, our capacities to form new dispositions and concepts will reach a limit. Perhaps, the objective requirements of availability will not be met. Those possibilities cannot be ruled out *a priori*. Thus, the possibility of skepticism is a serious one. It is not, as some have thought, only a philosopher's nightmare.[61] Here I side with Richard Foley who writes:

The way to respond to skeptical doubts is not to legislate against them metaphysically, and it is not to dismiss them as meaningless, self-defeating, or even odd ... It is to recognize what makes epistemology possible makes skeptical worries inevitable – namely, our ability to make our methods of inquiry themselves into an object of inquiry.[62]

Now, of course, I think there might be an infinite series of reasons available; and if so, our desire for a reason can be answered whenever it arises. Foley thinks that the lack of final guarantees implies that "the reality of our intellectual lives is that we are working without nets."[63] And I agree that there are no final guarantees. There is no final net of that sort.

Nevertheless, although I think the kind of "lifetime" guarantee that would settle things once and for all is not available, my view is that there are important, "limited" guarantees available; and there might be a limitless set of limited guarantees available. The limited guarantees are the reasons that we can find for our beliefs. We have a limited guarantee that p is true whenever we have a reason for p. Is this an airtight guarantee?

No. But, we do have limited guarantees. And, for all I know, there might be an infinite number of such limited guarantees. Thus, although no *a priori* argument is available whose conclusion is that there is an infinite regress of objectively and subjectively available reasons, as we have seen there is also no such argument for the claim that there is no such set of reasons available.

Thus, I would not characterize our epistemic predicament as one in which there are *no* nets. For there might be a net whenever we need one. Rather, I would characterize it as one in which it is possible, as Lewis Carroll would say, that there are nets all the way down.

Notes

1   The term "infinitism" is not original with me. To the best of my knowledge, the first use of a related term is in Paul Moser's paper "A Defense of Epistemic Intuitionism", *Metaphilosophy* (15.3), 1984, pp. 196–204, in which he speaks of "epistemic infinitism." Also, John Post in *The Faces of Existence* (Ithaca: Cornell University Press, 1987) refers to a position similar to the one I am defending as the "infinitist's claim." (p. 91) There is, however, an important difference between the view that Post correctly criticizes and my view that will become clear later when I discuss his objection to infinitism.

2   For example, Robert Audi in *The Structure of Justification* (New York: Cambridge University Press, 1993) uses the "regress problem in a way that brings out its role in motivating both

foundationalism and coherentism." (p. 10). He specifically eschews a "full-scale assessment" of the regress argument (p. 127). In addition, William Alston, in his *Epistemic Justification* (Ithaca: Cornell University Press, 1989) employs the regress argument to motivate a type of foundationalism. He, too, does not examine the argument in detail but says "I do not claim that this argument is conclusive; I believe it to be open to objection in ways I will not be able to go into here. But I do feel that it gives stronger support to foundationalism than any other regress argument." (p. 55) Finally, Laurence BonJour in his *The Structure of Empirical Knowledge* (Cambridge: Harvard University Press, 1985) says that the considerations surrounding the regress argument are "perhaps the most crucial in the entire theory of knowledge" (p. 18) but dismisses the infinite regress by alluding to the "finite mental capacity" of human beings. Indeed, he says "though it is difficult to state in a really airtight fashion, this argument [that humans have a finite mental capacity] seems to me an adequate reason for rejecting [the view that the structure of justificatory reasons is infinite]." (p. 24) We will, of course, consider the "finite mind" objection in due course. My point is that such a crucial issue in the theory of knowledge deserves careful consideration.

3   I might note in passing that Davidson's characterization of coherence theories – namely that "what distinguishes a coherence theory is simply the claim that nothing can count as a reason for holding a belief except another belief" might distinguish it from foundationalist theories, but it does not distinguish it from infinitism. See "Coherence Theory of Truth and Knowledge" in *Truth and Interpretation*, Ernest Lepore, ed., (New York: Blackwell, 1986), pp. 307–19. Citation from p. 310.

4   I take *traditional coherentism* to be the view that the structure of justification is such that some proposition, say x, provides some warrant for another proposition, say y, and y also provides some warrant for x. It is to be distinguished from another view, discussed later, which holds that coherence is a property of sets of propositions and individual propositions in the set are warranted because they

belong to such a set. In this *non-traditional coherentist* view, warrant attaches to beliefs because they are members of such a set. Unlike traditional coherentism, warrant is not a property transferred from one proposition to another.

5   Throughout I will be using single-strand chains of reasons. Nothing depends upon that. I do so in order to make the contrast between foundationalism and coherentism more readily evident.

6   Note that stating PAC this way does not entail that "being a reason for" is transitive. This avoids a valid criticism of an argument for infinitism. See John Post, "Infinite Regress Argument" in *Companion to Epistemology*, Jonathan Dancy and Ernest Sosa, eds, (New York: Blackwell, 1992), pp. 209–12. His criticism of infinitism depends upon my own argument against the transitivity of justification. See *Certainty* (Minneapolis: University of Minnesota Press, 1981), pp. 30–5. Those criticisms do not apply here because "being in the evidential ancestry of" is transitive.

7   Laurence BonJour in *The Structure of Empirical Knowledge* and Keith Lehrer in *Theory of Knowledge* (Boulder: Westview Press, 1990) develop accounts of what I call "non-traditional coherentism."

8   There are other necessary conditions of justification, but they are not important for the discussion here. For example, there must not be another proposition, d, available to S that overrides r (unless there is an ultimately non-overridden overrider of d). See my *Certainty*, pp. 44–70.

9   This is important to note since as I understand Ernest Sosa's objection to infinitism it is its supposed incompatibility with the supervenience of the normative on the non-normative that makes it unacceptable. See his "The Raft and the Pyramid", *Midwest Studies in Philosophy*, vol 5, (Minneapolis: University of Minnesota Press, 1980), pp. 3–25, especially section 7. James Van Cleve makes a similar point in his "Semantic Supervenience and Referential Indeterminacy", *Journal of Philosophy* LXXXIX, no. 7, (July 1992), pp. 344–61, especially pp. 350–1 and 356–7. Note that I am not asserting that the normative does, in fact, supervene on the non-normative. Indeed, I think the issue

might be misconceived. Perhaps there are some properties – the so-called "normative" properties of knowledge and justification – that are hybrid properties being neither normative nor non-normative. My claim is merely that as sketched in this paper, infinitism is compatible with the supervenience of the normative on the non-normative.

10 Thus, each one of these accounts of objective availability specifies a sufficient condition that entails that a belief is a reason. If the sufficient condition appeals only to non-normative properties, as some of them do, then what is unique to infinitism satisfies Van Cleve's requirement for epistemic supervenience. He says:

> One of the tasks of epistemology is to articulate *epistemic principles* – principles of the form "If ——, then subject S is justified in believing proposition p". Such principles divide into two classes. One class includes principles that warrant inference from already justified propositions to further propositions; the antecedents of such principles will specify that certain propositions already have some epistemic status for the subject. But not all epistemic principles can be like this. There must also be a class of epistemic principles that specify the nonepistemic conditions under which some beliefs come to have some epistemic status or other in the first place – the conditions, one might say, under which epistemic status is *generated* … [This] requirement is really just the requirement of epistemic supervenience – that there be some nonepistemic features that ultimately underlie the instantiation of any epistemic property. (Van Cleve, "Semantic Supervenience and Referential Indeterminacy," p. 350)

If I am right that the sufficient conditions for both subjective and objective availability can be specified in nonepistemic terms, then there is no reason for thinking that infinitism is incompatible with epistemic supervenience. For the conditions are sufficient for making beliefs into the required sort of reasons.

There are other conditions besides those specified in PAC and PAA that a belief must satisfy in order to be justified (see fn. 8), but if those also supervene on the non-normative facts, then infinitism is compatible with epistemic supervenience. Those other features are not unique to infinitism. The combination of PAC and PAA is what distinguishes infinitism from coherentism and foundationalism. My point is that what distinguishes infinitism is compatible with epistemic supervenience.

11 This is a paraphrase of an account developed by Roderick Chisholm, *Theory of Knowledge* (Englewood Cliffs, NJ: Prentice-Hall Inc., 1966). See especially fn. 22, p. 23.

12 For a development of the individualistically relativistic account of objective availability, see Richard Foley, *The Theory of Epistemic Rationality*, (Cambridge: Harvard University Press, 1987), especially pp. 68–154.

13 See, for example: David Lewis, "Scorekeeping in a Language Game," *Journal of Philosophical Logic* VIII (1979), pp. 339–59; L. Wittgenstein, *On Certainty*, G.E.M. Anscombe and G.H. von Wright, ed., (New York: Harper and Row, 1972). There are also hints at such a view in Aristotle. (*Metaphysics*, 1006a–1011b.)

14 This position is advocated by Linda Zagzebski in *Virtues of the Mind*, (Cambridge: Cambridge University Press, 1996).

15 One problem for some interpretations of objective availability needs to be avoided. Troy Cross has pointed out to me that *if* the probability of propositions diminishes as the chain of reasons lengthens, our beliefs might have such a low probability that they would not in any normal sense of "justified," in fact, be justified. There are four ways around that worry. The first is that there is an infinite number of probability gradations available given any required probability level of the putatively justified proposition. The second is that it is the proposition, itself, that is located in the chain rather than a proposition with a probability assigned. The third is to simply reject the reading of "objective probability" in frequency terms and treat "p is probable" as roughly synonymous with "p is acceptable and can be used to make other propositions acceptable." The fourth is simply to reject probability theory as providing an appropriate set of conditions for objective availability.

16 See, for example, the passage cited earlier in BonJour, *The Structure of Empirical Knowledge*. (See fn. 2.)

17 There is a deep problem with treating beliefs as dispositions to have thoughts *under the appropriately restricted circumstances*. For it appears that almost any proposition as well as its negation could count as believed under some range of "appropriately restricted circumstances." I do not have a settled view regarding the way to restrict the range of circumstances to avoid that consequence. Obviously, this is a general, difficult problem for a dispositional account of belief. There just seem to be too many beliefs. But, as we will see, the problem for the infinitist is just the opposite. For infinitism seems to require more beliefs than we can or do have. It would be nice to have a satisfactory dispositional account of belief. A fully developed infinitist theory must address this issue. Nevertheless, since my purpose here is merely to make infinitism a view worth exploring, we can proceed without solving this general problem concerning a dispositional account of beliefs.

18 Ernest Sosa makes a similar point in "The Raft and the Pyramid". It is reprinted in his book, *Knowledge in Perspective*, (New York: Cambridge University Press, 1991), pp. 165–91, see especially p. 178.

19 Dretske, "Two Conceptions of Knowledge: Rational Belief vs. Reliable Belief," *Grazer Philosophische Studien* 40 (1991), pp. 15–30, especially p. 18.

20 Alvin Goldman, "What is justified belief?," in *On Knowing and the Known*, Kenneth G. Lucy, ed., (Amherst, New York: Prometheus Books, 1996), p. 190.

21 Keith Lehrer, *Theory of Knowledge*, p. 164.

22 Ernest Sosa, *Knowledge in Perspective*, p. 95.

23 Laurence BonJour, *The Structure of Empirical Knowledge*, especially pp. 9–14.

24 See, for example, *Outlines of Pyrrhonism*, PH I, 114–17, 122–4.

25 See, for example, John Williams, "Justified Belief and the Infinite Regress Argument," *American Philosophical Quarterly* XVIII, no 1, (1981), pp. 85–8, especially p. 86.

26 William Alston, "Two types of Foundationalism," *Journal of Philosophy* LXXIII (1976), pp. 165–85. The article also appears as Essay 1, in Alston's book, *Epistemic Justification*, pp. 19–38.

27 Laurence BonJour, *The Structure of Empirical Knowledge*, pp. 108–9.

28 Donald Davidson also seems concerned to establish this sort of connection between coherence and truth:

> What is needed to answer the skeptic is to show that someone with a (more or less) coherent set of beliefs has a reason to suppose that his beliefs are not mistaken in the main. What we have shown is that it is absurd to look for a justifying ground for the totality of beliefs, something outside the totality which we can use to test or compare with our beliefs. The answer to our problem must then be to find a *reason* for supposing most of our beliefs are true that is not a form of *evidence*. (Davidson, "Coherence Theory of Truth and Knowledge", p. 314)

29 See Peter Klein and Ted Warfield, "What Price Coherence?," *Analysis* 54.3, (July 1994), pp. 129–32.

30 Steven Luper-Foy, "Arbitrary Reasons," in *Doubting: Contemporary Perspectives on Skepticism*, Michael Roth and Glenn Ross, eds, (Dordrecht: Kluwer Academic Publishers, 1990), pp. 39–55. Citation is from p. 45.

31 Luper-Foy, "Arbitrary Reasons," p. 40.

32 See "Questions Concerning Certain Faculties Claimed for Man," in the *Collected Papers of Charles Sanders Peirce*, Charles Hartshorne and Paul Weiss, eds, (Cambridge, MA: Belknap Press of Harvard University Press, 1965), Vol V, Bk II, pp. 135–55, especially pp. 152–3. There he writes:

> Question 7. *Whether there is any cognition not determined by a previous cognition.*
> 259. It would seem that there is or has been; for since we are in possession of cognitions, which are all determined by previous ones and these by cognitions earlier still, there must have been a *first* in this series or else our state of cognition at any time is completely determined according to logical laws, by our state at any previous time. But there are many facts against this last supposition, and therefore in favor of intuitive cognitions.

260. On the other hand, since it is impossible to know intuitively that a given cognition is not determined by a previous one, the only way in which this can be known is by hypothetic inference from observed facts. But to adduce the cognition by which a given cognition has been determined is to explain the determinations of that cognition. And it is a way of explaining them. For something entirely out of consciousness which may be supposed to determine it, can, as such, only be known and only adduced in the determinate cognition in question. So, that to suppose that a cognition is determined solely by something absolutely external, is to suppose its determinations incapable of explanation. Now, this is a hypothesis which is warranted under no circumstances, inasmuch as the only possible justification for a hypothesis is that it explains that facts, and to say that they are explained and at the same time to suppose them inexplicable is self-contradictory.

Peirce may, indeed, be arguing that only beliefs (cognitions) can provide a basis for other beliefs – nothing "external" can do so. He also might be arguing that the "meta-argument" referred to earlier can not succeed because one can always ask of the supposed meta-justification what justifies it. But I am not certain that either is what he is claiming. Further, if he is merely claiming that cognitions are infinitely revisable given new experiences, then he is not advocating infinitism.

33 John Williams, "Justified Belief and the Infinite Regress Argument," p. 85.

34 Williams, p. 86.

35 Richard Foley, "Inferential Justification and the Infinite Regress," *American Philosophical Quarterly* XV, no.4, (1978), pp. 311–16; quotation from pp. 311–12.

36 Williams, p. 86.

37 Robert Audi considers the set of beliefs: 2 is twice 1, 4 is twice 2, etc. Then, he says, "Surely, for a finite mind there will be some point or other at which the relevant proposition cannot be grasped." (See Audi's "Contemporary Foundationalism," in *The Theory of Knowledge: Classic and Contemporary Readings*, Louis Pojman, ed. (Belmont: Wadsworth, 1993), pp. 206–13. The quotation is from p. 209.)

The example is repeated in Audi's book, *The Structure of Justification*, (New York: Cambridge University Press, 1993), p. 127. My reply is that there are other examples of infinite series of beliefs (understood as dispositions) that do not involve increasingly difficult to grasp propositions (like the one about to be given in the main text).

38 I am indebted to Vann McGee for this point.

39 Richard Fumerton, "Metaepistemology and Skepticism," in *Doubting: Contemporary Perspectives on Skepticism*, pp. 57–68, quotation from p. 60. The same account of justification is given in Fumerton's book, *Metaepistemology and Skepticism* (Lanham, Maryland: Rowman & Littlefield Publishers, 1995), p. 36.

40 Richard Foley, "Inferential Justification and the Infinite Regress," esp. pp. 314–15.

41 There is a related point which I do think might be telling against the relatively thin view of justification I am proposing; and it might appear that this would jeopardize infinitism. Although it is clear that the requirement that S have a justification about what constitutes good reasoning is too strong a requirement of having a justification *simpliciter* or of paradigmatic forms of having a justification *simpliciter* for the reason just given, it is plausible to suggest that S must *believe*, at least dispositionally, that e makes p probable (to use Fumerton's terminology) whenever S is justified *simpliciter* in believing that p and S's available reason for p is e. That is a somewhat thicker notion of justification than the one I am proposing. It is plausible because the intuitions that inform the Truetemp case can be employed to support this moderately thick view. Suppose Mr. Truetemp believes it is 104 degrees and he also believes that he has an accurate thermometer-cum-temperature-belief-generator implanted in his head. On my "thin" view, if S believes that he has an accurate thermometer-cum-temperature-belief-generator implanted in his head, then S has a justification for the belief that it is 104 degrees, if, *ceteris paribus*, he has a good enough, non-question begging reason for believing that he has an accurate

thermometer-cum-temperature-belief-generator implanted in his head, and he has a reason for that reason, etc. But on my thin view, S might not believe that is his real reason. He might believe (dispositionally or occurrently) falsely, for example, that his reason is that it is Tuesday and that it is always 104 degrees on Tuesday. Of course, that is not a reason on my account because that belief, like the one offered in the Fish/Army Boots Case considered earlier, is not objectively available to Mr. Truetemp. I think such a case is best seen as one in which Mr. Truetemp does not know what his real reason is – but that he has a good enough reason available in both the objective and subjective sense. Thus, I think that, *ceteris paribus*, he has a justification *simpliciter* and that, *ceteris paribus*, he does know that the temperature is 104 degrees, but he does not know *how* he knows that the temperature is 104 degrees or even *that* he knows that. Nevertheless, I acknowledge the intuitive tug in the opposite direction – namely that he is not justified *simpliciter*, and hence does not know, because he would offer the "wrong" reason for his belief that it is 104 degrees.

Let me make the distinction between the three views of justification absolutely clear. The "thin" view (the one I think is correct) holds that *S has a justification for p on the basis of r* entails that (a) *S believes r* and (b) *r is a reason for p*. It does not require that, in addition, either (1) S believes that r is a reason for p or (2) S is justified in believing that r is a reason for p. The "moderately thick view" (the one I think is plausible) adds (1) to the thin view. The "extremely thick" view (the one I think cannot be correct) adds (2), and presumably (1) as well, to the thin view.

What is crucial to note is that, without jeopardizing infinitism, I can grant that S must dispositionally believe that e makes p probable in order for p to be justified by e for S. Of course on such a view, S would, at the next link in the chain, have to believe that e^1 makes e probable, and, at the next link believe that e^2 makes e^1 probable, etc. But note that granting that this thicker view of justification is correct would not force the infinitist into requiring that S have an implausibly complex belief. The beliefs at every step of the regress are no more complex than the one at the first step. So, the intuitive tug of this moderately thick view of justification can be allowed to modify the thin view without damaging my central claim. I resist the tug because I think it is the reasons available to S for p that determine whether S has a justification for p regardless of S's beliefs about those reasons.

42   There are some places in the *Posterior Analytics* where Aristotle *might* be claiming that it does follow from the fact that not all reasoning is the result of demonstration that the structure of reasons cannot be infinite:

> Our own doctrine is that not all knowledge is demonstrative: on the contrary, knowledge of the immediate premises is independent of demonstration. (The necessity of this is obvious: for since we must know the prior premises from which the demonstration is drawn, and since the regress must end in immediate truths, those truths must be indemonstrable.) [72b18–23] [*Basic Works of Aristotle*, Richard McKeon, ed., (New York: Random House, 1941)]

My point is that Aristotle's argument concerning the genesis of knowledge can be granted without granting that the structure of justification is finite. Demonstration cannot be required to bring about all knowledge. But it does not follow that reasons could not be given for all beliefs.

43   *Basic Works of Aristotle*, Richard McKeon, ed., 1011a1–14.

44   I. T. Oakley, "An Argument for Skepticism Concerning Justified Beliefs," *American Philosophical Quarterly* XIII, no. 3, (1976), pp. 221–8, especially pp. 226–7.

45   We said, in PAC, that for all x and for all y, if x is contained in the ancestry of y, y cannot be contained in the ancestry of x. Let "xCy" stand for "x is contained in the ancestry of y".

1. $(x)(y)(xCy \rightarrow \sim(yCx))$ 1. Premiss (PAC)
2. $aCa \rightarrow \sim(aCa)$ 2. UI (twice), 1
3. aCa 3. Assume, for reductio
4. $\sim(aCa)$ 4. 2,3 MP

5. ~(aCa)   5. CP (discharge), 3–4
6. (x)~(xCx)   6. UG, 5

46   In order to foreclose a possible objection, it is important to note that my claim that if every link contains q, the chain would be question begging does not have the unacceptable consequence that if S is justified in believing (p & q), then S is not justified in believing that q. My claim is merely that it is not always the case that (p & q) is an acceptable (i.e., non-question begging) reason for q. What typically occurs is that the chain of reasons includes p and includes q before including (p & q). But, of course, if the chain is of that form, then S would be justified in believing p and justified in believing q when S is justified in believing (p & q) because the justification of (p & q) depends upon the prior justification of p and the prior justification of q.

    I say "typically" in the preceding paragraph, because there do seem to be some chains of reasoning in which (p & q) precedes p and precedes q. Consider this one (where "xRy" stands for "x is a reason for y"):

Sally says "p & q" and whatever Sally says is true} **R** {(p & q)} **R** {q}

That chain does not appear to me to be question begging. The crucial point here is that my denial that (p & q) is always a reason for q (the presupposition of Oakley's argument), does not commit me to denying that justification distributes over conjunction.

47   I have condensed the argument a bit. In particular, there are other constraints besides the question begging one discussed by Post. But I believe that they are not relevant. See John Post, "Infinite Regress of Justification and of Explanation," *Philosophical Studies* XXXVIII, (1980), pp. 32–7, especially pp. 34–5. The argument, in a slightly revised form appears in Post's book, *The Faces of Existence*, (Ithaca: Cornell University Press, 1987), pp. 84–92.

48   I might note in passing that if PAA and PAC are necessary requirements of justification, both foundationalism and coherentism lead to the result that no contingent proposition is justified, since they advocate reasoning that violates those principles. I think any theory of justification that automatically leads to the view that *no* proposition is justified ought to be rejected as readily as a view that has the consequence that *all* contingent propositions are justified.

49   Ernest Sosa, "The Raft and the Pyramid," *Midwest Studies in Philosophy*, Section 5.

50   Post claims in *The Faces of Existence* that his new formulation of the *reductio* argument meets the objection by Sosa (see his fn. 21, p. 91). As I construe Sosa's objection, namely that more is required for a belief to have a justification than the mere existence of a series of beliefs which under some circumstances would provide a justification, Post's reformulation does not meet Sosa's objection. Post says that in such a series "justification is supposed to accumulate for [the first item in the series] merely as a result of [the person's] being able endlessly to meet the demand for justification simply by appealing to the next inferential justification in the [series]." (p. 90). My point is that there will not be such a series of available reasons for some beliefs.

51   The infinitist must be careful here not to fall into a trap laid by Paul Moser. He points out correctly that if the distinction between conditional (or potential) regresses and actual ones were that there is some external *information* that makes each step justified, then it could appear that the infinitist is committed to the view that the *reason* for believing any member of the chain is not the merely the antecedent in the chain but the antecedent *plus* the "external" information. That is, the external information would become an additional reason for holding the belief. See Paul Moser, "Whither Infinite Regresses of Justification," *The Southern Journal of Philosophy* XXIII, no. 1, (1985), pp. 65–74, especially p. 71.

    But the infinitist need not fall into the trap. The infinitist holds that there are some facts in virtue of which a belief is a reason. These facts are not part of the chain of reasoning.

52   Jonathan Dancy, *Introduction to Contemporary Epistemology*, (Oxford: Basil Blackwell, 1985) p. 55.

53   I use the term "provisional" justification rather than "conditional" justification (as used

by Dancy) because the term "provisional" more clearly underscores the fact that the reasons in the chains are replaceable.

54 *Outlines of Pyrrhonism*, PH I, 166.

55 Richard Fumerton, *Metaepistemology and Skepticism*, p. 57. Some of what follows repeats my comments on Fumerton's book in "Foundationalism and the Infinite Regress of Reasons," *Philosophy and Phenomenological Research* LVIII, No. 4 (1989), pp. 219–25.

56 Fumerton, p. 92.

57 A case similar to this one was discussed in a paper that Ernest Sosa presented at the Chapel Hill Philosophy Colloquium entitled "Two False Dichotomies: Foundationalism/ Coherentism and Internalism/Externalism" on 10/17/97.

58 BonJour makes a similar point this way:

> ... the fact that a clever person could invent an acceptable inferential justification on the spot when challenged to justify a hunch or arbitrary claim of some sort, so that the justification was in a sense available to him, would not mean that his belief was inferentially justified prior to that time ... (See BonJour, *The Structure of Empirical Knowledge*, p. 19)

59 Sosa, "Two False Dichotomies: Foundationalism/Coherentism and Internalism/Externalism," manuscript, p. 6.

60 It is crucial to note that I have been arguing that a necessary condition of S's being justified in believing that p is that S has an appropriate justification for p and having such a justification requires that there be an infinite number of non-repeating reasons available to S. I was not suggesting that was a sufficient condition for S's being justified or even having a justification (see fn. 8 above). So, Sosa's objection, even if valid, cannot be directed towards the main claim of this paper. Nevertheless, it is an important objection since the infinitist will at least have to show how it is possible for S to have a justified belief *according to the infinitist's account of justified belief*, if the distinctive type of adult human knowledge is to be shown to be

possible. Nevertheless, let us grant for the sake of argument that somehow it could be shown – either through philosophic argument, or perhaps even by cognitive science, that our beliefs do not (or can not) have the requisite causal history as required by infinitism (or foundationalism or coherentism, for that matter). What would be the consequences to infinitism (foundationalism or coherentism)? I think that is very far from clear-cut. The infinitist is claiming that a normatively acceptable set of reasons must be infinitely long and non-repeating if we are to avoid the pitfalls of foundationalism (arbitrariness) and coherentism (begging the question). If infinitism correctly specifies our current concept about what is required for a belief to have the appropriate normative pedigree and if it were to turn out that beliefs don't (or can't) have the requisite causal structure, then we have at least three choices: (1) We can revise our concept of the normative structure of good reasoning or (2) we can adopt a form of Pyrrhonism (withholding assent to any proposition requiring a justification) or (3) we can accept an antinomy. It would not follow that the normative constraints were incorrectly described – unless, perhaps, epistemic oughts imply epistemic cans. But that seems highly dubious. Would it not be possible for it to be the case that the rules of inference that are most truth conducive are such that we are not "wired" to employ them? If so, there is a perfectly good sense in which we ought to reason in some way that we can't.

61 See Michael Williams, *Unnatural Doubts* (Oxford, UK and Cambridge, MA: Blackwell, 1991).

62 Richard Foley, "Skepticism and Rationality," in *Doubting: Contemporary Perspectives on Skepticism*, cited earlier, pp. 69–81, quotation from p. 75.

63 Foley, "Skepticism and Rationality," p. 80. For a full development of the "no nets" view, see Richard Foley, *Working Without a Net: A Study of Egocentric Epistemology*, (New York: Oxford University Press, 1993).

PART III
Defining Knowledge

Introduction

The papers in this section are concerned with questions of analysis. An analysis, at least, provides informative, necessary, and sufficient conditions. Can knowledge be analyzed, and if so how?

Edmund Gettier's landmark paper successfully refuted the traditional analysis of knowledge as justified true belief. Through a series of examples, Gettier shows that one can believe what is true and be justified in so believing and yet fail to know. Justified true belief is not sufficient for knowledge.

What changes must be made to the traditional account, then, to escape the Gettier cases? One historically influential position requires that, to know that p, there must be no true proposition, q, such that, if q were to be become justified for S at t, p would no longer be justified for S at t. (Peter Klein, for example, has advocated such a position.) Gilbert Harman criticizes this sort of account, relying on an example based originally on one given by Keith Lehrer and Thomas Paxson, Jr. Suppose I see Tom steal a library book, and this is the testimony I give before the University Judicial Council. As it happens, later that day, after I have left the hearing room, Tom's mother testifies that Tom is thousands of miles away, but that his identical twin, Buck, who might well do such things, is in town. Suppose, further, that Tom's mother is a pathological liar and that this is clear to all in the courtroom. Myself, I know nothing about Tom's mother, brother, or any further testimony. Do I know that Tom stole the book? According to the historically influential position, the answer would be no. But Harman claims, intuitively, that it is yes.

Harman's suggested fourth condition for knowledge that p requires that "One's conclusion that p is not based solely on reasoning that essentially involves false intermediate conclusions." The problem posed by the example of Tom is then addressed as follows. First, reasoning is construed so as to involve a claim about the evidence one does not possess. Yet the construal is not so strong as to require that there be *no evidence whatever* that if known would destroy one's justification. Rather, the claim must be that there is no *undermining evidence* one does not possess. Although Harman admits he cannot provide criteria for distinguishing true propositions that constitute undermining evidence from those that are such that if known would render the person unjustified, he notes that there is an intuitive difference, and that this difference is at work in our judgments about Tom.

Linda Zagzebski doesn't offer a specific suggestion for a fourth condition on knowledge but does argue for a general constraint on responses to the Gettier problem. She argues that as long as an analysis of knowledge implies what she calls "warrant fallibilism," Gettier problems will be inescapable. Traditionally, epistemologists have granted a close connection between truth and justification (or warrant). For example, perhaps a justified belief is one in which the available evidence makes the truth of the belief very likely or perhaps a justified belief is one that was produced by faculties that are usually very reliable. But epistemologists have not insisted that this connection between justification and truth is a necessary one. In other words, epistemologists have favored *warrant fallibilism*, the view that it is possible for a belief to be justified (or warranted) but false. A Gettier case arises when an accident of bad luck that "disconnects" the justification of a belief from its usual close connection with truth is cancelled out by an accident of good luck that makes the belief true nonetheless. Zagzebski shows that both internalist and externalist accounts (including Plantinga's proper functional account) of justification are subject to Gettier problems, and she provides a two-step recipe for constructing a Gettier counter-example for any analysis of knowledge that implies warrant fallibilism. First, construct a case of a belief that includes a degree of justification (or warrant) sufficient for knowledge but ensure that some accident renders the belief false. Second, add another element of luck that makes the belief true in a way that leaves the degree of justification unchanged. *Voila*: a Gettier counter-example!

Timothy Williamson proposes a reorientation for epistemology – that we treat knowledge as unanalyzable and seek rather to understand epistemological phenomena generally (e.g., justified belief, evidence, warranted assertion) in terms of knowledge. This approach has come to be called *knowledge-first* epistemology. But why did we think knowledge was definable in the first place? We endorsed the following reasoning. Because knowing that p entails both the mental state of believing that p and the (typically) non-mental state of its being true that p, knowledge must be some sort of composite involving these two components. Williamson argues that this reasoning is incorrect. Just because something entails something non-mental as well as something mental does not mean that it has these as component parts. And surely our inability to complete the full factorization provides evidence that knowledge is not so factorizable. This frees us to affirm what seems plausible on its face, that knowledge itself is a mental state. Williamson goes on to argue that knowledge can be identified as the broadest factive mental state. (A mental state with a content p is factive if one can be in it only if p.)

Further Reading

Alston, William P., *Epistemic Justification* (Ithaca, NY: Cornell University Press, 1989).

Chisholm, Roderick, *Theory of Knowledge* (Englewood Cliffs: Prentice-Hall, 1966, 2nd edn 1977, 3rd edn 1989).

Craig, Edward, *Knowledge and the State of Nature* (Oxford: Clarendon Press, 1990).

Fogelin, Robert, *Pyrrhonian Reflections on Knowledge and Justification* (Oxford: Oxford University Press, 1997).

Goldman, Alvin, "A Causal Theory of Knowing," *Journal of Philosophy* 64 (1967), pp. 357–72.

——, *Epistemology and Cognition* (Cambridge, MA: Harvard University Press, 1986).

Lehrer, Keith, *Theory of Knowledge* (Boulder, CO: Westview Press, 1990).

Moser, Paul K., *Knowledge and Evidence* (Cambridge: Cambridge University Press, 1989).

Plantinga, Alvin, *Warrant and Proper Function* (Oxford: Oxford University Press, 1993).

Pollock, John, *Contemporary Theories of Knowledge* (Totowa, NJ: Rowman and Littlefield, 1986).

Roth, M. D. and L. Galis (eds), *Knowing: Essays in the Analysis of Knowledge* (New York: Random House, 1970).

Shope, Robert K., *The Analysis of Knowing* (Princeton: Princeton University Press, 1983).

Sosa, Ernest, *Knowledge in Perspective: Selected Essays in Epistemology* (Cambridge: Cambridge University Press, 1991).

Williamson, Timothy, *Knowledge and Its Limits* (Oxford: Oxford University Press, 2000).

Zagzebski, Linda Trinkhaus, *Virtues of the Mind: An Inquiry into the Nature of Virtue and the Ethical Foundations of Knowledge* (Cambridge: Cambridge University Press, 1996).

CHAPTER 15

Is Justified True Belief Knowledge?

Edmund Gettier

Various attempts have been made in recent years to state necessary and sufficient conditions for someone's knowing a given proposition. The attempts have often been such that they can be stated in a form similar to the following:[1]

(a)   S knows that *P IFF*   (i)   *P* is true,
  (ii)   S believes that *P*, and
  (iii)   S is justified in believing that *P*.

For example, Chisholm has held that the following gives the necessary and sufficient conditions for knowledge:[2]

(b)   S knows that *P IFF*   (i)   S accepts *P*,
  (ii)   S has adequate evidence for *P*, and
  (iii)   *P* is true.

Ayer has stated the necessary and sufficient conditions for knowledge as follows:[3]

(c)   S knows that *P IFF*   (i)   *P* is true,
  (ii)   S is sure that *P* is true, and
  (iii)   S has the right to be sure that *P* is true.

Originally published in *Analysis* (1963), pp. 121–3.

I shall argue that (a) is false in that the conditions stated therein do not constitute a *sufficient* condition for the truth of the proposition that S knows that *P*. The same argument will show that (b) and (c) fail if "has adequate evidence for" or "has the right to be sure that" is substituted for "is justified in believing that" throughout.

I shall begin by noting two points. First, in that sense of "justified" in which S's being justified in believing *P* is a necessary condition of S's knowing that *P*, it is possible for a person to be justified in believing a proposition which is in fact false. Second, for any proposition *P*, if S is justified in believing *P* and *P* entails Q and S deduces Q from *P* and accepts Q as a result of this deduction, then S is justified in believing Q. Keeping these two points in mind, I shall now present two cases in which the conditions stated in (a) are true for some proposition, though it is at the same time false that the person in question knows that proposition.

Case I

Suppose that Smith and Jones have applied for a certain job. And suppose that Smith has strong evidence for the following conjunctive proposition:

(d)   Jones is the man who will get the job, and Jones has ten coins in his pocket.

Smith's evidence for (d) might be that the president of the company assured him that Jones would in the end be selected, and that he, Smith, had counted the coins in Jones's pocket ten minutes ago. Proposition (d) entails:

(e) The man who will get the job has ten coins in his pocket.

Let us suppose that Smith sees the entailment from (d) to (e) and accepts (e) on the grounds of (d), for which he has strong evidence. In this case, Smith is clearly justified in believing that (e) is true.

But imagine, further, that unknown to Smith, he himself, not Jones, will get the job. And, also, unknown to Smith, he himself has ten coins in his pocket. Proposition (e) is then true, though proposition (d), from which Smith inferred (e), is false. In our example, then, all of the following are true: (*i*) (e) is true, (*ii*) Smith believes that (e) is true, and (*iii*) Smith is justified in believing that (e) is true. But it is equally clear that Smith does not *know* that (e) is true; for (e) is true in virtue of the number of coins in Smith's pocket, while Smith does not know how many coins are in Smith's pocket, and bases his belief in (e) on a count of the coins in Jones's pocket, whom he falsely believes to be the man who will get the job.

Case II

Let us suppose that Smith has strong evidence for the following proposition:

(f) Jones owns a Ford.

Smith's evidence might be that Jones has at all times in the past within Smith's memory owned a car, and always a Ford, and that Jones has just offered Smith a ride while driving a Ford. Let us imagine, now, that Smith has another friend, Brown, of whose whereabouts he is totally ignorant. Smith selects three place names quite at random and constructs the following three propositions:

(g) Either Jones owns a Ford, or Brown is in Boston.
(h) Either Jones owns a Ford, or Brown is in Barcelona.
(i) Either Jones owns a Ford, or Brown is in Brest-Litovsk.

Each of these propositions is entailed by (f). Imagine that Smith realizes the entailment of each of these propositions he has constructed by (f), and proceeds to accept (g), (h), and (i) on the basis of (f). Smith has correctly inferred (g), (h), and (i) from a proposition for which he has strong evidence. Smith is therefore completely justified in believing each of these three propositions. Smith, of course, has no idea where Brown is.

But imagine now that two further conditions hold. First, Jones does *not* own a Ford, but is at present driving a rented car. And second, by the sheerest coincidence, and entirely unknown to Smith, the place mentioned in proposition (h) happens really to be the place where Brown is. If these two conditions hold, then Smith does *not* know that (h) is true, even though (*i*) (h) *is* true, (*ii*) Smith does believe that (h) is true, and (*iii*) Smith is justified in believing that (h) is true.

These two examples show that definition (a) does not state a *sufficient* condition for someone's knowing a given proposition. The same cases, with appropriate changes, will suffice to show that neither definition (b) nor definition (c) do so either.

Notes

1 Plato seems to be considering some such definition at *Theaetetus* 201, and perhaps accepting one at *Meno* 98.
2 Roderick M. Chisholm, *Perceiving: A Philosophical Study* (Ithaca, NY: Cornell University Press, 1957), p. 16.
3 A. J. Ayer, *The Problem of Knowledge* (London: Pelican, 1976).

CHAPTER 16

Thought, Selections

Gilbert Harman

Knowledge and Probability

The lottery paradox

Some philosophers argue that we never simply
believe anything that we do not take to be certain.
Instead we believe it to a greater or lesser degree;
we assign it a higher or lower "subjective probability." If knowledge implies belief, on this view
we never know anything that isn't absolutely certain. That conflicts with ordinary views about
knowledge, since our degree of belief in some
things we think we know is greater than our
degree of belief in other things we think we
know.

We might count as believed anything whose
"subjective probability" exceeds .99. But that
would also conflict with ordinary views. We do
not suppose that a man inconsistently believes of
every participant in a fair lottery that the participant will lose, even though we suppose that the
man assigns a subjective probability greater than
.99 to each person's losing. If ordinary views are
to be preserved, belief must be distinguished from
high degree of belief.

A rule of inductive inference is sometimes
called a "rule of acceptance," since it tells us what
we can accept (i.e., believe), given other beliefs,

Originally published in G. Harman, *Thought* (Princeton:
Princeton University Press, 1973).

degrees of belief, etc. A purely probabilistic rule
of acceptance says that we may accept something
if and only if its probability is greater than .99.
Kyburg points out that such a rule leads to a
"lottery paradox" since it authorizes the acceptance of an inconsistent set of beliefs, each saying
of a particular participant in a lottery that he
will lose.[1]

It is true that no contradiction arises if conclusions are added to the evidence on whose basis
probabilities are calculated. Concluding that a
particular person will lose changes the evidential
probability that the next person will lose. When
there are only 100 people left, we cannot infer the
next person will lose, since the evidential probability of this no longer exceeds .99. But this does
not eliminate paradox. The paradox is not just
that use of a purely probabilistic rule leads to
inconsistent beliefs. It is not obviously irrational
to have inconsistent beliefs even when we know
that they are inconsistent. It has occasionally been
suggested[2] that a rational man believes that he has
at least some (other) false beliefs. If so, it follows
logically that at least one thing he believes *is* false
(if nothing else, then his belief that he has other
false beliefs); a rational man will know that. So a
rational man knows that at least one thing he
believes is false. Nevertheless it *is* paradoxical to
suppose that we could rationally believe of every
participant in a lottery that he will lose; and it is
just as paradoxical to suppose that we could

rationally believe this of all but 100 participants in a large lottery.

The lottery paradox can be avoided if a purely probabilistic rule of acceptance is taken to be relevant not to the acceptance of various individual hypotheses but rather to the set of what we accept. The idea is that the probability of the whole set must exceed .99. We are free to choose among various hypotheses saying that one or another participant in a lottery loses as long as the probability of the conjunction of all hypotheses accepted remains above .99. (The idea requires a distinction between what is simply accepted and what is accepted as evidence. If we could add new conclusions to the evidence, the lottery paradox would be generated as indicated in the previous paragraph.) However, although this version of a purely probabilistic rule does not yield the lottery paradox, it does not fit in with ordinary views, as I shall now argue.

Gettier examples and probabilistic rules of acceptance

In any Gettier example we are presented with similar cases in which someone infers h from things he knows, h is true, and he is equally justified in making the inference in either case.[3] In the one case he comes to know that h and in the other case he does not. I have observed that a natural explanation of many Gettier examples is that the relevant inference involves not only the final conclusion h but also at least one intermediate conclusion true in the one case but not in the other. And I have suggested that any account of inductive inference should show why such intermediate conclusions are essentially involved in the relevant inferences. Gettier cases are thus to be explained by appeal to the principle

> P Reasoning that essentially involves false conclusions, intermediate or final, cannot give one knowledge.

It is easy to see that purely probabilistic rules of acceptance do not permit an explanation of Gettier examples by means of principle P. Reasoning in accordance with a purely probabilistic rule involves essentially only its final conclusion. Since that conclusion is highly probable, it can be inferred without reference to any other

conclusions; in particular, there will be no intermediate conclusion essential to the inference that is true in one case and false in the other.

For example, Mary's friend Mr Nogot convinces her that he has a Ford. He tells her that he owns a Ford, he shows her his ownership certificate, and he reminds her that she saw him drive up in a Ford. On the basis of this and similar evidence, Mary concludes that Mr Nogot owns a Ford. From that she infers that one of her friends owns a Ford. In a normal case, Mary might in this way come to know that one of her friends owns a Ford. However, as it turns out in this case, Mary is wrong about Nogot. His car has just been repossessed and towed away. It is no longer his. On the other hand, Mary's friend Mr Havit does own a Ford, so she is right in thinking that one of her friends owns a Ford. However, she does not realize that Havit owns a Ford. Indeed, she hasn't been given the slightest reason to think that he owns a Ford. It is false that Mr Nogot owns a Ford, but it is true that one of Mary's friends owns a Ford. Mary has a justified true belief that one of her friends owns a Ford but she does not know that one of her friends owns a Ford. She does not know this because principle P has been violated. Mary's reasoning essentially involves the false conclusion that Mr. Nogot owns a Ford.[4]

But, if there were probabilistic rules of acceptance, there would be no way to exhibit the relevance of Mary's intermediate conclusion. For Mary could then have inferred her final conclusion (that one of her friends owns a Ford) directly from her original evidence, all of which is true. Mr Nogot *is* her friend, he *did* say he owns a Ford, he *did* show Mary an ownership certificate, she *did* see him drive up in a Ford, etc. If a purely probabilistic rule would permit Mary to infer from that evidence that her friend Nogot owns a Ford, it would also permit her to infer directly that one of her friends owns a Ford, since the latter conclusion is at least as probable on the evidence as the former. Given a purely probabilistic rule of acceptance, Mary need not first infer an intermediate conclusion and then deduce her final conclusion, since by means of such a rule she could directly infer her final conclusion. The intermediate conclusion would not be essential to her inference, and her failure to know that one of her friends owns a Ford could not be explained by appeal to principle P.

A defender of purely probabilistic rules might reply that what has gone wrong in this case is not that Mary *must* infer her conclusion from something false but rather that, from the evidence that supports her conclusion, she *could* also infer something false, namely that Mr Nogot owns a Ford. In terms of principle *P*, this would be to count as essential to Mary's inference any conclusion the probabilistic rule would authorize from her starting point. But given any evidence, some false conclusion will be highly probable on that evidence. This follows, e.g., from the existence of lotteries. For example, let *s* be a conclusion saying under what conditions the New Jersey State Lottery was most recently held. Let *q* say what ticket won the grand prize. Then consider the conclusion, *not both s and q*. Call that conclusion *r*. The conclusion *r* is highly probable, given evidence having nothing to do with the outcome of the recent lottery, but *r* is false. If such highly probable false conclusions were always considered essential to an inference, Mary could never come to know anything.

The problem is that purely probabilistic considerations do not suffice to account for the peculiar relevance of Mary's conclusion about Nogot. Various principles might be suggested; but none of them work. For example, we might suspect that the trouble with *r* is that it has nothing to do with whether any of Mary's friends owns a Ford. Even if Mary were to assume that *r* is false, her original conclusion would continue to be highly probable on her evidence. So we might suggest that an inferable conclusion *t* is essential to an inference only if the assumption that *t* was false would block the inference. That would distinguish Mary's relevant intermediate conclusion, that Nogot owns a Ford, from the irrelevant conclusion *r*, since if Mary assumed that Nogot does not own a Ford she could not conclude that one of her friends owns a Ford.

But again, if there is a purely probabilistic rule of acceptance, there will always be an inferable false *t* such that the assumption that it is false would block even inferences that give us knowledge. For let *h* be the conclusion of any inference not concerned with the New Jersey Lottery and let *r* be as above. Then we can let *t* be the conjunction *h & r*. This *t* is highly probable on the same evidence *e* on which *h* is highly probable; *t* is false; and *h* is not highly probable relative to the

evidence *e & (not t)*. Any inference would be undermined by such a *t*, given a purely probabilistic rule of acceptance along with the suggested criterion of essential conclusions.

The trouble is that purely probabilistic rules are incompatible with the natural account of Gettier examples by means of principle *P*. The solution is not to attempt to modify *P* but rather to modify our account of inference.

Knowledge and Explanation

A causal theory

Goldman suggests that we know only if there is the proper sort of causal connection between our belief and what we know.[5] For example, we perceive that there has been an automobile accident only if the accident is relevantly causally responsible, by way of our sense organs, for our belief that there has been an accident. Similarly, we remember doing something only if having done it is relevantly causally responsible for our current memory of having done it. Although in some cases the fact that we know thus simply begins a causal chain that leads to our belief, in other cases the causal connection is more complicated. If Mary learns that Mr Havit owns a Ford, Havit's past ownership is causally responsible for the evidence she has and also responsible (at least in part) for Havit's present ownership. Here the relevant causal connection consists in there being a common cause of the belief and of the state of affairs believed in.

Mary fails to know in the original Nogot–Havit case because the causal connection is lacking. Nogot's past ownership is responsible for her evidence but is not responsible for the fact that one of her friends owns a Ford. Havit's past ownership at least partly accounts for why one of her friends now owns a Ford, but it is not responsible for her evidence. Similarly, the man who is told something true by a speaker who does not believe what he says fails to know because the truth of what is said is not causally responsible for the fact that it is said.

General knowledge does not fit into this simple framework. That all emeralds are green neither causes nor is caused by the existence of the particular green emeralds examined when we come to know that all emeralds are green. Goldman handles such examples by counting logical connections among the causal connections. The belief that all emeralds are green is, in an extended sense, relevantly causally connected to the fact that all emeralds are green, since the evidence causes the belief and is logically entailed by what is believed.

It is obvious that not every causal connection, especially in this extended sense, is relevant to knowledge. Any two states of affairs are logically connected simply because both are entailed by their conjunction. If every such connection were relevant, the analysis Goldman suggests would have us identify knowledge with true belief, since there would always be a relevant "causal connection" between any state of true belief and the state of affairs believed in. Goldman avoids this reduction of his analysis to justified true belief by saying that when knowledge is based on inference relevant causal connections must be "reconstructed" in the inference. Mary knows that one of her friends owns a Ford only if her inference reconstructs the relevant causal connection between evidence and conclusion.

But what does it mean to say that her inference must "reconstruct" the relevant causal connection? Presumably it means that she must infer or be able to infer something about the causal connection between her conclusion and the evidence for it. And this suggests that Mary must make at least two inferences. First she must infer her original conclusion and second she must infer something about the causal connection between the conclusion and her evidence. Her second conclusion is her "reconstruction" of the causal connection. But how detailed must her reconstruction be? If she must reconstruct every detail of the causal connection between evidence and conclusion, she will never gain knowledge by way of inference. If she need only reconstruct some "causal connection," she will always know, since she will always be able to infer that evidence and conclusion are both entailed by their conjunction.

I suggest that it is a mistake to approach the problem as a problem about what else Mary needs to infer before she has knowledge of her original conclusion. Goldman's remark about reconstructing the causal connection makes more sense as a remark about the kind of inference Mary needs to reach her original conclusion in the first place. It has something to do with principle *P* and the natural account of the Gettier examples.

Nogot presents Mary with evidence that he owns a Ford. She infers that one of her friends owns a Ford. She is justified in reaching that conclusion and it is true. However, since it is true, not because Nogot owns a Ford, but because Havit does, Mary fails to come to know that one of her friends owns a Ford. The natural explanation is that she must infer that Nogot owns a Ford and does not know her final conclusion unless her intermediate conclusion is true. According to this natural explanation, Mary's inference essentially involves the conclusion that Nogot owns a Ford. According to Goldman, her inference essentially involves a conclusion concerning a causal connection. In order to put these ideas together, we must turn Goldman's theory of knowledge into a theory of inference.

As a first approximation, let us take his remarks about causal connections literally, forgetting for the moment that they include logical connections. Then let us transmute his causal theory of knowing into the theory that inductive conclusions always take the form *X causes Y*, where further conclusions are reached by additional steps of inductive or deductive reasoning. In particular, we may deduce either *X* or *Y* from *X causes Y*.

This causal theory of inferring provides the following account of why knowledge requires that we be right about an appropriate causal connection. A person knows by inference only if all conclusions essential to that inference are true. That is, his inference must satisfy principle *P*. Since he can legitimately infer his conclusion only if he can first infer certain causal statements, he can know only if he is right about the causal connection expressed by those statements. First, Mary infers that her evidence is a causal result of Nogot's past ownership of the Ford. From that she deduces that Nogot has owned a Ford. Then she infers that his past ownership has been causally responsible for present ownership; and she deduces that Nogot owns a Ford. Finally, she deduces that one of her friends owns a Ford. She fails to know because she is wrong when she infers that Nogot's past ownership is responsible for Nogot's present ownership.

Inference to the best explanatory statement

A better account of inference emerges if we replace "cause" with "because." On the revised account, we infer not just statements of the form *X causes Y* but, more generally, statements of the form *Y because X* or *X explains Y*. Inductive inference is conceived as inference to the best of competing explanatory statements. Inference to a causal explanation is a special case.

The revised account squares better with ordinary usage. Nogot's past ownership helps to explain Mary's evidence, but it would sound odd to say that it caused that evidence. Similarly, the detective infers that activities of the butler explain these footprints; does he infer that those activities caused the footprints? A scientist explains the properties of water by means of a hypothesis about unobservable particles that make up the water, but it does not seem right to say that facts about those particles cause the properties of water. An observer infers that certain mental states best explain someone's behavior; but such explanation by reasons might not be causal explanation.

Furthermore, the switch from "cause" to "because" avoids Goldman's *ad hoc* treatment of knowledge of generalizations. Although there is no causal relation between a generalization and those observed instances which provide us with evidence for the generalization, there is an obvious explanatory relationship. That all emeralds are green does not cause a particular emerald to be green; but it can explain why that emerald is green. And, other things being equal, we can infer a generalization only if it provides the most plausible way to explain our evidence.

We often infer generalizations that explain but do not logically entail their instances, since they are of the form, *In circumstances C, X's tend to be Y's*. Such generalizations may be inferred if they provide a sufficiently plausible account of observed instances all things considered. For example, from the fact that doctors have generally been right in the past when they have said that someone is going to get measles, I infer that doctors can normally tell from certain symptoms that someone is going to get measles. More precisely, I infer that doctors have generally been right in the past because they can normally tell from certain symptoms that someone is going to get measles. This is a very weak explanation, but it is a genuine one. Compare it with the pseudo-explanation, "Doctors are generally right when they say someone has measles because they can normally tell from certain symptoms that someone is going to get measles."

Similarly, I infer that a substance is soluble in water from the fact that it dissolved when I stirred it into some water. That is a real explanation, to be distinguished from the pseudo-explanation, "That substance dissolves in water because it is soluble in water." Here too a generalization explains an instance without entailing that instance, since water-soluble substances do not always dissolve in water.

Although we cannot simply deduce instances from this sort of generalization, we can often infer that the generalization will explain some new instance. The inference is warranted if the explanatory claim *that X's tend to be Y's will explain why the next X will be Y* is sufficiently more plausible than competitors such as *interfering factor Q will prevent the next X from being a Y*. For example, the doctor says that you will get measles. Because doctors are normally right about that sort of thing, I infer that you will. More precisely, I infer that doctors' normally being able to tell when someone will get measles will explain the doctor's being right in this case. The competing explanatory statements here are not other explanations of the doctor's being right but rather explanations of his being wrong – e.g., because he has misperceived the symptoms, or because you have faked the symptoms of measles, or because these symptoms are the result of some other disease, etc. Similarly, I infer that this sugar will dissolve in my tea. That is, I infer that the solubility of sugar in tea will explain this sugar's dissolving in the present case. Competing explanations would explain the sugar's not dissolving – e.g., because there is already a saturated sugar solution there, because the tea is ice-cold, etc.

Further examples[6]

I infer that when I scratch this match it will light. My evidence is that this is a Sure-Fire brand match, and in the past Sure-Fire matches have always lit when scratched. However, unbeknownst to me, this particular match is defective. It will not light unless its surface temperature can be raised to six hundred degrees, which is more than can be attained by scratching. Fortunately, as I scratch the match, a burst of Q-radiation (from the sun) strikes the tip, raising surface temperature to six hundred degrees and igniting the match. Did I know that the match would light? Presumably I did not know. I had justified true belief, but not knowledge. On the present account, the explanation of my failure to know is this: I infer that the match will light in the next instance because Sure-Fire matches generally light when scratched. I am wrong about that; that is not why the match will light this time. Therefore, I do not know that it will light.

It is important that our justification can appeal to a simple generalization even when we have false views about the explanation of that generalization. Consider the man who thinks that barometers fall before a rainstorm because of an increase in the force of gravity. He thinks the gravity pulls the mercury down the tube and then, when the force is great enough, pulls rain out of the sky. Although he is wrong about this explanation, the man in question can come to know that it is going to rain when he sees the barometer falling in a particular case. That a man's belief is based on an inference that cannot give him knowledge (because it infers a false explanation) does not mean that it is not also based on an inference that does give him knowledge (because it infers a true explanation). The man in question has knowledge because he infers not only the stronger explanation involving gravity but also the weaker explanation. He infers that the explanation of the past correlation between falling barometer and rain is that the falling barometer is normally associated with rain. Then he infers that this weak generalization will be what will explain the correlation between the falling barometer and rain in the next instance.

Notice that if the man is wrong about that last point, because the barometer is broken and is leaking mercury, so that it is just a coincidence that rain is correlated with the falling barometer in the next instance, he does not come to know that it is going to rain.

Another example is the mad-fiend case. Omar falls down drunk in the street. An hour later he suffers a fatal heart attack not connected with his recent drinking. After another hour a mad fiend comes down the street, spies Omar lying in the gutter, cuts off his head, and runs away. Some time later still, you walk down the street, see Omar lying there, and observe that his head has been cut off. You infer that Omar is dead; and in this way you come to know that he is dead. Now there is no causal connection between Omar's being dead and his head's having been cut off. The fact that Omar is dead is not causally responsible for his head's having been cut off, since if he had not suffered that fatal heart attack he still would have been lying there drunk when the mad fiend came along. And having his head cut off did not cause Omar's death, since he was already dead. Nor is there a straightforward logical connection between Omar's being dead and his having his head cut off. (Given the right sorts of tubes, one might survive decapitation.) So it is doubtful that Goldman's causal theory of knowing can account for your knowledge that Omar is dead.

If inductive inference is inference to the best explanatory statement, your inference might be parsed as follows: "Normally, if someone's head is cut off, that person is dead. This generalization accounts for the fact that Omar's having his head cut off is correlated here with Omar's being dead." Relevant competing explanatory statements in this case would not be competing explanations of Omar's being dead. Instead they would seek to explain Omar's not being dead despite his head's having been cut off. One possibility would be that doctors have carefully connected head and body with special tubes so that blood and air get from body to head and back again. You rule out that hypothesis on grounds of explanatory complications: too many questions left unanswered (why can't you see the tubes? why wasn't it done in the hospital? etc.). If you cannot rule such possibilities out, then you cannot come to know that Omar is dead. And if you do rule them out but they turn out to be true, again you do not come to know. For example, if it is all an elaborate psychological philosophical experiment, which however fails, then you do not come to know that Omar is dead even though he is dead.

Statistical inference

Statistical inference, and knowledge obtained from it, is also better explicated by way of the notion of statistical explanation than by way of the notion of cause or logical entailment. A person may infer that a particular coin is biased because that provides the best statistical explanation of the observed fraction of heads. His conclusion explains his evidence but neither causes nor entails it.

The relevant kind of statistical explanation does not always make what it explains very probable. For example, suppose that I want to know whether I have the fair coin or the weighted coin. It is equally likely that I have either; the probability of getting heads on a toss of the fair coin is 1/2; and the probability of getting heads on a toss of the weighted coin is 6/10. I toss the coin 10,000 times. It comes up heads 4,983 times and tails 5,017. I correctly conclude that the coin is the fair one. You would ordinarily think that I could in this way come to know that I have the fair coin. On the theory of inference we have adopted, I infer the best explanation of the observed distribution of heads and tails. But the explanation, that these were random tosses of a fair coin, does not make it probable that the coin comes up heads exactly 4,983 times and tails exactly 5,017 times in 10,000 tosses. The probability of this happening with a fair coin is very small. If we want to accept the idea that inference is inference to the best explanatory statement, we must agree that statistical explanation can cite an explanation that makes what it explains less probable than it makes its denial. In the present case, I do not explain why 4,983 heads have come up rather than some other number of heads. Instead I explain how it happened that 4,983 heads came up, what led to this happening. I do not explain why this happened rather than something else, since the same thing could easily have led to something else.

To return to an example I have used elsewhere, you walk into a casino and see the roulette wheel stop at red fifty times in a row. The explanation may be that the wheel is fixed. It may also be that the wheel is fair and this is one of those times when fifty reds come up on a fair wheel. Given a fair wheel we may expect that to happen sometimes (but not very often). But if the explanation is that the wheel is fair and that this is just one of those times, it says what the sequence of reds is the result of, the "outcome" of. It does not say why fifty reds in a row occurred this time rather than some other time, nor why that particular

series occurred rather than any of the $2^{50}-1$ other possible series.

This kind of statistical explanation explains something as the outcome of a chance set-up. The statistical probability of getting the explained outcome is irrelevant to whether or not we explain that outcome, since this kind of explanation is essentially pure nondeterministic explanation. All that is relevant is that the outcome to be explained is one possible outcome given that chance set-up. That is not to say that the statistical probability of an outcome is irrelevant to the explanation of that outcome. It is relevant in this sense: the greater the statistical probability an observed outcome has in a particular chance set-up, the better that set-up explains that outcome.

The point is less a point about statistical explanation than a point about statistical inference. I wish to infer the best of competing statistical explanations of the observed distribution of heads. This observed outcome has different statistical probabilities in the two hypothetical chance set-ups, fair coin or weighted coin. The higher this statistical probability, the better, from the point of view of inference (other things being equal). The statistical probability of an outcome in a particular hypothetical chance set-up is relevant to how good an explanation that chance set-up provides. Here a better explanation is one that is more likely to be inferable. For example, I infer that I have the fair coin. The statistical probability of 4,983 heads on 10,000 tosses of a fair coin is much greater than the statistical probability of that number of heads on 10,000 tosses of the weighted coin. From the point of view of statistical probability, the hypothesis that the coin is fair offers a better explanation of the observed distribution than the hypothesis that the coin is biased. So statistical probability is relevant to statistical explanation. Not that there is no explanation unless statistical probability is greater than 1/2. Rather that statistical probability provides a measure of the inferability of a statistical explanation.

According to probability theory, if initially the coin is just as likely to be the fair one or the weighted one and the statistical probability of the observed outcome is much greater for the fair coin than for the weighted coin, the probability that the coin is fair, given the observed evidence, will be very high. We might conclude that the statistical probability of the observed outcome given the fair or weighted coin is only indirectly relevant to my inference, relevant only because of the theoretical connections between those statistical probabilities and the evidential probabilities of the two hypotheses about the coin, given the observed evidence. But that would be to get things exactly backward. No doubt there is a connection between high evidential probability and inference; but, as we have seen, it is not because there is a purely probabilistic rule of acceptance. High probability by itself does not warrant inference. Only explanatory considerations can do that; and the probability relevant to explanation is statistical probability, the probability that is involved in statistical explanation. It is the statistical probabilities of the observed outcome, given the fair and weighted coins, that is directly relevant to inference. The evidential probabilities of the two hypotheses are only indirectly relevant in that they in some sense reflect the inferability of the hypotheses, where that is determined directly by considerations of statistical probability.

Suppose that at first you do not know which of the two coins I have selected. I toss it 10,000 times, getting 4,983 heads and 5,017 tails. You infer that I have the fair coin, and you are right. But the reason for the 4,983 heads is that I am very good at tossing coins to come up whichever way I desire and I deliberately tossed the coin so as to get roughly half heads and half tails. So, even though you have justified true belief, you do not know that I have the fair coin.

If statistical inference were merely a matter of infering something that has a high probability on the evidence, there would be no way to account for this sort of Gettier example. And if we are to appeal to principle *P*, it must be a conclusion essential to your inference that the observed outcome is the result of a chance set-up involving the fair coin in such a way that the probability of heads is 1/2. Given a purely probabilistic rule, that conclusion could not be essential, for reasons similar to those that have already been discussed concerning the Nogot–Havit case. On the other hand, if statistical inference is inference to the best explanation and there is such a thing as statistical explanation even where the statistical probability of what is explained is quite low, then your conclusion about the reason for my getting 4,983 heads is seen to be essential to your

inference. Since your explanation of the observed outcome is false, principle *P* accounts for the fact that you do not come to know that the coin is the fair coin even though you have justified true belief.

Conclusion

We are led to construe induction as inference to the best explanation, or more precisely as inference to the best of competing explanatory statements. The conclusion of any single step of such inference is always of the form *Y because X* (or *X explains Y*), from which we may deduce either *X* or *Y*. Inductive reasoning is seen to consist in a sequence of such explanatory conclusions.

We have been led to this conception of induction in an attempt to account for Gettier examples that show something wrong with the idea that knowledge is justified true belief. We have tried to find principles of inference which, together with principle *P*, would explain Gettier's deviant cases. Purely probabilistic rules were easily seen to be inadequate. Goldman's causal theory of knowing, which promised answers to some of Gettier's questions, suggested a causal theory of induction: inductive inference as inference to the best of competing causal statements. Our present version is simply a modification of that, with *explanatory* replacing *causal*. Its strength lies in the fact that it accounts for a variety of inferences, including inferences that involve weak generalizations or statistical hypotheses, in a way that explains Gettier examples by means of principle *P*.

Evidence One Does Not Possess

Three examples

Example (1)
While I am watching him, Tom takes a library book from the shelf and conceals it beneath his coat. Since I am the library detective, I follow him as he walks brazenly past the guard at the front door. Outside I see him take out the book and smile. As I approach he notices me and suddenly runs away. But I am sure that it was Tom, for I know him well. I saw Tom steal a book from the library and that is the testimony I give before the University Judicial Council. After testifying, I leave the hearing room and return to my post in

the library. Later that day, Tom's mother testifies that Tom has an identical twin, Buck. Tom, she says, was thousands of miles away at the time of the theft. She hopes that Buck did not do it; but she admits that he has a bad character.

Do I know that Tom stole the book? Let us suppose that I am right. It was Tom that took the book. His mother was lying when she said that Tom was thousands of miles away. I do not know that she was lying, of course, since I do not know anything about her, even that she exists. Nor does anyone at the hearing know that she is lying, although some may suspect that she is. In these circumstances I do not know that Tom stole the book. My knowledge is undermined by evidence I do not possess.[7]

Example (2)

Donald has gone off to Italy. He told you ahead of time that he was going; and you saw him off at the airport. He said he was to stay for the entire summer. That was in June. It is now July. Then you might know that he is in Italy. It is the sort of thing one often claims to know. However, for reasons of his own Donald wants you to believe that he is not in Italy but in California. He writes several letters saying that he has gone to San Francisco and has decided to stay there for the summer. He wants you to think that these letters were written by him in San Francisco, so he sends them to someone he knows there and has that person mail them to you with a San Francisco postmark, one at a time. You have been out of town for a couple of days and have not read any of the letters. You are now standing before the pile of mail that arrived while you were away. Two of the phony letters are in the pile. You are about to open your mail. I ask you, "Do you know where Donald is?" "Yes," you reply, "I know that he is in Italy." You are right about where Donald is and it would seem that your justification for believing that Donald is in Italy makes no reference to letters from San Francisco. But you do not know that Donald is in Italy. Your knowledge is undermined by evidence you do not as yet possess.

Example (3)

A political leader is assassinated. His associates, fearing a coup, decide to pretend that the bullet hit someone else. On nationwide television they announce that an assassination attempt has failed to kill the leader but has killed a secret service man by mistake. However, before the announcement is made, an enterprising reporter on the scene telephones the real story to his newspaper, which has included the story in its final edition. Jill buys a copy of that paper and reads the story of the assassination. What she reads is true and so are her assumptions about how the story came to be in the paper. The reporter, whose by-line appears, saw the assassination and dictated his report, which is now printed just as he dictated it. Jill has justified true belief and, it would seem, all her intermediate conclusions are true. But she does not know that the political leader has been assassinated. For everyone else has heard about the televised announcement. They may also have seen the story in the paper and, perhaps, do not know what to believe; and it is highly implausible that Jill should know simply because she lacks evidence everyone else has. Jill does not know. Her knowledge is undermined by evidence she does not possess.

These examples pose a problem for my strategy. They are Gettier examples and my strategy is to make assumptions about inference that will account for Gettier examples by means of principle *P*. But these particular examples appear to bring in considerations that have nothing to do with conclusions essential to the inference on which belief is based.

Some readers may have trouble evaluating these examples. Like other Gettier examples, these require attention to subtle facts about ordinary usage; it is easy to miss subtle differences if, as in the present instance, it is very difficult to formulate a theory that would account for these differences. We must compare what it would be natural to say about these cases if there were no additional evidence one does not possess (no testimony from Tom's mother, no letters from San Francisco, and no televised announcement) with what it would be natural to say about the cases in which there is the additional evidence one does not possess. We must take care not to adopt a very skeptical attitude nor become too lenient about what is to count as knowledge. If we become skeptically inclined, we will deny there is knowledge in either case. If we become too lenient, we will allow that there is knowledge in both cases. It is tempting to go in one or the other of these directions, toward skepticism or leniency, because it proves so difficult to see what general principles are involved that would mark the difference. But at least some difference between the cases is revealed by the fact that we are *more inclined* to say that there is knowledge in the examples where there is no undermining evidence a person does not possess than in the examples where there is such evidence. The problem, then, is to account for this difference in our inclination to ascribe knowledge to someone.

Evidence against what one knows

If I had known about Tom's mother's testimony, I would not have been justified in thinking that it was Tom I saw steal the book. Once you read the letters from Donald in which he says he is in San Francisco, you are no longer justified in thinking that he is in Italy. If Jill knew about the television announcement, she would not be justified in believing that the political leader has been assassinated. This suggests that we can account for the preceding examples by means of the following principle.

> One knows only if there is no evidence such that if one knew about the evidence one would not be justified in believing one's conclusion.

However, by modifying the three examples it can be shown that this principle is too strong.

Suppose that Tom's mother was known to the Judicial Council as a pathological liar. Everyone at the hearing realizes that Buck, Tom's supposed twin, is a figment of her imagination. When she testifies no one believes her. Back at my post in the library, I still know nothing of Tom's mother or her testimony. In such a case, my knowledge would not be undermined by her testimony; but if I were told only that she had just testified that Tom has a twin brother and was himself thousands of miles away from the scene of the crime at the time the book was stolen, I would no longer be justified in believing as I now do that Tom stole the book. Here I know even though there is evidence which, if I knew about it, would cause me not to be justified in believing my conclusion.

Suppose that Donald had changed his mind and never mailed the letters to San Francisco. Then those letters no longer undermine your

knowledge. But it is very difficult to see what principle accounts for this fact. How can letters in the pile on the table in front of you undermine your knowledge while the same letters in a pile in front of Donald do not? If you knew that Donald had written letters to you saying that he was in San Francisco, you would not be justified in believing that he was still in Italy. But that fact by itself does not undermine your present knowledge that he is in Italy.

Suppose that as the political leader's associates are about to make their announcement, a saboteur cuts the wire leading to the television transmitter. The announcement is therefore heard only by those in the studio, all of whom are parties to the deception. Jill reads the real story in the newspaper as before. Now, she does come to know that the political leader has been assassinated. But if she had known that it had been announced that he was not assassinated, she would not have been justified in believing that he was, simply on the basis of the newspaper story. Here, a cut wire makes the difference between evidence that undermines knowledge and evidence that does not undermine knowledge.

We can know that *h* even though there is evidence *e* that we do not know about such that, if we did know about *e*, we would not be justified in believing *h*. If we know that *h*, it does not follow that we know that there is not any evidence like *e*. This can seem paradoxical, for it can seem obvious that, if we know that *h*, we know that any evidence against *h* can only be misleading. So, later if we get that evidence we ought to be able to know enough to disregard it.

A more explicit version of this interesting paradox goes like this.[8] "If I know that *h* is true, I know that any evidence against *h* is evidence against something that is true; so I know that such evidence is misleading. But I should disregard evidence that I know is misleading. So, once I know that *h* is true, I am in a position to disregard any future evidence that seems to tell against *h*." This is paradoxical, because I am never in a position simply to disregard any future evidence even though I do know a great many different things.

A skeptic might appeal to this paradox in order to argue that, since we are never in a position to disregard any further evidence, we never know anything. Some philosophers would turn the argument around to say that, since we often know things, we are often in a position to disregard further evidence. But both of these responses go wrong in accepting the paradoxical argument in the first place.

I can know that Tom stole a book from the library without being able automatically to disregard evidence to the contrary. You can know that Donald is in Italy without having the right to ignore whatever further evidence may turn up. Jill may know that the political leader has been assassinated even though she would cease to know this if told that there was an announcement that only a secret service agent had been shot.

The argument for paradox overlooks the way actually having evidence can make a difference. Since I now know that Tom stole the book, I now know that any evidence that appears to indicate something else is misleading. That does not warrant me in simply disregarding any further evidence, since getting that further evidence can change what I know. In particular, after I get such further evidence I may no longer know that it is misleading. For having the new evidence can make it true that I no longer know that Tom stole the book; if I no longer know that, I no longer know that the new evidence is misleading.

Therefore, we cannot account for the problems posed by evidence one does not possess by appeal to the principle, which I now repeat:

> One knows only if there is no evidence such that if one knew about the evidence one would not be justified in believing one's conclusion.

For one can know even though such evidence exists.

A result concerning inference

When does evidence one doesn't have keep one from having knowledge? I have described three cases, each in two versions, in which there is misleading evidence one does not possess. In the first version of each case the misleading evidence undermines someone's knowledge. In the second version it does not. What makes the difference?

My strategy is to account for Gettier examples by means of principle *P*. This strategy has led us to conceive of induction as inference to the best explanation. But that conception of inference does not by itself seem able to explain these examples. So I want to use the examples in order to learn something more about inference, in particular about what other conclusions are essential to the inference that Tom stole the book, that Donald is in Italy, or that the political leader has been assassinated.

It is not plausible that the relevant inferences should contain essential intermediate conclusions that refer explicitly to Tom's mother, to letters from San Francisco, or to special television programs. For it is very likely that there is an infinite number of ways a particular inference might be undermined by misleading evidence one does not possess. If there must be a separate essential conclusion ruling out each of these ways, inferences would have to be infinitely inclusive – and that is implausible.

Therefore it would seem that the relevant inferences must rule out undermining evidence one does not possess by means of a single conclusion, essential to the inference, that characterizes all such evidence. But how might this be done? It is not at all clear what distinguishes evidence that undermines knowledge from evidence that does not. How is my inference to involve an essential conclusion that rules out Tom's mother's testifying a certain way before a believing audience but does not rule out (simply) her testifying in that way? Or that rules out the existence of letters of a particular sort in the mail on your table but not simply the existence of those letters? Or that rules out a widely heard announcement of a certain sort without simply ruling out the announcement?

Since I am unable to formulate criteria that would distinguish among these cases, I will simply *label* cases of the first kind "undermining evidence one does not possess." Then we can say this: one knows only if there is no undermining evidence one does not possess. If there is such evidence, one does not know. However, these remarks are completely trivial.

It is somewhat less trivial to use the same label to formulate a principle concerned with inference.

> *Q*   One may infer a conclusion only if one also infers that there is no undermining evidence one does not possess.

There is of course an obscurity in principle *Q*; but the principle is not as trivial as the remarks of the last paragraph, since the label "undermining evidence one does not possess" has been explained in terms of knowledge, whereas this is a principle concerning inference.

If we take principle Q, concerning inference, to be basic, we can use principle P to account for the differences between the two versions of each of the three examples described above. In each case an inference involves essentially the claim that there is no undermining evidence one does not possess. Since this claim is false in the first version of each case and true in the second, principle P implies that there can be knowledge only in the second version of each case.

So there is, according to my strategy, some reason to think that there is a principle concerning inference like principle Q. That raises the question of whether there is any independent reason to accept such a principle; and reflection on good scientific practice suggests a positive answer. It is a commonplace that a scientist should base his conclusions on all the evidence. Furthermore, he should not rest content with the evidence he happens to have but should try to make sure he is not overlooking any relevant evidence. A good scientist will not accept a conclusion unless he has some reason to think that there is no as yet undiscovered evidence which would undermine his conclusion. Otherwise he would not be warranted in making his inference. So good scientific practice reflects the acceptance of something like principle Q, which is the independent confirmation we wanted for the existence of this principle.

Notice that the scientist must accept something like principle Q, with its reference to "undermining evidence one does not possess." For example, he cannot accept the following principle,

> One may infer a conclusion only if one also infers that there is no evidence at all such that if he knew that evidence he could not accept his conclusion.

There will always be a true proposition such that if he learned that the proposition was true (and learned nothing else) he would not be warranted in accepting his conclusion. If h is his conclusion, and if k is a true proposition saying what ticket will win the grand prize in the next New Jersey State Lottery, then *either k or not h* is such a proposition. If he were to learn that it is true that *either k or not h* (and learned nothing else), *not h* would become probable since (given what he knows) k is antecedently very improbable. So he could no longer reasonably infer that h is true.

There must be a certain kind of evidence such that the scientist infers there is no as yet undiscovered evidence of that kind against h. Principle Q says that the relevant kind is what I have been labelling "undermining evidence one does not possess." Principle Q is confirmed by the fact that good scientific practice involves some such principle and by the fact that principle Q together with principle P accounts for the three Gettier examples I have been discussing.

If this account in terms of principles P and Q is accepted, inductive conclusions must involve some self-reference. Otherwise there would be a regress. Before we could infer that h, we would have to infer that there is no undermining evidence to h. That prior inference could not be deductive, so it would have to be inference to the best explanatory statement. For example, we might infer that the fact that there is no sign of undermining evidence we do not possess is explained by there not being any such evidence. But, then, before we could accept that conclusion we would first have to infer that there is no undermining evidence to *it* which one does not possess. And, since that inference would have to be inference to the best explanation, it would require a previous inference that there is no undermining evidence for its conclusion; and so on *ad infinitum*.

Clearly, we do not *first* have to infer that there is no undermining evidence to h and only then infer h. For that would automatically yield the regress. Instead, we must at the same time infer both h and that there is no undermining evidence. Furthermore, we infer that there is not only no undermining evidence to h but also no undermining evidence to the whole conclusion. In other words, all legitimate inductive conclusions take the form of a self-referential conjunction whose first conjunct is h and whose second conjunct (usually left implicit) is the claim that there is no undermining evidence to the whole conjunction.

Notes

1   Henry Kyburg, *Probability and the Logic of Rational Belief* (Middletown: Wesleyan University Press, 1961).
2   E.g., by Robert Nozick.
3   Edmond Gettier, "Is Justified True Belief Knowledge?", this vol., ch. 15.
4   Keith Lehrer, "Knowledge, Truth, and Evidence," *Analysis* 25 (1965), pp. 168–75.
5   Alvin Goldman, "A Causal Theory of Knowing," *Journal of Philosophy* 64 (1967), pp. 357–72.
6   Brian Skyrms, "The Explication of 'X knows that p,'" *Journal of Philosophy* 64 (1967), pp. 373–89.
7   Keith Lehrer and Thomas Paxson, Jr., "Knowledge: Undefeated Justified True Belief," *Journal of Philosophy* 66 (1969).
8   Here and in what follows I am indebted to Saul Kripke, who is, however, not responsible for any faults in my presentation.

CHAPTER 17

The Inescapability of Gettier Problems

Linda Zagzebski

Gettier problems arise in the theory of knowledge when it is only by chance that a justified true belief is true. Since the belief might easily have been false in these cases, it is normally concluded that they are not instances of knowledge.[1] The moral drawn in the thirty years since Gettier published his famous paper is that either justified true belief (JTB) is not sufficient for knowledge, in which case knowledge must have an "extra" component in addition to JTB, or else justification must be reconceived to *make it* sufficient for knowledge. I shall argue that given the common and reasonable assumption that the relation between justification and truth is close but not inviolable, it is not possible for either move to avoid Gettier counter-examples. What is more, it makes no difference if the component of knowledge in addition to true belief is identified as something other than justification, e.g., warrant or well-foundedness. I conclude that Gettier problems are inescapable for virtually every analysis of knowledge which at least maintains that knowledge is true belief plus something else.

Notice first that Gettier problems arise for both internalist and externalist notions of justification. On internalist theories the grounds for justification are accessible to the consciousness of the believer, and Gettier problems arise when there is

nothing wrong with the internally accessible aspects of the cognitive situation, but there is a mishap in something inaccessible to the believer. Since justification does not guarantee truth, it is possible for there to be a break in the connection between justification and truth, but for that connection to be regained by chance.

The original "Smith owns a Ford or Brown is in Barcelona" case is an example of this sort. Here we are to imagine that Smith comes to you bragging about his new Ford, shows you the car and the bill of sale, and generally gives you lots of evidence that he owns a Ford. Basing what you think on the evidence, you believe the proposition "Smith owns a Ford", and from that you infer its disjunction with "Brown is in Barcelona", where Brown is an acquaintance and you have no reason at all to think he is in Barcelona. It turns out that Smith is lying and owns no Ford, but Brown is by chance in Barcelona. Your belief "Smith owns a Ford or Brown is in Barcelona" is true and justified, but it is hardly the case that you know it.

In this case the problem arises because in spite of the fact that you have done everything to reach the truth from your point of view and everything that anyone could expect of you, your efforts do not lead you to the truth. It is mere bad luck that you are the unwitting victim of Smith's lies, and only an accident that a procedure that usually leads you to the truth leads you to believe the falsehood "Smith owns a Ford". The fact that you end up with a true belief anyway is due to a second

Originally published in *The Philosophical Quarterly* 44, No. 174 (1994), pp. 65–73.

accidental feature of the situation – a feature that has nothing to do with your cognitive activity. What generates the problem for JTB, then, is that an accident of bad luck is cancelled out by an accident of good luck. The right goal is reached, but only by chance.

Internalist theories are not the only ones afflicted with Gettier problems, contrary to a recent claim made by Alvin Plantinga.[2] Consider how the problem arises for reliabilism. In this group of theories believers are justified when their beliefs are formed in a reliable, or truth-conducive, manner. On this account also there is no guarantee that justified beliefs are true, and a breakdown in the connection between a reliable belief-forming process and the truth is possible. When that happens, even if you manage to hit on the truth anyway, you do not have knowledge.

The well-known fake barn case can be described as an example of this sort. Here we are to imagine that you are driving through a region in which, unknown to you, the inhabitants have erected three barn façades for each real barn in an effort to make themselves look more prosperous. Your eyesight is normal and reliable enough in ordinary circumstances to spot a barn from the road. But in this case the fake barns are indistinguishable from the real barns at such a distance. As you look at a real barn you form the belief "That's a fine barn". The belief is true and justified, but is not knowledge.

As in the first case, the problem arises because of the combination of two accidental features of the cognitive situation. It is only an accident that visual faculties normally reliable in this sort of situation are not reliable in this particular situation; and it is another accident that you happened to be looking at a real barn and hit on the truth anyway. Again the problem arises because an accident of bad luck is cancelled out by an accident of good luck.

Gettier problems cannot be avoided by Alvin Plantinga's new theory either. Plantinga calls the property that in sufficient quantity converts true belief into knowledge "warrant" rather than "justification". On his proposal warrant is the property a belief B has for believer S when B is produced in S by S's faculties working properly in the appropriate environment, according to a design plan successfully aimed at truth.[3] But Plantinga does not maintain that every warranted

belief is true any more than reliabilists maintain that every reliably formed belief is true or internalists maintain that every internally justified belief is true. Let us see if we can form a Gettier case for Plantinga's theory parallel to the other two cases we have considered. To do so we need to look for a situation in which S's faculties are working the way they were designed to in the appropriate environment, but S unluckily has a false belief. We can then add a second accident which makes the belief true after all.

Suppose that Mary has very good eyesight, but it is not perfect. It is good enough to allow her to identify her husband sitting in his usual chair in the living room from a distance of fifteen feet in somewhat dim light (the degree of dimness can easily be specified). She has made such an identification in these circumstances many times. Each time her faculties have been working properly and the environment has been appropriate for the faculties. There is nothing at all unusual about either her faculties or the environment in these cases. Her faculties may not be functioning perfectly, but they are functioning well enough, so that if she goes on to form the belief "My husband is sitting in the living room", that belief has enough warrant to constitute knowledge when true and we can assume that it is almost always true.

The belief is *almost* always true, we say. That is because warrant in the degree necessary for knowledge does not guarantee truth, according to Plantinga. If it *did* guarantee truth, of course, the component of truth in the analysis of knowledge would be superfluous. Knowledge would simply be warranted belief. So it is possible for Mary to make a mistake even though her faculties are functioning properly enough for knowledge and the environment is normal for the faculties. Let us look at one such case.

Suppose Mary simply misidentifies the chairsitter who is, let us suppose, her husband's brother. Her faculties may be working as well as they normally do when the belief is true and when we do not hesitate to say it is warranted in a degree sufficient for knowledge. It is not a question of their suddenly becoming defective, or at any rate, more defective than usual, nor is there a mismatch between her faculties and the environment. No one is dressing up as her husband to fool her, or anything like that, so the environment is not abnormal as the fake barn case is abnormal. Her degree of warrant is as high as it usually is when she correctly identifies her husband since even in those cases it is true that she *might* have misidentified the chair-sitter if it had been her husband's brother instead. Of course, she usually has no reason to suspect that it *is* her husband's brother and we can imagine that she has no reason to suspect so in this case either. Maybe she knows that her husband's brother looks a lot like him, but she has no reason to believe that he is in the vicinity, and, in fact, has strong reason to believe he has gone to Australia. So in the case we are considering, when Mary forms the false belief, her belief is as warranted as her beliefs normally are in these circumstances. In spite of well-functioning faculties and a benign environment, she just makes a mistake.

Now, of course, *something* has gone wrong here, and that something is probably in Mary rather than in the environment. It may even be correct to say that there is a minor defect in her faculties; perhaps she is not perfectly attentive or she is a little too hasty in forming her belief. But she is no less attentive and no more hasty than she usually is in such cases and usually it does not matter. People do not have to be perfectly attentive and perfectly cautious and have perfect vision to have beliefs sufficiently warranted for knowledge on Plantinga's theory. And this is not a *mistake* in Plantinga's theory. It would surely be unreasonable of him to expect perfectly functioning faculties in a perfectly attuned environment as his criteria for the warrant needed for knowledge. So Mary's defect need not be sufficient to bring her degree of warrant down below that needed for knowledge on Plantinga's account.

We can now easily emend the case as a Gettier example. Mary's husband could be sitting on the other side of the room, unseen by her. In that case her belief "My husband is sitting in the living room" is true and has sufficient warrant for knowledge on Plantinga's account, but she does not have knowledge.

In discussing Gettier problems Plantinga concludes: "What is essential to Gettier situations is the production of a true belief despite a relatively minor failure of the cognitive situation to match its design".[4] But this comment is problematic on his own account. As we have seen, Plantinga considers warrant a property that admits of degree,

but it is clear that the degree of warrant sufficient for knowledge does not require faculties to be working perfectly in an environment perfectly matched to them. In Gettier-style cases such as the case of Mary, either the degree of warrant is sufficient for knowledge or it is not. If it is not, then a multitude of beliefs we normally think are warranted are not, and there is much less knowledge in the world than Plantinga's numerous examples suggest. On the other hand, if the degree of warrant *is* sufficient for knowledge, then Plantinga's theory faces Gettier problems structurally identical to those of the other theories. Furthermore, even if some aspect of the Mary example makes it unpersuasive, there must still be cases of warranted false belief on Plantinga's theory if the component of truth in knowledge is not redundant. With such a case in hand a Gettier example can be constructed by adding a feature extraneous to the warrant of the believer which makes the belief true after all. In such a case the degree of warrant is unchanged, but it is not knowledge since it might just as well have been false.

It is not enough, then, to say that Gettier problems arise because of a minor mismatch between faculties and environment. What Plantinga should have said is that the problem is due to a relatively minor failure of the cognitive situation to connect to the truth. As long as the property that putatively converts true belief into knowledge is analysed in such a way that it is strongly linked with the truth, but does not guarantee it, it will always be possible to devise cases in which the link between such a property and the truth is broken but regained by accident. Such is the nature of Gettier cases.

The three examples we have considered suggest a general rule for the generation of Gettier cases. It really does not matter how the *particular* element of knowledge in addition to true belief is analysed. As long as there is a small degree of independence between this other element and the truth, we can construct Gettier cases by using the following procedure: start with a case of justified (or warranted) false belief. Make the element of justification (warrant) strong enough for knowledge, but make the belief false. The falsity of the belief will not be due to any systematically describable element in the situation, for if it were, such a feature could be used in the analysis of the components of knowledge other than true belief, and then truth would be entailed by the other components of knowledge, contrary to the hypothesis. The falsity of the belief is therefore due to some element of luck. Now emend the case by adding another element of luck, only this time an element which makes the belief true after all. The second element must be independent of the element of warrant so that the degree of warrant is unchanged. The situation might be described as one element of luck counteracting another. We now have a case in which the belief is justified (warranted) in a sense strong enough for knowledge, the belief is true, but it is not knowledge. The conclusion is that as long as the concept of knowledge closely connects the justification component and the truth component, but permits *some* degree of independence between them, justified true belief will never be sufficient for knowledge.

It is often observed that in typical Gettier cases the justified belief depends upon or otherwise "goes through" a false belief, so a way to handle these cases is to add what are commonly called "defeasibility conditions" to the analysis of knowledge. This move was especially popular during the sixties and seventies. It adds to the requirement that knowledge be justified true belief the restriction that the belief in question must also be justified in certain counterfactual situations. One way to define these conditions is in terms of the psychological effect on the subject, as in Steven Levy's definition of a defeasibility condition as "a requirement to the effect that for S to know that p there must be no other evidence against p strong enough to undermine S's belief that p, should this evidence come to S's attention".

The three cases I have just described do have the feature that there is a false belief in the neighbourhood of the belief in question which is such that, should the subject discover its falsehood, that would undermine the belief in the proposition in question. So your belief that either Smith owns a Ford or Brown is in Barcelona is undermined if you discover that Smith does not own a Ford. Your belief that this is a barn is undermined if you discover that most objects that look like barns in this vicinity are not real barns. Mary's belief that her husband is sitting in the living room is undermined if she discovers that that man sitting over *there* in a particular chair in the

living room is not her husband. In each case were S to be advised of the falsity of the underlying belief, S would retract the belief under discussion. The belief would be defeated by such new information.

This move puts a strain on the independence of the justification/defeasibility condition and the truth condition. If S's belief that p is false, there will obviously be many other propositions which are logically or evidentially connected to p which are false also. Should S become aware of any of these propositions, that may easily undermine S's belief that p, assuming S is rational. This means that the falsehood of p is incompatible with a strong defeasibility condition, contrary to the hypothesis that the justification and defeasibility components of knowledge do not entail the truth condition. This problem is even more apparent in statements of the defeasibility condition in terms of evidential support rather than a psychological requirement, as in Pappas and Swain's definition: "the evidence e must be sufficiently complete that no further additions to e would result in a loss of justification and hence a loss of knowledge".[6] Obviously, if the belief is *false*, further additions to e will result in a loss of justification, and hence a loss of knowledge.

Strong defeasibility conditions, then, threaten the assumption of independence between the justification (warrant) condition and the truth condition for knowledge. But weaker defeasibility conditions are subject to Gettier-style counterexamples following the pattern described above. In each case we find an example of a false belief which satisfies the justification and defeasibility conditions, and then make the belief true anyway due to features of the situation independent of the satisfaction of those conditions.

Suppose Dr Jones, a physician, has very good inductive evidence that her patient, Smith, is suffering from virus X. Smith exhibits all of the symptoms of this virus, and a blood test has shown that his antibody levels against virus X are extremely high. In addition, let us suppose that the symptoms are not compatible with any other known virus, all of the evidence upon which Jones bases her diagnosis is true, and there is no evidence accessible to her which counts significantly against the conclusion. The proposition that Smith is suffering from virus X really is extremely probable on the evidence.

In this case there is nothing defective in the justification of Dr Jones' belief that Smith has virus X and no false belief figures causally or evidentially in her justification, nor is there any false belief in the neighbourhood. Furthermore, she would have believed that Smith has virus X in a wide range of counterfactual situations. None the less, let us suppose that the belief is false. Smith's symptoms are due to a distinct and unknown virus Y and the fact that he exhibits high antibody levels to virus X is due to idiosyncratic features of his biochemistry which cause him to maintain unusually high antibody levels long after a past infection. In this case Dr Jones' belief that Smith is presently suffering from virus X is false, but it is both justified and undefeated. Of course, given that the belief is false, there must be *some* evidence against it accessible to her in some counterfactual circumstances, so if defeasibility conditions are strong enough, no false empirical belief passes the test. But as said above, that is to impose an unreasonably strong defeasibility condition, one that makes the justification/defeasibility condition entail truth. The most reasonable conclusion to draw in this case, then, is that Jones' belief is justified and undefeated, but false.

Now to construct a Gettier-style example we simply add the feature that Smith has very recently contracted virus X, but so recently that he does not yet exhibit symptoms caused by X, nor has there been time for a change in the antibody levels due to this recent infection. So while the evidence upon which Dr Jones bases her diagnosis does make it highly probable that Smith has X, the fact that Smith has X has nothing to do with that evidence. In this case, then, Dr Jones' belief that Smith has virus X is true, justified and undefeated, but it is not knowledge.

It appears, then, that no account of knowledge as true belief plus something else can withstand Gettier objections as long as there is a small degree of independence between truth and the other conditions of knowledge. What are our alternatives? We have already seen that one way to solve the problem is to give up the independence between the justification condition and the truth condition. Justification would be defined in such a way that no false belief can satisfy it. Since Gettier cases are based on situations in which the belief is true, but it might just as well have been false, all such cases would be excluded from the class of justified (warranted) beliefs. On this approach the element of truth in the account of knowledge is superfluous and knowledge is simply justified (warranted) belief. "S is justified in believing p" entails p. Few philosophers have supported this view.[7]

So Gettier problems can be avoided if there is no degree of independence at all between truth and justification. A second way to avoid them is to go to the opposite extreme and to make the justification condition and the truth condition almost completely independent. It could still be the case that justification puts the subject in the best position available for getting the truth, but if the best position is not very good, most justified beliefs will be false. Perhaps most justified scientific hypotheses since the world began have been false. Perhaps Plato, Spinoza, Kant and Hegel were justified in believing their metaphysical theories, but most of their theories (at least) were false. Still, if one of them is true, some theorists might be willing to call it knowledge. On this approach the element of luck permitted in the state of knowledge is so great that alleged counter-examples based on luck do not count against it. From this viewpoint, Gettier cases would simply be accepted as cases of knowledge. After all, if knowledge is mostly luck anyway, there will be nothing bothersome about a case in which the truth is acquired by luck.

Perhaps neither of these alternatives will appeal to most philosophers, who find the idea that there is a small but real degree of independence between justification and the acquisition of truth just too attractive to give up. A third reaction to the problem, then, is to accept the fact that no "true belief + x" account of knowledge will be sufficient, but that it will always be necessary to add the element of luck to the analysis. So knowledge is true belief + x + luck. This approach recognizes the fact that the concept we substitute for "x" ought to be one that has a strong general connection with the acquisition of truth, but that an inviolable connection would be unreasonable. On the other hand, it also recognizes the fact that we are much less forgiving with the concept of knowledge itself. The connection between justification or whatever it is we substitute for "x" and truth must exist in each and every particular case of knowledge. The notion of knowledge requires success, both in reaching the goal of truth, and in reaching it via the right cognitive path. The notion of justification or warrant is less stringent, requiring only that the right path is one that is *usually* successful at getting the truth. It is this difference between the notion of knowledge and the notion of justification that is responsible for Gettier problems.

Almost every contemporary theory of justification or warrant aims only to give the conditions for putting the believer in the best position for getting the truth. The best position is assumed to be very good, but imperfect, for such is life.

Properly functioning faculties need not be working perfectly, but only well enough; reliable belief-producing mechanisms need not be perfectly reliable, only reliable enough; evidence for a belief need not support it conclusively, but only well enough; and so on. As long as the truth is never assured by the conditions which make the state justified, there will be situations in which a false belief is justified. I have argued that with this common, in fact, almost universal assumption, Gettier cases will never go away.

Notes

1   "Is Justified True Belief Knowledge?", *Analysis* 23 (1963), pp. 121–3.

2   Alvin Plantinga, *Warrant and Proper Function*, (Oxford University Press, 1993), p. 48.

3   The wording I have used can be found in Plantinga's book *Warrant and Proper Function*. A very similar wording can be found in "Positive Epistemic Status and Proper Function", in J. E. Tomberlin (ed.), *Philosophical Perspectives 2: Epistemology* (Atascadero: Ridgeview, 1988), pp. 1–50. In that paper he calls "positive epistemic status" what he now calls "warrant".

4   "Positive Epistemic Status and Proper Function", p. 43.

5   Steven Levy, "Defeasibility Theories of Knowledge", *Canadian Journal of Philosophy* 7 (1977), p. 115.

6   George Pappas and Marshall Swain (eds), *Essays on Knowledge and Justification* (Ithaca and London: Cornell University Press, 1978), p. 27.

7   An exception is Robert Almeder, "Truth and Evidence", *The Philosophical Quarterly*, 24 (1974), pp. 365–8. Almeder's reason for maintaining that "S is justified in believing p" entails p is that the *determination* of the fact that a belief p is justified entails the determination of the fact that p is true. I find this implausible, since (1) there are many ways to determine the truth-value of a proposition p independently of the justification of a particular believer in believing p; and (2) even if the act of determining that a belief is justified included the determination of its truth, it does not follow that the fact that a belief is justified entails its truth.

CHAPTER 18

A State of Mind

Timothy Williamson

1 Factive Attitudes

Knowing is a state of mind. That claim is central to the account of knowledge developed in this book. But what does it mean?

A state of a mind is a mental state of a subject. Paradigmatic mental states include love, hate, pleasure, and pain. Moreover, they include attitudes to propositions: believing that something is so, conceiving that it is so, hoping or fearing that it is so, wondering whether it is so, intending or desiring it to be so. One can also know that something is so. This book concerns such propositional knowledge. If p is a proposition, we will understand knowing p not as merely being acquainted with p but as knowing that something is so, something that is so if and only if p is true. For example, if p is the proposition that it is cold, then one is acquainted with p in merely wondering whether it is cold; to know p is to know that it is cold. Knowing in that sense is a *factive* attitude; one knows p only if p is true, although one can be acquainted with the proposition p even if it is false. Other factive attitudes include perceiving that something is so, remembering that it is so, and regretting that is so. If attitudes are relations of subjects to propositions, then the claim is that

Originally published in Timothy Williamson, *Knowledge and Its Limits* (Oxford: Oxford University Press, 2000), pp. 21–48.

knowing itself is a mental relation such that, for every proposition p, having that relation to p is a mental state. Thus for some mental state S, being in S is necessary and sufficient for knowing p. We abbreviate that claim by saying that knowing is a mental state.

We may assume initially that knowing p entails believing p; section 5 considers that assumption in more depth. Someone might expect knowing to be a state of mind simply on the grounds that knowing p involves the paradigmatic mental state of believing p. If those grounds were adequate, the claim that knowing is a state of mind would be banal. However, those grounds imply only that there is a mental state being in which is *necessary* for knowing p. By contrast, the claim that knowing is a state of mind is to be understood as the claim that there is a mental state being in which is necessary *and sufficient* for knowing p. In short, knowing is *merely* a state of mind. This claim may be unexpected. On the standard view, believing is merely a state of mind but knowing is not, because it is factive: truth is a non-mental component of knowing.

Our initial presumption should be that knowing is a mental state. Prior to philosophical theory-building, we learn the concept of the mental by examples. Our paradigms should include propositional attitudes such as believing and desiring, if our conception of the mental is not to be radically impoverished. But factive attitudes have so many similarities to the non-factive attitudes that we should expect them to constitute mental states too; we expect a concept to apply to whatever sufficiently resembles its paradigms. It would be strange if there were a mental state of fearing but no mental state of regretting, or a mental state of imagining but no mental state of remembering. Indeed, it is not clear that there are any pretheoretic grounds for omitting factive attitudes from the list of *paradigmatic* mental states. That the mental includes knowing and other factive attitudes is built into the natural understanding of the procedure by which the concept of the mental is acquired. Of course, that does not exclude the subsequent discovery of theoretical reasons for drawing the line between the mental and the non-mental somewhere else. But the theory behind those reasons had better be a good one.

This chapter … eliminates some putative differences between knowing and non-factive attitudes that might be thought to disqualify knowing as a mental state. The supposed disqualifications concern constitutive dependence on the environment, first-person accessibility, and causal efficacy. In each case, the differences dissolve on inspection. Naturally, this form of argument cannot provide conclusive proof. We survey the current candidates and find them wanting. We can still wonder whether our list of potential differences is complete. But without good theoretical reasons to demote knowing from its pretheoretical status as a central case of a mental state, demotion is surrender to mere special pleading. Indeed, conceptions on which knowing is the wrong kind of state to count as mental are objectionable on independent grounds. We can best understand knowing by classifying it with other mental phenomena.

In this chapter, section 2 orients the claim that knowing is a mental state with respect to some traditional issues about scepticism and self-knowledge. Section 3 explains an incompatibility between the view of knowing as a factive mental state and standard analyses of the concept *knows* as a conjunction of the concepts *believes* and *true* (predicated of the proposition) and of other concepts; it blames the analyses. Section 4 presents a modest positive account of the concept *knows*, distinguishes it from analyses of the traditional kind, and indicates the possibility of understanding epistemology in terms of the metaphysics of

states. Section 5 discusses the relation between knowing and believing, and explores some implications for so-called disjunctive accounts of mental states.[1]

2   Mental states, First-Person Accessibility, and Scepticism

The conception of knowing as a mental state can look like a confusion between objective and subjective certainty. Someone might even diagnose that conception as Descartes' central mistake. Did he not seek a mental state sufficient for knowing *p*? Was not clearly and distinctly conceiving *p* his candidate? And does not the failure of his epistemological programme manifest the impossibility of a mental state of the required kind?

On the view to be developed here, if Descartes sought a mental state sufficient for knowing, his mistake lay elsewhere: perhaps in the view (if he held it) that one must always be in a position to know what mental state one is in. H. A. Prichard, who also took knowing to be a mental state, held that one is always in a position to know whether one knows or merely believes (Prichard 1950, p. 86). Few would now claim such powers of discrimination. Indeed, one cause of denials that knowing is a mental state may be the assumption that one must always be in a position to know whether one is in a given mental state.

One is surely not always in a position to know whether one knows *p* (for almost any proposition *p*), however alert and conceptually sophisticated one is. The point is most vivid when the subject believes *p* falsely. Consider, for example, the situation of a generally well-informed citizen N.N. who has not yet heard the news from the theatre where Lincoln has just been assassinated. Since Lincoln is dead, he is no longer President, so N.N. no longer knows that Lincoln is President (knowing is factive). However, N.N. is in no position to know that anything is amiss. He continues reasonably to believe that Lincoln is President; moreover, this seems to him to be just another item of general knowledge. N.N. continues reasonably to believe that he knows that Lincoln is President. Although N.N. does not know that Lincoln is President, he is in no position to know that he does not know that Lincoln is President (see also Hintikka 1962, 106 and section 8.2).

The argument as stated assumes that no a priori reasoning demonstrates that it is impossible to have knowledge about the external world, for such reasoning would make it unreasonable for N.N. to believe that he knows that Lincoln is President. Of course, if all knowledge is impossible then, for any proposition p whatsoever, one does not know p and is not in a position to know that one fails to know p; one is never in a position to know whether one knows p. A sceptic about the external world who is not a sceptic about everything might attempt to maintain that, for any informative proposition p about the external world, one is in a position to know that one does not know p. Let us assume for the time being that such a sceptic is wrong. …

We can also construct cases in which one knows p without being in a position to know that one knows p. They involve more delicate issues. It is enough for present purposes that one can fail to know p without being in a position to know that one fails to know p.

Let transparency be the thesis that for every mental state S, whenever one is suitably alert and conceptually sophisticated, one is in a position to know whether one is in S. Given transparency, knowing p is not a mental state, for almost any proposition p.

Transparency is false, however, and demonstrably so by reference to uncontentiously paradigmatic mental states. For example, one is sometimes in no position to know whether one is in the mental state of hoping p. I believe that I do not hope for a particular result to a match; I am conscious of nothing but indifference; then my disappointment at one outcome reveals my hope for another. When I had that hope, I was in no position to know that I had it. Indeed, it is hard to find a non-trivial mental state for which transparency holds. It fails for the state of believing p, for the difference between believing p and merely fancying p depends in part on one's dispositions to practical reasoning and action manifested only in counterfactual circumstances, and one is not always in a position to know what those dispositions are. Transparency is even doubtful for the state of being in pain; with too much self-pity one may mistake an itch for a pain, with too little one may mistake a pain for an itch. … But even if transparency does hold for a few mental states, it clearly fails for others; the premise of the argument

from transparency to the denial that knowing p is a mental state is false. Given that knowing p is a mental state, we will not expect knowing whether one is in it to be always easy.

It does not follow that there is no asymmetry at all between knowledge of one's own mental states and knowledge of the mental states of others. Perhaps failures of transparency could not be the normal case, although that claim would require extensive argument. A more plausible claim is that we have some non-observational knowledge of our own mental states and not of the mental states of others. But then the same may be said of knowing: we have some non-observational knowledge of our own knowledge and ignorance and not of the knowledge and ignorance of others. Any genuine requirement of privileged access on mental states is met by the state of knowing p. Knowing is characteristically open to first-person present-tense access; like other mental states, it is not perfectly open.

Some may object that knowing whether one knows p requires evaluating reasons for and against p in a way in which knowing whether one believes p does not. They distinguish knowing whether one currently believes p from deciding whether to continue believing p. Suppose for a moment that they are correct in taking knowing whether one believes p not to require one to evaluate reasons for and against p. Still, even on their view there is also the mental state of *rationally* believing p, on some appropriate concept of rationality. Knowing whether one rationally believes p does require one to evaluate reasons for and against p. Thus the need for such evaluation in order to know whether one knows p does not show that knowing p is not a mental state.

Could it be replied that knowing and rationally believing are not mental states in the way that believing is, because "know" and "rational" are normative terms? Belief attributions have a normative element too, for to have any mental attitude to a content one must in some sense grasp that content, and therefore have some minimal ability to deal rationally with it; the reply itself classifies "rational" as a normative term. In any sense in which "know" and "rational" are normative terms, ascriptions of mental states can be normative.

A different objection is that one's belief about whether one knows p is defeasible by new information in a way in which one's belief about whether one believes p is not. For example, the new information might show that p is false. But is one's belief about whether one believes p really indefeasible by new information? Someone might believe that he believes that the world will end next year, because he has joined a religious sect in which there is strong pressure to believe that the world will end next year, but his unwillingness to cash in his pension may suggest that he does not really believe that the world will end next year. When he reflects on his unwillingness to cash in his pension, he may come to that conclusion himself. But even if we forget such examples and suppose that one's belief about whether one believes p is not defeasible by further evidence, we must still acknowledge mental states such as being alert or thinking clearly about a problem. One's belief about whether one is alert or thinking clearly about a problem is defeasible by new information, for example about what drugs had been slipped into one's drink. Thus the defeasibility of beliefs about whether one knows p does not show that knowing p is not a mental state.

Once we consider the full variety of acknowledged mental states, it is clear that any general requirements of privileged access on mental states are very mild. Knowing satisfies those mild requirements.

The failure of transparency helps to clarify the relation between the thesis that knowing is a mental state and a traditional pattern of sceptical argument. The sceptic argues that a subject with a true belief could have been in exactly the same mental state (that is, in the same total set of mental states) even if the belief had been false. He concludes that, since the belief fails to constitute knowledge in the latter case, it fails equally to do so in the former. The sceptical argument assumes something like this: if one's mental state is exactly the same in two situations, then one's knowledge is also the same. On the account to be developed here, that assumption is correct, although not quite in the way that the sceptic imagines.

The sceptic supposes that a difference in knowledge would require some *prior* difference in mental state, which the subject could detect. On the present account, a difference in knowledge would *constitute* a difference in mental state. This difference need not be detectable by the subject who lacks knowledge. Thus the sceptic's assumption is correct for reasons that undermine his argument. He claims to have constructed a

case in which the belief is false although the mental state is exactly the same. But the most that he has really shown about the case is that the belief is false and one's situation is not discriminably different. He has not shown that one cannot be in different mental states in indiscriminable situations. Indeed, since we are sometimes in no position to know whether we are in a given mental state, as argued above, surely one can be in different mental states in situations between which one cannot discriminate (see McDowell 1982).

If knowing is a mental state, then the sceptical argument is not compelling. Indeed, such a view of knowledge need only be defensible for the sceptical argument not to be compelling. Thus *one* route into scepticism is blocked. It is not the purpose of this chapter to argue that all are. ...

If someone has already taken the route into scepticism offered by that fallacious argument, before it was blocked, and has become genuinely undecided, at least in principle, as to whether she is in a sceptical scenario, then the blocking of the route now comes too late to rescue her. Nothing said here should convince someone who has given up ordinary beliefs that they did in fact constitute knowledge, for nothing said here should convince her that they are true. The trick is never to give them up. This is the usual case with philosophical treatments of scepticism: they are better at prevention than at cure. If a refutation of scepticism is supposed to reason one out of the hole, then scepticism is irrefutable. The most to be hoped for is something which will prevent the sceptic (who may be oneself) from reasoning one into the hole in the first place.

The purpose of these remarks has been to give a feel for the view that knowing is a state of mind. The content of the view must now be examined more explicitly. The notion of a mental state will not be formally defined, for that would require a formal definition of the mental. Rather, reflection on the intuitive notion of a mental state will help to clarify its workings. Section 4 will provide a less informal account.

3   Knowledge and Analysis

To call knowing a mental state is to assimilate it, in a certain respect, to paradigmatic mental states such as believing, desiring, and being in pain. It is also to contrast it with various non-examples of mental states. Perhaps the most revealing contrast is between knowing and believing truly.

Believing *p* truly is not a mental state, at least, not when *p* is an ordinary contingent proposition about the external environment. Intuitively, for example, there is no mental state being in which is necessary and sufficient for believing truly that it is raining (that is, for believing while it is raining that it is raining), just as there is no mental state being in which is necessary and sufficient for believing while Rome burns that it is raining. There is a mental state of believing that it is raining, and there is – on the present account – a mental state of knowing that it is raining, but there is no intermediate mental state of believing truly that it is raining. Let S_1 be knowing that it is raining, S_2 be believing truly that it is raining, and S_3 be believing that it is raining. Then, we may assume, necessarily, everything that is in S_1 is in S_2; necessarily, everything that is in S_2 is in S_3. Nevertheless, on the present account, although S_1 and S_3 are mental states, S_2 is not a mental state.

That something sandwiched between two mental states need not itself be a mental state is not as paradoxical as it may sound. Consider an analogy: the notion of a geometrical property. For these purposes, we can understand geometrical properties to be properties possessed by particulars in physical space. Let π_1 be the property of being an equilateral triangle, π_2 the property of being a triangle whose sides are indiscriminable in length to the naked human eye, and π_3 the property of being a triangle. Necessarily, everything that has π_1 has π_2, because lines of the same length cannot be discriminated in length; necessarily, everything that has π_2 has π_3. Nevertheless, although π_1 and π_3 are geometrical properties, π_2 is not a geometrical property, because it varies with variations in human eyesight. Something sandwiched between two geometrical properties need not itself be a geometrical property. Similarly, there is no structural reason why something sandwiched between two mental states should itself be a mental state.

The point is general. If S is a mental state and C a non-mental condition, there need be no mental state S* such that, necessarily, one is in S* if and only if one is in S and C obtains. The non-existence of such an S* is quite consistent with the existence of a mental state S** such that, necessarily, one is in S** only if (but not: if) one is in S and C is met. A mental state can guarantee that conjunction only by guaranteeing more than that conjunction.

If the denial that believing truly is a mental state does not immediately convince, think of it this way. Even if believing truly is a mental state in some liberal sense of the latter term, there is also a more restrictive but still reasonable sense in which believing truly is not a mental state but the combination of a mental state with a non-mental condition. The present claim is that knowing is a mental state in *every* reasonable sense of that term: there is no more restrictive but still reasonable sense of "mental" in which knowing can be factored, like believing truly, into a combination of mental states with non-mental conditions. A sense of "mental" is reasonable if it is sufficiently close to an ordinary sense of the word in important respects. Although the present claim is therefore vague, it is at least clear enough to be disputed.

Strictly speaking, we must distinguish a conceptual and a metaphysical contrast. The conceptual contrast is that the concept *knows* is a mental concept while the concept *believes truly* is not a mental concept. The metaphysical contrast is that knowing is a mental state while believing truly is not a mental state.

The concept *mental state* can at least roughly be defined in terms of the concept *mental concept of a state*: a state is mental if and only if there could be a mental concept of that state. This definition does not in principle exclude the possibility of a non-mental concept of a mental state, for different concepts can be of the same state. We may reasonably assume that states S_1 and S_2 are identical if and only if necessarily everything is in S_1 if and only if it is in S_2. In a given context, distinct concepts may be necessarily coextensive. For example, since gold is necessarily the element with atomic number *79*, the state of having a tooth made of gold is the state of having a tooth made of the element with atomic number *79*, but the concept *has a tooth made of gold* is not the concept *has a tooth made of the element with atomic number 79*. Similarly, for any mental state S, the concept *is in S and such that gold is the element with atomic number 79* is necessarily coextensive with the concept *is in S*, so they are both concepts of S.

Of the conceptual and metaphysical contrasts, neither immediately entails the other. If the concept *knows* is mental while the concept *believes truly* is not, then it follows immediately that knowing is a mental state, but it does not follow immediately that believing truly is not a mental state, for perhaps there could also be a mental concept of the state of believing truly. Thus the conceptual contrast does not immediately entail the metaphysical contrast. If knowing is a mental state and believing truly is not a mental state, then it follows immediately that the concept *believes truly* is not mental, but it does not follow immediately that the concept *knows* is mental, for perhaps there could be a different concept of the state of knowing which was mental. Thus the metaphysical contrast does not immediately entail the conceptual contrast. Nevertheless, it is hard to see why someone should accept one contrast without accepting the other. If the concept *believes truly* is non-mental, its imagined necessary coextensiveness with a mental concept would be a bizarre metaphysical coincidence. If the concept *knows* were a non-mental concept of a mental state, its necessary coextensiveness with a mental concept would be an equally bizarre metaphysical coincidence. In practice, sloppily ignoring the distinction between the metaphysical and conceptual contrasts is unlikely to do very much harm. Nevertheless, it is safer not to ignore the distinction.

The concept *believes truly* is not a mental concept of a state. If the concept C is the conjunction of the concepts $C_1, ..., C_n$, then C is mental if and only if each C_i is mental. For example, the conjunctive concept *is sad and such that gold is the element with atomic number 79* is non-mental, simply because it has the non-mental conjunct *is such that gold is the element with atomic number 79*, although it is a concept of the state of sadness. Even a logically redundant non-mental component concept would make C a non-mental concept, although it would then be logically equivalent to a mental concept. By contrast, non-mental concepts in the content clause of an attitude ascription do not make the concept expressed non-mental; the concept *believes that there are numbers* can be mental even if the concept *number* is not. At least, all that is so in a reasonable sense of "mental", which one might express as "purely mental". Now the concept *believed truly* is the

conjunction of the concepts *believed* and *true*. The conjunct *true* is not mental, for it makes no reference to a subject. Therefore, the concept *believed truly* is non-mental. Similarly, the concept *believes truly* of subjects rather than propositions is non-mental. The metaphysical and conceptual contrasts turn on whether knowing is a mental state, and on whether *knows* is a mental concept.

Just as the concept *believes truly* is non-mental, so for a similar reason is the concept *has a justified true belief*. Indeed, such an argument applies to any of the concepts with which the concept *knows* is equated by conjunctive analyses of the standard kind. The argument can be generalized to analyses formed using logical connectives other than conjunction. It would not apply if those simpler concepts were all mental, but analyses of the concept *knows* of the standard kind always involve irredundant non-mental constituents, in particular the concept *true*. Consequently, the analysing concept is non-mental: that is, not purely mental. Given that the concept *knows* is mental, every analysis of it of the standard kind is therefore incorrect as a claim of concept identity, for the analysing concept is distinct from the concept to be analysed.

If a non-mental concept were necessarily coextensive with the mental concept *knows*, they would be concepts of the same mental state. The present account does not strictly entail that no analysis of the traditional kind provides correct necessary and sufficient conditions for knowing. But once we accept that the concept *knows* is not a complex concept of the kind traditionally envisaged, what reason have we to expect any such complex concept even to provide necessary and sufficient conditions for knowing?

Experience confirms inductively what the present account implies, that no analysis of the concept *knows* of the standard kind is correct. Indeed, the candidate concepts turn out to be not merely distinct from, but not even necessarily coextensive with, the target concept. Since Gettier refuted the traditional analysis of *knows* as *has a justified true belief* in 1963, a succession of increasingly complex analyses have been overturned by increasingly complex counterexamples, which is just what the present view would have led one to expect.[2]

Even if some sufficiently complex analysis never succumbed to counterexamples, that would not entail the identity of the analysing concept with the concept *knows*. Indeed, the equation of the concepts might well lead to more puzzlement rather than less. For knowing matters; the difference between knowing and not knowing is very important to us. Even unsophisticated curiosity is a desire to *know*. This importance would be hard to understand if the concept *knows* were the more or less ad hoc sprawl that analyses have had to become; why should we care so much about *that*?[3]

On quite general grounds, one would not expect the concept *knows* to have a non-trivial analysis in somehow more basic terms. Not all concepts have such analyses, on pain of infinite regress; the history of analytic philosophy suggests that those of most philosophical interest do not. "Bachelor" is a peculiarity, not a prototype. Attempts to analyse the concepts *means* and *causes*, for example, have been no more successful than attempts to analyse the concept *knows*, succumbing to the same pattern of counterexamples and epicycles. The analysing concept does not merely fail to be the same as the concept to be analysed; it fails even to provide a necessary and sufficient condition for the latter. The pursuit of analyses is a degenerating research programme.[4]

We can easily describe simple languages in which no necessary and sufficient condition for knowing can be expressed without circularity. Many fragments of English have that property. Why should we expect English itself to be different? Once "know" and cognate terms have been removed, what remains of our lexicon may be too impoverished to frame necessary and sufficient conditions for knowing.

The programme of analysis had its origin in great philosophical visions. Consider, for example, Russell's Principle of Acquaintance: "*Every proposition which we can understand must be composed wholly of constituents with which we are acquainted*" (Russell 1910–11, at Salmon and Soames 1988, p. 23). Russell calls the principle "the fundamental epistemological principle in the analysis of propositions containing descriptions". There may well be a reading on which it is correct. However, when the principle is combined with Russell's extremely intimate conception of acquaintance, it forces analysis to go deeper than the surface constituents of the evidently intelligible propositions of science and common sense, for our acquaintance with those surface constituents is not perfectly

intimate.[5] In such a context, the programme of analysis has a philosophical point. Now the philosophical visions which gave it a point are no longer serious options. Yet philosophers continued to pursue the programme long after the original motivation had gone. Correct deep analyses would doubtless still be interesting if they existed; what has gone is the reason to believe that they do exist.

While the general point is conceded, it might nevertheless be claimed that we have special reason to expect an analysis of *knows*. For we already have the necessary condition that what is known be true, and perhaps also believed; we might expect to reach a necessary and sufficient condition by adding whatever knowing has which believing truly may lack. But that expectation is based on a fallacy. If G is necessary for F, there need be no further condition H, specifiable independently of F, such that the conjunction of G and H is necessary and sufficient for F. Being coloured, for example, is necessary for being red, but if one seeks a further condition whose conjunction with being coloured is necessary and sufficient for being red, one finds only conditions specified in terms of "red": being red; being red if coloured.

There are other examples of the same phenomenon. Although x is a parent of y only if x is an ancestor of y, it does not follow that we implicitly conceptualize parenthood as the conjunction of ancestry with whatever must be added to ancestry to yield parenthood, or even that ancestry is conceptually prior to parenthood. Rather, x is an ancestor of y if and only if a chain of parenthood runs from x to y (more formally: if and only if x belongs to every class containing all parents of y and all parents of its members). Thus parents of y are automatically ancestors of y. If anything, parenthood is conceptually prior to ancestry; we use the necessary and sufficient condition for ancestry in terms of parenthood to explain why ancestry is necessary for parenthood.[6] Again, x is identical with y only if x weighs no more than y, but it does not follow that the concept *is identical with* is the conjunction of *weighs no more than* with whatever must be added to it to yield the former concept, or even that *weighs no more than* is prior to *is identical with*. In this case we explain the entailment by Leibniz's Law: if x is identical with y, whatever holds of x holds of y too, so since x weighs no more than x, x weighs no more than y. We grasp Leibniz's Law without considering all its instances. In principle one could grasp it before having acquired any concept of weight. Necessary conditions need not be conjuncts of necessary and sufficient conditions in any non-trivial sense.

More generally, the existence of conceptual connections is a bad reason to postulate an analysis of a concept to explain them. For example, the axiom of extensionality says that sets with the same members are identical; it has as good a claim to conceptual truth as the proposition that knowledge entails belief. Nevertheless, the axiom is not explained by an analysis of the concept *set*, if an analysis provides a non-circular statement of necessary and sufficient conditions.

The working hypothesis should be that the concept *knows* cannot be analysed into more basic concepts.[7] But to say that is not to say that no reflective understanding of it is possible.

4 Knowing as the Most General Factive Mental State

Knowing does not factorize as standard analyses require. Nevertheless, a modest positive account of the concept can be given, one that is not an analysis of it in the traditional sense. The one sketched below will appear thin by comparison with standard analyses. That may not be a vice. Indeed, its thinness will clarify the importance of the concept as more complex accounts do not.

The main idea is simple. A propositional attitude is factive if and only if, necessarily, one has it only to truths. Examples include the attitudes of seeing, knowing, and remembering. Not all factive attitudes constitute states; forgetting is a process. Call those attitudes which do constitute states *stative*. The proposal is that knowing is the most general factive stative attitude, that which one has to a proposition if one has any factive stative attitude to it at all. Apparent counterexamples to this conjecture are discussed below. The point of the conjecture is to illuminate the central role of the concept of knowing in our thought. It matters to us because factive stative attitudes matter to us.

To picture the proposal, compare the state of knowing with the property of being coloured, the colour property which something has if it has any colour property at all. If something is coloured, then it has a more specific colour property; it is red or green or. ... Although that specific colour may happen to lack a name in our language, we could always introduce such a name, perhaps pointing to the thing as a paradigm. We may say that being coloured is being red or green or ... if the list is understood as open-ended, and the concept *is coloured* is not identified with the disjunctive concept. One can grasp the concept *is coloured* without grasping the concept *is green*, therefore without grasping the disjunctive concept. Similarly, if one knows that A, then there is a specific way in which one knows; one can see or remember or ... that A. Although that specific way may happen to lack a name in our language, we could always introduce such a name, perhaps pointing to the case as a paradigm. We may say that knowing that A is seeing or remembering or ... that A, if the list is understood as open-ended, and the concept *knows* is not identified with the disjunctive concept. One can grasp the concept *knows* without grasping the concept *sees*, therefore without grasping the disjunctive concept.

We can give substance to the category of factive stative attitudes by describing its realization in a natural language. The characteristic expression of a factive stative attitude in language is a *factive mental state operator* (FMSO). Syntactically, an FMSO Φ has the combinatorial properties of a verb. Semantically, Φ is an unanalysable expression; that is, Φ is not synonymous with any complex expression whose meaning is composed of the meanings of its parts. A fortiori, Φ is not itself such an expression. Φ also meets three further conditions. For simplicity, they are stated here as conditions on an FMSO in English, although the general category is realized in other languages too. First, Φ typically takes as subject a term for something animate and as object a term consisting of "that" followed by a sentence. Second, Φ is factive, in the sense that the form of inference from "S Φs that A" to "A" is deductively valid (the scrupulous will read quotation marks as corner quotes where appropriate). Third, "S Φs that A" attributes a propositional attitude to S. On the present view, "know" and "remember" are typical FMSOs. Even with the following glosses, these remarks do not constitute a rigorous definition of "FMSO", but they should make its extension moderately clear.

First, "S Φs that A" is required to have "A" as a deductive consequence, not as a mere cancellable presupposition. There is a use of the verb "guess" on which "S guessed that A" in some sense presupposes "A". However, this presupposition is cancellable by context, as the logical and linguistic propriety of the following sentences shows:

(1) I guessed incorrectly that he was guilty.
(2) I guessed that he was guilty and you guessed that he was innocent.

In contrast, the substitution of "knew" for "guessed" in (1) or (2) yields a contradiction. Incidentally, therefore, the implication from "S does not know that A" to "A" is not like that from "S knows that A" to "A", for only the former is cancellable. The following sentences are logically and linguistically proper:

(3) I did not know that he was guilty, for he was innocent.
(4) I did not know that he was guilty and you did not know that he was innocent.

In contrast, the substitution of "knew" for "did not know" in (3) or (4) yields a contradiction. If Φ is an FMSO, the implication from "S Φs that A" to "A" is not cancellable (see Grice 1989, pp. 44–6 and 279–80 for cancellability and the presuppositions of "know" respectively).

Second, FMSOs are stative: they are used to denote states, not processes. This distinction is linguistically marked by the impropriety of progressive tenses. Consider:

(5) She is proving that there are infinitely many primes.
(6) The shoes are hurting her.
*(7) She is knowing that there are infinitely many primes.
*(8) She is believing that there are infinitely many primes.
*(9) The shoes are fitting her.

Sentences (7)–(9) are deviant because "know", "believe", and "fit" (on the relevant reading), unlike "prove" and "hurt", are stative. Of course, a verb may have both stative and non-stative readings, as in (10):

?(10) She is remembering that there are infinitely many primes.

On the salient reading of "remember", (10) is deviant, but it might correctly be used to say that she is in the process of recalling that there are infinitely many primes (see Vendler 1967, p. 104 for more on the linguistic marks of statives).

Third, an FMSO ascribes an attitude to a proposition to the subject. Thus "S Φs that A" entails "S grasps the proposition that A". To know that there are infinitely many primes, one must grasp the proposition that there are infinitely many primes, so "know" passes the test. A verb with a sense like "is responsible for its being the case that" would fail it. Thus, given that "see" and "remember" are FMSOs, one can see that Olga is playing chess or remember that she was playing chess only if one has a concept of chess. This is not to deny that one's perceptions and memories may have a content which one lacks the concepts to express; the point is just that the English constructions "see that A" and "remember that A" do not ascribe such content. Other constructions with those verbs behave differently; one does not need a concept of chess to see or remember Olga playing chess.

Fourth, an FMSO is semantically unanalysable. An artificial verb stipulated to mean the same as "believe truly" would not be an FMSO. A semantically analysable expression has a more complex semantic role than that of simply denoting an attitude; its proper treatment would require an account of the meanings from which its meaning is composed. Thus it is best at this stage to concentrate on semantically unanalysable expressions. Verbs such as "know" and "remember" will be assumed to be semantically unanalysable. However, an FMSO is not required to be syntactically unanalysable. In English and some other languages, for example, the addition of the auxiliary "can" often forms an FMSO (Vendler 1967, pp. 104–6). Consider the following pair:

(11) She felt that the bone was broken.
(12) She could feel that the bone was broken.

The "could" in (12) is not the "could" of ability; (12) does not mean anything like:

(13)   She had the ability to feel that the bone
       was broken.

A rough paraphrase of the salient reading of (11)
would be: "She intuitively believed that the bone
was broken." A rough paraphrase of the salient
reading of (12) would be: "She knew by the sense
of touch that the bone was broken". Sentence (12),
unlike (11), entails "The bone was broken." Thus
"could feel" differs from "felt" in two ways: it is
factive, and it is perceptual. Neither of these differences would occur if "could feel" were semantically analysable into "could" and "feel", for that
would assimilate "could feel" to "had the ability to
feel", which is neither factive nor perceptual.
"Could feel" is semantically fused. It is an FMSO;
"feel" is not.

   "Hear" is like "feel" in this respect. Consider:

(14)   She heard that the volcano was erupting.
(15)   She could hear that the volcano was
       erupting.

A rough paraphrase of the salient reading of (14)
would be: "She heard a report that the volcano
was erupting." A rough paraphrase of the salient
reading of (15) would be: "She knew by the sense
of hearing that the volcano was erupting."
Sentence (15), unlike (14), entails "The volcano
was erupting". Thus "could hear" differs from
"heard" in two ways: it is factive, and it is more
directly perceptual. Neither of these differences
would occur if "could hear" were semantically a
compound of "could" and "hear". "Could hear" is
an FMSO; "hear" is not.

   "Could see" differs from "see" in only one of
the two ways. Consider:

(16)   She saw that the stock market had
       crashed.
(17)   She could see that the stock market had
       crashed.

Both (16) and (17) entail "The stock market had
crashed"; there is no difference in factiveness.
However, they are naturally read in such a way
that (16) would be true and (17) false if she simply
saw a newspaper report of the crash; (17) might
be true if she saw investors lining the window
ledges. In such cases, one could insert "the news"
before "that" in (16) but not in (17) – not even

when she has inferred the crash from newspaper
reports of other events. In this way, "could see" is
more directly perceptual than "saw". This does
not prevent both from being FMSOs.

   The notion of an FMSO should by now be
clear enough to be workable; it can be projected
onto new cases. Moreover, it has been explained
without essential reference to the notion of knowing, although "know" is an example of an FMSO.
It will now be proposed that "know" has a special
place in the class of FMSOs.

   The proposal is that if Φ is any FMSO, then "S
Φs that A" entails "S knows that A". If you see that
it is raining, then you know that it is raining.
If you remember that it was raining, then you
know that it was raining. Such entailments are
plausible but not uncontroversial (see Unger 1972
and 1975, pp. 158–83 for useful discussion).

   It is sometimes alleged that one can perceive
or remember that A without knowing that A,
because one fails to believe or to be justified in
believing that A. Other evidence may give one
reason to think that one is only hallucinating
what one is in fact perceiving, or only imagining
what one is in fact remembering. One abandons
the belief, or retains it without justification;
either way, it is alleged, one fails to know (Steup
1992 is a recent example of such a view).
However, such cases put more pressure on the
link between knowing and believing or having
justification than they do on the link between
perceiving or remembering and knowing. If you
really do see *that* it is raining, which is not
simply to see the rain, then you know that it is
raining; seeing that A is a way of knowing that
A. You may not know that you see that it is raining, and consequently may not know that you
know that it is raining, but neither condition is
necessary for knowing that it is raining.
Similarly, if you really do remember *that* it was
raining, which is not simply to remember the
rain, then you know that it was raining; remembering that A is a way of knowing that A. You
may not know that you remember that it was
raining, and consequently may not know that
you know that it was raining, but neither condition is necessary for knowing that it is raining.
But it is far from obvious that you do see or
remember that it is or was raining in the cases
at issue, and an account will now be suggested
on which you do not.

There is a distinction between seeing that A and seeing a situation in which A. One difference is that only the former requires the perceiver to grasp the proposition that A. A normal observer in normal conditions who has no concept of chess can see a situation in which Olga is playing chess, by looking in the right direction, but cannot see *that* Olga is playing chess, because he does not know what he sees to be a situation in which Olga is playing chess. The present cases suggest another difference between the two notions of seeing. By looking in the right direction, you can see a situation in which it is raining. In the imagined case, moreover, you have enough concepts to grasp the proposition that it is raining. Nevertheless, you cannot see *that* it is raining, precisely because you do not know what you see to be a situation in which it is raining (given the unfavourable evidence). On this account, the case is a counterexample to neither the claim that seeing implies knowing nor the claim that knowing implies believing.

Similarly, there is a distinction between remembering that A and remembering a situation in which A. One difference is that only the former requires the rememberer to grasp the proposition that A. Someone whose memory is functioning normally but who has no concept of chess can remember a situation in which Olga was playing chess, but cannot remember *that* Olga was playing chess, because he does not know what he remembers to be a situation in which Olga was playing chess. The present cases suggest another difference between the two notions of remembering. You can remember a situation in which it was raining. In the imagined case, moreover, you have enough concepts to grasp the proposition that it was raining. Nevertheless, you cannot remember *that* it was raining, precisely because you do not know what you remember to be a situation in which it was raining (given the unfavourable evidence). On this account, the case is a counterexample to neither the claim that remembering implies knowing nor the claim that knowing implies believing.

The discussion of FMSOs may be summarized in three principles:

(18)   If Φ is an FMSO, from "S Φs that A" one may infer "A".

(19)   "Know" is an FMSO.

(20)   If Φ is an FMSO, from "S Φs that A" one may infer "S knows that A".

The latter two principles characterize the concept of knowing uniquely, up to logical equivalence, in terms of the concept of an FMSO. For let "schnow" be any term governed by (19') and (20'), the results of substituting "schnow" for "know" in (19) and (20) respectively. By (19) and (20'), from "S knows that A" one may infer "S schnows that A". Similarly, by (19') and (20), from "S schnows that A" one may infer "S knows that A". Thus "schnow" is logically equivalent to "know". Note that this argument would fail if (20) held only for *most* FMSOs. In simple terms, "know" is the most general FMSO, the one that applies if any FMSO at all applies.

In the material mode, the claim is that knowing is the most general stative propositional attitude such that, for all propositions p, necessarily if one has it to p then p is true. This is not quite to claim that, for all propositions p, knowing p is the most general mental state such that necessarily if one is in it then p is true. The latter claim fails for necessarily true propositions: every mental state is such that necessarily if one is in it then 5 + 7 = 12, but it does not follow that every mental state is sufficient for *knowing* that 5 + 7 = 12.

It is vital to this account of "know" that "believe truly" does not count as an FMSO. If it did, (20) would permit the invalid inference from "S believes truly that A" to "S knows that A". The mental state is believing that A, not believing truly that A. To entail knowing, the mental state itself must be sufficient for truth. The condition of semantic unanalysability ensures that "believe truly" does not count as an FMSO.

On this account, the importance of knowing to us becomes as intelligible as the importance of truth. Factive mental states are important to us as states whose essence includes a matching between mind and world, and knowing is important to us as the most general factive stative attitude. Of course, something needs to be said about the nature and significance of this matching, but that is a further problem. Someone who denied that the concept characterized by (18)–(20) is our concept *knows* might even think that it was more useful than the latter.

The states in question are general: different people can be in them at different times. No claim is made about the essences of their tokens; indeed, the idea of a token state is of doubtful coherence (Steward 1997, pp. 105–34). With respect to general states, the claims of necessity are *de re*, not just *de dicto*. Given that "knowing *p*" rigidly designates a mental state, the *de dicto* claim that the truth of *p* is necessary for knowing *p* implies the *de re* claim that for some mental state S the truth of *p* is necessary for S.

The account is explicitly not a decomposition of the concept *knows*; if "know" were semantically analysable, it would not be an FMSO. It would certainly be quite implausible to claim that everyone who thinks that John knows that it is raining thereby thinks that John has the most general stative propositional attitude such that, for all propositions *p*, necessarily if one has it to *p* then *p* is true, to the proposition that it is raining. What, then, is the status of the account?

Consider an analogy. Identity is uniquely characterized, up to logical equivalence, by the principles of reflexivity and Leibniz's Law, just as knowing is uniquely characterized, up to logical equivalence, by (19) and (20). However, it would be quite implausible to claim that everyone who thinks that Istanbul is Constantinople thereby thinks that Istanbul bears to Constantinople the reflexive relation that obeys Leibniz's Law. The metalogical concepts used in formulating Leibniz's Law are far more sophisticated than the concepts we use in thinking that Istanbul is Constantinople. In order to have the concept *is* (of identity), one must somehow be disposed to reason according to Leibniz's Law, but that does not require one to have the metalogical concepts used in formulating Leibniz's Law. If it did, there would be an obvious danger of an infinite regress. Similarly, in order to have the concept *knows*, one must somehow be disposed to reason according to (18)–(20), but that does not require one to have the metalinguistic concepts used in formulating (18)–(20).

It is no straightforward matter to say what it is for a subject to be disposed to reason according to rules which the subject cannot formulate. Such a subject may even consciously reject the rules; philosophers who mistakenly deny Leibniz's Law do not thereby cease to understand the "is" of identity. Nevertheless, some such notion does seem to be needed, independently of the account of knowing; the latter account can avail itself of that

notion, whatever exactly it proves to be. The present account of knowing is consistent with the main features of a theory of concepts such as that of Peacocke 1992, on which an account of a concept gives necessary and sufficient conditions for possession of the concept without any need to decompose the concept itself. However, the account is not committed to any general programme of Peacocke's kind in the theory of concepts.

The present account of knowing makes no use of such concepts as *justified*, *caused*, and *reliable*. Yet knowing seems to be highly sensitive to such factors over wide ranges of cases. Any adequate account of knowing should enable one to understand these connections. This challenge is not limited to the present account: standard accounts of knowing in terms of justification must enable one to understand its sensitivity to causal factors, and standard accounts of knowing in terms of causal factors must enable one to understand its sensitivity to justification; none of these tasks is trivial.

One way for the present account to meet the challenge is by exploiting the metaphysics of states. For example, a form of the essentiality of origins may apply to states; a necessary condition of being in some states may be having entered them in specific ways. States of perceiving and remembering have this feature, requiring entry along a specific kind of causal path. Thus the importance of causal factors in many cases of knowing is quite consistent with this account. More obviously, having an inferential justification of a specific kind may be essential to being in some mental states; having a proof is clearly a factive mental state. Thus the importance of justification in many cases of knowing is equally consistent with this account. Of course, these remarks merely adumbrate a strategy, without carrying it out. ... We can see epistemology as a branch of the philosophy of mind. If we try to leave epistemology out of the philosophy of mind, we arrive at a radically impoverished conception of the nature of mind.

5   Knowing and Believing

The account of knowing above makes no essential mention of believing. Formally, it is consistent with many different accounts of the relation between the two concepts. Historically, however, the view of knowing as a mental state has been associated with the view that knowing entails *not* believing. Prichard is a case in point (1950, pp. 86–8). On standard analyses of knowing, in contrast, knowing entails believing. On some intermediate views, knowing is consistent both with believing and with not believing. It is therefore natural to ask how far the present account of knowing constrains the relation between knowing and believing.

We have two schemas to consider:

(21)   If S knows that A then S believes that A.
(22)   If S knows that A then S does not believe that A.

If (21) is invalid, then the programme of analysing the concept *knows* as a conjunction of *believes* with *true* and other concepts is stillborn. Once the programme has been abandoned, (21) can be examined without prior need for its vindication.

The schema (22) is quite implausible. Whether I know that A on being told that A depends constitutively on whether my informant knew that A (amongst other factors). Whether I believe that A on being told that A does not depend constitutively on whether my informant knew that A; it would have to if knowing excluded believing. Of course, when one can describe someone as knowing that A, it is conversationally misleading simply to describe her as believing that A, but that is not to say that it is false. Not all believing is mere believing. We should reject (22).

The schema (21) does not sound *trivially* valid, as the schema "If S knows that A then A" does. When the unconfident examinee, taking herself to be guessing, reliably gives correct dates as a result of forgotten history lessons, it is not an obvious misuse of English to classify her as knowing that the battle of Agincourt was in 1415 without believing that it was. But intuitions differ over such cases; it is not very clear whether she knows and not very clear whether she believes. In a case in which she was taught incorrect dates and repeats them with equal unconfidence, she is in an at least somewhat belief-like state, which she is also in when she was taught the correct dates. We have no clear counterexamples to (21) (see Radford 1966, Armstrong 1973, pp. 138–49, and Shope 1983, pp. 178–87 for further discussion of such cases).

There is a wide grammatical divergence between the verbs "know" and "believe" not suggestive of closely connected terms. For example, in a context in which I have predicted that it will rain, "You know what I predicted" has a reading on which it is true if and only if you know that I predicted that it will rain, whereas "You believe what I predicted" has no reading on which it is true if and only if you believe that I predicted that it will rain. There are many further grammatical differences between "know" and "believe" (see Austin 1946, Vendler 1972, pp. 89–119, and Shope 1983, pp. 171–8, 191–2). One explanation of such facts, proposed by Vendler, is that "know" and "believe" take different objects: what one knows is a fact, what one believes a proposition, where a fact is not a true proposition. A contingently true proposition, unlike a contingent fact, could have been false and still have existed. If so, then knowing is not a *propositional* attitude, and much of the terminology of this book might need revision, although the substance of the account would remain. Vendler's explanation makes it hard to see why (21) should be valid. However, it is not strictly inconsistent with the validity of (21), since "that A" may refer to a fact in the antecedent and to a proposition in the consequent.

If "that A" refers to a fact in the context "S knows that A", then we might expect "that A" to suffer reference failure when "A" is false. Consequently, we might expect "S knows that A" and "S does not know that A" not to express propositions. But if "A" is false, "S knows that A" expresses a false proposition and "S does not know that A" a true one. Perhaps we could treat "that A" as elliptical for "the fact that A" and analyse it by a Russellian theory of definite descriptions. The reference of "fact that A" in the definite description is presumably determined by the proposition *p* expressed by "A"; it is therefore some function *f* of *p*. Thus to know that A is to know the *f(p)*, and hence to stand in a complex relation expressed by "know", "the", and "*f*" to the proposition expressed by "A". But then with only a slight change of meaning we could use the word "know" for that complex relation to a proposition. Thus, even on a view like Vendler's, knowing would still involve a propositional attitude. However, it is very doubtful that there are any such things as facts other than true propositions (see Williamson 1999 for an argument). Moreover, the propriety of remarks like "I always believed that you were a good friend; now I know it" and "Long before I knew those things about you I believed them" suggest that "believe" and "know" do take the same kind of object. Vendler's account is not accepted here.

The present account of knowing might be thought inconsistent with the validity of (21), on the grounds that it provides no basis for a conceptual connection between believing and knowing. That would be too quick. Section 3 already noted that not every conceptually necessary condition is a conjunct of a conjunctive analysis. It is a mistake to assume that (21) is valid only if that connection is explicable by an analysis of *knows* in terms of *believes*. Consider an analogy: it may be a priori that being crimson is sufficient for being red, but that implication need not be explained by an analysis of one colour concept in terms of the other. One can grasp either concept without grasping the other, by being shown examples of its application and non-application. Neither concept relies on the other in demarcating conceptual space. Nevertheless, the area demarcated by one concept might be so safely within the area demarcated by the other that one could know by a priori reflection that the former is sufficient for the latter. Similarly, the area demarcated by the concept *knows* might be so safely within the area demarcated by the concept *believes* that one could know (21) by a priori reflection. That is quite consistent with, although not entailed by, the account of knowing in section 4.

An alternative proposal is to reverse the direction of analysis, and validate (21) by an analysis of *believes* in terms of *knows*. The simplest suggestion is that the concept *believes* is analysable as a disjunction of *knows* with other concepts. The word "opine" will be used here as a term of art for the rest of the disjunction. On this analysis, one believes *p* if and only if one either knows *p* or opines *p*. Given that opining *p* is incompatible with knowing *p*, it follows that one opines *p* if and only if one believes *p* without knowing *p*. A similar view has been proposed by John McDowell (1982), building on the disjunctive account of perceptual experience developed by J. M. Hinton (1967 and 1973) and Paul Snowdon (1980–1 and 1990; see also Child 1994, pp. 143–64,

Dancy 1995, and Martin 1997). In McDowell's terminology, believing is not the highest common factor of knowing and opining. There is no such common factor. Rather, knowing and opining are radically different, mutually exclusive states, although instances of the latter are easily mistaken for instances of the former. Given a distinction between facts and true propositions, one could contrast knowing and opining somewhat as Vendler contrasts knowing and believing: to know is to be acquainted with a fact; to opine is to be acquainted with no more than a proposition. But the disjunctive conception does not require such an ontology of facts.

Not all those who advocate a disjunctive conception would claim that it provides a conceptual analysis. That claim faces difficulties additional to the generally dim prospects for conceptual analysis evoked in section 3. If the concept *believes* is the disjunction of *knows* and *opines*, then it must be possible to grasp the concept *opines* without previously grasping the concept *believes*. For otherwise, since grasping a disjunction involves grasping its disjuncts, it would be impossible to grasp the concept *opines* for the first time. Now "opine" was introduced as a term of art; how is it to be explained? The natural explanation is that to opine a proposition *p* is to have a mere belief *p*, which is presumably to believe *p* without knowing *p*, but that explanation uses the concept *believes*. It does not permit one to grasp *opines* without already grasping *believes*. The explanation that to opine *p* is to be of the opinion *p* does no better, for "be of the opinion" as ordinarily understood is just a rough synonym of "believe". In particular, once it is conceded – as it is by the disjunctive conception – that "know" implies "believe", little reason remains to deny that "know" implies "be of the opinion", too.

Can we explain "opine" in terms of "know"? A first attempt is this: one opines the proposition *p* if and only if one is in a state which one cannot discriminate from knowing *p*, in other words, a state which is, for all one knows, knowing *p*. That cannot be quite right, for if one cannot grasp the proposition *p* then one cannot discriminate one's state from knowing *p*; but one does not believe *p*, and therefore does not opine it. To avoid that problem, we can revise the definition thus: one opines *p* if and only if one has an attitude to the proposition *p* which one cannot discriminate from knowing, in other words, an attitude to *p* which is, for all one knows, knowing. However, that definition does not help a *disjunctive* analysis of believing. For if one knows *p*, then trivially one has an attitude to *p* which one cannot discriminate from knowing; one cannot discriminate something from itself. Thus the first disjunct, "One knows *p*", entails the second disjunct, "One opines *p*". The whole disjunction would therefore be equivalent to its second disjunct, and the disjunctive form of the definiens would be a mere artefact of conceptual redundancy. To tack the qualification "but does not know *p*" onto the end of the definition of "opine" would make no significant difference, for since "One either knows *p* or has an attitude to *p* which one cannot discriminate from knowing but does not know *p*" is still equivalent to "One has an attitude to *p* which one cannot discriminate from knowing *p*", the disjunctive form would remain a mere artefact.

Alternatively, "opine" might be explained as the disjunction of several more specific disjuncts, such as "be under the illusion", "be irrationally certain" and so on. However, it is very doubtful that, without using the concept *believes*, one could extend such a list to include all the different ways in which someone can believe without knowing. Those ways seem to be indefinitely various. How could one even specify, without using the concept *believes*, all the states in which someone can believe *p* falsely? If the list of disjuncts is open-ended, one could not grasp how to go on without realizing that one must list the ways in which someone can believe without knowing. Thus the explanation of "opine" illicitly relies on a prior grasp of the concept *believes*.

The phenomenon just noted also threatens more metaphysical disjunctive accounts which do not attempt conceptual analysis, instead making their claims only about the underlying facts in virtue of which the concepts apply. Such an account of believing might deny that believing is itself a unified state, insisting that it is necessary but not a priori that one believes *p* if and only if one is in either the state of knowing *p* or the state of opining *p*. Since conceptual analysis is no longer in question, the replacement of "opining" by "merely believing" is not objectionable on grounds of circularity. The trouble is rather that there is no *more* reason to regard merely believing *p* as a unified mental state than to regard believ-

ing *p* as such. What unifies Gettier cases with cases of unjustified false belief is simply that in both, the subject believes without knowing; a good taxonomy of believing would not classify them together on the basis of some positive feature that excludes knowing. Moreover, it is hard to see how such a taxonomy could describe every species of believing without using the concept *believes*. But if a good taxonomy of believing does use the concept *believes*, that undermines the denial that believing is a unified state. Similar objections apply to disjunctive accounts of perception, appearance, and experience. For example, there is no reason to postulate a unified mental state equivalent to its appearing to one that A while one does not perceive that A.

A strictly disjunctive account of belief is not correct at either the conceptual or the metaphysical level. However, the disjunctive account was brought into play as a simple means to reconcile the account of knowing in section 4 with the supposed validity of (21) (knowing entails believing). There are other means to that end. A non-disjunctive analysis of *believes* might also validate (21). For example, (21) is a corollary of an analysis of *believes* itself on the lines of the definition of *opines* above: one believes *p* if and only if one has an attitude to the proposition *p* which one cannot discriminate from knowing, in other words, an attitude to *p* which is, for all one knows, knowing. That definition suggestively makes knowing central to the account of believing. One attraction of such an account is that it opens the prospect of explaining the difficulty, remarked by Hume, of believing *p* at will in terms of the difficulty of knowing *p* at will. The analysis is also consistent with the account of knowing in section 4.

Although that analysis provides a reasonable approximation to our concept *believes*, it does not fully capture the concept. It incorrectly classifies as believing that food is present a primitive creature which lacks any concept of knowing and merely desires that food is present; for all the creature knows, its attitude to the proposition that food is present is knowing. Equally incorrectly, the account classifies as not believing that there is a god someone who consciously takes a leap of faith, knowing that she does not know that there is a god. Both examples, however, are compatible with the variant idea that to believe *p* is to treat *p* as if one knew *p* – that is, to treat *p* in ways similar to the ways in which subjects treat propositions which they know. In particular, a factive propositional attitude to a proposition is characteristically associated with reliance on it as a premise in practical reasoning, for good functional reasons; such reliance is crucial to belief. A creature which lacks a concept of knowing can still treat a proposition in ways in which it treats propositions which it knows. The primitive creature does not treat the proposition that food is present like that when merely desiring that food is present; it does not use the proposition as a premise in practical reasoning. By contrast, the person who genuinely believes that there is a god by a leap of faith does rely on that premise in such reasoning. The unconfident examinee who tentatively gives p as an answer is little disposed to rely on p as a premise, and for that reason does not clearly believe p, but for the same reason does not clearly know p. Although a full-blown exact conceptual analysis of *believes* in terms of *knows* is too much to expect, we can still postulate a looser connection along these lines.

If believing p is, roughly, treating p as if one knew p, then knowing is in that sense central to believing. Knowledge sets the standard of appropriateness for belief. That does not imply that all cases of knowing are paradigmatic cases of believing, for one might know p while in a sense treating p as if one did not know p – that is, while treating p in ways untypical of those in which subjects treat what they know. Nevertheless, as a crude generalization, the further one is from knowing p, the less appropriate it is to believe p. Knowing is in that sense the best kind of believing. Mere believing is a kind of botched knowing.[8] In short, belief aims at knowledge (not just truth). ...

Although the letter of disjunctive accounts has been rejected, the spirit may have been retained. For on the account in section 4, believing is not the highest common factor of knowing and mere believing, simply because it is not a factor of knowing at all (whether or not it is a necessary condition). Since that point is consistent with the claim that believing is common to knowing and mere believing, the claim is harmless. It no more makes the difference between knowing and mere believing extrinsic to a state than the point that continuity is common to straight and curved lines makes the difference between straight and curved extrinsic to a line. To know is not merely to believe while various other conditions are met; it is to be in a new kind of state, a factive one. What matters is not acceptance of a disjunctive account of believing but rejection of a conjunctive account of knowing.[9] Furthermore, the claim that belief is what aims at knowledge is consonant with the suggestion in disjunctive accounts that illusion is somehow parasitic on veridical perception. Properly developed, the insight behind disjunctive theories leads to a non-conjunctive account of knowledge and a non-disjunctive account of belief.

While belief aims at knowledge, various mental processes aim at more specific factive mental states. Perception aims at perceiving that something is so; memory aims at remembering that something is so. Since knowing is the most general factive state, all such processes aim at kinds of knowledge. If a creature could not engage in such processes without some capacity for success, we may conjecture that nothing could have a mind without having a capacity for knowledge.

Notes

1 McDowell 1995 and Gibbons 1998 defend closely related conceptions of knowing as a mental state. See also Guttenplan 1994 and Peacocke 1999, pp. 52–5.

2 See Shope 1983 for the history of a decade of research into the analysis of knowing after Gettier 1963; an equally complex book could be written on post-1983 developments. Not all this work aims to provide an analysis in the traditional sense; see Shope 1983, pp. 34–44.

3 Craig 1990 makes an interesting attempt to explain the point of the concept of knowledge in the light of the failure of analyses of the standard kind. However, on the present view it remains too close to the traditional programme, for it takes as its starting point our need for true beliefs about our environment (1990: 11), as though this were somehow more basic than our need for knowledge of our environment. It is no reply that believing

truly is as useful as knowing, for it is agreed that the starting point should be more specific than "useful mental state"; why should it be specific in the manner of "believing truly" rather than in that of "knowing"? …

4 For sophisticated but uncompelling defence of conceptual analysis see Jackson 1998 and Smith 1994, pp. 29–56, 161–4. However, the kind of analysis they defend constitutes little threat to the claim that knowing is a mental state in every reasonable sense of the latter term. They provide no reason to suppose that the concept *knows* can be non-trivially analysed in any sense in which paradigmatic mental concepts cannot be, or that it is somehow posterior in the order of analysis to the concept *believes*. See also Fodor 1998 for a discussion of the demise of definition.

5 We must also assume Russell's conception of propositions as at the level of reference rather than sense. In effect, Evans 1982 combines the Principle of Acquaintance with a conception of acquaintance much less extreme than Russell's. Of course, Russell's extremism here is no mere extraneous dogma; it is an attempt to solve puzzles about the identity and non-existence of denotation in intentional contexts.

Unfortunately, the cure is worse than the disease.

6 As noted in the Introduction, we cannot define "*x* is a parent of *y*" by "*x* is an ancestor of *y* and *x* is not an ancestor of an ancestor of *y*".

7 A further ground for suspicion of analyses of the concept *knows* in terms of the concept *believes* is that they seem to imply that the latter concept is acquired before the former. Data on child development suggest, if anything, the reverse order (see Perner 1993, pp. 145–203 for discussion of relevant work). Crudely: children understand ignorance before they understand error. Naturally, the data can be interpreted in various ways, and their bearing on the order of analysis depends on subtle issues in the theory of concepts.

8 See also Peacocke 1999, p. 34.

9 Martin 1997, pp. 88–90 questions whether a parallel account of perception and appearance will serve the purposes of naive realism, on the grounds that it does not entail the naive realist's distinctive claims about the phenomenology of perception. But a parallel account in terms of a factive mental state of conscious perceptual awareness may capture such claims.

References

Armstrong, D. M. 1973. *Belief, Truth and Knowledge* (Cambridge: Cambridge University Press).

Austin, J. L. 1946. "Other minds." *Proceedings of the Aristotelian Society*, supp. 20, pp. 148–87.

Child, T. W. 1994. *Causality, Interpretation and the Mind* (Oxford: Clarendon Press).

Craig, E. J. 1990. *Knowledge and the State of Nature: An Essay in Conceptual Synthesis* (Oxford: Clarendon Press).

Dancy, J. 1995. "Arguments from illusion." *Philosophical Quarterly* 45, pp. 421–38.

Evans, M. G. J. 1982. *The Varieties of Reference*, ed. J. H. McDowell (Oxford: Clarendon Press).

Fodor, J. A. 1998. *Concepts: Where Cognitive Science Went Wrong* (Oxford: Clarendon Press).

Gettier, E. 1963. "Is justified true belief knowledge?" *Analysis*, 23, pp. 121–3.

Gibbons, J. 1998. "Truth in action." Unpublished typescript.

Grice, H. P. 1989. *Studies in the Way of Words* (Cambridge, MA: Harvard University Press).

Guttenplan, S. 1994. "Belief, knowledge and the origins of content." *Dialectica* 48, pp. 287–305.

Hintikka, K. J. J. 1962. *Knowledge and Belief* (Ithaca, NY: Cornell University Press).

Hinton, J. M. 1967. "Visual experiences." *Mind* 76, pp. 217–27.

Howson, C. 1996. "Epistemic probability." *Proceedings of the Aristotelian Society*, supp. 70, pp. 63–77.

Jackson, F. 1998. *From Metaphysics to Ethics: A Defence of Conceptual Analysis* (Oxford: Oxford University Press).

McDowell, J. H. 1982. "Criteria, defeasibility, and knowledge." *Proceedings of the British Academy* 68, pp. 455–79. Partly reprinted with revisions in Dancy (ed.) 1988. *Perceptual Knowledge* (Oxford: Oxford University Press).

—— 1995. "Knowledge and the internal." *Philosophy and Phenomenological Research* 55, pp. 877–93.

Martin, M. G. F. 1997. "The reality of appearances." In R. M. Sainsbury (ed.) *Thought and Ontology* (Milan: FrancoAngeli).

Peacocke, C. A. B. 1992. *A Study of Concepts* (Cambridge, MA: MIT Press).

—— 1999. *Being Known* (Oxford: Clarendon Press).

Perner, J. 1993. "Fitch and intuitionistic knowability." *Analysis* 50, pp. 182–7.

Prichard, H. A. 1950. *Knowledge and Perception* (Oxford: Clarendon Press).

Radford, C. 1966. "Knowledge – by examples." *Analysis* 27, pp. 1–11.

Russell, J. B. A. W. 1910–11. "Knowledge by acquaintance and knowledge by description." *Proceedings of the Aristotelian Society* 11, pp. 108–28. Page reference to reprinting in Salmon and Soames 1988.

Salmon, N. U. and Soames, S. (eds) 1988. *Propositions and Attitudes* (Oxford: Oxford University Press).

Shope, R. K. 1983. *The Analysis of Knowing: A Decade of Research* (Princeton: Princeton University Press).

Smith, M. 1994. *The Moral Problem* (Oxford: Blackwell).

Snowdon, P. 1980–1. "Perception, vision and causation." *Proceedings of the Aristotelian Society* 81, pp. 175–92.

—— 1990. "The objects of perceptual experience." *Proceedings of Aristotelian Society*, supp. 64, pp. 121–50.

Steward, H. 1997. *The Ontology of Mind: Events, Processes and States* (Oxford: Clarendon Press).

Unger, P. 1972. "Propositional verbs and knowledge." *Journal of Philosophy* 69, pp. 301–12.

—— 1975. *Ignorance: A Case for Scepticism* (Oxford: Oxford University Press).

Vendler, Z. 1967. *Linguistics in Philosophy* (Ithaca, NY: Cornell University Press).

—— 1972. *Res Cogitans* (Ithaca, NY: Cornell University Press).

Williamson, T. 1999. "Truthmakers and the Converse Barcan Formula." *Dialectica* 53, pp. 253–70.

PART IV

Epistemic Closure

Introduction

It is a commonplace observation that deduction, or at least competent deduction, can extend our knowledge. We can expand our knowledge by figuring out what follows from it. This seems to be evidence for a kind of epistemic "closure" principle – a principle positing some strong connection between knowing something and knowing its implications. Moreover, it seems that skeptical reasoning quite often presupposes some such principle. For example, a skeptic might argue that because you don't know you're not a handless brain in a vat, you don't know you have hands. Getting clear on how our knowledge might be extended to the implications of what we know seems important, then, for evaluating skeptical reasoning.

It is plainly too strong to say that knowledge is closed under implication – that we know all that is implied by what we know – since one need have no idea that there is an implication. I might know that 2 + 2 is 4 but not know some very complicated mathematical proposition implied by it. A good first start for an epistemic closure takes knowledge to be closed under *known* implication:

> If S knows that p, and if S knows that p implies q, then S knows that q.

There is a lot to say in favor of this principle. For one thing, it seems clearly absurd to say, "I know that I'm awake, and I realize that my being awake implies my not dreaming, but I don't know I'm not dreaming." To use a term from Keith DeRose, such conjunctions seem *abominable*. The principle also seems to explain how deduction is a secure source of the transmission of knowledge. Nonetheless, the principle has difficulties. The selections in this section are all devoted either to making palatable the view that closure fails or to defending closure against the objections presented by its opponents.

Fred Dretske, for example, argues that it follows from the right conception of the semantics of "knows" that closure is violated. Suppose I have a reason to buy a car at Jones's used car lot – that it's the kind of car I'm looking for, and it's being sold cheaper at Jones's lot than anywhere else. This is a reason to buy my car at Jones's. But notice a logical consequence of my buying a car at Jones's. If I buy my car at Jones's, I don't steal my car at Jones's. My reason for buying my car at Jones's surely is not a reason not to steal a car at Jones's. My reasons for that lie elsewhere. According to Dretske, certain epistemic operators, like "R is a reason for …" and "E is an explanation for …," while truly applied to certain propositions, do not "penetrate" to all logical consequences of those propositions. And, according to Dretske, knowledge is a lot like "explains" and "is a reason for" in that the operator "S knows that" when applied to "p" does not penetrate to all logical consequences of p, even all those logical consequences which S knows about. This is just to say that closure fails in such cases. The reason is that to know something is to know it against a background of certain relevant alternatives, just as to have a reason for doing something is to have a reason for doing *it*, rather than some other specific alternative. In the case of certain standard skeptical arguments, Dretske proposes that we can fail to know that the skeptical alternatives don't obtain (e.g., we do not know that animals in the zebra pen at the zoo are not cleverly disguised mules) even while knowing what we originally said we knew (e.g., we do know that the animals in the zebra pen are zebras). Knowing, on Dretske's so-called *relevant alternatives theory*, requires ruling out all *relevant* alternatives, not *all* alternatives.

Gail Stine is also sympathetic to the relevant alternatives theory but, unlike Dretske, does not think that this approach requires the denial of closure. On her understanding of the theory, which alternatives are relevant can vary depending on the context of speech. If we are in a court of law or are discussing skepticism, alternatives can become relevant which aren't relevant in ordinary contexts. If we hold the speech context fixed, she claims, any relevant alternative to the conclusion of a (single-premised) valid argument will be a relevant alternative to its premise. Of course, by actually moving from asserting knowledge of the premises to asserting knowledge of the conclusion, we can alter the speech context, making new alternatives relevant, and so closure can appear to be violated. But this is mere appearance. For, in changing the speech context, one is in effect equivocating on 'knows.' We test a closure principle for truth by holding fixed the content of all terms involved, including 'knows,' and then seeing whether the antecedent can be true and the consequent false. But holding fixed the content of 'knows' requires holding fixed the class of relevant alternatives.

Like Dretske, Robert Nozick argues that a denial of closure falls out of the correct analysis of knowledge. Nozick, however, is not a relevant alternatives theorist. According to Nozick, the key to knowledge is tracking the truth. One knows through perception that there is a bird on the ledge because one wouldn't believe this if it weren't so. Moreover, one must be such that if things were slightly different and there was a bird on the ledge, one would still believe that this were so. Thus, we obtain the following preliminary account:

S knows that p iff
1 p is true.
2 S believes that p.
3 If p were not true, S would not believe that p.
4 If p were true, S would believe that p.

One of the great advantages of the account is that, if correct, it would defuse arguments for skepticism. For if Nozick is right about knowledge, it is not closed under known logical implication. There are cases in which one tracks the truth of p, tracks the truth of <p entails q> but fails to track the truth of q. The standard skeptical cases are prime examples: I track the truth of both <I have hands> and <<I have hands> entails

<I am not a brain in a vat deceived into thinking I have hands>>, but I don't track the truth of <I am not a brain in a vat deceived into thinking I have hands>. For had I been a brain in a vat so deceived, I would still believe I have hands, for my evidence would be just what it is. Thus, I know that I have hands, even though I don't know that I am not a brain in a vat deceived into thinking I have hands. The defeat of skepticism, as with Dretske, is provided by a denial of closure.

Ernest Sosa argues that we can defend Moorean common sense – and likewise, the closure principle – against Dretske and Nozick, based on an appeal to sensitivity (i.e., truth-tracking). Sosa understands Moore as arguing as follows: I know ordinary proposition O, and if I know O then I know the falsity of skeptical proposition H, and so I know ~H. Against this, it has been claimed that one can't know ~H because one is not sensitive to its truth. One can't know one isn't a brain in a vat, for example, because if one *were* a brain in a vat, one would still believe one was *not* a brain in a vat. Thus, to avoid the skeptical conclusion that one doesn't know ordinary propositions such as *I have hands*, the sensitivity theorist must either deny epistemic closure or appeal to some sort of contextual shift. Overlooked here is the distinction between sensitivity and a close relative of it, which Sosa calls *safety*. To say S's belief is safe is to say that if S were to believe p then p would be true. This is the contrapositive of sensitivity (and the converse of Nozick's condition 4). Some conditionals contrapose, but Sosa shows that contraposition fails for subjunctive conditionals. In fact, Sosa claims, the way in which it fails makes safety the better candidate for being a requirement of knowledge. (For example, I can know many propositions of the form *I do not falsely believe that p*, and in each case my belief is safe but not sensitive.) Replacing the sensitivity requirement with a safety requirement enables us to defend Moore. We do safely believe that we're not in a skeptical scenario H because were we to believe ~H we would be right. Finally, the close apparent connection between safety and sensitivity can help explain why we find the claim that we don't know ~H so tempting: we confuse safety with sensitivity.

Jonathan Vogel offers further defense of the closure principle generally and, in particular, those instances of the closure principle that figure in the skeptical arguments. Vogel argues that the intuitions which drive apparent counter-examples can be explained away in light of certain psychological tendencies to overestimate chances of error. Further, Vogel argues that even if the closure principle does fail in the face of certain lottery-like cases, this failure does not carry over to the contexts where the skeptic might appeal to the principle. Skeptical propositions – that you are a brain in a vat, etc. – do not have the characteristic features of lottery propositions.

Further Reading

Audi, Robert, "Deductive Closure, Defeasibility, and Scepticism: A Reply to Feldman," *Philosophical Quarterly* 45 (1995), pp. 494–9.

Brueckner, Anthony L., "Skepticism and Epistemic Closure," *Philosophical Topics* 13 (1985), pp. 89–117.

Cohen, Stewart, "Two Kinds of Skeptical Argument," *Philosophy and Phenomenological Research* 58 (1998), pp. 143–59.

Dretske, Fred, "The Case Against Closure," in Matthias Steup and Ernest Sosa (eds), *Contemporary Debates in Epistemology* (Oxford: Blackwell, 2005), pp. 13–25.

Feldman, Richard, "In Defence of Closure," *Philosophical Quarterly* 45 (1995), pp. 487–94.

Harman, Gilbert, *Change in View: Principles of Reasoning*, (Cambridge, MA: Massachusetts Institute of Technology Press, 1988).

Hawthorne, John, *Knowledge and Lotteries* (Oxford: Clarendon Press, 2004).

———, "The Case for Closure," in Matthias Steup and Ernest Sosa (eds), *Contemporary Debates in Epistemology* (Oxford: Blackwell, 2005), pp. 26–42.

Heller, Mark, "Relevant Alternatives and Closure," *Australasian Journal of Philosophy* 77 (1999), pp. 196–208.

Klein, Peter, "Closure Matters: Academic Skepticism and Easy Knowledge," *Nous* – supplement: *Philosophical Issues* 14 (2004), pp. 165–84.

Kvanvig, Jonathan, "Epistemic Closure," *Philosophy Compass* 1 (2006).

Nozick, Robert, *Philosophical Explanations* (Oxford: Oxford University Press, 1981).

Warfield, Ted A., "Deductive Closure and Relevant Alternatives," *Southwest Philosophical Studies* (1991), pp. 104–16.

CHAPTER 19

Epistemic Operators

Fred Dretske

Suppose Q is a necessary consequence of P. Given only this much, it is, of course, quite trivial that if it is true that P, then it must also be true that Q. If it is a fact that P, then it must also be a fact that Q. If it is necessary that P, then it is necessary that Q; and if it is possible that P, then it must also be possible that Q.

I have just mentioned four prefixes: "it is true that", "it is a fact that", "it is necessary that", and "it is possible that". In this paper I shall refer to such affixes as *sentential operators* or simply *operators*; when affixed to a sentence or statement, they operate on it to generate another sentence or statement. The distinctive thing about the four operators I have just mentioned is that, if Q is a necessary consequence of P, then the statement we get by operating on Q with one of these four operators is a necessary consequence of the statement we get by operating on P with the same operator. This may be put more succinctly if we let "O" stand for the operator in question and "O(P)" for the statement we get by affixing the operator "O" to the statement "P". We can now say that the above four operators share the following property: if P entails Q, then O(P) entails O(Q). I shall call any operator having this property a *penetrating operator* (or, when emphasis is required, a *fully penetrating operator*). In operating on P these

operators penetrate to every necessary consequence of P.

We are now in a position to ask ourselves a preliminary question. The answer to this question is easy enough, but it will set the stage for more difficult questions. Are all sentential operators fully penetrating operators? Are all operators such that if P entails Q, then O(P) entails O(Q)? If *all* operators are penetrating operators, then each of the following statements must be true (when P entails Q):

(1) You cannot have a reason to believe that P unless you have a reason to believe that Q.
(2) You cannot know that P unless you know that Q.
(3) You cannot explain why P is the case unless you can explain why Q is the case.
(4) If you assert that P, then you assert that Q.
(5) If you hope that P, then you hope that Q.
(6) If it is strange (or accidental) that P, then it must be strange (or accidental) that Q.
(7) If it was a mistake that P, then it was a mistake that Q.

This list begins with two epistemic operators, "reason to believe that" and "know that". Since I shall be concerned with these later in the paper, let me skip over them now and look at those appearing near the end of the list. They will suffice to answer our opening question, and their status is much less problematic than that of some of the other operators.

Originally published in *The Journal of Philosophy* LXVII, 24 (December 24, 1970), pp. 1007–23.

"She lost" entails "Someone lost". Yet, it may be strange that she lost, not at all strange that someone lost. "Bill and Susan married each other" entails that Susan got married; yet, it may be quite odd that (strange that, incredible that) Bill and Susan married each other but quite unremarkable, not at all odd that, Susan got married. It may have been a mistake that they married each other, not a mistake that Susan got married. Or finally, "I hit the bull's-eye" entails that I either hit the bull's-eye or the side of the barn; and though I admit that it was lucky that (accidental that) I hit the bull's-eye, I will deny that it was lucky, an accident, that I hit either the bull's-eye or the side of the barn.

Such examples show that not all operators are fully penetrating. Indeed, such operators as "it is strange that", "it is accidental that" and "it is a mistake that" fail to penetrate to some of the most elementary logical consequences of a proposition. Consider the entailment between "$P \cdot Q$" and "Q". Clearly, it may be strange that P and Q, not at all strange that P, and not at all strange that Q. A concatenation of factors, no one of which is strange or accidental, may itself be strange or accidental. Taken by itself, there is nothing odd or suspicious about Frank's holding a winning ticket in the first race. The same could be said about any of the other races: there is nothing odd or suspicious about Frank's holding a winning ticket in the nth race. Nonetheless, there is something very odd, very suspicious, in Frank's having a winning ticket in n races.

Therefore, not only are these operators *not* fully penetrating, they lie, as it were, on the other end of the spectrum. They fail to penetrate to some of the most elementary consequences of a proposition. I shall refer to this class of operators as *nonpenetrating* operators. I do not wish to suggest by this label that such operators are totally impotent in this respect (or that they are all uniform in their degree of penetration). I mean it, rather, in a rough, comparative sense: their *degree of penetration* is less than that of any of the other operators I shall have occasion to discuss.

We have, then, two ends of the spectrum with examples from both ends. Anything that falls between these two extremes I shall call a *semi-penetrating operator*. And with this definition I am, finally, in a position to express my main point, the point I wish to defend in the rest of this

paper. It is, simply, that all epistemic operators are semi-penetrating operators. There is both a trivial and a significant side to this claim. Let me first deal briefly with the trivial aspect.

The epistemic operators I mean to be speaking about when I say that all epistemic operators are semi-penetrating include the following:

(a) S knows that …
(b) S sees (or can see) that …
(c) S has reason (or a reason) to believe that …
(d) There is evidence to suggest that …
(e) S can prove that …
(f) S learned (discovered, found out) that …
(g) In relation to our evidence it is probable that …

Part of what needs to be established in showing that these are all semi-penetrating operators is that they all possess a degree of penetration greater than that of the nonpenetrating operators. This is the trivial side of my thesis. I say it is trivial because it seems to me fairly obvious that if someone knows that P and Q, has a reason to believe that P and Q, or can prove that P and Q, he thereby knows that Q, has a reason to believe that Q, or can prove (in the appropriate epistemic sense of this term) that Q. Similarly, if S knows that Bill and Susan married each other, he (must) know that Susan got married (married someone). If he knows that P is the case, he knows that P or Q is the case (where the "or" is understood in a sense which makes "P or Q" a necessary consequence of "P"). This is not a claim about what it would be appropriate to say, what the person himself thinks he knows or would say he knows. It is a question, simply, of what he knows. It may not be appropriate to *say* to Jim's wife that you know it was either her husband, Jim, or Harold who sent the neighbor lady an expensive gift *when you know it was Harold*. For, although you do know this, it is misleading to say you know it – especially to Jim's wife.

Let me accept, therefore, without further argument that the epistemic operators are not, unlike "lucky that", "strange that", "a mistake that", and "accidental that", nonpenetrating operators. I would like to turn, then, to the more significant side of my thesis. Before I do, however, I must make one point clear lest it convert my entire thesis into something as trivial as the first half of it. When we are dealing with the epistemic operators, it becomes crucial to specify whether the agent in question knows that P entails Q. That is to say, P may entail Q, and S may know that P, but he may not know that Q *because*, and perhaps *only* because, he fails to appreciate the fact that P entails Q. When Q is a simple logical consequence of P we do not expect this to happen, but when the propositions become very complex, or the relationship between them very complex, this might easily occur. Let P be a set of axioms, Q a theorem. S's knowing P does not entail S's knowing Q just because P entails Q; for, of course, S may not know that P entails Q, may not know that Q is a *theorem*. Hence, our epistemic operators will turn out *not* to be penetrating because, and perhaps *only* because, the agents in question are not fully cognizant of all the implications of what they know to be the case, can see to be the case, have a reason to believe is the case, and so on. Were we all ideally astute logicians, were we all fully apprised of all the necessary consequences (supposing this to be a well defined class) of every proposition, perhaps then the epistemic operators would turn into fully penetrating operators. That is, assuming that if P entails Q, we *know* that P entails Q, then every epistemic operator is a penetrating operator: the epistemic operators penetrate to all the *known* consequences of a proposition.

It is this latter, slightly modified, claim that I mean to reject. Therefore, I shall assume throughout the discussion that when Q is a necessary consequence of P, every relevant agent *knows that it is*. I shall be dealing with only the *known consequences* (in most cases because they are immediate and obvious consequences). What I wish to show is that, even under this special restriction, the epistemic operators are *only* semi-penetrating.

I think many philosophers would disagree with this contention. The conviction is that the epistemic worth of a proposition is hereditary under entailment, that whatever the epistemic worth of P, *at least* the same value must be accorded the known consequences of P. This conviction finds expression in a variety of ways. Epistemic logic: if S knows that P, and knows that P entails Q, then S knows that Q. Probability theory: if A is probable, and B is a logical consequence of A, then B is probable (relative to the same evidence, of course). Confirmation theory: if evidence e tends to confirm hypothesis h, then e indirectly confirms all the logical consequences of h. But perhaps the best evidence in favor of supposing that most philosophers have taken the epistemic operators to be fully penetrating is the way they have argued and the obvious assumptions that structure their arguments. Anyone who has argued in the following way seems to me to be assuming the thesis of penetrability (as I shall call it): if you do not know whether Q is true or not, and P cannot be true unless Q is true, then you (obviously) do not know whether P is true or not. A slightly more elaborate form of the same argument goes like this: If S does not know whether or not Q is true, then for all he knows it might be false. If Q is false, however, then P must also be false. Hence, for all S knows, P may be false. Therefore, S does not know that P is true. This pattern of argument is sprinkled throughout the epistemological literature. Almost all skeptical objections trade on it. S claims to know that this is a tomato. A necessary consequence of its being a tomato is that it is not a clever imitation which only looks and feels (and, if you will, tastes) like a tomato. But S does not know that it is *not* a clever imitation that only looks and feels (and tastes) like a tomato. (I assume here that no one is prepared to argue that anything that looks, feels, and tastes like a tomato to S *must be* a tomato.) Therefore, S does not know that this is a tomato. We can, of course, reply with G. E. Moore that we certainly *do* know it is a tomato (after such an examination) and since tomatoes are not imitations we know that this is not an imitation. It is interesting to note that this reply presupposes the same principle as does the skeptical objection: they both assume that if S knows that this is a P, and knows that every P is a Q, then S knows that this is a Q. The only difference is that the skeptic performs a modus tollens, Moore a modus ponens. Neither questions the principle itself.

Whether it be a question of dreams or demons, illusions or fakes, the same pattern of argument emerges. If you know this is a chair, you must know that you are not dreaming (or being deceived by a cunning demon), since its being a (real) chair entails that it is not simply a figment of your own imagination. Such arguments assume that the epistemic operators, and in particular the operator "to know", penetrate to all the known consequences of a proposition. If these operators were not penetrating, many of these objections might be irrelevant. Consider the following exchange:

S: How strange! There are tomatoes growing in my apple tree.
K: That isn't strange at all. Tomatoes, after all, are physical objects and what is so strange about physical objects growing in your apple tree?

What makes K's reply so silly is that he is treating the operator "strange that" as a fully penetrating operator: it cannot be strange that there are tomatoes growing in the apple tree unless the consequences of this (e.g., there are objects growing in your apple tree) are also strange. Similarly, it *may not* be at all relevant to object to someone who claims to know that there are tomatoes in the apple tree that he does not know, cannot be absolutely sure, that there are really any material objects. Whether or not this is a relevant objection will depend on whether or not this particular consequence of there being tomatoes in the apple tree is one of the consequences to which the epistemic operators penetrate. What I wish to argue in the remainder of this paper is that the traditional skeptical arguments exploit precisely those consequences of a proposition to which the epistemic operators do not penetrate, precisely those consequences which distinguish the epistemic operators from the fully penetrating operators.

In support of this claim let me begin with some examples which are, I think, fairly intuitive and then turn to some more problematic cases. I shall begin with the operator "reason to believe that" although what I have to say could be said as well with any of them. This particular operator has the added advantage that if it can be shown to be only semi-penetrating, then many accounts of knowledge, those which interpret it as a form of justified true belief, would also be committed to treating "knowing that" as a semi-penetrating operator. For, presumably, "knowing that" would not penetrate any deeper than one's "reasons for believing that".

Suppose you have a reason to believe that the church is empty. *Must* you have a reason to believe that it is a church? I am not asking whether you

generally have such a reason. I am asking whether one can have a reason to believe the church empty without having a reason to believe that it is a church which is empty. Certainly your reason for believing that the church is empty is not *itself* a reason to believe it is a church; or it *need not* be. Your reason for believing the church to be empty may be that you just made a thorough inspection of it without finding anyone. That is a good reason to believe the church empty. Just as clearly, however, it is not a reason, much less a good reason, to believe that what is empty is a church. The fact is, or so it seems to me, I do not have to have *any* reason to believe it is a church. Of course, I would never *say* the church was empty, or that I had a reason to believe that the church was empty, unless I believed, and presumably had a reason for so believing, that it *was* a church which was empty, but this is a presumed condition of my *saying* something, not of my having a reason to believe something. Suppose I had simply assumed (correctly as it turns out) that the building was a church. Would this show that I had no reason to believe that the church was empty?

Suppose I am describing to you the "adventures" of my brother Harold. Harold is visiting New York for the first time, and he decides to take a bus tour. He boards a crowded bus and immediately takes the last remaining seat. The little old lady he shouldered aside in reaching his seat stands over him glowering. Minutes pass. Finally, realizing that my brother is not going to move, she sighs and moves resignedly to the back of the bus. Not much of an adventure, but enough, I hope, to make my point. I said that the little old lady realized that my brother would not move. Does this imply that she realized that, or knew that, *it was my brother* who refused to move? Clearly not. We can say that S knows that X is Y without implying that S knows that *it is X* which is Y. We do not *have* to describe our little old lady as knowing that *the man* or *the person* would not move. We can say that she realized that, or knew that, *my brother* would not move (minus, of course, this pattern of emphasis), and we can say this because saying this does not entail that the little old lady knew that, or realized that, it was my brother who refused to move. She knew that my brother would not move, and she knew this despite the fact that she did not know something that was necessarily implied by what she did know – viz., that the person who refused to move was my brother.

I have argued elsewhere that to see that *A* is *B*, that the roses are wilted for example, is not to see, not even to be able to see, that they are roses which are wilted.[1] To see that the widow is limping is not to see that it is a widow who is limping. I am now arguing that this same feature holds for all epistemic operators. I can know that the roses are wilting without knowing that they are roses, know that the water is boiling without knowing that it is water, and prove that the square root of 2 is smaller than the square root of 3 and, yet, be unable to prove what is entailed by this – viz., that the number 2 *has* a square root.

The general point may be put this way: there are certain presuppositions associated with a statement. These presuppositions, although their truth is entailed by the truth of the statement, are not part of what is *operated on* when we operate on the statement with one of our epistemic operators. The epistemic operators do not *penetrate to* these presuppositions. For example, in saying that the coffee is boiling I assert that the coffee is boiling, but in asserting this I do not assert that *it is* coffee which is boiling. Rather, this is taken for granted, assumed, presupposed, or what have you. Hence, when I say that I have a reason to believe that the coffee is boiling, I am not saying that this reason applies to the fact that it is coffee which is boiling. This is *still* presupposed. I may have such a reason, of course, and chances are good that I do have such a reason or I would not have referred to what I believe to be boiling *as coffee*, but to have a reason to believe the coffee is boiling is not, thereby, to have a reason to believe it is coffee which is boiling.

One would expect that if this is true of the semi-penetrating operators, then it should also be true of the nonpenetrating operators. They also should fail to reach the presuppositions. This is exactly what we find. It may be accidental that the two trucks collided, but not at all accidental that it was two trucks that collided. Trucks were the only vehicles allowed on the road that day, and so it was not at all accidental or a matter of chance that the accident took place between two trucks. Still, it was an accident that the two trucks collided. Or suppose Mrs. Murphy mistakenly gives her cat some dog food. It need not be a mistake that she gave the food to *her* cat, or *some* food to *a*

cat. This was intentional. What was a mistake was that it was dog food that she gave to her cat.

Hence, the first class of consequences that differentiate the epistemic operators from the fully penetrating operators is the class of consequences associated with the presuppositions of a proposition. The fact that the epistemic operators do not penetrate to these presuppositions is what helps to make them semi-penetrating. And this is an extremely important fact. For it would appear that if this is true, then to know that the flowers are wilted I do not have to know that they are flowers (which are wilted) and, therefore, do not have to know all those consequences which follow from the fact that they are flowers, real flowers, which I know to be wilted.

Rather than pursue this line, however, I would like to turn to what I consider to be a more significant set of consequences – "more significant" because they are the consequences that are directly involved in most skeptical arguments. Suppose we assert that *x* is *A*. Consider some predicate, "*B*", which is incompatible with *A*, such that nothing can be both *A* and *B*. It then follows from the fact that *x* is *A* that *x* is not *B*. Furthermore, if we conjoin *B* with any other predicate, *Q*, it follows from the fact that *x* is *A* that *x* is not-(*B* and *Q*). I shall call this type of consequence a *contrast consequence*, and I am interested in a particular subset of these; for I believe the most telling skeptical objections to our ordinary knowledge claims exploit a particular set of these contrast consequences. The exploitation proceeds as follows: someone purports to know that *x* is *A*, that the wall is red, say. The skeptic now finds a predicate "*B*" that is incompatible with "*A*". In this particular example we may let "*B*" stand for the predicate "is white". Since "*x* is red" entails "*x* is not white" it also entails that *x* is not-(white and *Q*) where "*Q*" is any predicate we care to select. Therefore, the skeptic selects a "*Q*" that gives expression to a condition or circumstance under which a white wall would appear exactly the same as a red wall. For simplicity we may let "*Q*" stand for: "cleverly illuminated to look red". We now have this chain of implications: "*x* is red" entails "*x* is not white" entails "*x* is not white cleverly illuminated to look red". If "knowing that" is a penetrating operator, then if anyone knows that the wall is red he must know that it is not white cleverly illuminated to look red. (I assume here that the relevant parties know that if x is red, it cannot be white made to look red.) He must know that this particular contrast consequence is true. The question is: do we, generally speaking, know anything of the sort? Normally we never take the trouble to check the lighting. We seldom acquire any *special* reasons for believing the lighting normal although we can talk vaguely about there being no reason to think it unusual. The fact is that we habitually take such matters for granted, and although we normally have *good* reasons for making such routine assumptions, I do not think these reasons are sufficiently good, not without special precautionary checks in the particular case, to say of the particular situation we are in that we *know* conditions are normal. To illustrate, let me give you another example – a silly one, but no more silly than a great number of skeptical arguments with which we are all familiar. You take your son to the zoo, see several zebras, and, when questioned by your son, tell him they are zebras. Do you know they are zebras? Well, most of us would have little hesitation in saying that we did know this. We know what zebras look like, and, besides, this is the city zoo and the animals are in a pen clearly marked "Zebras." Yet, something's being a zebra implies that it is not a mule and, in particular, not a mule cleverly disguised by the zoo authorities to look like a zebra. Do you know that these animals are not mules cleverly disguised by the zoo authorities to look like zebras? If you are tempted to say "Yes" to this question, think a moment about what reasons you have, what evidence you can produce in favor of this claim. The evidence you *had* for thinking them zebras has been effectively neutralized, since it does not count toward their *not* being mules cleverly disguised to look like zebras. Have you checked with the zoo authorities? Did you examine the animals closely enough to detect such a fraud? You might do this, of course, but in most cases you do nothing of the kind. You have some general uniformities on which you rely, regularities to which you give expression by such remarks as, "That isn't very likely" or "Why should the zoo authorities do that?" Granted, the hypothesis (if we may call it that) is not very plausible, given what we know about people and zoos. But the question here is not whether this alternative is plausible, not whether it is more or less plausible than that there are real zebras in the pen, but whether *you know* that this alternative hypothesis

is false. I don't think you do. In this I agree with the skeptic. I part company with the skeptic only when he concludes from this that, therefore, you do not know that the animals in the pen are zebras. I part with him because I reject the principle he uses in reaching this conclusion – the principle that if you do not know that Q is true, when it is known that P entails Q, then you do not know that P is true.

What I am suggesting is that we simply admit that we do *not* know that some of these contrasting "skeptical alternatives" are *not* the case, but refuse to admit that we do not know what we originally said we knew. My knowing that the wall is red certainly entails that the wall is red; it also entails that the wall is not white and, in particular, it entails that the wall is not white cleverly illuminated to look red. But it does not follow from the fact that I know that the wall is red that I *know* that it is not white cleverly illuminated to look red. Nor does it follow from the fact that I know that those animals are zebras that I know that they are not mules cleverly disguised to look like zebras. These are some of the contrast consequences to which the epistemic operators do not penetrate.

Aside from asserting this, what arguments can be produced to support it? I could proceed by multiplying examples, but I do not think that examples alone will support the full weight of this view. The thesis itself is sufficiently counterintuitive to render controversial most of the crucial examples. Anyone who is already convinced that skepticism is wrong and who is yet troubled by the sorts of skeptical arguments I have mentioned will, no doubt, take this itself as an argument in favor of my claim that the epistemic operators are only semi-penetrating. This, however, hardly constitutes an argument against skepticism. For this we need *independent* grounds for thinking that the epistemic operators do not penetrate to the contrast consequences. So I shall proceed in a more systematic manner. I shall offer an analogy with three other operators and conclude by making some general remarks about what I think can be learned from this analogy. The first operator is "explains why" or, more suggestively (for the purposes of this analogy):

(A) R is the reason (explanatory reason) that (or why) ...

For example, the reason why S quit smoking was that he was afraid of getting cancer. The second operator has to do with reasons again, but in this case it is a reason which tends to *justify* one in doing something:

(B)   R is a reason for ... (S to do Y).[2]

For example, the fact that they are selling the very same (type of) car here much more cheaply than elsewhere is a reason to buy it here rather than elsewhere. The status of this as a reason will, of course, depend on a variety of circumstances, but situations can easily be imagined in which this would be a reason for someone to buy the car here. Finally, there is a particular modal relationship which may be construed as a sentential operator:

(C)   R would not be the case unless ...

For example, he would not have bid seven no-trump unless he had all four aces. I shall abbreviate this operator as "$R \rightarrow ...$"; hence, our example could be written "he bid seven no-trump $\rightarrow$ he had all four aces".

Each of these operators has features similar to those of our epistemic operators. If one retraces the ground we have already covered, one will find, I think, that these operators all penetrate deeper than the typical nonpenetrating operator. If R explains why (or is the reason that) P and Q are the case, then it explains why (is the reason that) Q is the case.[3] If I can explain why Bill and Harold are always invited to every party, I can explain why Harold is always invited to every party. From the fact that it was a mistake for me to quit my job it does not follow that it was a mistake for me to do something, but if I had a reason to quit my job, it does follow that I had a reason to do something. And if the grass would not be green unless it had plenty of sunshine and water, it follows that it would not be green unless it had water.

Furthermore, the similarities persist when one considers the presuppositional consequences. I argued that the epistemic operators fail to penetrate to the presuppositions; the above three operators display the same feature. In explaining why he takes his lunch to work, I do not (or need not) explain why he goes to work or why he works at all. The explanation may be obvious in some cases, of course, but the fact is I need not be able to explain why he works (he is *so* wealthy) to explain why he takes his lunch to work (the cafeteria food is *so* bad). The reason why the elms on Main Street are dying is *not* the reason there are elms on Main Street. I have a reason to feed my cat, no reason (not, at least, the same reason) to have a cat. And although it is quite true that he would not have known about our plans if the secretary had not told him, it does not follow that he would not have known about our plans if *someone other than the secretary* had told him. That is, (He knew about our plans) $\rightarrow$ (The secretary told him) even though it is *not* true that (He knew about our plans) $\rightarrow$ (It was the secretary who told him). Yet, the fact that *it was the secretary* who told him is (I take it) a presuppositional consequence of the fact that *the secretary* told him. Similarly, if George is out to set fire to the first empty building he finds, it may be true to say that George would not have set fire to the church unless it (the church) was empty, yet false to say that George would not have set fire to the church unless *it was a church*.

I now wish to argue that these three operators do not penetrate to a certain set of contrast consequences. To the extent that the epistemic operators are similar to these operators, we may then infer, by analogy, that they also fail to penetrate to certain contrast consequences. This is, admittedly, a weak form of argument, depending as it does on the grounds there are for thinking that the above three operators and the epistemic operators share the same logic in this respect. Nonetheless, the analogy is revealing. Some may even find it persuasive.[4]

(A) The pink walls in my living room clash with my old green couch. Recognizing this, I proceed to paint the walls a compatible shade of green. This is the reason I have, and give, for painting the walls green. Now, in having this explanation for why I painted the walls green, I do not think I have an explanation for two other things, both of which are entailed by what I do have an explanation for. I have not explained why I did not, *instead* of painting the walls green, buy a new couch or cover the old one with a suitable slip cover. Nor have I explained why, instead of painting the walls green, I did not paint them white and illuminate them with green light. The same effect would have been achieved, the same purpose would have been served, albeit at much greater expense.

I expect someone to object as follows: although the explanation given for painting the walls green does not, by itself, explain why the couch was not changed instead, it nonetheless succeeds as an explanation for why the walls were painted green only in so far as there is an explanation for why the couch was not changed instead. If there is no explanation for why I did not change the couch instead, there has been no real, no complete, examination for why the walls were painted green.

I think this objection wrong. I may, of course, have an explanation for why I did not buy a new couch: I love the old one or it has sentimental value. But then again I may not. It just never occurred to me to change the couch; or (if someone thinks that its not occurring to me *is* an explanation of why I did not change the couch) I may have thought of it but decided, for what reasons (if any) I cannot remember, to keep the couch and paint the walls. That is to say, I cannot explain why I did not change the couch. I thought of it but I did not do it. I do not know why. Still, I *can* tell you why I painted the walls green. They clashed with the couch.

(B) The fact that they are selling *X*s so much more cheaply here than elsewhere may be a reason to buy your *X*s here, but it certainly need not be a reason to do what is a necessary consequence of *buying* your *X*s here – viz., not *stealing* your *X*s here.

(C) Let us suppose that *S* is operating in perfectly normal circumstances, a set of circumstances in which it is true to say that the wall he sees would not (now) look green to him unless it was green (if it were any other color it would look different to him). Although we can easily imagine situations in which this is true, it does not follow that the wall would not (now) look green to *S* if it were white cleverly illuminated to look green. That is,

(i)   The wall looks green (to *S*) → the wall is green.
(ii) The wall is green *entails* the wall is not white cleverly illuminated to look green (to *S*).

are both true; yet, it is *not true* that

(iii) The wall looks green (to *S*) → the wall is not white cleverly illuminated to look green (to *S*).

There are dozens of examples that illustrate the relative impenetrability of this operator. We can truly say that *A* and *B* would not have collided if *B* had not swerved at the last moment and yet concede that they would have collided without any swerve on the part of *B* if the direction in which *A* was moving had been suitably altered in the beginning.[5]

The structure of these cases is virtually identical with that which appeared in the case of the epistemic operators, and I think by looking just a little more closely at this structure we can learn something very fundamental about our class of epistemic operators and, in particular, about what it means to know something. If I may put it this way, within the context of these operators no fact is an island. If we are simply rehearsing the facts, then we can say that it is a fact that Brenda did not take any dessert (though it was included in the meal). We can say this without a thought about what sort of person Brenda is or what she might have done had she ordered dessert. However, if we put this fact into, say, an explanatory context, if we try to explain this fact, it suddenly appears within a network of related facts, a network of possible alternatives which serve to define *what it is that is being explained*. What is being explained is a function of two things – not only the fact (Brenda did not order any dessert), but also the range of relevant alternatives. A relevant alternative is an alternative that might have been realized in the existing circumstances if the actual state of affairs had not materialized.[6] When I explain why Brenda did not order any dessert by saying that she was full (was on a diet, did not like anything on the dessert menu), I explain why she did not order any dessert *rather than, as opposed to, or instead of* ordering some dessert and *eating it*. It is this competing possibility which helps to define what it is that I am explaining when I explain why Brenda did not order any dessert. Change this contrast, introduce a different set of relevant alternatives, and you change what it is that is being explained and, therefore, what counts as an explanation, even though (as it were) the same fact is being explained. Consider the following contrasts: ordering some dessert and throwing it at the waiter; ordering some dessert and taking it home to a sick friend. With these contrasts none of the above explanations are any longer explanations of why Brenda did not order dessert. Anyone who really wants to know why Brenda did not order dessert and throw it at the waiter will not be helped by being told that she was full or on a diet. This is only to say that, within the context of explanation and within the context of our other operators, the proposition on which we operate must be understood as embedded within a matrix of relevant alternatives. We explain why *P*, but we do so within a framework of competing alternatives *A*, *B*, and *C*. Moreover, if the possibility *D* is not within this contrasting set, not within this network of relevant alternatives, then even though not-*D* follows necessarily from the fact, *P*, which we do explain, we do not explain why not-*D*. Though the fact that Brenda did not order dessert and throw it at the waiter follows necessarily from the fact that she did not order dessert (the fact that is explained), this necessary consequence is not explained by the explanation given. The only contrast consequences to which this operator penetrates are those which figured in the original explanation as relevant alternatives.

So it is with our epistemic operators. To know that *x* is *A* is to know that *x* is *A* within a framework of relevant alternatives, *B*, *C*, and *D*. This set of contrasts, together with the fact that *x* is *A*, serve to define what it is that is known when one knows that *x* is *A*. One cannot change this set of contrasts without changing what a person is said to know when he is said to know that *x* is *A*. We have subtle ways of shifting these contrasts and, hence, changing what a person is said to know *without changing the sentence that we use to express what he knows*. Take the fact that Lefty killed Otto. By changing the emphasis pattern we can invoke a different set of contrasts and, hence, alter what it is that *S* is said to know when he is said to know that Lefty killed Otto. We can say, for instance, that *S* knows that *Lefty* killed Otto. In this case (and I think this is the way we usually hear the sentence when there is no *special* emphasis) we are being told that *S* knows the identity of Otto's killer, that *it was Lefty* who killed Otto. Hence, we expect *S*'s reasons for believing that Lefty killed Otto to consist in facts that single out Lefty as the assailant *rather than* George, Mike, or someone else. On the other hand, we can say that *S* knows that Lefty *killed* Otto. In this case we are being told that *S* knows *what Lefty did to Otto*; he killed him *rather than* merely injuring him, killed

him *rather than* merely threatening him, etc. A good reason for believing that Lefty *killed* Otto (rather than merely injuring him) is that Otto is dead, but this is not much of a reason, if it is a reason at all, for believing that *Lefty* killed Otto. Changing the set of contrasts (from "Lefty rather than George or Mike" to "killed rather than injured or threatened") by shifting the emphasis pattern changes what it is that one is alleged to know when one is said to know that Lefty killed Otto.[7] The same point can be made here as we made in the case of explanation: the operator will penetrate *only* to those contrast consequences which form part of the network of relevant alternatives structuring the original context in which a knowledge claim was advanced. Just as we have not explained why Brenda did not order some dessert and throw it at the waiter when we explained why she did not order some dessert (although what we have explained – her not ordering any dessert – entails this), so also in knowing that Lefty *killed* Otto (knowing that what Lefty did to Otto was kill him) we do not *necessarily* (although we may) know that *Lefty* killed Otto (know that *it was Lefty* who killed Otto). Recall the example of the little old lady who knew that my brother would not move without knowing that it was my brother who would not move.

The conclusions to be drawn are the same as those in the case of explanation. Just as we can say that within the original setting, within the original framework of alternatives that defined what we were trying to explain, we *did explain* why Brenda did not order any dessert, so also within the original setting, within the set of contrasts that defined what it was we were claiming to know, we *did know* that the wall was red and *did know* that it was a zebra in the pen.

To introduce a novel and enlarged set of alternatives, as the skeptic is inclined to do with our epistemic claims, is to exhibit consequences of what we know, or have reason to believe, which we may not know, may not have a reason to believe; but it does not show that we did not know, did not have a reason to believe, whatever it is that has these consequences. To argue in this way is, I submit, as much a mistake as arguing that we have not explained why Brenda did not order dessert (within the original, normal, setting) because we did not explain why she did not order some and throw it at the waiter.

Notes

1   *Seeing and Knowing* (Chicago: University Press, 1969), pp. 93–112, and also "Reasons and Consequences," *Analysis* (April 1968).

2   Unlike our other operators, this one does not have a propositional operand. Despite the rather obvious differences between this case and the others, I still think it useful to call attention to its analogous features.

3   One must be careful not to confuse sentential conjunction with similar-sounding expressions involving a relationship between two things. For example, to say Bill and Susan got married (if it is intended to mean that they married *each other*), although it entails that Susan got married, does not do so by *simplification*. "Reason why" penetrates through logical simplification, *not* through the type of entailment represented by these two propositions. That is, the reason they got married is that they loved each oher; that they loved each other is not the reason Susan got married.

4   I think that those who are inclined to give a causal account of knowledge should be particularly interested in the operator "*R→...*" since, presumably, it will be involved in many instances of knowledge ("many" not "all," since one might wish to except some form of immediate knowledge – knowledge of one's own psychological state – from the causal account). If this operator is only semi-penetrating, then any account of knowledge that relies on the relationship expressed by this operator (as I believe causal accounts must) will be very close to giving a "semi-penetrating" account of "knowing that".

5   The explanation for why the modal relationship between R and P ($R→P$) fails to carry over (penetrate) to the logical consequences of P (i.e., $R→Q$ where Q is a logical consequence of P) is to be found in the set of circumstances that are taken as *given*, or *held fixed*, in subjunctive conditionals. There are certain logical consequences of P which, by bringing in a reference to circumstances tacitly held fixed in the original subjunctive ($R→P$), introduce a possible variation in these circumstances and, hence, lead to a *different*

framework of fixed conditions under which to assess the truth of $R→Q$. For instance, in the last example in the text, when it is said that A and B would not have collided if B had not swerved at the last moment, the truth of this conditional clearly takes it *as given* that A and B possessed the prior trajectories they in fact had on the occasion in question. *Given* certain facts, including the fact that they were traveling in the direction they were, they would not have collided if B had not swerved. Some of the logical consequences of the statement that B swerved do not, however, leave these conditions unaltered – e.g., B did not move in a perfectly straight line in a direction 2° counterclockwise to the direction it actually moved. This consequence "tinkers" with the circumstances originally taken *as given* (held fixed), and a failure of penetration will usually arise when this occurs. It *need not be true* that A and B would not have collided if B had moved in a perfectly straight line in a direction 2° counterclockwise to the direction it actually moved.

6   I am aware that this characterization of "a relevant alternative" is not, as it stands, very illuminating. I am not sure I can make it more precise. What I am after can be expressed this way: if Brenda *had* ordered dessert, she *would not* have thrown it at the waiter, stuffed it in her shoes, or taken it home to a sick friend (she has no sick friend). These are not alternatives that *might* have been realized in the existing circumstances if the actual state of affairs had not materialized. Hence, they are not relevant alternatives. In other words, the "might have been" in my characterization of a relevant alternative will have to be unpacked in terms of counterfactuals.

7   The same example works nicely with the operator "*R→...*". It may be true to say that Otto would not be dead unless Lefty *killed* him (unless what Lefty did to him was kill him) without its being true that Otto would not be dead unless *Lefty* killed him (unless it was Lefty who killed him).

CHAPTER 20

Skepticism, Relevant Alternatives, and Deductive Closure

Gail Stine

Discussions of skepticism, defined with varying degrees of precision, are of course perennial in philosophy. Some recent discussions of the issue[1] give prominence to the notion of "relevant alternatives", according to which a claim to know that p is properly made in the context of a limited number of competing alternatives to p; to be justified in claiming to know p (or simply to know p) it is sufficient to be able to rule out alternatives relevant to that context. This seems to me to be a correct and heartening development. Recent epistemological discussions have also brought up a relatively new subject, which is the validity of the general form of argument:

(A) a knows that p
   a knows that p entails q
   ∴ a knows that q

I shall call this the principle of epistemic deductive closure, or simply, in this paper, deductive closure.[2] What is interesting about recent comments on this principle is that it is perceived to have something to do with skepticism – in fact to lead to it – and hence is currently of very bad repute. And "relevant alternatives" views of knowledge vis-à-vis skepticism are supposed to show us the falsity of the principle.

Originally published in *Philosophical Studies* 29 (1976), pp. 249–61.

In this paper I propose to do three things. First, to give a qualified argument for deductive closure. Second, to give a qualified argument against skepticism which will make use of the relevant alternatives idea. It will be similar to others in leaving rather indeterminate the way in which the context determines what is taken to be a relevant alternative, although I shall distinguish different sources of this indeterminateness and draw some further conclusions. Third, I shall give an unqualified argument to the effect that the questions of the validity of the principle of epistemic deductive closure and skepticism are completely *irrelevant* to one another, and that in fact proper attention to the idea of relevant alternatives tends to confirm the principle. This, of course, puts me in direct conflict with the recent trend I have mentioned.

1. Epistemic Deductive Closure

I am in principle suspicious of all principles of epistemic logic on the general grounds that while the logic of a knower who is in some way simplified and idealized may be useful for limited purposes, what we are ultimately interested in are actual knowers who can be pretty obtuse and idiosyncratic, yet still lay claim to knowledge. For this, among other reasons, I have elsewhere been concerned with epistemic logic which eschews possible worlds semantics imposing strong constraints on knowers.[3] Certainly, I would reject the pattern which goes:

(B) a knows that p
       p entails q
       ∴ a knows that q

However, the pattern which I have labeled epistemic deductive closure does seem to represent a certain bare minimum. One looks naturally for counter-instances involving failure of belief where p and q are very complicated, but any such case I can imagine turns out to be apparent only because it invariably raises doubts about the truth of the second premise which are as strong as the doubts about the truth of the conclusion. The principle seems to be on a par with epistemic conjunction, to wit:

(C) a knows p
       a knows q
       ∴ a knows p and q

There have, of course, been problems in reconciling this principle with commitments to rational belief in terms of degrees of confirmation and knowledge in terms of rational belief,[4] but one feels strongly inclined to the view that the adjustment must be made in the area of these commitments and not in the principle of conjunction.

In addition to failure of belief, one may look for counter-examples to the principle of epistemic deductive closure in the area of failure of evidence or warrant. One's initial reaction to this idea is that if one's evidence is not sufficient for knowing q, it is not sufficient for knowing p, either, where p is known to entail q. I shall be returning to this subject later, for some philosophers to whom I have referred deny this point which seems, initially, fairly obvious and I shall argue that their reasons are mistaken.

Actually, if instead of (A) we adopt the stronger epistemic deductive closure principle:

(D) a knows p
       a knows q
       a knows $(p \cdot q$ entails $r)$
       ∴ a knows r

(A) and (C) may be seen as instances of a common principle, provided we allow "a knows $(p \cdot q$ entails $p \cdot q)$" as an uncontroversial instance of the third premise.[5] (D) is, ultimately, what we need, anyway to capture the idea of knowing the known logical consequences of what one knows, for (A) covers only the known consequences of the things one knows taken individually, not the known consequences of one's whole body of knowledge. And although (D) is stronger than (A), the arguments for (A) work just as strongly for (D), and, so far as I can see, there are no arguments that anyone might seriously offer against (D) which do not also apply to (A). However, for the sake of simplicity and conformity to other discussions in the literature, I shall continue to discuss deductive closure in the form of (A).

In summary, I am not absolutely convinced of the validity of the principle of epistemic deductive closure, as I am not absolutely convinced of the validity of the principle of epistemic conjunction, but in neither case can I think of an objection, and in both cases, apparent problems they lead to (skepticism, inconsistency) are either apparent only or are better handled by giving up other less obvious principles.

2.   Skepticism

In *Belief, Truth and Knowledge*, D. M. Armstrong argues:

> It is not a conclusive objection to a thermometer that it is only reliable in a certain sort of environment. In the same way, reliability of belief, but only within a certain sort of environment, would seem to be sufficient for the believer to earn the accolade of knowledge if that sort of environment is part of his boundary-conditions.[6]

For example, I know that the striped animal I see in the zoo is a zebra.[7] I know this despite the fact that I have no particular evidence that it is not a mule painted to look like a zebra (I have not looked for a paint can, tried paint remover on the animal, etc.). In this context – under normal circumstances, in zoos of integrity, etc. – that an animal on display has been deliberately disguised to fool trusting zoo-goers is just not a relevant hypothesis, one that I need trouble myself about rejecting. If the skeptic tries to persuade me to his position by stressing my lack of evidence against such an hypothesis, my proper response is to turn a deaf ear. He has ensnared me by improper means and is more than halfway to (illegitimately) winning his point if he gets me to agree that I must argue with him, go look for further evidence, etc.

This view, which I call the relevant alternative view, seems to me fundamentally correct. It does leave a lot of things unsaid. What are normal circumstances? What makes an alternative relevant in one context and not in another? However, in ordinary life, we do exhibit rather strong agreement about what is relevant and what is not. But there are grey areas. Alvin Goldman makes this point nicely with the following example which he attributes to Carl Ginet: if on the basis of visual appearances obtained under optimum conditions while driving through the countryside Henry identifies an object as a barn, normally we say that Henry knows that it is a barn. Let us suppose, however, that unknown to Henry, the region is full of expertly made papier-maché facsimiles of barns. In this case, we would not say Henry knows that the object is a barn, unless he has evidence against it being a papier-maché facsimile, which is now a relevant alternative. So much is clear, but what if no such facsimiles exist in Henry's surroundings, although they do in Sweden? What if they do not now exist in Sweden, but they once did? Are either of these circumstances sufficient to make the hypothesis relevant? Probably not, but the situation is not so clear.

Another area of obscurity resides not in the nature of the case but in the formulation of the view in question. Goldman seems to hold what I regard as the correct version of it, which is that:

(1)   an alternative is relevant only if there is some reason to think that it is true.

But there is also the view that:

(2)   an alternative is relevant only if there is some reason to think it *could* be true.

Clearly, the force of the "could" cannot be mere logical possibility, or the relevant alternative view would lose its distinguishing feature. However, if the "could" is read in some stronger way, we could still have a version of the relevant alternative view. Dretske's "Conclusive Reasons"[8] paper, espousing

a view according to which if one knows, then given one's evidence, one could not be wrong (he reads "could" as "physically possible") suggests that we should consider an hypothesis a live one unless it *could not* be true, given one's evidence. Hence any alternative would be relevant, in the sense of blocking knowledge, if one has not the evidence to rule it out, so long as it is physically possible, given one's evidence. Also, the passage in "Epistemic Operators" where Dretske says: "A relevant alternative is an alternative that *might* have been realized in the existing circumstances if the actual state of affairs had not materialized",[9] is more akin to (2) than (1), although so taking it depends on the force of his "might". This, I think, is the wrong way to take the relevant alternative view. First of all, however unclear it may be as to when there is some reason to think an alternative is true, it is much more unclear as to when there is reason to think it could be true. Certainly, if there is a difference between (1) and (2), (2) is weaker, allows more to count as a relative alternative. So possibly Descartes thought there was some reason to think that there *could*, in some sense stronger than logical possibility, be an evil genius. But it seems safe to say he was wrong if he thought that there was some reason to think that there *was* an evil genius. That is, the evil genius hypothesis is not a relevant alternative according to (1) but may be according to (2) (although I shall qualify this). But the whole thrust of the relevant alternative position, as I conceive it, is that such an hypothesis is not relevant. To allow it as relevant seems to me to preclude the kind of answer to the skeptic which I sketched in the opening paragraph of this section.

In truth, Dretske does combine a relevant alternative view with an answer to skepticism. But his account is tied in with a view of knowledge, which, although it does defeat skepticism, does so in a way which gives small comfort. On his account, we do know many things, i.e., there are many things about which given our evidence, we could not be wrong. However, he does not merely reject the view that knowing entails knowing that one knows.[10] He also seems committed to the view that one rarely, if ever, knows that one knows, for it is well high impossible on his account to defend the claim that one *knows*, given one's evidence, that one *could not* be wrong, in his sense of "could". Perhaps this is preferable to skepticism, but at best it is going from the fire into the frying pan.

Here some qualifications of this position that the relevant alternative view provides an answer to the skeptic are in order. In truth, *in some sense* skepticism is unanswerable. This rather supports the relevant alternative view, for the uncertainty which infects (1) as to when there is some reason to think an alternative true explains why this is so. The relevant alternative view does provide a kind of answer to the skeptic – the only kind of answer which can be given. But the skeptic has an entering wedge, and rightly so. It is an essential characteristic of our concept of knowledge that tighter criteria are appropriate in different contexts.[11] It is one thing in a street encounter, another in a classroom, another in a law court – and who is to say it cannot be another in a philosophical discussion? And this is directly mirrored by the fact we have different standards for judging that there is some reason to think an alternative is true, i.e., relevant. We can point out that some philosophers are very perverse in their standards (by *some* extreme standard, there is some reason to think there is an evil genius, after all) – but we cannot legitimately go so far as to say that their perversity has stretched the concept of knowledge out of all recognition – in fact they have played on an essential feature of the concept. On the other hand, a skeptical philosopher is wrong if he holds that *others* are wrong in any way – i.e., are sloppy, speaking only loosely, or whatever – when they say we know a great deal. And the relevant alternative view gives the correct account of why a skeptic is wrong if he makes such accusations.

3. Deductive Closure and Skepticism

Proponents of the relevant alternative view have tended to think that it provides grounds for rejecting deductive closure. Although many philosophers have recently taken this position, Dretske has provided the fullest published argument to this effect. He writes:

> To know that X is A is to know that X is A within a framework of relevant alternatives, B, C, and D. This set of contrasts together with the fact X is A, serve to define what it is that is known when one knows that X is A. One cannot change this set of contrasts without changing what a person is said to know when he is said to know that X is A. We

have subtle ways of shifting these contrasts and, hence, changing what a person is said to know *without changing the sentence that we use to express what he knows.*[12]

Consider the following instance of (A):

(E)   John knows that the animal is a zebra
       John knows that [*the animal is a zebra* entails *the animal is not a mule painted to look like a zebra*]
       $\therefore$ John knows that the animal is not a mule painted to look like a zebra

In Dretske's zoo example, the animal's being a mule painted to look like a zebra is not a relevant alternative. So what one means when one says that John knows the animal is a zebra, is that he knows it is a zebra, as opposed to a gazelle, an antelope, or other animals one would normally expect to find in a zoo. If, however, being a mule painted to look like a zebra became a relevant alternative, then one would literally mean something different in saying that John knows that the animal is a zebra from what one meant originally and that something else may well be false. Now, normally, in saying that one knows that p, one presupposes (in some sense) that not-p is a relevant alternative; hence one does not know p unless one has evidence to rule out not-p. This is in fact Dretske's view, for he holds that one does *not* know that the animal is not a mule painted to look like a zebra because one has no evidence to rule out the possibility that it is. However, according to Dretske, so long as the animal's being a mule painted to look like a zebra is not a relevant alternative, the fact that John does not know that it is not does not count against John's knowing that it is a zebra. Hence, deductive closure fails (we are assuming that John's knowing an animal's being a zebra entails his knowing that it is not a mule); i.e., (E) and hence (A), are invalid.

I submit that there is another account of this example on the relevant alternative view which does not entail giving up deductive closure. On this account, to say that John knows that p does normally presuppose that not-p is a relevant alternative. This is, however, a pragmatic, not a semantic presupposition.[13] That is, it is the speaker, not the sentence (or proposition) itself, who does the presupposing. Thus, the presupposition falls in the category of those which Grice labels "cancellable".[14] It is possible for "John knows that *p*" to be true even though a pragmatic presupposition, that not-*p* is a relevant alternative, is false. I would say that we may create some sort of special circumstance which cancels the normal presupposition when we utter the sentence in the course of making a deductive closure argument. After all, the utterance has got to be an odd case where we are given that not-*p* is not a relevant alternative to begin with – we can expect something unusual to happen, other than being forced to admit that it is a relevant alternative, after all. For even if we would not normally *affirm* "John knows that *p*" in such a situation, we would not normally *say* that John does *not* know that *p*, either. Or it may happen that stating a deductive closure argument affects normal presuppositions in another way. If we hesitate to say "John knows that the animal is not a mule painted to look like a zebra", we *may* well hesitate to affirm "John knows the animal is a zebra". If this is so, not being a mule painted to look like a zebra will have become a relevant alternative – we will have decided there is some reason to think it true – with respect to the latter sentence as well. Perhaps the mere utterance of the former sentence is enough to make us loosen up our notion of what counts as a relevant alternative.

Either way, my account holds the set of relevant alternatives constant from beginning to end of the deductive closure argument. This is as it should be; to do otherwise would be to commit some logical sin akin to equivocation. If the relevant alternatives, which have after all to do with the truth or falsity of the premises and conclusion, cannot be held fixed, it is hard so see on what basis one can decide whether the argument form is valid or not. And if the set of relevant alternatives is one thing for the first premise and another for the conclusion, how do we determine what it is for the second premise, and how does this affect the truth of the second premise? There is no reason for my account of the matter to make skeptics of us all. The skeptical argument goes: If you know it is a zebra, and you know its being a zebra entails its not being a painted mule, then you know it is not a mule painted to look like a zebra. But you do not know the last, so you do not know the first – i.e., you do not know it is a zebra. With our account in hand, let us see how the skeptic is to be treated. There are two possibilities. First, the skeptic may be up to something legitimate. He is beginning by suggesting that being a mule painted to look like a zebra is a relevant alternative – i.e., that there is some reason to think it is true. We point out to the skeptic that under normal circumstances, given what we know of people and zoos, etc., this is not the case. The skeptic may, however, persevere, playing on the looseness of "some reason to think true". At this point, while we cannot argue the skeptic out of his position, we are perfectly within our rights in refusing to adopt the skeptic's standards and can comfort ourselves by feeling that the skeptic, if not flatly wrong, is at least very peculiar. On the other hand, the skeptic may be up to something illegitimate. He may be trying to get us to doubt that we know it is a zebra without going through the hard work of convincing us that being a mule painted to look like a zebra is a relevant alternative. The skeptic seeks to persuade us of his conclusion by getting us to admit that we do not know it is not a mule painted to look like a zebra because we do not have evidence to rule out the possibility that it is. This is what Dretske believes and this is why he believes we must give up deductive closure to defeat the skeptic. I think this a wrong move. We do know it is not a mule painted to look like a zebra. Let us grant temporarily for the sake of this argument we do not have evidence. But Dretske is deluded by the fact that many knowledge claims require evidence on the part of the knower into thinking that all knowledge claims require evidence. Normally, as I have admitted, saying "*a* knows that *p*" presupposes that not-*p* is a relevant alternative. And it does sound odd to say that we know it is not a mule painted to look like a zebra when its being one is not a relevant alternative. But the fact that it sounds odd – is indeed perhaps misleading or even improper to say – does not mean as we have seen that the presupposition is not cancellable, and that the proposition in question is not true. We often get results which sound odd to *say* when we draw valid conclusions from true premises the utterance of which does not sound odd. "John knows that it is raining" may be true and quite in order to say to convey its literal meaning. But on the assumption of minimal logical competence on John's part and deductive closure, it entails "John knows that it is either raining or not raining". But this sentence, if uttered at all, is most likely to be used to suggest the negation of the first sentence. We might, in fact, say that the speaker presupposes it. Given knowledge of the first sentence, the latter is too obviously true to bother uttering at all, except for purposes of sarcasm, ironic effect, or some purpose other than conveying the information expressed by the literal meaning of the words. Yet, for all that, it is literally true. Or take a case with perhaps more analogies to our example. This is an example from Grice.[15] "My wife is in the kitchen" implies "My wife is in the kitchen or in the bedroom". Yet, the utterance of the latter, in normal circumstances, presupposes the speaker's ignorance of the former and is thus an improper or at best misleading thing for him to say if he knows the former. But for all that, the latter is true if the former is, and the presupposition is cancellable.

The logical consequences of knowledge claims which the skeptic draws by deductive closure of the sort Dretske discusses, are the sorts of propositions which, in normal circumstances, are such that their negations are not relevant alternatives. Thus they sound odd to say and often have the effect of suggesting that the circumstances are abnormal. It is indeed improper to utter them in normal circumstances unless one explicitly cancels the relevant alternative presupposition which they carry, because one misleads. Nevertheless, they are literally true in normal circumstances. I endorse here a view which I believe to be Austin's.[16] This view is adumbrated in the following passage:

> If, for instance, someone remarks in casual conversation, "As a matter of fact I live in Oxford", the other party to the conversation may, if he finds it worth doing, verify this assertion; but the *speaker*, of course, has no need to do this – he knows it to be true (or, if he is lying, false). ... Nor need it be true that he is in this position by virtue of having verified his assertion at some previous stage; for of how many people really, who know quite well where they live, could it be said that they have at any time *verified* that they live there? When could they be supposed to have done this? In what way? And why? What we have here, in fact, is an erroneous doctrine ... about evidence.[17]

The point is that one does know what one takes for granted in normal circumstances. I do know

that it is not a mule painted to look like a zebra. I do not need evidence for such a proposition. The evidence picture of knowledge has been carried too far. I would say that I do not have evidence that it is a zebra, either. I simply *see* that it is one. But that is perhaps another matter. The point I want to make here is simply that if the negation of a proposition is not a relevant alternative, then I know it – obviously, without needing to provide evidence – and so obviously that it is odd, misleading even, to give utterance to my knowledge. And it is a virtue of the relevant alternative view that it helps explain why it is odd.

There is another way in which (E) could be defended. This line could be to claim that John does, after all, in his general knowledge of the ways of zoos and people, etc., have evidence that the animal is not a mule painted to look like a zebra. The same would hold for other consequences of knowledge claims which the skeptic draws by deductive closure. This would involve a notion of evidence according to which having evidence is not just limited to cases in which one has a specific datum to which to point. Malcolm expresses this point of view when he says:

> ... The reason is obvious for saying that my copy of James's book does not have the characteristic that its print undergoes spontaneous changes. I have read millions of printed words on many thousands of printed pages. I have not encountered a single instance of a printed word vanishing from a page or being replaced by another printed word, suddenly and without external cause. Nor have I heard of any other person who had such an encounter. There is *overwhelming evidence* that printed words do not behave in that way. It is just as conclusive as the evidence that houses do not turn into flowers. That is to say, *absolutely conclusive evidence*[18] (italics mine).

It is true that in the last sentence of this passage Malcolm talks about evidence for a universal proposition to the effect that printed words do not behave in a certain way, but the thrust of his argument is such that he commits himself to the view that he also (thereby) has evidence that the printed words on his particular copy of James's book will not behave that way. I am not inclined towards such a view of what it is to have adequate evidence for the proposition that the print of my own particular copy of James's book did not undergo a spontaneous change. I am inclined to reject Malcolm's view, and others akin, in favor of the Austinian sort of one previously discussed – that is, that in such a case, evidence is not required to support a knowledge claim. I mention the view only as a possible alternative view of defending epistemic deductive closure in a way consonant with the relevant alternative view.

4. Summary

My view is that the relevant alternative position should be conceived of as in two parts:

(1) With respect to many propositions, to establish a knowledge claim is to be able to support it as opposed to a limited number of alternatives – i.e., only those which are relevant in the context.

(2) With respect to many propositions – in particular those which are such that their negations are not relevant alternatives in the context in question – we simply know them to be true and do not need evidence, in the normal sense, that they, rather than their negations, are true.

So conceived, the relevant alternative view neither supports the abandonment of deductive closure, nor is such abandonment in any way needed to provide the relevant alternative view with an answer to the skeptic, insofar as he can be answered.

Notes

1   I am partial to J. L. Austin's approach in "Other Minds" (*Philosophical Papers*, Oxford, 1961) and Chapter X of *Sense and Sensibilia* (Oxford, 1962). Other more recent and more explicitly developed accounts include those of Fred Dretske, most importantly in "Epistemic Operators", *Journal of Philosophy* LXVII (1970), pp. 1007–23, but also in "Contrastive Statements", *Philosophical Review* LXXXI (1972), pp. 411–30; D. M. Armstrong, *Belief, Truth and Knowledge* (Cambridge, 1973); Alvin Goldman, "Discrimination and Perceptual Knowledge", presented at the Annual Philosophy Colloquium, University of Cincinnati, 1973; James Cargile, "Knowledge and Deracination", presented at the Annual Philosophy Colloquium, University of Cincinnati, 1973; Norman Malcolm in "The Verification Argument" in *Knowledge and Certainty* (Prentice-Hall, 1963) is more concerned with certainty than knowledge but his discussion of when a proposition is "possible" is very much in accord with considerations which go towards making a proposition a "relevant alternative".

2   Dretske, "Epistemic Operators",; Cargile, "Knowledge and Deracination"; Goldman, "Discrimination and Perceptual Knowledge".

3   Cf. "Quantified Logic for Knowledge Statements", *Journal of Philosophy* LXXI (1974), and "Essentialism, Possible Worlds, and Propositional Attitudes", *Philosophical Review* LXXXII (1973), pp. 471–82.

4   Cf. discussions of the place of a principle of conjunction in an account of rational belief in, for example, Isaac Levi, *Gambling With Truth*, Knopf (1967); and in *Induction, Acceptance, and Rational Belief*, ed. by Swain, Reidel (1970) the following papers: Marshall Swain, "The Consistency of Rational Belief", Henry Kyburg, "Conjunctivitis", and Keith Lehrer, "Justification, Explanation, and Induction". This case for conjunction holding for rational belief is, of course, more problematic than the case for knowledge.

5   I owe this point to David Kaplan.

6   Armstrong, *Belief, Truth and Knowledge*, p. 174.

7   The example is Dretske's in "Epistemic Operators".

8   In *Australasian Journal of Philosophy* 49 (1971), pp. 1–22.

9   "Epistemic Operators", p. 1021.

10 This view has been criticized, for example, by Ronald DeSousa in "Knowledge, Consistent Belief, and Self-Consciousness", *Journal of Philosophy* (1970), against defenders of it such as Jaakko Hintikka in *Knowledge and Belief* (Cornell, 1962) and Keith Lehrer in "Belief and Knowledge", *Philosophical Review* (1968). The view is also rejected by Armstrong, *Belief, Truth and Knowledge* (p. 146), and at

least implicitly rejected on such accounts of knowledge as, for example, those of Alvin Goldman, "A Causal Theory of Knowing", *Journal of Philosophy* 64 (1967), pp. 357–72; Brian Skyrms, "The Explication of 'X Knows that P'", *Journal of Philosophy* 64 (1967), pp. 373–89; and Peter Unger, "An Analysis of Factual Knowledge", *Journal of Philosophy* 65 (1968), pp. 157–70.

11   Here I take a view directly opposed to that of Peter Unger, "A Defense of Skepticism", *Philosophical Review* (1971), according to which knowledge is an "absolute" concept, like the flatness of geometers.

12   "Epistemic Operators", p. 1022.

13   Here I distinguish pragmatic from semantic presuppositions in the manner of Robert Stalnaker, "Pragmatics", in *Semantics of Natural Language*, ed. by Davidson and Harman (Reidel, 1972), pp. 380–97. Attributing the notion of a semantic presupposition to Bas van Fraassen ("Singular Terms, Truth Value Gaps, and Free Logic", *Journal of Philosophy* 63 (1966), pp. 481–95, and "Presupposition, Implication, and Self Reference", *Journal of Philosophy* 65 (1968), pp. 136–51), Stalnaker says (p. 387):

According to the *semantic* concept, a proposition P presupposes a proposition Q if and only if Q is necessitated both by P and by *not*-P. That is, in every model in which P is either true or false, Q is true. According to the *pragmatic* conception, presupposition is a propositional attitude, not a semantic relation. People, rather than sentences or propositions are said to have, or make, presuppositions in this sense.

… In general, any semantic presupposition of a proposition expressed in a given context will be a pragmatic presupposition of the people in that context, but the converse clearly does not hold.

To presuppose a proposition in the pragmatic sense is to take its truth for granted, and to assume that others involved in the context do the same.

14   H. P. Grice, "The Causal Theory of Perception", *Proceedings of the Aristotelian Society*, Suppl. Vol. XXXV (1961).

15   *Ibid.*

16   In "Other Minds", *Loc. cit.*, and Chapter X of *Sense and Sensibilia*, Oxford (1962).

17   *Sense and Sensibilia*, pp. 117–18.

18   "The Verification Argument", p. 38.

CHAPTER 21

Knowledge and Skepticism

Robert Nozick

Knowledge

Conditions for knowledge

Our task is to formulate further conditions to go alongside

(1) p is true.
(2) S believes that p.

We would like each condition to be necessary for knowledge, so any case that fails to satisfy it will not be an instance of knowledge. Furthermore, we would like the conditions to be jointly sufficient for knowledge, so any case that satisfies all of them will be an instance of knowledge. We first shall formulate conditions that seem to handle ordinary cases correctly, classifying as knowledge cases which are knowledge, and as nonknowledge cases which are not; then we shall check to see how these conditions handle some difficult cases discussed in the literature.[1]

The causal condition on knowledge, previously mentioned, provides an inhospitable environment for mathematical and ethical knowledge; also there are well-known difficulties in specifying the type of causal connection. If someone floating in a tank oblivious to everything around

Originally published in R. Nozick, *Philosophical Explanations* (Cambridge MA: Harvard University Press, 1981), pp. 172–85, 197–217.

him is given (by direct electrical and chemical stimulation of the brain) the belief that he is floating in a tank with his brain being stimulated, then even though that fact is part of the cause of his belief, still he does not know that it is true.

Let us consider a different third condition:

(3) If p weren't true, S wouldn't believe that p.

Throughout this work, let us write the subjunctive "if-then" by an arrow, and the negation of a sentence by prefacing "not-" to it. The above condition thus is rewritten as:

(3) not-p → not-(S believes that p).

This subjunctive condition is not unrelated to the causal condition. Often when the fact that p, (partially) causes someone to believe that p, the fact also will be causally necessary for his having the belief – without the cause, the effect would not occur. In that case, the subjunctive condition 3 also will be satisfied. Yet this condition is not equivalent to the causal condition. For the causal condition will be satisfied in cases of causal overdetermination, where either two sufficient causes of the effect actually operate, or a back-up cause (of the same effect) would operate if the first one didn't; whereas the subjunctive condition need not hold for these cases.[2] When the two conditions do agree, causality indicates knowledge because it acts in a manner that makes the subjunctive 3 true.

The subjunctive condition 3 serves to exclude cases of the sort first described by Edward Gettier, such as the following. Two other people are in my office and I am justified on the basis of much evidence in believing the first owns a Ford car; though he (now) does not, the second person (a stranger to me) owns one. I believe truly and justifiably that someone (or other) in my office owns a Ford car, but I do not know someone does. Concluded Gettier, knowledge is not simply justified true belief.

The following subjunctive, which specifies condition 3 for this Gettier case, is not satisfied: if no one in my office owned a Ford car, I wouldn't believe that someone did. The situation that would obtain if no one in my office owned a Ford is one where the stranger does not (or where he is not in the office); and in that situation I still would believe, as before, that someone in my office does own a Ford, namely, the first person. So the subjunctive condition 3 excludes this Gettier case as a case of knowledge.

The subjunctive condition is powerful and intuitive, not so easy to satisfy, yet not so powerful as to rule out everything as an instance of knowledge. A subjunctive conditional "if p were true, q would be true," $p \rightarrow q$, does not say that p entails q or that it is logically impossible that p yet not-q. It says that in the situation that would obtain if p were true, q also would be true. This point is brought out especially clearly in recent "possible-worlds" accounts of subjunctives: the subjunctive is true when (roughly) in all those worlds in which p holds true that are closest to the actual world, q also is true. (Examine those worlds in which p holds true closest to the actual world, and see if q holds true in all these.) Whether or not q is true in p worlds that are still farther away from the actual world is irrelevant to the truth of the subjunctive. I do not mean to endorse any particular possible-worlds account of subjunctives, nor am I committed to this type of account.[3] I sometimes shall use it, though, when it illustrates points in an especially clear way.[4]

The subjunctive condition 3 also handles nicely cases that cause difficulties for the view that you know that p when you can rule out the relevant alternatives to p in the context. For, as Gail Stine writes,

what makes an alternative relevant in one context and not another? ... if on the basis of visual appearances obtained under optimum conditions while driving through the countryside Henry identifies an object as a barn, normally we say that Henry knows that it is a barn. Let us suppose, however, that unknown to Henry, the region is full of expertly made papier-mâché facsimiles of barns. In that case, we would not say that Henry knows that the object is a barn, unless he has evidence against it being a papier-mâché facsimile, which is now a relevant alternative. So much is clear, but what if no such facsimiles exist in Henry's surroundings, although they once did? Are either of these circumstances sufficient to make the hypothesis (that it's a papier-mâché object) relevant? Probably not, but the situation is not so clear.[5]

Let p be the statement that the object in the field is a (real) barn, and q the one that the object in the field is a papier-mâché barn. When papier-mâché barns are scattered through the area, if p were false, q would be true or might be. Since in this case (we are supposing) the person still would believe p, the subjunctive

(3)   not-$p \rightarrow$ not-(S believes that p)

is not satisfied, and so he doesn't know that p. However, when papier-mâché barns are or were scattered around another country, even if p were false q wouldn't be true, and so (for all we have been told) the person may well know that p. A hypothesis q contrary to p clearly is relevant when if p weren't true, q would be true; when not-$p \rightarrow q$. It clearly is irrelevant when if p weren't true, q also would not be true; when not $p \rightarrow$ not-q. The remaining possibility is that neither of these opposed subjunctives holds; q might (or might not) be true if p weren't true. In this case, q also will be relevant, according to an account of knowledge incorporating condition 3 and treating subjunctives along the lines sketched above. Thus, condition 3 handles cases that befuddle the "relevant alternatives" account; though that account can adopt the above subjunctive criterion for when an alternative is relevant, it then becomes merely an alternate and longer way of stating condition 3.[6]

Despite the power and intuitive force of the condition that if p weren't true the person would not believe it, this condition does not (in conjunction with the first two conditions) rule out every problem case. There remains, for example, the case of the person in the tank who is brought to believe, by direct electrical and chemical stimulation of his brain, that he is in the tank and is being brought to believe things in this way; he does not know this is true. However, the subjunctive condition is satisfied: if he weren't floating in the tank, he wouldn't believe he was.

The person in the tank does not know he is there, because his belief is not sensitive to the truth. Although it is caused by the fact that is its content, it is not sensitive to that fact. The operators of the tank could have produced any belief, including the false belief that he wasn't in the tank; if they had, he would have believed that. Perfect sensitivity would involve beliefs and facts varying together. We already have one portion of that variation, subjunctively at least: if p were false he wouldn't believe it. This sensitivity as specified by a subjunctive does not have the belief vary with the truth or falsity of p in all possible situations, merely in the ones that would or might obtain if p were false.

The subjunctive condition

(3) not-$p \rightarrow$ not-(S believes that p)

tells us only half the story about how his belief is sensitive to the truth-value of p. It tells us how his belief state is sensitive to p's falsity, but not how it is sensitive to p's truth; it tells us what his belief state would be if p were false, but not what it would be if p were true.

To be sure, conditions 1 and 2 tell us that p is true and he does believe it, but it does not follow that his believing p is sensitive to p's being true. This additional sensitivity is given to us by a further subjunctive: if p were true, he would believe it.

(4) $p \rightarrow$ S believes that p.

Not only is p true and S believes it, but if it were true he would believe it. Compare: not only was the photon emitted and did it go to the left, but (it was then true that): if it were emitted it would go to the left. The truth of antecedent and consequent is not alone sufficient for the truth of a subjunctive; 4 says more than 1 and 2.[7] Thus, we presuppose some (or another) suitable account of subjunctives. According to the suggestion tentatively made above, 4 holds true if not only does

he actually truly believe p, but in the "close" worlds where p is true, he also believes it. He believes that p for some distance out in the p neighborhood of the actual world; similarly, condition 3 speaks not of the whole not-p neighborhood of the actual world, but only of the first portion of it. (If, as is likely, these explanations do not help, please use your own intuitive understanding of the subjunctives 3 and 4.)

The person in the tank does not satisfy the subjunctive condition 4. Imagine as actual a world in which he is in the tank and is stimulated to believe he is, and consider what subjunctives are true in that world. It is not true of him there that if he were in the tank he would believe it; for in the close world (or situation) to his own where he is in the tank but they don't give him the belief that he is (much less instill the belief that he isn't) he doesn't believe he is in the tank. Of the person actually in the tank and believing it, it is not true to make the further statement that if he were in the tank he would believe it – so he does not know he is in the tank.[8]

The subjunctive condition 4 also handles a case presented by Gilbert Harman.[9] The dictator of a country is killed; in their first edition, newspapers print the story, but later all the country's newspapers and other media deny the story, falsely. Everyone who encounters the denial believes it (or does not know what to believe and so suspends judgment). Only one person in the country fails to hear any denial and he continues to believe the truth. He satisfies conditions 1 through 3 (and the causal condition about belief) yet we are reluctant to say he knows the truth. The reason is that if he had heard the denials, he too would have believed them, just like everyone else. His belief is not sensitively tuned to the truth, he doesn't satisfy the condition that if it were true he would believe it. Condition 4 is not satisfied.[10]

There is a pleasing symmetry about how this account of knowledge relates conditions 3 and 4, and connects them to the first two conditions. The account has the following form.

(1)
(2)
(3) not-1 $\rightarrow$ not-2
(4) 1 $\rightarrow$ 2

I am not inclined, however, to make too much of this symmetry, for I found also that with other conditions experimented with as a possible fourth condition there was some way to construe the resulting third and fourth conditions as symmetrical answers to some symmetrical looking questions, so that they appeared to arise in parallel fashion from similar questions about the components of true belief.

Symmetry, it seems, is a feature of a mode of presentation, not of the contents presented. A uniform transformation of symmetrical statements can leave the results nonsymmetrical. But if symmetry attaches to mode of presentation, how can it possibly be a deep feature of, for instance, laws of nature that they exhibit symmetry? (One of my favorite examples of symmetry is due to Groucho Marx. On his radio program he spoofed a commercial, and ended, "And if you are not completely satisfied, return the unused portion of our product and we will return the unused portion of your money.") Still, to present our subject symmetrically makes the connection of knowledge to true belief especially perspicuous. It seems to me that a symmetrical formulation is a sign of our understanding, rather than a mark of truth. If we cannot understand an asymmetry as arising from an underlying symmetry through the operation of a particular factor, we will not understand why that asymmetry exists in that direction. (But do we also need to understand why the underlying asymmetrical factor holds instead of its opposite?)

A person knows that p when he not only does truly believe it, but also would truly believe it and wouldn't falsely believe it. He not only actually has a true belief, he subjunctively has one. It is true that p and he believes it; if it weren't true he wouldn't believe it; if it weren't true he wouldn't believe it, and if it were true he would believe it. To know that p is to be someone who would believe it if it were true, and who wouldn't believe it if it were false.

It will be useful to have a term for this situation when a person's belief is thus subjunctively connected to the fact. Let us say of a person who believes that p, which is true, that when 3 and 4 hold, his belief *tracks* the truth that p. To know is to have a belief that tracks the truth. Knowledge is a particular way of being connected to the world, having a specific real factual connection to the world: tracking it.

One refinement is needed in condition 4. It may be possible for someone to have contradictory beliefs, to believe p and also believe not-p. We do not mean such a person to easily satisfy 4, and in any case we want his belief-state, sensitive to the truth of p, to focus upon p. So let us rewrite our fourth condition as:

(4) $p \to$ S believes that p and not-(S believes that not-p).[11]

As you might have expected, this account of knowledge as tracking requires some refinements and epicycles. Readers who find themselves (or me) bogged down in these refinements should move on directly to this essay's second part, on skepticism, where the pace picks up.

Ways and methods

The fourth condition says that if p were true the person would believe it. Suppose the person only happened to see a certain event or simply chanced on a book describing it. He knows it occurred. Yet if he did not happen to glance that way or encounter the book, he would not believe it, even though it occurred. As written, the fourth condition would exclude this case as one where he actually knows the event occurred. It also would exclude the following case. Suppose some person who truly believes that p would or might arrive at a belief about it in some other close situation where it holds true, in a way or by a method different from the one he (actually) used in arriving at his belief that p, and so thereby come to believe that not-p. In that (close) situation, he would believe not-p even though p still holds true. Yet, all this does not show he actually doesn't know that p, for actually he has not used this alternative method in arriving at his belief. Surely he can know that p, even though condition 4, as written, is not satisfied.

Similarly, suppose he believes that p by one method or way of arriving at belief, yet if p were false he wouldn't use this method but would use another one instead, whose application would lead him mistakenly to believe p (even though it is false). This person does not satisfy condition 3 as written; it is not true of him that if p were false he wouldn't believe it. Still, the fact that he would use another method of arriving at belief if p were false does not show he didn't know that p when he used this method. A grandmother sees her grandson is well when he comes to visit; but if he were sick or dead, others would tell her he was well to spare her upset. Yet this does not mean she doesn't know he is well (or at least ambulatory) when she sees him. Clearly, we must restate our conditions to take explicit account of the ways and methods of arriving at belief.

Let us define a technical locution, S knows, via method (or way of believing) M, that p:

(1) p is true.
(2) S believes, via method or way of coming to believe M, that p.
(3) If p weren't true and S were to use M to arrive at a belief whether (or not) p, then S wouldn't believe, via M, that p.
(4) If p were true and S were to use M to arrive at a belief whether (or not) p, then S would believe, via M, that p.

We need to relate this technical locution to our ordinary notion of knowledge. If only one method M is actually or subjunctively relevant to S's belief that p, then, simply, S knows that p (according to our ordinary notion) if and only if that method M is such that S knows that p via M.

Some situations involve multiple methods, however.

First Situation: S's belief that p is overdetermined; it was introduced (or reinforced) by two methods, each of which in isolation would have been sufficient to produce in S the belief that p. S's belief that p via one of these methods satisfies conditions 1–4. However, S's belief that p via the second method does not satisfy conditions 1–4, and in particular violates condition 3.

A case of this sort is discussed by Armstrong.[12] A father believes his son innocent of committing a particular crime, both because of faith in his son and (now) because he has seen presented in the courtroom a conclusive demonstration of his son's innocence. His belief via the method of courtroom demonstration satisfies 1–4, let us suppose, but his faith-based belief does not. If his son were guilty, he would still believe him innocent, on the basis of faith in his son. Thus, his belief that p (that his son is innocent) via faith in

his son violates condition 3. Looking at his belief alone, without mention of method, his belief that p violates the third condition (namely, if p were false S wouldn't believe that p), which made no mention of method.

Second Situation: S's belief that p via one method satisfies conditions 1–4. However, if p were false, S would not use that method in arriving at a belief about the truth value of p. Instead, he would use another method, thereby deciding, despite p's falsity, that p was true. S's actual belief that p is in no way based on the use of this second method, but if p were false he would believe p via the second method. (However, if p were false and S were to decide about its truth value by using the first method, then S would not believe that p. To be sure, if p were false S wouldn't decide about it by using that first method.) The truth value of p affects which method S uses to decide whether p.

Our earlier example of the grandmother is of this sort. Consider one further example, suggested to me by Avishai Margalit. S believes a certain building is a theater and concert hall. He has attended plays and concerts there (first method). However, if the building were not a theater, it would have housed a nuclear reactor that would so have altered the air around it (let us suppose) that everyone upon approaching the theater would have become lethargic and nauseous, and given up the attempt to buy a ticket. The government cover story would have been that the building was a theater, a cover story they knew would be safe since no unmedicated person could approach through the nausea field to discover any differently. Everyone, let us suppose, would have believed the cover story; they would have believed that the building they saw (but only from some distance) was a theater.

S believes the building is a theater because he has attended plays and concerts inside. He does not believe it is a theater via the second method of reading the government's cover story plus planted spurious theater and concert reviews. There are no such things. However, if it weren't a theater, it would be a nuclear reactor, there would be such cover stories, and S would believe still (this time falsely and via the second method) that the building was a theater. Nonetheless, S, who actually has attended performances there, knows that it is a theater.

To hold that a person knows that p if there exists at least one method M, satisfying conditions 1–4, via which he believes that p, would classify the father as knowing his son is innocent, a consequence too charitable to the father. Whereas it seems too stringent to require that all methods satisfy conditions 1–4, including those methods that were not actually used but would be under some other circumstances; the grandmother knows her grandson is well, and the person who has attended the concerts and plays knows the building is a theater. It is more reasonable to hold he knows that p if all the methods via which he actually believes that p satisfy conditions 1–4. Yet suppose our theatergoer also believes it is a theater partly because government officials, before they decided on which use they would put the building to, announced they were building a theater. Still, the theatergoer knows the building is a theater. Not all methods actually used need satisfy conditions 1–4, but we already have seen how the weak position that merely one such method is enough mishandles the case of the father.

We are helped to thread our way through these difficulties when we notice this father does not merely believe his son is innocent via the route of faith in his son; this defective route, not satisfying 1–4, also outweighs for him the method of courtroom demonstration. Even if courtroom demonstration (had it operated alone) would lead to the belief that his son is guilty, that not-p, still he would believe his son innocent, via faith in his son. Although it is the method of courtroom demonstration that gives him knowledge that p if anything does, for the father this method is outweighed by faith.[13] As a first try at delineating outweighing, we might say that method M is outweighed by others if when M would have the person believe p, the person believes not-p if the other methods would lead to the belief that not-p, or when M would have the person believe not-p, the person believes p if the other methods would lead to the belief that p.

This leads us to put forth the following position: S knows that p if there is some method via which S believes that p which satisfies conditions 1–4, and that method is not outweighed by any other method(s), via which S actually believes that p, that fail to satisfy conditions 3 and 4. According to this position, in some cases a person has knowledge even when he also actually believes via a method M_1 that does not satisfy 1–4, provided it is outweighed by one that does; namely, in the over-determination case, and in the case when M_1 alone would suffice to fix belief but only in the absence of a verdict from the M he also uses which does satisfy 1–4.

S knows that p if and only if there is a method M such that (a) he knows that p via M, his belief via M that p satisfies conditions 1–4, and (b) all other methods M_1 via which he believes that p that do not satisfy conditions 1–4 are outweighed by M.[14]

We have stated our outweighing requirement only roughly; now we must turn to refinements. According to our rough statement, in the over-determination case, method M_1, which satisfies 3 and 4 and which is what gives knowledge if anything does, wins out over the other method M_2 in all cases. The actual situation (Case I) is where M_1 recommends believing p as does M_2, and the person believes p. In this case we have made our answer to the question whether he knows that p depend on what happens or would happen in the two other cases where the methods recommend different beliefs (see Table 21.1). The first rough statement held that the person knows in Case I only if he would believe p in Case II and not-p in Case III. While this is sufficient for knowledge in Case I, it seems too stringent to be necessary for such knowledge.

An alternative and more adequate view would hold constant what the other method recommends, and ask whether the belief varies with the recommendation of M_1. Since M_2 actually

Table 21.1

	M_1 recommends	M_2 recommends	Does the person believe p or believe not-p?
Case I	believe p	believe p	believes p
Case II	believe p	believe not-p	?
Case III	believe not-p	believe p	?

recommends p (Case I), we need look only at Case III and ask: when M_2 continues to recommend p and M_1 recommends not-p, would the person believe not-p? Despite his faith, would the father believe his son guilty if the courtroom procedure proved guilt? That is the relevant question – not what he would believe if the courtroom showed innocence while (somehow) his method of faith led to a conclusion of guilty.

Consider how this works out in another simple case. I see a friend today; he is now alive. However, if he were not alive, I wouldn't have seen him today or (let us suppose) heard of his death, and so still would believe he was alive. Yet condition 3 is satisfied; it includes reference to a method, and the method M_1 of seeing him satisfies 3 with respect to p equals he is alive at the time. But there also is another method M_2 via which I believe he is alive, namely having known he was alive yesterday and continuing to believe it. Case III asks what I would believe if I saw the friend dead (though I knew yesterday he was alive); our position holds I must believe him dead in this case if I am to know by seeing him that he is alive in Case I. However, we need not go so far as to consider what I would believe if I had "learned" yesterday that he was dead yet "saw" him alive today. Perhaps in that case I would wonder whether it really was he I was seeing. Even so, given the result in Case III, I know (in Case I) he is alive. Thus, we hold fixed the recommendation of the other method, and only ask whether then the belief varies with the recommendation of method M_1.[15]

Our test of looking at Case III cannot apply if M_1 is a one-sided method, incapable of recommending belief in not-p; it either recommends belief in p or yields no recommendation. (Perhaps M_1 detects one of a number of sufficient conditions for p; not detecting this, M_1 remains silent as to the truth of p.) What are we to say about his knowing if a person's belief is overdetermined or jointly determined by a one-sided method M_1 plus another method M_2 which fails to satisfy condition 3? Should we now look at Case II, where M_1 recommends belief in p and M_2 recommends belief in not-p, and say that believing p in this case is sufficient to show that M_1 outweighs M_2? That does not seem unreasonable, but we had better be careful to stipulate that this Case II situation is a sufficient condition for M_1's outweighing M_2 only when the Case III situation is impossible, for otherwise we face the possibility of

divergent results. (For example, he believes p in Case II and in Case III, yet believes not-p when both methods recommend not-p; here the result in Case II indicates M_1 outweighs M_2 while the result in Case III indicates M_2 outweighs M_1.) It is Case III that should predominate.

One final remark about method. Suppose a method is good for some types of statements but not others; it satisfies 3 and 4 for the first type but not for the second. However, S believes the method is good for all types of statements and applies it indiscriminately. When he applies it to a statement of the first type which he thereby comes to believe, does he know that it is true? He does, if he satisfies conditions 3 and 4. Hesitation to grant him knowledge stems, I think, from the fact that if p were false and were of the second type, he might well still believe it. Whether or not this undercuts condition 3 for knowledge depends upon the disparity of the two types; the greater the gulf between the types, the more willing we are to say he knows a statement of the type where M works.

In explaining the nature of knowledge by reference to a method or way of believing, we leave large questions open about how to individuate methods, count them, identify which method is at work, and so on. I do not want to underestimate these difficulties, but neither do I want to pursue them here.[16] Still, some clarifying remarks are needed.

A person can use a method (in my sense) without proceeding methodically, and without knowledge or awareness of what method he is using. Usually, a method will have a final upshot in experience on which the belief is based, such as visual experience, and then (a) no method without this upshot is the same method, and (b) any method experientially the same, the same "from the inside," will count as the same method. Basing our beliefs on experiences, you and I and the person floating in the tank are using, for these purposes, the same method.

Some methods are supervenient on others, for example, "believing what seems to be true to you" or "believing what seems true given the weighting of all other methods." The account of outweighing is not to apply to such supervenient methods, otherwise there always will be such a one that outweighs all the others. There are various gerrymandered (Goodmanesque) methods that would yield the same resulting belief in the actual situation; which method a person actually is using will depend on which general disposition to acquire beliefs (extending to other situations) he actually is exercising.[17]

Although sometimes it will be necessary to be explicit about the methods via which someone believes something, often it will cause no confusion to leave out all mention of method. Furthermore, some statements play a central role in our continuing activities, or in our picture of the world or framework wherein we check other statements, for example, "I have two hands," "the world has existed for many years already"; it is misleading to think of our coming to believe them via some delimited method or methods.[18] So nested are these statements in our other beliefs and activities, and so do they nest them, that our belief or acceptance of them is (for almost all purposes) best represented apart from any particular methods. In considering our knowledge of them we may revert to the earlier simpler subjunctives

(3)   not-$p \rightarrow$ not-(S believes that p)
(4) $p \rightarrow$ S believes that p.

The very centrality of the specific p means that 4 will be satisfied without reference to a specific method or way of believing. In contrast, I know there is a pair of scissors on my desk (in front of me) now; but it is not accurate simply to say that if there were a pair of scissors there, I would believe there was. For what if I weren't looking, or hadn't looked, or were elsewhere now? Reference to the method via which I believe there are scissors on the desk is needed to exclude these possibilities. With the most central statements, however, there is no similar "what if"; their centrality ensures they will not escape notice.

Skepticism

The skeptic about knowledge argues that we know very little or nothing of what we think we know, or at any rate that this position is no less reasonable than the belief in knowledge. The history of philosophy exhibits a number of different attempts to refute the skeptic: to prove him wrong or show that in arguing against

knowledge he presupposes there is some and so refutes himself. Others attempt to show that accepting skepticism is unreasonable, since it is more likely that the skeptic's extreme conclusion is false than that all of his premises are true, or simply because reasonableness of belief just means proceeding in an anti-skeptical way. Even when these counterarguments satisfy their inventors, they fail to satisfy others, as is shown by the persistent attempts against skepticism.[19] The continuing felt need to refute skepticism, and the difficulty in doing so, attests to the power of the skeptic's position, the depth of his worries.

An account of knowledge should illuminate skeptical arguments and show wherein lies their force. If the account leads us to reject these arguments, this had better not happen too easily or too glibly. To think the skeptic overlooks something obvious, to attribute to him a simple mistake or confusion or fallacy, is to refuse to acknowledge the power of his position and the grip it can have upon us. We thereby cheat ourselves of the opportunity to reap his insights and to gain self-knowledge in understanding why his arguments lure us so. Moreover, in fact, we cannot lay the specter of skepticism to rest without first hearing what it shall unfold.

Our goal is not, however, to refute skepticism, to prove it is wrong or even to argue that it is wrong. Our task here is to explain how knowledge is possible, given what the skeptic says that we do accept (for example, that it is logically possible that we are dreaming or are floating in the tank). In doing this, we need not convince the skeptic, and we may introduce explanatory hypotheses that he would reject. What is important for our task of explanation and understanding is that *we* find those hypotheses acceptable or plausible, and that they show us how the existence of knowledge fits together with the logical possibilities the skeptic points to, so that these are reconciled within our own belief system. These hypotheses are to explain to ourselves how knowledge is possible, not to prove to someone else that knowledge *is* possible.[20]

Skeptical possibilities

The skeptic often refers to possibilities in which a person would believe something even though it was false: really, the person is cleverly deceived by others, perhaps by an evil demon, or the person is dreaming or he is floating in a tank near Alpha Centauri with his brain being stimulated. In each case, the p he believes is false, and he believes it even though it is false.

How do these possibilities adduced by the skeptic show that someone does not know that p? Suppose that someone is you; how do these possibilities count against your knowing that p? One way might be the following. (I shall consider other ways later.) If there is a possible situation where p is false yet you believe that p, then in that situation you believe that p even though it is false. So it appears you do not satisfy condition 3 for knowledge.

(3)   If p were false, S wouldn't believe that p.

For a situation has been described in which you do believe that p even though p is false. How then can it also be true that if p were false, you wouldn't believe it? If the skeptic's possible situation shows that 3 is false, and if 3 is a necessary condition for knowledge, then the skeptic's possible situation shows that there isn't knowledge.

So construed, the skeptic's argument plays on condition 3; it aims to show that condition 3 is not satisfied. The skeptic may seem to be putting forth

R: Even if p were false, S still would believe p.[21]

This conditional, with the same antecedent as 3 and the contradictory consequent, is incompatible with the truth of 3. If 3 is true, then R is not. However, R is stronger than the skeptic needs in order to show 3 is false. For 3 is false when if p were false, S might believe that p. This last conditional is weaker than R, and is merely 3's denial:

T: not-[not-p → not-(S believes that p)].

Whereas R does not simply deny 3, it asserts an opposing subjunctive of its own. Perhaps the possibility the skeptic adduces is not enough to show that R is true, but it appears at least to establish the weaker T; since this T denies 3, the skeptic's possibility appears to show that 3 is false.[22]

However, the truth of 3 is not incompatible with the existence of a possible situation where the person believes p though it is false. The subjunctive

(3)   not-p → not-(S believes p)

does not talk of all possible situations in which p is false (in which not-p is true). It does not say that in all possible situations where not-p holds, S doesn't believe p. To say there is no possible situation in which not-p yet S believes p, would be to say that not-p entails not-(S believes p), or logically implies it. But subjunctive conditionals differ from entailments; the subjunctive 3 is not a statement of entailment. So the existence of a possible situation in which p is false yet S believes p does not show that 3 is false;[23] 3 can be true even though there is a possible situation where not-p and S believes that p.

What the subjunctive 3 speaks of is the situation that would hold if p were false. Not every possible situation in which p is false is the situation that would hold if p were false. To fall into possible worlds talk, the subjunctive 3 speaks of the not-p world that is closest to the actual world, or of those not-p worlds that are closest to the actual world, or more strongly (according to my suggestion) of the not-p neighborhood of the actual world. And it is of this or these not-p worlds that it says (in them) S does not believe that p. What happens in yet other more distant not-p worlds is no concern of the subjunctive 3.

The skeptic's possibilities (let us refer to them as SK), of the person's being deceived by a demon or dreaming or floating in a tank, count against the subjunctive

(3)   if p were false then S wouldn't believe that p

only if (one of) these possibilities would or might obtain if p were false; only if one of these possibilities is in the not-p neighborhood of the actual world. Condition 3 says: if p were false, S still would not believe p. And this can hold even though there is some situation SK described by the skeptic in which p is false and S believes p. If p were false S still would not believe p, even though there is a situation SK in which p is false and S does believe p, provided that this situation SK wouldn't obtain if p were false. If the skeptic describes a situation SK which would not hold even if p were false then this situation SK doesn't show that 3 is false and so does not (in this way at least) undercut knowledge. Condition C acts to rule out skeptical hypotheses.

C: not-$p \to$ SK does not obtain.

Any skeptical situation SK which satisfies condition C is ruled out. For a skeptical situation SK to show that we don't know that p, it must fail to satisfy C which excludes it; instead it must be a situation that might obtain if p did not, and so satisfy C's denial:

not-(not-$p \to$ SK doesn't obtain).

Although the skeptic's imagined situations appear to show that 3 is false, they do not; they satisfy condition C and so are excluded.

The skeptic might go on to ask whether we know that his imagined situations SK are excluded by condition C, whether we know that if p were false SK would not obtain. However, typically he asks something stronger; do we know that his imagined situation SK does not actually obtain? Do we know that we are not being deceived by a demon, dreaming, or floating in a tank? And if we do not know this, how can we know that p? Thus we are led to the second way his imagined situations might show that we do not know that p.

Skeptical results

According to our account of knowledge, S knows that the skeptic's situation SK doesn't hold if and only if

(1) SK doesn't hold
(2) S believes that SK doesn't hold
(3) If SK were to hold, S would not believe that SK doesn't hold
(4) If SK were not to hold, S would believe it does not.

Let us focus on the third of these conditions. The skeptic has carefully chosen his situations SK so that if they held we (still) would believe they did not. We would believe we weren't dreaming,

weren't being deceived, and so on, even if we were. He has chosen situations SK such that if SK were to hold, S would (still) believe that SK doesn't hold – and this is incompatible with the truth of 3.[24]

Since condition 3 is a necessary condition for knowledge, it follows that we do not know that SK doesn't hold. If it were true that an evil demon was deceiving us, if we were having a particular dream, if we were floating in a tank with our brains stimulated in a specified way, we would still believe we were not. So, we do not know we're not being deceived by an evil demon, we do not know we're not in that tank, and we do not know we're not having that dream. So says the skeptic, and so says our account. And also so we say – don't we? For how could we know we are not being deceived that way, dreaming that dream? If those things *were* happening to us, everything would seem the same to us. There is no way we can know it is not happening for there is no way we could tell if it were happening; and if it were happening we would believe exactly what we do now – in particular, we still would believe that it was not. For this reason, we feel, and correctly, that we don't know – how could we? – that it is not happening to us. It is a virtue of our account that it yields, and explains, this result.

The skeptic asserts we do not know his possibilities don't obtain, and he is right. Attempts to avoid skepticism by claiming we do know these things are bound to fail. The skeptic's possibilities make us uneasy because, as we deeply realize, we do not know they don't obtain; it is not surprising that attempts to show we do know these things leave us suspicious, strike us even as bad faith.[25] Nor has the skeptic merely pointed out something obvious and trivial. It comes as a surprise to realize that we do not know his possibilities don't obtain. It is startling, shocking. For we would have thought, before the skeptic got us to focus on it, that we did know those things, that we did know we were not being deceived by a demon, or dreaming that dream, or stimulated that way in that tank. The skeptic has pointed out that we do not know things we would have confidently said we knew. And if we don't know these things, what can we know? So much for the supposed obviousness of what the skeptic tells us.

Let us say that a situation (or world) is doxically identical for S to the actual situation when if S were in that situation, he would have exactly the beliefs (*doxa*) he actually does have. More generally, two situations are doxically identical for S if and only if he would have exactly the same beliefs in them. It might be merely a curiosity to be told there are nonactual situations doxically identical to the actual one. The skeptic, however, describes worlds doxically identical to the actual world in which almost everything believed is false.[26]

Such worlds are possible because we know mediately, not directly. This leaves room for a divergence between our beliefs and the truth. It is as though we possessed only two-dimensional plane projections of three-dimensional objects. Different three-dimensional objects, oriented appropriately, have the same two-dimensional plane projection. Similarly, different situations or worlds will lead to our having the very same beliefs. What is surprising is how very different the doxically identical world can be – different enough for almost everything believed in it to be false. Whether or not the mere fact that knowledge is mediated always makes room for such a very different doxically identical world, it does so in our case, as the skeptic's possibilities show. To be shown this is nontrivial, especially when we recall that we do not know the skeptic's possibility doesn't obtain: we do not know that we are not living in a doxically identical world wherein almost everything we believe is false.[27]

What more could the skeptic ask for or hope to show? Even readers who sympathized with my desire not to dismiss the skeptic too quickly may feel this has gone too far, that we have not merely acknowledged the force of the skeptic's position but have succumbed to it.

The skeptic maintains that we know almost none of what we think we know. He has shown, much to our initial surprise, that we do not know his (nontrivial) possibility SK doesn't obtain. Thus, he has shown of one thing we thought we knew, that we didn't and don't. To the conclusion that we know almost nothing, it appears but a short step. For if we do not know we are not dreaming or being deceived by a demon or floating in a tank, then how can I know, for example, that I am sitting before a page writing with a pen, and how can you know that you are reading a page of a book?

However, although our account of knowledge agrees with the skeptic in saying that we do not know that not-SK, it places no formidable barriers before my knowing that I am writing on a page with a pen. It is true that I am, I believe I am, if I weren't I wouldn't believe I was, and if I were, I would believe it. (I leave out the reference to method.) Also, it is true that you are reading a page (please, don't stop now!), you believe you are, if you weren't reading a page you wouldn't believe you were, and if you were reading a page you would believe you were. So according to the account, I do know that I am writing on a page with a pen, and you do know that you are reading a page. The account does not lead to any general skepticism.

Yet we must grant that it appears that if the skeptic is right that we don't know we are not dreaming or being deceived or floating in the tank, then it cannot be that I know I am writing with a pen or that you know you are reading a page. So we must scrutinize with special care the skeptic's "short step" to the conclusion that we don't know these things, for either this step cannot be taken or our account of knowledge is incoherent.

Nonclosure

In taking the "short step," the skeptic assumes that if S knows that *p* and he knows that *p* entails *q* then he also knows that *q*. In the terminology of the logicians, the skeptic assumes that knowledge is closed under known logical implication; that the operation of moving from something known to something else known to be entailed by it does not take us outside of the (closed) area of knowledge. He intends, of course, to work things backwards, arguing that since the person does not know that *q*, assuming (at least for the purposes of argument) that he does know that *p* entails *q*, it follows that he does not know that *p*. For if he did know that *p*, he would also know that *q*, which he doesn't.

The details of different skeptical arguments vary in their structure, but each one will assume some variant of the principle that knowledge is closed under known logical implication. If we abbreviate "knowledge that *p*" by "K*p*" and abbreviate "entails" by the fish-hook sign $\prec$," we can write this principle of closure as the subjunctive principle

P: K(p $\prec$ q) & Kp → Kq.

If a person were to know that p entails q and he were to know that p then he would know that q. The statement that q follows by modus ponens from the other two stated as known in the antecedent of the subjunctive principle P; this principle counts on the person to draw the inference to q.

You know that your being in a tank on Alpha Centauri entails your not being in place X where you are. (I assume here a limited readership.) And you know also the contrapositive, that your being at place X entails that you are not then in a tank on Alpha Centauri. If you knew you were at X you would know you're not in a tank (of a specified sort) at Alpha Centauri. But you do not know this last fact (the skeptic has argued and we have agreed) and so (he argues) you don't know the first. Another intuitive way of putting the skeptic's argument is as follows. If you know that two statements are incompatible and you know the first is true then you know the denial of the second. You know that your being at X and your being in a tank on Alpha Centauri are incompatible; so if you knew you were at X you would know you were not in the (specified) tank on Alpha Centauri. Since you do not know the second, you don't know the first.[28]

No doubt, it is possible to argue over the details of principle P, to point out it is incorrect as it stands. Perhaps, though Kp, the person does not know that he knows that p (that is, not-KKp) and so does not draw the inference to q. Or perhaps he doesn't draw the inference because not-KK ($p \prec q$). Other similar principles face their own difficulties: for example, the principle that K($p \rightarrow q$) $\rightarrow$ (Kp $\rightarrow$ Kq) fails if Kp stops $p \rightarrow q$ from being true, that is, if Kp $\rightarrow$ not-($p \rightarrow q$); the principle that K($p \prec q$) $\rightarrow$ K(Kp $\rightarrow$ Kq) faces difficulties if Kp makes the person forget that ($p \prec q$) and so he fails to draw the inference to q. We seem forced to pile K upon K until we reach something like KK($p \prec q$) & KKp $\rightarrow$ Kq; this involves strengthening considerably the antecedent of P and so is not useful for the skeptic's argument that p is not known. (From a principle altered thus, it would follow at best that it is not known that p is known.)

We would be ill-advised, however, to quibble over the details of P. Although these details are difficult to get straight, it will continue to appear that something like P is correct. If S knows that "p

entails q" and he knows that p and knows that "(p and p entails q) entails q" and he does draw the inference to q from all this and believes q via the process of drawing this inference, then will he not know that q? And what is wrong with simplifying this mass of detail by writing merely principle P, provided we apply it only to cases where the mass of detail holds, as it surely does in the skeptical cases under consideration? For example, I do realize that my being in the Van Leer Foundation Building in Jerusalem entails that I am not in a tank on Alpha Centauri; I am capable of drawing inferences now; I do believe I am not in a tank on Alpha Centauri (though not solely via this inference, surely); and so forth. Won't this satisfy the correctly detailed principle, and shouldn't it follow that I know I am not (in that tank) on Alpha Centauri? The skeptic agrees it should follow; so he concludes from the fact that I don't know I am not floating in the tank on Alpha Centauri that I don't know I am in Jerusalem. Uncovering difficulties in the details of particular formulations of P will not weaken the principle's intuitive appeal; such quibbling will seem at best like a wasp attacking a steamroller, at worst like an effort in bad faith to avoid being pulled along by the skeptic's argument.

Principle P is wrong, however, and not merely in detail. Knowledge is not closed under known logical implication.[29] S knows that p when S has a true belief that p, and S wouldn't have a false belief that p (condition 3) and S would have a true belief that p (condition 4). Neither of these latter two conditions is closed under known logical implication.

Let us begin with condition

(3)   if p were false, S wouldn't believe that p.

When S knows that p, his belief that p is contingent on the truth of p, contingent in the way the subjunctive condition 3 describes. Now it might be that p entails q (and S knows this), that S's belief that p is subjunctively contingent on the truth of p, that S believes q, yet his belief that q is not subjunctively dependent on the truth of q, in that it (or he) does not satisfy:

(3')   if q were false, S wouldn't believe that q.

For 3' talks of what S would believe if q were false, and this may be a very different situation than the one that would hold if p were false, even though p entails q. That you were born in a certain city entails that you were born on earth.[30] Yet contemplating what (actually) would be the situation if you were not born in that city is very different from contemplating what situation would hold if you weren't born on earth. Just as those possibilities are very different, so what is believed in them may be very different. When p entails q (and not the other way around) p will be a stronger statement than q, and so not-q (which is the antecedent of 3′) will be a stronger statement than not-p (which is the antecedent of 3). There is no reason to assume you will have the same beliefs in these two cases, under these suppositions of differing strengths.

There is no reason to assume the (closest) not-p world and the (closest) not-q world are doxically identical for you, and no reason to assume, even though p entails q, that your beliefs in one of these worlds would be a (proper) subset of your beliefs in the other.

Consider now the two statements:

$p =$ I am awake and sitting on a chair in Jerusalem;

$q =$ I am not floating in a tank on Alpha Centauri being stimulated by electrochemical means to believe that p.

The first one entails the second: p entails q. Also, I know that p entails q; and I know that p. If p were false, I would be standing or lying down in the same city, or perhaps sleeping there, or perhaps in a neighboring city or town. If q were false, I would be floating in a tank on Alpha Centauri. Clearly these are very different situations, leading to great differences in what I then would believe. If p were false, if I weren't awake and sitting on a chair in Jerusalem, I would not believe that p. Yet if q were false, if I was floating in a tank on Alpha Centauri, I would believe that q, that I was not in the tank, and indeed, in that case, I would still believe that p. According to our account of knowledge, I know that p yet I do not know that q, even though (I know) p entails q.

This failure of knowledge to be closed under known logical implication stems from the fact that condition 3 is not closed under known logical implication; condition 3 can hold of one statement believed while not of another known

to be entailed by the first.[31] It is clear that any account that includes as a necessary condition for knowledge the subjunctive condition 3, not-$p \rightarrow$ not-(S believes that p), will have the consequence that knowledge is not closed under known logical implication.[32]

When p entails q and you believe each of them, if you do not have a false belief that p (since p is true) then you do not have a false belief that q. However, if you are to know something not only don't you have a false belief about it, but also you wouldn't have a false belief about it. Yet, we have seen how it may be that p entails q and you believe each and you wouldn't have a false belief that p yet you might have a false belief that q (that is, it is not the case that you wouldn't have one). Knowledge is not closed under the known logical implication because "wouldn't have a false belief that" is not closed under known logical implication.

If knowledge were the same as (simply) true belief then it would be closed under known logical implication (provided the implied statements were believed). Knowledge is not simply true belief, however; additional conditions are needed. These further conditions will make knowledge open under known logical implication, even when the entailed statement is believed, when at least one of the further conditions itself is open. Knowledge stays closed (only) if all of the additional conditions are closed. I lack a general nontrivial characterization of those conditions that are closed under known logical implication; possessing such an illuminating characterization, one might attempt to prove that no additional conditions of that sort could provide an adequate analysis of knowledge.

Still, we can say the following. A belief that p is knowledge that p only if it somehow varies with the truth of p. The causal condition for knowledge specified that the belief was "produced by" the fact, but that condition did not provide the right sort of varying with the fact. The subjunctive conditions 3 and 4 are our attempt to specify that varying. But however an account spells this out, it will hold that whether a belief that p is knowledge partly depends on what goes on with the belief in some situations when p is false. An account that says nothing about what is believed in any situation when p is false cannot give us any mode of varying with the fact.

Because what is preserved under logical implication is truth, any condition that is preserved under known logical implication is most likely to speak only of what happens when p, and q, are true, without speaking at all of what happens when either one is false. Such a condition is incapable of providing "varies with"; so adding only such conditions to true belief cannot yield an adequate account of knowledge.[33]

A belief's somehow varying with the truth of what is believed is not closed under known logical implication. Since knowledge that p involves such variation, knowledge also is not closed under known logical implication. The skeptic cannot easily deny that knowledge involves such variation, for his argument that we don't know that we're not floating in that tank, for example, uses the fact that knowledge does involve variation. ("If you were floating in the tank you would still think you weren't, so you don't know that you're not.") Yet, though one part of his argument uses that fact that knowledge involves such variation, another part of his argument presupposes that knowledge does not involve any such variation. This latter is the part that depends upon knowledge being closed under known logical implication, as when the skeptic argues that since you don't know that not-SK, you don't know you are not floating in the tank, then you also don't know, for example, that you are now reading a book. That closure can hold only if the variation does not. The skeptic cannot be right both times. According to our view he is right when he holds that knowledge involves such variation and so concludes that we don't know, for example, that we are not floating in that tank; but he is wrong when he assumes knowledge is closed under known logical implication and concludes that we know hardly anything.[34]

Knowledge is a real factual relation, subjunctively specifiable, whose structure admits our standing in this relation, tracking, to p without standing in it to some q which we know p to entail. Any relation embodying some variation of belief with the fact, with the truth (value), will exhibit this structural feature. The skeptic is right that we don't track some particular truths – the ones stating that his skeptical possibilities SK don't hold – but wrong that we don't stand in the real knowledge-relation of tracking to many other truths, including ones

that entail these first mentioned truths we believe but don't know.

The literature on skepticism contains writers who endorse these skeptical arguments (or similar narrower ones), but confess their inability to maintain their skeptical beliefs at times when they are not focusing explicitly on the reasoning that led them to skeptical conclusions. The most notable example of this is Hume:

> I am ready to reject all belief and reasoning, and can look upon no opinion even as more probable or likely than another ... Most fortunately it happens that since reason is incapable of dispelling these clouds, nature herself suffices to that purpose, and cures me of this philosophical melancholy and delirium, either by relaxing this bent of mind, or by some avocation, and lively impression of my senses, which obliterate all these chimeras. I dine, I play a game of backgammon, I converse, and am merry with my friends; and when after three or four hours' amusement, I would return to these speculations, they appear so cold, and strained, and ridiculous, that I cannot find in my heart to enter into them any farther. (*A Treatise of Human Nature*, Book I, Part IV, section VII)

> The great subverter of Pyrrhonism or the excessive principles of skepticism is action, and employment, and the occupations of common life. These principles may flourish and triumph in the schools; where it is, indeed, difficult, if not impossible, to refute them. But as soon as they leave the shade, and by the presence of the real objects, which actuate our passions and sentiments, are put in opposition to the more powerful principles of our nature, they vanish like smoke, and leave the most determined skeptic in the same condition as other mortals ... And though a Pyrrhonian may throw himself or others into a momentary amazement and confusion by his profound reasonings; the first and most trivial event in life will put to flight all his doubts and scruples, and leave him the same, in every point of action and speculation, with the philosophers of every other sect, or with those who never concerned themselves in any philosophical researches. When he awakes from his dream, he will be the first to join in the laugh against himself, and to confess that all his objections are mere amusement. (*An Enquiry Concerning Human Understanding*, Section XII, Part II)

The theory of knowledge we have presented explains why skeptics of various sorts have had such difficulties in sticking to their far-reaching skeptical conclusions "outside the study," or even inside it when they are not thinking specifically about skeptical arguments and possibilities SK.

The skeptic's arguments do show (but show only) that we don't know the skeptic's possibilities SK do not hold; and he is right that we don't track the fact that SK does not hold. (If it were to hold, we would still think it didn't.) However, the skeptic's arguments don't show we do not know other facts (including facts that entail not-SK) for we do track these other facts (and knowledge is not closed under known logical entailment.) Since we do track these other facts – you, for example, the fact that you are reading a book; I, the fact that I am writing on a page – and the skeptic tracks such facts too, it is not surprising that when he focuses on them, on his relationship to such facts, the skeptic finds it hard to remember or maintain his view that he does not know those facts. Only by shifting his attention back to his relationship to the (different) fact that not-SK, which relationship is not tracking, can he revive his skeptical belief and make it salient. However, this skeptical triumph is evanescent, it vanishes when his attention turns to other facts. Only by fixating on the skeptical possibilities SK can he maintain his skeptical virtue; otherwise, unsurprisingly, he is forced to confess to sins of credulity.

Skepticism and the conditions for knowledge

We have considered how the skeptic's argument from the skeptical possibilities SK plays off condition 3: if p weren't true S wouldn't believe that p. His argument gains its power by utilizing this condition ("but even if SK held, you still would believe it didn't, so you do not know it doesn't"); the deep intuitive force of the argument indicates that condition 3 (or something very much like it) is a necessary condition for knowledge. Similarly, are there any skeptical arguments or moves that play off condition 4: if p were true then S would believe that p (and wouldn't believe that not-p)? If condition 3 specifies how belief somehow should vary with the truth of what is believed, condition 4 specifies how belief shouldn't vary when the truth of what is believed does not vary. Condition 3 is a

variation condition, condition 4 is an adherence condition. Both conditions together capture the notion that S (who actually truly believes p) would have a true belief that p. He wouldn't have a false belief that p if p weren't true (condition 3), and he would have a true belief that p if p were true (condition 4). Just as the skeptic argued earlier that the belief wouldn't vary when it should, he also can argue that it would vary when it shouldn't, concluding both times that we don't have knowledge.

We would expect skeptical arguments playing off condition 4 to be less powerful and compelling than ones playing off 3. Condition 3 requires that we wouldn't falsely believe p, and we can be led to worry not only whether we might but whether we do. While condition 4 requires that we would truly believe p (and wouldn't falsely believe not-p), and though we might worry whether we might violate this, we need have no fear that we are – for we know we are believing p and are not believing not-p. Skeptical arguments playing off condition 4, unlike those with 3, cannot make us wonder also whether we violate the condition's indicative version.

Condition 4 is an adherence condition, so the relevant doubts concern how securely you are tied to the truth. For many (most?) of the things p you believe, if a group of people came and deceitfully told you not-p, you would believe them and stop believing p. (Relevant experiments frequently have been done by social psychologists.) So do you really know p? If physicists told you that Newton's theory turns out to have been correct after all, wouldn't (or mightn't) you believe them? So do you really know Newtonian theory is false?

But, as before, the mere possibility of its being true while you do not believe it is not sufficient to show you don't actually know it. That possibility must be one that might arise. Call this possibility of p's being true while you don't believe it: sk. (Lowercase "sk" is p's being true and your not believing it, while capital SK is p's being false and your believing p.) Possibility sk need not concern us when: if p were true, sk wouldn't hold; $p \rightarrow$ not-sk; sk is false throughout the first part of the p neighborhood of the actual world. It is fortunate for my knowing that p that there wouldn't be people who trick me, just as it is fortunate for my knowing I am in Emerson Hall that whatever would occur if I weren't there does not include people tricking or hypnotizing me into believing I am there.

Suppose I present a certain argument to someone who believes (truly) that p, and he is convinced by it and comes to believe not-p. Look how easily he can be moved from believing p to believing not-p. Suppose it happens that I do not present the argument to him, so he does not start to believe not-p, and he continues to believe p. Does he know that p? Is it merely the case that his knowledge is insecure, or does such instability show it is not knowledge after all?

A skeptic might argue that for almost each p we (think we) know, there is an argument or happening that would get us to believe not-p even though p was true. We reply to this skeptic as before – the fact that some possible argument or happening would get us to believe not-p when p doesn't show that it is false that 4: if p were true then S would believe p and S wouldn't believe not-p. To show the falsity of 4, the skeptic would have to refer to something that might occur if p were true; if it wouldn't hold if p were true, what he refers to is irrelevant.

Among the arguments that get people to stop believing things are the skeptic's arguments themselves. These arguments often puzzle people, sometimes they get people to stop believing they know that p. They do not know that they know. Should we describe this as a case of people who first know that they know but who, after hearing the skeptic's arguments, no longer know that they know because they no longer believe that they know (and knowledge entails belief)? Our present view is that such people did not know that they knew that p, even before hearing the skeptic. For their previous belief that they knew that p would vary when it shouldn't, so it violates condition 4. Similarly, some people who never have heard the skeptic's arguments would (if they heard them) become convinced that they don't know that p. It is pleasant to grant the skeptic a partial victory after all, one gained by the plausibility of his arguments, not their cogency. Because of the skeptical arguments, some people would falsely believe they don't know that p, and these people do not know they know it. The existence of skeptical arguments makes one type of skeptical conclusion (that we don't know we know things) true of some people – those the shoe fits have been wearing it.

Meno claimed he could speak eloquently about virtue until Socrates, torpedolike, began to question him. He did not know what virtue was, for Socrates' questions uncovered Meno's previously existing confusions. Even if it had been a sophist's questions that bewildered Meno, getting him to believe the opposite, what he previously had would not have been knowledge. Knowledge should be made of sterner stuff.[35]

Thus, some skeptical arguments play off condition 3, others off condition 4. In addition to these conditions, our (full) account of knowledge formulates a condition about outweighing to cover the situation when multiple methods, not all satisfying 3 and 4, give rise to the belief. Do any skeptical arguments play off this outweighing condition? Here, presumably, would fit various attempts at unmasking the dominant sources of our belief as methods that do not track: faith, prejudice, self-interest, class-interest, deep psychological motives. The outweighing view involves subjunctives, but does anything here correspond to the skeptic's focusing upon a possibility that is so far out that it wouldn't occur, even if p were false? Perhaps the following is comparable. Recall that it was not necessary for the tracking method to win out against the combined opposed weight of all other methods; the person's belief merely had to vary with the verdict of the tracking method when the recommendations of every other way used to arrive at belief were held fixed. (It was only Case III in the chart that needed to be examined.) Any actual split in the verdict of nontracking methods will be welcome support. The skeptic should not load the other methods against what tracking recommends, any more than they actually are; to suppose more counts as too far out.

Some skeptical arguments play off condition 3, some off condition 4, some (perhaps) off the outweighing condition when multiple methods are involved. Still other skeptical arguments play off the methods themselves, off the fact that knowledge is gained via methods or ways of believing. In the situations when we are aware of what methods we are using, do we know we are using those methods? To decide whether we know this, according to condition 3 we must consider what we would believe if we weren't using the methods. Would we then still believe we were? If so, condition 3 is violated, and so we did not actually know we were using the methods.

Along this pathway lies trouble. For if we weren't using that method, the very method we use to track various facts – a situation we have to contemplate in applying condition 3 – who knows what we would believe about what methods we are using? That method M we are using to track various facts may be the very method via which we believe that we are using method M. This is likely if (and only if) M is described widely and deeply enough, for example, as the sum total of our (rational or effective) methods. But then, how are we to treat the question of what we would believe if we weren't using that method M, a question condition 3 pushes at us in order to decide if we know we are using M? "If I weren't using M, would I still believe I was?" What methods of believing am I left by this question? After all, condition 3 when fully formulated says: not-p and S, via M, comes to a belief about the truth of $p \rightarrow$ not-(S believes that p). And the method M of condition 3 is the very one said to be actually utilized, in condition 2: S believes, via M, that p.

Yet now we face the situation where S believes of himself that he is applying method M, via an application of method M itself;[36] moreover, in this situation the statement p, which we are trying to decide whether S knows, is: S is using method M. The result of substituting this p in the full condition 3 is: If S weren't using method M, and S, via using M, were to decide about the truth of "S is using method M" then S would not believe "S is using method M." But the antecedent of this subjunctive is supposing both that S is not using method M (this supposition is the not-p of the antecedent of condition 3) and that S is using method M (he uses this method in 3 to decide whether or not p, since that is the method via which, in condition 2, he actually believes p). We have no coherent way to understand this.[37]

Yet if we cannot simply include the use of method M in determining what S would believe if he were not using M, neither can we simply suppose (for the purposes of condition 3) that S is using some other method to arrive at a belief about this matter. We saw earlier, in considering a range of examples, the great importance of holding the method fixed in deciding questions about knowledge. Recall the grandmother who sees her grandson visit her and so believes he is healthy and ambulatory; yet if he weren't ambulatory, other relatives would tell her he was fine to spare

her anxiety and upset. She sees her grandson walking; does she know he is ambulatory? According to condition 3 we must ask what she would believe if he weren't ambulatory. If the method via which she believes is not held fixed, the answer will be wrong. True, if he weren't ambulatory, she would then believe he was (via hearing about him from other relatives). But the relevant question is: what would she believe if he weren't ambulatory and (as before) she saw him and spoke to him. Thus, to reach the correct answer about her knowledge, the method must be held fixed – that is one of the reasons why we introduced explicit reference to the method or way of believing.

How then are we to treat the question of whether the person knows he is using method M, when he believes he is via that very method M? If he knows he is, then his belief that he is tracks the fact that he is, and varies with that fact. To determine whether it so varies, we must look to the question of what he would believe if p were false, that is, if he weren't using method M. How are we to understand this question? It seems we must hold fixed the method M via which he believes, in order to reach the correct answer about knowledge (as is shown by the case of the grandmother), and that we cannot hold the method M fixed, for then we have the (apparently) incoherent supposition that he is applying the method to the situation where he is not using it, in order to determine whether or not he is – and this supposes that he both is and isn't using the method.

This problem does not arise when we know via another method that we are using some particular method; it arises only for our knowledge of our use of our deepest methods, though not for shallower specifications of these methods in specific instances. Still, what should we say about our knowledge of these deepest methods or of the conditions in which we apply them. Do you know you are rational, do you know you are sane? If you were irrational or insane, mightn't you think you were rational and sane? Yes, but not by applying methods under (fixed) conditions of rationality and sanity. We cannot conclude simply that condition 3 is not satisfied so you don't know you are rational or sane; for that condition is not satisfied only when the method is allowed to vary. It would be best to be able coherently to discover whether or not that method is being used. I can use M to discover whether you are using M (if you weren't, I wouldn't believe, via M, that you were), or whether I was using M in the past (if I hadn't been, I wouldn't now believe, via M, that I had been). The difficulty is to make sense of saying that M, if currently used, would detect that it was not being used (if it weren't). And while I do not think this simply is incoherent, neither is it pellucidly clear.[38]

Questions about knowing one is rational or sane need not depend on varying the method used. If what we have to go on as we apply methods is the appearance of rationality and sanity, then mightn't we appear sane and rational to ourselves even if we are not? So how do we know we are? We do have more to go on than how we appear to ourselves; there also is the agreement with others. Let us leave aside the possibility that all those others also might be insane and irrational, or be engaged in a plot to convince me (falsely) that I was rational and sane. Neither of these is what (actually) would or might occur if I weren't rational or sane. Might an insane and irrational person also be mistaken about whether others are agreeing with him, though, interpreting their disagreement as concord? If a person were insane or irrational in this way then others would appear (to him) to agree with him, and so he would appear sane and rational to himself. Things would appear qualitatively indistinguishable to him from the situation where he rationally and sanely judges the world. There appears to be no shift in method here, at least insofar as how using the method is experienced internally by the user. Do you know, then, that you are not in that particular skeptical situation SK? Perhaps not, but (as before) from our not knowing that particular not-SK it does not follow that we don't know other things, including that we are being sane and rational in particular situations in particular ways. For if we weren't, we wouldn't believe we were; if we weren't then sane and rational in those particular ways, what would or might obtain is not this skeptic's possibility SK. These points emerge even more clearly if we consider positions skeptical not about (almost) all knowledge in general, but about particular kinds of knowledge.

Notes

1 Despite some demurrals in the literature, there is general agreement that conditions 1 and 2 are necessary for knowledge. (For some recent discussions, see D. M. Armstrong, *Belief, Truth and Knowledge* (Cambridge: Cambridge University Press, 1973), ch. 10; Keith Lehrer, *Knowledge* (Oxford: Oxford University Press, 1974), chs. 2, 3.) I shall take for granted that this is so, without wishing to place very much weight on its being belief that is the precise cognitive attitude (as opposed to thinking it so, accepting the statement, and so on) or on the need to introduce truth as opposed to formulating the first condition simply as: p.

   I should note that our procedure here does not stem from thinking that every illuminating discussion of an important philosophical notion must present (individually) necessary and (jointly) sufficient conditions.

2 Below, we discuss further the case where though the fact that p causes the person's belief that p, he would believe it anyway, even if it were not true. I should note here that I assume bivalence throughout this chapter, and consider only statements that are true if and only if their negations are false.

3 See Robert Stalnaker, "A Theory of Conditionals," in N. Rescher (ed.), *Studies in Logical Theory* (Oxford: Basil Blackwell, 1968); David Lewis, *Counterfactuals* (Cambridge: Harvard University Press, 1973); and Jonathan Bennett's critical review of Lewis, "Counterfactuals and Possible Worlds," *Canadian Journal of Philosophy* IV, 2 (Dec. 1974), pp. 381–402.

   Our purposes require, for the most part, no more than an intuitive understanding of subjunctives. However, it is most convenient to examine here some further issues, which will be used once or twice later. Lewis's account has the consequence that $p \rightarrow q$ whenever p and q are both true; for the possible world where p is true that is closest to the actual world is the actual world itself, and in that world q is true. We might try to remedy this by saying that when p is true, $p \rightarrow q$ is true if and only if q is true in all p worlds closer (by the metric) to the actual world than is any not-p world. When p is false, the usual accounts hold that $p \to q$ is true when q holds merely in the closest p worlds to the actual world. This is too weak, but how far out must one go among the p worlds? A suggestion parallel to the previous one is: out until one reaches another not-p world (still further out). So if q holds in the closest p world w_1 but not in the p world w_2, even though no not-p world lies between w_1 and w_2, then (under the suggestion we are considering) the subjunctive is false. A unified account can be offered for subjunctives, whatever the truth value of their antecedents. The p neighborhood of the actual world A is the closest p band to it; that is, w is in the p neighborhood of the actual world if and only if p is true in w and there are no worlds $w^{\bar{p}}$ and w^p such that not-p is true in $w^{\bar{p}}$ and p is true in w^p, and $w^{\bar{p}}$ is closer to A than w is to A, and w^p is at least as close to A as $w^{\bar{p}}$ is to A. A subjunctive $p \to q$ is true if and only if q is true throughout the p neighborhood of the actual world.

If it is truly a random matter which slit a photon goes through, then its going through (say) the right slit does not establish the subjunctive: if a photon were fired at that time from that source it would go through the right-hand slit. For when p equals A photon is fired at that time from that source, and q equals the photon goes through the right-hand slit, q is not true everywhere in the p neighborhood of the actual world.

This view of subjunctives within a possible-worlds framework is inadequate if there is no discrete p band of the actual world, as when for each positive distance from the actual world A, there are both p worlds and not-p worlds so distant. Even if this last is not generally so, many p worlds that interest us may have their distances from A matched by not-p worlds. Therefore, let us redefine the relevant p band as the closest spread of p worlds such that there is no not-p world intermediate in distance from A to two p worlds in the spread unless there is also another p world in the spread the very same distance from A. By definition, it is only p worlds in the p band, but some not-p worlds may be equidistant from A.

Though this emendation allows us to speak of the closest spread of p worlds, it no longer is so clear which worlds in this p band subjunctives (are to) encompass. We have said it is not sufficient for the truth of $p \to q$ that q hold in that one world in the p band closest to the actual world. Is it necessary, as our first suggestion has it, that q hold in all the p worlds in the closest p band to the actual world? Going up until the first "pure" stretch of not-p worlds is no longer as natural a line to draw as when we imagined "pure" p neighborhoods. Since there already are some not-p worlds the same distance from A as some members of the p band, what is the special significance of the first unsullied not-p stretch? There seems to be no natural line, though, coming before this stretch yet past the first p world. Perhaps nothing stronger can be said than this: $p \to q$ when q holds for some distance out in the closest p band to the actual world, that is, when all the worlds in this first part of that closest p band are q. The distance need not be fixed as the same for all subjunctives, although various general formulas might be imagined, for example, that the distance is a fixed percentage of the width of the p band.

I put forth this semantics for subjunctives in a possible-worlds framework with some diffidence, having little inclination to pursue the details. Let me emphasize, though, that this semantics does not presuppose any realist view that all possible worlds obtain. I would hope that into this chapter's subjunctively formulated theoretical structure can be plugged (without too many modifications) whatever theory of subjunctives turns out to be adequate, so that the theory of knowledge we formulate is not sensitive to variations in the analysis of subjunctives. In addition to Lewis and Stalnaker cited above, see Ernest W. Adams, *The Logic of Conditionals* (Dordrecht: Reidel, 1975); John Pollock, *Subjunctive Reasoning* (Dordrecht: Reidel, 1976); J. H. Sobel, "Probability, Chance and Choice" (unpublished book manuscript); and a forthcoming book by Yigal Kvart.

4   If the possible-worlds formalism is used to represent counterfactuals and subjunctives,

the relevant worlds are not those p worlds that are closest or most similar to the actual world, unless the measure of closeness or similarity is: what would obtain if p were true. Clearly, this cannot be used to explain when subjunctives hold true, but it can be used to represent them. Compare utility theory which represents preferences but does not explain them. Still, it is not a trivial fact that preferences are so structured that they can be represented by a real-valued function, unique up to a positive linear transformation, even though the representation (by itself) does not explain these preferences. Similarly, it would be of interest to know what properties hold of distance metrics which serve to represent subjunctives, and to know how subjunctives must be structured and interrelated so that they can be given a possible worlds representation. (With the same one space serving for all subjunctives?)

One further word on this point. Imagine a library where a cataloguer assigns call numbers based on facts of sort F. Someone, perhaps the cataloguer, then places each book on the shelf by looking at its call number, and inserting it between the two books whose call numbers are most nearly adjacent to its own. The call number is derivative from facts of type F, yet it plays some explanatory role, not merely a representational one. "Why is this book located precisely there? Because of its number." Imagine next another library where the person who places books on the shelves directly considers facts of type F, using them to order the books and to interweave new ones. Someone else might notice that this ordering can be represented by an assignment of numbers, numbers, from which other information can be derived as well, for example, the first letter of the last name of the principal author. But such an assigned number is no explanation of why a book in this library is located between two others (or why its author's last name begins with a certain letter). I have assumed that utility numbers stand to preferences, and closeness or similarity measures stand to subjunctives, as the call numbers do to the books, and to the facts of type F they exhibit, in the second library.

5   G. C. Stine, "Skepticism, Relevant Alternatives and Deductive Closure," *Philosophical Studies* 29 (1976), p. 252, who attributes the example to Carl Ginet.

6   This last remark is a bit too brisk, for that account might use a subjunctive criterion for when an alternative q to p is relevant (namely, when if p were not to hold, q would or might), and utilize some further notion of what it is to rule out relevant alternatives (for example, have evidence against them), so that it did not turn out to be equivalent to the account we offer.

7   More accurately, since the truth of antecedent and consequent is not necessary for the truth of the subjunctive either, 4 says something different from 1 and 2.

8   I experimented with some other conditions which adequately handled this as well as some other problem cases, but they succumbed to further difficulties. Though much can be learned from applying those conditions, presenting all the details would engage only the most masochistic readers. So I simply will list them, each at one time a candidate to stand alone in place of condition 4.

(a)   S believes that not-$p \rightarrow$ not-p.
(b)   S believes that not-$p \rightarrow$ not-p or it is through some other method that S believes not-p. (Methods are discussed in the next section.)
(c)   (S believes p or S believes not-p) $\rightarrow$ not-(S believes p, and not-p holds) and not-(S believes not-p, and p holds).
(d)   not-(S believes that p) $\rightarrow$ not-(p and S believes that not-p).
(e)   not-(p and S believes that p) $\rightarrow$ not-(not-p and S believes that p or p and S believes that not-p).

9   Gilbert Harman, *Thought* (Princeton: Princeton, University Press, 1973), ch. 9, pp. 142–54.

10   What if the situation or world where he too hears the later false denials is not so close, so easily occurring? Should we say that everything that prevents his hearing the denial easily could have not happened, and does not in some close world?

11   This reformulation introduces an apparent asymmetry between the consequents of conditions 3 and 4. Since we have rewritten 4 as

$p \rightarrow$ S believes that p and not-(S believes that not-p),
why is 3 not similarly rewritten as
not-$p \rightarrow$ not-(S believes that p) and S believes that not-p?

It is knowledge that p we are analyzing, rather than knowledge that not-p. Knowledge that p involves a stronger relation to p than to not-p. Thus, we did not first write the third condition for knowledge of p as: not-$p \rightarrow$ S believes that not-p; also the following is not true: S knows that $p \rightarrow$ (not-$p \rightarrow$ S knows that not-p).

Imagine that someone S knows whether or not p, but it is not yet clear to us which he knows, whether he knows that p or knows that not-p. Still, merely given that S knows that————, we can say:

not-$p \rightarrow$ not-(S believes that p)
$p \rightarrow$ not-(S believes that not-p).

Now when the blank is filled in, either with p or with not-p, we have to add S's believing it to the consequent of the subjunctive that begins with it. That indicates which one he knows. Thus, when it is p that he knows, we have to add to the consequent of the second subjunctive (the subjunctive that begins with p): S believes that p. We thereby transform the second subjunctive into:

$p \rightarrow$ not-(S believes that not-p) and S believes that p.

Except for a rearrangement of which is written first in the consequent, this is condition 4. Knowledge that p especially tracks p, and this special focus on p (rather than not-p) gets expressed in the subjunctive, not merely in the second condition.

There is another apparent asymmetry in the antecedents of the two subjunctives 3 and 4, not due to the reformulation. When actually p is true and S believes that p, condition 4 looks some distance out in the p neighborhood of the actual world, while condition 3 looks some distance out in the not-p neighborhood, which itself is farther away from the actual world than the p neighborhood.

Why not have both conditions look equally far, revising condition 3 to require merely that the closest world in which p is false yet S believes that p be some distance from the actual world. It then would parallel condition 4, which says that the closest world in which p yet p is not believed is some distance away from the actual world. Why should condition 3 look farther from the actual world than condition 4 does?

However, despite appearances, both conditions look at distance symmetrically. The asymmetry is caused by the fact that the actual world, being a p world, is not symmetrical between p and not-p. Condition 3 says that in the closest not-p world, not-(S believes that p), and that this "not-(S believes that p)" goes out through the first part of the not-p neighborhood of the actual world. Condition 4 says that in the closest p world, S believes that p, and that this "S believes that p" goes out through the first part of the p neighborhood of the actual world. Thus the two conditions are symmetrical; the different distances to which they extend stems not from an asymmetry in the conditions but from one in the actual world – it being (asymmetrically) p.

12 D. M. Armstrong, *Belief, Truth and Knowledge* (Cambridge: Cambridge University Press, 1973), p. 209; he attributes the case to Gregory O'Hair.

13 Some may hold the father is made more sure in his belief by courtroom proof; and hold that the father knows because his degree of assurance (though not his belief) varies subjunctively with the truth.

14 If there is no other such method M_1 via which S believes that p, the second clause is vacuously true.

Should we say that no other method used outweighs M, or that M outweighs all others? Delicate questions arise about situations where the methods tie, so that no subjunctive holds about one always winning over the other. It might seem that we should require that M outweigh (and not merely tie) the other methods; but certain ways of resolving the ties, such as not randomly deciding but keeping judgment suspended, might admit knowledge when a true belief is arrived at via a tracking method M which is not outweighed yet also doesn't (always) outweigh the others present. There is no special need to pursue the details here; the outweighing condition should be read here and below as a vague one, residing somewhere in the (closed) interval between "outweighs" and "not outweighed", but not yet precisely located. This vagueness stands independently of the refinements pursued in the text immediately below.

15 When a belief is overdetermined or jointly produced by three methods, where only the first satisfies conditions 3 and 4, the question becomes: what does the person believe when M_1 recommends believing not-p while the two others each recommend believing p? Notice also that in speaking of what would happen in Case III we are imposing a subjunctive condition; if there is no "would" about it, if in each instance of a Case III situation it is determined at random which method outweighs which, then that will not be sufficient for knowledge, even though sometimes M_1 wins out.

It is worrisome that in weakening our initial description of outweighing by looking to Case III but not to Case II, we seem to give more weight to condition 3 for tracking than to condition 4. So we should be ready to reconsider this weakening.

16 For example, in the case of the father who believes on faith that his son is innocent and sees the courtroom demonstration of innocence, does the father use two methods, faith and courtroom demonstration, the second of which does satisfy conditions 3–4 while the first (which outweighs it) does not satisfy 3–4; or does the father use only one method which doesn't satisfy 3–4, namely: believe about one's son whatever the method of faith tells one, and only if it yields no answer, believe the result of courtroom demonstration? With either mode of individuation, knowledge requires the negative existentially quantified statement (that there is no method …) somewhere, whether in specifying the method itself or in specifying that it is not outweighed.

17 One suspects there will be some gimmick whereby whenever p is truly believed a trivial

method M can be specified which satisfies conditions 3 and 4. If so, then further conditions will have to be imposed upon M, in addition to the dispositional condition. Compare the difficulties encountered in the literature on specifying the relevant reference class in probabilistic inference and explanation; see Henry Kyburg, *Probability and the Logic of Rational Belief* (Middletown: Wesleyan University Press, 1961), ch. 9; C. G. Hempel, *Aspects of Scientific Explanation* (New York: Free Press, 1965), pp. 394–405; also his "Maximal Specificity and Lawlikeness in Probabilistic Explanation," *Philosophy of Science* 35 (1968), pp. 116–33.

18 See Ludwig Wittgenstein, *On Certainty* (Oxford: Basil Blackwell, 1969), 83, 94, 102–10, 140–4, 151–2, 162–3, 166, 411, 419, 472–5.

19 There is an immense amount of literature concerning skepticism. See, for example, Sextus Empiricus, *Writings* (4 vols, Loeb Classical Library, Cambridge: Harvard University Press); Richard Popkin, *History of Skepticism from Erasmus to Descartes* (rev. edn, New York: Humanities Press, 1964); Arne Naess, *Skepticism* (New York: Humanities Press, 1968); René Descartes, *Meditations on First Philosophy* (New York: Liberal Arts Press, 1960); G. E. Moore, "Proof of an External World," "Four Forms of Scepticism," and "Certainty," this vol., chs 2, 3 and 4, and "A Defense of Common Sense," in his *Philosophical Papers* (Allen and Unwin, London, 1959); J. L. Austin, "Other Minds" in his *Philosophical Papers* (Oxford University Press, 1961); Wittgenstein, *On Certainty*; Keith Lehrer, "Why Not Skepticism?" (in Swain and Pappas (eds), *Essays on Knowledge and Justification*, pp. 346–63); Peter Unger, *Ignorance* (Oxford University Press, 1975), pp. 7–24; Michael Slote, *Reason and Skepticism* (London: Allen and Unwin, 1970); Roderick Firth, "The Anatomy of Certainty," *Philosophical Review* 76 (1967), pp. 3–27; Thompson Clarke, "The Legacy of Skepticism," *Journal of Philosophy* 69 (1972), pp. 754–69; Stanley Cavell, *The Claim of Reason* (Oxford University Press, 1979).

20 From the perspective of explanation rather than proof, the extensive philosophical discussion, deriving from Charles S. Peirce, of

whether the skeptic's doubts are real is beside the point. The problem of explaining how knowledge is possible would remain the same, even if no one ever claimed to doubt that there was knowledge.

21 Subjunctives with actually false antecedents and actually true consequents have been termed by Goodman *semi-factuals. R* is the semi-factual: not-$p \rightarrow$ S believes p.

22 Should one weaken condition 3, so that the account of knowledge merely denies the opposed subjunctive *R*? That would give us: not-(not-$p \rightarrow$ S believes p). This holds when 3 does not, in situations where if p were false, S might believe p, and also might not believe it. The extra strength of 3 is needed to exclude these as situations of knowledge.

23 Though it does show the falsity of the corresponding entailment, "not-p entails not-(S believes that p)."

24 If a person is to know that SK doesn't hold, then condition 3 for knowledge must be satisfied (with "SK doesn't hold" substituted for p). Thus, we get

(3) not-(SK doesn't hold) $\rightarrow$ not-(S believes that SK doesn't hold).

Simplifying the antecedent, we have

(3) SK holds $\rightarrow$ not-(S believes that SK doesn't hold).

The skeptic has chosen a situation SK such that the following is true of it:

SK holds $\rightarrow$ S believes that SK doesn't hold.

Having the same antecedent as 3 and a contradictory consequent, this is incompatible with 3. Thus, condition 3 is not satisfied by the person's belief that SK does not hold.

25 Descartes presumably would refute the tank hypothesis as he did the demon hypothesis, through a proof of the existence of a good God who would not allow anyone, demon or psychologist, permanently to deceive us. The philosophical literature has concentrated on the question of whether Descartes can prove this (without begging the question against

the demon hypothesis). The literature has not discussed whether even a successful proof of the existence of a good God can help Descartes to conclude he is not almost always mistaken. Might not a good God have his own reasons for deceiving us; might he not deceive us temporarily – a period which includes all of our life thus far (but not an afterlife)? To the question of why God did not create us so that we never would make any errors, Descartes answers that the motives of God are inscrutable to us. Do we know that such an inscrutable God could not be motivated to allow another powerful "demon" to deceive and dominate us?

Alternatively, could not such a good God be motivated to deceive itself temporarily, even if not another? (Compare the various Indian doctrines designed to explain our ignorance of our own true nature, that is, Atman-Brahman's or, on another theory, the purusha's nature.) Whether from playfulness or whatever motive, such a good God would temporarily deceive itself, perhaps even into thinking it is a human being living in a material realm. Can we know, via Descartes' argument, that this is not our situation? And so forth.

These possibilities, and others similar, are so obvious that some other explanation, I mean the single-minded desire to refute skepticism, must be given for why they are not noticed and discussed.

Similarly, one could rescrutinize the *cogito* argument. Can "I think" only be produced by something that exists? Suppose Shakespeare had written for Hamlet the line, "I think, therefore I am," or a fiction is written in which a character named Descartes says this, or suppose a character in a dream of mine says this; does it follow that they exist? Can someone use the cogito argument to prove he himself is not a fictional or dream character? Descartes asked how he could know he wasn't dreaming; he also should have asked how he could know he wasn't dreamed. See further my fable "Fiction," *Ploughshares* 6, 3 (Oct. 1980).

26 I say almost everything, because there still could be some true beliefs such as "I exist." More limited skeptical possibilities present

worlds doxically identical to the actual world in which almost every belief of a certain sort is false, for example, about the past, or about other people's mental states.

27   Let w_1 ..., w_n be worlds doxically identical to the actual world for S. He doesn't know he is not in w_1, he doesn't know he is not in w_2 ...; does it follow that he doesn't know he is in the actual world w_A or in one very much like it (in its truths)? Not if the situation he would be in if the actual world w_A did not obtain wasn't one of the doxically identical worlds; if the world that then would obtain would show its difference from the actual one w_A, he then would not believe he was in w_A.

However, probably there are some worlds not very different from the actual world (in that they have mostly the same truths) and even doxically identical to it, which might obtain if w_A did not. In that case, S would not know he was in w_A specified in all its glory. But if we take the disjunction of these harmless worlds (insofar as drastic skeptical conclusions go) doxically identical with w_A then S will know that the disjunction holds. For if it didn't, he would notice that.

28   This argument proceeds from the fact that floating in the tank is incompatible with being at X. Another form of the skeptic's argument, one we shall consider later, proceeds from the fact that floating in the tank is incompatible with knowing you are at X (or almost anything else).

29   Note that I am not denying that Kp & K(p ≺ q) → Believes q.

30   Here again I assume a limited readership, and ignore possibilities such as those described in James Blish, *Cities in Flight*.

31   Thus, the following is not a deductively valid form of inference.

$p \prec q$ (and S knows this)
not-$p \to$ not-(S believes that p)
Therefore, not-$q \to$ not-(S believes that q).

Furthermore, the example in the text shows that even the following is not a deductively valid form of inference.

$p \prec q$ (and S knows this)
not-$p \to$ not-(S believes that p)
Therefore, not-$q \to$ not-(S believes that p).

Nor is this one deductively valid:

$p \prec q$
not-$q \to r$
Therefore, not-$p \to r$.

32   Does this same consequence of nonclosure under known logical implication follow as well from condition 4: $p \to$ S believes that p? When p is not actually true, condition 4 can hold of p yet not of a q known to be entailed by p. For example, let p be the (false) statement that I am in Antarctica, and let q be the disjunction of p with some other appropriate statement; for example, let q be the statement that I am in Antarctica or I lost some object yesterday though I have not yet realized it. If p were true I would know it, p entails q, yet if q were true I wouldn't know it, for the way it would be true would be by my losing some object without yet realizing it, and if that happened I would not know it.

This example to show that condition 4 is not closed under known logical implication depends on the (actual) falsity of p. I do not think there is any suitable example to show this in the case where p is true, leaving aside the trivial situation when the person simply does not infer the entailed statement q.

33   Suppose some component of the condition, call it C', also speaks of some cases when p is false, and when q is false; might it then provide "varies with," even though C' is preserved under known logical implication, and is transmitted from p to q when p entails q and is known to entail q? If this condition C' speaks of some cases where not-p and of some cases where not-q, then C' will be preserved under known logical implication if, when those cases of not-p satisfy it, and p entails q, then also those cases of not-q satisfy it. Thus, C' seems to speak of something as preserved from some cases of not-p to some cases of not-p, which is preservation in the reverse direction to the entailment involving these, from not-q to not-p. Thus, a condition that is preserved under known logical implication and that also provides some measure of "varies with" must contain a component condition saying that something interesting (other than falsity) is preserved in the direction opposite to the

logical implication (for some cases); and moreover, that component itself must be preserved in the direction of the logical implication because the condition including it is. It would be interesting to see such a condition set out.

34 Reading an earlier draft of this chapter, friends pointed out to me that Fred Dretske already had defended the view that knowledge (as one among many epistemic concepts) is not closed under known logical implication. (See his "Epistemic Operators," *Journal of Philosophy* 67 (1970), pp. 1007–23, ch. 19 in this vol.) Furthermore, Dretske presented a subjunctive condition for knowledge (in his "Conclusive Reason," *Australasian Journal of Philosophy* 49, (1971), pp. 1–22), holding that S knows that *p* on the basis of reasons *R* only if: *R* would not be the case unless *p* were the case. Here Dretske ties the evidence subjunctively to the fact, and the belief based on the evidence subjunctively to the fact through the evidence. (Our account of knowledge has not yet introduced or discussed evidence or reasons at all. While this condition corresponds to our condition 3, he has nothing corresponding to 4.) So Dretske has hold of both pieces of our account, subjunctive and nonclosure, and he even connects them in a passing footnote (*Journal of Philosophy* 67, p. 1019, n. 4), noticing that any account of knowledge that relies on a subjunctive conditional will not be closed under known logical implication. Dretske also has the notion of a relevant alternative as "one that might have been realized in the existing circumstances if the actual state of affairs had not materialized" (p. 1021), and he briefly applies all this to the topic of skepticism (pp. 1015–16), holding that the skeptic is right about some things but not about others.

It grieves me somewhat to discover that Dretske also had all this, and was there first. It raises the question, also, of why these views have not yet had the proper impact. Dretske makes his points in the midst of much other material, some of it less insightful. The independent statement and delineation of the position here, without the background noise, I hope will make clear its many merits.

After Goldman's paper on a causal theory of knowledge (in *Journal of Philosophy* 64

(1967)), an idea then already "in the air," it required no great leap to consider subjunctive conditions. Some two months after the first version of this chapter was written, Goldman himself published a paper on knowledge utilizing counterfactuals ("Discrimination and Perceptual Knowledge," *Journal of philosophy* 78 (1976), pp. 771–91), also talking of relevant possibilities (without using the counterfactuals to identify which possibilities are relevant); and Shope's survey article has called my attention to a paper of L. S. Carrier ("An Analysis of Empirical Knowledge," *Southern Journal of Philosophy* 9 (1971), pp. 3–11) that also used subjunctive conditions including our condition 3. Armstrong's reliability view of knowledge (*Belief, Truth and Knowledge*, pp. 166, 169) involved a lawlike connection between the belief that *p* and the state of affairs that makes it true. Clearly, the idea is one whose time has come.

35 Is it a consequence of our view that of two people who know *p*, each believing he knows *p* and satisfying condition 3 for knowing he knows *p*, one may know he knows and the other not, because (although identical in all other respects) the second might encounter skeptical arguments while the first somehow lives hermetically sealed from the merest brush with them?

36 Our task now is not to wonder whether it is legitimate to use *M* to reach a belief that *M* is being used. What, after all, is the alternative? Presumably, an infinite regress of methods, or a circle, or reaching a method which is used but either is not believed to be used, or is believed to be though not via any method or way of believing.

37 Similar questions arise about our knowledge of other statements such that if they were false, we would not be using the methods via which we know they are true, for example, "there are eyes," "I am alive," "I am sentient," perhaps "I sometimes am tracking something."

38 Should we say for these cases discussed in the text that condition 3 does not apply, so that, as in the previous case of necessary truths, the whole weight of tracking devolves upon condition 4? The issue then simply turns on whether in similar situations where the person uses method *M*, he also would believe he does.

CHAPTER 22

How to Defeat Opposition to Moore

Ernest Sosa

What modal relation must a fact bear to a belief in order for this belief to constitute knowledge of that fact? Externalists have proposed various answers, including some that combine externalism with contextualism. We shall find that various forms of externalism share a modal conception of "sensitivity" open to serious objections. Fortunately, the undeniable intuitive attractiveness of this conception can be explained through an easily confused but far preferable notion of "safety." The denouement of our reflections, finally, will be to show how replacing sensitivity with safety makes it possible to defend plain Moorean common sense against the spurious advantages over it claimed by skeptical, tracking, relevant-alternative, and contextualist accounts.

A

A belief by S that p is "sensitive" iff were it not so that p, S would not believe that p. This concept is important in a line of thought developed by Dretske, Nozick, and DeRose, among others, each in his own way. It enables the following requirement.

> *Sensitivity* In order to constitute knowledge a belief must be sensitive.

Originally published in *Philosophical Perspectives* 13, Epistemology (1999), pp. 141–53.

(That the subject's belief be sensitive is sometimes required rather for correct *attribution* to that subject of corresponding "knowledge." Although we shall take little further notice of this formulation, much of what follows could be recast in its terms.)

An "alternative" to a proposition is any incompatible possibility. (Among the truths only the contingent have alternatives, since no "possibility" can be incompatible with a necessary truth.) To "rule out" such an alternative is to know that it is not the case. The following principle of exclusion now seems plausible:

> PE In order to know a fact P one must rule out (i.e., know to be false) every alternative that one knows to be incompatible with it.

That creates a problem for the sensitivity requirement. My belief that

(o)   here is a hand

might constitute knowledge even though my belief that

(~h)   I am not now fooled by a demon into believing incorrectly that here is a hand

is not sensitive, despite my knowing that <o> entails <~h>. But if my belief of <~h> is not sensitive, then the sensitivity requirement precludes my knowing <~h>, and precludes thereby my ruling out <h>, which, in combination with PE, precludes in turn my knowing <o>. Advocates of the "relevant alternatives" approach, relevantists, take this in stride by rejecting principle PE in its full generality. Instead they propose this:

> PE-rel In order to know a fact P one must rule out every *relevant* alternative that one knows to be incompatible with it.

Thus one might know that (o) here is a hand, despite being unable to rule out the hypothetical possibility that (h) one is being fooled by a demon, etc.; or so say relevantists. Replacing PE with PE-rel enables them to reject the demand to exclude alternative <h>, if they can marginalize that alternative as irrelevant. What then is the difference between relevant and irrelevant alternatives? What makes an alternative irrelevant? No answer is generally accepted, even among relevantists, and the notion of relevance remains obscure, no published account having yet much relieved this darkness. (I do not expect relevance theorists to disagree radically with this estimate; one thinker's debilitating drawback is another's challenging open problem, to be resolved in due course.)

Here is an alternative approach.

> Call a belief by S that p "safe" iff: S would believe that p only if it were so that p. (Alternatively, a belief by S that p is "safe" iff: S would not believe that p without it being the case that p; or, better, iff: as a matter of fact, though perhaps not as a matter of strict necessity, not easily would S believe that p without it being the case that p.)

Safety   In order to (be said correctly to) constitute knowledge a belief must be safe (rather than sensitive).

While akin to *Sensitivity*, *Safety* has important advantages.[1]

Principle PE, for example, does not give *Safety* the problem we saw it give *Sensitivity*. Suppose the belief <o> above to be a *safe* belief, and consider the paired skeptical proposition <~h> that one knows to be entailed by <o>. Although one's belief of <~h> is clearly not sensitive, it does seem

quite safe. In other words, unlike sensitivity, safety is preserved under this known entailment. No belief constitutes knowledge unless safe, we may now say, while leaving ourselves free to exclude such skeptical scenarios that we know to be incompatible with something we know. If you know that p, and you know that some such scenario <h> is necessarily incompatible with <o>, you are not precluded by the safety requirement from knowledgeably excluding that scenario.

Replacing the sensitivity requirement with the safety requirement may thus enable a unary conditionals-theoretic account of knowledge in need of no distinction between relevant and irrelevant alternatives. (This counters some at least of the rationale for the relevant alternatives tack.)

B.   The Skeptic Answered: Moore, Nozick, and DeRose

What follows will explore sensitivity-based opposition to plain Moorean common sense. We shall find that several of the most striking attacks on plainness rest essentially, in one way or other, on some assumed requirement of sensitivity. Replacing sensitivity with safety would in one stroke undercut all such attacks.

First some abbreviations:

> h   I am a handless brain in a vat being fed experiences as if I were normally embodied and situated.
> o   I now have hands.

Here now is the skeptic's "argument from ignorance" AI:

1.   I do not know that not-h.
2.   If 1, then c (below).
c.   I do not know that o.

That lays out the skeptic's stance. G. E. Moore for his part grants the skeptic premise 2, but rejects C and therefore 1. Nozick's stance is different. Like Moore, he rejects C. Like the skeptic, he affirms 1. So he must reject 2, which he does aided by his independently supported account of knowledge as tracking. Tracking is in fact not preserved by entailment, nor even by known entailment. One can perfectly well track a fact P and yet fail to track a fact Q that one knows to be entailed by P.

We already have an example: I know that O (above) entails not-H; but I track the former without tracking the latter.[2] It is not only Nozick who rejects closure under known entailment; so does the relevantist, for whom in order to know some fact X you need not know, and often cannot know, the negation of an alternative known to be incompatible with X, so long as it is not a "relevant" alternative.

Nozick's account implies a conjunction found "abominable" (one that would of course be no less "abominable" when derived from the relevant alternatives approach): namely, that I know O without knowing not-H.[3] Despite rejecting the account for that reason, DeRose draws from it a key concept for his own contextualist response to the skeptic, that of sensitivity. Again, one's belief of <p> is sensitive if, and only if, were it not so that p, one would not believe it. My belief that here before me now is a hand is a sensitive belief, since: did I *not* now have a hand before me, I would not believe that I did.[4]

To that the contextualist response now joins a second key concept, that of the "strength of one's epistemic position." One's epistemic position with respect to P is stronger the more remote are the least remote possibilities wherein one's belief as to whether p does not match the fact of that matter.[5]

These two concepts enable a distinctive response to argument AI. It is not enough, we are told, just to select some consistent stance on the three propositions involved: thus the Moorean stance, or the skeptic's, or Nozick's or that of relevant alternatives. Whatever stance one selects, a proper treatment of the paradox will require one to explain also why the argument is as plausible as it is.[6] In particular, one will need to explain why it is that the skeptic's premise 1 is so plausible. This requirement the Mooreans have not met. Nor has Nozick properly explained the appeal of his rejected premise, premise 2, which one can reject only at the cost of denying the closure of knowledge under known entailment (and deduction).

DeRose meets that explanatory requirement through his new contextualism, according to which S is correctly attributed knowledge that O only if S's belief of O is strong enough by the operative standards. And how strong is "strong enough"? What sets the threshold in any given context? One crucial consideration is a certain salience in that context of some proposition H which one must knowledgeably rule out in order to know O. In a context with H thus salient, S can be said correctly to "know" O only if S would avoid belief/fact mismatch re O up to and including the least remote possibilities where H (and not just not-O) is the case. But in the skeptic's scenario H, S would go wrong both in believing not-H and in believing O.[7]

Compatibly, it may still be true to say in *ordinary* contexts that one "knows" O: there one is at least free of any skeptical challenge. In such contexts more relaxed standards allow one an epistemic position strong enough to render true the claim to "know" O. For it is now required only that one avoid belief/fact mismatch strongly enough to make one's belief sensitive: i.e., one that would be right in any possibility up to and including the least remote possibilities in which O was false.

Recall the skeptic's "argument from ignorance" AI:

1. I do not know that not-h.
2. If 1, then c (below).
c. I do not know that o.

Three main positions have been adopted here:

Skeptic:	1, 2, c
Nozick, et al.:	1, ~c, ~2
Moore:	2, ~c, ~1

(Where Nozick represents those who deny closure under known entailment, which, again, includes those who opt for "relevant alternatives.") DeRose has something interestingly fresh to say about this dialectic by in effect distinguishing whether an argument is sound in itself, as an abstract argument, from whether it would be sound to endorse it.[8] An argument might be endorsed in any of at least three ways: (a) by public affirmation, (b) by conscious and occurrent thought, and (c) by implicit belief. DeRose's contextualism implies that Moore's argument could not correctly be endorsed at least in ways a and b, and perhaps not in way c either. However, this does not affect the soundness of the argument when unendorsed.

The unutterable soundness of Moore's argument is subtly interesting and quite similar to the unutterable truth of "I am silent." It may enable a fascinatingly attractive position on the skeptical paradox. According to DeRose's contextualism, the Moorean combination (2, ~c, ~1) may be the abstractly sound argument, as compared with its rival arguments favored respectively by Nozick and the skeptic; but it can remain so only at the cost of being unuttered and unthought.[9] Moore's position may hence be correct but unendorsable. If one must take a position on the paradox, one of the three laid out as the skeptic's, Nozick's, and Moore's, then the right option is rather the skeptic's. For DeRose it is only the skeptic's position that is ever endorsable, in whatever context, inasmuch as the very endorsing of that position so changes the context as to make its endorsement correct.[10]

C. There's A Better Way

1. Sensitivity not necessary for knowledge

The "sensitivity" of a belief that p – that were it not so that p one would not believe it – was rejected earlier as a necessary condition for the truth of the assertion that one "knows" P. What follows will support that rejection by showing how the sensitivity requirement runs against simple and striking counterexamples.

Suppose first we have two propositions as follows: (a) that p, and (b) that I do not believe incorrectly (falsely) that p. Surely no-one minimally rational and attentive who believes both of these will normally know either without knowing the other. Yet even in cases where one's belief of (a) is sensitive, one's belief of (b) could never be sensitive. After all, even if (b) were false, one would still believe it anyhow. Still it is quite implausible that the assertion that I know (b) could never be true, not even in the many situations where the assertion that I know (a) *would* be true.[11]

Second counterexample. On my way to the elevator I release a trash bag down the chute from my high rise condo. Presumably I know my bag will soon be in the basement. But what if, having been released, it still (incredibly) were not to arrive there? That presumably would be because it had been snagged somehow in the chute on the

way down (an incredibly rare occurrence), or some such happenstance. But none such could affect my predictive belief as I release it, so I would still predict that the bag would soon arrive in the basement. My belief seems not to be sensitive, therefore, but constitutes knowledge anyhow, and can correctly be said to do so.[12]

Thirdly, sensitivity is doubtful as a condition for our being correctly said to have knowledge of any apodictically necessary truth A, given how hard it would be to make sense of the supposition that not-A. This problem leads Nozick himself to abandon the requirement of sensitivity for such truths.

2. Better safe than sensitive

These problems for sensitivity do not affect our "safety." A belief is sensitive iff had it been false, S would not have held it, whereas a belief is *safe* iff S would not have held it without it being true. For short: S's belief B(p) is sensitive iff $\sim p \rightarrow \sim B(p)$, whereas S's belief is safe iff $B(p) \rightarrow p$. These are not equivalent, since subjunctive conditionals do not contrapose.[13]

DeRose gives a persuasive defense of the sensitivity idea common to the various forms of sensitivity-based opposition to Moore: namely, the skeptical, tracking, relevant-alternative, and contextualist approaches that share some form of commitment to that requirement. This idea supports the skeptic's correctness in affirming the first premise of AI. Ordinary claims to know can apparently be sustained only by distinguishing ordinary contexts in which such claims are made from contexts where the skeptic asserts his distinctive premise in the course of giving argument AI. With this difference in context comes a difference in standards, and because of this difference, it is incorrect to say in a skeptic's context that one knows O, correct though it may remain to say it in an ordinary context.

That response to the skeptic faces a problem. Nozick and DeRose argue that sensitivity is necessary for correct attributions of knowledge. The requirement that a belief must be sensitive if it is to be (correctly characterizable as) "knowledge" is found to be broadly *prima facie* plausible: in many cases it is found intuitively that the failure of a belief to be (correctly characterizable as) "knowledge" may be explained through the fact that the belief would remain in place even if false (in circumstances determined by the context of attribution). The problem for this way of arguing is that an alternative explanation is equally adequate for undisputed cases (undisputed, for example, between the Moorean who rejects the skeptic's distinctive premise 1 and the contextualist who is willing to affirm it). According to this alternative explanation, it is safety that (correct attribution of) "knowledge" requires, a requirement violated in the ordinary cases cited, wherein the subject fails to know. One fails to know in those cases, it is now said, because one's belief is not safe. Suppose this generalizes to all uncontentious cases adduced by the contextualist to favor his sensitivity requirement. Suppose in all such cases the condition required could just as well be safety as sensitivity. And suppose, moreover, that the problems for sensitivity briefly noted do not affect safety, as I have claimed. If so, then one cannot differentially support sensitivity as the right requirement, in support of the skeptic's main premise.

Here is the striking result: if we opt for safety as the right requirement then a Moorean stance is defensible, and we avoid skepticism.[14] That is to say, one does satisfy the requirement that one's belief of not-H be safe: after all, not easily *would* one believe that not-H (that one was not so radically deceived) without it being true (which is not to say that not possibly *could* one believe that not-H without it being true). In the actual world, and for quite a distance away from the actual world, up to quite remote possible worlds, our belief that we are not radically deceived matches the fact as to whether we are or are not radically deceived.[15]

D. A Moorean Stance Defended

One last job will complete our defense of the Moorean stance. Recall the compelling requirement that a fully adequate treatment of the paradox explain to us why the component of the paradox rejected by that treatment seems so plausible. We might try to meet this requirement by explaining how the skeptic is guaranteed to be right in affirming his distinctive premise (while we are pleasantly surprised that we can still ordinarily "know" that we have hands, etc.). This

is the approach of the contextualism just reviewed.

In his special context, with the raised standards, the skeptic's main premise turns out to be *true*. However, one *need not* explain plausibility in terms of *truth*. Many false things are plausible and we can explain why they are plausible without having to consider them true. We are said to face illusions at every turn, from the humble perceptual and cognitive illusions of interest to psychologists to the more momentous illusions alleged by Freud and Marx. In all such cases illusion may be said to explain plausibility. (One might however prefer to view illusion as misbegotten plausibility, so that the plausibility is *constitutive* of the illusion, which therefore cannot explain it really; still, in all such cases of illusion it may be explained why something strikes us as plausible despite being false.)

Consider, moreover, the need to explain how the skeptic's premise – that one does not know oneself not to be radically misled, etc. – is as plausible as it is. That requirement must be balanced by an equally relevant and stringent requirement: namely, that one explains how that premise is as *implausible* as it is.[16] To many of us it just does not seem so uniformly plausible that one cannot be said correctly to know that one is not at this very moment being fed experiences while envatted. So the explanatory requirement is in fact rather more complex than might seem at first. And given the distribution of intuitions here, the contextualist and the Nozickian, et al., still owe us an explanation.

Interestingly, our distinction between sensitivity and safety may help us meet the more complex explanatory demand, compatibly with the Moorean stance, which I adopt as my own. My preferred explanation may be sketched as follows.

a. It is safety that is required for knowledge (and for its correct attribution), not sensitivity. It is required that $B(p) \rightarrow p$, and not that $\sim p \rightarrow \sim B(p)$.[17]

b. Take our belief that we are not radically deceived as in a skeptical scenario such as H. Since that belief *is* safe, the skeptic cannot argue for his distinctive premise by alleging that here we violate the safety requirement.

c. Safety and sensitivity, being mutual contra-positives, are easily confused, so it is easy to confuse the correct requirement of safety (for knowledge and its correct attribution) with a requirement of sensitivity. It is easy to over-look that subjunctive conditionals do not contrapose.

d. Those who find the skeptic's distinctive premise plausible *on the basis of sensitivity considerations* may thus be confusing sensitiv-ity with safety, and may on that basis assess as correct affirmations of that premise. After all, the requirement of safety is well supported by the sorts of considerations adduced generally by the sensitivity-based opposition to Moore. Sensitivity being so similar to safety, so easy to confuse, it is no surprise that one would find sensitivity so plausible, enough to mislead one into assessing as correct affirmations of that premise.

e. The plausibility of the skeptic's premise is thus explained compatibly with its falsity, which fits the stance of the Moorean. Once that premise (premise 1 of AI) is thus rejected, finally, two other things are then avoidable: first, one can avoid "abominable" conjunctions and still pre-serve our ordinary knowledge; second, in doing so one can avoid both the semantic ascent and the contextualist turn favored by many recent treatments of the paradox.[18]

Thus may a Moorean epistemology defend itself against "sensitivity-based" objections, whether wielded by the skeptic, by the Nozickian et al., or by the contextualist. These three alternatives to a plain Moorean stance all require that in order to constitute knowledge a belief must first be "sensi-tive." We reject that requirement, and thereby support our preferred Moorean alternative.

Of course all we really need in order to explain the plausibility of the skeptic's premise is that it clearly enough follow from something plausible enough. And the sensitivity requirement may perhaps fulfill that role well enough independ-ently of whether it is confused with a safety requirement. But that would still leave the ques-tion of why sensitivity is so plausible if it is just false. And here there might still be a role for safety if it can function as a plausible enough requirement, one both true and defensible through reflection, and one that appeals to us

simply through our ability to discern the true from the false in such a priori matters. Compatibly with that, some of us may be misled into accept-ing the requirement of sensitivity because it is so easily confused with the correct requirement, that of safety, thus succumbing to cognitive illusion.[19]

E. Objections and Replies

Objection 1

We have before us an explanation for why it is that people find it as plausible as they do that we do not know ourselves to be free of such skeptical scenarios as that of the evil demon and that of the envatted brain. But how would we explain the extent to which people find it plausible to think that we do not know ordinary things such as that one has hands, once exposed to the skeptic's rea-soning? Does the contextualist have an advantage in that regard?

Reply

If people are persuaded that a belief can amount to knowledge only if sensitive, and they are also per-suaded that whatever follows obviously from the known must itself be known, then it is not surpris-ing that they may puzzle over how they can possi-bly know that they have hands if they do not know that they are not handlessly envatted, etc. Moreover, I do not see why our new contextualist should enjoy any advantage here, since he does accept that what follows obviously from the known must itself be known. So the new contextualist in fact grants us what we need for our explanation.

Objection 2

Doesn't the requirement of safety share with the requirement of sensitivity the drawback that it makes knowledge not closed under deduction? Could one not then know that p, deduce that q from one's premise that p, and yet not know thereby that q?

Reply

Yes, in fact this is one reason why our account of safety is only at best a first approximation. Here now is a closer approximation (or an initial sketch of one). What is required for a belief to be safe is not just that it would be held only if true, but rather that it be based on a reliable indication. What counts as such an indication? Indications are deliverances, as when you ostensibly perceive, or remember, or deduce something or other. A *deliverance* in the product sense is a proposition, i.e., what is delivered; in the process sense it is the delivering. A proposition is thus delivered to you when something inclines you to believe it, as in the ostensible perception, memory, or sound conclusion. Such a deliverance is an indication if and only if it would occur only if the delivered proposition were true. Again, a belief is safe if and only if it is based on a reliable indication. And it is this more complex safety that is required for knowledge, not the simpler one that I offered for comparison with the Nozick/DeRose sensitivity. Of course, that sensitivity requirement is itself also a first approximation, and Nozick has recourse to his "methods" in his fuller account. So there is no disadvantage in respect of complexity for safety as compared with sensitivity.[20]

Notes

1 Subjunctive conditionals do not contrapose, which makes safety inequivalent to sensitivity, as may be seen through counterexamples like the following.

First Argument.

Let   f = Water flows from
                           the faucet
                       o = The main valve is open
Then we have: (a) $f \rightarrow \sim(f\&\sim o)$
                       (b) $\sim[(f\&\sim o) \rightarrow \sim f]$

Both (a) and (b) seem intuitively right and hence constitute a prima facie counterexample to the general claim that the subjunctive conditional contraposes. If the subjunctive conditional contraposes, then we have to say that if (a) above is true then the following must also be true:

(c) $(f\&\sim o) \rightarrow \sim f$

But (c) seems intuitively unacceptable (while (a) seems still intuitively acceptable).

Second Argument.

Let   p = I am not wrong in
                           thinking that I have a hand
                           before me.

And let's imagine a normal situation, like Moore's, where, while awake, alert, etc., one holds one's hand before one. Then we have:

(a) $B(p) \rightarrow p$
(b) $\sim[\sim p \rightarrow \sim B(p)]$

Re (a): If I were to believe that I'm not wrong in thinking I have a hand before me, then I would not be wrong in so thinking surely, given the normal situation, the good light, the open eyes, etc. In such a situation one would believe that one was not wrong in thinking one had a hand before one, only if either (i) one did not have a hand before one and did not think one did, or (ii) one *did* have a hand before one and thought one *did* – therefore, only if one was not wrong in thinking that one had a hand before one. So we do get that $B(p) \rightarrow p$. Re (b): If I were to be wrong in thinking that I have a hand before me, would I then believe that I was wrong in so thinking? No, I would never believe that I was wrong in thinking that such and such, no matter what the "such and such" might be. Indeed, what I would believe is that I was *not* wrong in thinking that I had a hand before me. So in any case it would be false that $[\sim p \rightarrow \sim B(p)]$, and true rather that $\sim[\sim p \rightarrow \sim B(p)]$. This shows once again that the subjunctive conditional fails to contrapose.

2 Expressions of the form "<p>" will be short for corresponding expressions of the form "the proposition that p". Capitalization will also be used as an alternative device equivalent to such enclosing in angle brackets.

3 Keith DeRose, "Solving the Skeptical Problem," *The Philosophical Review* 104 (1995), pp. 1–52; p. 28.

4 DeRose often works with a stronger "insensitivity" idea than the Nozickian one (or the one I am using). His stronger understanding is this: that if it were not so that p, one *would* believe that p anyhow. The weaker one is

this: that it is false that if it were not so that p, one *would not* believe that p. (It seems to me that the stronger entails the weaker, but not conversely. However, DeRose does not distinguish these steadily, and tells me that he is inclined to think them equivalent.) I don't think this affects the dialectic to follow in any fundamental way.

5 "An important component of being in a strong epistemic position with respect to P is to have one's belief as to whether P is true match the fact of the matter as to whether P is true, not only in the actual world, but also at the worlds sufficiently close to the actual world. That is, one's belief should not only be true, but should be non-accidentally true, where this requires one's belief as to whether P is true to match the fact of the matter at nearby worlds. The further away one can get from the actual world, while still having it be the case that one's belief matches the fact at worlds that far away and closer, the stronger a position one is in with respect to P." *Ibid.*, p. 34.

6 Here and in his general framing of the skeptic's puzzle, DeRose acknowledges Stewart Cohen; see, e.g., Cohen's "How to be a Fallibilist," *Philosophical Perspectives* 2 (1988), pp. 91–123.

7 According to the "Rule of Sensitivity," restricted so as to make it most directly relevant to the skeptical paradox: "When it is asserted that some subject S knows (or does not know) some proposition P, the standards for knowledge (the standards for how good an epistemic position one must be in to count as knowing) tend to be raised, if need be, to such a level as to require S's belief in that particular P to be sensitive for it to count as knowledge." And this will also affect the standards for the evaluation of suitably related more ordinary propositions: "Where the P involved is to the effect that a skeptical hypothesis does not obtain, then this rule dictates that the standards will be raised to a quite high level, for, as we've seen, one must be in a stronger epistemic position with respect to a proposition stating that a skeptical hypothesis is false – relative to other, more ordinary, propositions – before a belief in such as proposition can be sensitive." (DeRose, "Solving the skeptical Problem," p. 36.)

8 His approach is fresh in appealing to threshold-setting within a dimension of *strength*, which distinguishes him from Stewart Cohen, who uses rather degree of *justification* as his dimension of relevant epistemic interest.

9 DeRose speaks of the components of AI as "propositions," presumably indexical propositions, which can be truth-evaluated relative to various standards. It is in some such way that one would understand the abstract soundness of an argument such as Moore's: ~C, 2; therefore, ~1.

10 Although it remains a bit unclear whether, for the contextualism under review, Moore's argument is unendorsable even through implicit belief, the general lines of the position staked out are at least vaguely discernible. There is one other issue on which the position is not quite clear and distinct, however, namely whether we are definitely to affirm that the Moorean combination is a sound argument. I do not find an unambiguous verdict on this. Is the sort of indirect endorsement that would be involved in such an affirmation to be countenanced by this new contextualism? In *saying* that Moore's combination (2, ~c, and ~1) constitutes a sound argument, we are at least indirectly highlighting proposition 1. And having done that, it seems no more correct to say that the Moorean argument is sound than it would be to give the argument itself affirmatively in speech or in thought.

That may make the skeptic's paradox even more deeply paradoxical than might at first appear, from the perspective of our new contextualism. We dimly see that an argument might be sound even though it could never be identified directly so as to attribute its soundness to it. Its soundness could perhaps be attributed to it were it identified only quite indirectly, perhaps as the argument laid out on such and such a page of Moore's *Philosophical Papers*, or in some such way. As soon as the argument is identified more directly in terms of its actual content, however, soundness may no longer be attributed correctly to it. (How "directly" may the argument be specified compatibly with thinking or calling it sound? That is an interesting issue that threatens to enmesh us in controversies of content externalism in philosophy of language and mind.)

11 See my "Postscript to 'Proper Functionalism and Virtue Epistemology'," in *Warrant in Contemporary Epistemology*, ed. Jonathan Kvanvig (Rowman & Littlefield, 1996), pp. 271–81. Can anyone find that consequence acceptable? In fact, DeRose is well aware of this problem, and waves it aside for future consideration, proposing in the meantime an ad hoc stopgap. This problem is also in Jonathan Vogel's "Tracking, Closure, and Inductive Knowledge," in S. Luper-Foy, ed., *The Possibility of Knowledge* (Rowman & Littlefield, 1987). Compare moreover: (c) p, and (d) if I'm not mistaken, p. Even when one tracks and thereby can know that p, one could never track the likes of (d), for the reason, precisely, that belief of (d) could not be sensitive. This sort of counterexample, unlike the one to follow, strikes me as conclusive.

12 This sort of problem is also presented by Vogel, "Tracking, Closure and Inductive Knowledge," and is endorsed by Stewart Cohen in his "Contextualist Solutions to Epistemological Problems: Skepticism, Gettier, and the Lottery," forthcoming in the *Australasian Journal of Philosophy*.

13 If water now flowed from your kitchen faucet, it would *not* then be the case that water so flowed while your main valve was closed. But the contrapositive of this true conditional is clearly false.

14 I mean that *we* in our reflection and in our discussions in journal and seminar, avoid skepticism; we can say right here and now that we do know various things, and not just that we say "I know" correctly in various contexts not now our own.

15 This sort of externalist move has been widely regarded as unacceptably circular, mistakenly, as I argue in "Philosophical Scepticism and Epistemic Circularity," *Proceedings of the Aristotelian Society*, supp. vol. 68 (1994), pp. 268–90, and in "Reflective Knowledge in the Best Circles," *Journal of Philosophy* 94 (1997), pp. 410–30.

16 Informal polling of my classes has revealed (of course defeasibly) that those who find it false outnumber those who find it true, and quite a few prefer to suspend judgment. At every stage people spread out in some such patters of three-way agreement-failure.

17 This is actually a first approximation that will need to be qualified. A closer approximation that preserves the spirit of safety and the opposition to sensitivity may be found in my "How Must Knowledge Be Modally Related to What is Known?" in the festschrift for Sydney Shoemaker forthcoming in *Philosophical Issues*. (I should emphasize that I use the arrow merely as an abbreviatory device. So "p → q" abbreviates the likes of "As a matter of fact, though perhaps not as a matter of strict necessity, it would not be so that p, without it being so that q"; etc.; or, perhaps better: "As a matter of fact, though perhaps not as a matter of strict necessity, not easily would it have been so that p without it being so that q.")

18 A turn found problematic in my "Contextualism and Skepticism," forthcoming in *Philosophical Issues*.

19 I need hardly say how much this work owes to writings of Fred Dretske, Robert Nozick, and Keith DeRose. Portions of it were read at the Conference on Methods meeting of May 1998, where Richard Feldman and Jonathan Vogel commented, and at the SOFIA meeting of June 1998, where Hilary Kornblith, Keith Lehrer, and James Tomberlin did so. (And the present paper overlaps in part my contribution to the proceedings of that conference.) David Sosa was helpful both editorially and philosophically, as was discussion in both my seminar and my dissertation group at Brown, and in the Gibbons/Unger seminar at NYU. Thank you all!

20 Actually, this second approximation is close but itself needs further improvement. This and related issues are taken up further in my "How Must Knowledge Be Modally Related to What is Known". For example, I favor requiring for one's belief to be knowledge that it be based on an indication, where an indication is in the way specified a reliable or itself "safe" delivering. (But in addition the delivering must be fundamentally through the exercise of an intellectual virtue. Thus the source that yields the deliverance must be virtuous, i.e., in a reliable or trustworthy

way a source of truth; and moreover, if it is a source that is based on a more fundamental source, then the most fundamental source involved must be thus virtuous. Thus if I normally infer from something's being a sea-creature that it is a mammal, and it is this that underlies my inference form something's being a whale to its being a mammal, then the latter source, despite being virtuous, is not a source of knowledge or apt belief.)

CHAPTER 23

Are There Counterexamples to the Closure Principle?

Jonathan Vogel

Very often, a person can't know a proposition without knowing various logical consequences of that proposition. So, for instance, if you know that your friend is wearing a yellow tie, you can't fail to know that your friend is wearing a tie, period. In this case, the relation of logical consequence is obvious. When the relation isn't obvious, a proposition you know may have a logical consequence you don't know – for example, a suitably obscure mathematical theorem. In light of these considerations, it seems plausible to hold that if a person knows a given proposition, that person must also know any logical consequence of that proposition which he or she recognizes as such. Putting it differently, we might say that knowledge is closed under known logical implication.[1]

The problem of skepticism about the external world gives this epistemic principle (hereafter, the "Closure Principle") a special interest. When the skeptic argues that we have no knowledge of the world because we don't know that we aren't massively deceived in some way, he or she appears to assume that knowledge has the closure property. But if it is possible to find clear examples demonstrating that closure sometimes fails, a crucial piece of support for skepticism will be

Originally published in M. D. Roth and G. Ross (eds), *Doubting* (Dordrecht: Kluwer Academic Publishers, 1990), pp. 13–27.

removed. The purpose of this paper is to show that even the strongest apparent counterexamples to closure don't hold up under scrutiny. To that extent, the problem of skepticism is still with us.

I Dretske's Zebra Case

In a widely read paper, Fred Dretske offered an intriguing example which is meant to show that the Closure Principle is invalid. It is worthwhile to quote Dretske's discussion at length:

> You take your son to the zoo, see several zebras, and when questioned by your son, tell him they are zebras. Do you know they are zebras? Well, most of us would have little hesitation in saying that we did know this. We know what zebras look like, and, besides, this is the city zoo and the animals are in a pen clearly marked "Zebras." Yet, something's being a zebra implies that it is not a mule and, in particular, not a mule cleverly disguised by the zoo authorities to look like a zebra. Do you know that these animals are not mules cleverly disguised by the zoo authorities to look like zebras? If you are tempted to say "Yes" to this question, think a moment about what reasons you have, what evidence you can produce in favor of this claim. The evidence you *had* for thinking them zebras has been effectively neutralized, since it does not count toward their *not* being mules cleverly disguised to look like zebras. You have some general uniformities on which you rely,

regularities to which you give expression by such remarks as "That isn't very likely" or "Why should the zoo authorities do that?" Granted, the hypothesis (if we may call it that) is not very plausible, given what we know about people and zoos. But the question here is not whether this alternative is plausible, not whether it is more or less plausible than that there are real zebras in the pen, but whether *you know* that this alternative hypothesis is false. I don't think you do.[2]

According to Dretske, the Zebra Case is a counterexample to closure because you know (a) the animals in the pen are zebras, but don't know a clear logical consequence of (a), namely, (b) the animals in the pen aren't cleverly disguised mules. I find this description of the situation implausible. Given what Dretske has said in laying out the example, I think it is more reasonable to conclude that if you know (a) you know (b) as well, and closure is preserved after all.

The reason you know that an animal in the pen is not a disguised mule (if you do know it's a zebra) is that you have a true belief to that effect backed up by good evidence. That evidence includes background information about the nature and function of zoos. You know that zoos generally exhibit genuine specimens, and that it would be a great deal of trouble to disguise a mule and to substitute it for a zebra. Only under the most unlikely and bizarre circumstances, if at all, would such a substitution be made, and there is no reason whatsoever to think that any such circumstances obtain. If you did feel there was a chance that a switch had been made, you would have reason to doubt that the animal you see is a *zebra*. You would not, then, know that it is a zebra, contrary to what was assumed.

Dretske's motivations for denying that you know you aren't seeing a disguised mule are not fully clear. He himself grants that the "hypothesis" that the animal is really a mule is "not very plausible", yet adds

> But the question here is not whether this alternative is plausible, not whether it is more or less plausible than that there are real zebras in the pen, but whether *you know* that this alternative is false.[3]

One might have thought that if a belief is much more plausible than its denial, a person would be

justified in accepting that belief. And, then, barring Gettier-like complications, that person's belief, if true, would be knowledge.[4]

Perhaps Dretske's point is this: When you look at the pen where the animal is, you have evidence that there is a zebra there, namely that the animal looks like a zebra. Your visual evidence does not, though, give any support to your belief that the animal you are seeing *isn't* a disguised mule. For, if it were a disguised mule, your visual experience would be just as it is. As Dretske says, "The evidence you *had* for thinking them zebras has been effectively neutralized, since it does not count toward their *not* being mules cleverly disguised to look like zebras".[5] The upshot is that you do know there is a zebra, since you have a true belief to that effect supported by evidence. You do *not* know that the animal isn't a disguised mule, since your belief in this case is true but not supported by available evidence. So, you know the first proposition, but don't know its clear logical consequence.

I indicated above why I think this analysis is incorrect. Your background knowledge does give you justification for denying that the animal is a mule, so you know that it isn't one. Still, it may appear that the possibility of failure for the Closure Principle arises out of the situation as I described it. It seems that the usual adequate evidence for the claim "It's a zebra" (i.e. visual evidence) is different from the background evidence which supports "It's not a cleverly disguised mule." If so, you could conceivably be in a position where you had the visual evidence and knew there was a zebra, but lacked the background knowledge, and hence didn't know there wasn't a disguised mule. In such circumstances, the Closure Principle would face a counterexample.

To my mind, this appraisal is based on an overly atomistic conception of evidence and justification. Your belief that the animal at the zoo is a zebra is justified in part by your visual evidence, but it is *also* supported by the background information that counts against the animal's being a disguised mule. By itself, the visual evidence wouldn't be sufficient to give you knowledge that there is a zebra. To see this, consider a case where the proper background knowledge is lacking. Imagine that you are driving through ranchland out West and for some reason or other stop by the roadside. Across the way you see a black and white striped equine creature tranquilly grazing in its pen. In a situation of this sort, it seems to me, it is far from clear that you could know the animal before you to be a zebra, even though it looks just as much like a zebra as the animal in the zoo does. The difference here is that you have no applicable background information which makes it more likely that a zebra-like animal really is a zebra rather than an oddly colored mule. So, even back at the zoo, your justification that what you see is a zebra depends on background information – just as the justification for your denial that it's a disguised mule would so depend.[6] There is no discrepancy here which provides grounds for thinking that the Closure Principle is false.

One might object that the defense of closure just given makes unrealistically high demands so far as evidence is concerned. A young child at the zoo, seeing an animal that resembles an illustration in a picture book might point and happily say "Zebra!". Despite the fact that the child knows nothing about how zoos work, doesn't that child know the animal is a zebra? The issues here are complex, but there are various reasons not to take this objection as decisive. First, even if it is granted that the child knows in the full sense that the animal is a zebra, if he or she isn't capable of drawing the inference about disguised mules, the child's case doesn't bear on the validity of the Closure Principle. Moreover, it's unclear that, under the circumstances, the child really ought to be described as knowing that the animal is a *zebra*. Suppose that the child can't conceptually distinguish between "looks like an zebra" and "is a zebra." Perhaps the child knows only that the animal it sees looks like a zebra, and wouldn't know that the animal is a zebra without acquiring further conceptual resources and information.[7]

II   Car Theft Cases

I have maintained that Dretske's Zebra Case does not furnish a counterexample to the Closure Principle. But what I have said so far bears largely on the particular details of the case as Dretske sets it up. His remarks point towards the formulation of examples which cannot be treated so straightforwardly. I call these "Car Theft Cases", for reasons which will become clear in a moment. It may be, in fact, that the Zebra Case properly understood is one of these.

Suppose you own a car which you parked a few hours ago on a side street in a major metropolitan area. You remember clearly where you left it. Do you know where your car is? We are inclined to say that you do. Now it is true that every day hundreds of cars are stolen in the major cities of the United States. Do you know that your car has not been stolen? Many people have the intuition that you would not know that. If this intuition is combined with the previous one, then it seems that the closure principle is violated. That is: You know the proposition (p) "My car is now parked on (say) Avenue A." You also know that that proposition entails (q) "My car has not been stolen and driven away from where it was parked." Yet, it seems, you do not know q, despite the fact that it is for you a clear logical consequence of p, which you do know. Since, in this instance, you (apparently) fail to know a clear logical consequence of a proposition you do know, the Closure Principle is (apparently) violated.

This example turns on a rather unusual feature of the clear logical consequence q. Given your evidence, that proposition is much more probable than not, and it is at least as likely to be true as p is. To that extent, it seems as though you should be as justified in believing q as you are in believing p. Nevertheless, even though your belief that p, if true, may be knowledge, your belief that q, if true, is not. You do not know that your car hasn't been stolen by someone and driven away, despite the high probability that your belief to that effect is true.

In this respect, your belief that q resembles someone's belief that a ticket, which he holds, will not win a fair lottery. No matter how high the odds that the ticket will not win, it strikes us that the ticket-holder doesn't *know* that his ticket will not win. In fact, the analogy between a subject's belief about holding a losing lottery ticket and one's belief that one's car has not been stolen goes even further than this and is quite illuminating.

A number of features of a lottery situation are especially relevant here. First, although winning a lottery on a particular ticket is unlikely or improbable, it would not be *abnormal* in some intuitive sense, for it to turn out that the ticket one holds happens to be a winner. Second, even though the weight of the evidence is certainly against any particular ticket's winning, there is still some *statistical* evidence in favor of the proposition that a certain particular ticket will win, i. e. there is some (small) reason to think a particular ticket-holder will win.[8]

A third important consideration is that, with respect to its chances of winning the lottery, each ticket is indistinguishable from every other one. So, any reason you have for thinking that your particular ticket will lose would be an equally good reason for believing of any other ticket in the lottery that it, too, will lose. Under these circumstances, it would be arbitrary to believe of some tickets (including your own) but not others that they will not win. So, if you are consistent rather than arbitrary, and you do conclude on the basis of the evidence available that *your* ticket will not win, you will conclude the same of every other lottery ticket. Nevertheless, you hold the belief that some ticket or other will win. On pain of arbitrariness, then, it seems that you can't justifiably hold both that your ticket will lose *and* that some ticket will win. *A fortiori*, you can't know that your ticket will lose and that some ticket will win.[9]

Now, in certain important ways, one's epistemic situation with respect to the lottery is like one's epistemic situation in the Car Theft Case.[10] In effect, when you park your car in an area with an appreciable rate of auto theft, you enter a lottery in which cars are picked, essentially at random, to be stolen and driven away. Having your car stolen is the unfortunate counterpart to winning the lottery. And, just as one doesn't know that one will *not* have one's number come up in the lottery, it seems one doesn't know that one's number won't come up, so to speak, for car theft.

To be more particular, believing that your car won't be stolen is like believing you won't win the lottery, in the ways just canvassed. (1) If you park your car in an area with a high rate of car theft, an area where it is virtually certain that some car like yours will be stolen, it would not be abnormal for your car to be stolen. (2) In the Car Theft Case, your knowledge that there is a considerable amount of auto theft gives you some real statistical reason to think you car will be stolen.[11] (3) It would be arbitrary of you to believe that your car, but not all the others relevantly similar to it, won't be stolen. In general, if a person fails to know a proposition because of considerations like these, I will call the proposition not known a *lottery proposition*.

The point of this extended comparison of the lottery and the Car Theft Case has been to try to characterize a family of apparent counterexamples to the Closure Principle. The essential feature of these examples is that they are cases in which the clear logical consequence of a known proposition is itself a lottery proposition meeting the criteria just discussed. What makes the Zebra Case, in my opinion, a weaker potential counterexample to the Closure Principle than the Car Theft Case, is just the fact that the clear logical consequence of the Zebra Case is harder to see as a lottery proposition. First, it *would* be abnormal for a disguised mule to be in a zoo enclosure marked "Zebras". Second, as Dretske describes the example, it isn't apparent that you have any reason (statistical or otherwise) to think that there might be a disguised mule in the zebra pen. These two weaknesses are related to the third: it is difficult to see the presence of a disguised mule in the zebra pen as the outcome of any lottery-like process. That is, it is not as though you know that a disguised mule has been placed in some zebra pen in some zoo chosen at random. In *that* case, any reason you had for thinking that the animal you happen to see isn't the disguised mule would apply in every other situation. You would, then, have to conclude that no zoo had a disguised mule running around – in contradiction with what you know to be the case, viz. there is a disguised mule in some zoo somewhere. However, this kind of lottery element isn't present in the Zebra Case as Dretske described it. So, it is unclear why, as Dretske maintains, you do not know that the striped animal before you isn't a disguised mule.[12]

III   Car Theft Cases and Skepticism

I would like to turn now to the implications of the Car Theft Case. That case is supposed to count as a counterexample to the Closure Principle. For, in the Car Theft Case, you seem to know a proposition about where your car is, but you apparently fail to know another proposition which is a clear logical consequence of the first one. I will maintain below that taking the Car Theft Case in this fashion, as a counterexample to closure, is not the only, or the best way, to understand it. But, suppose that the Car Theft Case does stand as a counterexample to closure; does that really help us with the problem of skepticism?

The thought was that the Car Theft Case would show that closure isn't valid in general. Then the skeptic's reliance on that principle in the course of the argument from deception would be illegitimate, and the argument wouldn't go through. However, what the Car Theft Case really shows about the Closure Principle, if it shows anything at all, is that that principle is invalid when the clear logical consequence involved is a lottery proposition *with the features mentioned above*. The Car Theft Case gives us no reason to think that closure fails to hold for clear logical consequences which don't satisfy those criteria.

The question at this point is whether the clear logical consequence in the skeptic's argument is a lottery proposition in the specified sense. The clear logical consequence the skeptic invokes is something like "I am not a brain in a vat thoroughly deceived by sinister neurophysiologists." And this is clearly *not* a lottery proposition satisfying the three criteria having to do with abnormality, reliance on statistical evidence, and non-arbitrariness. Let me take these out of order. (1) If the skeptic's logical consequence were a lottery proposition, I would have to be an indistinguishable member of a class of subjects of which it is known that at least one member is a brain in a vat (making it arbitrary for me to believe that I'm not such a brain). This is hardly the case, since I don't know that there are any brains in vats anywhere. The lottery-like element which was crucial to the structure of the Car Theft Case is therefore lacking here. (2) Moreover, since there is no reason to think that some brains are put into vats as a matter of course, it might well be abnormal, in an intuitive sense, for someone to turn out to be a brain in a vat. (3) Finally, given (1), there is no basis for assigning a real, positive statistical probability to the proposition that someone is a brain in a vat.

The force of these observations is that the situation in which the skeptic invokes closure cannot easily be assimilated to situations like the Car Theft Case, in which there is some reason to think closure fails. Hence, the Car Theft Case as such gives little support to the claim that the Closure Principle fails when the skeptic appeals to it. This means that the Car Theft Case provides no convincing basis for rejecting the Deceiver Argument.

It may be that, if Cartesian skepticism is the issue, no more needs to be said about the Zebra Case or the Car Theft Case. I will, however, pursue the question of whether the Car Theft Case is a genuine counterexample to the Closure Principle. Aside from whatever intrinsic interest that question may have, it is worth seeing that the results strengthen, rather than weaken, the conclusion that these examples do not undercut skepticism.

IV   The Interpretation of Intuitions about the Problem Cases

The Car Theft Case and its analogues provide counterexamples to the Closure Principle if we take our intuitions about such cases at face-value. For, then, it seems that in the circumstances described, a person may know some proposition (e.g. "My car is on Avenue A, where I parked it") yet not know a clear logical consequence of that proposition (e.g. "My car hasn't been stolen and driven away from where it was parked"). It's worth noting, though, that some additional reactions people have suggest that closure is preserved in these situations after all. Often, when faced with the possibility that their cars might have been stolen, people withdraw, at least temporarily, their initial claims to know where their cars are. Such a response is just what the Closure Principle would require.

Now, I think it must be admitted that the intuitions we have here are weak. It would be difficult to find decisive support for closure in the tendency people have to change their minds in the way just mentioned. Still, the fact that the Closure Principle seems to be respected to the extent that it is provides a motivation for analyzing that case in a way that doesn't presuppose the failure of closure.

The problem facing any such analysis is to accommodate or discredit the intuitions that produce the impression of closure failure in the first place. Those are the intuitions which lead us to say, first, that a person, under certain circumstances, would know some proposition, and, second, that the person doesn't know a clear logical consequence of that proposition. One way of trying to reconcile these intuitions with closure is to argue that some kind of shift takes place between these responses. The claim would then be that, for no *fixed* set of circumstances, do we regard a subject as knowing a proposition while failing to know one of its clear logical consequences.

Certain psychological studies provide independent reasons to believe that a shift of this kind takes place. These studies concern people's attitudes towards improbable events. They are relevant to the Car Theft Case because of the essential role played in that case by the unlikely possibility that your car has been stolen. If closure does fail here, it is because the possibility of theft, though highly improbable, undercuts the claim that you *know* that your car hasn't been stolen, even while that possibility somehow leaves intact your knowing that your car is at a certain spot. In the studies mentioned, it has been found that people may treat improbable events either as likelier than they really are or as having essentially no chance of occurring. Moreover, these assessments are unstable, and subjects can easily be influenced to grant a possibility more weight than otherwise, if that possibility is made salient to them.[13]

Such psychological considerations provide an explanation for our intuitions about the Car Theft Case. Initially and generally, in evaluating the knowledge claims in that case, we treat the chance of your car's being stolen as essentially zero. You can, then, be as sure as you need to be that your car is where you left it; you are fully justified in that belief. Thus, we are likely to say without hesitation that in the situation described you know where your car is. Later, however, when we dwell on the rate of car theft, the chance of your car's having been stolen is lent more weight. Given a (now) significant possibility that you may be wrong in believing that your car hasn't been stolen, we are no longer prepared to say that you *know* it hasn't been stolen. And, viewing the situation in this light, giving weight to the chance that the car isn't where you left it, we may be inclined to go on to say that you don't know where the car is after all. That is, there seems to be a motivation to deny your initial knowledge claim in a set of circumstances where you cannot claim to know a clear logical consequence of what you thought you knew. In that way, the Closure Principle is respected.

In short, the fact that at one time we would say that you know the location of your car, and that *shortly thereafter* we might say that you don't know your car hasn't been stolen, does not establish the invalidity of the Closure Principle. For, it may be that at no *one* time do we affirm that you know something yet fail to know one of its clear logical consequences. It is doubtful, then, that the Car Theft Case, when properly understood, provides a counterexample to the Closure Principle.

I have suggested that the anomalous character of our intuitions about the Car Theft Case may be due to some kind of epistemically important shift rather than to closure failure. My conjecture has been that the shift is a change in a probability assignment, but other mechanisms may be at work instead. An alternative explanation of our intuitions is that we are somehow induced to shift our sense of the degree of assurance knowledge requires. Thus, our estimation of the chance the subject could be wrong because of car theft would remain constant, but we would change our minds as to whether knowledge is consistent with that level of epistemic risk. There are still other forms the shift could take. It might even be that the movement in the Car Theft-type situations is between wholly distinct notions of knowledge embodying different sets of necessary and sufficient conditions.

For my purposes, the details of what actually occurs are relatively unimportant. The main point I wish to make is that there are explanations other than closure failure for our intuitions about the Car Theft Cases.[14] Or, to put it differently, a straightforward appeal to those intuitions is insufficient to establish that the Closure Principle does not hold without restriction.

V   The Problem of Semi-Skepticism

I have just argued that a simple inspection of our intuitions about the Car Theft Case does not conclusively refute the Closure Principle. The advocate of closure can claim that the Closure Principle only *appears* to fail, as the result of an epistemically important switch that takes place in the course of our thinking about the example. However, a claim of this sort leaves open what a subject, in fact, does and doesn't know in Car Theft-type situations. The Closure Principle faces a strong objection to the effect that it is incompatible with any acceptable account of what is known in Car Theft Cases.

If closure holds, and some uniform standard of knowledge applies across the board, either you don't know where your car is, or you do know that it hasn't been stolen. The latter claim seems hard to sustain. This impression is strengthened by the similarity between the Car Theft Case and a real lottery situation. Knowing that your car hasn't been stolen would be, in the ways I've mentioned, like knowing someone will lose a fair lottery. And *that* seems like the sort of thing one doesn't know. So, given the untenability of saying that you know your car hasn't been stolen, the Closure Principle will require that, contrary to what we might have thought, you don't know where your car is.

This result seems unwelcome, and things worsen quickly. It turns out that, of the propositions about the external world which we take ourselves to know, a great many entail lottery propositions as in the Car Theft Case. (The propositions with these consequences are, specifically, propositions about the current state of the world beyond our immediate environments.) To see the range of Car Theft-type cases consider some other examples:

Bush Case:

    Q.   Do you know who the current President of the United States is?
    A.   Yes, it's George Bush.
    Q.   Do you know that Bush hasn't had a fatal heart attack in the last five minutes?
    A.   No.

Luncheonette Case:

    Q.   Do you know where I can get a good hamburger?
    A.   Yes, there's a luncheonette several blocks from here.
    Q.   Do you know that a fire hasn't just broken out there?
    A.   No.

Meteorite Case:

    Q.   Do you know what stands at the mouth of San Francisco Bay?
    A.   Yes, the Bay is spanned by the Golden Gate Bridge.

    Q.   Do you know that the Bridge wasn't just demolished by a falling meteorite?
    A.   No.

It's apparent that variations on these cases can be constructed for any number of propositions about people, things, or activities. That is to say, all the propositions about such matters, which we take ourselves to know, entail lottery propositions which, it seems, we do not know. If closure holds, along with the intuition that we do not in fact know the clear logical consequences in question, the result is that we have a great deal less knowledge of the world than we had supposed. In other words, the Closure Principle leads, even without the argument from deception, to a fairly strong and unpalatable semi-skepticism. The case against closure appears that much the stronger.

But does the threat of semi-skepticism really count against the Closure Principle? The key idea here is that there is supposed to be some feature which the lottery propositions in Car Theft Cases share with propositions about genuine lotteries, in virtue of which we can't be correctly described as knowing those propositions. What is that feature? One answer is that, because of the statistical probability that your ticket may win in a genuine lottery, there is a "real" possibility of error in believing that you will lose. In other words, the crucial belief in these circumstances lacks a kind of certainty, and hence can't count as knowledge.[15] Similarly, the lottery propositions which figure in Car Theft Cases are such that a "real" possibility exists that they are false. Since, therefore, the subject can't be certain of the truth of these lottery propositions, the subject can't know them. By the Closure Principle, it would follow that the subject can't have knowledge of the propositions which he knows to entail those lottery propositions. This would result, as we have seen, in a pervasive semi-skepticism.

The important thing to realize about this way of viewing matters is that it doesn't really justify concluding that the Closure Principle is invalid. For, according to the objection, the lesson of the genuine lottery examples is that a belief can't be knowledge if there is a "real", and not merely logical, possibility that the subject is wrong about it. If this is correct, then semi-skepticism follows *without* the Closure Principle. After all, there is a "real" possibility that, e.g. you may be wrong in believing that your car is at a certain spot; it is possible that your car has been stolen. The same point applies, *mutatis mutandis*, to any other Car Theft Case. So, perhaps, there is a legitimate epistemological problem in the threat of a semi-skepticism derived from a certainty requirement for knowledge. However, since rejecting closure won't avoid that problem, that problem doesn't provide a reason for denying the Closure Principle's validity.

On another way of analyzing the lottery examples, the unknowability in these contexts of propositions like "My ticket will lose" is due to the arbitrariness of accepting any proposition of that form. By analogy, in the Car Theft Case, you wouldn't know the proposition "My car has not been stolen"; there is reason to think that some car or cars similar to yours will be stolen, and you have no non-arbitrary ground for believing that your car in particular won't be the one (or one of the ones) stolen. Once more, it looks as though *all* knowledge claims about lottery propositions in other Car Theft cases would be undercut by similar considerations. Then, semi-skepticism will be inevitable if closure holds.

Here again, though, I am inclined to think that there is no argument to be found against the Closure Principle as such. The analysis of the lottery effect now being entertained makes the following assumption: all other things being equal, it is unjustified to accept any member of a set of propositions L, such that the members of L are equiprobable and the subject knows (or has good reason to believe) that at least one member of L is false.[16]

It turns out that this principle is sufficient to establish semi-skepticism regardless of the validity of the Closure Principle. To see why this might be so, let's take the Car Theft Case as the basic model. The present attempt to attach the burden of semi-skepticism to the Closure Principle amounts to the claim that the non-arbitrariness requirement just stated defeats your claim to know the lottery proposition that your car hasn't been stolen – while it leaves intact your claim to know a proposition (i.e. "My car is on Avenue A, where I parked it") clearly entailing that lottery proposition. But the entailing proposition is itself a member of a set of equiprobable propositions which, you have good reason to believe, contains at least one falsehood. That set contains, along with "My car is on Avenue A, where I parked it," propositions like "My neighbor's car is where he

parked it," "The postman's car is where he parked it," and so on. You may not be able to state all the members of the set explicitly, but you still have very good reason to think that there is such a set L. By the non-arbitrariness requirement, it would follow that you don't know the original proposition "My car is on Avenue A, where I parked it."[17]

The same line of thought would seem to apply to any case of the Car Theft-type where knowledge of a lottery proposition is blocked by the non-arbitrariness constraint. So, if the non-arbitrariness condition is strong enough to establish ignorance across the board for lottery propositions, it is also strong enough to establish ignorance of the propositions which, in Car Theft cases, entail the lottery propositions. That is to say, if the non-arbitrariness condition *plus* closure generates semi-skepticism, so too does the non-arbitrariness condition alone. Therefore, the opponent of closure cannot use that condition as the basis for an argument that the Closure Principle is invalid because *it* would lead to semi-skepticism.

The preceding discussion makes clearer what would be required in order to make the case against closure work. The critic of the Closure Principle has to identify some way in which beliefs in lottery propositions are epistemically defective, and this defect must not be shared by the mundane beliefs whose contents, in Car Theft cases, are known to entail those lottery propositions. It isn't easy to see what such a defect would be, if not the ones just considered.[18]

In this section, I have tried to show that our anomalous intuitions about Car Theft Cases and the related threat of semi-skepticism really have little to do with closure. No attempt has been made here to give a fully acceptable positive account of what is really known in these cases, and I suspect that such an account may not be available at all. For it may be that the Car Theft Cases together with the problem of semi-skepticism reflect deep-seated, unresolved conflicts in the way we think about knowledge.[19]

VI   Car Theft Cases and Relevant Alternatives

It is tempting to think that the omission of a positive account of what we know could be made good by adopting a version of the relevant alternatives approach to knowledge.[20] This approach promises all the advantages, without the defects, of the treatment just given. In my view, a turn to the relevant alternatives approach is not advisable, but the proposal is interesting and deserves consideration.

According to the relevant alternatives theorist, the demands for knowledge are restricted and contextual. On one version of the theory, S knows that p just in case S possesses evidence which counts against all relevant alternatives to p; on another formulation, S knows that p just in case S would be right about p over some class of relevant alternative situations. A major problem for the relevant alternatives approach is to explicate the crucial notion of relevance it invokes. Relevance of alternatives will vary according to the subject's situation; it may also (depending on the details of the theory) be determined by the content of the subject's belief and the context of attribution for the knowledge claim. If the standard of relevance obeys certain constraints, the relevant alternatives theory may be used to explain intuitions about the Car Theft Cases in a way that doesn't deny the validity of the Closure Principle.

How would this go? Suppose the facts are as described in the Car Theft Case. Initially, we operate with a standard of relevance according to which the possibility of Car Theft is too remote to be considered. At this point, the fact that you would be wrong about the location of your car, had it been stolen,[21] doesn't impair the claim that you know where your car is. Moreover, since the possibility of car theft is remote, that possibility doesn't undercut the claim that you know your car hasn't been stolen. Closure is maintained. What produces the impression to the contrary? When the possibility of car theft is explicitly raised, somehow a new, more generous standard of relevance is instated, according to which the possibility of car theft *is* relevant. By this standard, you know neither where your car is nor that it hasn't been stolen. Closure is still preserved, as before.[22]

There are several drawbacks to analyzing the Car Theft Cases in this fashion. First, the supposed virtue of the analysis is that it provides an account of what you would and wouldn't know in the circumstances given. But in giving such an account, the relevant alternatives theorist must say that, in some sense or from some standpoint,

you would know that your car hasn't been stolen. This seems plainly wrong, and the intuition that it is wrong is just what makes it so hard to give an adequate treatment of the Car Theft Case and its analogues. The relevant alternatives approach really doesn't accommodate the body of our intuitions in an unforced, convincing way, contrary to what one might have hoped.

Let me turn to a further point. The relevant alternatives theorist hypothesizes that, in the problem cases, there is a shift in the standard of epistemic relevance. In the Car Theft Case specifically, the possibility of car theft is supposed to be, alternatively, too remote and not too remote to be relevant. It is natural to presume that "remoteness" here is to be understood in probabilistic terms. Thus, at one time, the chance of car theft is treated as small enough to be ignored; later, in a more scrupulous frame of mind, we find even that little probability of error sufficient to undercut knowledge. Relevance, then, is a function of an alternative's probability.

This probabilistic criterion of relevance seems attractive, but it leads to trouble, especially if knowledge requires having evidence that excludes relevant alternatives. Suppose you know a proposition k. Let l be an alternative probable enough to be relevant to k, and let m be any other alternative to k which should count as *ir*relevant. Consider, in addition, the disjunction $(l \lor m)$, which is logically incompatible with k. This disjunction is at least as probable as its disjunct l, so it is probable enough to be relevant to your knowing k. Now, since $(l \lor m)$ is relevant to your knowing k, you have to have good evidence against it. That is to say, you have to have good evidence for the negation of $(l \lor m)$, namely the conjunction $(not\text{-}l \ \& \ not\text{-}m)$.

Why is this a problem? If you have good evidence for $(not\text{-}l \ \& \ not\text{-}m)$, you presumably have good evidence for $not\text{-}m$ alone.[23] Thus, your being in this favorable position with respect to $not\text{-}m$ is a condition for your knowing k. So, m *isn't* irrelevant to your knowing k, contrary to what we originally supposed, and there is a threat of contradiction.[24] In the face of this objection, the relevant alternatives theorist may eschew a probabilistic criterion of relevance as such. Yet, it's hard to see what alternative, and otherwise satisfactory, standard of relevance would yield the desired conclusions about the Car Theft Cases, and the value of the relevant alternatives approach in dealing with such cases seems questionable.

An important motivation for pursuing that approach is the hope that this would contribute, down the line, to a solution of the problems raised by Cartesian skepticism. Typically, a relevant alternatives theorist takes the position that we can have knowledge of the external world even though we may be victims of massive sensory deception. On this view, the possibility of such deception leaves our knowledge of the world intact because, with respect to such knowledge, the possibility of deception is an irrelevant alternative. Of course, it won't help just to declare skeptical alternatives irrelevant – that evaluation has to be made in a principled way. Now, suppose that the relevant alternatives approach really did provide an acceptable account of the Car Theft Cases. Such success would mean that relatively pedestrian possibilities like car theft are, in some contexts at least, epistemically irrelevant. All the more reason, then, to hold that the outlandish possibilities raised by skeptics are irrelevant as well.

The envisioned anti-skeptical strategy is to try to assimilate the problem of skepticism to the problem of knowledge in the Car Theft Cases. Such an attempt seems misguided, in light of considerations raised above. The issues arising in the Car Theft Cases have to do with knowledge on the basis of statistical evidence and, perhaps, the requirement of non-arbitrariness in forming justified beliefs. As I have argued, these are not the issues raised by Cartesian skepticism, and there is no reason to expect that a solution to one set of problems will have any bearing on the other set. To be more specific, let's imagine that a preponderance of statistical evidence can create situations in which some alternatives are irrelevant. This is not the situation in which we confront the skeptic (i.e., it's not as though we know, antecedently, that just a handful of the sentient creatures in the universe are massively deceived). So, it isn't easy to see here any basis for the claim that the possibility raised by the skeptic is, for us now, an irrelevant alternative.

VII   Conclusions

I have argued for a number of points concerning the Closure Principle. First, Dretske's Zebra Case does not, on my view, provide a genuine counterexample to the Closure Principle. It seems more plausible that there is a violation of closure in examples like the Car Theft Case. However, even if the Closure Principle does fail in cases of that sort, there is, I maintain, no reason to believe that such a failure carries over to the contexts where the skeptic may appeal to closure. Finally, in my view, serious questions may be raised as to whether the Car Theft Cases really do demonstrate any failure of the Closure Principle at all.

Notes

1   This formulation stands in need of further refinements. For, suppose someone knows both p and (p entails q); if that person doesn't put these things together, he or she might fail to infer, and hence not know, q. This kind of complication doesn't affect what I want to say below, so I will disregard it. Where a logical consequence is properly recognized as such, I will call it a "clear" logical consequence.

2   Fred Dretske, [3], pp. 1015–16. Dretske also employs the example in his more recent [5], p. 130.

3   Dretske, [3], p. 1016.

4   The problem can't be that you aren't certain that what you see isn't a mule. For, any chance or possibility that the animal is a mule is a chance that it's not a zebra. If this chance makes you uncertain of "It's not a mule" it should make you equally uncertain of "It's a zebra".

5   Dretske, [3], p. 1016.

6   Someone might maintain that you don't need this sort of background in formation at the zoo; such information is required out West only because *there* you have information which conflicts with the claim that the animal is a zebra (viz. zebras aren't generally found on Western ranchland). My first response would be that the zoo and ranchland situations are still analogous. If you happen to be at, say, the Bronx Zoo, you have evidence that

conflicts with the claim that the animal in the pen is a zebra, namely, the information that zebras aren't native to New York City. In any case, the example could be further modified. Suppose you are in a situation where you mean to identify an animal by sight, but you have no information at all about whether such animals are found in your location, nor about the presence or absence of similar looking but different creatures in the area. Under those circumstances, I think, you couldn't know that the animal is of the sort you would take it to be. I am indebted here to Robert Audi.

7   For a discussion of these issues, see Robert Stalnaker, [10], especially pp. 63–8.

8   When I say that there is a statistical reason or statistical evidence in favor of the proposition, I mean roughly the following. Let us say that a statistical probability of an A's being a B is one that is assigned on the basis of relative frequencies, counting cases, and so forth. On the basis of such statistical probabilities, a statistical probability may be assigned by direct inference to the proposition "This A is a B". If this statistical probability, in turn, is not zero, we have, other things being equal, some reason – perhaps very small – to think that the A in question is a B. I am calling such a reason a statistical reason. (My usage here follows John Pollock, [10], pp. 231–52).

9   This analysis will seem misguided to those who doubt that justified acceptance is closed under conjunction. However, it might still be that the existence of the relevantly similar tickets, one of which is known to win, somehow undercuts justification (and knowledge) regardless of how things stand with conjunction. For such a view, see Laurence BonJour, [1]. The role of the non-arbitrariness constraint in situations like this is also clouded by the fact that someone may fail to know that his or her ticket will lose in lotteries in which the winning chances of the tickets are uneven. I hope to pursue these issues in a further paper; for now, it would be sufficient for my purposes if nothing beyond statistical probability and abnormality enters into the proper characterization of these examples. My conclusions below should remain unaffected by dropping any assumptions about the significance of non-arbitrariness in these contexts.

10   The connection between lottery-like situations and situations where closure (apparently) fails has also been noticed by Jeffrey Olen in [8], pp. 521–6. I am indebted to David Shatz for this reference.

11   Compare this set of circumstances with those of a crime-free small town. In a locale where cars are never stolen, you would have no reason at all to think that your car in particular has been stolen, and you can know that it's where you left it. Notice, too, that in such circumstances your car's being taken would be abnormal.

12   Interestingly enough, the Zebra Case can be made more convincing by filling it out so that a lottery element is introduced. The example could be developed in this way:

Q.   Do you know what the animal in the pen is?
A.   Sure, it's a zebra.
Q.   Do you know for a fact that members of some college fraternity didn't steal the zebra last night as a prank, leaving behind a disguised mule?

The reason one might hesitate to claim to know that such a prank wasn't carried out may be that there is some reason to think that successful, temporarily undetected college pranks are brought off from time to time. Then, in turn, you may not be entitled to say that you know that there isn't a cleverly disguised mule before you. So, it may be that, properly understood or properly filled out, Dretske's Zebra Case should be taken as a member of the family of cases for which the Car Theft Case was the paradigm.

13   These findings are summarized and discussed by Daniel Kahneman and Amos Tversky, [6].

14   Which is not to say, of course, that alternative explanations, involving closure failure, can't also be devised. I am indebted here to Richard Feldman.

15   By a "real" possibility, I mean just one for which there is a positive, even if small, statistical probability; this is a richer notion than plain logical possibility. The associated notion of certainty is the absence of any real possibility of error. This notion of certainty

is weaker than the conception of certainty according to which one must have evidence that entails the truth of a belief for that belief to be certain. It is questionable whether the stronger standard of certainty represents a condition for knowledge, since it *ipso facto* rules out the possibility of knowledge by induction. I should make it clear here, though, that I don't intend these glosses to serve as a substantive account of real possibility or of certainty.

16 The statement of this principle is rough, since it doesn't rule out that the members of L could be entirely unrelated in content. Some stipulation is needed to ensure that L be suitably natural or appropriate; this problem is, of course, closely related to that of choosing an appropriate reference class for direct inference about probabilities.

17 A similar point is made by BonJour, [1], p. 73n.

18 Jeffrey Olen suggests that you know the mundane proposition because there is a "nomic connection" between the state of affairs picked out by the propositions which are your evidence and the state of affairs you believe to obtain; in the case of your belief in the clear logical consequence, however, the connection is merely probabilistic and not nomic, and you don't know. Notice, though, that in the Car Theft Case, it is nomologically possible for you to have the evidence you have and yet be wrong in your belief about both the initial proposition and the clear logical consequence. So, it is at least obscure exactly how Olen means to draw the crucial distinction. See Olen, [8]. Another explanation of closure failure that would fit the Car Theft Cases is that you "track", in the sense discussed by Nozick, the truth of initial proposition but not that of the clear logical consequence. Nozick's account is presented in his *Philosophical Explanations* (Cambridge: Harvard University Press, 1981); however a discussion of Nozick's work lies outside the scope of this essay.

19 For more discussion of this possibility, see my doctoral dissertation "Cartesian Skepticism and Epistemic Principles" (Yale University, 1986), Chapter II.

20 Important early statements of the relevant alternatives theory are found in Fred Dretske, [3] and [4], and in Alvin Goldman [5].

21 Or, alternatively: the fact that your evidence doesn't exclude the possibility of car theft.

22 A sophisticated version of this line of thought has been developed by Stewart Cohen in [2].

23 The relevant-alternatives theorist can't balk at this point, since we're assuming that he or she endorses the Closure Principle.

24 A related argument may be given to show that the probabilistic criterion of relevance is unacceptable when the relevant alternatives theory is couched in terms of reliability over a range of counterfactual situations.

References

1 BonJour, Laurence. "The Externalist Conception of Knowledge", in P. French, T. Uchling, and H. Wettstein, eds, *Midwest Studies in Philosophy*, Vol. V: Studies in Epistemology (Minneapolis: University of Minnesota Press, 1980).

2 Cohen, Stewart. "How To Be A Fallibilist", in J. Tomberlin, ed. *Philosophical Perspectives*, Vol. II: Epistemology (Atascadero: Ridgeview Publishing Company, 1988).

3 Dretske, Fred. "Epistemic Operators", *The Journal of Philosophy* 69 (1970), pp. 1015–16.

4 Dretske, Fred. "The Pragmatic Dimension of Knowledge", *Philosophical Studies* 40 (1981), pp. 363–8.

5 Dretske, Fred. *Knowledge and the Flow of Information* (Cambridge: Bradford Books, 1981).

6 Goldman, Alvin. "Discrimination and Perceptual Knowledge", *The Journal of Philosophy* 73 (1976), pp. 771–91.

7 Kahneman, Daniel and Tversky, Amos. "Choices, Values, and Frames", *American Psychologist* 39 (1984), pp. 341–50.

8 Nozick, Robert. *Philosophical Explanations* (Cambridge: Harvard University Press), 1981.

9 Olen, Jeffrey. "Knowledge, Probability, and Nomic Connections", *The Southern Journal of Philosophy* 15 (1977), pp. 521–6.

10 Pollock, John. "Epistemology and Probability", *Synthese* 55 (1983), pp. 231–52.

11 Stalnaker, Robert. *Inquiry* (Cambridge: MIT Press, 1984).

PART V

Theories of Epistemic Justification

Introduction

The selections in this section attempt to answer the following question: "Under what general conditions is one epistemically justified in believing a proposition?" In answering this question, one must examine how justification relates both to truth and to criticizability.

One can plainly be justified in believing that p even if p is not true, but does being justified in believing that p at least make it objectively probable that p? If it doesn't, why should we care about justification? The question of whether having unjustified beliefs entails being criticizable might seem to be easily answered: yes, if one has an unjustified belief, then one ought not have that belief, and one can be rightly criticized for having a belief one ought not have. Yet, there is a basic problem with this response. Broadly speaking, epistemologists often use the term 'epistemic justification' to pick out a kind of positive value status related to gaining truth and avoiding error. The crucial point, emphasized by Richard Feldman and Earl Conee in their selection, is that deontological statuses of being obligated, being forbidden, etc., do not exhaust positive value statuses. It is often acknowledged in ethics, for example, that it is bad to have cruel instincts. One arguably does not deserve blame for having cruel instincts because that is not in one's power; rather, such instincts have a negative moral or ethical value. Depending on one's theory of value, this may be a matter of not being conducive to the production of states of pleasure, states of desire satisfaction, etc. Not all criticism, i.e., all normative assessment, amounts to praise or blame. Similarly, a natural proclivity toward wishful thinking, while not being something for which one deserves blame, merits criticism due to its epistemic disvalue.

Feldman and Conee argue in favor of evidentialism about justification. Whether a subject's doxastic attitude toward a proposition is justified is determined by whether taking that attitude fits the subject's evidence. Evidence here includes experiential as well as doxastic evidence. Feldman and Conee defend this view against reliabilist theories which connect justified belief essentially with objective probability of truth. They claim that important reliabilist intuitions can be captured in their framework by appealing to the notion of wellfoundedness, a notion which employs the evidentialist conception of justification together with the notion of a basing relation. S's doxastic attitude D toward p is well-founded if and only if having D toward p is justified and S has D toward p on the basis of a body of evidence E that meets the following conditions: (1) S has E as evidence; (2) having D toward p fits E; and (3) there is no more inclusive body of evidence I had by S such that having D toward p does not fit I. Here (3) is necessary to ensure that S has no undermining justification.

As do Feldman and Coney, Richard Foley insists there is a kind of positive epistemic status that is not essentially related to objective probability of truth. More generally, Foley sees a basic division of labor in epistemology. Some sorts of epistemic value depend on luck and some do not. Knowledge, for example, depends on a factor of luck, which explains why we cannot have a Cartesian guarantee that our beliefs about the world are true. Yet there is still a kind of luck-free epistemic value that epistemologists may investigate, a kind that depends only on that over which we have substantial, if not full, control. This is what Foley calls egocentric rationality. If I would believe that p upon deep reflection, then it is egocentrically rational for me to believe that p. Whether I am egocentrically rational in believing what I do is thus an epistemic good over which I have control. If I lack egocentric rationality, I am to be criticized, for egocentric rationality is something even a very hostile epistemic environment cannot strip from me. Why seek egocentric rationality, one might ask, if it provides no guarantee of truth or even of objective probability of truth? Foley's answer is that we believe by our best lights that it is effective to pursue our goal of having accurate and comprehensive beliefs by being egocentrically rational. We are working without nets, as Foley puts it, but this is the only way we can work, and it is a good way to work.

Several of the selections in this section concern so-called "epistemic externalism." It is perhaps useful to think of the varieties of epistemic externalism as denying one or more *internalist* theses. *Access* internalists claim the believer must have reflective epistemic access to certain facts relevant to her justification, whether these be facts about the reliability of her source of belief, facts about what she would have believed under various conditions, or perhaps only facts about what her reasons are for believing as she does. To use an example of Keith Lehrer's: Truetemp's merely having a reliable mechanism in his brain for producing accurate and highly discriminatory beliefs about the temperature doesn't by itself suffice to make any of his correct temperature judgments justified, since he has no reflective access to this mechanism or its reliability. *Ontological* internalists claim that justification is fixed by one's mental states, which, unlike Williamson, they typically take not to include states of *knowing*, and certainly not to include facts about reliability. Ontological internalism does not require access internalism, nor vice versa, though the two have often been thought to go together because mental states have been thought to be states to which we have reflective access.

In his selection, Alvin Goldman formulates an externalist theory of justification according to which a belief is justified if and only if it is produced by a reliable belief-forming process. This is eventually modified to take account of the difference between processes that take beliefs as inputs (belief-dependent processes) and those that do not (belief-independent processes). Thus, justification is specified recursively. According to Goldman, the principal intuitive benefit of reliabilism is that it explains why the way a belief is actually produced matters to justification. Wishful beliefs and hasty judgments lack justification because they are the products of unreliable ways of believing.

Goldman is also aware of several possible problems for his account, and he proposes solutions to each (some more tentative than others). Here are several of the problems his account faces. First, suppose wishful thinking is reliable in some world unlike ours. Would its products in such a world count as justified? Second, is the victim of a Cartesian evil demon totally lacking in justified belief merely owing to bad luck in having unreliable faculties of perception, testimony, and the rest? Third, it seems that someone who has excellent undermining evidence for a belief that, as it turns out, is reliably produced, cannot be justified in believing as he does, and yet reliabilism implies that he is justified.

Jonathan Vogel and Laurence BonJour offer internalist critiques of, respectively, reliabilism specifically and externalism more generally. According to Vogel, the two most commonly defended varieties of reliabilism about knowledge have false implications regarding higher-order knowledge (knowledge about what we know). According to *neighborhood reliabilism*, you know that *p* if and only if in some specified neighborhood of nearby possible worlds your believing that *p* implies that *p*. This is a safety condition. According to *counterfactual reliabilism*, you know that *p* if and only if the safety condition is met and if *p* were false, you would not believe that *p*. The second condition is a sensitivity condition. Vogel argues that both forms of reliabilism fail to account for our higher-order knowledge. Counterfactual reliabilism is too strong: it prohibits higher-order knowledge that we actually have. We often have higher-order knowledge of propositions of the form "I do not falsely believe that *p*." But were I to falsely believe that *p* I would believe I didn't falsely believe that *p*. Second, Vogel argues that neighborhood reliabilism is too weak: it grants us higher-order knowledge that we do not have. Neighborhood reliabilism seems to allow "bootstrapping," which amounts to using the beliefs generated by some process to establish the reliability of that very process. For example, a believer could come to know without any independent checks that a gas gauge was reliable simply by applying inductive reasoning to his reliably formed beliefs about what the gauge reads. Vogel notes that the only plausible solution to the bootstrapping objection strips reliabilism of one of its primary motivations: a solution to radical skepticism.

Laurence BonJour argues that no form of externalism can succeed, because justification requires a strong form of uncriticizability. At a minimum, Bonjour argues, a belief is epistemically justified for a subject only if he has adequate reason to think the belief is true. Without an adequate reason to think the belief is true, the belief is irresponsible or irrational. However, a belief can meet externalist conditions despite the fact that the believer has no adequate reason to think the belief is true. For example, suppose Norman – a completely reliable clairvoyant – comes to believe via his occult clairvoyant power that the president is in New York. By stipulation, Norman has no evidence for or against his clairvoyance and no evidence for or against the claim that the president is in New York. According to externalism, his belief is justified. Intuitively, it is not. BonJour strengthens this intuition by drawing parallels to justification in both morality and rationality. The lesson of his cases is simple: "external or objective reliability is not enough to offset subjective irrationality." And since it is subjectively irrational to accept beliefs which one has no reason to think true, externalistic theories of justification fail.

Goldman defends externalism against its deontological critics in his second contribution to this section. He reconstructs what he considers the most important argument given by internalists against externalism. Many internalists stress that the notion of justification is intimately tied to the problem of determining what to believe. They accept, in particular, the *guidance deontological conception of justification* (GD), according to which justification should guide us in our beliefs and it is our duty or responsibility to be so guided. Internalists then derive from GD the *knowability constraint* (KJ) upon the determiners of justification, according to which the only facts that qualify as justifiers are those which are knowable; for we can be guided by a fact only if we can know about it. Finally, internalists take KJ to imply that only internal conditions qualify as legitimate determiners of justification. Only if the determiners of justification are internally accessible, and therefore knowable, can they potentially guide our belief-formation in such a way that we are culpable for not being so guided. Among several problems which Goldman brings to light is that there is no cogent inferential route from the GD conception of justification to internalism via the knowability constraint. The simple version of the KJ constraint merely requires that facts about justification be readily knowable – and some readily knowable facts might be external rather than internal. The issue cannot be resolved, as has been attempted by some internalists, by making the constraint a direct knowability constraint. This is because GD implies that cognitive agents must know what justifiers are present, but no particular types of knowledge are intimated. So, GD cannot rationalize a restricted version of KJ.

According to Richard Fumerton, however, the difficulty with externalism is not so much that it severs the connection between justification and strong criticizability but that it is a naturalistic account. If some form of externalism were correct, normative epistemology would not lie within the province of philosophy. Scientists, rather than philosophers (qua philosophers), have the qualifications necessary for identifying and describing the causal/nomological features of beliefs with which externalists identify justification. But this is not Fumerton's principal criticism in the end. He objects most of all to externalism's consequence that there is nothing epistemically problematic in using a method of belief to show that it is reliable, that is, about bootstrapping. Given externalism, there simply wouldn't be a problem of epistemic circularity. As long as, say, perception is a reliable process, there would be nothing problematic about concluding that perception is reliable by using perception itself. Such a conclusion would end up justified on a reliabilist model (and similarly for other externalist views). Fumerton claims there is no philosophically interesting conception of justification that meets this description, a fact revealed by the impossibility of even getting skeptical arguments off the ground in an externalist framework. Higher-order questions of justification, under externalism, cannot be treated any differently than lower-order questions.

Finally, in their second contribution to this section, Feldman and Conee attempt to defend a form of ontological internalism from the contention that externalism is better able to deal with certain philosophical problems. Internalism is committed to the following theses – (S): the justificatory status of a person's doxastic attitudes strongly supervenes on the person's mental states, events and conditions, and (M): if two persons are mentally identical then the same beliefs are justified for them to the same extent. They deal with two main categories of objections – (1) that there are some justified beliefs for which there are no internal justifying states, and (2) that internalists cannot say anything definite about the connections between candidate internal justifiers and the beliefs they are supposed to justify. They argue that while some internalist theories may encounter problems with these objections, an approach which limits justifying states to currently conscious mental states or one which includes as potential justifiers anything that is retained in memory, can overcome them. Because these objections can be defeated, there is no reason to reject their form of ontological internalism.

Further Reading

Alston, William P., *Epistemic Justification* (Ithaca, NY: Cornell University Press, 1989).

——, *Beyond "Justification": Dimensions of Epistemic Evaluation* (Ithaca, NY: Cornell University Press, 2005).

Audi, Robert, *The Structure of Justification* (New York: Cambridge University Press, 1993).

Bergmann, Michael, *Justification without Awareness* (Oxford: Oxford University Press, 2006).

BonJour, Laurence and Ernest Sosa, *Epistemic Justification: Internalism vs. Externalism, Foundations vs. Virtues* (Oxford: Blackwell, 2003).

Conee, Earl and Richard Feldman, *Evidentialism* (Oxford: Oxford University Press, 2004).

Foley, R., *The Theory of Epistemic Rationality* (Cambridge, MA: Harvard University Press, 1987).

——, *Working Without a Net: A Study of Egocentric Epistemology* (Oxford: Oxford University Press, 1993).

Haack, Susan, *Evidence and Inquiry: Towards Reconstruction in Epistemology* (Oxford: Blackwell, 1993).

Lehrer, Keith, *Theory of Knowledge* (Boulder, CO: Westview Press, 1990).

Lycan, William, *Judgment and Justification* (Cambridge: Cambridge University Press, 1988).

Moser, Paul K., *Knowledge and Evidence* (Cambridge: Cambridge University Press, 1989).

Pappas, George S. (ed.), *Justification and Knowledge* (Dordrecht: Kluwer Academic Publishers, 1979).

Plantinga, Alvin, *Warrant: The Current Debate* (Oxford: Oxford University Press, 1993).

Pollock, John, *Contemporary Theories of Knowledge* (Totowa, NJ: Rowman and Littlefield, 1986).

Sosa, Ernest, *Knowledge in Perspective: Selected Essays in Epistemology* (Cambridge: Cambridge University Press, 1991).

Steup, Matthias, *Knowledge, Truth, and Duty: Essays on Epistemic Justification, Responsibility, and Virtue* (Oxford: Oxford University Press, 2004).

Swinburne, Richard, *Epistemic Justification* (Oxford: Oxford University Press, 2001).

CHAPTER 24

Evidentialism

Richard Feldman
and Earl Conee

I

We advocate evidentialism in epistemology. What we call evidentialism is the view that the epistemic justification of a belief is determined by the quality of the believer's evidence for the belief. Disbelief and suspension of judgment also can be epistemically justified. The doxastic attitude that a person is justified in having is the one that fits the person's evidence. More precisely:

> EJ Doxastic attitude D toward proposition p is epistemically justified for S at t if and only if having D toward p fits the evidence S has at t.[1]

We do not offer EJ as an analysis. Rather it serves to indicate the kind of notion of justification that we take to be characteristically epistemic – a notion that makes justification turn entirely on evidence. Here are three examples that illustrate the application of this notion of justification. First, when a physiologically normal person under ordinary circumstances looks at a plush green lawn that is directly in front of him in broad daylight, believing that there is something green before him is the attitude toward this proposition that fits his evidence. That is why the belief is

Originally published in *Philosophical Studies* 48 (1985), pp. 15–34.

epistemically justified. Second, suspension of judgment is the fitting attitude for each of us toward the proposition that an even number of ducks exists, since our evidence makes it equally likely that the number is odd. Neither belief nor disbelief is epistemically justified when our evidence is equally balanced. And third, when it comes to the proposition that sugar is sour, our gustatory experience makes disbelief the fitting attitude. Such experiential evidence epistemically justifies disbelief.[2]

EJ is not intended to be surprising or innovative. We take it to be the view about the nature of epistemic justification with the most initial plausibility. A defense of EJ is now appropriate because several theses about justification that seem to cast doubt on it have been prominent in recent literature on epistemology. Broadly speaking, these theses imply that epistemic justification depends upon the cognitive capacities of people, or upon the cognitive processes or information-gathering practices that led to the attitude. In contrast, EJ asserts that the epistemic justification of an attitude depends only on evidence.

We believe that EJ identifies the basic concept of epistemic justification. We find no adequate grounds for accepting the recently discussed theses about justification that seem to cast doubt on EJ. In the remainder of this paper we defend evidentialism. Our purpose is to show that it continues to be the best view of epistemic justification.

II

In this section we consider two objections to EJ. Each is based on a claim about human limits and a claim about the conditions under which an attitude can be justified. One objection depends on the claim that an attitude can be justified only if it is voluntarily adopted, the other depends on the claim that an attitude toward a proposition or propositions can be justified for a person only if the ability to have that attitude toward the proposition or those propositions is within normal human limits.

Doxastic voluntarism

EJ says that a doxastic attitude is justified for a person when that attitude fits the person's evidence. It is clear that there are cases in which a certain attitude toward a proposition fits a person's evidence, yet the person has no control over whether he forms that attitude toward that proposition. So some involuntarily adopted attitudes are justified according to EJ. John Heil finds this feature of the evidentialist position questionable. He says that the fact that we "speak of a person's beliefs as being warranted, justified, or rational ... makes it appear that ... believing something can, at least sometimes, be under the voluntary control of the believer."[3] Hilary Kornblith claims that it seems "unfair" to evaluate beliefs if they "are not subject" to "direct voluntary control."[4] Both Heil and Kornblith conclude that although beliefs are not under *direct* voluntary control, it is still appropriate to evaluate them because "they are not entirely out of our control either."[5] "One does have a say in the procedures one undertakes that lead to" the formation of beliefs.[6]

Doxastic attitudes need not be under any sort of voluntary control for them to be suitable for epistemic evaluation. Examples confirm that beliefs may be both involuntary and subject to epistemic evaluation. Suppose that a person spontaneously and involuntarily believes that the lights are on in the room, as a result of the familiar sort of completely convincing perceptual evidence. This belief is clearly justified, whether or not the person cannot voluntarily acquire, lose, or modify the cognitive process that led to the belief. Unjustified beliefs can also be involuntary. A paranoid man might believe without any supporting

evidence that he is being spied on. This belief might be a result of an uncontrollable desire to be a recipient of special attention. In such a case the belief is clearly epistemically unjustified even if the belief is involuntary and the person cannot alter the process leading to it.

The contrary view that only voluntary beliefs are justified or unjustified may seem plausible if one confuses the topic of EJ with an assessment of the *person*.[7] A person deserves praise or blame for being in a doxastic state only if that state is under the person's control.[8] The person who involuntarily believes in the presence of overwhelming evidence that the lights are on does not deserve praise for this belief. The belief is nevertheless justified. The person who believes that he is being spied on as a result of an uncontrollable desire does not deserve to be blamed for that belief. But there is a fact about the belief's epistemic merit. It is epistemically defective – it is held in the presence of insufficient evidence and is therefore unjustified.

Doxastic limits

Apart from the questions about doxastic voluntarism, it is sometimes claimed that it is inappropriate to set epistemic standards that are beyond normal human limits. Alvin Goldman recommends that epistemologists seek epistemic principles that can serve as practical guides to belief formation. Such principles, he contends, must take into account the limited cognitive capacities of people. Thus, he is led to deny a principle instructing people to believe all the logical consequences of their beliefs, since they are unable to have the infinite number of beliefs that following such a principle would require.[9] Goldman's view does not conflict with EJ, since EJ does not instruct anyone to believe anything. It simply states a necessary and sufficient condition for epistemic justification. Nor does Goldman think this view conflicts with EJ, since he makes it clear that the principles he is discussing are guides to action and not principles that apply the traditional concept of epistemic justification.

Although Goldman does not use facts about normal cognitive limits to argue against EJ, such an argument has been suggested by Kornblith and by Paul Thagard. Kornblith cites Goldman's work as an inspiration for his view that "having justified beliefs is simply doing the best one can in the light of the innate endowment one starts from."[10] Thagard contends that rational or justified principles of inference "should not demand of a reasoner inferential performance which exceeds the general psychological abilities of human beings."[11] Neither Thagard nor Kornblith argues against EJ, but it is easy to see how such an argument would go: A doxastic attitude toward a proposition is justified for a person only if having that attitude toward that proposition is within the normal doxastic capabilities of people. Some doxastic attitudes that fit a person's evidence are not within those capabilities. Yet EJ classifies them as justified. Hence, EJ is false.

We see no good reason here to deny EJ. The argument has as a premise the claim that some attitudes beyond normal limits do fit someone's evidence. The fact that we are limited to a finite number of beliefs is used to support this claim. But this fact does not establish the premise. There is no reason to think that an infinite number of beliefs fits any body of evidence that anyone ever has. The evidence that people have under ordinary circumstances never makes it evident, concerning every one of an infinite number of logical consequences of that evidence, that it is a consequence. Thus, believing each consequence will not fit any ordinary evidence. Furthermore, even if there are circumstances in which more beliefs fit a person's evidence than he is able to have, all that follows is that he cannot have at one time all the beliefs that fit. It does not follow that there is any particular fitting belief which is unattainable. Hence, the premise of the argument that says that EJ classifies as justified some normally unattainable beliefs is not established by means of this example. There does not seem to be any sort of plausible evidence that would establish this premise. While some empirical evidence may show that people typically do not form fitting attitudes in certain contexts, or that some fitting attitudes are beyond some individual's abilities, such evidence fails to show that any fitting attitudes are beyond normal limits.[12]

There is a more fundamental objection to this argument against EJ. There is no basis for the premise that what is epistemically justified must be restricted to feasible doxastic alternatives. It can be a worthwhile thing to help people to choose among the epistemic alternatives open to them. But suppose that there were occasions when forming the attitude that best fits a person's evidence was beyond normal cognitive limits. This would still be the attitude *justified* by the person's evidence. If the person had normal abilities, then he would be in the unfortunate position of being unable to do what is justified according to the standard for justification asserted by EJ. This is not a flaw in the account of justification. Some standards are met only by going beyond normal human limits. Standards that some teachers set for an "A" in a course are unattainable for most students. There are standards of artistic excellence that no one can meet, or at least standards that normal people cannot meet in any available circumstance. Similarly, epistemic justification might have been normally unattainable.

We conclude that neither considerations of doxastic voluntarism nor of doxastic limits provide any good reason to abandon EJ as an account of epistemic justification.

III

EJ sets an epistemic standard for evaluating doxastic conduct. In any case of a standard for conduct, whether it is voluntary or not, it is appropriate to speak of "requirements" or "obligations" that the standard imposes. The person who has overwhelming perceptual evidence for the proposition that the lights are on, epistemically ought to believe that proposition. The paranoid person epistemically ought not to believe that he is being spied upon when he has no evidence supporting this belief. We hold the general view that one epistemically ought to have the doxastic attitudes that fit one's evidence. We think that being epistemically obligatory is equivalent to being epistemically justified.

There are in the literature two other sorts of view about epistemic obligations. What is epistemically obligatory, according to these other views, does not always fit one's evidence. Thus, each of these views of epistemic obligation, when combined with our further thesis that being epistemically obligatory is equivalent to being epistemically justified, yields results incompatible with evidentialism. We shall now consider how these proposals affect EJ.

Justification and the obligation to believe truths

Roderick Chisholm holds that one has an "intellectual requirement" to try one's best to bring it about that, of the propositions one considers, one believes all and only the truths.[13] This theory of what our epistemic obligations are, in conjunction with our view that the justified attitudes are the ones we have an epistemic obligation to hold, implies the following principle:

> CJ Doxastic attitude D toward proposition p is justified for person S at time t if and only if S considers p at t and S's having D toward p at t would result from S's trying his best to bring it about that S believe p at t iff p is true.

Evaluation of CJ is complicated by an ambiguity in "trying one's best." It might mean "trying in that way which will in fact have the best result." Since the goal is to believe all and only the truths one considers, the best results would be obtained by believing each truth one considers and disbelieving each falsehood one considers. On this interpretation, CJ implies that believing each truth and disbelieving each falsehood one considers is justified whenever believing and disbelieving in these ways would result from something one could try to do.

On this interpretation CJ is plainly false. We are not justified in believing every proposition we consider that happens to be true and which we could believe by trying for the truth. It is possible to believe some unsubstantiated proposition in a reckless endeavor to believe a truth, and happen to be right. This would not be an "epistemically justified belief."[14]

It might be contended that trying one's best to believe truths and disbelieve falsehoods really amounts to trying to believe and disbelieve in accordance with one's evidence. We agree that gaining the doxastic attitudes that fit one's evidence is the epistemically best way to use one's evidence in trying to believe all and only the truths one considers. This interpretation of CJ makes it nearly equivalent to EJ. There are two relevant differences. First, CJ implies that one can have justified attitudes only toward propositions one actually considers. EJ does not have this

implication. CJ is also unlike EJ in implying that an attitude is justified if it would result from the *trying* to form the attitude that fits one's evidence. The attitude that is justified according to EJ is the one that as a matter of fact does fit one's evidence. This seems more plausible. What would happen if one tried to have a fitting attitude seems irrelevant – one might try but fail to form the fitting attitude.

We conclude that the doxastic attitudes that would result from carrying out the intellectual requirement that Chisholm identifies are not the epistemically justified attitudes.

Justification and epistemically responsible action

Another view about epistemic obligations, proposed by Hilary Kornblith, is that we are obligated to seek the truth and gather evidence in a responsible way. Kornblith also maintains that the justification of a belief depends on how responsibly one carried out the inquiry that led to the belief.[15] We shall now examine how the considerations leading to this view affect EJ.

Kornblith describes a case of what he regards as "epistemically culpable ignorance." It is an example in which a person's belief seems to fit his evidence, and thus it seems to be justified according to evidentialism. Kornblith contends that the belief is unjustified because it results from epistemically irresponsible behavior. His example concerns a headstrong young physicist who is unable to tolerate criticism. After presenting a paper to his colleagues, the physicist pays no attention to the devastating objection of a senior colleague. The physicist, obsessed with his own success, fails even to hear the objection, which consequently has no impact on his beliefs, Kornblith says that after this, the physicist's belief in his own theory is unjustified. He suggests that evidentialist theories cannot account for this fact.

Crucial details of this example are left unspecified, but in no case does it provide a refutation of evidentialism. If the young physicist is aware of the fact that his senior colleague is making an objection, then this fact is evidence he has against his theory, although it is unclear from just this much detail how decisive it would be. So, believing his theory may no longer be justified for him according to a purely evidentialist view. On the other hand, perhaps he remains entirely ignorant of the fact that a senior colleague is objecting to his theory. He might be "lost in thought" – privately engrossed in proud admiration of the paper he has just given – and fail to understand what is going on in the audience. If this happens, and his evidence supporting his theory is just as it was prior to his presentation of the paper, then believing the theory does remain justified for him (assuming that it was justified previously). There is no reason to doubt EJ in the light of this example. It may be true that the young physicist is an unpleasant fellow, and that he lacks intellectual integrity. This is an evaluation of the character of the physicist. It is supported by the fact that in this case he is not engaged in an impartial quest for the truth. But the physicist's character has nothing to do with the epistemic status of his belief in his theory.

Responsible evidence-gathering obviously has some epistemic significance. One serious epistemological question is that of how to engage in a thoroughgoing rational pursuit of the truth. Such a pursuit may require gathering evidence in responsible ways. It may also be necessary to be open to new ideas, to think about a variety of important issues, and to consider a variety of opinions about such issues. Perhaps it requires, as BonJour suggests, that one "reflect critically upon one's belief."[16] But everyone has some justified beliefs, even though virtually no one is fully engaged in a rational pursuit of the truth. EJ has no implication about the actions one must take in a rational pursuit of the truth. It is about the epistemic evaluation of attitudes given the evidence one does have, however one came to possess that evidence.

Examples like that of the headstrong physicist show no defect in the evidentialist view. Justified beliefs can result from epistemically irresponsible actions.

Other sorts of obligation

Having acknowledged at the beginning of this section that justified attitudes are in a sense obligatory, we wish to forestall confusions involving other notions of obligations. It is not the case that there is always a *moral* obligation to believe in accordance with one's evidence. Having a fitting attitude can bring about disastrous personal or social consequences. Vicious beliefs that lead to vicious acts can be epistemically justified. This rules out any moral obligation to have the epistemically justified attitude.[17]

It is also false that there is always a *prudential* obligation to have each epistemically justified attitude. John Heil discusses the following example.[18] Sally has fairly good evidence that her husband Burt has been seeing another woman. Their marriage is in a precarious condition. It would be best for Sally if their marriage were preserved. Sally foresees that, were she to believe that Burt has been seeing another woman, her resulting behavior would lead to their divorce. Given these assumptions, EJ counts as justified at least some measure of belief by Sally in the proposition that Burt has been seeing another woman. But Sally would be better off if she did not have this belief, in light of the fact that she would be best served by their continued marriage. Heil raises the question of what Sally's prudential duty is in this case. Sally's *epistemic* obligation is to believe that her husband is unfaithful. But that gives no reason to deny what seems obvious here. Sally *prudentially* ought to refrain from believing her husband to be unfaithful. It can be prudent not to have a doxastic attitude that is correctly said by EJ to be justified, just as it can be moral not to have such an attitude.

More generally, the causal consequences of having an unjustified attitude can be more beneficial in *any* sort of way than the consequences of having its justified alternative. We have seen that it can be morally and prudentially best not to have attitudes justified according to EJ. Failing to have these attitudes can also have the best results for the sake of *epistemic* goals such as the acquisition of knowledge. Roderick Firth points out that a scientist's believing against his evidence that he will recover from an illness may help to effect a recovery and so contribute to the growth of knowledge by enabling the scientist to continue his research.[19] William James's case for exercising "the will to believe" suggests that some evidence concerning the existence of God is available only after one believes in God in the absence of justifying evidence. EJ does not counsel against adopting such beliefs for the sake of these epistemic ends. EJ implies that the beliefs would be unjustified when adopted. This is not to say that the believing would do no epistemic good.

We acknowledge that it is appropriate to speak of epistemic obligations. But it is a mistake to think that what is epistemically obligatory, i.e., epistemically justified, is also morally or prudentially obligatory, or that it has the overall best epistemic consequences.

IV

Another argument that is intended to refute the evidentialist approach to justification concerns the ways in which a person can come to have an attitude that fits his evidence. Both Kornblith and Goldman propose examples designed to show that merely *having* good evidence for a proposition is not sufficient to make believing that proposition justified.[20] We shall work from Kornblith's formulation of the argument, since it is more detailed. Suppose Alfred is justified in believing *p*, and justified in believing if *p* then *q*. Alfred also believes *q*. EJ seems to imply that believing *q* is justified for Alfred, since that belief does seem to fit this evidence. Kornblith argues that Alfred's belief in *q* may still not be justified. It is not justified, according to Kornblith, if Alfred has a strong distrust of *modus ponens* and believes *q* because he likes the sound of the sentence expressing it rather than on the basis of the *modus ponens* argument. Similarly, Goldman says that a person's belief in *q* is not justified unless the belief is caused in some appropriate way.

Whether EJ implies that Alfred's belief in *q* is justified depends in part on an unspecified detail – Alfred's evidence concerning *modus ponens*. It is possible that Alfred has evidence against *modus ponens*. Perhaps he has just seen a version of the Liar paradox that seems to render *modus ponens* as suspect as the other rules and premises in the derivation. In the unlikely event that Alfred has such evidence, EJ implies that believing *q* is *not* justified for him. If rather, as we shall assume, his overall evidence supports *modus ponens* and *q*, then EJ does imply that believing *q* is justified for him.

When Alfred has strong evidence for *q*, his believing *q* is epistemically justified. This is the sense of "justified" captured by EJ. However, if Alfred's basis for believing *q* is not his evidence for it, but rather the sound of the sentence expressing *q*, then it seems equally clear that there is some sense in which this state of believing is epistemically "defective" – he did not arrive at the belief in the right way. The term "well-founded" is sometimes used to characterize an attitude that is epistemically both well-supported and properly arrived at. Well-foundedness is a second evidentialist notion used to evaluate doxastic states. It is an evidentialist notion because its application depends on two matters of evidence – the evidence one *has*, and the evidence one *uses* in forming the attitude. More precisely:

WF S's doxastic attitude *D* at *t* toward proposition *p* is well-founded if and only if

(i)   having *D* toward *p* is justified for S at *t*; and

(ii) S has *D* toward *p* on the basis of some body of evidence *e*, such that
   (a) S has *e* as evidence at *t*;
   (b) having *D* toward *p* fits *e*; and
   (c) there is no more inclusive body of evidence *é* had by S at *t* such that having *D* toward *p* does not fit *é*.[21]

Since the evidentialist can appeal to this notion of well-foundedness, cases in which a person has but does not use justifying evidence do not refute evidentialism. Kornblith and Goldman's intuitions about such cases can be accommodated. A person in Alfred's position *is* in an epistemically defective state – his belief in *q* is not well-founded. Having said this, it is reasonable also to affirm the other evidentialist judgment that Alfred's belief in *q* is in another sense epistemically right – it is justified.[22]

V

The theory of epistemic justification that has received the most attention recently is reliabilism. Roughly speaking, this is the view that epistemically justified beliefs are the ones that result from belief-forming processes that reliably lead to true beliefs.[23] In this section we consider whether reliabilism casts doubt on evidentialism.

Although reliabilists generally formulate their view as an account of epistemic justification, it is clear that in its simplest forms it is better regarded as an account of well-foundedness. In order for a belief to be favorably evaluated by the simple sort of reliabilism sketched above, the belief must actually be held, as is the case with WF. And just as with WF, the belief must be "grounded" in the proper way. Where reliabilism appears to differ from WF is over the conditions under which a belief is properly grounded. According to WF, this occurs when the belief is based on fitting evidence. According to reliabilism, a belief is properly grounded if it results from a belief-forming process that reliably leads to true beliefs. These certainly are *conceptually* different accounts of the grounds of well-founded beliefs.

In spite of this conceptual difference, reliabilism and WF may be extensionally equivalent. The question of equivalence depends on the resolution of two unclarities in reliabilism. One pertains to the notion of a belief-forming process and the other to the notion of reliability.

An unclarity about belief-forming processes arises because every belief is caused by a sequence of particular events which is an instance of many types of causal processes. Suppose that one evening Jones looks out of his window and sees a bright shining disk-shaped object. The object is in fact a luminous frisbee, and Jones clearly remembers having given one of these to his daughter. But Jones is attracted to the idea that extra-terrestrials are visiting the Earth. He manages to believe that he is seeing a flying saucer. Is the process that caused this belief reliable? Since the sequence of events leading to his belief is an instance of many types of process, the answer depends upon which of these many types is the relevant one. The sequence falls into highly general categories such as perceptually-based belief formation and visually-based belief formation. It seems that if these are the relevant categories, then his belief is indeed reliably formed, since these are naturally regarded as "generally reliable" sorts of belief-forming processes. The sequence of events leading to Jones's belief also falls into many relatively specific categories such as night-vision-of-a-nearby-object and vision-in-Jones's-precise-environmental-circumstances. These are not clearly reliable types. The sequence is also an instance of this contrived kind: process-leading-from-obviously-defeated-evidence-to-the-belief-that-one-sees-a-flying-saucer. This, presumably, is an unreliable kind of process. Finally, there is the maximally specific process that occurs only when physiological events occur that are exactly like those that led to Jones's belief that he saw a

flying saucer. In all likelihood this kind of process occurred only once. Processes of these types are of differing degrees of reliability, no matter how reliability is determined. The implications of reliabilism for the case are rendered definite only when the kind of process whose reliability is relevant is specified. Reliabilists have given little attention to this matter, and those that have specified relevant kinds have not done so in a way that gives their theory in intuitively acceptable extension.[24]

The second unclarity in reliabilism concerns the notion of reliability itself. Reliability is fundamentally a property of kinds of belief-forming processes, not of sequences of particular events. But we can say that a sequence is reliable provided its relevant type is reliable. The problem raised above concerns the specification of relevant types. The current problem is that of specifying the conditions under which a kind of process is *reliable*. Among possible accounts is one according to which a kind of process is reliable provided most instances of that kind until now have led to true beliefs. Alternative accounts measure the reliability of a kind of process by the frequency with which instances of it produce true beliefs in the future as well as the past, or by the frequency with which its instances produce true beliefs in possible worlds that are similar to the world of evaluation in some designated respect, or by the frequency with which its instances produce true beliefs in all possible worlds.[25]

Because there are such drastically different ways of filling in the details of reliabilism the application of the theory is far from clear. The possible versions of reliabilism seem to include one that is extensionally equivalent to WF. It might be held that all beliefs are formed by one of two relevant kinds of belief-forming process. One kind has as instances all and only those sequences of events leading to a belief that is based on fitting evidence; the other is a kind of process that has as instances all and only those sequences leading to a belief that is not based on fitting evidence. If a notion of reliability can be found on which the former sort of process is reliable and the latter is not, the resulting version of reliabilism would be very nearly equivalent to WF.[26] We do not claim that reliabilists would favor this version of reliabilism. Rather, our point is that the fact that this *is* a version shows that reliabilism may not even be a rival to WF.[27]

Evaluation of reliabilism is further complicated by the fact that reliabilists seem to differ
about whether they *want* their theory to have
approximately the same extension as WF in fact
has. The credibility of reliabilism and its relevance
to WF depend in part on the concept reliabilists
are really attempting to analyze. An example first
described by Laurence BonJour helps to bring out
two alternatives.[28] BonJour's example is of a
person who is clairvoyant. As a result of his clairvoyance he comes to believe that the President is
in New York City. The person has no evidence
showing that he is clairvoyant and no other evidence supporting his belief about the President.
BonJour claims that the example is a counter-
example to reliabilism, since the clairvoyant's
belief is not justified (we would add: and therefore
ill-founded), although the process that caused it is
reliable – the person really is clairvoyant.

The general sort of response to this example
that seems to be most commonly adopted by reliabilists is in effect to agree that such beliefs are
not well-founded. They interpret or revise reliabilism with the aim of avoiding the counter-
example.[29] An alternative response would be to
argue that the reliability of clairvoyance shows
that the belief *is* well-founded, and thus that the
example does not refute reliabilism.[30]

We are tempted to respond to the second alternative – beliefs such as that of the clairvoyant in
BonJour's example really are well-founded – that
this is so clear an instance of an ill-founded belief
that any proponent of that view must have in
mind a different concept from the one we are discussing. The clairvoyant has no reason for holding his belief about the President. The fact that
the belief was caused by a process of a reliable
kind – clairvoyance – is a significant fact about it.
Such a belief may merit some favorable term of
epistemic appraisal, e.g., "objectively probable."
But the belief is not well-founded.

There are, however, two lines of reasoning that
could lead philosophers to think that we must
reconcile ourselves to the clairvoyant's belief
turning out to be well-founded. According to one
of these arguments, examples such as that of
Alfred (discussed in Section IV above) show that
the evidentialist account of epistemic merit is
unsatisfactory and that epistemic merit must be
understood in terms of the reliability of belief-
forming processes.[31] Since the clairvoyant's belief

is reliably formed, our initial inclination to regard
it as ill-founded must be mistaken.

This argument is unsound. The most that the
example about Alfred shows is that there is a concept of favorable epistemic appraisal other than
justification, and that this other concept involves
the notion of the *basis* of a belief. We believe that
WF satisfactorily captures this other concept.
There is no need to move to a reliabilist account,
according to which some sort of causal reliability
is *sufficient* for epistemic justification. The Alfred
example does not establish that some version of
reliabilism is correct. It does not establish that the
clairvoyant's belief is well-founded.

The second argument for the conclusion that
the clairvoyant's belief is well-founded makes use
of the strong similarity between clairvoyance in
BonJour's example and normal perception. We
claim that BonJour's clairvoyant is not justified in
his belief about the President because that belief
does not fit his evidence. Simply having a spontaneous uninferred belief about the whereabouts of
the President does not provide evidence for its
truth. But, it might be asked, what better evidence
is there for any ordinary perceptual belief, say,
that one sees a book? If there is no relevant epistemological difference between ordinary perceptual beliefs and the clairvoyant's belief, then they
should be evaluated similarly. The argument continues with the point that reliabilism provides an
explanation of the crucial similarity between
ordinary perceptual beliefs and the clairvoyant's
belief – both perception and clairvoyance *work*, in
the sense that both are reliable. So beliefs caused
by each process are well-founded on a reliabilist
account. The fact that reliabilism satisfactorily
explains this is to the theory's credit. On the other
hand, in advocating evidentialism we have
claimed that perceptual beliefs are well-founded
and that the clairvoyant's belief is not. But there
appears to be no relevant evidential difference
between these beliefs. Thus, if the evidentialist
view of the matter cannot be defended, then reliabilism is the superior theory and we should
accept its consequence – the clairvoyant's belief is
well-founded.

One problem with this argument is that reliabilism has no satisfactory explanation of *anything*
until the unclarities discussed above are removed
in an acceptable way: What shows that perception
and clairvoyance are relevant and reliable types of

processes? In any event, there *is* an adequate evidentialist explanation of the difference between ordinary perceptual beliefs and the clairvoyant's belief. On one interpretation of clairvoyance, it is a process whereby one is caused to have beliefs about objects hidden from ordinary view without any conscious state having a role in the causal process. The clairvoyant does not have the conscious experience of, say, seeming to see the President in some characteristic New York City setting, and on that basis form the belief that he is in New York. In this respect, the current version of clairvoyance is unlike ordinary perception, which does include conscious perceptual states. Because of this difference, ordinary perceptual beliefs are based on evidence – the evidence of these sensory states – whereas the clairvoyant beliefs are not based on evidence. Since WF requires that well-founded beliefs be based on fitting evidence, and typical clairvoyant beliefs on the current interpretation are not based on any evidence at all, the clairvoyant beliefs do not satisfy WF.

Suppose instead that clairvoyance does include visual experiences, though of remote objects that cannot stimulate the visual system in any normal way. Even if there are such visual experiences that could serve as a basis for a clairvoyant's beliefs, still there is a relevant epistemological difference between beliefs based on normal perceptual experience and the clairvoyant's belief in BonJour's example. We have collateral evidence to the effect that when we have perceptual experience of certain kinds, external conditions of the corresponding kinds normally obtain. For example, we have evidence supporting the proposition that when we have the usual sort of experience of seeming to see a book, we usually do in fact see a book. This includes evidence from the coherence of these beliefs with beliefs arising from other perceptual sources, and it also includes testimonial evidence. This latter point is easily overlooked. One reason that the belief that one sees a book fits even a child's evidence when she has a perceptual experience of seeing a book is that children are taught, when they have the normal sort of visual experiences, that they are seeing a physical object of the relevant kind. This testimony, typically from people whom the child has reason to trust, provides evidence for the child. And of course testimony from others during adult life also gives evidence for the verdicality of normal visual

experience. On the other hand, as BonJour describes his example, the clairvoyant has no confirmation at all of his clairvoyant beliefs. Indeed, he has evidence against these beliefs, since the clairvoyant perceptual experiences do not cohere with his other experiences. We conclude, therefore, that evidentialists can satisfactorily explain why ordinary perceptual beliefs are typically well-founded and unconfirmed clairvoyant beliefs, even if reliably caused, are not. There is no good reason to abandon our initial intuition that the beliefs such as those of the clairvoyant in BonJour's example are not well-founded.

Again, reliabilists could respond to BonJour's example either by claiming that the clairvoyant's belief is in fact well-founded or by arguing that reliabilism does not imply that it is well-founded. We turn now to the second of these alternatives, the one most commonly adopted by reliabilists. This view can be defended by arguing either that reliabilism can be reformulated so that it lacks this implication, or that as currently formulated it lacks this implication. We pointed out above that as a general approach reliabilism is sufficiently indefinite to allow interpretations under which it does lack the implication in question. The only way to achieve this result that we know of that is otherwise satisfactory requires the introduction of evidentialist concepts. The technique is to specify the relevant types of belief-forming processes in evidentialist terms. It is possible to hold that the relevant types of belief-forming process are believing something on the basis of fitting evidence and believing not as a result of fitting evidence. This sort of "reliabilism" is a roundabout approximation of the straightforward evidentialist thesis, WF. We see no reason to couch the approximated evidentialist theory in reliabilist terms. Moreover, the reliabilist approximation is not exactly equivalent to WF, and where it differs it appears to go wrong. The difference is this: it seems possible for the process of believing on the basis of fitting evidence to be unreliable. Finding a suitable sort of reliability makes all the difference here. In various possible worlds where our evidence is mostly misleading, the frequency with which fitting evidence causes true belief is low. Thus, this type of belief-forming process is not "reliable" in such worlds in any straightforward way that depends on actual frequencies. Perhaps a notion of reliability that avoids this result can be found. We know of no such notion which does not create trouble elsewhere for the theory. So, the reliabilist view under consideration has the consequence that in such worlds beliefs based on fitting evidence are not well-founded. This is counterintuitive.[32]

In this section we have compared reliabilism and evidentialism. The vagueness of reliabilism makes it difficult to determine what implications the theory has and it is not entirely clear what implications reliabilists want their theory to have. If reliabilists want their theory to have approximately the same extension as WF, we see no better way to accomplish this than one which makes the theory an unnecessarily complex and relatively implausible approximation to evidentialism. If, on the other hand, reliabilists want their theory to have an extension which is substantially different from that of WF, and yet some familiar notion of "a reliable kind of process" is to be decisive for their notion of well-foundedness, then it becomes clear that the concept they are attempting to analyze is not one evidentialists seek to characterize. This follows from the fact that on this alternative they count as well-founded attitudes that plainly do not exemplify the concept evidentialists are discussing. In neither case, then, does reliabilism pose a threat to evidentialism.

VI

Summary and conclusion

We have defended evidentialism. Some opposition to evidentialism rests on the view that a doxastic attitude can be justified for a person only if forming the attitude is an action under the person's voluntary control. EJ is incompatible with the conjunction of this sort of doxastic voluntarism and the plain fact that some doxastic states that fit a person's evidence are out of that person's control. We have argued that no good reason has been given for thinking that an attitude is epistemically justified only if having it is under voluntary control.

A second thesis contrary to EJ is that a doxastic attitude can be justified only if having that attitude is within the normal doxastic limits of humans. We have held that the attitudes that are epistemically justified according to EJ are within these limits, and that even if they were not, that fact would not suffice to refute EJ.

Some philosophers have contended that believing a proposition, p, is justified for S only when S has gone about gathering evidence about p in a responsible way, or has come to believe p as a result of seeking a meritorious epistemic goal such as the discovery of truth. This thesis conflicts with EJ, since believing p may fit one's evidence no matter how irresponsible one may have been in seeking evidence about p and no matter what were the goals that led to the belief. We agree that there is some epistemic merit in responsibly gathering evidence and in seeking the truth. But we see no reason to think that epistemic justification turns on such matters.

Another thesis conflicting with EJ is that merely having evidence is not sufficient to justify belief, since the believer might not make proper use of the evidence in forming the belief. Consideration of this claim led us to make use of a second evidentialist notion, well-foundedness. It does not, however, provide any good reason to think that EJ is false. Nor do we find reason to abandon evidentialism in favor of reliabilism. Evidentialism remains the most plausible view of epistemic justification.

Notes

1   EJ is compatible with the existence of varying strengths of belief and disbelief. If there is such variation, then the greater the preponderance of evidence, the stronger the doxastic attitude that fits the evidence.
2   There are difficult questions about the concept of fit, as well as about what it is for someone to *have* something as evidence, and of what kind of thing constitutes evidence. As a result, there are some cases in which it is difficult to apply EJ. For example, it is unclear whether a person has as evidence propositions he is not currently thinking of, but could recall with some prompting. As to what constitutes evidence, it seems clear that this includes both beliefs and sensory states such

as feeling very warm and having the visual experience of seeing blue. Some philosophers seem to think that only beliefs can justify beliefs. (See, for example, Keith Lehrer, *Knowledge* (Oxford: Oxford University Press, 1974), pp. 187–8.) The application of EJ is clear enough to do the work that we intend here – a defense of the evidentialist position.

3   See "Doxastic agency," *Philosophical Studies* 43 (1983), pp. 355–64. The quotation is from p. 355.

4   See "The psychological turn," *Australasian Journal of Philosophy* 60 (1982), pp. 238–53. The quotation is from p. 252.

5   Ibid., p. 253.

6   Heil, "Doxastic agency," p. 363.

7   Kornblith may be guilty of this confusion. He writes, "if a person has an unjustified belief, that person is epistemically culpable," "The psychological turn," p. 243.

8   Nothing we say here should be taken to imply that any doxastic states are in fact voluntarily entered.

9   See "Epistemics: The regulative theory of cognition," *The Journal of Philosophy* LXXV (1978), pp. 509–23, esp. p. 510 and p. 514.

10 "Justified belief and epistemically responsible action," *The Philosophical Review* 92 (1983), pp. 33–48. The quotation is from p. 46.

11 Paul Thagard, "From the descriptive to the normative in psychology and logic," *Philosophy of Science* 49 (1982), pp. 24–42. The quotation is from p. 34.

12 Another version of this argument is that EJ is false because it classifies as justified for a person attitudes that are beyond *that person's* limits. This version is subject to similar criticisms.

13 See *Theory of Knowledge*, 2nd edn (Englewood Cliffs, NJ: Prentice-Hall, 1977), especially pp. 12–15.

14 Roderick Firth makes a similar point against a similar view in "Are epistemic concepts reducible to ethical concepts," in Alvin Goldman and J. Kim *Values and Morals* (Dordrecht: D. Reidel, 1978), pp. 215–29.

15 Kornblith defends this view in "Justified belief and epistemically responsible action." Some passages suggest that he intends to introduce a new notion of justification, one to be understood in terms of epistemically responsible action. But some passages, especially in Section II, suggest that the traditional analysis of justification is being found to be objectionable and inferior to the one he proposes.

16 Laurence BonJour, "Externalist theories of empirical justification," *Midwest Studies* V (1980), p. 63.

17 This is contrary to the view of Richard Gale, defended in "William James and the ethics of belief," *American Philosophical Quarterly* 17 (1980), pp. 1–14, and of W. K. Clifford who said, "It is wrong always, everywhere, and for every one, to believe anything upon insufficient evidence" (quoted by William James in "The will to believe," reprinted in J. Feinberg (ed.), *Reason and Responsibility*, (Belmont, California: Wadsworth Publishing Co., 1981) p. 100).

18 See "Believing what one ought," *Journal of Philosophy* 80, pp. 752ff.

19 See "Epistemic merit, intrinsic and instrumental," *Proceedings and Addresses of The American Philosophical Association* 55 (1981), pp. 5–6.

20 See Kornblith's "Beyond foundationalism and the coherence theory," *The Journal of Philosophy* 77 (1980), pp. 597–612, esp. pp. 601 ff. and Goldman's "What is justified belief?" this vol., ch. 26.

21 Clause (ii) of WF is intended to accommodate the fact that a well-founded attitude need not be based on a person's whole body of evidence. What seems required is that the person base a well-founded attitude on a justifying part of the person's evidence, and that he not ignore any evidence he has that defeats the justifying power of the evidence he does base his attitude on. It might be that his defeating evidence is itself defeated by a still wider body of his evidence. In such a case, the person's attitude is well-founded only if he takes the wider body into account.

WF uses our last main primitive concept – that of *basing* an attitude on a body of evidence. This notion is reasonably clear, though an analysis would be useful. See Note 22 below for one difficult question about what is entailed.

22 Goldman uses this sort of example only to show that there is a causal element in the concept of justification. We acknowledge that there is an epistemic concept – well-foundedness – that appeals to the notion of

basing an attitude on evidence, and this may be a causal notion. What seems to confer epistemic merit on basing one's belief on the evidence is that in doing one *appreciates* the evidence. It is unclear whether one can appreciate the evidence without being caused to have the belief by the evidence. But in any event we see no such causal requirement in the case of justification.

23   The clearest and most influential discussion of reliabilism is in Goldman's "What is justified belief?" One of the first statements of the theory appears in David Armstrong's *Belief, Truth and Knowledge* (London: Cambridge University Press, 1973). For extensive bibliographies on reliabilism, see Frederick Schmitt's "Reliability, objectivity, and the background of justification," *Australasian Journal of Philosophy* 62 (1984), pp. 1–15, and Richard Feldman's "Reliability and justification," *The Monist* 68 (1985), pp. 159–74.

24   For discussion of the problem of determining relevant kinds of belief-forming processes, see Goldman, "What is justified belief?", Schmitt, "Reliability, objectivity, and the background of justification," Feldman, "Reliability and justification," and Feldman, "Schmitt on reliability, objectivity, and justification," *Australasian Journal of Philosophy* 63 (1985), pp. 354–60.

25   In "Reliability and justified belief," *Canadian Journal of Philosophy* 14, (1984), pp. 103–15, John Pollock argues that there is no account of reliability suitable for reliabilists.

26   This version of reliabilism will not be exactly equivalent to WF because it ignores the factors introduced by clause (ii) of WF.

27   It is also possible that versions of reliabilism making use only of natural psychological kinds of belief-forming processes are extensionally equivalent to WF. Goldman seeks to avoid evaluative epistemic concepts in his theory of epistemic justification, so he would not find an account of justification satisfactory unless it appealed only to such natural kinds. See "What is justified belief?"

28   See "Externalist theories of empirical justification," p. 62.

29   See Goldman, "What Is Justified Belief?", this vol., p. 333, Kornblith, "Beyond foundationalism and the coherence theory," pp. 609–11, and Frederick Schmitt, "Reliability, objectivity, and the background of justification."

30   We know of one who has explicitly taken this approach. It seems to fit most closely with the view defended by David Armstrong in *Belief, Truth and Knowledge*.

31   We know of no one who explicitly defends this inference. In "The psychological turn," p. 241 ff., Kornblith argues that these examples show that justification depends upon "psychological connections" and "the workings of the appropriate belief forming process." But he clearly denies there that reliabilism is directly implied.

32   Stewart Cohen has made this point in "Justification and truth," *Philosophical Studies* 46 (1984), pp. 279–95. Cohen makes the point in the course of developing a dilemma. He argues that reliabilism has the sort of flaw that we describe above when we appeal to worlds where evidence is mostly misleading. Cohen also contends that reliabilism has the virtue of providing a clear explanation of how the epistemic notion of justification is connected with the notion of truth. A theory that renders this truth connection inexplicable is caught on the second horn of Cohen's dilemma.

Although Cohen does not take up evidentialism as we characterize it, the second horn of his dilemma affects EJ and WF. They do not explain how having an epistemically justified or well-founded belief is connected to the truth of that belief. Evidentialists can safely say this much about the truth connection: evidence that makes believing *p* justified is evidence on which it is *epistemically* probable that *p* is true. Although there is this connection between justification and truth, we acknowledge that there may be no analysis of epistemic probability that makes the connection to truth as close, or as clear, as might have been hoped.

Cohen argues that there must be a truth connection. This shows no flaw in EJ or WF unless they are incompatible with there being such a connection. Cohen does not argue for this incompatibility and we know of no reason to believe that it exists. So at most Cohen's dilemma shows that evidentialists have work left to do.

CHAPTER 25

Skepticism and Rationality

Richard Foley

Skeptical hypotheses have been allowed to set the terms of the epistemological debate. They convince no one. Yet they have an enormous influence. It is often influence by provocation. They provoke epistemologists into endorsing metaphysical and linguistic positions that antecedently would have seemed to have had little appeal. Skeptical hypotheses, it is said, cannot even be meaningfully asserted, or if they can, the nature of God or the nature of objects or the nature of thought makes it altogether impossible for them to be true. There are those who refuse to be provoked, but even their epistemologies tend to be dominated by skeptical hypotheses. The hypotheses push them into an overly defensive posture from which it can seem that the test of an epistemology is how well it would fare in a hostile environment. There must be a third way. There must be a way to think about skeptical hypotheses that is neither dismissive nor submissive.

The kind of skeptical challenge that is most familiar to us is the kind that concerned Descartes. To be sure, the skeptical tradition is an ancient one, but the challenges of the ancient skeptics had a different aim from those discussed by Descartes. The followers of Pyrrho of Elis, for example, saw skepticism as a way of life and a desirable one at

Originally published in M. D. Roth and G. Ross (eds), *Doubting* (Dordrecht: Kluwer Academic Publishers, 1990), pp. 69–81.

that. Suspending judgement about how things really are was thought to be a means to tranquillity. There is no hint of this in Descartes or in the Enlightenment philosophers who succeeded him. Descartes did think that skeptical doubt could be put to good use. It could help deliver us from prejudices and thereby help put our beliefs upon a secure foundation. But even for Descartes, skepticism was first and foremost a threat rather than an opportunity, and it remains so for us. However, Descartes thought that it was a threat that could be successfully met. He thought that by making rational use of our cognitive resources, we can be guaranteed of the truth. Correspondingly, he thought that error is something for which we are always responsible. We have the tools to avoid it. Knowledge is ours for the taking. We need only to be sufficiently reflective and sufficiently cautious. For if we are sufficiently reflective we will come to perceive clearly and distinctly the truth of various claims, and if we are sufficiently cautious we will refrain from believing anything else. Skeptical hypotheses were of interest for Descartes because they provided him with a dramatic way to illustrate these assumptions. They helped him to dramatize the potential power of reason. One need not rely upon tradition or authority for one's opinions. One can stand alone intellectually, deciding for oneself what to make of the world and what to make of one's tradition. And if in doing so one makes proper use of one's reason, one can be assured of knowledge.

An increasing specialization of intellectual labor has made us sensitive, in a way in which Descartes was not, about the extent to which we rely upon the opinions of others, just as a heightened appreciation of cultural relativity has made us more sensitive about the extent to which we are shaped by our traditions. Even so, we are as reluctant to rely uncritically upon our authorities and traditions as Descartes and his Enlightenment successors were upon theirs. We realize how difficult it is to distance ourselves intellectually from our surroundings, but we realize also that even our best scientists can be mistaken and that even our most venerable traditions can be misguided. As a result, we too feel the need to make up our own minds. This creates for us an intellectual predicament that is much like the one that Descartes describes at the beginning of the *Meditations*. It is an egocentric predicament, prompted by a simple question, "What am I to believe?" I cannot simply read off from the world what is true, nor can I unproblematically rely upon the acknowledged experts or the received traditions to guide me towards the truth. I instead must marshall my own resources. I must marshall them to determine by my own lights what is true and who is reliable and what if anything is defensible about the traditions of my community. In this respect the individualism of Descartes has won the day.

What we find unacceptable in Descartes is his optimism. We think it naive. We no longer think that by properly marshalling our resources we can be assured of the truth. Being sufficiently reflective and sufficiently cautious is no guarantee that we will avoid error. It is not even a guarantee of reliability. Even so, philosophical problems come down to us through time, and today we remain under the spell of the epistemological aspirations of Descartes, Locke, Hume, Kant and others. The cure is to remind ourselves that their aims need not be ours. What they took to be an intellectual problem in need of a solution we can appreciate as part of the human condition. Given the kind of creatures that we are, we cannot help but lack guarantees of the sort that they sought. This is no more a problem for us than is that of finding a way to do without oxygen. We just are creatures who need oxygen. Similarly, the lack of intellectual guarantees just is part of the human condition. The problem is one of how to react to that condition.

The reaction need not be one of abandoning egocentric epistemology. Reliabilism, for example, constitutes such an abandonment. The egocentric question is "What am I to believe?" To answer this question, I must marshall my resources in an effort to determine what methods of inquiry are reliable. So, from the egocentric perspective, it is altogether unhelpful to be told that I am to have beliefs that are the products of reliable methods. Of course, no sensible reliabilist would claim otherwise. The point, rather, is that reliabilists tend to be satisfied with an epistemology that does not address the problems of the egocentric predicament, despite the fact that such problems have been at the heart of the great epistemological projects of the past. My point, in turn, is that we need not be satisfied with such an epistemology. We can do better.

But if we are to do better, we must give up an assumption that has had a hold on epistemologists from Descartes through Gettier. According to Descartes, it is rational to believe just that which is clear and distinct for you, and what is clear and distinct for you is true. So, for Descartes rational belief always results in knowledge. This means that there are no Gettier problems within Cartesian epistemology. No one can rationally infer a truth from a rational but false belief, since there are no rational false beliefs. Today we standardly construe the link between rational belief and true belief in a looser manner than did Descartes. A rational belief can be false. So, Gettier problems do arise within our epistemologies. Even so, the difference between Cartesian and contemporary epistemologies is not so great, since within the latter it still is commonly assumed that a rational true belief absent Gettier problems is always knowledge. It is this assumption that must be abandoned. More exactly, it must be abandoned if the answer to the question "What is it rational for me to believe?" is to be relevant to the egocentric predicament. The assumption must be abandoned because it ties rational belief too closely with knowledge and, as a consequence, too closely with reliability. For if by being rational one cannot be assured of having mostly true beliefs, then, contrary to the assumption, a rational true belief need not be a good candidate for knowledge even absent Gettier problems.

Skeptical hypotheses can help illustrate this. Imagine a world in which a demon alters your environment so that you make massive errors about it. You regularly make perceptual mistakes. Even so, the demon allows you to have a few isolated true beliefs about your environment. Perhaps the demon permits the existence of only one chair and it is the one that you are now sitting upon. So, your belief that you are now sitting upon a chair is true. Yet almost all of your other beliefs about your environment are false. This true belief of yours is not a particularly good candidate for knowledge, but why not? There need not be Gettier problems here. You need not have inferred the truth that you are now sitting upon a chair from any falsehood. But then, on the assumption that rational true belief absent Gettier problems is knowledge, the explanation must be that your belief is not rational. But why isn't it rational? Again we seem to have little choice. The explanation must cite whatever it is that we think prevents you from having knowledge. So, if we think that you do not know that you are sitting upon a chair because your belief is the product of perceptual equipment that is unreliable in your current environment, this same fact must be what precludes your belief from being rational. The more closely rational belief is tied to knowledge, the more difficult it is to avoid this conclusion.

My counterproposal is that the prerequisites of rational belief are not so closely tied to the conditions of knowledge. More exactly, the proposal is that this is so for the sense of rational belief that presupposes the egocentric perspective. This is not the only sense of rational belief. On the contrary, we evaluate beliefs from a variety of perspectives, depending on the context and our purposes, and we tend to give expression to these evaluations using the language of rationality.[1] The more objective the perspective that is presupposed, the more plausible will be the idea that a rational true belief absent Gettier problems is always an instance of knowledge. However, this is not so for egocentrically rational belief. The evil demon or the scientist who envats your brain deprive you of knowledge, but they need not deprive you of the opportunity of being egocentrically rational. This is the real lesson of the evil demon and the brain in the vat. By hypothesis these are situations that you could not distinguish from what you take to be your current situation. From your skin in, everything about

these situations is as it is now. And yet, from your skin out, things are drastically different from what you take them to be in the current situation. Still, you would have egocentric reasons in such situations to believe exactly what you do now. The demon does not deprive you of these reasons. Rather, he alters your environment so that these reasons are no longer reliable indicators of truths. In so doing he deprives you of knowledge.

Knowledge, then, requires an element of luck, of good fortune. We cannot altogether eliminate the possibility of massive error by being egocentrically rational. We need the world to cooperate. This is what skeptical hypotheses teach us.[2] Knowledge is not within our control to the degree that egocentric rationality is. If contrary to what we think, the world or something in it conspires against us, then so much the worse for us as knowing creatures. Nothing that we can do with respect to getting our own house in order will succeed in bringing us knowledge. This is not a comforting thought. We like to think of knowledge as part of our birthright. The thought that it might not be is so discomforting that it makes an appeal to idealism in one of its many garbs attractive to some. This is an appeal to be resisted. It has all the advantages of metaphysics over a straightforward assessment of our situation. The better alternative is to give up success as a condition of egocentric rationality – to admit that this kind of rationality in and of itself is not enough to guarantee either truth or reliability.

Many of us will find it difficult to admit this, especially when doing philosophy. Among philosophers it is often taken for granted that the worst charge that we can make against others is that they are irrational. This attitude finds its way into our ethics as well as our epistemology. We resist the idea that egoists can be as rational as the rest of us. We think that we must prove that they are irrational, as if we would be at a loss as to how to criticize them if we could not do so. The remedy is to remind ourselves that not every failure need be one of rationality. There can be other explanations for moral failures. They might be the result of inadequate moral training, for example – a training that did not sufficiently develop our moral sensitivities. As a result, we might not be able to discriminate finely enough among the relevant features of morally difficult situations. Or more seriously, it may have left us with a fundamentally flawed character, one that has us caring for the wrong things.

Analogously, we may be tempted to think that someone who has massively mistaken beliefs must be irrational, as if this were the only possible explanation of their being so thoroughly misguided. But again, we need to remind ourselves that not every failure is a failure of rationality. There are other explanations for intellectual error, even widespread error. Like moral failure, it might be largely a matter of bad training. We might have been brought up in a culture whose intellectual traditions encourage error, a tradition that emphasizes magic, for example. Or more ominously, we might have inappropriate cognitive equipment. We might not be cognitively suited to detect truths in the environment in which we find ourselves. But whatever the explanation, the point is the same: Rationality in the theoretical sphere need be no more intimately tied to knowledge than it is to goodness in the practical sphere. Just as you can be rational and yet lacking in virtue, so too you can be rational and yet lacking in knowledge. Appreciating this can help cure the preoccupation with skepticism that has dominated modern epistemology. It can allow egocentric epistemology to be done non-defensively.[3]

A non-defensive epistemology is one that refuses to apologize for a lack of guarantees. There is no guarantee that by being rational you will avoid error. There is no guarantee that you will avoid massive error. It need not even be probable that you will avoid massive error. Much of the implausibility of the Cartesian project arises from its failure to recognize that this is part of our intellectual condition. It instead insists that by being rational we can be assured of success. This insistence has disastrous consequences for egocentric epistemology. For contrary to what Descartes thought, there is nothing that we can do with respect to marshalling our cognitive resources that will result in such guarantees. Marshall them as we please. We will still need the world to cooperate. Consider the trust that we place in our perceptual equipment. If unbeknownst to us there is a deceiving demon in this world, then many of our perceptual beliefs will be false. And if most other close worlds are also demon worlds, then trusting our perceptual equipment does not even make it probable that we will avoid massive error.[4] A non-defensive

epistemology refuses to be intimidated by this possibility. It refuses to be intimidated into making success or likely success a prerequisite of rationality. It allows that it might be rational for us to trust our perceptual equipment even if doing so, unbeknownst to us, is likely to result in massive error.

It is a mistake for an egocentric epistemology to insist upon any kind of guarantee whatsoever between rationality and truth or likely-truth. This is the deepest flaw in the Cartesian approach to epistemology. It is not just that Descartes tried to guarantee too much, although this too is so. He unrealistically insisted that by being egocentrically rational we can be altogether assured of avoiding error. He was thus forced to regard any skeptical conjecture, no matter how far-fetched, as a *prima facie* defeater, one which itself had to be conclusively defeated before a claim could be rationally believed. But of course, if this were so, not much of anything would be rational for us to believe.

It might seem that the solution is simply to weaken the guarantee, but this would still leave us with a defensive epistemology, and one that would face exactly the same problem that plagues Cartesian epistemology. This problem arises regardless of the strength of the guarantee, and it arises in exactly the same form as it did for Descartes. It arises if we say that by being rational we can be assured of having mostly true beliefs. It arises if we say more cautiously that by being rational we can at least be assured of avoiding the likelihood of massive error. It even arises if we say that by being rational we can be assured only that the likelihood of our avoiding error is greater than if we were not rational.[5] For regardless of the nature of the guarantee, there will be no non-question begging assurances that the way in which we are marshalling our cognitive resources generates beliefs that meet the guarantee. There will be no non-question begging assurances, in other words, that the way in which we are marshalling our resources is suitable for our environment.

After all, the search for such assurances will itself require us to marshall our cognitive resources. It will itself involve the use of methods about which we can sensibly have doubts, doubts that cannot be addressed without begging the question. Any attempt to address them will employ methods either that are themselves already at issue or that can be made so. There is a close analogy with the practical realm. There too self-directed inquiry can raise doubts that cannot be addressed without begging the question. I commit myself to various projects, ones that initially seem worthwhile, but if I examine my commitments and the values implicit in them, doubts can occur to me. I can ask whether I want to be the kind of person who makes these sorts of commitments. Can I endorse my being that kind of person? And even if I answer "yes," this does not definitively settle the doubts. I can go on and ask about the values implicit in this latest endorsement. Either they are values that were implicit in the commitments about which I originally had doubts or they are new values about which I can also raise doubts. It is hopeless to search for a non-question begging way to endorse all of our values, including the values implicit in the endorsement itself. Any search of this sort would be based on the assumption that there is a neutral position from which such endorsements can be made, but there isn't. Nor is there in epistemology. There is no neutral position from which to defend our intellectual commitments.

But if not, we must admit that egocentric epistemology cannot provide non-question begging assurances that we will avoid massive error by being rational. The search for such assurances is doomed from the start. It is one thing to insist that skeptical hypotheses are genuinely possible. It is another to insist that the rationality of our beliefs depends upon our having a non-question begging way to discharge them. We have no such way, and our rationality does not depend upon our having one.

Admitting this need not lead to quietism. One of our intellectual projects, arguably our most fundamental one, is to understand our own position in the world, including our position as inquirers. Within the context of such a project, it is natural to raise general doubts about our intellectual commitments. It is natural to entertain even radically skeptical doubts about them. Of course, making ourselves into an object of systematic inquiry is not an everyday occurrence. It requires some detachment from our ordinary concerns. You cannot with sanity raise general questions about your intellectual commitments when, say, discussing with your mechanic the problems you are having with your car.[6] Nor can

you raise them when you are doing physics or biology or geometry. But in the context of an inquiry into our place in the world, they arise without force. We make ourselves into the objects of our study, and we recognize that these objects that we are studying are creatures who have a rich interaction with their environment. They have various beliefs about it and various desires for it, all of which become intertwined in their projects. The intellectual projects that find expression in their sciences, for example, are intertwined with projects that are aimed at controlling their environment. These projects, we further recognize, can be conducted more or less successfully. In wondering about the relative success of their intellectual projects, we are raising general questions about their beliefs, questions that make it natural to entertain skeptical hypotheses. We are wondering whether their cognitive equipment and their ways of employing this equipment are sufficiently well-suited for their environment as to be prone to produce true beliefs about it. Even in wondering about the success of their non-intellectual projects, these same questions arise indirectly. For even if we grant that these creatures are mostly successful in controlling their environment, it is natural to want some explanation for this success. Is it by having largely accurate beliefs about their environment that they are able to exercise this control or is there some other explanation? But in wondering whether there might not be another explanation, we are once again taking skeptical possibilities seriously. It is perfectly natural for us to do so in this context.

So, it is not a mistaken philosophical tradition that leads us to skeptical thoughts.[7] It is our natural curiosity. We are curious about these creatures' place in the world, including their place as inquirers. We know that they take themselves to be accurately representing their world. It is natural for us to wonder whether they are right in thinking this or whether their representations might be distorted in some systematic way. The hypothesis of the evil demon and the brain in the vat are merely dramatic devices to express these kinds of thoughts in their most radical form.

There is, of course, something else that is unusual about these kinds of thoughts. They are about our beliefs, our presuppositions, our methods of inquiry. If we are to make these things the objects of concern, we must be able to distance ourselves from them in some way. This might make it seem as if the entertainment of skeptical hypotheses is inevitably an exercise in schizophrenia.

But if this be schizophrenia, it is of a common enough sort. Indeed, it is easy to come by even in the limiting case of belief, that which is indubitable for you. Such propositions are irresistible for you once you bring them clearly to mind. Clarity about them is enough to command your assent.[8] So, you cannot directly doubt the truth of such a proposition. I may be able to do that, but you cannot. Otherwise, it would not be genuinely indubitable for you. Even so, you can do the next best thing. You can raise questions about its truth indirectly. You can do so by considering in a general way whether that which is indubitable for you is really true. You can wonder whether you might not be the kind of creature who finds certain falsehoods impossible to doubt. Your wondering this does not prove that nothing is really indubitable for you. It does not prove that you really are capable of doubting that you exist and that $2 + 1 = 3$. These propositions can still be irresistible for you whenever you directly consider them. However, you can refuse to do this. You can refuse to bring them fully to mind, and by so refusing you gain the ability to suspend belief in them hypothetically. You need not cease believing them. You merely cease focusing your direct attention upon them. In doing this you can distance yourself even from that which is indubitable for you, and thus you can make even these propositions an object of skeptical concern. There is nothing mysterious about your doing so.[9] Similarly, there is nothing mysterious about your entertaining serious and general skeptical worries about the other propositions that you believe. You can doubt in a general way whether much of what of you believe is true, and you can do so without actually giving up those beliefs. It is enough for you to suspend them hypothetically.

To think that there is something inevitably puzzling about entertaining general skeptical doubts is to make human thought into something far less flexible than it is. Atheists can debate even theological questions with theists and they can do so without altering their beliefs. They hypothetically suspend for the duration of the discussion a good portion of what they believe. Similarly, the morally upright can appreciate, admire, and even enjoy the ingenuity and resourcefulness of literary villains even when that ingenuity and resourcefulness is put to repugnant purposes. They can do so by hypothetically suspending their moral scruples. There may be limits as to how much of our beliefs and values we can put into suspension, but the limits are at best distant ones. They are not so constraining as to prevent sensible discussion between atheists and theists, and they are not such as to preclude appreciation of the great literary villains. Nor are they so stringent as to rule out worries about the general reliability of our beliefs. We need not abandon our beliefs in order to entertain such worries. It is enough for us to suspend them hypothetically.[10]

The way to respond to skeptical doubts is not to legislate against them metaphysically, and it is not to dismiss them as meaningless, self-defeating, or even odd. It is rather to live with them. It is to recognize that what makes epistemology possible also makes skeptical worries inevitable – namely, our ability to make our methods of inquiry themselves into an object of inquiry. Within the context of such an inquiry, the worry that we might possibly have widely mistaken beliefs is as natural as it is ineradicable. If this illustrates our whimsical condition, then so be it,[11] but it is, after all, not so surprising. We want to be able to defend or at least explain the reliability of our methods of inquiry, but the only way to do so is within our own system of inquiry. We seek to use our methods to show that these same methods are to be trusted. This leaves us vulnerable to the charge that we are begging the question against the skeptic. If the only way to defend or to explain our general way of proceeding is by using that way of proceeding, then we will not have altogether ruled out the possibility that its products might be widely mistaken. This is no more than a generalization of the problem of the Cartesian circle, and it is a circle from which we can no more escape than could Descartes.

But if we too are caught in this circle, what's the point of inquiring into the reliability of our methods of inquiry? Why not relax and just assume that our fundamental methods are reliable? Why not encourage or at least tolerate intellectual complacency about these matters? Because striving to use our fundamental methods of inquiry to defend or to explain their own reliability is far from pointless. Besides, even if it were, it would not matter. We cannot help ourselves. Our curiosity compels us to seek such explanations. But in fact, it is not pointless to seek them, since they need not always be forthcoming. Not all methods of inquiry are even capable of begging the question in their own defense, even though this is the least we should expect from them. The least we should expect is that they be self-referentially defensible. What this means, for beginners, is that they be logically coherent. It must be possible to employ them in their own defense,[12] but possibility is not enough. In addition, the circumstances have to be favorable for such a defense, and the methods themselves might indicate that this is not so. It is sometimes suggested that the collection of procedures that we call "the scientific method" is self-referentially indefensible in just this way. The history of science, it is argued, is largely a history of error. We look back at the theories of even the best scientists of previous times and find much in those theories that is false and even silly. Moreover, there is no reason to think that future scientists won't think the same of our best current theories. In this way, the history of science might seem to give us good inductive grounds – grounds that are themselves acceptable given the methods of science – for thinking that the scientific method is unreliable.

This is a perfectly respectable argumentative strategy. If the use of the scientific method in our environment has been proven, in accordance with canons acceptable to that method, to generate mistaken theories with regularity, then so much the worse for it as a procedure to generate true theories. The least we should expect from a proposed method of inquiry is that it be abel to defend itself in its own terms. Much of recent philosophy of science can be read as trying to do just that. It can be read, that is, as trying to give a construal of the scientific method and a reading of the history of science that together constitute a response to this pessimistic induction. For example, there are those who claim that any fair look at the history of science reveals not so much a history of repudiation of past theories but rather a history in which past theories are largely incorporated into their successor theories. In addition, they claim that the immediate aim of scientific theorizing is not so much to generate theories that are strictly and thoroughly true but rather ones that are at least approximately true. The aim

is verisimilitude. They then point out that the history of science, so understood, provides no basis for an induction whose conclusion is that present theories are not even approximately true. On the contrary, that history is marked by ever increasing predictive success, and the best explanation of this is that those sciences are getting closer and closer to the truth. So, far from supporting a pessimistic induction, the history of science gives us good reason to think that the terms of our sciences, especially our more mature ones, typically do refer.[13]

It is tempting to dismiss arguments of this sort on the grounds that they beg the question. After all, the scientific method is a method that makes essential use of arguments to the best explanation. So, questions about its reliability are in large measure questions about the truth preservingness of such arguments. And yet, the response employs an argument to the best explanation in order to defend the scientific method. It is thus presupposing exactly that which it is trying to establish.

Even so, what I have been arguing is that some questions deserve to be begged. Questions about the reliability of our fundamental methods of inquiry are just such questions. It need not be a fault of the scientific method that it cannot be defended without begging the question. The fault would lie in there being no argument by which the method can be defended. If there is no way that the method can be defended, not even a question begging way, then it would fail even the minimum test for a method of inquiry. This is only the minimum, however. There are patently silly methods that can be used to defend themselves.[14] So, if the only thing that can be said in favor of the scientific method is that it can be used to defend itself, this is not much. It is certainly not enough to provide assurances of its reliability, as proponents of arguments to the best explanation sometimes hint. On the other hand, it is not altogether insignificant either, as their opponents sometimes hint.

Likewise, it is misguided to complain about the Cartesian circle, not because Descartes did not argue in a circle – he did – but rather because this is not the flaw in his strategy. The problem is not that he begs the question by appealing to what he takes to be clear and distinct considerations in order to show that clarity and distinctness assures us of truth. If a proposed method of rational inquiry is fundamental, it cannot help but be used in its own defense if it is to be defended at all. The problem, rather, is that Descartes thought that his strategy, if successful, could altogether extinguish serious skeptical worries. He was wrong about this. Suppose that Descartes had in fact provided a clear, distinct and hence irresistible proof of God's existence and had succeeded also in providing an irresistible proof that God would not allow that which is irresistible for us to be mistaken. This still would not have been enough to answer all of the skeptic's questions, although admittedly it perhaps would come as close as possible to doing so. In large part it is this that makes the Cartesian strategy such an appealing one. If the arguments work, would-be skeptics are forced to go to extreme lengths to keep their skeptical concerns alive, but they can do so. They will not be able to do so as long as they have Descartes' irresistible proofs clearly in mind, for as long as these proofs are clearly in mind even would-be skeptics cannot help but believe that irresistible propositions are true. But of course, they need not always have the proofs in mind. Thus, as with other propositions, they can suspend belief hypothetically in the proposition that irresistible propositions are true. They can distance themselves from the spell of the proofs' irresistibility and by so doing they can sensibly raise the question of whether irresistibility really is sufficient for truth. Descartes can urge them to recall his proofs, since by hypothesis this will dispel all of their doubts. However, and this is the most important point, while not under the influence of the irresistible proofs, the would-be skeptics can grant that recalling the proofs would have this effect upon them and yet still insist that this does not settle the issue of whether irresistibility really is sufficient for truth. And they would be right.[15]

Thus, there is nothing wrong with trying to appeal to clear and distinct and hence irresistible ideas in an attempt to argue that such ideas are true. One of the things we should expect of those proposing strategies of inquiry is that they be able to use these strategies to defend their own proposals. On the other hand, it is a mistake to think any such defense will be capable of altogether eliminating skeptical worries. Skeptical worries are ineradicable, and we might as well get ourselves used to this idea.

Doing so will involve admitting that it is alright to do epistemology, and egocentric epistemology in particular, non-defensively. The prerequisite of egocentric rationality is not truth or even reliability but rather the absence of any internal motivation for either retraction or supplementation of our beliefs. Egocentric rationality requires that we have beliefs that are to our own deep intellectual satisfaction – ones that do not merely satisfy us in a superficial way but that would do so even with the deepest reflection. So, to be egocentrically rational is to be invulnerable to a certain kind of self-condemnation. It is to have beliefs that in our role as truth-seekers we wouldn't criticize ourselves for having even if were to be deeply reflective. There are various ways of trying to say what exactly this amounts to,[16] but for the issue at hand these details are not important. What is important is that even if we are deeply satisfied with our beliefs, we cannot be assured of avoiding massive error. There are no such assurances. There are not even assurances of it being even likely that we will avoid massive error. The lack of assurances is built into us, and it is built into the nature of our inquiries. We must do epistemology with this in mind.

Even so, it is equally important to remember that being deeply satisfied with one's methods and beliefs is not everything. You might be deeply satisfied with them because you are dogmatic, for example. You might have views about your methods of inquiry that effectively protect them against self-directed challenges. You have ready explanations for any would-be oddity in your method or in the beliefs that they generate. Take astrology as a case in point. Most contemporary astrologers may be impostors, but suppose you are not. You are deeply convinced of its truth. No amount of disinterested reflection would prompt you to be critical of your methods or of the beliefs that they produce. Are your beliefs irrational? Not necessarily. Are they dogmatic and misguided? Of course.

Most of us are not afflicted with this kind of extreme dogmatism. If we are dogmatic, we are unlikely to be so all the way down. The deepest epistemic standards of even the most dedicated astrologers are not likely to be radically different from those of the rest of us. But if so, they are likely to be vulnerable to self-criticism. They themselves would be suspicious of their methods and their beliefs were they to be sufficiently impartial and sufficiently reflective.

There are those, no doubt, who will find this naive. Perhaps it is. But if so, the alternative is not to make all astrologers irrational by fiat. It is rather to admit that some might be rational albeit fundamentally misguided. The impulse to inject every intellectual desirable characteristic into the theory of rationality is one to be resisted. It is not inconceivable that someone can be dogmatic without being irrational. My approach is to explain as much dogmatism as possible internally. It is to rely upon our own characters as inquirers. Most dogmatists, I claim, are violating their own deepest standards. If there are some dogmatists left over, some who are not violating even their own deepest standards, they are to be dismissed as dogmatic and that is the end of the matter. It is a mistake to try to construct an objective theory of dogmatism and then to make the avoidance of that kind of dogmatism a prerequisite of rationality. Not every shortcoming is one of rationality.

Again, there is a useful analogy between the practical and the intellectual. There is no more unity among intellectually desirable characteristics than there is among non-intellectual ones. Our actions are egocentrically rational insofar as we lack internal motivations to be dissatisfied with them. Much immoral behavior can be criticized as being irrational in just this way. We do what we ourselves cannot sincerely endorse, given our own deepest values. But of course, this makes the irrationality of immorality contingent upon our characters. It makes it contingent upon our deepest values. If there are fanatics who lack even a deeply internal motivation to detach from their vicious behavior, then we must be content with regarding them as fanatics. Their problem, and ours, is that they have vicious characters. They need not be irrational.

This is not to say that there is not a looser kind of unity between egocentric rationality and morally desirable characteristics on the one hand and between egocentric rationality and intellectually desirable ones on the other. It may be that when we have no internal motivations, not even deep ones, to be dissatisfied with what we are doing, then in general we will be acting in a morally virtuous way, and it may be that when we are not acting virtuously, there generally will be some internal motivation for detachment that we have

ignored or not noticed. Our normal psychological make-up may ensure that in general this is so. As a result, it may be that egocentric rationality and morality go hand-in-hand except in situations that are bizarre or in people who are deranged.

Similarly for egocentric rationality and intellectually desirable characteristics. It may be that when we have no internal motivations to retract what we believe, then in general we are neither dogmatic nor thoroughly misguided. It likewise may be that when we are either dogmatic or misguided, there is in general some internal motivation for retraction that we have ignored. Thus, it may be that egocentric rationality and knowledge, like egocentric rationality and morality, go hand-in-hand except in situations that are bizarre or in people who are deranged. If so, it will also be the case that except in such situations or with such people, we can expect disagreements of opinion to be largely the result of differences of information. Or put the other way around, if our intellectual peers persist in disagreeing with our opinions despite the fact that they have access to the same information, this calls for some explanation. It won't do simply to say that they are wrong and we are right. On the contrary, unless there is some plausible way to explain away their opinion, the disagreement ordinarily will give us a good reason to be suspicious of our own opinions.

All these things may well be so. The mistake is to try to make these general truths, if that be what they are, into categorical ones. It is a mistake to make it a matter of necessity that being egocentrically rational is likely to bring us knowledge, and it is equally a mistake to assume that those who have fundamentally misguided beliefs – even those who are misguided to the point of being deranged – must of necessity also be irrational. Correspondingly, it is a mistake to make it a matter of necessity that rational people will agree with one another if they have the same information. One of the presuppositions of the Cartesian project was that rationality is what stands between us and "a chaotic disagreement in which anything goes."[17] However, this need not be our presupposition. We can say that what stands in the way of chaotic disagreement is not simply the nature of rationality but also the contingent fact that we are born with similar cognitive equipment and into similar environments, a contingent fact that makes it likely that the deep epistemic standards of one person will not be radically different from those of another.

This then is a sketch of a way to think about egocentric rationality. According to this conception, egocentric rationality brings with it no guarantees of truth or likely-truth, and as a result it brings with it no guarantees that rational people with access to the same information will agree with one another. Why, then, should we be interested in egocentric rationality? Because we are interested in having beliefs that are accurate and comprehensive and because by being egocentrically rational we will be pursuing this end in a way that by our own lights seems effective.

To be sure, this involves a leap of intellectual faith. It involves our having confidence in those intellectual methods that are deeply satisfying to us despite the fact that we cannot vindicate this confidence in a non-question begging way. This may be regrettable but it is also undeniable. The reality of our intellectual lives is that we are working without nets. No procedure, no amount of reflection, no amount of evidence gathering can guarantee that we won't fall into error, perhaps even massive error. We are thus forced to choose between proceeding in a way that we on reflection would take to be effective and proceeding in a way that we would not take to be effective. If we are rational, we opt for the former.

Notes

1 See Richard Foley, *The Theory of Epistemic Rationality* (Cambridge: Harvard University Press, 1987), especially sec. 2.8.

2 In his book *Philosophical Explanations* (Cambridge: Harvard University Press, 1981), Robert Nozick insists that for a belief to constitute knowledge, it must be non-accidentally true. At first glance this might seem to be at odds with what I am claiming, but in fact it isn't. Knowledge may very well require that truth and belief be non-accidentally related, so that given the belief that *P* it is not matter of luck that *P* is true, and vice-versa. Even so, we need an element of luck – we need the world to cooperate – in order for there to be this non-accidental relationship between truth and belief.

3 I have borrowed the phrase 'defensive epistemology' from Bas van Fraassen.

4 I assume here that if *p* is probable given *q*, then it cannot be the case that *p* is false in most close situations in which *q* is true.

5 Socrates argued that one never acts for the worse by having a virtue. The claim here is analogous; one never believes for the worse by being rational, where believing for the worse is a matter of believing in a way that is more likely to lead to error. Rationality, it is claimed, guarantees at least this much.

6 Descartes himself emphasized this, insisting that his method of doubt is not appropriate for use in ordinary life. See his *Discourse on Method*, in Descartes, *Philosophical Writings*, vol. I, eds. Haldane and Ross (Cambridge: Cambridge University Press, 1911), especially pp. 100–1.

7 See Richard Rorty, *Philosophy and the Mirror of Nature* (Princeton: Princeton University Press, 1979).

8 In the *Fifth Meditation*, Descartes says "… the nature of my mind is such that I would be unable not to assent to these things (which I clearly and distinctly perceive) so long as I clearly perceive them …" See Haldane and Ross, vol. I, p. 180.

9 Compare with Bernard Williams, *Descartes: The Project of Pure Inquiry* (Harmondsworth: Penguin Books, 1978), and "Descartes' Use of Skepticism," in M. Burnyeat (ed.), *The Skeptical Tradition* (Berkeley: University of California Press, 1983), pp. 337–52. See also Anthony Kenny's discussion of first-order doubt and second-order doubt in "The Cartesian Circle and the Eternal Truths," *The Journal of Philosophy* 67(1970), pp. 685–700; and James Van Cleve, "Foundationalism, Epistemic Principles, and the Cartesian Circle," *The Philosophical Review* 88 (1979), pp. 55–91 and E. Sosa and J. Kim (eds), *Epistemology: An Anthology* (Malden, MA; Oxford: Blackwell, 2000), pp. 242–60.

10 Contrast this with Hume, whose position does hint of schizophrenia. Hume reported

that while engaged in philosophical reflection he found himself forced to give up his ordinary beliefs about material objects, the future and the self, but that as soon as he left his study these reflections appeared strained to him and his ordinary beliefs returned. So, according to Hume, his beliefs changed dramatically depending upon which of his personalities was engaged, his philosophical one or his everyday one. The potential for schizophrenia here is made even more dramatic if we assume not only that the philosophical Hume knew that were he to quit reflecting he would begin believing but also that the everyday Hume knew (at least tacitly) that were he to begin reflecting he would cease believing.

11 "When [a Pyrrhonian] awakes from his dream, he will be the first to join in the laugh against himself, and to confess, that all his objections are mere amusement, and can have no other tendency than to show the whimsical condition of mankind, who must act and reason and believe; though they are not able, by their most diligent enquiry, to satisfy themselves concerning the foundations of these operations, or to remove the objections, which may be raised against them." David Hume, *An Enquiry Concerning Human Understanding*, ed. L. A. Selby-Bigge with text revised by P. H. Nidditch (Oxford: Oxford University Press, 1975), sec. XII, p. 128.

12 Alvin Plantinga claims that certain versions of classical foundationalism cannot possibly be used to defend themselves. See Plantinga, "Is Belief in God Rational?" in C. F. Delaney (ed.), *Rationality and Religious Belief* (Notre Dame: University of Notre Dame Press, 1979), pp. 7–27.

13 See, e.g. Hilary Putnam, *Reason, Truth and History* (Cambridge: Cambridge University Press, 1986); William Newton-Smith, *The Rationality of Science* (London: Routledge & Kegan Paul, 1981); Ernan McMullin, "The Fertility of Theory and the Unity of Appraisal in Science," in R. S. Cohen *et al.* (eds), *Boston Studies* 39 (1976), pp. 395–432.

14 Ernest Sosa gives the following example: "If a rule or principle contains the proposition that the earth is flat, then it is acceptable, as is the proposition that the earth is flat." See Sosa, "Methodology and Apt Belief," *Synthese* 74 (1988), p. 418.

15 Contrast with Bernard Williams: "So the believer can always recall the skeptic, unless the skeptic is willfully obstinate, to considering the existence and benevolence of God, and if the skeptic concentrates on those proofs, he will believe not only those propositions themselves but also something that follows from them – namely, that clear and distinct perceptions are reliable, and hence skepticism unjustified." Williams, "Descartes' Use of Skepticism," p. 349. My position, in turn, is that in this context, where the issue is precisely whether irresistible proofs might be mistaken, it is not mere obstinacy to refuse to recall the proofs. The skeptic's refusal to recall them is not unlike the alcoholic's refusal to enter the bar. In each case the refusal is motivated by a fear that one's weaknesses will be exploited.

16 For my suggestions, see *The Theory of Epistemic Rationality*.

17 The phrase is from Bernard Williams. See Williams, "Descartes' Use of Skepticism," p. 344.

CHAPTER 26

What Is Justified Belief?

Alvin I. Goldman

The aim of this essay is to sketch a theory of justified belief. What I have in mind is an explanatory theory, one that explains in a general way why certain beliefs are counted as justified and others as unjustified. Unlike some traditional approaches, I do not try to prescribe standards for justification that differ from, or improve upon, our ordinary standards. I merely try to explicate the ordinary standards, which are, I believe, quite different from those of many classical, e.g., "Cartesian," accounts.

Many epistemologists have been interested in justification because of its presumed close relationship to knowledge. This relationship is intended to be preserved in the conception of justified belief presented here. In previous papers on knowledge,[1] I have denied that justification is necessary for knowing, but there I had in mind "Cartesian" accounts of justification. On the account of justified belief suggested here, it *is* necessary for knowing, and closely related to it.

The term "justified," I presume, is an evaluative term, a term of appraisal. Any correct definition or synonym of it would also feature evaluative terms. I assume that such definitions or synonyms might be given, but I am not interested in them. I want a set of *substantive* conditions that specify when a belief is justified. Compare the

moral term "right." This might be defined in other ethical terms or phrases, a task appropriate to meta-ethics. The task of normative ethics, by contrast, is to state substantive conditions for the rightness of actions. Normative ethics tries to specify non-ethical conditions that determine when an action is right. A familiar example is act-utilitarianism, which says an action is right if and only if it produces, or would produce, at least as much net happiness as any alternative open to the agent. These necessary and sufficient conditions clearly involve no ethical notions. Analogously, I want a theory of justified belief to specify in non-epistemic terms when a belief is justified. This is not the only kind of theory of justifiedness one might seek, but it is one important kind of theory and the kind sought here.

In order to avoid epistemic terms in our theory, we must know which terms are epistemic. Obviously, an exhaustive list cannot be given, but here are some examples: "justified," "warranted," "has (good) grounds," "has reason (to believe)," "knows that," "sees that," "apprehends that," "is probable" (in an epistemic or inductive sense), "shows that," "establishes that," and "ascertains that." By contrast, here are some sample non-epistemic expressions: "believes that," "is true," "causes," "it is necessary that," "implies," "is deducible from," and "is probable" (either in the frequency sense or the propensity sense). In general, (purely) doxastic, metaphysical, modal, semantic, or syntactic expressions are not epistemic.

Originally published in G. S. Pappas (ed.), *Justification and Knowledge* (Dordrecht: D. Reidel, 1976), pp. 1–23.

There is another constraint I wish to place on a theory of justified belief, in addition to the constraint that it be couched in non-epistemic language. Since I seek an explanatory theory, i.e., one that clarifies the underlying source of justificational status, it is not enough for a theory to state "correct" necessary and sufficient conditions. Its conditions must also be appropriately deep or revelatory. Suppose, for example, that the following sufficient condition of justified belief is offered: "If S senses redly at t and S believes at t that he is sensing redly, then S's belief at t that he is sensing redly is justified." This is not the kind of principle I seek; for, even if it is correct, it leaves unexplained *why* a person who senses redly and believes that he does, believes this justifiably. Not every state is such that if one is in it and believes one is in it, this belief is justified. What is distinctive about the state of sensing redly, or "phenomenal" states in general? A theory of justified belief of the kind I seek must answer this question, and hence it must be couched at a suitably deep, general, or abstract level.

A few introductory words about my *explicandum* are appropriate at this juncture. It is often assumed that whenever a person has a justified belief, he knows that it is justified and knows what the justification is. It is further assumed that the person can state or explain what his justification is. On this view, a justification is an argument, defense, or set of reasons that can be given in support of a belief. Thus, one studies the nature of justified belief by considering what a person might *say* if asked to defend, or justify, his belief. I make none of these sorts of assumptions here. I leave it an open question whether, when a belief *is* justified, the believer *knows* it is justified. I also leave it an open question whether, when a belief is justified, the believer can *state* or *give* a justification for it. I do not even assume that when a belief is justified there is something "possessed" by the believer which can be called a "justification." I do assume that a justified belief gets its status of being justified from some processes or properties that make it justified. In short, there must be some justification-conferring processes or properties. But this does not imply that there must be an argument, or reason, or anything else, "possessed" at the time of belief by the believer.

I

A theory of justified belief will be a set of principles that specify truth-conditions for the schema ⌈S's belief in p at time t is justified⌉, i.e., conditions for the satisfaction of this schema in all possible cases. It will be convenient to formulate candidate theories in a recursive or inductive format, which would include (A) one or more base clauses, (B) a set of recursive clauses (possibly null), and (C) a closure clause. In such a format, it is permissible for the predicate "is a justified belief" to appear in recursive clauses. But neither this predicate, nor any other epistemic predicate, may appear in (the antecedent of) any base clause.[2]

Before turning to my own theory, I want to survey some other possible approaches to justified belief. Identification of problems associated with other attempts will provide some motivation for the theory I shall offer. Obviously, I cannot examine all, or even very many, alternative attempts. But a few sample attempts will be instructive.

Let us concentrate on the attempt to formulate one or more adequate base-clause principles.[3] Here is a classical candidate:

(1)   If S believes p at t, and p is indubitable for S (at t), then S's belief in p at t is justified.

To evaluate this principle, we need to know what "indubitable" means. It can be understood in at least two ways. First, "p is indubitable for S" might mean: "S has no *grounds* for doubting p." Since "ground" is an epistemic term, however, principle (1) would be inadmissible in this reading, for epistemic terms may not legitimately appear in the antecedent of a base clause. A second interpretation would avoid this difficulty. One might interpret "p is indubitable for S" psychologically, i.e., as meaning "S is psychologically incapable of doubting p." This would make principle (1) admissible, but would it be correct? Surely not. A religious fanatic may be psychologically incapable of doubting the tenets of his faith, but that doesn't make his belief in them justified. Similarly, during the Watergate affair, someone may have been so blinded by the aura of the presidency that even after the most damaging evidence against

Nixon had emerged he was still incapable of doubting Nixon's veracity. It doesn't follow that his belief in Nixon's veracity was justified.

A second candidate base-clause principle is this:

(2)   If S believes p at t and p is self-evident, then S's belief in p at t is justified.

To evaluate this principle, we again need an interpretation of its crucial term, in this case "self-evident." On one standard reading, "evident" is a synonym for "justified." "*Self*-evident" would therefore mean something like "directly justified," "intuitively justified," or "non-derivatively justified." On this reading "self-evident" is an epistemic phrase, and principle (2) would be disqualified as a base-clause principle.

However, there are other possible readings of "p is self-evident" on which it isn't an epistemic phrase. One such reading is: "It is impossible to understand p without believing it."[4] According to this interpretation, trivial analytic and logical truths might turn out to be self-evident. Hence, any belief in such a truth would be a justified belief, according to (2).

What does "it is *impossible* to understand p without believing it" mean? Does it mean "*humanly* impossible"? That reading would probably make (2) an unacceptable principle. There may well be propositions which humans have an innate and irrepressible disposition to believe, e.g., "Some events have causes." But it seems unlikely that people's inability to refrain from believing such a proposition makes every belief in it justified.

Should we then understand "impossible" to mean "impossible in principle," or "logically impossible"? If that is the reading given, I suspect that (2) is a vacuous principle. I doubt that even trivial logical or analytic truths will satisfy this definition of "self-evident." Any proposition, we may assume, has two or more components that are somehow organized or juxtaposed. To understand the proposition one must "grasp" the components and their juxtaposition. Now in the case of *complex* logical truths, there are (human) psychological operations that suffice to grasp the components and their juxtaposition but do not suffice to produce a belief that the proposition is

true. But can't we at least *conceive* of an analogous set of psychological operations even for simple logical truths, operations which perhaps are not in the repertoire of human cognizers but which might be in the repertoire of some conceivable beings? That is, can't we conceive of psychological operations that would suffice to grasp the components and componential-juxtaposition of these simple propositions but do not suffice to produce *belief* in the propositions? I think we can conceive of such operations. Hence, for any proposition you choose, it will be possible for it to be understood without being believed.

Finally, even if we set these two objections aside, we must note that self-evidence can at best confer justificational status on relatively few beliefs, and the only plausible group are beliefs in necessary truths. Thus, other base-clause principles will be needed to explain the justificational status of beliefs in contingent propositions.

The notion of a base-clause principle is naturally associated with the idea of "direct" justifiedness, and in the realm of contingent propositions first-person-current-mental-state propositions have often been assigned this role. In Chisholm's terminology, this conception is expressed by the notion of a "*self-presenting*" state or proposition. The sentence "I am thinking," for example, expresses a self-presenting proposition. (At least I shall *call* this sort of content a "proposition," though it only has a truth value given some assignment of a subject who utters or entertains the content and a time of entertaining.) When such a proposition is true for person S at time t, S is justified in believing it at t: in Chisholm's terminology, the proposition is "evident" for S at t. This suggests the following base-clause principle.

(3)   If p is a self-presenting proposition, and p is true for S at t, and S believes p at t, then S's belief in p at t is justified.

What, exactly, does "self-presenting" mean? In the second edition of *Theory of Knowledge*, Chisholm offers this definition: "h is self-presenting for S at $t = df.$ h is true at t; and necessarily, if h is true at t, then h is evident for S at t."[5] Unfortunately, since "evident" is an epistemic term, "self-presenting" also becomes an epistemic term on this definition, thereby disqualifying (3) as a legitimate base clause. Some other definition of self-presentingness must be offered if (3) is to be a suitable base-clause principle.

Another definition of self-presentation readily comes to mind. "Self-presentation" is an approximate synonym of "self-intimation," and a proposition may be said to be self-intimating if and only if whenever it is true of a person that person believes it. More precisely, we may give the following definition:

(SP)   Proposition p is self-presenting if and only if: necessarily, for any S and any t, if p is true for S at t, then S believes p at t.

On this definition, "self-presenting" is clearly not an epistemic predicate, so (3) would be an admissible principle. Moreover, there is initial plausibility in the suggestion that it is *this* feature of first-person-current-mental-state propositions – viz., their truth guarantees their being believed – that makes beliefs in them justified.

Employing this definition of self-presentation, is principle (3) correct? This cannot be decided until we define self-presentation more precisely. Since the operator "necessarily" can be read in different ways, there are different forms of self-presentation and correspondingly different versions of principle (3). Let us focus on two of these readings: a "*nomological*" reading and a "*logical*" reading. Consider first the nomological reading. On this definition a proposition is self-presenting just in case it is nomologically necessary that if p is true for S at t, then S believes p at t.[6]

Is the nomological version of principle (3) – call it "(3_N)" – correct? Not at all. We can imagine cases in which the antecedent of (3_N) is satisfied, but we would not say that the belief is justified. Suppose, for example, that p is the proposition expressed by the sentence "I am in brain-state B," where "B" is shorthand for a certain highly specific neural state description. Further suppose it is a nomological truth that anyone in brain-state B will ipso facto *believe* he is in brain-state B. In other words, imagine that an occurrent belief with the content "I am in brain-state B" is realized whenever one is in brain-state B.[7] According to (3_N), any such belief is justified. But that is clearly false. We can readily imagine circumstances in which a person goes into brain-state B and therefore has the belief in question, though this belief

is by no means justified. For example, we can imagine that a brain-surgeon operating on S artificially induced brain-state B. This results, phenomenologically, in S's suddenly believing – out of the blue – that he is in brain-state B, without any relevant antecedent beliefs. We would hardly say, in such a case, that S's belief that he is in brain-state B is justified.

Let us turn next to the logical version of (3) – call it "(3_L)" – in which a proposition is defined as self-presenting just in case it is logically necessary that if p is true for S at t, then S believes p at t. This stronger version of principle (3) might seem more promising. In fact, however, it is no more successful than (3_N). Let p be the proposition "I am awake" and assume that it is logically necessary that if this proposition is true for some person S and time t, then S believes p at t. This assumption is consistent with the further assumption that S frequently believes p when it is false, e.g., when he is dreaming. Under these circumstances, we would hardly accept the contention that S's belief in this proposition is always justified. Nor should we accept the contention that the belief is justified when it is *true*. The truth of the proposition logically guarantees that the belief is *held*, but why should it guarantee that the belief is *justified*?

The foregoing criticism suggests that we have things backwards. The idea of self-presentation is that truth guarantees belief. This fails to confer justification because it is compatible with there being belief without truth. So what seems necessary – or at least sufficient – for justification is that belief should guarantee truth. Such a notion has usually gone under the label of "*infallibility*" or "*incorrigibility*." It may be defined as follows:

(INC)   Proposition p is incorrigible if and only if: necessarily, for any S and any t, if S believes p at t, then p is true for S at t.

Using the notion of incorrigibility, we may propose principle (4).

(4)   If p is an incorrigible proposition, and S believes p at t, then S's belief in p at t is justified.

As was true of self-presentation, there are different varieties of incorrigibility, corresponding to different interpretations of "necessarily." Accordingly, we have different versions of principle (4). Once again, let us concentrate on a nomological and a logical version, (4_N) and (4_L) respectively.

We can easily construct a counterexample to (4_N) along the lines of the belief-state/brain-state counterexample that refuted (3_N). Suppose it is nomologically necessary that if anyone believes he is in brain-state B then it is true that he is in brain-state B, for the only way this belief-state is realized is through brain-state B itself. It follows that "I am in brain-state B" is a nomologically incorrigible proposition. Therefore, according to (4_N), whenever anyone believes this proposition at any time, that belief is justified. But we may again construct a brain-surgeon example in which someone comes to have such a belief but the belief isn't justified.

Apart from this counterexample, the general point is this. Why should the fact that S's believing p guarantees the truth of p imply that S's belief is justified? The nature of the guarantee might be wholly fortuitous, as the belief-state/brain-state example is intended to illustrate. To appreciate the point, consider the following related possibility. A person's mental structure might be such that whenever he believes that p will be true (of him) a split second later, then p is true (of him) a split second later. This is because, we may suppose, his believing it brings it about. But surely we would not be compelled in such a circumstance to say that a belief of this sort is justified. So why should the fact that S's believing p guarantees the truth of p precisely at the time of belief imply that the belief is justified? There is no intuitive plausibility in this supposition.

The notion of logical incorrigibility has a more honored place in the history of conceptions of justification. But even principle (4_L), I believe, suffers from defects similar to those of (4_N). The mere fact that belief in p logically guarantees its truth does not confer justificational status on such a belief.

The first difficulty with (4_L) arises from logical or mathematical truths. Any true proposition of logic or mathematics is logically necessary. Hence, any such proposition p is logically incorrigible, since it is logically necessary that, for any S and any t, if S believes p at t then p is true (for S at t). Now assume that Nelson believes a certain very complex mathematical truth at time t. Since such

a proposition is logically incorrigible, (4_L) implies that Nelson's belief in this truth at t is justified. But we may easily suppose that this belief of Nelson is not at all the result of proper mathematical reasoning, or even the result of appeal to trust-worthy authority. Perhaps Nelson believes this complex truth because of utterly confused reasoning, or because of hasty and ill-founded conjecture. Then his belief is not justified, contrary to what (4_L) implies.

The case of logical or mathematical truths is admittedly peculiar, since the truth of these propositions is assured independently of any beliefs. It might seem, therefore, that we can better capture the idea of "belief logically guaranteeing truth" in cases where the propositions in question are *contingent*. With this in mind, we might restrict (4_L) to *contingent* incorrigible propositions. Even this amendment cannot save (4_L), however, since there are counterexamples to it involving purely contingent propositions.

Suppose that Humperdink has been studying logic – or, rather, pseudo-logic – from Elmer Fraud, whom Humperdink has no reason to trust as a logician. Fraud has enunciated the principle that any disjunctive proposition consisting of at least 40 distinct disjuncts is very probably true. Humperdink now encounters the proposition p, a contingent proposition with 40 disjuncts, the 7th disjunct being "I exist." Although Humperdink grasps the proposition fully, he doesn't notice that it is entailed by "I exist." Rather, he is struck by the fact that it falls under the disjunction rule Fraud has enunciated (a rule I assume Humperdink is not *justified* in believing). Bearing this in mind, Humperdink forms a belief in p. Now notice that p is logically incorrigible. It is logically necessary that if anyone believes p, then p is true (of him at that time). This simply follows from the fact that, first, a person's believing anything entails that he exists, and second, "I exist" entails p. Since p is logically incorrigible, principle (4_L) implies that Humperdink's belief in p is justified. But surely, given our example, that conclusion is false. Humperdink's belief in p is not at all justified.

One thing that goes wrong in this example is that while Humperdink's belief in p logically implies its truth, Humperdink doesn't *recognize* that his believing it implies its truth. This might move a theorist to revise (4_L) by adding the requirement that S "recognize" that p is logically incorrigible. But this, of course, won't do. The term "recognize" is obviously an epistemic term, so the suggested revision of (4_L) would result in an inadmissible base clause.

II

Let us try to diagnose what has gone wrong with these attempts to produce an acceptable base-clause principle. Notice that each of the foregoing attempts confers the status of "justified" on a belief without restriction on *why* the belief is held, i.e., on what *causally initiates* the belief or *causally sustains* it. The logical versions of principles (3) and (4), for example, clearly place no restriction on causes of belief. The same is true of the nomological versions of (3) and (4), since nomological requirements can be satisfied by simultaneity or cross-sectional laws, as illustrated by our brain-state/belief-state examples. I suggest that the absence of causal requirements accounts for the failure of the foregoing principles. Many of our counterexamples are ones in which the belief is caused in some strange or unacceptable way, e.g., by the accidental movement of a brain-surgeon's hand, by reliance on an illicit, pseudo-logical principle, or by the blinding aura of the presidency. In general, a strategy for defeating a noncausal principle of justifiedness is to find a case in which the principle's antecedent is satisfied but the belief is caused by some faulty belief-forming process. The faultiness of the belief-forming process will incline us, intuitively, to regard the belief as unjustified. Thus, correct principles of justified belief must be principles that make causal requirements, where "cause" is construed broadly to include sustainers as well as initiators of belief (i.e., processes that determine, or help to overdetermine, a belief's continuing to be held).[8]

The need for causal requirements is not restricted to base-clause principles. Recursive principles will also need a causal component. One might initially suppose that the following is a good recursive principle: "If S justifiably believes q at t, and q entails p, and S believes p at t, then S's belief in p at t is justified." But this principle is unacceptable. S's belief in p doesn't receive justificational status simply from the fact that p is entailed by q and S justifiably believes q. If what causes S to believe p at t is entirely different, S's belief in p may well not be justified. Nor can the situation be remedied by adding to the antecedent the condition that S justifiably believes that q entails p. Even if he believes this, and believes q as well, he might not put these beliefs together. He might believe p as a result of some other wholly extraneous considerations. So once again, conditions that fail to require appropriate causes of a belief don't guarantee justifiedness.

Granted that principles of justified belief must make reference to causes of belief, what kinds of causes confer justifiedness? We can gain insight into this problem by reviewing some faulty processes of belief-formation, i.e., processes whose belief-outputs would be classed as unjustified. Here are some examples: confused reasoning, wishful thinking, reliance on emotional attachment, mere hunch or guesswork, and hasty generalization. What do these faulty processes have in common? They share the feature of *unreliability*: they tend to produce *error* a large proportion of the time. By contrast, which species of belief-forming (or belief-sustaining) processes are intuitively justification-conferring? They include standard perceptual processes, remembering, good reasoning, and introspection. What these processes seem to have in common is *reliability*: the beliefs they produce are generally true. My positive proposal, then, is this. The justificational status of a belief is a function of the reliability of the process or processes that cause it, where (as a first approximation) reliability consists in the tendency of a process to produce beliefs that are true rather than false.

To test this thesis further, notice that justifiedness is not a purely categorical concept, although I treat it here as categorical in the interest of simplicity. We can and do regard certain beliefs as more justified than others. Furthermore, our intuitions of comparative justifiedness go along with our beliefs about the comparative reliability of the belief-causing processes.

Consider perceptual beliefs. Suppose Jones believes he has just seen a mountain-goat. Our assessment of the belief's justifiedness is determined by whether he caught a brief glimpse of the creature at a great distance, or whether he had a good look at the thing only 30 yards away. His belief in the latter sort of case is (*ceteris paribus*) more justified than in the former sort of case.

And, if his belief is true, we are more prepared to say he *knows* in the latter case than in the former. The difference between the two cases seems to be this. Visual beliefs formed from brief and hasty scanning, or where the perceptual object is a long distance off, tend to be wrong more often than visual beliefs formed from detailed and leisurely scanning, or where the object is in reasonable proximity. In short, the visual processes in the former category are less reliable than those in the latter category. A similar point holds for memory beliefs. A belief that results from a hazy and indistinct memory impression is counted as less justified than a belief that arises from a distinct memory impression, and our inclination to classify those beliefs as "*knowledge*" varies in the same way. Again, the reason is associated with the comparative reliability of the processes. Hazy and indistinct memory impressions are generally less reliable indicators of what actually happened, so beliefs formed from such impressions are less likely to be true than beliefs formed from distinct impressions. Further, consider beliefs based on inference from observed samples. A belief about a population that is based on random sampling, or on instances that exhibit great variety, is intuitively more justified than a belief based on biased sampling, or on instances from a narrow sector of the population. Again, the degree of justifiedness seems to be a function of reliability. Inferences based on random or varied samples will tend to produce less error or inaccuracy than inferences based on non-random or non-varied samples.

Returning to a categorical concept of justifiedness, we might ask just *how* reliable a belief-forming process must be in order that its resultant beliefs be justified. A precise answer to this question should not be expected. Our conception of justification is *vague* in this respect. It does seem clear, however, that *perfect* reliability isn't required. Belief-forming processes that *sometimes* produce error still confer justification. It follows that there can be justified beliefs that are false.

I have characterized justification-conferring processes as ones that have a "tendency" to produce beliefs that are true rather than false. The term "tendency" could refer either to *actual* long-run frequency, or to a "propensity," i.e., outcomes that would occur in merely *possible* realizations of the process. Which of these is intended? Unfortunately, I think our ordinary conception

of justifiedness is vague on this dimension too. For the most part, we simply assume that the "observed" frequency of truth versus error would be approximately replicated in the actual long-run, and also in relevant counterfactual situations, i.e., ones that are highly "realistic" or conform closely to the circumstances of the actual world. Since we ordinarily assume these frequencies to be roughly the same, we make no concerted effort to distinguish them. Since the purpose of my present theorizing is to capture our ordinary conception of justifiedness, and since our ordinary conception is vague on this matter, it is appropriate to leave the theory vague in the same respect.

We need to say more about the notion of a belief-forming "*process*." Let us mean by a "process" a *functional operation* or procedure, i.e., something that generates a *mapping* from certain states – "inputs" – into other states – "outputs." The outputs in the present case are states of believing this or that proposition at a given moment. On this interpretation, a process is a *type* as opposed to a *token*. This is fully appropriate, since it is only types that have statistical properties such as producing truth 80 per cent of the time; and it is precisely such statistical properties that determine the reliability of a process. Of course, we also want to speak of a process as *causing* a belief, and it looks as if types are incapable of being causes. But when we say that a belief is caused by a given process, understood as a functional procedure, we may interpret this to mean that it is caused by the particular *inputs* to the process (and by the intervening events "through which" the functional procedure carries the inputs into the output) on the occasion in question.

What are some examples of belief-forming "processes" construed as functional operations? One example is reasoning processes, where the inputs include antecedent beliefs and entertained hypotheses. Another example is functional procedures whose inputs include desires, hopes, or emotional states of various sorts (together with antecedent beliefs). A third example is a memory process, which takes as input beliefs or experiences at an earlier time and generates as output beliefs at a later time. For example, a memory process might take as input a belief *at t_i* that Lincoln was born in 1809 and generate as output a belief *at t_n* that Lincoln was born in 1809.

A fourth example is perceptual processes. Here it isn't clear whether inputs should include states of the environment, such as the distance of the stimulus from the cognizer, or only events within or on the surface of the organism, e.g., receptor stimulations. I shall return to this point in a moment.

A critical problem concerning our analysis is the degree of generality of the process-types in question. Input–output relations can be specified very broadly or very narrowly, and the degree of generality will partly determine the degree of reliability. A process-type might be selected so narrowly that only one instance of it ever occurs, and hence the type is either completely reliable or completely unreliable. (This assumes that reliability is a function of *actual* frequency only.) If such narrow process-types were selected, beliefs that are intuitively unjustified might be said to result from perfectly reliable processes, and beliefs that are intuitively justified might be said to result from perfectly unreliable processes.

It is clear that our ordinary thought about process-types slices them broadly, but I cannot at present give a precise explication of our intuitive principles. One plausible suggestion, though, is that the relevant processes are *content-neutral*. It might be argued, for example, that the process of *inferring p whenever the Pope asserts p* could pose problems for our theory. If the Pope is infallible, this process will be perfectly reliable; yet we would not regard the belief-outputs of this process as justified. The content-neutral restriction would avert this difficulty. If relevant processes are required to admit as input beliefs (or other states) with *any* content, the aforementioned process will not count, for its input beliefs have a restricted propositional content, viz., "*the Pope* asserts *p*."

In addition to the problem of "generality" or "abstractness" there is the previously mentioned problem of the "*extent*" of belief-forming processes. Clearly, the causal ancestry of beliefs often includes events outside the organism. Are such events to be included among the "inputs" of belief-forming processes? Or should we restrict the extent of belief-forming processes to "*cognitive*" events, i.e., events within the organism's nervous system? I shall choose the latter course, though with some hesitation. My general grounds for this decision are roughly as follows. Justifiedness seems to be a function of how a cognizer deals with his environmental input, i.e., with the goodness or badness of the operations that register and transform the stimulation that reaches him. ("Deal with," of course, does not mean *purposeful* action, nor is it restricted to *conscious* activity.) A justified belief is, roughly speaking, one that results from cognitive operations that are, generally speaking, good or successful. But "*cognitive*" operations are most plausibly construed as operations of the cognitive faculties, i.e., "information-processing" equipment *internal* to the organism.

With these points in mind, we may now advance the following base-clause principle for justified belief.

> (5) If S's believing *p* at *t* results from a reliable cognitive belief-forming process (or set of processes), then S's belief in *p* at *t* is justified.

Since "reliable belief-forming process" has been defined in terms of such notions as belief, truth, statistical frequency, and the like, it is not an epistemic term. Hence, (5) is an admissible base clause.

It might seem as if (5) promises to be not only a successful base clause, but the only principle needed whatever, apart from a closure clause. In other words, it might seem as if it is a necessary as well as a sufficient condition of justifiedness that a belief be produced by reliable cognitive belief-forming processes. But this is not quite correct, given our provisional definition of "reliability."

Our provisional definition implies that a reasoning process is reliable only if it generally produces beliefs that are true, and similarly, that a memory process is reliable only if it generally yields beliefs that are true. But these requirements are too strong. A reasoning procedure cannot be expected to produce true belief if it is applied to false premises. And memory cannot be expected to yield a true belief if the original belief it attempts to retain is false. What we need for reasoning and memory, then, is a notion of "*conditional reliability*." A process is conditionally reliable when a sufficient proportion of its output-beliefs are true *given that its input-beliefs are true*.

With this point in mind, let us distinguish *belief-dependent* and *belief-independent* cognitive processes. The former are processes *some* of whose inputs are belief-states.[9] The latter are processes *none* of whose inputs are belief-states. We may then replace principle (5) with the following two principles, the first a base-clause principle and the second a recursive-clause principle.

(6_A)   If S's belief in *p* at *t* results ("immediately") from a belief-independent process that is (unconditionally) reliable, then S's belief in *p* at *t* is justified.

(6_B)   If S's belief in *p* at *t* results ("immediately") from a belief-dependent process that is (at least) conditionally reliable, and if the beliefs (if any) on which this process operates in producing S's belief in *p* at *t* are themselves justified, then S's belief in *p* at *t* is justified.[10]

If we add to (6_A) and (6_B) the standard closure clause, we have a complete theory of justified belief. The theory says, in effect, that a belief is justified if and only if it is "*well-formed*," i.e., it has an ancestry of reliable and/or conditionally reliable cognitive operations. (Since a dated belief may be over-determined, it may have a number of distinct ancestral trees. These need not all be full of reliable or conditionally reliable processes. But at least one ancestral tree must have reliable or conditionally reliable processes throughout.)

The theory of justified belief proposed here, then, is an *Historical* or *Genetic* theory. It contrasts with the dominant approach to justified belief, an approach that generates what we may call (borrowing a phrase from Robert Nozick) "*Current Time-Slice*" theories. A Current Time-Slice theory makes the justificational status of a belief wholly a function of what is true of the cognizer *at the time* of belief. An Historical theory makes the justificational status of a belief depend on its prior history. Since my Historical theory emphasizes the reliability of the belief-generating processes, it may be called "*Historical Reliabilism*."

The most obvious examples of Current Time-Slice theories are "Cartesian" Foundationalist theories, which trace all justificational status (at least of contingent propositions) to current mental states. The usual varieties of Coherence theories, however, are equally Current Time-Slice views, since they too make the justificational

status of a belief wholly a function of *current* states of affairs. For Coherence theories, however, these current states include all other beliefs of the cognizer, which would not be considered relevant by Cartesian Foundationalism. Have there been other Historical theories of justified belief? Among contemporary writers, Quine and Popper have Historical epistemologies, though the notion of "justification" is not their avowed *explicandum*. Among historical writers, it might seem that Locke and Hume had Genetic theories of sorts. But I think that their Genetic theories were only theories of ideas, not of knowledge or justification. Plato's theory of recollection, however, is a good example of a Genetic theory of knowing.[11] And it might be argued that Hegel and Dewey had Genetic epistemologies (if Hegel can be said to have had a clear epistemology at all).

The theory articulated by (6_A) and (6_B) might be viewed as a kind of "Foundationalism" because of its recursive structure. I have no objection to this label, as long as one keeps in mind how different this "diachronic" form of Foundationalism is from Cartesian, or other "synchronic" varieties of, Foundationalism.

Current Time-Slice theories characteristically assume that the justificational status of a belief is something which the cognizer is able to know or determine at the time of belief. This is made explicit, for example, by Chisholm.[12] The Historical theory I endorse makes no such assumption. There are many facts about a cognizer to which he lacks "privileged access," and I regard the justificational status of his beliefs as one of those things. This is not to say that a cognizer is necessarily ignorant, at any given moment, of the justificational status of his current beliefs. It is only to deny that he necessarily has, or can get, knowledge or true belief about this status. Just as a person can know without knowing that he knows, so he can have justified belief without knowing that it is justified (or believing justifiably that it is justified).

A characteristic case in which a belief is justified though the cognizer doesn't know that it's justified is where the original evidence for the belief has long since been forgotten. If the original evidence was compelling, the cognizer's original belief may have been justified, and this justificational status may have been preserved through memory. But since the cognizer no longer remembers how or why he came to believe, he may not know that the belief is justified. If asked now to justify his belief, he may be at a loss. Still, the belief *is* justified, though the cognizer can't demonstrate or establish this.

The Historical theory of justified belief I advocate is connected in spirit with the causal theory of knowing I have presented elsewhere.[13] I had this in mind when I remarked near the outset of the essay that my theory of justified belief makes justifiedness come out closely related to knowledge. Justified beliefs, like pieces of knowledge, have appropriate histories; but they may fail to be knowledge either because they are false or because they founder on some other requirement for knowing of the kind discussed in the post-Gettier knowledge-trade.

There is a variant of the Historical conception of justified belief that is worth mentioning in this context. It may be introduced as follows. Suppose S has a set B of beliefs at time t_0, and some of these beliefs are *un*justified. Between t_0 and t_1 he reasons from the entire set B to the conclusion p, which he then accepts at t_1. The reasoning procedure he uses is a very sound one, i.e., one that is conditionally reliable. There is a sense or respect in which we are tempted to say that S's belief in p at t_1 is "justified." At any rate, it is tempting to say that the *person* is justified in believing p at t. Relative to his antecedent cognitive state, he did as well as could be expected: the *transition* from his cognitive state at t_0 to his cognitive state at t_1 was entirely sound. Although we may acknowledge this brand of justifiedness – it might be called "*Terminal-Phase Reliabilism*" – it is not a kind of justifiedness so closely related to knowing. For a person to know proposition p, it is not enough that the *final phase* of the process that leads to his belief in p be sound. It is also necessary that some entire history of the process be sound (i.e., reliable or conditionally reliable).

Let us return now to the Historical theory. In the next section, I shall adduce reasons for strengthening it a bit. Before looking at these reasons, however, I wish to review two quite different objections to the theory.

First, a critic might argue that *some* justified beliefs do not derive their justificational status from their causal ancestry. In particular, it might be argued that beliefs about one's current phenomenal states and intuitive beliefs about elementary logical or conceptual relationships do not derive their justificational status in this way. I am not persuaded by either of these examples. Introspection, I believe, should be regarded as a form of retrospection. Thus, a justified belief that I am "now" in pain gets its justificational status from a relevant, though brief, causal history.[14] The apprehension of logical or conceptual relationships is also a cognitive process that occupies time. The psychological process of "seeing" or "intuiting" a simple logical truth is very fast, and we cannot introspectively dissect it into constituent parts. Nonetheless, there are mental operations going on, just as there are mental operations that occur in *idiots savants*, who are unable to report the computational processes they in fact employ.

A second objection to Historical Reliabilism focuses on the reliability element rather than the causal or historical element. Since the theory is intended to cover all possible cases, it seems to imply that for any cognitive process C, if C is reliable in possible world W, then any belief in W that results from C is justified. But doesn't this permit easy counterexamples? Surely we can imagine a possible world in which wishful thinking is reliable. We can imagine a possible world where a benevolent demon so arranges things that beliefs formed by wishful thinking usually come true. This would make wishful thinking a reliable process in that possible world, but surely we don't want to regard beliefs that result from wishful thinking as justified.

There are several possible ways to respond to this case, and I am unsure which response is best, partly because my own intuitions (and those of other people I have consulted) are not entirely clear. One possibility is to say that in the possible world imagined, beliefs that result from wishful thinking *are* justified. In other words, we reject the claim that wishful thinking could never, intuitively, confer justifiedness.[15]

However, for those who feel that wishful thinking couldn't confer justifiedness even in the world imagined, there are two ways out. First, it may be suggested that the proper criterion of justifiedness is the propensity of a process to generate beliefs that are true *in a non-manipulated environment*, i.e., an environment in which there is no purposeful arrangement of the world either to accord or conflict with the beliefs that are formed. In other words, the suitability of a belief-forming process is only a function of its success in "*natural*" situations, not situations of the sort involving benevolent or malevolent demons or any other such manipulative creatures. If we reformulate the theory to include this qualification, the counterexample in question will be averted.

Alternatively, we may reformulate our theory, or reinterpret it, as follows. Instead of construing the theory as saying that a belief in possible world *W* is justified if and only if it results from a cognitive process that is reliable in *W*, we may construe it as saying that a belief in possible world *W* is justified if and only if it results from a cognitive process that is reliable in *our world*. In short, our conception of justifiedness is derived as follows. We note certain cognitive processes in the actual world, and form beliefs about which of these are reliable. The ones we believe to be reliable are then regarded as justification-conferring processes. In reflecting on hypothetical beliefs, we deem them justified if and only if they result from processes already picked out as justification-conferring, or processes very similar to those. Since wishful thinking is not among these processes, a belief formed in a possible world *W* by wishful thinking would not be deemed justified, even if wishful thinking is reliable *in W*. I am not sure that this is a correct reconstruction of our intuitive conceptual scheme, but it would accommodate the benevolent demon case, at least if the proper thing to say in that case in that the wishful-thinking-caused beliefs are unjustified.

Even if we adopt this strategy, however, a problem still remains. Suppose that wishful thinking turns out to be reliable *in the actual world!*[16] This might be because, unbeknownst to us at present, there is a benevolent demon who, lazy until now, will shortly start arranging things so that our wishes come true. The long-run performance of wishful thinking will be very good, and hence even the new construal of the theory will imply that beliefs resulting from wishful thinking (in *our* world) are justified. Yet this surely contravenes our intuitive judgment on the matter.

Perhaps the moral of the case is that the standard format of a "conceptual analysis" has its shortcomings. Let me depart from that format and try to give a better rendering of our aim and the theory that tries to achieve that aim. What we really want is an *explanation* of why we count, or

would count, certain beliefs as justified and others as unjustified. Such an explanation must refer to our *beliefs* about reliability, not to the actual *facts*. The reason we *count* beliefs as justified is that they are formed by what we *believe* to be reliable belief-forming processes. Our beliefs about which belief-forming processes are reliable may be erroneous, but that does not affect the adequacy of the explanation. Since we *believe* that wishful thinking is an unreliable belief-forming process, we regard beliefs formed by wishful thinking as unjustified. What matters, then, is what we *believe* about wishful thinking, not what is *true* (in the long run) about wishful thinking. I am not sure how to express this point in the standard format of conceptual analysis, but it identifies an important point in understanding our theory.

III

Let us return, however, to the standard format of conceptual analysis, and let us consider a new objection that will require some revisions in the theory advanced until now. According to our theory, a belief is justified in case it is caused by a process that is in fact reliable, or by one we generally believe to be reliable. But suppose that although one of S's beliefs satisfies this condition, S has no reason to believe that it does. Worse yet, suppose S has reason to believe that his belief is caused by an *unreliable* process (although *in fact* its causal ancestry is fully reliable). Wouldn't we deny in such circumstances that S's belief is justified? This seems to show that our analysis, as presently formulated, is mistaken.

Suppose that Jones is told on fully reliable authority that a certain class of his memory beliefs are almost all mistaken. His parents fabricate a wholly false story that Jones suffered from amnesia when he was seven but later developed *pseudo-memories* of that period. Though Jones listens to what his parents say and has excellent reason to trust them, he persists in believing the ostensible memories from his seven-year-old past. Are these memory beliefs justified? Intuitively, they are not justified. But since these beliefs result from genuine memory and original perceptions, which are adequately reliable processes, our theory says that these beliefs are justified.

Can the theory be revised to meet this difficulty? One natural suggestion is that the actual reliability of a belief's ancestry is not enough for justifiedness; in addition, the cognizer must be *justified in believing* that the ancestry of his belief is reliable. Thus one might think of replacing (6_A), for example, with (7). (For simplicity, I neglect some of the details of the earlier analysis.)

>   (7)   If S's belief in *p* at *t* is caused by a reliable cognitive process, and S justifiably believes at *t* that his *p*-belief is so caused, then S's belief in *p* at *t* is justified.

It is evident, however, that (7) will not do as a base clause, for it contains the epistemic term "justifiably" in its antecedent.

A slightly weaker revision, without this problematic feature, might next be suggested, viz.,

>   (8)   If S's belief in *p* at *t* is caused by a reliable cognitive process, and S believes at *t* that his *p*-belief is so caused, then S's belief in *p* at *t* is justified.

But this won't do the job. Suppose that Jones believes that his memory beliefs are reliably caused despite all the (trustworthy) contrary testimony of his parents. Principle (8) would be satisfied, yet we wouldn't say that these beliefs are justified.

Next, we might try (9), which is stronger than (8) and, unlike (7), formally admissible as a base clause.

>   (9)   If S's belief in *p* at *t* is caused by a reliable cognitive process, and S believes at *t* that his *p*-belief is so caused, and this meta-belief is caused by a reliable cognitive process, then S's belief in *p* at *t* is justified.

A first objection to (9) is that it wrongly precludes unreflective creatures – creatures like animals or young children, who have no beliefs about the genesis of their beliefs – from having justified beliefs. If one shares my view that justified belief is, at least roughly, *well-formed* belief, surely animals and young children can have justified beliefs.

A second problem with (9) concerns its underlying rationale. Since (9) is proposed as a substitute for (6_A), it is implied that the reliability

of a belief's own cognitive ancestry does not make it justified. But, the suggestion seems to be, the reliability of a *meta-belief*'s ancestry confers justifiedness on the first-order belief. Why should that be so? Perhaps one is attracted by the idea of a "trickle-down" effect: if an n + 1-level belief is justified, its justification trickles down to an n-level belief. But even if the trickle-down theory is correct, it doesn't help here. There is no assurance from the satisfaction of (9)'s antecedent that the meta-belief itself is *justified*.

To obtain a better revision of our theory, let us re-examine the Jones case. Jones has strong evidence against certain propositions concerning his past. He doesn't *use* this evidence, but if he *were* to use it properly, he would stop believing these propositions. Now the proper use of evidence would be an instance of a (conditionally) reliable process. So what we can say about Jones is that he *fails* to use a certain (conditionally) reliable process that he could and should have used. Admittedly, had he used this process, he would have "worsened" his doxastic states: he would have replaced some true beliefs with suspension of judgment. Still, he couldn't have known this in the case in question. So he failed to do something which, epistemically, he should have done. This diagnosis suggests a fundamental change in our theory. The justificational status of a belief is not only a function of the cognitive process *actually* employed in producing it, it is also a function of processes that could and should be employed.

With these points in mind, we may tentatively propose the following revision of our theory, where we again focus on a base-clause principle but omit certain details in the interest of clarity.

>   (10)   If S's belief in *p* at *t* results from a reliable cognitive process, and there is no reliable or conditionally reliable process available to S which, had it been used by S in addition to the process actually used, would have resulted in S's not believing *p* at *t*, then S's belief in *p* at *t* is justified.

There are several problems with this proposal. First, there is a technical problem. One cannot use an additional belief-forming (or doxastic-state-forming) process *as well as* the original process if the additional one would result in a different doxastic state. One wouldn't be using the original process at all. So we need a slightly different formulation of the relevant counterfactual. Since the basic idea is reasonably clear, however, I won't try to improve on the formulation here. A second problem concerns the notion of "*available*" belief-forming (or doxastic-state-forming) processes. What is it for a process to be "available" to a cognizer? Were scientific procedures "available" to people who lived in pre-scientific ages? Furthermore, it seems implausible to say that all "available" processes ought to be used, at least if we include such processes as gathering *new* evidence. Surely a belief can sometimes be justified even if additional evidence-gathering would yield a different doxastic attitude. What I think we should have in mind here are such additional processes as calling previously acquired evidence to mind, assessing the implications of that evidence, etc. This is admittedly somewhat vague, but here again our ordinary notion of justifiedness is vague, so it is appropriate for our analysans to display the same sort of vagueness.

This completes the sketch of my account of justified belief. Before concluding, however, it is essential to point out that there is an important use of "justified" which is not captured by this account but can be captured by a closely related one.

There is a use of "justified" in which it is not implied or presupposed that there is a *belief* that is justified. For example, if S is trying to decide whether to believe *p* and asks our advice, we may tell him that he is "justified" in believing it. We do not thereby imply that he *has* a justified *belief*, since we know he is still suspending judgment. What we mean, roughly, is that he *would* or *could* be justified if he were to believe *p*. The justificational status we ascribe here cannot be a function of the causes of S's believing *p*, for there is no belief by S in *p*. Thus, the account of justifiedness we have given thus far cannot explicate *this* use of "justified." (It doesn't follow that this use of "justified" has no connection with causal ancestries. Its proper use may depend on the causal ancestry of the cognizer's cognitive state, though not on the causal ancestry of his believing *p*.)

Let us distinguish two uses of "justified": an *ex post* use and an *ex ante* use. The *ex post* use occurs when there exists a belief, and we say of *that belief* that it is (or isn't) justified. The *ex ante* use occurs when no such belief exists, or when we wish to ignore the question of whether such a belief exists. Here we say of the *person*, independent of his doxastic state vis-à-vis *p*, that *p* is (or isn't) suitable for him to believe.[17]

Since we have given an account of *ex post* justifiedness, it will suffice if we can analyze *ex ante* justifiedness in terms of it. Such an analysis, I believe, is ready at hand. S is *ex ante* justified in believing *p* at *t* just in case his total cognitive state at *t* is such that from that state he could come to believe *p* in such a way that this belief would be *ex post* justified. More precisely, he is *ex ante* justified in believing *p* at *t* just in case a reliable belief-forming operation is available to him such that the application of that operation to his total cognitive state at *t* would result, more or less immediately, in his believing *p* and this belief would be *ex post* justified. Stated formally, we have the following:

(11) Person S is *ex ante* justified in believing *p* at *t* if and only if there is a reliable belief-forming operation available to S which is such that if S applied that operation to this total cognitive state at *t*, S would believe *p* at *t*-plus-delta (for a suitably small delta) and that belief would be *ex post* justified.

For the analysans of (11) to be satisfied, the total cognitive state at *t* must have a suitable causal ancestry. Hence, (11) is implicitly an Historical account of *ex ante* justifiedness.

As indicated, the bulk of this essay was addressed to *ex post* justifiedness. This is the appropriate analysandum if one is interested in the connection between justifiedness and knowledge, since what is crucial to whether a person *knows* a proposition is whether he has an actual *belief* in the proposition that is justified. However, since many epistemologists are interested in *ex ante* justifiedness, it is proper for a general theory of justification to try to provide an account of that concept as well. Our theory does this quite naturally, for the account of *ex ante* justifiedness falls out directly from our account of *ex post* justifiedness.

Notes

1 "A Causal Theory of Knowing," *Journal of Philosophy* 64 (1967), pp. 335–72; "Innate Knowledge," in S. P. Stich (ed.), *Innate Ideas* (Berkeley: University of California Press, 1975); and "Discrimination and Perceptual Knowledge," *Journal of Philosophy* 73 (1976), pp. 771–99.

2 Notice that the choice of a recursive format does not prejudice the case for or against any particular theory. A recursive format is perfectly general. Specifically, an explicit set of necessary and sufficient conditions is just a special case of a recursive format, i.e., one in which there is no recursive clause.

3 Many of the attempts I shall consider are suggested by material in William P. Alston, "Varieties of Privileged Access," *American Philosophical Quarterly* 8 (1971), pp. 223–41.

4 Such a definition (though without the modal term) is given, for example, by W. V. Quine and J. S. Ullian in *The Web of Belief* (New York: Random House, 1970), p. 21. Statements are said to be self-evident just in case "to understand them is to believe them."

5 Ibid., 22.

6 I assume, of course, that "nomologically necessary" is *de re* with respect to "S" and "*t*" in this construction. I shall not focus on problems that may arise in this regard, since my primary concerns are with different issues.

7 This assumption violates the thesis that Davidson calls "The Anomalism of the Mental." Cf. "Mental Events" in L. Foster and J. W. Swanson (eds), *Experience and Theory* (Amherst: University of Massachusetts Press, 1970). But it is unclear that this thesis is a necessary truth. Thus, it seems fair to assume its falsity in order to produce a counterexample. The example neither entails nor precludes the mental–physical identity theory.

8 Keith Lehrer's example of the gypsy lawyer is intended to show the inappropriateness of a causal requirement (see *Knowledge* (Oxford: Clarendon Press, 1974), pp. 124–5.) But I find this example unconvincing. To the extent that I clearly imagine that the lawyer fixes his beliefs solely as a result of the cards, it seems intuitively wrong to say that he *knows* – or has a *justified belief* – that his client is innocent.

9 This definition is not exactly what we need for the purposes at hand. As Ernest Sosa points out, introspection will turn out to be a belief-dependent process, since sometimes the input into the process will be a belief (when the introspected content is a belief). Intuitively, however, introspection is not the sort of process which may be merely conditionally reliable. I do not know how to refine the definition so as to avoid this difficulty, but it is a small and isolated point.

10 It may be objected that principles (6_A) and (6_B) are jointly open to analogues of the lottery paradox. A series of processes composed of reliable but less-than-perfectly-reliable processes may be extremely unreliable. Yet applications of (6_A) and (6_B) would confer justifiedness on a belief that is caused by such a series. In reply to this objection, we might simply indicate that the theory is intended to capture our ordinary notion of justifiedness, and this ordinary notion has been formed without recognition of this kind of problem. The theory is not wrong *as* a theory of the ordinary (naive) conception of justifiedness. On the other hand, if we want a theory to do more than capture the ordinary conception of justifiedness, it might be possible to strengthen the principles to avoid lottery-paradox analogues.

11 I am indebted to Mark Pastin for this point.

12 Cf. *Theory of Knowledge*, 2nd edn, pp. 17, 114–16.

13 Cf. "A Causal Theory of Knowing." The reliability aspect of my theory also has its precursors in earlier papers of mine on knowing: "Innate Knowledge" and "Discrimination and Perceptual Knowledge."

14 The view that introspection is retrospection was taken by Ryle, and before him (as Charles Hartshorne points out to me) by Hobbes, Whitehead, and possibly Husserl.

15 Of course, if people in world *W* learn *inductively* that wishful thinking is reliable, and regularly base their beliefs on this inductive inference, it is quite unproblematic and straightforward that their beliefs are justified. The only interesting case is where their beliefs are formed *purely* by wishful thinking,

without using inductive inference. The suggestion contemplated in this paragraph of the text is that, in the world imagined, even pure wishful thinking would confer justifiedness.

16 I am indebted here to Mark Kaplan.

17 The distinction between *ex post* and *ex ante* justifiedness is similar to Roderick Firth's distinction between *doxastic* and *propositional* warrant. See his "Are Epistemic Concepts Reducible to Ethical Concepts?" in Alvin I. Goldman and Jaegwon Kim (eds), *Values and Morals, Essays in Honor of William Frankena, Charles Stevenson, and Richard Brandt* (Dordrecht: D. Reidel, 1978).

CHAPTER 27

Reliabilism Leveled

Jonathan Vogel

Max knows that the 6 o'clock train goes all the way to Montauk. He just asked at the information booth in the station, where the staffers are highly competent and have direct access to the master timetable. But suppose that, instead of asking at the booth, Max had consulted an old, out-of-date schedule, and that many of the routes and times listed there had changed. Even if the schedule happened to say that the 6 o'clock goes to Montauk, Max would not know that it does. Whether Max knows or not seems to turn on the fact that information provided at the booth is extremely reliable, while information provided by the out-of-date schedule is not. Accordingly, one might hold that knowledge just *is* a reliably true belief, or, alternatively, a belief that results from a process that reliably produces true beliefs.

To adopt such a view is to endorse reliabilism with respect to knowledge. Here, I distinguish two versions of this position, which I call *neighborhood reliabilism* and *counterfactual reliabilism*. I then raise the question of what reliabilists can and must say about reflective or higher-level knowledge (that is, knowledge about one's knowledge or beliefs). It will emerge that both versions of reliabilism encounter serious difficulties in this connection, and must be regarded as unsatisfactory. These results suggest that the traditional

Originally published in *The Journal of Philosophy* 97, 11 (2000), pp. 602–23.

justification requirement for knowledge cannot be supplanted by a reliability requirement, as many now are inclined to suppose.

I.   Reliability and Reliabilism

Reliabilism about knowledge takes different forms. To some extent, one can distinguish "reliable belief" accounts of knowledge from "reliable process" accounts. Roughly, according to the former, whether you know that *P* depends upon whether your *belief* that *P* is prone to error. According to the latter, whether you know that *P* depends upon whether the *process* that produced your belief that *P* is prone to error. Reliabilism about knowledge differs from reliabilism about justification, which seeks to explicate justification (rather than knowledge) in terms of reliability. The view I am considering involves no commitment to the notion that justification can be so understood.[1]

A principal motivation for adopting reliabilism is the idea that truth is the ultimate epistemic norm, and that besides truth, there are no others. We want what we believe to be true. Moreover, because truth is so important, we want our beliefs to be not just adventitiously true, but *securely* true. Knowledge, then, is securely true belief, and knowledge is compromised to the extent that there is falsehood or the possibility of falsehood. The greatest security one could have would be certainty or infallibility. A belief would be certain if it could not possibly be wrong. That is, in any possible world in which you believe X, X is true:

(1)   Necessarily, $B(X)$ implies X.

and, equivalently:

(2)   Necessarily, $\neg X$ implies $\neg B(X)$.

Similarly, a belief-forming process would be infallible if it could not possibly go wrong, and this conception can be spelled out along the lines of (1) and (2).

But such logical invulnerability to error is often an unattainably high standard. Whenever someone believes a contingent proposition as the result of an inductive inference, it is logically possible for the belief she arrives at to be wrong. Hence, it seems that knowledge must demand something less than certainty or infallibility – that is, something less than truth in any logically possible situation. Knowledge may require reliability instead. What is crucial is that reliability, whether it pertains to beliefs or to processes, need not be total or absolute. Something may do Y reliably, even if it would fail to do Y under very extreme or extraordinary conditions. An alarm clock may be reliable, despite the fact that it would not ring if the power went out, or if the ceiling collapsed on it. Accordingly, reliability as it pertains to knowledge may be understood as truth in all situations that could arise, *except* for extraordinary or outlandish ones that we do not, and need not, care about. Thus, perception, or particular beliefs formed by perception, may count as reliable, despite the fact that perception, or particular beliefs arrived at by perception, can go wrong under certain circumstances.

This understanding of epistemic reliability can be sharpened somewhat, as follows. Think of possible worlds as being farther away from the actual world to the extent that they differ from the actual world. A belief is reliable just in case it turns out to be true whenever it is held in a neighborhood N of worlds not too far away from the actual world; a process is reliable just in case it yields (mostly) true beliefs in a neighborhood N of worlds not too far away from the actual world. Proceeding in this vein, the reliabilist may set out as a condition of knowledge:

(3a)   In N, $B(X)$ implies X.[2]

or:

(3b)   In N, $B(X)$ by process P implies X.

or:

(3c)   In N, all or nearly all beliefs $B(X_i)$ formed by process P are such that $B(X_i)$ implies X_i.

Assume, at least for now, that the boundary of N is fixed. In particular, it does not vary with the content of the proposition believed, the process of belief formation, or pragmatic considerations.

(3a)–(3c) invoke one conception of reliability, but there are others. And, clearly, there will be different versions of reliabilism corresponding to the different conceptions of reliability one might adopt. Theorists such as David Armstrong, Fred Dretske, Robert Nozick, and Keith DeRose have held that knowledge requires satisfaction of a co-variation or tracking condition:

(4)   If X were false, then $\neg B(X)$.[3]

A belief might meet a version of condition (3) as stated, yet not meet condition (4). Here is why. Consider (3a) and (4). Given the standard Lewis–Stalnaker semantics for counterfactuals, instances of (4) are true if and only if the consequent is true in the closest possible world (or worlds) in which the antecedent holds. Which world that is, and how far it is from the actual world, depends upon what the value of X is. To illustrate, consider two propositions I know:

(5)   I am not carrying a pen with blue ink.
(6)   The Earth is not governed by cows.

Condition (4) makes my knowledge of (5) depend upon what I would believe in the closest possible world in which I was carrying a pen with blue ink, and it makes my knowledge of (6) depend upon what I would believe in the closest possible world in which the Earth was governed by cows. The closest $\neg$ (5) world – one in which I happen to be carrying a pen with blue ink – need not be very different from the actual world, in which I happen to be carrying a pen with black ink. That is, the closest ¬(5) world is very close to the actual world, and we may assume that it falls within the boundary of N. A possible world in which the Earth was governed by cows would, however, be very different from the actual world, so different that it might well lie beyond the boundary of N. We may suppose that my belief as to whether the Earth is governed by cows is always true inside N, and that I thereby satisfy condition (3a). It remains open that I am wrong about this matter in the nearest world where cows do govern, contrary to (4). Thus, satisfaction of condition (3a) with respect to a given proposition does not guarantee satisfaction of condition (4) with respect to that proposition.[4]

In light of the foregoing, we can distinguish two different versions of reliabilism. The first, which I shall call *neighborhood reliabilism* (NR), is the view that you know X, if and only if you have a true belief that X which satisfies some version of (3). The second, which I shall call *counterfactual reliabilism* (CR), is the view that you know X, if and only if you have a true belief that X which satisfies some version of both (3) and (4).

It is important to note what requirements these theories do *not* impose on knowledge. First, NR and CR eschew the traditional claim that one could not know a proposition without having justification for believing it. Let us say that to be justified in believing a proposition means something like having beliefs or nondoxastic states that provide good reasons for believing that proposition. Reliabilists who reject the justification condition sometimes argue as follows. The justification condition is independent of the reliability condition only if holding beliefs for good reasons is not necessarily truth conducive. In that case, the pursuit of rational belief and the pursuit of true belief could, at least in principle, diverge. But truth is the sole and ultimate epistemic value, so any substantive, independent justification condition has no place among the requirements for knowledge.[5]

That is one rationale for giving up the justification condition. A highly advertised benefit of doing so is that it immediately allows us to be rid of at least some forms of skepticism. According to a very familiar line of skeptical argument, I have no justification for believing that I am not a thoroughly deceived brain in a vat, and consequently I fail to know that I am not. Since I fail to know that I am not thoroughly deceived in this way, I have no knowledge of the external world. A reliabilist, or anyone else who rejects the justification condition, will balk at the first step. She may concede that I have no justification for believing that I am not a brain in a vat. Unless knowledge requires justification, however, it does not follow that I fail to know that I am not a brain in a vat, and the skeptical argument is blocked. I shall return to this issue later.

A second point is that reliability theorists typically reject various "higher-level" requirements on knowledge, such as:

(7) $K(X)$ entails $K(K(X))$.

and:

(8) $K(X)$ entails $K(R(X))$.[6]

The reliabilist has a number of motivations for denying (8), and, therefore, (7).

For one thing, a reliable belief or process is truth tropic regardless of whether it is *known* to be so. Hence, a requirement that, beyond being reliable, a belief or process has to be known to be reliable would not do anything to foster the epistemic norm of truth. Such a requirement, then, has no place in an account of knowledge.

Next, from the reliabilist standpoint, you know X in virtue of being reliable about X. X is one fact about the world; whether you are reliable about X is another, different fact about the world. You are reliable about X if, in your environment, you are suitably related to X. You may be so related to X without being so related to $R(X)$. Hence, you can be reliable about X but not reliable about $R(X)$. You would, then, know X, but not that you are reliable about X.

In addition, (8) as stated apparently requires an endless sequence of beliefs $B(R(X))$, $B(RR(X))$, $B(RRR(X))$, and so on, such that one is reliable about $R(X)$, $RR(X)$, $RRR(X)$, and so on. That is unattractive, certainly. And, if each of these beliefs has to be generated by distinct or additionally complex mechanisms or procedures, the regress is utterly vicious.[7]

Finally, the denial of (8) must be independently plausible, if reliabilism is to withstand one of the main criticisms which has been directed against it. This criticism, due to Laurence BonJour[8] and Keith Lehrer,[9] is presented by way of various examples. Here is BonJour's well-known "Norman" case:

> Norman, under certain conditions which usually obtain, is a completely reliable clairvoyant with respect to certain kinds of subject matter. He possesses no evidence or reasons of any kind for or against the general possibility of such a cognitive power, or for or against the thesis that he possesses it. One day Norman comes to believe the President is in New York City. … In fact the belief is true and results from his clairvoyant power under circumstances under which it is completely reliable (*op. cit.*, p. 62).

BonJour maintains that Norman does not know in this instance, and concludes that reliabilism is untenable. Even among those who find this example convincing, there is some difference of opinion as to what defect in reliabilism it brings to light. But one prominent reaction is that Norman does not know the president is in New York because he fails to satisfy some higher-level requirement on knowledge.[10] If Norman had verified that the deliverances of his clairvoyant power reliably report how things are, then he would know that the president is in New York. But, since he lacks this higher-level knowledge, Norman lacks the first-level knowledge that the president is in New York.

I am not sure exactly what to make of this discussion, since I tend to lose my bearings when clairvoyance is so much as mentioned.[11] I do think, however, that this much is relatively clear: it is possible for one to be reliable about *X* without knowing that one is. According to reliabilist accounts of knowledge, simply being reliable about *X* is supposed to be sufficient for knowing that *X*. If knowing that you are reliable about *X* is an additional necessary condition for your knowing *X*, then these reliabilist accounts are mistaken.[12]

To the reliabilists I have in mind, the big picture looks like this. We know a lot about the world. We are reliable about things we believe on the basis of perception, so we know all kinds of things by seeing, hearing, and so forth. In addition, we are competent reasoners, at least about relatively elementary matters. We are reliable when we arrive at beliefs by induction or deduction, and these beliefs also count as

knowledge. If we think about it, we probably believe that we are reliable about the things we believe on the basis of perception and inference. It is not apparent, however, whether these higher-level judgments are themselves reliable. If and when they are not, then we fail to know that we know. But, says the reliabilist, there is nothing wrong with that.

II. Counterfactual Reliabilism is Too Strong

I think the right picture is somewhat different. I agree that we know a lot about the world. I also agree that, when we form various beliefs, those beliefs or belief-forming processes may be reliable without our knowing that they are. Nevertheless, we often know that our beliefs about the world are true, not false. On some occasions we know, further, that we are reliable about what we believe. And, finally, there are many instances when we know that we know. It is incumbent upon reliabilists to get these facts about higher-level knowledge straight. I do not think they can.

Let me begin with CR. My treatment of it will be relatively brief, in part because I have discussed the status of (4) as a condition for knowledge elsewhere. (4) was the subject of intense scrutiny some years ago, and serious problems with it came to light. For one thing, it leads to unacceptable failures of what is known as the *closure principle for knowledge*:

(9)   If $K(P)$ & $K(P$ entails $Q)$, then $K(Q)$.

Also, there are unexceptional cases of inductive knowledge for which (4) does not hold, so (4) is too strong.[13] There is an additional difficulty: (4) is hard to square with a satisfactory account of higher-level knowledge.[14]

Consider the following example. You see your long-time friend Omar, who is a perfectly decent and straightforward sort of person. Noticing his shiny white footwear, you say, "Nice shoes, Omar, are they new?" Omar replies, "Yes, I bought them yesterday." I think the following things are true:

(10)   You know Omar has a new pair of shoes.

(11) You know that your belief that Omar has a new pair of shoes is true, or at least not false.[15]

(12) You know that your belief that Omar has a new pair of shoes is reliable.[16]

(13) Other things being equal, you know that you know that Omar has a new pair of shoes.

(13) and (12) depend upon (11), and (11) is certainly compelling in its own right. (13) entails (11), because to know X entails that you have a true belief that X. (12) entails (11), if your being reliable about X is understood to entail that your belief that X is actually true.

The prime question at this point whether CR can accommodate (11). Does CR allow you to know that your belief that Omar has a new pair of shoes is true, not false? In particular, does (11) meet the condition set by (4)? I think the answer is no. I shall try to say why somewhat loosely and informally, and then more carefully.

(4) requires that, if you know X, then you would not believe X, if X were false. As things actually are, you believe that your belief that Omar has new shoes is not false. What if it were? If somehow your belief that Omar has a new pair of shoes were false, you would still believe that your belief was true, not false. The alternative is hard to fathom. It is difficult to conceive of your not believing that something you believe is true, whenever the matter happens to cross your mind. So, if your belief that Omar has new shoes were false, you would still believe that your belief was true, not false. You thereby fail to satisfy condition (4). According to CR, then, you do not know that your belief that Omar has new shoes is true, not false.

Let me now go through the same point a little more carefully. Let O = "Omar has new shoes"; $B(O)$ = "You believe Omar has new shoes"; $B(\neg(B(O) \& \neg O))$ = "You believe that you do not believe falsely that Omar has new shoes."

(14) In the actual world, $B(\neg(B(O) \& \neg O))$.

Consider the nearest possible world W in which your higher-level belief is false, that is,

(15) In W, $\neg(\neg(B(O) \& \neg O))$.

Simplifying,

(16) In W, $((B(O) \& \neg O))$.

From (16),

(17) In W, $B(O)$.

If you believe O, you believe that you do not falsely believe O (see above). Hence,

(18) In W, $B(\neg(B(O) \& \neg O))$.

Given (15) and (18),

(19) In W, $(B(O) \& \neg O) \& B(\neg(B(O) \& \neg O))$.

That is, if your belief that O were false, you nevertheless would believe that it was not false. So, according to (4), you fail to know that you do not believe falsely that O. It follows, I take it, that you also fail to know that your belief is true.[17]

Note that the argumentation here is quite general. (4) makes it impossible for you to know that *any* of your beliefs is true, not false.[18] Thus, it also seems to exclude your knowing that any of your beliefs is reliable, or that any of your beliefs is knowledge. That is going far too far, in my book.[19] So, let us set CR aside, and move on to NR.[20]

III. Neighborhood Reliabilism is Too Weak

NR makes knowledge out to be true belief that satisfies some version of (3). The differences among the various formulations, and the forms of NR they give rise to, can be quite significant. The trend these days seems to be toward reliable-process theories, which run along the lines of (3c) rather than (3a) or (3b). Hence, in what follows, I shall consider the variant of NR that incorporates (3c), although what I shall have to say carries over to the other forms of NR as well.[21] As I have set things up, NR is generally weaker than CR, since NR forgoes condition (4) while CR includes it. I have maintained that CR is too strong. It stints us higher-level knowledge we actually have. Now, I shall argue that NR is too weak. It would allow us higher-level knowledge we do not have.

Once again, I shall proceed by considering an example, namely, the "gas-gauge case," due in its original form to Michael Williams.[22] Williams describes himself driving a car with a working, highly reliable gas gauge. Williams does not know, however, that the gauge is reliable. Let us stipulate that he has never checked it, he has never been told anything about its reliability, and he does not even have any background information as to whether gauges like his are likely to be working. He never takes any special steps to see whether the gauge is going up or down when it ought to be. Rather, without giving the matter a second thought, Williams simply goes by what the gauge says. The gauge reads "F," and Williams believes that his gas tank is full. According to NR, he *knows* that his tank is full. He has this knowledge because his belief results from a reliable process, that is, going by a well-functioning gas gauge. But Williams does not *know that he knows* that his tank is full. To have this higher-level knowledge, he would need to know that the gauge reliably registers the level of gas in his tank, and we have stipulated that he has no such information.[23]

No one should be distracted by the details of the case. Perhaps it is hard to imagine how, in the situation described, Williams could fail to have *any* background information about the reliability of his gas gauge. Then again, one might doubt whether the supposedly reliable process Williams uses is appropriately identified as "going by a well-functioning gas gauge." But what is essential here is just the claim that a subject might arrive at a belief by some reliable process, appropriately identified as *P*, yet not know that *P* is reliable. If particular features of my example create difficulties for you, let reading the gas gauge be a proxy for any such process *P*.

Now consider another driver, whom I shall call Roxanne. She is like Williams, in that she believes implicitly what her gas gauge says, without knowing that the gauge is reliable. But she undertakes the following, admittedly curious, procedure. She looks at the gauge often. Not only does she form a belief about how much gas is in the tank, but she also takes note of the state of the gauge itself. So, for example, when the gauge reads "F", she believes that, on this occasion, the tank is full. She also believes that, on this occasion, the gauge reads "F." Moreover, Roxanne combines these beliefs; she believes:

(20) On this occasion, the gauge reads "F" and *F*.

Certainly, the perceptual process by which Roxanne forms her belief that the gauge reads "F" is a reliable one. By hypothesis, her belief that the tank is full is also reached by a reliable process. Hence, there seems to be no good reason to deny that Roxanne's belief in (20) is the result of a reliable process, and the reliabilist will say that she knows (20).[24]

Now, it is a completely straightforward logical consequence of (20) that:

(21) On this occasion, the gauge is reading accurately.

Assume that Roxanne deduces (21) from (22). Deduction is certainly a reliable process, so there is no loss of reliability at this step. Consequently, it seems that Roxanne must be credited with knowing (21). She knows this, supposedly, despite the fact that she has no independent information at all about the reliability of the gauge – whether it is broken or likely to be broken, whether it is hooked up properly, and so on. She just looks at the gauge and immediately believes what it says.

Let us say further that Roxanne does this over and over again for a good while. At various times *t*, she looks at the gauge, which reads "*X*," and forms the belief that, on occasion *t*, the gauge says "*X*" and the tank is *X*. Given what has already been said, she comes to know that, on each of these occasions, the gauge was reading accurately. Then, putting these pieces of information together, Roxanne concludes by induction:

(22) The gauge reads accurately all the time.

Reliabilists generally accept that induction is a reliable belief-forming process. So they should concede that the transition from various beliefs like (21) to (22) is knowledge preserving. We can add that, from (22), Roxanne infers:

(23) The gauge is reliable.

If Roxanne knows that the gauge is reliable, then she can presumably deduce and know that the process by which she comes to believe that her gas tank is full is a reliable one. And with just a little more deduction, Roxanne can come to know that she knows that her gas tank is full.[25]

This extraordinary procedure, which I shall call *bootstrapping*, seems to allow one to promote many, if not all, of one's beliefs that were formed by reliable processes into *knowledge* that those beliefs were formed by reliable processes.[26] I assume that bootstrapping is illegitimate. Roxanne cannot establish that her gas gauge is reliable by the peculiar reasoning I have just described. The challenge to NR is that it may go wrong here. On the face of things, it does improperly ratify bootstrapping as a way of gaining knowledge.[27]

To sort this out, we need to get clear about what the defect in bootstrapping is. I shall consider some possible diagnoses, in a point-counterpoint format:

Point. It is obvious what Roxanne did wrong. Suppose the gauge had not been reliable. Roxanne would have gone through exactly the same procedure, and reached the false conclusion that her gauge was reliable. Hence, she does not know that the gauge is reliable.

Counterpoint. Say that if you like. But then you are really assuming that knowledge has to satisfy condition (4). In other words, you are abandoning NR in favor of CR, and we have already seen that CR fails.

Point. The problem with Roxanne's procedure is that it could not have possibly yielded any other result other than the one it did, namely, that the gauge is reliable.

Counterpoint. It is not clear that the putative defect really is one. The process by which I know I am conscious when I am is surely a reliable one, yet that process could not return a verdict other than that I am conscious.[28]

Point. Roxanne does not know that the gauge is reliable, because she reaches that conclusion by bootstrapping, and bootstrapping itself is an unreliable process. After all, you can apply bootstrapping to a great many underlying processes, some reliable, some not. Every time, though, bootstrapping will tell you that the underlying process is reliable. When the underlying process is unreliable, bootstrapping will yield the false belief that the underlying process is reliable. So, bootstrapping itself often generates false beliefs, and must be considered unreliable.

Counterpoint. So far as I can tell, this is the best answer for the reliabilist to give, but it still seems problematic in various respects. My first worry is

a methodological one. The response under consideration identifies the process leading up to Roxanne's belief in (23) as a token of a relatively wide process type, roughly *bootstrapping in general*. The failures of other tokens of this broad type are supposed to discredit Roxanne's undertaking, and the belief that results from it. Such a response is dissatisfying because it is generally possible to find a process type under which a given process token falls, such that the token counts as reliable, just as it is generally possible to find another process type under which the token falls, such that the token counts as unreliable. There is no agreed-upon, principled way of identifying which is the proper process type to consider in evaluating the epistemic status of a particular belief.[29]

The reliabilist herself may encounter some embarrassment on just this score. One might describe Roxanne's initially going by her gas gauge as "forming a belief by an *unauthenticated* process," that is, a process one does not know to be reliable. By parallel with the argument just given against bootstrapping, one might say that, if one forms beliefs by an unauthenticated process, often enough the token process one employs will be unreliable, and one's belief will be false. Hence, forming a belief by an unauthenticated process is generally unreliable, and beliefs that result from unauthenticated processes do not count as knowledge. Of course, the reliabilist rejects the demand that a process must be known to be reliable if it is to be a source of knowledge. She then has to find some basis for allowing the criticism of Roxanne's bootstrapping to stand, while rejecting the corresponding criticism of Roxanne's forming a belief by an unauthenticated process in the first place. Otherwise, the reliabilist's charge of guilt by association may boomerang.

Suppose we set this scruple aside, and accept that Roxanne's way of reaching (23) is unreliable. What makes it so? Where does the unreliability enter in? It will be useful to compare Roxanne's bootstrapping with a procedure that really would establish that a car's gas gauge is reliable. Imagine that Catherine periodically uses a dipstick to measure the level of gas in the tank of her car, and she verifies that the reading of the gauge matches that of the dipstick. Each time she does this, she comes to know an instance of:

(21*)   On occasion t, the gauge is reading accurately.

After enough repeated successes, we can agree, Catherine may know by induction that the gauge is accurate all the time, and she can properly reach the yet stronger (modalized) conclusion that the gauge is reliable. The crucial point is that this impeccable way of finding out that a gas gauge is reliable is identical to Roxanne's original procedure from a certain point onward. Both Catherine and Roxanne infer that their gauges are reliable from beliefs of the form given by (21*). So, it seems that any lapse in reliability on Roxanne's part must occur in the way that she arrives at such beliefs.

In each case, Roxanne deduces an instance of (21*) from a belief of the form:

(20*)   On occasion t, the gauge reads "X" and X.

As I said earlier, it would be hard to deny that Roxanne's beliefs about how the gas gauge reads are reliably formed. And, by hypothesis, Roxanne's beliefs about how much gas is in her car's tank are formed by a reliable process. So, the reliabilist seems committed to the claim that when Roxanne comes to believe instances of (20*), those beliefs result from reliable processes. Given what has already been said, the only point left at which some defect can enter into Roxanne's procedure has to be in her transition from instances of (20*) to belief in corresponding instances of (21*). But, since any instance of (20*) entails an instance of (21*), that instance of (21*) must be true if the corresponding instance of (20*) is! In that sense, there is no more risk of error with respect to the instances of (21*) than there is with respect to the instances of (20*). So, it is opaque how proceeding from instances of (20*) to corresponding instances of (21*) turns a reliable process into an unreliable one.[30]

Let us also waive *this* objection for the time being, and permit the proponent of NR to take refuge in the claim that bootstrapping is an unreliable process. Thus, her position will be that you cannot use the beliefs generated by some process to establish the accuracy or the reliability of that very process. Unfortunately for the reliabilist, such a response to the gas-gauge case disrupts the full-blooded, noncontextualist antiskepticism that reliabilists often regard as a great virtue of their position. For, while bootstrapping may seem absurd when it involves someone's gas gauge, it has been regarded as a sound response to Cartesian skepticism.[31]

This answer to skepticism is basically G. E. Moore's vintage commonsense response, transposed and fortified by the addition of some early twenty-first-century reliabilism. It goes as follows. You know you have a hand. Your belief that you have a hand was formed by perception, which is a reliable process. Hence, that belief counts as knowledge. Now, the proposition that you have a hand entails that you are not a brain in a vat, deceived into believing falsely that you have a hand. Hence, you can deduce that you are not a brain in a vat from the proposition that you have a hand. Your belief that you are not a brain in a vat qualifies as knowledge, because it, too, is formed by a reliable process. At least, that will be so if deduction from a belief arrived at by a reliable process itself counts as a reliable process.

The correspondence between this neo-Moorean argument and the rejected line of argument in the gas-gauge case emerges clearly if the former is reformulated slightly:

(A)   You know you have a hand.
(B)   You know that it appears to you as though you have a hand.

(B) holds, because we may assume that your beliefs about how things appear to you are generated by a reliable process. Continuing:

(C)   Therefore, you know that your appearance of having a hand is veridical.
(D)   Therefore, you know you are not a deceived brain in a vat.

For comparison:

(A′)   Roxanne knows that her gas tank is full.
(B′)   Roxanne knows that the gas gauge reads "F."
(C′)   Therefore, Roxanne knows that, on this occasion, her gas gauge is reading accurately.

Thus, the reliabilist version of Moore's refutation of skepticism sanctions the same kind of inference that created problems in connection with the gas-gauge case. Suppose we grant that the reliabilist is able to evade those problems by denying, either for principled reasons or by fiat, that bootstrapping can lead to knowledge. The upshot will be that reliabilism cannot provide a satisfactory response to skepticism along the lines just laid out.[32]

Let me return to the status of NR in general. I have taxed that view for allowing bootstrapping to count as a source of knowledge, or for not being able to explain what is wrong with it. In the example given above, the crux of the matter came down to the status of beliefs of the form:

(20*)   On occasion t, the gauge reads "X" and X.

and:

(21*)   On occasion t, the gauge is reading accurately.

It looked as though the reliabilist was committed to saying that Roxanne knows instances of (20*), but does not know corresponding instances of (21*), even though she deduces the second from the first. Now, contextualism about knowledge might appear to offer the reliabilist a way out of this uncomfortable situation. The contextualist will say that our standards for knowledge rise as we think through the example. That is, the neighborhood N which determines the reliability of processes expands. At first, when (20*) is under consideration, worlds in which the gas gauge fails are excluded from N. The gas gauge counts as reliable, and Roxanne is correctly judged to know both conjuncts of (20*), and (20*) itself. But overt consideration of (21*) brings questions about the accuracy of the gauge into the picture, and worlds in which the gauge is wrong come to be included in N. In this setting, the gauge no longer counts as reliable, so Roxanne does not know that her gas tank is full. Hence, she does not know one of the conjuncts of (20*), and she does not know (20*) as a whole. Nor does she know (21*), which she derived from (20*). Contextualism relieves the reliabilist's embarrassment of having to explain how reliability is lost in the course of Roxanne's deducing a proposition from another one that entails it.

I do not propose to enter into a full-blown discussion of contextualism here, but I shall make two brief points. First, if the standards of reliability and knowledge can be elevated in something like the manner just described, then we almost never know explicitly that we know anything. We also lose some seemingly impeccable first-order knowledge. To see this, recall the example in which you believe that Omar has new shoes. Say that you reflect upon your epistemic situation, and you believe that your belief that Omar has a new pair of shoes is the outcome of a reliable process. According to the contextualist revision of NR, considering the reliability of a belief-forming process expands the neighborhood N so that the process no longer counts as reliable. It follows that once you reflect upon the fact that your belief-forming process is reliable, you no longer know that Omar has a new pair of shoes. A fortiori, you do not know that you know that Omar has new shoes. Recourse to contextualism of this sort would make both first- and higher-order knowledge very fragile, unable to survive virtually any reflection at all. Such a result is hardly acceptable.[33]

My second thought is that adding a contextualist dimension to NR may be going to great lengths to save a view that does not want to be saved. I say this because a consequence of the contextualist maneuver is that, if it is possible to maintain low epistemic standards while the entire bootstrapping procedure is carried out, that procedure would be successful. Roxanne could convert knowledge of how much fuel is in the tank of her car into knowledge that her gas gauge is reliable. But, for the reliabilist, knowledge of how much fuel is in the tank is knowledge of one empirical fact, and knowledge that the gauge is reliable is knowledge of another, independent empirical fact. One should not be able to transmute the first into the second, as bootstrapping would allow one to do.[34] To put the same point another way: suppose a change in epistemic standards of the sort envisioned does thwart or suppress the bootstrapping procedure. Still, the standards' tendency to change would not eliminate the possibility of bootstrapping in principle or somehow make bootstrapping intrinsically more acceptable. To that extent, whatever relief contextualism provides will strike the reliabilist as cosmetic, not real.

IV. Some Conclusions

CR and NR, as I understand them, are meant to be general theories of what knowledge is. I have been arguing that both views encounter substantial difficulties when they have to deal with higher-level knowledge. CR allows:

(10)   You know that Omar has new shoes.

but not the higher-level:

(11)   You know that your belief that Omar has new shoes is true (not false).

NR got into trouble with the gas-gauge case. A proponent of NR has to say that Roxanne knows:

(20)   On this occasion, the gauge says "F" and *F*.

But if he goes on to grant that she knows:

(21)   On this occasion, the gauge is reading accurately.

it appears that she can proceed to knowledge of:

(23)   The gauge is reliable.

and beyond. This result is unacceptable, yet it is not clear how NR can avoid it.

What lessons should we draw? First, these phenomena provide some reason – not a conclusive reason, but some reason – to endorse the traditional view that knowledge requires justification. The traditional view handles the problem cases with relative ease. First, it offers a natural explanation of why (11) follows so closely on (10). Good evidence that Omar has new shoes is good evidence that a belief that Omar has new shoes is true, not false. If you have such evidence (and you believe that Omar has new shoes, and your belief is true, and there are no Gettier traps), then you are in a good position to have the knowledge reported in (10). Moreover, given that you have this evidence, you are also in a good position to have the higher-level knowledge reported in (11), so long as you recognize that you believe that Omar has new shoes, and you believe that your belief is true, not false.

Bringing justification into the picture also helps to explain what is wrong with Roxanne's bootstrapping. Given the way the example was framed, Roxanne has no justification for (23), nor, I think, for (22) or (21). If justification is necessary for knowledge, she does not know any of these, which seems correct. What about (20)? Since (20) directly entails (21), Roxanne would be justified in believing (21) if she is justified in believing (20). If, as I claim, she is not justified in believing (21), then she is not justified in believing (20), either. That, too, seems plausible. If Roxanne has no independent reason to believe that the position of the needle on the gauge is reliably correlated with how much gas is in the tank, I cannot see that she is justified in believing that her tank is full when she looks at the gauge. So the traditionalist can say that Roxanne does not know (20) or (21), since she lacks justification for both. There are no bootstraps for her to pull on.

Thus, re-instating a justification requirement for knowledge does make it easier to explain what is going on in the gas-gauge case. An objection is bound to arise, however. I have as much as said that for Roxanne to know how much gas she has by reading the gauge, she needs to have justification for thinking that the gauge is reliable. This claim seems to invite a version of the regress problem discussed in section I. Suppose that, in general, justification for believing that *X* always requires justification for the belief that the process by which you came to believe that *X* is reliable. It apparently follows that justification for any belief will require an endless hierarchy of further justified beliefs of level $(N + 1)$ as to the reliability of the way one's belief at level *N* was formed.[35] But to say that justification *sometimes* requires reason to believe that one's belief-forming process is reliable, as it does in Roxanne's situation, does not imply that justification *always* requires such higher-level support or supplementation. It is this second, stronger claim that creates the regress, and one can refuse to agree to it. Note, though, that one can maintain that knowledge always requires justification, without maintaining that justification always requires *further* justification for the higher-level belief that the process that led to the formation of one's initial belief was reliable.[36]

In sum, reliabilism encounters serious difficulties in accounting for reflective knowledge, difficulties that might well be avoided by a justificationist approach to knowledge. The question now arises whether the weakness in reliabilism that has come to light is confined to its treatment of reflective knowledge, or whether there is some deeper, more far-reaching problem with reliabilism which vividly shows itself when reflective knowledge is under consideration. Correlatively, one might ask whether the only essential work the justification condition does is to capture the relations between lower- and higher-level knowledge.

My own view, which I shall state but not argue for, is that the inability of reliabilism to account for reflective knowledge has its roots in a more basic deficiency. I take it that knowledge is a kind of human success. It is something we accomplish; we have to do our part. The justification requirement is an attempt to formulate what that part is. Reliabilism either loses sight of this aspect of knowledge, or tries, in effect, to substitute some kind of de facto alignment between belief and the world for the knower's own contribution.[37] As a consequence, reliabilist theories go wrong in their treatment of various cases, and these include the examples deployed above. Reliabilism has trouble accounting for reflective knowledge because it is defective as an account of knowledge in general. A consideration of reflective knowledge shows that knowledge in general is neither reliably true belief nor belief that results from a reliable process.

Notes

1   Rather, the reliabilist I have in mind denies that there is any independent, substantive justification condition for knowledge; see below. It may well be, though, that the arguments I shall present also tell against reliabilism about justified belief. I should mention that there is a hybrid of justificationist and reliabilist accounts, sometimes called the "reliable indicator theory." According to such a view, S knows that P only if S's belief that P is based on evidence E, where E is a reliable indicator of P. I shall not discuss this approach here.

2   Note that we do not want the converse condition for knowledge, namely, that in N, X implies $B(X)$.

3   Like (3), the tracking condition is subject to modification. (4) as stated corresponds to (3a) above. An analogue to (3b) would be:

(4b)   If X were false, then $\neg(B(X)$ by process $P)$.

where P is the process you actually used to arrive at your belief that X. Proponents of the tracking condition, like Nozick and DeRose, have in fact been led to include some reference to methods or processes in their accounts. But that has proved to be something of a quagmire; it is unclear how the relevant method or process is to be specified, and it is difficult to say exactly how reference to the process should figure in the account. For further comment on (4b), see footnote 18. I cannot think of any version of the tracking condition that corresponds neatly to (3c).

4   Another way to make the point: suppose you know the proposition that the actual world is in N. Evaluation of whether that belief satisfies (4) requires considering the truth of what you believe in worlds outside N.

5   For an argument in this spirit, see Alvin Goldman, *Epistemology and Cognition* (Cambridge: Harvard, 1986), pp. 97–103.

6   Read "$R(X)$" as "S is reliable about X." When I say "S is reliable about X," that locution is meant to stand in for whatever more specific reliabilist condition one might adopt. I shall assume, as a matter of terminology, that you are reliable about X only if you believe X and X is true. So, under this regimentation, $R(X)$ entails $B(X)$ and X. Moreover, for the reliabilist, $R(X)$ becomes equivalent to $K(X)$, and (7) become equivalent to (8).

7   See Goldman, "Naturalistic Epistemology and Reliabilism," in Peter A. French, Theodore E. Uehling, and Howard K. Wettstein, eds, *Midwest Studies in Philosophy*, Volume XIX (Minneapolis: Minnesota University Press, 1994), pp. 310–12. He claims that (7) and analogous principles create a vicious regress for nonreliabilist theories.

8 "Externalist Theories of Empirical Knowledge," in French, Uehling, and Wettstein, eds, *Midwest Studies in Philosophy*, Volume v (Minneapolis: Minnesota University Press, 1980), pp. 55–73.

9 *Theory of Knowledge* (Boulder: Westview, 1990).

10 This is BonJour's own conclusion (pp. 62–4; see also Lehrer, p. 165).

11 It seems to me, though, that a less far-fetched example to the same effect could be given. A few people have perfect pitch; they can immediately identify what absolute pitch they are hearing. I take it that whether someone does in fact have perfect pitch is not immediately apparent to that individual. To tell whether you have perfect pitch, you need to be tested. Let us suppose, then, that many people believe that they have perfect pitch, although they really do not. Now consider Norma, who has perfect pitch, but has never checked whether she does. She hears a tone, which she correctly takes to be an "A." Does she know that the tone is an "A"?

12 I should note that Goldman distinguishes "basic psychological *processes*" (my emphasis) of belief formation from *methods*, which are "various sorts of algorithms, heuristics, and learnable methodologies" – *Epistemology and Cognition*, p. 93. He also writes: "They are not part of the fixed, native architecture of the cognitive system. This is sufficient grounds for their not being basic processes" (p. 366). Goldman suggests that it is not enough for a method to be reliable to pass muster; it has to be acquired by a process or method that has higher-order reliability. That is, the first-order method needs to be acquired by a procedure that reliably leads to the acquisition of reliable methods (pp. 91–3). To this extent, a reliabilist account of knowledge modeled on Goldman's account of justification might recognize a higher-order requirement in the case of non-native, acquired belief-forming methods. But as Goldman himself acknowledges, the distinction between processes and methods is difficult to draw (p. 92 note 11). For example, the capacity to see requires maturation and stimulation in order to develop, but Goldman does not want perceptual beliefs to be subject

to higher-level requirements. A further qualm is that it is hard to see how instituting such a requirement for methods can be squared with the thought that all we should ask for from beliefs or ways of forming beliefs is reliable truth.

13 See my "Tracking, Closure, and Inductive Knowledge," in S. Luper-Foy, ed., *The Possibility of Knowledge: Nozick and His Critics* (Totowa, NJ: Rowman and Littlefield, 1987), pp. 197–215.

14 What follows is a more emphatic version of a criticism I originally directed against Nozick's account of knowledge (*ibid.*, p. 203). In his "Solving the Skeptical Problem," *The Philosophical Review*, CIV (1995), pp. 1–51, DeRose has defended something very like (4) (although, to be precise, DeRose's view is not that (4) is actually a condition for knowledge per se, but works instead to set the standards for correct knowledge attributions). DeRose takes note of the sort of problem I raised, for which he offers no solution (p. 22). He nevertheless retains confidence in a version of the counterfactual requirement, though on what basis I cannot see. For additional discussion of counterfactuals and knowledge, see my "Subjunctivitis," *Philosophical Studies* 134, 1 (May 2007), pp. 73–88.

15 Note, in addition, that any proposition X itself entails that a belief that X is not false: X entails $\neg(B(X) \,\&\, \neg X)$. So, to say that you know that Omar has new shoes, but you fail to know that you do not believe falsely that Omar has new shoes would be to reject the closure principle for knowledge.

16 Alternatively: you know that the process by which you arrived at that belief is reliable.

17 Unfortunately, this maneuvering is clumsy and roundabout. I did it this way in part to avoid complications about counterfactuals with disjunctive antecedents. Such technical hazards will arise any time one tries to apply (4) to knowledge of a conjunction. So far as I am concerned, that itself is good reason to be suspicious about (4).

18 Very much the same goes for the modification of (4) mentioned in footnote 3, namely, (4b). Suppose you believe O by some particular process P. It should be possible for

you to know that you do not falsely believe O by process P. That knowledge requires $B(\neg(P(O) \& \neg O))$, where "$P(O)$" now stands for the proposition that you believe O by way of process P. Suppose that your belief were false, that is, $(P(O) \& \neg O)$. Make the further, plausible assumption that your path from believing O by process P to a belief in the falsity of the conjunction would remain the same. Then, your belief in the falsity of the conjunction fails to satisfy condition (4b). In other words, you cannot know that you do not falsely believe O by process P.

19   This argument also cuts against reliabilism that accepts (4) without (3).

20   A proponent of CR might attempt to surmount this difficulty by adding to her account a stipulation that you know any propositions you deduce from other propositions you know. This step is fraught with difficulties, however. The revised account may be too weak, and fail for the same reason that NR does (see below). Moving in this direction would also exacerbate other problems facing CR, such as those raised by Saul Kripke in widely heard but unpublished lectures.

21   For a somewhat different taxonomy of reliabilist positions, and for some arguments that would favor what he calls a "global" process theory like (3c), see Goldman, *Epistemology and Cognition*, pp. 43–9. I am not sure that Goldman's official scheme has room for NR as I construe it, since he seems to assume that what he calls a "relevant alternatives" theory is a broadening of a "pure subjunctive theory" (p. 45). As I would put it, Goldman assumes the reliabilist accepts (4), and the open question is then whether to add some version of (3). I have set things up the other way around.

22   *Unnatural Doubts* (New York: Oxford, 1991), p. 347.

23   Williams himself says: "No item of knowledge guarantees full knowledge of its own reliability conditions: indeed this is just another way of stating the externalist point that knowing does not guarantee knowing that one knows" (*ibid.*, p. 348).

24   What I have said may provoke disquiet of the following sort. You might believe that A by way of a reliable process, and believe that B by way of a reliable process, yet your belief that $(A \& B)$ might not be the result of a reliable process. For one thing, the chances of error with respect to A may be just barely acceptable and the chances of error with respect to B may be just barely acceptable. The chances of error with respect to the conjunction may then come out to be higher than the chances of error with respect to the conjuncts, and so the belief in the conjunction may not count as reliable. Another problem is that the process by which one comes to believe that A may interfere with the process by which one comes to believe that B, or vice versa. For example, one might use one instrument to measure for A, and another to measure for B, yet the operation of the second instrument may disrupt the functioning of the first. So, I think it is true in general that $R(X)$ and $R(Y)$ do not entail $R(X \& Y)$. But it seems implausible that such a failure occurs in the situation under discussion.

25   There is a noteworthy similarity between the problem I am raising for reliabilism and a difficulty that faces co-variational accounts of semantic content. The former is an attempt to analyze knowledge in terms of the co-occurrence of beliefs and the facts; the latter is an attempt to analyze semantic content in terms of the co-occurrence of linguistic or mental tokens and the facts. A difficulty for the latter is that, if tokens of R co-occur with distal events X, they also co-occur with the proximate process P that links X's with R's. So, the result would be that the R's just as well represent P as X. See Fred Dretske, "Misrepresentation," reprinted in William Lycan, ed., *Mind and Cognition: A Reader* (New York: Oxford, 1992), pp. 129–43. The parallel problem I am raising is that, if the output of some belief-forming process P reliably co-occurs with X, that output also reliably co-occurs with instances of a reliable belief-forming process, namely, P itself. Thus, the result seems to be that P itself can give one knowledge that one is linked to X by way of a reliable process, that is, P can directly give one knowledge that one knows that X. The general lesson to be drawn is that

co-occurrence can obtain for a variety of reasons, and is of questionable value in understanding relations like representation and knowledge.

26 For definiteness, let us say that bootstrapping is the procedure that leads to beliefs, like (23), about the reliability of its underlying process. Bootstrapping may require that one be able to identify appropriately the underlying process by which one has arrived at a particular belief, and sometimes one may not meet that condition.

27 Richard Fumerton independently arrived at a somewhat similar point – *Metaepistemology and Skepticism* (Lanham, MD: Rowman and Littlefield, 1995), pp. 178–9.

28 Something like this objection is raised by William Alston, *The Reliability of Sense Perception* (Ithaca: Cornell, 1993), p. 17. He does want to allow, however, that introspection counts as a reliable process (p. 139).

29 This is the well-known "generality problem," which itself raises difficulties for reliabilism. See Richard Feldman, "Reliability and Justification," *The Monist*, LXVII (1985), pp. 159–74; and Feldman and Earl Conee, "The Generality Problem for Reliabilism," *Philosophical Studies*, XCIII (1997), pp. 1–29. In presenting my own objections to reliabilism here, I have tried my best to steer clear of problems of this sort, allowing the reliability of the underlying process to be a matter of stipulation. But at this point such complications may be unavoidable.

30 Williams insists that reliability cannot be lost through deduction (*Unnatural Doubts*, p. 328), leaving him little recourse at this point. Now, the thought may arise again that it is possible for processes to be reliable severally, but not in concatenation. One might then say that the process that led to Roxanne's belief in (20) is reliable, and that deduction is reliable, but that the combination of the two need not count as reliable. Goldman provides good reasons, however, for distinguishing processes that are reliable simpliciter (more precisely, "belief-independent J-rules") from those which are conditionally reliable ("belief-dependent J-rules"). The former generate (largely) true beliefs given nondoxastic inputs. The latter

take beliefs as input, and will generate (largely) true beliefs, if their inputs are true. It seems to me that genuine deduction would be a paradigm of a conditionally reliable process, notwithstanding the logical errors made by subjects in certain experimental situations. Goldman allows, as it seems he should, that a belief is reliably formed if it is the output of a conditionally reliable process whose inputs were the output of a reliable process or processes (*Epistemology and Cognition*, especially p. 83). Some care may be necessary here, but I think a reliable process theory must include some provision such as the one Goldman makes. Consequently, I have difficulty envisioning how the reliabilist can legitimately escape the difficulty raised in the text.

31 For an outline and discussion of reliabilism as an answer to skepticism, see Goldman, *Epistemology and Cognition*, especially pp. 55–7 (though he couches that discussion in terms of a reliabilist theory of justification). The bootstrapping aspect of such a response to skepticism emerges clearly in Alston, pp. 12–17, and in Williams, pp. 327ff. Alston endorses it reluctantly and with qualifications (pp. 138–40). Williams mistakenly believes that his own view avoids the kind of criticism I have raised. It is also noteworthy that reliabilists have embraced bootstrapping in mounting an inductive defense of induction. See, for example, James Van Cleve, "Reliabilism, Justification, and the Problem of Induction," in French, Uehling, and Wettstein, eds, *Midwest Studies in Philosophy*, Volume IX (Minneapolis: Minnesota University Press, 1984), pp. 555–67; and David Papineau, "Reliabilism, Induction, and Scepticism," *The Philosophical Quarterly*, XLII (1992), pp. 1–20.

32 One might think that the reliabilist can simply stand on the claim that we have perceptual knowledge of the external world, insofar as our perceptual beliefs are generated by a reliable process. We cannot, on this more minimal view, move on to knowledge that our experiences are veridical; that further step would allow for bootstrapping, which we have said is unreliable. One difficulty, among others, with such a position

is that it is inconsistent with the closure principle for knowledge.

33   To be sure, the contextualist scheme I have described is quite crude, and one might hope to find more satisfactory accounts of when and how epistemic standards get raised. But I am not aware of any worked-out proposal that would serve the reliabilist's purposes any better; see my "The New Relevant Alternatives Theory," *Philosophical Perspectives*, xiii (1999), pp. 155–80, especially section 3.

34   I suppose Roxanne also has reliable beliefs, and knowledge, about the outputs of the gauge. What she still lacks is any access to whether the gauge itself is accurate or reliable.

35   Some coherentists cheerfully accept this consequence.

36   For such a view, see Alston, "What's Wrong with Immediate Knowledge?" reprinted in his *Epistemic Justification: Essays in the Theory of Knowledge* (Ithaca: Cornell, 1989),

pp. 57–78. Another response would be to deny that the pertinent beliefs fall into the hierarchy of levels described in the text, setting off the regress. Perhaps first-order beliefs about how various mechanisms perform can justify beliefs about the reliability of those mechanisms, and about the reliability of belief-forming procedures that make use of those mechanisms. A view something like this was developed by Wilfrid Sellars, "Empiricism and the Philosophy of Mind," reprinted in *Science, Perception and Reality* (London: Routledge and Kegan Paul, 1963), pp. 127–96.

37   So-called "virtue epistemology" seeks to do justice to the contribution of the knower while retaining many of the central features of reliabilism. My impression is that the reliabilist component of such accounts prevents them from giving a proper treatment of the way a knower's *evidence* figures in knowledge, but I shall not pursue that issue here.

CHAPTER 28

Externalist Theories of Empirical Knowledge

Laurence BonJour

Of the many problems that would have to be solved by a satisfactory theory of empirical knowledge, perhaps the most central is a general structural problem which I shall call *the epistemic regress problem*: the problem of how to avoid an infinite and presumably vicious regress of justification in one's account of the justification of empirical beliefs. *Foundationalist* theories of empirical knowledge, as we shall see further below, attempt to avoid the regress by locating a class of empirical beliefs whose justification does not depend on that of other empirical beliefs. *Externalist* theories, the topic of the present paper, represent one species of foundationalism.

I

I begin with a brief look at the epistemic regress problem. The source of the problem is the requirement that beliefs that are to constitute knowledge must be *epistemically justified*. Such a requirement is of course an essential part of the "traditional" conception of knowledge as justified true belief, but it also figures in at least most of the revisions of that conception which

have been inspired by the Gettier problem. Indeed, if this requirement is understood in a sufficiently generic way, as meaning roughly that the acceptance of the belief must be epistemically rational, that it must not be epistemically irresponsible, then it becomes hard to see how any adequate conception of knowledge can fail to include it.

How then are empirical beliefs epistemically justified? Certainly the most obvious way to *show* that such a belief is justified is by producing a justificatory argument in which the belief to be justified is shown to follow inferentially from some other (perhaps conjunctive) belief, which is thus offered as a reason for accepting it. Beliefs whose justification would, if made explicit, take this form may be said to be *inferentially justified*. (Of course, such a justificatory argument would usually be explicitly rehearsed only in the face of some specific problem or challenge. Notice also that an inferentially justified belief need not have been *arrived at* through inference, though it often will have been.)

The important point about inferential justification, however, is that if the justificandum belief is to be genuinely justified by the proffered argument, then the belief that provides the premise of the argument must itself be justified in some fashion. This premise belief might of course itself be inferentially justified, but this would only raise a new issue of justification with respect to the premise(s) of this new justificatory argument,

Originally published in P. French, T. Uehling Jr., and H. Wettstein (eds), *Midwest Studies in Philosophy*, vol. 5 (Minneapolis: University of Minnesota Press, 1980), pp. 53–73.

and so on, so that empirical knowledge is threatened by an infinite and seemingly vicious regress of epistemic justification, with a thoroughgoing skepticism as the eventual outcome. So long as each new step of justification is inferential, it appears that justification can never be completed, indeed can never really even get started, and hence that there is no justification and no knowledge. Thus the epistemic regress problem.

What is the eventual outcome of this regress? There are a variety of possibilities, but the majority of philosophers who have considered the problem have believed that the only outcome that does not lead more or less directly to skepticism is *foundationalism*: the view that the regress terminates by reaching empirical beliefs (a) that are genuinely justified, but (b) whose justification is not inferentially dependent on that of any further empirical belief(s), so that no further issue of empirical justification is thereby raised. These non-inferentially justified beliefs, or *basic beliefs* as I shall call them, are claimed to provide the foundation upon which the edifice of empirical knowledge rests. And the central argument for foundationalism is simply that all other possible outcomes of the regress lead inexorably to skepticism.[1]

This argument has undeniable force. Nonetheless, the central concept of foundationalism, the concept of a basic belief, is itself by no means unproblematic. The fundamental question that must be answered by any acceptable version of foundationalism is: *how are basic beliefs possible?* How, that is, is it possible for there to be an empirical belief that is epistemically justified in a way completely independent of any believed premises that might provide reasons for accepting it? As Chisholm suggests, a basic belief seems to be in effect an epistemologically unmoved (or perhaps self-moved) mover. But such a status is surely no less paradoxical in epistemology than it is in theology.

This intuitive difficulty with the idea of a basic empirical belief may be elaborated by considering briefly the fundamental concept of epistemic justification. There are two points to be made. First, the idea of justification is generic, admitting in principle of many different species. Thus, for example, the acceptance of an empirical belief might be morally justified, or pragmatically justified, or justified in some still different sense. But a belief's being justified in one of these other senses will not satisfy the justification condition for knowledge. What knowledge requires is *epistemic* justification. And the distinguishing characteristic of this particular species of justification is, I submit, its internal relationship to the cognitive goal of *truth*. A cognitive act is epistemically justified, on this conception, only if and to the extent that is aimed at this goal – which means at a minimum that one accepts only beliefs that there is adequate reason to think are true.

Second, the concept of epistemic justification is fundamentally a normative concept. It has to do with what one has a duty or obligation to do, from an epistemic or intellectual standpoint. As Chisholm suggests, one's purely intellectual duty is to accept beliefs that are true, or likely to be true, and reject beliefs that are false, or likely to be false. To accept beliefs on some other basis is to violate one's epistemic duty – to be, one might say, *epistemically irresponsible* – even though such acceptance might be desirable or even mandatory from some other, non-epistemic standpoint.

Thus if basic beliefs are to provide a suitable foundation for empirical knowledge, if inference from them is to be the sole basis for the justification of other empirical beliefs, then that feature, whatever it may be, in virtue of which an empirical belief qualifies as basic, must also constitute an adequate reason for thinking that the belief is true. And now if we assume, plausibly enough, that the person for whom a belief is basic must *himself* possess the justification for that belief if *his* acceptance of it is to be epistemically rational or responsible, and thus apparently that he must believe *with justification* both (a) that the belief has the feature in question and (b) that beliefs having that feature are likely to be true, then we get the result that this belief is not basic after all, since its justification depends on that of these other beliefs. If this result is correct, then foundationalism is untenable as a solution to the regress problem.[2]

What strategies are available to the foundationalist for avoiding this objection? One possibility would be to grant that the believer must be in possession of the reason for thinking that his basic belief is true but hold that the believer's cognitive grasp of that reason does not involve further *beliefs*, which would then require justification, but instead cognitive states of a different and more rudimentary kind: *intuitions* or *immediate apprehensions*, which are somehow capable of conferring justification upon beliefs without themselves requiring justification. Some such view as this seems implicit in most traditional versions of foundationalism.[3]

My concern in the present paper, however, is with an alternative foundationalist strategy, one of comparatively recent innovation. One way, perhaps somewhat tendentious, to put this alternative approach is to say that according to it, though there must in a sense be a reason why a basic belief is likely to be true, the person for whom such a belief is basic need not have any cognitive grasp of this reason. On this view, the epistemic justification or reasonableness of a basic belief depends on the obtaining of an appropriate relation, generally causal or nomological in character, between the believer and the world. This relation, which is differently characterized by different versions of the view, is such as to make it either nomologically certain or else highly probable that the belief is true. It would thus provide, *for anyone who knew about it*, an undeniably excellent reason for accepting such a belief. But according to proponents of the view under discussion, the person for whom the belief is basic need not (and in general will not) have any cognitive grasp of any kind of this reason or of the relation that is the basis for it in order for this basic belief to be justified; all these matters may be entirely *external* to the person's subjective conception of the situation. Thus the justification of a basic belief need not involve any further beliefs (or other cognitive states) so that no further regress of justification is generated. D. M. Armstrong calls this an "externalist" solution to the regress problem, and I shall adopt this label.

My purpose in this paper is to examine such externalist views. I am not concerned with problems of detail in formulating a view of this kind, though some of these will be mentioned in passing, but rather with the overall acceptability of an externalist solution to the regress problem and thus of an externalist version of foundationalism. I shall attempt to argue that externalism is not acceptable. But there is a methodological problem with respect to such an argument which must be faced at the outset, since it determines the basic approach of the paper.

When viewed from the general standpoint of the western epistemological tradition, externalism represents a very radical departure. It seems safe to say that until very recent times, no serious philosopher of knowledge would have dreamed of suggesting that a person's beliefs might be epistemically justified simply in virtue of facts or relations that were external to his subjective conception. Descartes, for example, would surely have been quite unimpressed by the suggestion that his problematic beliefs about the external world were justified if only they were in fact reliably related to the world – whether or not he had any reason for thinking this to be so. Clearly his conception, and that of generations of philosophers who followed, was that such a relation could play a justificatory role only if the believer possessed adequate reason for thinking that it obtained. Thus the suggestion embodied in externalism would have been regarded by most epistemologists as simply irrelevant to the main epistemological issue, so much so that the philosopher who suggested it would have been taken either to be hopelessly confused or to be simply changing the subject (as I note below, this may be what some externalists in fact intend to be doing). The problem, however, is that this very radicalism has the effect of insulating the externalist from any very direct refutation: any attempt at such a refutation is almost certain to appeal to premises that a thoroughgoing externalist would not accept. My solution to this threatened impasse will be to proceed on an intuitive level as far as possible. By considering a series of examples, I shall attempt to exhibit as clearly as possible the fundamental intuition about epistemic rationality that externalism seems to violate. Although this intuition may not constitute a conclusive objection to the view, it is enough, I believe, to shift the burden of proof decisively to the externalist. In the final section of the paper, I shall consider briefly whether he can discharge this burden.

II

Our first task will be the formulation of a clear and relatively adequate version of externalism. The recent epistemological literature contains a reasonably large number of externalist and quasi-externalist views. Some of these, however, are not clearly relevant to our present concerns, either because they are aimed primarily at the Gettier problem, so that their implications for a foundationalist solution of the regress problem are not made clear, or because they *seem*, on the surface at least, to involve a repudiation of the very conception of epistemic justification or reasonableness as a requirement for knowledge. Views of the latter sort seem to me to be very difficult to take seriously ; but if they are seriously intended, they would have the consequence that the regress problem, at least in the form discussed here, would simply not arise, so that there would be no need for any solution, foundationalist or otherwise. My immediate concern here is with versions of externalism that claim to *solve* the regress problem and thus that also claim that the acceptance of beliefs satisfying the externalist conditions is epistemically justified or rational or warranted. Only such an externalist position genuinely constitutes a version of foundationalism, and hence the more radical views, if any such are in fact seriously intended, may safely be left aside for the time being.

The most completely developed externalist view of the sort we are interested in is that of Armstrong, as presented in his book, *Belief, Truth and Knowledge*.[4] Armstrong is explicitly concerned with the regress problem, though he formulates it in terms of knowledge rather than justification. And it seems reasonably clear that he wants to say that beliefs satisfying his externalist criterion are epistemically justified or rational, though he is not as explicit as one might like on this point.[5] In what follows, I shall in any case assume such an interpretation of Armstrong and formulate his position accordingly.

Another version of externalism, which fairly closely resembles Armstrong's except for being limited to knowledge derived from visual perception, is offered by Dretske in *Seeing and Knowing*.[6] Goldman, in several papers, also suggests views of an externalist sort,[7] and the view that Alston calls "Simple Foundationalism" and claims to be the most defensible version of foundationalism seems to be essentially externalist in character.[8] The most extreme version of externalism would be one that held that the external condition required for justification is simply the *truth* of the belief in question. Such a view could not be held in general, of course, without obliterating the distinction between knowledge and mere

true belief, thereby turning every lucky guess into knowledge. But it might be held with respect to some more limited class of beliefs. Such a view is mentioned by Alston as one possible account of privileged access,[9] and seems, surprisingly enough, to be advocated by Chisholm (though it is very hard to be sure that this is what Chisholm really means).[10]

Here I shall concentrate mainly on Armstrong's view. Like all externalists, Armstrong makes the acceptability of a basic belief depend on an external relation between the believer and his belief, on the one hand, and the world, on the other, specifically a law-like connection: "there must be a *law-like connection* between the state of affairs *Bap* [i.e., *a*'s believing that *p*] and the state of affairs which makes '*p*' true, such that, given *Bap*, it must be the case that *p*." [p. 166] This is what Armstrong calls the "thermometer-model" of non-inferential knowledge: just as the readings of a reliable thermometer lawfully reflect the temperature, so one's basic beliefs lawfully reflect the states of affairs that make them true. A person whose beliefs satisfy this condition is in effect a reliable cognitive instrument; and it is, according to Armstrong, precisely in virtue of this reliability that these basic beliefs are justified.

Of course, not all thermometers are reliable, and even a reliable one may be accurate only under certain conditions. Similarly, it is not a requirement for the justification of a basic belief on Armstrong's view that all beliefs of that general kind or even all beliefs of that kind held by that particular believer be reliable. Thus the law linking the having of the belief with the state of affairs that makes it true will have to mention properties, including relational properties, of the believer beyond his merely having that belief. Incorporating this modification yields the following schematic formulation of the conditions under which a non-inferential belief is justified and therefore basic: a non-inferential belief is justified if and only if there is some property *H* of the believer, such that it is a law of nature that whenever a person satisfies *H* and has that belief, then the belief is true. [p. 197][11] Here *H* may be as complicated as one likes and may include facts about the believer's mental processes, sensory apparatus, environment, and so on. But presumably, though Armstrong does not mention this point, *H* is not to include anything that would entail the truth of the belief; such a logical connection would not count as a law of nature.

Armstrong adds several qualifications to this account, aimed at warding off various objections, of which I shall mention only two. First, the nomological connection between the belief and the state of affairs that makes it true is to be restricted to "that of *completely reliable sign* to thing signified." [p. 182] What this is intended to exclude is the case where the belief itself *causes* the state of affairs that makes it true. In such a case, it seems intuitively that the belief is not a case of knowledge even though it satisfies the condition of complete reliability formulated above. Second, the property *H* of the believer which is involved in the law of nature must not be "too specific"; there must be a "real possibility" of a recurrence of the situation described by the law. What Armstrong is worried about here is the possibility of a "veridical hallucination," i.e., a case in which a hallucinatory belief happens to be correct. In such a case, if the state of affairs that makes the belief true happens to be part of the cause of the hallucination and if the believer and his environment are described in enough detail, it might turn out to be nomologically necessary that such a state of affairs obtain, simply because all alternative possible causes for the hallucinatory belief have been ruled out by the specificity of the description. Again, such a case intuitively should not count as a case of knowledge, but it would satisfy Armstrong's criterion in the absence of this additional stipulation. (Obviously this requirement of nonspecificity or repeatability is extremely vague and seems in fact to be no more than an *ad hoc* solution to this problem; but I shall not pursue this issue here.)

There are various problems of detail, similar to those just discussed, which could be raised about Armstrong's view, but these have little relevance to the main theme of the present paper. Here I am concerned with the more fundamental issue of whether Armstrong's view, or any other externalist view of this general sort, is acceptable as a solution to the regress problem and the basis for a foundationalist account of empirical knowledge. When considered from this perspective, Armstrong's view seems at the very least to be in need of considerable refinement in the face of fairly obvious counterexamples. Thus our first task will be to develop some of these counterexamples and suggest modifications in the view accordingly. This discussion will also lead, however, to a fundamental intuitive objection to all forms of externalism.

III

Although it is formulated in more general terms, the main concern of an externalist view like Armstrong's is obviously those non-inferential beliefs which arise from ordinary sources like sense-perception and introspection. For it is, of course, these beliefs which will on any plausible foundationalist view provide the actual foundations of empirical knowledge. Nevertheless, cases involving sense-perception and introspection are not very suitable for an intuitive assessment of externalism, since one central issue between externalism and other foundationalist and nonfoundationalist views is precisely whether in such cases a further basis for justification beyond the externalist one is typically present. Thus it will be useful to begin by considering the application of externalism to other possible cases of noninferential knowledge, cases of a less familiar sort where it will be easier to stipulate in a way that will be effective on an intuitive level that only the externalist sort of justification is present. Specifically, in this section and the next, our focus will be on possible cases of clairvoyant knowledge. Clairvoyance, the alleged psychic power of perceiving or intuiting the existence and character of distant states of affairs without the aid of any sensory input, remains the subject of considerable scientific controversy. Although many would like to dismiss out of hand the very idea of such a cognitive power, there remains a certain amount of evidence in favor of its existence which it is difficult to entirely discount. But in any case, the actual existence of clairvoyance does not matter at all for present purposes, so long as it is conceded to represent a coherent possibility. For externalism, as a general philosophical account of the foundations of empirical knowledge, must of course apply to all possible modes of non-inferential empirical knowledge, and not just to those that in fact happen to be realized.

The intuitive difficulty with externalism that the following discussion is intended to delineate and develop is this: on the externalist view, a person may be ever so irrational and irresponsible in accepting a belief, when judged in light of his own subjective conception of the situation, and may still turn out to be epistemically justified, i.e., may still turn out to satisfy Armstrong's general criterion of reliability. This belief may in fact be reliable, even though the person has no reason for thinking that it is reliable – or even though he has good reason to think that it is not reliable. But such a person seems nonetheless to be thoroughly irresponsible from an epistemic standpoint in accepting such a belief, and hence not justified, contrary to externalism. The following cases may help bring out this problem more clearly.

Consider first the following case:

Case I. Samantha believes herself to have the power of clairvoyance, though she has no reasons for or against this belief. One day she comes to believe, for no apparent reason, that the President is in New York City. She maintains this belief, appealing to her alleged clairvoyant power, even though she is at the same time aware of a massive amount of apparently cogent evidence, consisting of news reports, press releases, allegedly live television pictures, etc., indicating that the President is at that time in Washington, DC. Now the President is in fact in New York City, the evidence to the contrary being part of a massive official hoax mounted in the face of an assassination threat. Moreover, Samantha does in fact have completely reliable clairvoyant power, under the conditions that were then satisfied, and her belief about the President did result from the operation of that power.

In this case, it is clear that Armstrong's criterion of reliability is satisfied. There will be some complicated description of Samantha, including the conditions then operative, from which it will follow, by the law describing her clairvoyant power, that her belief is true.[12] But it seems intuitively clear nevertheless that this is not a case of justified belief or of knowledge: Samantha is being thoroughly irrational and irresponsible in disregarding cogent evidence that the President is not in New York City on the basis of a clairvoyant power which she has no reason at all to think that she possesses; and this irrationality is not somehow canceled by the fact that she happens to be right. Thus, I submit, Samantha's irrationality

and irresponsibility prevent her belief from being epistemically justified.

This case and others like it suggest the need for a further condition to supplement Armstrong's original one: not only must it be true that there is a law-like connection between a person's belief and the state of affairs that makes it true, such that given the belief, the state of affairs cannot fail to obtain, but it must also be true that the person in question does not possess cogent reasons for thinking that the belief in question is false. For, as this case seems to show, the possession of such reasons renders the acceptance of the belief irrational in a way that cannot be overridden by a purely externalist justification.

Nor is this the end of the difficulty for Armstrong. Suppose that the clairvoyant believer, instead of having evidence against the particular belief in question, has evidence against his possession of such a cognitive power, as in the following case:

Case II. Casper believes himself to have the power of clairvoyance, though he has no reasons for this belief. He maintains his belief despite the fact that on the numerous occasions on which he has attempted to confirm one of his allegedly clairvoyant beliefs, it has always turned out apparently to be false. One day Casper comes to believe, for no apparent reason, that the President is in New York City, and he maintains this belief, appealing to his alleged clairvoyant power. Now in fact the President is in New York City; and Casper does, under the conditions that were then satisfied, have completely reliable clairvoyant power, from which this belief in fact resulted. The apparent falsity of his other clairvoyant beliefs was due in some cases to his being in the wrong conditions for the operation of his power and in other cases to deception and misinformation.

Is Casper justified in believing that the President is in New York City, so that he then knows that this is the case? According to Armstrong's account, even with the modification just suggested, we must apparently say that the belief is justified and hence a case of knowledge: the reliability condition is satisfied, and Casper possesses no reason for thinking that the President is not in New York City. But this result still seems mistaken. Casper is being quite irrational and irresponsible from an epistemic standpoint in disregarding evidence that his beliefs of this sort are not reliable and should not be trusted. And for this reason, the belief in question is not justified.

In the foregoing case, Casper possessed good reasons for thinking that he did not possess the sort of cognitive ability that he believed himself to possess. But the result would be the same, I believe, if someone instead possessed good reasons for thinking that *in general* there could be no such cognitive ability, as in the following case:

> Case III. Maud believes herself to have the power of clairvoyance, though she has no reasons for this belief. She maintains her belief despite being inundated by her embarrassed friends and relatives with massive quantities of apparently cogent scientific evidence that no such power is possible. One day Maud comes to believe, for no apparent reason, that the President is in New York City, and she maintains this belief, despite the lack of any independent evidence, appealing to her alleged clairvoyant power. Now in fact the President is in New York City, and Maud does, under the conditions then satisfied, have completely reliable clairvoyant power. Moreover, her belief about the President did result from the operation of that power.

Again, Armstrong's criterion of reliability seems to be satisfied. But it also seems to me that Maud, like Casper, is not justified in her belief about the President and does not have knowledge. Maud has excellent reasons for thinking that no cognitive power such as she believes herself to possess is possible, and it is irrational and irresponsible of her to maintain her belief in that power in the face of that evidence and to continue to accept and maintain beliefs on this dubious basis.

Cases like these two suggest the need for a further modification of Armstrong's account: in addition to the law-like connection between belief and truth and the absence of any reasons against the particular belief in question, it must also be the case that the believer in question has no cogent reasons, either relative to his own case or in general, for thinking that such a law-like connection does *not* exist, i.e., that beliefs of that kind are not reliable.

IV

So far the modifications suggested for Armstrong's criterion are consistent with the basic thrust of externalism as a response to the regress problem. What emerges is in fact a significantly more plausible externalist position. But these cases and the modifications made in response to them also suggest an important moral which leads to a basic intuitive objection to externalism: external or objective reliability is not enough to offset subjective irrationality. If the acceptance of a belief is seriously unreasonable or unwarranted from the believer's own standpoint, then the mere fact that unbeknownst to the believer its existence in those circumstances lawfully guarantees its truth will not suffice to render the belief epistemically justified and thereby an instance of knowledge. So far we have been concerned only with situations in which the believer's subjective irrationality took the form of ignoring positive grounds in his possession for questioning either that specific belief or beliefs arrived at in that way. But now we must ask whether even in a case where these positive reasons for a charge of irrationality are not present, the acceptance of a belief where only an externalist justification is available cannot still be said to be subjectively irrational in a sense that rules out its being epistemically justified.

We may begin by considering one further case of clairvoyance, in which Armstrong's criterion with all the suggested modifications is satisfied:

> Case IV. Norman, under certain conditions that usually obtain, is a completely reliable clairvoyant with respect to certain kinds of subject matter. He possesses no evidence or reasons of any kind for or against the general possibility of such a cognitive power, or for or against the thesis that he possesses it. One day Norman comes to believe that the President is in New York City, though he has no evidence either for or against this belief. In fact the belief is true and results from his clairvoyant power, under circumstances in which it is completely reliable.

Is Norman epistemically justified in believing that the President is in New York City, so that his belief is an instance of knowledge? According to the modified externalist position, we must apparently say that he is. But is this the right result? Are there not still sufficient grounds for a charge of subjective irrationality to prevent Norman's being epistemically justified?

One thing that might seem relevant to this issue, which I have deliberately omitted from the specification of the case, is whether Norman *believes* himself to have clairvoyant power, even though he has no justification for such a belief. Let us consider both possibilities. Suppose, first, that Norman does have such a belief and that it contributes to his acceptance of his original belief about the President's whereabouts in the sense that were Norman to become convinced that he did not have this power, he would also cease to accept the belief about the President.[13] But is it not obviously irrational, from an epistemic standpoint, for Norman to hold such a belief when he has no reasons at all for thinking that it is true or even for thinking that such a power is possible? This belief about his clairvoyance fails after all to possess even an externalist justification. And if we say that the belief about his clairvoyance is epistemically irrational and unjustified, must we not say the same thing about the belief about the President which *ex hypothesi* depends upon it?[14]

A possible response to this challenge would be to add one further condition to our modified externalist position, *viz.*, that the believer not even *believe* that the law-like connection in question obtains, since such a belief will not in general be justified (or at least that his continued acceptance of the particular belief that is at issue not depend on his acceptance of such a general belief). In our present case, this would mean that Norman must not believe that he has the power of clairvoyance (or at least that his acceptance of the belief about the President's whereabouts not depend on his having such a general belief). But if this specification is added to the case, it now becomes more than a little puzzling to understand what Norman thinks is going on. From his standpoint, there is apparently no way in which he *could* know the President's whereabouts. Why then does he continue to maintain the belief that the President is in New York City? Why is not the mere fact that there is no way, as far as he knows or believes, for him to have obtained this information a sufficient reason for classifying this belief as an unfounded hunch and ceasing to accept it? And if Norman does not do this, is he not thereby being epistemically irrational and irresponsible?

For these reasons, I submit, Norman's acceptance of the belief about the President's whereabouts is epistemically irrational and irresponsible, and thereby unjustified, whether or not he believes himself to have clairvoyant power, so long as he has no justification for such a belief. Part of one's epistemic duty is to reflect critically upon one's beliefs, and such critical reflection precludes believing things to which one has, to one's knowledge, no reliable means of epistemic access.[15]

We are now face-to-face with the fundamental – and seemingly obvious – intuitive problem with externalism: *why* should the mere fact that such an external relation obtains mean that Norman's belief is epistemically justified, when the relation in question is entirely outside his ken? As remarked earlier, it is clear that one who knew that Armstrong's criterion was satisfied would be in a position to construct a simple and quite cogent justifying argument for the belief in question: if Norman has property *H* (being a completely reliable clairvoyant under the existing conditions and arriving at the belief on that basis), then he holds the belief in question only if it is true; Norman does have property *H* and does hold the belief in question; therefore, the belief is true. But Norman himself is by stipulation not in a position to employ this argument, and it is unclear why the mere fact that it is, so to speak, potentially available in the situation should justify *his* acceptance of the belief. Precisely what generates the regress problem in the first place, after all, is the requirement that for a belief to be justified for a particular person, not only is it necessary that there be true premises somehow available in the situation which could in principle provide a basis for a justification, but also that the believer in question know or at least justifiably believe some such set of premises and thus be in a position to employ the corresponding argument. The externalist position seems to amount merely to waiving this general requirement in a certain class of cases, and the question is why this should be acceptable in these cases when it is not acceptable generally. (If it were acceptable generally, then it seems likely that *any* true belief would be justified, unless some severe requirement is imposed as to how immediately available such premises must be. But any such requirement seems utterly arbitrary, once the natural one of actual access by the believer is abandoned.) Thus externalism looks like a purely *ad hoc* solution to the epistemic regress problem.

One reason why externalism may seem initially plausible is that if the external relation in question genuinely obtains, then Norman will in fact not go wrong in accepting the belief, and it is, *in a sense*, not an accident that this is so. But how is this supposed to justify Norman's belief? From his subjective perspective, it *is* an accident that the belief is true. Of course, it would not be an accident from the standpoint of our hypothetical external observer who knows all the relevant facts and laws. Such an observer, having constructed the justifying argument sketched above, would be thereby in a position to justify *his own* acceptance of the belief. Thus Norman, as Armstrong's thermometer image suggests, could serve as a useful epistemic instrument for such an observer, a kind of cognitive thermometer; and it is to this fact, as we have seen, that Armstrong appeals in arguing that a belief like Norman's can be correctly said to be reasonable or justifiable. [183] But none of this seems in fact to justify Norman's *own* acceptance of the belief, for Norman, unlike the hypothetical external observer, has no reason at all for thinking that the belief is true. And the suggestion here is that the rationality or justifiability of Norman's belief should be judged from Norman's own perspective, rather than from one that is unavailable to him.[16]

This basic objection to externalism seems to me to be intuitively compelling. But it is sufficiently close to being simply a statement of what the externalist wants to deny to make it helpful to buttress it a bit by appealing to some related intuitions.

First, we may consider an analogy with moral philosophy. The same conflict between perspectives which we have seen to arise in the process of epistemic assessment can also arise with regard to the moral assessment of a person's action: the agent's subjective conception of what he is doing may differ dramatically from that which would in principle be available to an external observer who had access to facts about the situation that are beyond the agent's ken. And now we can imagine an approximate moral analogue of externalism which would hold that the moral justifiability of an agent's action was, in certain cases at least, properly to be determined from the external perspective, entirely irrespective of the agent's own conception of the situation.

Consider first the moral analogue of Armstrong's original, unmodified version of externalism. If we assume, purely for the sake of simplicity, a utilitarian moral theory, such a view would say that an action might on occasion be morally justified simply in virtue of the fact that in the situation then obtaining, it would as a matter of objective fact lead to the best overall consequences – even if the agent planned and anticipated that it would lead to a very different, perhaps extremely undesirable, consequence. But such a view seems plainly mistaken. There is no doubt a point to the objective, external assessment: we can say correctly that it turns out to be objectively a good thing that the agent performed the action. But this is not at all inconsistent with saying that his action was morally unjustified and reprehensible, given his subjective conception of the likely consequences.

Thus our envisaged moral externalism must at least be modified in a way that parallels the modifications earlier suggested for epistemological externalism. Without attempting to make the analogy exact, it will suffice for our present purposes to add to the original requirement for moral justification, viz., that the action will in fact lead to the best overall consequences, the further condition that the agent not believe or intend that it lead to undesirable consequences. Since it is also, of course, not required by moral externalism that the agent believe that the action will lead to good consequences, the sort of case we are now considering is one in which an agent acts in a way that will in fact produce the best overall consequences, but has *no belief at all* about the likely consequences of his action. Although such an agent is no doubt preferable to one who acts in the belief that his action will lead to undesirable consequences, surely he is not morally justified in what he does. On the contrary, he is being highly irresponsible, from a moral standpoint, in performing the action in the absence of any evaluation of what will result from it. His moral duty, from our assumed utilitarian standpoint, is to do what will lead to the best consequences, but this duty is not satisfied by the fact that he produces this result willy-nilly, without any idea that he is doing so.[17] And similarly, the fact that a given sort of belief is objectively reliable, and thus that accepting it is in fact conducive to arriving at the truth, need not prevent our judging that the epistemic agent who accepts it without any inkling that this is the case violates his epistemic duty and is epistemically irresponsible and unjustified in doing so.

Second, we may appeal to the connection between knowledge and rational action. Suppose that Norman, in addition to the clairvoyant belief described earlier, also believes that the Attorney-General is in Chicago. This latter belief, however, is not a clairvoyant belief but is based upon ordinary empirical evidence in Norman's possession, evidence strong enough to give the belief some fairly high degree of reasonableness, but *not* strong enough to satisfy the requirement for knowledge.[18] Suppose further that Norman finds himself in a situation where he is forced to bet a very large amount, perhaps even his life or the life of someone else, on the whereabouts of either the President or the Attorney-General. Given his epistemic situation as described, which bet is it more reasonable for him to make? It seems relatively clear that it is more reasonable for him to bet the Attorney-General is in Chicago than to bet that the President is in New York City. But then we have the paradoxical result that from the externalist standpoint it is more rational to act on a merely reasonable belief than to act on one that is adequately justifed to qualify as knowledge (and which in fact *is* knowledge). It is very hard to see how this could be so. If greater epistemic reasonableness does not carry with it greater reasonableness of action, then it becomes most difficult to see why it should be sought in the first place. (Of course, the externalist could simply bite the bullet and insist that it is in fact more reasonable for Norman to bet on the President's whereabouts than the Attorney-General's, but such a view seems very implausible.)

I have been attempting in this section to articulate the fundamental intuition about epistemic rationality, and rationality generally, that externalism seems to violate. This intuition the externalist would of course reject, and thus my discussion does not constitute a refutation of the externalist position on its own ground. Nevertheless it seems to me to have sufficient intuitive force at least to place the burden of proof squarely on the externalist. In the final section of the paper, I shall consider briefly some of the responses that seem to be available to him.

V

One possible defense for the externalist in the face of the foregoing intuitive objection would be to narrow his position by restricting it to those commonsensical varieties of non-inferential knowledge which are his primary concern, viz., sense-perception and introspection, thereby rendering the cases set forth above strictly irrelevant. Such a move seems, however, utterly *ad hoc*. Admittedly it is more difficult to construct intuitively compelling counterexamples involving sense-perception and introspection, mainly because our intuitions that beliefs of those kinds are in fact warranted in *some* way or other are very strong. But this does nothing to establish that the externalist account of their warrant is the correct one. Thus unless the externalist can give some positive account of why the same conclusion that seems to hold for non-standard cases like clairvoyance does not also hold for sense-perception and introspection, this narrowing of his position seems to do him no good.

If the externalist cannot escape the force of the objection in this way, can he perhaps balance it with positive arguments in favor of his position? Many attempts to argue for externalism are in effect arguments by elimination and depend on the claim that alternative accounts of empirical knowledge are unacceptable, either because they cannot solve the regress problem or for some other reason. Most such arguments, depending as they do on a detailed consideration of the alternatives, are beyond the scope of the present paper. But one such argument depends only on very general features of the competing positions and thus can usefully be considered here.

The basic factual premise of this argument is that in very many cases that are commonsensically instances of justified belief and of knowledge, there seem to be no justifying factors explicitly present beyond those appealed to by the externalist. An ordinary person in such a case may have no idea at all of the character of his immediate experience, of the coherence of his system of beliefs, etc., and yet may still have knowledge. Alternative theories, so the argument goes, may describe correctly cases of knowledge involving a knower who is extremely reflective and sophisticated, but they are obviously too demanding and too grandiose when applied to these more ordinary cases. In these cases, *only* the externalist condition is satisfied, and this shows that no more than that is necessary for justification and for knowledge, though more might still be epistemically desirable.

Although the precise extent to which it holds could be disputed, in the main this factual premise must be simply conceded. Any non-externalist account of empirical knowledge that has any plausibility will impose standards for justification which very many beliefs that seem commonsensically to be cases of knowledge fail to meet in any full and explicit fashion. And thus on such a view, such beliefs will not *strictly speaking* be instances of adequate justification and of knowledge. But it does not follow that externalism must be correct. This would follow only with the addition of the premise that the judgments of common sense in this area are sacrosanct, that any departure from them is enough to demonstrate that a theory of knowledge is inadequate. But such a premise seems entirely too strong. There seems in fact to be no basis for more than a reasonably strong presumption in favor of the correctness of common sense, but one which is still quite defeasible. And what it would take to defeat this presumption depends in part on how great a departure from common sense is being advocated. Thus, although it would take very strong grounds to justify a very strong form of skepticism, not nearly so much would be required to make acceptable the view that what common sense regards as cases of justification and of knowledge are in fact only rough approximations to an epistemic ideal which *strictly speaking* they do not satisfy.

Of course, a really adequate reply to the externalist would have to spell out in some detail the precise way in which such beliefs really do approximately satisfy some acceptable alternative standard, a task which obviously cannot be attempted here. But even without such elaboration, it seems reasonable to conclude that this argument in favor of externalism fails to carry very much weight as it stands and would require serious buttressing in order to give it any chance of offsetting the intuitive objection to externalism: either the advocacy and defense of a quite strong presumption in favor of common sense, or a detailed showing that alternative theories cannot in fact grant to the cases favored by common sense even the status of approximations to justification and to knowledge.

The other pro-externalist argument I want to consider does not depend in any important way on consideration of alternative positions. This argument is hinted at by Armstrong [pp. 185–88], among others, but I know of no place where it is developed very explicitly. Its basic claim is that only an externalist theory can handle a certain version of the lottery paradox.

The lottery paradox is standardly formulated as a problem confronting accounts of inductive logic that contain a rule of acceptance or detachment, but we shall be concerned here with a somewhat modified version. This version arises when we ask how much or what degree of epistemic justification is required for a belief to qualify as knowledge, given that the other necessary conditions for knowledge are satisfied. Given the intimate connection, discussed earlier, between epistemic justification and likelihood of truth, it seems initially reasonable to take likelihood or probability of truth as a measure of the degree of epistemic justification, and thus to interpret the foregoing question as asking how likely or probable it must be, relative to the justification of one's belief, that the belief be true, in order for that belief to satisfy the justification requirement for knowledge. Most historical theories of knowledge tended to answer that knowledge requires *certainty* of truth, relative to one's justification. But more recent epistemological views have tended to reject this answer, for familiar reasons, and to hold instead that knowledge requires only a reasonably high likelihood of truth. And now, if this high likelihood of truth is interpreted in the obvious way as meaning that, relative to one's justification, the numerical probability that one's belief is true must equal or exceed some fixed value, the lottery paradox at once rears its head.

Suppose, for example, that we decide that a belief is adequately justified to satisfy the requirement for knowledge if the probability of its truth, relative to its justification, is 0.99 or greater. Imagine now that a lottery is to be held, about which we know the following facts: exactly 100 tickets have been sold, the drawing will indeed be held, it will be a fair drawing, and there will be only one winning ticket. Consider now each of the 100 propositions of the form:

Ticket number *n* will lose

where *n* is replaced by the number of one of the tickets. Since there are 100 tickets and only one winner, the probability of each such proposition is 0.99; and hence if we believe each of them, our individual beliefs will be adequately justified to satisfy the requirement for knowledge. And then, given only the seemingly reasonable assumptions, first, that if one has adequate justification for believing each of a set of propositions, one also has adequate justification for believing the conjunction of the members of the set, and, second, that if one has adequate justification for believing a proposition, one also has adequate justification for believing any further proposition entailed by the first proposition, it follows that we are adequately justified in believing that no ticket will win, contradicting our other information.

Clearly this is a mistaken result, but how is it to be avoided? In the first place, it will plainly do no good to simply increase the level of numerical probability required for adequate justification. For no matter how high it is raised, short of certainty, it will obviously be possible to duplicate the paradoxical result by simply choosing a large enough lottery. Nor do the standard responses to the lottery paradox, whatever their merits may be in dealing with other versions of the paradox, seem to be of much help here. Most of them are ruled out simply by insisting that we do know that empirical propositions are true, not merely that they are probable, and that such knowledge is not in general relative to particular contexts of inquiry. This leaves only the possibility of avoiding the paradoxical result by rejecting the two assumptions stated in the preceding paragraph. But this would be extremely implausible – involving in effect a denial that one may always justifiably deduce conclusions from one's putative knowledge – and in any case would still leave the intuitively unacceptable result that one could on this basis come to know separately the 99 true propositions about various tickets losing (though not of course the false one). In fact, it seems intuitively clear that I do not *know* any of these propositions to be true: if I own one of the tickets, I do not know that it will lose, even if in fact it will, and would not know no matter how large the total number of tickets might be.

At this stage, it may seem that the only way to avoid the paradox is to return to the traditional idea that any degree of probability or likelihood of truth less than certainty is insufficient for knowledge, that only certainty, relative to one's

justification, will suffice. The standard objection to such a view is that it seems to lead at once to the skeptical conclusion that we have little or no empirical knowledge. For it seems quite clear that there are no empirical beliefs, with the possible and extremely problematic exception of beliefs about one's own mental states, for which we have justification adequate to exclude all possibility of error. Such a solution seems as bad as the original problem.

It is at this point that externalism may seem to offer a way out. For an externalist position allows one to hold that the justification of an empirical belief must make it certain that the belief is true, while still escaping the clutches of skepticism. This is so precisely because the externalist justification need not be within the cognitive grasp of the believer or indeed of anyone. It need only be true that there is *some* description of the believer, however complex and practically unknowable it may be, which, together with *some* true law of nature, ensures the truth of the belief. Thus, e.g., my perceptual belief that there is a cup on my desk is not certain, on any view, relative to the evidence or justification that is in my possession; I might be hallucinating or there might be an evil demon who is deceiving me. But it seems reasonable to suppose that if the belief is indeed true, then there is *some* external description of me and my situation and *some* true law of nature, relative to which the truth of the belief is guaranteed, and if so it would satisfy the requirement for knowledge.

In some ways, this is a neat and appealing solution to the paradox. Nonetheless, it seems doubtful that it is ultimately satisfactory. In the first place, there is surely something intuitively fishy about solving the problem by appealing to an inprinciple guarantee of truth which will almost certainly in practice be available to no one. A second problem, which cannot be elaborated here, is that insisting on this sort of solution seems likely to create insuperable difficulties for knowledge of general and theoretical propositions. But in any case, the externalist solution seems to yield intuitively incorrect results in certain kinds of cases. A look at one of these may also suggest the beginnings of a more satisfactory solution.

Consider then the following case:

Case V. Agatha, seated at her desk, believes herself to be perceiving a cup on the desk. She also knows, however, that she is one of a group of 100 people who have been selected for a philosophical experiment by a Cartesian evil demon. The conditions have been so arranged that all 100 will at this particular time seem to themselves to be perceiving a cup upon their respective desks, with no significant differences in the subjective character of their respective experiences. But in fact, though 99 of the people will be perceiving a cup in the normal way, the last one will be caused by the demon to have a complete hallucination (including perceptual conditions, etc.) of a non-existent cup. Agatha knows all this, but she does not have any further information as to whether she is the one who is hallucinating, though as it happens she is not.

Is Agatha epistemically justified in her belief that there is a cup on the desk and does she know this to be so? According to the externalist view, we must say that she is justified and does know. For there is, we may assume, an external description of Agatha and her situation relative to which it is nomologically certain that her belief is true. (Indeed, according to Armstrong's original, unmodified view, she would be justified and would know even if she also knew instead that 99 of the 100 persons were being deceived by the demon, so long as she was in fact the odd one who was perceiving normally.) But this result is, I submit, intuitively mistaken. If Agatha knows that she is perceiving a cup, then she also knows that she is not the one who is being deceived. But she does not know this, for reasons that parallel those operative in the lottery case.

Is there then no way out of the paradox? The foregoing case and others like it seem to me to suggest the following approach to at least the present version of the paradox, though I can offer only an exceedingly brief sketch here. Intuitively, what the lottery case and the case of Agatha have in common is the presence of a large number of relevantly similar, alternative possibilities, all individually very unlikely, but such that the person in question *knows* that at least one of them will in fact be realized. In such a case, since there is no relevant way of distinguishing among these possibilities, the person cannot believe with adequate justification and *a fortiori* cannot know that any particular possibility will not be realized, even though the probability that it will not be realized may be made as high as one likes by simply increasing the total number of possibilities. Such cases do show that high probability is not by itself enough to satisfy the justification condition for knowledge. They do not show, however, that certainty is required instead. For what rules out knowledge in such a case is not merely the fact that the probability of truth is less than certainty but also the fact that the person *knows* that at least one of these highly probable propositions is false. It is a necessary condition for justification and for knowledge that this not be so. But there are many cases in which a person's justification for a belief fails to make it certain that the belief is true, but in which the person also does not know that some possible situation in which the belief would be false is one of a set of relevantly similar, alternative possibilities, at least one of which will definitely be realized. And in such a case, the lottery paradox provides no reason to think that the person does not know.[19]

An example may help to make this point clear. Consider again my apparent perception of the cup on my desk. I think that I do in fact know that there is a cup there. But the justification that is in my possession surely does not make it certain that my belief is true. Thus, for example, it seems to be possible, relative to my subjective justification, that I am being deceived by an evil demon, who is causing me to have a hallucinatory experience of the cup, together with accompanying conditions of perception. But it does not follow from this that I do not know that there is a cup on the desk, because it does not follow and I do not know that there is some class of relevantly similar cases in at least one of which a person is in fact deceived by such a demon. Although it is only probable and not certain that there is no demon, it is still possible for all I *know* that never in the history of the universe, past, present, or future, is there a case in which someone in a relevantly similar perceptual situation is actually deceived by such a demon. And, as far as I can see, the same thing is true of all the other ways in which it is possible that my belief might be mistaken. If this is so, then the lottery paradox provides no obstacle to my knowledge in this case.[20]

This response to the lottery paradox seems to me to be on the right track. It must be conceded, however, that it is in considerable need of further development and may turn out to have problems of its own. But that is a subject for another paper.[21]

There is one other sort of response, mentioned briefly above, which the externalist might make to the sorts of criticisms developed in this paper. I want to remark on it briefly, though a full-scale discussion is impossible here. In the end it may be possible to make intuitive sense of externalism only by construing the externalist as simply abandoning the traditional idea of epistemic justification or rationality and along with it anything resembling the traditional conception of knowledge. I have already mentioned that this may be precisely what the proponents of externalism intend to be doing, though most of them are anything but clear on this point.[22]

Against an externalist position that seriously adopts such a gambit, the criticisms developed in the present paper are of course entirely ineffective. If the externalist does not want even to claim that beliefs satisfying his conditions are epistemically justified or reasonable, then it is obviously no objection that they seem in some cases to be quite unjustified and unreasonable. But, as already noted, such a view, though it may possess some other sort of appeal, constitutes a solution to the epistemic regress problem or to any problem arising out of the traditional conception of knowledge only in the radical and relatively uninteresting sense that to reject that conception entirely is also, of course, to reject any problems arising out of it. Such "solutions" would seem to be available for any philosophical problem at all, but it is hard to see why they should be taken seriously.

Notes

1   For a fuller discussion of the regress argument, including a discussion of other possible outcomes of the regress, see my paper "Can Empirical Knowledge Have a Foundation?" *American Philosophical Quarterly* 15 (1978), pp. 1–13. That paper also contains a brief anticipation of the present discussion of externalism.

2   It could, of course, still be claimed that the belief in question was *empirically* basic, so long as both the needed justifying premises were justifiable on an *a priori* basis. But this would mean that it was an *a priori* truth that a particular empirical belief was likely to be true. In the present paper, I shall simply assume, without further discussion, that this seemingly unlikely state of affairs does not in fact obtain.

3   For criticism of this view, see the paper cited in note 1.

4   D. M. Armstrong, *Belief, Truth and Knowledge* (London, Press, 1973). Bracketed references in the text will be to the pages of this book.

5   The clearest passages are at p. 183, where Armstrong says that a belief satisfying his externalist condition, though not "based on reasons," nevertheless "might be said to be reasonable (justifiable), because it is a sign, a completely reliable sign, that the situation believed to exist does in fact exist"; and at p. 189, where he suggests that the satisfaction

of a slightly weaker condition, though it does not yield knowledge, may still yield rational belief. There is no reason to think that any species of rationality or reasonableness other than the epistemic is at issue in either of these passages. But though these passages seem to me to adequately support my interpretation of Armstrong, the strongest support may well derive simply from the fact that he at no point *disavows* a claim of epistemic rationality. (See also the parenthetical remark in the middle of p. 77.)

6   Fred I. Dretske, *Seeing and Knowing* (London, 1969), chap. III. Dretske also differs from Armstrong in requiring in effect that the would-be knower also believe that the externalist condition is satisfied, but not of course that this belief be justified.

7   Goldman does this most clearly in "Discrimination and Perceptual Knowledge," *Journal of Philosophy* 73 (1976), pp. 771–91; and in "What is Justified Belief?" forthcoming. See also "A Causal Theory of Knowing," *Journal of Philosophy* 64 (1967), pp. 355–72, though this last paper is more concerned with the Gettier problem than with a general account of the standards of epistemic justification.

8   William P. Alston, "Two Types of Foundationalism," *Journal of Philosophy* 73 (1976), pp. 165–85; see especially p. 168.

9 Alston, "Varieties of Privileged Access," in Roderick Chisholm and Robert Swartz, *Empirical Knowledge* (Englewood Cliffs, NJ, 1973), pp. 396–9. Alston's term for this species of privileged access is "truth-sufficiency."

10 See Chisholm, *Theory of Knowledge*, 2nd edn. (Englewood Cliffs, NJ, 1977), p. 22, where Chisholm offers the following definition of the concept of a state of affairs being *self-presenting*:

b is *self-presenting* for S at *t* = Df *b* occurs at *t*; and necessarily, if *b* occurs at *t* then *b* is evident [i.e., justified] for S at *t*.

Despite the overtones of the term "self-presentation," nothing in this passage seems to require that believer have any sort of immediate awareness of the state in question; all that is required is that it actually occur, i.e., that his belief be true. On the other hand, Chisholm also, in the section immediately preceding this definition, quotes with approval a passage from Leibniz which appeals to the idea of "direct awareness" and of the absence of mediation "between the understanding and its objects," thus suggesting the non-externalist variety of foundationalism (pp. 20–1).

11 Armstrong actually formulates the criterion as a criterion of knowledge, rather than merely of justification; the satisfaction of the belief condition is built into the criterion and this, with the satisfaction of the indicated justification condition, entails that the truth condition is satisfied.

12 This assumes that clairvoyant beliefs are caused in some distinctive way, so that an appropriately complete description of Samantha will rule out the possibility that the belief is a mere hunch and will connect appropriately with the law governing her clairvoyance.

13 This further supposition does not prevent the belief about the President's whereabouts from being non-inferential, since it is not in any useful sense Norman's reason for accepting that specific belief.

14 This is the basic objection to Dretske's version of externalism, mentioned above. Dretske's condition requires that one have an analogously unjustified (though true) belief about the reliability of one's perceptual belief.

15 The only apparent answer here would be to claim that the reasonable presumption is in favor of one's having such reliable means of access, unless there is good reason to the contrary. But it is hard to see why such a presumption should be thought reasonable.

16 Mark Pastin, in a critical study of Armstrong, has suggested that ascriptions of knowledge depend on the epistemic situation of the ascriber rather than on that of the ascribee at this point, so that I am correct in ascribing knowledge to Norman so long as *I* know that his belief is reliable (and hence also that the other conditions of knowledge are satisfied), even if Norman does not. But I can see no very convincing rationale for this claim. See Pastin, "Knowledge and Reliability : A Study of D. M. Armstrong's *Belief, Truth and Knowledge*," *Metaphilosophy* 9 (1978), pp. 150–62. Notice further that if the epistemic regress problem is in general to be dealt with along externalist lines, then my knowledge that Norman's belief is reliable would depend on the epistemic situation of a further external observer, who ascribes knowledge to me. And similarly for the knowledge of that observer, etc., *ad infinitum*. I do not know whether this regress of external observers is vicious, but it seems clearly to deprive the appeal to such an observer of any value as a practical criterion.

17 Of course there are cases in which one must act, even though one has no adequate knowledge of the likely consequences; and one might attempt to defend epistemic externalism by arguing that in epistemic contexts the analogous situation *always* obtains. But there are several problems with such a response. First, to simply assume that this is always so seems to be question-begging, and the externalist can argue for this claim only by refuting all alternatives to his position. Second, notice that in ethical contexts this situation usually, perhaps always, obtains only when not acting will lead definitely to bad consequences, not just to the failure to obtain good ones; and there seems to be no parallel to this in the epistemic case. Third, and most important, the justification for one's action

in such a case would depend not on the external fact, if it is a fact, that the action leads to good consequences, but simply on the fact that one could do no better, given the unfortunate state of one's knowledge; thus this position would not be genuinely a version of moral externalism, and analogously for the epistemic case.

18 I am assuming here, following Chisholm, that knowledge requires a degree of justification stronger than that required to make a belief merely reasonable.

19 I do not, alas, have any real account to offer here of the notion of *relevant similarity*. Roughly, the idea is that two possibilities are relevantly similar if there is no known difference between them that has a bearing on the likelihood that they will be realized. But this will not quite do. For consider a lottery case in which there are two tickets bearing each even number and only one for each odd number. Intuitively, it seems to me, this difference does not prevent all the tickets, odd and even, from being relevantly similar, despite the fact that it is twice as likely that an even ticket will be drawn.

20 But if this account is correct, I may still fail to know in many other cases in which common sense would say fairly strongly that I do. E.g., do I know that my house has not burned down since I left it this morning? Ordinarily we are inclined to say that we do know such things. But if it is true, as it might well be, that I also know that of the class of houses relevantly similar to mine, at least one will burn down at some point, then I do not, on the present account, *know* that my house has not burned down, however improbable such a catastrophe may be.

(On the other hand, knowledge would not be ruled out by the present principle simply because I knew that certain specific similar houses, *other than mine*, have in the past burned down or even that they will in the future burn down. For I know, *ex hypothesi*, that my house is not one of those. The force of the principle depends on my knowing that at least one possibility *which might for all I know be the one I am interested in* will be realized, not just on descriptively similar possibilities being realized.)

21 This response to the lottery paradox derives in part from discussions with C. Anthony Anderson.

22 The clearest example of such a position is in Goldman's paper "Discrimination and Perceptual Knowledge," cited above, where he rejects what he calls "Cartesian-style justification" as a requirement for perceptual knowledge, in favor of an externalist account. He goes on to remark, however, that one could use the term "justification" in such a way that satisfaction of his externalist conditions "counts as justification," though a kind of justification "entirely different from the sort of justification demanded by Cartesianism" (p. 790). What is unclear is whether this is supposed to be a purely verbal possibility, which would then be of little interest, or whether it is supposed to connect with something like the concept of epistemic rationality explicated in section I. Thus it is uncertain whether Goldman means to repudiate the whole idea of epistemic rationality, or only some more limited view such as the doctrine of the given (reference to which provides his only explanation of what he means by "Cartesianism" in epistemology).

CHAPTER 29

Internalism Exposed

Alvin I. Goldman

In recent decades, epistemology has witnessed the development and growth of externalist theories of knowledge and justification.[1] Critics of externalism have focused a bright spotlight on this approach and judged it unsuitable for realizing the true and original goals of epistemology. Their own favored approach, internalism, is defended as a preferable approach to the traditional concept of epistemic justification.[2] I shall turn the spotlight toward internalism and its most prominent rationale, revealing fundamental problems at the core of internalism and challenging the viability of its most popular rationale. Although particular internalist theories such as (internalist) foundationalism and coherentism will occasionally be discussed, those specific theories are not my primary concern.

The principal concern is rather the general architecture of internalism, and the attempt to justify this architecture by appeal to a certain conception of what justification consists in.

I. Deontology, Access, and Internalism

I begin with a certain rationale for internalism that has widespread support. It can be reconstructed in three steps:

(1) The *guidance-deontological* (GD) *conception of justification* is posited.

(2) A certain constraint on the determiners of justification is derived from the GD conception, that is, the constraint that all justification determiners must be *accessible to*, or *knowable by*, the epistemic agent.

(3) The accessibility or knowability constraint is taken to imply that only internal conditions qualify as legitimate determiners of justification. So justification must be a purely internal affair.[3]

What motivates or underlies this rationale for internalism? Historically, one central aim of epistemology is to guide or direct our intellectual conduct, an aim expressed in René Descartes's title, "Rules for the Direction of the Mind."[4] Among contemporary writers, John Pollock expresses the idea this way:

> I have taken the fundamental problem of epistemology to be that of deciding what to believe. Epistemic justification, as I use the term, is concerned with this problem. Considerations of epistemic justification guide us in determining what to believe. We might call this the "belief-guiding" or "reason-guiding" sense of "justification." (*Contemporary Theories of Knowledge*, p. 10)

The guidance conception of justification is commonly paired with the deontological conception

Originally published in *The Journal of Philosophy* 96, 6 (1999), pp. 271–93.

of justification. John Locke[5] wrote of a person's "duty as a rational creature" (*ibid.*, p. 413), and the theme of epistemic duty or responsibility has been echoed by many contemporary epistemologists, including Laurence BonJour (*The Structure of Empirical Knowledge*), Roderick Chisholm (*Theory of Knowledge*), Carl Ginet, Paul Moser, Matthias Steup, Richard Feldman, and Hilary Kornblith.[6] Chisholm defines cousins of the concept of justification in terms of the relation "more reasonable than", and he re-expresses the relation "p is more reasonable than q for S at t" by saying: "S is so situated at t that his intellectual *requirement*, his *responsibility* as an intellectual being, is better fulfilled by p than by q."[7] Similarly, Feldman says that one's epistemic duty is to "believe what is supported or justified by one's evidence and to avoid believing what is not supported by one's evidence" ("Epistemic Obligations," p. 254).

The guidance and deontological conceptions of justification are intimately related, because the deontological conception, at least when paired with the guidance conception, considers it a person's epistemic duty to guide his doxastic attitudes by his evidence, or by whatever factors determine the justificational status of a proposition at a given time. Epistemic deontologists commonly maintain that being justified in believing a proposition *p* consists in being (intellectually) required or permitted to believe *p*; and being unjustified in believing *p* consists in not being permitted, or being forbidden, to believe *p*. When a person is unjustified in believing a proposition, it is his duty not to believe it.

It is possible to separate the deontological conception from the guidance idea. In ethical theory, a distinction has been drawn between accounts of moral duty that aim to specify what makes actions right and accounts of moral duty that aim to provide practical decision procedures for what to do.[8] If an account simply aims at the first desideratum, it need not aspire to be usable as a decision guide. Similarly, accounts of epistemic duty need not necessarily be intended as decision guides. When the deontological conception is used as a rationale for epistemic internalism of the sort I am sketching, however, it does incorporate the guidance conception. Only if the guidance conception is incorporated can the argument proceed along the intended lines to the accessibility constraint, and from there to internalism. This is why I shall henceforth speak of the GD conception of justification.

I turn now to the second step of the argument for internalism. Following William Alston,[9] I shall use the term *justifiers* for facts or states of affairs that determine the justificational status of a belief, or the epistemic status a proposition has for an epistemic agent. In other words, justifiers determine whether or not a proposition is justified for an epistemic agent at a given time. It seems to follow naturally from the GD conception of justification that a certain constraint must be placed on the sorts of facts or states of affairs that qualify as justifiers. If a person is going to avoid violating his epistemic duty, he must know, or be able to find out, what his duty requires. By *know*, in this context, I mean only: have an *accurate*, or *true*, belief. I do not mean: have a *justified* true belief (or whatever else is entailed by the richer concept of knowledge). Admittedly, it might be possible to avoid violating one's duties by chance, without knowing (having true beliefs about) what one's duties are. As a practical matter, however, it is not feasible to conform to duty on a regular and consistent basis without knowing what items of conduct constitute those duties. Thus, if you are going to choose your beliefs and abstentions from belief in accordance with your justificational requirements, the facts that make you justified or unjustified in believing a certain proposition at a given time must be facts that you are capable of knowing, at that time, to hold or not to hold. There is an intimate connection, then, between the GD conception of justification and the requirement that justifiers must be accessible to, or knowable by, the agent at the time of belief. If you cannot accurately ascertain your epistemic duty at a given time, how can you be expected to execute that duty, and how can you reasonably be held responsible for executing that duty?[10]

The *knowability constraint on justifiers* which flows from the GD conception may be formulated as follows:

> KJ: The only facts that qualify as justifiers of an agent's believing *p* at time *t* are facts that the agent can readily know, at *t*, to obtain or not to obtain.

How can an agent readily know whether candidate justifiers obtain or do not obtain? Presumably, the agent must have a way of determining, for any candidate class of justifiers, whether or not they obtain. Such a way of knowing must be reliable, that is, it must generate beliefs about the presence or absence of justifiers that are usually (invariably?) correct. Otherwise, the agent will often be mistaken about what his epistemic duty requires. The way of knowing must also be "powerful," in the sense that when justifiers obtain it is likely (certain?) that the agent will believe that they obtain; at least he will believe this if he reflects on the matter or otherwise inquires into it.[11] As we shall soon see, internalists typically impose additional restrictions on how justifiers may be known. But the minimal, generic version of KJ simply requires justifiers to be the sorts of facts that agents have *some* way of knowing. In other words, justification-conferring facts must be the sorts of facts whose presence or absence is "accessible" to agents.[12]

Given the KJ constraint on justifiers, it becomes fairly obvious why internalism about justification is so attractive. Whereas external facts are facts that a cognitive agent might not be in a position to know about, internal facts are presumably the sorts of conditions that a cognitive agent can readily determine. So internal facts seem to be the right sorts of candidates for justifiers. This consideration leads to the third step of our rationale for internalism. Only internal facts qualify as justifiers because they are the only ones that satisfy the KJ constraint; at least so internalists suppose.

One possible way to criticize this rationale for internalism is to challenge the GD conception directly. This could be done, for example, by arguing that the GD conception of justification presupposes the dubious thesis of doxastic voluntarism, the thesis that doxastic attitudes can be "guided" by deliberate choices or acts of will. This criticism is developed by Alston,[13] and I have sympathy with many of his points. But the voluntarism argument against the GD conception is disputed by Feldman ("Epistemic Obligations") and John Heil,[14] among others. Feldman, for example, argues that epistemic deontologism is not wedded to the assumption of doxastic voluntarism. Many obligations remain in force, he points out, even when an agent lacks the ability to discharge them. A person is still legally obligated to repay a debt even when his financial situation makes him unable to repay it. Perhaps epistemic obligations have analogous properties.[15] Since the

complex topic of doxastic voluntarism would require article-length treatment in its own right, I set this issue aside and confine my attention to other issues. Although I do not accept the GD conception of justification, I take it as given for purposes of the present discussion and explore where it leads. In any case, what is ultimately crucial for internalism is the accessibility requirement that the GD conception hopes to rationalize. Even if the GD conception fails to provide a good rationale, internalism would be viable if some other rationale could be provided for a suitable accessibility requirement.

II. Direct Knowability and Strong Internalism

The initial KJ constraint was formulated in terms of knowability plain and simple, but proponents of internalism often add the further qualification that determinants of justification must be *directly* knowable by the cognitive agent. Ginet, for example, writes as follows:

> Every one of every set of facts about S's position that minimally suffices to make S, at a given time, justified in being confident that p must be *directly recognizable* to S at that time (*Knowledge, Perception, and Memory*, p. 34).

Similarly, Chisholm writes:

> [T]he concept of epistemic justification is ... internal and immediate in that one can *find out directly*, by reflection, what one is justified in believing at any time.[16]

Thus, Ginet and Chisholm do not endorse just the minimal KJ constraint as earlier formulated, but a more restrictive version, which might be written as follows:

> KJ_{dir}: The only facts that qualify as justifiers of an agent's believing *p* at time *t* are facts that the agent can readily know *directly*, at *t*, to obtain or not to obtain.

An initial problem arising from KJ_{dir} is this: What warrants the imposition of KJ_{dir} as opposed to the looser constraint, KJ? KJ was derived from the GD conception on the grounds that one cannot reasonably be expected to comply with epistemic duties unless one knows what those duties are. How does such an argument warrant the further conclusion that *direct* knowledge of justification must be available? Even indirect knowledge (whatever that is) would enable an agent to comply with his epistemic duties. So the second step of the argument for internalism cannot properly be revised to feature KJ_{dir} in place of KJ. Proponents of KJ_{dir} might reply that direct forms of knowledge are more powerful than indirect knowledge, but this reply is unconvincing. The power requirement was already built into the original version of KJ, and it is unclear how directness adds anything of significance on that score. Whether KJ_{dir} can be derived from GD is a serious problem, because the argument for internalism rests on something like the directness qualification. I shall say more about this later; for now I set this point aside in order to explore where KJ_{dir} leads.

What modes of knowledge count as direct? At least one form of direct knowledge is introspection. A reason for thinking that introspection is what Chisholm means by direct knowledge is that he restricts all determiners of justification to conscious states:

> A consequence of our "internalistic" theory of knowledge is that, if one is subject to an epistemic requirement at any time, then this requirement is imposed by the *conscious state* in which one happens to find oneself at that time (*ibid.*, pp. 59–60).

Since he restricts justifiers to conscious states, it is plausible to assume that direct knowledge, for Chisholm, means introspective knowledge, and knowledge by "reflection" coincides with knowledge by introspection.[17] At least in the case of Chisholm, then, KJ_{dir} might be replaced by:

KJ_{int}: The only facts that qualify as justifiers of an agent's believing *p* at time *t* are facts that the agent can readily know *by introspection*, at *t*, to obtain or not to obtain.

Now, the only facts that an agent can know by introspection are facts concerning what conscious states he is (or is not) currently in, so these are the

only sorts of facts that qualify as justifiers under KJ_{int}. This form of internalism may be called *strong internalism*:

> SI: Only facts concerning what conscious states an agent is in at time *t* are justifiers of the agent's beliefs at *t*.

Strong internalism, however, is an unacceptable approach to justification, for it has serious, skepticism-breeding, consequences. This is demonstrated by the *problem of stored beliefs*. At any given time, the vast majority of one's beliefs are stored in memory rather than occurrent or active. Beliefs about personal data (for example, one's social security number), about world history, about geography, or about the institutional affiliations of one's professional colleagues, are almost all stored rather than occurrent at a given moment. Furthermore, for almost any of these beliefs, one's conscious state at the time includes nothing that justifies it. No perceptual experience, no conscious memory event, and no premises consciously entertained at the selected moment will be justificationally sufficient for such a belief. According to strong internalism, then, none of these beliefs is justified at that moment. Strong internalism threatens a drastic diminution in the stock of beliefs ordinarily deemed justified, and hence in the stock of knowledge, assuming that justification is necessary for knowledge. This is a major count against this type of theory.

Feldman anticipates this problem because his own account of having evidence also implies that only consciously entertained factors have evidential force ("Epistemic Obligations, pp. 98–9). Feldman tries to meet the threat by distinguishing between occurrent and dispositional senses of epistemic terms. (He actually discusses knowledge rather than justification, but I shall address the issue in terms of justification because that is the target of our investigation.) Feldman is not simply restating the familiar point that "belief" has occurrent and dispositional senses. He is proposing that the term "justified" is ambiguous between an occurrent and a dispositional sense. Feldman apparently claims that in the case of stored beliefs, people at most have dispositional justification, not occurrent justification.

There are two problems with this proposal. First, if having a disposition to generate conscious evidential states qualifies as a justifier of a belief, why would this not extend from memorial to perceptual dispositions? Suppose a train passenger awakes from a nap but has not yet opened his eyes. Is he justified in believing propositions about the details of the neighboring landscape? Surely not. Yet he is *disposed*, merely by opening his eyes, to generate conscious evidential states that would occurrently justify such beliefs. So the dispositional approach is far too permissive to yield an acceptable sense of "justified".[18] Second, can an internalist, especially a strong internalist, live with the idea that certain dispositions count as justifiers? Having or not having a disposition (of the requisite type) is not the sort of fact or condition that can be known by introspection. Thus, the proposal to supplement the occurrent sense of "justified" with a dispositional sense of "justified" is simply the abandonment of strong internalism.

III. Indirect Knowability and Weak Internalism

The obvious solution to the problem of stored beliefs is to relax the KJ constraint: allow justifiers to be merely indirectly knowable. This yields:

KJ$_{ind}$: The only facts that qualify as justifiers of an agent's believing p at time t are facts that the agent can readily know at t, either directly or indirectly, to obtain or not to obtain.

The danger here is that indirect knowledge might let in too much from an internalist perspective. How are externalist forms of knowledge – for example, perceptual knowledge – to be excluded? Clearly, internalism must propose specific forms of knowledge that conform with its spirit. It is fairly clear how internalism should deal with the problem of stored beliefs: simply allow knowledge of justifiers to include memory retrieval. Stored evidence beliefs can qualify as justifiers because the agent can know that they obtain by the compound route of first retrieving them from memory and then introspecting their conscious contents. This yields the following variant of the KJ constraint:

KJ$_{int+ret}$: The only facts that qualify as justifiers of an agent's believing p at time t are facts that the agent can readily know, at t, to obtain or not to obtain, *by introspection and/or memory retrieval.*

This KJ constraint allows for a more viable form of internalism than strong internalism. We may call it *weak internalism*, and initially articulate it through the following principle:

WI: Only facts concerning what conscious and/or stored mental states an agent is in at time t are justifiers of the agent's beliefs at t.

WI will certify the justification of many stored beliefs, because agents often have other stored beliefs that evidentially support them. A person who believes that Washington, DC is the capital of the United States may have a stored belief to the effect that a map of the US he recently consulted showed Washington as the capital. The latter stored belief is what justifies the former one. So weak internalism is not plagued with the problem of stored justified beliefs. Weak internalism seems to be a legitimate form of internalism because even stored beliefs qualify, intuitively, as internal states.

Although weak internalism is better than strong internalism, it too faces severe problems. First is the *problem of forgotten evidence*.[19] Many justified beliefs are ones for which an agent once had adequate evidence that she subsequently forgot. At the time of epistemic appraisal, she no longer possesses adequate evidence that is retrievable from memory. Last year, Sally read a story about the health benefits of broccoli in the "Science" section of the *New York Times*. She then justifiably formed a belief in broccoli's beneficial effects. She still retains this belief but no longer recalls her original evidential source (and has never encountered either corroborating or undermining sources). Nonetheless, her broccoli belief is still justified, and, if true, qualifies as a case of knowledge. Presumably, this is because her past acquisition of the belief was epistemically proper. But past acquisition is irrelevant by the lights of internalism (including weak internalism), because only her current mental states are justifiers relevant to her current belief. All past events are "external" and therefore irrelevant according to internalism.

It might be replied that Sally does currently possess evidence in support of her broccoli belief.

One of her background beliefs, we may suppose, is that most of what she remembers was learned in an epistemically proper manner. So does she not, after all, now have grounds for the target belief? Admittedly, she has *some* evidence, but is this evidence sufficient for justification? Surely not. In a variant case, suppose that Sally still has the same background belief – namely, that most of what she remembers was learned in an epistemically proper manner – but she in fact acquired her broccoli belief from the *National Inquirer* rather than the *New York Times*. So her broccoli belief was never acquired, or corroborated, in an epistemically sound manner. Then even with the indicated current background belief, Sally cannot be credited with justifiably believing that broccoli is healthful. Her past acquisition is still relevant, and decisive. At least it is relevant so long as we are considering the "epistemizing" sense of justification, in which justification carries a true belief a good distance toward knowledge. Sally's belief in the healthfulness of broccoli is not justified in that sense, for surely she does not know that broccoli is healthful given that the *National Inquirer* was her sole source of information.

The category of forgotten evidence is a problem for weak internalism because, like the problem of stored beliefs facing strong internalism, it threatens skeptical outcomes. A large sector of what is ordinarily counted as knowledge are beliefs for which people have forgotten their original evidence.

In reply to the problem of forgotten evidence, Steup[20] offers the following solution. An additional requirement for memorial states to justify a belief that *p*, says Steup, is that the agent have adequate evidence for believing the following counterfactual: "If she had encountered *p* in a questionable source, she would not have formed the belief that *p*." Steup's suggestion is that in the *National Inquirer* variant, Sally fails to have adequate evidence for this counterfactual, and that is why her broccoli belief is not justified. My response to this proposal is twofold. First, the proposed requirement is too strong to impose on memorially justified belief. It is quite difficult to get adequate evidence for the indicated counterfactual. Second, the proposed requirement seems too weak as well. Sally might have adequate evidence for the counterfactual but still be unjustified in holding her broccoli belief. She might have adequate evidence for the counterfactual without

its being true; but if it is not true and the rest of the story is as I told it, her broccoli belief is not justified. So Steup's internalist-style solution does not work.

A second problem confronting weak internalism is what I call the *problem of concurrent retrieval*. Principle WI says that *only* conscious and stored mental states are justifiers, but it does not say that *all* sets or conjunctions of such states qualify as justifiers.[21] Presumably, which sets of such states qualify is a matter to be decided by reference to $KJ_{int+ret}$. If a certain set of stored beliefs can all be concurrently retrieved at time *t* and concurrently introspected, then they would pass the test of $KJ_{int+ret}$, and could qualify as justifiers under the principle of indirect knowability. But if they cannot all be concurrently retrieved and introspected at *t*, they would fail the test. Now it is clear that the totality of an agent's stored credal corpus at a time cannot be concurrently retrieved from memory. So that set of stored beliefs does not qualify as a justifier for purposes of weak internalism. Unfortunately, this sort of belief set is precisely what certain types of internalist theories require by way of a justifier. Consider holistic coherentism, which says that a proposition *p* is justified for person *S* at time *t* if and only if *p* coheres with *S*'s entire corpus of beliefs at *t* (including, of course, the stored beliefs). A cognitive agent could ascertain, at *t*, whether *p* coheres with her entire corpus only by concurrently retrieving all of her stored beliefs. But such concurrent retrieval is psychologically impossible.[22] Thus, the critically relevant justificational fact under holistic coherentism does not meet even the indirect knowability constraint, much less the direct knowability constraint. Here is a clash, then, between a standard internalist theory of justification and the knowability rationale under scrutiny. Either that rationale is indefensible, or a familiar type of internalism must be abandoned at the outset. Nor is the problem confined to coherentism. Internalist foundationalism might also require concurrent retrieval of more basic (or low-level) beliefs than it is psychologically feasible to retrieve.

IV.   Logical and Probabilistic Relations

As these last examples remind us, every traditional form of internalism involves some appeal to logical relations, probabilistic relations, or their ilk. Foundationalism requires that nonbasically justified beliefs stand in suitable logical or probabilistic relations to basic beliefs; coherentism requires that one's system of beliefs be logically consistent, probabilistically coherent, or the like. None of these logical or probabilistic relations is itself a mental state, either a conscious state or a stored state. So these relations do not qualify as justifiers according to either SI or WI. The point may be illustrated more concretely within a foundationalist perspective. Suppose that Jones possesses a set of basic beliefs at t whose contents logically or probabilistically support proposition p. This property of Jones's basic beliefs – the property of supporting proposition p – is not a justifier under WI, for the property itself is neither a conscious nor a stored mental state. Nor is the possession of this property by these mental states another mental state. So WI has no way of authorizing or permitting Jones to believe p. Unless WI is liberalized, no nonbasic belief will be justified, which would again threaten a serious form of skepticism.

Can this problem be remedied by simply adding the proviso that all properties of conscious or stored mental states also qualify as justifiers?[23] This proviso is unacceptably permissive for internalism. One property of many conscious and stored mental states is the property of *being caused by a reliable process*, yet surely internalism cannot admit this archetypically externalist type of property into the class of justifiers. How should the class of properties be restricted? An obvious suggestion is to include only formal properties of mental states, that is, logical and mathematical properties of their contents. But should *all* formal properties be admitted? This approach would fly in the face of the knowability or accessibility constraint, which is the guiding theme of internalism. Only formal properties that are knowable by the agent at the time of doxastic decision should be countenanced as legitimate justifiers under internalism. Such properties, however, cannot be detected by introspection and/or memory retrieval. So some knowing operations suitable for formal properties must be added, yielding a liberalized version of the KJ constraint.

How should a liberalized KJ constraint be designed? The natural move is to add some selected computational operations or algorithms, procedures that would enable an agent to ascertain whether a targeted proposition p has appropriate logical or probabilistic relations to the contents of other belief states he is in. Precisely which computational operations are admissible? Again, problems arise. The first is the *problem of the doxastic decision interval*.

The traditional idea behind internalism is that an agent is justified in believing p at time t if the evidential beliefs (and perhaps other, nondoxastic states) possessed *at t* have an appropriate logical or probabilistic relation to p. In short, justification is conferred simultaneously with evidence possession. Feldman makes this explicit: "For any person S and proposition p and time t, S epistemically ought to believe p at t if and only if p is supported by the evidence S has at t" ("Epistemic Obligations", p. 254). Once the knowability constraint is introduced, however, simultaneous justification looks problematic. If justification is contingent on the agent's ability to know what justifiers obtain, the agent should not be permitted to believe a proposition p at t unless she can know *by t* whether the relevant justifiers obtain. Since it necessarily takes some time to compute logical or probabilistic relations, the simultaneity model of justification needs to be revised so that an agent's mental states at t justify her in believing only p at $t + \epsilon$, for some suitable ϵ. The value of ϵ cannot be too large, of course, lest the agent's mental states change so as to affect the justificational status of p. But ϵ must be large enough to allow the agent time to determine the relevant formal relations.

These two conditions – (1) avoid mental change, but (2) allow enough time to compute formal relations – may well be jointly unsatisfiable, which would pose a severe problem for internalism. Mental states, including perceptual states that generate new evidence, change very rapidly and they could easily change before required computations could be executed. On the other hand, although mental states do change rapidly, the agent's belief system might not be epistemically required to reflect or respond to each change until interval ϵ has elapsed. Some doxastic decision interval, then, might be feasible.

Is there a short enough decision interval during which justificationally pertinent formal properties can be computed? Coherentism says that S is justified in believing proposition p only if

p coheres with the rest of S's belief system held at the time. Assume that coherence implies logical consistency. Then coherentism requires that the logical consistency or inconsistency of any proposition p with S's belief system must qualify as a justifier. But how quickly can consistency or inconsistency be ascertained by mental computation? As Christopher Cherniak[24] points out, determination of even tautological consistency is a computationally complex task in the general case. Using the truth-table method to check for the consistency of a belief system with 138 independent atomic propositions, even an ideal computer working at "top speed" (checking each row of a truth table in the time it takes a light ray to traverse the diameter of a proton) would take twenty billion years, the estimated time from the "big-bang" dawn of the universe to the present. Presumably, twenty billion years is not an acceptable doxastic decision interval!

Any reasonable interval, then, is too constraining for garden-variety coherentism. The knowability constraint again clashes with one of the stock brands of internalism.[25] Dyed-in-the-wool internalists might be prepared to live with this result. "So much the worse for traditional coherentism," they might say, "we can live with its demise." But this does not get internalism entirely off the hook. There threaten to be many logical and probabilistic facts that do not qualify as justifiers because they require too long a doxastic interval to compute. Furthermore, it is unclear what is a principled basis for deciding what is too long. This quandary confronting internalism has apparently escaped its proponents' attention.

A second problem for logical and probabilistic justifiers is the *availability problem*. Suppose that a particular set of *computational operations* – call it COMP – is provisionally selected for inclusion alongside introspection and memory retrieval. COMP might include, for example, a restricted (and hence noneffective) use of the truth-table method, restricted so as to keep its use within the chosen doxastic decision interval.[26] This yields a new version of the KJ constraint:

$KJ_{int+ret+COMP}$: The only facts that qualify as justifiers of an agent's believing p at time t are facts that the agent can readily know within a suitable doxastic decision interval *via* introspection, memory retrieval, and/or COMP.

Now, the KJ constraint is presumably intended to apply not only to the cleverest or best-trained epistemic agents but to all epistemic agents, including the most naive and uneducated persons on the street. After all, the point of the knowability constraint is that justifiers should be facts within the purview of every epistemic agent. Under the GD conception, compliance with epistemic duty or responsibility is not intended to be the private preserve of the logical or mathematical elite. It is something that ought to be attained – and should therefore be attainable – by any human agent. The truth-table method, however, does not seem to be in the intellectual repertoire of naive agents, so it is illegitimate to include COMP operations within a KJ constraint. Unlike introspection and memory retrieval, it is not available to all cognitive agents.

It may be replied that computational operations of the contemplated sort would be within the *capacity* of normal human agents. No superhuman computational powers are required. Computing power, however, is not the issue. A relevant sequence of operations must also be *available* in the agent's intellectual repertoire; that is, she must know which operations are appropriate to obtain an answer to the relevant (formal) question.[27] Since truth-table methods and other such algorithms are probably not in the repertoire of ordinary cognitive agents, they cannot properly be included in a KJ constraint.

A third problem concerns the proper methodology that should be used in selecting a KJ constraint that incorporates computational operations. As we see from the first two problems, a KJ constraint that conforms to the spirit of the GD rationale must reflect the basic cognitive skills or repertoires of actual human beings. What these basic repertoires consist in, however, cannot be determined a priori. It can only be determined with the help of empirical science. This fact fundamentally undermines the methodological posture of internalism, a subject to which I shall return in section VII.

Until now, I have assumed a *universal* accessibility constraint, one that holds for all cognitive agents. But perhaps potential justifiers for one agent need not be potential justifiers for another.

Justifiers might be allowed to vary from agent to agent, depending on what is knowable by the particular agent. If two agents have different logical or probabilistic skills, then some properties that do not qualify as justifiers for one might yet qualify as justifiers for the other. Indeed, the constraint $KJ_{int+ret+COMP}$ might be read in precisely this agent-relativized way. The subscripts may be interpreted as indicating knowledge routes that are available *to the agent in question*, not necessarily to all agents.

If KJ constraints are agent relativized as a function of differences in knowledge skills, this means that two people in precisely the same evidential state (in terms of perceptual situation, background beliefs, and so on) might have different epistemic entitlements. But if the two agents are to comply with their respective epistemic duties, each must *know* which knowledge skills she has. This simply parallels the second step of the internalist's original three-step argument. If one's epistemic duties or entitlements depend on one's knowledge skills (for example, on one's computational skills), then compliance with one's duties requires knowledge of which skills one possesses. There are two problems with this approach. First, it is unlikely that many people – especially ordinary people on the street – have this sort of knowledge, and this again threatens large-scale skepticism. Second, what is now required to be known by the agent is something about the *truth-getting* power of her cognitive skills – that is, the power of her skills in detecting justifiers. This seems to be precisely the sort of *external* property that internalists regard as anathema. How can they accept this solution while remaining faithful to the spirit of internalism?[28]

V. Epistemic Principles

When the KJ constraint speaks of justifiers, it is not clear exactly what these comprehend. Specifically, do justifiers include epistemic principles themselves? I believe that principles should be included, because epistemic principles are among the items that determine whether or not an agent is justified in believing a proposition, which is just how "justifiers" was defined. Furthermore, true epistemic principles are items an agent must know if she is going to

determine her epistemic duties correctly. Knowledge of her current states of mind and their properties will not instruct her about her epistemic duties and entitlements unless she also knows true epistemic principles.

How are epistemic principles to be known, according to internalism? Chisholm[29] says that central epistemic principles are normative supervenience principles, which (when true) are necessarily true. Since they are necessary truths, they can be known a priori – in particular, they can be known "by reflection."

> The internalist assumes that, merely by reflecting upon his own conscious state, he can formulate a set of epistemic principles that will enable him to find out, with respect to any possible belief he has, whether he is justified in having that belief.[30]

This passage is ambiguous as to whether (correct) epistemic principles are accessible on reflection just to epistemologists, or accessible to naive epistemic agents as well. The latter, however, must be required by internalism, because justifiers are supposed to be determinable by all epistemic agents.

Are ordinary or naive agents really capable of formulating and recognizing correct epistemic principles? This seems highly dubious. Even many career-long epistemologists have failed to articulate and appreciate correct epistemic principles. Since different epistemologists offer disparate and mutually conflicting candidates for epistemic principles, at most a fraction of these epistemologists can be right. Perhaps none of the principles thus far tendered by epistemologists is correct! In light of this shaky and possibly dismal record by professional epistemologists, how can we expect ordinary people, who are entirely ignorant of epistemology and its multiple pitfalls, to succeed at this task?[31] Nor is it plausible that they should succeed at this task purely "by reflection" on their conscious states, since among the matters epistemic principles must resolve is what computational skills are within the competence of ordinary cognizers. I do not see how this can be answered a priori, "by reflection."

A crippling problem emerges for internalism. If epistemic principles are not knowable by all naive agents, no such principles can qualify as justifiers under the KJ constraint. If no epistemic principles so qualify, no proposition can be justifiably believed by any agent. Wholesale skepticism follows.

VI.   The Core Dilemma for the Three-Step Argument

I raise doubts here about whether there is any cogent inferential route from the GD conception to internalism via an acceptable KJ constraint. Here is the core dilemma. The minimal, unvarnished version of the KJ constraint does not rationalize internalism. That simple constraint merely says that justifiers must be readily knowable, and some readily knowable facts might be external rather than internal. If all routes to knowledge of justifiers are allowed, then knowledge by perception must be allowed. If knowledge by perception is allowed, then facts of an external sort could qualify for the status of justifiers. Of course, no epistemologist claims that purely external facts should serve as justifiers. But partly external facts are nominated by externalists for the rank of justifiers. Consider properties of the form: being a reliable perceptual indicator of a certain environmental fact. This sort of property is at least partly external because reliability involves truth, and truth (on the usual assumption) is external. Now suppose that a certain auditory perceptual state has the property of being a reliable indicator of the presence of a mourning dove in one's environment. Might the possession of this reliable indicatorship property qualify as a justifier on the grounds that it is indeed readily knowable? If every route to knowledge is legitimate, I do not see how this possibility can be excluded. After all, one could use past perceptions of mourning doves and their songs to determine that the designated auditory state is a reliable indicator of a mourning dove's presence. So if unrestricted knowledge is allowed, the (partly) external fact in question might be perfectly knowable. Thus, the unvarnished version of the KJ constraint does not exclude external facts from the ranks of the justifiers.

The simple version of the KJ constraint, then, does not support internalism. Tacit recognition of this is what undoubtedly leads internalists to favor a "direct" knowability constraint. Unfortunately,

this extra rider is not rationalized by the GD conception. The GD conception at best implies that cognitive agents must know what justifiers are present or absent. No particular types of knowledge, or paths to knowledge, are intimated. So the GD conception cannot rationalize a restrictive version of the KJ constraint that unambiguously yields internalism.

Let me put the point another way. The GD conception implies that justifiers must be readily knowable, but are internal facts always more readily knowable than external facts? As discussed earlier, probabilistic relations presumably qualify as internal, but they do not seem to be readily knowable by human beings. An entire tradition of psychological research on "biases and heuristics" suggests that naive agents commonly commit probabilistic fallacies, such as the "conjunction fallacy," and use formally incorrect judgmental heuristics, such as the representativeness heuristic and the anchoring-and-adjustment heuristic.[32] If this is right, people's abilities at detecting probabilistic relationships are actually rather weak. People's perceptual capacities to detect external facts seem, by contrast, far superior. The unqualified version of the KJ constraint, therefore, holds little promise for restricting all justifiers to internal conditions in preference to external conditions, as internalism requires.[33]

VII.   The Methodology of Epistemology: Empirical or a Priori?

Internalism standardly incorporates the doctrine that epistemology is a purely a priori or armchair enterprise rather than one that needs help from empirical science. Chisholm puts the point this way:

> The epistemic principles that [the epistemologist] formulates are principles that one may come upon and apply merely by sitting in one's armchair, so to speak, and without calling for any outside assistance. In a word, one need only consider one's own state of mind.[34]

Previous sections already raised doubts about the merits of apriorism in epistemology, even in the context of the theoretical architecture presented here. I now want to challenge the viability of apriorism in greater depth.

Assume that, despite my earlier reservations, an internalist restriction on justifiers has somehow been derived, one that allows only conscious states and certain of their nonexternal properties to serve as justifiers. How should the epistemologist identify particular conscious states and properties as justifiers for specific propositions (or types of propositions)? In other words, how should specific epistemic principles be crafted? Should the task be executed purely a priori, or can scientific psychology help?

For concreteness, consider justifiers for memory beliefs. Suppose an adult consciously remembers seeing, as a teenager, a certain matinee idol. This ostensible memory could have arisen from imagination, since he frequently fantasized about this matinee idol and imagined seeing her in person. What clues are present in the current memory impression by which he can tell whether or not the recollection is veridical? This is precisely the kind of issue which internalist epistemic principles should address. If there are no differences in features of memory states that stem from perceptions of real occurrences versus features of states that stem from mere imagination, does this not raise a specter of skepticism over the domain of memory? If there are no indications by which to distinguish veridical from nonveridical memory impressions, can we be justified in trusting our memory impressions? Skepticism aside, epistemologists should surely be interested in identifying the features of conscious memory impressions by which people are made more or less justified (or prima facie justified) in believing things about the past.

Epistemologists have said very little on this subject. Their discussions tend to be exhausted by characterizations of memory impressions as "vivid" or "nonvivid." There is, I suspect, a straightforward reason for the paucity of detail. It is extremely difficult, using purely armchair methods, to dissect the microfeatures of memory experiences so as to identify telltale differences between trustworthy and questionable memories. On the other hand, empirical methods have produced some interesting findings, which might properly be infused into epistemic principles in a way entirely congenial to internalism. Important research in this area has been done by Marcia Johnson and her colleagues.[35] I shall illustrate my points by brief reference to their research.

Johnson calls the subject of some of her research *reality monitoring*. She tries to characterize the detectable differences between (conscious) memory traces derived from veridical perception of events versus memory traces generated by mere imaginations of events.[36] Johnson and Raye ("Reality Monitoring") propose four dimensions along which memory cues will typically differ depending on whether their origin was perceptual or imaginative. As compared with memories that originate from imagination, memories originating from perception tend to have (1) more perceptual information (for example, color and sound), (2) more contextual information about time and place, and (3) more meaningful detail. When a memory trace is rich along these three dimensions, this is evidence of its having originated through perception. Memories originating from imagination or thought, by contrast, tend to be rich on another dimension: they contain more information about the cognitive operations involved in the original thinkings or imaginings (for example, effortful attention, image creation, or search). Perception is more automatic than imagination, so a memory trace that originates from perception will tend to lack attributes concerning effortful operations. Johnson and Raye therefore suggest that differences in average value along these types of dimensions can form the basis for deciding whether the origin of a memory is perceptual or nonperceptual. A memory with a great deal of visual and spatial detail, and without records of intentional constructive and organizational processes, should be judged to have been perceptually derived.[37]

Epistemologists would be well-advised to borrow these sorts of ideas and incorporate them into their epistemic principles. A person is (prima facie) justified in believing in the real occurrence of an ostensibly recalled event if the memory trace is strong on the first three dimensions and weak on the fourth dimension. Conversely, an agent is unjustified in believing in the real occurrence of the recalled event if the memory trace is strong on the fourth dimension but weak on the first three dimensions. All of these dimensions, of course, concern features of conscious experience. For this reason, internalist epistemologists should be happy to incorporate these kinds of features into their epistemic principles.

Let me distinguish two categories of epistemologically significant facts about memory experience which empirical psychology might provide. First, as we have seen, it might identify types of representational materials which are generally available in people's memory experiences. Second, it might indicate which of these representational materials are either reliable or counter-reliable indicators of the veridicality of the ostensibly recalled events. Is the reliability of a memory cue a legitimate issue from an internalist perspective? It might be thought not, since reliability is usually classed as an external property. But epistemologists might use reliability considerations to decide which memory characteristics should be featured in epistemic principles. They need not insert reliability per se into the principles. There is nothing in our present formulation of internalism, at any rate, which bars the latter approach. Any KJ constraint provides only a necessary condition for being a justifier; it leaves open the possibility that additional necessary conditions, such as reliable indication, must also be met. Indeed, many internalists do use reliability as a (partial) basis for their choice of justifiers. BonJour (*op. cit.*, p. 7) says that the basic role of justification is that of a *means* to truth, and he defends coherence as a justifier on the ground that a coherent system of beliefs is likely to correspond to reality. This point need not be settled definitively, however. There are already adequate grounds for claiming that internalism cannot be optimally pursued without help from empirical psychology, whether or not reliability is a relevant consideration.

VIII.   Conclusion

Let us review the parade of problems infecting internalism which we have witnessed, though

not all in their order of presentation. (1) The argument from the GD conception of justification to internalism does not work. Internalism can be derived only from a suitably qualified version of the KJ constraint because the unqualified version threatens to allow external facts to count as justifiers. No suitably qualified version of the KJ constraint is derivable from the GD conception. (2) A variety of qualified KJ constraints are possible, each leading to a different version of internalism. None of these versions is intuitively acceptable. Strong internalism, which restricts justifiers to conscious states, is stuck with the problem of stored beliefs. Weak internalism, which allows stored as well as conscious beliefs to count as justifiers, faces the problem of forgotten evidence and the problem of concurrent retrieval. (3) The question of how logical and probabilistic facts are to be included in the class of justifiers is plagued by puzzles, especially the puzzle of the doxastic decision interval and the issue of availability. (4) Epistemic principles must be among the class of justifiers, but such principles fail internalism's knowability requirement. (5) The favored methodology of internalism – the armchair method – cannot be sustained even if we grant the assumption that justifiers must be conscious states.

Internalism is rife with problems. Are they all traceable to the GD rationale? Could internalism be salvaged by switching to a different rationale? A different rationale might help, but most of the problems raised here arise from the knowability constraint. It is unclear exactly which knowability constraint should be associated with internalism, and all of the available candidates generate problematic theories. So I see no hope for internalism; it does not survive the glare of the spotlight.

Notes

1   Prominent statements of externalism include D. M. Armstrong, *Belief, Truth and Knowledge* (New York: Cambridge, 1973); Fred Dretske, *Knowledge and the Flow of Information* (Cambridge: MIT, 1981); Robert Nozick, *Philosophical Explanations* (Cambridge: Harvard, 1981); my *Epistemology and Cognition* (Cambridge: Harvard, 1986); and Alvin Plantinga, *Warrant*

and Proper Function (New York: Oxford, 1993).
2   Major statements of internalism include Roderick Chisholm, *Theory of Knowledge* (Englewood Cliffs, NJ: Prentice-Hall, 1966, 1st edition; 1977, 2nd edition; 1989, 3rd edition); Laurence BonJour, *The Structure of Empirical Knowledge* (Cambridge: Harvard,

1985); John Pollock, *Contemporary Theories of Knowledge* (Totowa, NJ: Rowman and Littlefield, 1986); Richard Foley, *The Theory of Epistemic Rationality* (Cambridge: Harvard, 1987); and Keith Lehrer, *Theory of Knowledge* (Boulder: Westview, 1990). In addition to relatively pure versions of externalism and internalism, there are also mixtures of the two approaches, as found in William Alston, *Epistemic Justification* (Ithaca: Cornell, 1989); Ernest Sosa, *Knowledge in Perspective* (New York: Cambridge, 1991); and Robert Audi, *The Structure of Justification* (New York: Cambridge, 1993).

3 Plantinga also traces internalism to the deontological conception: "If we go back to the source of the internalist tradition … we can see that internalism arises out of deontology; a deontological conception of warrant … leads directly to internalism" (*Warrant and Proper Function*, pp. 24–5). Alston proposes a slightly different rationale for internalism, although his rationale also proceeds via the knowability constraint (*Epistemic Justification*, p. 236). He suggests that the concept of justification derives from the interpersonal practice of criticizing one another's beliefs and asking for their credentials. A person can appropriately respond to other people's demands for credentials only if he knows what those credentials are. So it is quite understandable, says Alston, that justifiers must meet the requirement of being accessible to the agent. Clearly, this is one way to derive the accessibility constraint without appeal to the deontological conception. But Alston is the only one I know of who advances this ground for the accessibility constraint. In any case, most of the problems I shall identify pertain to the accessibility constraint itself, which Alston's rationale shares with the deontological rationale.

4 *Philosophical Works of Descartes, Volume I*, Elizabeth Haldane and G. R. T. Ross, trans. (New York: Dover, 1955).

5 *An Essay Concerning Human Understanding*, Volume II, A. C. Fraser, ed. (New York: Dover, 1955).

6 Ginet, *Knowledge, Perception, and Memory* (Dordrecht: Reidel, 1975); Moser, *Empirical Justification* (Dordrecht: Reidel, 1985); Steup,

"The Deontic Conception of Epistemic Justification," *Philosophical Studies*, LIII (1988), pp. 65–84; Feldman, "Epistemic Obligations," in J. Tomberlin, ed., *Philosophical Perspectives*, Volume II (Atascadero, CA: Ridgeview, 1988), pp. 235–56; and Kornblith, "Justified Belief and Epistemically Responsible Action," *Philosophical Review*, XCII (1983), pp. 33–48.

7 *Theory of Knowledge*, 2nd edition, p. 14 (emphasis added).

8 For example, R. Eugene Bales distinguishes between two possible aims of act-utilitarianism: as a specifier of a right-making characteristic or as a decision-making procedure. See "Act-utilitarianism: Account of Right-making Characteristics or Decision-making Procedure," *American Philosophical Quarterly*, VIII (1971), pp. 257–65. He defends utilitarianism against certain critics by saying that it does not *have* to perform the latter function.

9 "Internalism and Externalism in Epistemology," reprinted in his *Epistemic Justification*, pp. 185–226, here p. 189.

10 Some internalists explicitly reject externalism on the grounds that it cannot be used as a decision guide. For example, Pollock says: "[I]t is in principle impossible for us to actually employ externalist norms. I take this to be a conclusive refutation of belief externalism" (*Contemporary Theories of Knowledge*, p. 134). He would not subscribe to the full argument for internalism I am discussing, however, because it is committed to the "intellectualist model" of epistemology, which he disparages.

11 For the distinction between reliability and power (phrased slightly differently), see my *Epistemology and Cognition*, chapter 6.

12 Jack Lyons points out that to comply with one's epistemic duty it suffices to know *that one has* (undefeated) justifiers for proposition *p*; one does not have to know *which* justifiers these are. So the argument is not entitled to conclude that knowledge of particular justifiers is required by epistemic duty. Practically speaking, however, it is difficult to see how a cognitive agent could know that relevant justifiers exist without knowing which particular ones exist. So I

shall pass over this objection to the internalist line of argument.

13 "The Deontological Conception of Justification," reprinted in his *Epistemic Justification*, pp. 115–52.

14 "Doxastic Agency," *Philosophical Studies*, XL (1983), pp. 355–64.

15 Feldman's response, however, undercuts the step from the GD conception of justification to the knowability constraint. If epistemic duty does not require that the agent be *able* to discharge this duty, there is no longer a rationale for the knowability constraint. A different line of response to the voluntarism worry is taken by Lehrer, who suggests that epistemological analysis should focus not on belief but on *acceptance*, where acceptance is some sort of action that is subject to the will – "A Self-Profile," in R. Bogdan, ed., *Keith Lehrer* (Dordrecht: Reidel, 1981), pp. 3–104.

16 *Theory of Knowledge*, 3rd edition, p. 7; emphasis added and original emphasis deleted.

17 Other epistemologists who restrict justifiers to conscious states or discuss access in terms of introspection include Moser, p. 174; Feldman, "Having Evidence," in D. Austin, ed., *Philosophical Analysis* (Dordrecht: Kluwer, 1988), pp. 83–104; and Audi, "Causalist Internalism," *American Philosophical Quarterly*, XXVI, 4 (1989), pp. 309–20.

18 Feldman might reply that there is an important distinction between memorial and perceptual dispositions; but it is not clear on what basis a principled distinction can be drawn.

19 This sort of problem is discussed by Gilbert Harman, *Change in View* (Cambridge: MIT, 1986); Thomas Senor, "Internalist Foundationalism and the Justification of Memory Belief," *Synthese*, XCIV (1993), pp. 453–76; and Audi, "Memorial Justification," *Philosophical Topics*, XXIII (1995), pp. 31–45.

20 His proposal was part of his commentary at the meeting where this paper was first read.

21 Obviously, one would need to reject the principle that the knowability of fact *A* and the knowability of fact *B* entail the knowability of the conjunctive fact, *A* & *B*.

22 The "doxastic presumption" invoked by BonJour (*The Structure of Empirical Knowledge*, pp. 101–6) seems to assume that this is possible, but this is simply an undefended assumption. Pollock (*Contemporary Theories of Knowledge*, p. 136) also raises the problem identified here, though in slightly different terms.

23 More precisely, the contemplated proviso should say that the possession of any property by a mental state (or set of mental states) qualifies as a justifier. This reading will be understood wherever the text talks loosely of "properties."

24 "Computational Complexity and the Universal Acceptance of Logic," *The Journal of Philosophy*, LXXXI, 12 (December 1984), pp. 739–58.

25 This computational difficulty for coherentism is identified by Kornblith, "The Unattainability of Coherence," in J. Bender, ed., *The Current State of the Coherence Theory* (Dordrecht: Kluwer, 1989), pp. 207–14.

26 Because of the contemplated restriction, there will be many questions about formal facts to which COMP cannot deliver answers. Thus, formal facts that might otherwise qualify as justifiers will not so qualify under the version of the KJ constraint that incorporates COMP.

27 Propositional (or "declarative") knowledge of the appropriate sequence of operations is, perhaps, an unduly restrictive requirement. It would suffice for the agent to have "procedural" skills of the right sort. But even such skills will be lacking in naive cognitive agents.

28 It might be argued that internalism's spirit leads to a similar requirement even for universal versions of a KJ constraint, not just for agent-relativized versions. Perhaps so; but so much the worse for the general form of internalism.

29 "The Status of Epistemic Principles," *Noûs*, XXIV (1990), pp. 209–15.

30 *Theory of Knowledge*, 3rd edition, p. 76; emphasis omitted.

31 A similar worry is expressed by Alston in "Internalism and Externalism in Epistemology," pp. 221–2.

32 See Amos Tversky and Daniel Kahneman, "Judgment under Uncertainty: Heuristics and Biases," in Kahneman, P. Slovic, and

Tversky, eds, *Judgment under Uncertainty* (New York: Cambridge, 1982), pp. 3–20; and Tversky and Kahneman, "Extensional versus Intuitive Reasoning: The Conjunction Fallacy in Probability Judgment," *Psychological Review*, xci (1983), pp. 293–315.

33 It is not really clear, moreover, why logical or probabilistic facts intuitively count as "internal" facts. They certainly are not internal in the same sense in which mental states are internal. This is an additional problem about the contours of internalism.

34 *Theory of Knowledge*, 3rd edition, p. 76.

35 See Johnson and Carol Raye, "Reality Monitoring," *Psychological Review*, lxxxviii (1981), pp. 67–85; and Johnson, Mary Foley, Aurora Suengas, and Raye, "Phenomenal Characteristics of Memories for Perceived and Imagined Autobiographical Events," *Journal of Experimental Psychology: General*, cxvii (1988), pp. 371–6.

36 Memory errors are not confined, of course, to confusions of actual with imagined events. There are also errors that arise from confusing, or blending, two actual events. But this research of Johnson's focuses on the actual/nonactual (or perceived versus imagined) problem.

37 They also recognize that people can compare a target memory with memories of contextually related events to assess the target's veridicality. This kind of "coherence" factor is a stock-in-trade of epistemology, however, and hence not a good example of the distinctive contributions psychology can make to this subject. I therefore pass over it.

CHAPTER 30

Externalism and Skepticism

Richard Fumerton

After examining a number of different controversies associated with the internalism/externalism debates in epistemology, I argued that two of the most fundamental issues separating internalists and externalists are the question of whether fundamental epistemic concepts can be "naturalized" and the question of whether one takes access to inferential connections to be a necessary condition for inferential justification. We introduced the labels "inferential internalism" and "inferential externalism" to refer to the two positions one might take on this last question.

In this chapter I am primarily interested in exploring the ways in which an externalist might respond to the classic skeptical arguments sketched previously. For convenience I focus primarily on reliabilism, but almost all of what I say will apply mutatis mutandis to other paradigmatic externalists. My first aim is simply to be clear about the framework within which a foundationalist version of externalism will face the skeptical challenge. I want to understand where externalism leaves the philosopher when it comes to approaching normative epistemological issues in general, and these issues as they relate to skepticism in particular. But, as I implied earlier, I think the very examination of the way in which

the philosophical externalist should approach skepticism may reveal the fundamental weakness of externalism as a metaepistemological account of concepts fundamental to *philosophical* concern with epistemology.

Externalism, Foundationalism, and the Traditional Skeptical Argument

Previously, I have tried to characterize what I take to be the fundamental structure of skeptical arguments. The skepticism I am most interested in is skepticism with respect to justified or rational belief. Furthermore, we are concerned, in the first place, with "local" rather than "global" skepticism. The skeptics we considered put forth arguments designed to establish that we have no justified beliefs with respect to certain *classes* of propositions. They offered skeptical arguments that concluded that we have no reason to believe propositions about the physical world, the past, other minds, the future, and so on. The traditional skeptic virtually always presupposed some version of foundationalism, presupposed that we do have noninferentially justified belief in at least some propositions. The presupposition was seldom stated explicitly, but one cannot read any of the important historical figures concerned with either advancing or refuting skepticism without reaching the conclusion that they took some propositions to be epistemically unproblematic, where

Originally published in R. Fumerton, *Metaepistemology and Skepticism* (Lanham, MD: Rowman and Littlefield, 1995), pp. 159–81.

their unproblematic character seemed to stem from the fact that one did not need to *infer* their truth from any other propositions believed. In both the rationalist and the empiricist tradition, at least some propositions about the content of one's current mental states were taken to have this unproblematic, noninferential character.

The first step, then, in advancing an argument for skepticism with respect to some kind of proposition is to establish that our access to the relevant truth is at best *indirect*. In the terminology we have developed, the skeptic begins by denying that we have noninferential knowledge, or noninferentially justified belief in the relevant sort of proposition. Thus, for example, skeptics with respect to the physical world deny that we have noninferential "direct" access to physical objects. The standard claim is that if we have justification for believing anything about the physical world, that justification reduces to what we can legitimately *infer* about the physical world from what we know about the character of our past and present sensations. The skeptic about the past claims that we have no direct – that is, noninferential – knowledge of the past. What we know or reasonably believe about the past is restricted to what we can legitimately infer about past events from what we know about the present state of our minds.

One of the primary advantages that paradigmatic externalist accounts have in the battle against skepticism is the ease with which they can deny the crucial first premise of skeptical arguments. The class of noninferentially justified beliefs is likely to be much larger given an externalist epistemology. Notice that I say "likely" to be much larger. As far as I can see, virtually all externalist epistemologies entail that it is a purely contingent question as to which beliefs are justified noninferentially and which are not. On the reliabilist's view, for example, the question of whether or not one is noninferentially justified in believing at least some propositions about the physical world is a question about the nature of the processes that yield beliefs about the physical world and the nature of their "input." If we have been programmed through evolution to *react* to sensory stimuli with certain representations of the world, and we have been lucky enough to have "effective" programming, then we will have noninferentially justified beliefs about the physical world. If Nozick is right and our beliefs track facts

about the physical world around us, and this tracking does not involve inference from other propositions, we will again have noninferentially justified beliefs about the physical world. If our beliefs about the physical world are acting like that reliable thermometer that Armstrong uses as his model for direct knowledge, if we are accurately registering the physical world around us with the appropriate representations, then again we have noninferential, direct knowledge of that world. Whether or not we have such noninferential justification for believing propositions describing the physical world, on any of these externalist ways of understanding noninferential justification, is a purely *contingent* matter.

That it is a contingent fact is not in itself surprising, nor is it a consequence peculiar to externalist epistemologies. It is certainly a contingent fact on the acquaintance theory that I am acquainted with the fact that I am in pain. It is a contingent fact that I am in pain and so obviously contingent that I am acquainted with it. It is less obvious on traditional foundationalisms that it is a contingent fact that we are *not* acquainted with certain facts. It might seem, for example, that one *could not* be acquainted with facts about the distant past, the future, or even the physical world if it is understood as a construct out of actual or possible experience or as the cause of certain actual and possible experience.[1] But even here it is difficult to claim that it is necessarily the case that conscious minds are not acquainted with such facts. There may be no God, but it is not obvious that the concept of a consciousness far greater than ours is unintelligible. If the concept of a specious present makes sense, such a consciousness may have the capacity to directly apprehend a much greater expanse of time than can finite minds. In any event, it is not *clear* that the class of facts with which *we* can be acquainted exhausts the facts with which all possible consciousness can be acquainted.

But even if the scope of noninferentially justified belief is contingent on both internalist and externalist versions of foundationalism, there are crucial differences. On traditional (internalist) versions of foundationalism, philosophers are at least in a position to address reasonably the question of the content of noninferentially justified belief. The philosopher is *competent*, at least as competent as anyone else, to address the questions of whether or not we have noninferentially justified beliefs in propositions about the physical world, for example. There are two sources of knowledge as to what we are noninferentially justified in believing. One is dialectical argument. The other is acquaintance itself. One can be directly acquainted with the fact that one is directly acquainted with certain facts.

On the classic externalist views, the facts that determine whether one is noninferentially justified in believing a proposition are complex nomological facts. Given paradigm externalism, it is not clear that a philosopher *qua philosopher* is even in a position to speculate intelligently on the question of whether or not we have noninferentially justified belief in any of the propositions under skeptical attack.[2] Because the externalist has reduced the question of what is noninferentially justified to questions about the nature of the causal interaction between stimuli and response, and particularly to the processes of the brain that operate on the stimuli so as to produce the response, the search for noninferential justification would seem to be as much in the purview of the neurophysiologist as the philosopher.[3] In the last two hundred years, the vast majority of philosophers simply have not had the training to do a decent job of investigating the hardware and software of the brain. But without this training, it hardly seems reasonable for philosophers to be speculating as to what is or is not a reliable belief-independent process. To be sure, some contemporary epistemologists are trying to "catch up" on developments in cognitive science and even neurophysiology, but I cannot help worrying that the experts in such fields will quite correctly regard these philosophers as simply dilettantes who, having tired of their a priori discipline, now want to get their hands dirty in the real-life work of science.

Given this possibility, it is ironic that so many philosophers find externalist analyses of epistemic concepts attractive precisely because they seem to capture the prephilosophical intuition that there *is* something direct about our knowledge of the physical world through sensations. Through sheer repetition of the arguments, many philosophers got used to talking about *inferring* the existence of a table from propositions about the character of sensation, or *inferring* propositions about the past from propositions describing present consciousness. But critics have correctly pointed out that if such claims are intended to be phenomenologically accurate descriptions of our epistemic relation to the world, they are hardly credible. Anyone who has tried to draw knows that it is very difficult to distinguish the world as it appears from the world as it is. That there is a conceptual distinction between phenomenological appearance and reality seems obvious. If the difficulty of artistic representation shows that we rarely reflect on appearances (as opposed to reality), it also shows that there is such a thing as appearance. A number of philosophers have argued that the most frequent use of "appears" terminology is not that of describing the phenomenological character of sensation, but rather that of expressing tentative belief.[4] When I say that he appears to be a doctor I am probably only indicating my tentative conclusion that he is a doctor.

But even if we recognize what Chisholm called the "epistemic" use of "appears," there is surely another use of the term that is designed to capture the intrinsic character of sensation. When I say that the people on the street below look like ants, I am not expressing the tentative conclusion that they are ants. Again, as Sellars pointed out, we cannot directly conclude from such examples that the descriptive use of "appears" gives us a "pure" description of experience uncontaminated by reference to the physical world. "Appears" sometimes has what Chisholm called a "comparative" use.[5] To say that X appears F in this sense is to say that X appears the way F things appear under some set of conditions. The people down below look like ants in the sense that they look something like the way ants look when you are relatively close to them under standard conditions. Such complex facts include reference to physical objects and their tendency to appear in certain ways under certain conditions, and consequently are implausible candidates for objects of direct acquaintance. But Sellars aside, it is difficult to avoid the conclusion that the comparative use of "appears" virtually presupposes some other way of understanding the phenomenological character of appearance. There is some way that things appear and it is that way of appearing that the artist must think about in trying to represent realistically some aspect of the world. But whether or not this "noncomparative"[6] use of appears exists and is intelligible, it does not alter the phenomenological fact that we do seldom, if ever, consciously infer propositions about the physical world from propositions describing the character of sensation.

We also seldom consciously infer propositions about the past from anything we might call a memory "experience." The very existence of memory "experience" is far from obvious. And it is relatively seldom that our commonplace expectations about the future are formed as a result of careful consideration of premises describing past correlations of properties or states of affairs. When I expect my next drink of water to quench my thirst instead of killing me, I do *not* first consider past instances of water quenching thirst. It is useful to reflect carefully on this fact, for even most externalists will view this kind of knowledge as involving inductive *inference*. We must, therefore, be cautious in reaching conclusions about the role of phenomenology in determining whether a *justification* is inferential or not. We must distinguish questions about the causal origin of a belief from questions about the justification available for a belief.

We must also distinguish between occurrent and dispositional belief. It may be that I have all sorts of dispositional beliefs that are causally sustaining my beliefs when I am completely unaware of the causal role these dispositional beliefs play. In introducing this discussion I suggested that it was ironic that externalists would find attractive the fact that their externalism can accommodate the apparent phenomenological fact that far fewer commonsense beliefs involve inference than are postulated by traditional foundationalism. The irony is that phenomenology should have no particular role to play for the externalist in reaching conclusions about what is or is not inferentially justified. According to the externalist, the epistemic status of a belief is a function of the nomological relations that belief has to various features of the world. These nomological facts are complex and are typically not the kinds of facts that have traditionally been thought to be under the purview of phenomenology. I suppose an externalist can define some belief-producing process as "phenomenological." But again, even if one can describe such a process, it will be a contingent question as to what beliefs such a process might justify, a contingent question that goes far beyond

the competency of most philosophers (and certainly most phenomenologists) to answer.

But perhaps I am being unfair in suggesting that the philosopher who is an externalist in epistemology has no particular *credentials* qualifying him to assess the question of whether the skeptic is right or wrong in denying the availability of noninferential justification for beliefs under skeptical attack. The skeptics, after all, had arguments in support of their conclusion that we have no non-inferentially justified beliefs in propositions about the physical world, the past, the future, other minds, and so on. The externalists can at least refute those arguments based on their a priori reasonings about the correct metaepistemological position. The most common way of supporting the conclusion that we do not have noninferentially justified beliefs about the physical world is to point out that we can imagine someone having the very best justification possible for believing that there is a table, say, before him, when the table is not in fact there. A person who is vividly hallucinating a table can have just as good reason to think that the table exists as you do. But we can easily suppose that there is no table present before the victim of hallucination. If *direct* epistemic access to the table is anything like a real relation, then it cannot be present when the table is not present. But if the victim of hallucination does not have direct access to the table, and the victim of hallucination has the same kind of justification you have for thinking that the table exists (when you take yourself to be standing before a table in broad daylight), then you do not have direct access to the table either.

The reliabilist will deny the association between noninferential justification and direct access to the table. To have a noninferentially justified belief about the table's existence is to have a belief about the table produced by an unconditionally reliable belief-independent process. The victim of hallucination has (or at least might have) a belief in the table's existence produced by an unconditionally reliable belief-independent process. It depends in part on how we define the relevant process. But if we think of the stimuli as something like sensations (which the hallucinator has), and the process as what goes on in the brain when sensation is assimilated and turned into representation, there is no reason why someone who is hallucinating cannot satisfy the conditions for having a noninferentially justified belief, assuming of course that the process in question really is unconditionally reliable. The reliabilist's metaepistemology allows at least a conditional response to the skeptic's attack. More precisely, the reliabilist can point out that a reliabilist metaepistemology entails that the skeptic's conclusion about the noninferential character of belief about the physical world does not follow. And, of course, everything the reliabilist says about the physical world applies to the past, other minds, and even the future. The reliabilist probably will not claim that beliefs about the future are noninferentially justified, but he should claim that there is no reason in principle why they could not be, and should continue to assert that the skeptic has no argument for the conclusion that we have no direct, that is, noninferentially justified, beliefs about the future.

Interestingly, not all externalists will reject the skeptic's claim about noninferential justification in the same way. Consider again the reliabilist's response to the argument from hallucination as a way of establishing that we have no noninferentially justified beliefs about the physical world. The crucial move for the reliabilist was to deny that we are forced to regard the hallucinatory situation as one in which the subject lacked a noninferentially justified belief. A causal theorist about direct knowledge, like Armstrong, might admit that in hallucinatory experience we lack noninferential knowledge, but continue to assert that in veridical experience we have such knowledge. This externalist is more likely to deny the skeptic's presupposition that we should say the same thing about the nature of the justification available to the victim of vivid hallucination and the person who has *qualitatively* indistinguishable veridical experiences. You will recall that there is one sense of "internalism" according to which the internalist holds that the conditions sufficient for justification are always states internal to the subject. If sensations are not themselves relations (a controversial claim, to be sure), and the sensory evidence of S and R is indistinguishable, and there is nothing else "inside their minds" to distinguish their epistemic state, then this internalist will insist that if the one has a certain kind of justification for believing something, then so does the other.

But a causal theorist thinks that the relevant question that determines the nature of the justification available for a belief involves the *origin* of the belief. The internal, that is, nonrelational, states of S and R can be qualitatively indistinguishable, but S's internal states can result in S's having a noninferentially justified belief by virtue of their being *produced* in the appropriate way. R's internal states might bring about the very same belief, but because they were not caused by the appropriate facts they will not result in the having of a noninferentially justified belief. In short, the hallucinator's belief cannot be traced via sensation back to the fact about the world that would make the belief true. The person lucky enough to have veridical experience typically has a belief that can be traced back to the fact that makes the belief true. This is a perfectly clear distinction, and there is nothing to prevent an epistemologist from arguing that this just is the distinction that determines whether or not someone has a justified or rational belief. Furthermore, the question of whether the justification is inferential has only to do with the kinds of links in the causal chain leading to the relevant belief. If the causal connection goes directly from some fact about the physical world, to the occurrence of sensory states, to representations about the physical world, then there are no other *beliefs* that crucially enter the story. The justification that results will be justification that does not logically depend on the having of other justified beliefs.[7] It will be noninferential justification. So again, we can see how an externalist metaepistemology can put one in a position to claim that the skeptic has not established the crucial premise concerning the inferential character of our belief in the propositions under skeptical attack.

Even if externalism allows one to point out that the skeptic has not established the crucial first premise of the argument, it does not follow, of course, that the externalist has given any positive reason to suppose that the skeptic is wrong in claiming that the propositions under skeptical attack are not the objects of noninferentially justified belief. Both skeptics and nonskeptics play on a level playing field. There is no "burden of proof" when it comes to fundamental issues in epistemology. If the philosopher wants to claim that we have noninferentially justified belief in certain propositions, then the philosopher can give us good reasons to think that such justification exists. The skeptic who wishes to deny that we have such justification can give us good reasons to think that it does not exist. The skeptic, however, also has a fall-back position. Without arguing that we have no noninferentially justified beliefs in propositions about the physical world, the past, other minds, and the future, the skeptic can move "up" a level and deny that we have any good reason to believe that we have noninferential justification for these beliefs. A strong access internalist can move from the proposition that we have no justification for believing that we have a non-inferentially justified belief that P to the conclusion that we do not have a noninferentially justified belief that P. But the externalist rejects just such an inference. Even if we abandon strong access internalism, however, we might find skepticism that maintains that we have no justification for believing that we have a justified belief that P just as threatening as skepticism that concludes that we are unjustified in believing P. Before we consider the question of whether skepticism will arise at the next level up within an externalist epistemology, let us briefly discuss the externalist approach to normative issues involving inferential justification.

Skepticism, Externalism, and Inferential Justification

Most of the general observations made about the externalist's response to skeptical challenges concerning the class of noninferentially justified beliefs will apply as well to inferential justification. If the skeptic were to succeed in convincing the externalist that we are not noninferentially justified in believing propositions about the physical world, for example, the externalist presumably would argue that such beliefs are inferentially justified. The reliabilist, for example, would argue that if our beliefs about the external world result from input that includes beliefs about the internal and external conditions of perceiving, or even beliefs about the qualitative character of sensation, the relevant belief-dependent processes are conditionally reliable and therefore produce (inferentially) justified beliefs, *provided that the input beliefs are themselves justified*. The proviso is crucial, of course, and reminds us that to establish that first-level skepticism is false, the externalist who concedes that the justification is

inferential in character must establish the existence of at least one unconditionally reliable process and at least one conditionally reliable process.

We noted in discussing the externalist's views about noninferentially justified belief that externalism has a potentially significant advantage in dealing with skepticism precisely because there are no restrictions on how large the class of non-inferentially justified beliefs might be. As I indicated, there is no a priori reason for the externalist to deny even that we have noninferentially justified beliefs about the past and the future. Evolution might have taken care of us rather well when it comes to reaching true conclusions about the world, and evolution might have accomplished this end without burdening our brains with too many conditionally reliable belief-forming processes. Nozick's tracking relations can in principle hold between any fact and any belief, and the tracking relations *need* not involve any intermediate beliefs.

Just as the externalist's class of noninferentially justified beliefs can be very large in comparison to those recognized by traditional foundationalists, so the class of inferences recognized as legitimate by the externalist can be equally large. Consider again the reliabilist's position. There are no a priori restrictions on how many different kinds of conditionally reliable belief-dependent processes there might be. Valid deductive inference is presumably the paradigm of a conditionally reliable belief-dependent process. Classical enumerative induction may satisfy the requirements as well, provided that we find some suitably restricted characterization of the inductive "process" that succeeds in denoting and that takes care of grue/green riddles of induction.[8] I suspect most externalists will be reluctant to include perceptual beliefs among the beliefs produced by belief-dependent processes, but there is no reason why a reliabilist could not be a sense-datum theorist or an appearing theorist who holds that we do have at least dispositional beliefs about the qualitative character of sensation and who further holds that such beliefs are processed by conditionally reliable belief-dependent processes that churn out commonsense beliefs about the physical world. In short, take any kind of inference that people actually make and the reliabilist could hold that it involves a conditionally reliable belief-dependent process. All one needs to do is to formulate a description of the process that takes the beliefs one relies on as premises (the input) and produces the beliefs that constitute the conclusion (the output). The description will have to be such that we succeed in picking out a *kind* of process that does play the causal role described, but it will not need to involve any reference to the "hardware" of the brain. Indeed, we can try to *denote* the relevant process by directly referring only to the kind of premises and conclusion with which it is associated. Roughly, the idea is that we can try to denote a belief-dependent process *X*, for example, using the description "the process (whatever it is) that takes premises like these and churns out conclusions like this." Of course, such a description is probably too vague to do the trick. The locution "like these" can hardly be said to characterize precisely enough a class of premises. One would need to characterize the relevant points of similarity to have a well-defined class of premises which could then enter into the definite description denoting the process that takes them as input.

If we consider any argument someone actually makes, there will be indefinitely many classes of propositions to which the premises and the conclusion belong, and that will enable us to formulate any number of different descriptions of belief-forming processes. This is *not* a difficulty for the reliabilist, for as long as we have a locution that succeeds in denoting a process playing a causal role, we can use conditionals to define the conditions under which it is or is not conditionally reliable. The fact that a single inference might be subsumed under a number of different reliable belief-dependent processes is hardly a problem. If the inference can be subsumed under the description of both a reliable and an unreliable process, the crucial question will be which process is causally determining the production of a belief. Thus, if someone trustworthy tells me today that it rained in New York, I can describe this as a case of processing testimony to reach a conclusion about the truth of what is testified to, or I can describe it as a case of taking a statement I hear involving the name "New York" and believing all of the noun clauses containing that name. The former, let us suppose, is a reliable belief-dependent process, whereas the latter is not. But you recall that in formulating descriptions of processes appealing to kinds of premises and conclusions, we are

merely *hoping* to denote some process (presumably a complex brain process) that does take input and causally produce output beliefs. It does not follow, of course, that every definite description we formulate will succeed in denoting. In the hypothetical situation we are discussing, it may be that there is no programming in the brain that takes the "New York" input and processes it in the way described. If there is nothing denoted by the description playing the relevant causal role, then we do not need to worry about the fact that such a process, *if used*, would be unreliable.

To emphasize the point made earlier, according to externalism there are indefinitely many candidates for legitimate inferential processes. There are no a priori restrictions on how many conditionally reliable belief-dependent processes might be operating in normal human beings. There are no a priori restrictions on how many belief-dependent tracking relations might exist between beliefs and the facts that they track. Furthermore, just as in the case of noninferential justification, the question of which inferential processes generate justified beliefs for the externalist will be a purely contingent fact of a sort inaccessible to most philosophers *qua* philosophers. The existence of conditionally reliable processes, tracking relations, and the like is something that could be discovered only as a result of empirical investigation into causal relations. Philosophers are not trained to engage in this sort of empirical investigation.

Externalism, Normative Epistemology, and the Limits of Philosophy

Based on the observations above, I argue that if externalist metaepistemologies are correct, then normative epistemology is an inappropriate subject matter for philosophy. Philosophers as they are presently trained have no special *philosophical* expertise enabling them to reach conclusions about which beliefs are or are not justified. Since the classic issues of skepticism fall under normative epistemology, it follows that if externalism were correct, philosophers should simply stop addressing the questions raised by the skeptic. The complex causal conditions that determine the presence or absence of justification for a belief are the subject matter of empirical investigations that would take the philosopher out of the easy chair and into the laboratory.

The realization that a good part of the history of epistemology becomes irrelevant to contemporary philosophy if we become metaepistemological externalists might cause a good many philosophers to reconsider externalism. I have always found the skeptical challenge to be fascinating and it has always seemed to me that I can address the relevant issues from my armchair (or my bed, depending on how lazy I happen to feel on a given day). If I had wanted to go mucking around in the brain trying to figure out the causal mechanisms that hook up various stimuli with belief, I would have gone into neurophysiology.

To rely on the philosopher's interest in skepticism and penchant for armchair philosophy as a rhetorical device to convert potential externalists, however, might be viewed as a new low in the art of philosophical persuasion. The mere fact that philosophers have been preoccupied with a certain sort of question does not mean that they were qualified to answer it. There are all kinds of perfectly respectable candidates for misguided philosophical investigations. Many philosophers, for example, have taken the question of whether every event has a cause to be a deep metaphysical issue in philosophy. As a good Humean, I would be the first to argue that it is a purely contingent question and if one wants to know the answer to it, one should not ask a philosopher.

Analogously, the fact that philosophers have been preoccupied with the skeptical challenge for literally thousands of years should not stop contemporary epistemologists from entertaining the thesis that the appropriate subject matter of epistemology ends with metaepistemology. After the metaepistemological analysis is complete, the externalist might argue, the only way to answer normative questions in epistemology is to engage in the kind of empirical investigation that contemporary philosophers have not been trained *by philosophy* to do.

In reaching this conclusion I should be careful to admit that the philosophical externalist can, of course, embed normative epistemological conclusions in the consequents of conditional assertions. One can talk about what one would be justified in believing were certain conditions to obtain. But these conditionals are still part of metaepistemology. Indeed, such conditionals are merely a way of illustrating the consequences of metaepistemological positions as they apply to particular hypothetical situations. A Nozick, for example, can discuss what one would or would not know about the external world *if* a tracking analysis of knowledge were correct and *if* our beliefs about the physical world track the facts that would make them true. Nozick's analysis of knowledge also has the interesting feature that we can apparently determine a priori that we do *not* know certain things, for example, that we do not know that there is no evil demon deceiving us. But there will be no positive normative claim with respect to empirical knowledge that Nozick is particularly competent to make *qua philosopher*. As we shall see in a moment, externalism does not prevent a philosopher from reaching rational conclusions about what one is justified in believing. My conclusion is only that a philosopher's philosophical expertise is nothing that helps in reaching such conclusions. To illustrate this claim more clearly, let us turn to the question of whether externalist metaepistemologies suggest that one should be a skeptic about whether or not one has justified belief.

Second-Level Skepticism and the Fundamental Problem with Externalism

It is tempting to think that externalist analyses of justified or rational belief and knowledge simply remove one *level* the traditional problems of skepticism. When one reads the well-known externalists, one is surely inclined to wonder why they are so sanguine about their supposition that our commensense beliefs are, for the most part, justified, if not knowledge. When Nozick, for example, stresses that interesting feature of his account allowing us to conclude consistently that we know that we see the table even though we do not know that there is no demon deceiving us, we must surely wonder *why* he is so confident that the subjunctives that on his view are sufficient for knowledge are true. Perception, memory, and induction *may* be reliable processes in Goldman's sense, and thus given his metaepistemological position we *may* be justified in having the beliefs they produce, but, the skeptic can argue, we have no reason to believe that these processes *are* reliable, and thus, even if we accept reliabilism, we have no reason to conclude that the beliefs they produce are justified.

In the previous section I emphasized that if externalism is true then philosophers *qua philosophers* may not be particularly competent to answer normative questions in epistemology. I did *not* assert that if externalism is true we have no reason to believe that we have justified belief in commonsense truths about the world around us. According to externalist epistemologies, it is a purely contingent question as to what kinds of beliefs are justified. The existence of justified beliefs depends on nomological features of the world – facts about the reliability of belief-producing processes, the existence of tracking relations, causal connections between facts and beliefs, and the like. There are no a priori restrictions on what one might be justified in believing. But it *follows* from this that there are also *no* a priori restrictions on second-level knowledge or justified belief. It will also be a purely contingent question as to whether we have knowledge of knowledge or justified beliefs about justified beliefs. If we accept the externalist's metaepistemological views, it *may* be true that not only do we know what we think we know, but we also know that we know these things. Similarly, we may not only have all the justified beliefs we think we have, but we might also be justified in believing that we have these justified beliefs. The processes that yield beliefs about reliable processes may themselves be reliable. The beliefs about the truth of the subjunctives that Nozick uses to define first-level knowledge might themselves be embedded in true subjunctive conditionals that, *given the metaepistemological view*, are sufficient for second-level knowledge. My belief that my belief that *P* tracks the fact that *P* might track the fact that my belief that *P* tracks the fact that *P*. And there is no greater problem in principle when we move up levels. A reliable process might produce a belief that a reliable process produced the belief that my belief that *P* was produced by a reliable process. There might be a tracking relation tracking the tracking relation that tracks the fact that my belief that *P* tracks the fact that *P*. To be sure, the sentences describing the conditions for higher levels of metajustification might look more like tongue-twisters than metaepistemological analyses but, as ugly as they are, they are perfectly intelligible, and there is no a priori reason why the conditions required for higher-level justified belief and knowledge might not be satisfied.

It is also important to note that according to the externalist, in order to be justified in believing that I have a justified belief that *P*, I need not know anything about the *details* of the nomological connections sufficient for knowledge. Consider again reliabilism. In order to be justified in believing that my belief that *P* is produced by a reliable process, I do not need to know the physiological details of the brain states linking stimuli and belief. I would need to believe that there is *some* process producing the belief and I would need to believe that the process is reliable, but I would not need to know very much about what that process is. As I indicated earlier, one can denote the processes that produce beliefs using definite descriptions that refer directly only to the kinds of premises and conclusions that are linked by the process. Of course, the definite descriptions might fail to denote, and the beliefs in propositions expressed using such definite descriptions will either be false or meaningless (depending on what one does with the truth value of statements containing definite descriptions that fail to denote). But the descriptions might be successful, and in any event the belief that there is a reliable process taking stimuli *S* and resulting in belief *P* might itself be produced by a reliable process.

All this talk about what would in principle be possible given an externalist metaepistemology is fine, the skeptic might argue. But *how* exactly would one justify one's belief that, say, perception and memory are reliable processes? The rather startling and, I think, disconcerting answer is that *if* reliabilism is true, and *if* perception happens to be reliable, we could *perceive* various facts about our sense organs and the way in which they respond to the external world. Again, *if* reliabilism is true, and *if* memory is reliable, we could use memory, in part, to justify our belief that memory is reliable. You want a solution to the problem of induction? There is potentially no difficulty for the externalist. If reliabilism is true, and if inductive inference is a conditionally reliable belief-dependent process, then we can inductively justify the reliability of inductive inference. Our inductive justification for the reliability of inductive inference might itself be reliable, and if it is, that will give us second-level justification that our inductive conclusions are justified. A solution to the problem of induction will be important because with induction giving us inferentially justified conclusions, we can use inductive inference with the deliverances of perception and memory to justify our belief that those processes are reliable. I can remember, for example, that I remembered putting my keys on the desk and I can remember the keys being on the desk. If memory is an unconditionally reliable belief-independent process, then both my belief that I remembered putting the keys on the desk and my belief that I put the keys on the desk will be justified. I now have a premise that can be used as part of an inductive justification for memory being reliable. The more occasions on which I can remember memory being reliable, the stronger my inductive argument will be for the general reliability of memory.

The skeptic could not figure out how to get from sensations to the physical world. Assume that perception is itself a belief-independent, unconditionally reliable process. Assume also that whatever perception involves, its specification involves reference to sensation, and assume further that we have "introspective" access to sensation. Introspective access might itself be another belief-independent, unconditionally reliable process. Given these suppositions, if reliabilism is true, then introspection can give us justified beliefs that we are perceiving, and perception can give us justified beliefs that physical objects are present. The two reliable processes together can furnish a premise that, when combined with others generated in a similar fashion, gives us inductive justification for believing that perception is reliable. So if both introspection and perception happen to be reliable, there seems to be no great obstacle to obtaining justified belief that they are reliable. Second-level justified belief is not much more difficult to get than first-level justified belief.

How successful *inductive* reasoning will be in answering second-level skeptical questions depends very much on how the externalist resolves some of the controversies discussed elsewhere, specifically on how narrowly the relevant belief-forming processes are characterized. I have pointed out that as long as reliability is not defined in terms of actual frequencies, there is no *conceptual* difficulty in a reliabilist positing the existence

of very narrowly defined, reliable belief-forming processes that have only a few, or even no, instances. Although there is no conceptual difficulty in supposing that there are such processes, it obviously creates problems for any *inductive* justification for believing that they exist and are reliable. As should be clear by now, however, the unavailability of inductive justification in no way implies that there is not some *other* reliable belief-forming process that will still yield second-level knowledge or justified belief.

This reminds us, of course, of Quine's injunction to naturalize epistemology.[9] Quine suggested that we give ourselves full access to the deliverances of science when it comes to understanding how we have knowledge of the world around us. Contemporary externalists have simply given us more detailed metaepistemological views which allow us to rationalize following the injunction to naturalize epistemology. If the mere reliability of a process, for example, is sufficient to give us justified belief, then *if* that process is reliable we can use it to get justified belief wherever and whenever we like.

All of this will, of course, drive the skeptic crazy. You cannot *use* perception to justify the reliability of perception! You cannot *use* memory to justify the reliability of memory! You cannot *use* induction to justify the reliability of induction! Such attempts to respond to the skeptic's concerns involve blatant, indeed pathetic, circularity. Frankly, this does seem right to *me* and I hope it seems right to *you*, but *if* it does, then I suggest that you have a powerful reason to conclude that externalism is false. I suggest that, ironically, the very ease with which externalists can deal with the skeptical challenge at the next level betrays the ultimate implausibility of externalism as an attempt to explicate concepts that are of *philosophical* interest. If a philosopher starts wondering about the reliability of astrological inference, the philosopher will not allow the astrologer to read in the stars the reliability of astrology. Even if astrological inferences happen to be reliable, the astrologer is missing the point of a *philosophical* inquiry into the justifiability of astrological inference if the inquiry is answered using the techniques of astrology. The problem is perhaps most acute if one thinks about first-person philosophical reflection about justification. If I really am interested in knowing whether astrological inference is legitimate, if I have the kind of philosophical curiosity that leads me to raise this question in the first place, I will not for a moment suppose that further use of astrology might help me find the answer to my question. Similarly, if as a philosopher I start wondering whether perceptual beliefs are accurate reflections of the way the world really is, I would not dream of using perception to resolve my doubt. Even if there is some sense in which the reliable process of perception might yield justified beliefs about the reliability of perception, the use of perception could never satisfy a *philosophical curiosity* about the legitimacy of perceptual beliefs. When the philosopher wants an answer to the question of whether memory gives us justified beliefs about the past, that answer cannot possibly be provided by memory.

Again, if one raises skeptical concerns understanding fundamental epistemic concepts as the externalist does, then there should be no objection to perceptual justifications of perception, inductive justifications of induction, and reliance on memory to justify the use of memory. If one is understanding epistemic concepts as the reliabilist suggests, for example, then one can have no objection in principle to the use of a process to justify its use. After all, the whole point of inferential externalism is to deny the necessity of having access to the probabilistic relationship between premises and conclusion in order to have an inferentially justified belief. The mere reliability of the process is sufficient to generate justified belief in the conclusion of an argument. There is no conceptual basis for the reliabilist to get cold feet when epistemological questions are raised the next level up. Either reliability alone is sufficient or it is not. If it is, then it is sufficient whether one is talking about justification for believing *P* or justification for believing that one has a justified belief that *P*.

It is both interesting and illuminating that even many access externalists seem to worry about the possibility of second-level justification in ways that they do not worry about the possibility of first-level justification. Alston explicitly rejects the idea that one needs access to the adequacy of one's grounds for believing *P* in order to be justified in believing *P*. But in *The Reliability of Sense Perception*, he also seems to reject the idea that one can use a "track record" argument (an inductive argument of the sort I sketched above)

to *justify* one's belief that perception and memory are reliable. Such arguments will inevitably presuppose the adequacy of the very grounds whose adequacy is at issue. In doing so the argument will be viciously circular.

But what exactly is Alston's complaint? To justify my belief that perception or memory is reliable, I need only find a good argument whose premises I justifiably accept and whose premises support the conclusion that these ways of forming beliefs are reliable. But if perception and memory are reliable *and there is no requirement of access to adequacy of grounds* in order for a belief to be justified, what is the problem? Why is it harder to justify my belief that my perceptual beliefs are justified than it is to have justified beliefs based on perception?

Much of the time Alston seems to admit everything I have just said, but the circular nature of the available arguments still clearly bothers him:

> *if sense perception is reliable* [Alston's emphasis], a track record argument will suffice to show that it is. Epistemic circularity does not in and of itself disqualify the argument. But even granting that point, the argument will not do its job unless we *are* justified in accepting its premises; and this is the case only if sense perception is in fact reliable.
> … But when we ask whether one or another source of belief is reliable, we are interested in *discriminating* those that can reasonably be trusted from those that cannot. Hence merely showing that if a given source is reliable it can be shown by its record to be reliable, does nothing to indicate that the source belongs with the sheep rather than with the goats. (p. 17)

But again, *as an externalist*, what does Alston want? He obviously thinks that in some sense all we could ever really conclude is that we *might* have justification for thinking that we have justified beliefs based on perception. And the contextual implication of this claim is that we also *might not*. But what "might" is this? Clearly, it is intended to refer to *epistemic* possibility. Let us say that *P* is epistemically possible for S when *P* is consistent with everything that S knows. Is it epistemically possible for us that perception is unreliable? Not if perception is reliable, because we will have inductive knowledge that it is not unreliable. But you are still just asserting a conditional, Alston will complain. For all we know, it is possible that perception is unreliable. But this claim about epistemic possibility is precisely the claim that Alston, as an externalist, has no business making. Can we *discriminate* (his word) between reliable and unreliable fundamental sources of belief? As an externalist he has no reason to deny that we can and do discriminate between reliable and unreliable processes (using, of course, reliable processes). Alston clearly wants to assert (and assert justifiably) a conclusion about epistemic possibility. But the concept of epistemic possibility he wants to apply at the second level is not one that can be understood within the framework of the externalism he embraces.

I agree, of course, with Alston's conclusion that one cannot use perception to justify one's belief that perception is reliable and memory to justify one's belief that memory is reliable. But that is only because the externalist is wrong in characterizing the concept of justification that even externalists are often interested in when they move up levels and start worrying about whether they can justify their belief that their beliefs are justified. The epistemic concept of discrimination that Alston invokes in the passage I quoted is precisely the concept that is at odds with his own attempt to defend an externalist understanding of epistemic concepts.

The fundamental objection to externalism can be easily summarized. If we understand epistemic concepts as the externalists suggest we do, then there would be no objection in principle to using perception to justify reliance on perception, memory to justify reliance on memory, and induction to justify reliance on induction. But there is no philosophically interesting concept of justification or knowledge that would allow us to use a kind of reasoning to justify the legitimacy of using that reasoning. Therefore, the externalist has failed to analyze a philosophically interesting concept of justification or knowledge.

The objection is by no means decisive. Obviously, many externalists will bite the bullet and happily embrace Quine's recommendation to naturalize epistemology. If the argument convinces anyone, it will be those who were initially inclined to suppose that externalism will inevitably encounter skepticism at the next level up. Maybe we have knowledge or justified belief as the externalist understands these concepts, some would argue, but we would never be in a position to know that we have knowledge or justified belief if the externalist is right. The only reason I can see for granting the first possibility but denying the second is that one is implicitly abandoning an externalist analysis of epistemic concepts as one moves to questions about knowledge or justification at the next level. But if when one gets philosophically "serious" one abandons the externalist's understanding of epistemic concepts, then, for philosophical purposes, one should not concede the externalist's understanding of epistemic concepts at the first level. Once you concede that according to the externalist we might have knowledge or justified belief about the past and the external world, you have also implicitly conceded that we might have knowledge that we have such knowledge, justified belief that we have such justified belief. And we might also have knowledge that we have knowledge that we have knowledge, and have justified beliefs that we have justified beliefs that we have justified beliefs. It seems to many of us that the externalist is simply missing the point of the philosophical inquiry when externalist analyses of epistemic concepts continue to be presupposed as the skeptical challenge is repeated at the metalevels. But the only explanation for this is that the externalist analysis of epistemic concepts never was adequate to a philosophical understanding of epistemic concepts.

Notes

1 For a detailed defense of this last view, see Fumerton, *Metaphysical and Epistemological Problems of Perception* (Lincoln, NE: University of Nebraska Press, 1985).

2 I stress "qua philosopher" for there is a real danger that I will be misunderstood on this point. Later in this chapter I argue that externalism is perfectly compatible with philosophers (and anyone else) having justified beliefs about whether or not they have justified beliefs. It will not, however, be their philosophical competence that yields such justification.

3 As I shall argue shortly, this claim might be misleading. In one sense the detailed character of belief-forming processes would be best discovered by neurophysiologists. But there is another sense in which anyone can form beliefs about such processes, even without any detailed knowledge of how the brain works.

4 See Wilfrid Sellars, *Science Perception and Reality* (London: Routledge and Kegan Paul, 1963), pp. 146–7.

5 Roderick M. Chisholm, *Perceiving* (Ithaca, NY: Cornell University Press, 1957), p. 49.

6 Again the terminology and the distinction is introduced by Chisholm in ibid., pp. 50–3.

7 It should go without saying that there may be causally necessary conditions for the existence of such non-inferential justification having to do with the capacity to form other beliefs. The dependency that concerns us, however, is logical. Justification is noninferential when no other belief is a *constituent* of the justification.

8 The allusion is, of course, to the problem discussed in Nelson Goodman, *Fact, Fiction and Forecast* (Indianapolis: Bobbs-Merrill, 1955), ch. 3.

9 W. V. Quine, *Ontological Relativity and Other Essays* (New York: Columbia University Press, 1969), ch. 3.

CHAPTER 31

Internalism Defended

Richard Feldman
and Earl Conee

Internalism in epistemology has been getting bad press lately. Externalism is ascendant, partly because insurmountable problems for internalism are supposed to have been identified.[1] We oppose this trend. In our view the purported problems pose no serious threat, and a convincing argument for internalism is untouched by the recent criticism.

Our main goal here is to refute objections to internalism. We begin by offering what we think is the best way to understand the distinction between internalism and externalism. We then present a new argument for internalism. This frees internalism from what we regard as suspect deontological underpinnings. Finally, we reply to what we take to be the most significant objections to internalism.

I.   What is Internalism?

Internalism and externalism are views about which states, events, and conditions can contribute to epistemic justification – the sort of justification that, in sufficient strength, is a necessary condition for knowledge. Use of the terms "internalist" and "externalist" to classify theories of justification is a recent development, and the terms are routinely

Originally published in *American Philosophical Quarterly* 38, 1 (2001), pp. 1–18.

applied to theories that predate their use. Thus, many proponents of theories of justification have not classified their views as internalist or externalist. The recent literature is, therefore, the best source of information about the nature of the distinction. Here are a few examples of how internalism has been identified. Laurence BonJour writes:

> The most generally accepted account … is that a theory of justification is *internalist* if and only if it requires that all of the factors needed for a belief to be epistemically justified for a given person be *cognitively accessible* to that person, internal to his cognitive perspective.[2]

Robert Audi writes:

> Some examples suggest that justification is grounded entirely in what is internal to the mind, in a sense implying that it is accessible to introspection or reflection by the subject—a view we might call *internalism about justification*.[3]

Alvin Plantinga writes:

> The basic thrust of internalism in epistemology, therefore, is that the properties that confer warrant upon a belief are properties to which the believer has some special sort of epistemic access.[4]

John Pollock writes that:

> Internalism in epistemology is the view that only internal states of the cognizer can be relevant in

determining which of the cognizer's beliefs are justified.[5]

Finally, Ernest Sosa characterizes one version of internalism this way:

> Justification requires only really proper thought on the part of the subject: if a believer has obtained and sustains his belief through wholly appropriate thought, then the believer is justified in so believing – where the appropriateness of the thought is a matter purely internal to the mind of the subject, and not dependent on what lies beyond.[6]

We find two distinct but closely related characterizations of internalism in passages such as these. One characterization uses a notion of access. What we shall call "accessibilism" holds that the epistemic justification of a person's belief is determined by things to which the person has some special sort of access. BonJour calls this access a "suitable awareness."[7] Audi says that the access is through "introspection or reflection." Others say that the access must be "direct."[8] The quotations from Pollock and Sosa suggest a somewhat different account. They suggest that internalism is the view that a person's beliefs are justified only by things that are internal to the person's mental life. We shall call this version of internalism "mentalism."[9] A mentalist theory may assert that justification is determined entirely by occurrent mental factors, or by dispositional ones as well. As long as the things that are said to contribute to justification are in the person's mind, the view qualifies as a version of mentalism.

We think it likely that philosophers have not separated mentalism from accessibilism because they have tacitly assumed that the extensions of the two do not differ in any significant way. They have assumed that the special kind of access on which many internalist theories rely can reach only mental items, and perhaps all mental items, or at least all that might be counted as playing a role in justification.

We think that simplicity and clarity are best served by understanding internalism as mentalism. "Internalism" is a recent technical term. It has been introduced to refer to a variety of theories in epistemology that share some vaguely defined

salient feature. Any definition of the term is to some extent stipulative. Mentalism codifies one standard way in which the word has been used.

Somewhat more precisely, internalism as we characterize it is committed to the following two theses. The first asserts the strong supervenience of epistemic justification on the mental:

> S.　The justificatory status of a person's doxastic attitudes strongly supervenes on the person's occurrent and dispositional mental states, events, and conditions.

The second thesis spells out a principal implication of S:

> M.　If any two possible individuals are exactly alike mentally, then they are exactly alike justificationally, e.g., the same beliefs are justified for them to the same extent.[10]

(M) implies that mental duplicates in different possible worlds have the same attitudes justified for them. This cross world comparison follows from the strong supervenience condition in (S).[11] Externalists characteristically hold that differences in justification can result from contingent non-mental differences, such as differing causal connections or reliability. Theories that appeal to such factors clearly deny (S) and (M). Thus, our way of spelling out the internalism/externalism distinction properly classifies characteristically externalist views.

One advantage of our way of understanding the distinction between internalism and externalism in epistemology is that it closely parallels the counterpart distinction in the philosophy of mind.[12] In the philosophy of mind case, the main idea is to distinguish the view that the contents of attitudes depend entirely on things within a person's own cognitive apparatus from the view that there are factors external to the person that help to determine attitudinal content. Mind internalism is naturally rendered as a supervenience thesis. Roughly, the thesis is that a person's mental content supervenes on the person's "purely internal" states, events, and conditions. The relevant supervenience base cannot be specified as "the mental," as we have done for epistemic internalism, since a person's mental states, events, and conditions are trivially sufficient for the person's attitudes with their specific contents. But the root idea is the same. The mind internalist is trying to exclude such plainly external factors as the environmental causal origins and the social milieu of the person's attitudes. Likewise, the epistemic internalist is principally opposed to the existence of any justification-determining role for plainly external factors such as the general accuracy of the mechanism that produces a given belief or the belief's environmental origin. Mentalism bears this out.

What internalism in epistemology and philosophy of mind have in common is that being in some condition that is of philosophical interest – being epistemically justified in certain attitudes, or having attitudes with certain contents – is settled by what goes on inside cognitive beings. The condition of interest is in this sense an "internal" matter, thus justifying the use of this term. Mentalism obviously captures this feature of internalism. Accessibilism captures it only when conjoined with the further thesis that what is relevantly accessible is always internal to something, presumably the mind.[13]

Thus, one modest asset of mentalism is that it renders readily intelligible the nominal connection of epistemic internalism to mind internalism. A much stronger consideration in favor of mentalism is that it turns out to be entirely defensible, as we shall try to show.

II. A Defense of Internalism

Our argument for internalism focuses on pairs of examples that we take to be representative. Either in one member of the pair someone has a justified belief in a proposition while someone else's belief in that proposition is not justified, or one person's belief is better justified than the other's. We contend that these contrasts are best explained by supposing that internal differences make the epistemic difference. Here are the examples.

Example 1) Bob and Ray are sitting in an air-conditioned hotel lobby reading yesterday's newspaper. Each has read that it will be very warm today and, on that basis, each believes that it is very warm today. Then Bob goes outside and feels the heat. They both continue to believe that it is very warm today. But at this point Bob's belief is better justified.

Comment: Bob's justification for the belief was enhanced by his experience of feeling the heat, and thus undergoing a mental change which, so to speak, "internalized" the actual temperature. Ray had only the forecast to rely on.

Example 2) A novice bird watcher and an expert are together looking for birds. They both get a good look at a bird in a nearby tree. (In order to avoid irrelevant complexities, assume that their visual presentations are exactly alike.) Upon seeing the bird, the expert immediately knows that it is a woodpecker. The expert has fully reasonable beliefs about what woodpeckers look like. The novice has no good reason to believe that it is a woodpecker and is not justified in believing that it is.

Comment: The epistemic difference between novice and expert arises from something that differentiates the two internally. The expert knows the look of a woodpecker. The novice would gain the same justification as the expert if the novice came to share the expert's internal condition concerning the look of woodpeckers.

Example 3) A logic Teaching Assistant and a beginning logic student are looking over a homework assignment. One question displays a sentence that they both know to express a truth and asks whether certain other sentences are true as well. The TA can easily tell through simple reflection that some of the other sentences express logical consequences of the original sentence and thus she is justified in believing that they are true as well. The student is clueless.

Comment: Again there is an internal difference between the two. The difference is that the TA has justification for her beliefs to the effect that certain propositions validly follow from the original one. She is expert enough to "see" that the conclusions follow without performing any computations. This case differs from example 2 in that here the mental difference concerns cognizance of necessary truths of logic whereas in example 2 the expert was cognizant of contingent facts about visual characteristics of woodpeckers. But just as in example 2, relevant internal differences make the difference. The beginning student could come to share the epistemic state of the TA by coming to share the TA's familiarity with the logical consequence relation.

Example 4) Initially, Smith has excellent reasons to believe that Jones, who works in his office, owns a Ford. Smith deduces that someone in the office owns a Ford. The latter belief is true, but the former is false. Smith's reasons derive from Jones pretending to own a Ford. Someone else in the office, unknown to Smith, does own a Ford. The fact that Jones is merely simulating Ford ownership keeps Smith from knowing that someone in his office is a Ford owner, but it does not prevent Smith from being justified or diminish his justification. At a later time Smith gains ample reason to believe that Jones is pretending. At that point Smith is not justified in believing either that Jones owns a Ford or that someone in his office owns a Ford.

Comment: Again the epistemic change occurs when a suitable external fact – this time, the fact that what Smith has seen is Jones pretending to own a Ford – is brought into Smith's mind. The difference between Smith being justified in believing that Jones owns a Ford (and that someone in the office owns a Ford) in the one case and not in the other is an internal change in Smith.

Example 5) Hilary is a brain in a vat who has been abducted recently from a fully embodied life in an ordinary environment. He is being stimulated so that it seems to him as though his normal life has continued. Hilary believes that he ate oatmeal for breakfast yesterday. His memorial basis for his breakfast belief is artificial. It has been induced by his "envatters." Here are two versions of relevant details.

5a) Hilary's recollection is very faint and lacking in detail. The meal seems incongruous to him in that it strikes him as a distasteful breakfast and he has no idea why he would have eaten it.

5b) Hilary's recollection seems to him to be an ordinary vivid memory of a typical breakfast for him.

Comment: Although in both (5a) and (5b) Hilary's breakfast belief is false and its basis is abnormal, the belief is not well justified in (5a) and it is well justified in (5b). Hilary in (5a) differs internally from Hilary in (5b). His mental states in (5b) include better evidence for the belief than he has in (5a).

In the first four of these examples the location of a relevant item of information – in the mind of a subject or outside of it – makes the epistemic difference. In the fifth example, a purely internal difference is decisive. It is reasonable to generalize from these examples to the conclusion that every

variety of change that brings about or enhances justification either internalizes an external fact or makes a purely internal difference. It appears that there is no need to appeal to anything extramental to explain any justificatory difference. These considerations argue for the general internalist thesis that these epistemic differences have an entirely mental origin.

In each case, it is natural to regard the mental difference as a difference in the evidence that the person has. Variations in the presence or strength of this evidence correspond to the differences in justification. Our favorite version of internalism, evidentialism, asserts that epistemic justification is entirely a matter of evidence.[14] However, our goal here is to defend internalism generally, and not just its evidentialist version.

We have no proof that there is no exception to the pattern exhibited by our examples. The argument does not establish that internalism is true. It does support internalism. Further support will emerge from successful replies to objections.[15]

III.   Objections and Replies

The objections we shall consider fall into two broad and overlapping categories. One sensible general description of internalist theories is that they say belief B is justified just in case there is some combination of internal states – typically featuring an experience or another justified belief – that is suitably related to B. Objections of the first sort focus on internal states that are supposed to justify beliefs, arguing that there are some justified beliefs for which there are no internal justifying states. Objections in the second group focus on the connections between candidate internal justifiers and the beliefs they are supposed to justify, arguing that internalists inevitably run into insurmountable difficulties when they attempt to say anything definite about the nature or status of the connections.

While some internalist theories may have trouble dealing with some of these objections, there are several internalist approaches that can deal adequately with all of them. We concentrate primarily on two approaches, one that limits justifying states to currently conscious mental states and one that also includes as potential justifiers whatever is retained in memory. Since theories of each sort surmount all of the objections, the internalist approach is in no danger of a general refutation.[16]

A.   Are there enough internal justifiers?

A1.   Impulsional evidence

Alvin Plantinga's objection focuses on evidentialist versions of internalism.[17] But the same sort of objection seems equally applicable against any prima facie plausible internalist view. Plantinga asserts that there are three views evidentialists can hold concerning what constitutes evidence, and he argues that each view renders evidentialism unsatisfactory. The three possibilities are: (1) evidence consists only of other beliefs (all evidence is propositional); (2) evidence consists only of beliefs and sensory states (all evidence is propositional or sensory); (3) evidence can also include the sense of conviction or confidence that accompanies beliefs (all evidence is propositional, sensory, or impulsional).

Plantinga uses knowledge of simple arithmetical facts to defend his objection. He asserts that we do not believe that $2 + 1 = 3$ on the basis of propositional or sensory evidence. So, if evidentialists adopt alternatives (1) or (2), their theory implies that this belief is not justified. Yet, of course, we do know that $2 + 1 = 3$. Plantinga claims there is a "felt attractiveness" about the content of that belief, and he says $2 + 1 = 5$ "feels wrong, weird, absurd, eminently rejectable."[18] He calls the "felt attractiveness" an "impulse" and classifies it as "impulsional evidence." So internalists might take Plantinga's third alternative and claim that this impulsional evidence is the internal factor that justifies simple mathematical beliefs.

Plantinga argues that there is a problem with this account. He claims that necessarily all beliefs would have similar justification: "You have impulsional evidence for p just in virtue of believing p. … It isn't even possible that you believe p but lack impulsional evidence for it: how could it be that you believe p although it does not seem to you to be true?"[19] He infers that on this view of evidence, the internalist justification condition for knowledge that consists in having evidence is implied by the belief condition. If Plantinga is right about this, then evidentialists who take alternative (3) are stuck with the unacceptable conclusion that all actual beliefs are justified. The other initially plausible internalist views, for instance, those that appeal to epistemic responsibility as the key to a belief's justification, seem equally susceptible to this sort of objection. The "felt attractiveness" seems equally to render believing the epistemically responsible course of action to take. So, again, all beliefs would be justified.

Even if Plantinga were right in claiming that the evidence for beliefs like $2 + 1 = 3$ is impulsional, however, he would be mistaken in thinking that all beliefs have any similar sort of evidential support. There are several internal states to distinguish here. Perhaps we feel attracted to the proposition that $2 + 1 = 3$ and we feel impelled to believe it. Not everything we believe feels attractive in this way or any other. For instance, some known propositions are believed reluctantly, on the basis of reasons, in spite of their seeming distinctly unattractive and implausible. Some beliefs result from fears. They need not seem in any way attractive. Correspondingly, the denials of things we believe do not always feel "weird" or "absurd," even if we think that they are false. There may be a sense of obviousness that accompanies belief in some propositions. This sense may contribute to their evidential support. But quite plainly not all believed propositions share that feature, or anything that resembles it. So it is not true that there is "impulsional evidence" for every believed proposition.

Furthermore, even if there were impulsional evidence for each belief, it would not follow that each belief satisfies any plausible evidential version of the justification condition for knowledge. The existence of a bit of supporting evidence is clearly not enough. A plausible evidential condition for knowledge requires something more, such as strong evidence on balance, or at least evidence undefeated by other evidence. An impulse to believe would not always qualify as strong evidence on balance, or undefeated evidence. Moreover, even if there were some impulsional evidence for all beliefs, it would not follow that all beliefs are justified to any degree. In some cases anything like impulsional evidence is decisively outweighed by competing evidence. Therefore, the existence of impulsional evidence for all beliefs would not render redundant a plausible evidential condition on knowledge and would not saddle internalists with the unacceptable result that all beliefs are justified.

Even with regard to the simplest of mathematical beliefs, impulsional evidence of the sort Plantinga mentions is not our only evidence. We have evidence about our success in dealing with simple arithmetical matters and knowledge of the acceptance our assertions about these matters enjoy. So, we have reason to think that our spontaneous judgments about simple mathematical matters are correct. Furthermore, we know that we learned these sorts of things as children and we have not had our more recent assertions about them contradicted by others. If we had been making mistakes about these kinds of things, it is very likely that problems would have arisen and we would have been corrected. Finally, at least according to some plausible views, we have a kind of a priori insight that enables us to grasp simple mathematical propositions. This insight provides us with some evidence for the truth of simple mathematical truths. Much of this evidence is retained in memory; some of it is conscious whenever such propositions are consciously apprehended. There seems to be plenty of additional evidence, whether or not justifiers are restricted to conscious states. Indeed, the suggestion that the only evidential bases for simple arithmetical beliefs are impulses to believe is extremely implausible.

Thus, Plantinga's objection makes no real trouble for evidentialism. Any other reasonable internalist view clearly has a similar response available to the counterpart objections.

A2. Stored beliefs

Alvin Goldman argues that internal states cannot account for the justification of stored beliefs.[20] The problem is this. At any given moment almost nothing of what we know is consciously considered. We know personal facts, facts that constitute common knowledge, facts in our areas of expertise, and so on. Since we know all these things, we believe them. These are stored beliefs, not occurrent beliefs. Since we know them, we are justified in believing them. But on what internalist basis can these beliefs be justified? As Goldman says, "No perceptual experience, no conscious memory event, and no premises consciously entertained at the selected moment will be justificationally sufficient for such a belief."[21] Internalists are stuck with the unacceptable result that these beliefs are not justified, unless something internal that justifies them can be found.

In formulating this objection Goldman assumes two propositions, either of which internalists can sensibly reject. On the one hand, he assumes that virtually all justified beliefs are stored beliefs. On the other hand, he assumes that internalists must find something conscious to serve as their justification. But internalists have good reason to reject this pair of propositions. One alternative is to argue that, in the most central sense, few beliefs are justified, and typically the ones that are justified are occurrent. The second option is to argue that other non-occurrent internal states can contribute to the justification of non-occurrent beliefs.

The first response relies on the idea that there are occurrent and dispositional senses of "justified," just as there are occurrent and dispositional senses of "belief." In the most fundamental sense of "justified," a belief can be justified for a person only by the person's current evidence, and one's current evidence is all conscious. In this sense, non-occurrent beliefs are typically not justified. However, in the same way that there are propositions in which one has stored belief, one can have "stored justifications" for these beliefs. That is, one can have in memory reasons that justify the belief.[22] Beliefs like this are dispositionally justified.[23] Thus, although stored beliefs are seldom justified in the most fundamental sense, they are often dispositionally justified.

Goldman objects to a proposal along these lines that one of us made previously.[24] He takes the general idea behind the proposal to be that a disposition to generate a conscious evidential state counts as a justifier. He then raises the following objection:

> Suppose a train passenger awakes from a nap but has not yet opened his eyes. Is he justified in believing propositions about the details of the neighboring landscape? Surely not. Yet he is *disposed*, merely by opening his eyes, to generate conscious mental states that would occurrently justify such beliefs.[25]

The idea behind the current proposal is not what Goldman criticizes here. It is not that any conscious mental state that one is disposed to be in counts as evidence. The idea is that some non-occurrent states that one is already in, such as non-occurrent memories of perceptual experiences, are stored evidence. Presently having this stored evidence justifies dispositionally some non-occurrent beliefs that one already has. The train passenger does not have the evidence that he would have received were he to open his eyes. The dispositional state that he is in, his disposition to see the landscape by opening his eyes, is not stored evidence for propositions about the landscape. It is a potential to acquire evidence, and that is crucially different.

The second solution to the problem of stored beliefs does not invoke a distinction between occurrent and dispositional justification. Internalists can plausibly claim that if we have numerous ordinary justified beliefs that we are not consciously considering, then there is no reason to exclude from what justifies these beliefs further stored beliefs or other memories. These stored justifications are internalist by the standard of M and they are plausibly regarded as evidence that the person has.[26]

The description presented here of the second internalist approach leaves open important questions about which stored internal states can justify beliefs and what relation these stored states must have to a belief to justify it. No doubt these are difficult questions. Versions of internalism will differ concerning which stored states they count as justifiers.[27] But there is no appearance that internalism lacks the resources to provide satisfactory answers to these questions.

However, one might think that external factors having to do with the actual source of a memory belief can affect its justification. In fact, Goldman himself describes something similar to our second internalist approach and claims that it fails for just this reason.[28] We turn next to this objection.

A3. *Forgotten evidence*
Several authors have raised objections involving forgotten evidence.[29] We will focus on an example Goldman provides:

> Last year Sally read about the health benefits of broccoli in a *New York Times* science-section story. She then justifiably formed a belief in broccoli's beneficial effects. She still retains this belief but no longer recalls her original evidential source (and has never encountered either corroborating or undermining sources). Nonetheless,

her broccoli belief is still justified, and, if true, qualifies as a case of knowledge.[30]

This example illustrates something that must be conceded to be common. We now know things for which we have forgotten our original evidence. The problem for internalism arises most clearly if we assume that Sally's original evidence is irretrievably lost and not part of any stored justification that Sally might have. Let us assume that Sally is occurrently entertaining her justified belief about broccoli and that the facts about the original source of the belief are not part of any internalist justification of it. Externalists might argue that the contingent merits of the external source of this belief account for its justification. How can internalists explain why this belief is currently justified?

One internalist answer to this question is that Sally's justification consists in conscious qualities of the recollection, such as its vivacity and her associated feeling of confidence. We see no fatal flaw in this response. It will be most attractive to internalists who hold that only what is conscious can justify a belief. We note that not all memory beliefs are justified according to this theory. Some memory beliefs are accompanied by a sense of uncertainty and a lack of confidence. Other memory beliefs are accompanied by a recognition of competing evidence. This competing evidence can render vivacious memory beliefs unjustified. These are plausible results, so this restrictive version of internalism does have the resources to deal with forgotten evidence.

Another defensible answer is available to internalists who think that not all evidence is conscious. If Sally is a normal contemporary adult, she is likely to have quite of a bit of readily retrievable evidence supporting her belief about broccoli. The healthfulness of vegetables is widely reported and widely discussed. Furthermore, her belief about broccoli is probably not undermined by any background beliefs she is likely to have. Finally, she, like most people, probably has supporting evidence consisting in stored beliefs about the general reliability and accuracy of memory. She knows that she is generally right about this sort of thing. So Sally would have justification for her broccoli belief, though it is not her original evidence. If Sally lacks any supporting background information and also lacks any reason to trust her memory, then we doubt that her belief about broccoli really is justified.

Goldman considers and rejects this second response on the basis of a new version of the example about Sally.[31] The crucial feature of the revised example is that the belief originally came from a disreputable source. Sally has the same belief about broccoli and the same background beliefs about the reliability of her relevant capacities. But now it is part of the story that Sally obtained the belief about broccoli from an article in the *National Inquirer*, a source Goldman assumes to be unreliable. Goldman claims that

> Sally cannot be credited with justifiably believing that broccoli is healthful. Her past acquisition is still relevant, and decisive. At least it is relevant so long as we are considering the "epistemizing" sense of justification, in which justification carries a true belief a good distance toward knowledge. Sally's belief in the healthfulness of broccoli is not justified in that sense, for surely she does not know that broccoli is healthful given that the *National Inquirer* was her sole source of information.[32]

We agree that Sally does not know that broccoli is healthful under these conditions. We also agree that facts about her acquisition of the belief determine this result. However, it does not follow that Sally's belief is not justified. The "epistemizing" sense of justification is said by Goldman to be a sense according to which a belief that is justified is one that has been carried "a good distance toward knowledge." This fits with our initial characterization of epistemic justification as the sort which is necessary for knowledge. But from the fact that Sally's belief falls short of knowledge, it does not follow that it has not been carried a good distance toward knowledge. Thus, an initial weakness in this objection is that its concluding inference is invalid.

A second fault is that the allegedly unjustified belief is actually a justified true belief that is not knowledge. It is a Gettier case. We endorse the following rule of thumb for classifying examples of true beliefs that are not knowledge:

RT.   If a true belief is accidentally correct, in spite of its being quite reasonably believed, then the example is a Gettier case.

RT helps to show that the second version of the example about Sally is a Gettier case. Sally believes that broccoli is healthful. She believes (presumably justifiably) that she learned this from a reliable source. She is wrong about her source but, coincidentally, right about broccoli. This fits exactly the pattern of Gettier cases, and RT classifies it as such. It is a quite reasonable belief on Sally's part which, in light of its unreliable source, is just accidentally correct. It is a justified true belief that is not knowledge.

Our view has an implication that may initially seem odd. When Sally first came to believe that broccoli is healthful, the belief was unjustified because Sally had reason to distrust her source. Yet we seem in effect to be saying that merely because she has forgotten about that bad source, the belief has become justified. We are not quite saying that. As we see it, when she forgets about the source she has lost a defeater of a justification for her broccoli belief. Assuming that Sally knows herself normally to be judicious about her sources, any belief she retains thereby has considerable internal support. Whatever beliefs she retains are justified by this, unless they are defeated. A belief is defeated in any case in which she has indications that impeach what it is reasonable for her to take to be the source of her belief. But when she no longer possesses any such indication, as in the present Sally case, the otherwise generally good credentials of her memorial beliefs support the belief and are undefeated.

Some confirmation of our analysis comes from comparing the case as described to a case in which Sally does remember the unreliability of her source but retains the belief anyway. It is clear that there would be something far less reasonable about her belief in that situation. This suggests that forgetting the source does make the belief better justified.

Further confirmation emerges from contrasting the example with yet another variation. Suppose Sally believes both that broccoli is healthful and that peas are healthful. Suppose that her source for the former is still the *National Inquirer* but her source for the latter belief is the reliable *New York Times*. Again she has forgotten her sources, but she correctly and reasonably believes that she virtually always gets beliefs like these from trustworthy sources. Goldman's objection requires differentiating these two beliefs in an unacceptable way. It counts the former belief as unjustified, on the basis of the unreliability of its forgotten source. Yet from Sally's present perspective, the two propositions are on a par. It would be completely unreasonable for her to give up one belief but not the other. The best thing to say is that both are justified, but the broccoli belief does not count as knowledge because it is a Gettier case.

We conclude that internalism does not have any difficulty finding adequate justification in cases of forgotten evidence.[33]

B. Links and connections

We turn next to two objections concerning the connections between perceptual experiences or other justified beliefs and the beliefs they are supposed to justify. There are difficult questions about exactly how these states manage to justify the beliefs they support. These are problems of detail, and internalists have reasonable choices concerning how to work out the details. As we shall show by responding to several related objections, there are no unresolvable problems here.

B1. The need for higher order beliefs

William Alston has argued that the considerations that support internalism equally support the imposition of what he calls a "higher order requirement" on justification. The idea is that if the argument that leads to the conclusion that only internal factors can serve as justifiers is sound, then there is also a sound argument to the conclusion that for a belief to be justified the believer must be able to tell which factors justify the belief. Alston writes:

> Suppose that the sorts of things that can count as justifiers are always accessible to me, but that it is not accessible to me which items of these sorts count as justifications for which beliefs. I have access to the justifiers but not to their justificatory efficacy. This will take away my ability to do what I am said to have an obligation to do just as surely as the lack of access to the justifiers themselves. To illustrate, let's suppose that experiences can function as justifiers, and that they are accessible to us. I can always tell what sensory experiences I am having at a given moment. Even so, if I am unable to tell what belief about the current physical environment is justified by a given sensory experience, I am thereby unable to regulate

my perceptual beliefs according as they possess or lack experiential justification.[34]

Alston goes on to argue that this higher level requirement is one that few of us are able to satisfy, and he rejects the requirement partly for this reason. Since the argument for the higher order requirement is clearly unsound, Alston concludes that the original argument for internalism is unsound as well.

The argument that Alston is considering relies on a deontological conception of justification according to which justification is a matter of conforming to duties one must be in a position to know about. Internalists are free to reject that conception.[35] They need not defend an identification of justification with any sort of duty fulfillment. They need not defend anything that makes having justified beliefs depend on having some way to know what justifies what. To cite our favorite instance, evidentialists hold that the possession of the right evidence by itself secures the justification of the corresponding beliefs. The justification supervenes on the internal possession of appropriate evidence. Neither epistemic evaluations nor duties need enter in at all.

It might be thought that evidentialism should be formulated in ways that require for justification not only supporting evidence but also knowledge of higher level principles about the justificatory efficacy of this evidence. Some internalists do seem to impose such a requirement.[36] We agree with Alston that any such theory is implausible, implying that few people have justified beliefs. However, we see no reason to think that evidentialists, or internalists generally, must endorse any higher order requirement. Having evidence can make for justification on its own.

The appearance that justifying relations pose a problem for internalism arises partly from formulating the debate between internalists and externalists as a debate over whether all "justifiers" are internal. For example, Goldman takes to internalists to require that all "justifiers" must be in some suitable way accessible.[37] This way of formulating the issue is problematic. Suppose that a person who believes q on the basis of believing p is justified in believing q. We might then say, as a first approximation, that the justifiers for q are (i) the belief that p together with its justification, and (ii) the fact that p justifies q. The fact in (ii) is not itself an internal state, and so it might be thought that internalists are faced with the difficult task of finding some internal representation of this state to serve as a justifier.[38]

There is a sense in which p's support for q is a "justifier." It is part of an explanation of the fact that the person's belief in q is justified. But this does not imply that internalists are committed to the view that there must be some internal representation of this fact. It may be that a person's being in the state described by (i) is sufficient for the belief that q to be justified. If so, then all individuals mentally alike in that they share that state are justified in believing q. The fact in (ii) may help to account for the justification without the person making any mental use of that fact.

General beliefs that relate evidence to a conclusion sometimes do make a justificatory difference. This occurs in some of the examples in our argument for internalism. But the sort of connecting information that the examples suggest to be necessary is nonepistemic information that justified believers typically have. The logic TA, for example, had justification for beliefs about implication relations that the student lacked. The expert bird watcher had justification for beliefs about what woodpeckers look like. This might take the form of various generalizations, e.g., any bird that looks like that is a woodpecker, any bird with that sort of bill is a woodpecker, etc.[39] The student and the novice bird watcher lacked these justifications. It would be a mistake, however, to argue from these cases to any universal "higher order requirement," especially to a higher order requirement to have epistemic information about what justifies what.

A fully developed internalist theory must state whether linking information of the sort possessed by the logic TA and the expert bird watcher is required in the case of simpler connections. Suppose that a person has a justified belief in some proposition, p. Suppose further that q is an extremely simple and intuitively obvious (to us) logical consequence of p. For q to be justified for the person, must he have additional evidence, analogous the TA's additional evidence, for the proposition that q follows from p?

One possible view is that the answer is "No". According to this view, there are certain elementary logical connections that are necessarily reflected in epistemic connections. The best candidates for this relation include cases where one proposition is a conjunction of which the other is a conjunct. The general idea is that some propositions, p and q, have a primitive or basic epistemic connection. If p and q have this connection, then, necessarily, if a person is justified in believing p, then the person is also justified in believing q. Perhaps it is part of understanding p that one grasps the connection between p and q. There is, then, no need for additional information about the link between p and q that a person who is justified in believing p might lack. By the test of the supervenience thesis asserted by S, internalists can accept this answer.

Internalists can also hold that the answer to the question above is "Yes." In this case, there is something resembling a higher order requirement. However, it is not any implausible requirement to the effect that one have beliefs about justification. It is merely a requirement that one have evidence that there is a supporting connection – for instance, the logical consequence relation – between what is ordinarily regarded as one's evidence and what it is evidence for. This evidence can come from direct insight or from any other source. This is evidence that people normally have in a variety normal situations.[40]

A similar question arises concerning perceptual beliefs about the qualities of the objects one is perceiving. We said above that the expert bird watcher has background information about the look of woodpeckers that justified the belief that he saw a woodpecker. The novice lacked that information. The new question concerns simpler qualities such as redness. Must a person with a clear view of a red object have evidence about the look of red things in order to be justified in believing that there is something red before him or is the mere experience of redness (in the absence of defeaters) sufficient for justification?

Again, it is not crucial to answer this question here. What is important for present purposes is that internalists have plausible options. If an experience of the phenomenal quality corresponding to redness automatically justifies the belief (absent any defeater), then people internally alike in that they share the experience will be justified in believing the same external world proposition. If information about the look of red objects is required, then people internally alike in that they share this information as well as the experience of red will have the same external world proposition justified. There is a problem for internalism here only if there is some reason to think that internal differences are inadequate to account for some difference in justification. We see no threat of that.

B2. *Justification of introspective beliefs*

Ernest Sosa raises a problem about how experiences justify introspective beliefs:

> Some experiences in a certain sense "directly fit" some introspective beliefs. But not all experiences directly fit the introspective beliefs that describe them correctly. Thus my belief that at the center of my visual field there lies a white triangle against a black background would so fit the corresponding experience. But my belief that my visual field contains a 23-sided white figure against a black background would *not* fit that experience.[41]

The question, then, is this: Why does having a suitable experience of a triangle justify the introspective belief that one is having that experience, while our experience of a 23-sided figure does not justify for us the belief that we are having that experience?

Internalism has resources to explain why the two experiences have different epistemic consequences. We can best explain the relevant internal features through consideration of some hypothetical person who does have the ability to identify 23-sided figures in his visual field and contrasting this person with ordinary people who lack that ability. According to one internalist option, someone who has the ability has an experience qualitatively different from the experiences of those who lack that ability. We will call the quality that underlies the ability "recognition." It can plausibly be held that recognition makes a justificatory difference. When our visual field contains a triangle that contrasts clearly with its surroundings, we recognize it as such. We do not similarly recognize 23-sided figures. The recognition is not a true belief linking the experience to a belief about its content.[42] It is, instead, a feature of experience itself. This experiential feature is what makes it true that triangles, optimally viewed, are generally seen as triangles, while 23-sided figures, even when optimally viewed, are not generally seen as being 23-sided. It is this aspect of the experience that provides evidential support for

the corresponding belief. For most of us, this sort of feature is present when we experience clearly discriminable triangles and not present when we experience 23-sided figures. But a person who did have that remarkable ability would have an experience qualitatively unlike ours.

Rather than appealing to any qualitative difference in experience, internalists can appeal instead to background information. Ordinary people have learned that the property of being a three-sided image is associated with a certain sort of visual appearance. They have not learned which sorts of visual appearances are associated with being a 23-sided image. On this view, only by learning some such association could a person have justification from experience for making these sorts of classifications of images. Internalists can plausibly appeal to this sort of background information as the internal difference that accounts for differences in justification in these cases. As in the cases considered in section B1, the information here is not epistemic information about what justifies what, information people typically lack. It is simply information about properties that are associated with experiences of certain types.

We conclude that Sosa is right to say that some but not all experiences lead to justification of introspective beliefs that correctly describe them. But internal differences, either in the experiences themselves or in background information, are available to account for the difference between those that do lead to justification and those that do not.

IV. Conclusion

We have defended internalism not just to praise it, but to move the debate beyond it. We have tried to show that no genuine problem for this category of theories has been identified. We have seen that even versions of internalism that depend on only conscious elements have not been refuted. Various less restrictive views about what determines justification have emerged entirely unscathed as well. On any account of what internalism is, including the one we have offered here, internalism is nothing more than a broad doctrine about the location of the determining factors for epistemic justification. Having argued that internalist views stand in no jeopardy of being generally refuted, we recommend that epistemological attention focus on more specific accounts that are more informative.

Notes

1   For a summary of the current state of epis-
    temology that illustrates this sort of view,
    see Philip Kitcher, "The Naturalists Return,"
    The Philosophical Review, vol. 101 (1992),
    pp. 53–114.

2   Laurence BonJour "Externalism/Internalism,"
    in *A Companion to Epistemology*, ed. Jonathan
    Dancy and Ernest Sosa (Oxford: Blackwell,
    1992), p. 132.

3   Robert Audi, *Epistemology: A Contemporary
    Introduction to the Theory of Knowledge* (New
    York: Routledge, 1998), pp. 233–4. Emphasis
    in the original.

4   Alvin Plantinga, *Warrant: The Current
    Debate* (Oxford: Oxford University Press,
    1993), p. 6. A very similar formulation
    appears in William Harper, "Paper Mache
    Problems in Epistemology: A Defense of
    Strong Internalism," *Synthese*, vol. 116
    (1998), pp. 27–49. See p. 28.

5   John Pollock, "At the Interface of Philosophy
    and AI," *The Blackwell Guide to Epistemology*,
    ed. John Greco and Ernest Sosa (Malden,
    MA: Blackwell, 1999) pp. 383–414. The quo-
    tation is from p. 394.

6   Ernest Sosa, "Skepticism and the Internal/
    External Divide," *The Blackwell Guide to
    Epistemology*, pp. 145–57. The quotation is from
    p. 147. Sosa goes on to describe another version
    of internalism that highlights accessibility.

7   Laurence BonJour, "The Dialectic of Found-
    ationalism and Coherentism," *The Blackwell
    Guide to Epistemology*, pp. 117–42. The quo-
    tation is from p. 118.

8   William Alston, "Internalism and Externalism
    in Epistemology," reprinted in William Alston,
    *Epistemic Justification: Essays in the Theory of
    Knowledge* (Ithaca, NY: Cornell University
    Press, 1989), pp. 185–222. See p. 186.

9   Pollock does not make explicit that the inter-
    nal states to which he refers must be mental
    states. However, it is reasonable to assume
    that this is what he has in mind.

10 It has become standard to distinguish between
    an existing belief (or other attitude) being jus-
    tified and a person being justified in believing
    (or having another attitude toward) a proposi-
    tion whether or not the person actually believes
    it (or has that attitude). We shall use phrases

such as "justified belief" to refer to beliefs that
are justified and we shall say of a person that
he or she is justified in believing a proposition
when we mean to say that the latter relation
obtains. This distinction will not play a significant role in the discussion that follows. As
stated, (S) and (M) are about the justification
of existing attitudes. They could easily be
reformulated to state internalist constraints on
the conditions under which a person is justified in having a particular attitude.

11 Whether (M) implies (S) depends upon
    details of the supervenience relation which
    we will not discuss here.

12 Not all philosophers who make this sort of
    comparison seek an account of internalism
    with this advantage. James Pryor takes inter-
    nalism to be accessibilism, notes that inter-
    nalism in the philosophy of mind is a
    supervenience thesis, and concludes that the
    two kinds of internalism are dissimilar. See
    "Highlights of Recent Epistemology," *The
    British Journal for the Philosophy of Science*
    52, 1 (March 2001), pp. 95–124.

13 In "Skepticism and the Internal/External
    Divide," Sosa considers and rejects an argu-
    ment that has mentalism as a premise and
    accessibilism as its conclusion. See pp. 146–8.

14 See Richard Feldman and Earl Conee,
    "Evidentialism," *Philosophical Studies* vol. 48
    (1985), pp. 15–34.

15 In describing and assessing the beliefs in the
    examples of Section II, we did not say any-
    thing about what the individuals had a duty
    or obligation to believe, what they were per-
    mitted to believe, or what they might be
    praised or blamed for believing. There might
    be deontological truths of these sorts. We
    reject arguments for internalism based on
    the idea that epistemic concepts are to be
    analyzed in these deontological terms.

16 Other versions of internalism could be con-
    sidered. For example, some internalists hold
    that a belief is justified only if the believer is
    able to formulate good reasons for it. We will
    not address the merits of these versions of
    internalism here. We note that a theory
    requiring for justified belief that the believer
    not only be able to formulate good reasons

but also be able to articulate those reasons or persuade others is not an internalist theory by our standards.

17 "Respondeo Ad Feldman" in *Warrant in Contemporary Epistemology: Essays in Honor of Plantinga's Theory of Knowledge*, ed. Jon Kvanvig (London: Rowman and Littlefield, 1996), pp. 357–61.

18 "Respondeo," p. 259.

19 "Respondeo," p. 360.

20 Alvin Goldman, "Internalism Exposed," *Journal of Philosophy*, vol. 96, no. 6 (1999), p. 278.

21 Ibid.

22 It may be that if one were to become conscious of the belief, one would also bring to mind some stored justification that one has for it. Thus, if these stored beliefs were occurrent, they would be justified in the fundamental sense. Whether this justification would happen to accompany an occurrent consideration of a belief does not seem crucial. What may be crucial to having a stored epistemic justification for a stored belief is being capable of recalling a conscious justification, or at least being capable of recalling the key confirming evidence in such a justification.

23 Though it is possible for a stored belief to be justified by one's current evidence, in the usual case, one's evidence for a stored belief will also be stored. It is also possible for an occurrent belief to have only dispositional justification.

24 Richard Feldman, "Having Evidence," in *Philosophical Analysis*, ed. David Austin (Dordrecht, the Netherlands: Kluwer, 1988), pp. 83–104.

25 Goldman, "Internalism Exposed," pp. 278–9.

26 It is, in the typical case, an internal state that is accessible to the believer, so accessibilist versions of internalism can accept this approach as well. We suspect that many internalists will find the second sort of approach to the problem of stored beliefs more appealing. By limiting evidence to current conscious states, the former view limits severely the number of justified beliefs a person has at any time. We do not regard this limitation as clearly unsatisfactory, given the availability of a dispositional notion of justification to account for the favorable epistemic status of many stored beliefs. We shall continue to present both approaches in the remainder of this paper.

27 For example, they can differ with respect to how readily accessible those states must be. It is also possible to hold that the degree of justification provided by a state is partly determined by how readily accessible it is.

28 Goldman, "Internalism Exposed," p. 279.

29 See, for example, Sosa, "Skepticism and the Internal/External Divide," pp. 145–57. The relevant example appears on pp. 152f. Goldman cites Gilbert Harman, Thomas Senor, and Robert Audi as having raised similar objections. See Gilbert Harman, *Change in View* (Cambridge: MIT Press, 1986); Thomas Senor, "Internalist Foundationalism and the Justification of Memory Belief," *Synthese*, vol. 94 (1993), pp. 453–76; and Robert Audi, "Memorial Justification," *Philosophical Topics*, vol. 23 (1995), pp. 31–45.

30 Goldman, "Internalism Exposed," p. 281.

31 The new example resembles one that Ernest Sosa presents involving a generally reasonable person who believes a conclusion as a result of a now-forgotten "tissue of fallacies." Sosa thinks this origin renders the belief unjustified, no matter what the person now thinks about the source of her belief or her general capacities. See Sosa, "Skepticism and the Internal/External Divide," p. 153.

32 Goldman, "Internalism Exposed," pp. 280–1.

33 A third problem Goldman poses for internalism is the problem of concurrent retrieval. It purports to affect only those internalist views that are versions of holistic coherentism. A person has a large set of stored beliefs at any time. Holistic coherentism says that a belief is justified only if it coheres with one's whole corpus of beliefs, including stored beliefs. This leads to a problem for a defender of holistic coherentism who also accepts the deontologically defended claim that one can always find out whether a belief is justified. Ascertaining whether one belief coheres with the rest by bringing them all consciously to mind at once is well beyond the capacities of any person.

This is a problem for holistic coherentism only when it is conjoined with the deontologically defended thesis just mentioned.

A holistic coherentist need not accept a deontological conception of epistemic justification, and can simply deny that epistemic status is something that one always can find out. The holist can also respond to Goldman's objection by denying that finding out epistemic status so as to comply with any relevant duty requires the simultaneous retrieval of all that the status depends on. It might be held to be sufficient for complying with a duty to find out whether belief B1 coheres with one's other beliefs simply to form a true belief, B2, that B1 coheres with the others, as long as B2 itself coheres with the rest of one's beliefs.

In any case, problems peculiar to holistic coherentism cast no doubt on internalism generally. There are, however, related questions concerning the accessibility of stored beliefs that might be raised for other internalist theories, including evidentialism. Here is one of them. Suppose that someone has a conscious belief that is supported by some currently conscious evidence. Suppose further that the person also has a large number of stored beliefs whose conjunction implies the falsity of the conscious belief. This conjunction is too complex for the person to entertain. Under these circumstances, what is the epistemic status of the current belief?

Internalists have ample resources to deal with cases like this, whatever the correct answer to this question is. If beliefs like these are justified, internalists can hold that only currently accessed evidence is relevant to the epistemic status of occurrently believed propositions. So, potentially defeating combinations of beliefs that are not accessed would not undermine justification. If beliefs like these are not justified, internalists can say instead that all stored beliefs are among the mental items relevant to justification and that any conjunction of them can serve as a defeater of the justification of current beliefs, regardless of whether the individual can consciously consider the conjunction. It is also consistent with M to say that justification supervenes on a restricted class of stored mental items. Perhaps items that are too complex to be

retrieved are excluded. In that case, an unbelievably complex conjunction of stored beliefs would not be a defeater. Perhaps only combinations of stored beliefs whose negative relevance to the belief in question has been or could readily be noticed or appreciated count as defeaters. Perhaps, as accessibilists hold, only mental items that are in one way or another accessible can be defeaters. The same variety of claims can be made about what constitutes supporting evidence that one has.

Some of these approaches seem to us to be more promising than others. For present purposes it is not necessary to defend any particular view. We are arguing here for the explanatory power and credibility of internalist theorists. The devil may lurk in the details, for all that we have shown. But in the absence of any good reason to think that internalists must make ad hoc or indefensible claims about stored beliefs, there is no reason to think that there is a general problem here.

34   Alston, "Internalism and Externalism in Epistemology," p. 221.

35   Feldman and Conee, "Evidentialism."

36   See, for example, Laurence BonJour, "Externalist Theories of Empirical Knowledge," *Midwest Studies in Philosophy*, vol. 5 (1980), p. 55. In "Epistemology c. 1988–2000," James Pryor calls the view that endorses the higher order requirement "Inferential Internalism" and identifies several of its proponents.

37   Goldman, "Internalism Exposed," Section I.

38   For instance, Michael Bergmann, "A Dilemma for Internalism," APA, Central Division, 2000.

39   Internalists who hold that all evidence is conscious can point to evidence such as the expert's feeling of confidence and sense of familiarity while making the judgment.

40   There is a non-evidentialist view that some internalists find attractive. The idea is that a mental fact about people is that they have fundamental inferential abilities. Perhaps this view could also be described in terms of the ability to see connections. But this view denies that this ability is, or leads to, differences in evidence. This is a mental difference, but not an evidential difference.

These two views can also be applied to the original example about the logic student. We said the TA can see that the original sentence has consequences that the student can't see. This is what accounts for the differences in what's justified for them. As we described the case, we interpreted these facts in an evidentialist way, taking the difference in what they can see as an evidential difference. The non-evidentialist internalist alternative agrees that there is a mental difference between the two, but it characterizes that difference in terms of an inferential skill rather a difference in evidence. It is not essential to a defense of internalism to select between these alternatives.

41   Ernest Sosa, "Beyond Skepticism, to the Best of our Knowledge," *Mind*, vol. 97 (1988), pp. 153–88. The quotation is from p. 171.

42   The term "recognize" suggests that the classification is accurate. There is no need to insist on an infallible capacity here. If there is some such phenomenon as seemingly recognizing a conscious quality while misclassifying it, then it is a seeming recognition which supplies the conscious evidence for the classification.

PART VI

Virtue Epistemology
and the Value of Knowledge

Introduction

The novelty of reliabilism is not simply that it makes the justifier of a belief some feature we need not have internal epistemic access to. Reliabilism also seems to imply that the epistemic value of a justified belief – if justification is a form of value – derives from the epistemic value of the faculty that produced it. Of course, the reliabilist thinks that the relevant value-conferring feature of such a faculty is its reliability. But one might want to deny that reliability is the basis of epistemic value while agreeing with the reliabilist that epistemic value is properly located first in the faculty of the believer, or perhaps in the believer herself, and only secondarily in the belief. To use a well-known example from Linda Zagzebski, a delicious espresso produced by a well-functioning espresso machine is no better than an equally delicious espresso produced (by luck) from a poor espresso machine.

Virtue epistemology and proper functionalism may be fairly regarded as attempts to improve on reliabilism. Both require, for knowledge, that one's belief be produced by a reliable process, but both deny this is sufficient. Virtue theory requires, at least, that the belief-producing process also be an *ability*, a stable disposition to acquire or maintain beliefs, and proper functionalism requires that it be a faculty functioning the way it was designed to function. These restrictive modifications of reliabilism are aimed in part at solving some of the well-known problems facing reliabilism, including what John Greco calls the problem of epistemic responsibility, viz., the problem posed by reliably produced beliefs that fall short of knowledge (justification) owing to the epistemic irresponsibility of the believer, and the new evil demon problem, viz., the problem of accounting for the justification possessed by victims of the evil demon, subjects whose faculties are unreliable.

In his selection, Alvin Plantinga outlines proper functionalism. Proper functionalism is a theory of *warrant*, viz., of that feature that turns true belief into knowledge. The account Plantinga provides notably works with the normative notion of a faculty's *functioning properly*, and thus is a departure from standard externalist accounts. To function properly a faculty must function as it ought to function, that is, as it is designed to function. Our cognitive design plan, importantly, has a segment devoted to the production of true beliefs. A belief is warranted, then, only if the faculty that produced it was aiming at truth. But this is not enough. The faculty must be reliable, perhaps not *tout court*, but in the kinds of environment for which the subject's faculties were designed. A human clairvoyant in an imagined situation in which clairvoyance is reliable employs a belief-forming process that hasn't been given a role in the design plan, and so his clairvoyant beliefs, however reliable, lack warrant. Although victims of an evil demon lack full-blown warrant on Plantinga's account, one can see that there is room for assigning to their beliefs some degree of positive epistemic status, since their faculties are functioning properly and would reliably produce true beliefs in the kinds of environments for which they were designed.

Plantinga makes the value of a cognitive faculty a matter of its operating in accordance with its design plan. Virtue epistemology makes the value of a cognitive faculty a matter of whether it is an epistemic virtue. But what is an epistemic virtue? Linda Zagzebski claims that a virtue, whether moral or intellectual, is an excellence, acquired through time and work, that contains both a motivational element and a success element. Correlated with every virtue is a motivation directed to some goal, and no ability can be a virtue unless its possessor succeeds in achieving that goal. The goal unifying the intellectual virtues is the understanding of reality. Reliable success at achieving this goal, moreover, isn't limited to the overall production of more truths than falsehoods. A virtue, such as originality or intellectual courage, may be reliable in the further sense of helping to advance understanding in a domain of inquiry. As long as such traits, working together with other virtues, operate to correct errors produced along the way, they serve the ultimate epistemic goal of understanding the world.

John Greco argues that in order to solve the problems facing virtue theories, internalist elements must be introduced. It is not enough to say that the victims of the evil demon are justified because their faculties would be reliable in our environment. Even supposing our faculties are unreliable, many of the beliefs we form using them are justified. Facts about the success of our faculties are simply irrelevant. Nor can the problem of epistemic responsibility be solved by adding the requirement of a perspective on one's ways of believing. To achieve the right results, perspectives must be specified in a complicated way that the ordinary knower cannot be expected to understand.

The problems can be solved, however, if we introduce the internalist notion of a subject's conformance to a norm she countenances. To countenance a norm is to be guided by it in conscientious reasoning. To be in conformance with norms one countenances is not merely to believe in accordance with them, but to believe *because* one countenances them. Epistemically irresponsible believers either flout norms they countenance or fail to be in conformance with them. Greco gives the example of a person, Mary, who unwittingly possesses a special non-experiential device for detecting tigers. Mary's belief formed using this device cannot count as knowledge, since in forming the belief, she has flouted norms she countenances, for among the norms she countenances are norms that forbid forming beliefs about the presence of tigers in the absence of any evidence to that effect. In connection with the victims of the evil demon, Greco argues that, although they lack warrant, they have justification, for their beliefs are in conformance with norms they countenance. This, moreover, is a feature they possess independently of facts about the reliability of our faculties.

Duncan Pritchard asks whether virtue theory enables us to explain how knowledge excludes certain sorts of luck. Some kinds of luck are incompatible with knowing.

If I randomly guess that the president is eating a ham sandwich, then this won't count as a case of knowing that the president is eating a ham sandwich. I was just lucky. Pritchard distinguishes two importantly different sorts of luck at issue in contemporary theories of knowledge. *Veritic epistemic luck* occurs when a state of affairs obtains by a fluke (although it may seem quite probable given one's evidence). It is this sort of luck present in Gettier cases. *Reflective epistemic luck* occurs when the truth of a state of affairs is "accidental" or a fluke given one's available evidence. Despite the contemporary popularity of virtue-theoretic analyses of knowledge, Pritchard argues that virtue theories are not well-suited to explain how knowledge excludes either veritic or reflective luck. We do better with the safety-based accounts (see the Sosa paper included in Part IV).

Virtue theorists take a particular stance on the source of the value of a justified belief (or instance of knowledge). This value derives from the value of the relevant faculty or person. Virtue theorists differ on whether the latter themselves have their value derivatively, perhaps by connection to some ultimate epistemic value, e.g., truth. The remaining selections in this section explore questions of epistemic value generally. In what sense, if any, is true belief valuable? Why should virtuously held true belief be more valuable than mere true belief? Does knowledge have its own distinctive value?

As intellectual beings we are said to want the truth, but what does this mean? Ernest Sosa offers us a taxonomy of distinct epistemic values which may all be understood through their various relations to truth. Since we prefer truth to falsehood even if it comes by happenstance, there is the value of bare true believing. There is the *praxical, extrinsic* value of true believing. There is the *eudaemonist, intrinsic* value of true believing – the value of the *eudaemonist virtue epistemologist* – where what matters most is the agent grasping the truth in a manner attributable to her intellectual virtues acting of the agent's belief in concert conducted by reason (the truth of the agent's belief is thus *attributable* to the agent). Finally, there is the *performance value* of good cognitive performance, even when poor positioning robs it of its reward. Because a state of knowing is one where the truth is grasped in a manner attributable to an epistemic agent's skills and virtues, Sosa argues that knowledge is more valuable than true belief. And in the case of the evil demon, the *performance value* ensures that the state of believing is still valued, although the beliefs held may not be true.

But is knowledge really more valuable than other cognitive states such as mere true belief or justified true belief? The question was asked long ago by Socrates (as portrayed in the *Meno*), and Jonathan Kvanvig presses the point in his selection. An answer to the question is important because traditional epistemology focuses on questions about the nature, extent, and importance of knowledge as opposed to other candidate epistemic states like true belief or understanding. But once we realize that knowledge does not imply infallibility, certainty, permanence, etc. (things that *are* valuable), it becomes difficult to see why knowledge is so valuable. Kvanvig considers a number of different cognitive goals that we might have as believers and argues that for any given goal, knowledge is no better (and sometimes *worse*) than some other epistemic state such as justified true belief for securing that goal. And if knowledge is not uniquely positioned to satisfy our cognitive goals, then it's unreasonable for epistemologists to focus on knowledge to the exclusion of intellectual virtues such as understanding and wisdom.

Many analytic epistemologists today would agree that truth is the fundamental epistemic value. But Catherine Elgin argues that even the best theories are not true (be they scientific, philosophical, or from some other discipline). Science relies on laws, models, idealizations and approximations which diverge from the truth – but whose divergences are often necessary for the understanding science delivers. Because we take science to be cognitively reputable, an adequate theory of epistemology should be able to explain what makes good science cognitively good. Rejecting *veritism*, or truth-centered epistemology, Elgin argues that rather than requiring beliefs to be justified and true, epistemic acceptability should turn on whether beliefs are *true enough*. Because different statements in a theory play different roles, whether a given sentence in the theory is true is not the only epistemically relevant factor. Some statements may be fictions that shed light on the phenomena they concern and thus contribute to our understanding. Assessing a theory requires determining whether the component sentences are true enough given the parts they are assigned to play.

Further Reading

Axtell, Guy, "Recent Work on Virtue Epistemology," *American Philosophical Quarterly* 34 (1997), pp. 1–26.

BonJour, Laurence and Ernest Sosa, *Epistemic Justification: Internalism vs. Externalism, Foundations vs. Virtues* (Oxford: Blackwell, 2003).

Code, Lorraine, *Epistemic Responsibility* (Hanover, NH: University Press of New England, 1987).

Fairweather, Abrol and Linda Zagzebski, *Virtue Epistemology: Essays on Epistemic Virtue and Responsibility* (Oxford: Oxford University Press, 2004).

Greco, John, "Internalism and Epistemically Responsible Belief," *Synthese* 85 (1990), pp. 245–77.

——, "Virtues and Vices of Virtue Epistemology," *Canadian Journal of Philosophy* 23 (1993), pp. 413–32.

——, "Knowledge As Credit for True Belief," in Michael DePaul (ed.), *Intellectual Virtue: Perspectives from Ethics and Epistemology* (Oxford: Oxford University Press, 2004), pp. 111–34.

Kawall, Jason, "Virtue Theory and Ideal Observers," *Philosophical Studies* 109 (2002), pp. 197–222.

Kvanvig, Jonathan L., *The Intellectual Virtues and the Life of the Mind* (Lanham, MD: Rowman and Littlefield, 1992).

——, *The Value of Knowledge and the Pursuit of Understanding* (Cambridge: Cambridge University Press, 2003).

Kvanvig, Jonathan L. (ed.), *Warrant in Contemporary Epistemology: Essays in Honor of Plantinga's Theory of Knowledge* (Lanham, MD: Rowman and Littlefield, 1996).

Montmarquet, James A., *Epistemic Virtue and Doxastic Responsibility* (Lanham, MD: Rowman and Littlefield, 1993).

Plantinga, Alvin, *Warrant and Proper Function* (Oxford: Oxford University Press, 1993).

Pritchard, Duncan, *Epistemic Luck* (Oxford: Oxford University Press, 2005).

Pritchard, Duncan and Michael Brady (eds), *Moral and Epistemic Virtues* (Oxford: Blackwell, 2004).

Reed, Baron, "Epistemic Agency and the Intellectual Virtues," *The Southern Journal of Philosophy* 39 (2001), pp. 507–26.

Riggs, Wayne, "Beyond Truth and Falsehood: The Real Value of Knowing that P," *Philosophical Studies* 107, 1, 2002, pp. 87–108.

Sosa, Ernest, *Knowledge in Perspective: Selected Essays in Epistemology* (Cambridge: Cambridge University Press, 1991).

Steup, Matthias (ed.), *Knowledge, Truth, and Duty: Essays on Epistemic Justification, Responsibility, and Virtue* (Oxford: Oxford University Press, 2004).

Zagzebski, Linda Trinkhaus, *Virtues of the Mind: An Inquiry into the Nature of Virtue and the Ethical Foundations of Knowledge* (Cambridge: Cambridge University Press, 1996).

CHAPTER 32

Warrant: A First Approximation

Alvin Plantinga

One thought emerging from our canvas of contemporary accounts of warrant in *Warrant: The Current Debate* is that there are many different valuable epistemic states of affairs – epistemic *values*, we might call them, giving that oft-abused word a decent sense; and different conceptions of warrant appeal to different epistemic values. For example, there is doing one's subjective epistemic duty, doing one's objective epistemic duty, and doing both; these figure prominently in classical internalism. There is having a set of beliefs that is coherent to one or another degree; there is also the *disposition* to have coherent beliefs; these things are what the coherentist is quite naturally enthusiastic about. There is having adequate evidence or good reasons for your beliefs; this goes with the evidentialism that has been a dominant feature of the epistemological tradition and is presently represented in different ways by Feldman and Conee,[1] and William Alston.[2] There is having a reliable set of faculties or belief-producing mechanisms, which of course goes with reliabilism of various sorts. There is also knowing that you have a reliable set of epistemic faculties. There is also Foley rationality; and there are the several varieties of Foley rationality, such as believing what you *think* would contribute to

your attaining your epistemic goal, believing what on reflection you *would* think would contribute to your attaining that goal, believing what *really would* contribute to your doing so, and so on. There is having a set of beliefs that contributes to your nonepistemic goals such as happiness, or living the good life, or living the moral life. There is having the *right* goals; there is *aiming* to have the right goals; and there is *knowing* that you have the right goals. There is believing what is true, and there is having true beliefs on important topics; there is accepting a given belief to the right degree. There is knowing that you know; there is being able to prove to the skeptic that you know. And there are a thousand other epistemic virtues.

I Proper Function

Now the notion of warrant is clearly connected with all of these epistemic values and more besides. (The problem here is to come up with a conception of warrant that gives to each its due and describes how each is connected with the others and with warrant.) As a first step toward developing a satisfying account of warrant, I should like to call attention to still another epistemic value: having epistemic faculties that *function properly*. The first thing to see, I think, is that this notion of proper function is the rock on which the canvassed accounts of warrant founder. Cognitive malfunction has been a sort of recurring

Originally published in A. Plantinga, *Warrant and Proper Function* (Oxford and New York: Oxford University Press, 1993), pp. 3–20.

theme. Chisholm's dutiful epistemic agent who, whenever he is appeared to redly, always believes that nothing is appearing redly to him, Pollock's cognizer who by virtue of malfunction has the wrong epistemic norms, the Coherent but Inflexible Climber, Dretske's epistemic agent whose belief that Spot emits ultraviolet radiation has been caused by the fact that Spot does indeed emit such radiation, Goldman's victim of the epistemically serendipitous lesion: all are such that their beliefs lack warrant for them. In each case the reason, I suggest, is *cognitive malfunction*, failure of the relevant cognitive faculties to function properly, to function as they ought to. Chisholm's agent meets Chisholm's conditions for warrant; his beliefs lack warrant, however, because they result from cognitive dysfunction due to a damaging brain lesion, or the machinations of an Alpha Centaurian scientist, or perhaps the mischievous schemes of a Cartesian evil demon. Something similar must be said for each of the others. In each case the unfortunate in question meets the conditions laid down for warrant by the account in question; in each case her beliefs fail to have warrant because of cognitive malfunction. Hence each of these accounts misfires, at least in part by virtue of its failure to take appropriate account of the notion of proper function.

I therefore suggest initially that a necessary condition of a belief's having warrant for me is that my cognitive equipment, my belief-forming and belief-maintaining apparatus or powers, be free of such malfunction. A belief has warrant for you only if your cognitive apparatus is functioning properly, working the way it ought to work, in producing and sustaining it. (Of course this isn't nearly sufficient, and I shall try to supply some of what is necessary to achieve sufficiency.)

The notion of proper function is one member of a connected group of interdefinable notions; some of the other members of the group are *dysfunction, design, function* (simpliciter), *normality* (in the normative nonstatistical sense), *damage*, and *purpose*. There is initial reason to doubt, I think, that this circle of concepts can be broken into from the outside – that is, reason to doubt that any of them can be defined without reference to the others. Here we have a situation like that with modality: possibility, contingency, necessity, entailment, and their colleagues form a circle of properties or concepts that can be defined or explained in terms of each other but cannot be defined in terms of properties outside the circle. (Of course that is nothing against these modal concepts.) The same goes here, I think.

You may nonetheless think there is a serious problem with this notion right from the start. Isn't the idea of proper function an extremely unlikely idea to appeal to in explaining the notion of warrant? Isn't it every bit as puzzling, every bit as much in need of explanation and clarification, as the notion of warrant itself? Perhaps so; but even if so, at least we can reduce our total puzzlement by explaining the one in terms of the other; and we can see more clearly the source and location of some of our perplexities about warrant. Further, the idea of proper function is one we all have; we all grasp it in at least a preliminary rough-and-ready way; we all constantly employ it. You go to the doctor; he tells you that your thyroid isn't functioning quite as it ought (its thyroxin output is low); he prescribes a synthetic thyroxin. If you develop cataracts, the lenses of your eyes become less transparent; they can't function properly and you can't see well. A loss in elasticity of the heart muscle can lead to left ventricular malfunction. If a bird's wing is broken, it typically won't function properly; the bird won't be able to fly until the wing is healed, and then only if it heals in such a way as not to inhibit proper function. Alcohol and drugs can interfere with the proper function of various cognitive capacities, so that you can't drive properly, can't do simple addition problems, display poor social judgment, get into a fist fight, and wind up in jail.

And it isn't just in rough-and-ready everyday commonsense contexts that the notion of proper function is important; it is deeply embedded in science.

We are accustomed to hearing about biological functions for various bodily organs. The heart, the kidneys, and the pituitary gland, we are told, have functions – things they are, in this sense *supposed to do*. The fact that these organs are supposed to do these things, the fact that they have their functions, is quite independent of what *me* think they are supposed to do. Biologists *discovered* these functions; they didn't invent or assign them. We cannot, by agreeing among ourselves, *change* the functions of these organs. … The same seems true for sensory systems, those organs by means of which highly sensitive and continuous dependencies are maintained between external, public events and internal, neural processes. Can there be a serious question about whether, in the same sense in which it is the heart's function to pump the blood, it is, say, the task or function of the noctuid moth's auditory system to detect the whereabouts and movements of its archenemy, the bat?[3]

According to David Baltimore, "many instances of blood disorders, mental problems, and a host of other disabilities are traceable to a malfunctioning gene."[4] According to the great Swiss child psychologist Jean Piaget, a seven-year-old child whose cognitive faculties are functioning properly will believe that everything in the universe has a purpose in some grand overarching plan or design; later on a properly functioning person, he said, will learn to "think scientifically" and realize that everything has either a natural cause or happens by chance.[5]

Biological and social scientists, furthermore – psychologists, medical researchers, neuroscientists, economists, sociologists, and many others – continually give accounts of how human beings or other organisms or their parts and organs function: how they work, what their purposes are, and how they react under various circumstances. Call these descriptions (following John Pollock)[6] *functional generalizations*. For example, whenever a person is appeared to redly under such and such conditions, she will form the belief that there is something red present; whenever a person considers an obvious *a priori* truth such as $2 + 1 = 3$, she will find herself firmly believing it; whenever a person desires something and believes so and so, he will do such and such. To strike a more sophisticated if no more enlightening note: whenever an organism of kind K is in state S_i and receives sensory input P_j, then there is a probability of r that it will go into state S_j and produce output O_j. Pollock makes the important point that if these functional generalizations are taken straightforwardly and at face value, as universal generalizations about people and other organisms and their parts, they are nearly always false. They don't hold of someone who is in a coma, having a stroke, crazed by strong drink, or has just

hit the ground after a fall off a cliff. Clearly these functional generalizations contain something like an implicit restriction to organisms and organs that are *functioning properly*, functioning as they ought to, subject to no malfunction or dysfunction. The notion of proper function, therefore, is presupposed by the idea of functional generalizations.

So the notion of proper function is a notion we have and regularly employ; I may therefore appeal to it in explaining warrant. Still, it needs exploration, clarification, and explication if it is to serve as the key notion in an account of warrant. Let us provisionally entertain the idea that a belief has warrant for me only if the relevant parts of my noetic equipment – the parts involved in its formation and sustenance – are functioning properly. It is easy to see, however, that proper function cannot be the whole story about warrant. You have just had your annual cognitive checkup at MIT; you pass with flying colors and are in splendid epistemic condition. Suddenly and without your knowledge you are transported to an environment wholly different from earth; you awake on a planet revolving around Alpha Centauri. There conditions are quite different; elephants, we may suppose, are invisible to human beings, but emit a sort of radiation unknown on earth, a sort of radiation that causes human beings to form the belief that a trumpet is sounding nearby. An Alpha Centaurian elephant wanders by; you are subjected to the radiation, and form the belief that a trumpet is sounding nearby. There is nothing wrong with your cognitive faculties; they are working quite properly; still, this belief has little by way of warrant for you. Nor is the problem merely that the belief is false; even if we add that a trumpet really *is* sounding nearby (in a soundproof telephone booth, perhaps), your belief will still have little by way of warrant for you.

To vary the example, imagine that the radiation emitted causes human beings to form the belief not that a trumpet is sounding, but that there is a large gray object in the neighborhood. Again, an elephant wanders by; while seeing nothing of any particular interest, you suddenly find yourself with the belief that there is a large gray object nearby. A bit perplexed at this discovery, you examine your surroundings more closely: you still see no large gray object. Your faculties are displaying no malfunction (you have your certificate from MIT); you are not being epistemically careless or slovenly (you are doing your epistemic best); nevertheless you don't know that there is a large gray object nearby. That belief has little or no warrant for you. Of course you may be justified, within your epistemic rights in holding this belief; you may be flouting no epistemic duty. Further, the belief may also be rational for you in every sensible sense of "rational."[7] But it has little warrant for you.

What this example is designed to show, of course, is that the proper function of your epistemic equipment is not (logically) sufficient for warrant: it is possible that your cognitive equipment be functioning perfectly properly but your beliefs still lack warrant for you. And the reason is not far to seek: it is that your cognitive faculties and the environment in which you find yourself are not properly attuned. The problem is not with your cognitive faculties; they are in good working order. The problem is with the environment – with your cognitive environment. In approximately the same way, your automobile might be in perfect working order, despite the fact that it will not run well at the top of Pike's Peak, or under water, or on the moon. We must therefore add another component to warrant; your faculties must be in good working order, and the environment must be appropriate for your particular repertoire of epistemic powers. It must be the sort of environment for which your faculties are designed – by God or evolution (or both). Perhaps there are creatures native to the planet in question who are much like human beings but whose cognitive powers fit that epistemic environment and differ from ours in such a way that Alpha Centaurian elephants are not invisible to them. Then their beliefs would have warrant where yours do not.

It is tempting to suggest that warrant *just* is (or supervenes upon) proper functioning in an appropriate environment, so that a given belief has warrant for you to the degree that your faculties are functioning properly (in producing and sustaining that belief) in an environment appropriate for your cognitive equipment: the better your faculties function, the more warrant. But this cannot be correct. Couldn't it happen that my cognitive faculties are working properly (in an appropriate environment) in producing and sustaining a certain belief in me, while nonetheless that belief enjoys less by way of warrant for me than some other belief? Say that a pair of beliefs are (for want of a better term) *productively equivalent* if they are produced by faculties functioning properly to the same degree and in environments of equal appropriateness. Then couldn't it be that a pair of my beliefs should be productively equivalent while nonetheless one of them has more by way of warrant – even a great deal more – than the other? Of course that could be; as a matter of fact it happens all the time. The belief that $7 + 5 = 12$, or the belief that I have a name, or the belief that I am more than seven years old – any of these has more by way of warrant for me than does the memory belief, now rather dim and indistinct, that forty years ago I owned a secondhand sixteen-gauge shotgun and a red bicycle with balloon tires; but all, I take it, are produced by cognitive faculties functioning properly in a congenial environment. Although both epistemic warrant and *being properly produced* come in degrees, there seems to be no discernible functional relationship between them: but then we can't see warrant as simply a matter of a belief's being produced by faculties working properly in an appropriate environment. We still have no real answer to the question *What is warrant*? That particular frog (with apologies to John Austin) is still grinning residually up from the bottom of the mug.

Fortunately there is an easy response. Not only does the first belief, the belief that $7 + 5 = 12$, have more by way of warrant for me than the second; it is also one I accept much more firmly. It seems *obviously* true, in a way in which the belief about the bicycle and shotgun do not. Among the things we believe, we believe some much more firmly than others. I believe that I live in Indiana, that $2 + 1 = 3$, that the sun is larger than the earth, that China has a larger population than India, and that Friesland used to be much larger than it is now; and I believe some of these things more firmly than others. Here I speak of full belief, not the partial beliefs of which Bayesians speak.[8] Following Ramsey, Bayesians sometimes suggest that my degrees of belief can be at least roughly determined by examining my betting behavior; the least odds at which I will bet on a proposition A measures the degree to which I believe A. If I am willing to bet at odds of 2:1 that the die will come up either 5 or 6 then I must believe to degree .667 that it will come up that way. This seems to me wrong. The truth is I believe it *probable* to degree .667 that the die will come up that way. And no doubt I fully believe *that*; that is, in this case I don't believe *anything* to degree .667 (strictly speaking, there is no such thing as believing something to degree .667), but I *do* believe (fully believe) that there is a .667 probability that the die will come up either 5 or 6. Suppose I buy a ticket in a thousand-ticket lottery I believe to be fair. Here it is false, I think, that I believe I will not win, or believe that to degree .999. What I do believe is that it is very *probable* (probable to degree .999) that I won't win.[9]

Return to the case in question, then: although I believe both 7 + 5 = 12 and *40 years ago I owned a secondhand 16-gauge shotgun and a red bicycle with balloon tires*, I believe the former more strongly than the latter; this is correlated with the fact that the former has more by way of warrant for me than the latter. I therefore conjecture that when my cognitive establishment is working properly, then in the typical case, the degree to which I believe a given proposition will be proportional to the degree it has of warrant – or if the relationship isn't one of straightforward proportionality, some appropriate functional relationship will hold between warrant and this impulse. When my faculties are functioning properly, a belief has warrant to the degree that I find myself inclined to accept it; and this (again, if my faculties are functioning properly and nothing interferes) will be the degree to which I *do* accept it.

Initially, and to (at most) a zeroeth approximation, therefore, we may put it like this: in the paradigm cases of warrant, a belief *B* has warrant for S if and only if that belief is produced in S by his epistemic faculties working properly in an appropriate environment; and if both *B* and *B** have warrant for S, *B* has more warrant than *B** for S iff S believes *B* more firmly than *B**. And knowledge requires both true belief, and a certain degree of warrant (a degree that may vary from context to context, so that knowledge may display a certain indexical character).[10]

Putting the matter thus imports what is at this stage at best a wholly spurious pretense of precision and completeness; and the rest of this chapter will be given over to some of the necessary qualifications, amplifications, and the like, including attention to the absolutely crucial notion of the design plan. To begin with some of the essential and obvious qualifications then: it is of first importance to see that this condition – that of one's cognitive equipment functioning *properly* – is not the same thing as one's cognitive equipment functioning *normally*, not, at any rate, if we take the term "normally" in a broadly statistical sense. Even if one of my systems functions in a way far from the statistical norm, it might still be functioning properly. (Alternatively, what we must see is that there is a distinction between a normative and statistical sense of "normal.") Carl Lewis is not defective with respect to jumping by virtue of the fact that he can jump much further than the average person. Perhaps most adult tomcats get into lots of fights and ordinarily move into late middle age with patches of fur torn out; it does not follow that an old tomcat with all of his fur suffers from some sort of tonsorial disorder. Perhaps most male cats get neutered; it does not follow that those that don't are incapable of proper function. If, by virtue of some nuclear disaster, we were nearly all left blind, it would not follow that the few sighted among us would have improperly functioning eyes. So your belief's being produced by your faculties working *normally* or in *normal* conditions – that is, the sorts of conditions that most frequently obtain – must be distinguished from their working *properly*.

Further, a belief has warrant for me only if my epistemic faculties are working properly in producing and sustaining it; but of course it isn't true that *all* of my cognitive faculties have to be functioning properly in order for a given belief to have warrant for me. Suppose my memory plays me tricks; obviously that does not mean that I can't have warrant for such introspective propositions as that I am appeared to redly. What must be working properly are the faculties (or subfaculties, or modules) involved in the production of the particular belief in question. And even they need not be working properly over the entire range of their operation. Suppose I cannot properly hear high notes: I may still learn much by way of the hearing ability I do have. Furthermore, a faculty that does not function properly *without outside aid* can nonetheless furnish warrant; I can have warrant for visual propositions even if I need glasses and can see next to nothing without them. Still further, even if my corrected vision is very poor, I can still have warrant for visual propositions; even if I can't perceive colors at all, I can still have warrant for the proposition that I perceive something round. Again, even if I can't perceive colors at all, I can still have visual warrant for the proposition that something is red; even if for me nothing appears redly (everything is merely black and white) I might still be able to see that something is red, in the way in which one can see, on a black and white television, which boxer is wearing the red trunks. And of course there will be many more qualifications of this sort necessary:[11] suppose my belief is based upon two different mechanisms and one but not the other is functioning properly; suppose the same process works properly over one part of its range of operation but not over another, and my belief is produced by its working over both of these parts of its range of operation; or suppose a process is not working properly over part of its range but produces in me in given circumstances the very same belief it would have if it were working properly; in these cases does my belief have warrant? These are good questions, but there isn't time to work out all the answers here.

Still further, proper functioning, of course, *comes in degrees*; or if it does not, then approximation to proper functioning does. Clearly the faculties relevant with respect to a given belief need not be functioning *perfectly* for me to have warrant for my belief; many of my visual beliefs may constitute knowledge even if my vision is not 20/20. Similarly, my faculties can function *properly* even if they do not function *ideally*, even if they do not function as well as those of some other actual or possible species (a point I discuss in chapter 6 of *Warrant: The Current Debate*). My locomotory equipment may be functioning properly even if I can't run as fast as a cheetah; my arithmetic powers may be in good working order even if I can't anywhere nearly keep up with a computer, or an angel, or an Alpha Centaurian. But how well, then, must such powers be functioning? Part of the answer here, of course, is that there is no answer; the ideas of knowledge and warrant are to some degree vague; hence there needs to be no precise answer to the question in question. What I hope is that the vaguenesses involved in my account of warrant vary with the vaguenesses we independently recognize in the notion of warrant. If warrant and proper function are properly tied together, then we may expect that they will waver together.

Similar comments and qualifications, of course, must be made about the environmental condition. For my beliefs to have warrant, the environment must be similar to that for which my epistemic powers have been designed; but just how similar must it be? Here, of course, we encounter vagueness; there is no precise answer. Further, suppose I *know* that the environment is misleading; and suppose I know in just which ways it is misleading. (I'm on a planet where things that look square are really round.) Then, clearly enough, the fact that my environment is misleading need not deprive my beliefs of warrant. And of course the same must be said for the requirement that my faculties be in good working order. Suppose (as in Castañeda's fantasy)[12] I suffer from a quirk of memory: whenever I read a history book, I always misremember the dates, somehow adding ten years to the date as stated: beliefs formed by way of reading history books – even beliefs about dates – can still have warrant for me; I can compensate for my erroneous tendency. What counts, of course, are uncorrected and uncompensated malfunctionings. Clearly there is need here for a good deal of Chisholming; let me postpone it, however, in order to turn to other more pressing matters.

II   The Design Plan

But aren't there cases in which our faculties function perfectly properly in the right sort of environment but the resulting beliefs still lack warrant? Surely there are. Someone may remember a painful experience as less painful than it was, as is sometimes said to be the case with childbirth.[13] You may continue to believe in your friend's honesty long after evidence and cool, objective judgment would have dictated a reluctant change of mind. I may believe that I will recover from a dread disease much more strongly than is justified by the statistics of which I am aware. William James's climber in the Alps, faced with a life or death situation, believed more strongly than the evidence warrants that he could leap the crevasse. In all of these cases, there is no cognitive dysfunction or failure to function properly; it would be a mistake, however, to say that the beliefs in question had warrant for the person in question.

I cannot forbear quoting a couple of Locke's examples:

> Would it not be an insufferable thing for a learned professor, and that which his scarlet would blush at, to have his authority of forty years standing wrought out of hard rock Greek and Latin, with no small expence of time and candle, and confirmed by general tradition, and a reverent beard, in an instant overturned by an upstart novelist? Can any one expect that he should be made to confess, that what he taught his scholars thirty years ago, was all errour and mistake; and that he sold them hard words and ignorance at a very dear rate?[14]

The professor's faculties may be functioning properly (there may be a properly functioning defense mechanism at work); but his belief that the young upstart is dead wrong would have little by way of warrant. Another of Locke's examples:

> Tell a man, passiounately in love, that he is jilted; bring a score of witnesses of the falsehood of his mistress, 'tis ten to one but three kind words of hers, shall invalidate all their testimonies. ... What suits our wishes, is forwardly believed is, I suppose, what every one hath more than once experiemented; and though men cannot always openly gain-say, or resist the force of manifest probabilities, that make against them; yet yield they not to the argument. (*Essay*, IV, xx, 12)

Now it was widely believed in the eighteenth century that love was or induced a sort of madness, so that the lover's epistemic faculties are not functioning properly. Even if that isn't so, however, even if we are designed to act and believe in extravagant fashion when in love, the lover's belief that his mistress is true to him has little by way of warrant.

Still another case: according to Freud, religious belief is "the universal obsessional neurosis of mankind"; religious belief consists in "illusions, fulfillments of the oldest, strongest, and most insistent wishes of mankind."[15] Rather similar sentiments are expressed by Marx, who holds that religious belief is produced by an unhealthy, perverted social order: "This State, this society,

produce religion, produce a perverted world consciousness, because they are a perverted world. ... Religion is the sigh of the oppressed creature, the feelings of a heartless world, just as it is the spirit of unspiritual conditions."[16] Now neither Freud nor Marx would be mollified if we pointed out that religion is very widespread among human beings, that is, "normal" in the statistical sense; what is statistically normal may still be a disease, a matter of malfunction, in this case a cognitive dysfunction. But there is a further subtlety here; Freud and Marx differ in a significant way. Marx seems to think that religion is a sort of perversion, something unhealthy; it is as if he says, "Let's call it an aberration and be done with it." Freud, on the other hand, is ambivalent. First, he says that religious belief is or stems from neurosis: that sounds like he thinks religious belief arises from a cognitive malfunction of some sort. But then he also says it is a matter of illusion, and arises from the "oldest and strongest and most insistent wishes of mankind." That suggests not that religious belief arises from malfunction or failure of some cognitive module to function properly, but instead by way of wish fulfillment. What one believes in *that* way isn't necessarily a product of malfunction; illusion and wish fulfillment also have their functions. According to Freud, they enable us to mask the grim, threatening, frightening visage of the world – a visage that would otherwise cause us to cower in terror or sink into utter and apathetic despair. On the second way of thinking, then, religious belief need not be a result of malfunction; it might be produced by faculties functioning just as they should. Even so, however – even if the wish fulfillment that produces religious belief does not result from cognitive malfunction – religious belief won't enjoy much by way of warrant.

So the proposed condition for warrant – proper function in an appropriate environment – isn't anywhere nearly sufficient for warrant. Why not? Well, consider the elements of our cognitive faculties responsible for beliefs of the above sorts – those produced by wishful thinking, or by the optimism that enables one to survive a deadly illness – one thinks that the purpose of *these* modules of our cognitive capacities is not to produce true beliefs. They are instead aimed at something else: survival, or the possibility of friendship, or (Freud thinks) the capacity to carry on in this bleak and nasty world of ours.

To get a better understanding of this matter, we must consider a notion of crucial importance: that of specifications, or blueprint, or *design plan*. Human beings are constructed according to a certain design plan. This terminology does not commit us to supposing that human beings have been literally designed – by God, for example. Here I use "design" the way Daniel Dennett (not ordinarily thought unsound on theism) does in speaking of a given organism as possessing a certain design, and of evolution as producing optimal design: "In the end, we want to be able to explain the intelligence of man, or beast, in terms of his design; and this in turn in terms of the natural selection of this design."[17] We take it that when the organs (or organic systems) of a human being (or other organism) function properly, they function *in a particular way*. Such organs have a *function* or *purpose*; more exactly, they have several functions or purposes, including both proximate and more remote purposes. The ultimate purpose of the heart is to contribute to the health and proper function of the entire organism (some might say instead that it is to contribute to the *survival* of the individual, or the species, or even to the perpetuation of the genetic material itself).[18] But of course the heart also has a much more circumscribed and specific function: to pump blood. Such an organ, furthermore, normally functions in such a way as to fulfill its purpose; but it also functions to fulfill that purpose in just one of an indefinitely large number of possible ways. Here a comparison with artifacts is useful. A house is designed to produce shelter – but not in just any old way. There will be plans specifying the length and pitch of the rafters, what kind of shingles are to be applied, the kind and quantity of insulation to be used, and the like. Something similar holds in the case of us and our faculties; we seem to be constructed in accordance with a specific set of plans. Better (since this analogy is insufficiently dynamic) we seem to have been constructed in accordance with a set of specifications, in the way in which there are specifications for, for example, the 1992 Buick. According to these specifications (I'm just guessing), after a cold start the engine runs at 1,500 RPM until the engine temperature reaches 190°F; it then throttles back to 750 RPM.

Similarly, there is something like a set of specifications for a well-formed, properly functioning human being – an extraordinarily complicated and highly articulated set of specifications, as any first-year medical student could tell you. *Something* like such a set: a copy of these specifications does not come with every newborn child, and we can't write to the manufacturer for a new copy to replace the one we have carelessly lost. Suppose we call these specifications a "design plan." It is natural to speak of organisms and their parts as exhibiting design, and such talk is exceedingly common: "According to Dr Sam Ridgway, physiologist with the US Naval Ocean Systems Center in San Diego, seals avoid the bends by not absorbing nitrogen in the first place. 'The lungs of marine mammals,' Dr Ridgway explains, 'are designed to collapse under pressure exerted on deep dives. Air from the collapsed lungs is forced back into the windpipe, where the nitrogen simply can't be absorbed by the blood.'"[19] Of course the design plan for human beings will include specifications for our *cognitive* system or faculties. Like the rest of our organs and systems, our cognitive faculties can work well or badly; they can malfunction or function properly. They too work in a certain way when they are functioning properly – and work in a certain way to accomplish their purpose. The purpose of the heart is to pump blood; that of our cognitive faculties (overall) is to supply us with reliable information: about our environment, about the past, about the thoughts and feeling of others, and so on. But not just any old way of accomplishing this purpose in the case of a specific cognitive process is in accordance with our design plan. It is for this reason that it is possible for a belief to be produced by a cognitive process or belief-producing mechanism that is *accidentally* reliable (as in the case of the processes I have cited as counterexamples to Goldman's version of reliabilism).[20] Although such belief-producing processes are in fact reliable, the beliefs they yield have little by way of warrant; and the reason is that these processes are pathologically out of accord with the design plan for human beings.

Our design plan, of course, is such that our faculties are highly responsive to circumstances. Upon considering an instance of *modus ponens*, I find myself believing its corresponding conditional;

upon being appeared to in the familiar way, I find myself with the belief that there is a large tree before me; upon being asked what I had for breakfast, I reflect for a moment, and the belief that what I had was eggs on toast is formed within me. In these and other cases I do not *deliberate*; I do not total up the evidence (I am being appeared to redly; on most occasions when thus appeared to I am in the presence of something red; so most probably in this case I am) and thus come to a view as to what seems best supported; I simply find myself with the appropriate belief. Of course in *some* cases I may go through such a weighing of the evidence; for example, I may be trying to evaluate the alleged evidence in favor of the theory that human life evolved by means of such mechanisms as random genetic mutation and natural selection from unicellular life (which itself arose by substantially similar mechanical processes from nonliving material); but in the typical case of belief formation nothing like this is involved.

Here I wish to note just a couple of its salient features. According to our design plan, obviously enough, *experience* plays a crucial role in belief formation. *A priori* beliefs, for example, are not, as this denomination mistakenly suggests, formed prior to or in the absence of experience. Thinking of the corresponding conditional of *modus ponens* somehow *feels* different from thinking of, say, the corresponding conditional of *affirming the consequent*; and this difference in experience is connected with our accepting the one and rejecting the other. Of course experience plays a different role here from the role it plays in the formation of perceptual beliefs; it plays a still different role in the formation of memory beliefs, moral beliefs, beliefs about the mental lives of other persons, beliefs we form on the basis of inductive evidence, and the like. In later chapters we shall look into these matters in more detail.

Further, our design plan is such that under certain conditions we form one belief *on the evidential basis* of others. I may form the belief that Sam was at the party on the evidential basis of other beliefs – perhaps I learn from you that Sam wasn't at the bar and from his wife that he was either at the bar or at the party. Of course (if our faculties are functioning properly) we don't form just *any* belief on the evidential basis of just any other. I won't form the belief that Feike is a

Catholic on the evidential basis of the propositions that nine out of ten Frisians are Protestants and Feike is a Frisian – not, at any rate, unless I am suffering from some sort of cognitive malfunction. And here too experience plays an important role. The belief about Sam *feels like* the right one; that belief about Feike (in those circumstances) feels strange, inappropriate, worthy of rejection, not to be credited. Still further, the design plan dictates the appropriate *degree* or firmness of a given belief in given circumstances. You read in a relatively unreliable newspaper an account of a 53-car accident on a Los Angeles freeway; perhaps you then form the belief that there was a 53-car accident on the freeway. But if you hold that belief as firmly as, for example, that $2 + 1 = 3$, then your faculties are not functioning as they ought to and the belief has little warrant for you. Again, experience obviously plays an important role. What we need is a full and appropriately subtle and sensitive description of the role of experience in the formation and maintenance of all these various types of beliefs. For the moment, we may rest satisfied simply to note the importance of experience in the economy of our cognitive establishment.

Now return to the examples that precipitated this excursus about the design plan – the cases of beliefs produced by wish fulfillment, or the optimism necessary to surviving a serious illness, or willingness to have more children, or the like. In these cases, the relevant faculties may be functioning properly, functioning just as they ought to, but nevertheless not in a way that leads to truth, to the formation of true beliefs. But then proper function in a right environment is not sufficient for warrant. Different parts or aspects of our cognitive apparatus have different purposes; different parts or aspects of our design plan are aimed at different ends or goals. Not all aspects of the design of our cognitive faculties need be aimed at the production of true belief; some might be such as to conduce to survival, or relief from suffering, or the possibility of loyalty, or inclination to have more children, and so on. What confers warrant is one's cognitive faculties working properly, or working according to the design plan *insofar as that segment of the design plan is aimed at producing true beliefs*. But someone whose holding a certain belief is a result of an aspect of our cognitive design that is aimed not at truth but at something else won't be such that the belief has warrant for him; he won't properly be said to know the proposition in question, even if it turns out to be true.

So there are cases where belief-producing faculties are functioning properly but warrant is absent: cases where the design plan is not aimed at the production of true (or verisimilitudinous) beliefs but at the production of beliefs with some other virtue. But then there will also be cases where cognitive faculties are not functioning properly, but warrant is present; these will be inverses, so to speak, of the cases of the preceding paragraph. Suppose our design demands that under certain special circumstances our ordinary belief-producing mechanisms are overridden by a mechanism designed to deal with that specific case: perhaps there is a sort of optimistic mechanism that cuts in when I am seriously ill, causing me to believe more strongly than the evidence indicates that I will survive the illness, thereby enhancing my chances to survive it. Suppose I am taken seriously ill, and suppose through some malfunction (induced, perhaps, by the illness itself) the operation of the optimistic mechanism is inhibited, so that, believing just in accord with the evidence, I form the belief that I probably will not survive. Then the relevant segment of my cognitive faculties is not functioning properly; that is, it is not functioning in accordance with the design plan; but doesn't my belief have warrant anyway?[21] Might I not have the degree of warrant that goes with the degree to which I believe that I probably won't survive, despite the fact that if my faculties were functioning properly, I would believe (to one or another degree of firmness) that I *will* survive? The answer, of course, is as before: those segments of my cognitive faculties (those modules, we might say) that are aimed at *truth* are functioning properly; my cognitive faculties are functioning in accord with the design plan insofar as the design plan is aimed at the production of true beliefs. There is malfunction only with respect to those cognitive modules aimed at something other than truth; so in this case the belief that I will not survive has the degree of warrant normally going with the degree of belief I display.

Many questions remain,[22] but I must leave them to the reader.

III   Reliability

According to the zeroeth approximation, a belief has warrant for me, speaking roughly, if it is produced by my cognitive faculties functioning properly in a congenial environment. We have just seen that these two together are insufficient: the segment of the design plan governing the production of the belief in question must also be aimed at truth. But this is still insufficient. For suppose a well-meaning but incompetent angel – one of Hume's infant deities,[23] say – sets out to design a variety of rational persons, persons capable of thought, belief, and knowledge. As it turns out, the design is a real failure; the resulting beings hold beliefs, all right, but most of them are absurdly false.[24] Here all three of our conditions are met: the beliefs of these beings are formed by their cognitive faculties functioning properly in the cognitive environment for which they were designed, and furthermore the relevant modules of the design plan are aimed at truth (the relevant modules of their cognitive equipment have the production of true beliefs as their purpose). But the beliefs of these pitifully deceived beings do not have warrant.[25] What must we add? That the design plan is a *good* one – more exactly, that the design governing the production of the belief in question is a good one; still more exactly, that the objective probability of a belief's being true, given that it is produced by cognitive faculties functioning in accord with the relevant module of the design plan, is high. Even more exactly, the module of the design plan governing its production must be such that it is objectively highly probable that a belief produced by cognitive faculties functioning properly according to that module (in a congenial environment) will be true or verisimilitudinous. This is the reliabilist constraint on warrant, and the important truth contained in reliabilist accounts of warrant.

It is easy to overlook this condition. The reason is that we ordinarily take it for granted that when our cognitive faculties – at any rate, those whose function it is to produce true beliefs – function properly in an appropriate environment, then for the most part the beliefs they produce are true. When our faculties function in accord with our design plan (in an appropriate environment), the beliefs they produce are for the most part true. Certainly we think so with respect to memory, perception, logical and arithmetical beliefs, inductively based beliefs, and so on. Further, we take it for granted that these faculties are *reliable*; they not only *do* produce true beliefs, but *would* produce true beliefs even if things were moderately different. (They produce true beliefs in most of the appropriately nearby possible worlds; that is, most of the appropriately nearby possible worlds *W* meet the following condition: necessarily, if *W* had been actual, then our cognitive faculties would have produced mostly true beliefs.) Still another way to put it: we take it for granted that the statistical or objective probability of a belief's being true, given that it has been produced by our faculties functioning properly in the cognitive environment for which they were designed, is high. Perhaps more specifically our presupposition is that in general (for a person S with properly functioning faculties in an appropriate environment, and given the cited qualifications) the more firmly S believes *p*, the more likely it is that *p* is true. Of course, we think some faculties more reliable than others, and think a given faculty is more reliable under some conditions than others. This assumption on our part is a sort of presumption of reliability. Of course, it *is* a presumption or an assumption; it isn't or isn't obviously[26] entailed by the notion of proper function itself. So the account of proper function must include it as another condition: if one of my beliefs has warrant, then the module of the design plan governing the production of that belief must be such that the statistical or objective probability of a belief's being true, given that it has been produced in accord with that module in a congenial cognitive environment, is high.

How high, precisely? Here we encounter vagueness again; there is no precise answer. It is part of the presumption, however, that the degree of reliability varies as a function of degree of belief. The things we are most sure of – simple logical and arithmetical truths, such beliefs as that I now have a mild ache in my knee (that indeed I have knees), obvious perceptual truths – these are the sorts of beliefs we hold most firmly, perhaps with the maximum degree of firmness, and the ones such that we associate a very high degree of reliability with the modules of the design plan governing their production. Even here, however, we are not immune from error: even what seems to be selfevident can be mistaken,

as Frege learned to his sorrow.[27] It may be worth noting, however, that Frege did not believe the offending "axiom" to the maximal degree; if he had, then he would have been no more likely to give up that "axiom" than to conclude that there really *is* a set that is and is not a member of itself.

I say the presupposition of reliability is a feature of our usual way of thinking about warrant; but of course this presupposition is not inevitable for us. The skeptic, for example, can often best be seen as questioning this presupposition. She may agree that there is indeed a perfectly proper distinction between cognitive proper function and malfunction, but be agnostic about the question whether there is any correlation at all between proper function and truth. Or she may think there is indeed such a correlation, but think it far too weak to support our ordinary claims to knowledge. Or she may think that since the long-run purpose of our beliefs, as she sees it, is to enable us to move about in the environment in such a way that we do not come to grief (or do not come to grief until we have had a chance to reproduce), there is no interesting correlation between a belief's being produced by faculties functioning properly and its being true.[28] Of course one can be a skeptic about one particular area as opposed to others: a rationalist may think sense perception less reliable than reason and may thus maintain that it is only reason, not perception, that gives us knowledge; an empiricist may see things the other way around. Philosophy itself is a good candidate for a certain measured skepticism: in view of the enormous diversity of competing philosophical views, one can hardly claim with a straight face that what we have in philosophy is *knowledge*; the diversity of views makes it unlikely that the relevant segments of the design plan are sufficiently reliable. (In a properly run intellectual establishment, therefore, most philosophical views will not enjoy anywhere nearly the maximal degree of belief.)

To return to warrant then: to a first approximation, we may say that a belief *B* has warrant for S if and only if the relevant segments (the segments involved in the production of *B*) are functioning properly in a cognitive environment sufficiently similar to that for which S's faculties are designed; and the modules of the design plan governing the production of *B* are (1) aimed at truth, and (2) such that there is a high objective probability that a belief formed in accordance with those modules (in that sort of cognitive environment) is true; and the more firmly S believes B the more warrant B has for S. This is at best a first approximation; it is still at most programmatic, a suggestion, an idea, a hint. Furthermore, it might be suggested (in fact, it *has* been suggested) that while it may be difficult to find counterexamples to the view, that is only because it is vague and imprecise. I have sympathies with both complaints, although I would implore those who make the second to heed Aristotle's dictum and seek no more precision than the subject admits. Maybe there isn't any neat formula, any short and snappy list of conditions (at once informative and precise) that are severally necessary and jointly sufficient for warrant; if so, we won't make much progress by grimly pursuing them.

Notes

1   "Evidentialism," this vol., ch. 24.
2   See his "Concepts of Epistemic Justification," *Monist* (January 1985), and "An Internalist Externalism," *Synthese* 74, no. 3 (1988); see also several of the articles collected in *Epistemic Justification* (Ithaca: Cornell University Press, 1989).
3   Fred Dretske, *Explaining Behavior* (Cambridge: MIT Press, 1988), p. 91.
4   "Limiting Science: a Biologist's Perspective," *Daedalus* (Summer 1988), p. 336.
5   *The Child's Conception of Physical Causality* (London: Kegan Paul, Trench, Trubner, 1930).
6   "How to Build a Person," in *Philosophical Perspectives, 1, Metaphysics, 1987*, ed. James Tomberlin (Atascadero, CA.: Ridgeview, 1987), p. 146.
7   See my *Warrant: The Current Debate* (New York: Oxford University Press, 1993), ch. 6, sec. 1, "The Varieties of Rationality."
8   See ibid., ch. 6, pp. 117 ff.
9   It is sometimes suggested that whenever I believe A no more firmly than not-A and not-A no more firmly than A, then I can be thought of as believing A (and not-A) to degree .5. This seems clearly mistaken. Consider a case where I have no idea at all whether the proposition in question is true. You ask me (a touch pedantically) "consider the proposition that the highest mountain on Mars is between ten and eleven thousand feet high and call it 'A'; do you think A is true?" I have no idea about A and do not believe it more likely than its denial; I also do not believe its denial more likely than it. Then on the Bayesian view, I must believe A to degree .5. You then ask me the same question about B: the proposition that the highest mountain on Mars is between eleven and twelve thousand feet high. Again, I have no idea; so on the Bayesian view I am considering, I must also believe B to degree .5. Now A and B are mutually exclusive; according to the probability calculus, therefore, I should believe their disjunction to degree 1. But of course I do not; for I also have no idea whether the highest mountain on Mars is between ten and twelve thousand feet high. And the problem is not that I am desperately incoherent. The problem is that we can't properly represent ignorance of this sort as believing the proposition in question to degree .5. There is a vast difference between the situation in which I think A probable to degree .5 (perhaps A is the proposition that the die will come up side 1, 2, or 3) and the situation in which I have no idea what the probability of A's being true might be.
10 See H. N. Castañeda's "The Indexical Theory of Knowledge," in Peter French, Theodore E. Uehling, Jr., and Howard Wettstein (eds), *Midwest Studies in Philosophy*, vol. V (Minneapolis: University of Minnesota Press, 1980).
11 Here I am indebted to Tom Senor.
12 "The Indexical Theory of Knowledge," p. 202.
13 "A woman giving birth to a child has pain because her time has come; but when her baby is born she forgets the anguish because of her joy that a child is born into the world." John 16:21.
14 *An Essay concerning Human Understanding*, ed. A. C. Fraser (New York: Dover, 1953), IV, xx, 11, hereafter referred to as *Essay*.

15 *The Future of an Illusion* (1927), trans. and ed. James Strachey (London: Norton, 1961), p. 30.

16 K. Marx, *Introduction to a Critique of the Hegelian Philosophy of Right*, in *Collected Works*, by K. Marx and F. Engels (London: Lawrence & Wishart, 1975), 3:175.

17 *Brainstorms* (Cambridge: Bradford Books, 1978), p. 12.

18 See Richard Dawkins, *The Selfish Gene* (Oxford: Oxford University Press, 1976).

19 *National Geographic* 171, no. 4 (April 1987), p. 489.

20 See my *Warrant: The Current Debate*, ch. 9.

21 I owe this example to Caleb Miller.

22 Some of which were forcibly brought to my attention by Dean Zimmerman.

23 *Dialogues Concerning Natural Religion*, Part V (1779), ed. N. K. Smith (Bobbs-Merrill, 1947), p. 169.

24 Some (Donald Davidson, for example) apparently hold that it is impossible that there be a sizeable community of believers most of whose beliefs are false; I disagree and explain why elsewhere.

25 This counterexample was called to my attention by Richard Swinburne, Ian Foster, and Thomas Senor.

26 I suppose it might sensibly be held that it is impossible that there be rational beings (beings capable of reasoning or belief) whose cognitive faculties function properly but who nonetheless hold predominantly false beliefs. Perhaps there are purposes or ends necessarily built into certain kinds of creatures. Then if a malevolent Cartesian demon were to design a race of rational creatures whose beliefs were nearly always mistaken, their cognitive faculties would not be functioning properly, even if they were functioning just as they were designed to. Instead, we should have to say that what this demon wanted to do was to design a race of cognitive beings that did not function properly.

27 Frege produced a set of axioms for set theory, including the famous or infamous proposition that for any property P there exists the set of just those things that have P. Russell showed him that this axiom (together with the others) yields a contradiction: if it is true, there will be a set of nonselfmembered sets, which both will and will not be a member of itself.

28 Thus Patricia Churchland: "Boiled down to essentials, a nervous system enables the organism to succeed in the four F's: feeding, fleeing, fighting and reproducing. The principal chore of nervous systems is to get the body parts where they should be in order that the organism may survive. ... Truth, whatever that is, definitely takes the hindmost" (*Journal of Philosophy* 84 (October 1987), p. 548).

CHAPTER 33

Virtues of the Mind, Selections

Linda Zagzebski

General Account of a Virtue

A serious problem in any attempt to give a general account of the nature of virtue is that our language does not contain a sufficient number of names that convey the full unified reality of each virtue. Some names pick out reactive feelings (empathy), some pick out desires (curiosity), some pick out motivations to act (benevolence), whereas others pick out patterns of acting that appear to be independent of feeling and motive (fairness). For this reason it is easy to confuse a virtue with a feeling in some cases (empathy, compassion), and with a skill in others (fairness). The result is that it is very difficult to give a unitary account of virtues using common virtue language. MacIntyre (1984) blames the problem on a defect in our culture,[1] but this cannot be an adequate explanation since Aristotle's list was no better in this respect than ours. When we examine Aristotle's virtues and vices we see that he had difficulty in finding names for some of them, and a few of his names seem forced, such as his term "*anaisthesia*," which he coins for the trait of insensibility to pleasure. Gregory Trianosky's response to this situation is to say that virtues are not all traits of the same general type.[2] Robert Roberts

Originally published in L. Zagzebski, *Virtues of the Mind* (Cambridge: Cambridge University Press, 1996), pp. 134–7, 166–84.

also concludes that there are several distinct kinds of virtue.[3] This response is understandable and it is possible that we will eventually be forced into it, but I believe it should only be taken as a last resort, and I see no reason to take it yet. It is more plausible that the problem derives from a defect in our virtue language rather than a division in the nature of virtue itself.

Let us begin by reviewing the features of virtue we have already identified. First, a virtue is an acquired excellence of the soul, or to use more modern terminology, it is an acquired excellence of the person in a deep and lasting sense. A vice is the contrary quality; it is an acquired defect of the soul. One way to express the depth required for a trait to be a virtue or a vice is to think of it as a quality we would ascribe to a person if asked to describe her after her death. Perhaps no quality is really permanent, or, at least, no interesting quality, but virtues and vices are in the category of the more enduring of a person's qualities, and they come closer to defining who the person is than any other category of qualities.

Second, a virtue is acquired by a process that involves a certain amount of time and work on the part of the agent. This is not to suggest that a person controls the acquisition of a virtue entirely; that is plainly false. Nevertheless, the time and effort required partly account for a virtue's deep and lasting quality, one that in part defines a person's identity and that leads us to think of her as responsible for it. This means that typically a virtue is acquired through a process of habituation, although the virtues of creativity may be an exception.

Third, a virtue is not simply a skill. Skills have many of the same features as virtues in their manner of acquisition and in their area of application, and virtuous persons are expected to have the correlative skills in order to be effective in action, but skills do not have the intrinsic value of virtues.

Fourth, a virtue has a component of motivation. A motivation is a disposition to have a certain motive, and a motive is an emotion that initiates and directs action to produce an end with certain desired features. Motivations can become deep parts of a person's character and provide her with a set of orientations toward the world that emerge into action given the appropriate circumstances. A motivation is best defined, not as a way of acting in circumstances specifiable in advance, but in terms of the end at which it aims and the emotion that underlies it. The easiest way to identify a motivation is by reference to the end at which it aims, but it also involves an emotion disposition, and that is harder to identify by name.

This brings us to another important feature of virtue: "Virtue" is a success term. The motivational component of a virtue means that it has an end, whether internal or external. A person does not have a virtue unless she is reliable at bringing about the end that is the aim of the motivational component of the virtue. For example, a fair person acts in a way that successfully produces a state of affairs that has the features fair persons desire. A kind, compassionate, generous, courageous, or just person aims at making the world a certain way, and reliable success in making it that way is a condition for having the virtue in question. For this reason virtue requires knowledge, or at least awareness, of certain nonmoral facts about the world. The nature of morality involves, not only wanting certain things, but being reliable agents for bringing those things about. The understanding that a virtue involves is necessary for success in bringing about the aim of its motivational component. This means that virtue involves a component of understanding that is implied by the success component.

A virtue therefore has two main elements: a motivational element, and an element of reliable success in bringing about the end (internal or external) of the motivational element. These elements express the two distinct aims of the moral project that we find in commonsense moral thinking. On the one hand, ordinary ways of thinking about morality tell us that morality is largely a matter of the heart, and we evaluate persons for the quality of their motivations. But morality is also in part a project of making the world a certain kind of place – a better place, we might say, or the kind of place good people want it to be. Because of the latter interest, we are impressed with moral success, not to the exclusion of an interest in people's cares and efforts, but in addition to it.

A virtue, then, can be defined as a deep and enduring acquired excellence of a person, involving a characteristic motivation to produce a certain desired end and reliable success in bringing about that end. What I mean by a motivation is a disposition to have a motive; a motive is an action-guiding emotion with a certain end, either internal or external.

This definition is broad enough to include the intellectual as well as the traditional moral virtues. It may also be broad enough to include virtues other than the moral or intellectual, such as aesthetic, religious, or perhaps even physical virtues, but I will not consider virtues in these other categories in this work. The definition may not apply to higher-order virtues such as integrity and practical wisdom, however.

The Motivation for Knowledge and Reliable Success

In this section I will argue that the individual intellectual virtues can be defined in terms of motivations arising from the general motivation for knowledge and reliability in attaining the aims of these motives. Since all of the intellectual virtues have the same foundational motivation and since all of the other moral virtues have different foundational motivations, this means that a distinction between an intellectual and a moral virtue can be made on the basis of the motivational component of the virtue. I maintain that this is the only theoretically relevant difference between intellectual virtues and the other moral virtues, and so there are good grounds for continuing to call these virtues "intellectual," even though I have argued that they are best treated as a subset of the moral virtues. It may be that at the deepest level the moral and intellectual virtues arise from the same motivation, perhaps a love of being in general.[4] If so, such a motivation would serve to unify all the virtues, but I will not analyze the relations among the virtuous motivations in this work.

The simplest way to describe the motivational basis of the intellectual virtues is to say that they are all based in the motivation for knowledge. They are all forms of the motivation to have cognitive contact with reality, where this includes more than what is usually expressed by saying that people desire truth. Understanding is also a form of cognitive contact with reality, one that has been considered a component of the knowing state in some periods of philosophical history. I will not give an account of understanding in this work, but I have already indicated that it is a state that includes the comprehension of abstract structures of reality apart from the propositional. I will assume that it either is a form of knowledge or enhances the quality of knowledge. Although all intellectual virtues have a motivational component that aims at cognitive contact with reality, some of them may aim more at understanding, or perhaps at other epistemic states that enhance the quality of the knowing state, such as certainty, than at the possession of truth per se. A few stellar virtues such as intellectual originality or inventiveness are related, not simply to the motivation for the *agent* to possess knowledge, but to the motivation to advance knowledge for the human race. We will also look at how the motivation to know leads to following rules and belief-forming procedures known by the epistemic community to be truth conducive, and we will see how the individual intellectual virtues are knowledge conducive.

The task of defining virtues immediately raises the question of how virtues are individuated and whether they are unified at some deeper level. I will not go very far into this matter, although it is an interesting one and ought to be pursued in a full theory of virtue. I have no position on the question of whether intellectual virtues that share a name with certain moral virtues are two different virtues or one. Even within the class of intellectual virtues it is difficult to demarcate the boundaries of the individual virtues if I am right

that they all arise out of the motivation for knowledge since that implies that all intellectual virtues are unified by one general motivation. But, of course, the same thing can be said about all the other moral virtues since they also can be unified by one general motivation for good, and knowledge is a form of good.

Let me address one more point before beginning. The definition of intellectual virtue in terms of the motivation for knowledge is circular if we then go on to define knowledge in terms of intellectual virtue. The thesis here must be formulated less succinctly but without circularity as the thesis that the individual intellectual virtues can be defined in terms of derivatives of the motivations for truth or cognitive contact with reality, where the motivation for understanding is assumed to be a form of the motivation for cognitive contact with reality. I am formulating the position in terms of the motivation for knowledge because I think that that is closer to the way people actually think of their own motives and the way those motives are described by others, but I am not wedded to this view. The formulation in terms of knowledge motivation is simpler, and, of course, it is only circular when the theory of virtue is combined with the theory of knowledge.

The motivation for knowledge

Intellectual virtues have been neglected in the history of philosophy, but there were discussions of them in the early modern period as part of the general critical examination of human perceptual and cognitive faculties that dominated that era. Both Hobbes and Spinoza connected the intellectual as well as the moral virtues with the passions, and both traced the source of these virtues to a single human motivation, the motivation for self-preservation or power. In the early part of this century John Dewey stressed the place of the intellectual virtues in what he called "reflective thinking," arising from the desire to attain the goals of effective interaction with the world. We will look first at some remarks by Hobbes and Dewey, and then I will turn to the contemporary treatment of the intellectual virtues by James Montmarquet in the course of giving my own argument for the derivation of the motivational components of intellectual virtues from the motivation to know.

Let us begin with the lively discussion of the causes of intellectual virtue and vice in Hobbes's *Leviathan*:

> The causes of this difference of wits are in the passions, and the difference of passions proceeded partly from the different constitution of the body and partly from different education. For if the difference proceeds from the temper of the brain and the organs of sense, either exterior or interior, there would be no less difference of men in their sight, hearing, or other sense than in their fancies and discretions.[5] It proceeds, therefore, from the passions, which are different not only from the difference of men's complexions, but also from their difference of customs and education.
>
> The passions that most of all cause the difference of wit are principally the more or less desire of power, of riches, of knowledge, and of honor. All which may be reduced to the first – that is, desire of power. For riches, knowledge and honor are but several sorts of power.
>
> And therefore a man who has no great passion for any of these things but is, as men term it, indifferent, though he may be so far a good man as to be free from giving offense, yet he cannot possibly have either a great fancy or much judgment. For the thoughts are to the desires as scouts and spies, to range abroad and find the way to the things desired, all steadiness of the mind's motion, and all quickness of the same, proceeding from thence; for as to have no desire is to be dead, so to have weak passions is dullness; and to have passions indifferently for everything, GIDDINESS and *distraction;* and to have stronger and more vehement passions for anything than is ordinarily seen in others is that which men call MADNESS.[6]

A couple of points in this passage are of interest to our present concern. First, the motivation for knowledge is not a basic motive but is a form of the motivation for power, according to Hobbes. Second, Hobbes's cognitively ideal person is not passionless, but cognitive defects can be traced to an excessively strong, excessively weak, or misplaced desire for power. I will not question the first point. I think Hobbes is probably wrong in his reduction of the desire for knowledge to the desire for power, but I will not dispute it here since even if he is right, the effect is simply to add

another motivational layer beneath the one I am proposing, and so it is no threat to the structure of the theory I am proposing. But I want to call attention to Hobbes's second point, which I find insightful. Hobbes says that cognitive virtues and vices arise from differences in a motivation, and that motivation is a passion that admits of excess, deficiency, and distortion of various sorts, and this seems to me to be generally right. I differ with Hobbes mainly in that I identify this motivation with the motivation for knowledge, whereas Hobbes includes several other forms of the motivation for power along with the motivation for knowledge.

If the human drive for knowledge naturally and inexorably led to success, there would be no need for intellectual virtues. But this motivation can be deficient or distorted in many ways, leading to intellectual vices. Deficiency is presumably one of the most common problems, and Ralph Waldo Emerson expresses a pessimistic view of the human drive for knowledge that illustrates how a natural human motivation can be affected by lethargy:

> God offers to every mind its choice between truth and repose. Take which you please, – you can never have both. Between these, as a pendulum, man oscillates. He in whom the love of repose predominates will accept the first creed, the first philosophy, the first political party he meets, – most likely his father's. He gets rest, commodity, and reputation; but he shuts the door to truth. He in whom the love of truth predominates will keep himself aloof from all moorings, and afloat. He will abstain from dogmatism, and recognize all the opposite negations between which, as walls, his being is swung. He submits to the inconvenience of suspense and imperfect opinion, but he is a candidate for truth, as the other is not, and respects the highest law of his being. ("Intellect," Essay 11)

In this passage Emerson describes how a deficiency in the desire for truth leads to such cognitive vices as lack of autonomy, closed-mindedness, and dogmatism. This may lead us to wonder whether an excess of the motivation for knowledge can also lead to intellectual vices, as Hobbes implies in the passage quoted above. This is parallel to the question of whether a person can be a moral fanatic: excessively motivated by a desire to do or to produce good. Since it is problematic whether this is possible, we will not examine it here.

Few philosophers have given positive directions on how to think that are intended to circumvent the pitfalls in forming beliefs. The stress has generally been on the mistakes. A well-known exception is Descartes in *Rules for the Direction of the Mind*, and another is John Dewey in *How We Think*. I will not discuss the former since it has been exhaustively examined many times, but I find Dewey intriguing if rather nonspecific. Although he does not discuss the motivation for knowledge directly, he does discuss the motivations to reach our goals in action and to make systematic preparations for the future and the desire to be free from the control of nature, all of which are closely connected with knowledge.[7] These values require the practice of what Dewey calls "reflective thinking," which he outlines in some detail:

> No one can tell another person in any definite way how he *should* think, any more than how he ought to breathe or to have his blood circulate. But the various ways in which we *do* think can be told and can be described in their general features. Some of these ways are better than others; the reasons why they are better can be set forth. The person who understands what the better ways of thinking are and why they are better can, if he will, change his own personal ways until they become more effective; until, that is to say, they do better the work that thinking can do and that other mental operations cannot do so well. The better way of thinking that is to be considered in this book is called reflective thinking. (p. 3)

The disclaimer in the first sentence of the above passage is surely too strong, but the rest of the paragraph is reasonable. Dewey goes on to say that reflective thinking requires not only certain skills, but also certain "attitudes":

> Because of the importance of attitudes, ability to train thought is not achieved merely by knowledge of the best forms of thought. Possession of this information is no guarantee for ability to think well. Moreover, there are no set exercises in correct thinking whose repeated performance will cause one to be a good thinker. The information and the exercises are both of value. But no individual realizes their value

except as he is personally animated by certain dominant attitudes *in his own character* [emphasis added]. It was once almost universally believed that the mind had faculties, like memory and attention, that could be developed by repeated exercise, as gymnastic exercises are supposed to develop the muscles. This belief is now generally discredited in the large sense in which it was once held. ...

> What can be done, however, is to cultivate those *attitudes* that are favorable to the use of the best methods of inquiry and testing. Knowledge of the methods alone will not suffice; there must be the desire, the will, to employ them. This desire is an affair of personal disposition. But on the other hand the disposition alone will not suffice. There must also be understanding of the forms and techniques that are the channels through which these attitudes operate to the best advantage. (pp. 29–30)

In this passage Dewey places special importance on the desire to employ better ways of thinking, claiming that knowledge of methods is not sufficient. He thus traces a path from our motivation to believe truly and to act effectively to the formation of "attitudes" or intellectual virtues that lead us to employ certain methods of thinking and forming beliefs. For my purposes, the salient point is that the foundation of these virtues is a motivation: the motivation to think more effectively.

The "attitudes" Dewey says one needs to cultivate are the following:

Open-mindedness. "This attitude may be defined as freedom from prejudice, partisanship, and such other habits as close the mind and make it unwilling to consider new problems and entertain new ideas" (p. 30).

Wholeheartedness. "When a person is absorbed, the subject carries him on. Questions occur to him spontaneously; a flood of suggestions pour in on him; further inquiries and readings are indicated and followed; instead of having to use his energy to hold his mind to the subject. ... the material holds and buoys his mind up and gives an onward impetus to thinking. A genuine enthusiasm is an attitude that operates as an intellectual force. A teacher who arouses such an enthusiasm in his pupils has done something that no amount of formalized method, no matter how correct, can accomplish" (pp. 31–2).

Responsibility. "Like sincerity or wholeheartedness, responsibility is usually conceived as a moral trait rather than as an intellectual resource. But it is an attitude that is necessary to win the adequate support of desire for new points of view and new ideas and of enthusiasm for and capacity for absorption in subject matter. These gifts may run wild, or at least they may lead the mind to spread out too far. They do not of themselves insure that centralization, that unity, which is essential to good thinking. To be intellectually responsible is to consider the consequences of a projected step; it means to be willing to adopt these consequences when they follow reasonably from any position already taken. Intellectual responsibility secures integrity; that is to say, consistency and harmony in belief" (p. 32).

In the contemporary literature Laurence BonJour and Hilary Kornblith[8] introduced a motivational element into the discussion of epistemic normativity in the notion of epistemic responsibility, defined by Kornblith as follows: "An *epistemically responsible agent* desires to have true beliefs, and thus desires to have his beliefs produced by processes which lead to true beliefs; his actions are guided by these desires" (p. 34). Although Kornblith does not specifically discuss intellectual virtues, he implies that a motivation or desire is at the root of the evaluation of epistemic agents, and that seems to me to be right. A more extensive treatment of epistemic virtue and its connection with motivation has been given by James Montmarquet[9] who connects a large set of intellectual virtues with the desire for truth, claiming that these virtues are qualities a person who wants the truth would want to acquire. However, it is not Montmarquet's intention to define intellectual virtues the way I am proposing here or to derive them all from the motivation for truth or from the motivation for knowledge. Still, Montmarquet's work has an obvious affinity with the theory I am proposing. I want to give it close attention.

Recall Montmarquet's classification of the epistemic virtues. Briefly, they are the virtues of impartiality, or openness to the ideas of others; the virtues of intellectual sobriety, or the virtues of the careful inquirer who accepts only what is warranted by the evidence, and the virtues of intellectual courage, which include perseverance

and determination. Notice that there is quite a bit of overlap between these sets of virtues and Dewey's. The major differences are in Dewey's virtue of wholeheartedness and Montmarquet's virtues of courage.

Montmarquet calls the desire for truth "epistemic conscientiousness" and argues that *some* intellectual virtues arise out of this desire.

> The first point to be made ... is that such qualities as open-mindedness are widely regarded as truth-conducive. In contrast to the highly controversial claims of various theories, the truth-conduciveness of qualities such as openness and intellectual sobriety is widely acknowledged to be a fact, not only by the expert (if there are "experts" on any such matter as this), but also by the average nonexpert individual (at least if he or she is suitably queried). Take openness. Unless one starts from the unlikely presumption that one has found the truth already and that the contrary advice and indications of others is liable, therefore, only to lead one astray, one can hardly possess a sincere love of truth, but no concern about one's own openness. Or take intellectual sobriety. Here, too, unless one starts from the unlikely presumption that one's immediate reactions and unchecked inferences are so highly reliable as not to be improved by any tendency to withhold full assent until they are further investigated, the virtue of sobriety will have to be acknowledged. Or, finally, take intellectual courage. Again, unless one makes an initially unappealing assumption that one's own ideas – true as they may seem to oneself – are so liable to be mistaken as to require not only deference to the opinions of others, but also a deep sense that these are opinions more liable to be correct than one's own (even when one cannot see how or why) [, unless] one makes such an initial assumption, one will have to acknowledge intellectual courage as a virtue.[10]

The reader should not be misled into thinking that this is an argument that these virtues are truth conducive; in fact, Montmarquet questions the truth conduciveness of openness and courage, as we will see. It is, instead, an argument that they are traits persons who *desire* the truth would want to have. I take this to mean that such persons would be *motivated* to act the way open-minded, intellectually sober, cautious, courageous, and persevering people act in their belief-forming processes. So if a person is motivated to get the truth, she would be motivated to consider the ideas of others openly and fairly, to consider the evidence with care, not to back down too quickly when criticized, and all the rest. This seems to me to be correct. It means that the motivation for knowledge gives rise to the motivation to act in ways that are distinctive of the various intellectual virtues Montmarquet mentions. Undoubtedly it also leads to the motivation to acquire Dewey's trait of intellectual responsibility; in fact, the motivation to be able to accurately predict consequences is a form of the motivation to know. The trait that Dewey calls "wholeheartedness," the attitude of enthusiasm, which moves us onward in thinking, is also a form of the motivation to know, in fact, an intensification of it. It is reasonable to conclude, then, that a wide range of intellectual virtues arise out of the same *general* motivation, the motivation for knowledge, and have the same general aim, knowledge.

The success component of the intellectual virtues

Intellectually virtuous motivations lead the agent to guide her belief-forming processes in certain ways. They make her receptive to processes known to her epistemic community to be truth conducive and motivate her to use them, even if it means overcoming contrary inclinations. As Dewey tells us, it is not enough to be aware that a process is reliable; a person will not reliably *use* such a process without certain virtues. At least this is the case with reliable processes that are not unconscious or automatic. Contemporary research in epistemology has focused extensively on the concept of a truth-conducive belief-forming process, as well as on many specific examples of these processes. I have no intention of duplicating or replacing this work here. My purpose is to point out that the motivation for knowledge leads a person to follow rules and belief-forming processes that are truth conducive and whose truth conduciveness she is able to discover and use by the possession of intellectual virtue.

Intellectually virtuous motivations not only lead to following reliable procedures but also lead to the development of particular skills suited to the acquisition of knowledge in a certain area. Skills are more closely connected to effectiveness in a particular area of life or knowledge than are virtues, which are psychically prior and provide the motivations to develop skills. Intellectual skills are sets of truth-conducive procedures that are acquired through habitual practice and have application to a certain area of truth acquisition. Since the path to knowledge varies with the context, the subject matter, and the way a community makes a division of intellectual labor, people with the same intellectual virtues will not all need to have the same skills, at least not to the same degree. Clearly the importance of fact-finding skills, skills of spatial reasoning, and skills in the subtler branches of logic are not equally important for all areas of the pursuit of knowledge. But all of these skills could arise in different people from the same intellectual virtues – for example, carefulness, thoroughness, and autonomy.

We have already seen that virtue is more than a motivation. Of course, we would expect many virtuous motivations to lead to success in carrying out the aims of the motive. So, for example, the motive to be careful or persevering probably leads somewhat reliably to success in being careful or persevering, but the correlation with success is probably much less in the case of such virtuous motives as the motive to be autonomous, the motive to be courageous, and perhaps even the motive to be open-minded. The weak connection between motive and success is also noticeable in Dewey's virtue of wholeheartedness (if it is a virtue), since it is surely naive to think that the motivation to be enthusiastic reliably leads to being enthusiastic. But even when the motivational component of a virtue is *generally* related to success, we do not call a person virtuous who is not reliably successful herself, whether or not most people who have the trait are successful in carrying out the aims of the virtue in question. So if she is truly open-minded, she must actually be receptive to new ideas, examining them in an evenhanded way and not ruling them out because they are not her own; merely being motivated to act in these ways is not sufficient. Similarly, if she is intellectually courageous, she must, in actual fact, refrain from operating from an assumption that the views of others are more likely to be true than her own and must be willing to withstand attack when she has good reason to think she is right, but not otherwise. Parallel remarks apply to the other intellectual virtues. It follows that each of these intellectual virtues has a motivational component arising out of the motivation to know and a component of reliable success in achieving the aim of the motivational component.

Most virtues are acquired by habituation and we only consider them virtues when they are entrenched in the agent's character. Entrenchment is a necessary feature of virtues because they are often needed the most when they encounter resistance. For example, the tendency to be motivated by compassion does not signify the existence of the *virtue* of compassion in a person who loses this motivation in the presence of physically unattractive persons in need, even if these circumstances do not arise very often. Similarly, the tendency to be motivated to fairly evaluate the arguments of others does not signify the existence of the virtue of intellectual fairness in a person who loses this motivation when confronted with arguments for unappealing conclusions, even if she is lucky enough not to encounter such arguments very often. So the motivational component of a virtue must be inculcated sufficiently to reliably withstand the influence of contrary motivations when those motivations do not themselves arise from virtues. The more that virtuous motivations and the resulting behavior become fixed habits, the more they are able to reliably achieve the ends of the virtue in those cases in which there are contrary tendencies to be overcome.

One way to distinguish among the truth-conducive qualities those that are virtues and those that are not is by the difference in the value we place on the entrenchment of these traits. Montmarquet mentions that we would not want the desire to uphold behaviorist psychology to be an entrenched trait even if it is truth conducive,[11] unlike the desire for the truth itself or, I would add, the desire to be open-minded, careful in evaluating evidence, autonomous, etc. The latter traits, when entrenched, lead to the truth partly *because* of their entrenchment, whereas the desire to uphold behaviorism is less likely to lead to the truth if it is entrenched than if it is not. The intellectual virtues are a subset of truth-conducive traits that are entrenched and whose entrenchment aids their truth conduciveness.[12] The value of the

entrenchment of a trait would, of course, depend partly on the environment in which it is entrenched.[13] Most of the qualities I have been calling intellectual virtues – traits such as open-mindedness, carefulness, and perseverance – are to a great extent environment neutral, but this does not mean that there are not other intellectual virtues that are more context sensitive.

Many intellectual virtues, including those mentioned by Dewey, not only arise from and serve the motivation to know the truth, but are also crucial in such activities as the arts, crafts, and games. The ultimate aim of these activities is not knowledge but something practical: creating an artistically superior sonnet, making a fine violin, winning a chess game.[14] These ends cannot be successfully achieved without knowledge in one of its senses, but probably not the kind of knowledge whose object is true propositions. At least, that sort of knowledge is not the one most fundamentally connected to success in these activities, which is more a matter of knowing-how rather than knowing-that. Still, some of the same virtues that arise out of the desire for knowledge and aid its successful achievement can also aid the achievement of these practical ends and, in some people, may arise more out of a desire for the practical end than out of a desire for knowledge. I do not claim, then, that intellectual virtues arise only from the motivation to know, much less do I claim they arise only from the motivation to have propositional knowledge, and I certainly do not claim that their exercise is properly directed only at knowledge. The value of intellectual virtues extends beyond their epistemic use. So not only is the distinction between intellectual and moral virtues highly artificial, but the distinction between intellectual virtues and the practical virtues needed for doing such things as creating sonnets, making violins, or winning chess games is artificial as well. Again, I will not discuss the problem of virtue individuation. There may be *some* difference between, say, the kind of openness displayed in writing a Shakespeare sonnet and the kind of openness displayed in pure scientific investigation. This difference may amount to a distinction in the virtues themselves if virtue identity is determined by the ultimate end of the virtue. The point is that even if this is the case, there are practical and intellectual virtues so similar to each other that they are very difficult to distinguish, and this means that it is highly implausible to maintain that intellectual virtues are fundamentally different in kind from the virtues needed for the kinds of practical activities just named.

Amelie Rorty points out that while the utility and success of intellectual virtues depend on their becoming habits that lead to action without prior deliberation, habits can become pathological or idiotic.[15] They become pathological, she says, when they become so habitual that their exercise extends to situations that no longer concern their internal aims. So generosity is pathological when it debilitates its recipients. The capacity to generate what Rorty calls "bravura virtuoso thought experiments" becomes pathological when it applies only to a very rare, narrow range of circumstances (p. 13). A virtuous habit becomes idiotic when its exercise resists a reasonable redirection of its aims, a redirection that is appropriate to changing circumstances. Rorty gives the example of courage when one is unable to make the transition from its military use to its use in political negotiation. In the intellectual sphere, the virtue of properly arguing from authority becomes idiotic when it is used to block the investigation of the legitimacy of the authority itself (p. 14). Some of these problems can be addressed by the function of the virtue of *phronesis*, but we do need to be reminded of the potential negative effects of habit. Nevertheless, these considerations do not falsify the claim that there is an element of habit in virtue. So far, then, our analysis of the components of intellectual virtue has identified a component of habitual motivation arising from the motive to know and a component of reliable success in achieving the aims of the virtue in question.

I have said that the primary motivation underlying the intellectual virtues is the motivation for knowledge. Such a motivation clearly includes the desire to have true beliefs and to avoid false ones, and we have looked at how such a motivation leads a person to follow rules or procedures of belief formation that are known to her epistemic community to be truth conducive. The motivation for knowledge also leads its possessor to acquire the motivational components distinctive of the individual intellectual virtues: open-mindedness, fair-mindedness, intellectual

flexibility, and so on. And the motivation to be, say, open-minded, will lead to acquiring patterns of behavior characteristic of the open-minded; the motivation to be fair-minded will lead to acquiring patterns of behavior characteristic of the intellectually fair; and so on. It is doubtful that such patterns of behavior are fully describable in terms of following rules or procedures. It is clear, then, that the following of truth-conducive procedures is not all that a knowledge-motivated person does, both because the motivation for truth leads to behavior that is not fully describable as the following of procedures, and because the motivation for knowledge includes more than the motivation for truth. The motivation for knowledge leads us to be aware of the reliability of certain belief-forming processes and the unreliability of others, but it also leads us to be aware that there are reliable belief-forming mechanisms whose unreliability is not yet known. And similarly, there are unreliable belief-forming mechanisms whose unreliability is not yet known. This is something we cannot ignore; otherwise, knowledge about knowledge would not progress. This means that intellectual virtues such as flexibility, open-mindedness, and even boldness are highly important. It also suggests that there is more than one sense in which a virtues can be truth conducive. In the sense most commonly discussed by reliabilists, truth conduciveness is a function of the *number* of true beliefs and the *proportion* of true to false beliefs generated by a process. There is another sense of truth conduciveness, however, which is important at the frontiers of knowledge and in areas, like philosophy, that generate very few true beliefs, no matter how they are formed. I suggest that we may legitimately call a trait or procedure truth conducive if it is a necessary condition for advancing knowledge in some area even though it generates very few true beliefs and even if a high percentage of the beliefs formed as the result of this trait or procedure are false. For example, the discovery of new reliable procedures may arise out of intellectual traits that lead a person to hit on falsehood many times before hitting on the truth. As long as these traits (in combination with other intellectual virtues) are self-correcting, they will eventually advance human knowledge, but many false beliefs may have to be discarded along the way. A person motivated to know would be motivated to act cognitively in a manner that is truth conducive in this sense, I would argue, in addition to acting in a way that is truth conducive in the more common sense.

The virtues of originality, creativity, and inventiveness are truth conducive in the sense just described. Clearly, their truth conduciveness in the sense of producing a high proportion of true beliefs is much lower than that of the ordinary virtues of careful and sober inquiry, but they are truth conducive in the sense that they are necessary for the advancement of human knowledge. If only 5 per cent of a creative thinker's original ideas turn out to be true, her creativity is certainly truth conducive because the stock of knowledge of the human race has increased through her creativity. The way in which these virtues are truth conducive is probably circuitous and unpredictable, and for this reason it is doubtful that they give rise to a set of rules, and, in fact, they may even defy those rules already established. Often creative people simply operate on intuition, which is usually what we call an ability when it works and we don't know how it works. Ernest Dimnet relates the story that Pasteur was constantly visited by intuitions that he was afterward at great pains to check by the ordinary canons of science (1928, p. 187).[16] Presumably, following the canons in the absence of his bold and original ideas would not have gotten him (or us) nearly as far. Dimnet tells another anecdote about the creative process in novelists. Apparently, when Sir Walter Scott hit upon the idea for a new novel, he would read volume after volume that had no reference to his subject, merely because reading intensified the working of his mind. Dimnet comments that this process did for Scott's power of invention what the crowds in the city did for Dickens's (p. 7). Of course, novelists are not aiming for truth in the sense that is the major focus of this book, but the same point could apply to creative work in philosophy, history, mathematics, and the sciences. The knowledge-motivated person will want to have the virtues of creativity to the extent that she is able, and that gives us another reason why the motive to know includes more than the motive to follow procedures known to be reliable. The division of epistemic labor probably limits the number of people who are strongly motivated in this way, but their existence is important for the knowledge of the whole community.[17]

In "The Doctrine of Chances," C. S. Peirce expressed the opinion that even the scientific method is truth conducive only in a sense similar to the one I have just described. Peirce says that the scientist must be unselfish because he is not likely to arrive at the truth for himself in the short run. Instead, his procedures are likely to lead the scientific community to better theories and more comprehensive truths in the long run.[18] If Peirce is right, the sense in which the virtues of originality and creativity are truth conducive is not clearly different from the way in which the virtues of careful scientific inquiry are truth conducive.

Another reason the motivation to know is not fully expressed by following well-known reliable belief-forming processes is that, as already remarked, the motivation to know includes the motivation for understanding. Knowledge has been associated with certainty and understanding for long periods of its history, but generally not with both at the same time.[19] The virtues that lead to the kind of knowledge that gives the possessor certainty may be different from the virtues that lead to understanding, and the following of belief-forming processes known to the epistemic community to be reliable may be insufficient for either one. For one thing, to aim at certainty is not just to aim at truth but to aim to have an awareness of truth that has a certain quality. To get an awareness with that quality it may not be enough to use processes known or truly believed by one's epistemic community to be reliable. One may need to be aware of how and why one's belief-forming process is justified, or at least how and why it is reliable and the degree of its reliability. The virtues that enable one to see how one's belief can stand up to attack contribute to certainty. Virtues that lead to clarity in one's grasp of a matter may also contribute to certainty. Aiming at understanding is even farther removed from using procedures known to be reliable, because understanding is not a property whose object is a single proposition. Those virtues that enable the agent to see connections among her beliefs – introspective attentiveness and insight in its various forms – are understanding conducive. All of these virtues deserve careful attention, and although I will not stop to investigate them individually, I hope that others will do so.

Notes

1　Alisdair MacIntyre, *After Virtue* (Notre Dame, IN: University of Notre Dame Press, 1984).

2　Gregory Trianosky, "Virtue, Action, and the Good Life: Towards a Theory of the Virtues," *Pacific Philosophical Quarterly* 68 (1987), pp. 124–47.

3　Robert C. Roberts, "Aristotle on Virtues and Emotions," *Philosophical Studies* 56 (1989), pp. 293–306.

4　In *Reason and the Heart: A Prolegomenon to a Critique of Passional Reason* (Ithaca, NY: Cornell University Press, 1996), ch. 2, William Wainwright discusses the love of being in general as an epistemic virtue recognized by Jonathan Edwards.

5　Hobbes implies here that people do not differ as much in their sensory faculties as in their virtues and vices. He also says that part of what leads us to call a quality a virtue is that it is uncommon. The Hobbesian approach would hesitate, then, in attributing anything virtuous to cases of simple perceptual beliefs that are produced by normally functioning faculties.

6　Thomas Hobbes, *Leviathan* (New York: Macmillan, 1958), pt. 1, ch. 8, pp. 68–9.

7　John Dewey, *How We Think* (Boston: D. C. Heath and Co., 1933), ch. 2, sec. 1; page numbers given in parenthesis in the text.

8　Laurence BonJour, "Externalist Theories of Empirical Knowledge," in *Studies in Epistemology. Midwest Studies in Philosophy*, vol. 5 (Notre Dame, IN: Notre Dame University Press, 1980); Hilary Kornblith, "Justified Belief and Epistemically Responsible Action," *Philosophical Review* 92 (1983), pp. 33–48.

9　James A. Montmarquet, "Epistemic Virtue," *Mind* 96 (1986), pp. 482–97; "Epistemic Virtue," in Jonathan Dancy and Ernest Sosa (eds), *A Companion to Epistemology* (Oxford: Basil Blackwell, 1992); *Epistemic Virtue and Doxastic Responsibility* (Lanham, MD: Rowman and Littlefield, 1993), ch. 2.

10　*Epistemic Virtue*, pp. 27–8.

11　Ibid., pp. 26–7.

12　Charles Young has suggested to me that a problematic case is the desire that the interesting be true, a quality whose entrenchment might have value, he suggests, independently of its capacity to reliably lead to the truth. There is a passage in the *Meno* (81de) in which Socrates seems to be saying that even if we have no rational grounds for preferring the religious story of 81ad to the eristic story of 80d, we are better off believing the former: it makes us energetic seekers, whereas the eristic story makes us lazy. I have noticed in myself and others the tendency to go for the more metaphysically exciting position on such issues as the nature of time or the existence of abstract objects, quite apart from a consideration of the weight of the argumentative evidence. Such a tendency is clearly dangerous, but it is not obviously a bad thing. There might even be value in its entrenchment.

13　I thank Hilary Kornblith for drawing my attention to this point.

14　I thank Charles Young for this point.

15　Amelie Rorty, "From Exasperating Virtues to Civic Virtues," *American Philosophical Quarterly* 38 (1996), pp. 303–14.

16　Ernest Dimnet, *The Art of Thinking* (New York: Simon and Schuster, 1928), p. 187.

17　A careful study of the psychology of creativity would probably show that motivation operates in a different way in the virtues of creativity and originality than it does in the other intellectual virtues. The motivation to be creative does not lead to being creative in the way the motivation to be careful leads to being careful. I imagine that creative people begin by being creative involuntarily and find it pleasant, exciting, even thrilling. These feelings give them the impetus to permit their creativity a certain latitude, which may lead them to ignore the established canons, at least temporarily. This means that the motivational component in creativity does not so much lead its possessors to *acquire* the trait as allow them to give it free rein, and this may lead to ignoring the dictates of certain other virtues.

18　Christopher Hookway has an interesting discussion of this position of Peirce and related views. See C. S. Peirce, *The Essential*

Peirce, vol. 1, ed. Nathan Houser and Christian Kloesel (Bloomington: Indiana University Press, 1992) and Christopher Hookway, "Mimicking Foundationalism: On Sentiment and Self-Control," *European Journal of Philosophy* 1:2 (1993), pp. 156–74.

19   See Mary Tiles and Jim Tiles, *An Introduction to Historical Epistemology* (Cambridge, MA: Basil Blackwell, 1993), and Stephen Everson, *Epistemology*, Companions to Ancient Thought, vol. 1 (Cambridge: Cambridge University Press, 1990), for historical discussions of the difference between the values of certainty and understanding in different periods of epistemological history.

CHAPTER 34

Virtues and Vices of Virtue Epistemology

John Greco

In this paper I want to examine the virtues and vices of virtue epistemology. My conclusion will be that the position is correct, when qualified appropriately. The central claim of virtue epistemology is that, Gettier problems aside, knowledge is true belief which results from a cognitive virtue. In section one I will clarify this claim with some brief remarks about the nature of virtues in general, and cognitive virtues in particular. In section two I will consider two objections to the theory of knowledge which results. In section three of the paper I will argue that virtue epistemology can be qualified so as to avoid the objections raised in section two.

Specifically, I will argue that not all reliable cognitive virtues give rise to knowledge. Rather, a cognitive virtue gives rise to knowledge only if (i) it is reliable, and (ii) the reliability of the virtue is the result of epistemically responsible doxastic practices. In cases of knowledge, reliability is grounded in responsible belief formation and maintenance. The resulting position has ramifications for the analysis of knowledge, the internalism–externalism debate concerning epistemic justification, and the problem of skepticism.

Originally published in *Canadian Journal of Philosophy* 23, 3 (1993), selections from pp. 413–32.

I   What is a Cognitive Virtue?

A virtue, in one important sense, is an ability. An ability, in turn, is a stable disposition to achieve certain results under certain conditions. Further, when we say that a subject S has an ability to achieve certain results, we imply that it is no accident that S achieves those results. S's disposition to achieve the relevant results is grounded in certain properties of S, such that under the appropriate conditions any subject with those properties would tend to achieve those results.

For example, Don Mattingly has the ability to hit baseballs. This means that Mattingly has a stable disposition to hit baseballs under appropriate conditions, although Mattingly will not hit the baseball every time under those conditions. Further, it is no accident that Mattingly tends to hit baseballs. Mattingly's tendency to hit baseballs is grounded in certain properties of Mattingly, such that anyone with those properties would also tend to hit baseballs with similar success in similar conditions.

A more exact definition of cognitive virtue is as follows:

(V)   A mechanism M for generating and/or maintaining beliefs is a cognitive virtue if and only if M is an ability to believe true propositions and avoid believing false propositions within a field of propositions *F*, when one is in a set of circumstances *C*.

According to the above formulation, what makes a cognitive mechanism a cognitive virtue is that it is reliable in generating true beliefs rather than false beliefs in the relevant field and in the relevant circumstances. It is correct to say, therefore, that virtue epistemology is a kind of reliabilism. Whereas generic reliabilism maintains that justified belief is belief which results from a reliable cognitive process, virtue epistemology puts a restriction on the kind of process which is allowed. Specifically, the cognitive processes which are important for justification and knowledge are those which have their bases in a cognitive virtue.

Let us use the term "positive epistemic status" to designate that property (whatever it may be) which turns true belief into knowledge, Gettier problems aside. Then an important corollary of virtue epistemology is as follows.

(VE) S's belief that *p* has positive epistemic status for S if and only if S's believing that *p* is the result of some cognitive virtue of S.

The claim embodied in (VE) has a high degree of initial plausibility. By making the idea of faculty reliability central, virtue epistemology explains nicely why beliefs caused by perception and memory often have positive epistemic status, while beliefs caused by wishful thinking and superstition do not. Second, the theory gives us a basis for answering certain kinds of skepticism. Specifically, we may agree that *if* we were brains in a vat, or victims of a Cartesian demon, then we would not have knowledge even in those rare cases where our beliefs turned out true. But virtue epistemology explains that what is important for knowledge is that our cognitive faculties are *in fact* reliable in the conditions we are in. And so we do have knowledge so long as we are in fact *not* victims of a Cartesian demon, or brains in a vat.

But although virtue epistemology has initial plausibility, it faces at least two substantial objections. I turn to those objections now.

II Objections to Virtue Epistemology

1 The evil demon problem for virtue epistemology

The first objection faced by virtue epistemology is that (VE) seems too strong. This objection arises if we think that positive epistemic status is closely related to epistemic justification. More specifically, it seems possible that an epistemic agent could be justified in believing that *p*, even when her intellectual faculties are largely unreliable. Suppose, for example, that Kathy is the victim of a Cartesian deceiver. Despite her best efforts almost none of Kathy's beliefs about the world around her are true. It is clear that in this case Kathy's faculties of perception are almost wholly unreliable. But we would not want to say that none of Kathy's perceptual beliefs are justified. If Kathy believes that there is a tree in her yard, and if she bases this belief on the kind of experience usually caused by trees, then it seems that she is as justified as we would be regarding a similar belief. The problem for virtue epistemology is to account for this intuition. There is something about Kathy's belief which is epistemically valuable, i.e., valuable in a way which is relevant for having knowledge. Yet it is clear that Kathy's belief is not the result of a cognitive virtue in the sense defined by (V).

Sosa's strategy for addressing the evil demon problem is to make justification relative to an environment. Thus Sosa recognizes that there is something valuable about Kathy's belief, even though that belief has its origin in wholly unreliable cognitive faculties. What is valuable about Kathy's belief, Sosa argues, is that it is produced by cognitive faculties which would be reliable in *our* environment.

> On the present proposal, aptness is relative to an environment. Relative to our actual environment A, our automatic experience-belief mechanisms count as virtues that yield much truth and justification and aptness. Of course, relative to the demonic environment D, such mechanisms are not virtuous and yield neither truth nor aptness. It follows that relative to D the demon's victims are not apt, and yet *relative to A their beliefs are apt.*[1]

The above proposal by Sosa is an interesting one, but some questions arise. First, couldn't we construct the example so that Kathy's cognitive mechanisms are *not* reliable relative to our environment? Thus suppose that Kathy is a brain in a vat, hooked up to a super computer which causes her to have experiences exactly similar to the experiences that I am having now. If in these circumstances Kathy forms the belief that there is a glass of water on the table in front of her, her belief should be as justified as is my belief that there is a glass of water on the table in front of me. But if Kathy were in my environment her cognitive faculties would not be reliable at all, and in fact would be incapable of connecting her with reality at all. For if Kathy were in my environment, rather than hooked up to a super computer, she would lack the faculties for producing experiences. She would be a helpless brain on a desk.

Or suppose that Kathy's powers of reasoning are *helped* by her vat environment. We may imagine that Kathy's natural reasoning mechanisms are defective, but that the fluids in the vat serve to correct the defect. Thus inside the vat environment Kathy is a flawless reasoner. But if Kathy were in a normal environment, i.e., inside a normal head with normal sensory apparatus, her reasoning mechanisms would be defective and thus unreliable. Now suppose that Kathy believes that the house in front of her was built before 1900, and that she believes this partly on the basis of her present experience and partly on the basis of her reasoning from this experience. It seems to me that Kathy could be perfectly justified in this belief, even though she is a brain in a vat and the cognitive mechanisms which produce her belief are not reliable. However, the mechanisms which produce Kathy's belief are not reliable relative to our environment either, since in our environment Kathy would lack the vat fluids which correct her cognitive defects.

Sosa might attempt to solve the problem as follows. We could define environments very specifically, so as to include being in a normal head, etc., and then define sets of circumstances in terms of experiential and doxastic inputs. Cognitive mechanisms would then be dispositions to form certain beliefs in a field, given certain experiential and doxastic inputs. We could then say that what is valuable about Kathy is not that she would *have* virtues if she were in our environment, but that the cognitive

mechanisms she does have in her environment would *be* virtues in our environment.[2]

I take it that there are at least two problems with the latest proposal: one for Sosa's positions in particular; and one for virtue epistemology in general. First, Sosa's position requires an epistemic perspective on one's own cognitive virtues in order to have reflective justification, and in order to solve the generality problem.[3] But it is implausible that the typical believer has such a perspective when virtues are defined in terms of experiential inputs. I take it that the experience-belief pairs that would describe a reliable mechanism must be very detailed regarding the quality of the experiences involved. But in the typical case there is no such detailed perspective on even our present experiences, much less the range of our possible experiences.

Second, Sosa's account of what is valuable about Kathy's belief assumes that Kathy's cognitive mechanisms would be reliable in our environment. But this assumes that *our* cognitive mechanisms are reliable in our environment. We think Kathy is reliable because she is like us in relevant respects, and we think we are reliable. But suppose we are victims of an evil deceiver, or that we are brains in a community vat. Then Kathy's mechanisms are no more reliable in our environment than they are in hers. And thus, according to Sosa's account, Kathy's beliefs are not justified relative to our environment. But this seems wrong – there seems to be something valuable about Kathy's beliefs whether or not she or we are victims of an evil deceiver. There is something epistemically important about the way her and our beliefs are formed, whether or not they are formed via cognitive faculties which are objectively reliable relative to our environment.

We can pursue this point by considering the second of our two objections to virtue epistemology.

2   The problem of epistemic irresponsibility

The second objection to be considered is that (VE) is too weak. Specifically, we can imagine cases where S's cognitive faculties are highly reliable with respect to his belief that *p*, but where S is epistemically irresponsible in believing that *p*. Such a case may arise when S has substantial but misleading evidence against his belief that *p*.

Consider the case of Mary, who is in most respects a normal human being. The relevant difference is that Mary's cognitive faculties produce the belief in her that there is a tiger nearby whenever there is a tiger nearby, and even in cases where Mary does not see, hear or otherwise perceive a nearby tiger. Mary's brain is designed so as to be sensitive to an electromagnetic field emitted only by tigers, thus causing her to form the relevant belief in the appropriate situation, and without any corresponding experience, sensory or otherwise. We can imagine that this cognitive feature was designed by natural processes of evolution, or that it was literally designed by a beneficent creator, one who realizes that tigers are dangerous to beings like Mary and who therefore wishes to equip her with a reliable warning device. Now suppose that a tiger is walking nearby, and that Mary forms the appropriate belief. Add that Mary has no evidence that there is a tiger in the area, nor any evidence that she has such a faculty. Rather, she has considerable evidence *against* her belief that there are tigers in the area. Clearly, Mary's belief that there is a tiger nearby does not have positive epistemic status in this situation, even though the belief is caused by properly functioning faculties in an appropriate environment. Mary does not *know* that there is a tiger nearby. Again, the explanation for this is that Mary's belief is epistemically irresponsible. Given the way things look from Mary's point of view, she *ought not* to believe that there is a tiger nearby.

Sosa's strategy for addressing this kind of example recognizes the importance of S's point of view by invoking S's epistemic perspective. Sosa makes a distinction between animal knowledge and reflective knowledge. For animal knowledge, it is sufficient that S's true belief be caused by a reliable faculty. For reflective knowledge, we must add that S has a true grasp of the fact that her belief is grounded in a reliable cognitive faculty. This grasp must in turn result from a faculty of faculties, which gives rise to the required epistemic perspective.

For one is able to boost one's justification in favor of *P* if one can see one's belief of *P* as in a field F and in circumstances C, such that one has a faculty (a competence or aptitude) to believe correctly in field F when in conditions C. … One thereby attributes to oneself some intrinsic state such that when there arises a question in field F and one is in conditions C, that intrinsic state adjusts one's belief to the facts in that field so that one always or very generally believes correctly.[4]

According to Sosa, to "see" one's belief that *p* as in a field and circumstances and to "attribute" to oneself reliability in that field and those circumstances, is to have true beliefs to that effect, where those true beliefs are themselves products of a cognitive virtue. And now we may see how this position can be applied to the case above. According to Sosa, Mary has animal knowledge but not reflective knowledge. Further, he can say that Mary's belief is reflectively unjustified, since her belief actually conflicts with her epistemic perspective on her faculties.

But the problem with this proposal is that we seldom have such beliefs about our beliefs and about our cognitive faculties. In the typical case, we have no beliefs at all about the sources of our beliefs, or about our reliability in particular fields and circumstances.

Or at least this is so for occurrent beliefs. Is it plausible that we typically have such beliefs dispositionally? Where we do have such a dispositional perspective, the field and circumstances that perspective specifies are probably the wrong ones. Specifically, to the extent that I attribute to myself certain cognitive faculties, those faculties are specified much too broadly to be of any use. For example, consider my belief that there is a glass of water on the table. In the typical case I have no occurrent beliefs about the source of this belief in a given cognitive virtue. Let me now consider any dispositional beliefs I might have. After considering the issue for a moment, it occurs to me that my belief about the glass is the result of sight. But if you ask me to get very specific about a field of propositions F, or a set of circumstances C, such that I am highly reliable in that field when in those circumstances, I am at a loss. I simply do not have very specific beliefs in this area, nor is it plausible that such beliefs are available dispositionally if only I think about it a little more.

We may conclude that in the typical case a believer will not have a true grasp of the inventory of cognitive faculties she possesses, nor will she have a perspective on which faculty is responsible for producing the particular belief in question. On the other hand, there does seem to be something importantly right about Sosa's proposal. I want to argue that Sosa is right to invoke S's point of view as an important element for having knowledge, but that he invokes S's point of view in the wrong sense. Below I will develop a different sense in which Mary's belief is correct or appropriate from her point of view, and I will argue that this is the sense which is relevant for having knowledge.

III   An Internalist Version of Virtue Epistemology

We have said that (VE) fails to take into account an important kind of epistemic value. Namely, (VE) fails to recognize the importance of S's belief being correct or appropriate from S's point of view. One way in which this lack presents itself is in the evil demon problem. Virtue epistemology fails to recognize an appropriate sense in which S's beliefs might be epistemically valuable, even if those beliefs result from wholly unreliable cognitive faculties. Another way in which this problem presents itself is in examples which show that (VE) is too weak. There are cases where S's true belief is the result of a reliable cognitive faculty, but where S lacks knowledge because S's belief is somehow inappropriate from S's point of view.

Sosa tries to address the latter problem by invoking the idea of an epistemic perspective. The problem with this proposal is that the relevant perspective is lacking in the typical case. It is implausible that believers typically have a true grasp of their cognitive faculties, or a true grasp of which faculty has produced a particular belief. Below I want to develop a different understanding of what it means for a belief to be correct or appropriate from S's point of view. I will then argue that virtue epistemology can be amended so as to incorporate this understanding, and I will defend the theory of knowledge which results.

1   Norm internalism

Norm internalism is the position that justified belief is the result of following correct epistemic norms, or correct rules of belief formation and maintenance. More exactly,

(NI)   S is epistemically justified in believing that p if and only if S's believing that p is in conformance with the epistemic norms which S countenances, and the history of S's belief has also been in conformance with those norms.[5]

It will be necessary to say more about two of the central notions involved in (NI): the notion of a belief being in conformance with an epistemic norm, and the notion of an epistemic norm being countenanced. I begin with the latter.

We may get an idea of what it is to countenance an epistemic norm if we consider the following example. Suppose that Jane, who is not very good at math, bases her belief in a complicated theorem on a set of axioms which do in fact support the theorem. But suppose that she does so not because she sees the supporting relation, but because she has reasoned invalidly from the axioms to the theorem. Obviously Jane is not justified in her belief that the theorem is correct.

What is required for Jane to be justified in believing the theorem? What is it that justification requires but Jane lacks? A plausible suggestion is that Jane must be sensitive to the inference relation between her theorem and the axioms on which she bases the theorem. Just what this sensitivity amounts to, however, is not easy to state. For although we are often "aware" that some set of evidence supports a conclusion, it is not easy to state what this awareness consists in.

One suggestion is that Jane must believe that her conclusion follows from her evidence. But this is obviously too weak. For Jane could believe that her conclusion follows from her evidence even if she has reasoned fallaciously and has no real insight into how her conclusion follows from her evidence. Alternatively, one might suggest that Jane must believe that the relevant general rule of inference is correct, and that her inference is an instance of the general rule. But this suggestion is too strong. Typically only logicians have beliefs about the deductive rules which govern our reasoning, and it is agreed on all sides that no one has successfully characterized the rules which govern our non-deductive reasoning. But if we typically do not have beliefs about the rules which govern correct reasoning, how are we to understand our sensitivity to such rules?

I suggest that although we do not typically have beliefs about such rules, we do *countenance* such rules in our reasoning. In other words, we follow such rules when we reason conscientiously, although the way in which we follow them does not involve having beliefs about them, either occurrent or dispositional. Thus the way in which we countenance rules of reasoning is analogous to the way we countenance other action-governing norms. The norms which govern good hitting in baseball, for example, are countenanced by good hitters when they are batting conscientiously. But this does not mean that all good hitters are capable of articulating those norms, or otherwise forming true beliefs about them. Not all good hitters make good hitting coaches. In fact, it is possible for a good hitter to form false beliefs about the norms which he countenances when he is actually playing.

So although we do not typically have beliefs about the norms which govern our beliefs, we do countenance certain norms and not others. The norms that we countenance are the norms that we follow when we reason conscientiously. And thus it makes perfect sense to say that someone is reasoning in a way that he does not countenance. This is in fact what happens when we form our beliefs hastily, or fall into wishful thinking, or are swayed by our prejudices.

I now turn to the notion of a belief's being in conformance with a norm. The notion can be made more clear by considering a distinction common in moral philosophy. It is common for moral philosophers to make a distinction between acting in accordance with one's duty and acting for the sake of one's duty. In the former case one's actions happen to coincide with one's duties. In the latter case one's actions are performed *because* one has certain duties. And now a similar distinction can be made with respect to our believings. While some of our beliefs are merely in accordance with the norms of belief formation which we countenance, others of our beliefs are in conformance with those norms in the following sense; they arise, at least partly, *because* we countenance certain norms and not others. The latter beliefs are accepted (at least partly) *because* we follow certain norms when we are reasoning conscientiously.[6]

Notice that the position articulated in (NI) is not subject to the objections raised against Sosa's

idea of an epistemic perspective. Thus the position does not require that S have beliefs *about* which norms she countenances, or about which norms are involved in the formation of a particular belief. All that is necessary is that S does in fact countenance the relevant norms, and that S's belief is in fact in conformance with those norms. Second, the present position explains what is valuable about the beliefs of the victim of the evil deceiver. In the case of the evil deceiver, Kathy's beliefs are justified because they are in conformance with the rules of belief formation and maintenance which Kathy countenances. Finally, the account explains why Mary's beliefs do not amount to knowledge. Even though Mary's belief results from a reliable tiger-detecting faculty, Mary's belief is not in accordance with the norms which Mary countenances. Presumably, Mary countenances norms which disallow believing that tigers are present in the absence of any evidence to that effect, or in cases where one has considerable evidence against that belief and no evidence in favor of it.[7]

2   Norm internalism applied to virtue epistemology

We may see how the present position can be used to amend virtue epistemology if we make a distinction between a virtue and the basis for that virtue. We have been understanding virtues as abilities, and we have been understanding abilities as stable dispositions to achieve certain results under certain conditions. But then the same virtue might have different bases in different subjects. Thus the ability to absorb oxygen into the blood has a different basis in fish than it does in human beings. Similarly, the ability to roll down an inclined plane has a different basis in a pencil than it does in a baseball. Now, according to Sosa, the basis for a cognitive virtue is the inner nature of the cognitive subject. Thus Sosa refers to the subject's inner nature explicitly in his latest account: "One has an intellectual virtue or faculty relative to an environment E if and only if one has an inner nature I in virtue of which one would mostly attain the truth and avoid error in a certain field of propositions F, when in certain conditions C."[8]

A different proposal would be that the basis for cognitive virtues, at least where knowledge is concerned, must be S's conformance to the epistemic norms which S countenances. On this proposal cognitive virtues relevant to knowledge are grounded in conscientious belief formation and maintenance, rather than in an unchanging inner nature.

Perhaps the following analogy will clarify the present proposal. Pitching machines and Nolan Ryan both have the ability to throw baseballs at high speeds. But the basis of this virtue in the pitching machine is different from the basis of the virtue in Ryan. Moreover, the basis for the virtue in the machine is the machine's inner nature; given the way that the machine is constructed and given the appropriate conditions, the machine throws baseballs at high speeds. The basis of the same virtue in Ryan is of a different sort; Ryan's ability to throw baseballs is based in Ryan's conformance to the norms governing good throwing. A person might have the same inner nature as Ryan and not have the ability to throw baseballs because that person fails to conform to the proper norms. Consider that Ryan himself would not throw baseballs at high speeds if he did not conform to the norms of good throwing.

The analogy should be obvious. I am suggesting that knowers are more like Ryan than like pitching machines. Specifically, I am suggesting that the virtues associated with knowledge have their bases in conformance to relevant norms rather than in a fixed inner nature.[9]

Applying norm internalism to virtue epistemology results in the following account of positive epistemic status:

(VEI) S's belief that p has positive epistemic status for S if and only if
  (i)   S believes that p;
  (ii) S's believing that p is the result of a reliable cognitive virtue V of S; and
  (iii) S's virtue V has its basis in S's conforming to epistemic norms which S countenances.

3   (VEI) defended

According to (VEI), knowledge is true belief which results from a cognitive virtue, where this virtue has its basis in S's conforming to epistemic norms which S countenances. Thus on the present account, knowledge is virtuous in both a subjective and an objective sense. Knowledge is virtuous in a subjective sense in that knowledge is belief which is correct or appropriate from S's point of view. And this means that in cases of knowledge S's belief is in conformance with the rules of belief formation and maintenance which S countenances. Knowledge is virtuous in an objective sense in that belief which is knowledge is the result of a reliable cognitive faculty. Further, the two ways in which knowledge is virtuous are related. In cases of knowledge, a belief is objectively virtuous *because* it is subjectively virtuous. In other words, in cases of knowledge the basis of S's objectively reliable cognitive virtue is in S's conformance to the epistemic norms which S herself countenances; reliability results from responsibility.

We may now see that (VEI) avoids the two objections raised against virtue epistemology as defined by (VE). Because (VEI) recognizes an internalist element in knowledge, (VEI) explains what is valuable about the beliefs of the victim of an evil deceiver. Namely, someone whose cognitive faculties are made wholly unreliable by an evil deceiver might nevertheless reason in conformance with the norms that she countenances. Thus the victim of an evil deceiver might have beliefs which are subjectively responsible, even if they are not objectively reliable. Second, (VEI) avoids the counterexamples which show that (VE) is too weak. Specifically, (VEI) *requires* epistemic responsibility for positive epistemic status. And this requires that S's belief be correct or appropriate from S's point of view, in the sense defined by norm internalism.

Thus (VEI) avoids the two objections raised against (VE). Does (VEI) still have the attractive features which we attributed to virtue epistemology at the beginning of the paper? (VEI) continues to explain nicely why beliefs caused by perception and memory often have positive epistemic status, while beliefs caused by wishful thinking and superstition do not. But it has the added advantage of explaining why not all reliable cognitive faculties give rise to positive epistemic status. Thus it explains why Mary's tiger-detecting faculties do not. Second, the theory continues to give us a basis for answering certain kinds of skepticism. Thus it continues to explain why we would lack knowledge *if* we were brains in a vat, or victims of a Cartesian demon, and why we do not lack knowledge so long as this is not the case. (VEI) in fact nuances our answer to skepticism by explaining what is epistemically valuable about the beliefs of victims trapped in the skeptical scenarios.

We may conclude that (VEI) retains all the advantages of (VE), while avoiding problems which (VE) cannot.

Notes

1   Ernest Sosa, "Intellectual Virtue in Perspective," in *Knowledge in Perspective: Collected Essays in Epistemology* (Cambridge: Cambridge University Press, 1991), p. 289.
2   Here I am indebted to Sosa, who suggested this response in conversation.
3   The notion of an epistemic perspective and its role in Sosa's account of reflective justification is discussed below.
4   Sosa, *Knowledge in Perspective*, p. 282. Sosa develops this strategy in "Intellectual Virtue in Perspective" and in "Reliabilism and Intellectual Virtue," both in *Knowledge in Perspective*.
5   This position is defended in detail in my "Internalism and Epistemically Responsible Belief," *Synthese* 85 (1990), pp. 245–77.
6   For a similar distinction, see John Pollock, *Contemporary Theories of Knowledge* (Totowa, NJ: Rowman and Littlefield 1986), p. 168.
7   Of course questions remain. For example, it is plausible that a person's norms will change and even conflict over time. How does this effect epistemic responsibility? There is also the problem of "norm schizophrenia," or the problem of conflicting norms at the same time. Finally, it might be thought that the above account leads to an unacceptable kind of epistemic relativism. I address all of these questions in my "Internalism and Epistemically Responsible Belief." There I conclude that a) responsibility concerns conformance to one's present norms; b) when present norms conflict responsibility requires that none of S's norms disallow S's belief; and c) the only kind of relativism involved is harmless, and should be expected given the analogy to moral responsibility.
8   Sosa, "Intellectual Virtue in Perspective," p. 284. See also Sosa's definitions on pp. 286–9.
9   Perhaps I should say "rather than *merely* in a fixed inner nature," since it is possible that S's conformance to relevant norms is itself based in a deeper inner nature.

Reason VEI Because it has objective & subjective sense

CHAPTER 35

Cognitive Responsibility and the Epistemic Virtues

Duncan Pritchard

Introduction

… [We can identify] two varieties of epistemic luck that pose problems for any theory of knowledge. The first variety – veritic epistemic luck – is the type of epistemic luck that is at issue in the Gettier-style counter-examples to the classical tripartite account of knowledge. It is the elimination of this kind of luck that is the focus of externalist epistemologies – particularly the paradigm case of an externalist epistemology, the safety-based neo-Moorean account. We also saw that there was another epistemologically problematic variety of epistemic luck – reflective epistemic luck – and that when commentators charged externalist epistemologies with being far too concessive in their treatment of epistemic luck, it was specifically this variety of luck that they had in mind. Given that externalist accounts of knowledge are unable to eliminate reflective epistemic luck, this presents us with prima facie grounds in favour of an internalist safety-based epistemological theory.

One explanation that might be offered for thinking that we need an epistemology that is able to eliminate relflective epistemic luck – and which would further support the case for adopting a safety-based internalist theory of knowledge – is

Originally published in Duncan Pritchard, *Epistemic Luck* (Oxford: Oxford University Press, 2005), pp. 181–201.

that it is only by proposing an epistemological theory that can eliminate reflective epistemic luck that one can adequately capture a conception of cognitive responsibility that is central to knowledge possession. In essence, the thought is that what is epistemically problematic about the knowledge putatively possessed by the (unenlightened) chicken-sexer is that she is unable to take cognitive responsibility for the truth of her beliefs in the kind of robust way that is at issue when we ascribe knowledge to agents. Crucially, for example, the naïve chicken-sexer is unable to properly *claim* her brute externalist knowledge.

The goal of this chapter is to examine this relationship between reflective epistemic luck and cognitive responsibility in more detail and, in so doing, look a little deeper into the issue of just what is involved in the idea of cognitive responsibility. To this end, we will be discussing the "virtue-theoretic" challenge that has recently been directed against early externalist accounts of knowledge and justification, and which has been used to motivate the kind of virtue epistemic theories that are currently popular in the literature. As I explain, this challenge largely concerns the difficulty that these externalist accounts have in eliminating epistemic luck and therefore in capturing the kind of cognitive responsibility that is necessary for knowledge. So understood, however, this complaint is ambiguous, and this explains why there are two very divergent types of virtue epistemology currently on offer in the literature – an epistemologically externalist version that models itself on process reliabilism, and an epistemologically internalist "neo-Aristotelian" version. Disentangling the various threads of motivation for virtue epistemology thus not only throws light on the issue of why we should seek to eliminate reflective luck from our knowledge (and hence on the epistemological externalist–internalist distinction), but also on the issue of the status of virtue epistemology itself. Indeed, as we will see, by factoring our discussion of epistemic luck into the debate regarding virtue epistemology we are able to identify a core problem facing all such theories of knowledge.

1. Epistemological Internalism and Cognitive Responsibility

What we have then are *two* epistemically problematic varieties of luck. It is important to note, however, that in granting that these types of luck are both epistemically problematic one does not *thereby* concede the truth of epistemological internalism, since there may be ways in which an agent's beliefs, whilst epistemically undesirable in some fashion, are nevertheless able to meet the standards for knowledge. That is, whilst it is clear that both of these types of luck are epistemically undesirable, and that veritic luck is incompatible with knowledge possession (such is the immediate moral of the post-Gettier literature), the further question of whether reflective luck is incompatible with knowledge is moot. There is certainly *something* epistemically deficient about the naïve chicken-sexer's beliefs, but it is not clear that this means that she lacks knowledge.

Indeed, it is important to remember that whilst no one seriously thinks that the agents in the Gettier-type cases whose beliefs are infected with veritic epistemic luck have knowledge, there *are* people – epistemological externalists – who think that the unenlightened chicken-sexer has knowledge, despite the presence of reflective epistemic luck. Indeed, such externalists will no doubt even grant that there is something epistemically lacking about the naïve chicken-sexer's beliefs. Nevertheless, they will contend that there is nothing epistemically lacking which is essential to knowledge possession. Accordingly, we cannot straightforwardly take the conclusion generated

by our observations on reflective epistemic luck that there is something epistemically amiss with pure externalist knowledge and convert this into a knock-down argument for epistemological internalism.

We have thus returned to the debate between epistemological externalism and internalism, in that the issue is whether the kind of internalist justification that would be needed to eliminate reflective luck should be made a necessary condition for knowledge. If you think that it should – that only "enlightened" chicken-sexers can have knowledge – then your intuitions side with the internalists, whilst if you think that it shouldn't, then your intuitions side with the externalists. We shouldn't expect an easy resolution to this issue. The endurance of the debate between the internalists and the externalists in the recent literature is evidence, if evidence were needed, that our intuitions about such examples are divided.

Nevertheless, the observation that epistemological internalists are more concerned about reflective epistemic luck than externalists does add something substantive to our understanding of this debate. In the first instance, it identifies one area about which internalists and externalists have managed to speak past one another. ... Linda Zagzebski argu[es] that the problem with pure externalist knowledge [is] that it [is] no better than a lucky guess. Although ... there [is] *some* truth in this, it [isn't] altogether an accurate description of the situation given that even the unenlightened chicken-sexer [is] forming beliefs that [are] safe, and hence which [are] not veritically lucky.

This failure to recognize the subtleties involved in the way that externalists and internalists respond to the problem posed by epistemic luck is common in the literature. Consider the following quotation from Zagzebski:

> The dispute between externalists and internalists looms large mostly because of ambivalence over the place of luck in normative theory. Theorists who resist the idea that knowledge ... is vulnerable to luck are pulled in the direction of internalism. ... Externalists are more sanguine about luck. ... There is lots of room for luck in externalist theories since the conditions that make it the case that the knower is in a state of knowledge are independent of her conscious access. (1996, p. 39)

Whilst superficially persuasive, this interpretation of the internalism–externalism debate is at best misleading. After all, it is just not true that externalists are sanguine about epistemic luck, since, like all post-Gettier epistemologists, they make the elimination of veritic epistemic luck an adequacy condition on their theory of knowledge. What they are sanguine about (if that's the right word) is only the presence of reflective epistemic luck, and even then it is entirely consistent with their position to concede that such luck is epistemically undesirable, if ultimately compatible with knowledge possession. (Indeed, I would suggest that any modest externalist epistemological theory would be inclined to allow that the naïve chicken-sexer's beliefs are epistemically problematic.)[1] In any case, the issue about conscious access is itself misleading, since even internalists will want to eliminate veritic epistemic luck and this goal, as we have seen, will have the consequence that they are obliged to incorporate an external epistemic condition into their theory, a condition which the agent lacks "conscious access" to. Thus, internalists are also in an important sense "sanguine" about epistemic luck as well (we will return to this point). So whilst Zagzebski's way of viewing the debate emphasizes the differences between the positions, focusing on the role of the two types of epistemically problematic luck in this debate brings out the common ground.[2]

My sympathies here are with the externalist, but I doubt that any definitive considerations can be offered which will decide the matter one way or the other. What is important for present purposes, however, is the issue of what is it about reflective epistemic luck that makes it an epistemically undesirable feature of one's beliefs. That is, why is it that we value beliefs that are internalistically justified, even if we don't also insist that meeting this constraint is necessary for knowledge? I think that the answer to this question relates to the fact that we tend to want beliefs that are more than just safe. That is, we don't just want agents to be forming beliefs in such a way that we can rely on the truth of those beliefs, we also want agents to be *cognitively responsible* for their beliefs, and this is only possible if they form beliefs in ways that are responsive to the reflectively accessible grounds that they have in favour of their beliefs. The naïve chicken-sexer may well be a reliable indicator of the truth regarding the subject matter at issue, but she is not in a position to take any credit for this reliability. Another way of putting this point is to say that whilst her safe true beliefs are in some minimal sense an achievement of hers, in that it is *her* cognitive trait that is giving rise to them, the achievement here is entirely at the sub-personal level. So whilst we might think that her chicken-sexing capacity is a good cognitive trait to have – it does, after all, enable one to form safe true beliefs about the subject matter in question – we would not think that the naïve chicken-sexer herself is deserving of any epistemic credit for forming beliefs in this way because in the relevant sense the safety of her beliefs has nothing to do with any epistemic act of hers. In contrast, the enlightened chicken-sexer is deserving of epistemic credit because by forming beliefs in response to the reflectively accessible evidence that she possesses she has acted in a way that is epistemically responsible.[3]

I think that this point becomes clearer once one considers how the enlightened chicken-sexer is in a position to properly claim knowledge of what she believes whereas this is not the case for her naïve counterpart. … Agents who do not meet internal epistemic conditions will typically be unable to properly claim to possess knowledge, even if one grants that what the agent would be asserting in making such a claim would be true. The reason for this is that a claim to know – especially one that is made explicitly via a locution of the form "I know that …" – carries the conversational implicature that one is able to offer relevant reflectively accessible grounds in support of that claim, and this is just what agents who don't meet internal epistemic conditions, such as naïve chicken-sexers, cannot do. The ability to properly claim the knowledge that one has is, however, a very desirable epistemic capacity. For whilst it might be useful to us to know that the naïve chicken-sexer is forming safe true beliefs, and thus know that she is a reliable indicator when it comes to the subject matter in question, she herself is not able to perform the role of being a reliable *informant* in this respect, since from her point of view she lacks any reason for thinking that she is forming beliefs in a safe fashion. But the ability to be a reliable informant, to put our knowledge to use in this way, is clearly something of tremendous value to us and thus it is little wonder that we find the kind of "knowledge" (if that's what it is) that the naïve chicken-sexer has as being so intellectually dissatisfying.

2. Process Reliabilism, Agent Reliabilism, and Virtue Epistemology

This intuition that the possession of knowledge demands that the agent should in some way be able to take credit for the truth of her belief gets expression in recent work by virtue epistemologists, as does the more fine-grained thought that there are different ways in which an agent's belief can be of credit to the agent.[4] In essence, what virtue epistemologists contend is that knowledge should actually be *defined* in terms of the epistemic virtues – such as conscientiousness or open-mindedness – and perhaps also in terms of our cognitive faculties as well, such as our perceptual faculties. What is radical about this proposal is that we would ordinarily identify a trait as being an epistemic virtue or a cognitive faculty by noting that it is knowledge-conducive, and thus we would be presupposing a prior theory of knowledge. Indeed, whilst it is part of the recent epistemological tradition to regard any adequate epistemology as needing to include some account of how it is that agents such as ourselves come to have knowledge – a story which will undoubtedly make essential reference to the epistemic virtues and the cognitive faculties – it does not normally *define* knowledge in terms of the epistemic virtues and cognitive faculties. Nevertheless, given the widespread intuition that we have noted concerning how the cognitive achievement involved in knowledge possession excludes luck (in some sense), if a virtue epistemology is able to do this then it will be one way (if not the only way) of capturing what is involved in an anti-luck epistemology. As we will see, I am sceptical that we need to endorse the radical claim that virtue epistemologists make – i.e. that knowledge must actually be *defined* in terms of the epistemic virtues and cognitive faculties. Nevertheless, tracing the motivations for the development of the view will cast some light upon the distinction we have made here between veritic and reflective epistemic luck.

The early forms of virtue epistemology that have been developed in the recent literature were generally modelled along reliabilist lines and grew out of a certain kind of dissatisfaction with process reliabilism. Consider a crude process reliabilist account of knowledge as being one which simply demanded, in essence, that one has knowledge if, and only if, one forms one's true belief via a reliable process (a process which ensures a high ratio of true beliefs relative to false beliefs). In terms of rather "low-grade" knowledge, such as basic perceptual knowledge, this is a fairly plausible account.[5] Intuitively, such beliefs count as knowledge just so long as they are formed in reliable ways which, as the products of our perceptual faculties in normal circumstances, we would expect them to be. Nothing more seems to be necessary to knowledge in this case than meeting such a condition. Such a view, however, at least if extended so that it applies to knowledge of contingent propositions in general, faces a number of difficulties.

For one thing, the position is clearly an externalist theory of knowledge that would allow ascriptions of knowledge to such agents as the naïve chicken-sexer, and we have already noted that there are those who would be unhappy about this consequence of the view. Moreover, there are notorious problems of formulation with process reliabilism, both in terms of the specification of reliability that is at issue and, relatedly, regarding the issue of how one individuates the relevant processes (the so-called "generality problem").[6] Although the early virtue epistemologists were naturally concerned with these kinds of familiar difficulties for the process reliabilist position,[7] their focus was not on these objections facing the process reliabilist position but rather on the manner in which process reliabilism seemed to allow that agents could possess knowledge even though the reliability in question in no way reflected a cognitive achievement on their part.

Consider the following two problems. First, there is the difficulty of how process reliabilism as it stands seems to leave it open as to whether the reliability in question has anything to do with the agent's beliefs tracking the world. For example, suppose that there was a benevolent demon who ensured that every time our protagonist formed a belief the world was adjusted to make it such that the belief was true. Clearly, this would be a highly reliable way of forming beliefs since it would never fail to result in a true belief. Nevertheless, our intuition in such a case is that the agent lacks knowledge since her reliably formed true beliefs do not reflect a cognitive achievement on her part at all. John Greco describes just such an example as follows:

> René thinks he can beat the roulette tables with a system he has devised. Reasoning according to the Gambler's Fallacy, he believes that numbers which have not come up for long strings are more likely to come up next. However, unlike Descartes' demon victim, our René has a demon helper. Acting as a kind of epistemic guardian, the demon arranges reality so as to make the belief come out as true. Given the ever present interventions of the helpful demon, René's belief forming process is highly reliable. But this is because the world is made to confirm to René's beliefs, rather than because René's beliefs conform to the world. (1999, p. 286)

Clearly here we would not regard René as having knowledge for the simple reason that the reliability that he is exhibiting in his beliefs is nothing to do with him, but rather reflects the interference of the demon helper.

Second, there is the problem that the process reliabilist account of knowledge seems to accord knowledge in cases where the reliability, whilst it might be "to do with the agent" in some basic causal sense, is not related to the agent's cognitive character in quite the right fashion. A good way to bring this point out is via examples of reliable "malfunctions". This is where an agent forms a belief in a reliable manner despite the fact that this reliability is the product of a malfunction. An example, due to Alvin Plantinga, concerns a rare brain lesion that causes the victim to believe that he has a brain lesion. He describes this scenario as follows:

> Suppose … that S suffers from this sort of disorder and accordingly believes that he suffers from a brain lesion. Add that he has no evidence at all for this belief: no symptoms of which he is aware, no testimony on the part of physicians or other expert witnesses, nothing. (Add if you like, that he has much evidence *against* it; but then add also that the malfunction induced by the lesion makes it impossible for him to take appropriate account of this evidence.) Then the relent [process] will certainly be reliable; but the resulting belief – that he has a brain lesion – will have little by way of warrant for S. (1993a, p. 199)

We have a strong intuition that there is something epistemically amiss about forming true beliefs via malfunctions in this way, even where those malfunctions happen to support a process of forming beliefs which is reliable. Although malfunction examples like this are different from the helpful demon case in that the reliability at issue has at least *something* to do with the agent (it is *his* brain lesion after all), it is nevertheless the case that the agent's true belief cannot be considered a cognitive achievement on his part because it is *in spite of himself* that he formed a true belief. If his cognitive faculties had been functioning properly, and thus had not been malfunctioning, then we would not have expected him to have formed a true belief in this proposition.

In response to problems of this sort, early virtue epistemologists argued that process reliabilism should be rejected in favour of a kind of reliabilism that specifically focuses on the reliable traits of the agents. This view has come to be known as "faculty" or "agent" reliabilism.[8] The basic idea is that it is not reliability per se that epistemologists should be attending to, but rather the particular kind of reliability that represents a cognitive achievement on the part of the agent, and this means a reliability that is tied to stable belief-forming traits of the agent such as her intellectual faculties and epistemic virtues. In general, then, agent reliabilists advocate a thesis along the following lines:

Agent reliabilism

For all agents, φ, an agent has knowledge of a contingent proposition, φ, if, and only if, that agent forms a true belief that φ as a result of the stable and reliable dispositions that make up that agent's cognitive character.

For example, think about the range of stable dispositions involved in the formation of our beliefs about our immediate environment that make up our faculty of sight. If this faculty is working properly and applied in the right conditions, then the beliefs that it generates will be highly reliable. Moreover, since this reliability is keyed into our cognitive character, forming a true belief in this way is a cognitive achievement on our part and will thus tend to be regarded as an instance of knowledge (though we will consider some Gettier-style complications in a moment).

In contrast, the reliability that might attach itself to a cognitive malfunction will not count as knowledge-conducive on this view because the belief-forming process involved is not a stable feature of our cognitive character at all, and thus the reliable true beliefs that result are of no credit to us. Indeed, as we noted above, it is *in spite of* the stable cognitive dispositions that make up the agent's cognitive character that he is reliable in the malfunction case that we looked at earlier, not because of them. Similarly, forming beliefs in a reliable fashion where that reliability has nothing to do with one's cognitive character, as in the case in the "benevolent demon" example, is also ruled out. The reliability at issue here cannot support knowledge because it represents no cognitive achievement at all on the part of the agent. Agent reliabilists are thus able to deal with a certain type of core objection that has been levelled against process reliabilism, and do so whilst staying within the general reliabilist framework.[9]

We noted above that these early virtue theorists were not primarily concerned with the problems of formulation facing process reliabilism, nor with its commitment to epistemological externalism, and this sketch of the agent reliabilist position should make it obvious why. To begin with, whilst we might have a better intuitive grasp of how we should individuate our intellectual faculties and our epistemic virtues than how we should individuate cognitive processes *simpliciter*, it remains that there will still be issues of formulation left over here. Recall the brain lesion case, for example. Although this example is defined in such a way that it won't count as a stable and reliable cognitive disposition that makes up the agent's cognitive character – for one thing, it is *defined* as a cognitive malfunction – it doesn't take too much imagination to think of a way in which this example could be understood so that it did appear to meet the agent reliabilist rubric. As Greco himself concedes:

[I]t is not clear why the man with the brain lesion does not have a cognitive virtue, and it is therefore not clear how virtue reliabilism addresses the case. Put another way, it is not clear why the process associated with the brain lesion is not part of reliable cognitive character. Thus we can imagine that the lesion has been there since birth,

and that the associated process is both stable and reliable in the relevant senses. (2003, pp. 356–7)[10]

The problems of formulation associated with process reliabilism thus resurface – albeit perhaps in a more manageable form – with agent reliabilism.

Similarly – and these points are related – agent reliabilism is also clearly an externalist account of knowledge and so is subject, just like process reliabilism, to the counter-intuitions put forward by the epistemological internalist. Whatever one might want to say about reliable brain lesions, it is certainly true that the naïve chicken-sexer discussed above is forming her true beliefs via stable and reliable dispositions that make up her cognitive character. As a result, on the agent reliabilist view the chicken-sexer comes out as having knowledge, something which the epistemological internalist will find unacceptable. Again, the agent reliabilist can weaken this objection slightly by arguing that the externalism on offer here is tempered by the fact that the reliability in question must be essentially related to the agent's cognitive character. Accordingly, they can claim that by advocating epistemological externalism they are not thereby allowing knowledge to be completely unconnected with cognitive responsibility. Nevertheless, the issue remains that in these cases the cognitive achievement is entirely at a sub-personal level, and in this sense the agent proper is not cognitively responsible for her reliably formed true beliefs at all. So whilst agent reliabilist accounts of knowledge might ensure that agents are able to take a very minimal form of cognitive responsibility for their beliefs, what the epistemic internalist will demand is a more robust form of cognitive responsibility – a type of cognitive responsibility that could legitimate a claim to know, for example.[11]

Indeed, this point dovetails with the further issue that it sounds odd, to the modern ear at least, to describe agent reliabilism as a *virtue*-theoretic account of knowledge at all. After all, although there is, admittedly, a historical precedent for thinking of the cognitive faculties as being epistemic virtues, our contemporary understanding of the virtues, and thus of the intellectual virtues, tends to regard them as very different to cognitive faculties.[12] Indeed, in terms of the modern usage of the term "virtue" I think the consensus would be to regard the naïve chicken-sexer as behaving in a way that exhibits an epistemic *vice* on the grounds that she is forming beliefs in the absence of any reflectively accessible evidence in favour of those beliefs. We will return to this point in the next section.

For now, the more pressing issue is how this account of knowledge ties in with the remarks we have made so far about epistemic luck. We have already noted the close relationship between cognitive achievement and the absence of epistemically problematic luck, so we should expect that the manner in which agent reliabilism constitutes an improvement on process reliabilism is directly related to how it eliminates luck of this sort. And, indeed, this is just what we find, since the counter-examples that the agent reliabilists direct against process reliabilism are all Gettier-style examples, in that they are instances of true belief where the agent has met the epistemic conditions demanded by the theory of knowledge in question, and yet the agent lacks knowledge because her belief is nevertheless veritically lucky.

Consider again the helpful demon example. Here we have an agent who would be forming beliefs in an unreliable fashion (via the Gambler's Fallacy) were it not for the fact that, as it happens, there is a helpful demon in town who not only has the capacity to ensure that any beliefs our agent forms in this regard are true, but also has the inclination to be helpful in this fashion. As a result, even though the agent has met the epistemic condition imposed by a basic form of process reliabilism – in that he is forming his true belief via a process which counts as reliable on this view – it is nevertheless also the case that his true belief is here being formed in a way that is subject to a substantive degree of veritic epistemic luck. That is, there will be a large class of nearby possible worlds in which this agent forms his belief in the same way as in the actual world – and this means in this case that he forms his belief via the Gambler's Fallacy – and his belief is false. After all, the class of possible worlds at issue here will include worlds where there is no demon, or where there is a demon but he is not being helpful, or where there is a demon who is being helpful, but who is not being helpful in this particular respect, and so on. Accordingly, since the belief in question is infected by veritic epistemic luck, it is therefore not safe, and so not an instance of knowledge in the light of a safety-based theory.

Next, consider the malfunction case. Again, as the example is described at any rate, we have a case of a true belief that is infected by a substantive degree of veritic epistemic luck. Whilst the agent has formed a true belief in the actual world via a causal process that meets the reliability condition imposed by a basic form of process reliabilism, in most nearby possible worlds we would expect the agent to form a false belief via this process. After all, if it is an incidental fact about the brain lesion that it supports a reliable belief-forming process about this subject matter in this way, then in most nearby possible worlds we would expect it to not be supporting a reliable belief-forming process and thus expect it to not lead the agent to true beliefs about whether or not he has a brain lesion. His belief is thus veritically lucky and hence not safe. Both these examples thus lend support to the Gettier-style contention that meeting the epistemic condition laid down by a basic process reliabilist account of knowledge does not suffice to eliminate veritic epistemic luck, and hence that such a theory of knowledge is highly questionable.

Of course, as we noted above, there is an added complication when it comes to the malfunction example in that there are alternative ways of understanding this case so that the reliability in question isn't incidental in the relevant way but is rather brought about by a stable cognitive disposition on the part of the agent. On this understanding of the example, the agent reliabilist response starts to look suspect, since now the agent *does* seem to be forming true beliefs as a result of stable and reliable traits that make up his cognitive character, at least given the agent reliabilist construal of "cognitive character" as including the cognitive faculties. The brain lesion case now becomes akin to the naïve chicken-sexer example in that it is an instance of *merely* externalist knowledge – i.e. knowledge where the agent has met no relevant internal justification condition.

By the same token, the agent's true belief on this construal of the example is no longer (at least obviously) infected by veritic epistemic luck, and thus it will be, prima facie at least, in accordance with the demands laid down by a safety-based theory of knowledge. Of course (as in the naïve chicken-sexer example), we would not be happy with the agent making self-ascriptions of knowledge in this case and there is clearly something important epistemically lacking about this agent's belief (it is, as we saw above in our discussion of the naïve chicken-sexer, a true belief that is subject to a substantive degree of reflective epistemic luck). Nevertheless, depending on the details of the example, if we knew that the agent was forming beliefs about this subject matter in a safe way then we might be inclined to ascribe knowledge of a very brute sort to the agent even if we did not think that the agent should be ascribing this knowledge to himself.

It seems then that the objection raised by agent reliabilism against process reliabilism is much the same objection that the proponent of an anti-veritic-luck epistemology would make against process reliabilism – that it cannot capture even a minimal sense in which knowledge is a cognitive achievement on the part of the agent because the rubric it sets down for knowledge does not exclude veritic epistemic luck. The two theses are not complementary, however, in that they end up defining knowledge in very different ways. For whilst the safety-based theorist might no doubt wish to tell an explanatory story about how creatures such as ourselves come to have safe true beliefs that makes essential reference to the cognitive faculties and the epistemic virtues, she does not *define* knowledge in terms of these cognitive traits as the agent reliabilist does. Thus, despite being motivated by similar concerns, agent reliabilism, being a virtue-theoretic theory, is offering a much more radical epistemological thesis.

The issue is therefore whether we need to endorse such a radical view in order to eliminate veritic epistemic luck, or whether we can simply advocate a safety-based view that incorporates an explanatory story that makes essential use of the cognitive faculties and epistemic virtues. It seems that we can do the latter, and ought to, for two reasons. The first reason concerns how the agent reliabilist account of knowledge is not necessary for the elimination of veritic epistemic luck. As we have just seen, the examples of veritic epistemic luck that agent reliabilism claims to be able to deal with in a way that other theories cannot – such as the helpful demon and the brain lesion cases – are examples where a safety-based view has direct application.

As it stands, this observation alone merely puts the two views on a theoretical par in this respect, and thereby only leaves a mere safety-based approach as a live – rather than a preferred – option.[13] There is a further consideration, however, which motivates a safety-based approach over an agent reliabilist alternative, and this is that the agent reliabilist theory of knowledge, unlike the safety-based theory, is not only unnecessary to deal with the problem of veritic luck, but is also *insufficient*. Consider the following Gettier-style counter-example to agent reliabilism:

> Mary has good eyesight, but it is not perfect. It is good enough to allow her to identify her husband sitting in his usual chair in the living room from a distance of fifteen feet in somewhat dim light. … Of course, her faculties may not be functioning perfectly, but they are functioning well enough that if she goes on to form the belief *My husband is sitting in the living room*, her belief has enough warrant to constitute knowledge when true. … Suppose Mary simply misidentifies the chair sitter, who is, we'll suppose, her husband's brother, who looks very much like him. … We can now easily amend the case as a Gettier example. Mary's husband could be sitting on the other side of the room, unseen by her. (Zagzebski 1996, pp. 285–7)

What is the agent reliabilist to say about such a case? Clearly, Mary is forming a true belief which meets the epistemic conditions laid down by the agent reliabilist, in that her true belief is a result of the stable and reliable dispositions that make up her cognitive character. Crucially, however, the belief in this case is not an instance of knowledge because of the veritic epistemic luck involved. After all, there will be a wide class of nearby possible worlds in which Mary forms her belief in the same way as in the actual world and yet continues to form a false belief as a result because her husband is not, as it happens, in the room in these worlds.

What is crucial about the fact that agent reliabilist views can be "Gettiered" in this way is that it completely undermines the agent reliabilist claim to be in a peculiarly good position to capture the sense in which knowledge is a cognitive achievement on the part of the agent. Whilst Mary is certainly deserving of some epistemic credit for forming the belief that she did, we would hardly regard it as a cognitive achievement on her part that she formed a true belief since the truth of her belief was largely due to luck. The inability of agent reliabilism to eliminate veritic epistemic luck means that it allows these Gettier-style cases where the agent meets the relevant epistemic rubric even whilst forming a veritically lucky true belief. Accordingly, the view legitimates a knowledge ascription even though the agent concerned is clearly not exhibiting anything like the kind of cognitive achievement (sub-personal or otherwise) that is necessary for knowledge.

Moreover, note that safety-based views will not have this problem since Mary's true belief, since it is veritically lucky, will not be safe and thus will not be accorded the status of knowledge by the lights of a safety-based thesis. The adoption of a safety-based view – unlike an agent reliabilist view – is thus sufficient for the elimination of veritic epistemic luck.

Furthermore, note that any safety-based account of knowledge that offered an explanatory story about how agents gain safe true beliefs – and thus are able to acquire knowledge – will no doubt make reference to the kinds of cognitive traits at issue in agent reliabilism. In this way, safety-based views can account for why Mary is deserving of some epistemic credit even though in this case she lacks knowledge because the cognitive faculties that she is employing in forming her belief are good ways in which to acquire safe beliefs. Nevertheless, since such a fully-fledged epistemological theory does not *define* knowledge in terms of the epistemic virtues and cognitive faculties, such an epistemology is still a safety-based theory rather than a virtue-theoretic account.

So whilst agent reliabilists are right to be troubled by veritic epistemic luck and thus to seek a theory of knowledge that eliminates such luck (thereby ensuring that knowing agents are able to take a minimal degree of cognitive responsibility for their beliefs), it remains that the way to achieve this is via a safety-based theory rather than via a virtue-theoretic account.

3.   Neo-Aristotelian Virtue Epistemology

Not all virtue-theoretic accounts of knowledge are modelled along reliabilist lines, however, and more recent work on virtue epistemology has tended to move towards an epistemologically internalist version of the thesis which understands the epistemic virtues in a way that is more in keeping with our ordinary conception of them, and which thus does not treat mere cognitive faculties as epistemic virtues. Such views are often called "responsibilist" or "neo-Aristotelian" and stress that agents should not only exhibit reliable cognitive traits but that they should also be in a position to take the kind of robust reflective responsibility for their true beliefs that is noticeably lacking in externalist views of knowledge. Since epistemic virtues are reliable cognitive traits which also demand a certain level of reflective responsibility on the part of the agent, they fit the bill perfectly.

Perhaps the most prominent and well-developed version of a thesis of this sort is due to Zagzebski,[14] who argues that mere reliability is not enough and that agents should have to meet internal epistemic conditions as well. On her view, the kind of sub-personal cognitive achievement that is present in, for example, naïve chicken-sexer cases, will not suffice for knowledge. For whilst the naïve chicken-sexer might be forming belief in ways that are reliable, she is not forming beliefs in ways that are epistemically virtuous (at least in the modern sense of the term). She is not, for example, forming her beliefs in a way that is epistemically conscientious, or, indeed, in a way that is responsive to the reflectively accessible evidence that she has in favour of her beliefs at all. (In fact, as we noted above, the naïve chicken-sexer is, if anything, forming her beliefs via an epistemic vice rather than a virtue, at least provided we understand the epistemic "virtues" in the standard way which excludes mere cognitive faculties.)

We saw above how Zagzebski also motivated her adoption of an internalist account of knowledge by claiming that such internalism was necessary to eliminate epistemic luck, but that the kind of epistemic luck that was at issue was, it turned out, specifically reflective epistemic luck rather than veritic epistemic luck. We would expect the motivation for most virtue epistemologies of this sort to be susceptible to the same diagnosis, in that their underlying concern regarding agent reliabilism is that whereas the reliabilist element of the view deals with veritic epistemic luck, and does so in a way that makes the reliability a product (in some sense) of the agent's cognitive character, since this form of "virtue" theory allows sub-personal traits of the agent to count as knowledge-conducive, it won't capture the fuller sense in which knowledge is a cognitive achievement of the agent. This "fuller sense" of cognitive achievement involves, of course, not just the elimination of veritic epistemic luck but also the elimination of reflective epistemic luck – hence the necessity of adding, via the focus on the epistemic virtues alone, an internal epistemic condition to the view.[15]

If one is persuaded by the general virtue-theoretic line and unpersuaded by the considerations in favour of epistemological externalism, then one will be inclined to adopt a virtue epistemology of this sort. As we will see in a moment, however, it is not at all clear that this new variant on the general virtue-theoretic approach adds anything which can help it evade the criticisms that we levelled against agent reliabilism above, since an internalized version of virtue epistemology doesn't appear to be in any better position to handle cases of veritic epistemic luck than an agent reliabilist view is. Accordingly, it appears that if one is troubled by the problem posed by reflective epistemic luck then one would be wiser to endorse an internalized version of a safety-based theory – i.e., a safety-based theory that also incorporated an internal epistemic condition – rather than a version of the more radical neo-Aristotelian virtue account.

In order to see this, consider again the Gettier-style example that we saw Zagzebski offering above which concerned an agent, Mary, who formed a true belief about whether or not her husband was in the room as a result of stable and reliable cognitive traits that made up her cognitive character, and yet who lacked knowledge because her belief was subject to a substantive degree of veritic epistemic luck (she was not looking at her husband, but her husband's brother). As it stands, this example doesn't demand that the agent should form her belief in a way that is epistemically virtuous rather than merely as a result of reliable and stable cognitive faculties, but we can easily understand the example along these lines. Suppose, for example, that Mary forms her belief in such a way that it is epistemically virtuous (she has been conscientious about forming her belief on the basis of adequate reflectively accessible evidence and so forth), and that the belief in question is therefore internalistically justified. Since her belief is true, and has been formed

via the stable and reliable epistemic virtues that make up her cognitive character, we would expect Mary to have knowledge about what she believes. Nevertheless, all these conditions could be met and her belief still be "Gettiered" because, as in the original example, she happens to be looking at her husband's brother whilst her husband is hidden from view elsewhere in the room. The belief is thus still veritically lucky and hence not a case of knowledge.

Interestingly, Zagzebski is quite willing to grant that she cannot meet the Gettier examples head-on via her theory of knowledge in this way. Instead, she tries to motivate a response to this problem by bringing additional resources to bear on the issue, albeit resources that are, she claims, consistent with her general virtue-theoretic approach. Essentially, her contention is that what is lacking about agents in Gettier cases is that whilst they have managed to acquire true beliefs by forming their beliefs in ways that are epistemically virtuous, they do not believe the truth *through* an act of epistemic virtue. Consider the following passage:

> [I]n the case of Mary's belief that her husband is in the living room, she may exhibit all the relevant intellectual virtues and no intellectual vices in the process of forming the belief, but she is not lead to the truth through those virtuous processes or motives. So even though Mary has the belief she has because of her virtues and the belief is true, she does not have the truth because of her virtues. (Zagzebski 1996, p. 297)

Zagzebski's claim is thus that it is not enough to merely form a true belief via one's stable and reliable epistemic virtues in order to have knowledge; rather one must form that true belief *because of* one's stable and reliable epistemic virtues.[16]

This distinction is obscure, however, since it is not at all clear what it involves. What is the difference between the case where Mary's belief hasn't been "Gettiered", and where she thus has knowledge, and the case under discussion in which she has been "Gettiered" and so lacks knowledge? Clearly, the difference does not relate to anything about Mary because, by hypothesis, Mary's cognitive character is exactly the same in both cases. Zagzebski thus seems to be implicitly supplementing her putatively virtue-theoretic account of knowledge with an extra non-virtue-theoretic condition that is able to rule out Gettier cases. Indeed, Zagzebski seems to have a modal claim in mind here. Not only should the agent form her true belief via her stable and reliable epistemic virtues, but she should also believe what she does because it is true where, intuitively, this means that were what is believed not true, then she would not form the belief that she did via her stable and reliable epistemic virtues. So construed, Zagzebski seems to be wanting to add a sensitivity condition to her virtue theory, such that the means by which the agent forms her true belief in the actual world should be via the epistemic virtues, and that in the nearest possible world or worlds in which the proposition in question is false the agent does not believe that proposition via this same method.

… [A]dding a sensitivity condition will do the trick in Gettier-type cases like this, at least provided that the principle is understood in the right kind of way. But recall that we also noted that if any modal condition is applicable here, then it is the safety principle, not only because it directly defuses the veritic epistemic luck at issue in Gettier-type cases, but also because, unlike the sensitivity principle, it isn't committed to allowing far-off possible worlds to be relevant to knowledge. Moreover, we also saw that once sensitivity is modified so as to deal with Gettier-type cases – such that it is concerned with a range of nearby possible worlds – then it no longer differs from safety in any substantive respect, and thus there cannot be anything to gain by opting for the sensitivity principle over the safety principle.

Presumably, then, Zagzebski ought to be happy to construe her modal requirement on knowledge along safety-based lines, and thus argue that the knowing agent should form her true belief via her epistemic virtues, and that her belief should, in addition, be safe. However, if this is what her response to Gettier amounts to then one could just as well adopt a safety-based view that deals with veritic epistemic luck – and thus the Gettier-style examples – directly and then supplement it, if need be, with an internal justification condition to deal with the additional problem posed by reflective epistemic luck. Crucially, however, such a theory of knowledge need make no essential mention of the epistemic virtues, even if an account of how agents gain internalistically justified safe

beliefs will no doubt incorporate a virtue-theoretic story. Again, then, we find that the case for the virtue-theoretic account of knowledge is moot.

The problem at issue here arises because even internalists need to advocate an external epistemic condition in order to eliminate veritic epistemic luck. The difficulty is that the only external epistemic condition that does the trick is a safety-type condition, and once one has made the crucial move to adopting a condition of this sort as part of one's theory of knowledge then one has thereby moved away from a virtue-theoretic account that defines knowledge in terms of the epistemic virtues because such a principle makes no essential reference to the epistemic virtues at all. It is not then as if Zagzebski is merely offering an internalized virtue-theoretic account that is supplemented by a safety-type condition, since the adoption of a safety-type condition makes the virtue-theoretic proposal obsolete. If one has externalist intuitions about knowledge, then one should seek a mere safety-based theory of knowledge that will, no doubt, be supplemented by a further explanatory story concerning the epistemic virtues and cognitive faculties that explains how agents gain safe beliefs that are not veritically lucky. Alternatively, if one has internalist intuitions about knowledge, then one should seek an internalist safety-based theory of knowledge that will, no doubt, be supplemented by a further explanatory story concerning the epistemic virtues that explains how agents gain safe and internalistically justified beliefs that are neither veritically nor reflectively lucky. Either way, one is left with a non-virtue-theoretic account of knowledge and, far from motivating the virtue-theoretic position in this regard, reflection on the role of epistemic luck merely highlights the juncture at which the virtue epistemological thesis goes awry.

One final point is in order. Recall that we saw Zagzebski arguing earlier that epistemological externalists, as opposed to internalists, were sanguine about epistemic luck, and we noted there that this was a misleading way of putting matters. This discussion of Zagzebski's response to the Gettier problem brings this point nicely to the fore. Zagzebski is just as concerned about the veritic epistemic luck that is at issue in the Gettier counter-examples as externalists are, and this is why she has a reliability condition in her account, one that is, moreover, implicitly coupled to a modal anti-veritic-luck condition for good measure. Moreover, we have also seen that an externalist theory of knowledge which eliminated veritic epistemic luck would capture one sense in which knowledge demands cognitive achievement, which is the minimal sense that the true belief in question is not gained via a matter of luck and so is, in this very limited sense, of credit to the agent.

Furthermore, it is worth emphasizing that it is not as if externalists are necessarily unconcerned about reflective epistemic luck either, since it is entirely consistent with their view that they regard such luck as being epistemically undesirable. What distinguishes epistemic internalists from externalists on this issue is thus not whether or not they are sanguine about epistemic luck *simpliciter*, but more specifically whether they think that the elimination of reflective epistemic luck should be a necessary condition for knowledge. The internalist thinks that it should be, and so adduces an internal epistemic condition, whereas the externalist disagrees.

4.   Concluding Remarks

Epistemological externalists and epistemological internalists thus have a tendency to "speak past" one another, and we have seen that this is caused, at least in part, by a failure to realize that they are each primarily concerned with advancing a theory of knowledge that is able to eliminate a *different* species of epistemic luck. Indeed, as we saw with our discussion of the two main types of virtue epistemology, this issue about eliminating epistemic luck also explains the different conceptions of cognitive responsibility that are at issue in debates between proponents of these two theses. Since we have already granted the internalist claim that the possession of an internalist justification for one's belief is epistemically desirable – where this epistemic desirability is reflected in how one is able to take cognitive responsibility for one's belief in a fuller sense than would be possible if such justification were lacking – it follows that we ought to be at least sympathetic to the theoretical aspirations of epistemological internalists. The issue therefore comes down to whether we are willing to allow that there are some instances in which agents might have knowledge in the "brute" externalist sense where the agent's cognitive responsibility for her beliefs is, at best, entirely sub-personal.

… [W]e cannot fully resolve this issue without returning to the problem of scepticism … since … the sceptical problem is, first and foremost a challenge to the very sort of cognitive responsibility that epistemological internalists aspire to and which is downplayed by externalist theories of knowledge. The sceptical problem is thus, at root, concerned with the issue of eliminating reflective epistemic luck from our beliefs.

Notes

1 For example, Foley (1987) argues that we should seek beliefs that are both internalistically justified *and* reliable, but that it is only the satisfaction of external epistemic conditions that is necessary for knowledge. According to Foley, internalists and externalists are engaged in two distinct projects. Internalists are trying to identify the conditions under which an agent"s beliefs are rational, whilst externalists are aiming to elucidate the conditions under which agents have knowledge. Crucially, according to Foley at any rate, one can meet the latter set of conditions without thereby having internalistically justified (and thus rational) true beliefs (and vice versa). As a result, the naïve chicken-sexer's beliefs are epistemically problematic, but not in a way that undermines her knowledge possession. See also Foley (1993).

2 It should be noted that Zagzebski characterizes the internalist–externalist distinction in a somewhat unorthodox fashion such that internalist epistemologies are theories that *only* advance internal epistemic conditions. In light of this understanding of the distinction, her own view comes out as being what she calls a "mixed" externalist thesis because it incorporates both internal and external epistemic conditions, whereas it would be an internalist view in light of the more orthodox

characterization of the distinction put forward here. There are a number of problems with the way in which Zagzebski draws the internalist–externalist distinction, but the most pressing is that on this understanding it is not clear who the opposition is supposed to be since hardly anyone in these post-Gettier days holds that knowledge is just internalistically justified true belief. The debate between internalists and externalists is thus trivialized.

3   Of course, agents might have reflectively accessible evidence and yet fail to take appropriate account of it, and it will be part of any theory of internalist justification to elucidate just what it means to take "appropriate" account of the evidence that one has reflectively available to one. I ignore this complication in what follows.

4   Indeed, Zagzebski's remarks cited in the last section were taken from a context in which she was discussing her own version of virtue epistemology, a version which we will discuss further below.

5   And, indeed, process reliabilism was primarily aimed at perceptual belief. For discussion of process reliabilism, see Armstrong (1973), Goldman (1976, 1979, 1986), and Talbott (1990).

6   For more on the generality problem, see Brandom (1998) and Conee and Feldman (1998).

7   Indeed, as we will see below, they thought that their view could at least contribute towards a satisfactory resolution of them. A third sort of problem facing process reliabilism, and which a virtue-theoretic reliabilism might also hope to resolve, is its failure to deal with certain Gettier-style examples. Again, this is an issue that we will return to below.

8   Versions of this thesis have been proposed by Sosa (1985, 1991, 1993), Goldman (1993) and Greco (1993, 1999, 2000). A related view in this respect is Plantinga's (1988, 1993b, 1993c) "proper functionalism", although he has explicity resisted any virtue-based interpretation of his view. For an overview of proposals of this sort, see Axtell (1997, especially §2).

9   Although I'm willing to grant the general point that agent reliabilism constitutes an improvement on process reliabilism, I think that the issue is somewhat more complicated than proponents of agent reliabilism sometimes suppose. In particular, I would argue that they tend to achieve their victory over process reliabilism rather cheaply by working with a very underdeveloped formulation of the process reliabilist position. I discuss this issue in more detail in Pritchard (2003), to which Axtell (2003) and Greco (2003) respond.

10 I develop this problem in Pritchard (2003c), and Greco was here responding to that objection. For more discussion of this issue, see the exchange between Plantinga (1993c) and Sosa (1993), and the references offered by Greco (2003, p. 357).

11 For an overview of the different ways in which the main virtue-theoretic forms of reliabilism try to meet the problems of formulation facing process reliabilism and deal with the more counter-intuitive aspects of its commitment to epistemological externalism, see Axtell (1997, §2).

12 Sosa defends his broad usage of the term "virtue" in the following passage:

> For example, it may be one's faculty of sight operating in good light that generates one's belief in the whiteness and roundness of a facing snowball. Is possession of such a faculty a "virtue"? Not in the narrow Aristotelian sense, of course, since it is no disposition to make deliberate choices. But there is a broader sense of "virtue", still Greek, in which anything with a function – natural or artificial – does have virtues. The eye does, after all, have its virtues, and so does a knife. And if we include grasping the truth about one's environment among the proper ends of a human being, then the faculty of sight would seem in a broad sense a virtue in human beings; and if grasping the truth is an intellectual matter then that virtue is also in a straightforward sense an intellectual virtue. (1991, p. 271)

13 Though one might argue, of course, that the safety-based view is the more minimal of the two proposals, and thus that when one is faced with an *impasse* of this sort it should be preferred.

14 See especially Zagzebski (1996). Views of this general sort have also been offered by Code

(1984, 1987), Montmarquet (1987, 1993), Kvanvig (1992), and Hookway (1994). For an overview of responsibilist virtue-theoretic theses in the recent literature (though one that invokes a broader understanding of this description than that employed here), see Axtell (1997, §4). For some of the recent literature on this topic that covers both this type of virtue theory and faculty-based accounts, see the papers collected in the following anthologies: Axtell (2000), Fairweather and Zagzebski (2001), DePaul and Zagzebski (2002), Steup (2002), and Brady and Pritchard (2003).

15   A secondary motivation that Zagzebski offers for preferring an internalist version of virtue-theory over an externalist version is that only the former can meet what she calls the "value problem" which, essentially, is the claim that only an internalist virtuetheoretic account of knowledge can explain what is valuable about knowledge. She develops this line in Zagzebski (2003; cf. Percival 2003). For some of the key recent discussions of the value problem, see Jones (1997), Kvanvig (1998, 2003, 2004), Greco (2002), Riggs (2002), and Axtell (2003).

16   See also Zagzebski (1999). This idea has also gained expression in the work of a number of other proponents of virtue epistemology. See, e.g., Riggs (2002) and Greco (2002, 2003).

References

Armstrong, D. M. (1973). *Belief, Truth and Knowledge* (Cambridge: Cambridge University Press).

Axtell, G. (1997). "Recent Work on Virtue Epistemology", *American Philosophical Quarterly* 34, pp. 1–26.

——— (2000). *Knowledge, Belief, and Character: Readings in Virtue Epistemology* (Lanham, MD: Roman & Littlefield).

——— (2003). "*Felix Culpa*: Luck in Ethics and Epistemology", *Metaphilosophy* 34, pp. 331–52; and reprinted in Brady and Pritchard (2003).

Brady, M. S., and Pritchard, D. H. (eds) (2003). *Moral and Epistemic Virtues* (Oxford: Blackwell).

Brandom, R. (1998). "Insights and Blindspots of Reliabilism", *The Monist* 81, pp. 371–92.

Code, L. (1984). "Toward a 'Responsibilist' Epistemology", *Philosophy and Phenomenological Research* 44, pp. 29–50.

——— (1987). *Epistemic Responsibility* (Hanover, NH: University Press of New England).

Cohen, S. (1998a). "Contextualist Solutions to Epistemological Problems: Scepticism, Gettier, and the Lottery", *Australasian Journal of Philosophy* 76: 289–306.

——— (1998b). "Two Kinds of Skeptical Argument", *Philosophy and Phenomenological Research* 58: 143–59.

——— (1999). "Contextualism, Skepticism, and the Structure of Reasons", *Philosophical Perspectives* 13: 57–90.

Conee, E., and Feldman, R. (1998). "The Generality Problem for Reliabilism", *Philosophical Studies* 89, pp. 1–29.

DePaul, M., and Zagzebski, L. (eds) (2002). *Intellectual Virtue: Perspectives from Ethics and Epistemology* (Oxford: Oxford University Press).

Fairweather, A., and Zagzebski, L. (eds) (2001). *Virtue Epistemology: Essays on Epistemic Virtue and Responsibility* (Oxford: Oxford University Press).

Foley, R. (1987). *A Theory of Epistemic Rationality* (Cambridge, MA: Harvard University Press).

——— (1993). *Working without a Net* (Oxford: Oxford University Press).

Goldman, A. (1976). "Discrimination and Perceptual Knowledge", *Journal of Philosophy* 73, pp. 771–91.

——— (1979). "What is Justified Belief?", in *Justification and Knowledge*, ed. G. S. Pappas (Dordrecht, Holland: D. Reidel).

——— (1986). *Epistemology and Cognition* (Cambridge, MA: Harvard University Press).

——— (1993). "Epistemic Folkways and Scientific Epistemology", *Philosophical Issues* 3, pp. 271–84.

Greco, J. (1993). "Virtues and Vices of Virtue Epistemology", *Canadian Journal of Philosophy* 23, pp. 413–32.

——— (1999). "Agent Reliabilism", *Philosophical Perspectives* 13, pp. 273–96.

——— (2002). "Knowledge as Credit for True Belief", in *Intellectual Virtue: Perspectives from Ethics and Epistemology*, ed. M. DePaul and L. Zagzebski (Oxford: Oxford University Press).

——— (2003). "Virtue and Luck, Epistemic and Otherwise", *Metaphilosophy* 34, pp. 353–66; and repr. in Brady and Pritchard (2003).

Hookway, C. (1994). "Cognitive Virtues and Epistemic Evaluations", *International Journal of Philosophical Studies* 2, pp. 211–27.

Jones, W. (1997). "Why Do We Value Knowledge?", *American Philosophical Quarterly* 34, pp. 423–40.

Kvanvig, J. (1992). *The Intellectual Virtues and the Life of the Mind: On the Place of the Virtues in Contemporary Epistemology* (Savage, MD: Rowman & Littlefield).

—— (1998). "Why Should Inquiring Minds Want to Know?", *The Monist* 81, pp. 426–51.

—— (2003). *The Value of Knowledge and the Pursuit of Understanding* (Cambridge: Cambridge University Press).

—— (2004). "Nozickian Epistemology and the Value of Knowledge", *Philosophical Issues* 14.

Montmarquet, J. (1987). "Epistemic Virtue", *Mind* 96, pp. 487–97.

—— (1993). *Epistemic Virtue and Doxastic Responsibility* (Lanham, MD: Rowman & Littlefield).

Percival, P. (2003). "The Pursuit of Epistemic Good", *Metaphilosophy* 34, pp. 29–47; and repr. in Brady and Pritchard (2003).

Plantinga, A. (1988). "Positive Epistemic Status and Proper Function", *Philosophical Perspectives* 2, pp. 1–50.

—— (1993a). *Warrant: The Current Debate* (New York: Oxford University Press).

—— (1993b). *Warrant and Proper Function* (New York: Oxford University Press).

—— (1993c). "Why We Need Proper Function", *Noûs* 27, pp. 66–82.

Pritchard, D. H. (2003). "Virtue Epistemology and Epistemic Luck", *Metaphilosophy* 34, pp. 106–30; and repr. in Brady and Pritchard (2003).

Riggs, W. (2002). "Reliability and the Value of Knowledge", *Philosophy and Phenomenological Research* 64, pp. 79–96.

Sosa, E. (1985). "Knowledge and Intellectual Virtue", *The Monist* 68, pp. 224–45.

—— (1988). "Beyond Skepticism, to the Best of our Knowledge", *Mind* 97: 153–89.

—— (1991). "Intellectual Virtue in Perspective", in his *Knowledge in Perspective: Selected Essays in Epistemology* (Cambridge: Cambridge University Press).

—— (1993). "Proper Functionalism and Virtue Epistemology", *Noûs* 27, pp. 51–65.

Steup, M. (ed.) (2002). *Knowledge, Truth, and Duty: Essays on Epistemic Justification, Responsibility, and Virtue* (Oxford: Oxford University Press).

Talbott, W. J. (1990). *The Reliability of the Cognitive Mechanism* (New York: Garland Publishing).

Zagzebski, L. (1996). *Virtues of the Mind: An Inquiry into the Nature of Virtue and the Ethical Foundations of Knowledge* (Cambridge: Cambridge University Press).

—— (1999). "What is Knowledge?", in *Epistemology*, ed. J. Greco and E. Sosa (Oxford: Blackwell).

—— (2003). "The Search for the Source of the Epistemic Good", *Metaphilosophy* 34, pp. 12–28; and repr. in Brady and Pritchard (2003).

CHAPTER 36

The Place of Truth in Epistemology

Ernest Sosa

... [Human] good turns out to be activity of soul in accordance with virtue, and if there are more than one virtue, in accordance with the best and most complete.
(Aristotle, *Nichomachean Ethics*, Bk I, sec. 7)

... With those who identify happiness [faring happily or well] with virtue or some one virtue our account is in harmony; for to virtue belongs virtuous activity. But it makes, perhaps, no small difference whether we place the chief good in possession or in use, in state of mind or in activity. For the state of mind may exist without producing any good result, as in a man who is asleep or in some other way quite inactive, but the activity cannot; for one who has the activity will of necessity be acting, and acting well. And as in the Olympic Games it is not the most beautiful and the strongest that are crowned but those who compete (for it is some of these that are victorious), so those who act win, and rightly win, the noble and good things in life.
(*Ibid.*, Bk I, sec. 8)

... [Of] the intellect which is contemplative, not practical nor productive, the good and the bad state are truth and falsity respectively (for this is the work of everything intellectual).
(*Ibid.*, Bk VI, sec. 2)[1]

I

In order to qualify as knowledge, a belief need only be both true and "apt." What then is such

Originally published in M. DePaul and L. Zagzebski (eds), *Intellectual Virtue: Perspectives from Ethics and Epistemology* (Oxford: Oxford University Press, 2003), pp. 155–79.

aptness and what role might truth play in determining it? Is a belief (epistemically) apt insofar as it promotes some truth-involving goal? If so, which goal?

If knowledge *is* better than mere true belief, moreover, in what way is it better? How does our conception of epistemic aptness help explain why it is better to have an *apt* true belief than a mere true belief?

A belief does not count as apt simply because it promotes the goal of having true beliefs. A belief that a certain book is a good source of information may be ill-grounded and inapt though in fact true and, when acted upon, a source of much further true belief. A belief can promote a massive acquisition of true beliefs without thereby becoming apt.

We do well to replace that diachronic goal, therefore, perhaps with a synchronic goal of *now* acquiring true beliefs (and no false ones). But this threatens a *reductio*: that all and only one's present true beliefs will then be epistemically rational, by promoting one's goal of *now* acquiring true beliefs.

We might try replacing the simple synchronic goal with a subjunctive synchronic goal such as

G   Being such that $(\forall x)$(One would now believe x if and only if x were true).

This avoids the *reductio*. Not every true belief is such that one *would* believe it only if true.

These truth goals nonetheless all share a problem: namely, how implausible it is to suppose that we either do or should have any such goal. We are, it is true, said to want the truth as intellectual beings. But what does this mean? It might mean that we want true beliefs, any true beliefs, since among the features that make a belief desirable is its plain truth. If so, is our time and energy always well used in acquiring true beliefs, *any* true beliefs? Is no true belief wholly ineffectual, even if we might then attain ends that we rightly value even more?

At the beach on a lazy summer afternoon, we might scoop up a handful of sand and carefully count the grains. This would give us an otherwise unremarked truth, something that on the view before us is at least a positive good, other things equal. This view I hardly understand. The number of grains would not interest most of us in the slightest. Absent any such antecedent interest, moreover, it is hard to see any sort of *value* in one's having that truth.[2]

Are we then properly motivated to acquire true beliefs *simply under the aspect of their being true*? More plausible seems the view that, for any arbitrary belief of ours, we would prefer that it be true rather than not true, other things equal. In other words,

(a)   so far as truth goes, we'd rather have it in any given belief that we actually hold.

However, this does not entail that

(b)   if all a belief has to be said for it is that it is true, then we prefer to have it than not to have it.

Nor does this follow even if we add that the belief is evaluatively neutral in every respect other than its truth.

To want the answer to a question, for its practical value or simply to satisfy our curiosity, is to want to know a truth. If I want to know whether p, for example, I want this: *to know that p, if p*, and *to know that not-p, if not-p*. And to want *to know that p, if p*, is to want *to know that it is true that p, if it is true that p*; and similarly for not-p. So our desire for truths is largely coordinate with our desire for answers to our various questions.

Just as we want the food we eat to be nutritious, so we want that the beliefs we hold be true, other things equal. Indeed, in pursuing the answer to a question we are automatically pursuing the truth on that question. But this does not mean we must value the truth *as* the truth, in the sense that, for any of the vast set of truths available, one must value one's having it at least in the respect that it is a truth. This no more follows for true propositions than does its correlate for nutritious food.

That distinction bears emphasis. I can want food that is nutritious, in this sense: that *if*, for whatever reason, because I find it savory, perhaps, I want to have – with my next meal, or just regularly and in general – bread, I would prefer that my bread be nutritious; which does not mean that I want, in itself and independently of its being food desired in other respects, that I have nutritious food simply for its nutritive value. In fact, of course, most of us do want regularly to eat nutritious food, as its own separable desideratum. Nevertheless, from (a) the premise that we want the food we eat to be nutritious rather than not, we cannot validly draw (b) the conclusion that we have a separable desire that we consume nutritious food, that we have an objective of next, or regularly, doing so, regardless of whatever *other* desires we may or may not have for sorts of food.

Similarly, we may want true beliefs, in this sense: that *if*, for whatever reason, we are interested in a certain question, we would prefer to believe correct rather than incorrect answers to that question; but this does not mean that we want, in itself and independently of our wanting these questions answered, for whatever independent reason, that we have true answers to them, simply for the truth this would give us.

What then of our belief formation? What do we hope for in that regard? Insofar as our belief formation is directed to answering questions we want answered, it is of course aimed at truth, trivially so, as we have seen. But which questions *should* we want answered, if any? Some questions we can hardly avoid: our very survival turns on them. Other questions we want answered for the sake of our comfort, and so on. Even once we put aside the most mundane questions, that still leaves a lot open. We shall be interested in a huge variety of questions, as family members, as citizens, and just as rational, naturally curious beings. Is there anything general to be said here? Can some general desire for the truth be recommended? It is hard to see what it could be. Remember, we have no desire for truths per se. When we have a desire for the truth, this is because that desire is implicated in our desire for an answer to a particular question or for answers to questions of some restricted sort. But our interest in the truth in such a case is just our interest in the question(s). If we can generalize beyond this to a recommendable desire for truth, accordingly, it must involve a generalization to a sort of question that *should* draw our interest. But is there such a thing? Can we at least pick out a *sort* of truth that *should* interest us (apart from the sort of "truths that should interest us" or variants of this)?

Your life goals may quite properly be different from mine once we move beyond the most abstract level of *living a good life* or *living a good life in the company of good fellow human beings in a good society*, or the like. Each of us may have such a goal, but great differences set in once we determine more specifically the shape of its realization in a life, given the constitution and context of that particular human being. Won't our intellectual goals be subject to this same kind of difficulty? Our interest in the truth is an interest in certain questions or in certain sorts of questions,

and properly viewed as such. What questions interest a given thinker may properly differ, moreover, from those that interest others.

It might be replied that we do or at least should have these goals, if only with near-vanishing intensity when the truth is unimportant enough. Take again the synchronic goal:

G   Being such that $(\forall x)$(One would now believe x if and only if x were true).

If the scope of the propositional variable here includes the multitude of trivial truths of vanishingly small interest and importance to us, this will presumably induce a correspondingly diminished desire that we satisfy *this* goal, as opposed to the goal that, for all *important* truths P, one would believe P iff P were true. And consider now the implication of this for the account of epistemic aptness through *pursuit of synchronic goal G*. If G is insignificant, the means to it cannot derive high epistemic status thereby. But the epistemic rationality and aptness of a belief in a triviality is *not* proportional to how well that belief furthers our goal G. The trivial truth may be one we only negligibly desire *to believe if and only if it were true*. Irrespective of that, however, it may be epistemically rational to the highest degree. The problem here is that the way in which the truth goal bears on our retail believing is wildly out of step with the degrees of epistemic justification of our unimportant beliefs. Accordingly, the epistemic normative status of *these* beliefs is not plausibly derivable from our interest in believing truths, or from any standing motive towards the truth.

Perhaps we should weaken goal G to G': $(\forall x)$(One would believe x only if x were true). This would be what elsewhere I call *safety* and defend as preferable to its contraposed *sensitivity*. A safe belief is thus one that you would have only if it were true, whereas a sensitive belief is one that you would *not* have if it were *not* true. So there is, I believe, a lot to be said for requiring safety of any belief candidate for the title of knowledge. Actually, the true requirement will have to be somewhat more complex, since a belief might be unsafe because overdetermined, and yet amount to knowledge.[3]

Regardless of how the safety goal is to be delineated, a sort of problem may remain. If the objective is to explain the epistemic rationality relevant to whether a belief amounts to knowledge, and if the goal-theoretic strategy is that of understanding such epistemic rationality as a variety of means-ends rationality, then it will be important that the goal be one that potential knowers in fact have and that it be plausible that the positive normative status of our beliefs be explicable through their promoting or being thought to promote the goal in question. But how does our hosting a belief promote the goal of having safe beliefs, goal G' above? It is quite obscure how one promotes such a goal by having any particular belief. Whether we have or do *not* have the belief seems irrelevant to whether we satisfy that goal with respect to the proposition believed. That is to say, whether or not one is such that (B(p) → p) seems independent of whether one does or does not actually believe p. Indeed *not* believing that p would seem *less* risky with regard to making sure one does not fall short of one's goal.

In any case, there is now this question: Why think of the epistemically normative status that turns a true belief into knowledge in terms of a *goal*? Why not just say that the belief needs to be safe in order to be knowledge, while making no commitment on whether safety is or is not anyone's goal?

II

Perhaps truth has a role to play *not* as a goal or as a component of a goal but more plausibly as a value in terms of which we can assess beliefs, whether anyone does or should have a corresponding goal or not. We come thus to the value that beliefs have in virtue of being true. And we suppose, for the sake of argument, that truth is the only distinctively cognitive or intellectual intrinsic value or, at least, the only such *fundamental* value. If so, then cognitive methods, processes, faculties, virtues, etc., will have value only derivatively, perhaps in virtue of their efficacy in yielding beliefs that are true. This approach to epistemology is distinctively "reliabilist." And now, it is argued, we may see how poorly such reliabilism fits our intuitive conviction that knowledge and epistemically rational true belief are more valuable than mere true belief. In brief the argument is as follows.

The antireliabilist argument[4]

1. To believe that p correctly *and* with epistemic rationality is more valuable than merely to believe that p and be right.
2. The additional value of epistemically rational belief over mere true belief would have to derive from the value imported by the belief's additional property of being thus rational.
3. According to reliabilist accounts of epistemic rationality, a belief is epistemically rational through deriving from a method, or process, or faculty, or virtue that is reliable, one that generally yields beliefs that are true.
4. But in that case how can being yielded by such a source add any further value to a belief over and above the value that it has simply in virtue of being true? How can a true belief obtain further value, beyond the value of its truth, by deriving from such a source, when the whole point of using the source is to get beliefs that are true? This would be as absurd as a hedonist supposing that pleasure from a reliable pleasure-source would be better than that pleasure of the same intensity, duration, etc., derived from an unreliable pleasure-source.

With this argument we focus on epistemic rationality, at most one component of epistemic aptness, of what a belief needs in order to qualify as knowledge. I will not here try to relate epistemic rationality more specifically to epistemic aptness. However these are related, since truth is by hypothesis the only fundamental epistemic value, the value of epistemic rationality must itself be explained in terms of truth.[5]

In considering our argument let us first reflect on some varieties of value. One may distinguish first between two sorts of value: the intrinsic and the instrumental. Let us assume monistic hedonism, and consider events Y and Z, each an instance of pleasure. Suppose event Y also brings about much future pleasure, while Z does not. Y is then better than Z, even if it is no better *intrinsically*. Moreover, an event X may not be an instance of pleasure, and hence *not* good intrinsically, while yet it is still good instrumentally, because of the pleasure it yields. All of this we may appreciate, as good hedonists, from a judicial, spectatorial stance that evaluates how matters stand, past, present, and future.

Take now two situations, or even two worlds, wherein the only evaluatively relevant aspects are as follows, for X, Y, and Z as described above. Both worlds contain this sequence: X occurs, then Y occurs, then Z occurs. In world W1 each member causes its successor if any. In world W2 no member causes any other member. Is world W1 better than world W2? Not according to hedonism, whose only source of intrinsic value is pleasure, for there is no more pleasure in W1 than in W2. And yet the X of W1, call it X1, is anyhow better than the X of W2, call it X2. X1 is better than X2 since X1 brings into the world the intrinsic value that it entrains by causing Y1 and, indirectly, Z1, whereas X2 entrains nothing. And so, X1 is better than X2, and Y1 is better than Y2. And Z1 is the same in value as Z2. And yet W1 is no better than W2. How can this be?

The explanation: Worlds are evaluated by total intrinsic value, but particular events are not. Particular events are also evaluated by their instrumental value, a sort of value with its own distinctive status. True, it is not a fundamental kind of value, since it involves rather the amount of intrinsic value that an event *causes*. So instrumental value is logically constituted by causation plus intrinsic value. The instrumental value of an event derives from the intrinsic value found in the causal progeny of that event. Nevertheless, events can have a distinctively instrumental value over and above any intrinsic value they may also have. When we assess an event from the judicial stance, we may assess it as intrinsically valuable, and also, separately, as instrumentally valuable.

An agent A may bring about an event E. The bringing about of E by A may then itself be assessed. This event, call it E', may not have any intrinsic value beyond the intrinsic value contained already in E, but it will have instrumental value proper to the special relation involved in E's happening because of E'. Call this special sort of instrumental value *praxical value*, the sort of instrumental value in actions of bringing about something valuable. Now, for the hedonist, an event of someone's being pleased does contain some measure of intrinsic value. Supposing that someone brings about that pleasure, is there also value in this further event?

There is of course no distinctive intrinsic value, no intrinsic value *beyond* that found in the pleasure brought about. But even a monistic hedonist may yet find in that action some degree of praxical value.

A world does not enhance its total value by containing not only intrinsically valuable but also instrumentally valuable states. Praxical value is in this respect just like any other variety of instrumental value. But, again, from this it does not follow that a particular event with praxical value is not itself valuable through the praxical value that it contains. Here again praxical value is like instrumental value in general. Instrumentally valuable events do have their proper value, their own sort of *instrumental* value.

III

Take a case of someone's knowing something in particular. *Do* we attribute to such knowledge any value over and above whatever value it has through being a true belief? When a thing has value it has it in respect of having a certain property or satisfying a certain condition. More precisely, then, our question is this: Does a bit of knowledge have value in a respect other than being a true belief? It would seem so, but how could you possibly explain this if you thought that any such additional value must derive from the belief's manifesting an intellectual virtue, understood as a psychological mechanism that would deliver a high enough preponderance of true beliefs (over false ones), at least in normal circumstances. This is hard to see as a respect in which a true belief could then be enhanced, any more than espresso itself is enhanced simply through the reliability of its source.

If persuaded that knowledge must have some value beyond that of its constitutive true belief, therefore, one may well take the Antireliabilist argument to refute the following sort of virtue epistemology:

VE (i) a belief's epistemic worth is constituted at least in important part through its deriving appropriately from an intellectual virtue, and

   (ii) what makes a feature of a subject's psychology an "intellectual virtue" is the reliable tendency of that feature to give rise to true beliefs on the part of that subject.

Is VE refuted by the value problem?

Within the sport of archery we aim to hit the bull's-eye, an end intrinsic to that sort of activity. When engaged in the activity, don't we also prefer to hit the bull's-eye by means of skill and not just by luck? A gust of wind might come along and guide our arrow to the bull's-eye, but this will not be as sweet a hit as one unaided by the lucky gust. Of course a hit that through skill compensates for the wind might be sweeter yet. So I see nothing unacceptable in a notion of a good, skillful shot that goes beyond that of a mere winning or accurate shot. A winning, accurate shot may have been just lucky and not at all skillful, and not in that sense a good shot. In archery we want accurate, winning shots, but we also want shots that are good and skillful. Are the goodness and skill that we want in our shots qualities that we want merely as means? Maybe so, but it seems unlikely. We would not be fully satisfied even with many accurate, winning shots, if they all derived from sheer luck, and manifested no skill, despite our gaining *some* satisfaction through hitting the mark (not to speak of prizes, fame, etc.).

Whether or not we want such goodness and skill only as means, anyhow, a perfectly understandable concept of a good, skillful shot includes *both* hitting the mark *and* doing so through skill appropriate to the circumstances. Can there be any doubt that we have such a concept concerning archery? Surely we do, along with many analogous concepts in other sports, *mutatis mutandis*. What precludes our conceiving of knowledge in a similar way, as a desideratum that includes an intrinsic success component, a hitting of the mark of truth, along with *how* one accomplishes that, how one succeeds in hitting the mark of truth? On this conception, knowledge is not just hitting the mark but hitting the mark somehow through means proper and skillful enough. There seems nothing "incoherent" in any pejorative sense in such a desideratum of "knowledge," and there are plenty of analogous desiderata throughout the wide gamut of human endeavors.

To recognize that, moreover, may not require us to think that only some additional *intrinsic* value could account for the value in the skillful shot over and above the mere hitting of the bull's-eye, nor need the additional value be fundamental. The further value might rather be just *praxical* value or the like. Can VE deal with the value problem by appealing thus to the praxical value of hitting the mark of truth through intellectual skill?

IV

In a *very* weak sense even a puppet "does" something under the control of the puppeteer, and even to stumble across a stage unintentionally is to "do" something. These are cases of "behavior" or even "acts" in correspondingly weak senses. Still a puppet's performance can be assessed. A puppet can be said to perform well or not, depending for example on whether its hinges are rusty and tend to stick. And the movements of the stumbling ballerina might be, as mere motions, indistinguishable from a lovely pas, though less admirable nonetheless.

Greater independence is displayed by a temperature control system consisting of a thermostat with two triggers, one for a heater and one for a cooler. The system normally keeps the temperature in a certain space within certain bounds. If it gets too hot, then the system triggers the cooler, if it gets too cool, it triggers the heater, and if the temperature is just right, then it idles. What makes it a good system for that space, moreover, is that it *would* perform thus in normal conditions. It is not enough that it *does* perform thus. That the system would perform thus relative to that space is due, finally, to two factors: (a) to its internal constitution and character, and (b) to its relation to the relevant space. In virtue of being stably thus constituted and related, therefore, the system is, at least in a minimal sense, a properly operative system of temperature control for that space.

If it is a sheer accident that it is thus constituted and thus related, then the system falls short in respect of how properly operative it is for that space. At least it falls short in a certain stronger sense of what is required in such a system. A properly operative temperature-control system for a certain space over a certain interval is not one that *accidentally* remains so constituted and related that it would keep the temperature in that space within the desired bounds.

We can of course assess the system independently of its relation to the space. We might naturally assess how well it *would* control the temperature of such spaces if suitably related to them (in a way perhaps in which one can standardly make such systems be related to such spaces). One can of course then assess such a system independently of whether it then happens to be appropriately installed. It might be sitting in a display room in a store. The evaluation would then focus on whether it is so constituted that, if also suitably installed, it would reliably control the temperature of that space.

Whether such a system performs well relative to a certain space would then go beyond whether by virtue of that performance it is or is not contributing causally to keeping the temperature within proper bounds. A good system might perform in such a way that it does so contribute, *not* because it is working right, however, but only because, although it does not then work right, luck enables it to cause the right outcome anyhow. Thus the system may suffer a glitch, while yet, coincidentally, an insect happens to alight on a crucial component of its internal mechanism so that the system does trigger the cooler as it should if it is to keep the temperature within the proper bounds. Only because of that bit of luck does the system then contribute causally to keeping the temperature within the proper bounds. Had it not been for the insect, then, it would not have triggered the cooler. So it would be false to say that it "worked right" on that occasion, when it just suffers a glitch. It is a good enough system nevertheless, since it does work right in the great majority of circumstances where it is normally called on to operate.[6]

This example shows that for a system to work right or perform well, in ways that are creditable, more is required than just (a) that it is a good system (in the relevant respects), and (b) that it then contribute causally to the desired outcome. For it may contribute causally to that outcome only through some fluke, in which case it then contributes despite *not* working right or performing well.

A system works right or performs well on a particular occasion, then, only if it unflukily enters a state that would lead in the relevant circumstances to the desired outcome. Accordingly, what the system does in entering that state, unaided by luck, must be sufficient to produce the desired outcome, given perhaps its normal relation to its relevant space. In our example the system did enter such a state, but only because of the insect in machina.

V

An artifact like our temperature control system that "does" things, that "works," might be evaluated variously, along with its performances. We might evaluate it by reference to how well it serves those it is expected to serve in certain characteristic ways. Or we might evaluate it independently of how well installed it is, if installed at all. Or we might evaluate its operation on a particular occasion: does it work right or perform well on that occasion? So there is the "agent" in a broad sense that includes mechanical agents of various degrees of sophistication, with various ranges of intended activity. There is the "performance" of that agent on a particular occasion. And sometimes there is also a performance-distinct situation or object or quantity of stuff that such an agent brings about or produces through its performance, a performance-distinct result that might also be performance-transcendent.

None of our three evaluations of aspects of such a situation, wherein an agent performs, uniquely determines any of the others. An agent could be a fine agent and perform poorly on a particular occasion, which in turn is compatible with the performance-distinct product being of high quality or of low quality or of any quality in between. Or the agent could be a mediocre or worse agent and yet perform well on a given occasion. It is even possible that a poor performance by a poor agent may lead to an excellent performance-distinct outcome. So the three dimensions of evaluation seem largely independent of each other – but not entirely, or so I now argue.

Performances relate in one direction to the agents involved, and in another direction to their performance-distinct products, if any. So they might be evaluated with a view towards one direction, or towards the other. An agent might be nearly incompetent and yet perform most effectively on a particular occasion. This evaluates the performance in the light of its wonderful outcome. Someone with a barely competent tennis serve may blast an ace past his opponent at 130 mph. This is a most effective serve given its outcome: a ball streaking past the receiver untouched, having bounced within the service court. But from another point of view it may not have been so positively evaluable after all. If the player is a rank beginner, for example, one most unlikely to reproduce that performance or anything close to it, then one may reasonably withhold one's encomium. It was still a wonderfully *effective* serve, but hardly a *skillful* one. Performances are in this way double-faced. So the evaluation of a performance seems not after all independent of the evaluation of the other two components of the performance situation. Either the evaluation is agent-involving or it is outcome-involving (or both). Performances that are creditable must be attributable to the agent's skills and virtues, and thus attributable to the agent himself.

VI

In evaluating the Antireliabilist Argument it will help to have in view the categories of praxis, of human doings and actions. To get something done you do not need much sophistication. Water flows downhill, for example, supermarket doors open when people approach, your knee jerks under the doctor's mallet, and so on. Distinctively human action is on a higher plane. A rational agent's action is controlled and informed by reason. At a minimum one must know what one is doing and must do it for a reason. Bees dance, it is true, perhaps guided not only by instincts but also by "reasons," unlike puppets. Higher up the animal kingdom, in any case, and well before we reach humanity, much behavior is less and less plausibly explained by appeal to mere instinct. Differences of degree are still differences, however, and the rational animal stands head and shoulders above the rest.

Three sorts of agency. The dimension of agency divides into at least three divisions, corresponding to at least three ways of ø'ing. First, there is *plain* ø'ing, however autonomously or informedly, or even attributively. Second, there is ø'ing intentionally, perhaps deliberately. Third, there is ø'ing *attributably*, in a way that makes one's ø'ing attributable to oneself as agent. Just as it is fallacious to

infer that an agent ø's intentionally from the fact that he ø's, since he might ø unintentionally, so it is a fallacy to infer that an agent ø's attributably from the fact that he ø's, since he might ø unattributably, as when someone *falls*, having been pushed off a roof. All intentional ø'ings are attributable, but the converse is false; and all attributable ø'ings are plain ø'ings, but again the converse is false.

Three forms of evaluation. With regard to instruments, tools, mechanisms, and useful artifacts, methods, and procedures in general, there are three interestingly different forms of evaluation, positive or negative, whether the evaluation takes the form of approval, favoring, or admiring, or the form of disapproval, disfavoring, or deploring. A useful cultural device is normally meant to help secure goods that we value independently of the device. Thus we value conveyance to one's destination, ambient temperature within certain bounds, savory and nourishing food, etc. And we also value devices whose normal operation will enable us to secure those goods, and also particular instances where the operation of the device secures one of its characteristic goods.

We favor and approve of good performance in our devices. We admire and even "praise" such performance. On the flip side, we disfavor and disapprove of malfunction, and deplore poor performance, and may even "blame" it on the device. Such evaluations of performance, whether positive or negative, go beyond the evaluation of goods produced by the performance, whether it be conveyance to one's destination, ambient temperature within certain bounds, savory and nutritious food, etc. And they also go beyond evaluation of the artifact and of its general reliability. The evaluation of a particular performance is distinct from the evaluation of the artifact that then performs and of any performance-transcendent product of the performance. A first-rate artifact may yield an excellent product despite the very low quality of its performance itself on that occasion.[7]

Why do we evaluate not only devices and their products, but also, separately, their performances? Well, why do we evaluate not only intrinsic value but also extrinsic value? Presumably we have concepts of instrumental value because it is useful for us to keep track of the levers of useful power. We bend nature to our ends, and in doing so we rely on what works, on what leads causally to our desiderata. Thus the importance of suitable concepts that help us keep track of what does work, of what has value through its causal powers. These are often states we can bring about more directly, whereby we secure more remote effects, as when we switch on the light by flipping the switch. But an extrinsically evaluable state need *not* be such a potential instrument relative to human capacities. A hurricane can be awful even if uncontrollable. The more general concept is the concept of what brings about value or disvalue; it is the more general concept of the extrinsically good or bad. Nevertheless, such a concept seems clearly important to agents whose wills must work indirectly in securing outcomes desired for their intrinsic worth and in avoiding those intrinsically unworthy. And it also seems important to those who need to adjust their conduct in the light of perceived danger, regardless of our ability to control that sort of situation. Thus the hurricane; we can at least control our relationship to it.

Tools, instruments, mechanisms, and other artifacts and devices, draw our interest primarily for the goods secured through their use. Efficiently smooth operation may of course be admired in its own right irrespective of its utilitarian implications. For the most part, nonetheless, what we care about in our artifacts is that they serve us well by helping produce the goods that we want from them.

Derivatively from that, we evaluate also the artifacts themselves in respect of how reliably they operate in the normal circumstances of their operation. We need to keep track of the reliability of our thermostats, cars, airplanes, etc., so we need concepts, including evaluative concepts, that enable us to discriminate the reliable from the unreliable. And we evaluate the *performances* of our artifacts, using similar categories of evaluation. What is the *point* of such evaluation? If we already know (a) that the performance-transcendent product of the performance has a certain value, and (b) that the performing artifact also is reliable up to a certain level, why then are we *also* interested in (c) how worthy the particular performance is?

It is hard to see what interest there could be in evaluations of artifactual performance except through the implications of such evaluations for assessment of the performing artifacts. Thus we have an important interest in the reliable quality of our artifacts, and from this interest derives rationally our interest in the quality of their particular performances. (Again I am leaving aside any purely aesthetic interest that artifactual performances may acquire.) Artifacts are "agents," however, only weakly, perhaps in an extended and even metaphorical sense. And this is of a piece with our treating them as mere means (except when we treat them as objects of aesthetic appreciation). Correlatively, our approval, admiration, and even praise for their performances is also qualified by the standing of the performers as mere tools at the service of our ends.

VII

Wise action. Suppose your raft glides downstream and comes to a fork. Down the right effluent there's treasure, down the left effluent only mud. Knowing this, and having control of the rudder, you take the right effluent and reach your reward. What you do and your attainment are then attributable to you, and properly admirable and praiseworthy. The reward is something you win through your own well-directed rational effort.

Consider now some ways one might fall short of that:

(a) The raft might be completely beyond one's control, either because someone else controls its rudder and disregards your preferences, or because it drifts rudderless.

(b) One might not know that one is going down the right effluent, or that it is better to take that direction.

If either (a) or (b) is true of you, then even if you *do* go down the right effluent and reach the prize, this will be something that *happens* to you, by luck; it will not be something properly attributable to you as your rational doing, as something properly admirable in you, or as something properly deserving of praise.

Again, in a *very* broad sense you *do* something when you "go down the right effluent tied down and blindfolded." You do something at least as does water when it flows, as does the knee when it jerks. Take an arbitrary "doing" of yours, in this very general sense. What conditions must such a doing satisfy in order to qualify as a proper subject not only of admiration (as one may admire the swelling flow of Niagara) but as a proper basis for praise or blame, credit or discredit? One condition would require that it be autonomous enough, another that it be sufficiently well informed.

What is true of our doings generally is true of our believings in particular. Belief, too, may be found up and down the evolutionary scale, and even below. A door may "think" somebody is approaching when a garbage can blows by. A dog may think it's about to be fed when it hears a clatter in the kitchen. Man is rational when his belief is controlled and informed by reason (and "adroit" through his properly operating cognitive systems). We may believe in the weakest sense, however, as when a belief is instilled through subliminal suggestion or through hypnosis or brainwashing. Such a belief is insufficiently derived from the exercise of the distinctively intellectual capacities and abilities, the faculties, cognitive methods, and intellectual virtues of the subject (irrespective of whether its adoption counts as *voluntary*). The believing is hence not attributable to the subject, not even in the way in which the circulation of the blood is attributable to the subject's heart and thereby, indirectly, to the subject as well. You may believe something, again, in a way that does not derive from the exercise of your intellectual excellences, but only from some external source not appropriately under your cognitive control. If so, then the believing in question may not be properly attributable to you as your doing. It may be something you *do* only as weakly as does the puppet dance when the puppeteer makes it do so.

VIII

Even when one does attributably bring about one's belief, one's believing something in particular, it remains to be seen whether its being a *true* believing is also attributable to oneself as one's own doing. The following is, again, fallacious:

1. Attributably to S as S's doing, S ø's.
2. S ø's in way W.
3. Therefore, attributably to S as S's doing, S ø's in way W.

Consider:

1a. Attributably to your heart as its doing, it pumps blood through your body.
2a. Your heart pumps blood in this building (pointing to the building where you are).
3a. Therefore, attributably to your heart as its doing, it pumps blood in this building.

Your heart's pumping blood in this building is perhaps your doing, since for one thing you could easily have been elsewhere, but that the pumping takes place in this building is not attributable to your heart as *its* doing.

Analogously, the following would also be fallacious.

1b. Attributably to you as your doing, you believe that p.
2b. You believe that p correctly (with truth).
3b. Therefore, attributably to you as you doing, you believe that p correctly.

So in order for *correct* belief to be attributable to you as your doing, the being true of your believing must derive sufficiently from "yourself," which involves its deriving from constitutive features of your cognitive character, and of your psychology more generally.

If truth has its own cognitive or intellectual value, then bringing about one's believing truly will have its corresponding praxical value, a distinctive sort of instrumental value. Compatibly with this, truth may still have a special role in explaining the normativity of belief. For the hedonist, similarly, pleasure has a special role in explaining the normativity of action, even if there are many things with value besides instances of pleasure. Eating savory food will have value instrumentally by promoting pleasure, for example, and the bringing about of pleasure will have its own distinctive value, different from the intrinsic value of the pleasure brought about, but value nonetheless, praxical value.

Does the bringing about of pleasure have value over and above the value of the contained pleasure? Well, it does have a different sort of value, one distinct from the value of the pleasure brought about. So a world where that pleasure is present uncaused will have the same intrinsic value as this one, but it will be missing something present here, which does here have value of a sort, praxical value. This is rather like the comparison between the world where the X–Y–Z sequence occurs unaided by any causation, and hence with no instrumental value in the X or the Y components, by comparison with the world where Y causes Z and X causes Y, wherein there is the same intrinsic value present in the three items, but wherein also (a) it's a good thing X happens, *not* because of any intrinsic value of its own but because of the intrinsic value that it yields by causing Y and Z, and (b) it's a good thing Y happens, not only because of its own intrinsic value but also because of the intrinsic value that it yields by causing Z.

Similarly, in the world where an agent brings about some pleasure, there is not only the intrinsic value of the pleasure but also the distinctive value of the agent's action. We can say about that action that it's good that it is done, at least in the respect that it brings about some pleasure, which is intrinsically good. So there is this praxically good action in the world in addition to the intrinsically good pleasure that it brings about.

Consider now a case where a true belief, a *true* believing is attributable to you as your doing. We may now say that, besides the epistemic good in that true belief, there is further the praxical good in your action of bringing it about. And this arguably involves your exercise of excellences constitutive of your cognitive character.

That is, it seems to me, a way in which truth can have a distinctively important and fundamental place in explaining epistemic normativity, compatibly with knowledge having epistemic worth over and above the worth of mere true belief. We can see the good proper to an epistemic action creditable to the agent, who brings about that good for himself, and is more than just the recipient of blind epistemic luck.[8]

IX

However, the account of the extra value of knowledge in terms of the praxical value that it contains does not go far enough. For this praxical value does not explain the fact that we would prefer a life of knowing, where we gain truth through our own intellectual performance, to a life where we are visited with just as much truth but through mere external agency (brainwashing, hypnosis,

subliminal suggestion, etc.). This might be the work of a less malevolent evil demon, who allows a world out there pretty much as we believe it to be, but one that fits our beliefs only through happenstance, the happenstance that the demon has deigned to give us just those beliefs although he might more easily have given us beliefs dissonant from our external reality.[9]

If we prefer a life in which we gain our truths through our own performances, then the value of our apt performances cannot be mere praxical value. For if it were merely praxical value, then the value of our performances would derive entirely from their causing the intrinsic value resident in the true believings that they would bring about. In that case, and if true believing is the only intrinsically valuable epistemic good, then two worlds containing the same true believings could hardly differ in overall value, regardless of the fact that in one of them there is a lot more praxical value. Compare the case of extrinsic value more generally, and the two X–Y–Z worlds above.

So if we rationally prefer a world in which our true beliefs derive from our own cognitive performances to one with the same true beliefs, now courtesy of the less malevolent demon, then there must be some further value involved in the first world not exhausted merely by the praxical value that it contains. What could this further value be?

When Aristotle speaks of the "chief good" as activity which goes beyond the state of mind that produces it since "the state of mind may exist without producing any good result" it seems clear that in his view performances creditable to an agent as their own are the components of eudaimonia, of human good or faring well, which "turns out to be activity of soul in accordance with virtue." In purely theoretical activity, moreover, truth and falsity are the good and bad state respectively, and the work of everything intellectual.

According to the Aristotelian view, then, passive reception of truth is not enough to count as human good, or at least not as the chief human good. Our preference is not just the presence of truth, then, however it may have arrived there. We prefer truth whose presence is the work of our intellect, truth that derives from our intellectual performance. We do not want just truth that is given to us by happenstance, or by some alien agency, where we are given a belief that hits the mark of truth *not* through our own performance, but in a way that represents no accomplishment creditable to us.[10]

We have reached the following result. Truth-connected epistemology might grant the value of truth, of *true believing*, might grant its intrinsic value, while allowing also the praxical extrinsic value of one's attributably hitting the mark of truth. This praxical extrinsic value would reside in such attributable intellectual deeds. But in addition to the extrinsic praxical value, we seem plausibly committed to the *intrinsic* value of such intellectual deeds. So the grasping of the truth central to truth-connected reliabilist epistemology is not just the truth that may be visited upon our beliefs by happenstance or external agency. We desire rather truth gained through our own performance, and this seems a reflectively defensible desire for a good preferable not just extrinsically but intrinsically. What we prefer is the deed of true believing, where not only the believing but also its truth is attributable to the agent as his or her own doing.

Does this adequately account in reliabilist terms for the value of knowledge over and above its contained true belief? Is the additional value simply the value contained in the attributable, creditable attaining of the truth, as opposed to the mere presence of truth (which might conceivably derive from happenstance or external agency)? The foregoing considerations go quite far, but *not* all the way to the required full account of epistemic value within reliabilist, truth-connected epistemology. At least one further step is needed and that is the aim of our next section.

X

Compare two evil demon victims. The first victim takes in quite fully and flawlessly the import of her sense experience and other states of consciousness, to an extent rarely matched by any human, and then reasons therefrom with equal prowess to conclusions beyond the reach of most people, and retains her results in memory well beyond the normal. The other victim is on the contrary extensively handicapped in her cognitive faculties and performs with singular ineptness. Clearly one of these victims is better off than the other; you would prefer to be and perform like the first and unlike the second. However, neither one attains truth at all, not even as a doing, through being visited with truth; much less does either one attain truth as a deed, by hitting the mark of truth through the excellence of their performance. So the epistemic value of the intellectual conduct of the first victim, the value that lifts her performance over that of the second victim, is not to be explained in the terms of our earlier account. Neither subject hits the mark of truth at all, whether attributably and creditably or not. So how can one of them still attain more value than the other? What sort of value can this be?

Recall the temperature-control device, with the two triggers. Suppose it is taken off the shelf in the display room for a demonstration, and a situation is simulated wherein it should activate the cooling trigger, and then a second situation is simulated wherein it should activate the warming trigger. In such a test the device might either perform well or not. But the quality of its performance is not to be assessed through how well it actually brings about the goods that it is meant to bring about in its normal operation. For in the display room it brings about neither the cooling nor the heating of any space. And yet we can and do assess the quality (and in a sense the "value") of its performance. What we are doing is quite obvious: we are assessing whether it performs in ways that would enable it to bring about the expected goods once it was properly installed, i.e., properly related to the target of its operation. We might call this sort of value "performance value." The performance value of a performance is the degree of positive or negative quality attained by that operation, measured by how well the performance enables the "agent" to operate, by entering various states in various circumstances, so as to be such that, when suitably installed, it would in fact bring about the expected goods in its target (where of course the "agent" and "target" might be the same).

It does not require an imaginative leap to conceive of our cognitive systems as devices that operate normally with the expected result: truths of certain sorts acquired by the host organism. There are various ways of conceptualizing this, but one way might include *the visual system, the auditory system,* and so on. Alternatively, we might have *the brain-including nervous system, together with sense organs.* Alternatively, we might have *the animal*, or *the human being*. In any case, there would be the system or organism on one side, and the normal environments in which it operates on the other. And we can evaluate the performances of the organism independently of its proper emplacement in a suitable environment. This would be similar to what we do in evaluating the performance of the temperature-control device in the display room. Consider then the deliverings of our cognitive systems, of whatever level of complexity we pick, including the top, total-human, level. Such deliverings can be assessed for performance value, through assessing how well the performance would enable the system to deliver the expected goods if it were "properly installed" in a suitable environment.

Recall the greater epistemic value, the higher epistemic quality, found in the performance of the first of our two victims of the less malevolent demon. We may now say that this higher value is performance value. It is like the higher value of the glitch-free performance of the temperature control device in the display room under simulation. If this is correct, then we have a way to understand the value of the epistemic justification that we find in the beliefs of the properly "perceiving" and reasoning victim of the evil demon. It is performance value, and what is good about this performance value is still to be understood in a truth-connected, reliabilist way. What is good about that performance value cannot be understood independently of the fundamental value of true believing, and especially of true believing that hits the mark of truth attributably to the agent. For *this* is the good that the relevant system is expected to deliver through its operation when "properly installed" in a suitable environment, and the good that may thus be credited to the organism as a whole, in virtue of the proper operation of its cognitive architecture.

Does that sufficiently identify the sorts of epistemic values that an adequate epistemology should be able to explain? We have identified: (a) the value of bare true believing (since we do prefer to be given truth rather than falsehood, even when it comes through happenstance or external agency); (b) the praxical, *extrinsic* value of true believing where the agent brings about the belief, and perhaps even hits the truth as his own doing; (c) the praxical, *intrinsic* value of true believing where the agent hits the mark of truth as his own

attributable deed, one which is hence creditable to the agent as his own doing; and (d) the performance value of a deliverance-induced believing, present even when the belief induced is false, so long as the performance is high on the quality scale for such performances, as measured by how well such performance would provide the expected goods, if the system were properly installed, in a suitable environment. Are we able to account for all our intuitions concerning epistemic evaluation, epistemic quality and value, in terms of these four concepts of epistemic normative or evaluative status?

It might be objected now again that our preference for the life of the first of the two demon victims, the one who "perceives" and reasons properly is not explained exhaustively merely through appeal to the performance value of the believings of that victim. For if it were mere performance value, then we would *not* hold that world and that life to be intrinsically better than the life and world of the other victim. But we do think it to be thus intrinsically better, do we not?

Surely we care about our devices performing well in display rooms not intrinsically (again, leaving aside aesthetic evaluation) but only because that shows them to be devices suitable for delivering the goods. But it is the goods to be delivered that we really care about. Of course the goods to be delivered need not be performance-transcendent. And indeed, on the Aristotelian view, in our intellectual lives the goods to be delivered by our cognitive systems are not performance-transcendent. The "chief" intellectual goods involve attributable truth-attainment, where one does hit the mark of truth through the quality of one's performance. Nevertheless, one cares about cognitive systems in good working order not for their own sake, but for the truth-attaining performances that they enable. Much less does one care about good performances by cognitive systems "in display rooms" isolated from the environments within which they would enable one attributably to attain the truth. Such good performances are valued presumably only for their implications about the worth of the operative systems, so their value is, it seems to me, partly epistemic; they manifest within our view the worth of the operative systems. But partly it is a distinctive value of its own, even independently of what they enable us to know. Even if there is no-one around to see it, the good performance by a system is somehow better than its poor performance; and this is presumably at least in part a matter of the more-than-accidental connection between the quality of the performance and the quality of the system. To the extent that the system performs poorly, to that extent is it a lesser system than it might be.

In any case, whether through its epistemic value or through its connection with the worth of the performing system, the value of simulational good performance is, like extrinsic value, not of fundamental, intrinsic import. The world with such good performances is no better epistemically on the whole than the one without them, so long as the two worlds contain all the same intrinsically valuable epistemic goods.

If so, then those who defend the fundamental status of truth or truth attainment at the basis of epistemic value would seem committed to denying that the good performance of the superior victim is of a higher intrinsic order than the poor performance of the other victim. They are different in quality, true enough, those two performances, but the difference is to be explained in terms of performance value, and hence not in terms of intrinsic value. That is how it would seem on the eudaimonistic account, and that is how it seems to me.[11]

Notes

1   My paper may amount to little more than a partial reading of these three passages by Aristotle (partial, perhaps, in more than one sense).

2   It might be replied that the value is indeed there though nearly indiscernibly slight. This I am not inclined to dispute, since what I have to say could be cast about as well in terms of vanishingly slight value, irrespective of whether its magnitude is epsilon or zero.

3   This point is due to Juan Comesaña. My "Reply to Critics" in *Philosophical Issues* 10 (2000) contains a further reason why a belief might amount to knowledge despite being unsafe.

4   The issues of epistemic normativity involved in this argument are discussed in a growing literature that includes the following, all of which I have found helpful and suggestive, as will be clear to those in the know. (Of course I would not have written this paper had I not been left with a question or two.) Ward E. Jones, "Why Do We Value Knowledge?" *American Philosophical Quarterly* 34 (1997), pp. 423–39; Jonathan L. Kvanvig, "Why Should Inquiring Minds Want to Know? *Meno* Problems and Epistemological Axiology," *The Monist* 81 (1998), pp. 426–51; Linda Zagzebski, "From Reliability to Virtue Epistemology," in G. Axtell, ed., *Knowledge, Belief, and Character* (Lanham, MD: Rowman & Littlefield, 2000), pp. 113–22; Marian David, "Truth as the Epistemic Goal," in M. Steup, ed., *Knowledge, Truth, and Duty* (Oxford: Oxford University Press, 2001), pp. 151–69; Michael DePaul, "Value Monism in Epistemology," in M. Steup, ed., *Knowledge, Truth, and Duty* (Oxford: Oxford University Press, 2001), pp. 170–83; Wayne D. Riggs, "Reliability and the Value of Knowledge," *Philosophy and Phenomenological Research* 64 (2002), pp. 79–96.

In the present paper I develop an approach sketched in "Beyond Skepticism, to the Best of Our Knowledge," *Mind* (1988) and in "Reflective Knowledge in the Best Circles," *Journal of Philosophy* (1997), reprinted in Steup, *Knowledge, Truth, and Duty*. John Greco also treats related issues in his paper for this conference, and I agree with a lot in his contextualist approach.

5   My value-monistic assumption is only a working assumption. I doubt that the value of understanding can be reduced to that of truth. I should also recognize that my use of "rationality" here is very broad, and does not pertain only to the proper operation of reason in any narrow sense. It pertains rather more broadly to the proper operation of one's cognitive systems, skin-inwards, or, better, mind-inwards. So epistemic "adroitness" might better capture my sense.

6   It might be replied that the system did work right ... *with the help of the insect.* And I am in some linguistic sympathy with this reply. Perhaps, I am willing to grant, "working right"

is at least ambiguous, and in one sense it does permit this reply. In any case, there would presumably remain the sense in which the system itself does not really work right, which is tantamount to its not working *well* on that occasion, and "working well" lends itelf less well to the present reply, as it seems less subject to the ambiguity that affects "working right."

7 And things can come unravelled in other ways too. Thus an excellent performance may have an unfortunate outcome due to unfavorable circumstances.

8 In fact the account here of praxical value is only a first approximation, perhaps sufficient unto the day. A more adequate account, in any case, would allow the possibility of a performance with praxical value that does *not* succeed in securing its characteristic inherent value. Even if some bad luck robs it of its expectable fruits, an action may still be a wonderful performance, and properly admirable, and correspondingly valuable, *praxically* valuable in our richer sense. (Delineating that sense should be within reach, and what follows is one attempt.)

9 Nor does the account explain how the virtuous bringing about of a true belief is better than the accidental bringing about of that belief even if the two bringings about are otherwise the same to the greatest possible extent.

10 When I presented these ideas at Notre Dame, Alvin Plantinga wondered what would be so bad about being the beneficiary of Divine revelation, where there are no special faculties, really, that set one apart; where one is just visited by the overpowering light of the revealed truth. In response it seemed to me that even if, with Aristotle, one finds the de facto chief human good in active virtuous attainments of one's own, this need not prevent one from granting that there may be other ways to the truth that might be just as desirable and even admirable. It seems to me that much of our epistemology and epistemic value theory could be isolated from such issues of rational theology.

11 Much of our reflection in epistemology seems applicable to ethics, mutatis mutandis.

CHAPTER 37

Why Should Inquiring Minds Want to Know?: *Meno* Problems and Epistemological Axiology

Jonathan L. Kvanvig

MENO: In that case, I wonder why knowledge should be so much more prized than right opinion, and indeed how there is any difference between them.
SOCRATES: Shall I tell you the reason for your surprise, or do you know it?
MENO: No, tell me.
SOCRATES: It is because you have not observed the statues of Daedalus. Perhaps you don't have them in your country.
MENO: What makes you say that?
SOCRATES: They too, if no one ties them down, run away and escape. If tied, they stay where they are put.
MENO: What of it?
SOCRATES: If you have one of his works untethered, it is not worth much; it gives you the slip like a runaway slave. But a tethered specimen is very valuable, for they are magnificent creations. And that, I may say, has a bearing on the matter of true opinions. True opinions are a fine thing and do all sorts of good so long as they stay in their place, but they will not stay long. They run away from a man's mind; so they are not worth much until you tether them by working out the reason. That process, my dear Meno, is recollection, as we agreed earlier. Once they are tied down, they become knowledge, and are stable. That is why knowledge is something more valuable than right opinion. What distinguishes one from the other is the tether.[1]

National Enquirer commercials tell us that some people want to know. I have no idea what such a desire has to do with reading tabloid journalism, but the avowal of wanting to know interests me. Maybe this desire is shared by all; at the very least, curiosity is universal. Curiosity may amount to a desire for knowledge, or perhaps it might be explained in other terms, such as a desire for understanding or for finding the truth. Perhaps

none of these, even. Maybe the desire is only one of being able to make sense of one's experience of the world. Or maybe the important matter is not the existence of any desire at all. Perhaps, that is, it is not *desire* as such that drives the search, but rather some *need* or *interest* or *purpose*.

The questions raised by these meandering thoughts all have to do with the internal, psychological constitution of typical human beings. Such psychological questions lead naturally to axiological ones, for we can wonder whether what we desire and value is really valuable or desirable. So, regardless of whether humans desire or seek knowledge,

Originally published in *The Monist* 81, 3 (1998), pp. 426–51.

is knowledge valuable? Or is merely getting to the truth the appropriate goal? Why should one value knowledge if one already has understanding, or what would be the use of knowledge about a phenomenon once one had made sense of it?

Such axiological questions appear first in the *Meno*, where Socrates addresses the question of what makes knowledge better than mere true belief. The question raises the possibility that knowledge isn't nearly so important as we might suppose. Here I will identify the discipline of epistemology with inquiry into the nature, extent, and importance of knowledge. Given this common understanding, the Socratic issue raises the specter that epistemology itself is not very important. Epistemology has long been a central subdiscipline of philosophy, but deserved centrality must be earned by argument, for there is no *a priori* certainty that the relationship between mind and world, the nature of cognition and the appropriate standards for evaluating it, should be addressed employing the concept of knowledge. Reflecting on philosophical inquiry into cognition might lead us to the conclusion that addressing epistemological questions is ancillary to the fundamental tasks of philosophy. The hypothesis that I want to consider and argue for is the hypothesis that epistemology is really not central to the fundamental philosophical tasks of understanding the relationships between mind, world, and language; that epistemology is born of confusion; that it arises when we legitimately desire or value some things which are confused with knowledge (things such as infallibility, incorrigibility, permanence, unrevisability, metaphysical certainty, or the capacity to stand in the face of any amount of further learning). The result is that we think knowledge important, thereby committing ourselves to the centrality of epistemology to philosophy, when knowledge is really not all that important nor is epistemology central to our philosophical interests.

Epistemological Axiology, Knowledge, and Truth

In the *Meno*, Socrates and Meno discuss the value placed on knowledge over true opinion, but there are other problems of epistemological axiology besides this one. One could have arisen for Socrates, for a presupposition of the problem he discusses is that the value of true belief should be obvious. It is easy to see, however, that there is a question to be answered here as well: what value does true belief have over false belief, over belief that is merely empirically adequate, or over beliefs that make sense of experience? Furthermore, once time has introduced Gettier, we have the further question of what makes knowledge better than justified true belief[2] (notice that this question is interesting and important even if one thinks that justification is not necessary for knowledge, for even if knowledge is, say, reliably produced true belief, we might have to conclude that it offers us nothing of value beyond justified true belief). The history of epistemology reveals much discussion of the question of the differences between truth and empirical adequacy, knowledge and true belief, justified true belief and true belief, and knowledge and justified true belief. But there is little attention paid to *Meno* problems, problems of epistemological axiology. It is on those problems that I want to focus here.

Let us begin, then, by asking what would justify the pre-eminence of knowledge, or what is the same thing, the pre-eminence of epistemology, in philosophical inquiry regarding cognition, regarding the connection between mind and world. What do we want out of cognition that would make us focus so quickly on knowledge? A quick and easy answer might be that it is knowledge itself that we want, but this answer is hasty. First, the history of epistemology is not on the side of this proposal, for it shows other concerns. Starting with Plato and Socrates, the importance of knowledge over true belief is explained, not on the basis of the intrinsic value of the former over the latter, but in other terms. For Plato, knowledge is "tethered," and true belief is not; for Descartes, knowledge is not open to doubt and cannot be undermined by further learning, whereas true belief is and can be. The history of epistemology suggests that knowledge is valuable because it is partially constituted by other properties that are obviously valuable. The problem for these defenses of the importance of knowledge is that the properties cited, properties such as incorrigibility, infallibility, permanence, "tetheredness," metaphysical certainty, and the like, though immensely valuable, simply are not among the constituents of knowledge. Such a history suggests that the focus on knowledge results from some sleight of hand whereby knowledge is confused with that which is truly valuable. Furthermore, some acquaintance with the literature spawned by Gettier should make us wonder why we should want knowledge, if knowledge is ungettiered justified true belief. What interest do we have in such? I want to get to the truth, and I want to be sure I have. I'm sure you're roughly the same in this regard, and it is important to notice that no mention of the concept of knowledge, especially no mention of anything ungettiered, need be made to understand such desires.

You might think I haven't tried very hard to find the importance of knowledge, so I'll work a bit harder at defending my thesis. First, I will consider what it would be like for cognition to be ideal, to be everything we could ever want out of it. This ideal, we shall see, may imply knowledge, but is not identical to it. So, the theory of knowledge is a mere footnote to what ideal cognition would get us. Of course, cognition is not ideal, and a bit more realistic approach to it might reveal an important place for epistemology, so I will consider what happens when we make adjustments for various features of the human condition that make this ideal impossible for us to achieve. Backing off of the ideal will help us grasp what types of interaction between mind and world we find most valuable, and whether the concept of knowledge ever plays a central role in the kinds of interactions that are to be valued most. I will argue that knowledge plays only an ancillary role at best, and hence that epistemology deserves no central place in philosophy.

Here's what I want: every time I consider a proposition, I want to be able to tell immediately whether or not it is true, and for every proposition whose truth value affects me in any way, I want to have considered that proposition and stored that information so that no cognitive mistake ever causes me not to get what I want. Well, not quite; I exaggerate a bit. There are some things I guess I prefer to remain ignorant of: the intimate details of my parents' sex life, for example. But the desire for ignorance here is a product of interests I have other than purely cognitive ones. If my only interests were purely cognitive ones, what I said earlier would be true. Of course, were I nothing more than a cognitive machine, I might want other things as well, such as omniscience, but this will do for a start.

Others might agree with the idea behind what I just wrote, but will balk at this way of putting

the desire. They may, for example, prefer to avoid the concept of truth altogether. They might argue that we have no interest in truth but only in that which is empirically adequate, or that which makes sense out of the entirety of our experience. I am somewhat sympathetic to such claims. At times, I think all that matters is having an understanding of things that can stand up to further testing. As any good student of scientific methodology knows, true hypotheses purportedly do just that, and so we are tempted to value true beliefs in virtue of their ability to withstand testing. But such thinking is confused. True beliefs are no more immune to defeat than false ones. Experts can deceive us, pockets of misleading evidence are commonplace, and auxiliary hypotheses confound out testing procedures.

There are other ways of attempting to secure the importance of truth, however, that I will only mention but not pursue here. Davidsonian arguments concerning the role of truth in interpretation,[3] and externalist theories of mental content[4] with their implications regarding the rarity of false belief come to mind. Alternatively, we might balk on theological grounds at the idea that truth is unimportant; if so, maybe epistemologists should be in Religious Studies departments! Since I don't want to focus here on these issues, I'll grant provisionally the value of truth, even though serious questions remain about the defense of this importance.

Putting aside the question of truth, let's return to the picture of cognitive ideality above. There I noted that I want to be able to tell immediately and directly, without any special effort, the truth value of any claim that has or will have any effect on my life. I want cognitive excellence of a certain sort with minimal effort. I don't think I'm idiosyncratic in this regard; I think we all want efficiency in producing desired output. We want a maximally efficient cognitive machine.

Alas, disappointment here is inevitable. One of the lessons of experience is that such machinery is simply unavailable. So if we can't have maximally efficient cognitive machinery, what might we want short of that? One answer is provided by Descartes. He wants some way of guaranteeing that his beliefs are true, and he wants to be able to secure such a guarantee without having to leave the comfort of his warm stove. A little less lazy than I, but not much. I like it.

Notice, however, that neither what Descartes nor I want should be confused with knowledge. In both cases, knowledge would be a mere by-product of getting what we want. So these desires provide no foundation for the centrality of epistemology to the philosophical enterprise. Hence, if these desires reflect what is valuable from a cognitive point of view, epistemology could become central only by confusing knowledge with something else distinct from it.

Recall, however, that we are supposed to be trucking in reality here, and Descartes's ideal is every bit as chimerical as my earlier ideal for the lazy. Our goal should not be to provide an account of cognitive ideality *simpliciter*; it should be, rather, to elucidate a *realistic* ideal, one that is humanly possible to achieve. Descartes's ideal simply cannot be achieved; there is nothing or almost nothing about which we can be metaphysically certain. So the epistemological heaven described by Descartes turns out to be mere fancy.

Cartesianism is attractive in part because, like Descartes, we all want some guarantee that we have the right beliefs. First, we abhor the double mindedness constituted by instability in the cognitive realm. We do not want to be in a condition in which we keep changing our minds from one moment to the next about what to believe, nor is it good for us to be continually in the Pyrrhonian state of suspension of belief. But mere stability of belief – fixation of belief – is not what we want either. We are all aware of the delusional capacities of human beings, and we don't want to live a lie. What we want is fixation on the right beliefs, not mere fixation of belief. We want fixed, *true* belief. If Descartes's ideal were humanly achievable, it would get us fixed, true belief. But it isn't. So we must ask, how do we retreat from Descartes?

Truth and Justification

Let's cut to the chase and see what can be made of the idea that an appropriate retreat from Descartes will lead us to the promised land of epistemology. Here's a try. If you want to fix true belief, you should want to be responsive to indicators of truth, or what is the same thing, to evidence of truth. When you are responsive to such, the beliefs on which you fix will be justified, or warranted.

This proposal attempts to sneak in a concept of evidence or justification or warrant in terms of truth indication or likelihood of truth, but the attempt should be rejected at this point. The defense of the theory of justification claims that if you desire fixed, true belief, you should want to be sensitive to indicators of truth. If the proposal means to include among such indicators signs that are only suggestive of truth, it would be rejected at this point. If I want chocolate, I'll want to go to a store that sells it. I won't be inclined to take counsel from those who tell me which stores *look* like they sell chocolate, or are *likely* to sell chocolate, over counsel from those who tell me which stores in fact sell chocolate. Recall that the only value we have identified is fixed, true belief. So all we are entitled to claim at this point is that if a belief is true and fixed, it is valuable, and if it is not true and fixed, it is not valuable. So, if a concept of evidence is legitimate here, the only things that will count as evidence are signs that imply the truth of what they signal. That is, no role has been found as yet for the epistemological pith of evidenced, false belief. Yet, if we have found a place for a concept of evidence, surely there must be such a role; so we should resist at this point the suggestion that the traditional epistemological concern with justification or warrant has found a place in our discussion.

One might claim that we have failed to find a place for warrant because we have ignored the difference between the single case and the long run. Truth may be all that matters in the single case, it might be claimed, but there is also the matter of what will happen in the long run. The strategies for battle taught at West Point might fail in a single case, but they are taught because they will generate more victories in the long run. Just so, the procedures, mechanisms, and methods that produce mostly true beliefs should be valued because they will produce more true beliefs over the long run than procedures, mechanisms and methods that produce beliefs unlikely to be true.

The response is unsuccessful. First, it does not follow from anything said so far, or anything that might reasonably be added, that more of one's beliefs will be true in the long run if one uses methods or procedures likely to get one to the truth. Second, and more important, the defense is irrelevant. For if there are methods, mechanisms, and procedures that make it likely that we will get to the truth by employing them, there are other methods, mechanisms, and procedures that are even better. Consider the mechanism operative when and only when I believe the truth; ponder the method employed when one believes p if and only if p is true; contemplate the procedure followed by accepting p just in case it is true. If we want focus on the long-term prospects of getting to the truth and if we want to adjust our counsel regarding strategies of belief-formation so as to maximize getting to the truth and avoiding error, why not prefer the very best strategies such as those just delineated? If we do, we get the earlier result that true belief is all that matters; justification drops entirely out of the picture.

One might argue that justification or warrant doesn't arise only when one adopts optimal methods for getting to the truth; satisfactory methods, when employed properly, can also generate warrant. This point, however true, is of no use whatsoever in our context. For we do not yet have any reason for thinking that justification is important. What I want to know is whether traditional epistemology is worth doing, and to this point all we have found is that true belief is valuable. So the project is not to construct a theory of justification or warrant; we are asking instead why anyone should undertake such a project at all. The attempt above was to argue that the project is important on the basis of a distinction between features of a single case and features of a long-run pursuit of truth. That attempt failed, and any attempt to avoid that argument by distinguishing between optimal and adequate results of inquiry is a complete *non sequitur*.

There are, however, two other ways I can think of to try to find a place for justification or warrant in a theory that grants the importance of true belief. One standard maneuver is to begin talking about means and ends, with truth as the end and justification as the means to it.[5] The other maneuver pessimistically resigns on the task of clarifying justification in terms of the goal of truth, claiming instead that it is itself valuable independently of any relation it might have to the goal of having fixed true beliefs.[6] I will begin with the more pessimistic approach.

The position that justification is valuable independently of the importance or value of truth ought to strike us as an utterly mysterious one. It is akin to developing statistical categories in baseball that have nothing to do with winning baseball games. We keep statistics on batting average, slugging percentage, numbers of home runs, stolen bases, earned run average, fielding percentage, etc., because each of these has something to do with success in the game, i.e., winning. But suppose we introduce a further category: what percentage of times you step on home plate as you begin running toward first base, and claim that the lower percentage, the better (left-handers have an obvious advantage in this category, which, this left-hander holds, is all for the good). Puzzled, you query why anyone should be interested in this statistic. What does it have to do with success in the game of baseball? I answer that there is no connection, it's just a valuable characteristic to have independently of any role it might play in winning games. You'd walk away perplexed by such a claim, I submit. I further submit that the same reaction is appropriate when it is claimed that justification has a value completely independent of the value of truth. The point of cognition is to get to the truth (so we have assumed here, at any rate), and the things we cite when we want to defend the *truth* of what we believe are usually (what we take to be) justifications of the truth. If that isn't what justification is, if it is not connected to the truth in any interesting way at all, I don't see why we'd be any more interested in it than in what percentage of times batters hit home plate on their way to first base.

If justification does not have intrinsic value, then perhaps it has instrumental value. Instead of thinking of justification as having value independently of truth, perhaps we will find its value in its relationship to truth: truth is the goal of inquiry and justification the means to it. There is even a way of seeing the first position, that justification must have intrinsic value, as arising out of this conception of the relationship between justification and truth. One gets forced into the intrinsic value position by assuming a restrictive account of what can count as a connection to truth. Once one restricts the possible connections, the next step is to become pessimistic about the prospects of connecting justification and truth on the restricted possibilities envisaged. Finally, uncomfortable with the idea that justification is unimportant, one decides that no connection at all is needed; justification is valuable in itself, and not on the basis of any connection to truth.

The undue restrictions on possible connections to truth come by ignoring other possibilities. In particular, an ambiguity gets ignored in the concept of a means to a goal. This concept is ambiguous between *intentional* means and *effective* means. In the arena of action, the first concept is instanced when a person performs a certain action with the intention of realizing a certain goal. If I am chosen to take a shot from halfcourt at a Chicago Bulls basketball game for one million dollars, I will perform certain actions as a means to the goal of making the shot. I will, for example, face the basket; I'll even shoot the ball. But I will perform no action that constitutes an *effective* means toward winning the million dollars. For, to be an effective means, the action must make it objectively likely that the goal is realized, or at least more likely than it would have been otherwise. In many cases, however, there simply are no effective means available. In the example, nothing I could do will make it likely that I make a shot from halfcourt, and nothing I could do will even raise the likelihood of my making such a shot. After all, I'm not as young as I used to be; maybe I'm beyond the point of even throwing the ball that far. Nonetheless, one would still try, and in trying, adopt some intentional means to the goal of making the basket.

When justification is conceived of as appropriately connected to the truth only when it is an *effective* way to truth, it is easy to become pessimistic about the prospects of a satisfactory account of the connection between justification and truth. I don't want to vouch for the correctness of any particular complaint here, but one of the most worrisome difficulties has come to be called the *New Evil Demon Problem*.[7] If justification must be an effective means to the truth, then inhabitants of evil demon worlds have hardly any justified beliefs. But how could that be? After all, the same is not true of us, even though they might, after all, *be us*. Or so the argument runs, at any rate. Plagued by this difficulty, one might simply give up on the idea that justification and truth are connected, resorting to the mysterious idea that justification is intrinsically valuable independently of any connection to the truth.

Notice that if we do not limit our conception of means to effective means but also countenance

intentional means, more can be said. Some goals cannot be achieved directly, requiring the adoption of some means in achieving them. In the case of winning a million dollars at a Bulls game, that goal cannot be achieved directly. The first means that I must adopt is that of making a basket from midcourt. So that becomes my secondary goal. But note that it too cannot be achieved directly, so I must adopt some means of achieving it. Notice that this process of developing means toward goals stops when I get to actions that I can control with relative ease. I can, pretty directly, turn and face the basket. If you're a fan of basic actions in action theory, you might want to insist that I go further, perhaps all the way to tryings: in order to reach the goal of turning and facing the basket, I must *try* to do so. But I didn't want to become mired in action theory here. I only want to point out that if we countenance intentional means to a goal, we can develop an account of when means should be adopted and how the ways in which we ordinarily approach such goals count as means to achieving them. If we talk only of effective means, nothing in the example is coherent. I have to make a basket in order to win a million dollars, but nothing I do is effective in making the basket. The only basis of evaluation available is, thus, whether or not I make the basket; no discussion of appropriate means can serve as a basis for positive evaluation in spite of missing my goal.

Care must be shown in extending this discussion, which is at home most in the arena of action to the arena of belief, for we do not want to assume that beliefs are voluntary in the way actions are.[8] Perhaps something like the following is what we are after. The goal of truth for belief is relatively remote; it is not a property we can always tell directly and immediately whether a belief has. So we should try to have, or value, beliefs with some other property, one that we can always tell directly and immediately whether a belief has. In order to count as an analogue of an intentional means to a goal in the arena of action, this property must be one that is appropriate (or the best we can do), by our own lights, for getting to the truth. Such a description generates the appropriate analogue in the arena of belief of a concept most at home in the arena of action, and it does so without requiring that beliefs are voluntary.

These points yield a lesson for those who wish to defend the importance of justification by appealing to the distinction between means and ends, or between intrinsic and instrumental value. The very first question such an approach must be able to answer is why the distinction between means and ends is introduced in the first place. The only adequate response must appeal in some way to the mediacy of the goal and the immediacy of the means, to our inability always to achieve the goal directly and immediately in the case of action, to our inability always to tell immediately and directly whether the goal has been achieved in the arena of belief. Yet, if only effective means count as means, this answer is unavailable. For no property a belief has is such that it is necessarily likely to attach to a true belief and also one that is easier to tell a belief has than the property of truth itself. Thus, the position that justification has a value derived from that of truth becomes indefensible when means are limited to effective means, for such a defense simply must be able to explain why the talk of means arises in the first place. Only by countenancing intentional means can such an explanation be developed, however.

So, if justification is instrumentally valuable in virtue of its relationship to the truth, that relationship must be conceived in terms of intentional means to the goal of truth rather than in terms of effective means. Intentional-means theorists can say that truth is not a property of a belief that we can always tell immediately and directly whether it is present, so we should adopt some means for getting to the truth. Moreover, in order to fulfill this motive for introducing the concept of a means to the truth, the property that results from following such means must be internalist in character – it must be such that one can always tell by reflection or introspection alone that a belief has that property; it must be a discernible property of a belief.[9]

Effective means-theorists might not succumb yet, however. They may want to insist that even if justification must be introduced into the discussion in the guise of intentional means to the goal of truth, we won't have justification unless the intentional means are also effective means. This ploy is not directly relevant to the question of the importance of justification, but I will make one brief comment about it. I would remind the reader that the most thorough investigation of

such an approach – Larry BonJour's[10] – ends in the deepest skepticism about the existence of justified beliefs, a skepticism strong enough to entail all other forms of skepticism about justification.

Effective-means theorists still have one complaint. They may complain that we are showing a prejudice against *approximations*. They may say, that is, that even if the very best would be for us to always and only get to the truth, some failures are closer approximations to that ideal than others, and hence more valuable. They may insist that we are exhibiting a kind of childish response of saying that if we can't have the very best, we don't want anything at all. A more mature approach would be to recognize the unmatched value of always finding the truth, and yet grant the value, albeit lower, of always holding beliefs that are highly likely to be true.

An appropriate retort to this insult is to point out that maturity often culminates in senility. Something like this culmination occurs here, I think. You might buy a TV that works half the time instead of one that works only ten percent of the time; but that decision gives you no reason to prize your acquisition. It gives you reason to prize your TV over the less reliable one, but that is a different point entirely. To say that x is more valuable than y simply does not imply that x is valuable. There is an old joke that close doesn't count except in hand-grenades, government work, and jazz. The point of the joke is not that approximations are sometimes valuable, but rather that, in certain areas, getting close to what would be the goal in other domains *just is* to have fulfilled the goal in other areas. That is, the goal is simply different, and easier to achieve, in some areas than in others. So the appeal to the value of approximations simply won't work.

There is, however, one appeal to approximations that would work. If we first established that the goal could not be achieved, or could not be achieved directly, then we could turn to ways of getting to the goal that might only yield approximations of the ideal rather than fulfillment of it. Yet, if it is the best we can do, no more could reasonably be expected, and the results of doing the best we can should be valued. If, for example, the best TV's only work half the time, then in purchasing such a machine, you've purchased something valuable (as long as there is something valuable in watching TV). Such a response, however, returns us to the land of internalism. The best we can do, the best processes to instantiate, the best methods to follow, must be understood first in terms of the doxastic analogue of intentional means to a goal. The moral of the story is that the centrality of epistemology to the philosophical enterprise presupposes the internalistic character of warrant or justification; without it, all we get is the value of truth over error.

Let me make it clear that I am not endorsing the internalist proposal here, for I think this approach faces difficulties of its own. For most theories, e.g., foundationalist, coherentist, reliabilist, or evidentialist, do not honor the metatheoretical constraint that justification or warrant must be a property of a belief that one can always tell, immediately and directly, whether a belief has it. If not, then no matter what else one might say about such theories, they are irrelevant to the task of defending the importance of epistemology. They may constitute theories of one requirement for knowledge, but they do nothing to show that there is anything cognitively important other than true belief.

The fact that standard theories of justification typically do not yield the result that justification is transparent to reflection may lead us to question the transparency defense of justification. We may decide, that is, that transparency is too strong a requirement on a theory of justification. Even if it is, however, there is a useful lesson here. The lesson of this result is that the appropriate focus for the question of the importance of epistemology as it relates to the theory of justification must focus on the prospects for a strong internalism, for there is simply no place in a defense of the importance of epistemology by appeal to the distinction between means and ends for externalist theories of justification. Such theories make use of a tow by internalism across the waters from philosophical ignominy toward the land of useful theory, only to eschew internalism on sighting land, failing to take into account that they drown without the tow. I'm not saying the internalist will make it to shore; the two may drown together. But the least the internalist has this to be said on his behalf: he was, after all, making a significant effort, the only one with any hope of success.

Knowledge and the Gettier Problem

Though I have not defended the acceptability of the internalist defense of the importance of justification, I want to grant the importance of both truth and justification for the rest of this paper. For even if both of these are important, the importance of epistemology has not yet been shown, since knowledge is more than justified true belief. Let me repeat that I do not mean to suggest that there is no such thing as knowledge or that it would be improper to develop a theory of it; what I'm questioning is the importance of doing so. Why should we care at all what knowledge is, even if it matters to us what truth and justification are and which of our beliefs have these properties?

This question becomes more poignant when we reflect on the difference between knowledge and justified true belief. Knowledge, it is said, is not accidental; the connection between belief and truth is not accidental and the connection between justification and truth is not accidental either. Why should we be interested in such a concept? Suppose all of your beliefs are justified and true; what difference would it make if you didn't have any knowledge, if all your justified true beliefs were only accidentally so? You would be an epistemological Mr. Magoo, accidentally getting things correct, right and left. But so what? Why should you care?

Of course, I don't doubt that some do care. But maybe we care, when we do, because we desire something even stronger than knowledge, perhaps something like the metaphysical certainty Descartes describes. We've been down this path already, however, and it is time for reality therapy to have its effect. Once we adopt more realistic desires, it is not clear that it matters at all whether we ever instance the ordinary concept of knowledge.

You might think something in the literature on the nature of knowledge might provide ammunition for defending the importance of knowledge. A brief look at some representative approaches suggests otherwise. What we will find is that the capacity to address axiological issues in an interesting way is strongly correlated with failure at solving the Gettier problem, but I must caution that my argumentation here will be sketchy at best. As our continental brethren might put the point, argumentation will appear in what follows in "the privative mode."

Some approaches to the Gettier problem focus on the role falsehoods play. According to such approaches, the absence of knowledge is a result of evidence that contains falsehoods, or presupposes falsehoods, or confirms falsehoods.[11] Such approaches suggest that knowledge might be important because it insulates us from error, beyond the object of belief itself. That viewpoint, however, is simply mistaken. First, among the lessons of the preface and fallibility paradoxes are that we nearly always have evidence in support of some false propositions: I also think that these same paradoxes can be used to show that the justifications for those aware of their own fallibility nearly always presuppose falsehoods. Second, the possibility of statistical knowledge undermines many of these approaches. A statistical sample can deviate in statistically significant ways from what it confirms about a population, and still be used to gather knowledge about that population. For example, a sample might give us knowledge that most swans are white even though the actual percentage of white swans is significantly different than our sample confirms. We can agree that insulation from error is important, but the lesson here is that one can't defend the importance of knowledge by citing perhaps unfortunate features of the human condition that knowledge has no power to displace.

Another approach to the nature of knowledge claims that if you don't have knowledge, then either your cognitive equipment is not functioning as it was designed to function or it is not operating in an environment suitable to that design. So suppose I regularly have justified true belief but no knowledge; then either I'm an engineering nightmare (perhaps, better put, an engineer's nightmare) or I'm not in Kansas anymore. Upset, I'm not; I'll just blissfully smile and bless the gods for my justified true beliefs while some epistemologists sing their lament. I'd join in the refrain if there were an argument that my condition will lead, or likely will lead, to failures of justified true belief in the future, but no such argument is available.

Another approach to the Gettier problem is the defeasibility approach,[12] and we might wonder whether there is some special value attaching to justified beliefs that are not defeated. I agree there is, but knowledge is not undefeated justified true belief. One of the lessons of that literature is that not all defeaters undermine knowledge; some defeaters are misleading ones and some are not[13] (perhaps because some defeaters are ultimately overridden by other information and others are not). So even if we value undefeated justification, that gives us no reason to value knowledge over justified true belief, for knowledge does not eliminate defeaters. And if there are defeaters present, I don't see how the distinction between defeaters that undermine knowledge and those that do not is of any significant importance to human interests, needs, or purposes. One might answer like this: when you are subject only to the misleading defeaters, you could learn everything epistemically relevant to your belief and still be justified in believing what you presently believe. That is true, but it is also true when you are subject to nonmisleading defeaters, for there aren't any justified truths that one with all the evidence would fail to be justified in believing.

Another approach to the Gettier problem imputes to knowers a truth-tracking power.[14] When you lack knowledge, on this approach, either you would still believe the claim if it were false or there are close counterfactual circumstances in which it is still true in which you would not believe it. Yet, these counterfactuals alone are of little interest to us. A benevolent demon might just devote himself to making the appropriate counterfactuals true so that I count as a truth-tracker; another, malevolent demon might make those same counterfactuals false regardless of the quality of my evidence. The truth or falsity of these counterfactuals alone is of no special interest to us, so if their truth is what makes the difference between justified true belief and knowledge, then knowledge is of no special importance either.

There is a reply here, that it is not the truth of the counterfactuals that interests us, but the *explanation* of their truth. We want the counterfactuals to be true in virtue of capacities or abilities we have at finding the truth, so even though the mere truth of the counterfactuals may not be important or valuable, their truth in virtue of our powers is. If the counterfactuals are true because of the activity of some demon, they don't interest us much; but if they are true in virtue of our cognitive powers, they do interest us, and properly so.

The question we must ask, however, is what all this has to do with knowledge. It is not hard to see that knowledge is not to be identified with justified true belief, even where the true belief occurs in virtue of our cognitive powers in such a way as to sustain the truth of the counterfactuals above. The closest such suggestion one can find in the literature is Nozick's truth-tracking theory, but this proposal is nothing more than Nozick's intuitive theory which he immediately amends in the face of obvious counterexamples.[15] These counterexamples imply that production of justified true belief by suitably impressive cognitive powers is neither necessary nor sufficient for knowledge. So even if we could defend the importance of impressive cognitive architecture as above, such a defense simply does not yield the conclusion that knowledge is important.

There is another problematic feature of this proposal. This reply ignores the role a suitable, cooperative environment plays in making the counterfactuals in question true. When the counterfactuals are true, they are never true *solely* in virtue of our cognitive powers. The environment itself must also be suitable for the operation of those powers. If we had infallible powers, we wouldn't need a cooperative environment, but we do not have such powers, and hence the cooperation or suitability of the environment is required for the truth of the counterfactuals in question.

What is attractive about the idea that we want to have a hold on the truth in virtue of our own abilities, I submit, is that we would like to be in control of the cognitive affairs in question so that our hold on the truth is not fortuitous or accidental. But once we see that it is never solely in virtue of our cognitive powers that we find the truth, we must grant that there is always a bit of fortuitousness present when we find the truth. Without a suitable environment, none of our powers would be sufficient. So if it is fortuitousness that we hope to eliminate, we are hoping for something that cannot be had short of possessing infallible powers of discernment. I grant that such powers are surely desirable and valuable, but any attempt to salvage the importance of epistemology that appeals to the value of infallible powers of discernment will surely fail.

Even if fortuity cannot be eliminated completely, one might still wonder why it wouldn't be valuable to eliminate some elements or kinds of it even if others can't be eliminated. So, since to know something is to eliminate a certain kind of fortuity regarding one's true belief, it is valuable to have knowledge.

One problem with this response is that it is simply not obvious that there is a distinctive kind of fortuity that is ruled out by knowledge, except by stipulating that the kind in question is just that kind eliminated by whatever closes the gap between justified true belief and knowledge. It is often pointed out that the reason that justified true beliefs can fail to be knowledge is that they can be accidentally true, but that gives us no reason to think that knowledge can be defined in terms of non-accidentally true, justified belief, nor in terms of justified true belief that possesses some particular kind of non-accidentality. No one taking himself to provide an analysis of knowledge also takes himself to be analyzing the notion of accidentality or some kind of it or trying to get at the fundamental nature of accidentality when giving an account of knowledge. Instead, what is being done is giving an account of knowledge on which the condition which plugs the gap between justified true belief and knowledge falls under the genus of non-accidentality. This characterization leaves entirely open whether there is any kind of fortuity or accidentality that is ruled out by knowledge, except where that kind is stipulatively picked out in terms of the species of non-accidentality that plugs the gap between justified true belief and knowledge.

If that is how we are conceiving of kinds of accidentality, however, I doubt there is any way to sustain the above claim that ruling out this kind of accidentality is valuable unless any other species of the genus in question is similarly valuable to eliminate. And this latter claim is highly dubious. Consider the fortuity I experience of having many more beliefs about a particular locale within the state of Texas than other locales. Eliminate that fortuity and I won't have more detailed information about any locale than any other, and, given our limited capacities for information, that implies that I would lose a certain depth of understanding that is valuable. So, eliminating fortuity of any kind whatsoever is not necessarily a good thing. And if it isn't, the proposal above stands in need of a defense of the claim that the particular kind of fortuity that knowledge rules out is valuable.

Moreover, as we've imagined the situation, we are considering individuals who are unusually blessed by luck, a kind of luck I'd love to have. For the situation we've imagined is one where one finds the fortuity of having only justified true beliefs and a broad range of them in spite of having no knowledge. What luck! Even more, I'd prefer this kind of luck to the absence of luck of those who know a lot. And for those who have the luck of knowing everything they believe, it is simply not obvious why the way in which they fail to be lucky is to be preferred over the luck possessed by those who only have justified true beliefs. They fail to be lucky in a way I would be, and they've eliminated a kind of fortuity that I haven't, but there simply is no uniform answer to the question about when fortuity or non-fortuity is valuable. Furthermore, once one notices that eliminating the fortuity involved in failing to know what one justifiedly and truly believes makes no difference at all for one's present or future, it is hard to see how eliminating it could serve any important human need, interest, or purpose. I conclude that it is very hard to see how the importance of knowledge could be defended in this way.

Knowledge, Assertion, and Understanding

There are, however, two other ways to try to answer the Gettierized version of the *Meno* problem that strike me as deeper and more interesting than the attempts considered so far. The first attempt claims that we should want to avoid accidentally true beliefs because they show that we lack an accurate picture of the interrelationship between things, that we lack an adequate understanding of the explanatory connections in nature. The second attempts to link the conditions for knowledge with speech-act theory. I turn first to the lack-of-understanding approach.

The lack-of-understanding approach insists that we should want to understand *what makes what true*, and having only accidentally justified true beliefs bars such understanding. This approach is interesting to me because it suggests that there are certain intellectual virtues that we will not possess if our beliefs are only accidentally true. Understanding is one such virtue; perhaps wisdom is another. This approach thus suggests

that the virtues themselves are important, and that mere justified true belief is no definitive mark of them. I agree on both counts, but unfortunately this emphasis on the virtues will not rescue epistemology, for such an approach to defending the importance of that discipline is at least too strong, and perhaps too weak as well. It is too strong because knowledge doesn't require explanatory understanding; instead, it is at most implied by this kind of understanding. One doesn't need to have any explanatory understanding of the phenomenon in order to learn (say, by testimony) of its occurrence. Thus, if explanatory understanding is what is crucially important beyond justified true belief, we'd have a reason for replacing epistemology with the project of constructing an adequate account of explanatory understanding. The theory of knowledge might compose an addendum to such a project, but the point would remain that we should spend less of our time doing epistemology and more time thinking about understanding. This viewpoint is one I am quite sympathetic with, but I will not defend it further here.

The answer may also be too weak, for I am unsure that explanatory understanding implies knowledge. It may be that a suitable range of true beliefs, or justified true beliefs, will be enough for explanatory understanding. If I can correctly answer all questions directly from information I possess about, say, the rise and fall of Comanche dominance of the southern plains of North America in the late seventeenth century through 1875, then, I'm inclined to think, I have some understanding of that phenomenon. Do I have knowledge? Maybe yes; maybe no. On behalf of knowledge ascription, there is ordinary language: if you heard me give all the answers, you would certainly say that I know a lot about the subject. Ordinary language, however, is far from decisive. All it shows for sure is that you'd have good evidence for concluding that I have knowledge. Furthermore, on the usual theories of knowledge, I could give all those answers from information possessed and still lack knowledge. I can answer in this way and lack justification, and I can answer in the way and still have only accidentally justified true beliefs.

Of course, such vagaries may lead you to wonder whether being able to answer questions on the basis of information possessed is enough for understanding. I grant the need for a good argument here, and I'm not sure there is one. But at least this much can be said. Whether a person *understands* seems to be principally a matter of that person seeing the relationships between various (true) propositions. The contrary suggestion would have to be, then, that though someone might correctly see the relationships in question, they don't understand because, perhaps, it is only accidental that they see these connections. That strikes me as strained; I'm inclined to conclude that, if it is only accidental that they see these connections, then it is only accidental that they have the understanding that they have. I grant that there is more by way of confession than argument here, but the response that strikes me as the most natural one is to posit the possibility of understanding by accident rather than insist that understanding implies knowledge.

Regardless of how that issue is resolved, the above appeal to loss of understanding when our justified true beliefs are only accidentally so doesn't justify a focus on knowledge, so let us turn to the speech-act attempt to see if it fares any better. The theory of speech acts posits conditions under which we are licensed to make various assertions – call these conditions "assertibility conditions." For your action of asserting p to be legitimate, you must satisfy the assertibility conditions for p. The speech-act rescue of epistemology posits that assertibility conditions include all the conditions for knowledge. First, you are required to believe p in order to assert it legitimately. We often reprimand each other's assertions by pointing out, "You don't really believe that," to which we might hear the reply, "Yes, you're right, I shouldn't have said that; I'm only feeling sorry for myself." Second, you must have good reasons for what you say, and what you say must be true. My father sometimes says that earthquakes are much more common in the twentieth century than in prior centuries. I question how he can say this since he has no evidence for it. His only reason for asserting it is that it fits his eschatological views quite well. (I'm going to assume without argument here that fitting his eschatological views is not reason enough for him to believe what he does. He agrees in this case; his sheepishness at admitting that he has no better reason confirms it.) It turns out that he's right, and there is available scientific confirmation of

what he thinks. But *he* didn't have the evidence, and so shouldn't have made the claim (stubborn cuss that he is, an inheritable trait by the way; he *won't* acknowledge the point, but that is another matter …). On the matter of truth, it is easy to elicit a retraction by showing that what a person said is false. I say, "Foley is not here," and you point him out, and I take it back. Finally, failure to satisfy the Gettier condition for knowledge engenders the same type of retraction. Consider the Nogot–Havit case, in which Nogot convinces you that he has a Ferrari, from which you infer that someone in the room owns a Ferrari. If you assert that someone in the room owns a Ferrari, we can get you to take it back by showing you that Nogot in fact does not own a Ferrari. You are required to withdraw your assertion as much as you are when the other conditions for knowledge fail.

Such considerations are supposed to convince us that epistemology is a central sub-discipline of philosophy because the conditions for knowledge are assertibility conditions on utterances.[16] I do not think the defense is successful, however. First, I'll engage in a bit of border skirmishing, to the effect that the connections between legitimate assertion and knowledge are weaker than the above suggests. Afterwards, I'll get to the main reason why the proposal fails.

Let's begin by being precise about the proposal. First, it claims a logical relationship between the assertibility of p and knowing p: p's being assertible by S entails S's knowing p, where p's being assertible is understood to mean that it is permissible for S to assert p. This claim is false. Consider someone who takes Pascal's advice of going to Mass and hoping for the best; in line with such advice, a person may sincerely avow that God exists even though that person does not (yet) believe it. Furthermore, no one in such a condition need be moved to retract the assertion upon complaint that the assertion is not backed by belief; at most, what you would get is an excuse for saying it, suggesting that the speaker understands that he or she has violated a condition on assertion that *normally* holds, but does not hold in this case. Or, again, consider someone, moved by William James's arguments,[17] who comes to believe that God exists and asserts it, all the while knowing that there is insufficient evidence to confirm this claim. Such a person need not retract the claim when the absence of evidence is noted;

at most, an excuse is needed. For a third case, imagine Churchland or Stich asserting, "I believe nothing that I assert," something their writings imply.[18] On the speech-act proposal, no such sentence is assertible, but it is easy to see that neither would be guilty of any impropriety in his assertion (I hesitate to say that an excuse is called for here, because there is no excuse for their views), even if it should turn out that they are philosophically mistaken in claiming that there are no beliefs. This latter case is a special instance of skeptical and Pyrrhonian assertion. (As an aside, such possibilities of appropriate assertion show that Moore's Paradox, the paradox that arises from a person's asserting that a certain proposition is true but that he or she doesn't believe it, is not always paradoxical; it is paradoxical only given certain assumptions about how standards for belief and standards for assertion are correlated.) Skeptics are quite comfortable asserting that knowledge is not possible, and Pyrrhonian skeptics not only assert that knowledge is not possible but that it is best not to hold any beliefs at all (though the interpretation of their belief/appearance distinction is quite subtle). In each of these cases, assertion is legitimate, even though the question of whether it is backed by knowledge is left open.

So it would appear that the most that can be claimed is that knowing p is *ordinarily* a requirement for legitimately asserting p. What, precisely, does such a claim mean, however? It is, of course, senseless to claim that one thing ordinarily entails another. Perhaps the notion of a requirement should be understood differently. Instead of thinking of requirement in terms of entailment, perhaps we should think of it as a defeasible relation, so that x can require y even though x&z does not require y. If we understand the notion of requirement in this way, we might still be able to claim that the assertibility of p requires knowing p even though in the unusual cases described above additional factors come into play so that the assertibility of p in those circumstances does not require knowledge.

Even such retrenchment cannot save the proposal, however. Recall the way in which the proposal began. We look for ways in which we can require a person to take back an assertion, and it turns out that the conditions for knowledge are among those ways. There are, however, two quite different things a person might be doing in taking back an assertion. The person might be taking back only *what is said*, or she might be taking back *the saying of it*. So, for example, if Joe says, "I don't know why I keep trying to be friendly, nobody likes me at all," and Mary says, "Joe, you don't really believe that; you're just upset," Joe might apologize for saying what he knows is false. Such cases support the view that belief is ordinarily a requirement on assertion because the retraction involves a taking back of the saying itself. Moreover, when people assert things without any good reason whatsoever, we reprove such utterances, realizing that, even though what is said might be true, *those individuals* have no business saying so. So once again, it is the saying itself that is at fault. But when new information is presented that undermines an assertion, only a retraction of what is said is in order. In the Nogot–Havit case,[19] pointing out that Nogot does not own a Ferrari should lead you to retract your claim that someone in the office owns one. It would be quite bizarre to hear you apologizing for having made the original claim; it is what was said, in your view, that was mistaken, not the saying of it. Again, if I assert what is false, and you show me that it is false, I'll retract my statement. But I wouldn't say that my uttering of it was out of order.

The distinction thus suggests that there is a better account of assertibility than the speech-act proposal aimed at rescuing epistemology. Instead of conditions of knowledge being assertibility conditions, only belief and justification are among such conditions. So here's the story we should tell about the connection between cognition and assertion. The appeal to knowledge to account for assertibility is superfluous, for all the explanatory work can be done by the concept of justified belief itself. When *the saying itself* is inappropriate, that is so in the ordinary case where standards of assertion and standards of belief converge because justified belief was not present when the assertion was made. When *what was said* must be retracted, that is so because justification for belief is no longer present. That is all the explanation that is needed, and no appeal to the concept of knowledge is involved in it.

There is, however, still a smidgen of a difficulty. For when you find out that you've been Gettiered, there is some residual embarrassment or regret for your assertion. If you assert that someone in this room owns a Ferrari on the basis of believing that Nogot owns one, and then are told that Nogot has deceived you, you might not only retract your statement, but experience some embarrassment or regret for the assertion. Are you thereby showing the inappropriateness of assertion in the absence of knowledge? No. You are showing that you dislike being duped, and one can be duped because of truths that undermine knowledge and because of truths that do not undermine knowledge. You'd experience the same embarrassment or regret if the defeater mentioned were a misleading one. The classic case involving misleading defeaters is the case of Tom stealing a book from the library.[20] You see Tom steal the book, and have a justified true belief that he stole it. But his mother, an inveterate liar, tells the police that it was his twin brother, Tim, who stole it. The police know the story is concocted; they know she is an inveterate liar and will say anything to protect Tom. They also know Tom has no twin. But you don't know all this, and if you were told what the mother said, you'd be every bit as inclined to take back the assertion that Tom stole the book and to experience some embarrassment or regret for having confidently claimed it. But the defeater is a misleading one; without having been told it, it does not undermine your knowledge, because it is so obviously farcical. Yet, even misleading defeaters, when discovered, undermine knowledge; that is what makes them defeaters in the first place. The lesson, then, is that your

embarrassment, shame, or regret is not an indicator that knowledge is a prerequisite of appropriate assertion. Instead, it is only a sign that none of us are comfortable with the existence of information we are not aware of that would undermine the justification of our beliefs. To have justifications that are immune from defeat is, of course, a valuable characteristic of a belief (provided justification itself is), for such justification has a kind of permanence to it – it is tethered, to use Socrates' metaphor, and will not fly away. To conclude, however, that one should never say anything for which one lacks immunity from defeat is, to paraphrase William James, to show a preoccupation with not being duped.[21]

Conclusion

So we have no good explanation as to why the philosophical inquiry concerning cognition should involve epistemology. Some of epistemology may be worthwhile, stemming from the force of the internalists' argument that we cannot pursue truth directly. But at most that only allows for a place for a theory of justification. I suggest the lesson is this: epistemologists should quit contemplating the nature and extent of knowledge as much as they do, and focus instead on the broader question of the nature of exemplary cognition, constrained perhaps by the possibilities of such for us, and the intellectual virtues such as understanding and wisdom that make for it.

Notes

1   Plato, *Meno* 97d–98a, in *Plato: The Collected Dialogues*, Edith Hamilton and Huntington Cairns, eds, (Princeton, NJ: Princeton University Press, 1961).

2   See Edmund Gettier's famous paper, "Is Justified True Belief Knowledge?" *Analysis*, vol. 23, June, 1963, pp. 121–3.

3   See Donald Davidson, "On the Very Idea of a Conceptual Scheme," *Inquiries into Truth and Interpretation*, pp. 183–98, (Oxford: Oxford University Press, 1984).

4   For a discussion, see Tyler Burge, "Individualism and the Mental," *Studies in*

Meta-physics, P. French, T. Uehling, and H. Wettstein, eds, (Minneapolis, MN: University of Minnesota Press, 1979).

5   Recent exponents of this view include Roderick Chisholm, Keith Lehrer, and Richard Foley, among others. See Chisholm, *Theory of Knowledge*, 2nd edn, Prentice-Hall, 1977; Lehrer, *Knowledge*, Clarendon Press, 1975; Foley, *The Theory of Epistemic Rationality* (Cambridge, MA: Harvard, 1985).

6   Roderick Firth suggests such a view in "Epistemic Merit, Intrinsic and Instrumental," *Proceedings and Addresses of the*

506 JONATHAN L. KVANVIG

American Philosophical Association 55 (1981), pp. 5–23.

7 I am not sure whom to credit with this difficulty, but an early statement of it can be found in Richard Foley, *The Theory of Epistemic Rationality*, pp. 72–3.

8 The most prominent critic of belief voluntarism is William P. Alston. See his *Epistemic Justification: Essays in the Theory of Knowledge*, (Ithaca, NY: Cornell University Press, 1989).

9 For discussion of the internalism/externalism distinction, see Richard Fumerton, "The Internalism/Externalism Controversy," *Philosophical Perspectives* 2, Epistemology, 1988.

10 Laurence BonJour, *The Structure of Empirical Knowledge*, (Cambridge, MA: Harvard University Press, 1985).

11 See, e.g., Roderick Chisholm, *Theory of Knowledge*, 2nd edn, ch. 6; Ernest Sosa, "Epistemic Presupposition," in George Pappas, ed., *Justification and Knowledge: New Studies in Epistemology*, (Dordrecht: D. Reidel, 1979), pp. 79–92.

12 See Keith Lehrer and Thomas D. Paxson, Jr., "Knowledge: Undefeated Justified True Belief," *The Journal of Philosophy*, vol. 66 (1969), pp. 225–37.

13 To my knowledge, Peter Klein first saw this. His own theory of the distinction is presented in *Certainty: A Refutation of Skepticism*, (Minneapolis, MN: University of Minnesota Press, 1981).

14 Robert Nozick is the most famous defender of this view, but the appeal to conclusive reasons first offered by Fred Dretske is another example. See Nozick, *Philosophical Explanations*, (Cambridge, MA: Harvard University Press, 1981); Dretske, "Conclusive Reasons," *Australasian Journal of Philosophy*, vol. 49 (1971), pp. 1–22.

15 See Robert Nozick, *Philosophical Explanations*, esp. pp. 179–85.

16 For a defense of this view, see Timothy Williamson, "Knowing and Asserting," *The Philosophical Review* 105, 4 (1996), pp. 489–523.

17 In "The Will to Believe," in *The Will to Believe and Other Essays in Popular Philosophy* (New York, 1897).

18 See Stephen Stich, *From Folk Psychology to Cognitive Science: The Case Against Belief* (Cambridge, MA; MIT Press, 1983); Paul Churchland, *Scientific Realism and the Plasticity of Mind*, (Cambridge: Cambridge University Press, 1979).

19 From Lehrer and Paxson, "Knowledge: Undefeated Justified True Belief."

20 Also from Lehrer and Paxson.

21 The actual quote is: "He who says 'Better go without belief forever than believe a lie!' merely shows his own preponderant private horror of becoming a dupe." William James, *Essays in Pragmatism*, (New York: Hafner, 1948), p. 100.

CHAPTER 38

True Enough

Catherine Z. Elgin

Epistemology valorizes truth. Sometimes practical, or prudential, or political reasons convince us to accept a known falsehood, but most epistemologists deny that we can have cognitively good reasons to do so. Our overriding cognitive objective, they maintain, is the truth, preferably the whole truth, and definitely nothing but the truth (Goldman 1999, p. 5; Lehrer 1986, p. 6; BonJour 1985, p. 9). If they are right, then at least insofar as our ends are cognitive, we should accept only what we consider true, take pains to insure that the claims we accept are in fact true, and promptly repudiate any previously accepted claims upon learning that they are false. I suggest, however, that the relation between truth and epistemic acceptability is both more tenuous and more circuitous than is standardly supposed. Sometimes, I contend, it is epistemically responsible to prescind from truth to achieve more global cognitive ends.

At first blush, this looks mad. To retain a falsehood merely because it has epistemologically attractive features seems the height of cognitive irresponsibility. Allegations of intellectual dishonesty, wishful thinking, false consciousness, or worse immediately leap to mind. But science routinely transgresses the boundary between truth and falsehood. It smoothes curves and ignores outliers. It develops and deploys simplified models that diverge, sometimes considerably, from the phenomena they purport to represent. Even the best scientific theories are not true. Not only are they plagued with anomalies and outstanding problems, but where they are successful, they rely on laws, models, idealizations and approximations that diverge from the truth. Truth-centered epistemology, or *veritism*, as Alvin Goldman calls it, easily accommodates anomalies and outstanding problems, since they are readily construed as defects. The problem comes with the laws, models, idealizations, and approximations which are acknowledged not to be true, but which are nonetheless critical to, indeed constitutive of, the understanding that science delivers. Far from being defects, they figure ineliminably in the success of science. If truth is mandatory, much of our best science turns out to be epistemologically unacceptable and perhaps intellectually dishonest. Our predicament is this: We can retain the truth requirement and construe science either as cognitively defective or as non-cognitive, or we can reject, revise, or relax the truth requirement and remain cognitivists about, and fans of, science.

I take it that science provides an understanding of the natural order. By this I do not mean merely that an ideal science *would* provide such an understanding or that in the end of inquiry science *will* provide one, but that much actual science has done so and continues to do so. I take it

Originally published in *Philosophical Issues* 14, Epistemology (2004), pp. 113–31.

then that much actual science is cognitively reputable. So an adequate epistemology should explain what makes good science cognitively good. Too strict a commitment to truth stands in the way. Nor is science the only casualty. In other disciplines such as philosophy, and in everyday discourse, we often convey information and advance understanding by means of sentences that are not literally true. An adequate epistemology should account for this as well. A tenable theory is a tapestry of interconnected sentences that together constitute an understanding of a domain.[1] My thesis is that some sentences that figure ineliminably in tenable theories make no pretense of being true, but are not defective on that account. If I am right, theories and the understandings they embed have a more intricate symbolic structure than we standardly suppose. Nevertheless, I do not think that we should jettison concern for truth completely. The question is what role a truth commitment should play in a holism that recognizes a multiplicity of sometimes conflicting epistemological desiderata.

Consensus has it that epistemic acceptability requires something like justified and/or reliable, true belief. The justification, reliability, and belief requirements involve thresholds. "[O]ne may need to be confident enough and well enough justified and one's belief must perhaps derive from a reliable enough source, and be little enough liable to be false" (Sosa 2000, p. 2). But truth, unlike the other requirements, is supposed to be an absolute matter. Either the belief is true or it is not. I suggest, however, that the truth requirement on epistemic acceptability involves a threshold too. I am not saying that truth itself is a threshold concept. Perhaps such a construal of truth would facilitate treatments of vagueness, but that is not my concern. My point is rather that epistemic acceptability turns not on whether a sentence is true, but on whether it is true enough – that is, on whether it is close enough to the truth. "True enough" obviously has a threshold.

I should begin by attempting to block some misunderstandings. I do not deny that (unqualified) truth is an intelligible concept or a realizable ideal. We readily understand instances of the (T) schema:

"Snow is white" is true ≡ snow is white
"Power corrupts" is true ≡ power corrupts

"Neutrinos have mass" is true ≡ neutrinos have mass

and so on. A disquotational theory of truth suffices to show that the criterion expressed in Convention (T) can be satisfied. One might, of course, want more from a theory of truth than satisfaction of Convention (T), but to make the case that the concept of truth is unobjectionable, a minimalist theory that evades the paradoxes suffices. Moreover, not only does it make sense to call a sentence true, we can often tell whether it is true. We are well aware not only that "Snow is white" is true ≡ snow is white, but also that "Newly fallen snow is white" is true. The intelligibility and realizability of truth, of course, show nothing about which sentences are true or which truths we can discover. Nevertheless, as far as I can see, nothing about the concept of truth discredits veritism. Since truth is an intelligible concept, epistemology can insist that only truths are epistemically acceptable. Since truth is a realizable objective, such a stance does not lead inexorably to skepticism. I do not deny that veritism is an available epistemic stance. But I think it is an unduly limiting one. It prevents epistemology from accounting for the full range of our cognitive achievements.

If epistemic acceptance is construed as belief, and epistemic acceptability as knowledge, the truth requirement seems reasonable. For cognizers like ourselves, there does not seem to be an epistemically significant gap between believing that p, and believing that p is true. Ordinarily, upon learning that our belief that p is false, we cease to believe that p. Moreover, we consider it cognitively obligatory to do so. One ought to believe only what is true. Perhaps a creature without a conception of truth can harbor beliefs. A cat, for example, might believe that there is a mouse in the wainscoting without believing that "There is a mouse in the wainscoting" is true.[2] In that case, the connection between believing that p and believing that p is true is not exceptionless. But whatever we should say about cats, it does not seem feasible for any creature that has a conception of truth to believe that p without believing that p is true. If epistemic acceptance is a matter of belief, acceptance is closely linked to truth. Assertion is too. Although asserting that p is not the same as asserting that p is true, it seems plain that one ought not to assert that p if one is prepared to deny that p is true or to suspend judgment about whether p is true; nor ought one assert that p is true if one is prepared to deny that p or to suspend judgment about whether p. Assertion and belief, then, seem committed to truth. So does knowledge. Whether or not we take knowledge to be equivalent to justified or reliably generated true belief, once we discover the falsity of something we took ourselves to know, we withdraw the claim to knowledge. We say, "I thought I knew it, but I was wrong", not "I knew it, but I was wrong".

Being skeptical about analyticity, I do not contend that a truth commitment is part of the meanings of "belief," "assertion," and "knowledge". But whatever the explanation, because the truth commitment tightly intertwines with our views about belief, assertion, and knowledge, it seems best to retain that connection and revise epistemology by making compensatory adjustments elsewhere. Once those adjustments are made, knowledge and belief turn out to be less central to epistemology than we standardly think. I do not then claim that it is epistemically acceptable to *believe* what is false or that it is linguistically acceptable to *assert* what is false. Rather, I suggest that epistemic acceptance is not restricted to belief (Cohen 1992). Analogously, uttering or inscribing seriously and sincerely for cognitive purposes – call it "professing" – is not limited to asserting. Understanding is often couched in and conveyed by symbols that are not, and do not purport to be, true. Where such symbols are sentential, I call them felicitous falsehoods. I contend that we cannot understand the cognitive contributions of science, philosophy, or even our ordinary take on things, if we fail to account for such symbols. Let's look at some cases:

Curve smoothing: Ordinarily, each data point is supposed to represent an independently ascertained truth. (The temperature at t_1, the temperature at t_2 ...) By interpolating between and extrapolating beyond these truths, we expect to discern the pattern they instantiate. If the curve we draw connects the data points, this is reasonable. But the data rarely fall precisely on the curve adduced to account for them. The curve then reveals a pattern that the data do not instantiate. Veritism would seem to require accepting the data only if we are convinced that they are true, and

connecting these truths to adduce more general truths. Unwavering commitment to truth would seem then to require connecting all the data points no matter how convoluted the resulting curve turned out to be. This is not done. To accommodate every point would be to abandon hope of finding order in most data sets, for jagged lines and complicated curves mask underlying regularities. Nevertheless, it seems cognitively disreputable simply to let hope triumph over experience. Surely we need a better reason to skirt the data and ignore the outliers than the fact that otherwise we will not get the kind of theory we want. Nobody, after all, promised that the phenomena would accommodate themselves to the kind of theory we want.

There are often quite good reasons for thinking that the data ought not, or at least need not be taken as entirely accurate. Sometimes we recognize that our measurements are relatively crude compared with the level of precision we are looking for. Then any curve that is within some δ of the evidence counts as accommodating the evidence. Sometimes we suspect that some sort of interference throws our measurements off. Then in plotting the curve, we compensate for the alleged interference. Sometimes the measurements are in fact accurate, but the phenomena measured are complexes only some of whose aspects concern us. Then in curve smoothing we, as it were, factor out the irrelevant aspects. Sometimes we have no explanation for the data's divergence from the smooth curve. But we may be rightly convinced that what matters is the smooth curve the data indicate, not the jagged curve they actually instantiate. Whatever the explanation, we accept the curve, taking its proximity to the data points as our justification. We understand the phenomena as displaying the pattern the curve marks out. We thus dismiss the data's deviation from the smooth curve as negligible.

Ceteris paribus claims: Many lawlike claims in science obtain only ceteris paribus.[3] The familiar law of gravity

$$F = Gm_1m_2/r^2$$

is not universally true, for other forces may be in play. The force between charged bodies, for example, is a resultant of electrical and gravitational forces. Nevertheless, we are not inclined to jettison the law of gravity. The complication that charge introduces just shows that the law obtains only ceteris paribus, and when bodies are charged, ceteris are not paribus. This is no news. "Ceteris paribus" is Latin for "other things being equal", but it is not obvious what makes for equality in a case like this. Sklar glosses it as "other things being normal" (Sklar 1999, p. 702), where "normal" seems to cash out as "typical" or "usual". Then a "ceteris paribus law" states what usually happens. In that case, to construe the law of gravity as a ceteris paribus law is to contend that although there are exceptions, bodies usually attract each other in direct proportion to the product of their masses and in inverse proportion to the square of the distance between them.

This construal does not always work. Some laws do not even usually hold. The law of gravity is one. Snell's law

$$n_1 \sin i = n_2 \sin r$$

which expresses the relation between the angle of incidence and the angle of refraction of a light ray passing from one medium to another, is a second.[4] As standardly stated, the law is perfectly general, ranging over every case of refraction. It is not true of every case, though; it obtains only where both media are optically isotropic. The law then is a ceteris paribus law. But it is not even usually true, since most media are optically anisotropic (Cartwright 1983, pp. 46–7). One might wonder why physicists don't simply restrict the scope of the law: "For any two optically isotropic media, $n_1 \sin i = n_2 \sin r$". The reason is Gricean: expressly restricting the scope of the law implicates that it affords no insight into cases where the restriction does not obtain. Snell's law is more helpful. Even though the law is usually false, it is often not far from the truth. Most media are anisotropic, but lots of them – and lots of the ones physicists are interested in – are nearly isotropic. The law supplies good approximations for nearly isotropic cases. So although explanations and calculations that rely on Snell's law do not yield truths, they are often not off by much.

The law is valuable for another reason as well. Sometimes it is useful to first represent a light ray as conforming to Snell's law, and later introduce "corrections" to accommodate anisotropic media.

If we were interested only in the path of a particular light ray, such a circuitous approach would be unattractive. But if we are interested in optical refraction in general, it might make sense to start with a prototypical case, and then show how anisotropy perturbs. By portraying anisotropic cases as perturbations, we point up affinities that direct comparisons would not reveal. The issue then is what sort of understanding we want. Showing how a variety of cases diverge from the prototypical case contributes valuable insights into the phenomenon we are interested in. And what makes the case prototypical is not that it usually obtains, but that it cleanly exemplifies the features we deem important.

Idealizations: Some laws never obtain. They characterize ideal cases that do not, perhaps cannot, occur in nature. The ideal gas law represents gas molecules as perfectly elastic spheres that occupy negligible space and exhibit no mutual attraction. There are no such molecules. Explanations that adduce the ideal gas law would be epistemically unacceptable if abject fidelity to truth were required. Since helium molecules are not dimensionless, mutually indifferent, elastic spheres, an account that represents them as such is false. If veritism is correct, it is epistemically unacceptable. But, at least if the explanation concerns the behavior of helium in circumstances where divergence from the ideal gas law is negligible (roughly, where temperature is high and pressure is low), scientists are apt to find it unexceptionable.

Stylized facts are close kin of ceteris paribus claims. They are "broad generalizations, true in essence, though perhaps not in detail" (Bannock et al. 1998, pp. 396–7). They play a major role in economics, constituting explananda that economic models are required to explain. Models of economic growth, for example, are supposed to explain the (stylized) fact that the profit rate is constant.[5] The unvarnished fact of course is that profit rates are not constant. All sorts of non-economic factors – such as war, pestilence, drought, and political chicanery – interfere. Manifestly, stylized facts are not (what philosophers would call) facts, for the simple reason that they do not obtain. It might seem then that economics takes itself to be required to explain why known falsehoods are true. (Voodoo economics, indeed!) This cannot be correct. Rather, economics is committed to the view that the claims it recognizes as stylized facts are in the right neighborhood, and that their being in the right neighborhood is something economic models need to account for. The models may show them to be good approximations in all cases, or where deviations from the economically ideal are slight, or where economic factors dominate non-economic ones. Or the models might afford some other account of their often being nearly right. The models may differ over what is actually true, or as to where, to what degree, and why the stylized facts are as good as they are. But to fail to acknowledge the stylized facts would be to lose valuable economic information (for example, the fact that if we control for the effects of non-economic interference such as wars, epidemics, and the president for life absconding with the national treasury, the profit rate is constant). Stylized facts figure in other social sciences as well. I suspect that under a less alarming description, they occur in the natural sciences too. The standard characterization of the pendulum, for example, strikes me as a stylized fact of physics. The motion of the pendulum that physics is supposed to explain is a motion that no actual pendulum exhibits. What such cases point to is this: The fact that a strictly false description is in the right neighborhood is sometimes integral to our understanding of a domain.

A fortiori arguments from limiting cases: Some accounts focus on a single, carefully chosen case and argue that what holds in that case holds in general. If so, it does no harm to represent the phenomena as having the features that characterize the exemplary case. Astronomy sometimes represents planets as point masses. Manifestly, they are not. But because the distance between planets is vastly greater than their size, their spatial dimensions can safely be neglected. Given the size and distribution of planets in the solar system, what holds for properly characterized point masses also holds for the planets. Another familiar example comes from Rawls. *A Theory of Justice* represents people as mutually disinterested. Rawls is under no illusion that this representation is accurate. He recognizes that people are bound to one another by ties of affection of varying degrees of strength, length, and resiliency. But, he believes, if political agents have reason to cooperate even under conditions of mutual disinterest, they will

have all the more reason to cooperate when ties of affection are present. I do not want to discuss whether Rawls is right. I just want to highlight the form of his argument. If what holds for the one case holds for the others, then it does no harm to represent people as mutually disinterested. That people are mutually disinterested is far from the truth. Conceivably, no one on Earth is wholly indifferent to the fates of every other person. But if Rawls is right, the characterization's being far from the truth does not impede its function in his argument.

The foregoing examples show that in some cognitive endeavors we accept claims that we do not consider true. But we do not indiscriminately endorse falsehoods either. The question then is what makes a claim acceptable? Evidently, to accept a claim is not to take it to be true, but to take it that the claim's divergence from truth, if any, is negligible. The divergence need not be small, but whatever its magnitude, it can be safely neglected. We accept a claim, I suggest, when we consider it true enough. The success of our cognitive endeavors indicates that we are often right to do so. If so, a claim is acceptable when its divergence from truth is negligible. In that case it is true enough.

In practical, political, or prudential contexts, both the acceptance and the acceptability of falsehoods are widely recognized. One can accept, and be right to accept, the dean's latest dictum, if what matters is that the dean hath said it, not that it is true. But epistemic contexts are supposed to be different. Many epistemologists contend that when our concerns are cognitive we should accept only what we consider true. I disagree. I suggest that *to accept* that p is to take it that p's divergence from truth, if any, does not matter. *To cognitively accept* that p, is to take it that p's divergence from truth, if any, does not matter cognitively. The falsehood is "as close as one needs for the purposes at hand" (Stalnaker 1987, p. 93). In what follows, I take "acceptance" to mean "cognitive acceptance".

This raises a host of issues. Perhaps the most pressing is to say something about what I mean by "cognitive". A familiar line is that for a consideration to be cognitive is for it to aim at truth or to be truth conducive. Plainly, I can say no such thing. I suggest rather that a consideration is cognitive to the extent that it figures in an understanding of how things are. This is admittedly vague, but I am not sure that it is any worse than untethered remarks about truth-conduciveness and the like.

It might seem that my characterization just postpones the evil day (and not for long enough!), since "an understanding of how things are" must itself be explicated in terms of truth or truth-conduciveness. To see the problem, compare three concepts – belief, thought, and understanding. Belief aims at truth. Roughly, a belief fulfills its goal in life only if it is true (Wedgwood 2002; Adler 2002). Thought, however, can be aimless. Musings, fantasies, and imaginings can be fully in order whether or not they are true. Understanding, the argument goes, is more like belief than like thought. Since there is such a thing as misunderstanding, understanding is subject to a standard of rightness. It has an aim. Misunderstanding evidently involves representing things as they are not. This suggests that the aim of understanding is truth. If so, it may seem, divergences from truth, even if unavoidable, are always cognitive defects.

The argument goes too fast. That misunderstanding involves representing things as they are not does not entail that whenever we represent things as they are not, we misunderstand them. At most it indicates that understanding is not indifferent to truth. But it does not follow that every sentence – or for that matter, any sentence – that figures in an understanding of how things are has its own truth as an objective. Understanding involves a network of commitments. It is not obvious that an aim of the network must be an aim of every, or indeed any, sentential node in the network. A goal of the whole need not be a goal of each of its parts. "Understanding" is a cognitive success term but, in my view, not a factive. I do not expect these sketchy remarks to persuade anyone that I am right to loosen the tie between understanding and truth. My hope is that they are enough to persuade you that the jig is not yet up, that a willing suspension of disbelief is still in order.

Let us turn then to acceptance. To accept that p, I said, is to take it that p's divergence from truth, if any, is negligible. In that case, p is true enough. Whether this is so is manifestly a contextual matter. A sentence can be true enough in some contexts but not in others. A variety of factors contribute constraints. Background assumptions play a role. "A freely falling body falls at a rate of 32 ft./sec.²" is true enough, assuming that the body is within the Earth's gravitational field, that nothing except the Earth exerts a significant gravitational force on the body, that the effects of non-gravitational forces are insignificant, and so on. But even when these assumptions are satisfied, the formula is not always true enough, since gravity varies slightly with longitude. Sometimes it matters where in the gravitational field the freely falling body is. Whether "G = 32 ft./sec.²" is true enough depends on what we want the formula for, what level of precision is needed for the calculation or explanation or account it figures in. There is no saying whether a given contention is true enough independently of answering, or presupposing an answer to the question "True enough for what?" So purposes contribute constraints as well. Whether a given sentence is true enough depends on what ends its acceptance is supposed to serve.

Function is critical too. If to accept that p is simply to take it that p's divergence from truth does not matter, it might seem that we accept all irrelevant propositions. None of my projects, cognitive or otherwise, is affected by the truth or falsity of the claim that Ethelred the Unready was a wise leader. So its divergence from truth, if any, does not matter to me. Since acceptance can be tacit, the fact that I have never considered the issue is not decisive. Nevertheless it seems wrong to say that my indifference makes the claim true enough. The reason is that the contention is idle. It performs no function in my cognitive economy. Owing to my indifference, there is no answer to the question "True enough for what?"

Context provides the framework. Purposes fix the ends. Function is a matter of means. The sentences that concern us tend not to have purposes or functions in isolation. Rather, they belong to and perform functions in larger bodies of discourse, such as arguments, explanations, or theories that have purposes. In accepting a sentence, then, we treat it in a given context as performing a function in a body of discourse which seeks to achieve some end. Whether "G = 32 ft./sec.²" is acceptable depends on whether the body of discourse it figures in serves its cognitive purpose – whether, that is, it yields the understanding of the domain that we seek.

A statement's divergence from truth is negligible only if that divergence does not hinder its performing its cognitive function. Hence whether a contention is true enough depends not just on its having a function, but on what its function is – on what role it plays in the account it belongs to. To determine whether a statement is true enough, we thus need to identify its function. It might seem that for cognitive purposes only one function matters. If the criterion for felicity is being true enough, one might think, the function of all felicitous falsehoods is to approximate. There is, as it were, a tacit "more or less" in front of all such claims. This will not do.

One reason is that the proposal is not sufficiently sensitive. Not all approximations perform the same function. Some are accepted simply because they are the best we can currently do. They are temporary expedients which we hope and expect eventually to replace with truths. We improve upon them by bringing them closer to the truth. Such approximations are, in Sellars's terms, promissory notes that remain to be discharged. The closer we get to the truth, the more of the debt is paid. They are, and are known to be, unsatisfactory. But not all approximations have this character. Some are preferable to the truths they approximate. For example, it is possible to derive a second-order partial differential equation that exactly describes fluid flow in a boundary layer. The equation, being non-linear, does not admit of an analytic solution. We can state the equation, but cannot solve it. This is highly inconvenient. To incorporate the truth into the theory would bring a line of inquiry to a halt, saying in effect: "Here's the equation; it is impossible to solve." Fluid dynamicists prefer a first-order partial differential equation, which approximates the truth, but admits of an analytical solution (Morrison 1999, pp. 56–60). The solvable equation advances understanding by providing a close enough approximation that yields numerical values that can serve as evidence for or constraints on future theorizing. The approximation then is more fruitful than the truth. There is no hope that future inquiry will remedy the situation, for it is demonstrable that the second-order equation cannot be solved numerically, while the first-order equation can.[6] That reality forces such a choice upon us may be disappointing, but under the circumstances it does not seem intellectually disreputable to accept and prefer the tractable first-order equation. One might say that

acceptance of the first-order approximation is only practical. It is preferable merely because it is more useful. This may be so, but the practice is a cognitive one. Its goal is to understand fluid flow in boundary layers. In cases like this, the practical and the theoretical inextricably intertwine. The practical value of the approximation is that it advances understanding of a domain. A felicitous falsehood thus is not always accepted only in default of the truth. Nor is its acceptance always "second best". It may make cognitive contributions that the unvarnished truth cannot match.

Moreover, not all felicitous falsehoods are approximations. Idealizations may be far from the truth, without thereby being epistemically inadequate. Political agents are not mutually disinterested. They are not nearly mutually disinterested. Nor is it the case that most political agents are mutually disinterested. There is no way I can see to construe Rawls's model as approximately true. Nevertheless, for Rawls's purposes, the characterization of political agents as mutually disinterested is felicitous if the features it highlights are constitutive of fair terms of cooperation underlying the basic structure of a democratic regime. There is no reason to think that in general the closer it is to the truth, the more felicitous a falsehood.

I suggest that felicitous falsehoods figure in cognitive discourse not as mistaken or inaccurate statements of fact, but as fictions. We are familiar with fictions and with reasoning about fictions. We regularly reason within the constraints dictated by a fiction, inferring, for example, that Hamlet may not have been mad, but Ophelia surely was. We also reason (with more trepidation) from a fiction to matters of fact. We may come to see a pattern in the facts through the lens that a fiction supplies. For example, we might understand the contemporary youth gang conception of being "dissed" by reference to the wrath of Achilles at Agamemnon's affront.[7] What is needed then is an account of how fictions can advance understanding.

David Lewis (1983) interprets fictional statements as descriptions of other possible worlds. We understand them in the same way that we understand ordinary statements of fact. For example, we understand the Sherlock Holmes stories in the same way we understand histories of Victorian England, the crucial difference being that the histories pertain to the actual world, while the stories pertain to other possible worlds. Lewis's realism about possible worlds is hard to countenance, but we need not enter into debates about it here. For even if we accept his metaphysics, a problem remains. It is puzzling how knowing what happens in another possible world can afford any insight into what happens in this world. Lewis measures the proximity of possible worlds in terms of similarity (Lewis 1973). The closest possible worlds are the ones most similar to the actual world. But even if one thinks that there is a non-question-begging way to assess the relative similarity of different possible worlds, the gap remains. It is hard to see how the knowledge that a nearby world is populated by rational economic agents should contribute to our understanding of the economic behavior of actual human agents.

Kendall Walton (1990) construes fiction as make-believe. To understand a fiction is to make believe or pretend that it is true. Stephen Yablo uses Walton's account to underwrite fictionalism in the philosophy of mathematics (1998; 2002). We can, Yablo maintains, avoid ontological commitment to mathematical entities by construing mathematics as an elaborate, highly systematic fiction. Then in doing mathematics, we make believe that there are such entities and make believe that they are related to one another in the ways the theorems say. Although at first glance this seems promising, it faces two serious problems. First, what it is to pretend is by no means clear. Exactly how one can pretend that power sets or cube roots exist if they do not, is not obvious. Second, the problem we saw with Lewis's theory also plagues Walton and Yablo. It is not at all clear how a pretense illuminates reality – how, for example, pretending that human beings are rational economic agents provides any insight into actual human economic behavior.

Philip Kitcher (1993) suggests that scientific idealizations are stories whose referents are fixed by stipulation. The scientific statements involving the idealizations are true by convention. The gap remains. If a story is to advance scientific understanding we need to know the connection between the story and the facts. Otherwise, the realization that certain relations among pressure, temperature, and volume are true by stipulation in the story of the ideal gas leaves us in the dark about the relations among pressure, temperature, and volume in actual gases.

The gap can be bridged by appeal to exemplification, the device by which samples and examples highlight, exhibit, display, or otherwise make manifest some of their features (Goodman 1968, pp. 45–67). To make this out requires a brief discussion of the device. A commercial paint sample consists of a patch of color on a card. The patch is not merely an instance of the color, but a telling instance – an instance that exemplifies the color. By so doing, the sample equips us to recognize the color, to differentiate it from similar shades. The sample then affords epistemic access to the color. Although the patch on the sample card has a host of other features – size, shape, location, and so on – it standardly does not exemplify them. Exemplification is selective. It brings out some features of an exemplar by over-shadowing, downplaying, or marginalizing others. Nothing in the nature of things dictates that the patch's color is worthy of selection, but its shape is not. What, if anything, an item exemplifies depends on its function. The very same item might perform any of a variety of functions. The patch on the sample card could be used to teach children what a rectangle is. In that case, it would exemplify its shape, not its color. The sample card could be used as a fan. Then the patch would not exemplify at all. Exemplification is not restricted to commercial and pedagogical contexts. Whatever an item exhibits, highlights, or displays, it exemplifies. A poem might exemplify its rhyme scheme, its imagery, or its style. A water sample might exemplify its mineral content, its flavor, or its impurities. Exemplification, I have argued elsewhere, is ubiquitous in art and science (Elgin 1996, pp. 171–83).

Treating paint samples as paradigmatic exemplars may encourage the idea that exemplified features are all like expanses of color – homogeneous qualities spread out before us, lacking depth and complexity, hence able to be taken in at a glance. Many are not like that. Pick up a rock containing iron ore. It might serve as a sample of iron, or of hematite, or of something that bears a striking resemblance to your high school algebra teacher. It can exemplify such features only where certain background assumptions are in place. Not just anyone looking at the rock could tell that it exemplified these features.

Moreover, although in principle any item can serve as an exemplar and any feature can be exemplified, a good deal of effort may be required to bring about the exemplification of a recondite feature. Some of that effort is mental. Just as we ignore the shape of the paint sample and focus on the color, we can ignore the fact that the rock looks like your algebra teacher and focus on its hardness. This is a start. But some irrelevant features so intricately intertwine with relevant ones that more drastic measures are called for. If we seek to exemplify recondite features of iron, mental agility alone may not be enough to bracket the effects of other minerals in the rock. So we refine the ore and filter out the impurities. The result of our efforts is pure iron. It is a product of a good deal of processing[8] which eliminates complicating factors and brings to the fore characteristics that are hard to detect and difficult to measure in nature. To facilitate the exemplification of the feature of interest, we do not just mentally sideline features we consider irrelevant, we physically remove some of them.

Even then, we do not just contemplate the bit of iron as we might a paint sample. We subject it to a variety of tests. We seek to produce circumstances where the features of interest stand out. We not only investigate the iron's behavior in standard conditions, we study what happens in extreme conditions – very high or low pressure or temperature, in a vacuum, under intense radiation, and so forth. Although we recognize that the test conditions do not ordinarily (or perhaps ever) obtain in nature, we take it that the behavior of the refined metal in the test conditions discloses something about the natural order. If so, by understanding what happens in the lab, we can understand something of what happens in the world. The connection is, of course, indirect. It involves a complicated extrapolation from situations and materials that are highly artificial and carefully contrived. One might argue that the lab itself is a fictional setting and the conclusions we draw about nature on the basis of our laboratory findings are projections from fiction to fact. I don't quite want to say that (although I suspect that Nancy Cartwright does). But I do want to point out that experimentation involves a lot of stage setting.

There is a tendency to think of experiments as processes that generate information, hence as ways to find things out. This of course is true. But it is worth noting that an experiment is not like an oracle,[9] or an anchorman, or a fortune cookie. It does not just issue a report stating its results. It displays them. It shows what happens to the magnetic properties of iron in conditions near the melting point. The experiment exemplifies its results.

No matter how carefully we set the stage, irrelevancies remain. We do not and ought not read every aspect of the experimental result back onto the world. Not only are there irrelevant features, there are issues about the appropriate vocabulary and level of precision for characterizing what occurs. The fact that the experiment occurred in Cleveland is unimportant. The fact that the sample has a certain mass or lattice structure may or may not be significant. The fact that the temperature is above 770° C may matter, while the fact that it was above 790° C does not. Some features of the iron in the experimental situation are telling features. Others are not. The telling features are the ones that the experiment discloses or makes manifest. By exemplifying certain features, the experiment brings them to light and affords epistemic access to them. That is its cognitive contribution. Other features, though equally real, are not exemplified. The experiment embodies an understanding of the phenomenon in question through its exemplification of telling features. By making these features manifest, it affords an understanding of the phenomenon.

If the cognitive contribution of an exemplar consists in the exemplification of select features, then anything that exemplifies exactly those features can, in a suitable context, make the same contribution. Return for a moment to the paint sample. I spoke of it as though it is a sample *of paint*, a telling instance of the stuff you might use to paint the porch. This is not true. The sample on the card does not consist of paint, but of an ink or dye of the same color as the paint whose color it exemplifies. If the sample were supposed to exemplify the paint itself, or the chemical features of the paint, the fact that it is not paint or has a different chemical composition would be objectionable. But since it exemplifies only the color, all that is needed is something that is the same color as the paint. The exemplar need not itself be paint. Similarly in scientific cases. Consider a DNA molecule that exemplifies its molecular structure. Anything that exemplifies the same structure has the capacity to perform the same function in our understanding of DNA. No more than the paint sample needs to consist of paint, does the exemplar of DNA's molecular structure need to consist of DNA. A schematic model that exemplifies the same features but has a different material (or even immaterial) substrate could to the job.

Here is where felicitous falsehoods enter the picture. Something other than paint can serve as a paint sample, affording epistemic access to a color also instantiated by the paint. Something other than a molecule can exemplify molecular structure, thereby affording epistemic access to a structure also instantiated by the molecule. A felicitous falsehood then is a fiction that exemplifies a feature in a context where the exemplification of that feature contributes to understanding. The utility of such a falsehood is plain. It is sometimes inconvenient, difficult, or even impossible to bring it about that the phenomena exemplify all and only the features that interest us. (DNA molecules are very small, charged pions are short lived.) If we introduce a falsehood that exemplifies those features – a bigger, longer-lasting model, for example – we can highlight them and display their significance for the understanding of the phenomenon in question. By exemplifying features it shares with the phenomena, a felicitous falsehood affords epistemic access to how things actually are. The camel's nose is now officially inside the tent.

There is more than one role that such fictions can play. Some serve as points of reference. We understand things in terms of them. In the simplest cases, like the model displaying the helical structure of the DNA molecule, they are simply schemata that exemplify factors they share with the phenomena they concern. They qualify as fictions because they diverge from the phenomena in unexemplified properties. (DNA molecules are not made of tinker toys.) In other cases, the connection to the facts is less direct. No real gas has the properties of the ideal gas. The model is illuminating though because we understand the properties of real gases in terms of their deviation from the ideal. In such cases, understanding involves a pattern of schema and correction. We represent the phenomena with a schematic model, and introduce corrections as needed to closer accord with the facts. Different corrections are needed to accord with the behavior of different gases. The fictional ideal then serves as a sort of least common denominator that facilitates reasoning about and comparison of actual gases. We "solve for" the simple case first, then introduce complications as needed.

Acknowledging the role of corrections might seem to suggest that the detour through fictions is just a circuitous route to the truth. Rather than a simple true description of the behavior of neon, we get a complicated truth that makes reference to deviations from some ideal. But the full cognitive contribution of the exercise resides in the truth, not the fiction. I don't think this is right for several reasons. The first is that sometimes the corrections that would be needed to yield a truth are unnecessary or even counter-productive. A fortiori arguments from limiting cases succeed because the corrections are unnecessary. If a consideration holds for one case, even if that case is a fiction, it holds for all. The multiple and complicated ways actual cases diverge from the fictive ideal make no difference. If Rawls's argument is sound, "correcting for" ties of affection just muddies the waters. Nor is this the only case where fidelity to the facts can prove a hindrance. It follows from the ideal gas law that as volume goes to zero, pressure becomes infinite. This would not happen. Given a fixed number of molecules, pressure increases as volume decreases – not to infinity, but only to the point where the container explodes. No one of course denies this. But to understand what would happen in the limit, we need to prescind from such material inconveniences and pretend that the walls of the container are infinitely strong. We need then to introduce not corrections that bring us back to the facts, but further idealizations. A second reason is that the requisite corrections often yield not truths, but more refined models. They supplant one falsehood with another. A third reason is that even where corrections yield truths, the fiction may be more than a *façon de parler*. It can structure our understanding in a way that makes available information we would not otherwise have access to. If, e.g., we draw a smooth curve that skirts the data, and construe the data as a complex of relevant and irrelevant factors (signal and noise), or construe a transaction in terms of an economic model overlaid with non-economic factors which skew the outcome, we impose an order on things, highlight certain aspects of the phenomena, reveal connections, patterns and discrepancies, and make possible insights that we could not otherwise obtain (Dennett 1991). We put ourselves in a position to see affinities between disparate occurrences by recognizing them as variations on a common theme.

Still, to say that felicitous falsehoods figure ineliminably in our understanding of certain phenomena is not to say that without them we would have no understanding whatsoever of those phenomena. Even without Snell's law, inspection and instantial induction would provide some insight into what happens when light passes between air and water, or between any other two specified media. What we would lack is a systematic understanding of how the several cases are alike. Felicitous falsehoods configure a domain, enabling us to characterize the phenomena in ways that would otherwise be unavailable. When, for example, we can construe seemingly divergent phenomena as variants of a common scheme, or as perturbations of a regular pattern, or as deviations from a simple norm, we see them and their relations to one another in a new light. We can discern systematic interconnections that direct inspection of the facts would not reveal. The fictions and the configurations of the domains that they engender provide conceptual resources for representing and reasoning about the phenomena in new and sometimes fruitful ways.

If I am right, not every theory is a conjunction of sentences, all of which are supposed to be true. Rather, a theory may be composed of both factual and fictional sentences, and the fictional sentences may play any of several different roles. This means that to understand what a theory conveys, and to understand the phenomena in terms of the theory requires sensitivity to the different roles the different sentences play. And to assess a theory requires determining whether the component sentences are true enough for the parts they are assigned to play. Yablo is investigating the metaphysical implications of the idea that fictions infuse even our most fundamental theories (Yablo 1998; 2002). I want to underscore the epistemological implications. One obvious consequence is that it is not plausible to think of an acceptable theory as a mirror of nature. Even if the goal of a

theory is to afford an understanding of a range of facts, it need not approach or achieve that goal by providing a direct reflection of those facts.

I have argued that a variety of components of cognitively acceptable theories neither are nor purport to be true. Rather, they are fictions that shed light on the phenomena they concern. They thereby contribute to our understanding of those phenomena. Even if my account makes sense of models and idealizations in science, a worry remains. My position threatens to make the world safe for postmodernist claptrap. If truth is not required for epistemic acceptability, why isn't a flagrantly false account acceptable? What is the objection to claiming that a theory attesting to the healing powers of crystals is as acceptable as the theories constituting mainstream crystallography? We seem to lose a valuable resource if we can't simply say, "Because it is false!" My seemingly wimpy requirement that an acceptable account must yield an understanding of how things are gives us what we need. An account that yields such an understanding must accommodate the facts in a domain. The accommodation may be indirect. Strictly false idealizations may be deployed. Detours through stylized facts may be made. The justification for the falsehoods is that they figure in accounts that make sense of the facts. A cognitively acceptable account sheds light on its subject. Where felicitous falsehoods are involved, the light may be oblique.

A theory can claim to make sense of a range of facts only if it is factually defeasible – only if, that is, there is some reasonably determinate, epistemically accessible factual arrangement which, if it were found to obtain, would discredit the theory. A felicitous falsehood is acceptable only if the theory or system of thought it belongs to accommodates the epistemically accessible facts. Exactly what this requires needs to be spelled out. The usual considerations about evidence, simplicity, scope, and so forth come into play. Even though some of the sentences in a theory are not supposed to be true, the way the world is constrains the acceptability of the theory they figure in. If, for example, evidence shows that friction plays a major role in collisions between gas molecules, then unless compensating adjustments are made elsewhere, theories that model collisions as perfectly elastic spheres will be discredited. An acceptable theory must be at least as good as any available alternative, when judged in terms of currently available standards of cognitive goodness. So such a theory would also be discredited by a theory that better satisfied those standards. Neither a defeated nor an indefeasible theory is tenable. Because it is indifferent to evidence, claptrap is indefeasible. Hence it is untenable. I said earlier that even in theories that include felicitous falsehoods truth plays a role. We see now what the role is. A factually defeasible theory has epistemically accessible implications which, if found to be false, discredit the theory. So a defeasible theory, by preserving a commitment to testable consequences retains a commitment to truth. My account then does not turn science into a genre of fiction. Quine said that the sentences of a theory face the tribunal of experience as a corporate body (Quine, 1961, p. 41). Although he recognized that not all the members of the corporation could be separately tested against experience, he probably believed that all were supposed to be fine, upstanding truths. I suggest that this is not so. An acceptable theory must make its case before the tribunal of experience. But the members of the corporation are more various and some a bit shadier than Quine suspected.

Notes

1   I use the term "theory" broadly, to comprehend the ways mature sciences and other disciplines account for the phenomena in their domains. Under my usage, a physical theory would include its models rather than being distinct from them.
2   I do not have strong intuitions about this case, but I do not think it is clearly wrong to say that the cat has such a belief.
3   Whether so-called ceteris paribus laws are really laws is a subject of controversy. See, for example, *Erkenntnis* 57, 2002, for a range of papers on the issue. Although for brevity I speak of them as laws, for my purposes, nothing hangs on whether the generalizations in questions really are laws, at least insofar as this is an ontological question. I am interested in the role such generalizations play in ongoing science. Whether or not they can (in some sense of "can") be replaced by generalizations where all the caveats and restrictions are spelled out, in practice scientists typically make no effort to do so. Nor, often, do they know (or care) how to do so.
4   i and r are the angles made by the incident beam to the normal and n_1 and n_2 are the refractive indices of the two media.
5   "The profit rate is the level of profits in the economy relative to the value of capital stock" (Bannock et al. 1998, p. 397).
6   Conceivably, of course, the equations in question will be superceded by some other understanding of the subject, but the fact that the equation we consider true does not have an analytical solution provides no reason to think so. Nor does it provide reason to think that the considerations that supersede it will be mathematically more tractable, much less that in the long run science will be free of all such irksome equations.
7   I am indebted to Amelie Rorty for this example.
8   This is why Nancy Cartwright thinks the laws of physics lie. The laws are developed on the basis of, and are strictly true only of, the processed samples, not their naturally occurring counterparts.
9   Actually, of course, I don't know how oracles are supposed to operate. I have always assumed that they simply emit true sentences like "Socrates is the wisest of men."

References

Adler, Jonathan. (2002) *Belief's Own Ethics*, Cambridge, MA: MIT.

Bannock, Graham, R.E. Baxter, Evan Davis. (1998) *Dictionary of Economics*, New York: John Wiley and Sons.

BonJour, Laurence. (1985) *The Structure of Empirical Knowledge*, Cambridge, MA: Harvard.

Cartwright, Nancy. (1983) *How the Laws of Physics Lie*, Oxford: Oxford.

Cohen, L. Jonathan. (1992) *An Essay on Belief and Acceptance*, Oxford: Clarendon.

Dennett, Daniel. (1991) "Real Patterns," *Journal of Philosophy* 88, pp. 27–51.

Elgin, Catherine Z. (1996) *Considered Judgment*, Princeton: Princeton.

Goldman, Alvin. (1999) *Knowledge in a Social World*, Oxford: Clarendon.

Goodman, Nelson. (1968) *Languages of Art*, Indianapolis: Hackett.

Kitcher, Philip. (1993) *The Advancement of Science*, Oxford: Oxford.

Lehrer, Keith. (1986) "The Coherence Theory of Knowledge," *Philosophical Topics* 14, pp. 5–25.

Lewis, David. (1983) "Truth in Fiction," *Philosophical Papers I*, Oxford: Oxford, pp. 261–81.

——. (1973) *Counterfactuals*, Cambridge, MA: Harvard.

Morrison, Margaret. (1999) "Models as Autonomous Agents," *Models as Mediators*, ed. Mary S. Morgan and Margaret Morrison, Cambridge: Cambridge, pp. 38–65.

Quine, W. V. (1961) "Two Dogmas of Empiricism," *From a Logical Point of View*, New York: Harper & Row, pp. 20–46.

Sklar, Lawrence. (1999) "Philosophy of Science," *Cambridge Dictionary of Philosophy*, ed. Robert Audi, Cambridge: Cambridge, pp. 700–4.

Sosa, Ernest. (2000) "Skepticism and Contextualism," *Skepticism*, ed. Ernest Sosa and Enrique Villanueva, Boston: Blackwell, pp. 1–18.

Stalnaker, Robert. (1987) *Inquiry*, Cambridge, MA: MIT Press.

Walton, Kendall. (1990) *Mimesis as Make-Believe*, Cambridge, MA: Harvard.

Wedgwood, Ralph. (2002) "The Aim of Belief," *Philosophical Perspectives* 16, pp. 267–97.

Yablo, Stephen. (2002) "Abstract Objects," *Philosophical Issues* 12, pp. 220–40.

——. (1998) "Does Ontology Rest on a Mistake?" *Proceedings of the Aristotelian Society*, Supplementary Volume 72, pp. 229–61.

PART VII

Naturalized Epistemology and the *A Priori*

Introduction

W. V. Quine is well known for urging the abandonment of epistemology, as tradition-ally pursued, in favor of the scientific project he calls "naturalized epistemology." Traditional epistemology, he claims, consists of two projects: one doctrinal and one conceptual. The doctrinal project aims to deduce our material object beliefs from premises about observations; the conceptual project aims to reduce material object concepts to sense experience concepts. Both projects are doomed to failure. Yet episte-mology, or something like it, "still goes on, though in a new setting and a clarified status." Epistemology becomes "a chapter of psychology and hence of natural science." Epistemology has always been concerned with the foundations of science, and rightly so, says Quine. But the relations between science and its foundations, the *evidence* on which it is based, viz. the totality of our sensory stimulations, are more usefully inves-tigated scientifically, causally. It is true that scientific theories explaining the relation between stimulation and theory themselves have their source ultimately in stimulation. Yet there is no circularity here, for there is no attempt, as there is in traditional episte-mology, to find a form of understanding better than our best science. We may legitimately use science to investigate its foundations.

One advantage of Quine's position is that it might be useful in addressing epistemo-logical questions important for feminist analysis. According to some theorists, main-stream epistemology is misguided because of its neglect of feminist epistemology. Louise Antony argues that much of the criticism by feminists of mainstream episte-mology depends upon a misreading of contemporary analytic philosophy and of the tradition from which it derives. Despite being a part of the contemporary analytic scene, Antony argues that Quine's naturalized epistemology – the view that the study of knowledge should be treated as an empirical investigation of knowers – serves as an adequate feminist epistemology. Quine's critique of epistemological foundationalism bears important similarities to contemporary feminist attacks on "modernist" concep-tions of objectivity and scientific rationality, and his positive views on the holistic nature of justification provide a theoretical basis for pressing the kinds of critical questions feminist critics are now raising. As a case study, Antony considers the bias paradox. On the one hand, feminists have been quick to challenge the liberal goal of impartiality. Not only does this ideal reinforce the power *status quo*, but it is also impossible to achieve. On the other hand, it is difficult to distinguish good from bad biases: if impartiality is impossible, then why criticize a theory or a believer for being biased? Naturalized epistemology, together with a traditional objective theory of truth, can help us make progress on these questions. We can distinguish good from bad biases by seeing which are conducive to truth and which are not. We don't see this by some form of completely unbiased, pure reason but by empirical inquiry. Of course, empirical inquiry, too, is biased but this does not mean it cannot be used to discover how things are. Empirical inquiry can expose the badness of the very androcentric biases feminists have revealed.

But naturalized epistemology has apparent difficulties. Jaegwon Kim argues that Quine is not entitled to think of naturalized epistemology as investigating the evidential foundations of science. Quine is urging us to dispense with the normative element in epistemology, yet evidence itself is a normative concept, distinct from and irreducible to the naturalistic concepts employed in science, e.g., the concepts of stimulation, causation, law, etc. Traditional epistemology asks what makes certain states, certain experiences and beliefs, evidence for other beliefs. Empirical psychology offers no help in answering this question, nor any other question about what confers positive epistemic value. Kim goes on to provide a Davidsonian argument for the claim that Quine is not even entitled to speak of naturalized epistemology as investigating the ancestry of *beliefs*. For to investigate this ancestry, one must identify beliefs, but the identification of beliefs is possible only on the assumption that one's subjects are rational, where rationality here is normative and includes epistemic rationality. If Quine's "successor subject" is to avoid the normative entirely, then *contra* Quine, it is a radically different subject from epistemology.

Kim ends his piece by providing an argument for the possibility of traditional normative epistemology. Epistemic properties, like all normative properties, are supervenient. If something is morally right, it is so because it possesses certain non-moral, ultimately non-normative, properties. There is thus a guarantee that there are correct normative epistemological principles, though not necessarily ones that admit of simple formulation, for there is a guarantee that there are non-epistemic, and ultimately non-normative, conditions that underlie epistemic properties.

So, one difficulty for naturalized epistemology is the challenge of accounting for epistemic normativity. Some philosophers worry, as well, about Quine's claim that there is no statement that is unrevisable in the face of some recalcitrant experience. On one traditional notion of the *a priori*, this is tantamount to rejecting the *a priori* entirely. Why might this be problematic? In a paper written prior to his contribution to this section, Hilary Putnam interpreted Quine's unrevisability thesis as claiming that *there are no truths that it would never be rational to give up*. (Putnam himself argued for this position on the basis of a theory of induction which, among other things, explained why certain statements *seem* to be *a priori*. The theory employed the notion of *contextual a priority*, which gives certain statements the status of being *a priori* relative to a body of knowledge.) Departing from his original sympathetic position, in the selection included here Putnam argues that there *is* at least one *a priori* truth – the Minimal Principle of Contradiction: that *not every statement is both true and false*. Putnam argues that this *a priori* truth cannot be counted as merely contextually *a priori*. In a separate note at the end of the paper Putnam challenges his own conclusion and returns to the Quinean position, above. In a final note, added some months after the last, Putnam considers his original argument, his initial recanting of the conclusion, and the epistemological value of the questions at issue.

Putnam's response to Quine grants the Quinean account of the *a priori* – that it must be immune from empirical revision – but denies that all statements are subject to empirical revision. But the nature of the *a priori* is not at all settled. Al Casullo emphasizes this point in defense of *a priori* knowledge against the Quinean challenge, firstly by showing that it is not the case that *a priori* knowledge entails rational unrevisability independent of any particular account of knowledge. *A priori* knowledge is a matter of the source of a belief, not what it takes to undermine the belief. Therefore, even if Quine is right that all statements are rationally revisable, this will not mean that there is no such thing as *a priori* knowledge. Secondly, Casullo explores the relationship between a specific account of knowledge – reliabilism – and the *a priori*. He suggests that the framework of reliabilism provides additional reasons for rejecting the thesis of rational unrevisability. Further, Casullo suggests that reliabilism is a useful account of knowledge for defending the existence of *a priori* knowledge.

A more traditional defense of *a priori* knowledge – though one consistent with Casullo's recommendation to adopt a kind of reliabilism, is provided by George Bealer's contribution. Bealer argues for two principles: (1) the thesis of the *autonomy of philosophy*, which holds that among the central questions of philosophy, most can be answered without relying on the sciences, and (2) the thesis of the *authority of philosophy*, which says that insofar as science and philosophy purport to answer the same philosophical questions, philosophy provides the better answer of the two. The method philosophers standardly use to answer philosophical questions involves canvassing and critiquing our intuitions (the procedure of *a priori* justification). Such intuitions, according to Bealer, are evidence, and modal reliabilism can explain why this is the case. Modal reliabilism states that something counts as a basic source of evidence relative to a given subject if and only if it is deemed to have a strong modal tie to the truth. But modal reliabilism implies the autonomy and authority of philosophy as long as scientific essentialism is no barrier (this being the concern that while cognitive conditions may improve, the scope of our intuitions could reach a limit). According to Bealer, however, scientific essentialism can be ruled out.

But should we place so much theoretical weight on our intuitions? Jonathan Weinberg, Shaun Nichols and Stephen Stich argue that recent empirical data concerning the diversity of epistemic intuitions should give us pause. The authors refer to the standard intuition-based methodology in contemporary philosophy as *Intuition Driven Romanticism*. The problem is that there is good reason to think that there is no such thing as "our" intuitions on the matter. Initial data suggests that intuitions regarding epistemic matters co-vary systematically with cultural and socio-economic factors. For example, people of East Asian origin are *far* more likely to grant knowledge in classic Gettier cases than those of Western descent. But if the conclusions of *Intuition Driven Romanticism* are so thoroughly affected by features such as culture, what is the normative force of these conclusions? Why should we care about epistemic principles that best explain the intuitions of a small class of epistemologists?

Not all naturalists are so skeptical about the value of intuitions. In Hilary Kornblith's selection, the first chapter of his book *Knowledge and its Place in Nature*, he argues that knowledge is a natural kind, to be investigated in the way natural kinds are investigated. This involves reliance on intuition especially early on in the investigation when it is important to pin down samples of the putative kind one wants to understand, whether it be a kind of rock or a kind of cognitive achievement. Intuitions, he emphasizes, shouldn't be understood as *a priori* insights but as a certain sort of empirical belief (exemplified in the classic cases such as Gettier cases, twin earth cases, etc.). Intuitions therefore do have their place. But they cannot reveal the nature of the kind. That is a job for theory. And theory can do this only through careful examination of the commonalties of the phenomenon.

Further Reading

Armstrong, D. M., *Belief, Truth, and Knowledge* (Cambridge: Cambridge University Press, 1973).

Boghossian, Paul, and Christopher Peacocke (eds.), *New Essays on the A Priori* (Oxford: Oxford University Press, 2001).

BonJour, Laurence, *In Defense of Pure Reason: A Rationalist Account of A Priori Justification* (Cambridge: Cambridge University Press, 1997).

Casullo, Albert, *A Priori Justification* (Oxford, Oxford University Press, 2003).

Casullo, Albert (ed.), *A Priori Knowledge* (Aldershot, UK: Ashgate, 1999).

Field, Hartry, "The A Prioricity of Logic," *Proceedings of the Aristotelian Society* 96 (1996), pp. 359–79.

——, "Epistemological Nonfactualism and the A Prioricity of Logic," *Philosophical Studies* 92 (1998), pp. 1–24.

——, "Apriority as an Evaluative Notion," in Paul Boghossian and Christopher Peacocke (eds.), *New Essays on the A Priori* (Oxford: Oxford University Press, 2000), pp. 117–49.

Foley, Richard, "Quine and Naturalized Epistemology," *Midwest Studies in Philosophy*, XIX (1994), pp. 243–61.

Goldman, Alvin, *Epistemology and Cognition* (Cambridge, MA: Harvard University Press, 1986).

——, *Liaisons: Philosophy Meets the Cognitive and Social Sciences* (Cambridge, MA: Massachusetts Institute of Technology Press, 1992).

——, "Epistemic Folkways and Scientific Epistemology," reprinted in Hilary Kornblith (ed.), *Naturalizing Epistemology*, 2nd edn (Cambridge, MA: Massachusetts Institute of Technology Press, 1994), pp. 219–315.

Haack, Susan, *Evidence and Inquiry: Towards Reconstruction in Epistemology* (Oxford: Blackwell, 1993).

Hookway, Christopher, *Quine* (Cambridge, UK: Polity Press, 1988), pt. IV.

Katz, Jerrold, *Realistic Rationalism* (Cambridge, MA: Massachusetts Institute of Technology Press, 1997).

Kitcher, Philip, "The Naturalists Return," *Philosophical Review* CI (1992), pp. 53–114.

Kornblith, Hilary, *Inductive Inference and Its Natural Ground: An Essay in Naturalized Epistemology* (Cambridge, MA: Massachusetts Institute of Technology Press, 1993).

——, *Knowledge and Its Place in Nature* (Oxford: Oxford University Press, 2005).

Kornblith, Hilary (ed.), *Naturalizing Epistemology*, 2nd edn (Cambridge, MA: Massachusetts Institute of Technology Press, 1994).

Plantinga, Alvin, *Warrant and Proper Function* (Oxford: Oxford University Press, 1993).

Quine, W. V. O., *Pursuit of Truth* (Cambridge, MA: Harvard University Press, 1992), ch. 1.

Ramsey, Michael R. and William DePaul (eds), *Rethinking Intuition* (Totowa, NJ: Rowman and Littlefield, 1999).

Sosa, Ernest, *Knowledge in Perspective: Selected Essays in Epistemology* (Cambridge: Cambridge University Press, 1991).

Stein, Edward, *Without good Reason: The Rationality Debate in Philosophy and Cognitive Science* (Oxford: Oxford University Press, 1996).

Stich, Stephen, *The Fragmentation of Reason: Preface to a Pragmatic Theory of Cognitive Evaluation* (Cambridge, MA: Massachusetts Institute of Technology Press, 1990).

Stich, Stephen and Richard Nisbett, "Justification and the Psychology of Human Reasoning," *Philosophy of Science* 47 (1980), pp. 188–202.

CHAPTER 39

Epistemology Naturalized

W. V. Quine

Epistemology is concerned with the foundations of science. Conceived thus broadly, epistemology includes the study of the foundations of mathematics as one of its departments. Specialists at the turn of the century thought that their efforts in this particular department were achieving notable success: mathematics seemed to reduce altogether to logic. In a more recent perspective this reduction is seen to be better describable as a reduction to logic and set theory. This correction is a disappointment epistemologically, since the firmness and obviousness that we associate with logic cannot be claimed for set theory. But still the success achieved in the foundations of mathematics remains exemplary by comparative standards, and we can illuminate the rest of epistemology somewhat by drawing parallels to this department.

Studies in the foundations of mathematics divide symmetrically into two sorts, conceptual and doctrinal. The conceptual studies are concerned with meaning, the doctrinal with truth. The conceptual studies are concerned with clarifying concepts by defining them, some in terms of others. The doctrinal studies are concerned with establishing laws by proving them, some on the basis of others. Ideally the more obscure concepts would be defined in terms of the clearer ones so as to maximize clarity, and the less obvious laws would be proved from the more obvious ones so as to maximize certainty. Ideally the definitions would generate all the concepts from clear and distinct ideas, and the proofs would generate all the theorems from self-evident truths.

The two ideals are linked. For, if you define all the concepts by use of some favored subset of them, you thereby show how to translate all theorems into these favored terms. The clearer these terms are, the likelier it is that the truths couched in them will be obviously true, or derivable from obvious truths. If in particular the concepts of mathematics were all reducible to the clear terms of logic, then all the truths of mathematics would go over into truths of logic; and surely the truths of logic are all obvious or at least potentially obvious, i.e., derivable from obvious truths by individually obvious steps.

This particular outcome is in fact denied us, however, since mathematics reduces only to set theory and not to logic proper. Such reduction still enhances clarity, but only because of the inter-relations that emerge and not because the end terms of the analysis are clearer than others. As for the end truths, the axioms of set theory, these have less obviousness and certainty to recommend them than do most of the mathematical theorems that we would derive from them. Moreover, we know from Gödel's work that no consistent axiom system can cover mathematics

Originally published in W. V. Quine, *Ontological Relativity and Other Essays* (New York: Columbia University Press, 1969), pp. 69–90.

even when we renounce self-evidence. Reduction in the foundations of mathematics remains mathematically and philosophically fascinating, but it does not do what the epistemologist would like of it: it does not reveal the ground of mathematical knowledge, it does not show how mathematical certainty is possible.

Still there remains a helpful thought, regarding epistemology generally, in that duality of structure which was especially conspicuous in the foundations of mathematics. I refer to the bifurcation into a theory of concepts, or meaning, and a theory of doctrine, or thruth; for this applies to the epistemology of natural knowledge no less than to the foundations of mathematics. The parallel is as follows. Just as mathematics is to be reduced to logic, or logic and set theory, so natural knowledge is to be based somehow on sense experience. This means explaining the notion of body in sensory terms; here is the conceptual side. And it means justifying our knowledge of truths of nature in sensory terms; here is the doctrinal side of the bifurcation.

Hume pondered the epistemology of natural knowledge on both sides of the bifurcation, the conceptual and the doctrinal. His handling of the conceptual side of the problem, the explanation of body in sensory terms, was bold and simple: he identified bodies outright with the sense impressions. If common sense distinguishes between the material apple and our sense impressions of it on the ground that the apple is one and enduring while the impressions are many and fleeting, then, Hume held, so much the worse for common sense; the notion of its being the same apple on one occasion and another is a vulgar confusion.

Nearly a century after Hume's *Treatise*, the same view of bodies was espoused by the early American philosopher Alexander Bryan Johnson.[1] "The word iron names an associated sight and feel," Johnson wrote.

What then of the doctrinal side, the justification of our knowledge of truths about nature? Here, Hume despaired. By his identification of bodies with impressions he did succeed in construing some singular statements about bodies as indubitable truths, yes; as truths about impressions, directly known. But general statements, also singular statements about the future, gained no increment of certainty by being construed as about impressions.

On the doctrinal side, I do not see that we are further along today than where Hume left us. The Humean predicament is the human predicament. But on the conceptual side there has been progress. There the crucial step forward was made already before Alexander Bryan Johnson's day, although Johnson did not emulate it. It was made by Bentham in his theory of fictions. Bentham's step was the recognition of contextual definition, or what he called paraphrasis. He recognized that to explain a term we do not need to specify an object for it to refer to, nor even specify a synonymous word or phrase; we need only show, by whatever means, how to translate all the whole sentences in which the term is to be used. Hume's and Johnson's desperate measure of identifying bodies with impressions ceased to be the only conceivable way of making sense of talk of bodies, even granted that impressions were the only reality. One could undertake to explain talk of bodies in terms of talk of impressions by translating one's whole sentences about bodies into whole sentences about impressions, without equating the bodies themselves to anything at all.

This idea of contextual definition, or recognition of the sentence as the primary vehicle of meaning, was indispensable to the ensuing developments in the foundations of mathematics. It was explicit in Frege, and it attained its full flower in Russell's doctrine of singular descriptions as incomplete symbols.

Contextual definition was one of two resorts that could be expected to have a liberating effect upon the conceptual side of the epistemology of natural knowledge. The other is resort to the resources of set theory as auxiliary concepts. The epistemologist who is willing to eke out his austere ontology of sense impressions with these set-theoretic auxiliaries is suddenly rich: he has not just his impressions to play with, but sets of them, and sets of sets, and so on up. Constructions in the foundations of mathematics have shown that such set-theoretic aids are a powerful addition; after all, the entire glossary of concepts of classical mathematics is constructible from them. Thus equipped, our epistemologist may not need either to identify bodies with impressions or to settle for contextual definition; he may hope to find in some subtle construction of sets upon sets of sense impressions a category of objects enjoying just the formula properties that he wants for bodies.

The two resorts are very unequal in epistemological status. Contextual definition is unassailable. Sentences that have been given meaning as wholes are undeniably meaningful, and the use they make of their component terms is therefore meaningful, regardless of whether any translations are offered for those terms in isolation. Surely Hume and A. B. Johnson would have used contextual definition with pleasure if they had thought of it. Recourse to sets, on the other hand, is a drastic ontological move, a retreat from the austere ontology of impressions. There are philosophers who would rather settle for bodies outright than accept all these sets, which amount, after all, to the whole abstract ontology of mathematics.

This issue has not always been clear, however, owing to deceptive hints of continuity between elementary logic and set theory. This is why mathematics was once believed to reduce to logic, that is, to an innocent and unquestionable logic, and to inherit these qualities. And this is probably why Russell was content to resort to sets as well as to contextual definition when in *Our Knowledge of the External World* and elsewhere he addressed himself to the epistemology of natural knowledge, on its conceptual side.

To account for the external world as a logical construct of sense data – such, in Russell's terms, was the program. It was Carnap, in his *Der logische Aufbau der Welt* of 1928, who came nearest to executing it.

This was the conceptual side of epistemology; what of the doctrinal? There the Humean predicament remained unaltered. Carnap's constructions, if carried successfully to completion, would have enabled us to translate all sentences about the world into terms of sense data, or observation, plus logic and set theory. But the mere fact that a sentence is *couched* in terms of observation, logic, and set theory does not mean that it can be *proved* from observation sentences by logic and set theory. The most modest of generalizations about observable traits will cover more cases than its utterer can have had occasion actually to observe. The hopelessness of grounding natural science upon immediate experience in a firmly logical way was acknowledged. The Cartesian quest for certainty had been the remote motivation of epistemology, both on its conceptual and its doctrinal side; but that quest was seen

as a lost cause. To endow the truths of nature with the full authority of immediate experience was as forlorn a hope as hoping to endow the truths of mathematics with the potential obviousness of elementary logic.

What then could have motivated Carnap's heroic efforts on the conceptual side of epistemology, when hope of certainty on the doctrinal side was abandoned? There were two good reasons still. One was that such constructions could be expected to elicit and clarify the sensory evidence for science, even if the inferential steps between sensory evidence and scientific doctrine must fall short of certainty. The other reason was that such constructions would deepen our understanding of our discourse about the world, even apart from questions of evidence; it would make all cognitive discourse as clear as observation terms and logic and, I must regretfully add, set theory.

It was sad for epistemologists, Hume and others, to have to acquiesce in the impossibility of strictly deriving the science of the external world from sensory evidence. Two cardinal tenets of empiricism remained unassailable, however, and so remain to this day. One is that whatever evidence there *is* for science *is* sensory evidence. The other, to which I shall return, is that all inculcation of meanings of words must rest ultimately on sensory evidence. Hence the continuing attractiveness of the idea of a *logischer Aufbau* in which the sensory content of discourse would stand forth explicitly.

If Carnap had successfully carried such a construction through, how could he have told whether it was the right one? The question would have had no point. He was seeking what he called a *rational reconstruction*. Any construction of physicalistic discourse in terms of sense experience, logic, and set theory would have been seen as satisfactory if it made the physicalistic discourse come out right. If there is one way there are many, but any would be a great achievement.

But why all this creative reconstruction, all this make-believe? The stimulation of his sensory receptors is all the evidence anybody has had to go on, ultimately, in arriving at his picture of the world. Why not just see how this construction really proceeds? Why not settle for psychology? Such a surrender of the epistemological burden to psychology is a move that was disallowed in earlier times as circular reasoning. If the epistemologist's goal is validation of the grounds of empirical science, he defeats his purpose by using psychology or other empirical science in the validation. However, such scruples against circularity have little point once we have stopped dreaming of deducing science from observations. If we are out simply to understand the link between observation and science, we are well advised to use any available information, including that provided by the very science whose link with observation we are seeking to understand.

But there remains a different reason, unconnected with fears of circularity, for still favoring creative reconstruction. We should like to be able to *translate* science into logic and observation terms and set theory. This would be a great epistemological achievement, for it would show all the rest of the concepts of science to be theoretically superfluous. It would legitimize them – to whatever degree the concepts of set theory, logic, and observation are themselves legitimate – by showing that everything done with the one apparatus could in principle be done with the other. If psychology itself could deliver a truly translational reduction of this kind, we should welcome it; but certainly it cannot, for certainly we did not grow up learning definitions of physicalistic language in terms of a prior language of set theory, logic, and observation. Here, then, would be good reason for persisting in a rational reconstruction: we want to establish the essential innocence of physical concepts, by showing them to be theoretically dispensable.

The fact is, though, that the construction which Carnap outlined in *Der logische Aufbau der Welt* does not give translational reduction either. It would not even if the outline were filled in. The crucial point comes where Carnap is explaining how to assign sense qualities to positions in physical space and time. These assignments are to be made in such a way as to fulfill, as well as possible, certain desiderata which he states, and with growth of experience the assignments are to be revised to suit. This plan, however illuminating, does not offer any key to *translating* the sentences of science into terms of observation, logic, and set theory.

We must despair of any such reduction. Carnap had despaired of it by 1936, when, in "Testability and Meaning,"[2] he introduced so-called

reduction forms of a type weaker than definition. Definitions had shown always how to translate sentences into equivalent sentences. Contextual definition of a term showed how to translate sentences containing the term into equivalent sentences lacking the term. Reduction forms of Carnap's liberalized kind, on the other hand, do not in general give equivalences; they give implications. They explain a new term, if only partially, by specifying some sentences which are implied by sentences containing the term, and other sentences which imply sentences containing the term.

It is tempting to suppose that the countenancing of reduction forms in this liberal sense is just one further step of liberalization comparable to the earlier one, taken by Bentham, of countenancing contextual definition. The former and sterner kind of rational reconstruction might have been represented as a fictious history in which we imagined our ancestors introducing the terms of physicalistic discourse on a phenomenalistic and set-theoretic basis by a succession of contextual definitions. The new and more liberal kind of rational reconstruction is a fictitious history in which we imagine our ancestors introducing those terms by a succession rather of reduction forms of the weaker sort.

This, however, is a wrong comparison. The fact is rather that the former and sterner kind of rational reconstruction, where definition reigned, embodied no fictitious history at all. It was nothing more nor less than a set of directions – or would have been, if successful – for accomplishing everything in terms of phenomena and set theory that we now accomplish in terms of bodies. It would have been a true reduction by translation, a legitimation by elimination. *Definire est eliminare*. Rational reconstruction by Carnap's later and looser reduction forms does none of this.

To relax the demand for definition, and settle for a kind of reduction that does not eliminate, is to renounce the last remaining advantage that we supposed rational reconstruction to have over straight psychology; namely, the advantage of translational reduction. If all we hope for is a reconstruction that links science to experience in explicit ways short of translation, then it would seem more sensible to settle for psychology. Better to discover how science is in fact developed and learned than to fabricate a fictitious structure to a similar effect.

The empiricist made one major concession when he despaired of deducing the truths of nature from sensory evidence. In despairing now even of translating those truths into terms of observation and logico-mathematical auxiliaries, he makes another major concession. For suppose we hold, with the old empiricist Peirce, that the very meaning of a statement consists in the difference its truth would make to possible experience. Might we not formulate, in a chapter-length sentence in observational language, all the difference that the truth of a given statement might make to experience, and might we not then take all this as the translation? Even if the difference that the truth of the statement would make to experience ramifies indefinitely, we might still hope to embrace it all in the logical implications of our chapter-length formulation, just as we can axiomatize an infinity of theorems. In giving up hope of such translation, then, the empiricist is conceding that the empirical meanings of typical statements about the external world are inaccessible and ineffable.

How is this inaccessibility to be explained? Simply on the ground that the experiential implications of a typical statement about bodies are too complex for finite axiomatization, however lengthy? No; I have a different explanation. It is that the typical statement about bodies has no fund of experiential implications it can call its own. A substantial mass of theory, taken together, will commonly have experiential implications; this is how we make verifiable predictions. We may not be able to explain why we arrive at theories which make successful predictions, but we do arrive at such theories.

Sometimes also an experience implied by a theory fails to come off; and then, ideally, we declare the theory false. But the failure falsifies only a block of theory as a whole, a conjunction of many statements. The failure shows that one or more of those statements is false, but it does not show which. The predicted experiences, true and false, are not implied by any one of the component statements of the theory rather than another. The component statements simply do not have empirical meanings, by Peirce's standard, but a sufficiently inclusive portion of theory does. If we can aspire to a sort of *logischer Aufbau der Welt* at

all, it must be to one in which the texts slated for translation into observational and logico-mathematical terms are mostly broad theories taken as wholes, rather than just terms or short sentences. The translation of a theory would be a ponderous axiomatization of all the experiential difference that the truth of the theory would make. It would be a queer translation, for it would translate the whole but none of the parts. We might better speak in such a case not of translation but simply of observational evidence for theories; and we may, following Peirce, still fairly call this the empirical meaning of the theories.

These considerations raise a philosophical question even about ordinary unphilosophical translation, such as from English into Arunta or Chinese. For, if the English sentences of a theory have their meaning only together as a body, then we can justify their translation into Arunta only together as a body. There will be no justification for pairing off the component English sentences with component Arunta sentences, except as these correlations make the translation of the theory as a whole come out right. Any translations of the English sentences into Arunta sentences will be as correct as any other, so long as the net empirical implications of the theory as a whole are preserved in translation. But it is to be expected that many different ways of translating the component sentences, essentially different individually, would deliver the same empirical implications for the theory as a whole; deviations in the translation of one component sentence could be compensated for in the translation of another component sentence. Insofar, there can be no ground for saying which of two glaringly unlike translations of individual sentences is right.[3]

For an uncritical mentalist, no such indeterminacy threatens. Every term and every sentence is a label attached to an idea, simple or complex, which is stored in the mind. When on the other hand we take a verification theory of meaning seriously, the indeterminacy would appear to be inescapable. The Vienna Circle espoused a verification theory of meaning but did not take it seriously enough. If we recognize with Peirce that the meaning of a sentence turns purely on what would count as evidence for its truth, and if we recognize with Duhem that theoretical sentences have their evidence not as single sentences but only as larger blocks of theory, then the indeterminacy of translation of theoretical sentences is the natural conclusion. And most sentences, apart from observation sentences, are theoretical. This conclusion, conversely, once it is embraced, seals the fate of any general notion of propositional meaning or, for that matter, state of affairs.

Should the unwelcomeness of the conclusion persuade us to abandon the verification theory of meaning? Certainly not. The sort of meaning that is basic to translation, and to the learning of one's own language, is necessarily empirical meaning and nothing more. A child learns his first words and sentences by hearing and using them in the presence of appropriate stimuli. These must be external stimuli, for they must act both on the child and on the speaker from whom he is learning.[4] Language is socially inculcated and controlled; the inculcation and control turn strictly on the keying of sentences to shared stimulation. Internal factors may vary *ad libitum* without prejudice to communication as long as the keying of language to external stimuli is undisturbed. Surely one has no choice but to be an empiricist so far as one's theory of linguistic meaning is concerned.

What I have said of infant learning applies equally to the linguist's learning of a new language in the field. If the linguist does not lean on related languages for which there are previously accepted translation practices, then obviously he had no data but the concomitances of native utterance and observable stimulus situation. No wonder there is indeterminacy of translation – for of course only a small fraction of our utterances report concurrent external stimulation. Granted, the linguist will end up with unequivocal translations of everything; but only by making many arbitrary choices – arbitrary even though unconscious – along the way. Arbitrary? By this I mean that different choices could still have made everything come out right that is susceptible in principle to any kind of check.

Let me link up, in a different order, some of the points I have made. The crucial consideration behind my argument for the indeterminacy of translation was that a statement about the world does not always or usually have a separable fund of empirical consequences that it can call its own. That consideration served also to account for the impossibility of an epistemological reduction of the sort where every sentence is equated to a sentence in observational and logico-mathematical terms. And the impossibility of that sort of epistemological reduction dissipated the last advantage that rational reconstruction seemed to have over psychology.

Philosophers have rightly despaired of translating everything into observational and logico-mathematical terms. They have despaired of this even when they have not recognized, as the reason for this irreducibility, that the statements largely do not have their private bundles of empirical consequences. And some philosophers have seen in this irreducibility the bankruptcy of epistemology. Carnap and the other logical positivists of the Vienna Circle had already pressed the term "metaphysics" into pejorative use, as connoting meaninglessness; and the term "epistemology" was next. Wittgenstein and his followers, mainly at Oxford, found a residual philosophical vocation in therapy: in curing philosophers of the delusion that there were epistemological problems.

But I think that at this point it may be more useful to say rather that epistemology still goes on, though in a new setting and a clarified status. Epistemology, or something like it, simply falls into place as a chapter of psychology and hence of natural science. It studies a natural phenomenon, viz., a physical human subject. This human subject is accorded a certain experimentally controlled input – certain patterns of irradiation in assorted frequencies, for instance – and in the fullness of time the subject delivers as output a description of the three-dimensional external world and its history. The relation between the meager input and the torrential output is a relation that we are prompted to study for somewhat the same reasons that always prompted epistemology; namely, in order to see how evidence relates to theory, and in what ways one's theory of nature transcends any available evidence.

Such a study could still include, even, something like the old rational reconstruction, to whatever degree such reconstruction is practicable; for imaginative constructions can afford hints of actual psychological processes, in much the way that mechanical simulations can. But a conspicuous difference between old epistemology and the epistemological enterprise in this new psychological setting is that we can now make free use of empirical psychology.

The old epistemology aspired to contain, in a sense, natural science; it would construct it somehow from sense data. Epistemology in its new setting, conversely, is contained in natural science, as a chapter of psychology. But the old containment remains valid too, in its way. We are studying how the human subject of our study posits bodies and projects his physics from his data, and we appreciate that our position in the world is just like his. Our very epistemological enterprise, therefore, and the psychology wherein it is a component chapter, and the whole of natural science wherein psychology is a component book – all this is our own construction or projection from stimulations like those we were meting out to our epistemological subject. There is thus reciprocal containment, though containment in different senses: epistemology in natural science and natural science in epistemology.

This interplay is reminiscent again of the old threat of circularity, but it is all right now that we have stopped dreaming of deducing science from sense data. We are after an understanding of science as an institution or process in the world, and we do not intend that understanding to be any better than the science which is its object. This attitude is indeed one that Neurath was already urging in Vienna Circle days, with his parable of the mariner who has to rebuild his boat while staying afloat in it.

One effect of seeing epistemology in a psychological setting is that it resolves a stubborn old enigma of epistemological priority. Our retinas are irradiated in two dimensions, yet we see things as three-dimensional without conscious inference. Which is to count as observation – the unconscious two-dimensional reception or the conscious three-dimensional apprehension? In the old epistemological context the conscious form had priority, for we were out to justify our knowledge of the external world by rational reconstruction, and that demands awareness. Awareness ceased to be demanded when we gave up trying to justify our knowledge of the external world by rational reconstruction. What to count as observation now can be settled in terms of the stimulation of sensory receptors, let consciousness fall where it may.

The Gestalt psychologists' challenge to sensory atomism, which seemed so relevant to epistemology forty years ago, is likewise deactivated.

Regardless of whether sensory atoms or Gestalten are what favor the forefront of our consciousness, it is simply the stimulations of our sensory receptors that are best looked upon as the input to our cognitive mechanism. Old paradoxes about unconscious data and inference, old problems about chains of inference that would have to be completed too quickly – these no longer matter.

In the old anti-psychologistic days the question of epistemological priority was moot. What is epistemologically prior to what? Are Gestalten prior to sensory atoms because they are noticed, or should we favor sensory atoms on some more subtle ground? Now that we are permitted to appeal to physical stimulation, the problem dissolves; A is epistemologically prior to B if A is causally nearer than B to the sensory receptors. Or, what is in some ways better, just talk explicitly in terms of causal proximity to sensory receptors and drop the talk of epistemological priority.

Around 1932 there was debate in the Vienna Circle over what to count as observation sentences, or *Protokollsätze*.[5] One position was that they had the form of reports of sense impressions. Another was that they were statements of an elementary sort about the external world, e.g., "A red cube is standing on the table." Another, Neurath's, was that they had the form of reports of relations between percipients and external things: "Otto now sees a red cube on the table." The worst of it was that there seemed to be no objective way of settling the matter: no way of making real sense of the question.

Let us now try to view the matter unreservedly in the context of the external world. Vaguely speaking, what we want of observation sentences is that they be the ones in closest causal proximity to the sensory receptors. But how is such proximity to be gauged? The idea may be rephrased this way: observation sentences are sentences which, as we learn language, are most strongly conditioned to concurrent sensory stimulation rather than to stored collateral information. Thus let us imagine a sentence queried for our verdict as to whether it is true or false, queried for our assent or dissent. Then the sentence is an observation sentence if our verdict depends only on the sensory stimulation present at the time.

But a verdict cannot depend on present stimulation to the exclusion of stored information. The very fact of our having learned the language evinces much storing of information, and of information without which we should be in no position to give verdicts on sentences however observational. Evidently then we must relax our definition of observation sentence to read thus: a sentence is an observation sentence if all verdicts on it depend on present sensory stimulation and on no stored information beyond what goes into understanding the sentence.

This formulation raises another problem: how are we to distinguish between information that goes into understanding a sentence and information that goes beyond? This is the problem of distinguishing between analytic truth, which issues from the mere meanings of words, and synthetic truth, which depends on more than meanings. Now I have long maintained that this distinction is illusory. There is one step toward such a distinction, however, which does make sense: a sentence that is true by mere meanings of words should be expected, at least if it is simple, to be subscribed to by all fluent speakers in the community. Perhaps the controversial notion of analyticity can be dispensed with, in our definition of observation sentence, in favor of this straightforward attribute of community-wide acceptance.

This attribute is of course no explication of analyticity. The community would agree that there have been black dogs, yet none who talk of analyticity would call this analytic. My rejection of the analyticity notion just means drawing no line between what goes into the mere understanding of the sentences of a language and what else the community sees eye-to-eye on. I doubt that an objective distinction can be made between meaning and such collateral information as is community-wide.

Turning back then to our task of defining observation sentences, we get this: an observation sentence is one on which all speakers of the language give the same verdict when given the same concurrent stimulation. To put the point negatively, an observation sentence is one that is not sensitive to differences in past experience within the speech community.

This formulation accords perfectly with the traditional role of the observation sentence as the court of appeal of scientific theories. For by our definition the observation sentences are the sentences on which all members of the community will agree under uniform stimulation. And what

is the criterion of membership in the same community? Simply, general fluency of dialogue. This criterion admits of degrees, and indeed we may usefully take the community more narrowly for some studies than for others. What count as observation sentences for a community of specialists would not always so count for a larger community.

There is generally no subjectivity in the phrasing of observation sentences, as we are now conceiving them; they will usually be about bodies. Since the distinguishing trait of an observation sentence is intersubjective agreement under agreeing stimulation, a corporeal subject matter is likelier than not.

The old tendency to associate observation sentences with a subjective sensory subject matter is rather an irony when we reflect that observation sentences are also meant to be the intersubjective tribunal of scientific hypotheses. The old tendency was due to the drive to base science on something firmer and prior in the subject's experience; but we dropped that project.

The dislodging of epistemology from its old status of first philosophy loosed a wave, we saw, of epistemological nihilism. This mood is reflected somewhat in the tendency of Polányi, Kuhn, and the late Russell Hanson to belittle the role of evidence and to accentuate cultural relativism. Hanson ventured even to discredit the idea of observation, arguing that so-called observations vary from observer to observer with the amount of knowledge that the observers bring with them. The veteran physicist looks at some apparatus and sees an x-ray tube. The neophyte, looking at the same place, observes rather "a glass and metal instrument replete with wires, reflectors, screws, lamps, and pushbuttons."[6] One man's observation is another man's closed book or flight of fancy. The notion of observation as the impartial and objective source of evidence for science is bankrupt. Now my answer to the x-ray example was already hinted a little while back: what counts as an observation sentence varies with the width of community considered. But we can also always get an absolute standard by taking in all speakers of the language, or most.[7] It is ironical that philosophers, finding the old epistemology untenable as a whole, should react by repudiating a part which has only now moved into clear focus.

Clarification of the notion of observation sentence is a good thing, for the notion is fundamental in two connections. These two correspond to the duality that I remarked upon early in this essay: the duality between concept and doctrine, between knowing what a sentence means and knowing whether it is true. The observation sentence is basic to both enterprises. Its relation to doctrine, to our knowledge of what is true, is very much the traditional one: observation sentences are the repository of evidence for scientific hypotheses. Its relation to meaning is fundamental too, since observation sentences are the ones we are in a position to learn to understand first, both as children and as field linguists. For observation sentences are precisely the ones that we can correlate with observable circumstances of the occasion of utterance or assent, independently of variations in the past histories of individual informants. They afford the only entry to a language.

The observation sentence is the cornerstone of semantics. For it is, as we just saw, fundamental to the learning of meaning. Also, it is where meaning is firmest. Sentences higher up in theories have no empirical consequences they can call their own; they confront the tribunal of sensory evidence only in more or less inclusive aggregates. The observation sentence, situated at the sensory periphery of the body scientific, is the minimal verifiable aggregate; it has an empirical content all its own and wears it on its sleeve.

The predicament of the indeterminacy of translation has little bearing on observation sentences. The equating of an observation sentence of our language to an observation sentence of another language is mostly a matter of empirical generalization; it is a matter of identity between the range of stimulations that would prompt assent to the one sentence and the range of stimulations that would prompt assent to the other.[8]

It is no shock to the preconceptions of old Vienna to say that epistemology now becomes semantics. For epistemology remains centered as always on evidence, and meaning remains centered as always on verification; and evidence is verification. What is likelier to shock preconceptions is that meaning, once we get beyond observation sentences, ceases in general to have any clear applicability to single sentences; also that epistemology merges with psychology, as well as with linguistics.

This rubbing out of boundaries could contribute to progress, it seems to me, in philosophically interesting inquiries of a scientific nature. One possible area is perceptual norms. Consider, to begin with, the linguistic phenomenon of phonemes. We form the habit, in hearing the myriad variations of spoken sounds, of treating each as an approximation to one or another of a limited number of norms – around thirty altogether – constituting so to speak a spoken alphabet. All speech in our language can be treated in practice as sequences of just those thirty elements, thus rectifying small deviations. Now outside the realm of language also there is probably only a rather limited alphabet of perceptual norms altogether, toward which we tend unconsciously to rectify all perceptions. These, if experimentally identified, could be taken as epistemological building blocks, the working elements of experience. They might prove in part to be culturally variable, as phonemes are, and in part universal.

Again there is the area that the psychologist Donald T. Campbell calls evolutionary epistemology.[9] In this area there is work by Hüseyin Yilmaz, who shows how some structural traits of color perception could have been predicted from survival value.[10] And a more emphatically epistemological topic that evolution helps to clarify is induction, now that we are allowing epistemology the resources of natural science.[11]

Notes

1 A. B. Johnson, *A Treatise on Language* (New York, 1836; Berkeley, 1947).

2 Carnap, *Philosophy of Science* 3 (1936), pp. 419–71; 4 (1937), pp. 1–40.

3 See Quine, *Ontological Relativity* (New York: Columbia University Press, 1969), pp. 2ff.

4 See ibid., p. 28.

5 Carnap and Neurath in *Erkenntnis* 3 (1932), pp. 204–28.

6 N. R. Hanson, "Observation and Interpretation," in S. Morgenbesser (ed.), *Philosophy of Science Today* (New York: Basic Books, 1966).

7   This qualification allows for occasional devi-
ants such as the insane or the blind.
Alternatively, such cases might be excluded by
adjusting the level of fluency of dialogue
whereby we define sameness of language. (For
prompting this note and influencing the
development of this essay also in more substantial ways I am indebted to Burton
Dreben.)

8   Cf. Quine, *Word and Object* (Cambridge, MA:
MIT Press, 1960), pp. 31–46, 68.

9   D. T. Campbell, "Methodological Suggestions from a Comparative Psychology of
Knowledge Processes," *Inquiry* 2 (1959),
pp. 152–82.

10 Hüseyin Yilmaz, "On Color Vision and a
New Approach to General Perception," in
E. E. Bernard and M. R. Kare (eds), *Biological
Prototypes and Synthetic Systems* (New York:
Plenum, 1962); "Perceptual Invariance and
the Psychophysical Law," *Perception and
Psychophysics* 2 (1967), pp. 533–8.

11 See Quine, "Natural Kinds," in *Ontological
Relativity*, ch. 5.

CHAPTER 40

What Is "Naturalized Epistemology"?

Jaegwon Kim

Epistemology as a Normative Inquiry

Descartes's epistemological inquiry in the *Meditations* begins with this question: What propositions are worthy of belief? In the First Meditation Descartes canvasses beliefs of various kinds he had formerly held as true and finds himself forced to conclude that he ought to reject them, that he ought not to accept them as true. We can view Cartesian epistemology as consisting of the following two projects: to identify the criteria by which we ought to regulate acceptance and rejection of beliefs, and to determine what we may be said to know according to those criteria. Descartes's epistemological agenda has been the agenda of Western epistemology to this day. The twin problems of identifying criteria of justified belief and coming to terms with the skeptical challenge to the possibility of knowledge have defined the central tasks of theory of knowledge since Descartes. This was as true of the empiricists, of Locke and Hume and Mill, as of those who more closely followed Descartes in the rationalist path.[1]

It is no wonder then that modern epistemology has been dominated by a single concept, that of *justification*, and two fundamental questions

Originally published in J. Tomberlin (ed.), *Philosophical Perspectives*, 2. Epistemology (Atascadero, CA: Ridgeview Publishing Co., 1988), pp. 381–405.

involving it: What conditions must a belief meet if we are justified in accepting it as true? and What beliefs are we in fact justified in accepting? Note that the first question does not ask for an "analysis" or "meaning" of the term "justified belief." And it is generally assumed, even if not always explicitly stated, that not just any statement of a necessary and sufficient condition for a belief to be justified will do. The implicit requirement has been that the stated conditions must constitute "criteria" of justified belief, and for this it is necessary that the conditions be stated *without the use of epistemic terms*. Thus, formulating conditions of justified belief in such terms as "adequate evidence," "sufficient ground," "good reason," "beyond a reasonable doubt," and so on, would be merely to issue a promissory note redeemable only when these epistemic terms are themselves explained in a way that accords with the requirement.[2]

This requirement, while it points in the right direction, does not go far enough. What is crucial is this: *the criteria of justified belief must be formulated on the basis of descriptive or naturalistic terms alone, without the use of any evaluative or normative ones, whether epistemic or of another kind.*[3] Thus, an analysis of justified belief that makes use of such terms as "intellectual requirement"[4] and "having a right to be sure"[5] would not satisfy this generalized condition; although such an analysis can be informative and enlightening about the interrelationships of these normative concepts, it will not, on the present conception, count as a statement of *criteria* of justified belief, unless of course these terms are themselves provided with nonnormative criteria. What is problematic, therefore, about the use of epistemic terms in stating criteria of justified belief is not its possible circularity in the usual sense; rather it is the fact that these epistemic terms are themselves essentially normative. We shall later discuss the rationale of this strengthened requirement.

As many philosophers have observed,[6] the two questions we have set forth, one about the criteria of justified belief and the other about what we can be said to know according to those criteria, constrain each other. Although some philosophers have been willing to swallow skepticism just because what we regard as correct criteria of justified belief are seen to lead inexorably to the conclusion that none, or very few, of our beliefs are justified, the usual presumption is that our answer to the first question should leave our epistemic situation largely unchanged. That is to say, it is expected to turn out that according to the criteria of justified belief we come to accept, we know, or are justified in believing, pretty much what we reflectively think we know or are entitled to believe.

Whatever the exact history, it is evident that the concept of justification has come to take center stage in our reflections on the nature of knowledge. And apart from history, there is a simple reason for our preoccupation with justification: it is the only specifically epistemic component in the classic tripartite conception of knowledge. Neither belief nor truth is a specifically epistemic notion: belief is a psychological concept and truth a semantical-metaphysical one. These concepts may have an implicit epistemological dimension, but if they do, it is likely to be through their involvement with essentially normative epistemic notions like justification, evidence, and rationality. Moreover, justification is what makes knowledge itself a normative concept. On the surface at least, neither truth nor belief is normative or evaluative (I shall argue below, though, that belief does have an essential normative dimension). But justification manifestly is normative. If a belief is justified for us, then it is *permissible* and *reasonable*, from the epistemic point of view, for us to hold it, and it would be *epistemically irresponsible* to hold beliefs

that contradict it. If we consider believing or accepting a proposition to be an "action" in an appropriate sense, belief justification would then be a special case of justification of action, which in its broadest terms is the central concern of normative ethics. Just as it is the business of normative ethics to delineate the conditions under which acts and decisions are justified from the moral point of view, so it is the business of epistemology to identify and analyze the conditions under which beliefs, and perhaps other propositional attitudes, are justified from the epistemological point of view. It probably is only an historical accident that we standardly speak of "normative ethics" but not of "normative epistemology." Epistemology is a normative discipline as much as, and in the same sense as, normative ethics.

We can summarize our discussion thus far in the following points: that justification is a central concept of our epistemological tradition, that justification, as it is understood in this tradition, is a normative concept, and in consequence that epistemology itself is a normative inquiry whose principal aim is a systematic study of the conditions of justified belief. I take it that these points are uncontroversial, although of course there could be disagreement about the details – for example, about what it means to say a concept or theory is "normative" or "evaluative."

The Foundationalist Strategy

In order to identify the target of the naturalistic critique – in particular, Quine's – it will be useful to take a brief look at the classic response to the epistemological program set forth by Descartes. Descartes's approach to the problem of justification is a familiar story, at least as the textbook tells it: it takes the form of what is now commonly called "foundationalism." The foundationalist strategy is to divide the task of explaining justification into two stages: first, to identify a set of beliefs that are "directly" justified in that they are justified without deriving their justified status from that of any other belief, and then to explain how other beliefs may be "indirectly" or "inferentially" justified by standing in an appropriate relation to those already justified. Directly justified beliefs, or "basic beliefs," are to constitute the foundation upon which the superstructure of "nonbasic" or "derived" beliefs is to rest. What beliefs then are directly justified, according to Descartes? Subtleties aside, he claimed that beliefs about our own present conscious states are among them. In what does their justification consist? What is it about these beliefs that makes them directly justified? Somewhat simplistically again, Descartes's answer is that they are justified because they are *indubitable*, that the attentive and reflective mind *cannot but assent* to them. How are nonbasic beliefs justified? By "deduction" – that is, by a series of inferential steps, or "intuitions," each of which is indubitable. If, therefore, we take Cartesian indubitability as a psychological notion, Descartes's epistemological theory can be said to meet the desideratum of providing nonepistemic, naturalistic criteria of justified belief.

Descartes's foundationalist program was inherited, in its essential outlines, by the empiricists. In particular, his "mentalism," that beliefs about one's own current mental state are epistemologically basic, went essentially unchallenged by the empiricists and positivists, until this century. Epistemologists have differed from one another chiefly in regard to two questions: first, what else belonged in our corpus of basic beliefs, and second, how the derivation of the nonbasic part of our knowledge was to proceed. Even the Logical Positivists were, by and large, foundationalists, although some of them came to renounce Cartesian mentalism in favor of a "physicalistic basis."[7] In fact, the Positivists were foundationalists twice over: for them "observation," whether phenomenological or physical, served not only as the foundation of knowledge but as the foundation of all "cognitive meaning" – that is, as both an epistemological and a semantic foundation.

Quine's Arguments

It has become customary for epistemologists who profess allegiance to a "naturalistic" conception of knowledge to pay homage to Quine as the chief contemporary provenance of their inspiration – especially to his influential paper "Epistemology Naturalized."[8] Quine's principal argument in this paper against traditional epistemology is based on the claim that the Cartesian foundationalist

program has failed – that the Cartesian "quest for certainty" is "a lost cause." While this claim about the hopelessness of the Cartesian "quest for certainty" is nothing new, using it to discredit the very conception of normative epistemology is new, something that any serious student of epistemology must contend with.

Quine divides the classic epistemological program into two parts: *conceptual reduction* whereby physical terms, including those of theoretical science, are reduced, via definition, to terms referring to phenomenal features of sensory experience, and *doctrinal reduction* whereby truths about the physical world are appropriately obtained from truths about sensory experience. The "appropriateness" just alluded to refers to the requirement that the favored epistemic status ("certainty" for classic epistemologists, according to Quine) of our basic beliefs be transferred, essentially undiminished, to derived beliefs, a necessary requirement if the derivational process is to yield knowledge from knowledge. What derivational methods have this property of preserving epistemic status? Perhaps there are none, given our proneness to err in framing derivations as in anything else, not to mention the possibility of lapses of attention and memory in following lengthy proofs. But logical deduction comes as close to being one as any; it can at least be relied on to transmit truth, if not epistemic status. It could perhaps be argued that no method can preserve certainty unless it preserves (or is known to preserve) truth; and if this is so, logical deduction is the only method worth considering. I do not know whether this was the attitude of most classic epistemologists; but Quine assumes that if deduction doesn't fill their bill, nothing will.

Quine sees the project of conceptual reduction as culminating in Carnap's *Der logische Aufbau der Welt*. As Quine sees it, Carnap "came nearest to executing" the conceptual half of the classic epistemological project. But coming close is not good enough. Because of the holistic manner in which empirical meaning is generated by experience, no reduction of the sort Carnap and others so eagerly sought could in principle be completed. For definitional reduction requires point-to-point meaning relations[9] between physical terms and phenomenal terms, something that Quine's holism tells us cannot be had. The second half of the program, doctrinal reduction, is in no better shape; in fact, it was the one to stumble first, for, according to Quine, its impossibility was decisively demonstrated long before the *Aufbau*, by Hume in his celebrated discussion of induction. The "Humean predicament" shows that theory cannot be logically deduced from observation; there simply is no way of deriving theory from observation that will transmit the latter's epistemic status intact to the former.

I don't think anyone wants to disagree with Quine in these claims. It is not possible to "validate" science on the basis of sensory experience, if "validation" means justification through logical deduction. Quine of course does not deny that our theories depend on observation for evidential support; he has said that sensory evidence is the only evidence there is. To be sure, Quine's argument against the possibility of conceptual reduction has a new twist: the application of his "holism." But his conclusion is no surprise; "translational phenomenalism" has been moribund for many years.[10] And, as Quine himself notes, his argument against the doctrinal reduction, the "quest for certainty," is only a restatement of Hume's "skeptical" conclusions concerning induction: induction after all is not deduction. Most of us are inclined, I think, to view the situation Quine describes with no great alarm, and I rather doubt that these conclusions of Quine's came as news to most epistemologists when "Epistemology Naturalized" was first published. We are tempted to respond: of course we can't define physical concepts in terms of sense-data; of course observation "underdetermines" theory. That is why observation is observation and not theory.

So it is agreed on all hands that the classical epistemological project, conceived as one of deductively validating physical knowledge from indubitable sensory data, cannot succeed. But what is the moral of this failure? What should be its philosophical lesson to us? Having noted the failure of the Cartesian program, Quine goes on:[11]

> The stimulation of his sensory receptors is all the evidence anybody has had to go on, ultimately, in arriving at his picture of the world. Why not just see how this construction really proceeds? Why not settle for psychology? Such a surrender of the epistemological burden to psychology is a

move that was disallowed in earlier times as circular reasoning. If the epistemologist's goal is validation of the grounds of empirical science, he defeats his purpose by using psychology or other empirical science in the validation. However, such scruples against circularity have little point once we have stopped dreaming of deducing science from observation. If we are out simply to understand the link between observation and science, we are well advised to use any available information, including that provided by the very science whose link with observation we are seeking to understand.

And Quine has the following to say about the failure of Carnap's reductive program in the *Aufbau*:[12]

> To relax the demand for definition, and settle for a kind of reduction that does not eliminate, is to renounce the last remaining advantage that we supposed rational reconstruction to have over straight psychology; namely, the advantage of translational reduction. If all we hope for is a reconstruction that links science to experience in explicit ways short of translation, then it would seem more sensible to settle for psychology. Better to discover how science is in fact developed and learned than to fabricate a fictitious structure to a similar effect.

If a task is entirely hopeless, if we know it cannot be executed, no doubt it is rational to abandon it; we would be better off doing something else that has some hope of success. We can agree with Quine that the "validation" – that is, logical deduction – of science on the basis of observation cannot be had; so it is rational to abandon this particular epistemological program, if indeed it ever was a program that anyone seriously undertook. But Quine's recommendations go further. In particular, there are two aspects of Quine's proposals that are of special interest to us: first, he is not only advising us to quit the program of "validating science," but urging us to take up another specific project, an empirical psychological study of our cognitive processes; second, he is also claiming that this new program replaces the old, that both programs are part of something appropriately called "epistemology." Naturalized epistemology is to be a kind of epistemology after all, a "successor subject"[13] to classical epistemology.

How should we react to Quine's urgings? What should be our response? The Cartesian project of validating science starting from the indubitable foundation of first-person psychological reports (perhaps with the help of certain indubitable first principles) is not the whole of classical epistemology – or so it would seem at first blush. In our characterization of classical epistemology, the Cartesian program was seen as one possible response to the problem of epistemic justification, the two-part project of identifying the criteria of epistemic justification and determining what beliefs are in fact justified according to those criteria. In urging "naturalized epistemology" on us, Quine is not suggesting that we give up the Cartesian foundationalist solution and explore others within the same framework[14] – perhaps, to adopt some sort of "coherentist" strategy, or to require of our basic beliefs only some degree of "initial credibility" rather than Cartesian certainty, or to permit some sort of probabilistic derivation in addition to deductive derivation of nonbasic knowledge, or to consider the use of special rules of evidence, like Chisholm's "principles of evidence,"[15] or to give up the search for a derivational process that transmits undiminished certainty in favor of one that can transmit diminished but still useful degrees of justification. Quine's proposal is more radical than that. He is asking us to set aside the entire framework of justification-centered epistemology. That is what is new in Quine's proposals. Quine is asking us to put in its place a purely descriptive, causal-nomological science of human cognition.[16]

How should we characterize in general terms the difference between traditional epistemological programs, such as foundationalism and coherence theory, on the one hand and Quine's program of naturalized epistemology on the other? Quine's stress is on the *factual* and *descriptive* character of his program; he says, "Why not see how [the construction of theory from observation] *actually proceeds? Why not settle for psychology?*";[17] again, "Better to *discover how science is in fact developed and learned than* …"[18] We are given to understand that in contrast traditional epistemology is not a descriptive, factual inquiry. Rather, it is an attempt at a "validation" or "rational reconstruction" of science. Validation, according to Quine, proceeds via deduction, and rational reconstruction via definition. However, their *point* is justificatory – that is, to rationalize our sundry knowledge claims. So

Quine is asking us to set aside what is "rational" in rational reconstruction.

Thus, it is normativity that Quine is asking us to repudiate. Although Quine does not explicitly characterize traditional epistemology as "normative" or "prescriptive," his meaning is unmistakable. Epistemology is to be "a chapter of psychology," a law-based predictive-explanatory theory, like any other theory within empirical science; its principal job is to see how human cognizers develop theories (their "picture of the world") from observation ("the stimulation of their sensory receptors"). Epistemology is to go out of the business of justification. We earlier characterized traditional epistemology as essentially normative; we see why Quine wants us to reject it. Quine is urging us to replace a normative theory of cognition with a descriptive science.

Losing Knowledge from Epistemology

If justification drops out of epistemology, knowledge itself drops out of epistemology. For our concept of knowledge is inseparably tied to that of justification. As earlier noted, knowledge itself is a normative notion. Quine's nonnormative, naturalized epistemology has no room for our concept of knowledge. It is not surprising that, in describing naturalized epistemology, Quine seldom talks about knowledge; instead, he talks about "science" and "theories" and "representations." Quine would have us investigate how sensory stimulation "leads" to "theories" and "representation" of the world. I take it that within the traditional scheme these "theories" and "representations" correspond to beliefs, or systems of beliefs; thus, what Quine would have us do is to investigate how sensory stimulation leads to the formation of beliefs about the world.

But in what sense of "lead"? I take it that Quine has in mind a causal or nomological sense. He is urging us to develop a theory, an empirical theory, that uncovers lawful regularities governing the processes through which organisms come to develop beliefs about their environment as a causal result of having their sensory receptors stimulated in certain ways. Quine says:[19]

[Naturalized epistemology] studies a natural phenomenon, viz., a physical human subject.

This human subject is accorded experimentally controlled input – certain patterns of irradiation in assorted frequencies, for instance – and in the fullness of time the subject delivers as output a description of the three-dimensional external world and its history. *The relation between the meager input and torrential output* is a relation that we are prompted to study for somewhat the same reasons that always prompted epistemology; namely, in order to see *how evidence relates to theory*, and in what ways one's theory of nature transcends any available evidence.

The relation Quine speaks of between "meager input" and "torrential output" is a causal relation; at least it is qua causal relation that the naturalized epistemologist investigates it. It is none of the naturalized epistemologist's business to assess whether, and to what degree, the input "justifies" the output, how a given irradiation of the subject's retinas makes it "reasonable" or "rational" for the subject to emit certain representational output. His interest is strictly causal and nomological: he wants us to look for patterns of lawlike dependencies characterizing the input–output relations for this particular organism and others of a like physical structure.

If this is right, it makes Quine's attempt to relate his naturalized epistemology to traditional epistemology look at best lame. For in what sense is the study of causal relationships between physical stimulation of sensory receptors and the resulting cognitive output a way of "seeing how evidence relates to theory" in an epistemologically relevant sense? The causal relation between sensory input and cognitive output is a relation between "evidence" and "theory"; however, it is not an *evidential relation*. This can be seen from the following consideration: the nomological patterns that Quine urges us to look for are certain to vary from species to species, depending on the particular way each biological (and possibly non-biological) species processes information, but the evidential relation in its proper normative sense must abstract from such factors and concern itself only with the degree to which evidence supports hypothesis.

In any event, the concept of evidence is inseparable from that of justification. When we talk of "evidence" in an epistemological sense we are talking about justification: one thing is "evidence"

for another just in case the first tends to enhance the reasonableness or justification of the second. And such evidential relations hold in part because of the "contents" of the items involved, not merely because of the causal or nomological connections between them. A strictly nonnormative concept of evidence is not our concept of evidence; it is something that we do not understand.[20]

None of us, I think, would want to quarrel with Quine about the interest or importance of the psychological study of how our sensory input causes our epistemic output. This is only to say that the study of human (or other kinds of) cognition is of interest. That isn't our difficulty; our difficulty is whether, and in what sense, pursuing Quine's "epistemology" is a way of doing epistemology – that is, a way of studying "how evidence relates to theory." Perhaps, Quine's recommendation that we discard justification-centered epistemology is worth pondering; and his exhortation to take up the study of psychology perhaps deserves to be heeded also. What is mysterious is why this recommendation has to be coupled with the rejection of normative epistemology (if normative epistemology is not a possible inquiry, why shouldn't the would-be epistemologist turn to, say, hydro-dynamics or ornithology rather than psychology?). But of course Quine is saying more; he is saying that an understandable, if misguided, motivation (that is, seeing "how evidence relates to theory") does underlie our proclivities for indulgence in normative epistemology, but that we would be better served by a scientific study of human cognition than normative epistemology.

But it is difficult to see how an "epistemology" that has been purged of normativity, one that lacks an appropriate normative concept of justification or evidence, can have anything to do with the concerns of traditional epistemology. And unless naturalized epistemology and classical epistemology share some of their central concerns, it's difficult to see how one could *replace* the other, or be a way (a better way) of doing the other.[21] To be sure, they both investigate "how evidence relates to theory." But putting the matter this way can be misleading, and has perhaps misled Quine: the two disciplines do not investigate the same relation. As lately noted, normative epistemology is concerned with the evidential relation properly so-called – that is, the relation

of justification – and Quine's naturalized epistemology is meant to study the causal – nomological relation. For epistemology to go out of the
business of justification is for it to go out of
business.

Belief Attribution and Rationality

Perhaps we have said enough to persuade ourselves that Quine's naturalized epistemology,
while it may be a legitimate scientific inquiry, is
not a kind of epistemology, and, therefore, that
the question whether it is a better kind of epistemology cannot arise. In reply, however, it might
be said that there was a sense in which Quine's
epistemology and traditional epistemology could
be viewed as sharing a common subject matter,
namely this: they both concern beliefs or "representations." The only difference is that the former
investigates their causal histories and connections
whereas the latter is concerned with their evidential or justificatory properties and relations. This
difference, if Quine is right, leads to another
(so continues the reply): the former is a feasible
inquiry, the latter is not.

I now want to take my argument a step further: I shall argue that the concept of belief is
itself an essentially normative one, and in consequence that if normativity is wholly excluded
from naturalized epistemology it cannot even be
thought of as being about beliefs. That is, if naturalized epistemology is to be a science of beliefs
properly so called, it must presuppose a normative concept of belief.

Briefly, the argument is this. In order to implement Quine's program of naturalized epistemology, we shall need to identify, and individuate,
the input and output of cognizers. The input, for
Quine, consists of physical events ("the stimulation of sensory receptors") and the output is said
to be a "theory" or "picture of the world" – that is,
a set of "representations" of the cognizer's environment. Let us focus on the output. In order to
study the sensory input–cognitive output relations for the given cognizer, therefore, we must
find out what "representations" he has formed as
a result of the particular stimulations that have
been applied to his sensory transducers. Setting
aside the jargon, what we need to be able to do is
to attribute *beliefs*, and other contentful

intentional states, to the cognizer. But belief attribution ultimately requires a "radical interpretation" of the cognizer, of his speech and intentional
states; that is, we must construct an "interpretive
theory" that simultaneously assigns meanings to
his utterances and attributes to him beliefs and
other propositional attitudes.[22]

Even a cursory consideration indicates that
such an interpretation cannot begin – we cannot
get a foothold in our subject's realm of meanings
and intentional states – unless we assume his total
system of beliefs and other propositional attitudes to be largely and essentially rational and
coherent. As Davidson has emphasized, a given
belief has the content it has in part because of its
location in a network of other beliefs and propositional attitudes; and what at bottom grounds
this network is the evidential relation, a relation
that regulates what is reasonable to believe given
other beliefs one holds. That is, unless our cognizer is a "rational being," a being whose cognitive
"output" is regulated and constrained by norms
of rationality – typically, these norms holistically
constrain his propositional attitudes in virtue of
their contents – we cannot intelligibly interpret
his "output" as consisting of beliefs. Conversely, if
we are unable to interpret our subject's meanings
and propositional attitudes in a way that satisfies
a minimal standard of rationality, there is little
reason to regard him as a "cognizer," a being that
forms representations and constructs theories.
This means that there is a sense of "rational" in
which the expression "rational belief" is redundant; every belief must be rational in certain minimal ways. It is not important for the purposes of
the present argument what these minimal standards of rationality are; the only point that matters
is that unless the output of our cognizer is subject
to evaluation in accordance with norms of rationality, that output cannot be considered as consisting of beliefs and hence cannot be the object of
an epistemological inquiry, whether plain or
naturalized.

We can separate the core of these considerations from controversial issues involving the
so-called "principle of charity," minimal rationality, and other matters in the theory of radical
interpretation. What is crucial is this: for the interpretation and attribution of beliefs to be possible,
not only must we assume the overall rationality of
cognizers, but also we must continually evaluate

and re-evaluate the putative beliefs of a cognizer in their evidential relationship to one another and other propositional attitudes. It is not merely that belief attribution requires the umbrella assumption about the overall rationality of cognizers. Rather, the point is that *belief attribution requires belief evaluation*, in accordance with normative standards of evidence and justification. If this is correct, rationality in its broad and fundamental sense is not an optional property of beliefs, a virtue that some beliefs may enjoy and others lack; it is a precondition of the attribution and individuation of belief – that is, a property without which the concept of belief would be unintelligible and pointless.

Two objections might be raised to counter these considerations. First, one might argue that at best they show only that the normativity of belief is an epistemological assumption – that we need to assume the rationality and coherence of belief systems when we are trying to *find out* what beliefs to attribute to a cognizer. It does not follow from this epistemological point, the objection continues, that the concept of belief is itself normative.[23] In replying to this objection, we can bypass the entire issue of whether the rationality assumption concerns only the epistemology of belief attribution. Even if this premise (which I think is incorrect) is granted, the point has already been made. For it is an essential part of the business of naturalized epistemology, as a theory of how beliefs are formed as a result of sensory stimulation, to *find out* what particular beliefs the given cognizers have formed. But this is precisely what cannot be done, if our considerations show anything at all, unless the would-be naturalized epistemologist continually evaluates the putative beliefs of his subjects in regard to their rationality and coherence, subject to the overall constraint of the assumption that the cognizers are largely rational. The naturalized epistemologist cannot dispense with normative concepts or disengage himself from valuational activities.

Second, it might be thought that we could simply avoid these considerations stemming from belief attribution by refusing to think of cognitive output as consisting of "beliefs," namely as states having propositional contents. The "representations" Quine speaks of should be taken as appropriate neural states, and this means that all we need is to be able to discern neural states of organisms. This requires only neurophysiology and the like, not the normative theory of rational belief. My reply takes the form of a dilemma: either the "appropriate" neural states are identified by seeing how they correlate with beliefs,[24] in which case we still need to contend with the problem of radical interpretation, or beliefs are entirely bypassed. In the latter case, belief, along with justification, drops out of Quinean epistemology, and it is unclear in what sense we are left with an inquiry that has anything to do with knowledge.[25]

The "Psychologistic" Approach to Epistemology

Many philosophers now working in theory of knowledge have stressed the importance of systematic psychology to philosophical epistemology. Reasons proffered for this are various, and so are the conceptions of the proper relationship between psychology and epistemology.[26] But they are virtually unanimous in their rejection of what they take to be the epistemological tradition of Descartes and its modern embodiments in philosophers like Russell, C. I. Lewis, Roderick Chisholm, and A. J. Ayer; and they are united in their endorsement of the naturalistic approach of Quine we have been considering. Traditional epistemology is often condemned as "aprioristic," and as having lost sight of human knowledge as a product of natural causal processes and its function in the survival of the organism and the species. Sometimes, the adherents of the traditional approach are taken to task for their implicit antiscientific bias or indifference to the new developments in psychology and related disciplines. Their own approach in contrast is hailed as "naturalistic" and "scientific," better attuned to significant advances in the relevant scientific fields such as "cognitive science" and "neuroscience," promising philosophical returns far richer than what the aprioristic method of traditional epistemology has been able to deliver. We shall here briefly consider how this new naturalism in epistemology is to be understood in relation to the classic epistemological program and Quine's naturalized epistemology.

Let us see how one articulate proponent of the new approach explains the distinctiveness of his position vis-à-vis that of the traditional episte-mologists. According to Philip Kitcher, the approach he rejects is characterized by an "apsy-chologistic" attitude that takes the difference between knowledge and true belief – that is, justi-fication – to consist in "ways which are independ-ent of the causal antecedents of a subject's states."[27] Kitcher writes:[28]

> we can present the heart of [the apsychologistic approach] by considering the way in which it would tackle the question of whether a person's true belief that p counts as knowledge that p. The idea would be to disregard the psychological life of the subject, looking just at the various propo-sitions she believes. If p is "connected in the right way" to other propositions which are believed, then we count the subject as knowing that p. Of course, apsychologistic epistemology will have to supply a criterion for propositions to be "con-nected in the right way' ... but proponents of this view of knowledge will emphasize that the criterion is to be given in *logical* terms. We are concerned with logical relations among proposi-tions, not with psychological relations among mental states.

On the other hand, the psychologistic approach considers the crucial difference between knowl-edge and true belief – that is, epistemic justifica-tion – to turn on "the factors which produced the belief," focusing on "processes which produce belief, processes which will always contain, at their latter end, psychological events."[29]

It is not entirely clear from this characteriza-tion whether a psychologistic theory of justifica-tion is to be *prohibited* from making *any* reference to logical relations among belief contents (it is difficult to believe how a theory of justification respecting such a blanket prohibition could suc-ceed); nor is it clear whether, conversely, an apsy-chologistic theory will be permitted to refer at all to beliefs qua psychological states, or exactly what it is for a theory to do so. But such points of detail are unimportant here; it is clear enough, for example, that Goldman's proposal to explicate justified belief as belief generated by a reliable belief-forming process[30] nicely fits Kitcher's char-acterization of the psychologistic approach. This account, one form of the so-called "reliability theory" of justification, probably was what Kitcher had in mind when he was formulating his general characterization of epistemological natu-ralism. However, another influential form of the reliability theory does not qualify under Kitcher's characterization. This is Armstrong's proposal to explain the difference between knowledge and true belief, at least for noninferential knowledge, in terms of "a *law-like connection* between the state of affairs [of a subject's believing that p] and the state of affairs that makes 'p' true such that, given the state of affairs [of the subject's believing that p], it must be the case that p."[31] There is here no reference to the causal *antecedents* of beliefs, something that Kitcher requires of apsychologistic theories.

Perhaps, Kitcher's preliminary characteriza-tion needs to be broadened and sharpened. However, a salient characteristic of the naturalis-tic approach has already emerged, which we can put as follows: justification is to be characterized in terms of *causal* or *nomological* connections involving beliefs as *psychological states* or *proc-esses*, and not in terms of the *logical* properties or relations pertaining to the *contents* of these beliefs.[32]

If we understand current epistemological nat-uralism in this way, how closely is it related to Quine's conception of naturalized epistemology? The answer, I think, is obvious: not very closely at all. In fact, it seems a good deal closer to the Cartesian tradition than to Quine. For, as we saw, the difference that matters between Quine's epis-temological program and the traditional program is the former's total renouncement of the latter's normativity, its rejection of epistemology as a normative inquiry. The talk of "replacing" episte-mology with psychology is irrelevant and at best misleading, though it could give us a momentary relief from a sense of deprivation. When one abandons justification and other valuational con-cepts, one abandons the entire framework of nor-mative epistemology. What remains is a descriptive empirical theory of human cognition which, if Quine has his way, will be entirely devoid of the notion of justification or any other evaluative concept.

As I take it, this is not what most advocates of epistemological naturalism are aiming at. By and large they are not Quinean eliminativists in regard to justification, and justification in its full-fledged normative sense continues to play a central role in their epistemological reflections. Where they differ from their nonnaturalist adversaries is the specific way in which criteria of justification are to be formulated. Naturalists and nonnaturalists ("apsychologists") can agree that these criteria must be stated in descriptive terms – that is, without the use of epistemic or any other kind of normative terms. According to Kitcher, an apsychologistic theory of justification would state them primarily in terms of *logical* properties and relations holding for propositional contents of beliefs, whereas the psychologistic approach advocates the exclusive use of *causal* properties and relations holding for beliefs as events or states. Many traditional epistemologists may prefer criteria that confer upon a cognizer a position of special privilege and responsibility with regard to the epistemic status of his beliefs, whereas most self-avowed naturalists prefer "objective" or "externalist" criteria with no such special privileges for the cognizer. But these differences are among those that arise within the familiar normative framework, and are consistent with the exclusion of normative terms in the statement of the criteria of justification.

Normative ethics can serve as a useful model here. To claim that basic ethical terms, like "good" and "right," are *definable* on the basis of descriptive or naturalistic terms is one thing; to insist that it is the business of normative ethics to provide *conditions* or *criteria* for "good" and "right" in descriptive or naturalistic terms is another. One may properly reject the former, the so-called "ethical naturalism," as many moral philosophers have done, and hold the latter; there is no obvious inconsistency here. G. E. Moore is a philosopher who did just that. As is well known, he was a powerful critic of ethical naturalism, holding that goodness is a "simple" and "nonnatural" property. At the same time, he held that a thing's being good "follows" from its possessing certain naturalistic properties. He wrote:[33]

> I should never have thought of suggesting that goodness was "non-natural," unless I had supposed that it was "derivative" in the sense that, whenever a thing is good (in the sense in question) its goodness ... "depends on the presence of certain non-ethical characteristics" possessed by the thing in question: I have always supposed that it did so "depend," in the sense that, if a thing is good (in my sense), then that it is so *follows*

from the fact that it possesses certain natural intrinsic properties ...

It makes sense to think of these "natural intrinsic properties" from which a thing's being good is thought to follow as constituting naturalistic criteria of goodness, or at least pointing to the existence of such criteria. One can reject ethical naturalism, the doctrine that ethical concepts are definitionally eliminable in favor of naturalistic terms, and at the same time hold that ethical properties, or the ascription of ethical terms, must be governed by naturalistic criteria. It is clear, then, that we are here using "naturalism" ambiguously in "epistemological naturalism" and "ethical naturalism." In our present usage, epistemological naturalism does not include (nor does it necessarily exclude) the claim that epistemic terms are definitionally reducible to naturalistic terms. (Quine's naturalism is eliminative, though it is not a definitional eliminativism.)

If, therefore, we locate the split between Quine and traditional epistemology at the descriptive vs. normative divide, then currently influential naturalism in epistemology is not likely to fall on Quine's side. On this descriptive vs. normative issue, one can side with Quine in one of two ways: first, one rejects, with Quine, the entire justification-based epistemological program; or second, like ethical naturalists but unlike Quine, one believes that epistemic concepts are naturalistically definable. I doubt that very many epistemological naturalists will embrace either of these alternatives.[34]

Epistemic Supervenience – Or Why Normative Epistemology Is Possible

But why should we think that there *must be* naturalistic criteria of justified belief and other terms of epistemic appraisal? If we take the discovery and systematization of such criteria to be the central task of normative epistemology, is there any reason to think that this task can be fruitfully pursued, that normative epistemology is a possible field of inquiry? Quine's point is that it is not. We have already noted the limitation of Quine's negative arguments in "Epistemology Naturalized," but is there a positive reason for thinking that normative epistemology is a viable program? One could consider a similar question about the possibility of normative ethics.

I think there is a short and plausible initial answer, although a detailed defense of it would involve complex general issues about norms and values. The short answer is this: we believe in the supervenience of epistemic properties on naturalistic ones, and more generally, in the supervenience of all valuational and normative properties on naturalistic conditions. This comes out in various ways. We think, with R. M. Hare,[35] that if two persons or acts coincide in all descriptive or naturalistic details, they cannot differ in respect of being good or right, or any other valuational aspects. We also think that if something is "good" – a "good car," "good drop shot," "good argument" – then that must be so "in virtue of" its being a "certain way," that is, its having certain "factual properties." Being a good car, say, cannot be a brute and ultimate fact: a car is good *because* it has a certain contextually indicated set of properties having to do with performance, reliability, comfort, styling, economy, etc. The same goes for justified belief: if a belief is justified, that must be so *because* it has a certain factual, non-epistemic properties, such as perhaps that it is "indubitable," that it is seen to be entailed by another belief that is independently justified, that it is appropriately caused by perceptual experience, or whatever. That it is a justified belief cannot be a brute fundamental fact unrelated to the kind of belief it is. There must be a *reason* for it, and this reason must be grounded in the factual descriptive properties of that particular belief. Something like this, I think, is what we believe.

Two important themes underlie these convictions: first, values, though perhaps not reducible to facts, must be "consistent" with them in that objects that are indiscernible in regard to fact must be indiscernible in regard to value; second, there must be nonvaluational "reasons" or "grounds" for the attribution of values, and these

"reasons" or "grounds" must be *generalizable* – that is, they are covered by *rules* or *norms*. These two ideas correspond to "weak supervenience" and "strong supervenience" that I have discussed elsewhere.[36] Belief in the supervenience of value upon fact, arguably, is fundamental to the very concepts of value and valuation.[37] Any valuational concept, to be significant, must be governed by a set of criteria, and these criteria must ultimately rest on factual characteristics and relationships of objects and events being evaluated. There is something deeply incoherent about the idea of an infinitely descending series of valuational concepts, each depending on the one below it as its criterion of application.[38]

It seems to me, therefore, that epistemological supervenience is what underlies our belief in the possibility of normative epistemology, and that we do not need new inspirations from the sciences to acknowledge the existence of naturalistic criteria for epistemic and other valuational concepts. The case of normative ethics is entirely parallel: belief in the possibility of normative ethics is rooted in the belief that moral properties and relations are supervenient upon nonmoral ones. Unless we are prepared to disown normative ethics as a viable philosophical inquiry, we had better recognize normative epistemology as one, too.[39] We should note, too, that epistemology is likely to parallel normative ethics in regard to the degree to which scientific results are relevant or useful to its development.[40] Saying this of course leaves large room for disagreement concerning how relevant and useful, if at all, empirical psychology of human motivation and action can be to the development and confirmation of normative ethical theories.[41] In any event, once the normativity of epistemology is clearly taken note of, it is no surprise that epistemology and normative ethics share the same metaphilosophical fate. Naturalized epistemology makes no more, and no less, sense than naturalized normative ethics.[42]

Notes

1   In making these remarks I am only repeating the familiar textbook history of philosophy; however, what *our* textbooks say about the history of a philosophical concept has much to do with *our* understanding of that concept.

2   Goldman 1979 explicitly states this requirement as a desideratum of his own analysis of justified belief. Chisholm's 1977 definition of "being evident" does not satisfy this requirement as it rests ultimately on an unanalyzed

epistemic concept of one belief being *more reasonable than* another. What does the real "criteriological" work for Chisholm is his "principles of evidence." See especially (A) on p. 73 of his 1977, which can usefully be regarded as an attempt to provide nonnormative, descriptive conditions for certain types of justified beliefs.

3 The basic idea of this stronger requirement seems implicit in Firth's notion of "warrant-increasing property" in his 1964. It seems that Alston 1976 has something similar in mind when he says, "like any evaluative property, epistemic justification is a supervenient property, the application of which is based on more fundamental properties" (at this point Alston refers to Firth's paper cited above) (the quoted remark occurs on p. 170). Although Alston doesn't further explain what he means by "more fundamental properties," the context makes it plausible to suppose that he has in mind non-normative, descriptive properties. See further below for more discussion.

4 See Chisholm 1977, p. 14. Here Chisholm refers to a "person's responsibility or duty *qua* intellectual being."

5 This term was used by Ayer 1956 to characterize the difference between lucky guessing and knowing, p. 33.

6 Notably by Chisholm in 1977, 1st edn, ch. 4.

7 See Carnap, 1936. We should also note the presence of a strong coherentist streak among some positivists; see, e.g., Hempel 1935.

8 In Quine 1969; see this vol., ch. 39. Also see his 1960; 1973; 1970; and especially 1975. See Schmitt's excellent bibliography on naturalistic epistemology in Kornblith 1985.

9 Or conformational relations, given the Positivists' verificationist theory of meaning.

10 I know of no serious defense of it since Ayer's 1940.

11 See Kornblith 1985a, pp. 19–20.

12 Ibid., p. 21.

13 To use an expression of Rorty's 1979, p. 11.

14 Sober 1978 makes a similar point: "And on the question of whether the failure of a foundationalist programme shows that questions of justification cannot be answered, it is worth noting that Quine's advice 'Since

Carnap's foundationalism failed, why not settle for psychology' carries weight only to the degree that Carnapian epistemology exhausts the possibilities of epistemology."

15 See Chisholm 1977, ch. 4.

16 "If we are seeking only the causal mechanism of our knowledge of the external world, and not a justification of that knowledge in terms prior to science …" Quine 1970, p. 2.

17 Ibid., p. 75. Emphasis added.

18 Ibid., p. 78. Emphasis added.

19 Ibid., p. 83. Emphasis added.

20 But aren't there those who advocate a "causal theory" of evidence or justification? I want to make two brief points about this. First, the nomological or causal input–output relations are not in themselves evidential relations, whether these latter are understood causally or otherwise. Second, a causal theory of evidence attempts to state *criteria* for "e is evidence for h" in causal terms; even if this is successful, it does not necessarily give us a causal "definition" or "reduction" of the concept of evidence. For more details see further below.

21 I am not saying that Quine is under any illusion on this point. My remarks are directed rather at those who endorse Quine without, it seems, a clear appreciation of what is involved.

22 Here I am drawing chiefly on Davidson's writings on radical interpretation. See Essays 9, 10, and 11 in his 1984. See also Lewis 1974.

23 Robert Audi suggested this as a possible objection.

24 For some considerations tending to show that these correlations cannot be lawlike, see my 1985.

25 For a more sympathetic account of Quine than mine, see Kornblith's introductory essay in his 1985.

26 See, for more details, Goldman 1986.

27 Kitcher 1983, p. 14.

28 Ibid.

29 Ibid., p. 13. I should note that Kitcher considers the apsychologistic approach to be an aberration of the twentieth-century epistemology, as represented by philosophers like Russell, Moore, C. I. Lewis, and Chisholm, rather than an historical characteristic of the

Cartesian tradition. Kornblith 1982 gives an analogous characterization of the two approaches to justification; he associates "justification-conferring processes" with the psychologistic approach and "epistemic rules" with the apsychologistic approach.

30 See Goldman 1979.

31 Armstrong 1973, p. 166.

32 The aptness of this characterization of the "apsychologistic" approach for philosophers like Russell, Chisholm, Lehrer, Pollock, etc. can be debated. Also, there is the issue of "internalism" vs. "externalism" concerning justification, which I believe must be distinguished from the psychologistic vs. apsychologistic division.

33 Moore, 1942, p. 588.

34 Rorty's claim, which plays a prominent role in his arguments against traditional epistemology, that Locke and other modern epistemologists conflated the normative concept of justification with causal-mechanical concepts is itself based, I believe, on a conflation of just the kind I am describing here. See Rorty, 1979, pp. 139ff. Again, the critical conflation consists in not seeing that the view, which I believe is correct, that epistemic justification, like any other normative concept, must have factual, naturalistic criteria, is entirely consistent with the rejection of the doctrine, which I think is incorrect, that justification *is*, or is *reducible* to, a naturalistic-nonnormative concept.

35 Hare 1952, p. 145.

36 See Kim 1984.

37 Sosa, too, considers epistemological supervenience as a special case of the supervenience of valuational properties on naturalistic conditions in his 1980, especially p. 551. See also Van Cleve's instructive discussion in his 1985, especially, pp. 97–9.

38 Perhaps one could avoid this kind of criteriological regress by embracing directly apprehended valuational properties (as in ethical intuitionism) on the basis of which criteria for other valuational properties could be formulated. The denial of the supervenience of valuational concepts on factual characteristics, however, would sever the essential connection between value and fact on which, it seems, the whole point of our valuational activities depends. In the absence of such supervenience, the very notion of valuation would lose its significance and relevance. The elaboration of these points, however, would have to wait for another occasion; but see Van Cleve's paper cited in the preceding note for more details.

39 Quine will not disagree with this: he will "naturalize" them both. For his views on values see 1978. For a discussion of the relationship between epistemic and ethical concepts see Firth 1978.

40 For discussions of this and related issues see Goldman 1986.

41 For a detailed development of a normative ethical theory that exemplifies the view that it is crucially relevant, see Brandt 1979.

42 An earlier version of this paper was read at a meeting of the Korean Society for Analytic Philosophy in 1984 in Seoul. An expanded version was presented at a symposium at the Western Division meetings of the American Philosophical Association in April, 1985, and at the epistemology conference at Brown University in honor of Roderick Chisholm in 1986. I am grateful to Richard Foley and Robert Audi who presented helpful comments at the APA session and the Chisholm Conference respectively. I am also indebted to Terence Horgan and Robert Meyers for helpful comments and suggestions.

References

Alston, William, 1976. "Two Types of Foundationalism," *Journal of Philosophy* 73, pp. 165–85.

Armstrong, David M., 1973. *Truth, Belief and Knowledge* (London: Cambridge University Press).

Ayer, A. J., 1940. *The Foundations of Empirical Knowledge* (London: Macmillan).

——, 1956. *The Problem of Knowledge* (London: Penguin Books).

Brandt, Richard, 1979. *A Theory of the Good and the Right* (Oxford: Clarendon Press).

Carnap, Rudolf, 1936. "Testability and Meaning," *Philosophy of Science* 3.

Chisholm, Roderick M., 1977. *Theory of Knowledge*, 2nd edn (Englewood Cliffs, NJ: Prentice-Hall).

Davidson, Donald, 1984. *Inquiries into Truth and Interpretation* (Oxford: Clarendon Press).

Firth, Roderick, 1964. "Coherence, Certainty, and Epistemic Priority," *Journal of Philosophy* 61, pp. 545–57.

——, 1978. "Are Epistemic Concepts Reducible to Ethical Concepts?" in A. I. Goldman and J. Kim (eds), *Values and Morals* (Dordrecht: Reidel).

Goldman, Alvin I., 1979. "What Is Justified Belief?" this vol., ch. 26.

——, 1986. *Epistemology and Cognition* (Cambridge, MA: Harvard University Press).

Hare, R. M., 1952. *The Language of Morals* (London: Oxford University Press).

Hempel, Carl G., 1935. "Some Remarks on 'Facts' and Propositions," *Analysis* 2, pp. 93–6.

Kim, Jaegwon, 1984. "Concepts of Supervenience," *Philosophy and Phenomenological Research* 45, pp. 153–76.

——, 1985. "Psychophysical Laws," in Ernest LePore and Brian McLaughlin (eds), *Actions and Events: Perspectives on the Philosophy of Donald Davidson* (Oxford: Basil Blackwell).

Kitcher, Philip, 1983. *The Nature of Mathematical Knowledge* (New York: Oxford University Press).

Kornblith, Hilary, 1982. "The Psychological Turn," *Australasian Journal of Philosophy* 60, pp. 238–53.

——, 1985. "What Is Naturalistic Epistemology?" in Hilary Kornblith (ed.), *Naturalizing Epistemology* (Cambridge, MA: MIT Press).

——, 1985a. *Naturalizing Epistemology* (Cambridge, MA: MIT Press).

Lewis, David, 1974. "Radical Interpretation," *Synthese* 27, pp. 331–44.

Moore, G. E., 1942. "A Reply to My Critics," in P. A. Schilpp (ed.), *The Philosophy of G. E. Moore* (Chicago & Evanston: Open Court).

Quine, W. V., 1960. *Word and Object* (Cambridge, MA: MIT Press).

——, 1969. *Ontological Relativity and Other Essays* (New York: Columbia University Press).

——, 1970. "Grades of Theoreticity," in L. Foster and J. W. Swanson (eds), *Experience and Theory* (Amherst, MA: University of Massachusetts Press).

——, 1973. *The Roots of Reference* (La Salle, IL: Open Court).

——, 1975. "The Nature of Natural Knowledge," in Samuel Guttenplan (ed.), *Mind and Language* (Oxford: Clarendon Press).

——, 1978. "The Nature of Moral Values," in Alvin I. Goldman and Jaegwon Kim (eds), *Values and Morals* (Dordrecht: Reidel).

Rorty, Richard, 1979. *Philosophy and the Mirror Of Nature* (Princeton, NJ: Princeton University Press).

Schmitt, Frederick, 1985. Bibliography, in Hilary Kornblith (ed.), *Naturalizing Epistemology*. Cambridge, MA: MIT Press.

Sober, Elliott, 1978. "Psychologism," *Journal of Theory of Social Behavior* 8, pp. 165–91.

Sosa, Ernest, 1980. "The Foundations of Foundationalism," *Nous* 14, pp. 547–64.

Van Cleve, James, 1985. "Epistemic Supervenience and the Circle of Belief," *The Monist* 68, pp. 90–104.

CHAPTER 41

Quine as Feminist: The Radical Import of Naturalized Epistemology

Louise M. Antony

The truth is always revolutionary.
Antonio Gramsci

I. Introduction

Do we need a feminist epistemology? This is a very complicated question. Nonetheless it has a very simple answer: yes and no.

Of course, what I should say (honoring a decades-old philosophical tradition) is that a great deal depends on what we *mean* by "feminist epistemology." One easy – and therefore tempting – way to interpret the demand for a feminist epistemology is to construe it as nothing more than a call for more theorists *doing* epistemology. On this way of viewing things, calls for "feminist political science," "feminist organic chemistry," and "feminist finite mathematics" would all be on a par, and the need for any one of them would be justified in exactly the same way, viz., by arguing for the general need for an infusion of feminist consciousness into the academy.

Construed in this way, an endorsement of "feminist epistemology" is perfectly neutral with respect to the eventual content of the epistemological theories that feminists might devise. Would it turn out, for example, that feminists as a group reject individualism or foundationalism? Would they favor empiricism over rationalism? Would they endorse views that privileged intui-

tion over reason or the subjective over the objective? We'd just have to wait and see. It must even be left open, at least at the outset, whether a feminist epistemology would be discernibly and systematically different from epistemology as it currently exists, or whether there would instead end up being exactly the same variety among feminists as there is now among epistemologists in general.

Now it might appear that the project of developing a feminist epistemology in this sense is one that we can all happily sign on to, for who could object to trying to infuse the disciplines with feminist consciousness? But now I must honor a some-what newer philosophical tradition than the one I honored earlier, and ask, "We, who?" For though the determined neutrality of this way of conceiving feminist epistemology – let me call it "bare proceduralism" – may give it the superficial appearance of a consensus position, it is in fact quite a partisan position. Even setting aside the fact that there are many people – yes, even some philosophers – who would rather be infused with bubonic plague than with feminist consciousness, it's clear that not everyone is going to like bare proceduralism. And ironically, it is its very neutrality that makes this an unacceptable reading of many, if not most, of the theorists who are currently calling for a feminist epistemology.[1]

To see the sticking point, consider the question of whether we should, as feminists, have an obligation to support *any* project whose

Originally published in L. Antony and C. Witt (eds), *A Mind of One's Own* (Boulder, CO: Westview, 1993), pp. 185–225.

participants represent themselves as feminists. Should we, for example, support the development of a "feminist sociobiology" or a "feminist military science," on the grounds that it's always a good idea to infuse a discipline, or a theory, with feminist consciousness, or on the grounds that there are people who are engaged in such projects who regard themselves as feminists and therefore have a claim on our sympathies? The answer to these questions, arguably, is no. Some projects, like the rationalization of war, may simply be *incompatible* with feminist goals; and some theories, like those with biological determinist presuppositions, may be *inconsistent* with the results of feminist inquiry to date.

Bare proceduralism, with its liberal, all-purpose, surely-there's-something-we-can-all-agree-on ethos, both obscures and begs the important question against those who believe that not all epistemological frameworks cohere – or cohere equally well – with the insights and aims of feminism. Specifically, it presupposes something that many feminist philosophers are at great pains to deny, namely the *prima facie* adequacy, from a feminist point of view, of those epistemological theories currently available within mainstream Anglo-American philosophy. At the very least, one who adopts the bare proceduralist standpoint with respect to feminist epistemology is making a substantive presupposition about where we currently stand in the process of feminist theorizing. To allow even that a feminist epistemology *might* utilize certain existing epistemological frameworks is to assert that feminist theorizing has not yet issued in substantive results regarding such frameworks.[2] Such a view, if not forthrightly expressed and explicitly defended, is disrespectful to the work of those feminists who claim to have already shown that those very epistemological theories are incompatible with feminism.

So we can't simply interpret the question, "Do we need a feminist epistemology?" in the bare proceduralist way and nod an enthusiastic assent. If we do, we'll be obscuring or denying the existence of substantive disagreements among feminists about the relation between feminism and theories of knowledge. One natural alternative to the bare proceduralist interpretation would be to try to give feminist epistemology a *substantive* sense – that is, take it to refer to a particular kind

of epistemology or to a particular theory within epistemology, one that is specifically feminist.

But this won't work either, for two good reasons. First, there simply is no substantive consensus position among feminists working in epistemology, so that it would be hubris for anyone to claim that his or her epistemology was *the* feminist one.[3] Second, many feminists would find the idea that there *should* be such a single "feminist" position repellent. Some would dislike the idea simply for its somewhat totalitarian, "PC" ring. (Me, I'm not bothered by that – it seems to me that one should strive to be correct in all things, including politics.) Some theorists would argue that variety in feminist philosophical positions is to be expected at this point in the development of feminist consciousness, and that various intra- and inter-theoretic tensions in philosophical inquiry reflect unprocessed conflicts among deeply internalized conceptions of reality, of ourselves as human beings, and of ourselves as women.[4] Still others would see the expectation or hope that there will *ever* be a single, comprehensive, "true" feminist position as nothing but a remnant of outmoded, patriarchal ways of thinking.[5]

Thus, while individual feminist theorists may be advertising particular epistemological theories as feminist theories, general calls for the development of a feminist epistemology cannot be construed as advocacy for any particular one of these. But recognition of this fact does not throw us all the way back to the bare proceduralist notion. It simply means that in order to decide on the need for a feminist epistemology, we need to look at details – both with respect to the issues that feminism is supposed to have raised for the theory of knowledge and with respect to the specific epistemological theories that have been proffered as answering to feminist needs.

This is where the yes-and-no comes in. If we focus on the existence of what might be called a "feminist agenda" in epistemology – that is, if the question, "Do we need a feminist epistemology?" is taken to mean, "Are there specific questions or problems that arise as a result of feminist analysis, awareness, or experience that any adequate epistemology must accommodate?" – then I think the answer is clearly yes. But if, taking for granted the existence of such an agenda, the question is taken to be, "Do we need, in order to accommodate these questions, insights, and projects, a specifically feminist alternative to currently available epistemological frameworks?" then the answer, to my mind, is no.

Now it is on this point that I find myself in disagreement with many feminist philosophers. For despite the diversity of views within contemporary feminist thought, and despite the disagreements about even the desiderata for a genuinely feminist epistemology, one theoretical conclusion shared by almost all those feminists who explicitly advocate the development of a feminist epistemology is that existing epistemological paradigms – particularly those available within the framework of contemporary analytic philosophy – are fundamentally unsuited to the needs of feminist theorizing.

It is this virtual unanimity about the inadequacy of contemporary analytic epistemology that I want to challenge. There is an approach to the study of knowledge that promises enormous aid and comfort to feminists attempting to expose and dismantle the oppressive intellectual ideology of a patriarchal, racist, class-stratified society, and it is an approach that lies squarely within the analytic tradition. The theory I have in mind is Quine's "naturalized epistemology" – the view that the study of knowledge should be treated as the empirical investigation of knowers.

It's both unfortunate and ironic that Quine's work has been so uniformly neglected by feminists interested in the theory of knowledge, because although naturalized epistemology is nowadays as mainstream a theory as there is, Quine's challenges to logical positivism were radical in their time, and still retain an untapped radical potential today. His devastating critique of epistemological foundationalism bears many similarities to contemporary feminist attacks on "modernist" conceptions of objectivity and scientific rationality, and his positive views on the holistic nature of justification provide a theoretical basis for pressing the kinds of critical questions feminist critics are now raising.

Thus my primary aim in this essay is to highlight the virtues, from a feminist point of view, of naturalized epistemology. But – as is no doubt quite clear – I have a secondary, polemical aim as well. I want to confront head-on the charges that mainstream epistemology is irremediably phallocentric, and to counter the impression, widespread among progressives both within and outside of the academy, that there is some kind of natural antipathy between radicalism on the one hand and the methods and aims of analytic philosophy on the other. I believe that this impression is quite false, and its promulgation is damaging not only to individual feminists – especially women – working within the analytic tradition, but also to the prospects for an adequate feminist philosophy.

The "bias" paradox

I think the best way to achieve both these aims – defending the analytic framework in general and showcasing naturalized epistemology in particular – is to put the latter to work on a problem that is becoming increasingly important within feminist theory. The issue I have in mind is the problem of how properly to conceptualize *bias*. There are several things about this issue that make it particularly apt for my purposes.

In the first place, the issue provides an example of the way in which feminist analysis can generate or uncover serious epistemological questions, for the problem about bias that I want to discuss will only be recognized as a problem by individuals who are critical, for one reason or another, of one standard conception of objectivity. In the second place, because of the centrality of this problem to feminist theory, the ability of an epistemological theory to provide a solution offers one plausible desideratum of a theory's adequacy as a feminist epistemology. Last of all, because the notions of bias and partiality figure so prominently in feminist critiques of mainstream analytic epistemology, discussion of this issue will enable me to address directly some of the charges that have led some feminist theorists to reject the analytic tradition.

But what is the problem? Within certain theoretical frameworks, the analysis of the notion of "bias" is quite straightforward. In particular, strict empiricist epistemology concurs with liberal political theory in analyzing bias as the mere possession of belief or interest prior to investigation. But for anyone who wishes to criticize the liberal/empiricist ideal of an "open mind," the notion of bias is enormously problematic and threatens to become downright paradoxical.

Consider feminist theory: On the one hand, it is one of the central aims of feminist scholarship to expose the male-centered assumptions and interests – the male *biases*, in other words – underlying so much of received "wisdom." But on the other hand, there's an equally important strain of feminist theory that seeks to challenge the ideal of pure objectivity by emphasizing both the ubiquity and the value of certain kinds of partiality and interestedness. Clearly, there's a tension between those feminist critiques that accuse science or philosophy of displaying male bias and those that reject the ideal of impartiality.

The tension blossoms into paradox when critiques of the first sort are applied to the concepts of objectivity and impartiality themselves. According to many feminist philosophers, the flaw in the ideal of impartiality is supposed to be that the ideal itself is biased: Critics charge either that the concept of "objectivity" serves to articulate a masculine or patriarchal viewpoint (and possibly a pathological one),[6] or that it has the ideological function of protecting the rights of those in power, especially men.[7] But how is it possible to criticize the partiality of the concept of objectivity without presupposing the very value under attack? Put baldly: If we don't think it's good to be *im*partial, then how can we object to men's being *partial*?

The critiques of "objectivity" and "impartiality" that give rise to this paradox represent the main source of feminist dissatisfaction with existing epistemological theories. It's charged that mainstream epistemology will be forever unable to either acknowledge or account for the partiality and locatedness of knowledge, because it is wedded to precisely those ideals of objective or value-neutral inquiry that ultimately and inevitably subserve the interests of the powerful. The valorization of impartiality within mainstream epistemology is held to perform for the ruling elite the critical ideological function of *denying the existence of partiality itself*.[8]

Thus Lorraine Code, writing in the *APA Newsletter on Feminism and Philosophy*,[9] charges that mainstream epistemology (or what she has elsewhere dubbed "malestream" epistemology[10]) has "defined 'the epistemological project' so as to make it illegitimate to ask questions about the identities and specific circumstances of these knowers." It has accomplished this, she contends,

by promulgating a view of knowers as essentially featureless and interchangeable, and by donning a "mask of objectivity and value-neutrality." The transformative potential of feminist – as opposed to a malestream – epistemology lies in its ability to tear off this mask, exposing the "complex power structure of vested interest, dominance, and subjugation" that lurks behind it.

But not only is it not the case that contemporary analytic epistemology is committed to such a conception of objectivity, it was analytic epistemology that was largely responsible for initiating the critique of the empiricistic notions Code is attacking. Quine, Goodman, Hempel, Putnam, Boyd, and others within the analytic tradition have all argued that a certain received conception of objectivity is untenable as an ideal of epistemic practice. The detailed critique of orthodox empiricism that has developed within the analytic tradition is in many ways more pointed and radical that the charges that have been leveled from without.

Furthermore, these philosophers, like many feminist theorists, have emphasized not only the *ineliminability* of bias but also the *positive value* of certain forms of it. As a result, the problems that arise for a naturalized epistemology are strikingly similar to those that beset the feminist theories mentioned above: Once we've acknowledged the necessity and legitimacy of partiality, *how do we tell the good bias from the bad bias?*

What kind of epistemology is going to be able to solve a problem like this? Code asserts that the specific impact of feminism on epistemology has been "to move the question '*Whose* knowledge are we talking about?' to a central place in epistemological discussion,"[11] suggesting that the hope lies in finding an epistemological theory that assigns central importance to consideration of the nature of the subjects who actually do the knowing. I totally agree: No theory that abjures empirical study of the cognizer, or of the actual processes by which knowledge develops, is ever going to yield insight on this question.

But more is required than this. If we as feminist critics are to have any basis for distinguishing the salutary from the pernicious forms of bias, we can't rest content with a *description* of the various ways in which the identity and social location of a subject make a difference to her beliefs. We need, in addition, to be able to make *normative* distinctions among various process of belief-fixation as well. Otherwise, we'll never escape the dilemma posed by the bias paradox: either endorse pure impartiality or give up criticizing bias.[12]

It is here that I think feminist philosophy stands to lose the most by rejecting the analytic tradition. The dilemma will be impossible to escape, I contend, for any theory that eschews the notion of *truth* – for any theory, that is, that tries to steer some kind of middle course between absolutism and relativism. Such theories inevitably leave themselves without resources for making the needed normative distinctions, because they deprive themselves of any conceptual tools for distinguishing the grounds of a statement's truth from the explanation of a statement's acceptance.

Naturalized epistemology has the great advantage over epistemological frameworks outside the analytic tradition (I have in mind specifically standpoint and postmodern epistemologies) in that it permits an appropriately realist conception of truth, viz., one that allows a conceptual gap between epistemology and metaphysics, between the world as we see it and the world as it is.[13] Without appealing to at least this minimally realist notion of truth, I see no way to even state the distinction we ultimately must articulate and defend. Quine simply, an adequate solution to the paradox must enable us to say the following: What makes the *good* bias good is that it facilitates the search for truth, and what makes the *bad* bias bad is that it impedes it.

Now that my absolutist leanings are out in the open, let me say one more thing about truth that I hope will forestall a possible misunderstanding of my project here. I do believe in truth, and I have *never* understood why people concerned with justice have given it such a bad rap. Surely one of the goals of feminism is to *tell the truth* about women's lives and women's experience. Is institutionally supported discrimination not a *fact*? Is misogynist violence not a *fact*? And isn't the existence of ideological denial of the first two facts *itself* a fact? What in the world else could we be doing when we talk about these things, *other* than asserting that the world actually *is* a certain way?

Getting at the truth is complicated, and one of the things that complicates it considerably is that powerful people frequently have strong motives for keeping less powerful people from getting at the truth. It's one job of a critical epistemology, in my view, to expose this fact, to make the mechanisms of such distortions transparent. But if we, as critical epistemologists, lose sight of what we're after, if we concede that there's nothing at stake other than the matter of whose "version" is going to prevail, then our projects become as morally bankrupt and baldly self-interested as Theirs.

This brings me to the nature of the current discussion. I would like to be clear that in endorsing the project of finding a "feminist epistemology," I do not mean to be advocating the construction of a serviceable epistemological ideology "for our side." And when I say that I think naturalized epistemology makes a good feminist epistemology, I don't mean to be suggesting that the justification for the theory is instrumental. A good *feminist* epistemology must be, in the first place, a good epistemology, and that means being a theory that is likely to be *true*. But of course I would not think that naturalized epistemology was likely to be true unless I also thought it explained the facts. And among the facts I take to be central are the long-ignored experiences and wisdom of women.

In the next section, I will explain in more detail the nature of the charges that have been raised by feminist critics against contemporary analytic epistemology. I'll argue that the most serious of these charges are basically misguided – that they depend on a misreading of the canonical figures of the Enlightenment as well as of contemporary epistemology. In the last section, I'll return to the bias paradox and try to show why a naturalized approach to the study of knowledge offers some chance of a solution.

II. What is Mainstream Epistemology and Why is It Bad?

One difficulty that confronts anyone who wishes to assess the need for a "feminist alternative" in epistemology is the problem of finding out exactly what such an epistemology would be an alternative to. What is "mainstream" epistemology anyway? Lorraine Code is more forthright than many in her willingness to name the enemy. According to her, "mainstream epistemology," the proper object of feminist critique, is "post-positivist empiricist epistemology: the epistemology that still dominates in Anglo-American philosophy, despite the best efforts of socialist, structuralist, hermeneuticist, and other theorists of knowledge to deconstruct or discredit it."[14]

By the "epistemology that still dominates in Anglo-American philosophy," Code would have to be referring to the set of epistemological theories that have developed within the analytic paradigm, for analytic philosophy has been, in fact, the dominant philosophical paradigm in the English-speaking academic world since the early twentieth century.[15] This means, at the very least, that the agents of sexism within academic philosophy – the individuals who have in fact been the ones to discriminate against women as students, job applicants, and colleagues – have been, for the most part, analytic philosophers, a fact that on its own makes the analytic paradigm an appropriate object for feminist scrutiny.

But this is not the main reason that Code and others seek to "deconstruct or discredit" analytic epistemology. The fact that the analytic paradigm has enjoyed such an untroubled hegemony within this country during the twentieth century – the period of the most rapid growth of American imperial power – suggests to many radical social critics that analytic philosophy fills an ideological niche. Many feminist critics see mainstream analytic philosophy as the natural metaphysical and epistemological complement to liberal political theory, which, by obscuring real power relations within the society, makes citizens acquiescent or even complicit in the growth of oppression, here and abroad.

What is it about analytic philosophy that would enable it to play this role? Some have argued that analytic or "linguistic" philosophy, together with its cognate fields (such as formal linguistics and computationalist psychology), is inherently male, "phallogocentric."[16] Others have argued that the analytic paradigm, because of its emphasis on abstraction and formalization and its valorization of elite skills, may be an instrument of cognitive control, serving to discredit the perspectives of members of nonprivileged groups.[17]

But most of the radical feminist critiques of "mainstream" epistemology (which, as I said, must denote the whole of analytic epistemology) are motivated by its presumed allegiance to the

conceptual structures and theoretical commitments of the Enlightenment, which provided the general philosophical background to the development of modern industrialized "democracies."[18] By this means, "mainstream" epistemology becomes identified with "traditional" epistemology, and this traditional epistemology becomes associated with political liberalism. Feminist theorists like Alison Jaggar and Sandra Harding, who have both written extensively about the connection between feminist political analysis and theories of knowledge, have encouraged the idea that acceptance of mainstream epistemological paradigms is tantamount to endorsing liberal feminism. Jaggar contends that the connection lies in the radically individualistic conception of human nature common to both liberal political theory and Enlightenment epistemology. In a chapter entitled "Feminist Politics and Epistemology: Justifying Feminist Theory," she writes:

> Just as the individualistic conception of human nature sets the basic problems for the liberal political tradition, so it also generates the problems for the tradition in epistemology that is associated historically and conceptually with liberalism. This tradition begins in the 17th century with Descartes, and it emerges in the 20th century as the analytic tradition. Because it conceives humans as essentially separate individuals, this epistemological tradition views the attainment of knowledge as a project for each individual on her or his own. The task of epistemology, then, is to formulate rules to enable individuals to undertake this project with success.[19]

Harding, in a section of her book called "A Guide to Feminist Epistemologies," surveys what she sees as the full range of epistemological options open to feminists. She imports the essentially conservative political agenda of liberal feminism, which is focused on the elimination of formal barriers to gender equality, into mainstream epistemology, which she labels "feminist empiricism": "*Feminist empiricism* argues that sexism and androcentrism are social biases correctable by stricter adherence to the existing methodological norms of scientific inquiry."[20] Harding takes the hallmark of feminist empiricism (which on her taxonomy is the only alternative to feminist standpoint and postmodernist epistemologies) to be commitment to a particular conception of objectivity, which, again, is held to be part of the legacy of the Enlightenment. In her view, acceptance of this ideal brings with it faith in the efficacy of "existing methodological norms of science" in correcting biases and irrationalities within science, in the same way that acceptance of the liberal ideal of impartiality brings with it faith in the system to eliminate political and social injustice.

In Harding's mind, as in Jaggar's, this politically limiting conception of objectivity is one that can be traced to traditional conceptions of the knowing subject, specifically to Enlightenment conceptions of "rational man." The message, then, is that mainstream epistemology, because it still operates with this traditional conception of the self, functions to limit our understanding of the real operations of power, and of our place as women within oppressive structures. A genuine feminist transformation in our thinking therefore requires massive overhaul, if not outright repudiation, of central aspects of the tradition.

This is clearly the message that political scientist Jane Flax gleans from her reading of feminist philosophy; she argues that feminist theory ought properly to be viewed as a version of postmodern thought, since postmodern theorists and feminist theorists are so obviously engaged in a common project:

> Postmodern philosophers seek to throw into radical doubt beliefs still prevalent in (especially American) culture but derived from the Enlightenment …;[21] feminist notions of the self, knowledge and truth are too contradictory to those of the Enlightenment to be contained within its categories. The way to feminist future(s) cannot lie in reviving or appropriating Enlightenment concepts of the person or knowledge.[22]

But there are at least two serious problems with this argument. The first is that the "tradition" that emerges from these critiques is a gross distortion and oversimplification of the early modern period. The critics' conglomeration of all classical and Enlightenment views into a uniform "traditional" epistemology obscures the enormous amount of controversy surrounding such notions as knowledge and the self during the seventeenth and eighteenth centuries, and encourages crude misunderstandings of some of the central

theoretical claims. Specifically, this amalgamation makes all but invisible a debate that has enormous relevance to discussions of bias and objectivity, viz., the controversy between rationalists and empiricists about the extent to which the structure of the mind might constrain the development of knowledge.[23]

The second problem is that the picture of analytic epistemology that we get once it's allied with this oversimplified "traditional" epistemology is downright cartoonish. When we look at the actual content of the particular conceptions of objectivity and scientific method that the feminist critics have culled from the modern period, and which they subsequently attach to contemporary epistemology, it turns out that these conceptions are precisely the ones that have been the focus of *criticism* among American analytic philosophers from the 1950s onward. The feminist critics' depiction of "mainstream" epistemology utterly obscures this development in analytic epistemology, and in glossing over the details of the analytic critique of positivism, misses points that are of crucial relevance to any truly radical assault on the liberal ideology of objectivity.[24]

The second problem is partly a consequence of the first. The feminist critics, almost without exception, characterize mainstream epistemology as "empiricist." But one of the chief accomplishments of the analytic challenge to positivism was the demonstration that a strictly empiricistic conception of knowledge is untenable. As a result, much of analytic epistemology has taken a decidedly rationalistic turn. Neglect of the rationalist/empiricist debate and misunderstanding of rationalist tenets make the critics insensitive to these developments and blind to their implications.

But the misreading of contemporary epistemology is also partly just a matter of the critics' failure to realize the extent to which analytic philosophy represents a *break* with tradition. I do not mean to deny that there were *any* important theoretical commitments common to philosophers of the early modern period. One such commitment, shared at least by classical rationalists and empiricists, and arguably by Kant, was an epistemological meta-hypothesis called "externalism." This is the view that the proper goal of epistemological theory is the rational *vindication* of human epistemic practice. But if externalism is regarded as the hallmark of "traditional epistemology," then the identification of analytic epistemology with traditional epistemology becomes all the more spurious.

It was the main burden of Quine's critique of positivism to demonstrate the impossibility of an externalist epistemology, and his suggested replacement, "naturalized epistemology," was meant to be what epistemology could be once externalist illusions were shattered. As a result of the analytic critique of externalism, the notions of objectivity and rationality available to contemporary analytic epistemologists are necessarily more complicated than the traditional conceptions they replace. This is so even for epistemologists who would not identify themselves as partisans of naturalized epistemology.

In what follows, I'll discuss in turn these two problems: first, the mischaracterization of the tradition, and then the caricature of contemporary analytic epistemology.

Rationalism v. empiricism: The importance of being partial

What I want to show first is that the "traditional epistemology" offered us by Jaggar and Flax grafts what is essentially a rationalist (and in some respects, specifically Cartesian) theory of *mind* onto what is essentially an empiricist conception of *knowledge*. This is a serious error. Although Jaggar and Flax claim that there are deep connections between the one and the other, the fact of the matter is that they are solidly opposed. The conception of objectivity that is ultimately the object of radical critique – perfect impartiality – is only supportable as an epistemic ideal on an empiricist conception of *mind*. Thus, I'll argue, the rationalistic conception of the self attacked by Jaggar and Flax as unsuitable or hostile to a feminist point of view actually provides the basis for a critique of the view of knowledge they want ultimately to discredit.

Much of what is held to be objectionable in "traditional epistemology" is supposed to derive from the tradition's emphasis on *reason*. But different traditional figures emphasized reason in different ways. Only the rationalists and Kant were committed to what I'll call "cognitive essentialism," a feature of the "traditional" conception of mind that comes in for some of the heaviest

criticism. I take cognitive essentialism to be the view (1) that there are certain specific properties the possession of which is both distinctive of and universal among human beings, (2) that these properties are cognitive in nature, (3) that our possession of these properties amounts to a kind of innate knowledge, and (4) that our status as moral agents is connected to the possession of these properties. Empiricists denied all these claims – in particular, they denied that reason had anything but a purely instrumental role to play in either normative or nonnormative activity, and tended to be opposed to any form of essentialism, cognitive or otherwise.

Although the purely instrumental conception of reason is also criticized by feminist scholars, cognitive essentialism is the focus of one specific set of feminist concerns. It is held to be suspect on the grounds that such a doctrine could easily serve to legitimate the arrogant impulses of privileged Western white men: first to canonize their own culture- and time-bound speculations as revelatory of the very norms of human existence, and then simultaneously to deny the very properties deemed "universal" to the majority of human beings on the planet.

Here's how it is supposed to work: Cognitive essentialism is supposed to engender a kind of fantasy concerning actual human existence and the actual prerequisites of knowledge. Because of its emphasis on *cognitive* characteristics, it's argued, the view permits privileged individuals to ignore the fact of their embodiment, and with that, the considerable material advantages they enjoy in virtue of their class, gender, and race.[25] To the extent that the characteristics they find in themselves are the result of their particular privileges instead of a transcendent humanity, the fantasy provides a basis for viewing less-privileged people – who well may lack such characteristics – as inherently less human. But since these characteristics have been lionized as forming the essence of moral personhood, the fantasy offers a rationale for viewing any differences between themselves and others as negative deviations from a moral norm.

Recall, for example, that the particular elements of Enlightenment thought that Flax finds inimical to feminist theory and praxis are the alleged universality, transcendence, and abstractness assigned to the faculty of reason:

The notion that reason is divorced from "merely contingent" existence still predominates in contemporary Western thought and now appears to mask the embeddedness and dependence of the self upon social relations, as well as the partiality and historical specificity of this self's existence....

In fact, feminists, like other postmodernists, have begun to suspect that all such transcendental claims reflect and reify the experience of a few persons – mostly White, Western males.[26]

But moreover, cognitive essentialism is supposed to lead to what Jaggar calls "individualism,"[27] the view that individual human beings are epistemically self-sufficient, that human society is unnecessary or unimportant for the development of knowledge. If the ideal "man of reason" is utterly without material, differentiating features, then the ideal knower would appear to be *pure* rationality, a mere calculating mechanism, a person who has been stripped of all those particular aspects of self that are of overwhelming human significance. Correlatively, as it is precisely the features "stripped off" the self by the Cartesian method that "traditional" epistemology denigrates as distorting influences, the ideally objective cognizer is also the man of reason. Knowledge is then achieved, it appears, not by active engagement with one's world and with the people in it, but by a pristine transcendence of the messy contingencies of the human condition.[28]

Lending support to Lorraine Code's grievance against "traditional" epistemology, Jaggar thus insists that it is this abstract and detached individualism that underwrites a solipsistic view of the construction of knowledge and precludes assigning any epistemological significance to the situation of the knower.

Because it conceives humans as essentially separate individuals, this epistemological tradition views the attainment of knowledge as a project for each individual on his or her own. The task of epistemology, then, is to formulate rules to enable individuals to undertake this project with success.[29]

It is here that the link is supposed to be forged between the Cartesian/Kantian conception of the self and the particular conception of objectivity –

objectivity as pure neutrality – that is thought to be pernicious.

But the individualism Jaggar takes to unite rationalists and empiricists is not in fact a view that *anyone* held. She derives it from a fairly common—indeed, almost canonical – misreading of the innate ideas debate. Significantly, Jaggar acknowledges the existence of disagreements within the early modern period, but avers that such issues as divided rationalists from empiricists are differences that make no difference. Both were foundationalists, she points out, and though the foundation for rationalists was self-evident truths of reason and the foundation for empiricists was reports of sensory experience, "in either case … the attainment of knowledge is conceived as essentially a solitary occupation that has no necessary social preconditions."[30]

The reading, in other words, is that whereas the empiricists thought all knowledge came from experience, the rationalists thought *all knowledge came from reason*. But the second element of this interpretation is simply wrong. It was no part of *Descartes's* project (much less Kant's) to assert the self-sufficiency of reason. Note that a large part of the goal of the exercise of hyperbolic doubt in the *Meditations* was to establish the reliability of sensory experience, which Descartes took to be essential to the development of adequate knowledge of the world. And although he maintained the innateness of many ideas, including sensory ideas, he carefully and repeatedly explained that he meant by this only that human beings were built in such a way that certain experiences would trigger these ideas and no others.[31]

Furthermore, Descartes himself explicitly endorses two of the very epistemic values his position is supposed to preclude. Not only does he clearly reject the sort of epistemic individualism Jaggar deplores, but he strongly upholds the necessity of acquainting oneself with the variety of human experience in order to form a just conception of the world. Expressing his contempt for the contradictions and sophistries of his learned and cloistered teachers, he recounts how, as soon as he was old enough to "emerge from the control of [his] tutors," he "entirely quitted the study of letters."

And resolving to seek no other science than that which could be found in myself, *or at least in the great book of the world* [my emphasis], I employed the rest of my youth in travel, in seeing courts and armies, in intercourse with men of diverse temperaments and conditions, in collecting varied experiences, in proving myself in the various predicaments in which I was placed by fortune, and under all circumstances bringing my mind to bear on the things which came before it, so that I might derive some profit from my experience.[32]

And far from recommending the divestiture of one's particular concerns as sound epistemic practice, Descartes affirms the importance of concrete engagement in finding the truth, pointing to the degradation of knowledge that can result from disinterestedness.

For it seemed to me that I might meet with much more truth in the reasonings that each man makes on the matters that specially concern him, and the issue of which would very soon punish him if he made a wrong judgment, than in the case of those made by a man of letters in his study touching speculations which lead to no result, and which bring about no other consequences to himself excepting that he will be all the more vain the more they are removed from common sense, since in this case it proves him to have employed so much the more ingenuity and skill in trying to make them seem probable.[33]

The bottom line is that rationalists, Descartes especially, did not hold the view that experience was inessential or even that it was unimportant; nor did they hold the view that the best epistemic practice is to discount one's own interests. The misreading that saddles Descartes with such views stems from a popular misconception about the innate ideas debate.

The disagreement between rationalists and empiricists was not simply about the existence of innate ideas. Both schools were agreed that the mind was natively structured and that that structure partially determined the shape of human knowledge. What they disagreed about was the *specificity* of the constraints imposed by innate mental structure. The rationalists believed that native structure placed quite specific limitations on the kinds of concepts and hypotheses the mind could form in response to experience, so that human beings were, in effect, natively *biased* toward certain

ways of conceiving the world. Empiricists, on the other hand, held that there were relatively few native constraints on how the mind could organize sensory experience, and that such constraints as did exist were *domain-general* and *content-neutral*.

According to the empiricists, the human mind was essentially a mechanism for the manipulation of sensory data. The architecture of the mechanism was supposed to ensure that the concepts and judgments constructed out of raw sense experience accorded with the rules of logic. This did amount to a minimal constraint on the possible contents of human thought – they had to be logical transforms of sensory primitives – but it was a highly general one, applying to every subject domain in precisely the same way. Thus, on this model, any one hypothesis should be as good as any other as far as the mind is concerned, as long as both hypotheses are logically consistent with the sensory evidence.[34] This strict empiricist model of mind, as it turns out, supports many of the elements of epistemology criticized by Code, Jaggar, and others (e.g., a sharp observation/theory distinction, unmediated access to a sensory "given," and an algorithmic view of justification). I'll spell this out in detail in the next section. For present purposes, however, the thing to note is that the model provides clear warrant for the particular conception of the ideal of objectivity – perfect neutrality – that is the main concern of Jaggar and the others and that is supposed to follow from cognitive essentialism. Here's how.

Because the mind itself, on the empiricist model, makes no substantive contribution to the contents of thought, knowledge on this model is *entirely* experience-driven: All concepts and judgments are held to reflect regularities in an individual's sensory experience. But one individual cannot see everything there is to see – one's experience is necessarily limited, and there's always the danger that the regularities that form the basis of one's own judgments are not general regularities, but only artifacts of one's limited sample. (There is, in other words, a massive restriction-of-range problem for empiricists.) The question then arises how one can tell whether the patterns one perceives are present in nature generally, or are just artifacts of one's idiosyncratic perspective.

The empiricists' answer to this question is that one can gauge the general validity of one's judgments by the degree to which they engender reliable expectations about sensory experience. But although this answer addresses the problem of how to tell whether one's judgments are good or bad, it doesn't address the problem of how to get good judgments in the first place. Getting good judgments means getting good data – that is, exposing oneself to patterns of sensations that are representative of the objective distribution of sensory qualities throughout nature.

This idea immediately gives rise to a certain ideal (some would say fantasy) of epistemic location – the best spot from which to make judgments would be that spot which is *least particular*. Sound epistemic practice then becomes a matter of constantly trying to maneuver oneself into such a location – trying to find a place (or at least come as close as one can) where the regularities in one's own personal experience match the regularities in the world at large. A knower who could be somehow stripped of all particularities and idiosyncrasies would be the best possible knower there is.

This is not, however, a fantasy that would hold any particular appeal for a rationalist, despite the image of detachment evoked by a cursory reading of the *Meditations*. The rationalists had contended all along that sensory experience *by itself* was insufficient to account for the richly detailed body of knowledge that human beings manifestly possessed, and thus that certain elements of human knowledge – what classical rationalists called *innate ideas* – must be natively present, a part of the human essence.

Because the rationalists denied that human knowledge was a pure function of the contingencies of experience, they didn't need to worry nearly as much as the empiricists did about epistemic location. If it is the structure of mind, rather than the accidents of experience, that largely determines the contours of human concepts, then we can relax about at least the broad parameters of our knowledge. We don't have to worry that idiosyncratic features of our epistemic positions will seriously distort our worldviews, because the development of our knowledge is not dependent upon the patterns that happen to be displayed in our particular experiential histories. The regularities we "perceive" are, in large measure, regularities that we're *built* to perceive.

"Pure" objectivity – if that means giving equal weight to every hypothesis consistent with the data, or if it means drawing no conclusions beyond what can be supported by the data – is thus a nonstarter as an epistemic norm from a rationalist's point of view. The rationalists were in effect calling attention to the *value* of a certain kind of partiality: if the mind were not natively biased – i.e., disposed to take seriously certain kinds of hypotheses and to disregard or fail to even consider others – then knowledge of the sort that human beings possess would itself be impossible. There are simply too many ways of combining ideas, too many different abstractions that could be performed, too many distinct extrapolations from the same set of facts, for a pure induction machine to make much progress in figuring out the world.

The realization that perfect neutrality was not necessarily a good thing, and that bias and partiality are potentially salutary, is thus a point that was strongly present in the early modern period, *pace* Jaggar and Flax. There was no single "traditional" model of mind; the model that can properly be said to underwrite the conceptions of rationality and objectivity that Jaggar brings under feminist attack is precisely a model to which Descartes and the other rationalists were *opposed*, and, ironically, the one that, on the face of it, assigns the most significance to experience. And although it is the cognitive essentialists who are charged with deflecting attention away from epistemically significant characteristics of the knower, it was in fact these same essentialists, in explicit opposition to the empiricists, who championed the idea that human knowledge was necessarily "partial."

Hume, Quine, and the break with tradition

Let me turn now to the second serious problem with the feminist criticisms of "mainstream" epistemology: To the extent that there really is a "tradition" in epistemology, it is a tradition that has been explicitly rejected by contemporary analytic philosophy.

If the rationalists solved one problem by positing innate ideas, it was at the cost of raising another. Suppose that there are, as the rationalists maintained, innate ideas that perform the salutary function of narrowing down to a manageable set the hypotheses that human minds have to consider when confronted with sensory data.

That eliminates the problem faced by the empiricists of filtering out idiosyncratic "distortions." But now the question is, How can we be sure that these biases – so helpful in getting us to *a* theory of the world – are getting us to the *right* theory of the world? What guarantees that our minds are inclining us in the right direction? Innate ideas lead us somewhere, but do they take us where we want to go?

The rationalists took this problem very seriously. A large part of their project was aimed at validating the innate constraints, at showing that these mental biases did not lead us astray. Descartes's quest for "certainty" needs to be understood in this context: The method of hyperbolic doubt should be viewed not as the efforts of a paranoid to free himself forever from the insecurity of doubt, but as a theoretical exercise designed to show that the contours imposed on our theories by our own minds were proper reflections of the topography of reality itself.

It is at this point that we're in a position to see what rationalists and empiricists actually had in common – not a conception of mind, not a theory of how knowledge is constructed, but a theory of *theories* of knowledge. If there is a common thread running through Enlightenment epistemologies, it is this: a belief in the possibility of providing a *rational* justification of the processes by which human beings arrive at theories of the world. For the empiricists, the trick was to show how the content of all knowledge could be reduced to pure reports of sensory experience; for the rationalists, it was showing the indubitability of the innate notions that guided and facilitated the development of knowledge. Philosophers in neither group were really on a quest for certainty – all they wanted was a reliable map of its boundaries.

But if one of the defining themes of the modern period was the search for an externalist justification of epistemic practice, then *Hume* must be acknowledged to be the first postmodernist. Hume, an empiricist's empiricist, discovered a fatal flaw in his particular proposal for justifying human epistemic practice. He realized that belief in the principle of induction – the principle that says that the future will resemble the past or that similar things will behave similarly – could not be rationally justified. It was clearly not a truth of reason, since its denial was not self-contradictory. But neither could it be

justified by experience: Any attempt to do so would be circular, because the practice of using past experience as evidence about the future is itself only warranted if one accepts the principle of induction.

Hume's "skeptical solution" to his own problem amounted to an abandonment of the externalist hopes of his time. Belief in induction, he concluded, was a *custom*, a tendency of mind ingrained by nature, one of "a species of natural instincts, which no reasoning or process of the thought and understanding is able, either to produce or to prevent."[35] For better or worse, Hume contended, we're stuck with belief in induction – we are constitutionally incapable of doubting it and conceptually barred from justifying it. The best we can do is to *explain* it.

Hume's idea was thus to offer as a replacement for the failed externalist project of rational justification of epistemic practice, the *empirical* project of characterizing the cognitive nature of creatures like ourselves, and then figuring out how such creatures, built to seek knowledge in the ways we do, could manage to survive and flourish. In this way, he anticipated to a significant degree the "postmodernist" turn taken by analytic philosophy in the twentieth century as the result of Quine's and others' critiques of externalism's last gasp – logical positivism.

Before fast-forwarding into the twentieth century, let me summarize what I take to be the real lessons of the modern period – lessons that, I've argued, have been missed by many feminist critiques of "traditional" epistemology. First, there is the essentially rationalist insight that perfect objectivity is not only impossible but undesirable, that certain kinds of "bias" or "partiality" are necessary to make our epistemic tasks tractable. Second, there is Hume's realization that externalism won't work, that we can never manage to offer a justification of epistemic norms without somehow presupposing the very norms we wish to justify. See this, if you will, as the beginning of the postmodern recognition that theory always proceeds from an "embedded" location, that there is no transcendent spot from which we can inspect our own theorizing.

The rationalist lesson was pretty much lost and the import of Hume's insight submerged by the subsequent emergence and development of neo-empiricist philosophy. This tradition, which involved primarily the British empiricists Mill and Russell, but also Wittgenstein and the Vienna Circle on the Continent, culminated in the school of thought known as logical positivism.[36] The positivists' project was, in some ways, an externalist one. They hoped to develop criteria that would enforce a principled distinction between empirically significant and empirically meaningless sentences. In the minds of some positivists (Schlick, arguably, and Ayer), this criterion would help to vindicate scientific practice by helping to distinguish science from "metaphysics," which was for positivists, a term of abuse.

The positivists were perfectly well aware of Hume's dilemma about the status of the principle of induction – similar problems about even more fundamental principles of logic and mathematics had come to light since his time. But the positivists in effect attempted to rehabilitate epistemological externalism by means of a bold move. They took all the material that was needed to legitimize scientific practice but that could not be traced directly to sensory experience, and relegated it to the *conventions* of human language. This tack had, at least *prima facie*, some advantages over Hume's nativist move: If our epistemic norms are a matter of convention, then (1) there's no longer any question of explaining how we got them – they're there because we *put* them there; and (2) there's no need to justify them because the parameter of evaluation for conventions is not truth but *utility*.

The positivists thus embarked on a program they called "rational reconstruction" – they wanted to show, in detail, how any empirically meaningful claim could be reduced, by the successive application of semantic and logical rules, to statements purely about sensory experience. If such reconstructions could be shown to be possible at least in principle, then all theoretical disagreements could be shown to be susceptible to resolution by appeal to the neutral court of empirical experience. And in all of this, the positivists were committed to basically the same series of assumptions that warranted the view of objectivity that I earlier associated with classical empiricism.

But there were two things absolutely essential to the success of this project. First, there had to be a viable distinction that could be drawn between statements whose truth depended on empirical contingencies (the contentful claims of a theory that formed the substance of the theory) and statements that were true "by convention" and thus part of the logical/semantic structure of the theory. Second, it would have to be shown that the reduction of empirically contentful statements to specific sets of claims about sensory experience could be carried out. But in the early 1950s, Quine (together with Hempel, Goodman, Putnam, and others) began producing decisive arguments against precisely these assumptions.[37] The ensuing changes in analytic epistemology were nothing short of radical.

Quine's main insight was that individual statements do not have any specific consequences for experience if taken individually – that it is only in conjunction with a variety of other claims that experiential consequences can even be derived. It follows from this that no single experience or observation can decisively refute any theoretical claim or resolve any theoretical dispute, and that all experimental tests of hypotheses are actually tests of *conjunctions* of hypotheses. The second insight – actually a corollary of the first point – was that no principled distinction can be drawn among statements on the basis of the grounds of their truth – there can be no distinction between statements made true or false by experience and those whose truth value depends entirely on semantic or logical conventions.

The implications of these two insights were far-reaching. Quine's arguments against the "two dogmas of empiricism" entailed, in the first place, that the confirmation relation could not be hierarchical, as the foundationalist picture required, but must rather be holistic. Because theories have to face "the tribunal of sensory experience as a corporate body" (to use Quine's military-industrial metaphor), there can be no evidentially foundational set of statements that asymmetrically confirm all the others – every statement in the theory is linked by some justificatory connections to every other.

It also meant that responses at the theoretical level to the acquisition of empirical data were not fully dictated by logic. If experimental tests were always tests of *groups* of statements, then if the prediction fails, logic will tell us only that *something* in the group must go, but not *what*. If logic plus data don't suffice to determine how belief is modified in the face of empirical evidence, then there must be, in addition to logic and sensory evidence, *extra-empirical* principles that partially govern theory selection. The "justification" of these principles can only be pragmatic – we are warranted in using them just to the extent that they work.[38]

But to say this is to say that epistemic norms – a category that must include any principle that in fact guides theory selection – are themselves subject to empirical disconfirmation. And indeed, Quine embraces this consequence, explicitly extending the lesson to cover not only pragmatic "rules of thumb," but to rules of logic and language as well. In short, any principle that facilitates the development of knowledge by narrowing down our theoretical options becomes itself a part of the theory, and a part that must be defended on the same basis as any other part. So much for the fact/value distinction.

The reasoning above represents another of the many routes by which Quine's attack on foundationalism can be connected with his critique of the analytic/synthetic distinction, so central to positivist projects. With the demonstration that any belief, no matter how apparently self-evident, could in principle be rejected on the basis of experience, Quine effectively destroyed the prospects for any "first philosophy" – any Archimedean fixed point from which we could inspect our own epistemic practice and pronounce it sound.

But his critique also pointed the way (as Hume's "skeptical solution" did to the problem of induction) to a different approach to the theory of knowledge. Epistemology, according to Quine, had to be "naturalized," transformed into the empirical study of the actual processes – not "rational reconstructions" of those processes – by which human cognizers achieve knowledge.[39] If we accept this approach, several consequences follow for our understanding of knowledge and of the norms that properly govern its pursuit.

The first lesson is one that I believe may be part of what the feminist critics are themselves pointing to in their emphasis on the essential locatedness of all knowledge claims. The lesson is that all theorizing *takes some knowledge for granted*. Theorizing about theorizing is no exception. The decision to treat epistemology as the empirical study of the knower requires us to presume that we can, at least for a class of clear cases, distinguish epistemic success from epistemic

failure. The impossibility of the externalist project shows us that we cannot expect to learn *from our philosophy* what counts as knowledge and how much of it we have; rather, we must begin with the assumption that we know certain things and figure out how that happened.

This immediately entails a second lesson. A naturalized approach to knowledge requires us to give up the idea that our own epistemic practice is transparent to us – that we can come to understand how knowledge is obtained either by *a priori* philosophizing or by casual introspection. It requires us to be open to the possibility that the processes that we actually rely on to obtain and process information about the world are significantly different from the ones our philosophy told us had to be the right ones.

Let me digress to point out a tremendous irony here, much remarked upon in the literature on Quine's epistemology and philosophy of mind. Despite his being the chief evangelist of the gospel that everything is empirical, Quine's own philosophy is distorted by his a prioristic commitment to a radically empiricistic, instrumentalist theory of psychology, namely psychological behaviorism. Quine's commitment to this theory – which holds that human behavior can be adequately explained without any reference to mental states or processes intervening between environmental stimuli and the organism's response – is largely the result of his philosophical antipathy to intentional objects, together with a residual sympathy for the foundationalist empiricism that he himself was largely responsible for dismantling.

Chomsky, of course, was the person most responsible for pointing out the in-principle limitations of behaviorism, by showing in compelling detail the empirical inadequacies of behaviorist accounts of the acquisition of language.[40] Chomsky also emphasized the indefensibility of the a prioristic methodological constraints that defined empiricistic accounts of the mind, appealing to considerations that Quine himself marshaled in his own attacks on instrumentalism in nonpsychological domains.[41]

Chomsky's own theory of language acquisition did not differ from the behaviorist account only, or even primarily, in its mentalism. It was also rationalistic: Chomsky quite self-consciously appealed to classical rationalistic forms of argument about the necessity of mental partiality in establishing the empirical case for his strong nativism. Looking at the actual circumstances of language acquisition, and then at the character of the knowledge obtained in those circumstances, Chomsky argued that the best explanation of the whole process is one that attributes to human beings a set of innate biases limiting the kinds of linguistic hypotheses available for their consideration as they respond to the welter of data confronting them.[42]

Chomsky can thus be viewed, and is viewed by many, as a naturalized epistemologist *par excellence*. What his work shows is that a naturalized approach to epistemology – in this case, the epistemology of language – yields an *empirical* vindication of rationalism. Since Chomsky's pathbreaking critique of psychological behaviorism, and the empiricist conception of mind that underlies it, nativism in psychology has flourished, and a significant degree of rationalism has been imported into contemporary epistemology.

A casual student of the analytic scene who has read only Quine could, of course, be forgiven for failing to notice this, given Quine's adamant commitment to an empiricist conception of mind; this may explain why so many of the feminist critics of contemporary epistemology seem to identify analytic epistemology with empiricism and to ignore the more rationalistic alternatives that have developed out of the naturalized approach. But I think, too, that the original insensitivity to the details of the original rationalist/empiricist controversy plays a role. Anyone who properly appreciates the import of the rationalist defense of the value of partiality will, I think, see where Quine's rejection of externalism is bound to lead.

So let's do it. I turn now to the feminist critique of objectivity and the bias paradox.

III. Quine as Feminist: What Naturalized Epistemology Can Tell Us About Bias

I've argued that much of the feminist criticism of "mainstream" epistemology depends on a misreading of both contemporary analytic philosophy, and of the tradition from which it derives. But it's one thing to show that contemporary analytic philosophy is not what the feminist critics think it is, and quite another to show that the contemporary analytic scene contains an

epistemology that can serve as an adequate *feminist* epistemology. To do this, we must return to the epistemological issues presented to us by feminist theory and see how naturalized epistemology fares with respect to them. I want eventually to show how a commitment to a naturalized epistemology provides some purchase on the problem of conceptualizing bias, but in order to do that, we must look in some detail at those feminist arguments directed against the notion of objectivity.

Capitalist science and the ideal of objectivity

As we've seen, one of the most prominent themes in feminist epistemology and feminist philosophy of science concerns the alleged ideological function of a certain conception of objectivity. Many feminist critics see a connection between radical (i.e., nonliberal) critiques of science and feminist critiques of "received" epistemology. Such critics take as their starting point the observation that science, as it has developed within industrialized capitalist societies like the United States, is very much an instrument of oppression: Rather than fulfilling its Enlightenment promise as a liberatory and progressive force, institutionalized science serves in fact to sustain and even to enhance existing structures of inequality and domination.[43]

Although all feminists agree that part of the explanation of this fact must be that modern science has been distorted by the sexist, racist, and classist biases it inherits from the society in which it exists, feminist theorists divide on the issue of whether some "deeper" explanation is required. Alison Jaggar's "liberal feminists" and Sandra Harding's "feminist empiricists" hold that society and science are both potentially self-correcting – that more equitable arrangements of power and more scrupulous enforcement of the rules of fairness would turn science back to its natural progressive course.

But Harding and Jaggar, together with Lorraine Code and Evelyn Fox Keller, disagree with this liberal analysis. They contend that the modern scientific establishment has not simply inherited its oppressive features from the inequitable society that conditions it. Rather, they claim, a large part of the responsibility for societal injustices lies deep within science itself, in the conception of knowledge and knowers that underlies "scientific method." These critics charge that the very ideals to which Western science has traditionally aspired – particularly rationality and objectivity – serve to sanction and promote a form of institutionalized inquiry uniquely suited to the needs of patriarchy. Thus, it's argued, feminist critique must not stop at exposing cases in which science has broken its own rules; it must press on to expose the androcentric bias inherent in the rules themselves.

Thus Evelyn Fox Keller claims that any critique that does not extend to the rules of scientific method allies itself with political liberalism in virtue of its epistemology. Any such critique, she argues, "can still be accommodated within the traditional framework by the simple argument that the critiques, if justified, merely reflect the fact that [science] is not sufficiently scientific." In contrast, there is "the truly radical critique that attempts to locate androcentric bias … in scientific ideology itself. The range of criticism takes us out of the liberal domain and requires us to question the very assumptions of rationality that underlie the scientific enterprise."[44]

All this seems to set a clear agenda for feminist philosophers who wish to be part of the struggle for a genuinely radical social transformation: If one's going to go deeper politically and criticize the presuppositions of liberal political theory, then one must coordinately go deeper *conceptually* and criticize the presuppositions of the epistemology and metaphysics that underwrite the politics.

But does this argument work? I think that it doesn't. To see why, we need to look more closely at the epistemological position that the feminist critics take to be allied with liberalism and look in more detail at the argument that is supposed to show that such a view of knowledge is oppressive.

The "traditional" epistemology pictured in the work of Flax, Code, and Jaggar, I've argued, is an unvigorous hybrid of rationalist and empiricist elements, but the features that are supposed to limit it from the point of view of feminist critique of science all derive from the empiricist strain. Specifically, the view of knowledge in question contains roughly the following elements:

(1) it is strongly foundationalist: It is committed to the view that there is a set of epistemically privileged beliefs, from which all knowledge is in principle derivable.
(2) it takes the foundational level to be constituted by reports of sensory experience, and views the mind as a mere calculating device, containing no substantive contents other than what results from experience.
(3) as a result of its foundationalism and its empiricism, it is committed to a variety of sharp distinctions: observation/theory, fact/value, context of discovery/context of justification.

This epistemological theory comes very close to what Hempel has termed "narrow inductivism,"[45] but I'm just going to call it the "Dragnet" theory of knowledge. To assess the "ideological potential" of the Dragnet theory, let's look first at some of the epistemic values and attitudes the theory supports.

To begin with, because of its empiricistic foundationalism, the view stigmatizes both inference and theory. On this view, beliefs whose confirmation depends upon logical relations to other beliefs bear a less direct, less "objective" connection to the world than reports of observations, which are supposed to provide us transparent access to the world. To "actually see" or "directly observe" is better, on this conception, than to infer, and an invidious distinction is drawn between the "data" or "facts" (which are incontrovertible) on the one hand and "theories" and "hypotheses" (unproven conjectures) on the other.

Second, the view supports the idea that any sound system of beliefs can, in principle, be rationally reconstructed. That is, a belief worth having is either itself a fact or can be assigned a position within a clearly articulated confirmational hierarchy erected on fact. With this view comes a denigration of the epistemic role of hunches and intuitions. Such acts of cognitive impulse can be difficult to defend "rationally" if the standards of defense are set by a foundationalist ideal. When a hunch can't be defended, but the individual persists in believing it anyway, that's *ipso facto* evidence of irresponsibility or incompetence. Hunches that happen to pay off are relegated to the context of discovery and are viewed as inessential to the justification of the ensuing belief. The distinction between context of discovery and context of justification itself follows from foundationalism: As long as it's possible to provide a rational defense of a belief *ex post facto* by demonstrating that it bears the proper inferential relation to established facts, we needn't give any thought to the circumstances that actually gave rise to that belief. Epistemic location becomes, to that extent, evidentially irrelevant.

Finally, the Dragnet theory is going to lead to a certain conception of how systematic inquiry ought to work. It suggests that good scientific practice is relatively mechanical: that data gathering is more or less passive and random, that theory construction emerges from the data in a relatively automatic way, and that theory testing is a matter of mechanically deriving predictions and then subjecting them to decisive experimental tests. Science (and knowledge-seeking generally) will be good *to the extent that* its practitioners can conform to the ideal of objectivity.

This ideal of objective method requires a good researcher, therefore, to put aside all prior beliefs about the outcome of the investigation, and to develop a willingness to be carried wherever the facts may lead. But other kinds of discipline are necessary, too. Values are different in kind from facts, on this view, and so are not part of the confirmational hierarchy. Values (together with the emotions and desires connected with them) become, at best, epistemically irrelevant and, at worst, disturbances or distortions. Best to put them aside, and try to go about one's epistemic business in as calm and disinterested a way as possible.

In sum, the conception of ideal epistemic practice yielded by the Dragnet theory is precisely the conception that the feminist critics disdain. Objectivity, on this view (I'll refer to it from now on as "Dragnet objectivity"), is the result of complete divestiture – divestiture of theoretical commitments, of personal goals, of moral values, of hunches and intuitions. We'll get to the truth, sure as taxes, provided everyone's willing to be rational and to play by the (epistemically relevant) rules. Got an especially knotty problem to solve? Just the facts, ma'am.

Now let's see how the Dragnet theory of knowledge, together with the ideal of objectivity it supports, might play a role in the preservation of oppressive structures.

Suppose for the sake of argument that the empirical claims of the radical critics are largely correct. Suppose, that is, that in contemporary US society institutionalized inquiry does function to serve the specialized needs of a powerful ruling elite (with trickle-down social goods permitted insofar as they generate profits or at least don't impede the fulfillment of ruling-class objectives). Imagine also that such inquiry is very costly, and that the ruling elite strives to socialize those costs as much as possible.

In such a society, there will be a great need to obscure this arrangement. The successful pursuit of the agendas of the ruling elite will require a quiescent – or, as it's usually termed, "stable" – society, which would surely be threatened if the facts were known. Also required is the acquiescence of the scientists and scholars, who would like to view themselves as autonomous investigators serving no masters but the truth and who would deeply resent the suggestion (as anyone with any self-respect would) that their honest intellectual efforts subserve any baser purpose.

How can the obfuscation be accomplished? One possibility would be to promote the idea that science is organized for the sake of *public* rather than *private* interests. But the noble lie that science is meant to make the world a better place is a risky one. It makes the public's support for science contingent upon science's producing tangible and visible public benefits (which may not be forthcoming) and generates expectations of publicity and accountability that might lead to embarrassing questions down the road.

An altogether more satisfactory strategy is to promote the idea that science is *value-neutral* – that it's organized for the sake of *no* particular interests at all! Telling people that science serves only the truth is safer than telling people that science serves *them*, because it not only hides the truth about who benefits, but deflects public attention away from the whole question. Belief in the value-neutrality of science can thus serve the conservative function of securing *unconditional* public support for what are in fact ruling-class initiatives. Any research agenda whatsoever – no matter how pernicious – can be readily legitimated on the grounds that it is the natural result of the self-justifying pursuit of truth, the more or less inevitable upshot of a careful look at the facts.

It will enhance the lie that science is objective, to augment it with the lie that scientists as individuals are especially "objective," either by nature or by dint of their scientific training. If laypersons can be brought to believe this, then the lie that scientific practice can transcend its compromised setting becomes somewhat easier to swallow. And if *scientists* can be brought to embrace this gratifying self-image, then the probability of *their* acquiescence in the existing system will be increased. Scientists will find little cause for critical reflection on their own potential biases (since they will believe that they are more able than others to put aside their own interests and background beliefs in the pursuit of knowledge), and no particular incentive to ponder the larger question of who actually is benefiting from their research.[46]

Now in such a society, the widespread acceptance of a theory of knowledge like the Dragnet theory would clearly be a good thing from the point of view of the ruling elite. By fostering the epistemic attitudes it fosters, the Dragnet theory helps confer special authority and status on science and its practitioners and deflects critical attention away from the material conditions in which science is conducted. Furthermore, by supporting Dragnet objectivity as an epistemic ideal, the theory prepares the ground for reception of the ideology of the objectivity of science.

In a society in which people have a reason to believe that science is successful in yielding knowledge, the Dragnet theory and the ideology of objectivity will in fact be mutually reinforcing. If one believes that science must be objective to be good, then if one independently believes that science is good, one must also believe that science *is objective!* The Dragnet theory, taken together with propagandistic claims that science is value-neutral, etc., offers an *explanation* of the fact that science leads to knowledge. Against the background belief that knowledge is actually structured the way the Dragnet theory says it is, the *success* of science seems to confirm the ideology.

We can conclude from all this that the Dragnet theory, along with the ideal of objectivity it sanctions, has clear ideological value, in the sense that their acceptance may play a causal role in people's acceptance of the ideology of scientific objectivity.

But we cannot infer from this fact either that the Dragnet theory is false or that its ideals are flawed. Such an inference depends on conflating what are essentially *prescriptive* claims (claims about how science ought to be conducted) with *descriptive* claims (claims about how science is in fact conducted). It's one thing to embrace some particular ideal of scientific method and quite another to accept ideologically useful assumptions about the satisfaction of that ideal within existing institutions.[47]

Note that in a society such as the one I've described, the ideological value of the Dragnet theory depends crucially on how successfully it can be promulgated *as a factual characterization* of the workings of the intellectual establishment. It's no use to get everyone to believe simply that it would be a good thing if scientists *could* put aside their prior beliefs and their personal interests; people must be brought to believe that scientists largely *succeed* in such divestitures. The ideological cloud of Dragnet objectivity thus comes not so much from the belief that science *ought* to be value-free, as from the belief that it *is* value-free. And of course it's precisely the fact that science is *not* value-free in the way it's proclaimed to be that makes the ideological ploy necessary in the first place.

If science as an institution fails to live up to its own ideal of objectivity, then the character of existing science entails nothing about the value of the ideal, nor about the character of some imagined science which *did* live up to it. In fact, notice that the more we can show that compromised science is *bad* science (in the sense of leading to false results), the less necessary we make it to challenge the Dragnet theory itself. A good part of the radical case, after all, is made by demonstrating the ways in which scientific research has been *distorted* by some of the very factors a Dragnet epistemologist would cite as inhibitors of epistemic progress: prejudiced beliefs, undefended hunches, material desires, ideological commitments.

There's no reason, in short, why a Dragnet theorist couldn't come to be convinced of the radical analysis of the material basis of science. Such a person might even be expected to experience a special kind of outrage at discovering the way in which the idea of objectivity is ideologically exploited in the service of special interests, much the way many peace activists felt when they first learned of some of the realities masked by US officials' pious avowals of their commitment to "human rights" and "democracy."

A materialist analysis of institutionalized science leads to awareness of such phenomena as the commoditization of knowledge, the "rationalization" of scientific research, and the proletarianization of scientists. Such phenomena make the limits of liberal reformism perfectly clear: Not even the most scrupulous adherence to prescribed method on the part of individual scientists could by itself effect the necessary transformations. But it's possible for even a Dragnet theorist to acknowledge these limits, and to do so without giving up the ideal of neutral objectivity.

I began by considering the claim, defended by several feminist theorists, that "traditional" epistemology limits the possibilities for exposing the machinations of the elite because it endorses the rules of the elite's game. On the contrary, I've argued; since a big part of the lie that needs exposing is the fact that capitalist science *doesn't follow* its own rules, the task of exposing the ideology of scientific objectivity needn't change the rules. A radical critique of science and society, *even if it* implicates certain ideals, *does not require repudiation of those ideals.*

Naturalized epistemology and the bias paradox

What I think I've shown so far is that if our only desideratum on an adequate critical epistemology is that it permits us to expose the real workings of capitalist patriarchy, then the Dragnet theory will do just fine, *pace* its feminist critics. But I certainly do not want to defend that theory; nor do I want to defend as an epistemic ideal the conception of objectivity as neutrality. In fact, I want to join feminist critics in rejecting this ideal. But I want to be clear about the proper basis for criticizing it.

There are, in general, two strategies that one can find in the epistemological literature for challenging the ideal of objectivity as impartiality. (I leave aside for the moment the question of why one might want to challenge an epistemic ideal, though this question will figure importantly in what follows.) The first strategy is to prove the *impossibility* of satisfying the ideal – this involves pointing to the *ubiquity* of bias. The second

strategy is to try to demonstrate the *undesirability* of satisfying the ideal – this involves showing the *utility* of bias. The second strategy is employed by some feminist critics, but often the first strategy is thought to be sufficient, particularly when it's pursued together with the kind of radical critique of institutionalized science discussed above. Thus Jaggar, Code, and others emphasize the essential locatedness of every individual knower, arguing that if all knowledge proceeds from some particular perspective, then the transcendent standpoint suggested by the ideology of objectivity is unattainable. All knowledge is conditioned by the knower's location, it is claimed; if we acknowledge that, then we cannot possibly believe that anyone is "objective" in the requisite sense.

But the appeal to the *de facto* partiality of all knowledge is simply not going to justify rejecting the ideal of objectivity, for three reasons. In the first place, the wanted intermediate conclusion – that Dragnet objectivity is impossible – does not follow from the truism that all knowers are located. The Dragnet conception of impartiality is perfectly compatible with the fact that all knowers start from some particular place. The Dragnet theory, like all empiricist theories, holds that knowledge is a strict function of the contingencies of experience. It therefore entails that differences in empirical situation will lead to differences in belief, and to that extent validates the intuition that all knowledge is partial.[48] Thus the neutrality recommended by the Dragnet theory does not enjoin cognizers to abjure the particularities of their own experience, only to honor certain strictures in drawing conclusions from that experience. Impartiality is not a matter of where you are, but rather how well you do from where you sit.

In the second place, even if it could be shown to be impossible for human beings to achieve perfect impartiality, that fact in itself would not speak against Dragnet objectivity *as an ideal.* Many ideals – particularly moral ones – are unattainable, but that does not make them useless, or reveal them to be inadequate as ideals.[49] The fact – and I have no doubt that it is a fact – that no one can fully rid oneself of prejudices, neurotic impulses, selfish desires, and other psychological detritus, does not impugn the moral or the cognitive value of attempting to do so. Similarly, the fact that no one can fully abide by the cognitive strictures imposed by the standards of strict impartiality doesn't entail that one oughtn't to try. The real test of the adequacy of a norm is not whether it can be realized, but (arguably) whether we get closer to what we want if we try to realize it.

But the third and most serious problem with this tack is that it is precisely the one that is going to engender the bias paradox. Notice that the feminist goal of exposing the structures of interestedness that constitute patriarchy and other forms of oppression requires doing more than just demonstrating that particular interests are being served. It requires criticizing that fact, showing that there's something wrong with a society in which science selectively serves the interests of one dominant group. And it's awfully hard to see how such a critical stand can be sustained without some appeal to the value of impartiality.

A similar problem afflicts the variation on this strategy that attempts to base a critique of the norm of objectivity on the androcentric features of its *source*. Even if it could be established that received epistemic norms originated in the androcentric fantasies of European white males (and I meant to give some reason to question this in section II), how is that fact supposed to be elaborated into a *critique* of those norms? All knowledge is partial – let it be so. How then does the particular partiality of received conceptions of objectivity diminish their worth?

The question that must be confronted by anyone pursuing this strategy is basically this: If bias is ubiquitous and ineliminable, then what's the good of exposing it? It seems to me that the whole thrust of feminist scholarship in this area has been to demonstrate that androcentric biases have distorted science and, indeed, distorted the search for knowledge generally. But if biases are distorting, and if we're all biased in one way or another, then it seems there could be no such thing as an *undistorted* search for knowledge. So what are we complaining about? Is it just that we want it to be distorted in *our* favor, rather than in theirs? We must say something about the badness of the biases we expose or our critique will carry no normative import at all.

We still have to look at the second of the two strategies for criticizing the ideal of objectivity, but this is a good place to pick up the question I bracketed earlier on: *Why* might one want to challenge an epistemic ideal? If my arguments have been correct up to this point, then I have shown that many of the arguments made against objectivity are not only unsound but ultimately self-defeating. But by now the reader must surely be wondering why we need *any* critique of the notion of objectivity as neutrality. If radical critiques of the ideology of scientific objectivity are consistent with respect for this ideal, and if we need some notion of objectivity anyway, why not this one?

The short answer is this: because the best empirical theories of knowledge and mind do not sanction pure neutrality as sound epistemic policy.

The fact is that the Dragnet theory is *wrong*. We know this for two reasons: First, the failure of externalism tells us that its foundationalist underpinnings are rotten, and second, current work in empirical psychology tells us that its empiricist conception of the mind is radically incorrect. But if the Dragnet theory is wrong about the structure of knowledge and the nature of the mind, then the main source of warrant for the ideal of epistemic neutrality is removed. It becomes an open question whether divestiture of emotions, prior beliefs, and moral commitments hinders, or aids, the development of knowledge.

The fact that we find ourselves wondering about the value of a proposed epistemic ideal is itself a consequence of the turn to a naturalized epistemology. As I explained in section II, Quine's critique of externalism entailed that epistemic norms themselves were among the presuppositions being subjected to empirical test in the ongoing process of theory confirmation. This in itself authorizes the project of *criticizing* norms – it makes coherent and gives point to a project which could be nothing but an exercise in skepticism, to an externalist's way of thinking.

Naturalized epistemology tells us that there is no presuppositionless position from which to assess epistemic practice, that we must take some knowledge for granted. The only thing to do, then, is to begin with whatever it is we think we know, and try to figure out how we came to know it: Study knowledge by studying the knower. Now if, in the course of such study, we discover that much of human knowledge is possible only because our knowledge seeking does not conform to the Dragnet model, then we will have good empirical grounds for rejecting perfect objectivity as an epistemic ideal. And so we come back to the second of the two strategies I outlined for challenging the ideal of objectivity. Is there a case to be made against the desirability of epistemic neutrality? Indeed there is, on the grounds that a genuinely open mind, far from leading us closer to the truth, would lead to epistemic chaos.

As I said in section II, empirical work in linguistics and cognitive science is making it increasingly clear how seriously mistaken the empiricist view of the mind actually is. From Chomsky's groundbreaking research on the acquisition of language, through David Marr's theory of the computational basis of vision, to the work of Susan Carey, Elizabeth Spelke, Barbara Landau, Lila Gleitman, and others in developmental psychology, the evidence is mounting that inborn conceptual structure is a crucial factor in the development of human knowledge.[50]

Far from being the streamlined, uncluttered logic machine of classical empiricism, the mind now appears to be much more like a bundle of highly specialized modules, each natively fitted for the analysis and manipulation of a particular body of sensory data. General learning strategies of the sort imagined by classical empiricists, if they are employed by the mind at all, can apply to but a small portion of the cognitive tasks that confront us. Rationalism vindicated.

But if the rationalists have turned out to be right about the structure of the mind, it is because they appreciated something that the empiricists missed – the value of partiality for human knowers. Whatever might work for an ideal mind, operating without constraints of time or space, it's clear by now that complete neutrality of the sort empiricists envisioned would not suit human minds in human environments. A completely "open mind," confronting the sensory evidence we confront, could never manage to construct the rich systems of knowledge we construct in the short time we take to construct them. From the point of view of an *unbiased* mind, the human sensory flow contains both too much information and too little: too much for the mind to generate *all* the logical possibilities, and too little for it to decide among even the relatively few that *are* generated.

The problem of paring down the alternatives is the defining feature of the human epistemic condition. The problem is partly solved, I've been arguing, by one form of "bias" – native conceptual structure. But it's important to realize that this problem is absolutely endemic to human knowledge seeking, whether we're talking about the subconscious processes by which we acquire language and compute sensory information, or the more consciously accessible processes by which we explicitly decide what to believe. The everyday process of forming an opinion would be grossly hampered if we were really to consider matters with anything even close to an "open mind."

This point is one that Quine has emphasized over and over in his discussions of the underdetermination of theory by data. If we had to rely on nothing but logic and the contingencies of sensory experience, we could never get anywhere in the process of forming an opinion, because we would have *too many choices*. There are an infinite number of distinct and incompatible hypotheses consistent with any body of data, never mind that there are always more data just around the corner, and never mind that we're logically free to reinterpret the "data" to save our hypotheses. If we really had to approach data gathering and theory building with a perfectly open mind, we wouldn't get anywhere.

This insight is also borne out by the history of science. As Thomas Kuhn has pointed out, science is at its least successful during the periods in its history when it most closely resembles the popular models of scientific objectivity. During a discipline's "pre-paradigm" phase, when there is no consensus about fundamental principles, nor even about what to count as the central phenomena, research is anarchic and unproductive. But progress accelerates dramatically when a discipline enters its mature period, marked by the emergence of a theory – a paradigm – capable of organizing the phenomena in a compelling enough way that it commands near-universal acceptance.

Kuhn emphasizes that one of the chief benefits a paradigm brings with it is a degree of closure about foundational issues, instilling in members of the community a principled and highly functional unwillingness to reconsider basic assumptions. The paradigm not only settles important empirical controversies, but also decides more methodological matters – what are the acceptable forms of evidence, what is the right vocabulary for discussing things, what are the proper standards for judging research. The fact is that all of these matters are disputable in principle – but a paradigm relieves its adherents of the considerable burden of having constantly to dispute them.

But what this means is that the practice and attitudes of scientists working within a paradigm will systematically deviate from the popular ideal of scientific objectivity: They will approach their research with definite preconceptions, and they will be reluctant to entertain hypotheses that conflict with their own convictions. Kuhn's point, however, is that the existence of such closed-mindedness among working scientists – what he calls "the dogmatism of mature science" – is not to be regretted; that it is actually beneficial to the course of scientific development: "Though preconception and resistance to innovation could very easily choke off scientific progress, their omnipresence is nonetheless symptomatic of characteristics upon which the continuing vitality of research depends."[51]

Once we appreciate these aspects of mature science, we can explain a great deal about how a fantasy of the pure objectivity of science can take hold independently of any ideological purposes such a fantasy might serve. (This is important if we want a serious, nuanced story about how ideologies work.) The fact that certain tenets of theory are, for all practical purposes, closed to debate can render invisible their actual status as hypotheses. Deeply entrenched theoretical principles, like the laws of thermodynamics or the principle of natural selection, become established "facts."[52] Similarly, the high degree of theoretical background required to translate various numbers and images into observations or data is forgotten by people accustomed to performing the requisite inferences on a daily basis.

Consensus and uniformity thus translate into objectivity. The more homogeneous an epistemic community, the more objective it is likely to regard itself, and, if its inquiries are relatively self-contained, the more likely it is to be viewed as objective by those outside the community. This suggests one fairly obvious explanation for the general perception that the physical sciences are more objective than the social sciences: Sociology, political science, economics, and psychology are disciplines that still lack paradigms in Kuhn's

technical sense. Because there is still public debate in these fields about basic theoretical and methodological issues, there can be no credible pretense by any partisan of having hold of the unvarnished truth.

The kind of bias that Kuhn is here identifying is, of course, different in several important respects from the kinds of biases that classical rationalists and contemporary cognitive psychologists are concerned with. For one thing, the biases that come with belief in a paradigm are acquired rather than innate; for another, there is an important social component in one case but not in the other. The lesson, however, is still the same: Human beings would know less, not more, if they were to actualize the Dragnet ideal.

What all this means is that a naturalized approach to knowledge provides us with *empirical* grounds for rejecting pure neutrality as an epistemic ideal, and for valuing those kinds of "biases" that serve to trim our epistemic jobs to manageable proportions. But it also seems to mean that we have a new route to the bias paradox – if biases are now not simply ineliminable, but downright *good*, how is it that *some* biases are *bad*?

I'm going to answer this question, honest, but first let me show how bad things really are. It's possible to see significant analogies between the function of a paradigm within a scientific community, and what is sometimes called a "worldview" within other sorts of human communities. Worldviews confer some of the same cognitive benefits as paradigms, simplifying routine epistemic tasks, establishing an informal methodology of inquiry, etc., and they also offer significant social benefits, providing a common sense of reality and fostering a functional sense of normalcy among members of the community.

But what about those outside the community? A shared language, a set of traditions and mores, a common sense of what's valuable and why – the very things that bind some human beings together in morally valuable ways – function simultaneously to exclude those who do not share them. Moreover, human communities are not homogeneous. In a stratified community, where one group of people dominates others, the worldview of the dominant group can become a powerful tool for keeping those in the subordinate groups in their places.

The real problem with the liberal conceptions of objectivity and neutrality begins with the fact that while they are unrealizable, it's possible for those resting comfortably in the center of a consensus to find that fact invisible. Members of the dominant group are given no reason to question their own assumptions: Their world-view acquires, in their minds, the status of established fact. Their opinions are transformed into what "everybody" knows.[53] Furthermore, these privileged individuals have the power to promote and elaborate their own worldview in public forums while excluding all others, tacitly setting limits to the range of "reasonable" opinion.[54]

Because of the familiarity of its content, the "objectivity" of such reportage is never challenged. If it were, it would be found woefully lacking *by liberal standards*. That's because the liberal ideal of objectivity is an *unreasonable* one; it is not just unattainable, but unattainable by a long measure. But because the challenge is *only* mounted against views that are aberrant, it is *only* such views that will ever be demonstrated to be "non-objective," and thus *only* marginal figures that will ever be charged with bias.[55]

Lorraine Code makes a similar point about the unrealistic stringency of announced standards for knowledge.[56] She rightly points out that most of what we ordinarily count as knowledge wouldn't qualify as such by many proposed criteria. I would go further and say that as with all unrealistically high standards, they tend to support the status quo – in this case, received opinion – by virtue of the fact that they will only be invoked in "controversial" cases, i.e., in case of challenge to familiar or received or "expert" opinion. Since the standards are unreasonably high, the views tested against them will invariably be found wanting; since the only views so tested will be unpopular ones, their failure to pass muster serves to add additional warrant to prevailing prejudices, as well as a patina of moral vindication to the holders of those prejudices, who can self-righteously claim to have given "due consideration" to the "other side."

But what are we anti-externalist, naturalized epistemologists to say about this? We can't simply condemn the members of the dominant class for their "bias," for their lack of "open-mindedness" about our point of view. To object to the hegemony of ruling-class opinion on this basis would be to tacitly endorse the discredited norm of neutral objectivity. "Biased" they are, but then, in a very deep sense, so are we. The problem with ruling-class "prejudices" cannot be the fact that they are deeply-held beliefs, or beliefs acquired "in advance" of the facts – for the necessity of such *kinds* of belief is part of the human epistemic condition.

The real problem with the ruling-class worldview is not that it is biased; it's that it is false. The epistemic problem with ruling-class people is not that they are closed-minded; it's that they hold too much power. The recipe for radical epistemological action then becomes simple: Tell the truth and get enough power so that people have to listen. Part of telling the truth, remember, is telling the truth about how knowledge is actually constructed – advocates of feminist epistemology are absolutely correct about that. We do need to dislodge those attitudes about knowledge that give unearned credibility to elements of the ruling-class worldview, and this means dislodging the hold of the Dragnet theory of knowledge. But we must be clear: The Dragnet theory is not false because it's pernicious; it's pernicious because it is false.

Whether we are talking in general about the ideology of scientific objectivity, or about particular sexist and racist theories, we must be willing to talk about truth and falsity. If we criticize such theories primarily on the basis of their ideological function, we risk falling prey to the very illusions about objectivity that we are trying to expose. I think this has happened to some extent within feminist epistemology. Because so much of feminist criticism has been oblivious to the rationalistic case that can be made against the empiricistic conceptions of mind at work in the Dragnet theory, empiricistic assumptions continue to linger in the work of even the most radical feminist epistemologists. This accounts, I believe, for much of the ambivalence about Dragnet objectivity expressed even by those feminist critics who argue most adamantly for its rejection.

This ambivalence surfaces, not surprisingly, in discussions about what to do about bad biases, where positive recommendations tend to fall perfectly in line with the program of liberal reformism. Lorraine Code's discussion of stereotypical thinking provides a case in point.[57] Code emphasizes, quite correctly, the degree to which stereotypical assumptions shape the interpretation of experience, both in science and in everyday life. But despite her recognition of the "unlikelihood of pure objectivity,"[58] the "unattainability of pure theory-neutrality,"[59] and her acknowledgment of the necessary role of background theory *in science*, her recommendations for reforming everyday epistemic practice are very much in the spirit of liberal exhortations to open-mindedness. She sees a difference between a scientist's reliance on his or her paradigm, and ordinary dependence on stereotypes:

> It is not possible for practitioners to engage in normal science without paradigms to guide their recognition of problems, and their problem-solving endeavours. Stereotype-governed thinking is different in this respect, for it is both possible and indeed desirable to think and to know in a manner *not* governed by stereotypes.[60]

But it's by no means clear that it *is* possible. I sense that Code has not appreciated the depth of human reliance on theories that cannot be shown to be "derived from the facts alone." In characterizing certain kinds of background belief and certain forms of "hasty generalization" *as stereotypes*, she is presupposing a solution to the very problem that must be solved: viz., telling which of the background theories that we routinely bring to bear on experience are *reliable* and which ones are not.

The liberal epistemological fantasy, still somewhat at work here, is that there will be formal marks that distinguish good theories from bad. The empiricist version of this fantasy is that the formal mark consists in a proper relation between theory and "fact." In this case, the good theories are supposed to be the ones that derive in the proper way from the data, whereas the bad ones – the biases, the prejudices, the stereotypes – are the ones that antedate the data. But once we realize that theory infects observation and that confirmation is a multidirectional relation, we must also give up on the idea that the good theories are going to look different from the bad theories. They can't be distinguished on the basis of their formal relation to the "facts," because (1) there are no "facts" in the requisite sense, and (2) there are too many good biases whose relation to the

data will appear as tenuous as those of the bad ones.

But what's the alternative?

A naturalized approach to knowledge, because it requires us to give up *neutrality* as an epistemic ideal, also requires us to take a different attitude toward bias. We know that human knowledge requires biases; we also know that we have no possibility of getting *a priori* guarantees that our biases incline us in the right direction. What all this means is that the "biasedness" of biases drops out as a parameter of epistemic evaluation. There's only one thing to do, and it's the course always counseled by a naturalized approach: *We must treat the goodness or badness of particular biases as an empirical question.*

A naturalistic study of knowledge tells us biases are good when and to the extent that they facilitate the gathering of *knowledge* – that is, when they lead us to the truth. Biases are bad when they lead us *away* from the truth. One important strategy for telling the difference between good and bad biases is thus to evaluate the overall theories in which the biases figure. This one point has important implications for feminist theory in general and for feminist attitudes about universalist or essentialist theories of human nature in particular.

As we saw in section II, much of the feminist criticism raised against cognitive essentialism focused on the fact that rationalist and Kantian theories of the human essence were all devised by men, and based, allegedly, on exclusively male experience. Be that so – it would still follow from a naturalized approach to the theory of knowledge that it is an *empirical* question whether or not "androcentrism" of that sort leads to bad theories. Partiality does not in general compromise theories; as we feminists ourselves have been insisting, all theorizing proceeds from *some* location or other. We must therefore learn to be cautious of claims to the effect that particular forms of partiality will inevitably and systematically influence the outcome of an investigation. Such claims must be treated as empirical hypotheses, subject to investigation and challenge, rather than as enshrined first principles.

So what about universalist or essentialist claims concerning human nature? I have argued that there really are no grounds for regarding such claims as antipathetic to feminist aspirations or even to feminist insights regarding the importance of embodiment or the value of human difference. Suggestions that essentialist theories reify aspects of specifically male experience, I argued, involve a serious misunderstanding of the rationalist strategy. But notice that even if such charges were true, the real problem with such theories should be their *falseness*, rather than their androcentrism. A theory that purports to say what human beings are like essentially must apply to *all human beings;* if it does not, it is wrong, whatever its origins.

In fact, I think there is excellent evidence for the existence of a substantial human nature and virtually no evidence for the alternative, the view that there is no human essence. But what's really important is to recognize that the latter view is as much a substantive empirical thesis as the Cartesian claim that we are essentially rational language-users. We need to ask ourselves *why* we ought to believe that human selves are, at the deepest level, "socially constructed" – the output of a confluence of contingent factors.[61]

Another thing that a naturalized approach to knowledge offers us is the possibility of *an empirical theory of biases*. As we've already seen, there are different kinds of biases – some are natively present, some are acquired. An empirical study of biases can refine the taxonomy and possibly tell us something about the reliability and the corrigibility of biases of various sorts. It may turn out that we can on this basis get something like a principled sorting of biases into good ones and bad ones, although it will be more likely that we'll learn that even a "good" bias can lead us astray in certain circumstances.[62]

One likely upshot of an empirical investigation of bias is a better understanding of the processes by which human beings design research programs. What we decide to study and how we decide to study it are matters in which unconscious biases – tendencies to see certain patterns rather than others, to attend to certain factors rather than others, to act in accordance with certain interests rather than others – play a crucial role. We can't eliminate the biases – we shouldn't want to, for we'd have no research programs left if we did – but we can identify the particular empirical presuppositions that lie behind a particular program of research so that we can subject them, if necessary, to empirical critique.

One important issue is the *saliency* of certain properties. Every time a study is designed, a decision is made, tacitly or explicitly, to pay attention to some factors and to ignore others. These "decisions" represent tacit or explicit hypotheses about the likely connection between various aspects of the phenomena under study, hypotheses that can be subjected to empirical scrutiny.

Imagine a study purporting to investigate the development of human language by examining a sample of two hundred preschoolers. Must the sample, to be a valid basis for extrapolation, contain boys and girls? Must it be racially mixed? How one answers this question will depend on the empirical assumptions one makes about the likely connection between parameters like gender and race, on the one hand, and the language faculty on the other. To think that gender or race must be controlled for in such studies is to make a substantive empirical conjecture – in this case, it is to deny the rationalistic hypothesis that human beings' biological endowment includes a brain structured in a characteristic way, and to make instead the assumption that cognitive development is sensitive to the kinds of differences that we *socially* encode as gender and race.

Such an assumption, laid out this baldly, seems pretty dubious. Indeed, it's hard to see what such an assumption is doing other than reflecting sexist, racist, and classist beliefs to the effect that social groupings are determined by biological groupings. Realizing this is a necessary first step to countering the genuinely pernicious "essentialist" theories of Jensen, Herrnstein, and the human sociobiologists and to exposing the racism and sexism inherent in their programs of "research." Such "research" is precisely at odds with rationalist methodology, which only invokes human essences as a way of explaining human *commonalities* – and then, only when such commonalities cannot plausibly be explained by regularities in the environment.

Consider, for example, the claims that blacks are "innately" less intelligent than whites.[63] In the first place, we must point out, as we do, that race is not a biological kind, but rather a *social* kind. That is to say that while there may be a biological explanation for the presence of each of the characteristics that constitute racial criteria – skin color, hair texture, and the like – the *selection of those characteristics as criteria* of membership in some category is *conventionally* determined. Here is where the empiricist notion of "nominal essence" has some work to do: race, in contrast to some other categories, *is* socially constructed.

The second step is to point out that if such classifications as race fail to reflect deep regularities in human biology, and reflect instead only historically and culturally specific interests, then there is no reason, *apart from racist ones*, to investigate the relation between race and some presumably biological feature of human beings. Again, it takes an extreme form of empiricism to believe that brute correlations between one arbitrarily selected characteristic and another constitutes *science* – but even from such a perspective it must be an arbitrary choice to investigate one set of such correlations rather than another. Why intelligence and *race*? Why not intelligence and number of hair follicles?

It is this point that really gives the lie to Herrnstein's repugnant invocation of "scientific objectivity" in defense of his racist undertakings.[64] The fact that there is no empirical grounding for the selection of race as a theoretical parameter in the study of intelligence utterly defeats the disingenuous defense that such "science" as Herrnstein is engaged in is simply detached fact gathering – callin' 'em like he sees 'em. The decision to use race as an analytical category betrays a host of substantive assumptions that would be exceedingly hard to defend once made explicit. How could one defend the proposition that race and intelligence are connected without confronting the embarrassing fact that there's no biologically defensible definition of "race"? And how could one defend the proposition that human "mating strategies" will receive their explanation at the biological level, without having to explicitly argue against the wealth of competing explanations available at the social and personal/intentional levels?[65]

In sum, a naturalized approach to knowledge requires us, as feminists and progressives, to be critical of the saliency such categories as gender and race have *for us*. The fact that such parameters have been egregiously overlooked in cases where they are demonstrably relevant shouldn't make us think automatically that they are always theoretically significant. The recognition that selection of analytical categories is an empirical matter, governed by both background theory and

consideration of the facts, is in itself part of the solution to the paradox of partiality.

The naturalized approach proceeds by showing the empirical inadequacy of the theory of mind and knowledge that makes perfect neutrality seem like a good thing. But at the same time that it removes the warrant for one epistemic ideal, it gives support for new norms, ones that will enable us to criticize some biases without presupposing the badness of bias in general. The naturalized approach can therefore vindicate all of the insights feminist theory has produced regarding the ideological functions of the concept of objectivity without undercutting the critical purpose of exposing androcentric and other objectionable forms of bias, when they produce oppressive falsehoods.

The End

I began this essay by asking whether we need a "feminist" epistemology, and I answered that we did, as long as we understood that need to be the need for an epistemology informed by feminist insight, and responsive to the moral imperatives entailed by feminist commitments. But I've argued that we do not necessarily need a conceptual transformation of epistemological theory in order to get a feminist epistemology in this sense. We need, in the first instance, a *political* transformation of the society in which theorizing about knowledge takes place. We've got to stop the oppression of women, eliminate racism, redistribute wealth, and *then* see what happens to our collective understanding of knowledge.

My bet? That some of the very same questions that are stimulating inquiry among privileged white men, right now in these sexist, racist, capitalist–imperialist times, are *still* going to be exercising the intellects and challenging the imaginations of women of color, gay men, physically handicapped high school students, etc.

I'm not saying that we should stop doing epistemology until after the revolution. That would of course be stupid, life being short. What I am saying is that those of us who think we know what feminism is, must guard constantly against the presumptuousness we condemn in others, of claiming as Feminist the particular bit of ground upon which we happen to be standing. We need to remember that part of what unites philosophers who choose to characterize their own work as "feminist" is the conviction that philosophy ought to matter – that it should make a positive contribution to the construction of a more just, humane, and nurturing world than the one we currently inhabit.

I have argued that contemporary analytic philosophy is capable of making such a contribution and that it is thus undeserving of the stigma "malestream" philosophy. But there's more at stake here than the abstract issue of mischaracterization. Attacks on the analytic tradition as "androcentric," "phallogocentric," or "male-identified" are simultaneously attacks on the feminist credentials of those who work within the analytic tradition. And the stereotyping of contemporary analytic philosophy – the tendency to link it with views (like the Dragnet theory) to which it is in fact antipathetic – has

turned feminists away from fruitful philosophical work, limiting our collective capacity to imagine genuinely novel and transformative philosophical strategies.

I acknowledge both the difficulty and the necessity of clarifying the implications of feminist theory for other kinds of endeavors. It's important, therefore, for feminist theorists to continue to raise critical challenges to particular theories and concepts. But surely this can be done without the caricature, without the throwaway refutations, in a way that is more respectful of philosophical differences.

Let's continue to argue with each other by all means. But let's stop arguing about which view is more feminist, and argue instead about which view is more likely to be true. Surely we can trust the dialectical process of feminists discussing these things with other feminists to yield whatever "feminist epistemology" we need.

Notes

1 A possible exception may be Jean Grimshaw, who comes closer than any other thinker I've encountered to endorsing what I'm calling a "bare proceduralist" conception of feminist philosophy: "There is no particular view, for example, of autonomy, of morality, of self, no one characterisation of women's activities which can be appealed to in any clear way as the woman's (or feminist) view. But I think nevertheless that feminism makes a difference to philosophy. The difference it makes is that women, in doing philosophy, have often raised new problems, problematised issues in new ways and moved to the centre questions which have been marginalised or seen as unimportant or at the periphery." From Grimshaw, *Philosophy and Feminist Thinking* (Minneapolis: University of Minnesota Press, 1986), p. 260.

2 Naomi Scheman made this point in a letter to members of the Committee on the Status of Women of the American Philosophical Association in 1988, when she and I were serving on the committee. Her letter was partly a response to a letter of mine raising questions about whether our charge as a committee should include the promotion of "feminist philosophy."

3 For discussions of epistemological frameworks available to feminists, see Sandra Harding, *The Science Question in Feminism*, (Ithaca, NY: Cornell University Press, 1986), especially pp. 24–9; Mary Hawkesworth, "Feminist Epistemology: A Survey of the Field," *Women and Politics* 7 (1987), pp. 112–24; and Hilary Rose, "Hand, Brain, and Heart: A Feminist Epistemology for the Natural Sciences," *Signs* 9, 11 (1983), pp. 73–90.

4 See Mary E. Hawkesworth, "Knowers, Knowing, Known: Feminist Theory and Claims of Truth," *Signs* 14, 3 (1989), pp. 533–57.

5 See, for example, Sandra Harding: "I have been arguing for open acknowledgement, even enthusiastic appreciation, of certain tensions that appear in the feminist critiques. I have been suggesting that these reflect valuable alternative social projects which are in opposition to the coerciveness and regressiveness of modern science. ... [S]table and coherent theories are not always the ones to be most highly desired; there are important understandings to be gained in seeking the social origins of instabilities and incoherences in our thoughts

and practices – understandings that we cannot arrive at if we repress recognition of instabilities and tensions in our thought" (*Science Question in Feminism*, pp. 243–4).

6 See Naomi Scheman, "Othello's Doubt/ Desdemona's Death: The Engendering of Skepticism," in *Power, Gender, Values,* ed. Judith Genova (Edmonton, Alberta: Academic Printing and Publishing, 1987); and also Scheman's essay in this volume. See also Evelyn Fox Keller, "Cognitive Repression in Physics," *American Journal of Physics* 47 (1979), pp. 718–21; and "Feminism and Science," in *Sex and Scientific Inquiry,* ed. S. Harding and J. O'Barr (Chicago: University of Chicago Press, 1987), pp. 233–46, reprinted in *The Philosophy of Science,* ed. Richard Boyd, Philip Gaspar, and John Trout (Cambridge, MA: MIT Press, 1991).

7 For example, see Catharine A. MacKinnon, *Towards a Feminist Theory of the State* (Cambridge, MA: Harvard University Press, 1989).

8 This is not quite right – the ideology of 'objectivity' is perfectly capable of charging those *outside* the inner circle with partiality, and indeed, such charges are also crucial to the preservation of the status quo. More on this below.

9 Lorraine Code, "The Impact of Feminism on Epistemology," *APA Newsletter on Feminism and Philosophy* 88, 2 (March 1989), pp. 25–9.

10 Lorraine Code, "Experience, Knowledge, and Responsibility," in *Feminist Perspectives in Philosophy*, ed. Morwenna Griffiths and Margaret Whitford (Bloomington: Indiana University Press, 1988), pp. 189ff.

11 Code, "Impact of Feminism on Epistemology," p. 25.

12 It might be objected that there is a third option – that we could criticize those biases that are biases against our interests and valorize those that promote our interests. But if we are in fact left with only this option, then we are giving up on the possibility of any medium of social change other than power politics. This is bad for two reasons: (1) As moral and political theory, egoism should be repugnant to any person ostensibly concerned with justice and human well-being;

and (2) as tactics, given current distributions of power, it's really stupid.

13 I have defended a kind of non-realist conception of truth, but one which maintains this gap. See my "Can Verificationists Make Mistakes?" *American Philosophical Quarterly* 24, 3 (July 1987), pp. 225–36. For a defense of a more robustly realist conception of truth, see Michael Devitt, *Realism and Truth* (Princeton, NJ: Princeton University Press, 1984). (2nd edn, 1997.)

14 Code, "Impact of Feminism on Epistemology," p. 25.

15 Significantly, these theories are not all empiricist, and the theories that are most "post-positivist" are the least empiricist of all. I'll have much more to say about this in what follows.

16 See, e.g., Helene Cixous, "The Laugh of the Medusa," tr. Keith Cohen and Paula Cohen, *Signs* 1, 4 (1976), pp. 875–93; Luce Irigaray, "Is the Subject of Science Sexed?" tr. Carol Mastrangelo Bove, *Hypatia* 2, 3 (Fall 1987), pp. 65–87; and Andrea Nye, "The Inequalities of Semantic Structure: Linguistics and Feminist Philosophy," *Metaphilosophy* 18, 3–4 (July/October 1987), pp. 222–40. I must say that for the sweepingness of Nye's claims regarding "linguistics" and "semantic theory," her survey of work in these fields is, to say the least, narrow and out-of-date.

17 See, e.g., Ruth Ginzberg, "Feminism, Rationality, and Logic" and "Teaching Feminist Logic," *APA Newsletter on Feminism and Philosophy* 88, 2 (March 1989), pp. 34–42 and 58–65.

18 Note that the term "Enlightenment" itself does not have any single, precise meaning, referring in some contexts to only the philosophers (and *philosophes*) of eighteenth-century France, in other contexts to any philosopher lying on the trajectory of natural-rights theory in politics, from Hobbes and Locke through Rousseau, and in still other contexts to all the canonical philosophical works of the seventeenth and eighteenth centuries, up to and including Kant. I shall try to use the term "early modern philosophy" to denote seventeenth-century rationalism and empiricism, but I may slip up.

19 In Alison Jaggar, *Feminist Politics and Human Nature* (Totowa, NJ: Rowman and Allenheld, 1983), p. 355.

20 In Harding, *Science Question in Feminism*, p. 24.

21 Jane Flax, "Postmodernism and Gender Relations in Feminist Theory," *Signs* 12, 4 (Summer 1987), p. 624.

22 Ibid., p. 627.

23 Never mind Kant, who, apart from this note, I'm going to pretty much ignore. Virtually nothing that Flax cites as constitutive of the Enlightenment legacy can be easily found in Kant. He was not a dualist, at least not a Cartesian dualist; his opinions regarding the possible existence of a mind-independent reality were complicated (to say the least), but he clearly thought that it would be impossible for human beings to gain knowledge of such a world if it *did* exist; and the reading of the Categorical Imperative – how does it go? "Treat others as ends-in-themselves, never merely as means"? – that has Kant coming out as ignorant or neglectful of human difference seems to me to be positively Orwellian.

24 Harding is an exception, since she acknowledges Quine, though nothing after Quine. Code does allude to there being some changes in mainstream epistemology since the heyday of positivism, but she says that the changes are not of the right nature to license the questions she thinks are central to feminist epistemology. The only contemporary analytic epistemologist Code ever cites in either of her two books is Alvin Goldman, whom she does not discuss.

This is ironic, because Goldman has been one of the chief advocates of a version of epistemology called reliabilism, that makes the actual circumstances of belief production an essential part of their justification. See his *Epistemology and Cognition* (Cambridge, MA: Harvard University Press, 1986). It is also terribly unfair. Goldman takes it to be a truism that knowledge has a social component and that the study of knowledge requires consideration of the social situation of the knower: "Most knowledge is a cultural product, channeled through language and social communication. So how could

epistemology *fail* to be intertwined with studies of culture and social systems?" I do not believe Goldman deserves the opprobrium Code heaps upon him.

Jaggar, too, acknowledges that positivism has lost favor, but says nothing about the shape of the theories that have succeeded it. See Jaggar, *Feminist Politics*.

25 Cognitive essentialism generally gets associated with another thesis singled out for criticism – namely, dualism, the view that the mind is separate from the body and that the self is to be identified with the mind. Although dualism is not exclusively a rationalist view (Locke is standardly classified as a dualist), it is most closely associated with Descartes, and it is Descartes's *a priori* argument for dualism in the *Meditations* that seems to draw the most fire. Cartesian dualism is seen as providing a metaphysical rationale for dismissing the relevance of material contingencies to the assessment of knowledge claims, because it separates the knowing subject from the physical body, and because it seems to assert the sufficiency of disembodied reason for the attainment of knowledge.

In fact, dualism is a red herring. It's an uncommon view in the history of philosophy. Many people classically characterized as dualists, like Plato, were surely not Cartesian dualists. And on top of that, the dualism does no work. Being a dualist is neither necessary nor sufficient for believing that the human essence is composed of cognitive properties.

26 Flax, "Postmodernism," p. 626.

27 "Individualism" as Jaggar uses it is rather a term of art. It has a variety of meanings within philosophical discourse, but I don't know of any standard use within epistemology that matches Jaggar's. In the philosophy of mind, the term denotes the view that psychological states can be individuated for purposes of scientific psychology, without reference to objects or states outside the individual. This use of the term has *nothing* to do with debates in political theory about such issues as individual rights or individual autonomy. A liberal view of the moral/political individual can work just as well (or as poorly) on an anti-individualist psychology

(such as Hilary Putnam's or Tyler Burge's) as on an individualist view like Jerry Fodor's.

28 See also Naomi Scheman's essay in this volume.

29 Jaggar, "Postmodernism," p. 355.

30 Ibid.

31 See, for example, the excerpts from *Notes Directed against a Certain Program*, in Margaret Wilson, ed., *The Essential Descartes* (New York: Mentor Press, 1969).

32 Ibid., p. 112.

33 Ibid. One passage from one work should, of course, not be enough to convince anyone, and Descartes is clearly fictionalizing his own history to some extent (like who doesn't?). I do not have the space here to provide a full defense of my interpretation, but I invite you to read the *Discourse* on your own.

34 A little qualification is necessary here: The empiricist's requirement that all concepts be reducible to sensory simples does count as a substantive restriction on the possible contents of thought, but it's one which is vitiated by the reductionist semantic theory favored by empiricists, which denies the meaningfulness of any term which cannot be defined in terms of sensory primitives. See the discussion of this point in Jerry Fodor, *Modularity of Mind: An Essay on Faculty Psychology* (Cambridge, MA: MIT Press, 1983).

Also, the empiricists did allow a kind of "bias" in the form of innate standards of similarity, which would permit the mind to see certain ideas as inherently resembling certain others. This innate similarity metric was needed to facilitate the operation of *association,* which was the mechanism for generating more complex and more abstract ideas out of the sensory simples. But the effects of a bias such as this were vitiated by the fact that associations could also be forged by the contiguity of ideas in experience, with the result once more that no effective, substantive limits were placed on the ways in which human beings could analyze the data presented them by sensory experience.

35 David Hume, *An Enquiry Concerning Human Understanding* (Indianapolis: Hackett, 1977), p. 30. For a different assessment of Hume's

potential contributions to a feminist epistemology, see Annette Baier's essay in L. Antony and C. Witt (eds), *A Mind of One's Own* (Boulder, CO: Westview, 1993).

36 I have been much chastised by serious scholars of early-twentieth-century analytic philosophy (specifically Warren Goldfarb, Neil Tennant, and Philip Kitcher) for here reinforcing the myth that logical positivism was a uniform "school of thought." I guess I should thank them. The view that I am labeling "positivism" is the usual received view of the movement, but it may have belonged to only some of the more flatfooted and marginal members of the group (like A. J. Ayer) and certainly was not the view of the most important philosopher in the movement, Rudolf Carnap.

Still, the version of positivism I am outlining is the version that Quine attributed to his predecessors, and the version that he was reacting against. Moreover, even if Carnap was not an externalist in the sense of seeking a metaphysical vindication of scientific practice (as Michael Friedman argues in "The Re-evaluation of Logical Positivism," *Journal of Philosophy* 88, 10 [October 1991], pp. 505–19), he still was committed to a sharp separation between contentful and merely analytic statements, which is enough to generate the kinds of difficulties that I'm claiming beset positivism generally. My thanks to Marcia Homiak for calling my attention to the Friedman article.

37 Here are some of the most important works: W. V. O. Quine, "Two Dogmas of Empiricism," reprinted in Quine, *From a Logical Point of View* (Cambridge, MA: Harvard University Press, 1953); Carl G. Hempel, "Problems and Changes in the Empiricist Criterion of Meaning," *Revue Internationale de Philosophie* 11 (1950), pp. 41–63, and "Empiricist Criteria of Cognitive Significance: Problems and Changes," in Hempel, *Aspects of Scientific Explanation and Other Essays in the Philosophy of Science* (New York: Free Press, 1965); Nelson Goodman, *Fact, Fiction, and Forecast* (Cambridge, MA: Harvard University Press, 1955); and Hilary Putnam, "What Theories Are Not," reprinted in Putnam, *Mathematics, Matter, and Method:*

Philosophical Papers, Vol. I (Cambridge: Cambridge University Press, 1975).

38 Quine and J. S. Ullian catalog these principles – which they refer to as the "virtues" of hypotheses – in an epistemological primer called *The Web of Belief* (New York: Random House, 1970). Quine and Ullian employ a strikingly Humean strategy in trying to explain the epistemological value of the virtues.

39 W. V. O. Quine, "Epistemology Naturalized," in Quine, *Ontological Relativity and Other Essays* (New York: Columbia University Press, 1969), pp. 69–90.

40 See Noam Chomsky, "Review of B. F. Skinner's *Verbal Behavior*," *Language* 35, 1 (1959), pp. 53–68.

41 See Noam Chomsky, "Quine's Empirical Assumptions," in *Words and Objections: Essays on the Work of W. V. Quine*, ed. D. Davidson and J. Hintikka (Dordrecht: D. Reidel, 1969). See also Quine's response to Chomsky in the same volume.

I discuss the inconsistency between Quine's commitment to naturalism and his *a prioristic* rejection of mentalism and nativism in linguistics in "Naturalized Epistemology and the Study of Language," in *Naturalistic Epistemology: A Symposium of Two Decades*, ed. Abner Shimony and Debra Nails (Dordrecht: D. Reidel, 1987), pp. 235–57.

42 For an extremely helpful account of the Chomskian approach to the study of language, see David Lightfoot's *The Language Lottery: Toward a Biology of Grammars* (Cambridge, MA: MIT Press, 1984).

43 I take this to be an established fact. There's a mountainous body of scholarship on this issue, much of it the result of feminist concerns about specific ways in which women have been excluded from and damaged by institutionalized science. The whole area of biological determinist theorists provides an excellent case study of the ways in which science both supports and is distorted by social stratification. *Genes and Gender II*, ed. by Ruth Hubbard and Marian Lowe (New York: Gordion Press, 1979), is a collection of now classic articles critically examining alleged biological and ethological evidence for the genetic basis of gender differences. For a more current analysis of similar research in neurophysiology and endocrinology, see Helen Longino, *Science as Social Knowledge* (Princeton, NJ: Princeton University Press, 1990), ch. 6. Two excellent general discussions of the interactions among politics, economics, ideology, and science as exemplified by the growth of biological determinist theories are Stephen Jay Gould, *The Mismeasure of Man* (New York: W. W. Norton, 1981); and R. C. Lewontin, Steven Rose, and Leon J. Kamin, *Not in Our Genes* (New York: Pantheon Books, 1984).

44 Evelyn Fox Keller, "Feminism and Science," in Boyd, Gaspar, and Trout, eds, *Philosophy of Science*, p. 281. In this passage, Keller is also remarking on the tendency of (what she views as) the liberal critiques to focus on the "softer" biological and social sciences, and to leave alone the "harder" sciences of math and physics.

45 Carl R. Hempel, *Philosophy of Natural Science* (Englewood Cliffs, NJ: Prentice-Hall, 1966). See especially pp. 10–18.

46 There's a good case to be made that scientists actually have *disincentives* to ponder such questions. The structure of incentives in academia necessitates rapid generation and publication of research, and research requires securing long-term funding, usually from a government agency or a private corporate foundation. Scientific research is thus heavily compromised at the outset, whatever the ideals and values of the individual scientist. For a detailed discussion of the ways in which academic and economic pressures systematically erode "objectivity" in science, see William Broad and Nicholas Wade, *Betrayers of the Truth: Fraud and Deceit in the Halls of Science* (New York: Simon and Schuster, 1982).

47 This follows from a general point emphasized by Georges Rey in personal conversation: It's important in general to distinguish people's theories of human institutions from the actual character of those institutions.

48 This despite the fact that the Dragnet theory supports a strong context of discovery/context of justification distinction. On empiricist theories, the justification of an individual's belief is ultimately a relation

between the belief and the sensory experience of that individual. Location matters, then, because the same belief could be justified for one individual and unjustified for another, precisely because of the differences in their experiences.

49 This is not to say that there are no puzzling issues about moral ideals that are in some sense humanly unattainable. One such issue arises with respect to the ideals of altruism and supererogation, ideals which it would be, arguably, *unhealthy* for human beings to fully realize. See Larry Blum, Marcia Homiak, Judy Housman, and Naomi Scheman, "Altruism and Women's Oppression," in *Women and Philosophy*, ed. Carol C. Gould and Marx W. Wartofsky (New York: G. P. Putnam, 1980), pp. 222–47. On the question of whether it would be good for human beings to fully realize *any* moral ideal, see Susan Wolf, "Moral Saints," *The Journal of Philosophy* 79, 8 (August 1982), pp. 419–39.

50 Jerry Fodor, *Modularity of Mind* (Cambridge, MA: MIT Press, 1983); Noam Chomsky, *Reflections on Language* (New York: Random House, 1975); David Marr, *Vision: A Computational Investigation Into the Human Representation and Processing of Visual Information* (San Francisco: W. H. Freeman, 1982); Susan Carey, *Conceptual Change in Childhood* (Cambridge, MA: MIT Press, 1985); Elizabeth Spelke, "Perceptual Knowledge of Objects in Infancy," in J. Mehler, E. C. T. Walker, and M. Garrett, eds, *Perspectives on Mental Representations* (Hillsdale, NY: Erlbaum, 1982); Barbara Landau and Lila Gleitman, *Language and Experience: Evidence from the Blind Child* (Cambridge, MA: Harvard University Press, 1985); Steven Pinker, *Learnability and Cognition: The Acquisition of Argument Structure* (Cambridge, MA: MIT Press, 1989).

51 Thomas S. Kuhn, "The Function of Dogma in Scientific Research," (1963), reprinted in Janet A. Kourany, *Scientific Knowledge* (Belmont, CA: Wadsworth, 1987), pp. 253–65. Quotation is from p. 254.

52 This phenomenon affects even as sensitive and sophisticated a critic of science as Stephen Jay Gould. Responding to creationist charges that evolution is "just a theory,"

Gould insists: "Well, evolution *is* a theory. It is also a fact. And facts and theories are different things, not rungs in a hierarchy of increasing certainty. Facts are the world's data. Theories are structures of ideas that explain and interpret facts. Facts do not go away while scientists debate rival theories for explaining them. ... [H]uman beings evolved from apelike ancestors whether they did so by Darwin's proposed mechanism or by some other, yet to be discovered." Stephen Jay Gould, "Evolution as Fact and Theory," *Hen's Teeth and Horse's Toes* (New York: W. W. Norton, 1980), pp. 253–62. Quotation from p. 254.

Gould's point, I believe, is that the world is as it is independently of our ability to understand it – a position I share. But if facts are part of the mind-independent world, they cannot also be "the world's data." "*Data*" is the name we give to that *part* of our theory about which we can achieve a high degree of interpersonal and intertheoretic agreement; however, there can be as much contention about "the data" as about "the theory." Gould concedes as much in the next paragraph when he writes: "Moreover, 'fact' does not mean 'absolute certainty.' ... In science, 'fact' can only mean 'confirmed to such a degree that it would be perverse to withhold provisional assent.'" If *that's* what "facts" are, then they can and do sometimes "go away while scientists debate rival theories for explaining them." Ibid., p. 255.

53 Notice that we don't have to assume here that anyone is knowingly telling lies. Clearly, in the real world, members of the ruling elite *do* consciously lie, and they do it a lot. But here I'm trying to point out that some of the mechanisms that can perpetuate oppressive structures are epistemically legitimate.

54 See Edward Herman and Noam Chomsky, *Manufacturing Consent* (New York: Pantheon, 1988); Noam Chomsky, *Necessary Illusions: Thought Control in Democratic Society* (Boston: South End Press, 1989), esp. ch. 3 ("The Bounds of the Expressible"); and Martin A. Lee and Norman Solomon, *Unreliable Sources: A Guide to Detecting Bias in News Media* (New York: Carol Publishing Group, 1990).

55 This explains some of what's going on in the so-called "debate" about so-called "political correctness." Most of what's going on involves pure dishonesty and malice, but to the extent that there are some intelligent and relatively fair-minded people who find themselves worrying about such issues as the "politicization" of the classroom, or about "ideological biases" among college professors, these people are reacting to the *unfamiliarity* of progressive perspectives. Those foundational beliefs that are very common within the academy – belief in a (Christian) god, in the benignity of American institutions, in the viability of capitalism – generally go without saying and are thus invisible. *Our* worldviews are unfamiliar, and so must be articulated and acknowledged. Precisely because we are willing and able to do that, while our National Academy of Scholars colleagues are not, we become open to the charge of being "ideological."

It's the very fact that there are so *few* leftist, African-American, Hispanic, openly gay, feminist, female persons in positions of academic authority that accounts for all this slavish nonsense about our "taking over."

56 Lorraine Code, "Credibility: A Double Standard," in *Feminist Perspectives*, ed. Code, Mullett, and Overall, pp. 65–6.

57 Ibid.

58 Ibid., p. 71.

59 Ibid., p. 73.

60 Ibid., p. 72.

61 Ironically, the preference among many feminist theorists for "thin" theories of the self, like postmodernist constructivist theories, is itself a vestige of an incompletely exorcised empiricism in contemporary feminist thought. It is a specifically empiricist position that the groupings of objects into kinds effected by human cognition are not keyed to "real essences," but are rather reflections of superficial regularities in experience that persist only because of their pragmatic utility.

62 We know, for example, that some of the built-in rules that make it possible for the human visual system to pick out objects from their backgrounds – so-called structure from motion rules – also make us subject to certain specific kinds of visual illusions. See A. L. Yuille and S. Ullman, "Computational Theories of Low-Level Vision," in *Visual Cognition and Action,* ed. Daniel N. Osherson, Stephen M. Kosslyn, and John M. Hollerbach, vol. 2 of *An Invitation to Cognitive Science,* ed. Daniel N. Osherson (Cambridge, MA: MIT Press, 1990), pp. 5–39.

63 I am here reiterating the arguments Chomsky mounted against Herrnstein's apologia for Jensen's theory of race and intelligence. See Noam Chomsky, "Psychology and Ideology," reprinted in Chomsky, *For Reasons of State* (New York: Random House, 1973), pp. 318–69; excerpted and reprinted as "The Fallacy of Richard Herrnstein's IQ," in *The IQ Controversy,* ed. Ned Block and Gerald Dworkin (New York: Random House, 1976), pp. 285–98.

64 See Herrnstein's reply to Chomsky, "Whatever Happened to Vaudeville?" in Block and Dworkin, eds, *IQ Controversy,* esp. pp. 307–9.

65 These considerations also help defeat the charge, hurled against critics of biological determinist theories, that we progressives are the ones guilty of "politicizing" the debate about nature and nurture. The Herrnsteins and E. O. Wilsons of this world like to finesse the meticulously arrayed empirical criticisms of their work by accusing their critics of the most pathetic kind of wishful thinking – "Sorry if you don't *like* what my utterly objective and bias-free research has proven beyond a shadow of a doubt. You must try to be big boys and girls and learn to cope with the unpleasant truth." For examples, see Herrnstein, "Whatever Happened to Vaudeville?" in Block and Dworkin, eds, *IQ Controversy;* and E. O. Wilson, "Academic Vigilantism and the Political Significance of Sociobiology," reprinted in *The Sociobiology Debate,* ed. Arthur L. Caplan (New York: Harper and Row, 1978), pp. 291–303.

CHAPTER 42

There is at Least One A Priori Truth

Hilary Putnam

In a number of famous publications (the most famous being the celebrated article "Two Dogmas of Empiricism", *Philosophical Review*, 1951) Willard van Orman Quine has advanced the thesis that there is no such thing as an (absolutely) *a priori* truth. (Usually he speaks of "analyticity" rather than apriority; but his discussion clearly includes both notions, and somewhere – I don't have the reference at the moment – he has explicitly said that what he is rejecting is the idea that any statement is completely *a priori*. For a discussion of the different threads in Quine's arguments, see my paper "Two Dogmas Revisited", in *Contemporary Aspects of Philosophy*, ed. Gilbert Ryle, Oriel Press, 1977). Apriority is identified by Quine with *unrevisability*. But there are at least two possible interpretations of unrevisability: (Interpretation One) A *behavioral* interpretation, *viz.* an unrevisable statement is one we would never give up (as a sheer behavioral fact about us); and (Interpretation Two) an *epistemic* interpretation, *viz.* an unrevisable statement is one we would never be *rational* to give up (perhaps, even a statement that it would never be rational to even *think* of giving up). On the first interpretation, the claim that we might revise even the laws of logic becomes merely the claim that certain phenomena might cause us to give up our belief in some of the laws of logic; there would be no claim being made that doing so would be rational. Rather the notion of rationality itself would have gone by the board.

I don't know if Quine actually intended to take so radical a position as this, but, in any case, I think that most of his followers understood him to be advocating a more moderate doctrine. This more moderate doctrine was, in any case, put forward by me, for example, in a paper I titled "It Ain't Necessarily So". The moderate doctrine, unlike the more radical doctrine, employs the notion of rationality. The claim of the moderate doctrine is that there are no truths which it would never be rational to give up; for every truth or putative truth, there are circumstances under which it would be rational to accept its denial. This position was itself argued for, on the basis of an induction from the history of science. It was not itself supposed to be an *a priori* truth. Thus the cheap shot, which consists in arguing that the anti-apriorist position is self-refuting because if it were correct then there would still be one *a priori* truth, namely that there are no *a priori* truths, doesn't work. But the induction from the history of science was a somewhat complicated affair. It was not a simple Baconian induction; rather, a theory was put forward, a theory which was intended, among other things, to explain why certain statements *seem* to be *a priori*.

I want to emphasize this point. The moderate Quinean position tries to "save the appearances".

Originally published in *Erkenntnis* 13 (1978), pp. 153–70.

It does not deny that there at least appear to be *a priori* truths, it does not deny that certain truths have a special status, it tries to explain why that is so. More precisely, it says that those truths really do have a special status, only the status has been misconceived. The key notion here was the notion I called "contextual apriority". The idea is that we can grant that certain truths, and even, at certain times, certain falsehoods, have a special status, but that we don't have to concede that that status is good old-fashioned apriority. The status these truths and falsehoods have, as long as they have it, is contextual apriority – apriority relative to the body of knowledge. And the thesis that there are no *a priori* truths becomes the thesis that there are no absolutely *a priori* truths. What still seems to me to be right about this is the idea that there is such a status as contextual apriority, and the idea that contextual apriority has sometimes been mistaken for absolute apriority, that is, for the status that a statement has if indeed it could never be rational to revise it.

There is an important difference between such statements as "the leaves always turn in October", which can be refuted by just well-confirmed observations, and such statements as the statements which comprise non-Euclidean geometry as a theory of actual space (or space–time) which can only be established when a whole new body of theory, not just geometrical theory, but physical theory and experimental interpretation, is put forward. Prior to the development of general relativity theory, most people, even most scientists, could not imagine any experiences that would lead them to give up, or that would make it rational to give up, Euclidean geometry as a theory of actual space; and this is what led to the illusion that Euclidean geometry was *a priori*. What I no longer think is that all cases of apparent apriority can be explained in this fashion.

Even the case of Euclidean vs. non-Euclidean geometry involves features that were glossed over in my previous account. It is not the case that every mathematician regarded non-Euclidean geometry as *a priori* impossible, as a description of actual physical space, prior to the development of general relativity. Indeed, Lobachevskii always regarded the question of which geometry describes actual physical space as an empirical question. And it isn't just the possibility of giving an operational interpretation to non-Euclidean

geometry that is important, although this was naturally stressed by empiricists like Lobachevskii but it is also important that one can give a coherent model for a non-Euclidean world within Euclidean mathematics. Mathematicians were led by a very straightforward analogy to grant the conceivability of Euclidean spaces of four and even more dimensions. A three-dimensional, non-Euclidean world – or at least a world whose intrinsic geometry, whose geometry viewed from within, is that of a three-dimensional non-Euclidean world, can be pictured as a curved hyper-surface in a four-dimensional Euclidean space. Of course, this doesn't explain the possibility of a non-Euclidean world which is *not* embedded in a higher-dimensional Euclidean space!

What I want to do today is to argue that there is at least one *a priori* truth in exactly the sense that Quine and I denied; that is, at least one truth that it would never be rational to give up. My example, not surprisingly, is going to be taken from the laws of logic. In the past I have argued that the laws of logic are revisable and that, in fact, the proper interpretation of quantum mechanics requires that we give up the distributive laws. Nothing that I say today will go against this position. It is after all perfectly possible that not all the traditional laws of logic are *a priori*, but that only some of them are. Indeed, even if, as I think, the notion of apriority has to be revived, that does not mean that we should go back to the old confident way of using it. To try to understand the epistemology of all of logic and classical mathematics in terms of a single notion of *a priori* truth would be, I think, a serious mistake. The law of logic I want to consider is a very weak version of the Principle of Contradiction. The Principle of Contradiction says that no statement is both true and false, or in the notation of propositional calculus, $\sim (p. \sim p)$.

The example of quantum logic suggests one way in which the revision of this principle might be suggested. Namely, it might be suggested that the principle holds only for *ordinary* statements about *ordinary* macro-observable properties of *ordinary* macro-observable objects, e.g., "the cat is on the mat", and it might be suggested that there is some class of recherché statements about waves and particles or whatnot for which the principle fails. Perhaps "the electron is a particle" is both true and false, or "the electron is a wave" is both true and false. This move might be avoided by considering what we may call the *Typical Principle of Contradiction*, that is, the principle that *ordinary macro-observable statements*, ordinary statements about macro-observables, *are not both true and false*, or by considering the principle that *most statements are not both true and false*, or some combination of these moves; but I shall consider the weakest possible version of the Principle of Contradiction, which I shall call the Minimal Principle of Contradiction. This is simply the principle that *not every statement is both true and false*. The denial of this principle is, of course, the claim that *every statement is both true and false*. If every statement is such that under some circumstances it might be rational to revise it, then under some circumstances it might be rational to accept that *every statement is both true and false*. Is this the case? Well, it certainly doesn't seem to be the case. And if it is not the case, if, indeed, there are no circumstances under which it would be rational to give up our belief that *not every statement is both true and false*, then there is at least one *a priori truth*. And one is all we need.

My argument is in this respect like Descartes'. I believe that one of the several things that Descartes wanted to do with his *cogito* was to establish precisely that there are *a priori* truths. And for the purpose of making this point, one needs only one example. Is, then, the statement that not every proposition is both true and false not an example of an absolutely, unconditionally, truly, actually *a priori* truth?

Recall that part of the strategy of what I called the moderate Quinean position was to save the appearances by showing that what we mistake for absolute apriority is a status which some propositions truly have, a status which is truly different from ordinary, garden-variety contingency, but which is not an absolute apriority. This is the status of contextual apriority. Is it possible that the Minimal Principle of Contradiction is then only a contextually *a priori* truth which we are tempted to mistake for an absolutely *a priori* truth?

The suggestion would be this: that there is some weird physical theory T which we have not yet thought of, but which implies the denial of the Minimal Principle of Contradiction and that someday when some scientist – some future Einstein – invents the theory T and shows us what beautiful predictions it leads to, and how much it enhances our understanding and control of nature to accept the theory T, then we will all be converted and by a kind of 'gestalt switch' we will go over to accepting the theory T and to denying the Minimal Principle of Contradiction.

But there is an obvious problem with this line. The problem is that it's quite obvious what the theory T will have to be. If we ever give up the Minimal Principle of Contradiction, that is, if we ever come to believe that every statement is both true and false, then its perfectly obvious what the theory T will have to be. The theory T will have to be the theory which consists of every statement and its negation! That is the theory T will have to consist of such statements as "the earth is round", "the earth is not round", "two and two are four", "two and two are not four", "the moon is made of green cheese", "the moon is not made of green cheese", "there are quarks", "there are no quarks", etc., etc., etc. … For once we are in the happy position of being able to say exactly what the 'surrounding theory' will have to be if we come to revise a particular contextually *a priori* statement.

Of course, my move here might be challenged. One might, for example, suggest that we will give up the Minimal Principle of Contradiction and the Law of Double Negation at the same time. Then we might accept *it is not the case that it is not the case that every statement is both true and false*, without accepting that every statement is both true and false. However, in that case the statement "every statement is both true and false" would still have the status of being *a priori* false, even if the statement of which it was the negation isn't *a priori* true. And to concede the existence of such a status as *a priori* falsity is, I think, as much as to concede the existence of such a status as *a priori* truth. I assume, therefore, that I am dealing with an opponent who maintains not merely that we might accept the double negation of the statement that *every statement is both true and false*, but that we might accept that statement itself.

Again, it might be suggested that we will assert "every statement is both true and false", while at the same time giving up the Principle of Universal Instantiation, which enables us to infer particular instances from an all-statement. Then we would say the words "every statement is both true and false", but for no particular statement would we be committed to saying of it that *it* is both true and false. But this would clearly be playing verbal games. If I say the words "every statement is both true and false", but I don't conclude that "the earth is round" is both true and false, or that "two and two equals five" is both true and false, then I simply don't mean what is normally meant, or anything what is like what is normally meant by "every statement is both true and false".

In the case of geometry, when we went over to non-Euclidean geometry we didn't change the meaning of the words, or at any rate we didn't *merely* change the meaning of the words. We discovered that a state of affairs which we had mistakenly regarded as inconceivable is, in fact, conceivable and quite probably actual. For example, we used to regard it as inconceivable that a three dimensional world should be both finite and unbounded. We now think it is conceivable and quite probably the case that the whole three-dimensional universe is both finite and unbounded. The question is whether, in the same way, the state of affairs that we now regard as being inconceivable, the state of affairs that "the earth is round" and at the same time "the earth is not round", that "the moon is made of green cheese", and at the same time that "the moon is not made of green cheese", that "two and two are five" and at the same time "two and two are not five", and so on, is really conceivable and will perhaps someday turn out to obtain. Could it be rational to think someday that "the moon is made of green cheese", and "the moon is not made of green cheese", that "two and two are five", and "two and two are not five", that "the earth is round", and "the earth is not round", and so on? That is our question. And I repeat, if that ever happens then we know exactly what the "theory" will be that we shall be accepting. It will have to consist of every statement and its negation.

Let me refer to the statement that *Euclidean geometry is true* – the statement we gave up when we went over to non-Euclidean physics – as the *critical statement*, and to the theory of the basis of which we decided that the critical statement was false – the General Theory of Relativity – as the *Embedding Theory*. What I've said so far is that if we take the Minimal Principle of Contradiction as our critical statement, then we know exactly what the Embedding Theory has to be. It has to

consist of every statement and its negation. But it may still be argued that there is a disanalogy between accepting non-Euclidean geometry on the basis of the General Theory of Relativity and accepting the denial of the Minimal Principle of Contradiction on the basis of the theory which consists of every statement together with its negation. The disanalogy is that the General Theory of Relativity leads to testable predictions, whereas the Embedding Theory which consists of every statement together with its negation leads to no testable predictions. But this is not the case either. The Embedding Theory in the latter case leads, for example, to the prediction that "my hand has five fingers", and to the prediction that "my hand has seven fingers". It also leads to the prediction that "my hand does not have five fingers", and to the prediction that "my hand does not have seven fingers". It leads to a *lot* of predictions! But, it may be objected, these are not genuine predictions for we don't know what it would be like for them all to come true. We can imagine all of the predictions of non-Euclidean physics coming true, even if we happen to be Euclidean physicists. But we don't know what it would be like for all the predictions of the theory that consists of every statement together with its negation to come true. I think this is right, but I think that this observation only poses the problem of apriority and does not solve it.

(Takes out box) In this box there is a sheet of paper. Suppose I predict that when I open the box you will see that the sheet of paper is red, and the sheet of paper is not red. Suppose I explain that I don't mean that the sheet of paper is red on one side and white on the other side, or anything like that. When I say that the sheet of paper is red, I mean that it's red on both sides – a nice, normal dye which doesn't look red from one angle and some other color from a different angle, or red to some people and a different color to other people, or anything like that. And when I say that the sheet of paper is red, and the sheet of paper is not red, I mean that the statement that "the sheet of paper is red" understood as just indicated, is both definitely true and definitely false. Now it's quite true that in a certain sense we don't know what it would be like for that prediction to be verified, and that's our reason for denying that it is a genuine prediction about what will be seen when the box is opened. But one has to be careful here.

The kind of inconceivability that is relevant is not mere unintuitability. Let me say that we can intuit a state of affairs if we can actually visualize it. (I want to stick to a notion of intuition that's close to perception.) Now, we can predict that something will happen which we cannot intuit, although we can, in a sense, conceive of it happening. For example, I might predict that when I open the box you will see that the sheet of paper is a shade of red that none of you has ever seen. I think that you'd all accept that as a perfectly good prediction, even though you can't intuit what it would be like for that prediction to come true. It's enough that we should be sure that that's a possible state of affairs or at least a state of affairs that we could recognize if it turned out to be actual. Similarly, if I predict that when I open the box you will see that the sheet of paper is a color – and I mean now a major color – that you've never seen before, I think that that would be a perfectly good prediction. It's true that such a prediction would upset a certain amount of physical theory, namely the physical theory that says that color is determined by lambda, the wavelength of the light reflected from the paper. For if that theory is true, and it's also true that we've correctly mapped out which lambdas correspond to which colors, and which lambdas the human eye is sensitive to, then there is no room, in the sense of no room in the theory, for another major color. Nevertheless, it would be absurd to say that someone who predicted that there was another major color and who claimed to have predicted that when we opened the box and looked at the paper we would see a major color we hadn't seen before, hadn't made a prediction just because we couldn't intuit the state of affairs that would obtain if his prediction turned out to be correct.

Actually the situation is more complicated than I'm suggesting because, in fact, the physical theory that I just mentioned, although it still appears in many textbooks, is certainly false, and the work of Jerome Letvin and of Irwin Land shows that color depends in a very complicated way on many factors besides lambda, and as far as I know it would not be the case that the discovery of a new major color tomorrow would very much mess up physical theory – there just isn't a good physical theory of color to mess up. For example, standard theory doesn't really account for the color "brown". But even if the lambda theory were not already suspect, I think that the fact remains that the prediction of a new major color would have to be counted as a prediction, even if we knew that verification of that prediction would mess up a certain amount of well-established theory.

Now, what do we mean when we say that we don't understand what it would be like for the prediction, that when I open this box you will see that the sheet of paper that it contains is both red and not red, to turn out to be true? We mean at least that we cannot intuit what it would be like for an observational situation to obtain which would *clearly* be describable by saying that the sheet of paper is red, in the sense I explained before, and also the sheet of paper is not red; but we had better mean more than that, otherwise this counts as a perfectly good prediction. Just as the sheet of paper is a shade of red that you have never seen before, and the shade of paper is a major color that you have never seen before both count as perfectly good predictions.

On the other hand, it isn't that "the sheet of paper is red" and "the sheet of paper is not red" is literally unintelligible in the way in which "wa'arobi besnork gavagai" is literally unintelligible, although some philosophers have tried to assimilate the unintelligibility of contradictions to the unintelligibility of what is literally without sense in the language. "This sheet of paper is red and this sheet of paper is not red" isn't unintelligible at all. It simply asserts what cannot possibly be the case. And the reason that *when I open the box you will see that the sheet of paper is red and the sheet of paper is not red* does not count as a prediction, is that we know – know *a priori* – that it can't possibly turn out to be the case. But this remark doesn't explain the phenomenon of *a priori* knowledge, it only points to its existence.

If what I've said so far is correct, then the theory that what is happening, what gives rise to the illusion of apriority, is that we mistake one status for another – mistake the status of contextual apriority for the status of absolute apriority – doesn't work in this case. That was what was going on in the case of non-Euclidean geometry. But to explain the special status of the Principle of Contradiction, or at least of the Minimal Principle of Contradiction, in terms of contextual apriority, is a loser.

At this point there is a rather tough line that we might take. We might say that if every statement is both true and false, then in particular the statement "my hand has five fingers" (or your favorite observation report) is both true and false. But I see that my hand has five fingers is true and I see that it is not false. So I *observe* that at least one statement is not both true and false, and this is enough to verify the Minimal Principle of Contradiction. This is a tough line to take because it amounts to giving up the search for a *special status* for the minimal Principle of Contradiction. It amounts to saying that the Minimal Principle of Contradiction is an *observation report* or is grounded upon a number of observation reports. But this is clearly wrong. It might turn out that there are not five fingers on my hand. For example, my hand may have been amputated and what I'm looking at may be a plastic substitute (of course we'd have to tell some story about why I don't realize that I'm not looking at my own hand, but that is not impossible, as we all know). But even if it turned out that I don't have a hand, or that my hand has only four fingers, or seven fingers, or whatever, discovering that I was wrong about the observation report would not at all shake my faith in my belief that that observation report is not both true and false. Even if I couldn't discover how many fingers there are on my right hand (imagine a drunken man looking at his hand), this would not shake my faith in my belief that it's not both true and false that the number is five. We seem to be struck with at least one *a priori* truth – really, actually, truly *a priori*, and not just contextually *a priori*.

If we cannot successfully deny that there are *a priori* truths then it has seemed to many that we can give a conventionalist account of how *a priori* truth is possible. According to a typical such account, it is simply a *rule of language* that one must not assert both a statement and its negation, or to ascend to the meta-language, that one must not apply both the predicates "true" and "false" to the same statement. Moreover, these rules are seen as constituting the meanings of negation and of falsity, or as partially constituting the meanings of negation and of falsity, respectively. Anyone who both asserts a sentence and its syntactic negation other than for special purposes, e.g., to call attention to an ambiguity in the situation, is going against the meaning of the negation

idiom. Thus if I say "It is raining and it is not raining", and I don't mean simply to call attention to the fact that the particular situation leaves some room for discretion in the application of the description "it is raining", or something of that kind, then I am going against the meaning of the words. And this is *why* the Principle of Contradiction is correct.

This account has a very fundamental defect which seems, strangely, not to have been noticed. *It explains much too much*. The problem with this account and with a number of other attempted accounts is that if it were correct, it wouldn't merely explain the status of the Principle of Contradiction in our *knowledge*, it would explain the Principle of Contradiction itself. It wouldn't just provide a reason that we know the Principle of Contradiction, it would provide a reason that the Principle of Contradiction is true. But it is easy to see that there cannot be such a reason. The Principle of Contradiction is prior to anything that might be offered as an explanation for its truth. For example, suppose the Principle of Contradiction were not true. Suppose that even the Minimal Principle of Contradiction were not true. Then every statement would be both true and false. Then of course it would be true that the Principle of Contradiction is true by convention. But it would also be true that the Principle of Contradiction is not true by convention. It would be true that our laying down certain linguistic stipulations does not cause the Principle of Contradiction to be true. To put it bluntly, you can't make the Principle of Contradiction true by convention unless it's *already* true. This objection, the objection of explaining too much, also applies to other historic empiricist attempts, and even non-empiricist attempts, to explain the laws of logic. For example, that they are the laws of thought, or that they arise from relations of our ideas.

Of course one might try a moderate conventionalism. That is, one might try saying that the laws of logic, or at least the Principle of Contradiction, or at least the Typical Principle of Contradiction, or at least the Minimal Principle of Contradiction are just true, and one might agree that the truth can't sensibly be explained in terms of anything else, but one might hold that what is a matter of convention is not the truth of these laws but their necessity or the rationality of believing them. This, however, does not seem very appetizing. To take the latter proposal first, if it's simply true by convention that it's rational to believe the laws of logic and this convention is simply the convention constituting the conventional use of the tri-syllabic English word "rational", then what we have is the somewhat notorious ordinary language solution to Hume's problem, only now proposed as the solution to the problem of deduction. With respect to the former, that is the appeal to ordinary language as a solution to Hume's problem, Wesley Salmon once remarked that all this amounts to is the claim that if you use induction then you have the right to apply to yourself the noise "rational", *and isn't that nice*. Professor Strawson replied to Salmon by observing that our propensity to make inductions need not be thought of as either arbitrary on the one hand, nor as conventional on the other; it may be *natural*. I take it that by "natural" Strawson meant something like "innate". Now, whatever the virtue may be of regarding our propensity to make inductions as simply an innate tendency that we have, it does seem as if in this respect deduction is different from induction. To say that our faith in the most fundamental principles of deductive logic, our faith in the Principle of Contradiction itself, is simply an innate propensity and that it has no need of justification just because it is an innate propensity, is to obliterate totally the distinction between reason and blind faith. Of course, I'm not accusing either Peter Strawson or David Hume of making this move; they would both restrict their nativist account to induction, and not deduction. Nor can I accept the view that the necessity of the laws of logic, that is the fact that they hold in all possible worlds not only in the actual world, the fact that even if we accept the laws of logic as true in the actual world, we cannot go on and say "but of course they might not have been true", or at least we cannot say "it might have been that every statement was both true and false", is accounted for by convention.

It is true that there are accounts of logical truths, notably Quine's, according to which such a schema as $\sim(p. \sim p)$, if valid at all, is *ipso facto* necessary, that is to say there's no difference on Quine's account between saying that every instance of $\sim(p. \sim p)$ is true in the actual world, and saying that it is necessary that $\sim(p. \sim p)$; but

this seems to me to be wrong. For one thing this assumes what we may call a Humean account of the modalities, that is it assumes that what is true in possible worlds is totally determined by what is true in the actual world plus our conventions. If this is right then there cannot be two possible worlds in which the *same* events take place, but which are such that *if* a certain experiment had been performed, which never was performed in either world, then different things would have happened in the two worlds. Now ask yourself this question: Can you imagine two worlds in neither of which the experiment is performed. The experiment just requires too much energy and the government won't let the physicist use so much energy in one experiment. Exactly the same events happen in both worlds but it is the case that *if* the experiment had been performed, *if* a certain particle had been submitted to much, much higher energies than were ever concentrated in a small space, then in *one* of the two worlds the particle would have split and in the other it would not have split? In other words, does the totality of facts about what events *actually* take place determine the truth value of all statements of the form "it is *possible* that p"? To me, at least, it seems that the answer is "no", and if the answer is "no", then both Quinean accounts of logical necessity and Humean accounts of causality have to be wrong. But I don't want to discuss this here, I simply want to point out that anyone who shares my modal-realist intuitions has to reject the claim that the *necessity* of the principles of logic is any *more* a matter of convention than their truth is. If any one is tempted to hold it, the form of moderate conventionalism that consists in saying that the laws of logic are *just* true in the actual world, but that *given* that they're true in the actual world it's a matter of our convention that they're true in all *possible* worlds seems to me quite untenable.

Incidently, the claim that physical possibility statements are translatable into statements about what actually happens seems to me in no better shape than the claim that statements about material objects are translatable into statements about sense data; and if physical possibility statements are not disguised statements about what actually happens then it is hard to see how logical possibility statements can be. There is however an account which goes part of the way towards explaining the special status of at least some of the laws of logic. A version of this account was, I believe, offered by Saul Kripke in a seminar at Princeton in which he criticized my published views on quantum logic; and the root idea of the account is to be found already in Aristotle's remarks about the laws of logic.

The idea is that the laws of logic are so central to our thinking that they define what a rational argument is. This may not show that we could never change our mind about the laws of logic, that is that no causal process could lead us to vocalize or believe different statements; but it does show that we could not be brought to change our minds *by a rational argument*. Let me spell this out a little. Typical rational arguments either have the form of chains of deduction of the familiar "if *a*, then *b*" form, or they have the form of inferences to the best explanation. But the latter sort of inductive arguments of the form "if *a* then *b*"; "*b*, so probably or plausibly *a*" also rely on properties of the connective "if then", specifically upon *modus ponens*. Both in inductive reasoning and in deductive reasoning we make use of the fact that our language contains a connective which satisfies transitivity and *modus ponens*. This does not show that these two rules of inference are separately or jointly unrevisable; but it does show that if somebody rejected both of them then we would have no way of arguing with him. And indeed, Aristotle remarks that if anyone pretends to disbelieve one of the laws of logic and undertakes to argue with us, we can easily convince him that his own argument presupposes the very laws of logic that he is objecting to.

Neither Aristotle nor Kripke make the mistake, however, of offering this account as an account of why the laws of logic are true in the first place. All this account says is that part of their very special epistemic character is explained by what Quine would call their *centrality*. That is, they're presupposed by so much of the activity of argument itself that it is no wonder that we cannot envisage their being overthrown, or all of them being overthrown, by rational argument. But we should be clear about what the centrality argument does not show. It does not show that a putative law of logic, for instance the Principle of Contradiction, could not be overthrown by *direct observation*. Presumably I would give up the Principle of Contradiction if I ever had a sense datum which was both red and not red, for example. And the centrality argument sheds no light on how we know that this could never happen.

Note

This is a first draft of a paper I never finished. I no longer agree with the conclusion for a number of reasons, but I think the arguments are still of interest. One way I would begin to meet some of the arguments in this paper is by distinguishing two senses of "revise". A statement may be "revised" by *negating* it – e.g., saying "this is not white", where formerly we said "this is white"; or it may be revised by *challenging a concept it contains*. My present position – February 18, 1977 – is that there are statements that cannot be revised in the *first* way (in this I think the foregoing paper is completely right), but that every statement is eligible for revision in the second way.

The question raised in the last paragraph – how do we know that a *direct observation* might not in the future contradict the principle of Contradiction – assumes that *what we now say* and *what is the case* are totally independent. (The stance I referred to as "metaphysical realism" in my Presidential Address to the APA) Even if we grant that we may in the future *say* "this sheet of paper is white and this sheet of paper is not white", we don't have to grant that we might be *right*. It may be that under our *present* conceptual scheme it is *mandatory* to find some explanation of that *future* utterance under which it is *not literally correct*. In Quine's terminology, it may be that homophonic translation (taking the future utterances at "face value") is inadmissible in this case. When I wrote the foregoing paper, I would have replied: "even if we refuse to say now that the future sheet of paper might be both red and not red, that doesn't *of itself* make it true that the future sheet of paper *won't* be both red and not red. How do we know it doesn't just make *us* stubborn?" This assumes that there is an intelligible distinction *within* our conceptual system between what it is possible to conceive of within that system and what is really (independently of all conceptual systems) the case. This is just what I criticize in the address referred to.

On the other hand, I am not urging that we regard all logical and mathematical truth as simply the product of our translation-practices (let alone of "convention"). I have long urged that there is an irreducible *factual* element in logic and mathematics (e.g., the *consistency* of a set of conventions is not itself a convention); which is not to deny that there is also a conventional *component* to logic and mathematics. I think it is right to say that, within our present conceptual scheme, the Minimal Principle of Contradiction is *so* basic that it cannot significantly be "explained" at all. But that doesn't make it an "absolutely *a priori* truth", in the sense of an absolutely unrevisable truth. Mathematical Intuitionism, for example, represents one proposal for revising even the Minimal Principle of Contradiction – not by saying that it is *false*, but by denying the applicability of the classical concepts of truth and falsity at all. Of course, then there would be a *new* "Minimal Principle of Contradiction" – e.g., "no statement is both proved and disproved" (where "proof" is taken to be a concept which does *not* presuppose the classical notion of "truth" by the Intuitionists); but this is not the Minimal Principle of Contradiction. Every statement is subject to revision; but not in every *way*.

Note to Supersede (Supplement?) the Preceding Note

Added December 23, 1977
As I continue to think about these matters, it now seems to me that the preceding note does not do justice to what was *right* in the original paper. Rather than simply revise it, I have chosen to supplement the original paper-plus-note-which-I-added-later with yet *another* note for a meta-philosophical reason: it seems to me, and it has also been remarked by another philosopher I respect, that we philosophers are frequently torn in just the fashion that I am torn now between opposing considerations, but we very infrequently show it in *print*. What we do is let ourselves be torn in private until we finally "plonk" for one alternative or the other; then the published paper only shows what we plonked for, and not the being torn. For once, the present paper-plus-potentially-infinite-series-of-notes *will* show the "being torn".

The preceding note tried to rescue what I called the "moderate Quinean" position by taking the line that "every statement is revisable but not in every *way*". Specifically, a distinction was drawn between giving up a statement by accepting its negation, and giving up a statement by giving up concepts which occur in the statement (as somehow defective).

I don't think this works. Consider the statement I used in the original paper to show that there exists *at least one a priori truth*. This was the statement: "Not *every* statement is *both* true and false". In the previous Note, I said we might give this up by giving up the *classical* notions of truth and falsity – e.g., by going over to Intuitionist logic and metatheory. But surely if we did *that* we wouldn't view it as *giving up* the concepts of truth and falsity; rather we would view it as giving up an incorrect *analysis* of those notions.

Here it seems Quine has an easy rejoinder. He can say "See! It's just as I told you. You can't draw a non-arbitrary line between changing the meaning of the words and changing collateral beliefs. And for that very reason you can't tell if the original statement is still being expressed by the sentence 'Not every statement is both true and false'. Lacking any meaningful notion of synonymy, that is of statement identity, the question of whether some *statement* (not, *sentence*!) is immune from revision lacks all sense."

But, as I have argued in the papers cited at the beginning, Quine isn't just arguing against the notion of *synonymy*. (If he were, then if linguists were to come up with a well-motivated proposal for assigning sentences to synonymy classes, Quine's work would lose all interest.) Much of Quine's argument – specifically, his historical argument from the succession of past scientific revolutions – was *independent* of the question of whether there is a good criterion for sentence synonymy. Quine excited philosophers because he put forward a picture of epistemology in which there was no *room* for apriority (miscalled "analyticity" by Quine *and* his positivist opponents). He excited philosophers by putting forward a view of epistemology in which "no statement is immune from revision" – a very different claim from the claim that the question, "Is every statement immune from revision?" is *meaningless*. It is this view of epistemology that I am now criticizing.

Moreover, we can finesse the question of whether adopting Intuitionism would or would not be to change the meaning of "true" and "false". If it is true, as I argued in the preceding Note, that we can't give up the critical statement except by changing the meaning of "true" and "false" (i.e., "giving up the concepts"), then the following hypothetical must be *absolutely* unrevisable:

If the classical notions of truth and falsity do not have to be given up, then not every statement is both true and false.

(In general, as Gareth Evans once remarked to me, to say that a statement is revisable, but only in a certain way, is to say that a certain conditional is *un*revisable.)

Again, look at the situation the following way: Consider the following Rule of Inference (call it "the Absolutely Inconsistent Rule"): *from any and all premise-sets, including the null set of premises, to infer every p.* The argument of the previous paper was that, whatever might be said about everything being up for revision in the big spiderweb (or field of force, or whatever your favorite metaphor may be) of beliefs, at least one thing is sure: it can never be rational to accept the Absolutely Inconsistent Rule. And this seems right.

Does this mean that we have to go back to the idea of fixed unchanging canons of rationality, which Quine so persuasively attacked? I don't think it does. It seems right to me that we use our scientific method to devise a better scientific method at every stage. (Reichenbach, who stressed this idea in much of his writing, compared this to all use of tools. The first crude tools were fashioned with our hands; then we used crude tools to fashion more refined tools, and so on.) We started with a "method" which evolution has "hard wired in' to our brains, and we used that "method" to discover (after how many thousand of years?) some principles of deduction and induction, which, after more thousands of years, have begun

to be explicitly formalized, at least in part, and to be ever more mathematically sophisticated. And these principles will undoubtedly guide us in the search for still better principles (together with the method "hard wired in" to our brains, which we still have to fall back on more than we like to admit). But the fact that the canons of rationality are themselves evolving doesn't mean they don't exist (*pace* Feyerabend, *pace* Foucault!), nor does it mean that, in the course of the evolution, *anything whatsoever* (including acceptance of the Absolutely Inconsistent Rule) might occur. Evolution, in the domain of *instruments*, doesn't imply total, protean, lack of definite structure.

But, after all, just how important is it that Quine is wrong in his *total* rejection of the *a priori*? In one way it is not very important. We do not have a good *theory* of rationality, and are unlikely to have one in the forseeable future. Lacking the "rigid designator" of rationality, the theoretical definition which tells us what rationality is in every possible world (as "water is H_2O" tells us what water is in every possible world), it is virtually hopeless to show with any semblance of good argument that any specific statement is such that it would be irrational to ever give it up (apart from special examples, such as the one I constructed). Nor do we really need a proof that a statement is *a priori* in this sense (rationally unrevisable) very often. If a statement has the property that *we cannot now describe* any circumstances under which it would be rational to give it up, that will surely suffice for most purposes of philosophical argument. But, if it is always dangerous to take on the burden of trying to show that a statement is absolutely *a priori*, the foregoing reflections show that it is not just dangerous but actually wrong to make the quick leap from the fact that it is dangerous to claim that any statement is absolutely *a priori* to the absolute claim that there are no *a priori* truths.

CHAPTER 43

Revisability, Reliabilism, and A Priori Knowledge

Albert Casullo

Proponents of a priori knowledge face two formidable tasks: (1) providing an illuminating characterization of the concept of a priori knowledge; and (2) providing cogent reasons for believing that some of our knowledge is indeed a priori. There have been two general approaches to defending the existence of a priori knowledge. Some begin by providing a general characterization of such knowledge and then show that there are plausible examples of knowledge which satisfy the conditions in the characterization.[1] On this approach, the defense of the *existence* of such knowledge depends on the *analysis* of the *concept* of a priori knowledge. The second approach treats these issues independently. In particular, it is argued that certain classes of statements, such as mathematical statements or necessary statements, cannot be known on the basis of experience and, hence, are known a priori *without* any attempt to offer a general characterization of a priori knowledge.[2]

Recent critics of the a priori fall into two similar camps. Some attempt to argue against the *existence* of a priori knowledge without presupposing any particular analysis of the *concept*. Paul Benacerraf, for example, adopts this approach by raising doubts about the existence of the cognitive faculty of intuition which is often invoked by

Originally published in *Philosophy and Phenomenological Research* 49, 2 (Dec. 1988), pp. 187–213.

proponents of the a priori as the source of such knowledge.[3] The second prominent line of attack, which has been forcefully developed by Hilary Putnam, begins by analyzing the *concept* of a statement known a priori as one which is rationally unrevisable.[4] Peirce's celebrated thesis of fallibilism is then invoked in support of the claim that no statements are rationally unrevisable. Philip Kitcher has extended this line of argument by incorporating it within the more general framework of reliabilism with devastating results.[5]

The primary focus of this paper is the second line of attack and divides into two parts. The first examines the plausibility of the Putnam–Kitcher thesis that a priori knowledge entails rational unrevisability independently of any general account of knowledge. Two versions of this thesis are distinguished and it is argued that both should be rejected. This result vitiates their general argument against the existence of a priori knowledge. The second part of the paper examines Kitcher's attempt to incorporate the unrevisability thesis within the more general framework of a psychologistic account of knowledge. Since reliabilism is the leading psychologistic account presently available, the implications of reliabilism for issues regarding the a priori are explored. It is argued, first, that reliabilism does not support the thesis that a priori knowledge entails rational unrevisability and, second, that reliabilism does not offer much promise of providing an informative characterization of the *concept* of a priori knowledge. In conclusion, an attempt is made to show that reliabilism offers proponents of the a priori some resources for defending the *existence* of such knowledge.

I.   Revisability and A Priori Knowledge

Our primary concern in this part of the paper is with the following question: Is there any good reason for supposing that a priori knowledge entails rational unrevisability? In order to bring out this issue more clearly, let us begin by assuming that

(1)   If S knows that p, then the statement that p is rationally unrevisable[6]

is false. For if (1) were true, then

(2)   If S knows that p a priori, then the statement that p is rationally unrevisable

would not be a distinctive thesis regarding the a priori but rather a trivial consequence of the general concept of knowledge. Furthermore, the conjunction of (1) with the doctrine of fallibilism entails the skeptical conclusion that there is *no* knowledge. But proponents of the second line of argument have wanted to maintain both (i) that science is our paradigm of knowledge; and (ii) that it is an essential feature of the scientific enterprise that all statements are subject to rational revision in light of future evidence. Hence, the leading premise of the second line of attack, the Unrevisability Thesis, is better cast as

(UT) If S is justified in believing that p a priori then the statement that p is rationally unrevisable

where "justified" is understood to designate a degree of justification sufficient for knowledge.

(UT) is a puzzling claim. Proponents of the a priori maintain that a *certain type of justification exists* which is intuitively characterized as non-experiential. Since they also maintain that there is a priori *knowledge*, they are committed to a thesis about the *strength* of such justification. Proponents of the a priori are committed to the thesis that such justification is sufficient for knowledge. (UT) also entails a thesis about the strength of such justification. It entails, very roughly, that such justification is strong enough to resist any potential future disconfirmation. The latter thesis is *stronger* than the former thesis for according to (1) justification sufficient for knowledge does *not* entail rational unrevisability. Hence, what is puzzling is how the proponent of (UT) moves from the uncontroversial premise that a priori justification is sufficient for knowledge to the stronger conclusion that such justification is unrevisable.

The problem can be succinctly captured by considering the following set of statements:

(3)   A priori justification is nonexperiential justification.

(4)   The existence of a priori knowledge entails that there is nonexperiential justification sufficient for knowledge.

(5)   The general concept of knowledge does not require that justification sufficient for knowledge entail rational unrevisability.

(6)   It is not the case that if S is justified in believing that p a priori then the statement that p is rationally unrevisable.

(3), (4) and (5) are uncontroversial. (6), which is the negation of (UT), is consistent with {(3), (4), (5)}. This establishes that (UT) is *not* a consequence of uncontroversial premises regarding a priori justification and the degree of justification sufficient for knowledge. Therefore, additional support is necessary to establish that the concept of a priori knowledge entails (UT).

The primary conclusion of Part I is that no additional support is forthcoming and, hence, (UT) must be rejected. This conclusion will be supported in two ways. First, it will be argued that adoption of (UT) leads to some unwanted consequences. Second, it will be shown that the primary motivation for adopting (UT) rests on an untenable principle regarding epistemic justification. But before we proceed to our more detailed examination of (UT), we need to distinguish between a strong and weak version of the thesis:

(SUT) If S is justified in believing that p a priori then the statement that p is rationally unrevisable in light of *any* future evidence.

(WUT) If S is justified in believing that p a priori then the statement that p is rationally unrevisable in light of any future *experiential* evidence.

Clearly, (WUT) is more plausible than (SUT). For suppose that S's belief that p is justified on the basis of nonexperiential evidence and it is acknowledged that p might be rationally revised in light of further *nonexperiential* evidence. In such a case it does not appear plausible to maintain that S's justification is *not* a priori. (WUT) is more promising since one can argue that if S's belief that p is revised in light of *experiential* evidence then that belief is not independent of experience in the requisite sense.

IA

Let us begin by examining (SUT) in more detail in order to bring out explicitly its consequences. Suppose that Mary is a college student who has had some training in logic. As a result, she is able to discriminate reliably between valid and invalid elementary inferences on the basis of reflective thought. Today Mary wonders whether "$p \supset q$" entails "$\sim p \supset \sim q$". She reflects upon the statements in question and on the basis of this reflection concludes that the former does indeed entail the latter. After she assents to this conclusion, a counterexample occurs to her. The occurrence of the counterexample results in her rejecting her former conclusion and coming to believe that "$p \supset q$" entails "$\sim q \supset \sim p$". The salient features of the example are as follows: (a) Mary's initial belief is based on a nonexperiental process which is reliable but not infallible; (b) a process of the *same type* leads Mary to conclude that the initial belief is mistaken and to arrive at the correct conclusion; and (c) Mary's conclusions as stated in (b) are justified beliefs. Now for some more controversial claims: (d) Mary's original belief that "$p \supset q$" entails "$\sim q \supset \sim p$" is also a *justified* belief; and (e) Mary's original belief is *justified a priori* despite having been revised.

What can be said in favor of (d) and (e)? (d) appears to be similar in all relevant respects to the following case. Mary sees a sheet of paper on the table and on that basis forms the belief that it is

square. A second closer visual examination reveals that two of the sides are slightly longer than the other two. On this basis, Mary rejects her former belief about the shape of the paper and comes to believe that it is rectangular. Since the circumstances under which Mary perceived the page were normal and Mary is a reliable discriminator of shapes, her initial belief is justified. The fact that our discriminatory powers sometimes fail us does not entail that beliefs based on shape perception are not justified. Furthermore, if such beliefs are typically justified, we don't single out particular cases as unjustified *merely* in virtue of the fact that they are false. Some other relevant difference must be cited such as that the perceiver was impaired or the environment was gerrymandered. Hence, the routine failure of Mary's otherwise reliable shape discriminating ability does not entail that her belief that the paper is square is unjustified despite the fact that it is false. Similarly, the routine failure of Mary's otherwise reliable ability to discriminate valid inferences does not entail that her belief that "$p \supset q$" entails "Œp ⊃ ~q" is unjustified despite the fact that it is false.

The only question which remains at this point is whether Mary's original belief is justified a priori or a posteriori. Note that a proponent of (SUT) must maintain that the belief is justified a posteriori *merely* in virtue of the fact that it was revised. This point can be brought out more clearly by introducing the notion of a "self-correcting process":

(SCP) A process φ is self-correcting for S just in case, for any false statement p, if φ produces in S the belief that p, then S has available from φ other beliefs which would justify S in believing that p is false.

(SUT) entails

(7)   If a process φ is self-correcting for S and there is a false belief that p which φ justifies for S then φ does not justify for S the belief that p a priori.

But this is an implausible restriction on the notion of a priori justification. For the intuitive basis of the distinction between a priori and a posteriori justification lies in the distinction between experiential and nonexperiential evidence. (7), however, is completely insensitive to the central question of whether the justificatory process in question is experiential or non-experiential. Hence, to endorse (7) is to divorce the notion of a priori justification from the notion of independence from experiential evidence. It is more plausible to reject (7) on the grounds that both Mary's original belief as well as the belief which led her to revise the original belief were based on nonexperiential evidence. Since experiential evidence plays no role either in the original justification or in the subsequent revision of Mary's belief, if it is justified, it is justified a priori. Once we reject (7), (SUT) must also be rejected.

Our rejection of (SUT) has been based on a single case. This case may appear questionable since it involves the controversial claim that there can be a priori justification for a false belief. In order to reinforce our conclusion, let us consider a second example which does not involve this claim. Suppose Charlie believes that p entails q on the basis of a valid proof P_1. Since the proof is the result of a process of reflective thought, Charlie's belief is justified nonexperientially. But now let us suppose that (a) there exists a pseudo-proof, P_2, from p to $\sim q$; and (b) if this pseudo-proof were brought to Charlie's attention, he would not be able to detect any flaws in it or to discount it in any other fashion. Given that the pseudo-proof never comes to Charlie's attention his belief remains justified despite the fact that *were* it to be brought to his attention his justification *would* be defeated. (SUT) entails that Charlie's belief is not justified a priori despite the fact that (i) it is justified; (ii) it is based on nonexperiential evidence; and (iii) the potential defeating evidence, if it were to become available to Charlie, would also be based on a process of reflective thought. Given that (SUT) entails that Charlie's belief is *not* justified a priori despite the fact that experiential evidence plays no role in either the original justification for Charlie's belief or its possible subsequent defeat, it is evident that (SUT) divorces the notion of a priori justification from the notion of nonexperiential justification. Instead, (SUT) bases its claim that Charlie's belief is not justified a priori solely on the following consideration:

(8)   The justification conferred on Charlie's belief by the process of reflective thought is defeasible

which is clearly a thesis about the *strength* of the justification conferred on the belief by the process of reflective thought. But (8) is not a sufficient reason for maintaining that Charlie's belief is not justified a priori. For it fails to take into account whether the beliefs which are the potential defeaters for Charlie's justified belief are experiential or nonexperiential. Hence, (SUT) must be rejected.[7]

(SUT) is implausible because it overlooks the fact that revision can take place on the basis of a priori considerations. Hence, one cannot argue that the justification conferred on a belief by a process is not a priori simply on the basis of the fact that the process is self-correcting or that the justification which it provides is defeasible. A similar observation is germane to evaluating the claim of Hilary Putnam that the presence of quasi-empirical methods in mathematics shows that mathematics is not a priori.[8] By "quasi-empirical" methods, Putnam has in mind

methods that are analogous to the methods of the physical sciences except that the singular statements which are "generalized by induction", used to test "theories", etc., are themselves the product of proof or calculation rather than being "observation reports" in the usual sense.[9]

Among the numerous examples of the use of quasi-empirical methods in mathematics Putnam discusses, Zermelo's introduction of the axiom of choice is the most striking. For Zermelo is quite explicit in maintaining that his justification for this move is "intuitive self evidence" and "necessity for science."[10] By necessity for science, Zermelo has in mind the indispensability of the axiom for proving certain theorems. So, in effect, the justification is akin to the use of the hypothetico-deductive method in scientific reasoning. What are the implications of Zermelo's justification for the issue of the alleged apriority of mathematics?

Suppose that T is a mathematical theory and that $\{p_1,...,p_n\}$ is a set of statements belonging to T each of whose members is accepted on the basis of nonexperiential evidence – i.e., either intuitive self-evidence or deductive proof. Suppose that we now introduce p_{n+1} which we recognize to be neither self-evident nor formally derivable from T. But from p_{n+1} we can derive $\{p_1,...,p_n\}$ and, in addition, some other principles which are neither self-evident nor provable from T but which prove fruitful in furthering research in this area of mathematics. Putnam regards two features of the example as salient: (1) no formal proof exists for p_{n+1} and (2) theoretical considerations might lead to a rejection of p_{n+1} (1), however, is of little independent significance. It appears that Putnam stresses (1) because he assumes that if there exists a formal proof of p_{n+1}, then p_{n+1} is rationally unrevisable. But this assumption overlooks the possibility of misleading evidence. As we saw in our earlier example, the fact that Charlie's belief that p entails q was based on a valid formal proof did not preclude the rational revisability of the belief. Once we recognize that formal proof does not preclude revisability, (2) does not appear to introduce any novel considerations with respect to the apriority of mathematics. For the set of statements $\{p_1,...,p_n\}$ is known independently of experience. When one confirms p_{n+1}, one derives formally the members of the set $\{p_1,...,p_n\}$ Additional confirmation comes from the fact that other statements, $\{p_{n+2},...p_{n+i}\}$, are derivable from p_{n+1} taken in conjunction with T which are both fruitful and not derivable from T alone. Hence, the only mode of justification involved is formal proof. Consequently, no novel form of justification has been introduced at this point. What about the circumstances which would lead to a rejection of p_{n+1}? Given the fruitfulness of p_{n+1} there seem to be only two circumstances in which it would be rejected: (a) if it is shown that although T is consistent, (T & p_{n+1}) is inconsistent; or (b) (T & p_{n+1}) but not T alone entails some p_i and ~p_i is independently well-supported. But, in either case, the only mode of justification involved is formal proof. Consequently, the use of hypothetico-deductive reasoning in mathematics has no tendency to show that mathematical knowledge is not a priori.[11] It would do so only if (a) the method of proof itself is not a priori; or (b) the members of the set $\{p_1,...p_n\}$ which form the confirmation base for p_{n+1} are justified experientially.

IB

At this point let us turn our attention to (WUT). (WUT) avoids the primary problem with (SUT).[12] It distinguishes between revisions based on experiential evidence as opposed to revisions based on nonexperiential evidence and maintains that it is only revision based on experiential evidence that is incompatible with a priori justification. Despite the initial plausibility of this claim, I believe that it is mistaken. In support of this contention, we will examine a prominent argument in support of (WUT). This examination will bring to light the principle regarding justification which motivates (WUT). An argument against this principle will be presented followed by two counterexamples to (WUT).

The most prominent recent proponent of (WUT) has been Philip Kitcher. In support of the thesis he argues

> We can say that a proposition is unrevisable for a person at a time just in case there is no possible continuation of that person's experience after that time which would make it reasonable for her to change her attitude to the proposition. The explication makes it apparent why one might think that propositions which a person knows a priori are unrevisable for that person. If you have a priori knowledge that p, then you have an a priori warrant for a belief that p. Assuming that the warrant is available independently of time, then, given any continuation of your experience, you would have available to you a warrant which would continue to support belief. Hence, it would never be reasonable for you to abandon p in favor of its negation. Whatever trickery your experience may devise for you, you will always be able to undergo a process which will sustain the belief.[13]

The strength of Kitcher's argument in support of (WUT) is that it is based on an uncontroversial feature of alleged a priori warrants, their availability independently of time. Thus, if this feature entails (WUT) the argument is unassailable. In order to assess it more carefully, let us first reconstruct it:

(1) If you have a priori knowledge that p, then you have an a priori warrant for the belief that p.

(2) If you have an a priori warrant for the belief that p, then the warrant is available independently of time.

(3) Therefore, if you have an a priori warrant for the belief that p, then given any continuation of your experience, you

would have available to you a warrant which would continue to support the belief that p.

(4)   Therefore, if you have a priori knowledge that p, then there is no possible continuation of your experience which would make it reasonable to abandon the belief that p.

It is crucial to recognize that the phrase "the warrant is available independently of time" is ambiguous since it can be read in either of the following ways:

(a)   the *process* which warrants the belief that p at t is available given any continuation of S's experiences;

(b)   the *warrant* which the process confers on the belief that p at t is available given any continuation of S's experiences.

If the phrase is taken in sense (b) then (3) follows from (2) but premise (2) is question-begging. If (3) is to be derived from some *independent* feature of a priori warrants, the phrase must be taken in sense (a). But when premise (2) is taken in this sense, the argument is no longer valid. For if we add the following additional premise which is consistent with (2):

(5)   Given some continuations of S's experience, there are other warrants available to S which either defeat or override the original warrant S had for the belief that p

the expanded set of premises entails the negation of (3). So we can*not* conclude from the fact that there exists a process which warrants a belief p at t_1 and is available at another time t_2 that it will also warrant p at t_2.

One might respond at this point that our argument against Kitcher is of little consolation to the apriorist. For in granting that the warrant conferred on a belief that p can be defeated or overridden by experience we have, *ipso facto*, conceded that the belief is based at least in part on an experiential warrant. This intuition provides the strongest motivation for endorsing (WUT). Let

us begin by noting that this intuition presupposes the following symmetry between confirming evidence and disconfirming evidence:

(ST)   If evidence of kind A can defeat or override the warrant conferred on S's belief that p by evidence of kind B, then the belief that p is based on evidence of kind A.

For suppose we begin with the idea that a priori justification is nonexperiential justification and consider S's belief that p which is justified by nonexperiential evidence at t_1. Let us also grant that the warrant conferred on p by this nonexperiential evidence can be either defeated or overridden by experiential evidence at some later time t_2. The conclusion that S's belief that p is based in part on experiential evidence and, hence, is not justified a priori at t_1 can be reached only if (ST) is assumed.

(ST), however, is not very plausible. Consider, for example, our knowledge of our own bodily sensations such as pains and itches. *At present* such knowledge is based on introspection. Traditionally, it was maintained that introspective knowledge is indubitable. One *could not* have any rational grounds for doubting the truth of an introspective belief about one's bodily sensations. This claim has been challenged by the so-called EEG argument[14] The basic idea is that although introspection provides *at present* our only evidence for bodily sensations, neurophysiology may evolve to the point where electroencephalograph readings will provide an alternative source of evidence. Furthermore, in suitably chosen circumstances, the EEG readings may override introspective evidence. Our purpose here is not to evaluate the argument. Suppose we grant

(6)   Neurophysiological evidence can defeat or override the warrant conferred on a belief about one's bodily sensations by introspection.

Clearly, it does not follow that my present justified belief that I have a mild headache is based on neurophysiological evidence. Consequently, (ST) must be rejected.

One might object that the intuition which motivates (WUT) does not depend on (ST) and offer the following argument in support of this contention.[15] Suppose that S believes that p on the basis of nonexperiential evidence and that the warrant which the nonexperiential evidence confers on p can be defeated by some experiential evidence. It follows that the nonexperiential evidence can warrant S's belief that p only in the *absence* of the potential defeating evidence. Hence, in order for S to be justified in believing that p, S must be justified in believing that the defeating evidence does not obtain. But such justification can come only from experience.

This line of argument presupposes a thesis analogous to (ST):

(ST*) If evidence e_1 can defeat or override the warrant conferred on S's belief that p by e_2, then e_2 does not justify S's belief that p unless S is justified in believing that $\sim e_1$.

(ST*) runs up against a problem similar to that faced by (ST). Suppose that we grant that (6) is true. It does not follow that my present introspective belief that I have a mild headache is justified only if I have some justified beliefs about my present neurophysiological state. Consequently, (ST*) must also be rejected.

Once (ST) is rejected, however, plausible counterexamples to (WUT) can be offered. Before providing the cases, a word of caution is in order. The issue of whether those beliefs traditionally alleged to be justified a priori, such as mathematical and logical beliefs, are rationally revisable in light of experiential evidence is controversial. Although I believe that the cases to be presented support the claim that such beliefs are revisable in light of experiential evidence, the truth of this claim is not necessary for our present concerns. For our purpose here is to argue that even *if* it is granted that such beliefs are open to experiential disconfirmation, it does not follow that they are *not* justified a priori.

Suppose that Phil is a working logician who regularly and consistently arrives at interesting results. Phil, however, is bothered by the fact that although he is a *reliable* producer of interesting proofs, he is not an *infallible* producer of such proofs. As it turns out, he has a colleague, Maria, who has done pioneering work in the neurophysiological basis of cognitive processes. As a radical means to self-improvement, Phil asks Maria to conduct a study of his efforts at constructing

proofs in order to see if she can uncover some, hopefully reversible, neurophysiological cause for his infrequent erroneous proofs. The investigation reveals that (a) a particular interference pattern is present in Phil's brain when and only when he constructs an erroneous proof; (b) whenever Phil constructs a proof under the influence of this pattern and the pattern is subsequently erradicated by neurophysiological intervention, he is able to see the flaw in the original proof and go on to correct it. Finally, there is an accepted body of neurophysiological theory available which supports the hypothesis that such a pattern should cause cognitive lapses. Now suppose that Phil believes that p entails q on the basis of constructing a proof which he carefully scrutinizes and finds acceptable. Despite his careful scrutiny, the proof is flawed. He later discovers in a subsequent meeting with Maria that (a) she had been monitoring his brain activity at the time the proof was constructed with a remote sensor; (b) the sensor indicated that the interference pattern was present; and (c) standard tests indicated that all of the equipment was functioning properly. Phil is still unable to uncover the flaw in the proof on his own but nevertheless concludes, on the basis of Maria's empirical findings, that there is a flaw in his proof that p entails q.

The salient features of the example are: (a) Phil's belief that p entails q was based on a process of reflective thought which is, *prima facie*, a source of a priori justification; (b) Phil's belief is justified since this process regularly and reliably produces correct proofs; and (c) the justification which the process of reflective thought conferred on the belief was subsequently defeated by the empirical evidence indicating that the interference pattern was present. (a) is uncontroversial. (b) is more controversial since it involves the claim that there can be a priori justification for a false belief. This claim was defended earlier when we discussed the Mary example. Finally, we propose to grant (c) for purposes of assessing (WUT). Hence, the only remaining question is whether it follows from (a), (b), and (c) that (d) Phil's belief that p entails q is not justified a priori. Note that the belief is justified and the process which produced it is a nonexperiential process. This appears sufficient to establish that the belief in question is justified a priori. A proponent of (WUT) can resist this conclusion only by insisting that since experiential evidence defeated the justification conferred on the belief by the process of reflective thought, the belief is based on experiential evidence. But this move involves embracing (ST) which we rejected earlier. There is no more plausibility in maintaining that Phil's belief that p entails q is based on neurophysiological evidence than there is in maintaining that his present belief that he has a headache is based on such evidence.

One might balk at this example since, like the Mary example of the previous section, it involves the claim that there can be a priori justification for a false belief. But this feature can easily be eliminated, as in the Charlie example, by introducing misleading evidence. Let us suppose that Phil's proof that p entails q is in fact correct but that Maria's sensor has malfunctioned, erroneously indicating the presence of the interference pattern. The standard tests, however, fail to detect the malfunction. Finally, let us suppose that *were* Phil to become aware that (a) the sensor had indicated the presence of the interference pattern, and (b) the standard tests indicated that the sensor was functioning correctly, he *would* conclude that his proof that p entails q is erroneous. Nevertheless, since Maria never reveals to Phil her observations, his belief remains justified. (WUT) entails that Phil's belief is not justified a priori despite the fact that (i) it is justified; and (ii) it is based on a process of reflective thought. Clearly, in order to substantiate the claim that Phil's belief is based on experiential evidence, the proponent of (WUT) must again appeal to (ST). Since (WUT) cannot be defended without appeal to (ST), it should be rejected.

It has been argued that neither (SUT) nor (WUT) is plausible. Hence, the concept of a priori justification is not tied to the concept of rational unrevisability. The most important consequence of this result is that it establishes that a very widespread line of argument against the a priori is unfounded. One cannot simply adopt Peirce's doctrine of fallibilism as an easy stepping stone to rejecting the a priori. Instead, attention must be focused on the crucial notion of nonexperiential evidence. The traditional problem of providing a general characterization of such evidence still, remains. Our investigation raises two additional salient questions which need to be addressed: a) the strength of a priori justifications; and b) the relationship between a priori and a posteriori

justifications for the same belief. Further investigation of these issues is more likely to clarify our understanding of the a priori than further investigation of the notion of rational unrevisability.

II.   Reliabilism and A Priori Knowledge

We have found reason to be sceptical about the alleged connection between the a priori and the rationally unrevisable. Our considerations, however, have proceeded at a very general level. We have considered the concept of a priori knowledge apart from any particular general account of knowledge. This raises the possibility that a specific theory of knowledge might provide some support for (UT) that has not emerged in our earlier discussion. Our primary purpose here is to examine whether (UT) is any more plausible when embedded in a reliabilist theory of knowledge. It will be argued that the framework of reliabilism actually provides independent reason for rejecting (UT) but offers little help in providing a positive characterization of a priori knowledge. We shall conclude by briefly outlining how reliabilism provides some resources for defending the existence of a priori knowledge.

IIA

Philip Kitcher's recent work attempts to characterize a priori knowledge within the more general framework of a *psychologistic* analysis of knowledge. The leading idea of such an analysis is that what differentiates mere true belief from knowledge is the *causal ancestry* of the belief in question. So we have

(1)   X knows that p if and only if p and X's belief that p was produced by a process which is a warrant for it

where "warrant" refers to those processes which produce beliefs in a manner suitable to justify them.[16] In order to complete this account, some further information must be provided about what types of processes warrant the beliefs they produce. Although Kitcher proposes to remain neutral on this issue, it is difficult, if not impossible, to assess his account of a priori warrant without some general characterization of warrant conferring processes. Since Alvin Goldman's version of process reliabilism is the most articulated psychologistic account presently available, and Kitcher endorses it as the best available account, we shall adopt it in our critical evaluation of Kitcher's analysis of a priori warrant.

Kitcher approaches the problem of analyzing the notion of an a priori warrant by attempting to isolate the general characteristics of belief forming processes which have led to their being classified as a priori. In order to produce knowledge which is independent of experience, a process must satisfy three conditions: (i) it must be *available* independently of experience; (ii) it must produce *warranted* belief independently of experience; and (iii) it must produce *true* belief independently of experience. These general ideas are spelled out more precisely in the following account of a priori knowledge:

(2)   X knows a priori that *p* if and only if X knows that *p* and X's belief that *p* was produced by a process which is an a priori warrant for it.

(3) α is an a priori warrant for X's belief that *p* if and only if α is a process such that, given any life *e*, sufficient for X for *p*,

   (a)   some process of the same type could produce in X a belief that *p*
   (b)   if a process of the same type were to produce in X a belief that *p*, then it would warrant X in believing that *p*
   (c)   if a process of the same type were to produce in X a belief that *p*, then *p*.[17]

Kitcher goes on to discuss in more detail the modal and conditional notions he employs as well as making some interesting observations about the classification of types of processes. Since these issues are not germane to our concerns, we can forego the details.

Let us proceed by examining individually each condition in Kitcher's account. Condition (a) is intended to capture the intuitive idea that a priori warrants are available independently of experience. The intuitive idea appears uncontroversial. When we turn to Kitcher's technical formulation

of the idea, however, some difficult questions arise. In order to address them directly, let us begin with a statement of the condition

(3a)   If α is an a priori warrant for X's belief that *p* then α is a process such that, given any life *e*, sufficient for X for *p*, some process of the same type could produce in X a belief that *p*.

A life is sufficient for X for *p* just in case X could have had that life and gained sufficient understanding to believe that p.[18] But what is involved in gaining sufficient understanding to believe a proposition?

Kitcher's informal discussion of the Kantian process of pure intuition as an example of an alleged a priori warrant provides some clarification:

> According to the Kantian story, if our life were to enable us to acquire the appropriate concepts … then the appropriate kind of pure intuition would be available to us. We could represent a triangle to ourselves, inspect it, and so reach the same beliefs.[19]

It appears that gaining sufficient understanding to believe that *p* consists in acquiring the concepts involved in *p*. Once one has acquired the requisite concepts, one can engage in the further process of constructing and inspecting the triangle which results in the belief that *p*.

The first condition appears to be too strong. Consider a belief forming process such as perception. This process consists of a complex series of events internal to the believer which is initiated by a retinal stimulation and results in a belief. The realization of such a process is nomologically dependent upon a large array of neurophysiological features of the believer. For example, such a process is not available to a person with a severed optic nerve or badly damaged retinas. Let us call the complex neurophysiological state of a person which is nomologically necessary for a process to produce beliefs in that person the *standing condition* for that process. (3a) implausibly requires that a priori processes be independent of their standing conditions.

In order to see this consider the following example. Suppose that in the actual world S forms the belief that no two sides of a triangle are parallel through a process of pure intuition. Let us also suppose that there is a single neural condition, N, of S's brain which is nomically necessary in order for S to form and inspect a mental representation of a triangle. Now consider a different world, W*, whose nomological structure down to the neurophysiological level is identical to that of the actual world. Let us also suppose that in W* N is *not* a necessary condition for acquiring the concepts involved in the belief that no two sides of a triangle are parallel. Finally, suppose that in W* S acquires these concepts but lacks N. Hence, in W* S has a life sufficient for the belief that no two sides of a triangle are parallel yet the process of pure intuitions is *not* available to S. Nevertheless, it seems implausible to maintain, solely on the basis of this fact, that the process of pure intuition does not provide an a priori warrant in the actual world for S's belief that no two sides of a triangle are parallel.

The source of Kitcher's difficulty with condition (3a) is that he tries to explicate the manner in which a priori processes are available *independently* of experience in terms of the manner in which they *depend* on experience. The key idea involved in the notion of a process being available independently of experience is

(4)   No experiences other than those *necessary* to acquire the concepts are *necessary* for the process to be available.

Kitcher analyzes this idea along the following lines:

(5)   A life which includes experiences *sufficient* to acquire the concepts is *sufficient* for the process to be available.

But (5) is clearly stronger than (4) since the latter is compatible with *other* conditions, such as neurophysiological conditions, being necessary for the availability of the process while (5) is not. Hence, (3a) needs to be revised along the following lines

(3a*)   If α is an a priori warrant for X's belief that p then α is a process such that, given any life e, sufficient for X for p, no further experiences are necessary for some process of the same type to produce in X a belief that p.

(3a*) is not open to the problem faced by (3a) since it allows that some *nonexperiential* conditions might be necessary for the belief in question to be produced.

Let us now turn to Kitcher's second condition on a priori warrants. He claims that such processes must produce warranted beliefs independently of experience. This claim can be put as follows

(3b)   If α is an a priori warrant for X's belief that p then α is a process such that, given any life e, sufficient for X for p, if a process of the same type were to produce in X a belief that p, then it would warrant X in believing that p.

(3b), in effect, places a very strong defeasibility condition on a priori warrants. It entails that

(DC) If α is an a priori warrant for X's belief that p then the warrant which α confers on p cannot be defeated by any experiences compatible with S's acquiring the concepts involved in p.

(DC) is, in effect, a close relative of (WUT).

This condition should have little plausibility for anyone who subscribes to a reliabilist account of warrant. For it follows from very general requirements of the reliability theory that *no* process can satisfy this condition. Let us begin by noting that there are two different ways in which the warrant a process α confers on a belief that p can be defeated by experience:

(a)   experience may provide reason to believe that α is not a reliable belief forming process;

(b)   experience may provide reason to believe that p is false.

I shall refer to experiences of the first sort as *indirect* defeaters and to experiences of the second sort as *direct* defeaters.[20] It is important to recognize that the experiences which are indirect defeaters for a belief that p are *not* typically also direct defeaters for that belief and vice-versa. Suppose, for example, that I form the belief that there is a cup on the desk via perception and the results of a neurological examination show that I am prone to hallucinations. Although the exam results defeat the warrant conferred on *my* belief by the process of perception, they do not provide evidence that there is not a cup on the desk. This is shown by the fact that no one else would be less warranted in believing that there is a cup on the desk were they to become aware of the results of my neurological examination.

If we now return to (DC), we can see that there is some plausibility to this principle if we consider only *direct* defeaters. For it can be plausibly argued that if one has constructed a valid proof for a particular theorem then the warrant conferred on the theorem by the process of constructing the proof cannot be defeated by experiences such as the testimony of authorities or the results of a computer program. If one has a proof in hand then one is warranted in being suspect about the sincerity or competence of the alleged authorities and computer programmers. But when we turn to *indirect* defeaters the situation changes radically. First of all, it is generally granted by proponents of reliabilism that the warrant which a reliable process confers on S's belief that *p* is defeated if S has reason to believe that the process is *not* a reliable one.[21] Secondly, the reliability of any cognitive process is a matter which is open to empirical investigation. Hence, there is some set of *possible* experiences which would justify us in believing that it is unreliable. Here it is crucial to recognize that even if a belief forming process is in fact reliable, it does not follow that the *available* evidence will warrant us in believing that the process is reliable. We may lack the technical sophistication to uncover the evidence which would establish the reliability of the process and the evidence which we have uncovered may point in the other direction. Furthermore, it is always possible that our experiences include *misleading* evidence. Such evidence, despite being misleading, would nevertheless defeat the warrant conferred on a belief by a reliable process.[22] Hence, (DC) requires that for a reliable belief forming process α to confer an a priori warrant on S's belief that *p*, there be *no* possible worlds in which S acquires the concepts involved in *p* and also has evidence, perhaps misleading, that α is *not* a reliable process. But, on the face of it, there appears to be no inconsistency in the supposition that such worlds exist. Therefore, no process can satisfy (DC). Since no process can satisfy (DC) and condition (3b) entails (DC), (3b) should also be rejected.

Even though we have argued that (3b) should be rejected, it does appear to be a plausible principle. Furthermore, it is widely accepted. Indeed, since (3b) is a variant of (WUT), it would be accepted by any proponent of (UT). I want to suggest, however, that (3b) and (WUT) derive whatever plausibility they have from confusing two different issues:

(a)   the *existence* of a priori warrants

and

(b)   the *strength* of a priori warrants.

In order to substantiate this claim, let us consider an analogous situation in the case of a posteriori warrants. It is generally granted that introspection is the primary source of knowledge of one's psychological states. Yet it is also recognized that behavioral evidence warrants beliefs about psychological states. It follows that the process of observing one's own behavior also warrants beliefs about one's own psychological states. Nevertheless, one rarely utilizes perceptual warrants since introspection alone can warrant such beliefs. Hence, it is widely held that

(6)   Introspection produces warranted beliefs independently of perception.

Some, however, have maintained that the beliefs formed by introspection have a special epistemic status. Such beliefs are indubitable. Let us put this claim as follows

(7)   If S's belief that *p* is formed by a process of introspection, then there is no future event such that if S were to become justified in believing that it occurred, then S would be less warranted in believing that *p*.

On the other hand, it has been argued in the recent literature that if neurophysiology were to advance to the point where there is (a) a well supported theory correlating neurophysiological states with psychological states and (b) a means of reliably ascertaining the state of person's central nervous system, then perceptual evidence could provide grounds for rejecting one's introspective beliefs.[23] If one grants that the scenario described is possible, it follows that

(8)   The warrant conferred on a belief by intro-
        spection can be defeated by perception.

(8) is clearly incompatible with (7). If (8) were
correct, it would follow that the *strength* of the
warrant claimed for introspection is exaggerated.
But is (8) also incompatible with (6)? No. For (6)
only claims that introspection can warrant a belief
in the *absence* of perceptual evidence. (8) does not
deny this. It tells us that (a) perceptual, *as well as*
introspective, evidence is relevant to the justification of beliefs about one's experiential states; and
(b) the warrant conferred on such beliefs by introspection is not strong enough to override all conflicting perceptual evidence. These points can be
made more explicit by analyzing (6) as follows

(6*)   If S's belief that *p* is produced by intro-
        spection and S has no beliefs produced
        by any perceptual processes regarding
        either the subject matter of *p* or the
        process which produced *p* then S's belief
        that *p* is warranted by introspection.

(6*) has the virtue of preserving the central idea
that introspection, unaided by perception, can
warrant beliefs without appearing to imply that
such beliefs are completely immune from perceptual disconfirmation.

The upshot of this discussion is that the intuitive idea that

(9)   A priori processes produce warranted
        beliefs independently of experience

should be analyzed in the same fashion as (6) was
analyzed. (6*) suggests that (3b) be revised as follows

(3b*)   If α is an a priori warrant for X's belief
          that *p* then α is a process such that,
          given any life *e*, sufficient for X for *p*
          and in which S has no beliefs pro-
          duced by any experiential processes
          regarding either the subject matter of
          p or the process which produced *p*, if
          a process of the same type were to
          produce in X a belief that *p*, then it
          would warrant X in believing that *p*.

(3b*) implies that a priori processes can warrant
beliefs in the absence of experiential processes

without implying that such warrants cannot be
defeated by experience.

Let us conclude by considering Kitcher's third
condition on a priori warrants:

(3c)   If α is an a priori warrant for X's belief
          that *p* then α is a process such that,
          given any life *e*, sufficient for X for *p*, if
          a process of the same type were to pro-
          duce in X a belief that *p*, then *p*.

(3c) requires of a priori warrants that they
have the highest degree of reliability. They
must not produce any false beliefs. Kitcher
motivates this strong condition by the following
consideration:

> to generate *knowledge* independently of experi-
> ence, a priori warrants must produce warranted
> true belief in counterfactual situations where
> experiences are different.[24]

This claim, however, is puzzling. It is uncontroversial that knowledge entails truth. But since
Kitcher is providing an account of a priori *warrant* rather than a priori *knowledge*, it is not clear
why he is at all concerned with the requirement of
truth. On the face of it, the mere fact that a process generates some false beliefs does not entail
that it does not warrant the beliefs that it produces. There are two possibilities here. Perhaps
the reliabilist account of *warrant* requires a strong
connection with truth. On the other hand, perhaps it is the notion of an a priori warrant which
necessitates the connection. Let us explore each
of these alternatives.

Does the reliabilist account of warrant require
that warrant conferring processes never produce
false beliefs? It appears not. Consider, for example, Goldman's account:

> A J-rule system R is right if and only if R permits
> certain (basic) psychological processes, and the
> instantiation of these processes would result in a
> truth ratio of beliefs that meets some specific
> high threshold (greater than .50).[25]

Goldman does not fix the threshold value and is
content to leave his account with this degree of
vagueness since he maintains that the ordinary
concept of justification is similarly vague. Hence,
reliabilism does not *in general* require that belief

forming processes be maximally reliable in order to produce warranted beliefs.

If it is granted that reliabilism does not *in general* require that a belief forming process be maximally reliable in order to warrant beliefs produced by it, is there any reason to suppose that a priori processes be maximally reliable? Kitcher does not explicitly argue in support of this claim but he does endorse an intuition which supports it:

> if a person is entitled to ignore empirical information about the type of world she inhabits then that must be because she has at her disposal a method of arriving at belief which guarantees *true* belief. (This intuition can be defended by pointing out that if a method which could produce false belief were allowed to override experience, then we might be blocked from obtaining knowledge which we might have otherwise gained.) In my analysis, the intuition appears as (3c).[26]

This intuition rests on very shaky grounds. The *existence* of a priori warrants does not entitle a person to ignore empirical information about the world. For such processes may warrant beliefs only in the absence of conflicting evidence derived from empirical sources. In order to be entitled to ignore empirical information about the world, one would have to be committed not only to the view that a priori warrants *exist* but also to the following thesis regarding the *strength* of such warrants:

(10)   The warrant conferred on a belief by an a priori process can neither be defeated nor overridden by experience.

But, as we argued earlier, (10) should be rejected. Once (10) is rejected then we are in a position to recognize that rather than *blocking* a person from obtaining knowledge she might have otherwise had via experience, a priori warrants which do *not* guarantee truth provide a person with an *additional* way of obtaining knowledge. Hence, we can conclude that (3c) should be revised along the following lines:

(3c*)   If α is an a priori warrant for X's belief that *p* then α is a process such that, given any life *e*, sufficient for X for *p*, if

a process of the same type were to produce beliefs in X, then a preponderance of those beliefs would be true.

Although (3c*) does not indicate what constitutes a "preponderance" of true beliefs in a life, it does make clear that a priori warrants need *not* guarantee truth.

We are now in a position to summarize our conclusions and to draw out their more general implications. Condition (3a) was rejected because it required that a priori processes be independent of their standing conditions. (3b) and (3c), on the other hand, conflated the *existence* of a priori warrants with the *strength* of such warrants. Revised necessary conditions were proposed to remedy these shortcomings. But are our revised necessary conditions jointly sufficient for analyzing the notion of an a priori warrant? (3c) provides a sufficient condition for a process to be a warrant. The burden of distinguishing between a priori and a posteriori warrants falls on (3a*) and (3b*). (3a*) tells us that in the case of a priori warrants, the only experiences necessary for producing a belief are those necessary for acquiring the requisite concepts. Hence (3a*) provides information about the *availability* of warrants but does not provide information about the *nature* of such warrants. This key role is left to (3b*). Unfortunately, (3b*) does not appear to be adequate for the role. For it simply states in reliabilist jargon the traditional idea that a priori warrants produce warranted beliefs independently of experience. It provides *no* account of what *differentiates* experiential warrants from nonexperiential warrants. But, of course, this is the chief obstacle to providing an *illuminating* characterization of a priori knowledge. For example, it is uncontroversial that knowledge based on either memory or perception is not a priori. But introspection has proved to be controversial. Some have maintained that there is introspective a priori knowledge of one's psychological states while others have denied this. On the other hand, proponents of the view that intuition is an a priori source of mathematical knowledge often maintain that it is a faculty akin to sense perception. What remains unclear, however, is the basis for maintaining that knowledge based on the former but not the latter is a priori. (3b*) is of little use in resolving these problems. So, in the end, the route through reliabilism has made little progress in demarcating the a priori.

IIB

It has been argued that reliabilism provides little help in elucidating the notion of a priori knowledge. In particular, it does not offer much illumination regarding the central notion of non-experiential warrant. Despite this shortcoming, reliabilism can be of significant value to a proponent of the a priori. For the account allows one to address what have been come to be regarded as "standard" objections to the existence of a priori knowledge. These objections fall into three broad categories: 1) a priori knowledge is incompatible with fallibilism; 2) a priori knowledge is at odds with the requirements of epistemology naturalized; and 3) proponents of the a priori cannot offer plausible answers to questions about second level justification.

The doctrine of fallibilism has been presented in various different forms. For our purposes let us understand fallibilism as the view that we should hold every belief, no matter how strongly it is supported, in an open minded spirit which acknowledges the possibility that future evidence may require us to abandon it. A priori knowledge is incompatible with the doctrine of fallibilism only if one adopts an analysis of the concept of the a priori which entails that such knowledge is rationally unrevisable. Such an analysis, however, should have little attraction for a reliabilist. For, as our discussion of Kitcher's principle (3b) indicates, rationally unrevisable beliefs are not even *possible* within a reliabilist framework. In order for a belief to be rationally unrevisable it must satisfy a strong defeasability constraint such as (DC). The process which warrants the belief must be such that no *possible* future evidence could defeat the warrant which that process confers on the belief in question. But, as we argued above, there always exists the possibility of evidence, even if it is only misleading evidence, which would justify one in believing that a belief forming process is unreliable. Such evidence would defeat the warrant which the process confers on the beliefs that it produces. Once this point is appreciated, it becomes evident that a reliabilist who analyzes the *concept* of a priori knowledge in terms of rational unrevisability cannot address the issue of the *existence* of such knowledge in a nontrivial fashion. The issue is settled by stipulation. Hence, any reliabilist who wishes to address

nontrivially the issue of the existence of a priori knowledge *cannot* adopt an account of such knowledge which is at odds with the doctrine of fallibilism.

The classical formulation of the tension between the alleged existence of a priori knowledge and epistemology naturalized is due to Paul Benacerraf.[27] The question he poses is how processes such as mathematical intuition can provide knowledge of mathematical entities if such entities are causally inert? Although a number of authors have attempted to respond to the question by arguing that abstract entities are *not* causally inert,[28] a reliabilist need not make this move. For reliabilism reduces the issue from the level of a *conceptual* problem to a *factual* issue. Reliabilism requires of a warranted belief that it be produced by a process that is *in fact* reliable. Although processes such as perception, which involve a causal relation between the believer and the objects of belief, are our present paradigms of reliable belief forming processes, it remains a *contingent* matter whether other sorts of belief forming processes are reliable. Since warrant requires reliability rather than causal connection, the alleged causal inertness of the objects of the beliefs formed by the process of mathematical intuition is not a conceptual bar to such beliefs being warranted.[29] Hence, if mathematical intuition is in fact a reliable belief forming process then the mathematical beliefs produced by this process are warranted (provided, of course, that the warrant conferred on those beliefs is not defeated or overridden by warrants from other processes).

Finally, let us turn to those problems which we have classified under the category of second level justification. It is a distinctive feature of reliabilism that in order for a reliable process to warrant a belief which it produces in a cognizer, the cognizer need not be aware that the belief was produced by a particular process, let alone that the process is a reliable one. So, in order for the process of mathematical intuition to warrant one's belief that $2 + 2 = 4$, it is not necessary that one be aware of the source of the belief. It is this feature of reliabilism which is rejected by internalists. For example, Laurence BonJour maintains that "For a belief to be epistemically justified for a particular person requires that this person be himself in cognitive possession of such a reason."[30] But it is precisely this requirement of internalist accounts that leads to the problems of second-level justification. Suppose that one comes to believe that 2 + 2 = 4 on the basis of intuiting that 2 + 2 = 4. According to the internalist, the mere fact that the belief is produced by the reliable process of intuition is not sufficient to warrant the belief. One must stand in some cognitive relation to the intuition. Presumably, one must justifiably believe that one intuits that 2 + 2 = 4. Now, of course, the appeal to further justificatory beliefs must stop at some point if an infinite regress of justification is to be avoided. So the question which naturally arises is whether the belief that one intuits that 2 + 2 = 4 is an appropriate point for justification to come to an end. The problem we face in addressing this question is that proponents of intuitionism diverge on their views regarding our knowledge of the existence of intuitions.[31] Some, like Gödel, seem to view the faculty of intuition as something which must be *posited* on theoretical grounds in order to explain mathematical knowledge.[32] On this view one's justification for believing that there are mathematical intuitions is *indirect*. Others, like Pollock, seem to think that the existence of such intuitions is uncontroversial.[33] On this view, one can be *directly* justified in believing that there are mathematical intuitions. But now the internalist is faced with a dilemma. If one's knowledge that one is intuiting that 2 + 2 = 4 is *indirect*, then the justification of mathematical beliefs cannot rest solely on intuition. Some account must be provided of how one is justified in believing that one is having the requisite intuition. And it begins to appear as though only those versed in the epistemology of mathematics will be in a position to provide an answer. Hence, the account severely restricts the scope of mathematical knowledge. But suppose the internalist claims, instead, that one can be *directly* justified in believing that there are mathe-matical intuitions. It then becomes difficult to explain why other proponents of intuitionism do not have this direct access to their intuitions. Given that they are favorably disposed toward intuitionism, why do they believe that the existence of intuitions can be justified only indirectly? Reliabilism, however, avoids the dilemma. Since cognitive access to the process which forms a belief is not a requirement for justification, the reliabilist is not forced to embrace either option. For if the belief in question is formed by the process of intuition and the process is a reliable one, it matters not whether the subject of the belief recognizes, or can justify the belief, that intuition is the operative faculty.

We have tried to indicate some ways in which the resources of reliabilism can be of use to a proponent of the a priori. The advantages offered by reliabilism, however, are realized at the level of defending the *existence* of a priori knowledge rather than at the level of *characterizing* such knowledge. In some ways, this result is not surprising. For although reliabilism offers the promise of advancing epistemology by incorporating advances in cognitive science and other relevant empirical disciplines, work in these areas is still at a sufficiently rudimentary stage that the conceptual scheme of folk psychology remains in place. Consequently, there is no theoretically informed replacement available for our intuitive distinction between experiential and nonexperiential belief forming processes. On the other hand, the introduction of reliability theories was to a large extent motivated by traditional epistemological problems such as the regress of justification and the failure of causal theories to solve the Gettier problem. These general epistemological problems, however, also arise within the more restricted domain of the a priori. Consequently, to the extent that reliabilism is successful in dealing with these general issues, it will be of use to a proponent of the a priori.

Notes

1 See, for example, Panayot Butchvarov, *The Concept of Knowledge* (Evanston, 1970), Part 2; and R. M. Chisholm, *Theory of Knowledge*, 2nd edn (Englewood Cliffs, 1977), chapter 3.

2 See, for example, John Pollock, *Knowledge and Justification* (Princeton, 1974), chapter 10; Mark Steiner, *Mathematical Knowledge* (Ithaca, 1975), chapter 4; and Jaegwon Kim, "Some Reflections on Perception and *A Priori*

Knowledge," *Philosophical Studies* 40 (1981), pp. 355–62.

3   Paul Benacerraf, "Mathematical Truth," *Journal of Philosophy* 70 (1973), pp. 661–79. For a further discussion of this issue, see Mark Steiner, *Mathematical Knowledge* (Ithaca, 1975), chapter 4; and W. H. Hart "Review of *Mathematical Knowledge*," *Journal of Philosophy* 74 (1977), pp. 118–29.

4   For a lucid summary of his anti-apriorism position, see Putnam's "'Two Dogmas' Revisited." Putnam has more recently expressed some misgivings about his earlier position. These are to be found in "There Is At Least One A Priori Truth," and "Analyticity and Apriority: Beyond Quine and Wittgenstein." All three papers are reprinted in Putnam's *Philosophical Papers*, Vol. 3: Realism and Reason (Cambridge, 1983).

5   Philip Kitcher, *The Nature of Mathematical Knowledge* (Oxford, 1983). His analysis of the concept of a priori knowledge orginally appeared in "A Priori Knowledge," *Philosophical Review* 89 (1980), pp. 3–23.

6   Following Putnam, I shall interpret the notion of unrevisability *epistemically*: "an unrevisable statement is one we would never be *rational* to give up ..." (*Realism and Reason*, p. 98). Hence, "the statement that *p* is rationally unrevisable" is shorthand for the more cumbersome "*S* would never be justified in rejecting the statement that *p*".

7   It is worth noting that two recent proponents of the a priori, John Pollock and Mark Steiner, acknowledge that beliefs based on intuition are defeasible but, nevertheless, maintain that such beliefs are justified a priori. See Pollock's discussion of "prima facie reasons" in chapter 10 of *Knowledge and Justification* and Steiner's discussion of "checking procedures" in chapter 4 of *Mathematical Knowledge*. Hence, (SUT) rules out *by stipulation* a feature which some proponents of the a priori have attempted to build into their accounts.

8   Hilary Putnam, "What Is Mathematical Truth?" in *Philosophical Papers*, Vol. 1: Mathematics, Matter and Method, 2nd edn. (Cambridge, 1979).

9   Ibid., p. 62.

10   E. Zermelo, "A New Proof of the Possibility of a Well Ordering," reprinted in J. van Heijenoort (ed.), *From Frege to Gödel* (Cambridge, 1967) and quoted in H. Putnam, "What Is Mathematical Truth?"

11   This argument can be extended to the cases of inductive justification that Polya has brought to our attention such as Euler's discovery that the sum of the series $1/n^2$ is $\pi^2/6$. See G. Polya, *Induction and Analogy in Mathematics* (Princeton, 1954). Since the statements which confirm the inductive generalization are known nonexperientially, there is no reason to suppose that the generalization is not known a priori. The epistemological significance of inductive procedures in mathematics is stressed by both Putnam in "What is Mathematical Truth?" and Steiner in *Mathematical Knowledge*, chapter 3.

12   Aron Edidin has argued, in "A Priori Knowledge for Fallibilists," *Philosophical Studies* 46 (1984), pp. 189–97, that (WUT) entails (SUT). If this were the case, then no additional argument would be required in order to reject (WUT). I have argued, however, in "A Note on Fallibilism and A Priori Knowledge" (manuscript), that Edidin's argument in support of this claim involves a premise which is not available to all proponents of a priori knowledge. Hence, those who cannot accept this premise will require further argument to reject (WUT).

13   P. Kitcher, "How Kant Almost Wrote 'Two Dogmas of Empiricism' and Why He Didn't," *Philosophical Topics* 12 (1981), p. 222.

14   See for example, D. M. Armstrong, "Is Introspective Knowledge Incorrigible?," *Philosophical Review* 72 (1963), pp. 417–32; and K. Parsons, "Mistaking Sensations," *Philosophical Review* 79 (1970), pp. 201–13.

15   This objection is due to an anonymous referee.

16   Kitcher, *The Nature of Mathematical Knowledge*, p. 17.

17   Ibid., p. 24.

18   Ibid., p. 22.

19   Ibid., p. 23.

20   This distinction is analogous to John Pollock's distinction between type I and type

II defeaters. See his *Knowledge and Justification*, pp. 42–3.

21 This point was recognized very early by Alvin Goldman in "What Is Justified Belief?" in G. Pappas (ed.), *Justification and Knowledge* (Dordrecht, 1979). It led him to move from the following straightforward formulation of a base-clause principle for justified belief:

(1) If S's believing *p* at *t* results from a reliable cognitive belief-forming process (or set of processes), then S's belief in *p* at *t* is justified.

to the more complicated

(2) If S's belief in *p* at *t* results from a reliable cognitive process, and there is no reliable or conditionally reliable process available to S which, had it been used by S in addition to the process actually used, would have resulted in S's not believing *p* at *t*, then S's belief in *p* at *t* is justified.

Note that (2) makes the justification of a belief depend not only on the process which actually produced the belief but also on processes that could and should be employed. The basic idea is that the proper use of evidence is a conditionally reliable process. So one who has evidence that a belief forming process is unreliable and uses that evidence will not place credence in beliefs produced by that process. Goldman offers a different way of handling this problem in *Epistemology and Cognition* (Cambridge, 1986), p. 63. I have argued in "Causality, Reliability, and Mathematical Knowledge" (manuscript) that the new account cannot handle the problem and must be replaced with an account in the spirit of (2).

22 Laurence BonJour has stressed this point in his criticism of reliability theories. See, for example, *The Structure of Empirical Knowledge* (Cambridge, 1985), chapter 3.

23 See the papers cited in footnote 14.

24 Kitcher, *The Nature of Mathematical Knowledge*, p. 24.

25 Alvin Goldman, *Epistemology and Cognition* (Cambridge, 1986), p. 106.

26 Kitcher, *The Nature of Mathematical Knowledge*, p. 30.

27 Paul Benacerraf, "Mathematical Truth," pp. 671–5.

28 Penelope Maddy, "Perception and Mathematical Intuition," *Philosophical Review* 89 (1980), pp. 163–96; and Jaegwon Kim, "Some Reflections on Perception and A Priori Knowledge."

29 Penelope Maddy makes a similar point in "Mathematical Epistemology: What is the Question?," *Monist* 67 (1984), pp. 46–55. This issue, however, is more complex than her paper suggests. Some of these complexities are discussed in detail in my "Causality, Reliability, and Mathematical Knowledge."

30 BonJour, *The Structure of Empirical Knowledge*, p. 32. R. M. Chisholm endorses a similar position in *Theory of Knowledge*, 2nd edn, p. 17.

31 Kitcher discusses this issue in chapter 3 of *The Nature of Mathematical Knowledge*.

32 Kurt Gödel, "What is Cantor's Continuum Problem?," reprinted in P. Benacerraf and H. Putnam (eds), *Philosophy of Mathematics*, 2nd edn (Cambridge, 1983), pp. 483–5.

33 Pollock, *Knowledge and Justification*, pp. 318–20.

CHAPTER 44

A *Priori* Knowledge and the Scope of Philosophy

George Bealer

Must philosophy rely substantively on science? If philosophy and science conflict, could philosophy ever have greater authority? I wish to recommend two theses which, though currently unfashionable, have been the dominant view historically:

The Autonomy of Philosophy Among the central questions of philosophy[1] that can be answered by one standard theoretical means or another, most can in principle be answered by philosophical investigation and argument without relying substantively on the sciences.

The Authority of Philosophy Insofar as science and philosophy purport to answer the same central philosophical questions, in most cases the support that science could in principle provide for those answers is not as strong as that which philosophy could in principle provide for its answers. So, should there be conflicts, the authority of philosophy in most cases can be greater in principle.

There are two largely independent defenses of the Autonomy and Authority of Philosophy – the Argument from Evidence and the Argument from Concepts.[2] The latter offers an analysis of what it is to possess a concept determinately, an analysis which, together with the fact that the central

concepts of philosophy can be possessed determinately, implies Autonomy and Authority. In this paper I will explain and defend (all too briefly, I am afraid) the Argument from Evidence:

(1) Intuitions are evidence.
(2) Modal reliabilism is the correct explanation of why intuitions are evidence.
(3) Modal reliabilism implies the Autonomy and Authority of Philosophy as long as scientific essentialism is no barrier.
(4) Scientific essentialism is no barrier.
∴ The Autonomy and Authority of Philosophy hold.

Modal reliabilism, if correct, would provide the foundation of a general account of *a priori* knowledge. That, however, lies beyond the scope of this paper.

1. Intuitions are Evidence

Our Standard Justificatory Procedure. I begin by reviewing some plain truths about the procedure we standardly use to justify our beliefs and theories. The first point is that we standardly use various items – for example, experiences, observations, testimony – as evidence. Now at one time many people accepted the doctrine that knowledge is justified true belief. But today we have good evidence to the contrary, namely, our intuitions that

Originally published in *Philosophical Studies* 81 (1996), pp. 121–42.

situations like those described in the Gettier literature are possible and that the relevant people in those situations would not know the things at issue. This and countless other examples show that, according to our standard justificatory procedure, *intuitions* are used as evidence (or as reasons). The evidential use of intuitions is ubiquitous in philosophy; recall just as few further examples: Chisholm's perceptual-relativity refutation of phenomenalism, Putnam's perfect-pretender refutation of behaviorism, all the various twin-earth examples, Burge's arthritis example, multiple-realizability, etc., etc. Each of these involves the evidential use of intuitions about certain possibilities and about whether relevant concepts apply to those possibilities.

Among our various theoretical beliefs, some are deemed to have *a priori* justification. This occurs for beliefs arrived at by a procedure that suitably approximates the following idealization: (1) canvassing intuitions; (2) subjecting those intuitions to dialectical critique; (3) constructing theories that systematize the surviving intuitions; (4) testing those theories against further intuitions; (5) repeating the process until equilibrium is approached.[3] The method philosophers standardly use to establish answers to central philosophical questions closely resembles this procedure of *a priori* justification. Perhaps the most important difference is that philosophers make occasional use of empirical evidence – specifically, we invoke actual "real-life" examples and actual examples from (the history of) science. In virtually all cases, however, use of such examples can be "modalized away."[4] That is, such examples can, at least in principle, be dropped and in their place one can use *a priori* intuitions affirming corresponding (not to say identical) *possibilities* which have equivalent philosophical force. (I will return to this point in section 4.)

Phenomenology of Intuitions. My next step is to say something about what is meant by intuition in this context. We do not mean a magical power or inner voice or anything of the sort. For you to have an intuition that A is just for it to *seem* to you that A. Here "seems" is understood, not as a cautionary or "hedging" term, but in its use as a term for a genuine kind of conscious episode. For example, when you first consider one of de Morgan's laws, often it neither seems to be true nor seems to be false; after a moment's reflection,

however, something happens: it now seems true; you suddenly "just see" that it is true. Of course, this kind of seeming is *intellectual*, not sensory or introspective (or imaginative). The subject here is *a priori* (or rational) intuition.

Intuition must be distinguished from belief: belief is not a seeming; intuition is. For example, there are many mathematical theorems that I believe (because I have seen the proofs) but that do not *seem* to me to be true and that do not *seem* to me to be false; I do not have intuitions about them either way. Conversely, I have an intuition – it still *seems* to me – that the naive comprehension axiom of set theory is true; this is so despite the fact that I do not believe that it is true (because I know of the set-theoretical paradoxes).[5] This case evidently shows that the classical modern infallibilist theory of intuition is incorrect. There is a rather similar phenomenon in sensory (vs. intellectual) seeming. In the Müller-Lyer illusion, it still *seems* to me that one of the arrows is longer than the other; this is so despite the fact that I do not believe that it is (because I have measured them). In each case, the seeming (intellectual or sensory) persists in spite of the countervailing belief.

This brings up a closely related distinction between belief and intuition. Belief is highly plastic. Using (false) appeals to authority, cajoling, intimidation, brainwashing, and so forth, you can get a person to believe almost anything, at least briefly. Not so for intuitions. Although there is disagreement about the degree of plasticity of intuitions (some people believe they are rather plastic; I do not), it is clear that they are inherently far more resistant to such influences than beliefs. Intuitions are also distinct from judgments, guesses, and hunches. There are significant restrictions on the propositions concerning which one can have intuitions; by contrast, there are virtually no restrictions on the propositions concerning which one can make a judgment or a guess or have a hunch. For related reasons, intuition is also different from common sense.

(Incidentally, the work of cognitive psychologists such as Wason, Johnson-Laird, Eleanor Rosh, Richard Nisbett, D. Kahneman and A. Tversky tells us little about intuition in the restricted use of the term relevant here; they have simply not been concerned with intuitions in this sense.)

The Argument from Epistemic Norms. Granted that our standard justificatory practice presently *uses* intuitions as evidence, why should this move radicals who just boldly deny that intuitions really *are* evidence? In "The Incoherence of Empiricism" I argued that denying that intuitions have evidential weight leads one to epistemic self-defeat. The purpose of this style of argument is to persuade even those under the spell of radicalism. To give a feel for this style of argument I will now sketch one of three such arguments against radical empiricism, the view that *only* (phenomenal) experiences and/or observations have genuine evidential weight.[6]

Consider an absurd position like *visualism*, the view that countenances only visual experience as evidence and that arbitrarily excludes nonvisual experiences (tactile, auditory, etc.). How is radical empiricism relevantly different? To avoid begging the question, radical empiricists must answer *from within* the standard justificatory procedure. The question to consider, therefore, is this: when one implements the standard justificatory procedure's mechanism of self-criticism, does intuition – in contrast to nonvisual experience – get excluded as a source of evidence?

In relation to "three *cs*" – *consistency, corroboration,* and *confirmation* – intuition is quite unlike spurious sources of evidence such as tea leaves, tarot, oracles, the stars, birds, and the like. First, a person's concrete-case intuitions are largely consistent with one another. (We confine ourselves to concrete-case intuitions, for it is to these that the standard justificatory procedure assigns primary evidential weight.) To be sure, a given person's concrete-case intuitions occasionally appear to be inconsistent with one another, but so do our observations and even our pure sense experiences. This is hardly enough to throw out observation and sense experience as sources of evidence. Moreover, for each of these sources – including intuition – most apparent conflicts can be reconciled by standard rephrasal techniques (for an example, see section 4). Second, although different people do have conflicting intuitions from time to time, there is an impressive corroboration by others of one's elementary logical, mathematical, conceptual, and modal intuitions. The situation is much the same with observation: different people have conflicting observations from time to time, but this is hardly enough to throw out

observation as a source of evidence. Third, unlike tea-leaf reading, intuition is seldom, if ever, disconfirmed by our experiences and observations. The primary reason is that the contents of our intuitions – whether conceptual, logical, mathematical, or modal – are by and large independent of the contents of our observations and experiences. The one potential exception involves our modal intuitions, but virtually no conflicts arise there because our intuitions about what experiences and observations are logically (metaphysically) possible are so liberal.

There is another kind of conflict, namely, conflict between certain *theories* and certain intuitions (e.g., intuitions about simultaneity and Euclidean geometry). Do such conflicts overturn intuition as a source of evidence? No, for there are analogous conflicts between certain theories and certain observations (e.g., observations that the sun is about the same size as the moon and that it moves across the sky). Likewise, experience and testimony come into conflict with certain theories. Such conflicts are not enough to overturn either of these sources of evidence. As a matter of fact, however, most of our elementary conceptual, logical, and numerical intuitions are not in conflict with, but are actually affirmed by, our empirical theories. And modal and higher mathematical intuitions, while not affirmed by our empirical theories, are for the most part not inconsistent with them. Moreover, our best comprehensive theory based on *all* standard sources of evidence, *including intuition,* affirms most of our modal and higher mathematical intuitions. This should be no surprise since it begins by including intuitions as evidence.

If radical empiricists are to try to overthrow intuition by means of the standard justificatory procedure's mechanism for self-criticism, they have only one alternative. They must invoke the comprehensive theory that one would formulate if one admitted only those sources of evidence *other than* intuition. Characterized more abstractly, this method of challenging standard sources of evidence goes as follows. One formulates one's best comprehensive theory on the basis of the standard sources of evidence that one is not challenging. If the resulting theory deems the omitted sources not to be reliable, then they are discounted as sources of evidence.

This method is appropriate in some cases, for example, to challenge as a source of evidence the hitherto uncritically accepted pronouncements of an established political authority (reminiscent of the Wizard of Oz). However, there are cases in which this method does not work. For example, it may not be used by "visualists" to challenge other modes of experience (tactile, auditory, etc.) as sources of evidence. Neither vision nor touch may be used in this way to override the other as a source of evidence. To be a source of evidence, neither requires affirmation by the best comprehensive theory based on other sources of evidence.

The difference between the political-authority case and the visualism case is plain. The political authority is *intuitively not as basic* a source of evidence as the sources of evidence that are being used to eliminate it (i.e., experience, observation, etc.). By contrast, vision and touch are *intuitively equally basic* sources of evidence. The standard justificatory procedure permits us to apply the present method against a currently accepted source of evidence if and only if *intuitively* that source is not as basic as the sources of evidence being used to challenge it.[7]

So in the radical empiricists' effort to eliminate intuition as a source of evidence, the standard justificatory procedure would warrant this move only if we had intuitions to the effect that intuition is a less basic source of evidence than experience and/or observation, one requiring auxiliary support from the best comprehensive theory based exclusively on these other sources of evidence. But when we consider relevant cases, we see that we do not have such intuitions. For example, suppose a person has an intuition, say, that if P then not not P; or (in your favorite Gettier example) that the person in question would not know; or that a good theory must take into account *all* the evidence; and so forth. Nothing more is needed. Intuitively, these intuitions are evidentially as basic as evidence gets. They are intuitively as basic as experiences, much as tactile experiences are intuitively as basic as visual experiences. In consequence, the present method for challenging a source of evidence cannot be used against intuition, any more than it can be used against, say, touch or vision.[8]

Thus, intuition survives as a genuine source of evidence when one applies the standard justificatory procedure's mechanism for self-criticism. We have not been able to find a relevant difference

between radical empiricism, which excludes intuition as a source of evidence, and various preposterous theories (e.g., visualism) that arbitrarily exclude other standard sources of evidence (e.g., touch). But, surely, these preposterous theories are not justified. So radical empiricism is not justified, either.

There is a way to strengthen this argument. Suppose that in our justificatory practices we were to make an arbitrary departure from our epistemic norms. There would then be *prima facie* reason to doubt that the theories we would formulate by following the non-standard procedure are justified. Since radical empiricists make an arbitrary departure form our epistemic norms, what can they do to overcome this reasonable doubt in their own case? They are caught in a fatal dilemma. On the one hand, they could invoke theories arrived at by following the standard justificatory procedure, with its inclusion of intuitions as evidence. But, by the radical empiricists' own standards, these theories are not justified. So this avenue is of no help. On the other hand, they could invoke theories arrived at by following their radical empiricist procedure. But this would be of no help, either. For, as we have seen, there is reasonable doubt that, by following that procedure, one obtains justified theories. To overcome this doubt, one may not invoke the very theories about whose justification there is already reasonable doubt. That would only beg the question. Either way, therefore, radical empiricists are unable to overcome the reasonable doubt that their procedure leads to justified theories. So the reasonable doubt stands.

Our epistemic situation is in this sense "hermeneutical": when one makes an arbitrary departure from it, reasonable doubts are generated, and there is in principle no way to overcome them. This is the fate of radical empiricism. Only the standard justificatory procedure escapes this problem: because it conforms to – and, indeed, constitutes – the epistemic norm, there is no *prima facie* reason to doubt that the theories it yields are justified; so the problem never arises.

2. Explanation of Why Intuitions are Evidence

What explains why intuitions are evidence? In "Philosophical Limits of Scientific Essentialism"

I argued that the only adequate explanation is some kind of truth-based, or reliabilist, explanation. In *Philosophical Limits of Science* I develop this argument in detail, dealing there with various alternative explanations – pragmatist, coherentist, conventionalist, and rule-based (or practice-based). In the present context, I will assume that these arguments are successful and that we must turn to a truth-based explanation.

Reliabilism has been associated with analyses of knowledge and justification, analyses which most philosophers today reject. Our topic, however, is not knowledge or justification but rather evidence. This difference is salutary, for here reliabilism promises to be less problematic. But not as a *general* theory of evidence: sources of evidence traditionally classified as derived sources are subject to counterexamples much like those used against reliabilist theories of justification. For example, testimony would still provide a person with evidence (reasons to believe) even if it were really just systematic undetectable lying. So reliability is not a necessary condition for something's qualifying as a source of evidence. Nor is reliability a sufficient condition for something's qualifying as a source of evidence: as in the case of justification, such things as nomologically reliable clairvoyance, telepathy, dreams, hunches, etc. are *prima facie* counterexamples.

The natural response to these counterexamples is to demand only that *basic* sources of evidence be reliable: something is a derived source of evidence relative to a given subject iff it is deemed (perhaps unreliably) to have a reliable tie to the truth by the best comprehensive theory based on the subject's basic sources of evidence.[9] Let us suppose that experience and intuition are our basic sources[10] and that all other sources are derived. The above counterexamples would not then fault this analysis of derived sources of evidence. In the case of undetectable lying, testimony would now rightly be counted as a source of evidence, for the subject's best comprehensive theory based on basic sources (experience and intuition) would deem it to have a reliable tie to the truth (even if it in fact does not because of the envisaged lying). In the case of spurious derived sources (reliable clairvoyance, telepathy, dreams, hunches, etc.), if one has not affirmed their reliability by means of one's best comprehensive theory based

on one's basic sources, their deliverances would rightly not qualify as evidence.

In this setting, reliabilism is restricted to basic sources of evidence: something is a basic source of evidence iff it has a certain kind of reliable tie to the truth. The fundamental question then concerns the character of this tie. Is it a contingent (nomological or causal) tie? Or is it some kind of strong necessary tie?

Contingent Reliabilism. On this account, something counts as a basic source of evidence iff there is a nomologically necessary, but nevertheless contingent, tie between its deliverances and the truth. This account, however, is subject to counterexamples of the sort which faulted the original sufficiency condition above (nomologically reliable telepathy, clairvoyance, guesses, hunches, etc.). Consider a creature who has a capacity for making reliable telepathically generated guesses. Phenomenologically, these guesses resemble those which people make in blind-sight experiments. The guesses at issue concern necessary truths of some very high degree of difficulty. These truths are known to the beings on distant planet who have arrived at them by ordinary *a priori* means (theoretical systematization of intuitions, proof of consequences therefrom, etc.). These beings have intelligence far exceeding that of our creature or anyone else coinhabiting his planet. Indeed, the creature and his coinhabitants will never be able to establish any of these necessary truths (or even assess their consistency) by ordinary *a priori* means. Finally, suppose that the following holds as a matter of nomological necessity: the creature guesses that p is true iff p is a necessary truth of the indicated kind and the creature is trying to make a guess as to whether p is true or false. But, plainly, guessing would not qualify as a basic source of evidence for the creature, contrary to contingent reliabilism.[11]

Modal Reliabilism. Given that contingent reliabilism fails, we are left with modal reliabilism, according to which something counts as a basic source iff there is some kind of strong modal tie between its deliverances and the truth. This thesis provides an invitation to search for the weakest modal tie to the truth sufficiently rich to explain the evidential status of our basic sources of evidence. In this paper I will attempt this only approximately and only for the case of intuitions.[12]

The explanation of the evidential status of intuitions requires a modal tie between intuitions and the truth which is strong enough to block counterexamples, such as those which beset contingent reliabilism. At the same time, if there is a modal tie which does this and which is weaker than infallibilism, we should adopt it. This suggests that we make the strong modal tie to the truth *dialectical and holistic* rather than local:

> For suitably good cognitive conditions, it is necessary that, if while in such conditions a subject goes through the whole procedure of *a priori* justification (described in section 1), then most of the propositions derivable from the resulting comprehensive theoretical systematization of the subject's intuitions would have to be true.

My hypothesis is that something like this modal tie is the sort we are seeking. Of course, this modal tie would be vacuous and the associated explanation of the evidential status of intuitions would fail if it were not possible for some subjects to be in cognitive conditions of the quality indicated. This possibility, and the associated modal tie to the truth, will be important in what follows next.

3. Derivation of the Authority and Autonomy of Philosophy

It is *necessary* that the comprehensive theoretical systematization of a subject's intuitions in cognitive conditions of the indicated quality is largely true (i.e., most of the propositions derivable from it are true). No such necessity ever holds for science. No matter how good the cognitive conditions, it is always *possible* that scientific theories arrived at in those conditions are largely mistaken. Why? For all the standard reasons – undetectably unrepresentative samples, non-simple natural laws, distorting perceptual media – not to mention too few or malfunctioning sense organs, hallucinations, vats, etc. Because of this, a comprehensive theoretical systematization of intuitions in the indicated cognitive conditions would have an in principle greater epistemic authority. But the methods by which that theoretical systematization would have been arrived at are just the standard methods of philosophy; they include no substantive reliance on science. Now suppose

that the indicated theoretical systematization of intuitions would include answers to most of the central questions of philosophy that can be answered by one standard theoretical means or another. Then, given that the epistemic support for this theoretical systematization is greater in principle than anything science could achieve in support of its theories, the thesis of the Authority of Philosophy would hold.

This argument is based on the supposition that the indicated theoretical systematization of intuitions would include answers to most of the central questions of philosophy which can be answered by one standard theoretical means or another. This supposition is basically the thesis of the Autonomy of Philosophy. The Argument from Concepts will provide perhaps the most conclusive defense of this thesis. But we are able to mount an independent defense right now.

Consider the intuitions that are the inputs when a subject engages in the indicated process. They include a wide range of intuitions about matters bearing on central questions of philosophy. What level of cognitive conditions would be required to insure the strong modal tie – that is, to insure that, necessarily, most of the propositions derivable from the resulting theoretical systematisation would be true? Presumably, it would be a high level. But as cognitive conditions (notably, attentiveness and intelligence) improve, the scope of one's intuitions increases. As a result, at the indicted high level of cognitive conditions, the scope of the intuitions that would be the inputs for the process would be very wide. It is extremely plausible that they would have implications for most central questions of philosophy. (In fact, our own intuitions already do.) What, then, could prevent the resulting theoretical systematization from giving answers to these questions? I know of nothing that could. But there are two nagging worries, namely, that inevitable limitations on intelligence and/or scientific essentialism might somehow constitute barriers.

Consider the worry about limitations on intelligence. Most of the central questions of philosophy do not seem to be the sort of questions requiring infinitary intelligence (e.g., for doing infinitary proofs, infinitary computations, etc.); some finite level (perhaps well beyond ours) ought to suffice. (In the Argument from Concepts I give a positive theoretical argument which insures that, no matter how high, the requisite level of intelligence must be possible, so this finiteness point is not essential.) If this is right, the issue comes down to the question of what level of finitary intelligence would be required (for having a sufficiently wide range of intuitions) to yield Autonomy. Is the level of intelligence needed to underwrite the Authority of Philosophy enough for this? Since the intelligence needed for Authority is very high, it seems to me that it ought to be enough. But suppose not; suppose some higher but nevertheless finite level of intelligence is needed. Intuitively, however, for any finite level of intelligence, it is possible for some being to be that intelligent. So, if there were a barrier to Autonomy, it would have to be something other than intelligence. Someone might respond that this intuition ought not be honored. But on what ground? There is no even faintly credible ground besides one associated with scientific essentialism, namely, that this intuition is really only an intuition of the kind of epistemic possibility which is so central to the defense of scientific essentialism. But this intuition is expressed in semantically stable terms, so scientific essentialists are committed to accepting it at face value, as I will argue in the next section.

This leaves us with the general scientific essentialist worry. Perhaps, as cognitive conditions (intelligence, attentiveness, etc.) improve, the scope of intuitions reaches a limit (or even narrows). Questions beyond that limit are scientific questions epistemically on a par with the question of the chemical composition of water, the analysis of heat, etc. In the next section I will argue that this is completely mistaken. If the argument is successful, we will be entitled to conclude that there is no barrier to having intuitions of sufficiently wide scope to underwrite the Autonomy of Philosophy.

4.   Scientific Essentialism is No Barrier

Scientific essentialism (SE) is the doctrine that there are necessities (e.g., that water = H_2O) that are knowable only with the aid of empirical science. The arguments supporting SE rely on intuitions; without them SE would be unjustified. (I defend this claim in detail in "Philosophical Limits of Scientific Essentialism".) For example,

the famous twin-earth intuition concerning water, H_2O, and XYZ. But there is a problem. Before the advent of SE, we had a host of anti-SE intuitions, for example, the intuition that it could have turned out that some samples of water contained no hydrogen. What are we to make of the conflict between pro-and anti-SE intuitions?

Rephrasal Strategies. Proponents of SE have two responses. First, they could simply declare that anti-SE intuitions are mistaken whereas their own pro-SE intuitions are correct. But critics of SE could simply meet this response by stating that things are the other way around. The result would be a stalemate. To avoid it, proponents of SE must turn to the second response, according to which widespread conflict among our intuitions is only an appearance. All, or most, of our intuitions are correct. Despite their correctness, however, many are *misreported*. When we rephrase our (apparently) anti-SE intuitions to make them consistent with our pro-SE intuitions, we succeed. But when we try to rephrase the latter to make them consistent with the former, we fail. Accordingly, the stalemate is broken in favor of SE.

According to Kripke, when we report our pro-SE intuitions, what we say is strictly and literally true, and we are reporting ordinary possibilities. But when we report our apparently anti-SE intuitions, we confuse ordinary possibility with the possibility of a certain kind of epistemic situation (see Kripke, pp. 103–4). Consider an example. When we say "It could have turned out that some samples of water contained no hydrogen", what we say is strictly and literally false. The intuition is true but incorrectly reported. The correct report would be something like this: it is possible for there to be a language group which is in an epistemic situation qualitatively identical to ours but which uses the expressions "water" and/or "hydrogen" to mean something other than what we do. This possibility is consistent with the SE thesis that, necessarily, water = H_2O. At the same time, when anti-scientific-essentialists try to use this rephrasal strategy to deflate pro-SE intuitions (e.g., the twin-earth intuition), they fail. (This matter is discussed at length in my "Mental Properties.") This and other examples lead to the following general schema for applying the rephrasal strategy: ⌜It could have turned out that A⌝ is to be rephrased as ⌜It is possible that a language group in an epistemic situation qualitatively identical to ours would make a true statement by asserting ⌜A⌝ with normal literal intent⌝.

Semantic Stability. The rephrasal strategy suggests a distinction between *semantically stable* and *semantically unstable* expressions. An expression is semantically stable iff, necessarilly, in any language group in an epistemic situation qualitatively identical to ours, the expression would mean the same thing. An expression is semantically unstable iff it is possible for it to mean something different in some language group whose epistemic situation is qualitatively identical to ours. Of course, "qualitatively identical epistemic situation" must be understood in the intended way.[13]

Presumably an expression is semantically unstable iff the external environment makes some contribution to its meaning. Natural kind terms are paradigmatic – "water", "gold", "heat", "beech", "elm", etc. Logical, mathematical, and a great many philosophical terms, by contrast, are semantically stable: the external environment makes no such contribution. For example, "some", "all", "and", "if", "is identical to", "is", "necessarily", "possibly", "true", "valid", "0", "1", "+", "÷", "*e*"; "property", "quality", "quantity", "relation", "proposition", "state of affairs", "object", "category", etc. It seems clear that all these are semantically stable: any language group in an epistemic situation qualitatively identical to ours would mean what we mean by these "formal" expressions.

How is the list to be continued? My hypothesis is that most, if not all, of the central terms of philosophy are semantically stable: "conscious", "sensation", "pleasure", "pain", "emotion", "think", "believe", "desire", "decide", "know", "reason", "evidence", "justify", "understand", "explain", "purpose", "good", "fair", "ought". Case by case, each of these intuitively is semantically stable. Consider "pain", for example. If there were a language group in an epistemic situation *qualitatively identical* to ours, they would use "pain" to mean pain. "Pain" is a term for a certain felt quality; our counterparts in a language group whose epistemic situation is *qualitatively identical* would have to be using "pain" for the *identical quality*.

Notice that I did not say that *all* central philosophical terms are semantically stable. It might be held that there are uses of "time", "space", "probable", "cause", and "matter" which are semantically

unstable. Even if there are, however, there exist other uses – seen in expressions like "a kind of time", "a kind of space", etc. – which are semantically stable. These *generic* uses occur in sentences such as "Euclidean space is a possible kind of space", "Newtonian time is a possible kind of time", etc. which are semantically stable sentences. In any language group in an epistemic situation qualitatively identical to ours, these sentence would mean the same as they mean for us and presumably would be true, just as they are for us. These generic uses are sufficient, I believe, to underwrite a general philosophy of space and time, probability, etc.

With this qualification in mind, we can state my hypothesis thus: most of the central terms of philosophy are semantically stable or else have generic uses which are semantically stable. Case by case, intuitions support this hypothesis. To deny it would be *ad hoc* unless accompanied by argument; I know of none which is not tendentious or question-begging. Unless and until a successful argument is found, we should accept the hypothesis.

Limits of Scientific Essentialism. This hypothesis is coupled with a second, namely, that scientific essentialism holds only for semantically unstable expressions. There are several arguments for the second hypothesis. The first, which I will now sketch, is a generalization on the argument from "Mental Properties" and has to do with the way one argues for SE in the case of particular expressions. (Another argument is that the most plausible explanation of certain puzzling patterns in our intuitions, including in particular pro- and anti-SE intuitions, implies the hypothesis. A third is that the analysis of what it is to possess a concept determinately implies the hypothesis. I discuss these two lines of defense in "Philosophical Limits of Scientific Essentialism".)

Consider how one argues for SE in a particular case, for example, the cogent SE argument that, necessarily, water = H_2O. The argument consists of two steps. First, pro-SE intuitions supporting the identity are elicited: in all known cases, these intuitions either are or can be reworked into twin-earth style intuitions. Second, it is shown that the rephrasal strategy can be used to deflate the force of our anti-SE intuitions but that, when anti-scientific-essentialists attempt to use it to deflate the force of our pro-SE intuitions (i.e., the intuitions elicited in step one), they fail. Because both steps evidently succeed, one may conclude that SE holds for "water".

Now consider some semantically stable term t. To show that SE holds for t, one would need to go through both steps. The problem is that *both steps fail* for all semantically stable terms t. In connection with the first step, consider the t-analogue of the twin-earth argument for "water". We are to contemplate the possibility of another planet (or possible world) macroscopically like earth but microscopically different. We are to consider items here to which t applies, and we are then to ask whether, intuitively, t would fail to apply to the corresponding items on the hypothetical planet (in the possible world). The question is outlandish if t is a "formal" term, that is, an expression of the following sort: "is identical to", "is", "necessarily", "possibly", "true", "property", "quality", "quantity", "relation", "proposition", "state of affairs", "substance", "event", "category", etc. For example, there are properties here; could there fail to be properties there?!

What about semantically stable expressions that are not "formal" but rather "contentful"? Consider "conscious", for example. The following would be the "conscious"-analogue of the original twin-earth argument for "water". Suppose that on earth all and only things that are conscious have a certain microstructure, say, "Con-fibers" (which are composed ultimately of hydrogen, oxygen, carbon, etc.). Consider a twin earth on which our Doppelgängers display "consciousness"-behavior exactly like ours. It turns out, however, that, whereas our consciousness – and our associated "consciousness"-behavior – co-occurs with firing Con-fibers, the "consciousness"-behavior of our Doppelgängers co-occurs instead with firing Con_{te}-fibers (composed ultimately of X, Y, Z, etc.). Would we say that these creatures are conscious? To be sure, we would not be *certain* that they are conscious; macroscopic behavioral criteria never entail that a mental predicate applies. Nevertheless, *it would not be counterintuitive to say that they are conscious*. Note the contrast with water. It would be counterintuitive to say that samples of XYZ on twin earth are samples of water. This intuition is the essential first step of the SE argument concerning "water". The analogous intuition

concerning "conscious" is simply *missing*! Accordingly, the essential first step of the argument that SE applies to "conscious" cannot even get off the ground.

I come now to the second step in the SE argument, namely, that anti-SE intuitions can be neutralized by means of the rephrasal strategy. My argument against this has two stages.

First, suppose that the intuitions in questions are expressed using *only* semantically stable terms. Then they will retain their original force even upon rephrasal. Suppose, for example, that an intuition is originally reported with a sentence ⌜It is possible that S⌝ consisting entirely of semantically stable expressions. Then (by the definition of semantic stability) any language group in an epistemic situation qualitatively identical to ours would mean what we mean by ⌜S⌝. Therefore, the rephrasal ⌜It is possible for there to be a language group in an epistemic situation qualitatively identical to ours who would make a true statement by asserting ⌜S⌝⌝ would imply ⌜It is possible that S⌝. So the force of the original intuition is not deflated.

Second, suppose that the intuitions in question are "mixed" – that is, expressed with a combination of semantically stable and unstable terms. Because of the semantically unstable terms, the force of these intuitions shifts upon rephrasal. But for the purpose of investigating central philosophical questions, there is a strategy for dealing with this. The idea is to find a new intuition with the philosophical import of the original but expressed entirely in semantically stable terms. To do this, we construct an appropriate semantically stable "counterpart" for each of the semantically unstable terms. In some cases, there may be no exact (i.e., necessarily equivalent) counterpart. But we can always find a counterpart which is as close to the semantically unstable original as is philosophically important. To illustrate this strategy, consider the chauvinistic identity-thesis that being conscious = having firing Con-fibers. A multiple-realizability argument against this thesis might invoke the intuition that it is possible for something to be conscious and not have Con-fibers. This intuition is "mixed": even though the expressions "something", "have", "not", and "conscious" are semantically stable, "Con-fibers" is not. (And presumably "Con-fibers" lacks an exact semantically stable counterpart, for there is evidently no semantically stable way to capture, e.g., relevant matters of scale.) The intuition therefore would not retain its original force upon rephrasal. The philosophical import of the intuition, however, is that it is possible for there to be consciousness in the absence of a certain highly specific nested complex of inter-related nonmetal parts (ultimately hydrogen, oxygen, carbon, etc.). We can get as close as we want to this notion using expressions from pure mathematics and other semantically stable expressions such as "part", "relation", "non", and "mental". Even though what is "left over" might be of scientific interest, it would not be relevant to the philosophical point (i.e., refuting the chauvinistic identity thesis). Because the new counterpart intuition is expressed with semantically stable expressions, it will (by the considerations of the previous paragraph) retain its original force upon rephrasal. Although this is only an illustration, it suggests how, for more complicated "mixed" intuitions, we can find counterpart intuitions which have the same philosophical import as the originals and which are expressible with semantically stable expressions. These counterpart intuitions would thus not be deflated upon rephrasal.

These considerations indicate that the second step in the SE argument fails even in the case of "mixed" intuitions. The general conclusion, therefore, is that both steps in the SE argument fail for semantically stable expressions. Hence, there is no reason whatsoever to think that SE generalizes from semantically unstable expressions to semantically stable expressions and, in turn, to think that SE is a barrier to the Autonomy and Authority of Philosophy.

5.   Concluding Remark

I have outlined my reasons for accepting the four premises of the Argument from Evidence, and as we saw, that argument implies Autonomy and Authority. It is of course another matter whether it is nomologically possible for human beings to be in sufficiently good cognitive conditions to achieve the kind of autonomy and authority asserted as a mere possibility in these two theses. Whether this is nomologically possible is a question on which I take no stand here. My personal belief, however, is that collectively, over historical time, undertaking philosophy as a civilization-wide project, we can do so closely enough to obtain authoritative answers to a substantial number of central philosophical questions.

Notes

1   Three criteria help to identify the central questions of philosophy. They are *universal* in that, regardless of the context (biological, historical, etc.), they would be of significant interest to philosophers, in their role as philosophers, at least once they had grasped the underlying concepts and their interrelations. These questions are *general* in that they do not pertain to this or that individual, species, historical event, etc. And they are *necessary* in that they call for answers that hold necessarily: it would not be enough to know that piety happened to be what Euthyphro exhibited; a philosopher wants to know what it must be.

Many philosophical questions of pressing *importance* to humanity lack one or more of the three features, I believe, however, that the relation between these questions and the central questions may be understood on analogy with the distinction between applied mathematics and pure mathematics. In most if not all cases, the answers to noncentral questions are immediate consequences of answers to central questions plus auxiliary (usually empirical) propositions having little philosophical content in and of themselves.

2   Developed in my *Philosophical Limits of Science*, forthcoming.

3   This procedure resembles the procedure of seeking "reflective equilibrium" but differs from it crucially. In the latter procedure, an equilibrium among all beliefs – including empirical beliefs – is sought. In the *a priori* process, an equilibrium based on *a priori* intuitions is sought. Empirical beliefs – and the experiences and observations upon which they are based – are sometimes used to raise

and to resolve doubts about the quality of the background cognitive conditions (intelligence, etc.). But these empirical resources play no role in the procedure of *a priori* justification itself. *A priori* intuitions – not empirical beliefs – constitute the grist for its mill. When I speak of not needing to rely *substantively* on empirical science, this is one of the points I have in mind.

As indicated, this procedure is an idealization. In real life, various stages are pursued at once, and they are performed only partially. The results are usually provisional and are used as "feedback" to guide subsequent efforts. These efforts are typically collective, and the results of past efforts – including those of past generations – are used liberally. The fact that speech and writings are used does not disqualify these collective efforts as *a priori*, at least not according to the central use of "*a priori*" I am employing. Experience and/or observation can be used to raise – and also to resolve – doubts about the quality of the communication conditions (speaker and author sincerity, reliability of the medium of transmission, accuracy of interpretation, etc.). But these empirical resources play no role in the procedure of the *a priori* justification itself. When I speak of not needing to rely substantively on empirical science, this is another one of the points I have in mind.

4   For certain phenomenal possibilities (e.g., certain Gestalt phenomena), perhaps the actual experience is required in order to know that that kind of experience is possible. This would not upset my main theses, for such use of experience would differ markedly from the use science makes of experience. When I say that philosophy need not rely substantively on science, another one of my intentions is to allow the use of experience to establish mere phenomenal possibilities. Despite this, I will sometimes talk as if the method of answering central philosophical questions is purely *a priori*. Perhaps this is not quite right, and appropriate adjustments might need to be made.

5   I am indebted to George Myro for this example and for the point it illustrates, namely, that it is possible to have an intuition without having the corresponding belief.

6   Of course, it is the *contents* of one's experiences and observations that are held to be evidential. Note that there is a more moderate empiricism which, like Hume's, deems (the contents of) intuitions of relations of ideas – that is, intuitions of analyticities – to be evidence but which excludes as evidence all intuitions of nonanalyticities. This view is also self-defeating, but for somewhat different reasons.

7   Someone might think that, rather than consulting intuition on the question of relative basicness, one should consult the simplest overall theory that takes as its evidence the deliverances of all of one's currently accepted sources of evidence. But this approach yields the wrong results. For example, according to it, the political authority, with just a bit of cleverness, would be as immune to challenge as, say, sense experience. But despite this, it would be appropriate to reject the political authority as a special source of evidence. The way we would do this, according to the standard procedure, would be to fall back on our intuitions about relative basicness.

8   This diagnosis is not circular: intuitions about relative basicness of candidate sources are not being used as evidence here; their use here is a prescribed step in the standard procedure of self-critique.

Someone might hold that being intuitively basic is necessary but not sufficient for a candidate source to withstand critique. For sufficiency, something additional is required, namely, that our best explanation of the candidate source should entail that its deliverances (tend to) be true. Using this idea, radical empiricists might hold that our best explanation of our (reports of) experiences and/or observations entail that they (tend to) be true but that this is not so for our best explanation of our intuitions. From this, the radical empiricist might conclude that, although experience and/or observation withstand critique, intuition does not. This, however, is question-begging. For advocates of intuitions may counter that the best explanation of intuition must invoke the analysis of what it takes to possess concepts determinately, and, according to that analysis, a necessary condition of determinate concept possession is that intuitions involving the concept (tend to) be true. Why accept this theory? Well, if (certain compelling) intuitions are admitted as evidence, its superiority over competing theories can be shown. Given this prospect, it would be question-begging for radical empiricists to reject this style of explanation in favor of their own candidate: their candidate could be defended only by disregarding a significant body of evidence (or at least what is counted as evidence according to our epistemic norms).

Is it question-begging for advocates of intuitions to invoke intuitions in support of this theory of determinate concept possession? No. It is standard justificatory practice to use intuitions evidentially. We are in a dialectical context in which radicals are trying to produce a *reason* for departing from this standard practice. No such reason is forthcoming; instead, radical empiricists only disregard a theory based on all the evidence in favor of a theory based on a circumscribed body of evidence. The conclusion is that this way of trying to undermine the argument in the text is unsuccessful.

9   This account of derived sources should be viewed as an idealization. Note that I need not commit myself to it; for an alternative account, see note 7 in my Replies [in Bealer 1996a]. What is important is that there be some account consistent with a reliabilist account of basic sources.

10   Might intuition be a derived source? No. First, intuitively, intuition is as basic as experience (or any source of evidence). Second, as Quine has shown us, our best overall purely empirical theory does not affirm that our modal intuitions have a reliable tie to the truth and, hence, would not explain their evidential status. Within the general explanatory strategy, there is no alternative but no identify intuition as a basic source of evidence. (This point is developed in greater detail in section 6, pp. 323–8, of my "Philosophical Limits of Scientific Essentialism".)

11   An analogous counterexample could be constructed around "hardwired" dispositions to guess. Of course, by sophisticated maneuvers, contingent reliabilists might try to avoid these and other problems, but as far as

I can tell, such efforts do not escape the underlying difficulties.

12   I will not attempt to state my final general analysis; that requires having various preliminaries which emerge in the course of the Argument from Concepts, alluded to earlier as the second pillar of my argument. In the finished version, the modal tie invoked in the analysis of evidence is constitutive of determinate concept possession. Determinate concept possession governs both *a priori* intuitions and "phenomenal intuitions," and insures their tie to the truth. Note that in the present proposal I require only that *most* derivable consequences of the indicated *a priori* theory be true. I do not say *all*, for I do not want to rule out unresolvable logical and philosophical antinomies.

13   As Kripke intended it (p. 103), this expression must be so understood that the rephrasal strategy can be successfully applied to "It could have turned out that water had no hydrogen in it" but not to "It could have turned out that the four color theorem is false". Other points of clarification: By saying that semantically stable expressions must mean the same in the indicated language group, I mean that they must make the same contribution to the propositions expressed by sentences in which they occur. This is meant to rule out indexicals as semantically stable. Note also that these definitions are indexed to *our* language group. Corresponding absolute notions can be defined. The resulting absolute notions mesh neatly with the Autonomy and Authority of Philosophy since these are modal theses concerning the possibility of autonomous, authoritative philosophical theories. At a few points my discussion will need the absolute notion; it should be clear when it is in effect. Note furthermore that by defining semantic stability in terms of whole language groups, rather than particular individuals, Burge-like phenomena would not by themselves render an expression semantically unstable; semantic instability has to do with the effects of the external environment. Of course, it is an expression *in one of its senses* that is semantically stable or unstable: there could be an ambiguous expression which is stable in one

of its senses and unstable in another. Note finally that the notion of semantic stability applies to expressions; there is a correspond- ing object-language notion of a semantically stable concept. In a finished formulation this object-language notion might be preferable.

References

Bealer, G.: 1987, "Philosophical limits of scientific essentialism", *Philosophical Perspectives* 1 (Ridgeview, Atascadero), pp. 289–365.

Bealer, G.: 1992, "The incoherence of empiricism", *The Aristotelian Society, Supplementary Volume* 66, pp. 99–138.

Bealer, G.: 1994, "Mental properties", *The Journal of Philosophy* 91, pp. 185–208.

Bealer, G.: 1996a, "*A Priori* Knowledge: Replies to William Lycan and Ernest Sosa," *Philosophical Studies* 81, 2–3, pp. 163–74.

Bealer, G.: 1996b, "On the possibility of philosophical knowledge", *Philosophical Perspectives* 10 (Basil Blackwell, Oxford).

Bealer, G.: (forthcoming), *Philosophical Limits of Science.*

Hirsch, E.: 1986, "Metaphysical necessity and conceptual truth", *Midwest Studies in Philosophy* 11, pp. 243–56.

Kripke, S.: 1980, *Naming and Necessity* (Harvard, Cambridge).

CHAPTER 45

Normativity and Epistemic Intuitions

Jonathan M. Weinberg, Shaun Nichols, and Stephen Stich

1. Introduction

In this paper we propose to argue for two claims. The first is that a sizeable group of epistemological projects – a group which includes much of what has been done in epistemology in the analytic tradition – would be seriously undermined if one or more of a cluster of empirical hypotheses about epistemic intuitions turns out to be true. The basis for this claim will be set out in Section 2. The second claim is that, while the jury is still out, there is now a substantial body of evidence suggesting that some of those empirical hypotheses *are* true. Much of this evidence derives from an ongoing series of experimental studies of epistemic intuitions that we have been conducting. A preliminary report on these studies will be presented in Section 3. In light of these studies, we think it is incumbent on those who pursue the epistemological projects in question to either explain why the truth of the hypotheses does not undermine their projects, or to say why, in light of the evidence we will present, they nonetheless assume that the hypotheses are false. In Section 4, which is devoted to Objections and Replies, we'll consider some of the ways in which defenders of the projects we are criticizing might reply to our challenge. Our goal, in all of this, is not to offer a

conclusive argument demonstrating that the epistemological projects we will be criticizing are untenable. Rather, our aim is to shift the burden of argument. For far too long, epistemologists who rely heavily on epistemic intuitions have proceeded as though they could simply ignore the empirical hypotheses we will set out. We will be well satisfied if we succeed in making a plausible case for the claim that this approach is no longer acceptable.

To start, it will be useful to sketch a brief – and perhaps somewhat idiosyncratic – taxonomy of epistemological projects. With the aid of this taxonomy we will try to "locate in philosophical space" (as Wilfrid Sellars used to say) those epistemological projects which, we maintain, are threatened by the evidence we will present. There are at least four distinct, though related, projects that have occupied the attention of epistemologists. Following Richard Samuels,[1] we'll call them the Normative Project, the Descriptive Project, the Evaluative Project and the Ameliorative Project.

The Normative Project, which we're inclined to think is the most philosophically central of the four, attempts to establish norms to guide our epistemic efforts. Some of these norms may be explicitly regulative, specifying which ways of going about the quest for knowledge should be pursued and which should not. This articulation of regulative norms is one of the more venerable of philosophical undertakings, going back at least

Originally published in *Philosophical Topics* 29, 1 and 2 (2001), pp. 429–60.

to Descartes's *Regulae* and evident in the work of Mill, Popper and many other important figures in the history of philosophy; and it continues in philosophy today. For example, when Alvin Goldman chastises internalism for being unable to provide us with "Doxastic Decision Principles," he is challenging the ability of internalism to pull its weight in this aspect of the Normative Project.[2] The Normative Project also aims to articulate what might be called *valuational* norms, which attempt to answer questions like: What is our epistemic good? and How should we prefer to structure our doxastic lives? One may not be able to generate regulative principles from the answers provided; rather, the answers tell us at what target the regulative principles should aim.

The Descriptive Project can have a variety of targets, the two most common being epistemic concepts and epistemic language. When concepts are the target, the goal is to describe (or "analyze") the epistemic concepts that some group of people actually invoke. When pursued by epistemologists (rather than linguists or anthropologists), the group in question is typically characterized rather vaguely by using the first person plural. They are "our" concepts, the ones that "we" use. Work in this tradition has led to a large literature attempting to analyze concepts like knowledge, justification, warrant, and rationality.[3] When language is the focus of the Descriptive project, the goal is to describe the way some group of people use epistemic language or to analyze the meaning of their epistemic terms. Here again, the group is almost invariably "us".

Many epistemologists think that there are important links between the Normative and Descriptive Projects. Indeed, we suspect that these (putative) links go a long way toward explaining why philosophers think the Descriptive Project is so important. In epistemology, knowledge is "the good stuff" and to call a belief an instance of knowledge is to pay it one of the highest compliments an epistemologist can bestow.[4] Thus terms like "knowledge," "justification," "warrant", etc. and the concepts they express are themselves plausibly regarded as implicitly normative. Moreover, many philosophers hold that sentences invoking epistemic terms have explicitly normative consequences. So, for example, "S's belief that p is an instance of knowledge" might plausibly be taken to entail "*Ceteris paribus*, S ought to believe

that p" or perhaps "*Ceteris paribus*, it is a good thing for S to believe that p."[5] For reasons that will emerge, we are more than a bit skeptical about the alleged links between the Descriptive and Normative Projects. For the time being, however, we will leave the claim that the two projects are connected unchallenged.

The Evaluative Project tries to assess how well or poorly people's actual belief forming practices accord with the norms specified in the Normative Project. To do this, of course, another sort of descriptive effort is required. Before we can say how well or poorly people are doing at the business of belief formation and revision, we have to say in some detail how they actually go about the process of belief formation and revision.[6] The Ameliorative Project presupposes that we don't all come out with the highest possible score in the assessment produced by the Evaluative Project, and asks how we can improve the way we go about the business of belief formation. In this paper our primary focus will be on the Normative Project and on versions of the Descriptive Project which assume that the Descriptive and Normative Projects are linked in something like the way sketched above.

2.   Intuition Driven Romanticism and The Normativity Problem

2.1   Epistemic romanticism and intuition driven romanticism

A central question that the Normative Project tries to answer is: *How ought we to go about the business of belief formation and revision?* How are we to go about finding an answer to this question? And once an answer has been proposed, how are we to assess it? If two theorists offer different answers, how can we determine which one is better? Philosophers who have pursued the Normative Project have used a variety of methods or strategies. In this section we want to begin by describing one very influential family of strategies.

The family we have in mind belongs to a larger group of strategies which (just to be provocative) we propose to call *Epistemic Romanticism*. One central idea of 19th-century Romanticism was that our real selves, the essence of our identity, is implanted within us, and that to discover who we really are we need but let that real identity emerge. Epistemic Romanticism assumes something rather similar about epistemic norms. According to Epistemic Romanticism, knowledge of the correct epistemic norms (or information that can lead to knowledge of the correct norms) is implanted within us in some way, and with the proper process of self-exploration we can discover them. As we read him, Plato was an early exponent of this kind of Romanticism about matters normative (and about much else besides). So *Epistemic Platonism* might be another (perhaps equally provocative) label for this group of strategies for discovering or testing epistemic norms.

There are various ways in which the basic idea of Epistemic Romanticism can be elaborated. The family of strategies that we want to focus on all accord a central role to what we will call *epistemic intuitions*. Thus we will call this family of strategies *Intuition Driven Romanticism* (or IDR). As we use the notion, an epistemic intuition is simply a spontaneous judgment about the epistemic properties of some specific case – a judgment for which the person making the judgment may be able to offer no plausible justification. To count as an Intuition Driven Romantic strategy for discovering or testing epistemic norms, the following three conditions must be satisfied:

(i)   The strategy must take epistemic intuitions as data or input. (It can also exploit various other sorts of data.)

(ii)   It must produce, as output, explicitly or implicitly normative claims or principles about matters epistemic. Explicitly normative claims include regulative claims about how we ought to go about the business of belief formation, claims about the relative merits of various strategies for belief formation, and evaluative claims about the merits of various epistemic situations. Implicitly normative claims include claims to the effect that one or another process of belief formation leads to justified beliefs or to real knowledge or that a doxastic structure of a certain kind amounts to real knowledge.

(iii)   The output of the strategy must depend, in part, on the epistemic intuitions it takes as input. If provided with significantly different intuitions, the strategy must yield significantly different output.[7]

Perhaps the most familiar examples of Intuition Driven Romanticism are various versions of the reflective equilibrium strategy in which (to paraphrase Goodman slightly) "a [normative] rule is amended if it yields an inference we are [intuitively] unwilling to accept [and] an inference is rejected if it violates a [normative] rule we are [intuitively] unwilling to amend."[8] In a much discussed paper called "Can Human Irrationality Be Experimentally Demonstrated," L. J. Cohen proposes a variation on Goodman's strategy as a way of determining what counts as rational or normatively appropriate reasoning.[9] It is of some importance to note that there are many ways in which the general idea of a reflective equilibrium process can be spelled out. Some philosophers, including Cohen, advocate a "narrow" reflective equilibrium strategy. Others advocate a "wide" reflective equilibrium strategy. And both of these alternatives can be elaborated in various ways.[10] Moreover, the details are often quite important since different versions of the reflective equilibrium strategy may yield different outputs, even when provided with exactly the same input.

Another example of the IDR strategy can be found in Alvin Goldman's important and influential book, *Epistemology and Cognition* (1986). A central goal of epistemology, Goldman argues, is to develop a theory that will specify which of our beliefs are epistemically justified and which are not, and a fundamental step in constructing such a theory will be to articulate a system of rules or principles evaluating the justificatory status of beliefs. These rules, which Goldman calls *J-rules*, will specify permissible ways in which cognitive agents may go about the business of forming or updating their beliefs. They "permit or prohibit beliefs, directly or indirectly, as a function of some states, relations, or processes of the cognizer."[11] But, of course, different theorists may urge different and incompatible sets of J-rules. So in order to decide whether a proposed system of J-rules is correct, we must appeal to a higher criterion – Goldman calls it "a criterion of rightness" – which will specify a "set of conditions that are necessary and sufficient for a set of J-rules to be right."[12] But now the theoretical disputes emerge at a higher level, for different theorists have suggested very different criteria of rightness. Indeed, as Goldman notes, an illuminating taxonomy of epistemological theories can be generated by classifying them on the basis of the sort of criterion of rightness they endorse. So how are we to go about deciding among these various criteria of rightness? The answer, Goldman maintains, is that the correct criterion of rightness is the one that comports with the conception of justification that is "embraced by everyday thought and language."[13] To test a criterion, we consider the judgments it would entail about specific cases, and we test these judgments against our "pretheoretic intuition." "A criterion is supported to the extent that implied judgments accord with such intuitions and weakened to the extent that they do not."[14, 15]

The examples we have mentioned so far are hardly the only examples of Intuition Driven Romanticism. Indeed, we think a plausible case can be made that a fair amount of what goes on in normative epistemology can be classified as Intuition Driven Romanticism. Moreover, to the extent that it is assumed to have normative implications, much of what has been written in descriptive epistemology in recent decades also counts as Intuition Driven Romanticism. For example, just about all of the vast literature that arose in response to Gettier's classic paper uses intuitions about specific cases to test proposed analyses of the concept of knowledge.[16]

For many purposes, the details of an IDR strategy – the specific ways in which it draws inferences from intuitions and other data – will be of enormous importance. But since our goal is to raise a problem for all IDR strategies, the exact details of how they work will play no role in our argument. Thus, for our purposes, an IDR strategy can be viewed as a "black box" which takes intuitions (and perhaps other data) as input and produces implicitly or explicitly normative claims as output. The challenge we are about to raise is, we claim, a problem for IDR accounts no matter what goes on within the black box.

2.2   The normativity problem

Reflective equilibrium strategies and other Intuition Driven Romantic strategies all yield as outputs claims that putatively have normative force. These outputs tell us how people ought to

go about forming and revising their beliefs, which belief forming strategies yield genuinely justified beliefs, which beliefs are warranted, which count as real knowledge rather than mere opinion, etc. But there is a problem lurking here – we'll call it the *Normativity Problem*: What reason is there to think that the output of one or another of these Intuition Driven Romantic strategies has real (as opposed to putative) normative force? Why should we care about the normative pronouncements produced by these strategies? Why should we try to do what these outputs claim we ought to do in matters epistemic? Why, in short, should we take any of this stuff seriously?

We don't think that there is any good solution to the Normativity Problem for Intuition Driven Romanticism or indeed for any other version of Romanticism in epistemology. And because there is no solution to the Normativity Problem, we think that the entire tradition of Epistemic Romanticism has been a very bad idea. These, obviously, are very big claims and this is not the place to mount a detailed argument for all of them. We do, however, want to rehearse one consideration, first raised in Stich's book, *The Fragmentation of Reason*.[17] We think it lends some plausibility to the claim that satisfying solutions to the Normativity Problem for Intuition Driven Romanticism are going to be hard to find. It will also help to motivate the empirical studies we will recount in the section to follow.

What Stich noted is that the following situation seems perfectly possible. There might be a group of people who reason and form beliefs in ways that are significantly different from the way we do. Moreover, these people might also have epistemic intuitions that are significantly different from ours. More specifically, they might have epistemic intuitions which, when plugged into your favorite Intuition Driven Romantic black box yield the conclusion that *their* strategies of reasoning and belief formation lead to epistemic states that are rational (or justified, or of the sort that yield genuine knowledge – pick your favorite normative epistemic notion here). If this is right, then it looks like the IDR strategy for answering normative epistemic questions might sanction any of a wide variety of regulative and valuational norms. And that sounds like bad news for an advocate of the IDR strategy, since the strategy doesn't tell us what we really want to know. It doesn't tell us how we should go about the business of forming and revising our beliefs. One might, of course, insist that the normative principles that should be followed are the ones that are generated when we put *our* intuitions into the IDR black box. But it is less than obvious (to put it mildly) how this move could be defended. Why should we privilege our intuitions rather than the intuitions of some other group?

One objection that was occasionally raised in response to this challenge focused on the fact that the groups conjured in Stich's argument are just philosophical fictions.[18] While it may well be logically possible that there are groups of people whose reasoning patterns and epistemic intuitions differ systematically from our own, there is no reason to suppose that it is nomologically or psychologically possible. And without some reason to think that such people are psychologically possible, the objection continued, the thought experiment does not poses a problem that the defender of the IDR strategy needs to take seriously. We are far from convinced by this objection, though we are prepared to concede that the use of nomologically or psychologically impossible cases in normative epistemology raises some deep and difficult issues. Thus, for argument's sake, we are prepared to concede that a plausible case might be made for privileging normative claims based on actual intuitions over normative claims based on intuitions that are merely logically possible. But what if the people imagined in the thought experiment are not just logically possible, but psychologically possible? Indeed, what if they are not merely psychologically possible but real – and to all appearances normal and flourishing? Under those circumstances, we maintain, it is hard to see how advocates of an IDR strategy can maintain that their intuitions have any special standing or that the normative principles these intuitions generate when plugged into their favorite IDR black box should be privileged over the normative principles that would be generated if we plugged the other people's intuitions into the same IDR black box. In the section to follow we will argue that these "what ifs" are not *just* "what ifs." There really are people – normal, flourishing people – whose epistemic intuition are systematically different from "ours".

3. Cultural Variation in Epistemic Intuitions

3.1 Nisbett and Haidt: Some suggestive evidence

Our suspicion that people like those imagined in Stich's thought experiment might actually exist was first provoked by the results of two recent research programs in psychology. In one of these, Richard Nisbett and his collaborators have shown that there are large and systematic differences between East Asians and Westerners[19] on a long list of basic cognitive processes including perception, attention and memory. These groups also differ in the way they go about describing, predicting and explaining events, in the way they categorize objects and in the way they revise beliefs in the face of new arguments and evidence. This work makes it very plausible that the first part of Stich's thought experiment is more than just a logical possibility. There really are people whose reasoning and belief forming strategies are very different from ours. Indeed, there are over a billion of them!

Though space does not permit us to offer a detailed account of the differences that Nisbett and his colleagues found, a few brief notes will be useful in motivating the studies we will describe later is this section. According to Nisbett and his colleagues, the differences "can be loosely grouped together under the heading of holistic vs. analytic thought." Holistic thought, which predominates among East Asians, is characterized as "involving an orientation to the context or field as a whole, including attention to relationships between a focal object and the field, and a preference for explaining and predicting events on the basis of such relationships." Analytic thought, the prevailing pattern among Westerners, is characterized as "involving detachment of the object from its context, a tendency to focus on attributes of the object in order to assign it to categories, and a preference for using rules about the categories to explain and predict the object's behavior."[20] One concomitant of East Asian holistic thought is the tendency to focus on chronological rather than causal patterns in describing and recalling events. Westerners, by contrast, focus on causal patterns in these tasks.[21] Westerners also have a stronger sense of agency and independence, while East

Asians have a much stronger commitment to social harmony. In East Asian society, the individual feels "very much a part of a large and complex social organism … where behavioral prescriptions must be followed and role obligations adhered to scrupulously."[22]

The second research program that led us to suspect there might actually be people like those in Stich's thought experiment was the work Jonathan Haidt and his collaborators.[23] These investigators were interested in exploring the extent to which moral intuitions about events in which no one is harmed track judgments about disgust in people from different cultural and socioeconomic groups. For their study they constructed a set of brief stories about victimless activities that were intended to trigger the emotion of disgust. They presented these stories to subjects using a structured interview technique designed to determine whether the subjects found the activities described to be disgusting and also to elicit the subjects' moral intuitions about the activities. As an illustration, here is a story describing actions which people in all the groups studied found (not surprisingly) to be quite disgusting:

> A man goes to the supermarket once a week and buys a dead chicken. But before cooking the chicken, he has sexual intercourse with it. Then he cooks it and eats it.

The interviews were administered to both high and low socioeconomic status (SES) subjects in Philadelphia (USA) and in two cities in Brazil. Perhaps the most surprising finding in this study was that there are large differences in moral intuitions between social classes. Indeed, in most cases the difference between social classes was significantly greater than the difference between Brazilian and American subjects of the same SES. Of course we haven't yet told you what the differences in moral intuitions were, though you should be able to predict them by noting your own moral intuitions. (Hint: If you are reading this article, you count as high-SES.) Not to keep you in suspense, low SES subjects tend to think that the man who has sex with the chicken is doing something that is seriously morally wrong; high SES subjects don't. Much the same pattern was found with the other scenarios used in the study.

3.2   Four hypotheses

For our purposes, Haidt's work, like Nisbett's, is only suggestive. Nisbett gives us reason to think that people in different cultural groups exploit very different belief forming strategies. Haidt's work demonstrates that people in different SES groups have systematically different moral intuitions. Neither investigator explored the possibility that there might be differences in *epistemic* intuitions in different groups. However, the results they reported were enough to convince us that the following pair of hypotheses *might* be true, and that it was worth the effort to find out:

> *Hypothesis 1*: Epistemic intuitions vary from culture to culture.
> *Hypothesis 2*: Epistemic intuitions vary from one socioeconomic group to another.

To these two experimentally inspired hypotheses we added two more that were suggested by anecdotal rather than experimental evidence. It has often seemed to us that students' epistemic intuitions change as they take more philosophy courses, and we have often suspected that we and our colleagues were, in effect, teaching neophyte philosophers to have intuitions that are in line with those of more senior members of the profession. Or perhaps we are not modifying intuitions at all but simply weeding out students whose intuitions are not mainstream. If either of these is the case, then the intuitions that "we" use in our philosophical work are not those of the man and woman in the street, but those of a highly trained and self-selecting community. These speculations led to:

> *Hypothesis 3*: Epistemic intuitions vary as a function of how many philosophy courses a person has had.

It also sometimes seems that the order in which cases are presented to people can have substantial effects on people's epistemic intuitions. This hunch is reinforced by some intriguing work on neural networks suggesting that a variety of learning strategies may be "path dependent."[24] If this hunch is correct, the pattern of intuitions that people offer on a series of cases might well differ systematically as a function of the order in which the cases are presented. This suggested our fourth hypothesis:

> *Hypothesis 4*: Epistemic intuitions depend, in part, on the order in which cases are presented.

Moreover, it might well be the case that some of the results of order effects are very hard to modify.[25]

If any one of these four hypotheses turns out to be true then, we maintain, it will pose a serious problem for the advocate of Intuition Driven Romanticism. If all of them are true, then it is hard to believe that any plausible case can be made for the claim that the normative pronouncements of Intuition Driven Romanticism have real normative force – that they are norms that we (or anyone else) should take seriously.

3.3   Some experiments exploring cultural variation in epistemic intuitions

Are any of these hypotheses true? To try to find out we have been conducting a series of experiments designed to test Hypotheses 1 and 2. While the results we have so far are preliminary, they are sufficient, we think, to at least shift the burden of argument well over in the direction of the defender of IDR strategies. What our results show, we believe, is that the advocates of IDR can no longer simply ignore these hypotheses or dismiss them as implausible, for there is a growing body of evidence which suggests that they might well be true.

In designing our experiments, we were guided by three rather different considerations. First, we wanted our intuition probes – the cases that we would ask subjects to judge – to be similar to cases that have actually been used in the recent literature in epistemology. Second, since the findings reported by Nisbett and his colleagues all focused on differences between East Asians (henceforth EAs) and European Americans (henceforth Ws, for "Westerners"), we decided that would be the obvious place to look first for differences in epistemic intuitions. Third, since Nisbett and his colleagues argue that Ws are significantly more individualistic than EAs, who tend to be much more interdependent and "collectivist" and thus much more concerned about community harmony and consensus, we tried to construct some

intuition probes that would tap into this difference. Would individualistic Ws, perhaps, be more inclined to attribute knowledge to people whose beliefs are reliably formed by processes that no one else in their community shares. The answer, it seems, is yes.

3.3.1   Truetemp cases

An issue of great moment in recent analytic epistemology is the internalism/externalism debate. Internalism, with respect to some epistemically evaluative property, is the view that *only* factors within an agent's introspective grasp can be relevant to whether the agent's beliefs have that property. Components of an agent's doxastic situation available to introspection are internalistically kosher; other factors beyond the scope of introspection, such as the reliability of the psychological mechanisms that actually produced the belief, are epistemically external to the agent. Inspired by Lehrer (1990), we included in our surveys a number of cases designed to explore externalist/internalist dimensions of our subjects' intuitions. Here is one of the questions we presented to our subjects, all of whom were undergraduates at Rutgers University.[26]

> One day Charles is suddenly knocked out by a falling rock, and his brain becomes re-wired so that he is always absolutely right whenever he estimates the temperature where he is. Charles is completely unaware that his brain has been altered in this way. A few weeks later, this brain re-wiring leads him to believe that it is 71 degrees in his room. Apart from his estimation, he has no other reasons to think that it is 71 degrees. In fact, it is at that time 71 degrees in his room. Does Charles really know that it was 71 degrees in the room, or does he only believe it?
>
> REALLY KNOWS   ONLY BELIEVES

Although Charles' belief is produced by a reliable mechanism, it is stipulated that he is completely unaware of this reliability. So his reliability is epistemically external. Therefore, to the extent that a subject population is unwilling to attribute knowledge in this case, we have evidence that the group's "folk epistemology" may be internalist. We found that while both groups were more likely to deny knowledge, EA subjects were much more

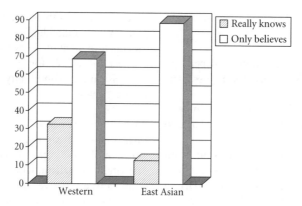

Figure 45.1   Individualistic Truetemp Case

likely to deny knowledge than were their W class-mates. The results are shown in Figure 45.1.[27]

After finding this highly significant difference, we began tinkering with the text to see if we could construct other "Truetemp" cases in which the difference between the two groups would disappear. Our first thought was to replace the rock with some socially sanctioned intervention. The text we used was as follows:

> One day John is suddenly knocked out by a team of well-meaning scientists sent by the elders of his community, and his brain is re-wired so that he is always absolutely right whenever he estimates the temperature where he is. John is completely unaware that his brain has been altered in this way. A few weeks later, this brain re-wiring leads him to believe that it is 71 degrees in his room. Apart from his estimation, he has no other reasons to think that it is 71 degrees. In fact, it is

at that time 71 degrees in his room. Does John really know that it was 71 degrees in the room, or does he only believe it?

REALLY KNOWS   ONLY BELIEVES

As we had predicted, the highly significant difference between the two groups disappeared. The results are shown in Figure 45.2.

Encouraged by this finding we constructed yet another version of the "Truetemp" case in which the mechanism that reliably leads to a true belief is not unique to a single individual, but rather is shared by everyone else in the community. The intuition probe read as follows:

> The Faluki are a large but tight knit community living on a remote island. One day, a radioactive meteor strikes the island and has one significant effect on the Faluki – it changes the chemical

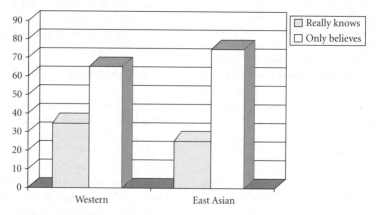

Figure 45.2   Truetemp: The Elders Version

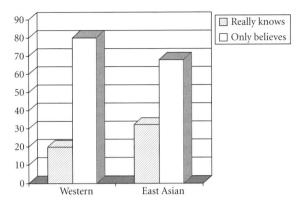

Figure 45.3 Community Wide Truetemp Case ("Faluki")

make-up of their brains so that they are always absolutely right whenever they estimate the temperature. The Faluki are completely unaware that their brains have been altered in this way. Kal is a member of the Faluki community. A few weeks after the meteor strike, while Kal is walking along the beach, the changes in his brain lead him to believe that it is 71 degrees where he is. Apart from his estimation, he has no other reasons to think that it is 71 degrees. In fact, it is at that time exactly 71 degrees where Kal is. Does Kal really know that it is 71 degrees, or does he only believe it?

As predicted, on this case too there was no significant difference between Ws & EAs. (See Figure 45.3.)

Intriguingly, though the difference is not statistically significant, the percentage of EAs who answered "Really Knows" in this case was *greater* than the percentage of Ws who gave that answer, reversing the pattern in the individualistic "hit by a rock" case. Figure 45.4, which is a comparison of the three Truetemp cases, illustrates the way in which the large difference between Ws and EAs in the Individualistic version disappears in the Elders version and looks to be reversing direction in the Faluki version.

REALLY KNOWS   ONLY BELIEVES

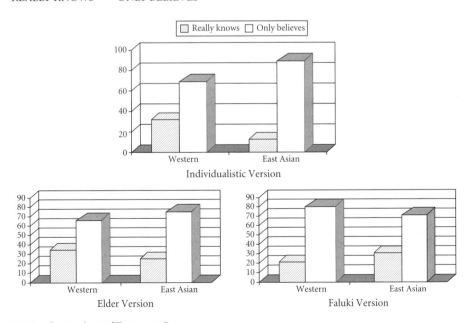

Figure 45.4 Comparison of Truetemp Cases

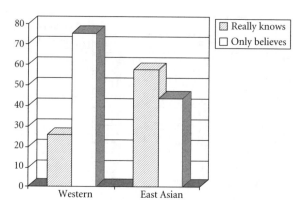

Figure 45.5   Gettier Case: Western & East Asian

3.3.2 Gettier cases

A category of examples that has loomed large in the recent epistemology literature are "Gettier cases," in which a person has good (though, as it happens, false, or only accidentally true, or in some other way warrant-deprived) evidence for a belief which is true. These cases are, of course, by their very construction in many ways quite similar to unproblematic cases in which a person has good and true evidence for a true belief. As Norenzayan and Nisbett have shown, EAs are more inclined than Ws to make categorical judgments on the basis of similarity. Ws, on the other hand, are more disposed to focus on causation in describing the world and classifying things.[28] In a large class of Gettier cases, the evidence that *causes* the target to form a belief turns out to be false. This suggest that EAs might be much less inclined than Ws to withhold the attribution of knowledge in Gettier cases. And, indeed, they are.

The intuition probe we used to explore cultural differences on Gettier cases was the following:

Bob has a friend, Jill, who has driven a Buick for many years. Bob therefore thinks that Jill drives an American car. He is not aware, however, that her Buick has recently been stolen, and he is also not aware that Jill has replaced it with a Pontiac, which is a different kind of American car. Does Bob really know that Jill drives an American car, or does he only believe it?

REALLY KNOWS   ONLY BELIEVES

The striking finding in this case is that a large majority of Ws give the standard answer in the philosophical literature, viz. "Only Believes." But amongst EAs this pattern is actually *reversed*! A majority of EAs say that Bob really knows. The results are shown in Figure 45.5.

3.3.3 Evidence from another ethnic group

The experiments we have reported thus far were done in lower division classes and large lectures at Rutgers. Since Rutgers is the State University of New Jersey and New Jersey is home to many people of Indian, Pakistani, and Bangladeshi descent, in the course of the experiments we collected lots of data about these people's intuitions. Initially we simply set these data aside since we had no theoretical basis for expecting that the epistemic intuitions of people from the Indian sub-continent (hereafter SCs) would be systematically different from the epistemic intuitions of Westerners. But, after finding the extraordinary differences between Ws and EAs on the Gettier case, we thought it might be interesting to analyze the SC data as well. We were right. It turns out that the epistemic intuitions of SCs are even more different from the intuitions of Ws than the intuitions of EAs are. The SC results on the Gettier case are shown in Figure 45.6. If these results are robust, then it seems that what counts as knowledge on the banks of the Ganges does not count as knowledge on the banks of the Mississippi!

There were two additional intuition probes that we used in our initial experiments which did not yield statistically significant differences between Ws and EAs. But when we analyzed the SC data, it turned out that there were significant differences between Ws and SCs. The text for one of these probes, the *Cancer Conspiracy* case, was as follows:

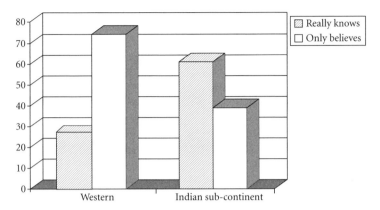

Figure 45.6 Gettier Case: Western & Indian

It's clear that smoking cigarettes increases the likelihood of getting cancer. However, there is now a great deal of evidence that just using nicotine by itself without smoking (for instance, by taking a nicotine pill) does not increase the likelihood of getting cancer. Jim knows about this evidence and as a result, he believes that using nicotine does not increase the likelihood of getting cancer. It is possible that the tobacco companies dishonestly made up and publicized this evidence that using nicotine does not increase the likelihood of cancer, and that the evidence is really false and misleading. Now, the tobacco companies did not actually make up this evidence, but Jim is not aware of this fact. Does Jim really know that using nicotine doesn't increase the likelihood of getting cancer, or does he only believe it?

REALLY KNOWS   ONLY BELIEVES

The results are shown in Figure 45.7.

The other probe that produced significant differences is a version of Dretske's *Zebra-in-Zoo* case (Dretske, 1970):

Mike is a young man visiting the zoo with his son, and when they come to the zebra cage, Mike points to the animal and says, "that's a zebra." Mike is right – it is a zebra. However, as the older people in his community know, there are lots of ways that people can be tricked into believing things that aren't true. Indeed, the older people in the community know that it's possible that zoo authorities could cleverly disguise mules to look just like zebras, and people viewing the animals would not be able to tell the difference. If the animal that Mike called a zebra had really been such a cleverly painted mule, Mike still would have thought that it

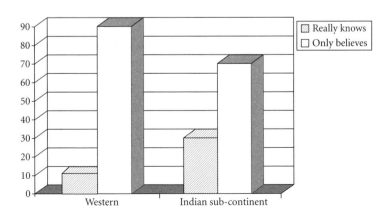

Figure 45.7 Conspiracy Case

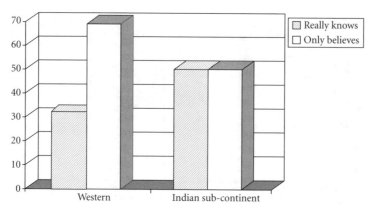

Figure 45.8   Zebra Case: Western & Indian

was a zebra. Does Mike really know that the animal is a zebra, or does he only believe that it is?

REALLY KNOWS   ONLY BELIEVES

The results are shown in Figure 45.8.

What's going on in these last two cases? Why do SCs and Ws have different epistemic intuitions about them. The answer, to be quite frank, is that we are not sure how to explain these results. But, of course, for our polemical purposes, an explanatory hypothesis is not really essential. The mere fact that Ws, EAs and SCs have different epistemic intuitions is enough to make it plausible that IDR strategies which take these intuitions as inputs would yield significantly different normative pronouncements as output. And this, we think, puts the ball squarely in the court of the defenders of IDR strategies. They must either argue that intuitive differences of the sort we've found would not lead to diverging normative claims, or they must argue that the outputs of an IDR strategy are genuinely normative despite the fact that they are different for different cultures. Nor is this the end of the bad news for those who advocate IDR strategies.

3.3.4   Epistemic intuitions and socioeconomic status

Encouraged by our findings in these cross-cultural studies, we have begun to explore the possibility that epistemic intuitions might also be sensitive to the socioeconomic status of the people offering the intuitions. And while our findings here are also quite preliminary, the apparent answer is that SES does indeed have a major impact on subjects' epistemic intuitions.

Following Haidt (and much other research in social psychology) we used years of education to distinguish low and high SES groups. In the studies we will recount in this section, subjects were classified as low SES if they reported that they had never attended college. Subjects who reported that they had one or more years of college were coded as high SES. All the subjects were adults; they were approached near various commercial venues in downtown New Brunswick, New Jersey, and (since folks approached on the street tend to be rather less compliant than university undergraduates in classrooms) they were offered McDonald's gift certificates worth a few dollars if they agreed to participate in our study.

Interestingly, the two intuition probes for which we found significant SES differences both required the subjects to assess the importance of possible states of affairs that do not actually obtain. Here is the first probe, which is similar to the Dretske-type case discussed above:

> Pat is at the zoo with his son, and when they come to the zebra cage, Pat points to the animal and says, "that's a zebra." Pat is right – it is a zebra. However, given the distance the spectators are from the cage, Pat would not be able to tell the difference between a real zebra and a mule that is cleverly disguised to look like a zebra. And if the animal had really been a cleverly disguised mule, Pat still would have thought that it was a zebra. Does Pat really know that the animal is a zebra, or does he only believe that it is?

REALLY KNOWS   ONLY BELIEVES

The results are shown in Figure 45.9.

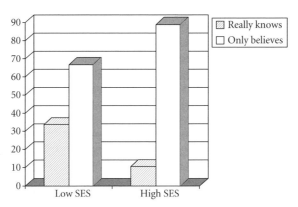

Figure 45.9 Zebra Case: Low & High SES

The second probe that produced significant (indeed enormous) differences between our two SES groups was the Cancer Conspiracy case that also generated differences between Western subjects and subjects from the Indian sub-continent. The results are shown in Figure 45.10. (For the text see 3.3.3.)

Why are the intuitions in these two SES groups so different? Here again we do not have a well worked out theoretical framework of the sort that Nisbett and his colleagues have provided for the W vs. EA differences. So any answer we offer is only a speculation. One hypothesis is that one of the many factors that subjects are sensitive to in forming epistemic intuitions of this sort is the extent to which possible but non-actual states of affairs are relevant. Another possibility is that high SES subjects accept much weaker knowledge-defeaters than low SES subjects because low SES

subjects have lower minimum standards for knowledge. More research is needed to determine whether either of these conjectures is correct. But whatever the explanation turns out to be, the data we've reported look to be yet another serious embarrassment for the advocates of IDR. As in the case of cultural difference, they must either argue that these intuitive differences, when plugged into an IDR black box, would not lead to different normative conclusions, or they must bite the bullet and argue that diverging normative claims are genuinely normative, and thus that the sorts of doxastic states that ought to be pursued by relatively rich and well educated people are significantly different from the sorts of doxastic states that poor and less well educated folks should seek. We don't pretend to have an argument showing that neither of these options is defensible. But we certainly don't envy the

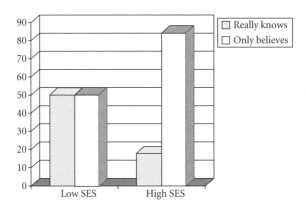

Figure 45.10 Cancer Conspiracy Case

predicament of the IDR advocate who has to opt for one or the other.

4.   Objections and Replies

In this section we propose to assemble some objections to the case against IDR that we've set out in the preceding sections along with our replies.

4.1   What's so bad about epistemic relativism?

Objection:

Suppose we're right. Suppose that epistemic intuitions *do* differ in different ethnic and SES groups, and that because of this IDR strategies will generate different normative conclusions depending on which group uses them. Why, the critic asks, should this be considered a problem for IDR advocates? At most it shows that different epistemic norms apply to different groups, and thus that epistemic relativism is true. But why, exactly, is that a problem? What's so bad about epistemic relativism? "Indeed," we imagine the critic ending with an *ad hominem* flourish, "one of the authors of this paper has published a book that *defends* epistemic relativism."[29]

Reply:

We certainly have no argument that could show that *all* forms of epistemic relativism are unacceptable, and the one avowed relativist among us is still prepared to defend some forms of relativism. But if we are right about epistemic intuitions, then the version of relativism to which IDR strategies lead would entail that the epistemic norms appropriate for the rich are quite different from the epistemic norms appropriate for the poor, and that the epistemic norms appropriate for white people are different from the norms appropriate for people of color.[30] And that we take to be quite a preposterous result. The fact that IDR strategies lead to this result is, we think, a very strong reason to think that there is something very wrong with those strategies. Of course, a defender of an IDR strategy might simply bite the bullet, and insist that the strategy he or she advocates is the right one for uncovering genuine epistemic norms, despite the fact that it leads to a relativistic consequence that many find implausible. But the IDR advocate who responds to our data in this way surely must offer some *argument* for the claim

that the preferred IDR strategy produces genuine epistemic norms. And we know of no arguments along these lines that are even remotely plausible.

4.2   There are several senses of "knowledge"

Objection:

The next objection begins with the observation that epistemologists have long been aware that the word "knows" has more than one meaning in ordinary discourse. Sometimes when people say that they "know" that something is the case, what they mean is that they have a strong sense of subjective certainty. So, for example, someone at a horse race might give voice to a strong hunch by saying: "I just know that Ivory Armchair is going to win." And even after Lab Bench comes in first, this colloquial sense of "know" still permits them to say, "Drat! I just knew that Ivory Armchair was going to win." At other times, though, when people use "know" and "knowledge" the sense they have in mind is the one that is of interest to epistemologists. The problem with our results, this objection maintains, is that we did nothing to ensure that when subjects answered "Really Know" rather than "Only Believe" the sense of "know" that they had in mind was the one of philosophical interest rather then the subjective certainty sense. "So," the critic concludes, "for all you know, your subjects might have been offering you philosophically uninteresting judgments about people's sense of subjective certainty."

Reply:

It is certainly possible that some of our subjects were interpreting the "Really Know" option as a question about subjective certainty. But there is reason to think that this did not have a major impact on our findings. For all of our subject groups (W, EA and SC in the ethnic studies and high and low SES in the SES study) we included a question designed to uncover any systematic differences in our subjects' inclination to treat mere subjective certainty as knowledge. The question we used was the following:

> Dave likes to play a game with flipping a coin. He sometimes gets a "special feeling" that the next flip will come out heads. When he gets this "special feeling", he is right about half the time, and wrong about half the time. Just before the next flip, Dave gets that "special feeling", and the feeling leads

him to believe that the coin will land heads. He flips the coin, and it does land heads. Did Dave really know that the coin was going to land heads, or did he only believe it?

REALLY KNOWS   ONLY BELIEVES

As shown in Figure 45.11, there was no difference at all between the high and low SES groups on this question; in both groups almost none of our subjects judged that this was a case of knowledge. The results in the ethnic studies were basically the same.[31]

This might be a good place to elaborate a bit on what we are and are not claiming about epistemic intuitions and the psychological mechanisms or "knowledge structures" that may subserve them. For polemical purposes we have been emphasizing the diversity of epistemic intuitions in different ethnic and SES groups, since these quite different intuitions, when plugged into an IDR black box will generate different normative claims. But we certainly do not mean to suggest that epistemic intuitions are completely malleable or that there are no constraints on the sorts of epistemic intuitions that might be found in different social groups. Indeed, the fact that subjects from all the groups we studied agreed in not classifying beliefs based on "special feelings" as knowledge suggests that there may well be a universal core to "folk epistemology." Whether this conjecture is true and, if it is, how this common core is best characterized, are questions that will require a great deal more research. Obviously, these are not issues that can be settled from the philosopher's armchair.

4.3 The effect size we've found is small and philosophically uninteresting

Objection:
If it were the case that virtually all Ws judged various cases in one way and virtually all EAs or SCs judged the same cases in a different way, that might be genuine cause for concern among epistemologists. But that's not at all what you have found. Rather, what you've shown is merely that in various cases there is a 20% or 30% difference in the judgments offered by subjects in various groups. So, for example, a majority in all of your groups withhold knowledge attributions in all the Truetemp cases that were designed to test the degree to which subjects' intuitions reflected epistemic internalism. Since the majority in all groups agree, we can conclude that the correct account of epistemic norms is internalist. So it is far from clear why epistemologists should find the sort of cultural diversity you've found to be at all troubling, or even interesting.

Reply:
Here we have two replies. First, the sizes of the statistically significant group differences that we've reported are quite comparable with the size of the differences that Nisbett, Haidt and other social psychologists take to show important differences between groups. The second reply is more important. While in some cases what we've been reporting are just the brute facts that intuitions in different groups differ, in other cases what we've found is considerably more interesting. The differences between Ws

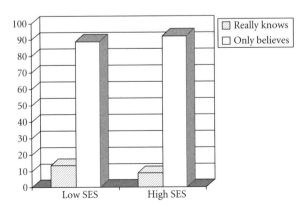

Figure 45.11   "Special Feeling" Case

and EAs look to be both systematic and explainable. EAs and Ws appear to be sensitive to different features of the situation, different *epistemic vectors*, as we will call them. EAs are much more sensitive to communitarian factors, while Ws respond to more individualistic ones. Moreover, Nisbett and his colleagues have given us good reason to think that these kinds of differences can be traced to deep and important differences in EA and W cognition. And we have no reason to think that equally important differences could not be found for SCs. Our data also suggests that both high and low SES Westerners stress the individualistic and non-communitarian vector, since there was no difference between high and low SES groups on questions designed to emphasize this vector. What separates high and low SES subjects is some quite different vector – sensitivity to mere possibilities, perhaps. What our studies point to, then, is more than just divergent epistemic intuitions across groups; the studies point to divergent epistemic *concerns* – concerns which appear to differ along a variety of dimensions. It is plausible to suppose that these differences would significantly affect the output of just about any IDR process.

4.4   We are looking at the wrong sort of intuitions; the right sort are accompanied by a clear sense of necessity

Objection:
The central idea of this objection is that our experiments are simply not designed to evoke the right sort of intuitions – the sort that the IDR process really requires. What we are collecting in our experiments are unfiltered spontaneous judgments about a variety of cases. But what is really needed, this objection maintains, are data about quite a different kind of intuitions. The right sort of intuitions are those that have modal import and are accompanied by a clear sense of necessity. They are the kind of intuitions that we have when confronted with principles like: If p, then not-not-p. Unless you show cultural or SES diversity in these sorts of intuitions, this objection continues, you have not shown anything that an IDR advocate needs to be concerned about, since you have not shown that the right sort of intuitions are not universal.[32]

Reply:
It is true that the sorts of intuitions that our experiments collect are not the sorts that some IDR theorists would exploit. However, our findings do raise serious questions about the suggestion that intuitions which come with a clear sense of necessity and modal import – *strong intuitions*, as we propose to call them – are anything close to universal. Many epistemologists would no doubt insist that their own intuitions about many cases are strong intuitions. Simple Gettier case intuitions are a good example. Indeed, if these intuitions, which led a generation of epistemologists to seek something better than the traditional justified true belief analysis of knowledge, are not strong intuitions, then it is hard to believe that there are enough strong intuitions around to generate epistemic norms of any interest. But if philosophers' intuitions on simple Gettier cases *are* strong intuitions, then our data indicate that strong intuitions are far from universal. For, while our experiments cannot distinguish strong from weak intuitions, they do indicate that almost 30% of W subjects do not have either strong or weak intuitions that agree with those of most philosophers, since almost 30% of these subjects claim that, in our standard Gettier scenario, Bob really knows that Jill drives an American car. Among EA subjects, over 50% of subjects have the intuition (weak or strong) that Bob really knows, and among SC subjects the number is over 60! It may well be that upper middle class, Westerners who have had a few years of graduate training in analytic philosophy do indeed all have strong, modality-linked intuitions about Gettier cases. But since most of the world's population apparently does not share these intuitions, it is hard to see why we should think that these intuitions tell us anything at all about the modal structure of reality, or about epistemic norms or indeed about anything else of philosophical interest.

4.5   We are looking at the wrong sort of intuitions; the right sort require at least a modicum of reflection

Objection:
We have also heard a rather different objection about the type of intuitions examined in our study.[33] The proper input intuitions for the IDR strategy, the critics maintain, are not "first-off"

intuitions – which may be really little better than mere guesses. Rather, IDR requires what might be called *minimally reflective intuitions* – intuitions resulting from some modicum of attention, consideration, and above all reflection on the particulars of the case at hand as well as one's other theoretical commitments. We have, this objection continues, done nothing to show that such minimally reflective intuitions would exhibit the sort of diversity we have been reporting, and until we show something along those lines, the IDR theorist need not worry.

Reply:
This objection is right as far as it goes, since we have not (yet) examined intuitions produced under conditions of explicit reflection. But the objection really does not go very far, and certainly not far enough to allow IDR theorists to rest easy. First of all, many of our subjects clearly did reflect at least minimally before answering, as evidenced in the many survey forms on which the subjects wrote brief explanatory comments after their answers. Moreover, as we stressed in Reply 4.2, it is not just that we found group differences in epistemic intuition; much more interestingly, Western and East Asian subjects' intuitions seem to respond to quite different epistemic vectors. It is extremely likely that such differences in sensitivities would be recapitulated – or even strengthened – in any reflective process. If EA subjects have an inclination to take into account factors involving community beliefs, practices, and traditions, and W subjects do not have such an inclination, then we see no reason to expect that such vectors will not be differentially present under conditions of explicit reflection. IDR theorists who want to make use of any purported difference between first-off and minimally reflective intuitions had better go get some *data* showing that such differences would point in the direction they would want.

4.6 We are looking at the wrong sort of intuitions; the right sort are those that emerge after an extended period of discussion and reflection

Objection:
The last objection we'll consider was proposed (though not, we suspect, endorsed) by Philip Kitcher. What IDR strategies need, this objection maintains, is neither first-off intuitions nor even minimally reflective intuitions, but rather the sorts of intuitions that people develop after a lengthy period of reflection and discussion – the sort of reflection and discussion that philosophy traditionally encourages. Kitcher suggested that they be called *Austinian intuitions*. Your experiments, the objection insists, do nothing to show that Austinian intuitions would exhibit the sort of cultural diversity you've found in first-off intuitions, or, indeed, that they would show any significant diversity at all. When sensible people reflect and reason together, there is every reason to suppose that they will ultimately reach a meeting of the minds.

Reply:
We certainly concede that we have not shown that Austinian intuitions would not ultimately converge. However, to echo the theme of our previous reply, in the absence of any evidence we don't think there is any reason to suppose that the sorts of marked cultural differences in sensitivity to epistemic vectors that our experiments have demonstrated would simply disappear after reflection and discussion. Moreover, even if these cultural differences do dissipate after extended reflection, it might well be the case that they would be replaced by the sorts of order effects suggested in our Hypothesis 4. If that hypothesis is correct, then the Austinian intuitions on which a group of reflective people would converge would depend, in part, on the order in which examples and arguments happened to be introduced. And different groups might well converge on quite different sets of Austinian intuitions which then proved quite impervious to change. Experiments demonstrating the sort of path dependence that we suggest in Hypothesis 4 are much harder to design than experiments demonstrating cultural differences in initial intuitions. In the next stage of our ongoing empirical research on intuitions, we hope to run a series of experiments that will indicate the extent to which the evolution of people's intuitions is indeed a function of the order in which examples and counter-examples are encountered. Neither those experiments nor any of the evidence we've cited in this paper will suffice to demonstrate that Austinian intuitions or IDR processes that propose to use

them will fail to converge. But, to end with the theme with which we began, our goal has not been to establish that IDR strategies *will* lead to very different (putatively) normative conclusions, but simply to make it plausible that they *might*. The assumption that they won't is an empirical assumption; it is not an assumption that can be made without argument.

Our data indicate that when epistemologists advert to "our" intuitions when attempting to characterize epistemic concepts or draw normative conclusions, they are engaged in a culturally local endeavor – what we might think of as *ethno-epistemology*. Indeed, in our studies, some of the most influential thought experiments of 20th-century epistemology elicited different intuitions in different cultures. In light of this, Intuition Driven Romanticism seems a rather bizarre way to determine the correct epistemic norms. For it is difficult to see why a process that relies heavily on epistemic intuitions that are local to one's own cultural and socioeconomic group would lead to genuinely normative conclusions. Pending a detailed response to this problem, we think that the best reaction to the High-SES, Western philosophy professor who tries to draw normative conclusions from the facts about "our" intuitions is to ask: What do you mean "we"?

Notes

1   Samuels (in preparation).
2   Goldman (1980).
3   The literature on conceptual analysis in epistemology is vast. For an elite selection, see the essays assembled in Sosa (1994).
4   This is a view with a venerable history. In Plato's *Protagoras*, Socrates says that "knowledge is a noble and commanding thing," and Protagoras, not to be out done, replies that "wisdom and knowledge are the highest of human things." (1892/1937, p. 352)
5   Perhaps the most important advocate of extracting normative principles from analyses of our epistemic terms is Roderick Chisolm (1977). This approach is shared in projects as otherwise dissimilar as BonJour (1985) and Pollock and Cruz (1999).
6   For further discussion of the Evaluative Project, see Samuels, Stich and Tremoulet (1999); Samuels, Stich and Bishop (2002); Samuels, Stich and Faucher (2004). These papers are available on the web site of the Rutgers University Research Group on Evolution and Higher Cognition: http://ruccs.rutgers.edu/ArchiveFolder/Research%20Group/research.html.
7   Note that as we've characterized them, epistemic intuitions are spontaneous judgments about *specific cases*. Some strategies for discovering or testing epistemic norms also take intuitions about general epistemic or inferential principles as input. These will count as Intuition Driven Romantic strategies provided that the output is suitably sensitive to the intuitions about specific cases that are included in the input.
8   Goodman (1965), p. 66.
9   Cohen, L. (1981). For a useful discussion of the debate that Cohen's paper provoked, see Stein (1996), Ch. 5.
10 See, for example, Elgin, C. (1996), Chapter IV, and Stein (1996), Chs 5 and 7.
11 Goldman (1986), p. 60.
12 Goldman (1986), p. 64.
13 Goldman, (1986), p. 58.
14 Goldman (1986), p. 66.
15 In an insightful commentary on this paper, presented at the Conference in Honor of Alvin Goldman, Joel Pust notes that in his recent work Goldman (1992, 1999, Goldman and Pust 1998) has offered a rather different account of how epistemic intuitions are to be used:

> Very roughly, Goldman's more recent view treats the targets of philosophical analysis as concepts in the psychological sense of "concept," concrete mental representations causally implicated in the production of philosophical intuitions. On this new view, intuitions serve primarily as reliable evidence concerning the intuitors internal psychological mechanisms. ... Especially interesting in the context of [the Weinberg, Nichols and Stich paper] is the fact that Goldman *explicitly disavows* the common assumption of "great uniformity in epistemic subjects" judgments about cases, noting that this

assumption may result from the fact that philosophers come from a "fairly homogeneous subculture." (Goldman 1992, p. 160).

This new psychologistic account makes it easier to explain why intuitions are reliable evidence of some sort. However, this reliability is gained by deflating the evidential pretensions of intuitions so that they are no longer treated as relevant to the *non-linguistic* or *non-psychological* question which is the central concern of the Normative Project: "What makes a belief epistemically justified?" While Goldman's approach solves *a* problem about the reliability of intuitions by telling us that *the fact that people have* certain intuitions is a reliable indicator of their psychological constitution, it does not resolve the problem which motivated Stich's argument since *that* problem was whether we are justified in treating *the content of* our epistemic intuitions as a reliable guide to the nature of justified belief. So, while Goldman's use of intuitions in his new project seems to me largely immune to [the criticisms in the paper by Weinberg, Nichols and Stich], this is because that project has aspirations quite different from those of traditional analytic epistemology.

16 Gettier, E. (1963). For a review of literature during the first two decades after Gettier's paper appeared, see Shope, (1983). For more recent work in this tradition, see Plantinga (1993a) and (1993b) as well as the follow-up collection of papers in Kvanvig (1996).

17 Stich (1990), Sec. 4.6.

18 Cf. Pollock and Cruz (1999), p. 150.

19 The East Asian subjects were Chinese, Japanese and Korean. Some of the experiments were conducted in Asia, others used East Asian students studying in the United States or first and second generation East Asian immigrants to the United States. The Western subjects were Americans of European ancestry.

20 Nisbett et al. (2001), MS, p. 11.

21 Nisbett (personal communication). Watanabe, M. (1999), Abstract. See also Watanabe (1998).

22 Nisbett et al. (2001), MS, pp. 4–5.

23 Haidt, J., Koller, S. and Dias. M. (1993). We are grateful to Christopher Knapp for bringing Haidt's work to our attention.

24 See Clark, A. (1997), pp. 204–7.

25 Nisbett and Ross's work on "belief perseverance" shows that, sometimes at least, once a belief is formed, it can be surprisingly impervious to change. See, for example, Nisbett and Ross (1980), Ch. 8.

26 In classifying subjects as East Asian or Western, we relied on the same ethnic identification questionnaire that Nisbett and his colleagues had used. We are grateful to Professor Nisbett for providing us with a copy of the questionnaire and for much helpful advice on its use.

27 The numerical data for all the experiments reported in this paper are assembled in the Appendix.

28 Norenzayan, Nisbett, Smith, and Kim (1999).

29 Stich (1990). See especially Ch. 6.

30 Though there is very little evidence on the point, we don't think the differences we've found are innate. Rather, we suspect, they are the product of deep differences in culture.

31 Another possible interpretation of "Really Knows" in our intuition probes would invoke what Ernest Sosa has termed merely "animal" or "servo-mechanical" knowledge. (Sosa, 1991, p. 95) We sometimes say that a dog knows that it's about to be fed, or that the thermostat knows the temperature in the room. But we philosophers are hunting different game – fully normative game which, the critic maintains, these surveys might not capture. However, if our subjects had this notion in mind, one would predict that they would overwhelmingly attribute such knowledge in the Truetemp cases, since the protagonists in each of the stories clearly has a reliable, thermostat-like information-registering capacity. Yet they did not do so – in none of the Truetemp cases did a majority of subjects opt for "Really Knows". So this rival gloss on "knows" will not help the IDR theorist to explain our data away.

32 See, for example, Bealer (1999) who insists that "the work of cognitive psychologists such as Wason, Johnson-Laird, Nisbett, Kahneman and Tversky tells us little about intuitions in our [philosophical] sense" (p. 31).

33 This objection was offered by Henry Jackman, Ram Neta, and Jonathan Schaffer.

References

Austin, J. L. (1964). *Sense and Sensibilia*. London: Oxford University Press.

Bealer, G. (1999). "A Theory of the *A Priori*," *Philosophical Perspectives* 13, Epistemology, pp. 29–55.

BonJour, L. (1985). *The Structure of Empirical Knowledge* (Cambridge, MA: Harvard University Press).

Cha, J.-H. and K. Nam (1985). "A Test of Kelley's Cube Theory of Attribution: A Cross-Cultural Replication of McArthur's Study." *Korean Social Science Journal* 12, pp. 151–80.

Chisolm, R. (1977). *Theory of Knowledge* (Englewood-Cliffs, NJ: Prentice-Hall).

Clark, A. (1997). *Being There: Putting Brain, Body and World Together Again* (Cambridge, MA: MIT Press).

Cohen, L. (1981). "Can human irrationality be experimentally demonstrated?," *Behavioral and Brain Sciences* 4, pp. 317–70.

Dretske, F. (1970). "Epistemic Operators," *Journal of Philosophy* 67(24), pp. 1007–23. Reprinted in Dretske, F. (2000) *Perception, Knowledge, and Belief* (Cambridge, UK: Cambridge University Press).

Elgin, C. (1996). *Considered Judgment* (Princeton, NJ: Princeton University Press).

Feldman, R. and E. Conee (1985). "Evidentialism," *Philosophical Studies* 48, pp. 15–34.

Gettier, E. (1963). "Is Justified True Belief Knowledge?," *Analysis* 23, pp. 121–3.

Goldman, A. (1980). "The Internalist Conception of Justification," in P. A. French, T. E. Uehling, and H. K. Wettstein (eds) *Midwest Studies in Philosophy*, V: Epistemology, (Minneapolis: University of Minnesota Press).

Goldman, A. (1986). *Epistemology and Cognition* (Cambridge, MA: Harvard University Press).

Goldman, A. (1992). "Epistemic Folkways and Scientific Epistemology," in A. Goldman, *Liaisons: Philosophy Meets the Cognitive and Social Sciences* (Cambridge, MA: MIT Press).

Goldman, A. (1999). "A Priori Warrant and Naturalistic Epistemology," in James Tomberlin (ed.), *Philosophical Perspectives* (a supplement to *Noûs*) 13, 1999.

Goldman, A. and J. Pust (1998). "Philosophical Theory and Intuitional Evidence," in M. DePaul and W. Ramsey (eds), *Rethinking Intuition* (Lanham, MD: Rowman & Littlefield).

Goodman, N. (1965). *Fact, Fiction and Forecast* (Indianapolis: Bobbs-Merrill).

Haidt, J., S. Koller and M. Dias (1993). "Affect, Culture and Morality," *Journal of Personality and Social Psychology* 65, 4, pp. 613–28.

Jackson, F. (1998). *From Metaphysics to Ethics: A Defence of Conceptual Analysis* (Oxford: Oxford University Press).

Klein, P. (1999). "Human Knowledge and the Infinite Regress of Reasons," *Philosophical Perspectives*, 13, Epistemology, pp. 297–325.

Kvanvig, J. ed. (1996). *Warrant in Contemporary Epistemology: Essays in Honor of Plantinga's Theory of Knowledge* (Lanham, MD: Rowman & Littlefield).

Lehrer, K. (1990). *Theory of Knowledge* (Boulder, CO and London: Westview Press and Routledge).

Lehrer, K. (1997). *Self-Trust: A Study of Reason, Knowledge, and Autonomy* (Oxford: Oxford University Press).

Morris, M., R. Nisbett and K. Peng (1995). "Causal understanding across domains and cultures," in D. Sperber, D. Premack, and A. J. Premack (eds), *Causal Cognition: A Multidisciplinary Debate* (Oxford: Oxford University Press).

Nisbett, R., K. Peng, I. Choi and A. Norenzayan (2001). "Culture and Systems of Thought: Holistic vs. Analytic Cognition," *Psychological Review* 108, pp. 291–310.

Nisbett, R. and L. Ross (1980). *Human Inference: Strategies and Shortcomings of Social Judgment* (Englewood Cliffs, NJ: Prentice-Hall).

Norenzayan, A., R. E. Nisbett, E. E. Smith and B. J. Kim (1999). *Rules vs. Similarity as a Basis for Reasoning and Judgment in East and West* (Ann Arbor: University of Michigan).

Plantinga, A. (1993a). *Warrant: The Current Debate* (Oxford: Oxford University Press).

Plantinga, A. (1993b). *Warrant and Proper Function* (Oxford: Oxford University Press).

Plato (1892/1937). *The Dialogues of Plato*, translated by B. Jowett. New York: Random House.

Pollock, J. and J. Cruz (1999). *Contemporary Theories of Knowledge* (Lanham, MA: Rowman & Littlefield).

Samuels, R. (in preparation). "Naturalism and Normativity."

Samuels, R., S. Stich and M. Bishop (2002). "Ending the Rationality Wars: How to Make Disputes About Human Rationality Disappear," in Renee Elio, (ed.), *Common Sense, Reasoning and Rationality*, Vancouver Studies in Cognitive Science, vol. 11 (Oxford: Oxford University Press).

Samuels, R, S. Stich and L. Faucher (2004). "Reasoning and Rationality," in I. Niiniluoto, M. Sintonen, and J. Wolenski (eds) *Handbook of Epistemology* (Dordrecht: Kluwer).

Samuels, R., S. Stich and P. Tremoulet (1999). "Rethinking Rationality: From Bleak Implications to Darwinian Modules," in E. LePore and Z. Pylyshyn (eds) *What Is Cognitive Science?* (Oxford: Blackwell), pp. 74–120.

Shope, R. (1983). *The Analysis of Knowing* (Princeton, NJ: Princeton University Press).

Sosa, E. (1991). *Knowledge in Perspective* (Cambridge: Cambridge University Press).

Sosa, E. ed. (1994). *Knowledge and Justification* (Brookfield, VT: International Research Library of Philosophy, Dartmouth Publishing Company Limited).

Stein, E. (1996). *Without Good Reason: The Rationality Debate in Philosophy and Cognitive Science* (Oxford: Clarendon Press).

Stich, S. (1990). *The Fragmentation of Reason* (Cambridge, MA: MIT Press).

Watanabe, M. (1998). "Styles of Reasoning in Japan and the United States: Logic of Education in Two Cultures," paper presented at the American Sociological Association Annual Meeting, San Francisco, August, 1998.

Watanabe, M. (1999). "Styles of Reasoning in Japan and the United States: Logic of Education in Two Cultures," unpublished PhD thesis, Columbia University.

Appendix

The Fisher Exact test was used to calculate statistical significance between groups.

Individualistic Truetemp Case (Figure 45.1)

	Really knows	Only believes
Western	61	128
East Asian	3	22

The p-exact = 0.020114

Elders Truetemp Case (Figure 45.2)

	Really knows	Only believes
Western	77	140
East Asian	5	15

The p-exact = 0.131784

Community Wide Truetemp Case (Figure 45.3)

	Really knows	Only believes
Western	2	8
East Asian	10	21

The p-exact = 0.252681

Gettier Case: Western & East Asian (Figure 45.5)

	Really knows	Only believes
Western	17	49
East Asian	13	10

The p-exact = 0.006414

Gettier Case: Western & Indian (Figure 45.6)

	Really knows	Only believes
Western	17	49
Indian subcontinental	14	9

The p-exact = 0.002407

Cancer Conspiracy Case: Western & Indian (Figure 45.7)

	Really knows	Only believes
Western	7	59
Indian subcontinental	7	16

The p-exact = 0.025014

Zebra-in-Zoo Case: Western & Indian (Figure 45.8)

	Really knows	Only believes
Western	19	43
Indian subcontinental	12	12

The p-exact = 0.049898

Zebra-in-Zoo Case: Low & High SES (Figure 45.9)

	Really knows	Only believes
Low SES	8	16
High SES	4	30

The p-exact = 0.038246

Cancer Conspiracy Case: Low & High SES (Figure 45.10)

	Really knows	Only believes
Low SES	12	12
High SES	6	29

The p-exact = 0.006778

Special Feeling Case: Low & High SES (Figure 45.11)

	Really knows	Only believes
Low SES	3	32
High SES	3	21

The p-exact = 0.294004

Special Feeling Case: Western & East Asian (no figure)

	Really knows	Only believes
Western	2	59
East Asian	0	8

The p-exact = 0.780051

CHAPTER 46

Investigating Knowledge Itself

Hilary Kornblith

Not so long ago, philosophy was widely understood to consist in an investigation of our concepts. There were books with titles such as *The Concept of Mind*;[1] *The Concept of a Person*;[2] *The Concept of Law*;[3] *The Concept of Evidence*;[4] and *The Concept of Knowledge*.[5] The idea that philosophy consists in, or, at a minimum, must begin with an understanding and investigation of our concepts is, I believe, both natural and very attractive. It is also, I believe, deeply mistaken. On my view, the subject matter of ethics is the right and the good, not our concepts of them. The subject matter of philosophy of mind is the mind itself, not our concept of it. And the subject matter of epistemology is knowledge itself, not our concept of knowledge. In this book, I attempt to explain what knowledge is.

My insistence that epistemology should not concern itself with our concept of knowledge requires that I depart, in important ways, from some common practices. I will not, for the most part, be comparing my account of knowledge with my intuitions about various imaginary cases; I will not be considering whether we would be inclined to say that someone does or does not have knowledge in various circumstances. I do not believe that our intuitions, or our inclinations to say various things, should carry a great deal of

weight in philosophical matters. But if we abandon these traditional philosophical tools, then how are we to proceed? How are we to go about investigating knowledge itself, rather than our concept of knowledge? Indeed, what could it even mean to suggest that there is such a thing as knowledge itself apart from our concept of it?

In this chapter, I focus on issues of method. Conceptual analysis, the use of imaginary examples and counterexamples, and appeals to intuition are the stock-in-trade of many philosophers. Indeed, George Bealer[6] has described the appeal to intuitions as part of "the standard justificatory procedure" in philosophy, and, as a simple sociological matter, I believe that Bealer is right; appeals to intuition are standard procedure. More than this, Bealer detects the use of this standard procedure in philosophers who otherwise differ on a wide range of issues; even philosophers who favor a naturalistic epistemology, Bealer argues, make use of appeals to intuition.[7] This is a special problem for naturalists, as Bealer sees it, because naturalists are committed to an epistemology that makes no room for appeals to intuition. So much the worse, Bealer argues, for naturalism. The very practice of philosophy is incompatible with a naturalistic epistemology.

Now the kind of epistemology I favor, and the kind I will argue for here, is a form of naturalism, and Bealer's argument is thus directly relevant to the conduct of this enquiry. If Bealer is right, a naturalistic epistemology is self-undermining.

Originally published in H. Kornblith, *Knowledge and its Place in Nature* (Oxford: Clarendon, 2002), pp. 1–27.

Bealer is not the only one to have made this sort of argument. Similar arguments have been made by Laurence BonJour,[8] Frank Jackson,[9] Mark Kaplan,[10] and Harvey Siegel.[11] Naturalistic epistemology, on this view, proclaims allegiance to a theory that is fundamentally at odds with the philosophical practice of its adherents. A naturalistic epistemology is thereby shown to be untenable.

The clarity and force with which Bealer and others have presented this argument requires that it be given a fair hearing. A naturalistic epistemology has far greater resources, I will argue, than these philosophers have given it credit for. In the course of responding to this argument, I hope to explain how it is that philosophical theorizing may flourish while assigning a significantly smaller role to appeals to intuition than do the critics of naturalism. And in providing an account of philosophical theory construction from a naturalistic point of view, I hope to explain how it is that one may reasonably hope to give an account of knowledge itself, and not just the concept of knowledge.

1   Appeals to Intuition: The Phenomenon

First, let us get clear about the phenomenon. Although any characterization of the phenomenon will be highly contentious, there is no difficulty in giving examples of the practice at issue. We will thus do our best to pin down the practice by way of examples, examples of what we hereby dub "appeals to intuition"; later we may address the question of what it is these examples are examples of.

There are substantial bodies of literature in philosophy that are driven in large part by frankly acknowledged appeals to intuition and are motivated by a desire to formulate accounts that square with those intuitions. Thus, in epistemology, there is the literature on the analyses of knowledge and justification, and especially would-be solutions to the Gettier problem. Imaginary cases are described, involving Brown and his travels in Spain; Nogot, Havit, and their vehicles; Tom Grabit and his kleptomaniacal proclivities at the library; gypsy lawyers; Norman the clairvoyant; barn façades in the countryside; and a host of others. In each of the cases described,

there is a good deal of agreement about whether, under the described conditions, a subject knows, or is justified in believing, something to be the case. Intuitions about these cases are then used to clarify the conditions under which various epistemic notions rightly apply. No empirical investigation is called for, it seems. Each of us can just tell, immediately and without investigation of any kind, whether the case described involves knowledge, or justified belief, or neither.

But epistemologists are not the only ones to use this method. In philosophy of language, there is the literature on the Gricean account of meaning, replete with subjects and their self-referential intentions, including the American soldier who hopes to convince his Italian captors that he is German by uttering the one German sentence he knows, "Kennst du das Land wo die Zitronen bluhen?"; not to mention a character who intends to clear a room with his rendition of "Moon Over Miami", at least in part, of course, in virtue of his audience recognizing that very intention. Here we have quite clear intuitions about when it is that a subject means something by an utterance, and when a subject merely means to achieve a certain effect without meaning anything by the utterance at all. There is also the literature on the causal or historical theory of reference, with the cases of Gödel, Schmidt, and the goings-on on Twin Earth.

There is the literature on personal identity, with its cases of brain transplantation, memory loss, and duplication. And there is the literature in moral philosophy involving children who amuse themselves by pouring gasoline on cats and igniting them; the woman who wakes up one morning to find herself an essential part of the life-support system for an ailing violinist; and a very large number of people unaccountably loitering on trolley tracks.

This method of appeal to intuitions about cases has been used in every area of philosophy, and it has often been used with subtlety and sophistication. There are those – and I count myself among them – who believe that there are substantial limitations to this method, and that some of these bodies of literature have diverted attention from more important issues. Even we, however, must acknowledge not only that the method of appeal to intuitions plays an important role in actual philosophical practice, but also that it has been used to achieve some substantial insights in a wide range of fields. We need an account of how it is that this method may achieve such results.

2 Bealer's Account of Intuition and the Standard Justificatory Procedure

Now George Bealer offers us precisely such an account, and he uses this account to argue that naturalism[12] is self-defeating. In order to see how Bealer's argument proceeds, we must begin with his characterization of the phenomenon.

Bealer describes what he calls "the standard justificatory procedure" (pp. 164–7). As Bealer notes, "we standardly use various items – for example, experiences, observations, testimony – as *prima facie* evidence for things, such as beliefs and theories" (p. 164). After describing a typical Gettier example, Bealer notes that intuitions as well count as prima facie evidence. But what are intuitions? According to Bealer, "When we speak of intuition, we mean '*a priori* intuition'" (p. 165).

Although use of the term "intuition" varies widely among philosophers, Bealer is careful to make his use of the term clear. "Intuition", Bealer tells us, "must … be distinguished from common sense … common sense is an amalgamation of various widely shared, more or less useful empirical beliefs, practical wisdom, *a priori* intuitions, and physical intuitions. Common sense certainly cannot be *identified* with *a priori* intuition" (p. 167). This distinction, Bealer tells us, is "obvious once [it] is pointed out" (ibid.).

Once this account of the standard justificatory procedure is in place, with its reliance on intuition in Bealer's sense,[13] the route to an indictment of naturalism is clear. Naturalists subscribe to a principle of empiricism: "A person's experiences and/or observations comprise the person's *prima facie* evidence" (p. 163). This rules out intuition as a legitimate source of evidence, and thus flies in the face of the standard justificatory procedure. Naturalists themselves make use of intuitions; they too subscribe, in practice, to the standard justificatory procedure. So naturalistic theory is belied by naturalistic practice. Indeed, if consistently followed in practice, Bealer argues, natural-

istic theory would not only rule out philosophy generally as illegitimate, but, given the role intuition plays in "following rules and procedures – for example, rules of inference" (p. 167), a consistent naturalist would have little room left for legitimate belief of any sort at all.

Bealer argues that some naturalists face an additional problem as well. Those who wish to make use of, rather than eliminate, epistemic terminology will find, Bealer argues, that their theory is at odds with their practice in yet another way. What Bealer calls "the principle of naturalism" holds that "the natural sciences … constitute the simplest comprehensive theory that explains all, or most, of a person's experiences and/or observations" (p. 163). Naturalists also endorse what Bealer calls "the principle of holism": "A theory is justified … for a person if and only if it is, or belongs to, the simplest comprehensive theory that explains all, or most, of the person's prima facie evidence" (ibid.). When these two principles are added to the principle of empiricism, which limits our source of prima-facie evidence to observation, naturalists are forced to eschew all epistemic terminology, because "the familiar terms 'justified,' 'simplest,' 'theory,' 'explain,' and '*prima facie* evidence' … do not belong to the primitive vocabulary of the simplest regimented formulation of the natural sciences" (p. 180). Not only is naturalistic theory at odds with naturalistic practice, but the very terms in which naturalistic theory is formulated, Bealer argues, are disallowed as illegitimate by that very theory. Naturalism is thus found to be self-defeating twice over.

There is more to naturalism, I believe, than is to be found in Bealer's account of it. There is room within a naturalistic epistemology for the practice of appeals to intuition, suitably understood, and also for the use of epistemic terminology. What I wish to do is explain how the naturalist may accommodate these phenomena. Much of what I say will be familiar; the story I have to tell, I believe, is at least implicit in the work of a number of investigators working within the naturalistic tradition.[14] But in squarely addressing these charges against naturalistic epistemology, we may not only put them to rest, but we may also lay the foundation for a deeper understanding of proper method in philosophical theorizing.

3   A Naturalistic Account of Appeals to Intuition

Naturalists and their opponents have divergent views about how philosophy ought to be practiced. At the same time, however, there is a great deal more agreement in actual practice than there is in theory about that practice. I do not believe that these differences are insignificant, and later in this chapter I will want to say something about what those differences are and why they matter. But for now, I want to focus on the areas of agreement in practice between naturalists and anti-naturalists, and I will assume that the characterization Bealer gives of the standard justificatory procedure accurately characterizes that common practice. That is, I will assume, with Bealer, that philosophers of all sorts assign prima-facie weight to experience, observation, testimony, *and intuition*, although I will not assume, with Bealer, that intuition here comes down to "a priori intuition". Instead, I will take intuition to be pinned down by the paradigmatic examples of it given above in sect. 1.

How should naturalists regard the standard justificatory procedure? The first thing to say about the intuitions to which philosophers appeal is that they are not idiosyncratic; they are widely shared, and – to a first approximation—must be so, if they are to do any philosophical work. Some philosophers will say, "I'm just trying to figure out what *I* should believe; I'm just trying to get my own intuitions into reflective equilibrium." But even philosophers who say this sort of thing must recognize that wholly idiosyncratic intuitions should play no role even in figuring out what they themselves ought to believe. If I attempt to offer a philosophical account of knowledge by drawing on my intuitions, and it should turn out that crucial intuitions upon which my account relies are had by no one but me, then this will not only dramatically reduce the interest of my account for others; it ought, as well, reduce the interest of my account for me. If my intuitions are wildly idiosyncratic, then most likely the project of accommodating them is no longer one that is engaged with the phenomenon others are attempting to characterize. Unless I can show that others have been somehow misled, what I ought to conclude is that I am probably the one who has been misled, and I ought to focus my attention on correcting my own errors, rather than taking my intuitive judgments at face value. The intuitions of the majority are not definitive, but they do carry substantial epistemic weight, at least in comparison with the intuitions of any single individual, even oneself.

Why is it that the intuitions of the majority carry such weight? It is not, of course, that we merely wish to be engaged in the project, whatever it may be, that other philosophers are engaged in. This would make philosophy into a shallow enterprise, a kind of intellectual imitation game in which the participants seek to engage one another in what they are doing, without any regard for what that might be. Instead, we must be assuming that disagreement with the majority is some evidence of error, and now the question is how that error should be characterized.

Now it is at this point that many philosophers will be tempted to bring in talk of concepts and conceptual analysis: in appealing to our intuitions, it will be said, we come to understand the boundaries of our shared concepts. But I don't think this way of seeing things is illuminating. By bringing in talk of concepts at this point in an epistemological investigation, we only succeed in changing the subject: instead of talking about knowledge, we end up talking about our concept of knowledge.

As I see it, epistemologists should be trying to understand what knowledge is. There is a robust phenomenon of human knowledge, and a presupposition of the field of epistemology is that cases of knowledge have a good deal of theoretical unity to them; they are not merely some gerrymandered kind, united by nothing more than our willingness to regard them as a kind. More than this, if epistemology is to be as worthy of our attention as most epistemologists believe, and if knowledge is to be as worthy of our pursuit, then certain deflationary accounts of knowledge had better turn out to be mistaken. What I have in mind here is those social constructivist accounts which, while granting a substantial theoretical unity to cases of knowledge, see that unity as residing in the social role that knowledge plays. Knowledge, on this kind of view, is merely a vehicle of power. Knowledge may well play some such social role, but its ability to play such a role, if I am right, is explained by a deeper fact, and it is this deeper fact about knowledge that gives it its theoretical unity.[15]

Now one of the jobs of epistemology, as I see it, is to come to an understanding of this natural phenomenon, human knowledge. Understanding what knowledge is, if the project turns out as I expect it will, will also, simultaneously, help to explain why knowledge is worthy of pursuit. When we appeal to our intuitions about knowledge, we make salient certain instances of the phenomenon that need to be accounted for, and that these are genuine instances of knowledge is simply obvious, at least if our examples are well chosen. What we are doing, as I see it, is much like the rock collector who gathers samples of some interesting kind of stone for the purpose of figuring out what it is that the samples have in common. We begin, often enough, with obvious cases, even if we do not yet understand what it is that provides the theoretical unity to the kind we wish to examine. Understanding what that theoretical unity is is the object of our study, and it is to be found by careful examination of the phenomenon, that is, something outside of us, not our concept of the phenomenon, something inside of us. In short, I see the investigation of knowledge, and philosophical investigation generally, on the model of investigations of natural kinds.

This point is quite important, for what it means is that a good deal of the work involved in defining the subject matter under investigation is actually done by the world itself rather than the investigator. The subject matter of the rock collector's investigation is the natural kind, whatever it may be, which (most of) the samples picked out are members of; but the investigator need not be in a position to characterize the essential features of that kind. The investigator's concept of that kind, therefore, because it may be quite incomplete or inaccurate, need not itself do very much of the work of defining the subject matter under study.

This is contrary, of course, to what defenders of conceptual analysis claim. Frank Jackson, for example, nicely lays out the traditional view about the importance of concepts in defining subject matter.

The role of intuitions about possible cases so distinctive of conceptual analysis is precisely to make explicit our implicit folk theory and, in particular, to make explicit which properties are really central to [the subject matter under study]. For surely it *is* possible to change the subject, and how else could one do it other than by abandoning what is most central to defining one's subject? Would a better way of changing the subject be to abandon what is *less* central?[16]

But surely a central point in favor of the causal or historical theory of reference is the observation that reference may remain stable even in the face of substantial changes in belief. It is not that subject matter is changed, as Jackson rhetorically suggests, by changing less central rather than more central defining features, for what is central or peripheral to our concept plays little role in defining subject matter in the first place. Rather, subject matter is defined by way of connections with real kinds in the world, and what we regard as central or defining features does not determine the reference of our terms.

When philosophical investigation is viewed on the model of the investigation of natural kinds, the method of appeal to intuitions is, I believe, easily accommodated within a naturalistic framework. The examples that prompt our intuitions are merely obvious cases of the phenomenon under study. That they are obvious, and thus uncontroversial, is shown by the wide agreement that these examples command. This may give the resulting judgments the appearance of a priority, especially in light of the hypothetical manner in which the examples are typically presented. But on the account I favor, these judgments are no more a priori than the rock collector's judgment that if he were to find a rock meeting certain conditions, it would (or would not) count as a sample of a given kind.[17] All such judgments, however obvious, are a posteriori, and we may view the appeal to intuition in philosophical cases in a similar manner.[18]

What should we say about the rock collector's judgments at early stages of investigation, i.e. prior to any deep theoretical understanding of the features that make his samples samples of a given kind? Such judgments are, of course, corrigible, and they will change with the progress of theory. What seemed to be a clear case of a given kind in the absence of theoretical understanding may come to be a paradigm case of some different kind once the phenomena are better understood. At the same time, it would be a mistake to see these initial naïve judgments as wholly independent of background theory. Our rock collector is naïve, but he is not a tabula rasa. Background knowledge will play a substantial role in determining a first-pass categorization of samples. Judgments about which features of the rocks are even deemed relevant in classification – hardness, for example, but not size perhaps – are themselves theory-mediated, although the operation of theory here is unselfconscious and is better revealed by patterns of salience than it is by overt appeal to principle. The extent to which naïve investigators agree in their classifications is not evidence that these judgments somehow bypass background empirical belief, but rather that background theory may be widely shared.

So too, I want to say, with appeals to intuition in philosophy. These judgments are corrigible and theory-mediated. The extent of agreement among subjects on intuitive judgments is to be explained by common knowledge, or at least common belief, and the ways in which such background belief will inevitably influence intuitive judgment, although unavailable to introspection, are none the less quite real.

Indeed, I want to push this analogy considerably further. The judgments of rock collectors at early stages of investigation are substantially inferior, epistemically speaking, to those at later stages, when theoretical understanding is further advanced. We should not say that initial judgments are of no evidential value, for were this the case progress in theory would be impossible. Our untutored judgment must have some purchase on the phenomenon under investigation; but, that said, it must also be acknowledged that judgment guided by accurate background theory is far superior to the intuitions of the naïve. Intuition must be taken seriously in the absence of substantial theoretical understanding, but once such theoretical understanding begins to take shape, prior intuitive judgments carry little weight unless they have been endorsed by the progress of theory. The greater one's theoretical understanding, the less weight one may assign to untutored judgment.

All this applies equally well to the case of appeals to intuition in philosophy. We sometimes hear philosophers speak of some intuitions as "merely" driven by theory, and thus to be ignored. While it is certainly true that judgments driven by

bad theories are not to be taken seriously, the solution is not to try to return to some pure state of theory-independent judgment, before the fall, as it were; rather the solution is to get a better theory. Intuition in the absence of theory does not count for nothing, especially if no credible theory is available. But this is not to award high marks to intuitive judgment before the arrival of successful theory, let alone after, when the initially low value of such judgment drops still lower.

Now if this account is correct, why do philosophers spend so much time scrutinizing their intuitions, that is, looking inward, if, on my view, what they are really interested in is external phenomena? I have two things to say about this. First, if I am asked a question about rocks, for example, one way to answer the question is to ask myself what I believe the answer is. Although I am asked a question about rocks, I answer it by enquiring into what I believe. This is a perfectly reasonable thing to do if I have good reason to think that my current beliefs are accurate, or if I do not have access to a better source of information. By looking inward, I answer a question about an external phenomenon. This, to my mind, is what we do when we consult our intuitions.

At the same time, however, I do not think that this can be the whole story here, and this is where the difference between the practice of naturalists and that of anti-naturalists comes into play. If my account is correct, then what we ought to be doing is not just consulting the beliefs we already have, but more directly examining the external phenomena; only then would appeals to intuition be given what, on my view, is their proper weight. Thus, appeal to intuition early on in philosophical investigation should give way to more straightforwardly empirical investigations of external phenomena. This is, to my mind, just what we see in the practice of naturalistically minded philosophers. Just a few decades ago, the philosophical practice of naturalistically minded epistemologists, for example, was almost indistinguishable from that of their more traditionally minded colleagues. Examples and counterexamples were used to motivate various accounts of knowledge and justification, and the progress of these accounts was shepherded along by a succession of appeals to intuition. This was, by my lights, a good thing to do at that stage of the investigation. Important insights were gained, which, given the absence of available explicitly articulated theory, could not have been gained by any other means. But now, as theory has progressed, more straightforwardly empirical investigation should be called upon; and this, of course, is just what we see. There is work on the psychology of inference, concept formation, cognitive development, and so on. Similarly, at the social level there is work on the distribution of cognitive effort, and, more generally, the social structures of science that underwrite and make scientific knowledge possible. As theory has advanced here, raw appeals to intuition have declined. Just look at the difference between early papers by Fred Dretske and Alvin Goldman, for example, and their more recent work. Similar results may be found by looking at naturalistically minded work in philosophy of mind, and even in ethics, where work in cognitive science and anthropology have been shaping the work of contemporary naturalists. The difference in methodology between naturalists and their more traditional colleagues has, to my mind, been paying substantial dividends for those willing to draw on empirical work. But even those who disagree with me here will have to agree that naturalistic methodology is now importantly different from that of other philosophers, even if not very long ago it would have been difficult to separate the naturalists from the non-naturalists by looking at their methods.

From a naturalistic perspective, there are substantial advantages to looking outward at the phenomena under investigation rather than inward at our intuitions about them. Most obviously, since it is some external phenomenon that we are interested in, we should approach it by the most direct means possible, rather than the more indirect approach of looking at what we currently believe about it. Aside from being indirect, the approach of examining our intuitions clearly robs us of the best available source of correctives for current mistakes. Moreover, the appeal to imaginable cases and what we are inclined to say about them is both overly narrow and overly broad in its focus. It is overly narrow because serious empirical investigation of a phenomenon will often reveal possibilities which we would not, and sometimes could not, have imagined before. It is overly broad because many imaginable cases are not genuine possibilities and need not be accounted for by our theories. We might be able

to imagine a rock with a certain combination of color, hardness, malleability, and so on, and such a rock, were it to exist, might be difficult or impossible to fit into our current taxonomy. But this raises no problem at all for our taxonomic principles if the imagined combination of properties is nomologically impossible. On the naturalistic view, the same may be said for testing our philosophical views against merely imaginable cases.

The suggestion that our intuitions about knowledge might actually be mistaken in the ways in which our intuitions about, say, gold can be will strike some philosophers as implausible. It is important, however, to realize that our intuitions about knowledge are, in important ways, historically conditioned. Descartes's idea that knowledge required certainty was surely a product of his view that things firm and lasting in the sciences could only be achieved if scientific claims could be given an absolute guarantee. As it turned out, Descartes was wrong about this. In ways Descartes could never have anticipated, the sciences have gone on to achieve levels of ever-increasing explanatory and predictive success coupled with technological applications crucially dependent upon the approximate truth of their theoretical claims. These successes, producing things "firm and lasting in the sciences", of just the sort Descartes hoped to achieve, did not depend in any way on the sort of certainty Descartes took to be a prerequisite for knowledge. The view that knowledge requires certainty is no longer widely held; it is an intuition that very few people have any more. In retrospect, this change in people's intuitions about the relationship between knowledge and certainty can be seen as a byproduct of the ways in which scientific success has actually been achieved. It is now just obvious to almost everyone that knowledge is possible without certainty. But it would be a mistake to see this realization as a matter of a priori insight into the nature of knowledge. Properly understood, it is, however indirectly, a claim empirically justified by the manner in which knowledge has in fact been gained.

Now all of this would make little difference if our intuitions responded to relevant empirical evidence in a timely fashion. Consulting our intuitions would be just as accurate as looking directly at the relevant phenomena if only our intuitions were suitably responsive to appropriate evidence.

But there is no reason to think that our intuitions are suitably responsive to available evidence. Changing a society's intuitions about a particular subject matter takes a good deal of time. It is one thing for the scientific community to make an important discovery; quite another for that discovery to become common knowledge. It takes still longer before our whole conception of a phenomenon comes to seem so obvious that we can no longer even remember what it was like to conceive of it in another way. But if we take the long historical view, this is exactly what happens with our intuitions when important discoveries are made. If we wish to understand a phenomenon accurately, we thus cannot merely seek to elucidate our current intuitive conception of it; we must examine the phenomenon itself. And this applies as much to understanding the nature of knowledge as it does to understanding the nature of gold.

One might seek a middle ground here. Alvin Goldman has suggested that there is room both for conceptual analysis of our folk epistemological concepts as well as a more scientific epistemology that would develop epistemological concepts that depart in important ways from our folk notions. But why, on this view, do the folk notions take on any epistemological import at all, especially in light of the fact that they are bound to build in, as Goldman himself points out, false presuppositions? On Goldman's view, there must be substantial continuity between the folk notions and the more scientific ones if there is to be such a thing as epistemology at all. Without such continuity, Goldman argues, we are just changing the subject. Now I have already argued that this account of what is involved in changing the subject, an account that Goldman shares with Jackson, is not correct. Continuity of concept is merely one way to mark commonality of subject matter; causal theorists of reference have another (and to my mind, better) account. Goldman does not consider the possibility of such an account in the case of knowledge, since he regards it as simply obvious that knowledge is not a natural kind. "Whatever one thinks about justice or consciousness as possible natural kinds, it is dubious that knowledge or justificational status are natural kinds."[19] ...

Although I do not agree with Goldman that there must inevitably be the degree of continuity he requires between our folk concepts and those of a properly scientific epistemology, I do not wish to exaggerate my disagreement with him either. After all, the account of knowledge I endorse is, in the end, a reliability account very similar to the one Goldman himself offers. Even if, however, we should discover that there is a tremendous amount of continuity between our folk epistemological notions and those of a proper scientific epistemology, it remains to be shown why our folk epistemological notions are of *epistemological* interest in their own right. Why should our folk epistemological notions be of any more interest to epistemologists than our folk chemical notions are to chemists?

Goldman responds to this challenge: "even if one rejects the plea for continuity, a description of our epistemic folkways is in order. How would one know what to criticize, or what needs to be transcended, in the absence of such a description? So a first mission of epistemology is to describe our folkways."[20] But if knowledge truly is a natural kind, then this sort of response is inadequate. We would hardly think that the chemist's first job is an elucidation of folk chemical notions (especially if this required extraordinary effort by the entire community of chemists over a period of millennia) so that we would know what chemical views need to be transcended. In the case of chemistry, we can simply skip straight to the project of understanding the real chemical kinds as they exist in nature. My suggestion here is that we should take seriously the possibility that a similar strategy might be equally fruitful in epistemology.

I do not mean to suggest that on the naturalistic view we will ever be able wholly to avoid appealing to our intuitions. I do think that appeals to intuition will continue to play a role in the development of philosophical views, even as theory progresses. I noted earlier that the actual practice of naturalistically minded philosophers has changed with the progress of theory so that now there is a good deal more empirical examination of various phenomena rather than an exclusive reliance on appeals to intuition. But this does not mean that appeals to intuition simply drop out of the picture. Thus, for example, in philosophy of mind not so many years ago there was a good deal of discussion about whether creatures who failed to exhibit certain sorts of characteristic behavior might nevertheless be in pain. These discussions did not involve much of a look at the empirical literature on pain; instead, they relied exclusively on appeals to intuition.[21] Now, although work in philosophy of mind involves a great deal of examination of the empirical literature, we still see appeals to intuition playing a role, although the intuitions are about more esoteric matters. For example, there is discussion of what magnetosomes represent, whether it be the presence of certain sorts of magnetic fields or, instead, the presence of anaerobic conditions.

The intuitions that naturalists currently appeal to, intuitions about matters far more esoteric than what is known about Brown in Barcelona, present clear cases of theory-mediated judgment, judgment which is rightly influenced by a large body of background belief. At the same time, these judgments are phenomenologically basic; their inferential heritage is not introspectively available. More than this, these judgments are typically far less well integrated with our best available theories, and thus not nearly so well justified,[22] as our more explicitly theory-guided judgments. As the scope of our theories expands, the use of such weakly founded judgments is a necessary stepping stone to better theory. The use of intuitive judgment does not disappear at any stage of theorizing. Instead, old intuitions give way to well-integrated theoretical judgments, and, in addition, to new intuitions about matters not yet fully captured in explicit theory.

We may thus respond to the first of Bealer's objections to naturalism by pointing out that appeals to intuition do not require some non-natural faculty or a priori judgment of any sort. Bealer's argument gets off on the wrong foot by assuming that intuitions are a priori; more than this, Bealer says, the distinction between common-sense empirical judgment and intuition is "obvious" (p. 165). Obvious it may be to those opposed to naturalism, but the appeal to a priority is, of course, contentious in this context. Bealer is right to think that naturalists owe us an explanation of their practice of appealing to intuition, especially in light of their rejection of the a priori. At the same time, I hope I have shown that this explanation is one that naturalists may easily provide. The practice of appealing to intuition has no non-natural ingredients.

4 Naturalism and Rules of Inference

Bealer argues that naturalists are not only unable to account for their own philosophical practice, but that naturalistic scruples leave little room for legitimate belief about any subject, since "following rules and procedures – for example, rules of inference" (p. 167) requires an acknowledgement of the force of a priori intuition. And Laurence BonJour comments, "the practice of even those who most explicitly reject the idea of substantive *a priori* justification inevitably involves tacit appeal to insights and modes of reasoning that can only be understood as *a priori* in character, if they are justified at all."[23] As BonJour points out, this leaves naturalists in an unenviable position: "we see that the repudiation of all *a priori* justification is apparently tantamount to the repudiation of argument or reasoning generally, thus amounting in effect to intellectual suicide."[24] But naturalists do not see the following of rules and procedures, in particular, the role of rules of inference, in the way in which Bealer and BonJour do.

Naturalists, of course, make inferences, and they need to account for the legitimacy of this practice, at least in those cases in which it is legitimate. The legitimacy of an inference, on the naturalist view, is dependent upon its reliability: reliable inferential practices are epistemically legitimate; those which are unreliable are not. We must thus engage in a project of self-examination, in which we scrutinize our own epistemic practice. We wish to examine the inferential rules that underlie our practice of belief acquisition, and to the extent that we find unreliable inference patterns at work, we need to re-examine and modify our own practice. The empirical work involved in understanding our inferential habits is well underway, as is the assessment of its epistemological importance.

Reliability is the naturalist's standard here. Meeting a priori standards is simply irrelevant. Rules of inference that tend to produce true beliefs in the kinds of environments that human beings occupy may fail to live up to a priori standards of cogency, but they are none the worse for that. By the same token, rules of inference that do meet a priori standards may be unworkable in practice or hopelessly mired in problems of computational complexity. These kinds of problems are not in any way ameliorated if the rules do meet a priori standards of cogency. A priori standards thus drop out of the picture entirely as simply irrelevant to proper epistemic practice. They fail to bear on the conduct of enquiry.[25]

A naturalistic account of proper belief acquisition thus does not need to appeal to a priori intuition of appropriate principles of inference. Recognition of appropriate inferential patterns is an empirical affair for the naturalist. More than this, justified belief, on at least one widely held naturalistic account, is a matter of reliable belief production and does not itself require recognition of that reliability. Naturalistic scruples about appropriate belief production thus leave room for a great deal of knowledge.

5   Naturalism and Epistemic Terminology

Let me turn then to the last of Bealer's charges against naturalism, that in eschewing a priori intuition, naturalism leaves no room for epistemic terminology. This charge too, I believe, falls short of its mark. While the account naturalists give of epistemic terminology is anything but uncontroversial, it should not be controversial that naturalists have an account of that terminology that satisfies their own epistemic standards. The suggestion that naturalism is self-defeating is thus turned aside.

Epistemology, according to naturalism, investigates a certain natural phenomenon, namely, knowledge, and the term "knowledge" and other epistemic idioms gain their reference in much the same way that natural-kind terms do. Now supposing that terms like "knowledge" gain their reference in this way is not without its presuppositions, as I pointed out earlier. The phenomenon we call knowledge must have a certain degree of theoretical unity if reference is to be secured. Were we to discover that there is no more theoretical unity to the various items we call knowledge than there is to the set consisting of ships and shoes and sealing wax, then a presupposition of the introduction of the term would be undermined, and the view that there is no such thing as knowledge would be sustained. But naturalists, and indeed, most non-naturalists, do not think that such a possibility is at all likely.[26] Indeed, almost all epistemologists believe that

there is a great deal of unity to the phenomenon of human knowledge. If there is indeed such a unity, one goal of epistemology is to say what it consists in. And of course if it should turn out there is no such unity, then one goal of epistemology would be to make that fact plain.

The investigation of the phenomenon of knowledge, on the naturalist's view, is an empirical investigation, and the legitimacy of epistemic terminology depends on its properly latching on to genuine, theoretically unified kinds. That is all that naturalistic scruples require. Because epistemology thus conceived is a wholly empirical investigation, naturalists have nothing here to apologize for. Their terminology earns its keep in just the way that chemical or biological or physical terminology earns its keep: it must be part of a successful empirical theory. The fact that terms such as "knowledge" are not part of physics or chemistry does not show that they are not naturalistically acceptable. Rather, the question for naturalists is whether knowledge turns out to be a theoretically unified phenomenon, and this gives every appearance of being a legitimate and tractable empirical question.

Some will say that this enterprise, because it is descriptive, fails to engage the normative dimension of epistemological theorizing. They will argue that it is only by removing knowledge from the empirical realm, and making it the object of a priori investigation, that its normative character may emerge. … [F]or now it is possible to say something brief that will go some distance toward responding to this challenge. The empirical investigation of knowledge may well reveal a phenomenon worthy of our pursuit. Surely such a suggestion does not require a degree of optimism ungrounded in fact. But this is all the normativity that our epistemic notions require. We should not suppose that the investigation of knowledge must be non-empirical if we are to be able to explain why knowledge is worth having.[27]

Epistemic terminology, and, indeed, philosophical terminology in general, must be grounded in the world if it is to be naturalistically legitimate. This does not require that such terminology appear in our physical theories, for naturalists need not accept any sort of reductionism. Once we regard epistemology as the investigation of a certain natural phenomenon, we clear the way for distinctively epistemic terminology.

Naturalism would only threaten to eliminate epistemic terminology as illegitimate if there were no prospect of discovering theoretically unified epistemic phenomena. But there is little reason, I believe, to think that this is currently a genuine possibility. Moreover, if there were reason to worry on this account, it would spell the demise not only of naturalistic epistemology, but epistemology generally. Bealer's final objection, that naturalists are not entitled to the very epistemic terminology they make use of, thus ultimately fails.

6 The Autonomy of Philosophy

I want to close this chapter by addressing one further issue, a concern that, I believe, motivates Bealer's attack on naturalism, and this has to do with the autonomy of philosophy. In a lengthy attack[28] on the kind of scientific essentialism I favor, Bealer begins by suggesting that naturalism raises the possibility that science will somehow "eclipse" philosophy. Naturalism threatens the autonomy of philosophical enquiry, Bealer argues, and it is thus only by rejecting naturalism that we may make room for a distinctively philosophical enterprise. BonJour has a similar conception of philosophical endeavors: "philosophy is *a priori* if it is anything (or at least if it is anything intellectually respectable)".[29] But then the naturalistic rejection of the a priori results immediately in a repudiation of philosophy itself. As Bealer and BonJour see it, if naturalism is right, we should all give up doing philosophy and take up science instead.

Now I myself have a high regard for philosophy. Although I am a naturalist, I do not believe that philosophy must be eliminated. Naturalists do not regard philosophy as illegitimate, nor do they see it as in any way threatened by the progress of science. At the same time, we do not wish to grant philosophy the degree of autonomy that Bealer, BonJour, and other opponents of naturalism would favor. There are important issues here, and it is worth making clear just where naturalism stands on them.

Questions about knowledge and justification, questions about theory and evidence, are, to my mind, legitimate questions, and they are ones in which philosophy has a special stake. The questions that philosophers wish to ask about these topics are different from those addressed by historians, sociologists, and psychologists, but no less important or intellectually respectable. If the autonomy of a discipline consists in its dealing with a distinctive set of questions, or in approaching certain phenomena with a distinctive set of concerns, then philosophy is surely an autonomous discipline. There is no danger that these questions and concerns will somehow be co-opted by other disciplines.

When Bealer raises the issue of philosophy's autonomy, however, he has in mind something quite different from this. For Bealer, the autonomy of philosophy is identified with the claim that philosophical knowledge is a priori, entirely independent of anything the empirical sciences have to offer. Now this, of course, is a claim any naturalist will want to reject. On the naturalist's view, philosophical questions are continuous with the empirical sciences. Work in the empirical sciences is deeply relevant to philosophical questions, and our philosophical theories are constrained and guided by results in other disciplines. It is worth noting that the special sciences are not autonomous in anything like Bealer's sense, i.e. they are not wholly independent of work in other disciplines. Work in biology is not wholly independent of chemistry; sociology is not wholly independent of psychology; and so on. But the loss of this sort of autonomy does not rob these disciplines of their legitimacy, nor does it threaten the special sciences with the loss of their distinctive subject matter. Biologists need not fear that their field will be taken away from them by chemists once it is recognized that chemistry is relevant to biological concerns.

So too with philosophy. In recognizing that philosophy is continuous with the sciences, we need not fear that philosophy will thereby be "eclipsed" by science. The constraints that science presents for philosophical theorizing should be welcomed, for philosophical theorizing unconstrained by empirical fact loses its connection with the very phenomena which we, as philosophers, seek to understand. Philosophy is an autonomous discipline, in the sense that it addresses a distinctive set of questions and concerns, and in this respect it is no more nor less autonomous than physics or chemistry or biology. This is surely all the autonomy we should want. It is, in any case, all the autonomy that we may have.

7 Conclusion

Bealer's multi-count indictment of naturalism is not supported by the facts. We can make perfectly good sense of a thoroughly empirical philosophy, one that does not assign either the weight or the provenance to intuition that Bealer and others do. Epistemology is fully naturalized when it regards knowledge as a natural phenomenon, an object of study with a substantial degree of theoretical unity to it. ...

Notes

1   Gilbert Ryle, *The Concept of Mind* (Barnes & Noble, 1949).

2   A.J. Ayer, *The Concept of a Person and Other Essays* (Macmillan, 1964).

3   H. L. A. Hart, *The Concept of Law* (Oxford University Press, 1961).

4   Peter Achinstein, *The Concept of Evidence* (Oxford University Press, 1983).

5   Panayot Butchvarov, *The Concept of Knowledge* (Northwestern University Press, 1970).

6   See George Bealer, "The Philosophical Limits of Scientific Essentialism", *Philosophical Perspectives*, 1 (1987), pp. 289–365; "The Incoherence of Empiricism", in S. Wagner and R. Warner (eds), *Naturalism: A Critical Appraisal* (Notre Dame University Press, 1993), pp. 163–96; and "Intuition and the Autonomy of Philosophy", in M. DePaul and W. Ramsey (eds), *Rethinking Intuition: The Psychology of Intuition and Its Role in Philosophical Inquiry* (Rowman & Littlefield, 1998), pp. 201–39. Page numbers in parentheses refer to "The Incoherence of Empiricism".

7   See also Frank Jackson, *From Metaphysics to Ethics: A Defense of Conceptual Analysis* (Oxford University Press, 1998), p. vii: "And, as you might expect, if I am right about our need for it, conceptual analysis is very widely practiced – though not under the name of conceptual analysis. There is a lot of 'closet' conceptual analysis going on."

8   Laurence BonJour, "Against Naturalistic Epistemology", *Midwest Studies in Philosophy*, 19 (1994), pp. 283–300, and *In Defense of Pure Reason* (Cambridge University Press, 1998).

9   Frank Jackson, *From Metaphysics to Ethics*.

10 Mark Kaplan, "Epistemology Denatured", *Midwest Studies in Philosophy*, 19 (1994), pp. 350–65.

11 Harvey Siegel, "Empirical Psychology, Naturalized Epistemology and First Philosophy", *Philosophy of Science*, 51 (1984), pp. 667–76.

12 Bealer has argued against a number of different targets, including naturalism, scientific essentialism, and empiricism. There are, of course, numerous versions of each of these views, and one may consistently subscribe to more than one of them. Indeed, the view I favor, and that I defend here, may rightly be described as falling under each of these three headings. It is for this reason that I feel called upon to answer Bealer's attacks on all these positions.

13 I don't mean to suggest that Bealer's usage here is idiosyncratic; it isn't. Compare, for example, BonJour's notion of intuition: "judgments and convictions that, though considered and reflective, are not arrived at via an explicit discursive process and thus are (hopefully) uncontaminated by theoretical or dialectical considerations" (*In Defense of Pure Reason*, p. 102).

14 For example, Michael Devitt remarks, in a footnote to his "The Methodology of Naturalistic Semantics", *Journal of Philosophy*, 91 (1994), pp. 545–72: "The naturalist does not deny 'armchair' intuitions a role in philosophy but denies that their role has to be seen as a priori: the intuitions reflect an empirically based expertise at identification" (564 n. 27). Devitt refers there to Bealer's work. The present chapter may be seen as an attempt to expand on this remark of Devitt's. After completing a draft of this chapter, my attention was drawn to the work of Terry Horgan which has many points of contact with the views expressed here. See Horgan's "The Austere Ideology of Folk Psychology", *Mind and Language*, 8 (1993), pp. 282–97, and Terence Horgan and George Graham, "Southern Fundamentalism and the End of Philosophy", *Philosophical Issues*, 5 (1994), pp. 219–47.

Finally, see also Richard Boyd's "How to Be a Moral Realist", in Geoffrey Sayre-McCord (ed.), *Essays on Moral Realism*, esp. pp. 192–3.

15 I have discussed this point at greater length in "A Conservative Approach to Social Epistemology", in Fred Schmitt (ed.), *Socializing Epistemology* (Rowman & Littlefield, 1994), pp. 93–110, and in "Naturalistic Epistemology and Its Critics", *Philosophical Topics*, 23 (1995), pp. 237–55.

16 Jackson, *From Metaphysics to Ethics*, p. 38.

17 What of the claim that something is a natural kind? Is that too known empirically? I believe that it is. Consider, again, the case of gold. What caught our attention and resulted in the introduction of the term, let us suppose, was a collection of salient features such as the color, reflectance pattern, malleability, and so on of a number of samples of rock. It was an empirical discovery that these constituted a natural kind, i.e. that these samples were not, from a theoretical perspective, merely heterogeneous, but rather that they shared some deep, underlying properties responsible for the more superficial properties that initially attracted our attention. The same is true of natural-kind terms generally. While a person introducing a term may well believe, at the time the term is introduced, that the referent of the term is a natural kind, subsequent investigation may reveal that this belief is false. By the same token, a term may be introduced for a property that is, in fact, a natural kind, without the person introducing the term recognizing that fact.

18 Here I simply take for granted a causal or historical account of the reference of natural-kind terms. While the details of such a theory remain to be established, the general outline is, I believe, perfectly clear in the foundational work of Kripke and Putnam. The following points should be agreed upon by all sides: (1) The initial samples that prompt the introduction of a natural-kind term need not all be members of the kind in order for reference to occur; (2) The most central beliefs about a kind held by early investigators may turn out to be false without thereby undermining reference. These points are not so much argued in the text as taken for granted. What I do argue is that

reference to knowledge may work in precisely the same way as reference to, for example, gold, and that there are no problems specific to the case of knowledge beyond those already addressed in the work on more paradigmatic natural kinds.

19 Goldman, "Psychology and Philosophical Analysis", in *Liaisons: Philosophy Meets the Cognitive and Social Sciences* (MIT Press, 1992), p. 144.

20 Goldman, "Epistemic Folkways and Scientific Epistemology", ibid., p. 156.

21 For a valuable discussion of the state of the art on this issue, see Colin Allen, "Animal Pain", manuscript.

22 I do not mean to be diverging here from a reliabilist account of justification. Rather, I mean only to be pointing out that allowing one's judgments to be influenced by accurate theory tends to be a source of increased reliability.

23 BonJour, *In Defense of Pure Reason*, p. ix.

24 Ibid., p. 5.

25 It is thus particularly ironic that Mark Kaplan both criticizes naturalistic epistemology as irrelevant to the conduct of enquiry and simultaneously defends the importance of a priori standards of cogent argument. See Kaplan, "Epistemology Denatured", pp. 350–65.

26 But see Michael Williams, *Unnatural Doubts: Epistemological Realism and the Basis of Skepticism* (Princeton University Press, 1996).

27 Nor is it clear why a non-empirical investigation, if such were possible, would go any distance at all toward addressing the normativity issue. Much of the criticism of naturalism on this score has been, I believe, entirely beside the point. While it is correctly pointed out that it is hard to see how an empirical investigation could address our normative concerns, critics of naturalism take this to count in favor of some sort of a priori investigation. But neither is it clear how an a priori investigation could address those concerns. The appropriate conclusion, I believe, is that we simply don't currently see how normative concerns can be addressed at all. This does not count for or against any particular view.

28 Bealer, "The Philosophical Limits of Scientific Essentialism".

29 BonJour, *In Defense of Pure Reason*, p. ix.

PART VIII

Knowledge and Context

Introduction

Consider the basic form of the skeptical argument as formulated by Keith DeRose, with "*H*" standing in for some sentence describing a skeptical hypothesis and "*O*" for a sentence describing an ordinary state of affairs:

1 I don't know that not-*H*.
2 If I don't know that not-*H*, then I don't know that *O*. So,
C I don't know that *O*.

In reply to the skeptic, the contextualist refuses to deny either of the premises and indeed does not deny the conclusion. This is the concession. Yet the skeptic is charged with the error of not seeing the implications of the context-sensitivity of knowledge claims, of supposing that knowledge claims are false in all contexts, even in ordinary contexts quite apart from any skeptical challenge. The truth of the matter, says the contextualist, is that the skeptic's dialectical challenge raises the standards for truly attributing knowledge. Still, in many ordinary contexts, lower standards are in place, allowing premise (1) to be false and thus allowing many ordinary knowledge attributions to be true. (Compare to Gail Stine's piece in Part IV of this volume.)

This is the contextualist reply to the skeptic, in broad outline. As is pointed out effectively by DeRose, putting flesh on the bones of this view requires describing the mechanisms by which the standards for truly ascribing knowledge are raised and lowered. The task of providing such descriptions, of course, introduces a danger of generating incorrect predictions regarding the truth-values of knowledge claims in various hypothetical situations. In his contribution, Stewart Cohen argues that this is the sort of difficulty that undermines David Lewis's recent contextualist account.

Keith DeRose takes as his starting point Robert Nozick's insight that knowledge is importantly connected to sensitivity. (See Nozick's selection in Part IV of this volume.) Why am I unable to know my lottery ticket is a loser regardless of how large the lottery pool is – unable, that is, *until* I hear the official announcements of the winner? The probability that my ticket is a loser given that it is one of a million (or more) is much *greater* than the probability that the announcer is telling the truth. Nozick answers: before but not after you hear the announcement your belief is insensitive; had your ticket not been a loser, you would have still believed it was.

Nonetheless, DeRose shies away from the pure sensitivity account because it fails to rule out, and even licenses, what he calls "abominable conjunctions." These are conjunctions of the form "I know that p, but I don't know that not-q," where p entails not-q. "Straight" solutions to the skeptical problem, which give up (2) in the argument opening this section, are forced to admit the truth of the abominable "I know that O, but I don't know that not-H." These fly in the face of our intuitions and should be regarded as false in every context. DeRose is therefore constrained not to locate the source of the context-dependence in the conditional premise, (2). He locates the source, instead, in the assertion of (1) itself. The effect of denying knowledge is to require thereafter a stronger epistemic position for knowledge than was required before. It is this notion of *strength of epistemic position* that receives an account in terms of sensitivity. We judge relative strength of epistemic positions when we judge the truth-values of conditionals of the form "If I know that p, then I know that q" e.g., "If I know that I own a cat, then I know that I own an animal," as well as those of their converses. What guides us in judging such conditionals true or false, moreover, are facts about the distance from actuality (if any) that would be required for the belief/fact link to be broken. Thus, a cat-owner S's epistemic position with respect to "I know I own an animal" will be stronger than his epistemic position with respect to "I know I own a cat," since one would have to look farther from actuality to find a possible world in which S believes falsely that he has a cat than one would to find a world in which S believes falsely that he has an animal. Sensitivity then enters as a limit to which the standards for strength of epistemic position can be raised. This is precisely the contextual feature that the skeptic exploits. By claiming that one lacks knowledge, say, that one is not a brain in a vat, the skeptic raises the contextual standards so high as to require sensitivity to the truth of the proposition that one is not a brain in a vat. But once the sphere of relevant worlds is so far extended, one's belief that one has hands will not match the facts across all the worlds. One's epistemic position with respect to one's belief that one has hands, after all, is not as strong as it is with respect to one's belief that one is not a brain in a vat. (This is a noteworthy claim in light of the fact that Dretske, Nozick, and others insist that while we may know that we have hands, we certainly do not know that we are not brains in vats.)

David Lewis's contextualism takes off from the intuitive infallibilist claim that one knows that p just in case one's evidence eliminates all possibilities in which not-p. This does not lead to skepticism (in all contexts), however, because the scope of "all" is taken to be contextually restricted. Thus, Lewis adds to this biconditional, *soto voce*, " – Psst! – except for those possibilities that we are properly ignoring." A significant portion of Lewis's paper is then devoted to listing rules that determine at least partially what can and cannot be properly ignored. Corresponding to the traditional triad of requirements for knowledge – truth, belief, and justification – we encounter a pair of rules: the actuality and the belief rules. If a possibility is actual it cannot properly be ignored. This rule thus guarantees that only what is true is known. If it is, or ought to be, believed by the subject to be actual, it cannot be properly ignored. This rule doesn't guarantee that only what is believed and justified can be knowledge, but it does make belief and justification relevant to whether one knows (e.g., if one believes or is justified in believing that what one sees is a painted mule, then one doesn't know that what one sees is a zebra). Prominent among the other rules listed are the rules of resemblance and attention. The rule of resemblance states that if a possibility saliently resembles another possibility, then if one cannot be properly ignored, neither can the other. The rule of attention states that if a possibility is attended to, it cannot be properly ignored. This framework is then applied to three kinds of problem: skepticism, the lottery problem, and the Gettier problem. The application to skepticism appeals to the rule of attention. To truly claim that S knows that p after the mention of the appropriate skeptical possibility, S's evidence would have to eliminate the skeptical possibility attended to, which it will not do. For the lottery and Gettier cases, the rules of actuality and resemblance do the required work. Since the possibility in which S has the winning ticket is saliently similar to actuality (whatever actuality may be), the possibility of having a winner is not properly ignored. Thus, the knowledge attribution will be false. Similarly, since the possibility in which neither Nogot nor Havit owns a Ford saliently resembles actuality, it is not properly ignored. Here, too, the knowledge attribution will be false.

Stewart Cohen argues that Lewis's rules wrongly assimilate the Gettier problem to the lottery problem and skepticism. The salient-resemblance requirement is appropriate in regard to the latter two problems, but not the former. To establish this, Cohen first distinguishes between *speaker-sensitive* and *subject-sensitive* rules for properly ignoring possibilities, noting that the rule of salient resemblance is both speaker- and subject-sensitive. He then examines the consequences. Suppose S sees a sheep-shaped rock on a hill, and taking the rock to be a sheep, comes to believe that there is a sheep on the hill. As it turns out, there is in fact a sheep behind the rock, out of S's view. Now an attributor who knows all these facts will find the possibility that S sees a sheep-shaped rock on a sheepless hill salient, but one who views the scene from a different angle may not realize that S is in fact seeing a rock. The second attributor will not find salient the possibility just mentioned, nor any other possibility like it. In fact, then, the second attributor can truly attribute knowledge to S. Since facts about salience vary from attributor to attributor, facts about whether it's true to say of someone in a Gettier case that she has knowledge, too, will vary.

Cohen argues that this result is implausible in the face of our stable disposition to deny knowledge to subjects in Gettier cases. A contextualist theory should appeal to speaker-sensitive rules only when our intuitions vacillate. We do vacillate about the truth of skeptical claims and about the truth of knowledge attributions in certain lottery cases, such as that of Lewis's Poor Bill: "Pity poor Bill! He squanders all his spare cash on the pokies, the races, and the lottery. He will be a wage slave all his days. We know he will never be rich. But if he wins the lottery (if he wins big), then he will be rich." We don't vacillate about Gettier cases.

The contextualist takes certain intuitively non-epistemic or non-truth-conductive factors, e.g., salience of possibilities of error or the cost of being wrong, to make a difference to the truth-conditions of knowledge-attributions. But most contextualists do not take such pragmatic factors to make a difference to whether anyone knows. It is perhaps part of the appeal of contextualism that it is consistent with what Jason Stanley dubs 'intellectualism.' Intellectualism claims that the differences between true belief and knowledge have to do strictly with matters of theoretical rationality and never practical rationality. Stanley argues that the alleged context-sensitivity of 'knows' has no parallel among the class of uncontroversial context-sensitive expressions. Therefore, the most reasonable hypothesis is that knowledge attributions are not context-sensitive in any distinctively epistemological way (they may of course inherit any context-sensitivity involved in tense or vagueness). If this is right, then the contextualist's examples instead show that the intellectualist assumption is false. Knowledge is not a purely epistemic notion: pragmatic factors – and in particular facts about the costs of being wrong – are relevant to whether one knows.

Stanley argues against intellectualism on the basis of the intuitions we have in response to certain contextualist examples. Jeremy Fantl and Matthew McGrath argue for a similar conclusion on the basis of certain epistemic principles. The first and most crucial step in their argument is that if you know that p and you know that if p then act A is best, then you know that act A is best, and so you are rational to do A. This step involves an application of a closure principle together with a principle connecting knowledge to action: if you know that A is best, you are rational to do A. If these two principles are accepted, they claim, the argument can be strengthened to deliver a pragmatic condition on justification: S is justified in believing that p only if S is rational to act (and prefer) as if p. But what a subject is rational to do depends crucially on her practical situation: what S wants or values, what options are available to S, etc. Therefore, holding fixed a subject's evidence for a proposition p, we can vary her practical situation in such a way as to falsify the evidentialist thesis according to which two subjects with the same evidence for p will either both be justified in believing that p or neither will be.

A third sort of argument for a practical role in knowledge is provided by John Hawthorne. Suppose you have a ticket in a very large lottery with a very large payout (such that the expected utility of keeping your ticket is greater than a penny). You are offered a penny. If you knew your ticket would lose, you could reason like this: "My ticket will lose. Therefore, if I keep it, I will get nothing. If I sell it, I'll get a penny. Therefore, I should sell it." Hawthorne thinks this sort of reasoning is "intuitively awful." But how to explain its awfulness? Best, he thinks, to introduce what he calls "The Practical Environment Constraint," according to which knowledge is the norm of practical reasoning, i.e., one can legitimately use p in practical reasoning (if and) only if one knows that p. The intuitive awfulness of the above reasoning indicates that you do not know the premise that your ticket will lose. However, it seems that by varying a subject's practical situation in certain ways – e.g., by varying how much she has at stake in being right about p – we can vary whether the subject can legitimately use p in practical reasoning. Thus, it appears that Hawthorne, like Fantl and McGrath, would be sympathetic to what Stanley calls anti-intellectualism.

Hawthorne dubs his favored position 'sensitive moderate invariantism' and claims that, suitably elaborated, it allows us to satisfy the bulk of the constraints on a checklist of constraints we want any theory of knowledge to meet. Among these are a Moorean anti-skeptical constraint, an epistemic closure requirement, a need to respect a disquotational schema for 'knows,' and an Epistemic Possibility Constraint – that knowledge requires that there be no epistemic possibility of error. In particular, sensitive moderate invariantism is preferable to contextualism in its performance on this scorecard. It offers the best hope for respecting the intuitive links between knowledge, assertion, and practical reasoning.

The first six selections in this section advocate either contextualism about knowledge-attributions – according to which the truth of knowledge-attributions shifts with the attributor's context – or sensitive invariantism about knowledge attributions – according to which the truth of knowledge-attributions shifts only with the subject's context. John

MacFarlane begins his critique of both sorts of views with a helpful taxonomy of standard views about the apparent shiftiness of knowledge attributions: strict invariantism (no semantic variability of epistemic standards), sensitive invariantism (variability depending on the subject's circumstance or circumstance of evaluation), and contextualism (variability depending on the context of use). Our use of 'knows' seems to belie all three views. As against strict invariantism, we seem to employ different epistemic standards in different contexts. Yet, as against sensitive invariantism, in any fixed context of use, it appears we employ one and the same epistemic standard, not different standards for subjects in different sorts of situations. As against contextualism, we seem to treat second-order claims about whether a knowledge-attribution is true no differently than we treat the first-order question of whether a subject knows.

MacFarlane argues that there is a neglected fourth view which fits all the data: assessment relativism. The main components of MacFarlane's final view are: (1) 'knows' expresses the same relation K in all contexts of use (contrary to contextualism), (2) whether K holds between a subject and a proposition is independent of the subject's non-epistemic circumstances (contrary to sensitive invariantism), but (3) things stand in K only relative to an epistemic standard determined by the context of assessment. These three features lead to the following truth-conditions (this is a rough approximation): "S knows that p" is true relative to C_A iff S bears K to p relative to the epistemic standard determined by C_A. So consider the "stolen car" case, in which we begin by asserting "I know where my car is," and then later retract this, saying "I guess I don't know where my car is." According to MacFarlane, in our retraction we are denying the very proposition we asserted earlier, and yet we are right to do so in both cases, just as – assuming, with orthodoxy, that propositions are true relative to times – we are right to first assert and later deny the same proposition in saying "I am hungry" at t1 and then saying "I am not hungry" at t2.

Further Reading

Annis, David, "A Contextualist Theory of Epistemic Justification," *American Philosophical Quarterly* 15 (1978), pp. 213–19.

Austin, J. L., "Other Minds," in Austin, *Philosophical Papers*, 3rd edn (Oxford: Clarendon Press, 1979), pp. 76–116.

Brown, Jessica, "Adapt or Die: The Death of Invariantism?," *The Philosophical Quarterly* 55 (2005), pp. 263–85.

Cohen Stewart, "How to be a Fallibilist," *Philosophical Perspectives* 2 (1988), pp. 81–123.

——, "Skepticism and Everyday Knowledge Attributions," in Roth and Ross (eds.), *Doubting: Contemporary Perspectives on Skepticism* (Dordrecht: Kluwer Academic Publishers, 1990), pp. 161–9.

——, "Contextualism, Skepticism and the Structure of Reasons," *Philosophical Perspectives* 13 (1999), pp. 57–89.

——, "Knowledge, Speaker, and Subject," *Philosophical Quarterly* 55 (2005), pp. 199–212.

DeRose, Keith, "Contextualism and Knowledge Attributions," *Philosophy and Phenomenological Research* 52 (1992), pp. 913–29.

——, "Contextualism: An Explanation and Defense," in *The Blackwell Guide to Epistemology* (Oxford: Blackwell, 1999), pp. 187–206.

——, "Contextualism Defended: Comments on Richard Feldman's 'Skeptical Problems, Contextualist Solutions,'" *Philosophical Studies* 103 (2001), pp. 87–98.

——, "Knowledge, Assertion, and Context," *The Philosophical Review* 111, No. 2 (2002), pp. 167–203.

——, "The Ordinary Language Basis for Contextualism, and the New Invariantism," *The Philosophical Quarterly* 55 (2005), pp. 172–98.

Dretske, Fred, "The Pragmatic Dimension of Knowledge," *Philosophical Studies* 40 (1981), pp. 363–78.

Fantl, Jeremy and Matthew McGrath, "Knowledge and the Purely Epistemic: In Favor of Pragmatic Encroachment," *Philosophy and Phenomenological Research* (forthcoming).

Feldman, Richard, "Skeptical Problems, Contextualist Solutions," *Philosophical Studies* 103 (2001), pp. 61–85.

Fogelin, Robert, *Pyrrhonian Reflections on Knowledge and Justification* (Oxford: Oxford University Press, 1997).

Hambourger, Robert, "Justified Assertion and the Relativity of Knowledge," *Philosophical Studies* 51 (1987), pp. 241–69.

Hawthorne, John, *Knowledge and Lotteries* (Oxford: Clarendon Press, 2004).

Lewis, David, "Scorekeeping in a Language Game," *Journal of Philosophical Logic* 8 (1979), pp. 339–59, esp. Example 6, "Relative Modality," pp. 354–5.

MacFarlane, John, "Knowledge Laundering: Testimony and Sensitive Invariantism," *Analysis* 65 (2005), pp. 132–38.

Neta, Ram, "Contextualism and the Problem of the External World," *Philosophy and Phenomenological Research* 66 (2003), pp. 1–31.

Schaffer, Jonathan, "From Contextualism to Contrastivism," *Philosophical Studies* 119 (2004), pp. 73–103.

——, "The Irrelevance of the Subject: Against Subject-Sensitive Invariantism," *Philosophical Studies* 127 (2006), pp. 87–107.

Schiffer, Stephen, "Contextualist Solutions to Scepticism," *Proceedings of the Aristotelian Society* 96 (1996), pp. 249–61.

Sosa, Ernest, "Chisholm's Epistemology and Epistemic Internalism," in Lewis Hahn (ed.), *The Philosophy of Roderick Chisholm* (Chicago: Open Court, 1997), pp. 267–87.

——, "Contextualism and Skepticism," *Philosophical Issues* 10 (1999), pp. 94–107.

Stanley, Jason, *Knowledge and Practical Interests* (Oxford: Oxford University Press, 2005).

Unger, Peter, *Philosophical Relativity* (Minneapolis: University of Minnesota Press, 1984).

——, "The Cone Model of Knowledge," *Philosophical Topics* 14 (1986), pp. 125–78.

Weatherson, Brian, "Can we do without Pragmatic Encroachment?," *Philosophical Perspectives* 19 (2005), pp. 417–43.

Williamson, Timothy, "Contextualism, Subject-Sensitive Invariantism, and Knowledge of Knowledge," *Philosophical Quarterly* 55 (2005), pp. 213–35.

Wittgenstein, Ludwig, *On Certainty* (New York: Harper and Row, 1972).

CHAPTER 47

Solving the Skeptical Problem

Keith DeRose

1 The Puzzle of Skeptical Hypotheses

Many of the most celebrated, intriguing, and powerful skeptical arguments proceed by means of skeptical hypotheses. Brutally pared to their barest essentials, they are roughly of the following form, where "*O*" is a proposition about the external world one would *ordinarily* think one knows (e.g., I have hands[1]) and "*H*" is a suitably chosen skeptical *hypothesis* (e.g., I am a bodiless brain in a vat who has been electrochemically stimulated to have precisely those sensory experiences I've had, henceforth a "BIV"[2]):

> *The Argument from Ignorance* (AI)[3]
> 1. I don't know that not-*H*.
> 2. If I don't know that not-H, then I don't know that *O*. So,
> C. I don't know that *O*.[4]

Setting aside the distracting side issues that immediately threaten from all directions, and keeping AI in this stark, uncomplicated form, I will, in what follows, present and defend, at least in broad outline, the correct solution to the puzzle AI confronts us with. And AI does present us with a puzzle, because, for reasons we'll investigate in later sections, each of its premises is initially plausible,

Originally published in *The Philosophical Review* 104, 1 (1995), pp. 1–7, 17–52.

when *H* is well chosen. For however improbable or even bizarre it may seem to suppose that I am a BIV, it also seems that I don't know that I'm not one. How *could* I know such a thing? And it also seems that if, for all I know, I am a BIV, then I don't know that I have hands. How could I know that I have hands if, for all I know, I'm bodiless (and therefore handless)? But, at the same time, it initially seems that I do know that I have hands. So two plausible premises yield a conclusion whose negation we also find plausible. So something plausible has to go. But what? And equally importantly, how?

To be sure, the premises are only plausible, not compelling. Thus, we will always have recourse to the Moorean reaction to this argument: Declare that it is more certain that one knows that one has hands than it is that either of the premises of the argument is true (much less that their conjunction is true), and therefore reject one of those premises, rather than accept the conclusion. But also available is the skeptical reaction, which is to accept the conclusion.

But we should hope for a better treatment of the argument than simply choosing which of the three individually plausible propositions – the two premises and the negation of the conclusion – seems least certain and rejecting it on the grounds that the other two are true. In seeking a solution to this puzzle, we should seek an explanation of how we fell into this skeptical trap in the first place, and not settle for making a simple choice among three distasteful ways out of the trap. We must explain how two premises that together yield a conclusion we find so incredible can themselves seem so plausible to us. Only with such an explanation in place can we proceed with confidence and with understanding to free ourselves from the trap.

Many of those working on AI in recent years seem to have understood this.[5] And I have good news to report: Substantial progress towards finally solving this skeptical puzzle has been made along two quite different fronts. The bad news is that, as I shall argue, neither approach has solved the puzzle. But the culminating good news is that, as I will also argue, the new solution I present here, which incorporates important aspects of each of the two approaches, *can* finally solve this perennially thorny philosophical problem. While more details and precision will be called for in the resulting solution than I will provide, there will be enough meat on the bones to make it plausible that the fully articulated solution lies in the direction I point to here.

In sections 2–4 of this paper, I explore the contextualist approach to the problem of skepticism, and show why it has thus far fallen short of solving the puzzle. In sections 3–7, I turn to Robert Nozick's attempt to solve our puzzle. Since the shortcomings of Nozick's treatment of knowledge and skepticism have been, at least to my satisfaction, duly demonstrated by others, it will not be my purpose here to rehearse those shortcomings, but rather to explore and expand upon the substantial insight that remains intact in Nozick's account. In sections 8–14, I present and defend my own contextualist solution, which I argue is the best solution to our puzzle. Since, as I argue in sections 12–14, the skeptic's own solution, according to which we accept AI's conclusion, is among the solutions inferior to the one I present, AI does not successfully support that conclusion.

2   Contextualist Solutions: The Basic Strategy

Suppose a speaker A (for "*attributor*") says, "S knows that *P*," of a subject S's true belief that *P*. According to contextualist theories of knowledge attributions, how strong an epistemic position S must be in with respect to *P* for A's assertion to be

true can vary according to features of A's conversational context.[6]

Contextualist theories of knowledge attributions have almost invariably been developed with an eye toward providing some kind of answer to philosophical skepticism. For skeptical arguments like AI threaten to show, not only that we fail to meet very high requirements for knowledge of interest only to misguided philosophers seeking absolute certainty, but that we don't meet even the truth conditions of ordinary, out-on-the-street knowledge attributions. They thus threaten to establish the startling result that we never, or almost never, truthfully ascribe knowledge to ourselves or to other mere mortals.

But, according to contextualists, the skeptic, in presenting her argument, manipulates the semantic standards for knowledge, thereby creating a context in which she can *truthfully* say that we know nothing or very little.[7] Once the standards have been so raised, we *correctly* sense that we only could falsely claim to know such things as that we have hands. Why then are we puzzled? Why don't we simply accept the skeptic's conclusion and henceforth refrain from ascribing such knowledge to ourselves or others? Because, the contextualist continues, we also realize this: As soon as we find ourselves in more ordinary conversational contexts, it will not only be true for us to claim to know the very things that the skeptic now denies we know, but it will also be wrong for us to deny that we know these things. But then, isn't the skeptic's present denial equally false? And wouldn't it be equally true for us now, in the skeptic's presence, to claim to know?

What we fail to realize, according to the contextualist solution, is that the skeptic's present denials that we know various things are perfectly compatible with our ordinary claims to know those very propositions. Once we realize this, we can see how both the skeptic's denials of knowledge and our ordinary attributions of knowledge can be correct.

Thus, it is hoped, our ordinary claims to know can be safeguarded from the apparently powerful attack of the skeptic, while, at the same time, the persuasiveness of the skeptical argument is explained. For the fact that the skeptic can invoke very high standards that we don't live up to has no tendency to show that we don't satisfy the more relaxed standards that are in place in more ordinary conversations and debates.

Three important points about contextualist strategies as described above should be made before I move on. First, this type of strategy will leave untouched the timid skeptic who purports by AI merely to be establishing the weak claim that in some (perhaps "high" or "philosophical") sense (perhaps induced by the presentation of AI) we don't know the relevant *O*, while not even purporting to establish the bold thesis that our ordinary claims to know that same proposition are false. Whether such a timid skeptical stance is of any interest is a topic for another paper. The contextualist strategy is important because AI initially seems to threaten the truth of our ordinary claims – it threatens to boldly show that we've been wrong all along in thinking and saying that we know this and that. For it doesn't seem as if it's just in some "high" or "philosophical" sense that AI's premises are true: They seem true in the ordinary sense of "know." In fact, one is initially tempted to say that there's *no* good sense in which I know that I'm not a BIV or in which I can know I have hands if I don't know that I'm not a BIV. How (and whether) to avoid the bold skeptical result is puzzle enough.

Second, in presenting the contextualist strategy, I have above assumed a skeptic-friendly version of contextualism – one according to which the philosophical skeptic can (fairly easily), and does, succeed in raising the standards for knowledge in such a way as to make her denials of knowledge true. Some contextualists may think that it's not so easy to so raise the standards for knowledge, and that a determined opponent of the skeptic can, by not letting the skeptic get away with raising them, keep the standards low. But the important point is to identify the mechanism by which the skeptic at least threatens to raise the standards for knowledge. Whether the skeptic actually succeeds against a determined opponent in so raising the standards is of little importance. To safeguard ordinary claims to know while at the same time explaining the persuasiveness of the skeptical arguments (which is the goal of his strategy), the contextualist can provisionally *assume* a skeptic-friendly version of contextualism, leaving it as an open question whether and under which conditions the skeptic actually succeeds at raising the standards. The contextualist's ultimate point will then be this: To the extent that the skeptic *does* succeed, she does so only by raising the standards

for knowledge, and so the success of her argument has no tendency to show that our ordinary claims to know are in any way defective.

Third, AI can be puzzling even when one is not in the presence of a skeptic who is presenting it. The argument has about the same degree of intuitive appeal when one is just considering it by oneself, without anybody's *saying* anything. But the contextualist explanation, as described above, involves the standards for knowledge being changed by what's being said in a conversation.[8] For the most part, I will frame the contextualist explanation in terms of such conversational rules, largely because that's what been done by my contextualist predecessors, with whom I want to make contact. But we must realize that the resulting solution will have to be generalized to explain why the argument can be so appealing even when one is considering it in solitude, with nothing being said. The basic idea of the generalization will take either or both of the following two forms. First, it can be maintained that there is a rule for the changing of the standards for knowledge that governs the truth conditions of our *thoughts* regarding what is and is not known that mirrors the rule for the truth conditions of what is *said* regarding knowledge. In that case, an analogue of the contextualist solution can be given for thought, according to which the premises and conclusion of AI are truly thought, but my true thought that, say, I don't know that I have hands, had when in the grip of AI, will be compatible with my thought, made in another context, that I do know that very thing. Second, our judgment regarding whether something can or cannot be truly asserted (under appropriate conditions) might be held to affect our judgment regarding whether it's true or false, even when we make this judgment in solitude, with nothing being said at all. That the premises of AI could be truly asserted, then, makes them (at least) seem true even when they're just being thought.

My own solution will employ the basic contextualist strategy explained in this section. But, as should be apparent already, we haven't explained the persuasiveness of AI, and thus haven't solved our puzzle, if we haven't located and explained the conversational rule or mechanism by which the skeptic raises (or threatens to raise) the standards for knowledge. And here contextualists have had little to offer.

3   The Subjunctive Conditionals Account (SCA) of the Plausibility of AI's First Premise

The main stumbling block of other contextualist solutions has been a failure to explain what it is about skeptical hypotheses that makes it so plausible to suppose that we don't know that they're false. This point of weakness in the contextualist solutions is the particular point of strength of Nozick's treatment of AI in his *Philosophical Explanations* (1981). In this and the following three sections I'll present and defend the *Subjunctive Conditionals Account* (SCA) of the plausibility of AI's first premise, which I've abstracted from Nozick's account of knowledge and skepticism.

According to SCA, the problem with my belief that I'm not a BIV – and I do have such a belief, as do most of us – is that I would have this belief (that I'm not a BIV) even if it were false (even if I were one). It is this that makes it hard to claim to *know* that I'm not a BIV. For, according to SCA, we have a very strong general, though not exceptionless, inclination to think that we don't know that *P* when we think that our belief that *P* is a belief we would hold even if *P* were false. Let's say that S's belief that *P* is *insensitive* if S would believe that *P* if *P* were false. SCA's generalization can then be restated as follows: We tend to judge that S doesn't know that *P* when we think S's belief that *P* is insensitive.

As is well worth noting, this general inclination explains the operation of nonphilosophical skeptical hypotheses that are far less radical than the BIV hypothesis or even the painted mule hypothesis. Just so, it serves to explain why, even though I feel inclined to say that I know the Bulls won their game last night because I read the result in a single newspaper, I still feel strongly pulled toward admitting the (mildly) skeptical claim that I don't know that the paper isn't mistaken about which team won: I realize that my belief that the paper isn't mistaken is a belief I would hold even if it were false (even if the paper were mistaken).

Indeed, after encountering a couple of instances of AI with different skeptical hypotheses plugged into the "*H*" slot (for example, the BIV, the painted mules, and the mistaken paper hypotheses), one develops a sense of what makes

for an effective skeptical hypothesis and, thus, an ability to construct convincing instances of AI oneself. To make AI's second premise convincing, it is usually sufficient (though not necessary) that *H* be incompatible with *O*. But what about the first premise? To make *it* convincing, we instinctively look for a hypothesis that elicits in the listener both the belief that the hypothesis doesn't obtain and an acknowledgement that this belief is one she would hold even if the hypothesis *did* obtain.

Upon hearing the hypothesis, typically one can't help but projecting oneself into it. How would things seem to me if that situation obtained? Well, pretty much (or sometimes exactly) as they actually seem to me. And, so, what would I believe if such a "strange" situation obtained? Pretty much (or exactly) what I actually believe. For example, and in particular, if I *were* a BIV, I would believe every bit as firmly as I actually do that I *wasn't* one. But if this belief is one I would hold even if it were false, how can I be in a position to tell that, or discern that, or *know* that, it's true?

As I've just hinted, a similar explanation, in terms of subjunctive conditionals, can explain the plausibility of the other ways we feel inclined to describe our seemingly limited epistemic position vis-à-vis effective skeptical hypotheses. Consider especially the description involving "ruling out." In a normal zoo setting, most of us would take ourselves to know that the animals in the zebra cage are zebras. From this, it seems, we should be able to infer that they're not cleverly painted mules, since zebras aren't mules. So why are we reluctant to count our seeing the zebras and performing this inference as a case of ruling out the painted mule hypothesis? Because, the explanation goes, even after performing the inference, it still seems we would believe the observed animals weren't painted mules if they were precisely that. Why does it seem we can't tell that they're not painted mules? Because we would believe they weren't even if they were. Ditto for why we seemingly can't discern that they're not and why it seems we can't distinguish their being cleverly painted mules from their not being such, etc.

Also worth noting is the usefulness of SCA in explaining our reluctance to ascribe knowledge in certain lottery situations. Even where the odds of your being a loser are astronomically high (there are 20 million tickets, only one of which is a winner, and you have but one ticket), it can seem that you don't know that you're a loser of a fair lottery if the winner hasn't yet been announced. SCA accounts for this seeming: Your belief that you're a loser is one you would hold even if you were the winner.

SCA is a powerful explanation. But there are problems. As I suggested above, there are exceptions to the general inclination to which SCA appeals: There are cases in which it seems to us that some S does know that P even though we judge that S would believe that P even if P were false. Some of these exceptions will be quickly discussed in sections 4 and 5 below. The first and main point to make regarding such exceptions, of course, is that this very general inclination needn't be exceptionless to perform the explanatory role SCA assigns it. In section 6 we will see strong grounds for endorsing SCA as being at least on the right track despite the exceptions to the generalization to which it appeals. But these exceptions are still worth examining, for they will indicate certain important directions in which SCA can be improved, even though we won't be in a position to make SCA ideally precise here.

4   SCA, Grandmothers, and Methods

First, then, consider a case discussed by Nozick:

> A grandmother sees her grandson is well when he comes to visit; but if he were sick or dead, others would tell her he was well to spare her upset. Yet this does not mean she doesn't know he is well (or at least ambulatory) when she sees him. (1981, p. 179)

Here, it seems, the grandmother knows her grandson is well, though it can seem that she doesn't satisfy the third condition of a preliminary form of Nozick's analysis of S knows that P, which is:

(3) If p weren't true, S wouldn't believe that p.

Nozick's response is to relativize this third condition to the method by which S has come to believe that P, yielding:

(3)   If p weren't true and S were to use M to arrive at a belief whether (or not) p, then S wouldn't believe, via M, that p (179),

where "M" is the method by which S has come to believe that P.[9]

Unlike Nozick, I'm not presenting an analysis of propositional knowledge. But his grandmother case also seems to be an exception to the general inclination SCA appeals to: Here we're not at all inclined to think the grandmother doesn't know her grandson is well, even though it can seem that if he weren't well, she would still believe he was. The generalization SCA utilizes says that we tend to judge that S doesn't know where S does not satisfy Nozick's third condition for knowledge. One possibility here is to follow Nozick *very* closely by modifying that generalization so that it refers to Nozick's modified, rather than his original, third condition, and thus, like Nozick, explicitly relativizing our account to the method by which S believes that P.

Often, though, context takes care of this for us. Even to one aware of the likelihood that the grandmother's family would have kept her in the dark about her grandson's condition were he not well, it *can* seem that even Nozick's initial formulation of the third condition for knowledge is met by the grandmother. On one way of evaluating that simple conditional, it seems that if the grandson were not well, the grandmother would *not* believe he was well. After all, she's looking right at him! The standard possible-worlds semantics for counterfactual conditionals can illuminate what's going on here. When one searches for the possible worlds most similar to the actual world in which the grandson is not well, the respects in which the possible worlds are to resemble the actual world is a highly context-sensitive matter. Especially where the context focuses one's attention on the grandmother and her cognitive and recognitional abilities, one *can* place heavy weight upon similarity with respect to the method she is using to arrive at her belief, and then it can seem that in the closest world in which the grandson is not well, she's looking right at him and seeing that he's not well, and so does *not* believe he is well. On this way of evaluating the conditional, the grandmother *does* satisfy even the initial formulation of Nozick's third condition, and she's no counter-example to the generalization utilized by SCA. But, in evaluating that simple conditional, one can also stress other similarities, particularly ones involving the propensities and plans of the various family members (or whatever facts ground the judgment that if her grandson weren't well, the grandmother would be effectively lied to), to reach the verdict that if he were not well, she *would* believe that he was well.

We can sharpen SCA by specifying that we tend to judge that S doesn't know when she fails to satisfy Nozick's initial formulation of (3), where (3) is evaluated in such a way that heavy emphasis is put upon similarity with respect to the method of belief formation utilized by S, or, following Nozick, we can insert a specification of the method into the antecedent of (3).[10] But in neither case is this to make a very precise modification; rather, it merely indicates the direction in which a more precise account might lie, for any such use of the notion of *methods* of belief formation in our account invites a host of questions (many of which Nozick wrestles with) involving how such methods are to be specified and individuated.

5   SCA and Some Skeptical Hypotheses That Don't Work

Certain instances of AI aren't very persuasive. The first premise of the argument can be quite unconvincing despite the fact that SCA predicts that we'd find it plausible. Suppose, for instance, that in an attempt to show by AI that I don't know I have hands, a skeptic utilizes, instead of the BIV hypothesis, the following simple *H*: I falsely believe that I have hands. The resulting instance of AI seems to pack little or no more punch than a simple skeptic's unsupported claim that I don't know I have hands. It's at the first premise that this ill-fated instance of AI fizzles. But my belief that I don't falsely believe that I have hands is insensitive: If this belief were false (if I did falsely believe that I have hands) I would still believe it was true (I'd still believe that I don't falsely believe that I have hands). Likewise insensitive is my belief that the following hypothesis is false: I'm an intelligent dog who's always incorrectly thinking that I have hands. If this belief of mine were false (if I were such a deluded intelligent dog) I'd still

believe it was true (I'd still believe that I wasn't such a creature). So SCA, as it has so far been formulated, predicts that it will seem to us that the above beliefs don't amount to knowledge and that we'll find plausible the first premise of AI that results when the above hypotheses are used. But in fact these instances of AI's first premise are far from convincing. As opposed to the BIV hypothesis, it seems that one *does* know that the deluded dog hypothesis and the simple false belief hypothesis are false.

Again, the main point to make here is that SCA's generalization needn't be exceptionless to be explanatory. While a more precisely Chisholmed refinement of SCA might not have the negations of these ineffective *H*'s as instances of those propositions it says we tend to judge we don't know, I'll here just make a preliminary observation as to what might be going wrong. Part of the problem with these "hypotheses" is that they don't give us much of an idea of *how* I come to have the false belief they assign to me. Hypotheses are supposed to explain; skeptical hypotheses should explain how we might come to believe something despite its being false. The first of these hypotheses simply stipulates that I'm wrong about my having hands, without indicating how I came to be so sadly mistaken. The second adds to the first that I'm a dog, which adds little to our understanding of how my mistake about having hands came about. By contrast, when we encounter effective skeptical hypotheses, we have some understanding of how (if *H* is true) we have come to falsely believe that *O*. If either of our ineffective hypotheses is filled in so as to make it clear to us how I came to falsely believe I have hands, it becomes effective.

SCA's generalization was this: We tend to judge that S doesn't know that *P* when we think that S's belief that *P* is insensitive (when we think that S would believe *P* even if *P* were false). The limitation of SCA's generalization that's suggested by these cases is this: We *don't* so judge ourselves ignorant of *P* where not-*P* implies something we take ourselves to know to be false, without providing an explanation of how we came to falsely believe this thing we think we know. Thus, *I falsely believe that I have hands* implies that I don't have hands. Since I do take myself to know that I have hands (*this* belief isn't insensitive), and since the above italicized proposition doesn't explain how I went wrong with respect to my having hands, I'll judge that I do know that proposition to be false. But this again is just a preliminary statement, and there's room for a lot more refinement here. What we need now is some assurance that we're headed in the right direction.

6   SCA Confirmed

Such assurance is to be found by considering what it would take to make it seem to us that we *do* know skeptical hypotheses to be false.

But let's first reconsider the lottery case. As noted above in section 3, we are puzzling reluctant to claim knowledge in certain lottery situations. The explanation provided by SCA for this phenomenon is intuitively appealing: It does seem that the fact that we would believe that we were losers even if we were winners is largely what's behind our judgment that we don't know we're losers. SCA receives further powerful support when we consider the grounds that *do* seem to us sufficient for knowledge of one's being a loser. In the lottery situation, even a very minute chance of being wrong seems to deprive one of knowledge. But if we're going to worry about even such minute chances of error, then why does it seem that you do know you're a loser after the winning number has been announced on the radio and you've compared the numbers on your ticket with the sadly different numbers announced? After all, radio announcements *can* be in error; what you're hearing *may* not be a real radio announcement but the voice of a friend who's rigged up a practical joke; you *might* be suffering from some weird momentary visual illusion and misreading the numbers on your ticket; and so forth. All very remote possibilities, to be sure. But, since we're already countenancing even the most minute chances of error, why don't these possibilities rob us of knowledge even after the announcement has been made and heard?

SCA's explanation of why we don't think we know *before* the announcement is made is that we at that time judge that if we weren't losers, we'd still believe that we were. Note that once you've heard the announcement of the winning numbers and compared them with the numbers on your ticket, it *no longer* seems that if you had been the winner, you'd believe you were a loser. Rather,

we judge that in that case you'd now believe you were the winner or would at least be suspending judgment as you frantically double-checked the match. It's very impressive that the very occurrence that would suffice to make it seem to us that you do know you're a loser (the radio announcement) also reverses our judgment regarding the truth of the conditional appealed to in SCA to explain why it seems to us that you don't know before the announcement is made. The occurrence which gets us to judge that we know here also removes what SCA posits as the block to our judging that we know. This is an indication that SCA has correctly identified the block.

SCA similarly provides a very intuitively appealing explanation for why it seems to us that we don't know that skeptical hypotheses are false, as was also noted in section 3. It again receives powerful further confirmation as we look to cases in which one seemingly does know that a skeptical hypothesis doesn't obtain (cases in which skeptical hypotheses that are ordinarily effective fail to be effective). The boastful zoologist I have introduced elsewhere [who invokes his extensive knowledge of zebra and mule anatomy], it seems, knows that the animals in the zebra cage are not cleverly painted mules, while I, it seems, do not. But the very anatomical knowledge that seemingly enables him to know they're not painted mules also has the consequence that if the animals *were* cleverly painted mules, the zoologist, unlike me, would *not* believe that they weren't. And although I don't seem to know they're not painted mules simply by looking at them, I could, it seems, get to know this if I undertook some special investigation – perhaps, as has been suggested in the literature (Stine 1976, p. 252), one involving paint remover. *Which* special investigations would do the trick (and under which circumstances would they)? A survey of various scenarios yields an impressive correlation: The investigations that would seemingly allow me to know that the animals aren't painted mules would also affect our judgment as to the truth value of the subjunctive conditional so critical to SCA. Once I have completed the investigation, it seems that I, like the zoologist, would *not* believe that the animals weren't painted mules if in fact they were. Likewise, by checking appropriately independent sources, I could get myself into a position in which I seemingly *would* know that the newspaper isn't mistaken about whether the Bulls won last night. But the checks that would seemingly allow this knowledge would also make it seem that if the paper were mistaken, I would *not* believe it wasn't. Again and again, SCA posits a certain block to our judging that we know, and the changes that would clear the way for our judging that we know also remove this block. This makes it difficult not to believe that SCA is at least roughly correct.

In the case of the BIV hypothesis, it's hard to test SCA in this way, for it's difficult to imagine a situation in which it seems a subject does know that she's not a BIV. But this only confirms SCA: While it's difficult to imagine a situation in which one seems to know that one's not a BIV, it's likewise difficult to imagine circumstances in which the block SCA posits is removed. It's difficult, that is, to imagine a situation in which someone believes they're not a BIV but in which the conditional *If S were a BIV, then S would believe she wasn't a BIV* isn't true. For, as the BIV hypothesis is formulated, one's brain is electrochemically stimulated so that one has precisely those sensory experiences one actually has had. But wouldn't one then have formed precisely those beliefs that one actually has formed, including the belief that one's not a BIV?

It seems that this explanation, SCA, for the plausibility of AI's first premise must be (at least roughly) correct and, therefore, that it points to part of the solution to our puzzle.

Indeed, some readers will wonder why I have claimed only that our general tendency not to count insensitive beliefs as instances of knowledge explains that premise's plausibility and have stopped short of accepting sensitivity as a necessary condition for knowledge[11] and therefore simply endorsing that first premise as true. But while we've just seen strong grounds for simply accepting AI's first premise, there are also strong grounds for accepting AI's second premise and for accepting the denial of its conclusion. We have to stop short somewhere; we can't simply accept all three members of this triad as true. To solve this puzzle, I'll claim that AI's first premise, while not *simply* true, is true according to unusually high standards for knowledge. But, I'll argue, my solution explains why that premise seems true and, more generally, why sensitivity seems necessary for knowledge. If my solution provides the

best explanation for how all three members of our puzzling triad seem true, that will be good reason for stopping short where my solution tells us to, rather than where one of its inferior rivals – bold skepticism, for example – tells us to.

7 Nozick's Own Solution and the Abominable Conjunction

Nozick's own treatment of AI, from which SCA was abstracted, fails. This treatment is based on Nozick's account of knowledge as true, *sensitive* belief, where, very roughly, one's true belief that *P* is sensitive to the truth value of *P* if one would not have believed that *P* if *P* had been false.[12] Thus, Nozick's treatment of AI involves accepting the skeptic's first premise. But, at the same time, and much more unfortunately, it also involves denying the second. You *don't* know that you're not a BIV, Nozick claims, because any belief you might have to this effect is insensitive: You would have held this belief even if it were false (even if you were a BIV). By contrast, Nozick claims, your belief that you have hands *is* a sensitive belief: If *it* were false – if you didn't have hands – you would not hold it. So you do know you have hands even though you don't know that you're not a BIV. The skeptic's mistake – the second premise – is supposing that you can know you have hands only if you also know that you're not a BIV.

Or so Nozick claims. This is not the place for a general evaluation of Nozick's analysis of propositional knowledge, so let us confine ourselves to the results of this analysis as applied to the beliefs in question in AI. Here Nozick's account does very well in issuing the intuitively correct verdict for the relevant particular judgments regarding what is known and what is not. Most of us would judge that we do know such things as that we have hands, and this is Nozick's verdict. And, when a skeptical hypothesis is well chosen, it does seem quite plausible to most of us that we don't know that it doesn't obtain. But there are three relevant issues to our puzzle: Is the first premise of AI true? Is the second premise true? Is the conclusion true? And it's easy to endorse the intuitively correct answer to two out of the three questions if you're willing to take the implausible stand on the remaining one.

Nozick takes his implausible stand on the issue of the second premise, denying it in the face of its evident intuitive appeal.[13] Accepting his treatment involves embracing the abominable conjunction that while you don't know you're not a bodiless (and handless!) BIV, still, you know you have hands. Thus, while his account does quite well on the relevant particular intuitions regarding what is and isn't known, it yields an intuitively bizarre result on the comparative judgment the second premise embodies.[14]

As promised, I won't here rehearse the powerful objections to Nozick's analysis of propositional knowledge that have been put forward,[15] but, assuming that this analysis isn't independently convincing before we turn to the problem of skeptical hypotheses,[16] we're left with little reason to follow Nozick in choosing to take an implausible stand precisely where he has rather than someplace else.

This leaves us in a bind. For, as we saw in sections 3 and 6 above, SCA is quite powerful. That explanation is that we realize that any belief we might have to the effect that an (effective) skeptical hypothesis doesn't obtain is insensitive, and we're inclined to think that insensitive beliefs don't constitute knowledge. How can we appropriate that explanation without following Nozick in having to implausibly deny the second premise of AI and embrace the abominable conjunction?

8 Strength of Epistemic Position and AI's Second Premise

Here's how: by incorporating SCA into a contextualist solution to our puzzle that avoids such a fumbling of AI's second premise. Indeed, I propose a *very* strong endorsement of that second premise.

Recall that according to contextualist theories of knowledge attributions, how strong a subject's epistemic position must be to make true a speaker's attribution of knowledge to that subject is a flexible matter that can vary according to features of the speaker's conversational context. Central to contextualism, then, is the notion of *(relative) strength of epistemic position*. In presenting and defending contextualism, I've found that most listeners feel that they understand pretty well what's meant when I claim, for instance, that

sometimes the standards for knowledge are higher than usual, or that in some conversational situations one's epistemic position must be stronger than in others to count as knowing. But it would be good to clarify this important notion of strength of epistemic position as best we can by, for instance, supplying an intuitive test for when one epistemic position is stronger than another. The best such device is that of *comparative conditionals*. One can have a variety of grounds for assenting to conditionals like *If Mugsy is tall, then Wilt is tall*, and *If Wilt is not tall, then Mugsy is not tall*. But one very good basis for assenting to these conditionals is the comparative knowledge that Wilt is at least as tall as Mugsy. Likewise, where S is a putative subject of knowledge, P is a true proposition that S believes, and A and B are situations in which S is found, we can have similarly comparative grounds for assenting to conditionals of the form *If S knows that P in A, then S knows that P in B*. In such a case, the comparative grounds for our assent is our realization that S is in *at least as strong* an epistemic position with respect to P in situation B as he is in with respect to that same proposition in situation A, and this comparative conditional serves as a good intuitive test for that comparative fact: It brings that fact to light.

So, for instance, to borrow some examples from Alvin Goldman (1976), let Henry be our subject, and let *What Henry is seeing is a barn* be the thing Henry putatively knows. Both in situation F (for "fakes") and in situation N ("no fakes"), Henry is driving through the countryside and, having no reason to think there's anything unusual going on, very firmly believes, and takes himself to know, that the object he's seeing is a barn. And indeed, in both cases, it is a barn. But in F, unbeknownst to him, Henry is in an area that is filled with very convincing fake barns – papier-mâché barn façades. In fact, we may suppose that Henry has just been fooled more than twenty times by such fakes, although he's now looking at the only actual barn for miles around, and so this time truly believes that what he's seeing is a barn. N is exactly like F, except that there are no fakes in the area – the things Henry has taken to be barns have all actually been barns. With regard to these examples, the conditional *If Henry knows in F, then he knows in N* seems to get the comparison right, indicating that Henry's in at least as strong an epistemic position in situation N as he is in situation F. The evident failure of *If Henry knows in N, then he knows in F* to get the comparison right shows that Henry's not in as strong a position to know in F as in N. Together, these results indicate that Henry's in a stronger epistemic position in N than in F.

As is important to our discussion of AI's second premise, comparative conditionals can similarly be used to test the relative strength of epistemic position of a single subject with respect to *different propositions* that subject believes in the same situation: Thus, the intuitive correctness of *If S knows that P, then S knows that Q* and *If S doesn't know that Q then S doesn't know that P* can indicate that S is in at least as strong an epistemic position with respect to Q as she's in with respect to P.[17]

Sometimes no clear verdict results when we attempt to evaluate a conditional in this comparative way, for the good reason that it's unclear how the two epistemic positions we're evaluating compare with one another. Thus, if we compare a situation in which Henry has a good look at the barn but in which there are a couple of fake barns several miles away that Henry hasn't encountered with a situation in which there are no fakes at all in Henry's vicinity but in which he doesn't have quite as good a look at the barn, the relevant conditionals can be difficult to evaluate. But, in many instances, some of the relevant conditionals *are* clearly true on comparative grounds.

Such is the case with instances of AI's second premise, where the skeptical hypothesis is well chosen. They seem true and *are* true, I suggest, for just this comparative reason: As we realize, we *are* in at least as good a position to know that the hypothesis is false as we're in to know the targeted piece of presumed ordinary knowledge.[18] Let's look briefly at some instances. Recall the following epistemologically perplexing pairs of propositions:

not-H	O
I'm not a BIV.	I have hands.
Those animals aren't just cleverly painted mules.	Those animals are zebras.
The paper isn't mistaken about whether the Bulls won last night.	The Bulls won last night.

Given natural background assumptions, we can sense that the following comparative fact holds for each of the above pairs: I am in no better a position to know that O than I am in to know that not-H. This comparative fact is revealed in each case by the highly plausible conditional that is AI's second premise: If I don't know that not-H, then I don't know that O. Closely tied to that comparative fact in each case is the related and intuitively compelling realization that it would be no wiser to bet one's immortal soul on O's being true than to bet it on not-H's being true.

I propose then to accept the relevant conditional with respect to each of the above pairs, and to accept other convincing instances of AI's second premise. Indeed, these conditionals are true *regardless of how high or low the standards for knowledge are set*. Just as the comparative fact that Wilt is at least as tall as Mugsy has the result that the conditional *If Wilt is not tall, then Mugsy is not tall* will be true regardless of how high or low the standards for tallness are set so the comparative fact that I'm in at least as strong an epistemic position with respect to not-H as I'm in with respect to O will result in *If I don't know that not-H, then I don't know that O* being true regardless of how high or low the standards for knowledge are set. Thus, we will never have to follow Nozick in accepting the abominable conjunction: that conjunction is false at any epistemic standard.

With that ringing endorsement of AI's second premise anchored firmly in place, we can return to the first premise, hoping to incorporate SCA into a contextualist account of that premise's plausibility.

9   Strength and Sensitivity

As has become very apparent, two notions that are central to my attempt to solve our puzzle are, on the one hand, the Nozickean notion of the sensitivity of beliefs and, on the other, the notion of strength of epistemic position. While both notions stand in need of a good deal of sharpening and explanation (only some of which they'll receive here), we've already obtained interesting results applying them to the epistemologically perplexing pairs of propositions displayed above. In each case, one's belief in O is sensitive, while one's belief in not-H is insensitive. Yet, at the same time, one is in at least as strong an epistemic position with respect to not-*H* as one is in with respect to *O*.

For each of the second and third pairs of propositions, one could gather further evidence, strengthen one's epistemic position with respect to both not-*H* and *O*, and *make* even one's belief that not-*H* sensitive. But even before this further evidence is gathered, one's belief that *O* is *already* sensitive, despite the fact that one is in no stronger an epistemic position with respect to this *O* than one is in with respect to not-*H*. (With respect to the first pair of propositions, it is difficult to imagine a situation in which one is in such a strong position with respect to one's not being a BIV that this belief is sensitive.)

This leads us to an important insight regarding skeptical hypotheses: One's epistemic position with respect to propositions to the effect that skeptical hypotheses don't hold must be stronger than it is with respect to other, more ordinary propositions (e.g., our above *O*s) if belief in such propositions is to be sensitive.

An explanation of our two central notions in terms of possible worlds will provide a partial and quite rough-and-ready, but still somewhat enlightening, picture of how this situation can arise. An important component of being in a strong epistemic position with respect to *P* is to have one's belief as to whether *P* is true match the fact of the matter as to whether *P* is true, not only in the actual world, but also at the worlds sufficiently close to the actual world. That is, one's belief should not only be true, but should be non-accidentally true, where this requires one's belief as to whether *P* is true to match the fact of the matter at nearby worlds. The further away one can get from the actual world, while still having it be the case that one's belief matches the fact at worlds that far away and closer, the stronger a position one is in with respect to *P*. (Recalling the results of section 4, we should remember either to restrict our attention solely to those worlds in which the subject uses the same method of belief-formation she uses in the actual world, or to weigh similarity with respect to the subject's method very heavily in determining the closeness of possible worlds to the actual world.) If the truth-tracking of one's belief as to whether *P* extends far enough from actuality to reach the closest not-*P* worlds, then one doesn't believe that

P in those closest not-*P* worlds, and one's belief that *P* is sensitive. But how far from actuality must truth-tracking reach – how strong an epistemic position must one be in – to make one's belief that *P* sensitive? That, of course, depends on how distant from actuality the closest not-*P* worlds are.

Consider my belief that I have hands. I believe this at the actual world, and it's true. What's more, in the other nearby worlds in which I have hands, I believe that I do. There are also, at least in my own case, some alarmingly close worlds in which I don't have hands. These include worlds in which I lost my hands years ago while working on my uncle's garbage truck. In the closest of these not-*P* worlds, I'm now fully aware of the fact that I'm handless, and my belief as to whether I have hands matches the fact of the matter. My belief as to whether I have hands doesn't match the fact in various worlds in which I'm a BIV, of course, but these are *very* distant. While there are closer worlds in which the match fails, it seems that in a fairly wide range of worlds surrounding the actual world, my belief as to whether I have hands does a good job of matching the fact of the matter. Thus, I'm in a pretty strong epistemic position with respect to that matter.

Now let *P* be *I'm not a BIV*. Where not-*P* (here, *I am a BIV*) is quite remote, one can be in a quite strong epistemic position with respect to *P* merely by believing that *P* in all the nearby worlds. As I do believe this *P* in such nearby worlds, I'm in a pretty strong epistemic position with respect to this *P*. This can occur, and in my case, does occur, even though one's belief as to whether *P* doesn't match the fact of the matter in the closest not-*P* worlds: Since even the closest of the not-*P* worlds are quite distant, one's belief as to whether *P* needn't match the fact of the matter that far from the actual world for one to be in a quite strong position with respect to *P*.

But for one's belief that *P* to be sensitive, one must *not* believe that *P* in the closest not-*P* worlds. Since skeptical hypotheses tend to fasten on somewhat remote (and sometimes very remote) possibilities, then, one can be in a relatively (and sometimes a very) strong position with respect to beliefs to the effect that they don't obtain (since one's belief as to whether they obtain matches the fact of the matter over a wide range of worlds closest to the actual world), while these beliefs remain insensitive (since one would still believe that the hypotheses didn't obtain in the closest worlds in which they do obtain). By contrast, where P is such that there are both P and not-P worlds very close to the actual world, one's belief that P must be sensitive (one must not believe that P in the closest not-P worlds) in order for one to be in even a minimally strong epistemic position with respect to P, and, conversely, one needn't be in a very strong position for one's belief to be sensitive.

10 The Rule of Sensitivity and the Beginnings of a New Contextualist Solution

The important insight regarding skeptical hypotheses – that one's epistemic position with respect to propositions to the effect that skeptical hypotheses don't hold must be stronger than it is with respect to other propositions before beliefs in such propositions can be sensitive – suggests a new contextualist account of how, in presenting AI, the skeptic raises the standards for knowledge. Let's call the conversational rule this new account posits as the mechanism by which the skeptic raises the standards for knowledge the "Rule of Sensitivity." Although a more general formulation of this rule is desirable, I will here state it in such a way that it applies only to attributions (and denials) of knowledge, since such applications are what's needed to address the present puzzle.[19] So limited, our rule is simply this: When it is asserted that some subject S knows (or does not know) some proposition P, the standards for knowledge (the standards for how good an epistemic position one must be in to count as knowing) tend to be raised, if need be, to such a level as to require S's belief in that particular P to be sensitive for it to count as knowledge. Where the P involved is to the effect that a skeptical hypothesis does not obtain, then this rule dictates that the standards will be raised to a quite high level, for, as we've seen, one must be in a stronger epistemic position with respect to a proposition stating that a skeptical hypothesis is false – relative to other, more ordinary, propositions – before a belief in such a proposition can be sensitive.

A story in terms of possible worlds again provides a rough-and-ready, but still perhaps enlightening, picture of how the Rule of Sensitivity operates. Context, I've said, determines how strong an epistemic position one must be in to count as knowing. Picture this requirement as a contextually determined sphere of possible worlds, centered on the actual world, within which a subject's belief as to whether P is true must match the fact of the matter in order for the subject to count as knowing. (Given the results of section 4, we must again remember either to restrict our attention solely to those worlds in which the subject uses the same method of belief formation she uses in the actual world, or to weigh similarity with respect to the subject's method very heavily in determining the closeness of possible worlds to the actual world.) Call this sphere the sphere of epistemically relevant worlds. As the standards for knowledge go up, the sphere of epistemically relevant worlds becomes larger – the truth-tracking of one's belief must extend further from actuality for one to count as knowing. Given this picture, the Rule of Sensitivity can be formulated as follows: When it's asserted that S knows (or doesn't know) that P, then, if necessary, enlarge the sphere of epistemically relevant worlds so that it at least includes the closest worlds in which P is false.

A powerful solution to our puzzle results when we follow the basic contextualist strategy (see section 2) and utilize this Rule of Sensitivity to explain how the standards for knowledge are raised by the skeptic's presentation of AI. While many noteworthy features and virtues of this solution are best explained by comparing it with the other proposed solutions to our puzzle, as I'll do in following sections, the basic idea of the present solution is this. In utilizing AI to attack our putative knowledge of O, the skeptic instinctively chooses her skeptical hypothesis, H, so that it will have these two features: (1) We will be in at least as strong a position to know that not-H as we're in to know that O, but (2) Any belief we might have to the effect that not-H will be an insensitive belief (a belief we would hold even if not-H were false – that is, even if H were true). Given feature (2), the skeptic's assertion that we don't know that not-H, by the Rule of Sensitivity, drives the standards for knowledge up to such a point as to make that assertion true. By the Rule of Sensitivity, recall, the standards for knowledge are raised to such a level as to require our belief that not-H to be sensitive before it can count as knowledge. Since our belief that not-H isn't sensitive (feature (2)), the standards are driven up to such a level that we don't count as knowing that not-H. And since we're in no stronger an epistemic position with respect to O than we're in with respect to not-H (feature (1)), then, at the high standards put in place by the skeptic's assertion of AI's first premise, we also fail to know that O. At these high standards, the skeptic truthfully asserts her second premise (which, recall, is also true at lower standards), and then truthfully asserts AI's conclusion that we don't know that O.[20] This accounts for the persuasiveness of AI. But since, on this account, the skeptic gets to truthfully state her conclusion only by raising the standards for knowledge, AI doesn't threaten the truth of our ordinary claims to know the very Os our knowledge of which the skeptic attacks. For the fact that the skeptic can install very high standards that we don't live up to has no tendency to show that we don't satisfy the more relaxed standards that are in place in more ordinary conversations and debates.

11 Our New Contextualist Solution Clarified and Compared with the Straightforward Solution

The puzzle of skeptical hypotheses, recall, concerns the premises of AI together with the negation of its conclusion:

1. I don't know that not-H.
2. If I don't know that not-H, then I don't know that O.

not-C. I do know that O.

A solution to the puzzle must, of course, issue a verdict as to the truth of each of these three, but it must also explain why we find all of them plausible.

Let's be clear about what our present contextualist solution has to say about each of these. Our verdict regarding (2) is that it's true regardless of what epistemic standard it's evaluated at, so its plausibility is easily accounted for. But this, combined with a similarly enthusiastic endorsement of (1), would land us in bold skepticism. We avoid that fate by endorsing (1) as true, not at all standards, but only at the unusually inflated

standards conducive to skepticism. Thus, on our solution, we do know, for instance, that we're not BIVs, according to ordinary low standards for knowledge. But, though (1) is false when evaluated according to those ordinary low standards, we're able to explain its plausibility, as we've seen, by means of the fact that the high standards at which (1) is true are precisely the standards that an assertion or denial of it put into play. Since attempts to assert (1) are bound to result in truth, and attempts to deny it are destined to produce falsehood,[21] it's no surprise that we find it so plausible.

But what of (not-C)? On the present solution, claims to know ordinary propositions are true according to ordinary low standards but false according to the highly inflated standards that, by the Rule of Sensitivity, are put in place by the assertion of (1). (Not-C) seems plausible because it's true when evaluated at the standards most normally applied to it. But, it will be asked, why do we find these claims to know plausible even when we're in a context in which the skeptic has raised the standards to such a level that these claims are false? A little caution is in order here. It's controversial just how intuitively correct (not-C) does seem to us in such a context. Most of us feel some ambivalence. Such ambivalence is to be expected whenever we're dealing with a puzzle consisting of mutually inconsistent propositions, all of which are individually plausible. For when the propositions are considered together, one will have this good reason for doubting each of them: that the others seem true. And it's difficult to distinguish the doubt of (not-C) that arises from this very general source (that its falsehood follows from other things one finds plausible) from that which arises from the fact that the standards are high. At any rate, the very strong pull that (not-C) continues to exert on (at least most of) us even when the standards are high is explained in the manner outlined in section 2: Even while we're in a context governed by high standards at which we don't count as knowing that O, we at the same time realize that as soon as we find ourselves in more ordinary conversational contexts, it will not only be true for us to claim to know these very Os that the skeptic now denies we know, but it will also be wrong for us to deny that we know these things. It's easy, then, to think that the skeptic's present denial must be equally false and that it would be equally true for us now, in the skeptic's presence, to claim to know that O.

The verdicts the present solution issues regarding the truth values of the members of the triad are complicated by the fact that ours is a contextualist solution. Only (2) receives the same verdict regardless of what the epistemic standards are; the truth values of (1) and (not-C) vary with context. It's just this variance that our solution so essentially relies on in explaining how we fall into our puzzling conflict of intuitions. Noncontextualist (henceforth, "straightforward") solutions, on the other hand, must choose one of the members of this triad to deny, claiming this loser to be false according to the invariant epistemic standards that govern all attributions and denials of knowledge: The "Moorean" solution in this way denies (1),[22] the "Nozickean" (2), and the "Bold Skeptical" solution thus denies (not-C), accepting that we speak falsely whenever, even in ordinary, nonphilosophical discussions, we claim to know the O in question.

From the perspective of our present contextualist solution, each of these straightforward solutions results in part, of course, from a failure to see the truth of contextualism. But which straightforward solution an invariantist confusedly adopts will depend on the standards that dominate her evaluation of our beliefs in O and in not-H. If her evaluation is dominated by the relatively low standards that govern our ordinary, out-on-the-street talk of knowledge, she will end up a Moorean. If she evaluates the beliefs in question according to the high standards that are put into place by the skeptic's presentation of AI, bold skepticism is the result. The Nozickean solution ensues from evaluating each belief according to the standards that would most often be used in evaluating that belief. For reasons we've seen, a claim to know (or an admission that one doesn't know) that a skeptical hypothesis is false will, by the Rule of Sensitivity, tend to invite a very high reading, at which the admission is true and the claim is false. But a claim to know that O doesn't so demand a high reading. From the present perspective, the Nozickean is reacting to the fact that one can usually truthfully claim that one does know that O and can usually truthfully claim not to know that not-H. What the Nozickean misses is how difficult it is to make these two claims together: once you have admitted that you don't

know that not-H, it seems the reverse of intuitively correct to claim to know that O, at least until the conversational air is cleared.

To succeed, a straightforward solution must explain what leads our intuitions astray with respect to the unlucky member of the triad which that solution denies. Otherwise, we'll have little reason for denying just that member of the triad. Nozick himself provides no such explanation with respect to (2), parenthetically leaving this vital task to "further exploration,"[23] and other Nozickeans, if any there be, have not, to the best of my knowledge, progressed any farther along this front. Mooreans, to the best of my knowledge, have fared no better in explaining why we're so reluctant to claim the status of knowledge for our insensitive beliefs. It's the defenders of bold skepticism who've made the most progress here. In the remaining sections, I'll explain why our contextualist solution is superior to that of the bold skeptic.

12   Bold Skepticism and the Warranted Assertability Maneuver

Almost of all of the time, it seems to almost all of us that we do know the Os that the skeptic claims we don't know. According to the bold skeptic, whenever we say or think that we know these things, we say or think something false. The bold skeptic thus implicates us, speakers of English, in systematic and widespread falsehood in our use, in speech and in thought, of our very common word "know." Equally paradoxically, the bold skeptic holds that we're speaking the truth whenever we say that someone doesn't know these Os, even though it seems to most of us that we'd then be saying something quite false. What leads us astray? Peter Unger and Barry Stroud have suggested on behalf of bold skepticism that although we don't know these Os, it's often useful for us to claim that we do know them, and we are therefore often warranted or justified in making such claims. What then leads us astray is this: We mistake this useful/justified/warranted assertability of knowledge ascriptions for truth.[24] On the other side of the coin, presumably, we're mistaking the useless/unwarranted/unjustified assertability of denials of knowledge for falsehood.

Two serious problems emerge for the bold skeptic at this point. The first is that such "warranted assertability maneuvers" could be attempted by advocates of the other solutions as well. Warranted assertability indeed can be mistaken for truth, and unwarranted assertability for falsehood, but this by itself does not favor the bold skeptic's solution over the other straightforward approaches. Each of the straightforward approaches denies a member of the triad constituting our puzzle, and each it seems could claim that the reason this loser they've chosen seems true, though it's in fact false, is that we're often warranted in asserting it, and we mistake this warranted assertability for truth. Thus, the Moorean, for instance, could claim that although we do indeed know that H is false, we're not warranted in claiming that we know this (though this claim would be true), but are rather warranted in saying that we don't know (though this latter is false). Simply attributing apparent truth to warranted assertability is a game almost any party to this dispute can fairly easily play.[25] That this line of thought would eventually work out any better for the bold skeptic than for his opponents would take some showing.[26]

It's at (1) that the skeptic has his best hope of gaining an advantage over my solution, for that premise indeed does seem true, and, unlike the skeptic, I've stopped short of fully endorsing it, making do with an explanation of its plausibility. But the skeptic's other problem lurks here. Usually, while solving a philosophical puzzle consisting of a set of individually plausible but mutually inconsistent claims, one only has to explain (away) the plausibility of those members of the set one denies, and one is relieved of the burden of explaining the plausibility of those members that one endorses, their truth and our ability to recognize that truth being explanation enough of their apparent truth. But truth does not suffice to explain apparent truth where one makes us out to be absolutely horrible judges of truths of the kind in question. Thus, the skeptic's second big problem is that, because he holds that we're subject to constant and radical error as to the scope of our knowledge, consistently thinking we know things when we don't, the skeptic, although he thinks (1) is true, owes us an explanation for its plausibility. Given that our habit of mistaking our ignorance

for knowledge is so pervasive, why doesn't it seem to us *here* that we know what, in fact, we don't – that these skeptical hypotheses are false? Why does our lack of knowledge, which we're so pervasively blind to, shine through so clearly to us just where the issue is whether we know a skeptical hypothesis to be false?

The skeptic's initial answer will certainly be that we're *not* warranted in claiming to know that skeptical hypotheses don't obtain, and thus can't mistake warranted assertability for truth here. But then, to see why skeptical hypotheses are effective, we must be told why we're not warranted in claiming to know that skeptical hypotheses are false, given that, according to the skeptic, we are warranted in claiming to know all manner of other things that in fact we don't know. And here skeptics have little to offer. But if the results of sections 3 and 6 above are correct, the answer must involve the lack of sensitivity enjoyed by our beliefs that skeptical hypotheses don't obtain. The skeptic's use of SCA will take this form: Although we know nothing (or very little), it's when our beliefs are insensitive that we're not even warranted in asserting that we know and we therefore recognize our lack of knowledge. But the skeptic must now also address AI's second premise, making sure his endorsement of SCA is made in such a way as to account for our intuitions here. Indeed, whether or not he buys into SCA, the skeptic faces this question: If, as he claims, we're usually under the delusion that we know that O, but we customarily recognize that we don't know that not-H, why aren't we happy to conjoin this error with that insight and embrace the abominable conjunction?

This may look like a difficult question, but the skeptic has a ready answer. His problem is that the warranted assertability maneuver by itself didn't really solve our puzzle, but rather reintroduced it in a new form. And the only way I've seen to incorporate SCA into a treatment of AI that also handles the other pieces of our puzzle is to employ the idea that contextually sensitive epistemic standards govern our use of "know," and to posit the Rule of Sensitivity as the mechanism by which the AI skeptic drives those standards up, as I've advocated here. But wise invariantists typically accept that contextually varying standards govern our use of ascriptions and denials of knowledge. The sensible invariantist will admit that, of course, what passes for knowledge in some contexts won't so pass in others. Being an invariantist, he'll deny that the truth conditions of knowledge attributions vary in the way the contextualist claims they do. But the clever invariantist will maintain that the varying epistemic standards that the contextualist supposes govern the truth conditions of these sentences in fact govern their conditions of warranted assertability.[27]

This allows the bold skeptic to mimic any contextualist solution, and in particular the solution I'm advocating here, by means of a simple twist. With respect to my solution, the bold skeptic can maintain that the Rule of Sensitivity is a rule for the raising of the epistemic standards governing our use of sentences ascribing knowledge to subjects, alright, but insist that it governs the warranted assertability conditions of these sentences, rather than their truth conditions, which, he'll maintain, remain constant at a level beyond the reach of mere mortals to satisfy. The warranted assertability maneuver can then be employed: We mistake warranted assertability for truth (and unwarranted assertability for falsehood). Thus, since we're never warranted in claiming to know that skeptical hypotheses don't obtain (due to the operation of the twisted Rule of Sensitivity), we're led to judge (correctly) that such claims to knowledge would be false. And since AI's second premise is always warranted, we judge (again correctly) that this premise is true. But since a claim to know some O is usually warranted, due to the low standards for warranted assertability that would ordinarily be applied to such a claim, we judge (incorrectly) that we know this O. Thus, my solution, like other contextualist solutions, can be easily adapted to suit the purposes of the bold skeptic. The result is a theory parallel to my own contextualist solution, which differs in its semantics of "know": According to this parallel invariantist theory, the context-sensitive varying epistemic standards we've discovered govern the warranted assertability conditions of attributions and denials of knowledge, rather than their truth conditions, which are held to be invariant.[28] How shall we rationally decide between a contextualist solution, and in particular the one I'm here defending, and the bold skeptic's analogue of it?[29]

13 Bold Skepticism and Systematic Falsehood

Like its contextualist relatives, our new solution is designed largely with the goal in mind of crediting most of our attributions of knowledge with truth. And no wonder. We in general take it as a strike against a theory of a common term of a natural language that it involves the speakers of that language in systematic and widespread falsehood in their use of that term. Let's borrow an example and suppose, for instance, that a crazed philosopher claimed that there are no physicians, because, in addition to holding a medical degree, a necessary condition for being a physician is that one be able to cure any conceivable illness.[30] On what grounds should we reject this bizarre conjecture in favor of a more traditional and less demanding account of what it is to be a physician? Our language certainly could have been such that S's having the ability to cure any conceivable illness was a truth condition of "S is a physician" (although the word "physician" would not have been very useful in that case). In virtue of what is our language in fact such that the strange theory is not true of it? I'm of course not in a position to give a complete answer to this question, but it's eminently reasonable to suppose that such facts as these, regarding our use, in thought and in speech, of the term "physician" are involved: that we take to be physicians many licensed practitioners of medicine who don't satisfy the demanding requirement alleged; that we seriously describe these people as being physicians; that we *don't deny* that these people are physicians; etc. It's no doubt largely in virtue of such facts as these that the traditional view, rather than the conjecture of our crazed philosopher, is true of our language. (The correctness of the traditional view largely *consists* in such facts.) And these facts also provide us with our best reasons or evidence for accepting the traditional, rather than the strange, hypothesis regarding the semantics of "physician." In this case, that the peculiar theory implicates us in systematic and widespread falsehood in our speech and thought involving "physicians" is a (constitutive and evidential) strike against the theory that proves quite decisive.

If our crazed philosopher tried to account for the above facts regarding our use of the term "physician" via the quick and easy conjecture that the less demanding requirements that are more traditionally assigned to "physician," while they don't accurately specify the truth conditions of sentences involving that term, do articulate these sentences' warranted assertability conditions, we should not, on the basis of this maneuver, suspend our judgment against his contention. That his theory involves us in systematic falsehood continues to constitute a strike against it, and in the absence of quite weighty counterbalancing considerations that favor the strange theory over the traditional one, this strike remains decisive.

Of course, the problem with this hopeless non-starter of a theory is that there don't seem to be any such counterbalancing considerations in its favor. By contrast, bold skepticism can appear to be supported by skeptical arguments like AI. Though the bold skeptic's resolution of our puzzle involves us in systematic falsehood because of its unwavering acceptance of AI's conclusion, it at the same time can seem to make sense of *other* pieces of the puzzle (that we're inclined to say that we don't know that skeptical hypotheses are false and to say that we don't know various ordinary things if we don't know these hypotheses to be false), making the warranted assertability maneuver seem more motivated here than it is in the hands of our imagined crazed philosopher. But, as we saw in the previous section, this appearance is deceptive. Bold skepticism, by itself, does not explain the plausibility of AI's premises. To help the skeptic solve the puzzle, I've had to ascribe to him an analogue of our new solution.[31] But once we see that the skeptical puzzle can be solved just as well without the bold skeptic's systematic falsehood, we're left with no reason for paying that high price for a solution.[32] Indeed, since the bold skeptical solution and our new contextualist solution under consideration closely parallel each other, there's not much difference in how they solve the puzzle. That the bold skeptical resolution involves us in systematic falsehood is one of the few differences to be found here, and it's a weighty consideration against that resolution. And, with there being little room for weighty compensating advantages for this resolution over the contextualist's (given how similar they are in other respects), this consideration proves decisive. So, as with the crazed philosopher's theory of "physician," the bold skeptic's resolution of AI should be rejected because it involves us in systematic and widespread falsehood in our use of a common term of our language.

14 Begging the Question Against the Skeptic?

If skeptics are allowed to play King of the Mountain – they start off on top (never mind how they got there) and it's the anti-skeptics' job to knock them off – displacing them can be a very difficult task. How difficult depends on several factors, one of which is what premises the anti-skeptic is allowed to appeal to in an argument designed to dethrone the skeptic. If the skeptic won't allow any premises to be available, then, as Thomas Reid noted, "It would be impossible by argument to beat him out of this stronghold; and he must even be left to enjoy his scepticism" (1895, p. 447).[33] If, to make the game a bit more interesting, a slim range of claims is allowed to pass inspection and be available for use in the anti-skeptical campaign, then (as Reid again recognized) it's often difficult to say what, if anything, of importance would follow from the fact that the skeptic can or cannot be knocked from his perch by arguments from premises of that particular type.

I have little interest in playing King of the Mountain. But skeptical arguments like AI threaten to show that the skeptic needn't just play this game, but can *gain* the top of the mountain – that starting from our own beliefs and intuitions, he can give us better reasons for accepting his skepticism than we have for rejecting it. I've here argued that the bold skeptic cannot win *this* battle – that of providing the best resolution of our puzzling conflict of intuitions. Although AI's premises are initially plausible, the best resolution for the conflict of intuitions generated by AI is not that of the bold skeptic.

Along the way, I've been assuming certain things that we believe but that the skeptic claims we can't know, thereby perhaps raising the concern that I'm begging the question against the skeptic. For instance, in claiming that my belief that I have hands is sensitive, I betray my conviction that I'm not a BIV, either in the actual world or in any nearby worlds. Indeed, I'm ready to admit to the skeptic that if I am a BIV, then I don't know I have hands, according to any standards for knowledge. But, of course, as I firmly believe, I'm not a BIV.

Is it legitimate for me to use this conviction in a debate against the skeptic? Not if we're playing King of the Mountain. But if the skeptic is marshalling deeply felt intuitions of ours in an attempt to give us good reasons for accepting his skepticism, it's legitimate to point out that other of our beliefs militate against his position, and ask why we should give credence to just those that favor him. And if we can further show that those

beliefs that seem to favor his solution can be accommodated in our solution better than he can accommodate those of our beliefs that are hostile to him, the best conclusion we can draw is that we're *not* ordinarily mistaken when we claim or ascribe knowledge, despite the bold skeptic's attempt to show that we are. Instead, the main insights to be drawn from a study of AI involve the context-sensitivity of attributions of knowledge, and the role that the Rule of Sensitivity plays in changing the epistemic standards that govern these attributions.

Notes

1 I choose this O partly for its historical connections to Descartes's First Meditation, and also because I think it *is* an exemplary case of something we ordinarily think we know. But while we would ordinarily think we know this O, we'd seldom have occasion to *say* that we know it, because cases in which such a claim to knowledge would be conversationally in order are quite rare. (Exception: A teacher begins an epistemology lecture by matter-of-factly listing various things she knows, and that any plausible theory of knowledge should make her come out to know. In the course of this listing, she says, "And I know that I have hands.") For this and various related reasons, some might not like my choice of O. Such readers are invited to supply their own favorite exemplary cases of things we know as the skeptic's target.

2 Those who think that Hilary Putnam may have already disarmed BIV-inspired skepticism should understand the BIV hypothesis to be the hypothesis that one's brain has been *recently* envatted after many years of normal embodiment. For even if Putnam is right in claiming that the content of the beliefs of the BIVs of his scenario is such that these BIVs aren't massively deceived, it seems that recently envatted BIVs are so deceived.

3 AI takes its name primarily from its first premise. But since one of AI's best formulations (to which I hereby refer readers seeking a good version of AI that has not been so brutally pared) is in chapter 1 of Peter Unger's book *Ignorance: A Case for Skepticism* (1975),

it is in more than one sense that it is an argument "from ignorance."

4 I actually haven't pared AI to its *barest* essentials. It could be further pared to a one-premise argument: I don't know that not-H; so, I don't know that O. The second, "bridge" premise has been added to facilitate my treatment of the argument, nicely dividing those issues that impact on the acceptability of the first premise from those germane to the second.

AI is the first and great argument by skeptical hypothesis. And the second, like unto it, is *The Argument from Possibility* (AP), which like AI, takes its name from its first premise, and which has this form:

1. It is possible that H_{ind}.
2. If it is possible that H_{ind}, then it is possible that not-O_{ind}. So,
3. It is possible that not-O_{ind}.
4. If it is possible that not-O_{ind}, then I don't know that O. So,
C. I don't know that O.

(The subscript "ind" indicates that what occurs in the scope of "It is possible that" is to be kept in the indicative mood, so that the possibility expressed will be an epistemic one. The "bridge" premises, 2 and 4, can be omitted.) In this paper I address only AI, but let me quickly indicate how AP should be handled. Premise 4, which initially strikes many as AP's weakest link, is actually correct (DeRose 1991, section G). Thus, the AP skeptic must be stopped *before* she reaches step 3. Fortunately, the treatment of AI that I present in this paper can be generalized to handle the initial phase (steps 1–3) of AP as well. This treatment of AP is left here as an exercise for the reader, but is explained in chapter 3, especially section K, of my 1990.

5 This is especially true of Stewart Cohen, to whom I'm indebted for his general setup of the puzzle as a conflict of intuitions, a satisfactory solution of which requires an explanation of why the puzzle arises. See Cohen 1988, pp. 93–4.

6 For a bit more on the nature of contextualist theories, see my 1992. The notion of (comparative) strength of epistemic position, central to my characterization of contextualism, will be explicated below in sections 8 and 9.

   For exemplary contextualist treatments of the problem of skepticism, see especially Unger 1986 and Cohen 1988.

7 This is at least so according to *skeptic-friendly* versions of contextualist solutions, as will be explained later in this section.

8 Thanks to Richard Grandy and to Peter Unger for pressing this point.

9 Precisely, what Nozick does is this: He analyzes the technical locution "S knows, via method *M*, that *p*," and then in turn analyzes the relation of S's knowing that *p* in terms of this technical locution. The revised third condition I've displayed is part of Nozick's attempt to analyze the technical locution.

10 These are not identical modifications. On the first option, similarity with respect to method is weighted heavily, but can be outweighed by other factors. Thus, even so evaluated, the most similar world(s) in which the antecedent of the original (3) are true may be worlds that diverge from the actual world with respect to the method by which S came to believe that *P*. By contrast, on the second option, since the method by which S believes that *P* becomes part of the antecedent of the conditional we're evaluating (the modified (3)), the closest possible world(s) in which that antecedent is true cannot be worlds that diverge from the actual world with respect to method.

11 Or, given the exceptions to the general tendency that we've discussed in sections 4 and 5, why I haven't accepted that some properly Chisholmed refinement of the sensitivity requirement (which has as instances of it convincing instances of AI's first premise) is necessary for knowledge.

12 Though this statement of Nozick's account of knowledge is rough, that will not affect my treatment, which would apply equally well to Nozick's full account. I've skipped entirely Nozick's fourth condition for knowledge, but I believe this fourth condition to be redundant, anyway: It automatically holds whenever true belief is present. Also, as I've already noted, Nozick takes account of the method of belief formation in his final version of the third condition. The same thing happens with the fourth.

13 At pp. 205–6 Nozick admits this appeal, and later he writes, "Thus, if our notion of knowledge was as strong as we naturally tend to think (namely, closed under known logical implication) then the skeptic would be right. (But why do we naturally think this? Further exploration and explanation is needed of the intuitive roots of the natural assumption that knowledge is closed under known logical implication)" (p. 242).

   Nozick is quite hard on anti-skeptics who choose rather to deny the first premise; he writes: "The skeptic asserts we do not know his possibilities don't obtain, and he is right. Attempts to avoid skepticism by claiming we do know these things are bound to fail. The skeptic's possibilities make us uneasy because, as we deeply realize, we do not know they don't obtain; it is not surprising that attempts to show we do know these things leave us suspicious, strike us even as bad faith" (p. 201). But similar remarks could be made about Nozick. As Nozick himself admits, the second premise has its own intuitive appeal. So why not say that what we "deeply realize" is that if you don't know that you're not a BIV, then you don't know you have hands, and that the skeptic is right about *this*? Nozick's denial of the second premise leaves me about as "suspicious" as does a denial of the first, and though Nozick's denial doesn't strike me as an instance of bad faith, denials of the first premise seem no better candidates for that charge.

14   What are Nozick's grounds for rejecting the second premise? Nozick notes that the premise is an instance of a very general principle to the effect that knowledge is closed under known implication (see note 18, below). After admitting that the closure principle *seems* true (pp. 205–6), Nozick claims that it's wrong, and his reasons for this claim are made entirely from within his analysis of knowledge: Given his analysis knowledge won't be closed (see especially pp. 206–8). So Nozick is relying on his analysis to show us that the second premise is false despite its intuitive appeal. And indeed, Nozick has developed and defended his analysis of knowledge (in part I of chapter 3) before he applies it to the issue of skepticism (in part 2).

15   Unfortunately, what is perhaps the most powerful attack on Nozick's theory of knowledge, made by Saul Kripke in lectures, circa 1985, has not, to the best of my knowledge, found its way into print. For those interested in critical literature on Nozick, a good place to start is with Forbes 1984 and several of the essays in Luper-Foy 1987. For still further reading, Luper-Foy 1987 contains an excellent bibliography.

16   As remarked in note 14, Nozick depends heavily on the independent plausibility of this analysis to provide the momentum for his treatment of AI.

17   And, of course, such conditionals can be used to make all manner of other comparisons: comparative strength of the epistemic positions of two *different subjects* with respect to the same proposition or with respect to different propositions, the strength of the epistemic position of a subject with respect to one proposition in one situation as compared with that same subject's epistemic position with respect to a different proposition in a different situation, etc.

18   As is well known, instances of AI's second premise are often instances of the principle that knowledge is closed under known logical implication: $Kp \,\&\, K\,(p \text{ entails } q) \rightarrow Kq$. (In the next paragraph I explain why this is not always the case, at least when the

closure principle isn't strengthened as there described.) As is also well known, there are exceptions to the principle so formulated, and it might take a lot of tinkering to get it exactly right. But, as Nozick, the arch denier of closure, puts it, "We would be ill-advised, however, to quibble over the details of P [the principle that knowledge is closed under known logical implication]. Although these details are difficult to get straight, it will continue to appear that something like P is correct" (1981, p. 205). Nozick goes on to claim that this appearance is deceiving. I believe that something like P is correct, but that doesn't compete with my present account of AI's second premise: When a conditional is an instance of the properly formulated closure principle, the relevant comparative fact involving strength of epistemic position holds. See Brueckner 1985 for arguments that the denial of knowledge closure principles "is not a fruitful anti-skeptical project" (p. 112).

While restrictions will have to be put on the closure principle that will weaken it in certain respects, there may be other respects in which it can be strengthened. Some instances of AI's second premise are convincing even though H is compatible with O. For instance, the BIV hypothesis seems to undermine my putative knowledge of *I'm in Houston* as well as of *I have hands*, but, of course, that I'm a bodiless BIV is compatible with my being in Houston. Perhaps if S is to know that P, then S must know that not-Q for any Q (but here restrictions must be added) such that if Q were true, S would not know that P. Thus, the range of Qs that must be known not to obtain may be broadened so as to include not only propositions that are incompatible with P, but also others such that if they were the case, then S wouldn't know that P. Those Qs that *are* incompatible with P itself will then be seen as special cases of those that are at odds with S's knowing that P. Barry Stroud discusses a stronger closure principle such as this in his 1984 (pp. 25–30).

19   Introducing a skeptical hypothesis into a conversation in any number of ways other than in attributions and denials of knowledge can seem to raise the standards for

knowledge. For instance, instead of arguing, "You don't know that the paper isn't mistaken about the result of last night's game; therefore, you don't know that the Bulls won," a skeptic may urge, "Consider this proposition: The newspaper is mistaken about who won the game. Now, keeping that proposition clearly in mind, answer me this: Do you *really* know that the Bulls won?" Of course, not just *any* mention of a skeptical hypothesis seems to trigger the mechanism for raising the standards of knowledge I'm about to articulate.

20 Again, I'm here assuming a skeptic-friendly version of contextualism. See the second important point made at the end of section 2.

21 But for cases in which it seems one *can* truthfully say "S knows that not-*H*," despite the fact that S's belief that not-*H* is insensitive, see chapter 3, section J ("Low-Strength Claims to Know that Skeptical Hypotheses Do Not Obtain") of my 1990. In such cases, given certain features of the conversational situation, the Rule of Sensitivity does not operate. These consitute exceptions to the rule that one cannot truthfully call an insensitive belief knowledge. As I explain there, I welcome these exceptions, and would actually be a bit worried if there weren't such exceptions. For it's a feature of my treatment of AI that we do know skeptical hypotheses to be false according to low epistemic standards. I would find it a bit embarrassing if we could never *claim* to have such knowledge by means of simple knowledge attributions, and I'm reassured by the result that in special conversational circumstances, it seems we *can* truthfully claim to know that not-*H*, despite the fact that our belief that not-*H* is insensitive.

22 This is called the "Moorean" solution because Moore responded in this way to the dream argument. It's far from certain that Moore would have so responded to other instances of AI that utilize different skeptical hypotheses.

23 See the first paragraph of note 13, above.

24 This is the basic line Unger takes in his defense of bold skepticism in his 1975; see especially pp. 50–4. Stroud, though not himself advocating bold skepticism, does seek to defend the bold skeptic along these lines in ch. 2 of his 1984; see especially pp. 55–82.

25 By contrast, our new contextualist solution attributes the apparent truth of (1) to (1)'s *truth* (and not just its warranted assertability) at the very standards its assertion invokes.

26 For my own part, for reasons I can't go into here, I think the resulting Moorean position would be slightly more defensible; thus, if I had to reject contextualism and adopt a straightforward solution, I'd be a Moorean.

27 Stroud thus claims that on the skeptic's conception of our practices, we operate under certain "practical constraints" (1984, p. 75) in our everyday uses of "know", and asserts that our standards for saying we know vary from case to case (pp. 65–6). Thus, on the skeptic's conception, the standards for ascribing knowledge that we employ in everyday use depend upon our "aims and interests at the moment" (p. 65). According to contextualism, these varying standards reflect a corresponding variation in the truth conditions for attributions of knowledge. But on Stroud's skeptic's conception, when we ascribe knowledge in everyday situations, we are typically saying something literally false, although "the exigencies of action" justify these false attributions. The best exploration of this type of idea is provided by Unger in his 1984.

28 Going back to the bold skeptic's first problem, note that all this maneuvering can be mimicked by the Moorean, who can also hold that a Rule of Sensitivity governs the warranted assertability conditions of knowledge ascriptions. Like the bold skeptic, the Moorean can hold that the truth conditions of such attributions of knowledge remain invariant, but in the Moorean's hands, these constant epistemic standards will be meetably low.

29 Readers of Unger's 1984 will see the strong influence of that excellent book on my procedure here, though I come to very different conclusions than he does in that work. (But see his more recent 1986.)

30 See Stroud (1984, p. 40), who in turn borrowed the example from elsewhere.

31 Of course, skeptics are free to refuse this help and propose other solutions. Like practically any claim to have provided the best explanation of something, my claim here is hostage to the possible future development of a better explanation coming along.

32 Well, little reason. In his 1984, as part of his case for his relativist conclusion that there's no fact of the matter as to whether contextualism or skeptical invariantism is correct, Unger tries to balance this relative disadvantage of skeptical invariantism against contextualism's relative disadvantage that it does not make the truth conditions of knowledge attributions appropriately independent from the current intents and interests of those who happen to be speaking on a given occasion (p. 37). In part 3 of my 1992, I argue that contextualism can handle the most serious consequences one might suspect would follow from this lack of independence. Whatever

independence concerns might remain with contextualism seem quite swamped by the cost of the bold skeptic's solution, which, as I've here argued, is quite high indeed.

In his review of Unger 1984, Brueckner, relating the advantages of invariantism, writes, "In particular, speakers' intuitions concerning the correct use of 'know' seem to conform to the closure principle for knowledge asserted by the invariantist yet denied by the contextualist" (1986, p. 512). If invariantism, but not contextualism, upheld closure, I would take this to be a very important advantage for invariantism – perhaps even weighty enough to make the contest between the two theories interesting. But, as I've argued, contextualism need not, and, properly developed, does not, take an implausible stand on the issue of closure. (See section 8 and especially note 18, above.)

33 I discuss this in section II.B of my 1989.

References

Brueckner, Anthony I., 1985. "Skepticism and Epistemic Closure," *Philosophical Topics* 13, pp. 89–117.

——, 1986. "Review of Unger, *Philosophical Relativity*," *Journal of Philosophy* 83, pp. 509–17.

Cohen, Stewart, 1988. "How to Be a Fallibilist," *Philosophical Perspectives* 2, pp. 91–123.

DeRose, Keith, 1989. "Reid's Anti-Sensationalism and His Realism," *Philosophical Review* 98, pp. 313–48.

——, 1990. "Knowledge, Epistemic Possibility, and Scepticism," PhD diss., University of California, Los Angeles.

——, 1991. "Epistemic Possibilities," *Philosophical Review* 100, pp. 581–605.

——, 1992. "Contextualism and Knowledge Attributions," *Philosophy and Phenomenological Research* 52, pp. 913–29.

Forbes, Graeme. 1984. "Nozick on Scepticism," *Philosophical Quarterly* 34, pp. 43–52.

Goldman, Alvin I. 1976. "Discrimination and Perceptual Knowledge," *Journal of Philosophy* 73, pp. 771–91.

Luper-Foy, Stephen (ed.), 1987. *The Possibility of Knowledge: Nozick and his Critics* (Totowa, NJ: Rowman and Littlefield).

Nozick, Robert, 1981. *Philosophical Explanations* (Cambridge, MA: Harvard University Press).

Reid, Thomas, 1895. *The Works of Thomas Reid*, 8th edn, ed. William Hamilton (Edinburgh: James Thin).

Stine, Gail C., 1976. "Skepticism, Relevant Alternatives, and Deductive Closure," *Philosophical Studies* 29, pp. 249–61.

Stroud, Barry, 1984. *The Significance of Philosophical Scepticism* (Oxford: Oxford University Press).

Unger, Peter, 1975. *Ignorance: A Case for Scepticism* (Oxford: Oxford University Press).

——, 1984. *Philosophical Relativity* (Minneapolis: University of Minnesota Press).

——, 1986. "The Cone Model of Knowledge," *Philosophical Topics* 14, pp. 125–78.

CHAPTER 48

Elusive Knowledge

David Lewis

We know a lot. I know what food penguins eat. I know that phones used to ring, but nowadays squeal, when someone calls up. I know that Essendon won the 1993 Grand Final. I know that here is a hand, and here is another.

We have all sorts of everyday knowledge, and we have it in abundance. To doubt that would be absurd. At any rate, to doubt it in any serious and lasting way would be absurd; and even philosophical and temporary doubt, under the influence of argument, is more than a little peculiar. It is a Moorean fact that we know a lot. It is one of those things that we know better than we know the premises of any philosophical argument to the contrary.

Besides knowing a lot that is everyday and trite, I myself think that we know a lot that is interesting and esoteric and controversial. We know a lot about things unseen: tiny particles and pervasive fields, not to mention one another's underwear. Sometimes we even know what an author meant by his writings. But on these questions, let us agree to disagree peacefully with the champions of "post-knowledgeism". The most trite and ordinary parts of our knowledge will be problem enough.

For no sooner do we engage in epistemology – the systematic philosophical examination of

Originally published in *Australasian Journal of Philosophy* 74, 4 (1996), pp. 549–67.

knowledge – than we meet a compelling argument that we know next to nothing. The sceptical argument is nothing new or fancy. It is just this: it seems as if knowledge must be by definition infallible. If you claim that S knows that *P*, and yet you grant that S cannot eliminate a certain possibility in which not-*P*, it certainly seems as if you have granted that S does not after all know that *P*. To speak of fallible knowledge, of knowledge despite uneliminated possibilities of error, just *sounds* contradictory.

Blind Freddy can see where this will lead. Let your paranoid fantasies rip – CIA plots, hallucinogens in the tap water, conspiracies to deceive, old Nick himself – and soon you find that uneliminated possibilities of error are everywhere. Those possibilities of error are far-fetched, of course, but possibilities all the same. They bite into even our most everyday knowledge. We never have infallible knowledge.

Never – well, hardly ever. Some say we have infallible knowledge of a few simple, axiomatic necessary truths; and of our own present experience. They say that I simply cannot be wrong that a part of a part of something is itself a part of that thing; or that it seems to me now (as I sit here at the keyboard) exactly as if I am hearing clicking noises on top of a steady whirring. Some say so. Others deny it. No matter; let it be granted, at least for the sake of the argument. It is not nearly enough. If we have only that much infallible knowledge, yet knowledge is by definition infallible, then we have very little knowledge indeed – not the abundant everyday knowledge we thought we had. That is still absurd.

So we know a lot; knowledge must be infallible; yet we have fallible knowledge or none (or next to none). We are caught between the rock of fallibilism and the whirlpool of scepticism. Both are mad!

Yet fallibilism is the less intrusive madness. It demands less frequent corrections of what we want to say. So, if forced to choose, I choose fallibilism. (And so say all of us.) We can get used to it, and some of us have done. No joy there – we know that people can get used to the most crazy philosophical sayings imaginable. If you are a contented fallibilist, I implore you to be honest, be naive, hear it afresh. "He knows, yet he has not eliminated all possibilities of error." Even if you've numbed your ears, doesn't this overt, explicit fallibilism *still* sound wrong?

Better fallibilism than scepticism; but it would be better still to dodge the choice. I think we can. We will be alarmingly close to the rock, and also alarmingly close to the whirlpool, but if we steer with care, we can – just barely – escape them both.

Maybe epistemology is the culprit. Maybe this extraordinary pastime robs us of our knowledge. Maybe we do know a lot in daily life; but maybe when we look hard at our knowledge, it goes away. But only when we look at it harder than the sane ever do in daily life; only when we let our paranoid fantasies rip. That is when we are forced to admit that there always are uneliminated possibilities of error, so that we have fallible knowledge or none.

Much that we say is context-dependent, in simple ways or subtle ways. Simple: "it's evening" is truly said when, and only when, it is said in the evening. Subtle: it could well be true, and not just by luck, that Essendon played rottenly, the Easybeats played brilliantly, yet Essendon won. Different contexts evoke different standards of evaluation. Talking about the Easybeats we apply lax standards, else we could scarcely distinguish their better days from their worse ones. In talking about Essendon, no such laxity is required. Essendon won because play that is rotten by demanding standards suffices to beat play that is brilliant by lax standards.

Maybe ascriptions of knowledge are subtly context-dependent, and may be epistemology is a context that makes them go false. Then epistemology would be an investigation that destroys its own subject matter. If so, the sceptical argument might be flawless, when we engage in epistemology – and only then![1]

If you start from the ancient idea that justification is the mark that distinguishes knowledge from mere opinion (even true opinion), then you well might conclude that ascriptions of knowledge are context-dependent because standards for adequate justification are context-dependent. As follows: opinion, even if true, deserves the name of knowledge only if it is adequately supported by reasons; to deserve that name in the especially demanding context of epistemology, the arguments from supporting reasons must be especially watertight; but the special standards of justification that this special context demands never can be met (well, hardly ever). In the strict context of epistemology we know nothing, yet in laxer contexts we know a lot.

But I myself cannot subscribe to this account of the context-dependence of knowledge, because I question its starting point. I don't agree that the mark of knowledge is justification.[2] First, because justification is not sufficient: your true opinion that you will lose the lottery isn't knowledge, whatever the odds. Suppose you know that it is a fair lottery with one winning ticket and many losing tickets, and you know how many losing tickets there are. The greater the number of losing tickets, the better is your justification for believing you will lose. Yet there is no number great enough to transform your fallible opinion into knowledge – after all, you just might win. No justification is good enough – or none short of a watertight deductive argument, and all but the sceptics will agree that this is too much to demand.[3]

Second, because justification is not always necessary. What (non-circular) argument supports our reliance on perception, on memory, and on testimony?[4] And yet we do gain knowledge by these means. And sometimes, far from having supporting arguments, we don't even know how we know. We once had evidence, drew conclusions, and thereby gained knowledge; now we have forgotten our reasons, yet still we retain our knowledge. Or we know the name that goes with the face, or the sex of the chicken, by relying on subtle visual cues, without knowing what those cues may be.

The link between knowledge and justification must be broken. But if we break that link, then it is not – or not entirely, or not exactly – by raising the standards of justification that epistemology destroys knowledge. I need some different story.

To that end, I propose to take the infallibility of knowledge as my starting point.[5] Must infallibilist epistemology end in scepticism? Not quite. Wait and see. Anyway, here is the definition. Subject S *knows* proposition P iff P holds in every possibility left uneliminated by S's evidence; equivalently, iff S's evidence eliminates every possibility in which not-P.

The definition is short, the commentary upon it is longer. In the first place, there is the proposition, P. What I choose to call "propositions" are individuated coarsely, by necessary equivalence. For instance, there is only one necessary proposition. It holds in every possibility; hence in every possibility left uneliminated by S's evidence, no matter who S may be and no matter what his evidence may be. So the necessary proposition is known always and everywhere. Yet this known proposition may go unrecognised when presented in impenetrable linguistic disguise, say as the proposition that every even number is the sum of two primes. Likewise, the known proposition that I have two hands may go unrecognised when presented as the proposition that the number of my hands is the least number n such that every even number is the sum of n primes. (Or if you doubt the necessary existence of numbers, switch to an example involving equivalence by logic alone.) These problems of disguise shall not concern us here. Our topic is modal, not hyperintensional, epistemology.[6]

Next, there are the possibilities. We needn't enter here into the question whether these are concreta, abstract constructions, or abstract simples. Further, we needn't decide whether they must always be maximally specific possibilities, or whether they need only be specific enough for the purpose at hand. A possibility will be specific enough if it cannot be split into sub-cases in such a way that anything we have said about possibilities, or anything we are going to say before we are done, applies to some sub-cases and not to others. For instance, it should never happen that proposition P holds in some but not all sub-cases; or that some but not all sub-cases are eliminated by S's evidence.

But we do need to stipulate that they are not just possibilities as to how the whole world is; they also include possibilities as to which part of the world is oneself, and as to when it now is. We need these possibilities *de se et nunc* because the propositions that may be known include propositions *de se et nunc*.[7] Not only do I know that there are hands in this world somewhere and somewhen. I know that *I* have hands, or anyway I have them *now*. Such propositions aren't just made true or made false by the whole world once and for all. They are true for some of us and not for others, or true at some times and not others, or both.

Further, we cannot limit ourselves to "real" possibilities that conform to the actual laws of nature, and maybe also to actual past history. For propositions about laws and history are contingent, and may or may not be known.

Neither can we limit ourselves to "epistemic" possibilities for S – possibilities that S does not know not to obtain. That would drain our definition of content. Assume only that knowledge is closed under strict implication. (We shall consider the merits of this assumption later.) Remember that we are not distinguishing between equivalent propositions. Then knowledge of a conjunction is equivalent to knowledge of every conjunct. P is the conjunction of all propositions not-W, where W is a possibility in which not-P. That suffices to yield an equivalence: S knows that P iff, for every possibility W in which not-P, S knows that not-W. Contraposing and cancelling a double negation: iff every possibility which S does not know not to obtain is one in which P. For short: iff P holds throughout S's epistemic possibilities. Yet to get this far, we need no substantive definition of knowledge at all! To turn this into a substantive definition, in fact the very definition we gave before, we need to say one more thing: S's epistemic possibilities are just those possibilities that are uneliminated by S's evidence.

So, next, we need to say what it means for a possibility to be eliminated or not. Here I say that the uneliminated possibilities are those in which the subject's entire perceptual experience and memory are just as they actually are. There is one possibility that actually obtains (for the subject and at the time in question); call it *actuality*. Then a possibility W is *uneliminated* iff the subject's perceptual experience and memory in W exactly match his perceptual experience and memory in actuality. (If you want to include other alleged forms of basic evidence, such as the evidence of our extrasensory faculties, or an innate disposition to believe in God, be my guest. If they exist, they should be included. If not, no harm done if we have included them conditionally.)

Note well that we do not need the "pure sense-datum language" and the "incorrigible protocol statements" that for so long bedevilled foundationalist epistemology. It matters not at all whether there are words to capture the subject's perceptual and memory evidence, nothing more and nothing less. If there are such words, it matters not at all whether the subject can hit upon them. The given does not consist of basic axioms to serve as premises in subsequent arguments. Rather, it consists of a match between possibilities.

When perceptual experience E (or memory) eliminates a possibility W, that is not because the propositional content of the experience conflicts with W. (Not even if it is the narrow content.) The propositional content of our experience could, after all, be false. Rather, it is the existence of the experience that conflicts with W: W is a possibility in which the subject is not having experience E. Else we would need to tell some fishy story of how the experience has some sort of infallible, ineffable, purely phenomenal propositional content ... Who needs that? Let E have propositional content P. Suppose even – something I take to be an open question – that E is, in some sense, fully characterized by P. Then I say that E eliminates W iff W is a possibility in which the subject's experience or memory has content different from P. I do *not* say that E eliminates W iff W is a possibility in which P is false.

Maybe not every kind of sense perception yields experience; maybe, for instance, the kinaesthetic sense yields not its own distinctive sort of sense-experience but only spontaneous judgements about the position of one's limbs. If this is true, then the thing to say is that kinaesthetic evidence eliminates all possibilities except those that exactly resemble actuality with respect to the subject's spontaneous kinaesthetic judgments. In saying this, we would treat kinaesthetic evidence

more on the model of memory than on the model of more typical senses.

Finally, we must attend to the word "every". What does it mean to say that every possibility in which not-P is eliminated? An idiom of quantification, like "every", is normally restricted to some limited domain. If I say that every glass is empty, so it's time for another round, doubtless I and my audience are ignoring most of all the glasses there are in the whole wide world throughout all of time. They are outside the domain. They are irrelevant to the truth of what was said.

Likewise, if I say that every uneliminated possibility is one in which P, or words to that effect, I am doubtless ignoring some of all the uneliminated alternative possibilities that there are. They are outside the domain, they are irrelevant to the truth of what was said.

But, of course, I am not entitled to ignore just any possibility I please. Else true ascriptions of knowledge, whether to myself or to others, would be cheap indeed. I may properly ignore some uneliminated possibilities; I may not properly ignore others. Our definition of knowledge requires a *sotto voce* proviso. S *knows* that P iff S's evidence eliminates every possibility in which not-P – Psst! – except for those possibilities that we are properly ignoring.

Unger suggests an instructive parallel.[8] Just as P is known iff there are no uneliminated possibilities of error, so likewise a surface is flat iff there are no bumps on it. We must add the proviso: Psst! – except for those bumps that we are properly ignoring. Else we will conclude, absurdly, that nothing is flat. (Simplify by ignoring departures from flatness that consist of gentle curvature.)

We can restate the definition. Say that we *presuppose* proposition Q iff we ignore all possibilities in which not-Q. To close the circle: we *ignore* just those possibilities that falsify our presuppositions. *Proper* presupposition corresponds, of course, to proper ignoring. Then S knows that P iff S's evidence eliminates every possibility in which not-P – Psst! – except for those possibilities that conflict with our proper presuppositions.[9]

The rest of (modal) epistemology examines the *sotto voce* proviso. It asks: what may we properly presuppose in our ascriptions of knowledge? Which of all the uneliminated alternative possibilities may not properly be ignored? Which ones are the "relevant alternatives"? – relevant, that is, to what the subject does and doesn't know?[10] In reply, we can list several rules.[11] We begin with three prohibitions: rules to tell us what possibilities we may not properly ignore.

First, there is the *Rule of Actuality*. The possibility that actually obtains is never properly ignored; actuality is always a relevant alternative; nothing false may properly be presupposed. It follows that only what is true is known, wherefore we did not have to include truth in our definition of knowledge. The rule is "externalist" – the subject himself may not be able to tell what is properly ignored. In judging which of his ignorings are proper, hence what he knows, we judge his success in knowing – not how well he tried.

When the Rule of Actuality tells us that actuality may never be properly ignored, we can ask: *whose* actuality? Ours, when we ascribe knowledge or ignorance to others? Or the subject's? In simple cases, the question is silly. (In fact, it sounds like the sort of pernicious nonsense we would expect from someone who mixes up what is true with what is believed.) There is just one actual world, we the ascribers live in that world, the subject lives there too, so the subject's actuality is the same as ours.

But there are other cases, less simple, in which the question makes perfect sense and needs an answer. Someone may or may not know who he is; someone may or may not know what time it is. Therefore I insisted that the propositions that may be known must include propositions *de se et nunc*; and likewise that the possibilities that may be eliminated or ignored must include possibilities *de se et nunc*. Now we have a good sense in which the subject's actuality may be different from ours. I ask today what Fred knew yesterday. In particular, did he then know who he was? Did he know what day it was? Fred's actuality is the possibility *de se et nunc* of being Fred on September 19th at such-and-such possible world; whereas my actuality is the possibility *de se et nunc* of being David on September 20th at such-and-such world. So far as the world goes, there is no difference: Fred and I are worldmates, his actual world is the same as mine. But when we build subject and time into the possibilities *de se et nunc*, then his actuality yesterday does indeed differ from mine today.

What is more, we sometimes have occasion to ascribe knowledge to those who are off at other possible worlds. I didn't read the newspaper yesterday. What would I have known if I had read it? More than I do in fact know. (More and less: I do in fact know that I left the newspaper unread, but if I had read it, I would not have known that I had left it unread.) I-who-did-not-read-the-newspaper am here at this world, ascribing knowledge and ignorance. The subject to whom I am ascribing that knowledge and ignorance, namely I-as-I-would-have-been-if-I-had-read-the-newspaper, is at a different world. The worlds differ in respect at least of a reading of the newspaper. Thus the ascriber's actual world is not the same as the subject's. (I myself think that the ascriber and the subject are two different people: the subject is the ascriber's otherworldly counterpart. But even if you think the subject and the ascriber are the same identical person, you must still grant that this person's actuality *qua* subject differs from his actuality *qua* ascriber.)

Or suppose we ask modal questions about the subject: what must he have known, what might he have known? Again we are considering the subject as he is not here, but off at other possible worlds. Likewise if we ask questions about knowledge of knowledge: what does he (or what do we) know that he knows?

So the question "whose actuality?" is not a silly question after all. And when the question matters, as it does in the cases just considered, the right answer is that it is the subject's actuality, not the ascriber's, that never can be properly ignored.

Next, there is the *Rule of Belief*. A possibility that the subject believes to obtain is not properly ignored, whether or not he is right to so believe. Neither is one that he ought to believe to obtain – one that evidence and arguments justify him in believing – whether or not he does so believe.

That is rough. Since belief admits of degree, and since some possibilities are more specific than others, we ought to reformulate the rule in terms of degree of belief, compared to a standard set by the unspecificity of the possibility in question. A possibility may not be properly ignored if the subject gives it, or ought to give it, a degree of belief that is sufficiently high, and high not just because the possibility in question is unspecific.

How high is "sufficiently high"? That may depend on how much is at stake. When error would be especially disastrous, few possibilities may be properly ignored. Then even quite a low degree of belief may be "sufficiently high" to bring the Rule of Belief into play. The jurors know that the accused is guilty only if his guilt has been proved beyond reasonable doubt.[12]

Yet even when the stakes are high, some possibilities still may be properly ignored. Disastrous though it would be to convict an innocent man, still the jurors may properly ignore the possibility that it was the dog, marvellously well-trained, that fired the fatal shot. And, unless they are ignoring other alternatives more relevant than that, they may rightly be said to know that the accused is guilty as charged. Yet if there had been reason to give the dog hypothesis a slightly less negligible degree of belief – if the world's greatest dog-trainer had been the victim's mortal enemy – then the alternative would be relevant after all.

This is the only place where belief and justification enter my story. As already noted, I allow justified true belief without knowledge, as in the case of your belief that you will lose the lottery. I allow knowledge without justification, in the cases of face recognition and chicken sexing. I even allow knowledge without belief, as in the case of the timid student who knows the answer but has no confidence that he has it right, and so does not believe what he knows.[13] Therefore any proposed converse to the Rule of Belief should be rejected. A possibility that the subject does not believe to a sufficient degree, and ought not to believe to a sufficient degree, may nevertheless be a relevant alternative and not properly ignored.

Next, there is the *Rule of Resemblance*. Suppose one possibility saliently resembles another. Then if one of them may not be properly ignored, neither may the other. (Or rather, we should say that if one of them may not properly be ignored *in virtue of rules other than this rule*, then neither may the other. Else nothing could be properly ignored; because enough little steps of resemblance can take us from anywhere to anywhere.) Or suppose one possibility saliently resembles two or more others, one in one respect and another in another, and suppose that each of these may not properly be ignored (in virtue of rules other than this rule). Then these resemblances may have an additive effect, doing more together than any one of them would separately.

We must apply the Rule of Resemblance with care. Actuality is a possibility uneliminated by the subject's evidence. Any other possibility W that is likewise uneliminated by the subject's evidence thereby resembles actuality in one salient respect: namely, in respect of the subject's evidence. That will be so even if W is in other respects very dissimilar to actuality – even if, for instance, it is a possibility in which the subject is radically deceived by a demon. Plainly, we dare not apply the Rules of Actuality and Resemblance to conclude that any such W is a relevant alternative – that would be capitulation to scepticism. The Rule of Resemblance was never meant to apply to *this* resemblance! We seem to have an *ad hoc* exception to the Rule, though one that makes good sense in view of the function of attributions of knowledge. What would be better, though, would be to find a way to reformulate the Rule so as to get the needed exception without *ad hoc*ery. I do not know how to do this.

It is the Rule of Resemblance that explains why you do not know that you will lose the lottery, no matter what the odds are against you and no matter how sure you should therefore be that you will lose. For every ticket, there is the possibility that it will win. These possibilities are saliently similar to one another: so either every one of them may be properly ignored, or else none may. But one of them may not properly be ignored: the one that actually obtains.

The Rule of Resemblance also is the rule that solves the Gettier problems: other cases of justified true belief that are not knowledge.[14]

(1) I think that Nogot owns a Ford, because I have seen him driving one; but unbeknownst to me he does not own the Ford he drives, or any other Ford. Unbeknownst to me, Havit does own a Ford, though I have no reason to think so because he never drives it, and in fact I have often seen him taking the tram. My justified true belief is that one of the two owns a Ford. But I do not know it; I am right by accident. Diagnosis: I do not know, because I have not eliminated the possibility that Nogot drives a Ford he does not own whereas Havit neither drives nor owns a car. This possibility may not properly be ignored. Because, first, actuality may not properly be ignored; and, second, this possibility saliently resembles actuality. It resembles actuality perfectly so far as

Nogot is concerned; and it resembles actuality well so far as Havit is concerned, since it matches actuality both with respect to Havit's carless habits and with respect to the general correlation between carless habits and carlessness. In addition, this possibility saliently resembles a third possibility: one in which Nogot drives a Ford he owns while Havit neither drives nor owns a car. This third possibility may not properly be ignored, because of the degree to which it is believed. This time, the resemblance is perfect so far as Havit is concerned, rather good so far as Nogot is concerned.

(2) The stopped clock is right twice a day. It says 4:39, as it has done for weeks. I look at it at 4:39; by luck I pick up a true belief. I have ignored the uneliminated possibility that I looked at it at 4:22 while it was stopped saying 4:39. That possibility was not properly ignored. It resembles actuality perfectly so far as the stopped clock goes.

(3) Unbeknownst to me, I am travelling in the land of the bogus barns; but my eye falls on one of the few real ones. I don't know that I am seeing a barn, because I may not properly ignore the possibility that I am seeing yet another of the abundant bogus barns. This possibility saliently resembles actuality in respect of the abundance of bogus barns, and the scarcity of real ones, hereabouts.

(4) Donald is in San Francisco, just as I have every reason to think he is. But, bent on deception, he is writing me letters and having them posted to me by his accomplice in Italy. If I had seen the phoney letters, with their Italian stamps and post-marks, I would have concluded that Donald was in Italy. Luckily, I have not yet seen any of them. I ignore the uneliminated possibility that Donald has gone to Italy and is sending me letters from there. But this possibility is not properly ignored, because it resembles actuality both with respect to the fact that the letters are coming to me from Italy and with respect to the fact that those letters come, ultimately, from Donald. So I don't know that Donald is in San Francisco.

Next, there is the *Rule of Reliability*. This time, we have a presumptive rule about what *may* be properly ignored; and it is by means of this rule that we capture what is right about causal or reliabilist theories of knowing. Consider processes whereby information is transmitted to us: perception, memory, and testimony. These processes are fairly reliable.[15] Within limits, we are entitled to take them for granted. We may properly presuppose that they work without a glitch in the case under consideration. Defeasibly – *very* defeasibly! – a possibility in which they fail may properly be ignored.

My visual experience, for instance, depends causally on the scene before my eyes, and what I believe about the scene before my eyes depends in turn on my visual experience. Each dependence covers a wide and varied range of alternatives.[16] Of course, it is possible to hallucinate – even to hallucinate in such a way that all my perceptual experience and memory would be just as they actually are. That possibility never can be eliminated. But it can be ignored. And if it is properly ignored – as it mostly is – then vision gives me knowledge. Sometimes, though, the possibility of hallucination is not properly ignored; for sometimes we really do hallucinate. The Rule of Reliability may be defeated by the Rule of Actuality. Or it may be defeated by the Rules of Actuality and of Resemblance working together, in a Gettier problem: if I am not hallucinating, but unbeknownst to me I live in a world where people mostly do hallucinate and I myself have only narrowly escaped, then the uneliminated possibility of hallucination is too close to actuality to be properly ignored.

We do not, of course, presuppose that nowhere ever is there a failure of, say, vision. The general presupposition that vision is reliable consists, rather, of a standing disposition to presuppose, concerning whatever particular case may be under consideration, that we have no failure in that case.

In similar fashion, we have two permissive *Rules of Method*. We are entitled to presuppose – again, very defeasibly – that a sample is representative; and that the best explanation of our evidence is the true explanation. That is, we are entitled properly to ignore possible failures in these two standard methods of non-deductive inference. Again, the general rule consists of a standing disposition to presuppose reliability in whatever particular case may come before us.

Yet another permissive rule is the *Rule of Conservatism*. Suppose that those around us normally do ignore certain possibilities, and it is common knowledge that they do. (They do, they expect each other to, they expect each other to expect each other to ...) Then – again, very defeasibly! – these generally ignored possibilities may properly be ignored. We are permitted, defeasibly, to adopt the usual and mutually expected presuppositions of those around us.

(It is unclear whether we need all four of these permissive rules. Some might be subsumed under others. Perhaps our habits of treating samples as representative, and of inferring to the best explanation, might count as normally reliable processes of transmission of information. Or perhaps we might subsume the Rule of Reliability under the Rule of Conservatism, on the ground that the reliable processes whereby we gain knowledge are familiar, are generally relied upon, and so are generally presupposed to be normally reliable. Then the only extra work done by the Rule of Reliability would be to cover less familiar – and merely hypothetical? – reliable processes, such as processes that relied on extrasensory faculties. Likewise, *mutatis mutandis*, we might subsume the Rules of Method under the Rule of Conservatism. Or we might instead think to subsume the Rule of Conservatism under the Rule of Reliability, on the ground that what is generally presupposed tends for the most part to be true, and the reliable processes whereby this is so are covered already by the Rule of Reliability. Better redundancy than incompleteness, though. So, leaving the question of redundancy open, I list all four rules.)

Our final rule is the *Rule of Attention*. But it is more a triviality than a rule. When we say that a possibility *is* properly ignored, we mean exactly that; we do not mean that it *could have been* properly ignored. Accordingly, a possibility not ignored at all is *ipso facto* not properly ignored. What is and what is not being ignored is a feature of the particular conversational context. No matter how far-fetched a certain possibility may be, no matter how properly we might have ignored it in some other context, if in *this* context we are not in fact ignoring it but attending to it, then for us now it is a relevant alternative. It is in the contextually determined domain. If it is an uneliminated possibility in which not-*P*, then it will do as a counter-example to the claim that *P* holds in every possibility left uneliminated by S's evidence. That

is, it will do as a counter-example to the claim that S knows that *P*.

Do some epistemology. Let your fantasies rip. Find uneliminated possibilities of error everywhere. Now that you are attending to them, just as I told you to, you are no longer ignoring them, properly or otherwise. So you have landed in a context with an enormously rich domain of potential counter-examples to ascriptions of knowledge. In such an extraordinary context, with such a rich domain, it never can happen (well, hardly ever) that an ascription of knowledge is true. Not an ascription of knowledge to yourself (either to your present self or to your earlier self, untainted by epistemology); and not an ascription of knowledge to others. That is how epistemology destroys knowledge. But it does so only temporarily. The pastime of epistemology does not plunge us forevermore into its special context. We can still do a lot of proper ignoring, a lot of knowing, and a lot of true ascribing of knowledge to ourselves and others, the rest of the time.

What is epistemology all about? The epistemology we've just been doing, at any rate, soon became an investigation of the ignoring of possibilities. But to investigate the ignoring of them was *ipso facto* not to ignore them. Unless this investigation of ours was an altogether atypical sample of epistemology, it will be inevitable that epistemology must destroy knowledge. That is how knowledge is elusive. Examine it, and straightway it vanishes.

Is resistance useless? If you bring some hitherto ignored possibility to our attention, then straightway we are not ignoring it at all, so *a fortiori* we are not properly ignoring it. How can this alteration of our conversational state be undone? If you are persistent, perhaps it cannot be undone – at least not so long as you are around. Even if we go off and play backgammon, and afterward start our conversation afresh, you might turn up and call our attention to it all over again.

But maybe you called attention to the hitherto ignored possibility by mistake. You only suggested that we ought to suspect the butler because you mistakenly thought him to have a criminal record. Now that you know he does not – that was the *previous* butler – you wish you had not mentioned him at all. You know as well as we do that continued attention to the possibility you brought up impedes our shared conversational purposes. Indeed, it may be common knowledge between you and us that we would all prefer it if this possibility could be dismissed from our attention. In that case we might quickly strike a tacit agreement to speak just as if we were ignoring it; and after just a little of that, doubtless it really would be ignored.

Sometimes our conversational purposes are not altogether shared, and it is a matter of conflict whether attention to some far-fetched possibility would advance them or impede them. What if some far-fetched possibility is called to our attention not by a sceptical philosopher, but by counsel for the defence? We of the jury may wish to ignore it, and wish it had not been mentioned. If we ignored it now, we would bend the rules of cooperative conversation; but we may have good reason to do exactly that. (After all, what matters most to us as jurors is not whether we can truly be said to know; what really matters is what we should believe to what degree, and whether or not we should vote to convict.) We would ignore the far-fetched possibility if we could – but can we? Perhaps at first our attempted ignoring would be make-believe ignoring, or self-deceptive ignoring; later, perhaps, it might ripen into genuine ignoring. But in the meantime, do we know? There may be no definite answer. We are bending the rules, and our practices of context-dependent attributions of knowledge were made for contexts with the rules unbent.

If you are still a contented fallibilist, despite my plea to hear the sceptical argument afresh, you will probably be discontented with the Rule of Attention. You will begrudge the sceptic even his very temporary victory. You will claim the right to resist his argument not only in everyday contexts, but even in those peculiar contexts in which he (or some other epistemologist) busily calls your attention to far-fetched possibilities of error. Further, you will claim the right to resist without having to bend any rules of cooperative conversation. I said that the Rule of Attention was a triviality: that which is not ignored at all is not properly ignored. But the Rule was trivial only because of how I had already chosen to state the *sotto voce* proviso. So you, the contented fallibilist, will think it ought to have been stated differently. Thus, perhaps: "Psst! – except for those possibilities we *could* properly have ignored." And then you will insist that those

far-fetched possibilities of error that we attend to at the behest of the sceptic are nevertheless possibilities we could properly have ignored. You will say that no amount of attention can, by itself, turn them into relevant alternatives.

If you say this, we have reached a standoff. I started with a puzzle: how can it be, when his conclusion is so silly, that the sceptic's argument is so irresistible? My Rule of Attention, and the version of the proviso that made that Rule trivial, were built to explain how the sceptic manages to sway us – why his argument seems irresistible, however temporarily. If you continue to find it eminently resistible in all contexts, you have no need of any such explanation. We just disagree about the explanandum phenomenon.

I say S knows that P iff P holds in every possibility left uneliminated by S's evidence – Psst! – except for those possibilities that *we* are properly ignoring. "We" means: the speaker and hearers of a given context; that is, those of us who are discussing S's knowledge together. It is our ignorings, not S's own ignorings, that matter to what we can truly say about S's knowledge. When we are talking about our own knowledge or ignorance, as epistemologists so often do, this is a distinction without a difference. But what if we are talking about someone else?

Suppose we are detectives; the crucial question for our solution of the crime is whether S already *knew*, when he bought the gun, that he was vulnerable to blackmail. We conclude that he did. *We* ignore various far-fetched possibilities, as hardheaded detectives should. But S does not ignore them. S is by profession a sceptical epistemologist. He never ignores much of anything. If it is our own ignorings that matter to the truth of our conclusion, we may well be right that S already knew. But if it is S's ignorings that matter, then we are wrong, because S never knew much of anything. I say we may well be right; so it is our own ignorings that matter, not S's.

But suppose instead that we are epistemologists considering what S knows. If we are well-informed about S (or if we are considering a well-enough specified hypothetical case), then if S attends to a certain possibility, we attend to S's attending to it. But to attend to S's attending to it is *ipso facto* to attend to it ourselves. In that case, unlike the case of the detectives, the possibilities we are properly ignoring must be among the possibilities that S himself ignores. We may ignore fewer possibilities than S does, but not more.

Even if S himself is neither sceptical nor an epistemologist, he may yet be clever at thinking up far-fetched possibilities that are unelimilated by his evidence. Then again, we well-informed epistemologists who ask what S knows will have to attend to the possibilities that S thinks up. Even if S's idle cleverness does not lead S himself to draw sceptical conclusions, it nevertheless limits the knowledge that we can truly ascribe to him when attentive to his state of mind. More simply: his cleverness limits his knowledge. He would have known more, had he been less imaginative.[17]

Do I claim you can know P just by presupposing it?! Do I claim you can know that a possibility W does not obtain just by ignoring it? Is that not what my analysis implies, provided that the presupposing and the ignoring are proper? Well, yes. And yet I do not claim it. Or rather, I do not claim it for any specified P or W. I have to grant, in general, that knowledge just by presupposing and ignoring *is* knowledge; but it is an *especially* elusive sort of knowledge, and consequently it is an unclaimable sort of knowledge. You do not even have to practise epistemology to make it vanish. Simply *mentioning* any particular case of this knowledge, aloud or even in silent thought, is a way to attend to the hitherto ignored possibility, and thereby render it no longer ignored, and thereby create a context in which it is no longer true to ascribe the knowledge in question to yourself or others. So, just as we should think, presuppositions alone are not a basis on which to *claim* knowledge.

In general, when S knows that P some of the possibilities in which not-P are eliminated by S's evidence and others of them are properly ignored. There are some that can be eliminated, but cannot properly be ignored. For instance, when I look around the study without seeing Possum the cat, I thereby eliminate various possibilities in which Possum is in the study; but had those possibilities not been eliminated, they could not properly have been ignored. And there are other possibilities that never can be eliminated, but can properly be ignored. For instance, the possibility that Possum is on the desk but has been made invisible by a

deceiving demon falls normally into this class (though not when I attend to it in the special context of epistemology).

There is a third class: not-P possibilities that might either be eliminated or ignored. Take the far-fetched possibility that Possum has somehow managed to get into a closed drawer of the desk – maybe he jumped in when it was open, then I closed it without noticing him. That possibility could be eliminated by opening the drawer and making a thorough examination. But if unelimilated, it may nevertheless be ignored, and in many contexts that ignoring would be proper. If I look all around the study, but without checking the closed drawers of the desk, I may truly be said to know that Possum is not in the study – or at any rate, there are many contexts in which that may truly be said. But if I did check all the closed drawers, then I would know *better* that Possum is not in the study. My knowledge would be better in the second case because it would rest more on the elimination of not-P possibilities, less on the ignoring of them.[18, 19]

Better knowledge is more stable knowledge: it stands more chance of surviving a shift of attention in which we begin to attend to some of the possibilities formerly ignored. If, in our new shifted context, we ask what knowledge we may truly ascribe to our earlier selves, we may find that only the better knowledge of our earlier selves still deserves the name. And yet, if our former ignorings were proper at the time, even the worse knowledge of our earlier selves could truly have been called knowledge in the former context.

Never – well, hardly ever – does our knowledge rest entirely on elimination and not at all on ignoring. So hardly ever is it quite as good as we might wish. To that extent, the lesson of scepticism is right – and right permanently, not just in the temporary and special context of epistemology.[20]

What is it all for? Why have a notion of knowledge that works in the way I described? (Not a compulsory question. Enough to observe that we do have it.) But I venture the guess that it is one of the messy short-cuts – like satisficing, like having indeterminate degrees of belief – that we resort to because we are not smart enough to live up to really high, perfectly Bayesian, standards of rationality. You cannot maintain a record of exactly which possibilities you have eliminated so far, much as you might like to. It is easier to keep track of which possibilities you have eliminated if you – Psst! – ignore many of all the possibilities there are. And besides, it is easier to list some of the propositions that are true in *all* the uneliminated, unignored possibilities than it is to find propositions that are true in *all and only* the uneliminated, unignored possibilities.

If you doubt that the word "know" bears any real load in science or in metaphysics, I partly agree. The serious business of science has to do not with knowledge *per se*; but rather, with the elimination of possibilities through the evidence of perception, memory, etc., and with the changes that one's belief system would (or might or should) undergo under the impact of such eliminations. Ascriptions of knowledge to yourself or others are a very sloppy way of conveying very incomplete information about the elimination of possibilities. It is as if you had said:

> The possibilities eliminated, whatever else they may also include, at least include all the not-*P* possibilities; or anyway, all of those except for some we are presumably prepared to ignore just at the moment.

The only excuse for giving information about what really matters in such a sloppy way is that at least it is easy and quick! But it *is* easy and quick; whereas giving full and precise information about which possibilities have been eliminated seems to be extremely difficult, as witness the futile search for a "pure observation language". If I am right about how ascriptions of knowledge work, they are a handy but humble approximation. They may yet be indispensable in practice, in the same way that other handy and humble approximations are.

If we analyse knowledge as a modality, as we have done, we cannot escape the conclusion that knowledge is closed under (strict) implication.[21] Dretske has denied that knowledge is closed under implication; further, he has diagnosed closure as the fallacy that drives arguments for scepticism. As follows: the proposition that I have hands implies that I am not a handless being, and *a fortiori* that I am not a handless being deceived by a demon into thinking that I have hands. So, by the closure principle, the proposition that I know

I have hands implies that I know that I am not handless and deceived. But I don't know that I am not handless and deceived – for how can I eliminate that possibility? So, by *modus tollens*, I don't know that I have hands. Dretske's advice is to resist scepticism by denying closure. He says that although having hands *does* imply not being handless and deceived, yet knowing that I have hands *does not* imply knowing that I am not handless and deceived. I do know the former, I do not know the latter.[22]

What Dretske says is close to right, but not quite. Knowledge *is* closed under implication. Knowing that I have hands *does* imply knowing that I am not handless and deceived. Implication preserves truth – that is, it preserves truth in any given, fixed context. But if we switch contexts midway, all bets are off. I say (1) pigs fly; (2) what I just said had fewer than three syllables (true); (3) what I just said had fewer than four syllables (false). So "less than three" does not imply "less than four"? No! The context switched midway, the semantic value of the context-dependent phrase "what I just said" switched with it. Likewise in the sceptical argument the context switched midway, and the semantic value of the context-dependent word "know" switched with it. The premise "I know that I have hands" was true in its everyday context, where the possibility of deceiving demons was properly ignored. The mention of that very possibility switched the context midway. The conclusion "I know that I am not handless and deceived" was false in *its* context, because that was a context in which the possibility of deceiving demons was being mentioned, hence was not being ignored, hence was not being properly ignored. Dretske gets the phenomenon right, and I think he gets the diagnosis of scepticism right; it is just that he misclassifies what he sees. He thinks it is a phenomenon of logic, when really it is a phenomenon of pragmatics. Closure, rightly understood, survives the test. If we evaluate the conclusion for truth not with respect to the context in which it was uttered, but instead with respect to the different context in which the premise was uttered, then truth is preserved. And if, *per impossibile*, the conclusion could have been said in the same unchanged context as the premise, truth would have been preserved.

A problem due to Saul Kripke turns upon the closure of knowledge under implication. *P* implies that any evidence against *P* is misleading. So, by closure, whenever you know that *P*, you know that any evidence against *P* is misleading. And if you know that evidence is misleading, you should pay it no heed. Whenever we know – and we know a lot, remember – we should not heed any evidence tending to suggest that we are wrong. But that is absurd. Shall we dodge the conclusion by denying closure? I think not. Again, I diagnose a change of context. At first, it was stipulated that S knew, whence it followed that S was properly ignoring all possibilities of error. But as the story continues, it turns out that there is evidence on offer that points to some particular possibility of error. Then, by the Rule of Attention, that possibility is no longer properly ignored, either by S himself or by we who are telling the story of S. The advent of that evidence destroys S's knowledge, and thereby destroys S's licence to ignore the evidence lest he be misled.

There is another reason, different from Dretske's, why we might doubt closure. Suppose two or more premises jointly imply a conclusion. Might not someone who is compartmentalized in his thinking – as we all are? – know each of the premises but fail to bring them together in a single compartment? Then might he not fail to know the conclusion? Yes; and I would not like to plead idealization-of-rationality as an excuse for ignoring such cases. But I suggest that we might take not the whole compartmentalized thinker, but rather each of his several overlapping compartments, as our "subjects". That would be the obvious remedy if his compartmentalization amounted to a case of multiple personality disorder; but maybe it is right for milder cases as well.[23]

A compartmentalized thinker who indulges in epistemology can destroy his knowledge, yet retain it as well. Imagine two epistemologists on a bushwalk. As they walk, they talk. They mention all manner of far-fetched possibilities of error. By attending to these normally ignored possibilities they destroy the knowledge they normally possess. Yet all the while they know where they are and where they are going! How so? The compartment in charge of philosophical talk attends to far-fetched possibilities of error. The compartment in charge of navigation does not. One compartment loses its knowledge, the other retains its knowledge. And what does the entire compartmentalized

thinker know? Not an altogether felicitous question. But if we need an answer, I suppose the best thing to say is that S knows that *P* iff any one of S's compartments knows that *P*. Then we can say what we would offhand want to say: yes, our philosophical bushwalkers still know their whereabouts.

Context-dependence is not limited to the ignoring and non-ignoring of far-fetched possibilities. Here is another case. Pity poor Bill! He squanders all his spare cash on the pokies, the races, and the lottery. He will be a wage slave all his days. We know he will never be rich. But if he wins the lottery (if he wins big), then he will be rich. Contrapositively: his never being rich, plus other things we know, imply that he will lose. So, by closure, if we know that he will never be rich, we know that he will lose. But when we discussed the case before, we concluded that we cannot know that he will lose. All the possibilities in which Bill loses and someone else wins saliently resemble the possibility in which Bill wins and the others lose; one of those possibilities is actual; so by the Rules of Actuality and of Resemblance, we may not properly ignore the possibility that Bill wins. But there is a loophole: the resemblance was required to be salient. Salience, as well as ignoring, may vary between contexts. Before, when I was explaining how the Rule of Resemblance applied to lotteries, I saw to it that the resemblance between the many possibilities associated with the many tickets was sufficiently salient. But this time, when we were busy pitying poor Bill for his habits and not for his luck, the resemblance of the many possibilities was not so salient. At that point, the possibility of Bill's winning was properly ignored; so then it was true to say that we knew he would never be rich. Afterward I switched the context. I mentioned the possibility that Bill might win, wherefore that possibility was no longer properly ignored. (Maybe there were two separate reasons why it was no longer properly ignored, because maybe I also made the resemblance between the many possibilities more salient.) It was true at first that we knew that Bill would never be rich. And at that point it was also true that we knew he would lose – but that was only true so long as it remained unsaid! (And maybe unthought as well.) Later, after the change in context, it was no longer true that we knew he would lose. At that point, it was also no longer true that we knew he would never be rich.

But wait. Don't you smell a rat? Haven't I, by my own lights, been saying what cannot be said? (Or whistled either.) If the story I told was true, how have I managed to tell it? In trendyspeak, is there not a problem of reflexivity? Does not my story deconstruct itself?

I said: S knows that *P* iff S's evidence eliminates every possibility in which not-*P* – Psst! – except for those possibilities that we are properly ignoring. That "psst" marks an attempt to do the impossible – to mention that which remains unmentioned. I am sure you managed to make believe that I had succeeded. But I could not have done.

And I said that when we do epistemology, and we attend to the proper ignoring of possibilities, we make knowledge vanish. First we do know, then we do not. But I had been doing epistemology when I said that. The uneliminated possibilities were *not* being ignored – not just then. So by what right did I say even that we used to know?[24]

In trying to thread a course between the rock of fallibilism and the whirlpool of scepticism, it may well seem as if I have fallen victim to both at once. For do I not say that there are all those uneliminated possibilities of error? Yet do I not claim that we know a lot? Yet do I not claim that knowledge is, by definition, infallible knowledge?

I did claim all three things. But not all at once! Or if I did claim them all at once, that was an expository shortcut, to be taken with a pinch of salt. To get my message across, I bent the rules. If I tried to whistle what cannot be said, what of it? I relied on the cardinal principle of pragmatics, which overrides every one of the rules I mentioned: interpret the message to make it make sense – to make it consistent, and sensible to say.

When you have context-dependence, ineffability can be trite and unmysterious. Hush! [moment of silence] I might have liked to say, just then, "All of us are silent". It was true. But I could not have said it truly, or whistled it either. For by saying it aloud, or by whistling, I would have rendered it false.

I could have said my say fair and square, bending no rules. It would have been tiresome, but it could have been done. The secret would have been to resort to "semantic ascent". I could have taken great care to distinguish between (1) the language I use when I talk about knowledge, or whatever, and (2) the second language that I use to talk about the semantic and pragmatic workings of the first language. If you want to hear my story told that way, you probably know enough to do the job for yourself. If you can, then my informal presentation has been good enough.

Notes

1 The suggestion that ascriptions of knowledge go false in the context of epistemology is to be found in Barry Stroud, "Understanding Human Knowledge in General", in Marjorie Clay and Keith Lehrer (eds), *Knowledge and Skepticism* (Boulder: Westview Press, 1989); and in Stephen Hetherington, "Lacking Knowledge and Justification by Theorising About Them" (lecture at the University of New South Wales, August 1992). Neither of them tells the story just as I do, however it may be that their versions do not conflict with mine.

2 Unless, like some, we simply define "justification" as "whatever it takes to turn true opinion into knowledge" regardless of whether what it takes turns out to involve argument from supporting reasons.

3 The problem of the lottery was introduced in Henry Kyburg, *Probability and the Logic of Rational Belief* (Middletown, CT: Wesleyan University Press, 1961), and in Carl Hempel, "Deductive-Nomological vs. Statistical Explanation", in Herbert Feigl and Grover Maxwell (eds), *Minnesota Studies in the Philosophy of Science*, vol. II (Minneapolis: University of Minnesota Press, 1962). It has been much discussed since, as a problem both about knowledge and about our everyday, non-quantitative concept of belief.

4 The case of testimony is less discussed than the others; but see C. A. J. Coady, *Testimony: A Philosophical Study* (Oxford: Clarendon Press, 1992), pp. 79–129.

5 I follow Peter Unger, *Ignorance: A Case for Skepticism* (New York: Oxford University

Press, 1975). But I shall not let him lead me into scepticism.

6   See Robert Stalnaker, *Inquiry* (Cambridge, MA: MIT Press, 1984), pp. 59–99.

7   See my "Attitudes *De Dicto* and *De Se*", *The Philosophical Review* 88 (1979), pp. 513–43; and R. M. Chisholm, "The Indirect Reflexive", in C. Diamond and J. Teichman (eds), *Intention and Intentionality: Essays in Honour of G. E. M. Anscombe* (Brighton: Harvester, 1979).

8   Peter Unger, *Ignorance*, chapter II. I discuss the case, and briefly foreshadow the present paper, in my "Scorekeeping in a Language Game", *Journal of Philosophical Logic* 8 (1979), pp. 339–59, esp. pp. 353–5.

9   See Robert Stalnaker, "Presuppositions", *Journal of Philosophical Logic* 2 (1973), pp. 447–57; and "Pragmatic Presuppositions", in Milton Munitz and Peter Unger (eds), *Semantics and Philosophy* (New York: New York University Press, 1974). See also my "Scorekeeping in a Language Game".

    The definition restated in terms of presupposition resembles the treatment of knowledge in Kenneth S. Ferguson, *Philosophical Scepticism* (Cornell University doctoral dissertation, 1980).

10 See Fred Dretske, "Epistemic Operators", *The Journal of Philosophy* 67 (1970), pp. 1007–22, and "The Pragmatic Dimension of Knowledge", *Philosophical Studies* 40 (1981), pp. 363–78; Alvin Goldman, "Discrimination and Perceptual Knowledge", *The Journal of Philosophy* 73 (1976), pp. 771–91; G. C. Stine, "Skepticism, Relevant Alternatives, and Deductive Closure", *Philosophical Studies* 29 (1976), pp. 249–61; and Stewart Cohen, "How to be A Fallibilist", *Philosophical Perspectives* 2 (1988), pp. 91–123.

11 Some of them, but only some, taken from the authors just cited.

12 Instead of complicating the Rule of Belief as I have just done, I might equivalently have introduced a separate Rule of High Stakes saying that when error would be especially disastrous, few possibilities are properly ignored.

13 A. D. Woozley, "Knowing and Not Knowing", *Proceedings of the Aristotelian Society* 53 (1953), pp. 151–72; Colin Radford, "Knowledge – By Examples", *Analysis* 27 (1966), pp. 1–11.

14 See Edmund Gettier, "Is Justified True Belief Knowledge?", this vol., ch. 15. Diagnoses have varied widely. The four examples below come from: (1) Keith Lehrer and Thomas Paxson Jr., "Knowledge: Undefeated True Belief", *The Journal of Philosophy* 66 (1969), pp. 225–37; (2) Bertrand Russell, *Human Knowledge: Its Scope and Limits* (London: Allen and Unwin, 1948), p. 154; (3) Alvin Goldman, "Discrimination and Perceptual Knowledge"; (4) Gilbert Harman, *Thought* (Princeton, NJ: Princeton University Press, 1973), p. 143.

    Though the lottery problem is another case of justified true belief without knowledge, it is not normally counted among the Gettier problems. It is interesting to find that it yields to the same remedy.

15 See Alvin Goldman, "A Causal Theory of Knowing", *The Journal of Philosophy* 64 (1967), pp. 357–72; D. M. Armstrong, *Belief, Truth and Knowledge* (Cambridge: Cambridge University Press, 1973).

16 See my "Veridical Hallucination and Prosthetic Vision", *Australasian Journal of Philosophy* 58 (1980), pp. 239–49. John Bigelow has proposed to model knowledge-delivering processes generally on those found in vision.

17 See Catherine Elgin, "The Epistemic Efficacy of Stupidity", *Synthese* 74 (1988), pp. 297–311. The "efficacy" takes many forms; some to do with knowledge (under various rival analyses), some to do with justified belief. See also Michael Williams, *Unnatural Doubts: Epistemological Realism and the Basis of Scepticism* (Oxford: Blackwell, 1991), pp. 352–5, on the instability of knowledge under reflection.

18 Mixed cases are possible: Fred properly ignores the possibility W_1 which Ted eliminates; however Ted properly ignores the possibility W_2 which Fred eliminates. Ted has looked in all the desk drawers but not the file drawers, whereas Fred has checked the file drawers but not the desk. Fred's knowledge that Possum is not in the study is better in one way, Ted's is better in another.

19 To say truly that X is known, I must be properly ignoring any uneliminated possibilities in which not-X; whereas to say truly that Y is better known than X, I must be attending to some such possibilities. So I cannot say both in a single context. If I say "X is known, but Y is better known", the context changes in midsentence: some previously ignored possibilities must stop being ignored. That can happen easily. Saying it the other way around – "Y is better known than X, but even X is known" – is harder, because we must suddenly start to ignore previously unignored possibilities. That cannot be done, really; but we could bend the rules and make believe we had done it, and no doubt we would be understood well enough. Saying "X is flat, but Y is flatter" (that is, "X has no bumps at all, but Y has even fewer or smaller bumps") is a parallel case. And again, "Y is flatter, but even X is flat" sounds clearly worse – but not altogether hopeless.

20 Thanks here to Stephen Hetherington. While his own views about better and worse knowledge are situated within an analysis of knowledge quite unlike mine, they withstand transplantation.

21 A proof-theoretic version of this closure principle is common to all "normal" modal logics: if the logic validates an inference from zero or more premises to a conclusion, then also it validates the inference obtained by prefixing the necessity operator to each premise and to the conclusion. Further, this rule is all we need to take us from classical sentential logic to the least normal modal logic. See Brian Chellas, *Modal Logic: An Introduction* (Cambridge: Cambridge University Press, 1980), p. 114.

22 See Dretske, "Epistemic Operators".

23 See Stalnaker, *Inquiry*, pp. 79–99.

24 Worse still: by what right can I even say that we used to be in a position to say truly that we knew? Then, we were in a context where we properly ignored certain uneliminated possibilities of error. Now, we are in a context where we no longer ignore them. If *now* I comment retrospectively upon the truth of what was said *then*, which context governs: the context now or the context then? I doubt there is any general answer, apart from the usual principle that we should interpret what is said so as to make the message make sense.

CHAPTER 49

Contextualist Solutions to Epistemological Problems: Scepticism, Gettier, and the Lottery

Stewart Cohen

Among the many problems discussed in the epistemological literature, three that figure prominently are scepticism, the Gettier problem, and the lottery. In a recent paper, David Lewis proposes a theory of knowledge designed to solve all three problems.[1] Each, argues Lewis, can be handled by appealing to certain mechanisms of context-sensitivity – what he calls "rules of relevance".

While others, myself among them, have proposed contextualist solutions to the problems of scepticism and the lottery, Lewis proposes to extend his contextualist approach to the Gettier problem.[2] I will argue that in so doing, Lewis's contextualism overreaches – an appeal to context-sensitivity cannot solve the Gettier problem. The difference in this respect, between the Gettier problem, on the one hand, and scepticism and the lottery, on the other, will provide some insight into what motivates a contextualist treatment of an epistemological problem.

I Contextualism

While various kinds of epistemological theories have been called contextualist, I am here concerned with theories according to which the truth-value of a knowledge ascription is sensitive

to certain facts about the speaker and hearers of the context. Accordingly, for a particular subject S, and proposition P, one speaker could truly say "S knows P" while at the same time another speaker in a different context truly says, "S does not know P".

This way of viewing knowledge ascriptions is similar to a natural way of viewing flatness ascriptions.[3] On this view, the truth-value of a flatness ascription is sensitive to context. For some particular X, one speaker could truly say "X is flat" while at the same time, a speaker in another context could truly say "X is not flat". For example, a group of (western) Coloradans may truly say that a particular road is flat while, at the same time in a different context, a group of Kansans with stricter standards may truly deny that the same road is flat.

We can think of the context-sensitivity of knowledge ascriptions in this way: For each context of ascription, there is a standard for how strong one's epistemic position with respect to a proposition P must be in order for one to know P.[4] Where two contexts differ with respect to this standard, a speaker in one context may truly say "S knows P", while a speaker in the other truly says "S does not know P". To complete the account, we need to specify how the standard for epistemic strength gets determined for each context. (More about this later.)

There are various ways of analysing this notion of the strength of one's epistemic position. One

Originally published in *Australasian Journal of Philosophy* 76, 2 (1998), pp. 289–306.

could think of it as determined, at least in part, by the strength of one's reasons or justification for believing P. On this view, the context-sensitivity of knowledge ascriptions derives from the context-sensitivity of standards for justification.

Consider again the analogy with flatness. We can think of a surface as being flat to varying degrees and we can also think of a surface as being flat *simpliciter*. What is the standard for how flat a surface must be to count as flat *simpliciter*? In different contexts, there can be different standards. Typically, when the topic of conversation is, e.g., roads, there will be a much stricter standard in contexts where the speaker and hearers are Kansans than when the speaker and hearers are Coloradans.

Analogously, we can think of a belief as being justified to various degrees and we can think of a belief as being justified *simpliciter*. On many views, being justified *simpliciter* is a necessary condition for a belief to be an instance of knowledge.[5] What is the standard for how justified a belief must be to count as justified *simpliciter*? For the contextualist view, in different contexts, there can be different standards.

Because Lewis thinks justification is not a component of knowledge, he rejects this account of the context-sensitivity of knowledge ascriptions.[6] To understand Lewis's account, consider another analogy with flatness ascriptions. We could view flatness ascriptions as involving a kind of implicit quantification: X is flat iff X has no bumps.[7] We could then view the context as restricting the domain of quantification. In the Coloradans context, small hills do not count as bumps whereas in the Kansans context, they do.

For Lewis, knowledge ascriptions as well involve a kind of implicit quantification:

S knows P iff S's evidence eliminates every possibility in which not-P – Psst! – except for those possibilities that we are properly ignoring. (p. 554)[8]

Which possibilities can we properly ignore, i.e., what is the domain of "every" in the definition? That is determined by the context. So on Lewis's view, the context determines how strong one's epistemic position must be with respect to P, i.e., the range of not-P possibilities one's evidence must eliminate, in order to know P.[9]

Which facts about the context determine which possibilities count – which possibilities must be eliminated and which can be properly ignored? Here Lewis provides a list of rules. In the language of relevant alternative theories, the rules tell us which alternatives are relevant – "relevant, that is, to what the subject does and doesn't know" (p. 554).

For our purposes, it is important to see that for some of the rules, what can be properly ignored depends on facts about the speaker and hearers of the context. As an example, we can consider the *Rule of Attention*. According to Lewis, if we are attending to a possibility, we are not properly ignoring it, for the simple reason that we are not ignoring it. So any possibility we are attending to is relevant in that very context. And as Lewis notes,

"We" [in the above definition] means: the speaker and hearers of a given context; that is, those of us who are discussing S's knowledge together. It is our ignorings not S's own ignorings, that matter to what we can truly say about S's knowledge. (p. 561)

So any possibility the speakers and hearers of a context are attending to is relevant in that very context.

Now just as there can be differences between what the speaker and hearers ignore, and what the subject ignores, so there can be differences between what the speaker and hearers of one context ignore and what the speaker and hearers of another context ignore. It follows that a possibility relevant in one context of ascription, may not be relevant in another. So on Lewis's view, a sentence ascribing knowledge to a particular subject at a particular time, can be true in the mouth of a speaker in one context and false in the mouth of another speaker in a distinct context.

II Scepticism

Contextualists argue that by appealing to context-sensitivity we can provide a satisfactory response to sceptical arguments. One strength of the contextualist approach is that it can account for the truth of our everyday knowledge ascriptions while still explaining the force of sceptical arguments. The basic idea is this: the sceptic's appeal to hypotheses (involving brains-in-a-vat, evil demons, etc.) creates a context where the standards for knowledge, i.e., the standards for how strong an epistemic position one must be in in order to know, are stricter than the standards that govern typical everyday contexts. In those "sceptical" contexts, we fail to know anything. So the contextualist concedes that there is some truth to scepticism. But a contextualist can limit the damage in a crucial way. For it remains true that we know many things in the typical everyday contexts where the standards are lower.[10] In this way, the contextualist can explain the appeal of sceptical arguments while preserving the truth of our everyday knowledge ascriptions.

As we have seen, particular contextualist theories may differ with respect to how they conceive of the strength of one's epistemic position. They can also differ with respect to the mechanism that brings about the contextual shifts in the standards. On Lewis's version, the sceptic raises the standards for knowledge ascriptions by expanding the range of alternatives that must be eliminated. The sceptic brings this about by calling our attention to sceptical possibilities, thereby making them relevant (by the Rule of Attention). In those very contexts where we are attending to sceptical possibilities, we in fact fail to know many of the things we ordinarily take ourselves to know.

But sceptical possibilities are not relevant in every context. Most importantly, they are not relevant in everyday contexts, where we are not attending to sceptical possibilities. In those contexts, the standards for what must be eliminated are lower. So in these contexts, we can truly say of ourselves and others, that we know.

My aim, in this paper, is not to dispute Lewis's contextualist treatment of scepticism. I have defended a similar approach.[11] Rather I will take issue with Lewis's application of his contextualism to the Gettier problem, and his assimilation of the Gettier problem to the lottery problem. Lewis suggests that the lottery is a special case of the Gettier problem and argues that both can be solved by the same contextualist rule. Though I endorse a contextualist treatment of the lottery problem, I will argue that contextualism can shed no light on the Gettier problem. I argue that the lottery problem is of a piece with scepticism, not the Gettier problem.

III   The Gettier Problem and the Lottery

The Gettier problem is (at least) to give a general account of why it is that certain cases of justified true belief fall short of knowledge. The lottery problem is to explain why it is (or perhaps merely seems) that no matter how great the number of tickets in a lottery, i.e., no matter how great the odds are you will lose, you nonetheless fail to know you will lose.[12] We can sharpen the lottery problem by nothing that, without knowing anything about the number of tickets, you can come to know you lose the lottery by reading the results of the drawing in the newspaper. This is puzzling because by simply increasing the number of tickets, we can make the odds of your losing conditional on the number of tickets, greater than the odds of your losing conditional on the newspaper report.

To solve these problems, Lewis appeals to two rules of relevance – the *Rule of Actuality* and the *Rule of Resemblance*. The Rule of Actuality states that "the possibility that actually obtains is never properly ignored" (p. 554); The Rule of Resemblance states that if "one possibility saliently resembles another [, t]hen if one of them may not be properly ignored, neither may the other" (p. 556).

Now consider Lewis's application of these rules to a standard Gettier case:

> The stopped clock is right twice a day. It says 4:39, as it has done for weeks. I look at it at 4:39; by luck I pick up a true belief. I've ignored the uneliminated possibility that I looked at it at 4:22 while it was stopped saying 4:39. That possibility was not properly ignored. It resembles actuality perfectly so far as the stopped clock goes. (p. 557)

By the Rule of Actuality, he cannot ignore the possibility that he looked, at 4:39, at the clock while it was stopped saying 4:39. And that possibility resembles – well enough – the possibility that he was looking at the clock at 4:22, while it was stopped saying 4:39. So, by the Rule of Resemblance, he cannot properly ignore this latter possibility either. Since this possibility is not eliminated by his evidence, he fails to know the time is 4:39.

Lewis wants to assimilate the lottery problem to the Gettier problem. He notes that though the lottery problem is a case of justified, true, belief that is not knowledge, it is not normally treated as a Gettier case. Yet, as he further notes, on his view it yields to the same treatment:

> For every ticket, there is the possibility that it will win. These possibilities are saliently similar to one another; so either every one of them may be properly ignored, or else none may. But one of them may not properly be ignored; the one that actually obtains. (p. 557)

So I cannot, by the Rules of Actuality and Resemblance, ignore the possibility, for any ticket, that it wins. In particular, I cannot ignore the possibility that my ticket wins. Since my evidence does not eliminate that possibility, I fail to know my ticket loses.

Is the lottery a kind of Gettier case? It is, of course, if by "Gettier case" we mean "a case of justified true belief that is not knowledge". But the more interesting issue is whether Lewis is correct in claiming that the lottery yields to the same solution as the standard Gettier cases. I will argue that it does not. While the lottery problem is fundamentally a problem of context-sensitivity, the Gettier problem is not.

IV Two Kinds of Rules and the Status of the Rule of Resemblance

We can begin by examining a distinction between two kinds of rules for proper ignoring (rules of relevance) in Lewis's account. Some of Lewis's rules dictate that what can be properly ignored depends on facts about the speaker and hearers of the context. We saw this in the case of the Rule of Attention: what the speaker and hearers of the context are attending to affects what can be properly ignored.

But others of Lewis's rules are not like this. The Rule of Actuality says that the actual world is never properly ignored. But the rule does not refer to the actuality of the speaker of the context. Rather, Lewis insists, it is the actuality of the subject that is never properly ignored (p. 555). This distinction will matter only in cases where we are considering whether subjects know in worlds other than our own. But this is precisely what we are doing when we give our intuitive responses to

merely possible cases, e.g., when we are considering the standard Gettier cases. So in those cases, the Rule of Actuality dictates that the subject's actuality cannot be ignored.

The Rule of Actuality does the work the truth condition does in traditional analyses of knowledge. It captures our intuition that you can not know P, if P is false. For our purposes, the important thing to note is that the operation of the Rule of Actuality does not depend on who the speakers and hearers of the context are.

Let us call rules of relevance whose operation depends on facts about the speaker (and hearers) of the context, "speaker-sensitive", and call rules of relevance whose operation depends on facts about the subject, "subject-sensitive". (As we shall see, a rule may be both subject-sensitive and speaker-sensitive.) Any theory that involves speaker-sensitive rules is contextualist in the sense I am concerned with.

Which kind of rule is the Rule of Resemblance? Consider its application to the lottery. Suppose we are considering whether S knows his ticket loses. The possibility that S's ticket wins resembles actuality not because of anything pertaining to us, the speakers (and hearers) of the context. Rather the resemblance exists because of facts about S, the subject of the knowledge ascription. It depends on the fact that he holds a ticket in a fair lottery. This means that the Rule of Resemblance is subject-sensitive.

But there is more to the story. The Rule of Resemblance says that a possibility that *saliently* resembles actuality (or any possibility that is relevant by some rule other than Resemblance) cannot be properly ignored. The need for this qualification arises in connection with a variation of the lottery problem discussed by Lewis:[13]

> Pity poor Bill! – He squanders all his spare cash on the pokies, the races, and the lottery. He'll be a wage slave all his days. We know he'll never be rich. (p. 565)

As Lewis suggests, intuitively, we know poor Bill will never get rich. But, intuitively, we do not know he loses the lottery. The problem is that his never getting rich, plus other things we know, entails that he loses the lottery. So if we do not know poor Bill loses the lottery, how can we know he'll never be rich?[14]

On Lewis's account, the Rules of Actuality and Resemblance determine that we fail to know poor Bill loses the lottery. "But there is a loophole", according to Lewis,

> ... the resemblance was required to be salient. Salience as well as ignoring, may vary between contexts. Before, when I was explaining how the Rule of Resemblance applied to the lotteries, I saw to it that the resemblance between the many possibilities associated with the many tickets was sufficiently salient. But this time, when we were busy pitying poor Bill for his habits and not for his luck, the resemblance of the many possibilities was not so salient. At that point, the possibility of Bill's winning was properly ignored; so then it was true to say that we knew he'd never be rich. Afterward, I switched the context. I mentioned the possibility that Bill might win, wherefore that possibility was no longer properly ignored ... It was true at first that we knew that Bill would never be rich. And at that point it was also true that we knew he'd lose – but that was only true so long as it remained unsaid. Later after the change in context, it was no longer true that we knew he'd lose. At that point, it was also no longer true that we knew he'd never be rich. (pp. 565–6)

So in contexts where the lottery resemblances are not salient to us, we can properly ignore the possibility that poor Bill's ticket wins. And so in those contexts, we can know poor Bill will never get rich and that he will not win the lottery. But in contexts where the resemblances are salient, we can not properly ignore the possibility that Bill's ticket wins and so we do not know either of these things.[15]

When Lewis says the resemblances are required to be salient, does he mean "salient to the subject of the ascription", or "salient to the speaker ascribing knowledge"? In the case of poor Bill, this is a distinction without a difference. The way Lewis describes it, we are both ascribers and subjects. The issue for us is – What do we know about Bill? But when subject and speaker are distinct, we can see that Lewis must require that the resemblances be salient to the *speaker* (and hearers) of the context. Consider again how he applies the Rule of Resemblance to the Gettier cases. There the resemblances that undermine knowledge are not salient to the subject. Recall the subject S who by

luck happens to be staring at a stopped clock at the very time, 4:39, displayed on the clock. According to Lewis, S fails to know the time because the possibility that he is looking at the clock at 4:22 while it is stopped saying 4:39, cannot be properly ignored. This possibility cannot be properly ignored because it resembles perfectly, as far as the stopped clock goes, the possibility that actually obtains. But this resemblance is not salient *for* S. If it were, this would not be a Gettier case since S would not even be justified in believing what the clock says. The resemblance is salient for those of us who know S is in a Gettier situation, *viz.*, the speaker and hearers of the context. That is why we cannot ignore the possibility that the time is 4:22, with the clock stopped saying 4:39. And this explains why we cannot ascribe knowledge to S.

Because of the salience qualification, the Rule of Resemblance is speaker-sensitive. (We have seen that it is also subject-sensitive). This means that features of the context of ascription – facts concerning what resemblances are salient to the speaker (and hearers) – will determine which possibilities cannot, by this rule, be properly ignored. This aspect of the Rule of Resemblance, I shall argue, leads to a serious difficulty for Lewis's treatment of the Gettier problem.

V   The Rule of Resemblance and Scepticism

Before returning to Lewis's treatment of the Gettier problem, I want to digress to show how the speaker-sensitivity of the Rule of Resemblance provides a way out of a problem Lewis raises for the application of this rule. "We must apply the Rule of Resemblance with care", notes Lewis.

> Actuality is a possibility uneliminated by the subject's evidence. Any other possibility W that is likewise uneliminated by the subject's evidence thereby resembles actuality in one salient respect: namely, in respect of the subject's evidence. That will be so even if W is in other respects very dissimilar to actuality – even if, for instance, it is a possibility in which the subject is radically deceived by a demon. Plainly, we dare not apply the Rules of Actuality and Resemblance to conclude that any such W is a relevant alternative – that would be capitulation to scepticism. (p. 556)

In response to this problem, Lewis makes an *ad hoc* stipulation that resemblances in respect of the subject's evidence alone do not count:

> The Rule of Resemblance was never meant to apply to this resemblance! We seem to have an *ad hoc* exception to the Rule, though one that makes good sense in view of the function of attributions of knowledge. What would be better, though, would be to find a way to reformulate the Rule so as to get the needed exception without *ad hoc*ery. I do not know how to do this. (pp. 556–7)

But there is a way for Lewis to avoid this sceptical problem without resorting to *ad hoc*ery. Possibilities that resemble actuality in respect of the subject's evidence are not, by the Rule of Resemblance, automatically relevant; they must *saliently* resemble actuality. That is the whole point of the Poor Bill case. But then scepticism does not threaten – that is, it does not threaten any more than a defender of context-sensitivity readily concedes. In normal, everyday contexts, where it is not salient that sceptical possibilities resemble actuality (in respect of the subject's evidence), those possibilities will not be relevant. Of course, the sceptic can make the resemblances salient to us and in that new context, the sceptical alternatives will be relevant. But this much the contextualist grants to the sceptic. This is how the contextualist explains the force of sceptical arguments. So in effect, Lewis is forced into his *ad hoc* restriction because he here treats the Rule of Resemblance as if it were merely subject-sensitive. But the rule's speaker-sensitivity enables us to avoid the threat of scepticism without resorting to *ad hoc*ery.

VI The Gettier Problem and Speaker-Sensitivity

Because the Rule of Resemblance is speaker-sensitive, it can both handle the Poor Bill variation of the lottery and avoid the threat of scepticism. But this very aspect of the rule undermines its applicability to the Gettier cases. Recall that according to Lewis's strategy for handling the Gettier cases, the subject fails to know *P* because there is an uneliminated not-*P* possibility that resembles

actuality.[16] But again, this by itself is not sufficient for the Rule of Resemblance to dictate that the not-*P* possibility cannot be properly ignored; the resemblance must be salient. The problem for Lewis is that there is nothing to guarantee that the resemblance will be salient. In some contexts the resemblance will be salient, but in others it will not. And in those contexts where the resemblance is not salient, the not-*P* possibility will be properly ignored and the subject will know.[17]

Surely this consequence of Lewis's theory is incorrect. To focus our intuitions, let's consider a particular Gettier case:

> S sees what appears to be a sheep on the hill. But what S actually sees is a rock that looks, from that distance, to be a sheep. It happens though, that behind the rock, out of S's view, is a sheep.

In this case, the subject S has a justified true belief that there is a sheep on the hill, but S does not know there is a sheep on the hill.[18] Why according to Lewis's account does S fail to know there is a sheep on the hill? Following Lewis's treatment of the stopped clock case, we can say that the possibility that there is no sheep on the hill but only a rock that looks like a sheep, resembles actuality. It resembles actuality perfectly with respect to the sheep-shaped rock. Thus by the Rules of Resemblance and Actuality, this possibility cannot be properly ignored.

Now consider A, standing next to S, who is unaware that S sees only a rock. The resemblance between the possibility that S sees a rock that looks like a sheep and actuality is not salient for A. A is not aware that S is in a Gettier situation of any kind. So according to Lewis's view, in A's context of ascription, the possibility that S sees merely a sheep-shaped rock can be properly ignored. Thus on Lewis's view, A truly ascribes knowledge to S. A can truly say "S knows there is a sheep on the hill".[19]

This strikes me as a strongly counterintuitive result. Surely it is very strange to suppose that there is any context of ascription in which one can truly say of S that he knows there is a sheep on the hill. The sentence, "S knows there is a sheep on the hill" looks false (at that world and time), regardless of who happens to be uttering it. Consider again S's situation. S mistakenly thinks the rock he is seeing is a sheep. Surely S cannot in this way come to know there is a sheep on the hill, even if by luck, there happens to be a sheep on the hill hidden from view behind the rock. But again, if the resemblance relations that otherwise falsify ascriptions of knowledge are not salient in A's context, Lewis must hold that A's ascription of knowledge to S is true.[20]

Does Lewis have a way to respond to this problem? One strategy he might adopt here is to bite the bullet and say that in A's context, A's ascription of knowledge to S is correct – and perhaps this would not be so difficult a bullet for him to bite. For as a contextualist, he can appeal to speaker-sensitivity to explain away the intuition that A cannot truly ascribe knowledge to S. He can hold that our own context, at which knowledge cannot be truly ascribed to S, runs interference on our evaluation of what A says in his context. We confuse what can be properly ignored by us in our context of ascription with what can be properly ignored by A in his context of ascription. So the fact that we cannot truly say S knows there is a sheep on the hill prevents us from seeing that A can truly say S knows there is a sheep on the hill.

There would be nothing *ad hoc* about Lewis explaining away our intuition in this way. On the contrary, we could view it as a natural extension of the contextualist treatment of both the lottery and scepticism. A contextualist treatment of these problems must explain away certain of our intuitions as resulting from our confusing distinct contexts of ascription. The contextualist, while holding that our everyday knowledge ascriptions are correct, must acknowledge that when we are in the grips of a sceptical argument, those ascriptions seem mistaken. But, according to the contextualist, this intuition is misleading. It results from our confusing what we can truly say in the sceptical context we are in as we consider sceptical arguments, with what we can truly say in everyday contexts.[21]

And the same considerations apply to the Poor Bill variation of the lottery. We can truly ascribe knowledge that Bill loses the lottery (and that he will never get rich) in contexts where the resemblances that otherwise undermine knowledge are not salient. Nonetheless, in contexts where the resemblances are salient, it seems wrong to say that in other contexts where the resemblances are not salient, we can truly ascribe knowledge that

Bill loses the lottery. Here again the contextualist must say that this intuition is misleading. It results from our confusing what can truly be said in our own context where the resemblances are salient, with what can truly be said in those contexts where the resemblances are not salient.

Now consider again our intuition that A's ascription to S of knowledge that there is a sheep on the hill is mistaken. In the very same way, Lewis can explain away our intuition as resulting from our confusing what can be truly ascribed in our own context where the relevant resemblance is salient with what can be truly ascribed in A's context, where the resemblance is not salient. This general strategy is central to the general contextualist view he is defending.

Of course, some may find contextualism to be implausible in general. For those who take this view, the application of this strategy to the Gettier case would be just another example of the kind of implausible line the theory takes in the cases of scepticism and the lottery. But I, as a proponent of a contextualist treatment of scepticism and the lottery, do not want to endorse this position. Still, I find it very implausible that we can truly ascribe knowledge in the Gettier case in *any* context. Thus, I will argue that this kind of contextualist approach, even if correct in the cases of scepticism and the lottery, cannot be extended to the Gettier problem.

VII   The Scope of Speaker-Sensitivity

On Lewis's view, the Rule of Resemblance is central to solving the Gettier problem. We can think of this rule as corresponding, roughly, to the Gettier or fourth condition in a standard analysis of knowledge. As we noted earlier, the Rule of Actuality corresponds to the truth condition.

Now consider Lewis's *Rule of Belief*:

> A possibility that the subject believes to obtain is not properly ignored, whether or not he is right to so believe. *Neither is one that he ought to believe to obtain – one that evidence and arguments justify him in believing – whether or not he does so believe.* [my emphasis] (p. 555)

The second part of this rule corresponds roughly to some of the phenomena that motivate the justification condition in a standard analysis of knowledge.

So each of the Rules of Actuality, Belief, and Resemblance corresponds to some element in a traditional analysis of knowledge. But on Lewis's view, there is an asymmetry in the way these rules are applied. This asymmetry results from the fact that of the three, only the Rule of Resemblance is speaker-sensitive. Note that the Rule of Belief, like the Rule of Actuality, is only subject-sensitive. According to this rule, we cannot ignore a possibility the subject believes, or merely ought to believe, to obtain.

Compare three cases. S_1 is looking at a sheep-shaped rock that happens to have a sheep behind it. S_2 is actually looking at a sheep under normal conditions, though he has evidence that justifies him in believing he is in fact looking at a sheep-shaped rock on a sheepless hill. S_3 is in fact looking at sheep-shaped rock on a sheepless hill. All three subjects believe there is a sheep on the hill. But none of these subjects knows there is a sheep on the hill. From the standpoint of traditional analyses of knowledge, S_1 fails to know because though he has a justified true belief that there is a sheep on the hill, he is in a Gettier situation. S_2 fails to know because his evidence justifies him in believing that, despite the appearances, there is no sheep on the hill, making his belief that there is a sheep on the hill unjustified. And S_3 fails to know because his belief that there is a sheep on the hill is false.

On Lewis's view, in each case, the failure of the subject to know there is a sheep on the hill is explained by the rules of relevance. We cannot truly ascribe knowledge to any of them, because in each case we may not properly ignore the possibility that there is only a sheep-shaped rock on the hill. S_1 is in a situation where that possibility saliently (for us) resembles actuality. So by the Rules of Resemblance and Actuality, we cannot properly ignore it. S_2 ought to believe that possibility obtains. So by the Rule of Belief, we cannot properly ignore it. And for S_3, that possibility is actual. So, by the Rule of Actuality, we cannot properly ignore it.

The rules of relevance deliver the same result for what we, in our context, can truly say about each subject: In each case, we are correct in denying that the subject knows there is a sheep on the hill. But suppose we consider whether it is correct

to ascribe knowledge to these subjects in certain contexts of ascription other than our own. Consider speaker A who is not aware that S_1 is in a Gettier situation; A thinks S_1 is, in fact, looking at a sheep. Nor is A aware that S_2 has evidence that justifies him in believing that there is no sheep on the hill. Nor is A aware that S_3 merely seems to see a sheep. Given only what is *salient* in A's context, all three subjects appear to be in the same epistemic situation, *viz.*, looking at a sheep under normal conditions. This leads A to say all three subjects know there is a sheep on the hill.

Are A's ascriptions of knowledge to S_1, S_2, and S_3, true? (We can assume hearers with the same information as A.) Consider first A's ascription of knowledge to S_1. Though the possibility that S_1 sees a rock with no sheep behind it resembles actuality (S_1's actuality), that resemblance is not salient for A. So, as we noted in section VI, as far as the Rule of Resemblance goes, A can properly ignore that possibility. Thus A can truly ascribe knowledge to S_1.

But matters are different for A's ascriptions to S_2 and S_3. S_2 ought to believe he sees a rock that looks like a sheep. So by the Rule of Belief, A may not properly ignore that possibility. Though it is not salient in A's context that S_2 ought to believe he sees merely a rock, the Rule of Belief does not require that it be salient. Thus A cannot truly ascribe knowledge to S_2.

Analogously, in the case of S_3. A may not ignore the possibility that S_3 sees merely a sheep-shaped rock. For that possibility is actual and so by the Rule of Actuality. A cannot properly ignore it. Though it is not salient in A's context that this possibility is actual, the Rule of Actuality does not require that it be salient. Thus A cannot truly ascribe knowledge to S_3.

Why should there be this asymmetry between knowledge ascriptions to S_1, on the one hand, and knowledge ascriptions to S_2 and S_3, on the other? The asymmetry results from the fact that the Rule of Resemblance is speaker-sensitive whereas the rules of Belief and Actuality are not. Because of this, the truth-value of knowledge ascriptions to S_1 can vary with the speaker whereas the truth-value of knowledge ascriptions to S_2 and S_3 cannot. This seems right for S_2 and S_3. Intuitively, neither S_2 nor S_3 knows there is a sheep on the hill, regardless of what is salient to the speaker (and hearers) of the context – S_2, because his evidence justifies him in believing there is no sheep on the hill and S_3 because his belief that there is a sheep on the hill is false. Our intuitions here provide a basis for thinking it is part of the fixed (across contexts) truth conditions for "S knows P" that P is true and that S's evidence does not justify him in believing not-P. If so, then we have a rationale for holding that knowledge ascriptions to S_2 and S_3 are false (at those worlds and times), regardless of who is making the ascription. But analogously, our intuitions provide the same kind of rationale for taking it as part of the fixed truth conditions for "S knows P" that S is not in the kind of Gettier situation S_1 is in. Intuitively, because of his situation, S_1 fails to know he sees a sheep, regardless of what is salient to the speaker of the context. Thus we have equally good reason to hold that, contrary to what Lewis's theory entails, knowledge ascriptions to S_1 are false, regardless of who is making them. This suggests that in order for the Rule of Resemblance to solve the Gettier problem, it should be construed as speaker-*insensitive*. This would require that the salience qualification be eliminated.[22]

Of course an asymmetry can be eliminated from either direction. Suppose we do have as good a rationale for holding that S_1 fails to know, irrespective of the speaker, as we do for holding that S_2 and S_3 fail to know, irrespective of the speaker. We could still reject that rationale for all three cases. After all, we saw in section IV how Lewis could employ a contextualist strategy to reject the rationale in the case of S_1. This strategy seeks to explain away the intuition that S_1 fails to know in contexts like A's as resulting from a confusion of contexts. We confuse contexts like A's, where the resemblance between actuality and the possibility at which there is only a sheep-shaped rock, is not salient, with contexts like our own where this resemblance is salient. Since in our context, S_1 fails to know, we mistakenly think S_1 fails to know in A's context as well.

Now we could, in the same way, seek to explain away our intuition that S_2 and S_3 fail to know regardless of the speaker. We could do this by construing the Rules of Belief and Actuality as speaker-sensitive, on the model of the Rule of Resemblance. Viewed in this way, the Rule of Belief would say that a possibility that the subject *saliently* believes, or saliently ought to believe, to obtain cannot be properly ignored. And the Rule

of Actuality would say that when a possibility is *saliently* actual, it cannot be properly ignored. On this view, when we consider whether S_2 knows, we cannot properly ignore the possibility that there is only a sheep-shaped rock on the hill. In our context, it is salient that S_2 ought to believe this possibility obtains. Nor can we ignore this possibility when we consider whether S_3 knows. In our context, it is salient that this possibility is actual (for S_3). But in A's context, neither of these facts is salient. So, in each case, A can properly ignore this possibility. So construing the rules in this way would allow that A could truly say that each of S_2 and S_3 knows there is a sheep on the hill. Our intuition that A, in his context, falsely ascribes knowledge to both S_2 and S_3 results from our confusing our own context with A's. This strategy strikes me as no less plausible in the cases of S_2 and S_3 than in the case of S_1.

So there are two options for eliminating the asymmetry between the way Lewis's theory handles the case of S_1 and the way his theory handles the cases of S_2 and S_3. We could eliminate the salience qualification from the Rule of Resemblance thereby making it speaker-insensitive. Or we could add a salience qualification to the Rules of Belief and Actuality thereby making them speaker-sensitive. Is there any reason to prefer one option to the other? I think that the best explanation for our intuition that A is mistaken in ascribing knowledge to all three subjects is that *even relative to A's context*, each of them in fact fails to know – S_1 because he is looking at a sheep-shaped rock with a sheep behind it, S_2 because his evidence justifies him in believing there is no sheep, and S_3 because he is looking at a hill with no sheep on it. A *mistakenly* ascribes knowledge to each of them for the simple reason that he is unaware, in each case, of the knowledge-defeating circumstance. So, I would hold that none of the three rules is speaker-sensitive, that all three subjects, S_{1-3}, fail to know there is a sheep on the hill, regardless of what is salient to the speaker.

But how do I reconcile taking this view for these cases with my defence of the contextualist approach to scepticism (and the Poor Bill variation of the lottery)? If what I say is the correct explanation for our intuition that A is mistaken in ascribing knowledge to S_1, S_2, and S_3, why should we not say the same thing about our sceptical intuitions toward our everyday knowledge ascriptions? As we have noted, when in the grips of a sceptical argument, we feel the strong intuitive pull of saying that our knowledge ascriptions are mistaken, even those we make in everyday contexts. But here the contextualist denies that our sceptical intuitions indicate that our everyday knowledge ascriptions are mistaken – that sceptical possibilities are relevant even in contexts where they are not salient to us. Rather the contextualist appeals to speaker-sensitivity to explain away those intuitions as resulting from a confusion of contexts.

So on what basis do I claim that we should invoke speaker-sensitivity to explain away our sceptical intuitions toward our everyday knowledge ascriptions, but not our "sceptical" intuitions toward ascriptions of knowledge to S_1, S_2, and S_3? If we take these latter intuitions at face value, as indicating that A's ascriptions of knowledge to S_1, S_2, and S_3 are mistaken even in A's context, why not take our sceptical intuitions at face value, as indicating that our everyday knowledge ascriptions are false, even in everyday contexts? This would mean viewing sceptical possibilities as relevant to any knowledge ascription regardless of what is salient to the speaker. Then, just as we explain A's mistaken ascriptions of knowledge to S_{1-3} as resulting from A's ignorance of certain features of the subject's epistemic situation, so the sceptic could explain why we have been mistakenly ascribing knowledge to ourselves in everyday contexts as resulting from our ignorance (prior to our initiation to sceptical arguments) of certain facts concerning our epistemic situation, viz., that our evidence does not eliminate sceptical possibilities.

As it turns out, there is an important difference between our sceptical intuitions and our intuitions about S_{1-3} – a difference that provides a rationale for appealing to speaker-sensitivity in the explanation of our sceptical intuitions, but not in the explanation of our intuitions toward knowledge ascriptions to S_{1-3}. Consider first our sceptical intuitions. Strong as they sometimes may be, they conflict with other strong intuitions we have, viz., our common sense intuitions concerning what we know. As Lewis notes:

We have all sorts of everyday knowledge, and we have it in abundance. To doubt that would be absurd. At any rate, to doubt in any serious and

lasting way would be absurd; and even philosophical and temporary doubt, under the influence of argument, is more than a little peculiar. (p. 549)

Of course, Lewis does not mean to be denying that there is any problem of scepticism. He acknowledges that, when considering sceptical arguments, we often feel a strong pull toward saying that our knowledge ascriptions are false. His theory is designed, in part, to explain these intuitions. It's just that these sceptical intuitions are not stable. We also find, while still engaged in philosophical reflection, that we have a tendency to shift to a perspective from which that conclusion is difficult to accept – "How could it be that I fail to know I have a hand? … Surely I know that!" But then I can again be overcome by the pull of the sceptical arguments and begin to doubt that I do know anything – even that I have hands. But this time around, the sceptical intuition is no more stable than before. This kind of vacillation is a fairly robust feature of our intuitions about scepticism. When we think about scepticism, we find ourselves pulled in inconsistent directions – we find ourselves shifting back and forth between thinking we fail to know and thinking that this conclusion is absurd.

This contrasts starkly with our intuitions toward ascriptions of knowledge to S_{1-3}. S_1 is looking at a sheep-shaped rock that happens to have a sheep behind it. Here we have a strong and stable intuition that S_1 does not know there is a sheep on the hill. In no way does it seem "absurd" or "more than a little peculiar" to deny that S_1 knows there is a sheep on the hill. We deny unequivocally that S_1 knows. Even if previously, because of our ignorance of S_1's situation, we were inclined to say he knows there is a sheep on the hill, once we learn that he actually sees only a rock, we would not be inclined, in the least, to say he knows. We would not find ourselves vacillating between saying that S_1 does not know and saying that he does.

Similarly we have a strong and stable intuition about ascriptions of knowledge to S_2 and S_3. Intuitively each fails to know there is a sheep on the hill, S_2 because his evidence justifies him in believing there is no sheep on the hill, and S_3 he is looking at a sheepless hill. In neither case do we find our intuitions pulled in opposing directions.[23]

But again, this kind of stability is lacking in the intuitions we have in contexts where we are considering sceptical arguments; these intuitions are notoriously unstable. Thus while nothing stands in the way of taking our intuitions toward S_{1-3} at face value, taking our sceptical intuitions at face value is problematic.

Here then is the opening for the contextualist to explain away our sceptical intuitions toward our everyday knowledge ascriptions by appealing to speaker-sensitivity. According to the contextualist, when we are in a sceptical frame of mind, we are in a context where sceptical possibilities are relevant. But again we are of two minds. We can also find it compelling that we know many things. This is because even though in our own context, sceptical possibilities are relevant, we can still evaluate knowledge ascriptions relative to other contexts where sceptical possibilities are not relevant. So even when a sentence ascribing knowledge is false in our own mouths, we can still evaluate it as true in the mouths of others (or our own mouths in other contexts). Thus, the instability of our intuitions toward our everyday knowledge ascriptions results from our alternatively evaluating them relative to our current sceptical contexts and other non-sceptical contexts.[24]

A similar phenomenon occurs in the Poor Bill version of the lottery. It seems intuitive to say we know he will never get rich. Yet we also find it intuitive that we do not know he will lose the lottery. But these intuitions take us in opposing directions. We know he'll never get rich only if we know he'll lose the lottery. Thus we find ourselves vacillating between thinking we know he'll never get rich and so that he'll lose the lottery, and thinking we know neither of these things. The contextualist holds that our opposing intuitions result from our evaluating these knowledge ascriptions relative to different contexts. In some contexts, we know he'll never get rich (and that he'll lose the lottery). In others, we fail to know that he'll never get rich (and that he'll lose the lottery).

Of course an appeal to speaker-sensitivity is not the only way to explain the instability of our intuitions. There are various sceptical explanations, as well, e.g., ones that appeal to force of habit. Which explanation is the best is not an issue we need confront in this paper.[25] The point

is that an appeal to speaker-sensitivity has at least some initial plausibility as an explanation for why our intuitions are unstable. This provides a motivation for appealing to speaker-sensitivity in our treatment of scepticism and the lottery. Where no such instability exists, as with our intuitions toward A's knowledge ascriptions to S_{1-3}, this motivation for appealing to speaker-sensitivity is absent. In these cases there is nothing for an appeal to speaker-sensitivity to explain. This makes it much more plausible to take at face-value our strong intuition that A's ascriptions of knowledge to S_{1-3} are simply mistaken.

VIII   The Gettier Problem, the Lottery, and the Rule of Resemblance

I have been arguing that it is considerably more plausible to appeal to speaker-sensitivity for knowledge ascriptions when our intuitions regarding them are unstable. As it turns out, Lewis's analysis is consonant with this view insofar as scepticism, the Poor Bill version of the lottery, and A's ascriptions of knowledge to S_2 and S_3 are concerned. In the cases of scepticism and poor Bill, where our intuitions are unstable, the operative rules of relevance – the Rule of Attention and the Rule of Resemblance – are speaker-sensitive. This allows the truth-value of knowledge ascriptions to vary in ways that explain the instability of our intuitions. In the cases of S_2 and S_3, where our intuitions are stable, the operative rules of relevance – the Rule of Belief and the Rule of Actuality – are not speaker-sensitive. This prevents the truth-value of the knowledge ascription from shifting with the context, thus explaining the stability of our intuitions.

But as we have seen, Lewis's analysis diverges from this view in the (Gettier) case of S_1. Here, even though our intuitions are stable, the operative rule of relevance – the Rule of Resemblance – is speaker-sensitive. If the argument of the previous section is correct, Lewis is mistaken in trying to handle this case with a speaker-sensitive rule. More generally, it is problematic to use a speaker-sensitive rule of relevance to solve the Gettier problem. There is no reason not to view the subject's failure to know in these Gettier cases as fixed across contexts of ascription – as holding regardless of who the speaker is.

So any rule that solves the Gettier problem must be speaker-insensitive. Thus, for the Rule of Resemblance to solve the Gettier problem, the salience qualification must be eliminated. But this would raise two problems. First, without the salience qualification, the sceptical consequences of the rule return. Recall that sceptical possibilities resemble actuality perfectly with respect to the subject's evidence. So, as Lewis notes, the Rule of Resemblance would seem to entail that sceptical possibilities are relevant, i.e., that they cannot be properly ignored. I argued in section V that, because of the salience qualification, the Rule of Resemblance can avoid this consequence. For in everyday contexts, the resemblances between sceptical possibilities and actuality are not salient. Without the salience qualification, this response is no longer available.

Lewis's own response to this difficulty was to make an *ad hoc* stipulation that these resemblances do not count. But this is really to concede that the rule does not solve the problem. Solving the Gettier problem requires either further revision of the Rule of Resemblance or perhaps a different rule altogether.

A second problem for eliminating the salience qualification from the Rule of Resemblance is that doing so would render the rule unable to handle the poor Bill variation of the lottery problem. For it would rule out our knowing of someone that he loses the lottery, in any context of ascription. But then it rules out our knowing, in any context of ascription, anything that entails of someone that he loses the lottery.[26] But it does seem that we can know many things that entail that a certain person loses the lottery. For example, we can know, in some contexts anyway, that poor Bill will never get rich.[27] The whole point of the salience qualification was to make the rule speaker-sensitive thereby allowing knowledge in some contexts that a certain person loses the lottery.

These two problems for the unqualified Rule of Resemblance show that resemblance is too pervasive a phenomenon to be appealed to in an unrestricted way. As we have seen, a natural move is to invoke speaker-sensitivity and restrict the rule by salience. But this very feature of the rule makes it incapable of solving the Gettier problem.[28]

We can now see that there is good reason to reject Lewis's assimilation of the lottery to the Gettier problem. Lewis notes that though the lottery seems to be a case of justified, true, belief that is not knowledge, it is not normally counted as a Gettier case. But according to Lewis, it can be solved by the same rule he invokes to handle the traditional Gettier cases, *viz.*, the Rule of Resemblance. We have just seen that this claim is doubtful. The lottery (given the poor Bill variation) requires speaker-sensitivity whereas the Gettier problem requires speaker-*in*sensitivity. The contextualist, as we have seen, invokes speaker-sensitivity to solve the problem of scepticism. The fact that an adequate treatment of the lottery requires an appeal to speaker-sensitivity as well suggests that the lottery has more in common with scepticism than with the Gettier problem.

Notes

1 [10] All Lewis page references are to this paper.

2 For other contextualist accounts, see Unger [12], [13], Cohen [2], [3], [4], and DeRose [5].

3 See [9], [13], [6]. I would argue for this kind of contextualism for many predicates, e.g., "happy", "tall", "old", "rich" …

4 I argue for such a view in [2]. There I talk about how strong our epistemic position must be with respect to alternatives to P in order for us to know P. Also see DeRose [5].

5 So for a belief to be justified *simpliciter*, it must be justified to the minimum degree necessary for knowledge. I do not claim that this is the only notion of justification *simpliciter*.

6 Lewis does not subscribe to this account of context-sensitivity because he holds that justification is neither necessary nor sufficient for a true belief to be knowledge. But I do not find his reasons for this view to be very convincing.

Justification is not necessary for knowledge, according to Lewis, because no "argument supports our reliance on perception, on memory, and on testimony. Yet we do gain knowledge by these means" (p. 551). But most accounts of justification for perception, memory, and testimony do not require our having anything like a supporting argument. Here, Lewis seems to rely on an overly restrictive conception of justification.

Justification is not sufficient for a true belief to be knowledge, according to Lewis, because in a lottery, one does not know one loses regardless of the number of tickets. Yet the greater the number of tickets, the greater one's justification (p. 551). This argument is somewhat puzzling. Since Gettier, few epistemologists think of justification as sufficient for a true belief to be knowledge. And Lewis suggests that the lottery is a kind of Gettier case. (I argue against this in section VIII). More importantly, Lewis ultimately allows that one can know, in certain contexts, that one loses the lottery. But then I see no reason why we should not say that in those contexts, one's justification is sufficient for one to know.

As we shall see, for Lewis, knowing P is a matter of one's evidence eliminating some alternatives to P and one's being able to properly ignore the rest of the alternatives. Certainly one's evidence eliminating alternatives is a component of justification as it is construed by many epistemologists. Moreover, whether or not one can properly ignore certain alternatives turns out to depend on one's evidence. This is true for the Rule of Resemblance and the Rule of Belief. So, though he denies it, I think it is fair to say Lewis's analysis of knowledge involves standards for justification – as many epistemologists think of justification, anyway.

7   Dretske [6], Unger [13].

8   Lewis says, "… a possibility W is uneliminated iff the subject's perceptual experience and memory in W exactly match his perceptual experience and memory in actuality" (p. 553).

9   On Lewis's view, the extent to which one's evidence eliminates possibilities is only part of what constitutes the strength of one's epistemic position. Some of the conditions that determine whether or not one can properly ignore a not-P possibility can be viewed as contributing to the strength of one's epistemic position, as well. This holds, in particular, for the rule of resemblance and the rule of belief.

10 For stylistic reasons, following Lewis, I will not always be careful about formulating the contextualist thesis metalinguistically. So instead of saying that a sentence containing the knowledge predicate can be true in one context and false in the other, I will say that whether we know can vary across contexts. Strictly speaking, though, the metalinguistic formulation should be used.

11 See [2]. On my version of contextualism, the standard governs justification and the mechanism is a Rule of Salience which is very similar, and perhaps equivalent to, Lewis's Rule of Attention. On DeRose's version in [5], the standard governs what he calls "truth tracking" and the mechanism is the Rule of Sensitivity.

12 There are, of course, other problems involving lotteries, see [10].

13 Gilbert Harman discusses a case like this in [7].

14 Lewis endorses the principle that knowledge is closed under strict implication (p. 564). A weaker principle says that knowledge is closed under known implication. Either way, the problem of poor Bill arises. I defend the closure principle in [2].

15 In Lewis's discussion, he notes that the possibility that poor Bill wins is also made relevant by the Rule of Attention, since Lewis mentions that possibility.

16 In some Gettier cases, the explanation appeals to the Rule of Resemblance working in conjunction with some other rule. See p. 557.

17 The possibility will be properly ignored, at least so far as the Rule of Resemblance goes. And Lewis says the Rule of Resemblance explains why the subject fails to know in a Gettier situation. Moreover, none of Lewis's other rules seem applicable.

18 This example is taken from Chisholm [1]. Nothing I say hinges on using this case rather than the stopped clock case. I use the former only because, by my lights, the intuition that the subject fails to know in this case is even more vivid than in the latter.

19 We might be able to construe salience in a way that results in the resemblance being salient.

Let's say the resemblance is strongly salient if it is salient that the possibility resembles actuality, and the resemblance is weakly salient if the features in virtue of which the possibility resembles actuality are salient. A possibility can be weakly salient without being strongly salient. Consider the feature in virtue of which the possibility that S sees a sheep-shaped rock with no sheep behind it resembles actuality, viz., the sheep-shaped rock. If A himself is looking at the sheep-shaped rock (thinking that it is a sheep), then the resemblance is weakly salient for A but not strongly salient. But of course, nothing guarantees that in Gettier cases, the relevant resemblances will be even weakly salient. A may not be looking at the sheep-shaped rock.

As another example, consider the bogus barn case. The possibility that S sees a bogus barn resembles actuality in virtue of the abundance of bogus barns in the vicinity of the actual barn. But this need not be salient to someone ascribing knowledge to S. Moreover, if we formulate the rule of resemblance in terms of weak salience, then the sceptical implications of the rule return. For the features in virtue of which, e.g., the brain-in-a-vat hypothesis resembles actuality are salient in everyday contexts. So these possibilities will (weakly) saliently resemble actuality in those contexts.

20   Given what he says in footnote 24, Lewis would hold that there is no general answer to whether we can say in the object language that A is in a position to truly say S knows. Of course we can avoid whatever problem there may be here if we, as Lewis suggests at the end of the paper, ascend semantically, i.e., describe the case metalinguistically.

21   I take this line in [2], [3], and [4].

22   We would then need a different rule to handle the Poor Bill version of the lottery. More about this in section VIII.

23   It may be that if we later forget that e.g., S_3 is looking at a sheepless hill, we will then find it intuitive that he knows. This is also true of scepticism – if we forget about sceptical possibilities we will find it intuitive that we know. But once it is pointed out to us that S_3 is seeing only a sheep-shaped rock, we will again think,

unequivocally, that we made a mistake. Our sceptical intuitions are not like that.

24   It also may be that our vacillations toward our knowledge ascriptions indicate that through subtle changes in ourselves as speakers and hearers, changes in our intentions, focus, purposes, etc. we bring about shifts in the set of relevant possibilities, i.e., we ourselves shift contexts. Sometimes we can indicate such a shift in our intentions and purposes by speaking in a certain tone of voice: "C'mon, you know you're not a brain-in-a-vat!" If this is correct, we would have to treat the rule of attention as defeasible. See Lewis's discussion of bending the rules of co-operative conversation, p. 560.

25   I defend the contextualist explanation over sceptical explanations in [4].

26   This assumes the deductive closure principle. See my footnote 14.

27   An example given by Harman in [7] is perhaps even more compelling. We can know S will be in New York tomorrow, even though if he wins the lottery he will be in New Jersey instead, collecting his winnings, i.e., even though knowing S will be in New York involves knowing S will lose the lottery.

28   I argue in [2] that both scepticism and the lottery can be handled by appealing to the same rule – a rule of salience. Though space considerations preclude a full discussion here, it may be that even on Lewis's view both problems can be solved by the same rule. According to Lewis, both problems result from speaker-sensitivity. And though on Lewis's view, both are handled by speaker-sensitive rules, each is handled by a different rule – skepticism, by the Rule of Attention, and the lottery, by the Rule of Resemblance. But it is not clear why Lewis needs to appeal to the Rule of Resemblance to solve the lottery problem. For it looks as if any possibility relevant by the Rule of Resemblance will also be relevant by the Rule of Attention.

Recall that for a possibility W to become relevant by the Rule of Resemblance, two conditions must be met. First, W must resemble actuality (or some other possibility relevant by some other rule). And second, the resemblance between W and actuality must be salient in the context. But if the resemblance between *W* and actuality is salient in the context, then *W* itself is salient in that context. For example, because it is a fair lottery, the possibility that my ticket wins (as well as the possibility for every other losing ticket, that it wins) resembles the possibility that (the winning ticket) *T* wins with respect to the set-up of the lottery. Now if it is salient that the possibility that my ticket wins resembles the possibility that *T* wins, then trivially the possibility that my ticket wins (along with the possibility that *T* wins) is salient as well. More generally, if possibilities saliently resemble one another in a context, then those possibilities themselves are salient in that context.

Does it follow that if possibilities saliently resemble one another in a context, then those possibilities are being attended to in that context? What exactly is the relationship between salience and attention? These issues are too large to explore here. Suffice it to say that for Lewis, salience is a kind of psychological notion closely related to attention. Though something can be salient without actually being attended to – think of the cartoon character, Mr Magoo – it is not clear why this difference should matter for whether an alternative is relevant in a context.

References

1. Roderick Chisholm, *Theory of Knowledge*, 2nd edn (Englewood Cliffs, NJ: Prentice-Hall, 1977).
2. Stewart Cohen, "How to be a Fallibilist", *Philosophical Perspectives* 2 (1988), pp. 581–605.
3. Stewart Cohen, "Skepticism, Relevance, and Relativity", in *Dretske and his Critics* (Oxford: Basil Blackwell, 1991), pp. 17–37.
4. Stewart Cohen, "Skepticism and Everyday Knowledge Attributions", in *Doubting* (Dordrecht: Kluwer, 1990), pp. 161–70.
5. Keith DeRose, "Solving the Sceptical Problem", this vol., ch. 47.
6. Fred Dretske, "The Pragmatic Dimension of Knowledge", *Philosophical Studies* 40 (1981), pp. 363–78.
7. Gilbert Harman, *Thought* (Princeton: Princeton University Press, 1974).
8. Henry Kyburg, "Conjunctivitis", in *Induction, Acceptance, and Rational Belief* (Dordrecht: Reidel, 1970), pp. 55–82.
9. David Lewis, "Scorekeeping in a Language Game", *Journal of Philosophical Logic* 8 (1979), pp. 339–59.
10. David Lewis, "Elusive Knowledge", this vol., ch. 48.
11. Gail Stine, "Skepticism, Relevant Alternatives, and Deductive Closure", *Philosophical Studies* 29 (1976), pp. 249–61.
12. Peter Unger, "The Cone Model of Knowledge", *Philosophical Topics* 14 (1986), pp. 125–78.
13. Peter Unger, *Philosophical Relativity* (Minneapolis: University of Minnesota Press, 1984).

CHAPTER 50

Knowledge and Practical Interest, Selections

Jason Stanley

Introduction

A central part of epistemology, as traditionally conceived, consists of the study of the factors in virtue of which someone's true belief is an instance of knowledge. The factors that have been proposed in epistemology are typically ones that are *truth-conducive*, in the sense that their existence makes the belief more likely to be true, either objectively or from the point of view of the subject. Much of epistemology has been devoted to debates between advocates of differing truth-conducive factors. For example, epistemic internalists have argued that the additional truth-conducive factors are other beliefs. Epistemic externalists have argued that the relevant truth-conducive factors include the fact that the belief is the product of a reliable belief-forming mechanism. All of these debates are between theorists who hold that only truth-conducive factors are relevant to the question of what makes it the case that someone's true belief is an instance of knowledge.

It is no surprise that epistemologists have widely shared the assumption that the additional factors that make a true belief into knowledge are uniformly truth conducive (either objectively or from the point of view of the subject). The

Originally published in J. Stanley, *Knowledge and Practical Interest* (New York: Oxford University Press, 2005), pp. 1–15, 47–73.

differences between true belief and knowledge are matters that fall within the purview of theoretical rationality, which many philosophers hold to be guided solely by the normative purpose of discovering the truth. My purpose in this book is to challenge this conception of knowledge. I will argue that the factors that make true belief into knowledge include elements from practical rationality. One consequence of my arguments is that the distinction between practical and theoretical rationality is less clear than one might wish.

Someone's practical investment in the truth or falsity of her belief is completely irrelevant to truth conduciveness in any sense. From the traditional perspective, then, when someone has a true belief, whether that belief is genuine knowledge is independent of *the costs of being wrong*. My aim is to provide a systematic case against this thesis. I join several recent authors in arguing that our *practical interests* have epistemic significance.[1] There are cases in which two people are similarly situated, but one has knowledge, whereas the other does not, because one has greater practical investment in the truth or falsity of her beliefs. What makes true belief into knowledge is not entirely an epistemic matter.

This conclusion is bound to sound somewhat paradoxical, because there are two senses in which epistemologists are prone to use the term "epistemic". On one use of "epistemic", it denotes truth-conducive factors, in the broad sense in which I have sketched above. On the other understanding of "epistemic", it has to do with factors relevant to whether a true belief is knowledge. The thesis of this book is that, contrary to epistemological orthodoxy, these two usages of the term do not coincide. Using "epistemic" in the first of these ways, then, the thesis of the book is that what makes true belief into knowledge is not entirely an epistemic matter.

The book is short, because many of the elements of my argument have already been set in place by those with different goals. In particular, *contextualists* about knowledge ascriptions have discovered many of the examples that suggest that whether a true belief is knowledge depends not just upon truth-conducive features of a situation, but on what is practically at stake.[2] However, contextualists generally share the widely held assumption that knowledge is not a matter of practical interests. So they have used these examples, together with the assumption, to argue for the thesis that a predicate such as "knows that penguins waddle" denotes different knowledge properties on different occasions of use. Each of the resulting semantic contents is a property, possession of which does not depend upon practical interests. But which such property is denoted by a knowledge-attributing predicate depends upon practical factors, such as how much is at stake. In this way, the contextualist can explain the examples without violating the commonly shared assumption that knowledge is not a matter of practical interests.

Contextualists have generally been interested in establishing the context-sensitivity of knowledge ascriptions in order to use the insight in the resolution of various traditional philosophical problems, such as explaining away the persuasive force of skeptical arguments. They have tended not to consider explicitly the assumption that what makes true belief into knowledge is purely a matter of truth-conducive factors, in the sense described above. But the interest of the examples they have employed to argue for the context-sensitivity of knowledge ascriptions is precisely that, when taken at face value, they do suggest the falsity of this assumption. Once we see that knowledge ascriptions are not context-sensitive in any distinctively epistemological way, we are led by such examples to reject the common assumption that knowledge (to put it tendentiously) is a purely epistemic notion.

Here are the examples I will focus upon; they have largely been made famous by others.

Low Stakes. Hannah and her wife Sarah are driving home on a Friday afternoon. They plan to stop at the bank on the way home to deposit their paychecks. It is not important that they do so, as they have no impending bills. But as they drive past the bank, they notice that the lines inside are very long, as they often are on Friday afternoons. Realizing that it isn't very important that their paychecks are deposited right away, Hannah says, "I know the bank will be open tomorrow, since I was there just two weeks ago on Saturday morning. So we can deposit our paychecks tomorrow morning."

High Stakes. Hannah and her wife Sarah are driving home on a Friday afternoon. They plan to stop at the bank on the way home to deposit their paychecks. Since they have an impending bill coming due, and very little in their account, it is very important that they deposit their paychecks by Saturday. Hannah notes that she was at the bank two weeks before on a Saturday morning, and it was open. But, as Sarah points out, banks do change their hours. Hannah says, "I guess you're right. I don't know that the bank will be open tomorrow."

Low Attributor–High Subject Stakes. Hannah and her wife Sarah are driving home on a Friday afternoon. They plan to stop at the bank on the way home to deposit their paychecks. Since they have an impending bill coming due, and very little in their account, it is very important that they deposit their paychecks by Saturday. Two weeks earlier, on a Saturday, Hannah went to the bank, where Jill saw her. Sarah points out to Hannah that banks do change their hours. Hannah utters, "That's a good point. I guess I don't really know that the bank will be open on Saturday." Coincidentally, Jill is thinking of going to the bank on Saturday, just for fun, to see if she meets Hannah there. Nothing is at stake for Jill, and she knows nothing of Hannah's situation. Wondering whether Hannah will be there, Jill utters to a friend, "Well, Hannah was at the bank two weeks ago on a Saturday. So she knows the bank will be open on Saturday."

Ignorant High Stakes. Hannah and her wife Sarah are driving home on a Friday afternoon. They plan to stop at the bank on the way home to deposit their paychecks. Since they have an impending bill coming due, and very little in their account, it is very important that they deposit their paychecks by Saturday. But neither Hannah nor Sarah is aware of the impending bill, nor of the paucity of available funds. Looking at the lines, Hannah says to Sarah, "I know the bank will be open tomorrow, since I was there just two weeks ago on Saturday morning. So we can deposit our paychecks tomorrow morning."

High Attributor–Low Subject Stakes. Hannah and her wife Sarah are driving home on a Friday afternoon. They plan to stop at the bank on the way home to deposit their paychecks. Since they have an impending bill coming due, and very little in their account, it is very important that they deposit their paychecks by Saturday. Hannah calls up Bill on her cell phone, and asks Bill whether the bank will be open on Saturday. Bill replies by telling Hannah, "Well, I was there two weeks ago on a Saturday, and it was open." After reporting the discussion to Sarah, Hannah concludes that, since banks do occasionally change their hours, "Bill doesn't really know that the bank will be open on Saturday".

Suppose that, in all five situations, the bank will be open on Saturday. Here, I take it, are the intuitive reactions we have about these cases. In Low Stakes, our reaction is that Hannah is right: her utterance of "I know the bank will be open" is true. In High Stakes, our reaction is that Hannah is also right. Her utterance of "I don't know that the bank will be open" is true. In Low Attributor–High Subject Stakes, our intuition is that Jill's utterance of "she knows the bank will be open on Saturday" is false. In Ignorant High Stakes, our reaction is that Hannah's utterance of "I know the bank will be open tomorrow" is false. In High Attributor–Low Subject Stakes, our reaction is that Hannah's utterance of "Bill doesn't really know that the bank will be open on Saturday" is true.

The *practical facts* about a situation are facts about the costs of being right or wrong about one's beliefs. All five cases involve people with the same non-practical basis for the belief the bank will be open the next morning (in the first four, Hannah, and in the fifth, Bill). But the facts as to whether the relevant attributor can truly ascribe the predicate "knows that the bank will be open"

to the relevant subject vary. Furthermore, the facts vary in accord with the *importance* to some person – either the knowledge attributor or the putative knower – of the bank's being open. This provides a prima facie case for the thesis that knowledge is not just a matter of non-practical facts, but is also a matter of *how much is at stake.*

I will call the thesis that knowledge does not depend upon practical facts *intellectualism.*[3] Intellectualism is a wide orthodoxy. So conservatism demands the exploration of alternative paths. For example, one might attempt to explain away the force of the intuitions behind these scenarios, by arguing that, when someone recognize that the costs of being wrong are particularly high, his or her confidence is shaken. The result of having one's confidence shaken is either to reduce one's degree of belief below the threshold required for knowledge or to defeat the evidence one has for one's belief in some other manner. This explanation provides an elegant account of the second scenario, where Hannah's awareness of the costs of being wrong undermines her confidence in her belief.[4]

However, this line of defense falters when one considers Ignorant High Stakes. In this case, Hannah's confidence that the bank will be open is not shaken, because she is ignorant of the potential costs of not depositing her check. So the defender of this line of defense would have to adopt the position that Hannah does not know that the bank will be open in the second scenario, but *does* know that the bank will be open in the fourth scenario. And this is an odd position. After all, Hannah is more knowledgeable about her situation in the second scenario than she is in the fourth scenario. It does not seem correct that adding a little ignorance increases knowledge. In short, if Hannah does not know in the second scenario, it seems she also does not know in the fourth scenario. If so, then appealing to loss of confidence does not help in evading the consequence that practical interests can have epistemic consequences.

This line of defense also does not account for our intuitions concerning High Attributor–Low Subject Stakes. We may suppose that Bill's confidence that the bank will be open is not affected by Hannah and Sarah's situation. So the account does not provide an explanation of our intuition that Hannah and Sarah are correct to deny knowledge to Bill. So some other explanation is required.

Another strategy that proponents of intellectualism commonly appeal to in the face of these examples is to argue that in certain cases our responses are sensitive not to whether the subject knows, but to whether the subject *knows* that she knows. According to advocates of this strategy, Hannah knows that the bank will be open in Low Stakes, High Stakes, and Ignorant High Stakes, and Bill knows that the bank will be open in High Attributor–Low Subject Stakes. Our judgments to the contrary in the latter three cases are to be explained by the fact that the relevant subjects do not *know that they know* in any of these cases. According to this line of reasoning, knowing that one knows that *p* requires having more evidence for *p* than knowing that *p*. When we are aware that the stakes are particularly high for a subject, we tend to require not just that the subject knows the propositions upon which she bases her actions, but that she knows that she knows those propositions. Our awareness of the raised stakes for Hannah in High Stakes leads us to think that she needs to know that she knows that the bank will be open, and not merely know that the bank will be open. Since she does not face a potentially hazardous predicament in Low Stakes, we are not led to make the error of thinking that she does not know that the bank will be open.

I am inclined to reject the KK thesis that knowing that *p* entails knowing that one knows that *p*. But I have difficulty seeing how the falsity of that thesis can be brought to bear to explain away these intuitions. First, the proponent of this way of rejecting our intuitions about these cases must explain why the fact that an agent does not know that she knows that *p* would lead us to deny that the agent knows that *p*. This requires an entirely independent explanation. Secondly, the proponent of this response must give some good reason to believe that in each case in which someone in a "low-stakes" situation (such as Hannah in Low Stakes) seems to know that *p*, whereas someone with comparable evidence in a "high-stakes" situation does not seem to know that *p*, the person in the low-stakes situation does not know that she knows that *p*.

I am skeptical that a good justification for the second claim can be provided. Most ordinary assertions of knowledge are made on such a basis

that we can envisage someone in a higher-stakes situation (often a much higher-stakes situation), whom we would not think of as possessing that knowledge, given similar evidence. The proponent of this response would have to argue that, in all such cases, the person in the low-stakes situation knows that *p*, but does not know that she knows that *p*. This leads to widespread failure of knowledge of knowledge. It is one thing to deny that knowledge entails knowing that one knows, but it is quite another to license such a wholesale denial of knowledge of knowledge.[5]

A third reaction one might have when confronted by these cases is to explain them away as various types of *framing effects*, of the sort familiar from recent psychological studies of rationality. It has been established that our judgments about the rationality of various inferences are highly dependent upon idiosyncratic facts about how the background situation is described. It would be unwise to put very much weight upon this evidence in claims about the nature of rationality. Similarly, one might think that the intuitions we have in the above cases are also due to psychological framing effects. If so, they are unlikely to be helpful in inquiry into the nature of the knowledge relation.

However, the above cases reveal intuitions that are not analogous to the framing effects we see in ordinary speakers' judgments about rationality. The latter sort of judgment does not follow a discernible pattern that reflects any plausible general claim about rationality. In contrast, the intuitions we have in the above cases are just the intuitions we would expect to have, if certain antecedently plausible conceptual connections between knowledge and practical reasoning were true. As other anti-intellectuals have argued (Fantl and McGrath 2002, and especially Hawthorne 2004), it is immensely plausible to take knowledge to be constitutively connected to action, in the sense that *one should act only on what one knows*.[6] For various theoretical reasons, this immensely plausible claim has not traditionally been accepted by those studying practical reasoning. But rejecting this claim devalues the role of knowledge in our ordinary conceptual scheme.

A standard use of knowledge attributions is to justify action. When I am asked why I went to the store on the left, rather than the store on the right, I will respond by saying that I knew that the store on the left had the newspaper I wanted, but I did not know whether the store on the right did. When my wife asks me why I turned left rather than going straight, I reply that I knew that it was the shortest direction to the restaurant. When it turns out that it was not a way to go to the restaurant at all, my wife will point out that I only *believed* that it was the shortest way to the restaurant. To say that an action is only based on a belief is to criticize that action for not living up to an expected norm; to say that an action is based on knowledge is to declare that the action has met the expected norm.

The fact that knowledge is thus connected to action is obscured by several points. First, *assertion* is also conceptually connected to knowledge; asserting that *p* implicates that one knows that *p*. So, in defending an action based upon one's knowledge that *p*, it is enough simply to assert that *p*. Secondly, in certain special circumstances, we do occasionally act on our knowledge that there is a *chance* that *p*, rather than our knowledge that *p*.[7] For example, there are lotteries in which it is rational for me to buy a ticket, even though I do not know that I will win; when pressed to defend my purchase, I will respond that there is a chance I will win. But this is just to say that there are certain types of action that I perform on the basis of beliefs about chances. In order for these actions to be acceptable, such beliefs must still constitute knowledge.

The intuitions we have in the above cases are best explained by appeal to our commitment to the principle that one should act only upon what one knows. For example, in High Stakes, we think it is mistaken for Hannah to act on her belief that the bank will be open on Saturday, and wait until Saturday to go there. The obvious reason why Hannah should not wait until Saturday to go to the bank is that she does not know that the bank will be open. The same is true for Ignorant High Stakes. Indeed, the intuitions in virtually all of the above cases are exactly the ones we would expect to have if it is true that knowledge is connected to action in the above sense.[8] The intuitions therefore provide powerful intuitive evidence for an antecedently plausible principle concerning the relation between knowledge and action.

It is odd to assert instances of the schema "P, but I don't know that P" (Moore's Paradox). The oddity of asserting instances of Moore's

Paradox is often taken to be strong evidence for the intuitive connection between assertion and knowledge (e.g. Williamson 2000, pp. 253–5), that *one ought only to assert what one knows*. It is highly unlikely that the oddity of Moore's Paradox is due to a psychological framing effect. For a similar reason, the reactions we have to virtually all of the cases I have discussed are not random noise. They are rather natural reflections of the conceptual connections between knowledge and action, of our intuitive adherence to the principle that one should act only upon what one knows.

So there is no easy intellectualist strategy for explaining away the intuitions. This leaves the intellectual with the following quandary. If the thesis that one's knowledge of one of one's true beliefs depends only upon non-practical facts is correct, then it cannot both be the case that (for example) Hannah knows that the bank will be open in Low Stakes, and does not know that the bank is open in the other three relevant situations. For, by stipulation, the non-practical facts for Hannah are the same in all of these cases, and she even has the same degree of confidence in her belief (at least in Low Stakes and Ignorant High Stakes). So, either the thesis must be rejected, or some other natural assumption.

Here are the options available to one who wishes to preserve the independence of knowledge from practical facts:

(a) One can challenge the claim that these are the intuitions we have in these cases.

(b) One can reject the semantic significance of one of the intuitions. For example, one could deny semantic significance to the intuition that the proposition semantically expressed by Hannah's utterance in Low Stakes is true. Alternatively, one could deny semantic significance to the intuition that the proposition semantically expressed by Hannah's utterance in High Stakes is true (or reject the semantic significance of either of the intuitions in the other two cases).

(c) One can deny that the proposition expressed by Hannah's utterance in Low Stakes is really the denial of the proposition expressed by Hannah's utterance in High Stakes (and make similar maneuvers for the other two cases).

Though I certainly do not take all of the intuitions we have in the above cases as indefeasible, I will not discuss except in passing the first of these options. The role of these intuitions is not akin to the role of observational data for a scientific theory. The intuitions are instead intended to reveal the powerful intuitive sway of the thesis that knowledge is the basis for action. Someone who denies that we have many of these intuitions is denying the pull of the link between knowledge to action. But the *value* of knowledge is explicable in part by its links to action; it is for this reason that skepticism threatens agency. Those who deny these intuitions are in effect maintaining that some other notion, such as appropriately confident belief, is intuitively the genuinely valuable one. It is because I find this reaction so implausible that I will not seriously consider rejecting these intuitions. Nevertheless, while my central interest is to evaluate accounts that make as much sense of these intuitions as possible, the central claims of this book hold, even if some of the above intuitions are less robust than others. I will leave it to the reader to decide which arguments in the book are strengthened or weakened by her particular pattern of intuitions.

As far as the second of these options is concerned, the most obvious way to develop it is to appeal to a certain view about the relation between semantics and pragmatics. According to this view, our intuitions about what is said by utterances of sentences are not in general reliable guides to the semantic contents of sentences in context, even relative to perfectly clear hypothetical circumstances like the ones described above. On this view, our intuitions about what is said by a sentence are often influenced by pragmatic, post-semantic content conveyed by the act of asserting that sentence.

For example, one might argue that we are wrong to think that Hannah's utterance in Low Stakes expresses a true proposition, because "know" expresses a relation that holds between a person and only a very few select propositions, those for which (say) she has deductive valid arguments from a priori premises. But knowledge ascriptions may pragmatically convey that the subject stands in some epistemically looser relation with the proposition. One could then "explain" the mistaken intuition on the hypothesis that we often confuse what an assertion of a

sentence pragmatically conveys with the semantic content of that sentence relative to a context.

Giving pragmatic explanations of apparently semantic intuitions is a standard maneuver in philosophy. While this strategy is certainly occasionally called for, it must be applied with great circumspection. For example, DeRose (1999) considers a crazed theorist who defends the view that "bachelor" just expresses the property of being a man. This theorist holds that the intuition that "is a bachelor" cannot be truly predicated of a married man has no semantic significance; it is due rather to (say) pragmatic felicity conditions governing the use of the term "bachelor". DeRose's point in considering such examples is that the tendency philosophers have to give pragmatic rather than semantic explanations of apparently semantic intuitions threatens to undermine the whole enterprise of giving semantic explanations. As he writes (1999, p. 198), concerning pragmatic explanations of speakers' apparently semantic intuitions about the cases that motivate his favored view:

> It's an instance of a general scheme that, if allowed, could be used to far too easily explain away the counterexamples marshaled against any theory about the truth-conditions of sentence forms in natural language. Whenever you face an apparent counterexample – where your theory says that what seems false is true, or when it says that what seems true is false – you can very easily just ascribe the apparent truth (falsehood) to the warranted (unwarranted) assertability of the sentence in the circumstances problematic to your theory. If we allow such maneuvers, we'll completely lose our ability to profitably test theories against examples.

By undermining the data for semantic theory, this kind of strategy threatens to undermine the semantic project.

Of course, there are cases in which it is legitimate to provide pragmatic explanations of apparent semantic intuitions. Again, to borrow an example from DeRose (1999, pp. 196 ff.), if someone clearly knows that p, it seems extremely odd to say that p is epistemically possible for that person. But there is a clear explanation from Gricean principles for the oddity in question. There is a general conversational principle to the effect that one should always assert the most informative proposition one is in a position to assert. If x asserts "It is possible that p", then x implicates, via this maxim, "I do not know that p". Our sense that such an assertion is odd, or seems false, is due to the fact that x is implicating something known to be false. The problem with many pragmatic explanations of apparently semantic intuitions is that there is no such clear explanation from general conversational principles.

Denying the semantic significance of apparently semantic intuitions is a significant cost, one that we should be reluctant to bear in the absence of a clear explanation of these intuitions from general conversational principles. Since I am not aware of such an explanation, I think that the most fruitful way to pursue preserving intellectualism is by appeal to the third option. And this leads us to the thesis of contextualism. [...]

Knowledge Ascriptions and Context-Sensitivity

I have argued that knowledge ascriptions are not intuitively gradable. There are two morals to the discussion. First, if one is a contextualist, one should avoid adopting a version of contextualism that makes knowledge semantically scalar. Secondly, the contextualist thesis about knowledge ascriptions is not supportable by appeal to an analogy to gradable expressions. In this section, I will argue that the alleged context-sensitivity of knowledge ascriptions has no other parallel among the class of uncontroversial context-sensitive expressions. During the course of these arguments, we will also see that some of the alleged theoretical benefits of contextualism are illusory. The way I will support this final thesis is by arguing that, if knowledge ascriptions are context-sensitive, then we would expect them to behave in ways that run counter to the contextualist's claims.

Contextualists have generally chosen to implement their claims semantically via the view that the verb "know" is an indexical:

> Thus the theory I wish to defend construes "knowledge" as an indexical. As such, one speaker may attribute knowledge to a subject while another speaker denies knowledge to that subject, without contradiction. (Cohen 1988, p. 97)

Citing this passage, DeRose (1992, pp. 920–1) writes:

> This lack of contradiction is the key to the sense in which the knowledge attributor and the knowledge denier mean something different by "know". It is similar to the sense in which two people who think they are in the same room but are in fact in different rooms talking to each other over an intercom mean something different by "this room" when one claims, "Frank is not in this room" and the other insists, "Frank is in this room – I can see him!" There is an important sense in which both do mean the same thing by "this room", in which they are using the phrase in the same sense. But there is also an important sense in which they do not mean the same thing by the phrase; this is the sense by which we can explain the lack of contradiction between what the two people are saying. To use David Kaplan's terminology, the phrase is being used with the same character, but with different content. Similarly, in [a bank case] ... when, in the face of my wife's doubt, I admit that I don't know that the bank will be open on Saturday, I don't contradict an earlier claim to know that I might have made before the doubt was raised and before the issue was so important because, in an important sense, I don't mean the same thing by "know" as I meant in the earlier claim: While "know" is being used with the same *character*, it is *not* being used with the same *content*. Or so the contextualist will claim.

Similarly, Lewis (1996, p. 564) writes:

> in the skeptical argument the context switched midway, and the semantic-value of the context-dependent word "know" switched with it.

So, Cohen, DeRose, and Lewis have all implemented their contextualist claims via the view that the verb "know" is an indexical in Kaplan's sense, having different semantic values relative to different contexts.[9] In recent years, however, some contextualists have moved beyond the model of contextualism that treats the word "know" itself as an indexical expression, like "here" or "now" (e.g. Schaffer 2004; Ludlow 2005). My purpose in this section is to provide some empirical arguments to show that, if instances of "know that p" are context-sensitive in a distinctively epistemological way, their context-sensitivity is not "detectable" by means that would detect the context-sensitivity of a range of other expressions. Some of the arguments I provide below suggest that the indexical model of "know" is not correct. But I will not confine myself to considering only the indexical model of "know". Instead, I seek to show disanalogies between knowledge ascriptions and a wide variety of context-sensitive constructions.

At the outset, I should confess to some skepticism about the existence of a single property that all context-sensitive expressions have, and all non-context-sensitive expressions lack (other than the property of context-sensitivity). The attempts that I am aware of for establishing such tests fail rather dramatically at their intended task. It is instructive to look at one test recently proposed by Herman Cappelen and Ernie Lepore, which they call *The Collective Description Test*. According to Cappelen and Lepore (2005, pp. 99):

> If for a range of true utterances of the form "A v-s" and "B v-s" we obviously can describe what they have in common by using "v" (i.e. by using "A and B v"), then that's evidence in favor of the view that "v" in these different utterances has the same semantic content, and hence, is not context-sensitive.

Cappelen and Lepore use the Collective Description Test to argue that a range of apparently context-sensitive constructions are not after all context-sensitive. For example, they use it to argue that "is tall" is not context-sensitive. Suppose that John utters "Jill is tall" and Bill utters "Mary is tall". One can conclude from the two premises they provide that "Both Jill and Mary are tall". By the collective description test, then, "is tall" is not context-sensitive. Similarly, suppose John utters "Jill knows that penguins waddle", and Bill utters "Mary knows that penguins waddle". One can conclude from the two premises they provide that Jill and Mary know that penguins waddle, and hence, if the Collective Description Test is reliable, that "knows that penguins waddle" is not context-sensitive.

Consider two sisters, Jill and Mary. John utters "Jill loves her mother" and Bill utters "Mary loves her mother". One can conclude from the

two premises offered that "Each sister loves her mother." Since one can describe what Jill and Mary have in common by the verb phrase "loves her mother", it follows that Cappelen and Lepore's test falsely predicts that "loves her mother" is not context-sensitive. Similarly, suppose Jill utters "I love my mother" and Mary utters "I love my mother". Jill and Mary can now conclude in unison, "We love our mothers". Cappelen and Lepore's test appears falsely to predict that "loves my mother" is not context-sensitive.[10]

Cappelen and Lepore might understandably respond by arguing that "loves her mother" in John and Bill's utterance is not context-sensitive, but is rather a case of controlled anaphora, where "her" is *bound* (by some higher operator, e.g. a lambda operator associated with the verb phrase). They could also give the same response for "love my mother", in Jill and Mary's utterances of "I love my mother". But this claim, though well motivated, is not open to Cappelen and Lepore. For then their opponents can give the *very same response* to defuse Cappelen and Lepore's application of the Collective Description Test to their favored examples.

For example, one of their targets is the view, espoused in Ludlow (1989) and Stanley (2000; 2002), that predicative uses of adjectives, such as "is tall", are associated with comparison class variables. But, if Cappelen and Lepore are allowed to give the above response to defend their test, advocates of such a view could give the exact same response to explain why one can, from utterances of "Jill is tall" and "Mary is tall" draw the conclusion "Both Jill and Mary are tall".[11]

So, either Cappelen and Lepore's test fails as a test of context-sensitivity, or it cannot be employed against their intended targets. I think it is no accident that their test fails. I doubt that there is one test that perspicuously divides all context-sensitive terms into one category, and all non-context-sensitive terms into another category. There are too many different classes of context-sensitive expressions. But what I am in a position to provide is a good inductive case that knowledge ascriptions are not context-sensitive in a distinctively epistemological way, as the contextualist would have it. In the realm of the empirical, a good inductive case is all we can expect.

There are a few tests that detect the context-sensitivity of a range of context-sensitive expressions that do not detect the alleged context-sensitivity of instances of "know that p". These tests involve speech-act reports and propositional anaphora. It would be a mistake to place excessive weight upon these tests. For the context-sensitivity of certain constructions that are clearly context-sensitive is also not detectable by these tests. I include these tests, not because "passing" them is a necessary condition for context-sensitivity, but because they are one part of the larger inductive argument that instances of "knows that p" are not context-sensitive. I will then try to motivate a more general property of context-sensitive expressions, and conclude by arguing that instances of "know that p" lack this more general property.

Here is the first kind of argument. Suppose A and B are at the zoo. A is a non-philosopher, and B is a philosophy professor, trying to explain what epistemology is to A. B asks A to give her an example of a proposition that A takes herself to know, in response to which B will explain how to give a skeptical undermining of A's knowledge. Here is a discourse in this situation that should, if "know" is like a core indexical such as "I", "here", and "now", sound perfectly reasonable (certainly, according to the contextualist, every statement in the discourse is true):

ZOO

A. (looking at a zebra in a normal zoo). I know that is a zebra.
B. But can you rule out its being a cleverly painted mule?
A. I guess I can't rule that out.
B. So you admit that you don't know that's a zebra, and so you were wrong earlier?
A. I didn't say I did. I wasn't considering the possibility that it could be a cleverly painted mule.

A's final utterance, according to the contextualist's semantics, is perfectly true. But this seems a very strange result. It is extremely difficult to make sense of A's denial except as a lie. But instead the contextualist predicts that it is clearly true.

The behavior of "know" in this kind of discourse contrasts with some other clearly context-sensitive expressions. For example, modal expressions are context-sensitive. In the first instance, there are what some philosophers have thought of as different "senses" of possibility, such as physical possibility, logical possibility, epistemic possibility, and metaphysical possibility.[12] But, even fixing upon one sense of modality, there are different readings of a modal term such as "could", depending upon the context of use. For example, where "could" is interpreted as physical possibility, one might mean physical possibility in a more or less restricted sense. Suppose A is in a conversation with a group of people talking about innovations in flight that have not been marketed to the public. B overhears A's comment, without knowing the background conversation:

TECHNOLOGY

A. It's possible to fly from London to New York City in 30 minutes.
B. That's absurd! No flights available to the public today would allow you to do that. It's not possible to fly from London to New York City in 30 minutes.
A. I didn't say it was. I wasn't talking about what's possible given what is available to the public, but rather what is possible given all existing technology.

In contrast to the last line of ZOO, A's final comment in TECHNOLOGY seems perfectly appropriate, and indeed true. The worry for the contextualist is that the discourse in ZOO should be as plausible and coherent as the discourse in TECHNOLOGY. But it clearly is not. This is a good minimal pair that shows that the alleged context-sensitivity of instances of "know that p" is considerably less accessible to us than the context-sensitivity of modals. This should lead us to doubt models according to which the context-sensitivity of "know" is modeled upon the context-sensitivity of modal expressions.

One should be clear about the strategy here. I am not arguing, as others have, that the infelicity of a discourse such as ZOO by itself undermines contextualism. By providing the contrasting minimal pair ZOO and TECHNOLOGY, my purpose is just to reveal differences between some uncontroversial context-sensitive expressions, such as modals, with instances of "know that p". The contrast between ZOO and TECHNOLOGY is not an anti-contextualist silver bullet, but rather one piece of the overall inductive argument for the thesis that the only evidence for the context-sensitivity of instances of "know that p" is the cases discussed in the Introduction.

Contextualism also makes some strange predictions about propositional anaphora. Consider the following discourses:

(1) If I have hands, then I know that I have hands. But come to think of it, I might be a brain in a vat, in which case I would believe I have hands, but wouldn't. Now that I'm considering such a skeptical possibility seriously, even if I have hands, I don't know that I do. But what I said earlier is still true.[13]

According to the contextualist semantics, there should be a clearly true reading of all the sentences in these two discourses. But they are very difficult to grasp. In particular, the only interpretation for the expression "what I said" in the final sentence is the proposition whose truth is being denied in the previous sentence.[14]

The case is again markedly different with uncontroversial context-sensitive expressions, such as genuine indexicals:

(2) It is raining here. Had I been inside, what I said still would have been true. But now that I am in fact inside, it is not raining here.

When informed of the facts, there is a clear reading of all of the sentences in (2) where they are true.

So, certain tests that detect the context-sensitivity of modal expressions and obvious indexicals are blind to the alleged context-sensitivity of instances of "knows that p". Mark Richard (2004, p. 236) presses the worry, in response to the above arguments, that these tests are also blind to the context-sensitivity of obvious context-sensitive constructions, such as those involving comparative adjectives. Commenting on my contrast between zoo and TECHNOLOGY, Richard writes:

The following dialogue is exactly as bizarre…
A. He is rich.
B. He can't afford a house on the Vineyard.
A. I see your point.
B. So you admit you were wrong when you said he was rich.
A. I said no such thing.

I agree with Richard that the above considerations may very well not be infallible indicators of context-sensitivity. But I disagree with Richard's particular example. I do think that the tests are successful in detecting the context-sensitivity of constructions involving gradable adjectives. For Richard's exchange with "rich" is simply not parallel to zoo and TECHNOLOGY. In the cases of zoo and TECHNOLOGY, background context is provided to make A's final assertion more palatable. For example, in the case of zoo, A adds to "I didn't say I did", the helpful explanation "I wasn't considering the possibility that it could be a cleverly painted mule". In the case of TECHNOLOGY, A adds to "I didn't say it was", the helpful explanation "I wasn't talking about what's possible given what is available to the public, but rather what is possible given all existing technology". The additional background context rescues the felicity of A's assertion in TECHNOLOGY, but does nothing to rescue the felicity of A's assertion in zoo. Adding similar background context to Richard's "rich" dialogue rescues the felicity of A's final assertion:

RICH

A. He is rich.
B. He can't afford a house on the Vineyard.
A. I see your point.
B. So you admit you were wrong when you said he was rich.
A. I didn't say that. I wasn't considering that level of wealth.

Perhaps the background context in RICH does not make A's assertion "I didn't say that" as smooth as A's assertion "I didn't say it was" in TECHNOLOGY. But RICH is still far more similar to TECHNOLOGY than it is to zoo. In zoo, A's final assertion is wellnigh incoherent to the ordinary speaker, whereas RICH is perfectly coherent to everyone.

So, I do not think that Richard has succeeded in undermining these tests as reliable indicators of context-sensitivity. Nevertheless, I am prepared to admit that the above tests are not perfectly reliable indicators, for the simple reason that I doubt that there are *any* perfectly reliable indicators of context-sensitivity. The next piece of my inductive argument against the contextualist is not such a test for context-sensitivity, but rather a generalization about the nature of semantic context-sensitivity. I am not certain whether this generalization is true. But it seems both empirically well confirmed, and motivated by general considerations about the nature of semantic context-sensitivity. And, if it is a true generalization, it provides further evidence against contextualism as a position in epistemology.

In the first instance, it is individual words that are context-sensitive, not sentences or discourses. For example, the semantic context-sensitivity of the sentence "I am human" is traceable to the semantically context-sensitive word "I". Similarly, the semantic context-sensitivity of "She is tired" is traceable to the word "She", which is context-sensitive, and the present tense. In some constructions, the semantic context-sensitivity is traceable to an unpronounced element in the syntactic structure of a sentence. For example, the semantic context-sensitivity of "John is tall" may be traceable to an unpronounced element in the syntactic structure of the predicate "is tall", say a comparison class variable associated with the adjective "tall" (see Stanley 2000). But in these instances, too, context-sensitivity is traceable to an individual element in the sentence uttered, albeit one that is not pronounced.

This suggests the following generalization. Since semantic context-sensitivity is traceable to an individual element, multiple occurrences of that element in a discourse should be able to take on differing values. In the case of an utterance such as "This is larger than this", where two different objects are pointed to by the person uttering the sentence, this feature is obviously confirmed. But it is present in a broader range of constructions.

For example, suppose John, who is very small for his age, identifies with small things. He has a picture on the wall in his bedroom of an elephant fighting off a much larger elephant. He also has a framed tiny butterfly on his wall. When he is asked why he has both things hung up, he says:

(3)   That butterfly is small, and that elephant is small.

John in fact also has a fondness for flat things. On his wall is a picture of a field in Kansas, and on his desk is a rock. When asked why he has both, he replies:

(4)   That field is flat, and this rock is flat.

Now imagine a picture of a butterfly that is surrounded by much smaller butterflies; it is huge for a butterfly. It is next to a picture of an elephant that is surrounded by much larger elephants. The following is a good description of the situation:

(5)   That butterfly is large, but that elephant isn't large.[15]

There are different possible explanations of why the two different occurrences of "large" in (5) express different semantics values. For example, one might argue that the comparison class property for the first occurrence of "large" is determined linguistically by the noun "butterfly", and the second occurrence of "large" is determined linguistically by the noun "elephant" (see Ludlow 1989). Alternatively, one might think that "large" is associated with different comparison class properties by free contextual assignment, in much the same way that unbound pronouns such as "he" and "she" have their denotations determined in context. The generalization is independent of either of these explanations. For the generalization is that, in the case of any context-sensitive expression, different occurrences of that expression can receive different values within a discourse by *whatever* mechanism, be it binding or contextual supplementation. And that is what we have seen to be the case for comparative adjectives.

It is worth expending a little more space on this example, since the proper interpretation of comparative adjectives is a vexed matter. In other work (Stanley 2002), I have argued for the following account of predicative uses of comparative adjectives. The syntactic structure of a predicate such as "is tall" or "is smart" contains a variable position, which can be either bound or free. When it is free, its value, relative to a context, is a comparison class property. Comparison class properties can be determined by the head noun, as in a reading of "That butterfly is large", where it expresses the proposition that the butterfly in question is a large butterfly. Comparison class properties can also be determined by assorted extralinguistic factors.

Comparison class properties do not need to be kind properties. Though she would not construe them this way, Graff (2000) provides examples in which the comparison class for "is old" can either be the property of *being a dog,* or be the property of *being an old dog* (suppose we are confronted with a 20-year-old dog; compared with several 14-year-old dogs, the 20-year-old dog is old, i.e. old for an old dog). Another example Graff (2000, p. 67) provides is as follows:

> it can be appropriate for me to say, when I see my young nephew for the first time in months at a family gathering, "Derek, you're so tall". It can be appropriate for me to say this even though I know that my nephew has always been and still is short for his age. What I am saying is that he has significantly more height than I expected him to have, given what his height was the last time I saw him.

In this example, the comparison class property is the property of *being a height that Delia expected her nephew to be.* What Graff says, in uttering "Derek, you're so tall", is that Derek is tall relative to the height that Graff expected her nephew to be.[16]

So, on the theory of gradable adjectives that I favor, they are associated with variables for comparison class properties. Examples such as (3)–(5) show that different occurrences of the same gradable adjective within a sentence can be associated with different comparison class properties. But the point that different occurrences of the same gradable adjective can be associated with different standards can be made on other accounts of gradable adjectives. For example, if one holds that gradable adjectives are associated with degrees on a scale, then examples such as (3)–(5) show that different occurrences of the same gradable adjective can be associated with different degrees on the relevant scale.[17]

This sort of shift is present in a variety of context-sensitive expressions other than gradable adjectives. For example, we see this behavior with demonstratives, context-sensitive determiners, and quantified noun phrases. For the first, as we have already seen, there is the example:

(6)   That is larger than that.

For the second, consider:

(7)   In Atlanta, there are many serial killers but not many unemployed men.

In this case, the contextual determinants for the denotation of "many" change within a clause. The first occurrence of "many" denotes a more distinct determiner meaning than the second occurrence of "many", since (7) may be true even though there are many more unemployed men than serial killers. The same phenomenon occurs with quantified expressions, as (8) can express the proposition that every sailor on one ship waved to every sailor on another (Stanley and Williamson 1995, p. 294):

(8)   Every sailor waved to every sailor.

It is no surprise that different occurrences of one and the same context-sensitive expression can have different values within the same discourse. For context-sensitivity is linked not to the *discourse,* but to a particular context-sensitive *term.* So what one is speaking about when one speaks of the "standard of tallness" relevant for evaluating a particular use of "is tall" is simply the degree of tallness that is associated with the expression "tall" by whatever semantic mechanism one exploits.

Let us see how this point applies to the version of contextualism advocated in Lewis (1996). According to Lewis, the semantics of the word "know" invokes universal quantification over possibilities. Lewis then exploits facts about natural language universal quantification to motivate contextualism about "know":

> Finally, we must attend to the word "every". What does it mean to say that every possibility in which not-P is eliminated? An idiom of quantification, like "every", is normally restricted to some limited domain. If I say that every glass is empty, so it's time for another round, doubtless I and my audience are ignoring most of all the glasses there are in the whole wide world throughout all of time. They are outside the domain. They are irrelevant to the truth of what was said.
>
> Likewise, if I say that every uneliminated possibility is one in which P, or words to that effect, I am doubtless ignoring some of all the uneliminated alternative possibilities that there are. They are outside the domain. They are irrelevant to the truth of what was said. (Lewis 1996, p. 553)

So, Lewis deduces contextualism about "know" first, from the claim that "know" involves universal quantification over possibilities, and secondly, from the fact that natural language quantification is typically restricted. But (as (8) demonstrated) it is a well-established fact that different occurrences of the same quantified expression within a discourse can be associated with different domains (Soames 1986, p. 357; Stanley and Williamson 1995, p. 294; Stanley and Szabo 2000, p. 249). Lewis's contextualism flows in part from facts about natural language quantification. So, two different occurrences of "know" within the same discourse should be able to be associated with different sets of possibilities (say, a set including quite remote possibilities, and a set including only quite close possibilities).

Distinct occurrences of the same context-sensitive term can have different interpretations within a discourse. We should therefore expect distinct occurrences of the instances of "know that p" to allow for the possibility of distinct interpretations within a discourse. But this opens the contextualist up to a number of objections that she does not otherwise face. Furthermore, if this is so, some of what contextualists say about the virtues of their theories over other theories falls by the wayside. I will substantiate these points in turn.

If instances of "know that p" behave like comparative adjectives, quantifier phrases, context-sensitive determiners, or modals, then we would expect it to be smoothly acceptable to associate different standards of knowledge with different occurrences of the "know that p", just as we associate different degrees of height with different occurrences of the predicate "is tall". So, if contextualism were true, we should expect the following to be fine:

(9)   If there is an external world, many normal non-philosophers know that there is, but, by contrast, no epistemologists know that there is.

If "know that there is an external world" could be associated with different standards, then one would expect an utterance of (9) to be felicitous and true, just as utterances of (3)–(8) are. For "is large" means one thing when predicated of a butterfly, and quite another when predicated of an elephant. Similarly, "many" means one thing when it occurs

with "unemployed men", and quite another when it occurs with "serial killers". So, if "know that there is an external world" is context-sensitive in a similar manner, one would naturally expect it to have different contents when predicated of non-epistemologists and epistemologists.[18]

In responding to various objections, contextualists have exploited the view that distinct occurrences of "know" within a discourse must be associated with the same standard. For example, this view is at work in the solution contextualists have provided to puzzles like the "Now You Know it, Now You Don't" concern (Yourgrau 1983; DeRose 1992; 2000). This concern is that the contextualist semantics would allow for discourses such as:

KNOWLEDGE SHIFT

A.   If that is a zebra, I know it is a zebra.
B.   But can you rule out its being merely a cleverly painted mule?
A.   No, I can't.
B.   So you admit you didn't know it was a zebra?
A.   If that is a zebra, then I knew it was a zebra. But now, after your question, even if it is a zebra, I don't know it is a zebra.[19]

DeRose (1992, p. 925) writes in response to a similar objection (similar because not in conditional form):

How shall the contextualist respond? The objection … is based upon a mistake. The contextualist believes that certain aspects of the context of an attribution or denial of knowledge attribution affect its content. … If in the context of the conversation the possibility of painted mules has been mentioned, and if the mere mention of this possibility has an effect on the conditions under which someone can be truly said to "know", then any use of "know" (or its past tense) is so affected, even a use in which one describes one's past condition.

This response presupposes that distinct occurrences of "know" within a discourse must all be associated with the same standard. But the analogous claim is incorrect for uncontroversial context-sensitive expressions.

Consider, for example, a gradable adjective such as "tall". The parallel claim for "tall" to

DeRose's claim about "know" would be that merely mentioning, for example, basketball players would so affect the conditions under which someone can be truly said to be "tall", that any use of "tall" is so affected, even a use in which one describes one's past condition. But this is clearly false for "tall", as the following discourse suggests. Suppose that A was the tallest member of his seventh-grade class. But A didn't grow over the summer, and most of his classmates did. B is the eighth-grade teacher:

TALLNESS SHIFT

B. OK, A, you're average height, so you sit in the middle.
A. But last year, I was tall and I got used to sitting in the back.

In the case of a predicate such as "is tall", one can clearly shift the standard governing it from a higher standard to a lower past standard. If the expression "know that p" is context-sensitive, one should expect the very same behavior. That is, one should expect KNOWLEDGE SHIFT to be felicitous. DeRose's account of the infelicity of KNOWLEDGE SHIFT therefore presupposes that "know" must be associated with the same standards throughout a discourse.

Shifting to Lewis's restricted quantification model of contextualism does not help to substantiate the contextualist's claim that raising a possibility to salience affects all future uses of "know". The parallel claim for quantification would be that once one introduces a domain of a certain size, a future use of a quantifier within that discourse cannot be understood to be restricted to a subset of that domain.[20] But this claim is quite clearly false:

QUANTIFIER SHIFT

A. Every Van Gogh painting is in the Dutch National Museum.
B. That's a change. When I visited last year, I saw every Van Gogh painting, and some were definitely missing.

The domain for the first occurrence of the quantifier phrase "every Van Gogh painting" is (if you like) maximally large. But we can, with no difficulty at all, understand the domain for the second occurrence to be a subset of this domain, restricted to last year's collection in the Dutch National Museum.[21] Lewis (1983, p. 247) claims that "the boundary readily shifts outward if what is said requires it, but does not so readily shift inward if what is said requires that". This claim, so important to his account of skepticism, is clearly false for domain restriction, the model upon which his account of "know" is based.

DeRose (1992) also appeals to a direct analogy between the indexical "here" and "know" to defend his claim concerning the pragmatics of "know":

Knowledge claims, then, can be compared to other sentences containing other context-sensitive words, like "here". One hour ago, I was in my office. Suppose I truly said, "I am here". Now I am in the word processing room. How can I truly say where I was an hour ago? I cannot truly say, "I was here", because I wasn't here; I was there. The meaning of "here" is fixed by the relevant contextual factors (in this case, my location) of the utterance, not by my location at the time being talked about.

The values of core indexicals, unlike most other context-sensitive expressions, are sometimes held to be fixed by facts about the context of utterance that are independent of speaker intentions (e.g. Wettstein (1984) on "pure indexicals"). So, for example, the value of "here" is fixed (in part) by the place of utterance, and the value of "I" is fixed by the person who utters it. Perhaps then, by analogy, the standard of knowledge (unlike the standard of tallness) is fixed by a fact about the context of utterance that is independent of the intentions of the person making the knowledge ascription.

The analogy is of little help to the contextualist. First, as we have already demonstrated, the analogy between "know" and core indexicals is poor. The context-sensitivity of core indexicals is easily demonstrable by a variety of tests, none of which detects the context-sensitivity of knowledge ascriptions. Secondly, the fact that the analogy is poor is problematic for the contextualist, since arguably core indexicals are the only expressions whose values are fixed (to some degree) independently of the intentions of the speaker. Third, it is not a semantic fact about core indexicals that they generally have the same denotation within a short discourse. It is rather a consequence of mundane physical facts about humans. Different occurrences of "here" within a discourse tend to have the same denotation, because most of our conversations occur while remaining in the same location.[22] Different occurrences of "I" within a single sentence tend to have the same denotation, because speakers rarely change mid-sentence. There is no reason to think that analogous mundane physical facts determine the same standard of knowledge throughout a discourse.

Once one abandons the contextualist claim that distinct occurrences of instances of "know that p" in a single discourse must be associated with the same standards, the contextualist is open to the objection that, by contextualist lights, infelicitous discourses such as KNOWLEDGE SHIFT should be acceptable. On my view, this is not a terrible concession. For the contextualist has no response to the infelicity of very similar discourses, such as (1), even assuming her model of context-sensitivity to be correct. But the situation is worse for the contextualist. If the model of context-sensitivity assumed by the contextualist is wrong, some of what contextualists say about the virtues of their theories over other theories is vitiated.

If different occurrences of instances of "knows that p" can be associated with different epistemic standards within a discourse, some of the paradigm sentences the infelicity of which supposedly motivates their accounts over rival accounts turn out to be felicitous and potentially true by contextualist lights. For example, if we have similar behavior to many other context-sensitive expressions, one would expect the following to be felicitous:

(10)   Bill knows that he has hands, but Bill does not know that he is not a bodiless brain in a vat.

(11)   Bill does not know that he is not a bodiless brain in a vat, but Bill knows he has hands.

As we have seen above, DeRose takes the persistent infelicity of utterances of the sentences in (10) and (11) to undermine alternative accounts on the grounds that they allow for acceptable utterances of these sentences. But, if instances of "knows that p" are context-sensitive, then one would expect there to be contexts in which the

sentences in (10) and (11) could be felicitously uttered. Someone who uttered sentence (10) would intend "knows that he has hands" to be associated with lower standards, and "know that he is not a bodiless brain in a vat" to be associated with higher standards. Someone uttering sentence (11) would be lowering standards across a conjunction.

With other context-sensitive expressions, we do find constructions analogous to those in (10) and (11) that can be felicitously uttered. For instance, consider again:

(7)   In Atlanta, there are many serial killers but not many unemployed men.

"Many" is analogous to the indexical contextualist's view that "know" is itself a context-sensitive term, which denotes different relations relative to different contexts of use. But in (7), the two semantic values of "many" are different, despite the fact that they occur within the same clause. The occurrence of the expression "serial killer" leads us to interpret the first occurrence of "many" in one way, whereas the occurrence of the expression "unemployed men" leads us to interpret the second occurrence in another way. Similarly, if the contextualist were right, one might wonder why the occurrence of "he has hands" should not lead us to interpret the relevant occurrences of "know" in one way (as denoting low-standards knowledge relations), while the occurrence of "he is not a bodiless brain in a vat" leads us to interpret the other occurrences of "know" in (10) and (11) in another way (as denoting high-standards knowledge relations).

According to the versions of contextualism developed in Schaffer (2004) and Ludlow (2005), instances of the predicate "know that p" are context-sensitive, because there is an epistemologically significant context-sensitive element associated with "know" in the predicate (though the lexical item "know" is not context-sensitive). But consider:

(12)   That mountain is tall for Michigan, but not tall for Colorado.

In (12), we find that different occurrences of the same adjective can be associated with different values for their contextually sensitive parameters within the same clause. So we would expect different occurrences of "know" to be able to be associated with distinct values for their associated contextually sensitive parameters within the same clause.

The contextualist might respond that the reason that (12) can be felicitously uttered is that we have devices that make explicit the comparison class properties for gradable adjectives, as in "for Michigan" and "for Colorado". Perhaps the infelicity of uttering the sentences in (10) and (11) is due to the inability we have to articulate the shifting standards associated with our knowledge claims, and when we cannot articulate the shift, extralinguistic context cannot do the task of shifting the standards for us.

This line of enquiry does not advance the contextualist's cause very far. For if there is no way to articulate the changing standards, as there is in the case of comparison class properties for gradable adjectives (or quantifier domains for quantifiers), that should simply raise more worry about the contextualist's thesis that epistemic vocabulary is context-sensitive in the way she describes. For with other context-sensitive constructions, we do find ways to articulate what is sometimes provided by context. If the epistemic standards cannot be smoothly linguistically articulated, that should lead us to worry that they are not there.

A perhaps more promising path for the contextualist to pursue is the one urged by Peter Ludlow (2005). Ludlow calls attention in his paper to the presence of standards operators in epistemic talk, as in examples such as:

(13)   John doesn't know that water is liquid by the standards of chemistry.

(14)   Copernicus didn't know that the sun was the center of the solar system by today's standards of knowledge.

Ludlow takes expressions such as "by the standards of chemistry" and "by today's standards of knowledge" to play an analogous function to the expressions "for Michigan" and "for Colorado", which articulate comparison class properties. Such expressions make explicit the standard of knowledge relative to which an ascription of knowledge is true or false.

Contextualism is the thesis that knowledge ascriptions are context-sensitive in an epistemologically distinctive way. Ludlow takes the presence of expressions in English such as "by the standards of chemistry" or "by today's standards of knowledge" to show that *unembellished* knowledge ascriptions, ones that do not contain explicit standards operators, nevertheless contain an unpronounced position for epistemic standards. That is, Ludlow takes the existence of such expressions to show that, in a sentence such as "John knows that he has hands", there is an unpronounced position in the verb phrase "knows that he has hands" that, relative to a context, receives an epistemic standard as a value. That is how Ludlow proposes to derive contextualism from the felicity and potential truth of sentences such as (13) and (14).

Ludlow is indisputably correct in his observation that people regularly utter sentences such as (13) and (14). However, the phenomenon he discusses is not specifically epistemic in character. Expressions such as "by loose standards", "by strict standards", and "by the standards of chemistry" regularly occur appended to sentences that contain no epistemic vocabulary at all (cf. Lewis 1981, p. 84):

(15)   By strict standards, France is not hexagonal.

(16)   By loose standards, this table is square.

(17)   By the standards of chemistry, what is in the Hudson River isn't water.

Expressions such as "by strict standards", "by loose standards" and "by the standards of chemistry" cannot be used to derive a conclusion about specifically epistemic context-sensitivity. The pattern of usage of these expressions is considerably more general in character. It has something to do with the phenomenon that is called *loose use*.

Even abstracting from the fact that (as I will argue [later]) appeal to loose use is not of help to the contextualist, there are other objections to Ludlow's proposed inference. If Ludlow takes the felicity and potential truth of sentences such as (13) and (14) to license the postulation of epistemic standards variables in unembellished knowledge ascriptions, then, by parity of reasoning, he needs to take the felicity and potential truth of sentences such as (15)–(17) as licensing the postulation of various kinds of standards positions in sentences such as "this is water", "this is square", and "this is hexagonal". Indeed, there are more than just considerations from parity of reasoning at work here, since one can conjoin knowledge attributions and non-epistemic statements in the scope of expressions such as "by the standards of chemistry", as in:

(18) By the standards of chemistry, what is in the Hudson River isn't water, and John doesn't know that water is liquid.

(19) By loose standards, this table is square and John knows that water is a liquid.

Since there is only one occurrence of a standards expression in (18) and (19), its effect on the embedded non-epistemic sentence must be the same as its effect on the epistemic sentence. If it binds a standards parameter in the epistemic sentence, it binds a standards parameter in the non-epistemic sentence. It follows that, if one takes the felicity and potential truth of (13) and (14) to license the postulation of epistemic standards variables, one would need standards positions in the syntax for *virtually every predication*. This is deeply implausible. Furthermore, the conclusion, even if it were plausible, is of no help to the theorist who wishes to establish that knowledge ascriptions have a specifically *epistemological* kind of context-sensitivity. So the contextualist should certainly reject Ludlow's position.[23]

Ludlow's view that knowledge ascriptions contain an implicit reference to standards cannot be pressed into service to rescue the contextualist from the charge that knowledge ascriptions behave quite differently from other context-sensitive expressions. Contextualists do in general claim that there are special rules governing the context-sensitivity of instances of "know

that *p*". In particular, once a skeptical possibility has been raised, they say, that has ramifications for the evaluation of future uses of instances of "know that *p*" within that discourse. But there are two worries for this strategy. First, it leaves the oddity of (10) unexplained. Secondly, as I have emphasized, it stipulates a certain pragmatic constraint about the context-sensitivity of instances of "know that *p*" that has no parallel with pragmatic principles governing the interpretations of other context-sensitive expressions. Thus, these kinds of claims about how raising skeptical scenarios change the discourse look like stipulations to save the theory from having similar uncomfortable consequences as rival theories.

I have argued that the contextualist needs knowledge ascriptions to have very different properties from familiar context-sensitive constructions. These arguments leave open the possibility that the alleged context-sensitivity of instances of "know that *p*" could be modeled on the context-sensitivity of some other kind of expression, one that does not allow for standard shifts within a clause, and is undetectable by the above tests involving propositional anaphora and assertion reports.[24]

A complete case against the contextualist would involve canvassing every kind of context-sensitive expression, and showing some clear disanalogy between the behaviors of expressions of that kind and instances of "know that *p*". This is obviously a task that cannot be accomplished here. However, the above arguments are not thereby rendered idle. Before such a task is undertaken, one might think that there are surely some context-sensitive expressions that behave like knowledge ascriptions. But the above discussions show that there is no familiar kind of context-sensitivity upon which to base the alleged context-sensitivity of knowledge ascriptions. The burden of proof is therefore on the contextualist to produce one.

Notes

1   See Fantl and McGrath (2002) and Hawthorne (2004: ch. 4).

2   In particular, most of the examples have been discovered by Stewart Cohen and Keith DeRose.

3   Thanks to Earl Conee for suggesting this term.

4   Jon Kvanvig (on the blog Certain Doubts) suggested this as an account of these sorts of cases.

5   Here is another point against the knowledge of knowledge maneuver, due to unpublished work by Kripke. Suppose that Hannah, in the

low-stakes bank case, knows that the bank will be open. Suppose Bill has the same evidence as Hannah, and is also in a low-stakes situation. Then Bill can felicitously and truly utter the sentence "I know that Hannah knows that the bank will be open". It seems bizarre to hold, as the advocate of this maneuver must, that Bill knows that Hannah knows that the bank will be open, but Hannah does not know that Hannah knows that the bank will be open, despite the fact that they have the same evidence that the bank will be open.

6   John Hawthorne (2004, p. 30) puts the principle as "one ought only to use that which one knows as a premise in one's deliberations", which is a good way to elucidate the relevant sense of "act on". Hawthorne writes, concerning this principle: "There are complications that call for *ceteris paribus* style qualifications. In a situation where I have no clue what is going on, I may take certain things for granted in order to prevent paralysis, especially when I need to act quickly." But *ceteris paribus* style qualifications are needed only insofar as they are needed in all normative claims. A similar point holds for the knowledge rule for assertion, discussed below.

7   Thanks to Jim Pryor for discussion here.

8   I say "virtually all the cases", because the one intuition that remains mysterious from this perspective is the intuition we have in High Attributor–Low Subject Stakes. It is fine for the person in Low Stakes to act on his or her belief that the bank will be open.

9   DeRose provides a reason for contextualists to advocate an indexical treatment of "know". According to him, so doing allows the contextualist to respond to the charge that she is committed to the truth of utterances of sentences such as "I don't know that I have hands, but I used to know that I have hands." (cf. DeRose 1992, pp. 924–8; 2000). I challenge DeRose's arguments below.

10 One cannot complain that "love their mother" is not the same verb phrase as "loves my mother" (because "their" is plural case and "my" is singular case). For in some of Cappelen and Lepore's target examples, we find the exact same situation. For example,

"know that penguins waddle" is plural, in "Jill and Mary know that penguins waddle", whereas "knows that penguins waddle" is singular, in "Jill knows that penguins waddle". But Cappelen and Lepore still infer from the fact that one can collect with "know that penguins waddle", to the conclusion that "knows that penguins waddle" is not context-sensitive.

11 For example, in Stanley (2002), I argue that predicative uses of adjectives, such as "is tall", have the syntactic structure "is tall $f(i)$". In these representations, "f" denotes a function from objects to comparison classes, whose value is supplied by context, and "i" denotes an individual, relative to a context. Both "f" and "i" can be bound by higher operators. So an utterance of the sentence "Jill is tall" is really of the form "Jill$_1$ is tall $f(i)$", and an utterance of the sentence "Mary is tall" is really of the form "Mary$_1$ is tall $g(i)$." On the envisaged response from Cappelen and Lepore, variables inside a verb phrase can be bound by operators attaching to the Verb Phrase (this is what they would have to say to defend the view that "her" and "my" are instances of bound anaphora). So, the reason one could conclude "Both Jill and Mary are tall" from an utterance of "Jill is tall" and "Mary is tall" is because it is of the form "Both Jill and Mary λx (are tall $h(x)$)", where the value of "h", relative to the envisaged context, is a function that takes Jill onto $f(\text{Jill})$, and takes Mary onto $g(\text{Mary})$.

12 The degree to which this marks genuine ambiguity or a kind of indexicality is subject to dispute; see Kratzer (1977).

13 The reason I have placed the initial sentence in conditional form is that, if the initial sentence was just "I know that I have hands", the contextualist could explain the infelicity of the final utterance by appeal to the knowledge account of assertion. Let us use "know-L" for the lower-standards knowledge relation and "know-H" for the higher-standards knowledge relation. Suppose that the initial sentence were just "I know that I have hands". Asserting that one's previous claim to know-L that one has hands is still true clearly entails that one has hands. By the

knowledge account of assertion (the norm for assertion is knowledge), I could assert in the higher standard's context that my previous knowledge claim is still true only if I know-H that I know-L that I have hands. But this requires that I know-H that I have hands (by an uncontroversial application of single-premise epistemic closure). But, by stipulation, I do not know-H that I have hands. So a contextualist could explain the infelicity of the final utterance by appeal to the knowledge account of assertion. By placing the original sentence in conditional form, I have blocked this maneuver.

14   DeRose appears to concede the point that, on his view, a metalinguistic version of this discourse is fine. Speaking of just such a case, DeRose (1992, p. 925) writes: "[one] *can* say, 'My previous knowledge claim was true,' just as one can say, 'My previous location claim was true.' Or so I believe. But saying these things would have a point only if one were interested in the truth-value of the earlier claim, rather than in the question of whether in the present contextually determined sense one knew and knows, or didn't and doesn't."; But it does not seem that semantic ascent helps here.

15   It is worth mentioning that one can felicitously assign different standards to different occurrences of the same adjective, even when predicated of the same object; consider: "In Michigan, that mountain is tall, but in Colorado, it would not be tall".

16   I am using Graff's examples for a purpose she explicitly repudiates, since Graff herself (2000, p. 55) thinks that "it is not the case that variation of the standards in use for a vague expression is always attributable to some comparison class". However, Graff assumes that comparison classes must be kinds of some type, an assumption I reject.

17   On my favored account of predicate uses of gradable adjectives (such as "John is tall" or "Mary is rich"), the degree on the scale is determined by the comparison class property. Many people have argued that the degree on the scale is not so determined (e.g. Richard 2004), but I am not convinced by these arguments.

18   Again, it is irrelevant whether the mechanism that would so affect the interpretation of the two distinct occurrences of "know" is due to a parameter associated with "know" being controlled by the noun phrases "many normal non-philosophers" and "no epistemologists", or due rather to a shift in free contextual assignment initiated by the use of these noun phrases.

19   Again, I have placed this discourse in conditional form to avoid appeal to the knowledge account of assertion in explaining the infelicity of asserting in a higher-standards context that one's previous knowledge claim is true.

20   This is, in essence, the parallel pragmatic principle to Lewis's "Rule of Attention" (1996, pp. 559 ff.) for quantifier domain restriction.

21   Of course, many Van Gogh paintings are housed in the Van Gogh museum in Amsterdam.

22   There is a commercial for McDonald's that shows a woman driving with her children, which begins with the children requesting. "Can we go to McDonald's now?", which is answered in the negative. Every subsequent few seconds, the children make their request again, taking advantage of the fact that "now" can change its denotation over a discourse.

23   There are a number of other reasons to question the inference Ludlow draws. First, there are similar inferences that are clearly invalid (a "bad-company" objection). From the truth of "according to John, chocolate is made of gold", we cannot conclude that the unembellished sentence "chocolate is made of gold" contains a reference to persons. It is similarly unclear what legitimates Ludlow's inference. More theoretically, on a very natural construal of these operators, they are adjuncts and not arguments. If so, they are only optionally present, and not present when phonologically unarticulated. In response, Ludlow rejects the argument-adjunct distinction. He argues that many expressions that we think of as adjuncts really mark positions that are linguistically active, even when unpronounced. Ludlow suggests e.g. that there is a position for an instrument (such as "with a knife") in a

sentence such as "John cut the salami". On this view, even when this position is not explicitly articulated (as it is in "John cut the salami with a knife") its value may be contextually supplied. But there is no position for instruments in "John cut the salami" that can be contextually supplied (see Stanley (2005)). If Bill utters "John cut the salami with a knife", Frank can deny his assertion by uttering "No he didn't; he cut it with a spoon". But if Bill utters only "John cut the salami", no matter what information is salient in extralinguistic context, it is never felicitous to follow his assertion with "No he didn't; he cut it with a spoon". So Ludlow's argument that "with a knife" is present even when unpronounced fails.

24   Barbara Partee (p.c.) pointed out to me that the relational term "enemy" does not easily allow for shifts in interpretation within a clause. An utterance of the sentence "John is an enemy and Bill is an enemy, but they are not enemies of the same person" is decidedly odd. Similarly, though one can switch from the "can" of physical possibility to the "can" of permissibility within a clause (as in "John can lift the table that Mary says he can"), it is harder to switch the domain of modals such as "can", fixing a sense of possibility. But I have provided other arguments to distinguish these expressions from knowledge ascriptions. The examples from propositional anaphora, and examples such as TECHNOLOGY, were so intended.

References

Cohen, Stewart (1988). "How to Be a Fallibilist", in J. Tomberlin (ed.), *Epistemology* (Philosophical Perspectives, 2, Atascadero, CA: Ridgeview), pp. 91–123.

DeRose, Keith (1992). "Contextualism and Knowledge Attributions", *Philosophy and Phenomenological Research*, 52/4, pp. 913–29.

—— (1999). "Contextualism: An Explanation and Defense", in J. Greco and E. Sosa (eds), *The Blackwell Guide to Epistemology* (Oxford: Blackwell), pp. 187–205.

—— (2000). "Now You Know It, Now You Don't", *Proceedings of the Twentieth World Congress of Philosophy*, v. *Epistemology* (Bowling Green, OH: Philosophy Documentation Center), pp. 91–106.

—— (2002)."Assertion, Knowledge, and Context", *Philosophical Review*, 111, pp. 167–203.

Fantl, Jeremy and McGrath, Matthew (2002). "Evidence, Pragmatics, and Justification", *Philosophical Review*, 111/1, pp. 67–94.

Graff, Delia (2000). "Shifting Sands: An Interest-Relative Theory of Vagueness" *Philosophical Topics*, 28/1, pp. 45–81.

Hawthorne, John (2004). *Knowledge and Lotteries* (Oxford: Oxford University Press).

Kratzer, Angelika (1977). "What 'Must' and 'Can' Must and Can Mean", *Linguistics and Philosophy*, 1, pp. 337–55.

Lewis, David (1983). "Scorekeeping in a Language Game", in Lewis, *Philosophical Papers* (New York: Oxford University Press), i, pp. 233–49.

—— (1996). "Elusive Knowledge", *Australasian Journal of Philosophy*, 74, pp. 549–67.

Ludlow, Peter (1989). "Implicit Comparison Classes", *Linguistics and Philosophy*, 12, pp. 519–33.

—— (2005). "Contextualism and the New Linguistic Turn in Epistemology", in G. Preyer and G. Peters (eds), *Contextualism in Philosophy*, (Oxford: Oxford University Press).

Richard, Mark (2004). "Contextualism and Relativism", *Philosophical Studies*, 119/1–2, pp. 215–41.

Schaffer, Jonathan (2004). "From Contextualism to Contrastivism", *Philosophical Studies*, 119/1–2, pp. 73–103.

Soames, Scott (1986). "Incomplete Definite Descriptions", *Notre Dame Journal of Formal Logic*, pp. 349–75.

—— (2000). "Context and Logical Form", *Linguistics and Philosophy*, 23/4, pp. 391–434.

—— (2002). "Nominal Restriction", in G. Peters and G. Preyer, *Logical Form and Language* (Oxford: Oxford University Press), pp. 365–88.

—— (2005). "Semantics in Context", in Gerhard Preyer and G. Peter (eds), *Contextualism* (Oxford: Oxford University Press).

——and Szabo, Z. (2000). "On Quantifier Domain Restriction", *Mind and Language*, 15, pp. 219–61.

——and Williamson, T. (1995). "Quantifiers and Context-Dependence", *Analysis*, 55, pp. 291–5.

Williamson, Timothy (2000). *Knowledge and its Limits* (Oxford: Oxford University Press).

Yourgrau, Palle (1983). "Knowledge and Relevant Alternatives", *Synthese*, 55, pp. 175–90.

CHAPTER 51

Evidence, Pragmatics, and Justification

Jeremy Fantl and Matthew McGrath

Train Case 1. You're at Back Bay Station in Boston preparing to take the commuter rail to Providence. You're going to see friends. It will be a relaxing vacation. You've been in a rather boring conversation with a guy standing beside you. He, too, is going to visit friends in Providence. As the train rolls into the station, you continue the conversation by asking, "Does this train make all those little stops, in Foxboro, Attleboro, etc?" It doesn't matter much to you whether the train is the "Express" or not, though you'd mildly prefer it was. He answers, "Yeah, this one makes all those little stops. They told me when I bought the ticket." Nothing about him seems particularly untrustworthy. You believe what he says.

Intuitively, in Train Case 1, you have good enough evidence to know that the train stops in Foxboro. You are epistemically justified in believing that proposition.[1]

Train Case 2. You absolutely need to be in Foxboro, the sooner the better. Your career depends on it. You've got tickets for a south-bound train that leaves in two hours and gets into Foxboro in the nick of time. You overhear a conversation like that in Train Case 1 concerning the train that just rolled into the station and leaves in 15 minutes. You think, "That guy's

information might be wrong. What's it to him whether the train stops in Foxboro? Maybe the ticket-seller misunderstood his question. Maybe he misunderstood the answer. Who knows when he bought the ticket? I don't want to be wrong about this. I'd better go check it out myself."

Intuitively, in Train Case 2, you do not have good enough evidence to know that the train stops in Foxboro. You are not justified in believing that proposition. When so much is at stake, a stranger's casual word isn't good enough. You should check further.[2]

Suppose these intuitions are correct: you are justified in Train Case 1 but not in Train Case 2. What follows is that epistemic justification is not simply a matter of the evidence one has. You have the same evidence in each case. But in one case you are justified; in the other you are not. So, if these intuitions are correct, a proposition's justification does not supervene on one's evidence for or against it; that is, evidentialism is false.[3]

> *Evidentialism.* For any two subjects S and S′, necessarily, if S and S′ have the same evidence for/against p, then S is justified in believing that p iff S′ is, too.

How surprising this conclusion is depends on how broad a notion of evidence is employed. Under an internalist conception of evidence, the falsity of evidentialism is of some interest, but

Originally published in *The Philosophical Review* 111, 1 (Jan. 2002), pp. 67–94.

might only reveal the weaknesses of internalism, and similarly for externalist versions of evidentialism. The term "evidence," however, is not a technical term requiring a stipulated meaning. In considering the Train Cases, we use "evidence" to mean what it ordinarily does. That is to say, we employ a broad intuitive concept of evidence, which internalists and externalists might analyze in different ways. It is difficult to say much that is helpful about the ordinary concept of evidence without taking up a particular theory. But it ought to be common ground between theories of evidence that having a lot at stake in whether p is true does not, by itself, provide evidence for or against p. Evidence for p ought to raise the probability of p's truth (in some appropriate sense of "probability"). But having a lot at stake in whether p is true doesn't affect its probability, except in rare cases in which one possesses special background information. For this reason, it seems that all candidate theories of evidence ought to allow that you have the same evidence in the Train Cases. So if the intuitions about the Train Cases are correct, then even when "evidence" is understood as expressing the broad intuitive notion, evidentialism is false. The conclusion that evidentialism, so understood, is false, is therefore surprising. If it is false, we suspect many forms of reliabilism, virtue theory, and deontologism are false as well.

We reject evidentialism, but we feel that the above argument is not enough to do the job. The intuitions in the Train Cases, though ultimately correct, are not strong enough to count as data in a decisive argument against evidentialism. Evidentialism is not so easily refuted.

Denying evidentialism seems tantamount to denying the undeniable distinction between epistemic and pragmatic justification. We usually distinguish the two by noting that the former has a special relationship to truth-acquisition and falsehood-avoidance that the latter lacks. Put one way, pragmatic justification has to do with all of our goals, while epistemic justification has to do only with our special truth-related goals. Consequently, if evidence for p, construed broadly, just is a matter of what serves our truth-related goals in respect of p, then epistemic justification will be a matter of evidence and nothing more.

Because of its apparent connection with this distinction, evidentialism is not defeated simply by noting that we often take (and ought to take) non-evidential considerations into account before forming or acting on a belief. Richard Rudner, for example, claims that "[h]ow sure we need to be before we accept a hypothesis will depend on how serious a mistake would be" (1953, p. 2). This might seem to require that justification be at least partly a pragmatic matter. But one could accept Rudner's claim without giving up evidentialism, if one distinguishes, as Richard Foley (2000) does, between a notion of responsible belief and a notion of epistemically rational belief. The latter, for Foley, is the epistemologically central notion, the notion that foundationalists, coherentists, and reliabilists dispute. It is an idealized notion, concerned with a "very specific goal, that of now having accurate and comprehensive beliefs" (p. 181). But as examples such as the Train Cases make clear, "in reality all of us have many goals" (p. 181). The notion of responsible belief takes account of these other goals. One *responsibly believes that p*, according to Foley, if one has an epistemically rational belief that one's procedures with respect to p have been acceptable given the limitations on one's time and capacities and given all one's goals (p. 183). The evidential standards for responsible belief "slide up or down with the significance of the issue" (p. 185); not so, for epistemically rational belief. For Foley, the subjects in the Train Cases are alike with respect to epistemic rationality (either both or neither would be epistemically rational to believe that p), and so presumably with respect to epistemic justification as well, but they differ with respect to responsibility.

If Foley is right, evidentialism is consistent with Rudner's claim that whether we ought to accept a hypothesis depends at least partly on how much is at stake, as long as the "ought" is one of responsibility, not epistemic rationality. So, it seems that evidentialists need not take intuitions about cases like the Train Cases as decisive against their view. They can respond by arguing that the intuitions at work, though real, are misdescribed. This is Foley's strategy, and the strategy of Keith Lehrer as well, who suggests that, properly construed, the intuitions reveal conversational rather than semantic constraints:[4]

When the context is one in which a great deal hinges on whether or not p is true, one should be cautious about giving one's word or authority for the truth of p. Consequently, it might be inappropriate to say, "I know that p," in such contexts even though one does know that p. (2000, p. 33)

In light of these sorts of evidentialist responses, one cannot refute evidentialism by a simple appeal to the Train Cases. But this is not our plan. Rather, we aim to provide a theoretical basis for rejecting evidentialism by defending a "pragmatic" necessary condition on epistemic justification. If our proposed condition is necessary for justification, it becomes reasonable to see the intuitions at work in cases like the Train Cases as intuitions about justification, rather than conversational dynamics or responsible belief. This is because our necessary condition, if correct, explains how differences in pragmatic factors – in facts about preferences – can make a difference to justification. Thus, we do not merely refute evidentialism. We show *that*, *why*, and *how* a subject's pragmatic situation may affect her justification.

We are not alone in rejecting views that fail to give pragmatic factors an epistemic role. In a recent book, David Owens offers the following argument against evidentialism.

[My case against evidentialism] can be made simply by asking: how are you going to tell us, in purely evidential terms, what level of evidence is needed to justify belief? Unless this question can be answered, evidentialism (internalist and externalist) must be abandoned. (2000, p. 26)

Something in addition to evidence must "complete" the justification. "How," he asks, "could this something be anything other than the (perceived) needs and interests of the believer?" (p. 26).

We join Owens in rejecting evidentialism, but we will not be making use of his argument. Though he does seem correct that the evidentialist does not provide us with a way to determine how much evidence is required for justification, we don't seem much closer to solving this problem after Owens's argument. We're told that our needs and interests are relevant. But we're not told how they bear on the evidence required for justification. What we're missing, even after Owens's argument, is a non-arbitrary rule telling us that in

such and such a pragmatic situation (specified in terms of needs and interests), such and such an amount of evidence is required for justification. In the absence of such a rule, the question of what level of evidence, given such-and-such stakes, is required for justification seems no less urgent for the opponent of evidentialism than the question of what level of evidence is required for justification is for the evidentialist. Therefore, because of evidentialism's initial plausibility, plus its resilience in the face of apparent counterexamples, until a better argument comes along, evidentialism has the upper hand.

This article is divided into three parts. In the first, we argue for a pragmatic necessary condition on epistemic justification that predicts and explains the intuitions we have about the Train Cases and their ilk. In the second, we apply our account to test cases, thereby showing how it avoids some of the pitfalls of other accounts that give pragmatics a role in epistemic justification. In the third, we consider an objection to our argument against evidentialism.

1. A Pragmatic Condition on Epistemic Justification

How might pragmatic factors affect whether, given one's evidence, one is justified in believing something? Let us begin with the more intuitive concept, knowledge.

If you know that p, then it shouldn't be a problem to act as if p. If it is a problem to act as if p, you can explain why by saying that you don't know that p. Suppose you are faced with some decision – do A or do B – where which of these is better depends on whether p. You know that if p, A is the thing to do, but that if not-p, B is. To say in one breath, "I know that p" and in the next breath, "But I'd better do B anyway, even though I know that A is the thing to do if p" seems incoherent. If you really know that p, and you know that if p, A is the thing to do, then it's hard to see how you could fail to know that A is the thing to do in fact. But then you ought to do A.

This seems to work both from the first-person and third-person perspectives. If S knows that p, then it shouldn't be a problem for S to act as if p. If it is a problem for S to act as if p, we can explain why by saying that S doesn't know that p. Suppose

S is faced with the above choice situation. S knows that if p, A is the thing to do, but that if not-p, B is. To say in one breath, "S knows that p" and in the next breath, "But S had better do B anyway, even though S knows that A is the thing to do if p" seems incoherent. If S really knows that p, and S knows that if p, A is the thing to do, then it's hard to see how S could fail to know that A is the thing to do in fact. But then S ought to do A.

This reasoning can be generalized into a two-part argument. The first part is a general closure argument:

(1) S knows that p.
(2) S knows that if p, then A is the thing to do.

Therefore,

(3) S knows that A is the thing to do.

Depending on how "the thing to do" is interpreted, different conclusions follow from (3). But if "the thing to do" is interpreted in terms of what would be the best thing one can do in light of all one's goals, then something quite interesting follows. We can add a second part to our argument relating knowledge to rationality of action:[5]

(3) S knows that A is the best thing she can do (in light of all her goals).

Therefore,

(4) S is rational to do A.

Combining the two parts into a whole, and interpreting "the thing to do" as "the best thing one can do (in light of all ones goals)" we arrive at:

(1′) S knows that p.
(2′) S knows that if p, then A is the best thing she can do.

Therefore,

(3′) S is rational to do A.

We can express our commitment to this argument in the form of a principle:

S knows that p only if, for any act A, if S knows that if p, then A is the best thing she can do, then S is rational to do A.

We think this is a good start. But there is an even stronger sense in which pragmatic factors have epistemic relevance. We can strengthen the principle in no fewer than four ways.

First, there is no need to restrict the original closure argument either to acts or to judgments of what is best. If you know that p, and you know that if p then A is better for you than B, then you know that A is better for you than B. Consequently, it's rational for you to prefer A to B.[6] Here, A and B may be any states of affairs, where acts can be treated as merely one kind of state of affairs.[7] Thus, we may strengthen the consequent of our principle to reach:

S knows that p only if, for any states of affairs A and B, if S knows that if p, then A is better for her than B, then S is rational to prefer A to B.[8]

Second, we may strengthen our principle to apply to cases in which, although one has good reason, one neither knows nor is justified in believing that one state of affairs will be better for her than another. We often have good evidence for thinking one state of affairs will be better for us than another, while lacking evidence good enough for knowledge. Suppose you're playing the card game *Hearts*. You've got both the ace and the two of diamonds. It is early in the game. You don't know – and aren't justified in believing – that if diamonds are led, it will be better to play the ace than the two. After all, you might well get stuck with the queen of spades if a fellow player has no diamonds. But it seems wiser, given that diamonds are led, to get rid of your ace than to waste your two (since it's pretty likely everyone has at least one diamond). In our terms: you are rational to prefer playing the ace to playing the two, given that diamonds are led. That is, you are rational to prefer the state of affairs in which diamonds are led and you play the ace to the state of affairs in which diamonds are led and you play the two. Now suppose you come to know that diamonds are being led; the person to your right leads the five of diamonds. What should you prefer: playing your ace or playing your two? Surely, you should prefer playing your ace. If you know that diamonds are led, and you are rational to prefer playing your ace to playing your two, given that diamonds are led, then you must be rational to prefer playing your ace to playing your two in fact. More generally, if you know that p, and if you are rational to prefer one state of affairs to another, given p, then you will be rational to prefer that state of affairs to the other in fact. Thus, we may improve upon our argument (1′)–(3′) as follows:

(1″)   S knows that p.
(2″)   S is rational to prefer A to B, given p.

Therefore,

(3″)   S is rational to prefer A to B in fact.

Correspondingly, our necessary condition on knowledge becomes:

S knows that p only if, for any states of affairs A and B, if S is rational to prefer A to B, given p, then S is rational to prefer A to B, in fact,

where *S is rational to prefer A to B, given p* is equivalent to *S is rational to prefer A&p to B&p*.[9]

Third, we can strengthen our principle by making it a requirement on justification, not simply on knowledge. So modified, (1″)–(3″) becomes

(1‴)   S is justified in believing that p.
(2‴)   S is rational to prefer A to B, given p.

Therefore,

(3‴)   S is rational to prefer A to B in fact.

Suppose that a subject, S, is justified in believing that p, but does not know that p. Suppose further that S is rational to prefer A to B, given p. Compare S to a second subject, S′, who has the same evidence and fundamental preferences as S but who knows that p. S′ is rational to prefer A to B. What one is rational to prefer is determined by one's evidence and fundamental preferences. Since S and S′ have the same evidence and fundamental preferences, they will be rational to prefer the same states of affairs. Thus, S, too, is rational to prefer A to B. Whatever it is rational for a knower to prefer is also rational for an otherwise identical subject who is merely justified in believing to prefer. Therefore, if (1″)–(3″) is valid, so is (1‴)–(3‴).

We can therefore strengthen our principle thus:

S is justified in believing that p only if, for any states of affairs A and B, if S is rational to prefer A to B, given p, then S is rational to prefer A to B in fact.

Now for the final strengthening. As it stands, the consequent of our principle is simply a conditional, rather than a biconditional. That is, our principle leaves open whether being justified in believing that p ensures that for states of affairs A and B, if S is rational to prefer A to B in fact, then S is rational to prefer A to B, given p. We now argue this issue should be closed. Assume you're justified in believing that the train goes to Foxboro (p). And assume that you are, in fact, rational to prefer boarding (B) the train to waiting (W) for the next train. Could it turn out that you are not rational to prefer B to W, given p? No. There are two ways you might fail to be rational to prefer B to W, given p. First, you could be rational to be indifferent between B and W, given p. In this case, since you would be justified in believing that p, then it seems that you would be rational to be indifferent between B and W in fact, which, by hypothesis, you are not. Second, you could be rational to prefer W to B, given p. Again, since you would be justified in believing that p, it seems that you would be rational to prefer W to B in fact, which, by hypothesis, you are not. Thus, we can strengthen our principle by making its consequent a biconditional: for any states of affairs A and B, S is rational to prefer A to B, given p, iff S is rational to prefer A to B, in fact.[10] When you satisfy this condition with respect to p, we will say that you are rational to *prefer as if p*. We express our principle compactly as a pragmatic necessary condition on epistemic justification:

(PC) S is justified in believing that p only if S is rational to prefer as if p.

Our view relates epistemic justification to rational preferences generally, and not merely to rational preferences about how to act. However, PC does entail a condition relating epistemic justification to acts and, in particular, to the act(s) that it is rational for S to do, given p.[11]

S is justified in believing that p only if, for all acts A, S is rational to do A, given p, iff S is rational to do A, in fact.

We may think of the consequent of this principle as making precise the intuitive notion of *acting as if p*. Thus, the principle may be formulated more simply as:

(PCA) S is justified in believing that p only if S is rational to act as if p.[12]

Two clarifications are in order. First, we have arrived at (PC) by converting an *argument pattern* $((1''')–(3'''))$ into a principle.[13] Our argument for (PC), then, is one and the same as our argument for the validity of the corresponding argument pattern. Our argument for the latter is based on a series of strengthenings of our original argument, $(1')–(3')$, which is the combination of two arguments, a closure argument $(1)–(3)$ and an argument linking knowledge to rational action $(3)–(4)$. Thus, our argument for (PC) does not appeal to intuitions about particular cases, such as the Train Cases. We are not proposing a condition for justification and then seeing if it fares well by the method of example and counterexample, but rather providing a theoretical argument for a condition on justification.

Second, it might seem that we are imposing an unduly severe restriction on justification and therefore knowledge. There will be some cases in which in order to have knowledge, one will need to have absolute certainty, or something close to it.[14] These will be cases in which something of great importance hinges on whether a belief is true.[15] Doesn't this make the requirements for knowledge too demanding? Can't we have knowledge without absolute certainty?

We can. Nor does our view entail otherwise. After all, in Train Case 1, our view is consistent with the claim that you know that the train is going to Foxboro, even though you have only the evidence of casual testimony. There are many cases – in fact, most cases are like this – in which we have knowledge without having a strong form of certainty. Requiring certainty in these cases would be otiose. Our account requires certainty for knowledge only in cases in which certainty is important – its importance consisting in the fact that it is required for being rational to prefer and act as if the relevant proposition is true. This should give the skeptic no consolation.

2. Illustrations and Test Cases

We can illustrate our view by applying it to the original Train Cases.[16] In Train Case 1, you don't much care about whether the train will stop in Foxboro. In Train Case 2, it is desperately important to you that it will.

Suppose that, in each Train Case, the same two options are available to you. You can inquire further to make sure that the train really will stop in Foxboro. Or you can board the train without inquiring further. PC entails that you are justified in believing that the train will stop in Foxboro only if you are rational to prefer as if the train will stop in Foxboro. In Train Case 1, what you are rational to prefer, given that the train will stop in Foxboro, is boarding the train. You are rational to prefer this to inquiring, since the latter will involve some cost to you, and you don't much care if the train will stop in Foxboro. You are also rational to prefer this in fact, for the very same reason. What it is rational for you to prefer, given that the train will stop in Foxboro, is also what you are rational to prefer in fact. That is, you are rational to prefer as if the train will stop in Foxboro. So PC is satisfied and you may have enough evidence for justification.

In Train Case 2, on the other hand, you are not rational to prefer as if p. For, in fact, you are not rational to prefer boarding the train to inquiring further. It is extremely important to you that the train will stop in Foxboro. If you board it, and it will not stop in Foxboro, things will go very badly for you. You need to inquire further to make sure that the train will stop in Foxboro. In fact, you are rational to prefer inquiring to boarding. Given that the train will stop in Foxboro, on the other hand, you are rational to prefer boarding to inquiring, since boarding will get you to Foxboro, and inquiring further involves a small cost to you.

Therefore, what you are rational to prefer, given that the train will stop in Foxboro, is not what you are rational to prefer in fact. That is, you are not rational to prefer as if the train will stop in Foxboro. So, PC is not satisfied. You are not justified in believing (and, hence, do not know) that the train will stop in Foxboro.

Let us see how our view handles some further cases. These cases will show how our account differs from, and improves upon, other accounts that find an epistemic role for pragmatic factors.

The first class of cases concerns the relation between justification and the costs/benefits of inquiry. Since our account provides only a necessary condition, the test cases for our account will be ones in which a subject has excellent evidence for a proposition but the cost of further inquiry is prohibitively high.

> *Case of the Time-Consuming Call.* You're at home. You're taking the train to New York tomorrow. You have a distinct recollection from making your reservation by phone that your train leaves at 5 pm. You are not worried about being wrong. You have good evidence, and in any case, if you miss the 5 pm, you'd take the 7 pm. Calling up Amtrak again would mean waiting on the phone for 35 minutes or so.

Intuitively, it seems that the cost of inquiring further doesn't have a bearing on whether you are justified in this case. You don't need to inquire further in order to be justified. Our account confirms this. What you are rational to prefer, given that the train leaves at 5 pm is what you are rational to prefer in fact. You are rational to prefer not inquiring to inquiring, both in fact, and given that your train leaves at 5 pm. Similarly, for other states of affairs.

However, you might still think that the costs/benefits of inquiry are of special concern in determining whether one is justified. Our view does give the costs/benefits of inquiry a somewhat special role, since it will often be the case that inquiry will, with little cost, raise the probability that p to a level at which it will be rational to prefer as if p. But, our view, you might think, does not give one's rational preferences for further inquiry as critical a role as they deserve. You might even think that, any time it is rational to inquire further, one must lack justification. This seems to be the view of D. S. Clarke Jr., who posits the following principle: "(BC) S rationally believes in p relative to e only if S believes the cost to him of acquiring additional evidence e′ is greater than what S believes to be the cost of p's being mistaken" (1985, p. 460).

This sort of view gives the costs/benefits of inquiry too prominent a place in determining justification. Suppose I offer to reward you handsomely for inquiring further about whether today is Tuesday (or whatever day of the week it is). You have plenty of evidence that it is Tuesday, but you haven't been dwelling on the fact too much, and nothing much hinges on which day of the week it is. Now there are no costs of inquiry whatsoever, only benefits, and great ones. Thus, the believed cost of inquiry to you is less than the believed cost of being mistaken. So, on Clarke's view, you are not rational (and therefore, presumably, not justified) in believing, no matter how much evidence you have. This seems wrong. On our view, what is rational to prefer, given p, is the same as what is rational to prefer in fact. You are rational to prefer inquiring in both cases. Therefore, our view, as articulated in PC, does not preclude you from being justified in believing that it's Tuesday.[17]

The second class of cases concerns the costs/benefits of believing a certain proposition. Since our account provides only a necessary condition for justification, the test cases are ones in which there is a high cost to believing something for which you have excellent evidence. We will discuss two such cases. The first is the:

> *Case of the Threat not to Believe.* Suppose you are threatened not to believe that George W. Bush is president. If you continue believing it, you will suffer great pain.

Intuitively, although you ought to try to get yourself to give up the belief that Bush is president, you are justified in believing it. Our account accommodates this intuition. What you are rational to prefer, given that Bush is president, is what you are rational to prefer in fact: you are rational to prefer not believing that Bush is president to believing he is. One might even say: you ought not to believe that Bush is president. This "ought," however, is the "ought" of rational preferability, not epistemic justification.

Robert Nozick gives us a more realistic case in this class:

Case of the Miserable Belief. It would be extremely hard for you to go on if you believed your son was guilty of the crime of which he is accused. The belief would result in intense misery and pain, whether or not he is in fact guilty. You have good evidence that he is guilty.

Intuitively, you are not justified in thinking your son is innocent, since all the evidence is against it. Are you justified in thinking he is guilty? Let us ask what our account implies. Is what you are rational to prefer given that your son is guilty the same as what you are rational to prefer in fact? It seems so. Even given that your son is guilty, you are rational to prefer not believing he is guilty to believing he is guilty. And this is what you are rational to prefer in fact. This seems to hold for all states of affairs. Our account therefore leaves open the possibility that you are justified in believing that your son is guilty. Here we differ from Nozick, who claims that the rule below expresses a constraint on rational belief (and so presumably on justified belief):

Rule 2: Believe (an admissible)[18] *h* only if the expected utility of believing *h* is not less than the expected utility of having no belief about *h*. (1993, p. 86)

This seems to yield unacceptable results. Indeed it seems that no matter how much evidence you have that your son is guilty, you are not rational to believe he is, given Rule 2. He could be staring you in the face, confessing the crime to you, and explaining precisely how he did it. You might even have caught him in the act. So long as believing he is guilty is so crushing, you are not rational to believe, and so not justified.[19]

As the last two cases show, our view does not surrender the distinction between epistemic and pragmatic justification. If our view is correct, then epistemic justification for p requires the rationality of preferring as if p. But this does not mean that epistemic justification for p requires pragmatic justification for believing p. As we have seen, one can be rational to prefer not believing that Bush is president, even though one is rational to prefer as if Bush is president, and one can be

rational to prefer not believing that one's son is guilty, even though one is rational to prefer as if he is. These are not isolated cases. Often there are costs to believing that p even when one is rational to prefer as if p. When those costs are high, you may not be pragmatically justified in believing that p (so believing won't best serve your general goals), and yet you may still be epistemically justified.

We noted earlier that acceptance of the epistemic/pragmatic justification distinction appears to commit one to evidentialism. How else to distinguish epistemic justification than by its taking into account only one's truth-related goals? And if it takes into account only one's truth-related goals, it seems it must be solely a matter of evidence. We can now see that this reasoning is fallacious. Epistemic justification can take into account our non-truth-related goals and still be distinguished from pragmatic justification.

3.   The Argument against Evidentialism

If our account is correct, that is, if PC states a pragmatic necessary condition on epistemic justification, then evidentialism must be false. If PC is true, then there could be two subjects, identical with respect to their evidence for/against p, one of whom should act (and generally prefer) as if p and one of whom should not. Train Cases 1 and 2 involve two such subjects.

This argument is too quick. Outright rejection of PC is implausible, as we hope to have made clear in previous sections. However, the evidentialist has another alternative. We will formulate a more careful approach in our response to this alternative.

Suppose an evidentialist reasons as follows: "I do accept your closure arguments and all the variations on them. This leads me to accept PC. However, I do not think that PC conflicts with my main evidentialist thesis that a proposition's justification supervenes on evidence for that proposition. All PC commits us to is the claim that if a subject is justified in believing that p, then she had better be rational to prefer as if p. But we can simply set the standard of evidence required for justification high enough to avoid pairs of subjects that have the same evidence but are such that one is rational to prefer as if p while the other is not. Two people with the same evidence for/against a proposition p will thus not differ in justification for p. In Train Case 1 you wouldn't count as justified, but that's not so hard to accept."

This response seems to commit the evidentialist to a kind of pragmatic condition on justification, namely:

(EPC) S is justified in believing that p only if anyone with S's evidence for p, no matter what the stakes, would be rational to prefer as if p.

EPC isn't merely *a* way for the evidentialist to embrace PC; it's the only way. For suppose evidentialism and PC are true, but EPC is false. Then there is a case in which a subject S is justified in believing that p, but it's not true that anyone with S's evidence would be rational to prefer as if p. Thus, there must be some subject S′ in a further case, who has the same evidence as S, but for whom the stakes are different, and who therefore isn't rational to prefer as if p. If evidentialism is true then, since S and S′ have the same evidence for/against p, and S is justified, so is S′. But then, PC is violated: S′ is justified, but it is not rational for S′ to prefer as if p.

For the evidentialist, then, a lot turns on the acceptability of EPC. We want to make several claims about this principle. First, given that EPC itself proposes a pragmatic condition on epistemic justification, the truth of EPC would support our general claim that there is a pragmatic element in epistemic justification, even if it would not support our claim against evidentialism. Second, we agree that it might be useful to put a common label to a kind of epistemic status – a kind of "justification" – subject to EPC. If you know that you have justification satisfying EPC, then you know that you are safe in preferring – and, hence, acting – as if p, and will be safe so long as your evidence regarding p remains unchanged, no matter what happens to your fundamental preferences. Third, though, we think that PC is true of the justification required for knowledge, while EPC is not. EPC is too strong. It doesn't allow for many cases of justification based on induction, testimony, memory, rational intuition, and perhaps even direct perception. In many cases in which we are justified in believing a proposition p we would not be rational to prefer as if

p, were the stakes radically higher. Train Cases 1 and 2 are meant to be instances of this general fact. But there are many other examples. (Bayesians have an arsenal; see Kaplan 1996, pp. 102–3.) In an ordinary case, when the stakes are low – you're sitting in your front room relaxing – you are justified in believing, on the basis of memory and induction, that your car is parked in your driveway. But if you were to have this same evidence concerning the where-abouts of your car when your action would save or jeopardize lives depending on whether your car was there or not, and you had time to check before acting, you ought to go check. Similar examples can be constructed for your normally low-stakes justified beliefs such as: *the local post office is open until noon on Saturdays, your cousin lives in San Diego, you have a Tuesday–Thursday schedule next semester, the Yankees won the World Series two years ago.* Maybe even your evidence for I have hands isn't sufficient for justification however high the stakes may be.[20]

Note that evidentialists cannot avoid this conclusion by accepting contextualism. To combine contextualism with evidentialism is to hold that, if subjects S and S′ have the same evidence, then within any fixed speaker context "S is justified" and "S′ is justified" have the same truth value, although across speaker contexts, these sentences can have different truth values. So, a contextualist might claim that, despite the fact that the subjects in the Train Cases have the same evidence, when we discuss Train Case 1, we correctly attribute "justified" to the subject, but when we discuss Train Case 2, we correctly attribute "unjustified" to the subject. Our speaker context switches.

Understanding the Train Cases in this way, however, commits one to a broader contextualism – not merely a contextualism about justification but a contextualism about rational preference. Here is why. Since contextualist evidentialists, like all evidentialists, must accept EPC, they must maintain that if "In Train Case 1, you are justified in believing that the train stops in Foxboro" is true in a given speaker context, then so is "In Train Case 2, you are rational to prefer as if the train stops in Foxboro." But, of course, as soon as we think about the latter, we judge it false. So, to save intuitions, while resisting skepticism, the contextualist must hold that "rational to prefer as if" is context-sensitive.

Recall that we defined "S is rational to prefer as if p" to mean *For any states of affairs A and B, S is rational to prefer A to B, given p, iff S is rational to prefer A to B, in fact.* Thus, the contextualist must hold that the relation "is rational to prefer x to y," too, is context-sensitive. There seems little merit to this theory. Intuitively, we do not vacillate about whether the subject in Train Case 2 is rational to prefer checking further to immediately boarding. We stably judge the subject rational to prefer checking further. The best explanation for our stable judgments about cases like this is that "rational to prefer x to y" expresses, across speaker contexts, a single relation that holds in virtue of the subject's evidence and fundamental preferences.

Furthermore, there is a fundamental difficulty for contextualism about rational preference. Contextualists about justification claim that what varies from context to context is not what degree of evidence a subject has, but whether that degree of evidence is enough for justification. What varies, that is, is the threshold for justification. The same holds good for contextualism about flatness, emptiness, tallness, etc. When it comes to rational preference, however, the question of a threshold does not arise. Rational preference is purely relational. Whether S is rational to prefer A to B is simply a matter of the relative positions of A and B in S's rational preference ordering, not a matter of meeting a threshold of "rational preferability."

If contextualism about rational preference is unacceptable, then "In Train Case 2, you are rational to prefer as if the train stops in Foxboro" will be false in all contexts. So if EPC is true in all contexts, it follows that the statement "In Train Case 1, you are justified in believing that the train stops in Foxboro" will have to be false in all contexts, too. Thus, the evidentialist cannot avoid skepticism by accepting contextualism.

Given that EPC is too strong, and given the truth of PC, it follows that evidentialism is false.

4. Conclusion

Our argument against evidentialism can be summarized succinctly. First, we argued for a pragmatic condition on epistemic justification.

(PC) S is justified in believing that p only if it is rational for S to prefer as if p.

(Recall that *it is rational for S to prefer as if p* abbreviates *for any states of affairs A and B, S is rational to prefer A to B, given p, iff S is rational to prefer A to B, in fact.*) We then showed that, if PC is true, then evidentialism could be true only if a strong pragmatic condition on justification holds, namely:

(EPC) S is justified in believing that p only if anyone with S's evidence, no matter what the stakes, would be rational to prefer as if p.

But, as we saw, EPC is too strong. It does not square with intuitions that one can be justified on the basis of a stranger's testimony about directions, train routes, etc., or on the basis of induction that one's cousin lives in San Diego, etc. Our conclusion: evidentialism is false.

Given that PC is correct and EPC is not, we have not only shown *that* differences in what's at stake for subjects can affect justification, we've shown *how*. Consider Owens's argument against evidentialism (discussed at the end of section 1, above). The key premise of his argument is that the evidentialist cannot simply set a threshold, since any threshold would be arbitrary. There is something wrong with the evidentialist's simply saying, "If you have this much evidence, your belief is justified." Owens suggests we need to appeal to pragmatic factors to secure a non-arbitrary threshold. Yet it seems no less arbitrary for Owens simply to say, "When the stakes are this high, then when you have this much evidence, your belief is justified." Why do these stakes require this amount of evidence, rather than some other amount? Owens does not answer this question. Not so in our case. It is clear how stakes play a role in the amount of evidence required for justification. We require at least as much evidence as is needed to make it rational to prefer as if the proposition in question is true. And this requirement is not arbitrary, as it would be if adopted by those who subscribe to Owens's argument. It is a direct result of theoretical arguments based on essential features (for example, closure) of knowledge and justification.

Epistemic justification isn't purely a matter of evidence. A subject is justified in believing something just in case she has evidence that is good enough for her to know. But what is "good enough" will not itself be a matter of evidence. Owens is correct in this at least. One subject (S) might have better evidence than another (S') along a purely evidential dimension of evaluation even while S isn't justified but S' is. Suppose Nozick's *credibility values* provide such a purely evidential dimension of evaluation of propositions. Here is Nozick:

> Let us imagine a network that incorporates a weighting of many factors – including Bayesian probabilities, explanatory value (as represented by the Causalized Bayesian formula). Popperian methodological maxims, and an assessment of undercuttings – and feeds forward to result in a *credibility value* for a statement *h*. View this as an ideal assessment that duly weights all of the reasons for and against *h*. (1993, p. 84)

Our conclusion, reformulated in terms of credibility values, is that no specific credibility value is both necessary and sufficient for justification, independently of all pragmatic factors. There is a credibility value sufficient for justification, namely, whatever credibility value satisfies EPC. And presumably there is a credibility value necessary for justification, that is, a credibility value that all justified propositions must exceed in credibility: the credibility value zero. But there is no such thing as a pragmatics-independent credibility value *threshold* for justification. For S to be justified in believing a proposition p, p's credibility value for S must exceed a threshold, but the threshold is determined in part by relevant features of S's pragmatic situation.

Appendix I

In cases in which one has no reason to believe that how one acts will causally affect whether p is true, our closure arguments are unproblematic. There are, however, cases in which one does have such reason. In these cases, argument (1')–(3') seems subject to a peculiar logical difficulty. Consider the following train case: You need to get to Foxboro. But you know that the train conductor is your sworn enemy and will bypass Foxboro if you board the train (and that is the only way he will thwart your aims). You also know that, if you do not board the train, the conductor will definitely take the train to Foxboro. You decide, therefore, not to board the train. The following modus ponens argument would then be available to you:

  (I)   The train will go to Foxboro.
 (II)   If the train will go to Foxboro, then taking the train is the best thing for me to do.

Therefore,

(III)   Taking the train is the best thing for me to do.

However, (III) seems not to be true in your case, even though (I) and (II) are (if you stick with your decision not to take the train). After all, if you take the train, it won't end up going to Foxboro. If it is questionable whether modus ponens fails in this cases, then *a fortiori* it is also questionable whether our closure argument (1')–(3') fails here. You know that (I) is true (given your decision and its efficacy), and you know that (II) is true, but it does not seem that you know that (III) is true. We need to restrict our closure arguments (1')–(3') to secure the unquestionable validity of the embedded instances of modus ponens. Moreover, it seems that, since we are closing knowledge under modus ponens, we must require that the relevant subject S have no reason to think that the validity of the embedded modus ponens argument is questionable. Restricting S/p/A combinations in our closure argument (1')–(3') so that S has no reason to believe that whether she does A will causally affect whether p is true serves our purpose adequately. We use a similar restriction for S/p/A/B combinations in our closure arguments and principles that involve comparisons between states of affairs.

It should be noted that the logical difficulties that we have mentioned raise questions about the validity of argument forms other than simple modus ponens. Consider the notorious Henry V argument (paraphrased from Shakespeare's account of Henry's speech to his badly outnumbered troops on the eve of battle):

(i) Either we will win or we will lose.
(ii) If we will win, it is better for us to be outnumbered (since there will be greater glory, etc.).
(iii) If we will lose, it is better for us to be outnumbered (since at least we will avoid shame).

Therefore,

(iv) It is better for us to be outnumbered.

(i)–(iii) seem true, but (iv) false. This seems to be a counterexample to the argument schema:

Either p or q.
If p, then A is better than B.
If q, then A is better than B.

Therefore,

A is better than B.

which is apparently valid insofar as it is subsumed under disjunction elimination.

Problems disappear here, as with (I)–(III) above, provided we impose a restriction about causal influence – provided, in particular, we require that whether A, as opposed to B, obtains will not causally affect whether p, as opposed to q, is true. (To say that the arguments seem wrong when and only when there exist such causal connections is not to answer the logical questions, Are arguments (i)–(iv) and (I)–(III) really invalid? Are modus ponens and disjunction elimination invalid?)[21]

Appendix II

Our condition on justification is supported by intuitions about the closure of knowledge under modus ponens. It is incumbent upon us, then, to show that our condition itself has this closure property.[22] For suppose our condition isn't closed under modus ponens. The worry would arise whether the truth of our account would undermine its support. Although the failure of closure for a necessary condition on justification doesn't entail the failure of closure for justification (and therefore knowledge), all the same, it would be cause for concern. We would need to appeal to further elements of the concept of justification in order to show how justification could have the closure property even though a necessary condition of it didn't.

We therefore seek to show that our condition is closed under modus ponens, or in other words, that the following argument is valid:[23]

(1′′′′) S is rational to prefer as if p.
(2′′′′) S is rational to prefer as if (p→q).

Therefore,

(3′′′′) S is rational to prefer as if q.

Our proof uses the following definitions:

D1: S is rational to prefer X to Y, given p $=_{def}$ S is rational to prefer X&p to Y&p.

D2: S is rational to prefer as if p =$_{def}$ for any states of affairs X and Y, S is rational to prefer X to Y, given p, iff S is rational to prefer X to Y, in fact.

1.	S is rational to prefer as if p.	Assumption
2.	S is rational to prefer as if (p→q).	Assumption
3.	S is rational to prefer A to B.	Assumption for Conditional Proof
4.	S is rational to prefer A to B, given p.	1,3,D2
5.	S is rational to prefer A&p to B&p.	4,D1
6.	S is rational to prefer A&q&p to B&q&p.	See subproof below
7.	S is rational to prefer A&q to B&q, given p.	6,D1
8.	S is rational to prefer A&q to B&q	1,7,D2
9.	S is rational to prefer A to B, given q.	8,D1
10.	If S is rational to prefer A to B then, S is rational to prefer A to B, given q.	3,9
11.	S is rational to prefer A to B, given q.	Assumption for Conditional Proof
12.	S is rational to prefer A&q to B&q.	11,D1
13.	S is rational to prefer A&q to B&q, given p.	1,12,D2
14.	S is rational to prefer A&q&p to B&q&p.	13,D1
15.	S is rational to prefer A&p to B&p.	See subproof below
16.	S is rational to prefer A to B, given p.	15,D1
17.	S is rational to prefer A to B.	1,16,D2
18.	If S is rational to prefer A to B, given q, then S is rational to prefer A to B.	11,17
19.	S is rational to prefer A to B, given q, iff S is rational to prefer A to B.	10,18
20.	S is rational to prefer as if q.	19,D2

We offer the following justifications for steps 6 and 15.

Justification for 6:

5.1	S is rational to prefer A&p to B&p, given (p→q).	2,5,D2
5.2	S is rational to prefer A&p&(p→q) to B&p&(p→q).	5,1,D1
5.3	A&q&p&(p→q) = A&p&(p→q) and B&q&p&(p→q) = B&p&(p→q).	Statements of Proposition Identity
5.4	S is rational to prefer A&q&p&(p→q) to B&q&p&(p→q).	5.2,5.3
5.5	S is rational to prefer A&q&p to B&q&p, given (p→q).	5.4,D1
6.	S is rational to prefer A&q&p to B&q&p.	2,5.5,D2

Justification for 15:

14.1	S is rational to prefer A&q&p to B&q&p, given (p→q).	2,14,D2
14.2	S is rational to prefer A&q&p&(p→q) to B&q&p&(p→q)	14,1,D1
14.3	A&q&p&(p→q) = A&p&(p→q) and B&q&p&(p→q) = B&p&(p→q).	Statements of Proposition Identity
14.4	S is rational to prefer A&p&(p→q) to B&p&(p→q).	14.2, 14.3

14.5   S is rational to prefer A&p to B&p,   14.4,D1
        given (p→q).
15.   S is rational to prefer A&p to B&p.   14.5,D2

Steps 5.3 and 14.3 are inessential. If the relevant propositions aren't identical, then they are trivi-ally equivalent, in which case it is rational to be indifferent between them. This is enough to secure 5.4 and 14.4.

Notes

1   We use "S is justified in believing that p" throughout the paper, in *a* standard way, to mean that S has good enough evidence to know that p. On our usage, you might have good undefeated evidence for p (have a good bit of "justification" for believing that p) and yet not be justified *simpliciter*, owing to the fact that your evidence isn't good enough for knowledge. Thus, at least on one standard intuition, before the lottery winner is announced, you aren't justified (in our sense) in believing that your ticket is a loser, even though you may have substantial justification on the basis of probabilistic reasoning. (The lottery case was never construed as a Gettier case – that is, as a case in which one had justi-fied true belief but failed to know.)

    What is it for evidence to be good enough for knowledge? To say that S's evidence is good enough to know that p isn't to say that S's having that evidence entails S's knowing that p. It is to say that, if S fails to know, it is not for S's lack of evidence. We take this con-dition not to be vacuous, since we assume that one cannot know without evidence.

2   This pair of cases is modeled after Stewart Cohen's airport case. In Cohen's case, it is not entirely clear that the two subjects share the same evidence. Our pair of cases ensures this. Cf. (Cohen 1999, p. 58). However, our cases inherit the ambiguity of planes or trains "stopping" at such and such places. Is the proposition *This train stops in Foxboro* equiv-alent to the proposition *This train (type) is scheduled to make a stop in Foxboro as part of its normal route?* Or is it, rather, equivalent to *This train (token) will stop in Foxboro?* This ambiguity does not seem to affect intuitions about justification. Intuitively, in cases like Train Case 1, one is justified in believing both

such propositions, while in Train Case 2, one is justified in believing neither.

3   For a defense of evidentialism, see Feldman and Conee 1985. They write:

What we call evidentialism is the view that the epistemic justification of a belief is determined by the quality of the believer's evidence for that belief. (p. 15)

    David Owens defines a broader notion of evidentialism: "Evidentialism is the doctrine that epistemic norms invoke only evidential considerations" (2000, p. 24).

4   See also Rysiew 2001.

5   To avoid making controversial commitments about certain peculiar cases, we here-after restrict S/p/A combinations in our closure arguments and principles so that S has no reason to believe that whether she does A will causally affect whether p is true. See Appendix 1 for discussion of the peculiar cases.

6   One might object as follows. Couldn't you know that A is better for you than B and yet not be rational to prefer A to B, because some-one is standing nearby (make this being a demon, if necessary) who will kill you iff you prefer A to B? It would seem, then, that you ought not to prefer A to B.

    In response, we want to extend a distinc-tion of Nozick's (1993. p. 70) to apply in the domain of rational preference. He distin-guishes between *p being the rational thing to believe* and *believing p being the rational thing to do*. We distinguish, correspondingly, between A *being rationally preferable to B* and *preferring A to B being the rational thing to do*. There is a clear sense in which, in the objec-tor's example above. A is rationally preferable to B for S (since, in light of S's evidence and basic preferences. A can be expected to have better results), though preferring A over B might not be the rational thing for S to do. See also Heil 1983, p. 758. When we say "S is rational to prefer A to B," we mean "A is rationally preferable to B, for S".

7   For acts as states of affairs (as "propositions") see Jeffrey 1983, pp. 83–4. Hereafter we assume that an act (A) is rational for S just in case A is available to S and there is no available competitor B such that it is rational for S to prefer doing B to doing A. On this definition, if two or more acts are tied for best, both are rational.

8   Two restrictions are needed here. First, we strengthen our earlier restriction on S/p/A combinations. Our proposal bears only on S/p/A/B combinations that are such that S has no reason to believe that whether A as opposed to B obtains will causally affect whether p is true.

Second, the inference

(1*)   S knows that p
(2*)   S knows that if p, then A is better for her than B.

Therefore,

(3*)   S knows that A is better for her than B.

Therefore,

(4*)   S is rational to prefer A to B.

is valid only when restricted to instances in which premises (1*) and (2*), if true, would still be true were S to face the choice of whether to make A true or make B true. To have a handier expression, we may formulate the restriction thus: the premises (1*) and (2*) must be robust (to borrow a term from Roy Sorensen (1988)) with respect to the choice situation *Make A true or Make B true*. The need for this restriction can be seen as follows. Suppose (1*) and (2*) (and so (3*)) are true in a particular case. Why think that (4*) must be true as well? (4*) is true, we may assume, only if S would be rational to prefer making A true to making B true when faced with the choice. Now if (1*) and (2*) are robust with respect

to the choice situation in question, then we can see that S would be rational to prefer making A true when faced with the choice: if you're in a choice situation with respect to A and B, and you know that A is the better of the two, then clearly you should choose A over B. However, suppose the robustness restriction is unsatisfied. Suppose, that is, that although (1*) and (2*) are true, they wouldn't both be true were S faced with the choice situation. Then there would be no guarantee that (3*) is true – that is, no guarantee that S would still know, in the choice situation, that A is better for her than B – and so no guarantee that S would be rational to choose A over B. Thus, the mere truth of (1*) and (2*) does not guarantee the truth of (4*). To derive (4*), we need the assurance that both premises are robust with respect to the A/B choice situation.

Some philosophers and decision theorists might have reservations about the assumption that if a person is rational to prefer a state of affairs A to a state of affairs B, then the person would be rational to prefer making A true to making B true when faced with the choice. A standard alternative to this approach is Jeffrey's "good news" approach, under which you are rational to prefer A to B iff you would welcome the news that A is true more than you would welcome the news that B is true (1983, p. 82–3). All the same, we need a similar restriction on (1*)–(4*) in this decision-theoretic setting. Suppose that, were you to get the news that A is true, not both of (1*) and (2*) would be true. Then there would be no guarantee that you would still know that A is better for you than B, and so no guarantee that you wouldn't wish the news had been B instead. But if we impose the restriction that (1*) and (2*) be robust with respect to your learning the news that A is true (or that B is true), then the conclusion is obtained: were you to learn that A is true, you wouldn't wish the news had been B instead.

For each of the remaining strengthenings of our original argument (1)–(4), we hereby impose a corresponding robustness restriction. We require that the premises of each such argument be robust with respect to the choice situation Make A true or Make B true (or alternatively with respect to your learning the news that A (or that B)). (When such arguments are converted into principles, our restriction requires the robustness of the antecedent of the embedded conditional with respect to the A/B choice situation.)

The second restriction is not covered by the first. Even if one lacks a reason for thinking that whether A or B obtains will causally affect whether p is true, it doesn't follow that if one knows both that p and that if p, then A is better than B, then one's knowledge would survive being faced with the A/B choice situation. If, as we shall argue, knowledge depends on stakes, then we should expect to find cases in which one knows that p even though, were one in a high-stakes choice situation, one would not know that p.

9   Here, as in note 6, one might object in the following way. Suppose A would bring great joy to you, B misery, and you know as much. Suppose also you know that p. These suppositions, moreover, are jointly consistent with your knowing that there is a demon nearby who is prepared to kill you iff you prefer A to B. In this case, you know that p, you're rational to prefer A to B, given p, but you're not rational to prefer A to B, in fact.

Our response here is similar to our earlier response in note 6. We distinguish the question of whether A is rationally preferable to B from that of whether having a preference for A over B is the rational thing to do. This distinction becomes especially plain if we think of rational preferability in terms of expected utility. A could have a higher expected utility than B, even though preferring A to B might have a lower utility than being indifferent or having the opposite preference (and vice versa). Assuming, in addition, that the rationality of acts is judged by expected utility, we would have the following situation: A is rationally preferable to B for S, but preferring A to B is not the rational thing to do.

As before, we use "S is rational to prefer A to B" to mean that A is rationally preferable to B for S.

10   Given that the preference-or-indifference relation is both transitive and connected, our revised principle implies that, in order for you to be justified in believing that p, the preference ordering it is rational for you to have, given p, must be the same as the preference ordering it is rational for you to have in fact.

11   A is rational for S to do, given p iff A is available to S and there is no state of affairs of the form B&p, where B is an available competitor to A, that S is rational to prefer to A&p.

12   In a brief discussion, Christopher Hookway seems to endorse something in the neighborhood of PCA. He writes:

[The fact that beliefs are among the antecedents of action] may help to explain our standards of cognitive evaluation. For example, our understanding of the amount of evidence we require in support of an hypothesis before we can describe it as justified may reflect the degree of support that is required before we can feel that we are acting responsibly when we act upon it. This promises to explain some of the relativities involved in our concept of justified belief; the greater the disaster if our actions fail to achieve their purpose, the more evidence we require before we regard the belief as properly justified: the greater the risks attaching to inaction, the readier we are to act on limited evidence. (1990, p. 139)

We think that Hookway's speculation is correct. Our argument for (PCA) can be thought of as a way of showing how essential features of justification bear out Hookway's speculation.

There is also a Bayesian account of belief analogous in some respects to PCA. Mark Kaplan calls it "The Contextualized Act View." Under this view, "you count as believing that P in a given context just if you are disposed in that context to act as if P is true" (1996, p. 105 n. 101). See Nozick 1993, pp. 93–100 for such a view. Our proposal differs from this one in two important ways. First, ours presents a condition, not on belief, but on justification in believing. Second, ours requires that you be rational to prefer as if p is true (and consequently to act as if p is true), rather than that you be disposed to act as if p is true.

13   To be exact, we have converted at once two argument patterns into a principle. These are (1‴)–(3‴) and the argument pattern

which uses (1‴) and (3‴) as premises, and (2‴) as the conclusion.

14   Here, we mean epistemic, rather than psychological, certainty. We have absolute epistemic certainty for p only if we have the highest possible degree of justification for p – perhaps something akin to infallibility.

15   Here is an example: *The World is at Stake.* Suppose *somehow* the desirability matrix for your sole available options doing A and doing B were as follows:

	p	not-p
Do A	small gain	$-\infty$
Do B	smaller gain	0

And suppose *somehow* you were justified in believing that whether you do A as opposed to B would not causally affect whether p is true. You'd be only a little better off doing A than B if p is true, but you'd be infinitely worse off doing A than B if not-p is true. Our account entails that if the probability of p is less than 1 for you – if p does not have the highest certainty for you – then you will not be epistemically justified in believing that p. Suppose p is the proposition that you have hands. Each of us believes he has the strongest form of certainty for p. If we were somehow certain we were faced with the choice between doing A (say, trying to make a fist) or B (not trying to make a fist), and that the desirability matrix were as it is above, we think we would be rational to do A. But the probability of *I have hands* might be less than 1 for someone else (S). S would therefore not be rational to try to make a fist. Therefore, by an application of PC, S would not be justified in believing that she has hands. We find this result correct.

16   Note that in each Train Case, our two restrictions delineated in note 8 are satisfied. In neither Case 1 nor Case 2 is it the case that whether A (boarding) or B (inquiring)

obtains is causally related to whether p (the train will stop in Foxboro) is true. Nor is it the case, in either Train Case, that actually being faced with the choice situation (board or inquire) would change what you know (or are justified in believing). You *are* faced with the choice situation.

17   For another account that treats justification as related to the costs/benefits of inquiry, see Owens 2000, 25–7.

18   An admissible *h* is a proposition that has a higher credibility value than any of its contraries (this is Rule 1) and has a "high enough" credibility value (this is Rule 3). See Nozick 1993, pp. 85–93.

19   Nozick means "rational" in an epistemic sense, since his rules are meant to be rules about when a proposition that p is the rational thing to believe rather than when believing p is the rational thing to do. For more on this distinction, see Nozick 1993, p. 70.

20   See note 15.

21   Plausibly, *If p, then A is better than B* is equivalent to *A&p is better than B&p.* If this is right, the Henry V argument is equivalent to a dominance argument. Its flaws, then, would receive ready diagnosis. However, such an equivalence would not imply that the argument's steps (ii) and (iii) weren't genuine conditionals. That is to say, the problem with disjunction elimination would not disappear. Similarly, the problem with modus ponens exemplified in (I)–(III) would not disappear if the constituent conditional were treated as equivalent to *One's doing A&p is better than any other state of affairs of the form One's doing B&p, where B is an available competitor to A.*

22   We extend special thanks to Robert Howell for making us recognize the need for this demonstration.

23   Here as before we impose our restriction on S/p/A/B combinations.

References

Clarke, D. S., Jr. 1985. "Ignoring Available Evidence." *Southern Journal of Philosophy* 22, pp. 453–67.

Cohen, Stewart. 1999. "Contextualism, Skepticism, and the Structure of Reasons." In *Philosophical*

Perspectives, ed. J. Tomberlin, pp. 57–89. Cambridge: Blackwell.

Feldman, Richard, and Earl Conee. 1985. "Evidentialism." *Philosophical Studies* 48, pp. 15–34.

Foley, Richard. 2000. "Epistemically Rational Belief and Responsible Belief." In *Proceedings of the Twentieth World Congress of Philosophy*, ed. R. Cobb-Stevens, pp. 181–8. Bowling Green. OH: Philosophy Documentation Center.

Heil, John, 1983. "Believing What One Ought." *Journal of Philosophy* 80, pp. 752–65.

Hookway, Christopher. 1990. *Scepticism*. London: Routledge.

Jeffrey, Richard, 1983. *The Logic of Decision*. Chicago: University of Chicago Press.

Kaplan, Mark. 1996. *Decision Theory as Philosophy*. Cambridge: Cambridge University Press.

Lehrer, Keith. 2000. "Sensitivity, Indiscernibility and Knowledge." In *Philosophical Issues*, ed. Ernest Sosa and Enrique Villanueva, pp. 33–7. Boston: Blackwell.

Nozick, Robert. 1993. *The Nature of Rationality*. Princeton: Princeton University Press.

Owens, David. 2000. *Reason without Freedom: The Problem of Epistemic Normativity*. London: Routledge.

Rudner, Richard. 1953. "The Scientist *Qua* Scientist Makes Value Judgments." *Philosophy of Science* 20, pp. 1–6.

Rysiew, Patrick. 2001. "The Context-Sensitivity of Knowledge Attributions." *Noûs* 35, pp. 477–514.

Sorensen, Roy. 1988. "Dogmatism, Junk Knowledge, and Conditionals." *Philosophical Quarterly* 38, pp. 433–54.

CHAPTER 52

Sensitive Moderate Invariantism

John Hawthorne

1 From Ascriber-Dependence to Subject-Dependence

The contextualist invited us to suppose that variations in the ascriber can affect the truth value of knowledge ascriptions even if we hold fixed the subject of the ascription. Thus, on her account, the relation expressed by the verb "know" on an occasion of use will depend upon, *inter alia*, what is salient to the ascriber and perhaps also upon what the interests of the ascriber are; upon whether there is a good deal at stake for the ascriber that turns on the truth value of the proposition that figures in the knowledge ascription; and so on. It is this ascriber-dependence that forces the thesis of context-dependence. For it forces the conclusion that two ascribers may be looking at a single subject at the same time and one truly say "He knows that *p*", another "He doesn't know that *p*". Contradiction is avoided by claiming that the verb "know" expresses different relations in the mouths of each ascriber.

It is worth inquiring whether there really are pressing grounds for admitting ascriber-dependence. For suppose instead that the kinds of factors that the contextualist adverts to as making for ascriber-dependence – attention,

Originally published in J. Hawthorne, *Knowledge and Lotteries* (Oxford: Clarendon, 2004), pp. 157–91.

interests, stakes, and so on – had bearing on the truth of knowledge claims only insofar as they were the attention, interests, stakes, and so on of the subject.[1] Then the relevance of attention, interests, and stakes to the truth of knowledge ascriptions would not, in itself, force the thesis of semantic context-dependence. Here is the picture. Restricting ourselves to extensional matters, the verb "know" picks out the same ordered triples of subject, time, and proposition in the mouths of any ascriber. However, whether a particular subject–time–proposition triple is included in the extension of "know" depends not merely upon the kinds of factors traditionally adverted to in accounts of knowledge – whether the subject believes the proposition, whether that proposition is true, whether the subject has good evidence, whether the subject is using a reliable method, and so on – but also upon the kinds of factors that in the contextualist's hands make for ascriber-dependence. These factors will thus include (some or all of) the attention, interests, and stakes of that subject at that time. In what follows, I wish to explore this picture – call it "sensitive moderate invariantism" – in a preliminary way, indicating how it may help with our puzzles.[2] I shall describe two sorts of mechanisms that arguably bear on the truth of knowledge claims, ones that are akin to contextualist machinery, except that they are conceived of as making for subject-sensitivity.[3]

2 Salience[4]

A contextualist challenge

Our contextualist claimed that if a kind of mistake is salient to the ascriber, then there is a default presumption that it is relevant to the knowledge ascription. Let us transform this into a claim about subjects. In its strongest form, a subject-sensitive salience constraint might take the following form: If S thinks that p, but a certain counterpossibility is salient to S, then S does not know that p. A weaker version would insert "*ceteris paribus*" into the consequent. I do not propose to quibble over these details just now.

Let us begin with a thought experiment raised by Stewart Cohen in support of contextualism and briefly adverted to earlier. On the basis of a printed itinerary, Smith believes that a certain flight has a layover in Chicago. John and Mary observe Smith consulting the itinerary, and hear him assert that he knows that the flight stops in Chicago. But it matters a great deal to John and Mary whether or not the flight will stop there. Worried that the itinerary contains a misprint or has been recently changed, they decide to check further. Let us accept Cohen's contention that they are prudent to do so.

One diagnosis of the case that Cohen considers is that the claim "Smith knows that the flight stops in Chicago" is straightforwardly true. But against this he complains:

> Yet if Smith knows on the basis of the itinerary that the flight stops in Chicago, what *should* they have said? "Okay, Smith knows that the flight stops in Chicago, but still, we need to check further." To my ear, it is hard to make sense of that claim. Moreover, if what is printed in the itinerary is a good enough reason for Smith to know, then it is a good enough reason for John and Mary to know. Thus John and Mary should have said, "Okay, *we* know the plane stops in Chicago, but still, we need to check further." Again, it is hard to make sense of such a claim. (1999, pp. 58–9)[5]

Let us look at the case through the lens of a subject-sensitive salience rule. Clearly, certain counterpossibilities to the proposition that the flight stops in Chicago are salient to John and Mary but not to Smith. Assume that Smith knows

the proposition. It might still be the case that John and Mary do not know it on account of the fact that certain possibilities are salient to them. So from the assumption that Smith knows, it hardly follows, *pace* Cohen, that John and Mary should have said "Okay, we know …". But isn't the first segment of Cohen's complaint still pertinent? Doesn't this view imply that John and Mary ought to say "Okay, Smith knows that the flight stops in Chicago, but still, we need to check further", or, worse still, that they ought to say "Smith knows and we don't"? It does not. If we cling to the idea that knowledge is the norm of assertion, then if John and Mary are to properly assert "Smith knows that the flight stops in Chicago", they will have to know that Smith knows that the flight stops in Chicago. Since knowledge is factive, they will then have to know (or at least be in a position to know by simple deduction) that the flight stops in Chicago. But, by hypothesis, they do not know that the flight stops in Chicago (since certain counterpossibilities are salient to them). A similar diagnosis accounts for the prudence of their checking further: Since they do not know that the flight stops in Chicago, they are not in a position to use "The flight stops in Chicago" as a premise in their practical deliberations. So Cohen's suggestion that the case provides something like a proof that contextualism is the only serious option to skepticism can be challenged.

Anxiety-provoking inferences

Let us now consider our puzzles directly. When we deploy parity reasoning, certain counterpossibilities to lottery propositions and to those ordinary propositions that entail lottery propositions become salient. According to the current perspective, this will place us in a position where we know neither the relevant lottery propositions, nor the ordinary propositions that entail them. Thus, once the possibility of his winning the lottery becomes salient to someone (remember – salience is not mere attention), then that person knows neither that he will lose the lottery nor that he will not be able to afford an African safari. Does this make trouble for closure? It does not. Suppose someone knows at t_1 that he will not be able to afford an African safari in the near future. Single-Premise Closure says that if he performs a competent deduction, thereby believing at some later time, t_2, that he will not win the lottery, *retaining all along* his knowledge that he will not be able to afford an African safari, then that person knows at t_2 that he will lose the lottery. But if the counterpossibility of winning the lottery becomes salient to him sometime during the reasoning process, then knowledge of the relevant premise gets destroyed. In that case, Single-Premise Closure does not entail that the person knows he will lose the lottery, even if the latter can be deduced from something that he currently believes.

Generalizing, we can say that certain inferences are what we might call *anxiety-provoking* for certain subjects. In certain settings, as a matter of psychological fact, certain kinds of counterpossibilities are made salient to us. And in these circumstances, the current brand of sensitive invariantism predicts that performing the relevant inference will destroy knowledge of the premises, rather than producing knowledge of the conclusion.[6] Insofar as someone knows an ordinary proposition, but finds the inference to some entailed lottery proposition anxiety-provoking in this sense, that person will know the premise but be incapable of coming to know the conclusion.

This is not to say, of course, that *anyone* who believes a lottery proposition is such that certain counterpossibilities will be salient. It is open to the proponent of this position to allow that in certain contexts, one can know a lottery proposition. (Perhaps these include some of those settings described earlier, where people are happy to assert a lottery proposition, and are untroubled by counterpossibilities.)[7]

Suppose that thinking about lotteries makes a certain counter-possibility to the African safari proposition salient. Should I now say "Up to five minutes ago, I knew I wouldn't have enough money to go on an African safari, but not any more"? The points raised against Cohen apply with equal force here. If at the later time I don't know the ordinary proposition, then I cannot assert that I used to know it, since knowledge is the norm of assertion. To properly assert that one used to know that p, one needs to know p now. The sentence "I used to know that I would not be able to afford to go on an African safari" may in fact be true, but it is not proper for me to assert it.

Note that it is extremely intuitive to suppose that someone who is in the midst of parity reasoning about a lottery proposition is not in a position to assert that proposition; and that he does not at that point know the lottery proposition would seem to be a natural and compelling explanation for this normative datum. Our current version of moderate invariantism, unlike simple moderate invariantism (with or without Harman's refinements) can embrace this explanation with open arms. It also seems clear that in the context of a conversation where some counterpossibility to a lottery proposition has been made salient, one is in no position to assert an ordinary proposition that entails it; and it seems that the obvious explanation is that one does not at that point know that the ordinary proposition is true. Once again, this explanation can be endorsed by the current view.

Pessimism and projection

This is not to say, of course, that there are no counterintuitive consequences to this version of sensitive invariantism. As far as I can see, every candidate story about our puzzle has counterintuitive results. This is no exception.

There is one way that *all* moderate invariantisms will depart from ordinary practice. Once we have gotten ourselves into the frame of mind of thinking "I do not in fact know whether or not I'll be able to afford the safari", as we frequently do when we use parity reasoning, we are not only unwilling to say "However I used to know that"; we are positively willing to say "I never did know that". And, if pressed, we are willing, moreover, to say that "I was mistaken in thinking that I did know that". But moderate invariantism allows that ordinary people do know all sorts of ordinary propositions – so it is inevitable that any form of moderate invariantism will be committed to saying that reflection on lottery propositions induces an excessively skeptical frame of mind. The moderate invariantist holds that we often *do* know things of the form "That table will be there for a while", and, correlatively, that the cast of mind I get in when I use parity reasoning drawn from quantum mechanics (one in which I say that no one knows what the future will bring) is a cast of mind in which I am excessively pessimistic about what people know. The contextualist, of course, is not so committed: she can maintain that in the so-called "pessimistic" frame of mind, our standards are high, and so we are exactly right to say "No one knows things like that". For the contextualist, the mistake arises only when we go to say to ourselves "So ordinary people are wildly mistaken in their knowledge ascriptions".[8]

Despite this departure from ordinary practice, subject-sensitive moderate invariantism has the beginnings of an explanation about why we are sometimes excessively pessimistic in our attributions of knowledge. After all, on such a view, when certain counterpossibilities are salient to us, it is perfectly correct to say *of ourselves* that we do not know the relevant propositions. What we need to account for in addition is our tendency to over-project our own lack of knowledge to others. In so doing, we might helpfully appeal to the psychological literature on heuristics and biases.

Psychologists in that tradition emphasize the role played by the "availability" heuristic as a distorting influence on our judgments of risk: in many cases, our estimation of the likelihood of an event is affected by the case with which we can recall or imagine it.[9] So, for example, when a certain scenario is made vivid, the perceived risk of that scenario may rise dramatically. In this regard, it is a widely documented phenomenon that "a recent disaster or a vivid film" may, as Slovic, Fischhoff, and Lichtenstein emphasize, "seriously distort risk judgments" as, for example, when "Recently experienced floods appear to set an upward bound to the size of loss with which managers believe they ought to be concerned."[10] They go on to note that a "particularly important implication of the availability heuristic is that discussion of a low-probability hazard may increase its memorability and imaginability and hence its perceived riskiness" (1982, p. 465).[11] Applied to the issue at hand, the availability heuristic may help to explain our tendency to skeptical overprojection. When certain non-knowledge-destroying counterpossibilities are made salient, we overestimate their real danger; as a result, we may find ourselves inclined to deny knowledge to others in cases where there is in fact no real danger of error.[12]

Whatever our favorite conjectures about the psychological mechanisms at work (I do not wish to speculate further here), one thing seems clear and very important: we do have some tendency to suppose that, as more and more possibilities of error become salient to us, we are reaching an ever more enlightened perspective. Thus when we consider someone who is not alive to these possibilities, we have a tendency to let our (putatively) more enlightened perspective trump his.[13] This tendency, when left unchecked, leads to skepticism. And even if we are convinced that skepticism is not correct, it is far from clear that we are capable of fully eradicating our tendency to find it compelling. Given this unhappy circumstance, it seems likely that our cognitive relationship to a nonskeptical semantics will always be a complicated one (as the last few thousand years of epistemology would seem to confirm).[14]

Note that the picture we have been considering yields a rather different picture of conversational dynamics than the one embraced by contextualists. Suppose I voice a set of knowledge ascriptions. As the conversation unfolds, counterpossibilities are made salient by my interlocutor, so that I come to give voice to a new, apparently conflicting and more skeptical set of knowledge ascriptions. Here are three candidate descriptions of the conversational dynamics. (*a*) Semantic accommodation.[15] I begin by assigning one semantic value to "know", but as time proceeds, I shift to a new semantic assignment in order that my ways of talking line up better with that of my interlocutor(s). (*b*) Testimonial accommodation. My interlocutor represents himself as knowing that I might be wrong. I am in general disposed to trust my interlocutors, so I come to believe that I might be wrong about this or that and bring my beliefs about what is known into line with these newly formed beliefs about epistemic modality. (*c*) Availability. My interloctutor paints an extremely vivid picture of certain kinds of error. I come to believe that I might be wrong, not because I trust the interlocutor, but because my tendency to make use of the availability heuristic lies beyond my conscious control.

The contextualist uses (*a*) to explain the conversational dynamics. It is far from clear that this is preferable to an explanation that proceeds by way (*inter alia*) of one or both of (*b*) and (*c*).

Residual costs

Let me now turn to examining the costs of the current approach. I have earlier indicated some ways in which a moderate invariantism that exploits salience may have an edge over simple moderate invariantism. This is not to deny that there are, intuitively speaking, special oddities to the former view. We don't normally embrace thoughts along the lines of "Just maybe, the only thing stopping me knowing is that I am worrying too much". Nor, having come to know p, do we embrace thoughts of the form "If I had been less anxious back then, more committed to p, less worried about alternatives, I would have known p back then". Nor, having got worried about p, do we think to ourselves "If p is true then I knew p before I got worried".[16] But on the current view, such thoughts are often warranted.[17,18] We may also note that insofar as the sensitive moderate invariantist embraces the Epistemic Possibility Constraint, he will likely find it difficult to accommodate van Fraassen's somewhat appealing Reflection Principle, which tells us that expected epistemic probability should equal current epistemic probability. Suppose that certain counterpossibilities are currently salient and hence my epistemic probability that p is merely .8. Suppose I know that after I dine and play backgammon, such possibilities will no longer be salient to me. Of course I do not now know that I will know p then, since I do not know p now. But, from the current perspective, I may well be highly confident that if p is true, I will know it at that point. For I may think that *if p is true*, the only thing stopping me from knowing it now is, crudely, anxiety. In short it may be that I assign roughly .8 to the proposition that my epistemic probability will be 1 post-backgammon. If p is false, I will still expect to have some non-zero epistemic probability of p post-backgammon: after all, conditional on p being false, it may well be quite unlikely that at that time I will be in a position to know that it is. So my expected epistemic probability will outstrip my current epistemic probability. I leave it to readers to judge for themselves whether such a violation of Reflection is altogether disastrous.

Note finally that one may complain that the kind of view that we are considering is unfair to thinking people: the philosopher who worries about being a brain in a vat, etc., will know less than the dullard who doesn't. The worry is finessed by the contextualist, who can claim that it turns on a conflation of use and mention. Not

so for the sensitive moderate invariantist. One can certainly soften the blow by pointing out that the philosopher is not in a position to *assert* that the dullard knows something he does not. Moreover, intuitions about rather similar cases often deviate from the ones maintained by the objector. Consider the "thinking person" who worries that his memory is deceiving him and that he has forgotten to turn the stove off. Is it so strained to suppose that, owing to self-induced anxiety, he no longer knows that he has turned the stove off? Consider, meanwhile, the "dullard" who does not suffer from such anxiety. Is it so strained to suppose that he retains knowledge of having turned off the stove?[19] The case against the view we are considering is certainly far from one-sided.

Another vexed issue is this: To what extent does salience of counterpossibility, anxiety, and so on, merely render one's knowledge temporarily unavailable for practical and theoretical reasoning (as opposed to destroying it)?[20] After all, it is not so strained to describe many of the cases under consideration as ones where one merely has anxiety-induced reluctance to put what one knows to work in one's cognitive labors. When is knowledge rendered inert owing to a (perhaps irrational) unwillingness to put something that one knows to use? When instead is it destroyed? I shall not attempt to resolve these questions here.

3   What is Salience?

I turn now to an issue that has been largely suppressed but that is nevertheless extremely important. What is it for the possibility of error to be salient anyway? … [I]t is not helpful in this context to identify the salience of error with the mere entertaining of an error-describing proposition.

It is plausible that salient counterpossibility of error is a certain kind of intellectual seeming. Some proposition seems to be true. (That is not to say I automatically believe it: we do not doxastically endorse all intellectual seemings.) But what proposition is it that seems to be true when the possibility of error by some subject S is salient? Not some proposition of metaphysical modality, to the effect there is some metaphysically possible world where an error is made. Rather, I would suggest, it is a claim of epistemic possibility that is tied to the epistemic subject. The content of the intellectual seeming associated with the salient possibility of error is basically this: For all the subject knows, p! There is now nothing puzzling whatsoever about the claim that the salience of the possibility of error induces retraction of a knowledge claim. This is just a special case of the claim that its intellectually seeming that p induces us to retract propositions that are incompatible with p.[21] (Notice that on this construal, contextualist proposals about salience as the mechanism whereby semantic shifts occur are fairly uninformative: they amount to the proposal that, other things being equal, if a negated knowledge ascription seems true, it is true.)

With this conception of salience in place, we can refine on our earlier discussion by distinguishing *three* different ways in which one might try to explicate the knowledge-undermining role of salience.[22]

(i) *The Belief Removal Model.* First, salience might destroy knowledge that p by destroying belief that p. It seems to one that it might be that not-p (where the "might" is here one of epistemic modality). This in turn induces one to stop believing that p, which, if knowledge requires belief, entails that one now does not know that p. So long as knowledge requires belief, there is no doubt that knowledge can be destroyed in this way; the question is whether belief is extinguished in the cases that we are considering, and thus whether this mechanism is the one that explains the veridicality (assuming for now they are veridical) of many ordinary claims of the form "I do not know whether or not I will win the lottery". On the face of it, this is not so plausible, since there seems to be a perfectly reasonable sense of "belief" in which one believes one will lose a lottery even when the possibility of error is salient in the relevant sense.

There is a variant on the current proposal that is worth considering. Suppose that an especially strong kind of conviction – something like *being sure*[23] – is a condition for knowledge.[24] One might think that insofar as the possibility of a certain kind of error is salient, this erases the kind of flat-out conviction required for knowledge. If all that were right, it would be natural to suppose that it explains why knowledge is absent in cases where the possibility of error is salient.[25]

(ii) *The Evidential Model.*[26] Its seeming to me perceptually that p provides me with evidence for p.[27] Similarly, if it seems to me that I might be wrong (in the sense explained) then, plausibly, that very seeming provides me with evidence that I might be wrong, and thus evidence that I do not know that p. Perhaps, even if I knew that p, the seeming provides evidence that destroys knowledge.[28] Here is the rough and ready principle at work:

> *Defeat.* If, at t, I get evidence that I do not know that p, and I have no effective means for rebutting that evidence, then I do not know that p at t.

(This of course must be distinguished from a weaker principle according to which, when I get evidence that I do not know that p, and cannot "rebut" it, then I do not know that I know that p.[29])

The Defeat Principle, as stated, does not strike me as particularly plausible.[30] Suppose a student is presented with an argument to the effect that he knows nothing and cannot rebut that argument. Is it really plausible that at that time, he does not know anything? If someone on a train presents me with Zeno's arguments that motion is impossible and, while not knowing how to answer them, I choose to ignore them, do I then not know that I am moving? When the possibility that I have left the cooker on becomes salient and yet I ignore it, shaking off the anxiety without trying to justify this to myself, is my knowledge really disturbed? The answer in all three cases seems to be "No"; it seems that one can know p while having nothing very useful to say about certain counterconsiderations that one recognizes as having some evidential force.[31]

While offering a somewhat elegant diagnosis of our puzzles, it remains unclear whether any model of knowledge in the vicinity of Defeat will fit well with our intuitions about cases. But it remains true that there are plenty of cases where we think knowledge *is* destroyed by excellent counterevidence. Given that an intellectual seeming that one does not know p is at least some evidence that one does not know p, we should not dismiss entirely the idea that salience destroys knowledge by providing counterevidence. I shall not pursue the matter further here.

(iii) *Authority*. It may be suggested that our negative verdicts about knowledge in our own case are decisive on account of a constitutive first-person authority. If I believe of myself that I do not know, then, automatically as it were, I do not know. On this model, the relevant intellectual seeming (that it might be that not-*p*) requires doxastic endorsement to destroy knowledge, but once that endorsement occurs, loss of knowledge inevitably follows. It might be suggested that this is a case of a more general phenomenon where our first-person negative verdicts have authority: If one thinks one isn't happy, one isn't happy, if one thinks one doesn't believe that *p*, one doesn't. And so on. The claimed constitutive authority for first-person verdicts does not seem at all plausible to me, and especially so in the knowledge case. (Consider the simple case of someone who believes that he doesn't know what the answer to a question is and yet quickly discovers that he has known the answer all along.) Perhaps the relevant authority claim can be weakened enough to make it plausible without rendering it utterly vacuous.[32] I shall not, however, pursue the authority idea further here.

4   Practical Environment

I earlier introduced the sensitive moderate invariantist as one who claimed that the extension of "know" "depends not merely upon the kinds of factors traditionally adverted to in accounts of knowledge – whether the subject believes the proposition, whether that proposition is true, whether the subject has good evidence, whether the subject is using a reliable method, and so on – but also upon the kinds of factors that in the contextualist's hands make for ascriber-dependence". Our discussion of salience has not proved to be a particularly promising way of making good on that view. For it may well be that the most promising version of a subject-dependent version of the thesis that salience destroys knowledge proceeds via that idea that salience destroys belief (or whatever kind of conviction is required for knowledge). This idea hardly takes us beyond the factors traditionally adverted to in accounts of knowledge, given the centrality of the belief condition to standard accounts. From this perspective, the only mistake made by the simple

moderate invariantist is to suppose that belief of the suitable type is invariably present in the puzzle cases we have been considering.

More importantly still, I do not think it plausible to suppose that an appeal to salience will, at least by itself, resolve our puzzles. Here is one way to make this especially clear. Suppose someone is dogmatic. When he infers lottery propositions, counterpossibilities are not salient to him (on any of our candidate glosses of "salience"). He infers that he will lose the lottery on the basis of some ordinary proposition and does not worry about alternatives. He then uses the conclusion of that inference as a basis for his assertoric and deliberative practices. Surely there is something out of line with such a dogmatist. But the account so far provides us with no resources for explaining why. The sensitive moderate invariantist should concede the limitations of the salience framework.

There is an analogy to be drawn here with the contextualist. Lewis is aware that the truth of a knowledge ascription has to depend not merely on what an ascriber is ignoring, but also on what he *ought* to be ignoring. Likewise in the case of subject-sensitive knowledge ascriptions: whether a subject knows some proposition depends not merely on which counterpossibilities he *does* ignore, but also on what he *should* ignore, and the problem with the dogmatist is that he ignores things he should not. But what is to be said, at least in a preliminary way, about the matter of which counterpossibilities ought to be ignored by a subject? Here I turn to the second kind of mechanism that I wish to discuss.

When introducing the connection between knowledge and practical reasoning, we noted a case where a lottery proposition serves as a premise for a manifestly bad piece of practical reasoning, and where it seems quite obvious that the explanation for why the practical reasoning is bad is that one does not know the premise to be true. Recall, then, the following case of an intuitively awful piece of practical reasoning:

(i)   You are offered a cent for a lottery ticket that cost a dollar, in a 10,000 ticket lottery with a $5,000 first prize and reason as follows:

I will lose the lottery.
If I keep the ticket I will get nothing.

If I sell the ticket, I will get a cent.
So I ought to sell the ticket.

It is important to notice that one can easily construct analogous cases where it is an ordinary proposition and not a lottery proposition which figures as the key premise. Thus consider the following:

(ii) You are offered a lottery ticket in the above lottery for the price of a penny and reason as follows:

I will not have enough money to go on an African safari this year.
So, if I buy the lottery ticket I will lose.
So I should not buy the lottery ticket.

Or again:

(iii) You are offered life insurance and reason:

I will be going to Blackpool next year.
So I won't die beforehand.
So I ought to wait until next year before buying life insurance.[33,34]

Two points of clarification. First, consider the following reasoning:

(iv) Someone dares you to eat poisonous toadstools and you reason as follows:

I will be going to Blackpool next year.
So if I take the $10,000 dare to eat those poisonous toadstools they won't kill me.
So I ought to take the dare.

Someone who reasons as (iv) describes is using the belief that she is going to Blackpool in a way that makes it likely to be false. By contrast, someone who, say, turns down lottery tickets on the basis described in (ii) is not using the African safari belief in a way that is likely to render it false. Indeed, in some sense it makes the belief more likely to be true if one uses it as a basis for turning down lottery tickets.

Second, our sense that these instances of practical reasoning are bad has nothing to do with assuming that certain counterpossibilities are salient to the reasoner. If the reasoner is so dogmatic as to ignore such counterpossibilities in these practical settings, that hardly makes us think better of the reasoning.

In these deliberative settings, then, it is intuitive to suppose that the practical reasoning is flawed and that this is because the premise – whether it is an ordinary proposition or a lottery proposition – is not known.[35] How can we respect this intuition without embracing skepticism? Only by allowing what we might call "practical environment" to make a difference to what one knows. We now have before us the outlines of a second mechanism that may be introduced by the sensitive moderate invariantist. The basic idea is clear enough. Insofar as it is unacceptable – and not merely because the content of the belief is irrelevant to the issues at hand – to use a belief that *p* as a premise in practical reasoning on a certain occasion, the belief is not a piece of knowledge at that time. Thus when offered a penny for my lottery ticket, it would be unacceptable to use the premise that I will lose the lottery as my grounds for making such a sale. So on that occasion I do not know that I will lose. Meanwhile, when you are offered life insurance, it would be unacceptable for you to use your belief that you are going to Blackpool as grounds for refusal.[36] So on that occasion you do not know that you are going to Blackpool.

Allowing such a mechanism will make knowledge come and go with ease.[37] One is offered a lottery ticket. At that point one doesn't know that one will be unable to afford a trip to Mauritius. One buys the ticket, forgets about the lottery, and goes to the bookstore. One chooses the "local destination guide" over the much more expensive "worldwide guide", reasoning from the premise "I won't be able to afford to go to an exotic destination". At that point you do know that you will be unable to afford a trip to Mauritius. Someone comes and offers you a penny for the lottery ticket. At that point you don't know. And so on.[38,39,40]

Of course it is very tempting to give the following explanation: the difference between the bookstore decision and the other decisions is that in the bookstore case the chance for the subject that he will win is small enough so as to be irrelevant to the practical issues at hand: he can safely disregard the small epistemic chance that he would win. Tempting indeed, But if there is always a chance for the subject that he will win, then – assuming the Epistemic Possibility Constraint – one *never* knows one will lose. Skepticism triumphs. If we are to avoid yielding to skepticism, then we must either adumbrate a notion of epistemic chance that is not tied to knowledge in the way that the Epistemic Possibility Constraint describes, or else resist the gloss just given, insisting that, when in the bookstore, there is no epistemic chance for you that you will be able to afford a trip to Mauritius.

There are thus two ways to develop the practical environment constraint. One approach gives up the Epistemic Possibility Constraint, allowing that knowledge that p is compatible with a small epistemic chance that not-p. There is a natural way to spell out the practical environment constraint on such a picture: if there is a small epistemic chance that not-p, one knows p only if one is in a practical environment where the difference between a small epistemic chance that not-p and zero epistemic chance that not-p is irrelevant to the matters at hand. A second option is one that cleaves to the Epistemic Possibility Constraint: when one knows p, there is zero epistemic chance that not-p. In that case, glosses of the practical environment idea in terms of epistemic chance will be circular and uninformative. Instead, one will consider the question of what kinds of practical reasoning we ought and oughtn't to engage in as sufficiently fundamental to be intractable in terms of a prior notion of epistemic probability. One's goal, in that case, will not be to offer an analysis of knowledge in terms of epistemic probability and decision-making. Rather it will be to insist that, contra the simple moderate invariantist, changes in deliberative environment can make a difference to whether one knows a given proposition. One will learn to live with a circle: In a deliberative environment where one ought to use p as a premise, one knows p. When one knows p, the epistemic chance for not-p is zero. When the epistemic chance of not-p is nonzero, one shouldn't use p as a premise in practical reasoning. Why should this circle require a more basic anchor?[41]

It is worth drawing attention to a theme that is by now familiar. One advantage of this version of sensitive moderate invariantism over (standard) contextualism is clear enough: suppose S uses "I will be in Blackpool next year" as a premise in

(illegitimate) practical reasoning. An ascriber, unaware of the practical reasoning to which that premise is being put, asserts "S knows that he will be in Blackpool next year". By standard contextualist lights, that ascription is true. Further, if the ascriber says "If S is now acting on the premise that he will be in Blackpool next year, he is acting on the basis of something he knows to be true", she will have said something true. The reason for this is that the practical environment of the subject is not given any constitutive role to play in the truth conditions for knowledge ascriptions. The connection between good practical reasoning and the truth of knowledge ascriptions has been lost. Not so for our sensitive moderate invariantist.

Meanwhile, considerations of practical environment provide one clue as to why we may be overly pessimistic in our knowledge ascriptions. When we claim that no one can know that he or she will lose the lottery, part of what is going on is that we realize that no one is in a position, in advance of the lottery draw, to acceptably sell a lottery ticket for miminal return. We sense well enough that in that kind of deliberative setting, the cognitive division into subcases typified by parity reasoning is recommended, and that brute reliance on a lottery proposition in one's deliberations is out of the question. And it is extremely natural to think that if anyone did know that he was going to lose the lottery in advance of the draw, that person would be in a position to reasonably sell the ticket whatever the sale price. If the practical environment idea is right, then that line of thought, while very natural, is flawed: if knowledge is destroyed by certain practical environments, any thought that knowledge will bring with it the capacity to perform certain cogent pieces of reasoning in those environments will be incorrect. For those will count among some of the very environments in which such knowledge would be destroyed.[42]

We now have the beginnings of a diagnosis for our epistemological puzzlement. We underestimate the contribution of practical environment to the truth of knowledge ascriptions. The picture just given is compatible with the idea that most ordinary knowledge claims come out true. But when we reflect as philosophers, it does not occur to us that issues about practical environment may be relevant to the truth of those ordinary ascriptions. We are insensitive, and attempt to evaluate knowledge ascriptions out of context. In particular, we fail to consider the deliberative context of the subject.[43] No wonder we get confused.[44]

5 Practical Reasoning and Misleading Evidence[45]

… [A] puzzle associated with Saul Kripke … uses Single-Premise Closure to generate the odd-sounding result that if I know that p, I can know that all future evidence against p will be misleading. [Elsewhere (Hawthorne 2004, p. 71)] I … endorse a solution to that puzzle that relies on treating that knowledge as "junk knowledge".

But there is a residual puzzle concerning practical reasoning. Suppose I am offered a pill that will make me ignore future evidence against p. If I know that p, it would seem that I can reason as follows: All future evidence against p will be misleading. So I would do well to ignore it. So I should take the pill.

But there is, intuitively, something wrong with this exercise of practical reasoning. Contrast two cases. (i) A pill has been developed that immunizes takers against propaganda against p. The pill gives the brain special powers – that of recognizing misleading counter-evidence to p. I know that p and to protect my knowledge, I take the pill. (ii) A pill has been developed that immunizes takers against *all* evidence against p. I know that p and reason that all evidence against p is misleading. On that basis, I reason that the effect of the pill will be to immunize me against propaganda against p. I take the pill.

Intuitively, the pill-taker in case (i) is acting acceptably – but not the pill-taker in case (ii). How is this to be explained? Accept the framework described in the last section and, at least schematically, a solution is ready at hand: in the practical environment described by case (ii), one does not know that p. Consider the reasoning: "p. But the pill will cause me to ignore all evidence against p. So all evidence that the pill will cause me to ignore will be misleading evidence. So (unless the pill has no other untoward effects) it would be a good thing for me to take the pill". Intuitively, this would be an acceptable piece of practical reasoning if the premise was known. Intuitively, the reasoning is unacceptable. The

"practical environment" framework has the advantage of respecting both intuitions.

6 Multi-Premise Closure

Do these reflections help to salvage Multi-Premise Closure (MPC)? The path is still a difficult one. Let us grant that all sorts of ordinary propositions can be known in the appropriate practical environments and with appropriate salience requirements satisfied. MPC suggests that on those occasions, if one competently deduces long conjunctions of those ordinary propositions, one can come to know those long conjunctions. After all, why should the mere activity of conjunction introduction destroy knowledge of the conjuncts?[46]

There are at least two objections that we ought to consider. First, there is the objection based on what might be called the *Preface Intuition*: for almost any long conjunction of empirical beliefs that one might have, one is in a position to know on inductive grounds that the conjunction is likely to be false. For the moderate invariantist, MPC does not sit well with the Preface Intuition. For if MPC is correct, one can come to know some long conjunction p. If the Preface Intuition is correct, one can come to know that p is probably false. But it seems altogether bizarre to suppose that one can come to know both that p and that p is probably false. The Preface Intuition has to be explained away. Second, we can make special trouble for MPC via certain lottery-style cases. Suppose it is allowed that in the appropriate practical setting, I can know that Amelia will never get rich and know that Bartholomew will never get rich and so on, for 5,000 friends, each of whom has a ticket in a 5,001 ticket lottery where only ticket #7 is owned by a nonfriend. Assume MPC and I will be able to know a conjunction that will be true only if #7 wins. But isn't it outrageous to suppose that anyone can know such a thing in advance of the lottery draw? Better, it seems, to endorse the skeptical hypothesis that no one ever really knows any of the conjuncts.

How, then, could the moderate invariantist hold onto MPC? A first step will be to maintain the Epistemic Possibility Constraint. For if knowledge is compatible with small epistemic chances of mistake, there is no prospect whatever of MPC being correct, since small epistemic chances add up. As for the twin arguments of the last paragraph, the best hope, I think, is to lean heavily on the idea of practical environment. In those settings where we intuitively think of putting long conjunctions to work – where some practical issue at hand turns on the whole long conjunction – knowledge is destroyed. So in any setting where the long conjunction is of practical relevance, we do know that it is probably false. It is only when our knowledge is idle that we know long conjunctions through MPC. And so the intuition that we know all such long conjunctions to be probably false (where "probably" is being used as an epistemic modal) is an understandable overprojection from practical cases.[47] A parallel diagnosis is offered for the second case, though here the pill is even harder to swallow. In any circumstance where we imagine the conjunction of "loser" beliefs being put to work (say, as a basis for spending a lot on lottery ticket #7), knowledge of the conjunction is destroyed. But in cases where it is idle, we do have such knowledge.

But it is not clear that an appeal to practical environment can do all the work. Begin with a thought that drives Preface intuitions: knowledge is destroyed when someone is given excellent evidence against p, even if the evidence turns out to be misleading. This does not turn on whether the recipient of the evidence is responsive to it. If someone ignores the evidence and carries on believing the relevant proposition, knowledge is still destroyed. Return to the APA case of Chapter 1, in the version where someone comes in and announces "I'm not going to tell you who, but one of the people on the list has just died". Suppose I hear that and ignore it, even though I have every reason to trust the informant (who is in fact speaking falsely on this occasion). I deduce and come to believe the long conjunction that says of 150 on the list that they will be at the APA. Given that excellent counterevidence (misleading or not) destroys knowledge, I do not know the conjunction. But what of my knowledge of the conjuncts? It seems something of a stretch to suppose that my knowledge of each individual conjunct is destroyed, especially in the case at hand, where my conviction is intact. Consider, similarly, a case where someone shows me a list of 1,000 propositions, each of which I in fact know, and gives me misleading evidence that one item on the list is false (without telling me which). Assuming that my conviction in each of the 1,000 propositions remains intact, it seems farfetched to suppose that my knowledge of each is destroyed. But my knowledge of the conjunction is certainly destroyed. Allow that I might have come to believe the conjunction by deduction from the conjuncts, and we seem to have a counterexample to MPC.

Suppose one were to treat MPC as an analytic girder. What is one to say here? I can think of only one promising strategy, borrowing from discussions of vagueness: the news that destroys the knowledge of the conjunction renders it determinate that one does not know all of the conjuncts, but for each conjunct, it is indeterminate whether the news destroys knowledge of that conjunct (where "determinate" and "indeterminate" are to be understood in accord with one's favorite theory of vagueness). This cluster of claims, note, is compatible (given standard logics of determinacy) with the further claim that it is determinate that I know nearly all of the *conjuncts*. MPC is retained without wholesale skeptical concession.[48,49,50]

For anyone drawn to such a line, a further embarrassment lies in wait, one that relies on the idea that small risks add up to big risks, using this time the concept of objective chance in place of epistemic chance. Suppose, as nonskeptics, we allow that knowing p is compatible with there being a small objective chance that not-p. If MPC is correct, then since small objective chances add up to large objective chances, we shall have to allow for truths of the form "S knows that p and it is overwhelmingly objectively likely that not-p"! Suppose, to illustrate, there are $2^{10,000,000}$ coin-flippers $f_1 \ldots f_n$. Each is poised to flip a fair coin a million times. I consider each coin-flipper in turn and form the belief that he will not toss heads a million times in a row. In fact, things are such that none of the coin-flippers will toss heads a million times in a row. Assuming MPC and my knowledge of each premise … I can know a conjunction that claims of each coin-flipper that she will not flip heads a million times in a row. While in any particular case, it would be very surprising that a coin-flipper toss a million heads, it is, by contrast, both objectively unlikely and intuitively quite remarkable that none of the coin-flippers tosses heads a million times in a row – certainly not the kind of thing that one can know.[51]

Whatever one says, certain deeply held intuitions will have to yield: I shall not adjudicate here whether, all things considered, it is MPC that should be relinquished.

7 Scorecard

Sensitive moderate invariantism has a fairly promising scorecard. It respects the Moorean Constraint and Single-Premise Closure. It offers the best hope yet for respecting the intuitive links between knowledge, assertion, and practical reasoning. And it offers *some* prospect for maintaining Multi-Premise Closure. As a species of invariantism, it can respect the disquotational schema for "knows". As we have seen, it can also be developed in a way that respects the Epistemic Possibility Constraint. We should acknowledge, though, that if developed so as to respect the Epistemic Possibility Constraint, it will have a hard time with the Objective Chance Principle. For assume both the Epistemic Possibility Constraint and the Objective Chance Principle. Then, supposing we know there are small objective chances of pretty much any description of the future, we will not know ordinary propositions about the future.

The Objective Chance Principle is not the only sticking point for the sensitive moderate invariantist. We have, along the way, noted a range of intuitive oddities that such a view will yield – and there will no doubt be many more that I have not brought to the fore.

8 Concluding Remarks

Closing reflections

It is striking that the puzzles with which we are struggling do not disturb us very much in ordinary life. Why is this? After all, as we have seen, ordinary common sense delivers apparently inconsistent verdicts across conversational contexts. Why does this not bother us? In broad outline, the answer is obvious enough. When we find ourselves in one practical environment, we do not look back to what we said in very different practical environments for guidance in forming our current epistemic verdicts. When offered life

insurance, I do not feel the force of my earlier claims to know things about my own future. It's not that I look back on those claims and evaluate them as incorrect; it's that I am so constituted as to simply ignore them. And this tendency is even more striking in the reverse case. When I say that I do know *p* although my earlier self, concerned with life insurance, claimed not to know *p* (or some *q* entailed by *p*), it's not that I evaluate my previous self as having been overcautious – I simply ignore him.

What I have been trying to do in the current work is to achieve some kind of unified semantic perspective on knowledge claims made in myriad settings: Which apparent inconsistencies are genuine? Which knowledge ascriptions are actually correct? This attempt to take in the gamut of knowledge ascriptions in one sweep, as it were, is precisely what we don't do in ordinary life. This is why the puzzlement that grips us here eludes us (for the most part) there. The smooth functioning of ordinary epistemic discourse in a person's life, despite apparent diachronic inconsistencies, is indeed a striking fact. But it is not one that by itself solves our puzzles, nor one that unmasks them as mere pseudo-puzzles.

So which of the views presented here is the right one? Some readers, faced with the range of competitors, will be inclined to think that there is no fact of the matter as to which is correct, embracing some kind of noncognitivism that denies statements of knowledge any truth value. They will perhaps, insist that the concept of knowledge is incoherent[52] – strictly speaking, tokenings of the verb "know" are deprived of an extension. Such a reaction would be unwise. Careful investigation will reveal analogous complexities and tensions for many or most of the concepts belonging to the manifest image: repeated solace in noncognitivism will almost certainly result in cognitive suicide. And it does not seem that there is *special* reason for noncognitivism in the case of "know".

So which view is correct? Our question does not by any means reduce to: "Contextualism: for or against?" For recall that even if contextualism is true, it may not provide the key to our puzzles. My best guess, indeed, is that it is not the key. Put a gun to my head and I will opt for a treatment of the puzzles built around the materials of the "Practical Environment" section above. But I am far from confident that this is the correct way to proceed. There is then the further question as to whether to embed those ideas within an invariantist semantical framework for "know"[53]. Here, though more tentatively still, I would opt for invariantism over contextualism.

My own opinions should not matter much at this stage, however. I prefer to think of these pages as forming a helpful basis for the reader to conduct her own investigation of the puzzles at hand. To think it vital that I embrace some particular view would be to seriously misunderstand the nature of the philosophical enterprise.

A concluding parable

Let me close with a story.

Once upon a time there was a tribe that shared deeply conflicting tendencies. On the one hand, whenever they reflected on the many ways that people can and do make mistakes, they found skeptical thoughts altogether natural and compelling. Such moments of reflection seemed to provide great enlightenment. And during such moments, it seemed utterly manifest how little people know. On the other hand, the people in the tribe endowed the concept of knowledge with great normative significance. It provided the normative framework for the giving and requesting of information, and also for practical deliberation.

Now the members of the tribe, like everyone else, had to speak and act. Given these exigencies, even the reflective ones regularly found themselves drawing lines between what is known and what isn't known, lines that corresponded hardly at all to the one they propounded in their skeptical moments. Even within this realm, there was instability: as interests and purposes shifted, so too did their sense of the line between what is known and what is not known. But rarely, if ever, did a near-global skepticism seem very compelling in the practical realm.

A dispute broke out among the tribespeople. One group called themselves the Theoreticians. They took the reflective moments very seriously. "How could you not take those moments seriously?" they argued. "Anyone who takes the time to think hard about it, secluded in their study, will find skepticism utterly natural!" And they were right: this tribe was indeed so constituted that,

when so secluded, skepticism was an utterly natural thought. Another group formed that called themselves the Practicians. They were insistent on the normative significance of knowledge. "It is a condition of deliberating and of asserting", they argued, "that one treats certain propositions as known, others not. Isn't it quite obvious that we generally act and deliberate just as we ought to? Concede this normative point, and the view of the Theoreticians is unsustainable. Given the connections between knowledge and normativity, it makes no sense to say that we assert and act as we ought but know next to nothing."

Debate raged. Theoreticians divided into global and near-global skeptics. Practicians discussed how the facts of knowledge were to be conceived given shifting practical environments in the life of a tribesperson. But the clash between the Practicians and the Theoreticians remained the most visible. And secretly, each felt very uneasy. The Practicians felt uneasy because, when secluded in their studies, they themselves felt the very natural compulsions that the Theoreticians had given voice to. In those moments they felt alienated from their own intellects, given the deliverances that their intellects were apt to press upon them. In those moments, they had to concentrate extremely hard on their favorite normative arguments, rehearsing them as a kind of mantra in order to stop the compulsions towards skepticism from overwhelming them. The Theoreticians felt uneasy too. They detected hidden claims to know in their own thoughts of understanding, insight, and enlightenment. And they too felt the need to talk and act and, just as the Practicians predicted, lapsed into nonskeptical thoughts and speeches when those exigencies took hold. When speaking about the Theoretical position itself, they found themselves with especially peculiar conflicting pressures. The need to speak induced tendencies to extend their sense of what is known to include their own speeches, but the content of the speeches reinforced their tendency to a skeptical point of view. Some of them lapsed into silence, as certain of their Ancient precursors had done.

The Practicians and Theoreticians searched for some common ground. "You will at least agree," contended the Theoreticians, "that you don't know which is correct, the Practical or the Theoretical vantage point." But the Practicians felt that this was already to prejudice matters in favor of the Theoretician. "If the voice of the Practician is to be heard on the matter of what we know, it is also to be heard on the matter of what we know we know. The practical perspective encourages us to think that any tribesperson knows that any other tribesperson knows quite a lot. And if he knows this about any other tribesperson, surely he knows the same about himself." The attempt to find reconciliation at the second level was a failure. Both the Practicians and Theoreticians remained uneasily attached to their respective positions.

Other groups sprang up. One group – a sort of epistemological cult – claimed not to find skeptical thoughts compelling, not even in quiet moments. "You just haven't analyzed 'knowledge' carefully enough," they said. "Once you do, your intellect will no longer be gripped by skepticism, not even in the study." Neither the Practicians nor the Theoreticians believed them. Nor, in their heart of hearts, did the members of the group itself. The group disbanded, remembered as a historical curiosity. Another group, the Variantists, came along. "You've all been speaking past one another," they said. "When you Theoreticians say 'know' you are talking about one thing. When you Practicians say 'know' you are talking about another." This greatly disturbed both the Theoreticians and the Practicians. The one piece of common ground they had enjoyed was a tacit recognition that they had not be talking past one another.

Both attacked the Variantists, though for different reasons. The Theoreticians could not reconcile Variantism with their own sense of enlightenment vis-à-vis those other tribespeople caught up in the rough and tumble of life. The Practicians, meanwhile, could not reconcile Variantism with the normative lie of the land. But the Variantists remained. And everyone continued to feel uneasy. When in the study, the Practicians continued to feel the natural compulsions described by the Theoreticians. And when speaking and acting, the Theoreticians continued to feel the natural compulsions described by the Practicians. The Variantists continued to struggle to reconcile their Variantism with both these compulsions, and with their own natural compulsion to see everyone as talking about the same thing.

Debates continued. Conflicting tendencies remained. Each side offered its own explanation of how, despite these inner conflicts, buildings got built and books got written. But each group told a different story, narrated from an opinionated vantage point. (When reading *this* history of the tribe, Theoreticians complained that it had been written by a Practician, what with its talk of seeing that this, and recognizing that that.) Each group mused about what God would do when he came across a tribe with such conflicting tendencies. "How would God interpret 'know' in our mouths?" they wondered. "When would God say 'know' was used to express truths, when falsehoods?" Each quickly realized that no neutral perspective was possible on this question either. Its answer turned on the very questions they were debating. Debates raged on. The strands of the tribe's conflicting natures alternately took hold. Each camp remained uneasy.

Perhaps that tribe is very much like us.

Notes

1 Cohen (1998) is clear about the distinction between rules of relevance that are "speaker-sensitive" and those that are "subject-sensitive" – indeed I have borrowed the terminology of sensitivity from him – but doesn't explore the possibility of transforming the speaker-sensitive rules offered by the contextualist into subject-sensitive rules.

2 There are likely to be principled limits to what can be said here. The verb "know" is a lexical and conceptual primitive for which no traditional analysis is likely (though that is not to deny that interesting necessary conditions on knowledge may be discovered). Moreover, any temptation to use the notion of probability in exploring our current subject will likely be unhelpful or circular insofar as we keep to the Epistemic Possibility Constraint. More generally, it is confused to think that a relatively manageable theory of the detailed semantic workings of our language is cognitively available to us.

3 Mechanisms for what? For the contextualist, the candidate mechanisms are mechanisms

for shifting the semantic value for "know". For the sensitive moderate invariantist, the candidate mechanisms are mechanisms for making knowledge come and go.

4 Conversations with Stewart Cohen were particularly helpful in writing this section.

5 Similar issues are raised by DeRose's "Bank Cases" (see DeRose 1992).

6 Note that in the American Model Penal Code the risk that salience may affect matters is somewhat averted by stipulatively defining "known" as "practically certain" (see American Law Institute, Model Penal Code, 2.02 (2)(b)(ii)). The role of the concept of knowledge in legal settings is well worth extensive investigation.

7 The same may be true of brain in a vat hypotheses. The preacher who asserts "We are beings whose lives make a difference to each other. We are not the beings of the Matrix, isolated in pods from one another, who merely imagine that we are making a difference to each other's lives" may well be one who entertains the brain in a vat hypothesis without it thereby standing as a salient counterpossibility.

8 Note also that if we were to discover that someone had sold a lottery ticket, and had asserted "I know it will lose", then we have a very strong intuition not merely that it is correct for us to say "He didn't know that" but, moreover, that he himself said something false. Standard contextualism does a good job at accommodating the first intuition, but has to explain the second one away by appeal to semantic blindness.

9 Similar suggestions are canvassed by Vogel (1990, p. 52). I do not at all intend that availability take up all the explanatory burden (nor, I presume, did Vogel).

10 Kates, quoted in Slovic, Fischhoff, and Lichtenstein (1982, p. 465).

11 See also Johnson, Hershy, and Meszaros (2000), who found that people were willing to pay more for flight insurance that provided life insurance in case of terrorism than for flight insurance that provided that same amount of life insurance in case of death "for any reason", remarking that "events associated with 'terrorism' ... would be more vivid and available than events suggested by the inclusive phrase 'any reason'" (p. 228).

12 For related discussion, see Vogel (1990). This kind of diagnosis will seem particularly natural to those who are happy to insist on a conceptual tie between the concept of knowledge and such concepts as being safe from error and being in danger of error. (See Williamson 2000; Sosa 2000.)

13 We of course have something of this tendency with "flat", "disgusting", "empty", and "solid", but it is far less entrenched in these cases ... The relevant similarity and differences certainly deserve further investigation.

14 I have heard similar thoughts voiced in conversation by Stewart Cohen, Richard Fumerton, and Timothy Williamson.

15 See Lewis (1983).

16 Stewart Cohen, Troy Cross, and Cian Dorr all pressed this point in conversation. Suppose I'm a contestant in a spelling bee. I do know the spelling of the word before I'm asked, but under pressure my confidence wilts. I might well think with respect to the spelling about which I'm now unsure that, if it's right, I knew it when I was more confident of it than I now am. By contrast, when I muse about lottery success, I'm not inclined to say that when, in the past, I was sure I would never get rich this year, I knew that I wouldn't. A natural picture is that in the spelling bee case, one is merely worried that one does not and never did know, but in the lottery case, once parity reasoning kicks in, one positively thinks one does not know and never did. (Thanks to Jonathan Vogel here.)

17 In *On Certainty* Wittgenstein writes "When we say we *know* that such and such, we mean that any reasonable person in our position would also know it, that it would be a piece of unreason to doubt it" (1969, p. 325). If the salience of a counterpossibility does not manifest unreason but does destroy knowledge, then it would seem that the sensitive moderate invariantist would have to dispute this albeit natural thought.

18 Another worry, raised by Stewart Cohen, merits further consideration: If the current approach is correct, then in order to know that S now knows that p, I would have to be in a position to know whether or not some counterpossibility to p is now salient to S.

But do I really have to be able to do the latter in order to know propositions of the former sort? If S thinks about skeptical alternatives from time to time, but is not now doing so, am I now precluded from knowing that S knows some humdrum proposition on account of the fact that I am in no position to know whether now is one of the times when S happens to be entertaining skeptical possibilities?

19 Suppose, by analogy, there were an oracle who could resolve skeptical doubts. The philosopher goes running to the oracle to find out if the world was created, complete with pseudo-memories, five minutes earlier. Is it really so strange to suppose that the philosopher, before arriving at the oracle, does not know he has been around for a while even though the dullard does know? (Informants varied wildly in their reactions to such cases.)

20 I am grateful for discussions with Adam Sennet here.

21 There is also a success sense of "salience", which will require that the intellectual seeming be veridical.

22 Conversations with and comments from Jim Pryor were helpful here.

23 Cf. Ayer (1956).

24 As a further variant on the current theme, one might consider Williamson's (2002) distinction between outright belief and high subjective probability. Perhaps some case could be made that outright belief is often destroyed by the salient possibility of error even though subjective confidence is not.

25 Insofar as one defends this kind of view, one has to confront the fact that we are often willing to ascribe knowledge to someone even when they vacillate or hesitate in consciously endorsing the proposition that they are claimed to know. In response, it might be suggested that we do often adopt a tiered conception of the human mind, allowing that there may be an underlying certainty, complete conviction in a proposition, below the surface of conscious indecision. Radford (1966) describes a librarian who has never made a mistake about the location of a book but who dithers about her answer, hesitating, unsure. It may be

argued that it is only because we suppose utter conviction at some level that we are willing to ascribe knowledge. If we learned that no matter how deeply we go into the librarian's psyche, we find nothing more than credence slightly above .5 in all the correct answers that she had given, that may well shake our willingness to ascribe knowledge. On the other hand, if one thinks that knowledge requires being sure (at some level), then one will be somewhat hard pressed to make sense of such locutions from daily life as "know with some confidence", "know with some reasonable certainty", "know with reasonable confidence", "know with reasonable certainty" (where it seems, for example, that if S knows with reasonable confidence that p, then S knows that p). Philosophers rarely use such locutions but ordinary people do. I shall not explore the issue further here. (I am grateful to Peter Ludlow for discussion on these points.)

26 I am particularly grateful to Jim Pryor here.

27 At least assuming that I know that that is how things seem to me.

28 Epistemologists often distinguish different kinds of "defeaters" for a belief that p. Sometimes one gets evidence that is directly suggestive of the falsity of p, and this in turn destroys knowledge that p. Sometimes, instead, one gets evidence that one's relevant epistemic mechanisms are inadequate, and this in turn destroys knowledge that p. Presumably, if the salience of error (in the sense given) is a defeater for my knowing that p, it is a defeater of the second sort (though of the first sort with respect to my knowing that I know that p).

29 For the record, I don't even find the weaker principle very plausible (unless knowing p automatically counts as "rebuttal", which is hardly the intended meaning of the principle).

30 Again, I assume that "rebutting" is not to be read in such a way that knowing p automatically counts as a rebuttal of evidence against p.

31 Of course if knowledge delivers probability 1, then one has to be careful. If I know p and q is purported evidence against p, then the conditional evidential probability of not-p

on q will be zero. In what sense then is q evidence against p? This is just a special case of the problem of "old evidence" familiar in discussions of Bayesian epistemology. I shall not undertake to examine solutions to that problem here.

32 Though I doubt it.

33 Of course, if the belief about a Blackpool vacation is true, then the life insurance will not come in handy. But this is beside the point. Such a belief, whether true or not, should not be used in practical reasoning of that sort. I assume that the reader shares that intuition very strongly, at least on one very obvious reading of "should". (There may be a reading of "should" where this is not so. When all the evidence suggests that the Cadillac is behind door A and I later find that it is behind door B, I might later say "I should have taken B", and perhaps there is a reading on which that is true.)

34 Supposing the quantum-mechanical chance of a desk evolving into a desk façade in the next two seconds is a trillion to one. Ten trillion people are each offered a bet such that one person (drawn at random from the pool of 10 trillion people) gets a cent if the desk in front of the bet-taker isn't a façade and everyone in the pool loses a dollar if it is. If every person in the pool takes the bet and one loses, should we say that all but the latter were epistemically laudable for taking the bet?

35 Of course, the reasoning also manifests tendencies that would be likely to get the reasoner into trouble in other situations, and reveals a flaw in the reasoner in that way too. But this additional observation does not seem to lessen our confidence that the premise is not known in this situation.

36 This should be distinguished from a different phenomenon, namely one where the offering of a bet straightforwardly provides one with relevant evidence for or against a proposition. When I claim to be healthy and my doctor says "Let's make a wager on that", the offer of a bet obviously gives me evidence against my good health. Not so when I am offered life insurance. Indeed, if anything, that is a sign of good health – if I had seemed to be at death's door, the insurance agent might well have been less willing to provide the insurance.

37 It is also worth reflecting on the fact that for pretty much any proposition of which we are convinced, we will be inclined to accept a bet against it given the right odds and reckon ourselves perfectly rational in doing so. (For example, I would happily bet a penny against a billion dollars on not having being born in England, and on the falsity of the law of noncontradiction.) In exploring these issues further, we should consider whether knowledge of any proposition can be destroyed by environments in which a suitable bet is offered. One option, of course, is to think that the sketched connection between knowledge and practical reasoning is only roughly correct, where this might still allow it to do work along the lines sketched in the body of the text. Readers are welcome to explore such middle ground.

38 Note that in such a setting I might make comparative likelihood assessments of pairs of propositions that I would ordinarily say I know to be false: "I'm more likely to go on an African safari than on the QE II since even if I won the lottery, there's the problem that my wife gets seasick ..." (Thanks to Richard Fumerton here.)

39 Of course there will be lots of indeterminacy besetting questions about when, exactly, knowledge comes and goes, and, more generally, about the cutoff between the practical environments that destroy knowledge and those that do not. One should here deploy one's favorite theory of vagueness.

40 As Timothy Williamson pointed out to me, this picture makes for some intuitively odd counterfactuals. There will be cases where someone does not know that p, but we can assert "If the stakes had been lower, he would have known that p" or "If he hadn't been offered a penny for his lottery ticket, he would have known that p"; and so on. There is no denying the intuitive cost. The question is whether, all things considered, it is a price worth paying. (Consider, in this connection, the following counterfactual, said of a person looking at a barn in fake barn country: "If there hadn't been those fake barns nearby, he would have known that he

was looking at a barn". Hear it afresh and you will certainly find this counterfactual odd as well.) Note also that contextualism will, for its part, likely make for the truth of such odd-sounding *indicative* conditionals as "If my stakes are low, he knows, but if they are not, he does not".

41 I should note in passing that while the practical environment constraint might be combined with a salience constraint of the sort described in the previous section, it need not be. Those that are unconvinced of, say, the destructive powers of salient counterpossibilities as such might still reckon practical environment a source of subject-sensitivity.

42 The reader may note some analogy here to the topic of "junk knowledge", discussed earlier.

43 Shades of pragmatism? I leave pursuit of such analogies to others.

44 Be that as it may, there is no avoiding the intuitive cost of this kind of view. As Stewart Cohen urged in conversation, it seems that the view will have to allow that I can truly say "I know that I won't be able to afford an African safari but you don't know that you won't", simply on account of the fact that you are right now being offered a lottery ticket and I am not (I have already bought mine). Can I even know that to be true? (If so, we cannot mollify the objector by claiming that the relevant truth is unassertable.) Perhaps attending to your environment will raise the possibility of my winning a lottery prize to salience. But what if I am dogmatic? (Recall that mere attention to a possibility should not be enough to destroy knowledge.) Another possibility: If we are not sufficiently discriminating to be able to gauge whether a contextualist or subject-sensitive treatment is true in these cases, then even if the subject-sensitive account is right, we are unable to know that it is right and hence unable to know that "know" applies to us in those cases which turn on the difference between rival accounts. So perhaps I am unable to know that I know in Cohen's case, owing to my lack of discriminatory abilities with regard to the concept of knowledge. I leave it to others to explore these matters further.

45 I am grateful for discussions with Stewart Cohen and Ram Neta here.

46 Those who think of knowledge in terms of safety – freedom from error in close worlds (see Williamson 2000; Sosa 2000) – can supplement all this with the simple logical consideration that if there are no close worlds where one makes a mistake about p and no close worlds where one makes a mistake about q then there are no close worlds where one deduces the conjunction from the conjuncts and is mistaken about the conjunction.

47 Think back to the faulty intuitions generated by cases of "junk knowledge".

48 If knowledge of some of the conjuncts was much safer than others, one might refine the proposal by allowing that the safer knowledge was unimpugned: it is determinate that knowledge of some conjunct is destroyed and determinate that it is not one of the safer pieces of knowledge.

49 One interesting issue is whether one should treat the case differently when the conjunction is not believed on the basis of deduction from the conjuncts. Might one make a case here that no knowledge of the individual conjuncts is destroyed? Perhaps so, if the only reason in the original case for claiming that it is determinate that one's knowledge of some conjunct is destroyed is that one was determined to treat MPC as a fixed point, a "penumbral connection" (in Fine's 1975 sense).

50 Assuming that indeterminate propositions cannot be known, this approach would lead one to suppose that in the cases we are considering, one cannot, for any conjunct, know that one knows it. But that would seem to be a happy consequence of the approach.

51 One might try the indeterminacy-based salvage here too. Hold MPC fixed and add the rule that when it is objectively likely that the conjunction is false, it is determinate that one does not know one of the conjuncts, though indeterminate which conjunct is not known.

52 Consider Chomsky's (1980) remark "In fact, it is not at all clear that the ordinary concept of "knowledge" is even coherent, nor would it be particularly important if it were shown not to be" (p. 82).

53 It is easy enough to see how some of those materials might be integrated into a contextualist framework. For example, as Jonathan

Schaffer pointed out in correspondence, one might happily add something like the following rule to Lewis's laundry list – The Rule of Praxis: possibilities which ought not to be ignored in any practical reasoning undertaken by the subject are relevant – and then make heavy appeal to that rule in the face of our puzzle. (Note though that the rule intuitively requires a context-invariant "ought".) A solution to the puzzles might, for example, blend an ascriber-sensitivity grounded in salience with a subject-sensitivity grounded in praxis. I do not wish to endorse a fusion of that kind here. Nor do I wish to rule it out.

References

Ayer, G. J. (1956), *The Problem of Knowledge* (London: Macmillan).

Chomsky, Noam (1980), *Rules and Representations* (New York: Columbia University Press).

Cohen, Stewart (1998), "Contextualist Solutions to Epistemological Problems: Skepticism, Gettier, and the Lottery", *Australasian Journal of Philosophy* 76, pp. 289–306.

—— (1999), "Contextualism, Skepticism, and the Structure of Reasons", *Philosophical Perspectives* 13, pp. 57–89.

DeRose, Keith (1992), "Contextualism and Knowledge Attributions", *Philosophy and phenomenological Research* 52, pp. 913–29.

Fine, Kit (1975), "Vagueness, Truth and Logic", *Synthese* 30, pp. 265–300.

Hawthorne, John (2004), *Knowledge and Lotteries* (Oxford: Clarendon Press).

Johnson, E., Hershey, J., Meszaros, J., and Kunreuther, H. (2000), "Framing, Probability Distortions, and Insurance Decisions", in Kahneman, Daniel, and Tversky, Amos, *Choices, Values and Frames* (Cambridge: Cambridge University Press).

Lewis, David (1983), "Scorekeeping in a Language Game", in Lewis, *Philosophical Papers*, vol. I (Oxford: Oxford University Press).

Radford, Colin (1966), "Knowledge – by Examples", *Analysis* 27, pp. 1–11.

Slovic, Paul, Fischhoff, Baruch and Lichtenstein, Sarah (1982), "Fact Versus Fears: Understanding Perceived Risk", in Kahneman, Daniel et al., *Judgment under Uncertainty: Heuristics and Biases* (Cambridge: Cambridge University Press).

Sosa, Ernest (2000), "Skepticism and Contextualism", *Philosophical Issues* 10, pp. 1–18.

Vogel, Jonathan (1990), "Are there Counterexamples to the Closure Principle?", in M. Roth and G. Ross (eds), *Doubting: Contemporary Perspectives on Skepticism* (Dordrecht: Kluwer).

Williamson, Timothy (2000), *Knowledge and its Limits* (Oxford: Oxford University Press).

Wittgenstein, Ludwig (1969), *On Certainty* (Oxford: Blackwell).

CHAPTER 53

The Assessment Sensitivity of Knowledge Attributions

John MacFarlane

Recent years have seen an explosion of interest in the semantics of knowledge-attributing sentences, not just among epistemologists but among philosophers of language seeking a general understanding of linguistic context sensitivity. Despite all this critical attention, however, we are as far from consensus as ever. If we have learned anything, it is that each of the standard views – invariantism, contextualism, and sensitive invariantism – has its Achilles' heel: a residuum of facts about our use of knowledge attributions that it can explain only with special pleading. This is not surprising if, as I will argue, there is a grain of truth in each of these views.

In this paper, I propose a semantics for "know" that combines the explanatory virtues of contextualism and invariantism. Like the contextualist, I take the extension of "know" to be sensitive to contextually determined epistemic standards. But where the contextualist takes the relevant standards to be those in play at the context of *use*, I take them to be those in play at the context of *assessment*: the context in which one is assessing a particular use of a sentence for truth or falsity. Thus, I can agree with the invariantist that "know" is not sensitive to the epistemic standards in play at the context of use, while still acknowledging a

kind of contextual sensitivity to epistemic standards. The proposed semantics for "know" is contextualist along one dimension (contexts of assessment) and invariantist along another (contexts of use).[1]

In the first part of the paper, I motivate my proposal by considering three facts about our use of "know" (§2) that collectively cause trouble for *all* of the standard views about the semantics of "know" (taxonomized in §1). I argue that the usual attempts to explain away the anomalies by appeal to pragmatics or to speaker error are unpersuasive (§3). In §4, I show how standard semantic frameworks must be modified to make room for my "relativist" semantics, and I show how the proposed semantics makes sense of the features of our use of "know" that proved puzzling on the standard views. Finally, in §5, I respond to worries about the coherence of relativist semantics by describing the role assessment-relative truth plays in a normative account of assertion.

1 A Taxonomy

For our purposes, the standard views about the semantics of "know" can be divided into three main classes. *Strict invariantists* hold that "know" is associated with a fixed epistemic standard, in much the same way as "six feet apart" is associated with a fixed standard of distance. A person

Originally published in T. S. Gendler and J. O'Leary-Hawthorne (eds), *Oxford Studies in Epistemology*, vol. 1 (Oxford: Clarendon, 2005).

and a fact satisfy "*x* knows *y*" just in case the person's epistemic position with respect to the fact is strong enough to meet this fixed epistemic standard. *Sensitive invariantists* allow the epistemic standard to vary with the subject and the *circumstances of evaluation* (in the sense of Kaplan 1989), in much the same way as the standard of distance expressed by "as far apart as Mars and Jupiter" varies with the circumstances (for instance, the time) of evaluation. And *contextualists* allow the epistemic standard to vary with the *context of use*, like the standard of distance expressed by "as far apart as my two hands are right now." The differences are summed up in Figure 53.1.

This is of course only one way of carving up the range of positions that have been taken, and it lumps together positions that may seem very different, even from a semantic point of view.[2] The advantage of this taxonomy is that it will allow us to see in a perspicuous way what is wrong with *all* of the views it encompasses. Because a "formal" taxonomy will be enough for our purposes, I leave it completely open here what an epistemic position is, how an epistemic standard might be specified, and what features determine which epistemic standard is relevant in a given context or circumstance. In particular, although I will sometimes talk of "high" and "low" standards, I wish to leave it open whether standards vary on a linear scale – from "low" to "high" – or in a more complex and qualitative way, as on "relevant alternatives" theories. Different views in each of our

formal categories will cash out these notions in different ways. The arguments that follow abstract from these details.

The differences between contextualism and sensitive invariantism tend to be obscured when we consider first-person, present-tense knowledge attributions. For in these cases the epistemic standards in play at the context of use will coincide with those in play for the subject at the circumstances of evaluation. To see the differences, we need to vary the context of use while keeping the circumstances of evaluation constant – say, by considering "On Tuesday, Joe knew that whales are mammals" as uttered by Sally on Wednesday and by Fred on Thursday – and vary the circumstances of evaluation while keeping the context of use constant – say, by considering both "On Tuesday, Joe knew that whales are mammals" and "On Wednesday, Joe knew that whales are mammals" as uttered by Fred on Thursday. Contextualism predicts that the epistemic standard one must meet in order to count as "knowing" should shift as we shift the context of use (even if the circumstances of evaluation are kept fixed), while sensitive invariantism predicts that it should shift as we shift the circumstances of evaluation (even if the context of use is kept fixed). Thus we may aptly describe a contextualist semantics for "know" as *use-variable* and a sensitive invariantist semantics as *circumstance-variable*. Standard versions of contextualism are *circumstance-invariant*, and

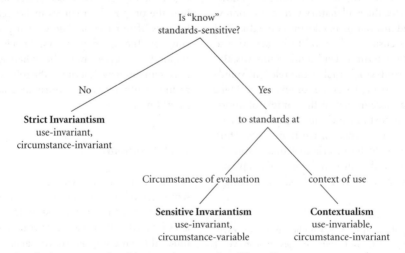

Figure 53.1   Standard taxonomy of positions on the semantics of "know"

standard versions of sensitive invariantism are *use-invariant* – though of course one might also have a hybrid view that was both use-variable and circumstance-variable. Strict invariantism is both use-invariant and circumstance-invariant.

2   Some Facts about Our Use of "Know"

I now want to look at three facts about our use of knowledge attributions that have figured prominently in discussions of the semantics of "know."

2.1   Variability of standards

Normally, I am perfectly happy to say that I know that my car is parked in my driveway. I will say this even when I'm at work, several miles away. But if someone asks me how I know that my car has not been stolen (and driven away), I will admit that I do not know this. And then I will have to concede that I do not know that my car is in my driveway: after all, if I knew this, then I would be able to deduce, and so come to know, that it has not been stolen.

How should we think of my shift from claiming to know to denying that I know? It doesn't seem right to describe me as having learned something, or as correcting a mistake. If I have learned something, what exactly have I learned? It's not as if I was unaware of the existence of car thieves when I made my original knowledge claim. Besides, the next day I will go right back to saying that I know that my car is in my driveway. Am I so dense as never to learn from my mistakes?

Nor does it seem right to say that when I claimed to know, I didn't mean it literally. I would have said the same thing in a forum where non-literal speech is discouraged, like a courtroom. And I would have said the same thing if I had been instructed to say just what I meant, without exaggeration, artifice, or innuendo. Indeed, I would have said the same thing in a crowd of epistemologists, so it was not just a matter of "speaking with the vulgar."

Perhaps my mistake lies in conceding that I don't know that the car is in the driveway. Perhaps the fact that I cannot rule out auto theft is actually irrelevant to whether I know. But what, then, *should* I say when the possibility is floated? Should I ignore it or dismiss it as irrelevant? That might

be the right response to certain far-fetched sceptical worries – say, "how do you know that the matter in your car has not spontaneously reorganized to form a giant lizard?" – but it hardly seems appropriate in response to a perfectly mundane worry about thieves. Should I say "Although I know that the car is in my driveway, there's always a chance that it has been stolen and is not in my driveway"? This sounds close to contradictory. Or should I say "Since I know that the car is in my driveway, I know that it hasn't been stolen"? That too seems wrong. I am not in a position to know that the car has not been stolen. If I am making a mistake, it is not one that ordinary speakers recognize as a mistake.

If I was speaking literally both times and didn't make a mistake, then presumably the standards I must meet in order to count as "knowing" must have changed. I met the laxer standards that were in play at the time of my first knowledge claim, but not the stricter ones that came into play after the mention of car thieves.

Examples like this can easily be multiplied. They form the basis of standard arguments for contextualism and sensitive invariantism.

2.2   Embedded occurrences of "know"

Temporal and modal operators shift the circumstances of evaluation. But we seem to use the same epistemic standard in evaluating "know" when it is embedded in the scope of temporal or modal operators as we do when it occurs unembedded. We don't seem to *mix* different standards at a single context of use, even when we're considering putative knowers in very different circumstances.

To take up the example from the last section, when I concede that I don't know that my car is parked in the driveway, I won't insist that I *did* know this two minutes ago, before the bothersome question raised the standards. I will say that I did not know it then either. In deciding whether I knew it then, I use the standards in play now, not the standards that were in play then.

Relatedly, we do not say things like "Before the possibility that he might win the lottery became relevant, John knew that he would not be able to afford health insurance, but now he does not know this (though he still believes it)," or "John knows that he won't be able to afford health

insurance, but if he were discussing the possibility that he might win the lottery, he would not
know this." If the judge asks Doris whether she
knew on January 13 that her car was in the driveway, it would be positively bizarre for her to answer
"I don't know: I can't remember whether I was
worried about car thieves that day" or "Remind
me: what epistemic standards were in play at that
time?" All this suggests that at any given context of
use, we hold the standards that one must meet in
order to count as "knowing" constant over all
circumstances of evaluation. Observations such
as these form the basis of standard arguments
against sensitive invariantism.[3]

2.3   Truth ascriptions and retraction

When standards have been raised, I will say not
only that I don't know that my car is in my driveway, and that I *didn't* know this earlier, but that my
earlier assertion of "I know that my car is in the
driveway" was *false*.[4] In part, this is because we tend
to report knowledge claims homophonically,
even when they were made in very different epistemic contexts.[5] Thus, I will report myself as having
asserted that I knew that my car was in the driveway. Since I now take myself not to have known
this, I must reckon my earlier assertion false.

I won't just *say* that it was false; I will *treat* it as
false. If challenged, I will *retract* my earlier claim,
rather than reformulating it in a way that shows it
to be consistent with my current claim – for
example, by saying, "What I asserted was merely
that I met the standard for 'knowing' that was in
place *when I was making the claim*."[6] I will have
correlative expectations about when others ought
to retract their knowledge claims. If yesterday
Sally asserted "I know that the bus will be on
time," and today she admits that she didn't know
yesterday that the bus would be on time, I will
expect her to retract her earlier assertion. I will
find it exceedingly bizarre if she replies by saying
that her assertion was true, even if she adds "by
the standards that were in place yesterday."

In these respects "know" functions very differently from ordinary indexicals like "here" and
from other expressions generally regarded as
context-sensitive, like "flat" and "tall."[7] Suppose
I'm on a moving train. At 3:30 we pass some big
factories and tenement houses, and I say "It's very
urban here." By 3:31 we have passed into suburbs,

and I say "It's not very urban here." I *won't* retract
my earlier claim. If it is challenged, I'll say: "When
I said a minute ago 'It's very urban here,' what I
said was true, and I stand by that, even though it's
not very urban *here*." To avoid confusion, I may
reformulate my earlier claim: "What I asserted
was that it was very urban where we were a
minute ago." Similarly, if I find myself in a scientific context where tiny bumps and ridges are
important, I might assert "The table is not flat,"
but I would not regard this as any reason to withdraw my assertion, made earlier in an everyday
context, of "The table is flat." If pressed, I would
say: "I only committed myself to the table's being
flat by everyday standards."

If we are correct in ascribing truth and falsity
to our earlier knowledge claims in light of present
standards, and retracting or standing by them
accordingly, then it seems that we do not take the
epistemic standards one must meet in order to
count as "knowing" to vary across contexts of use.
This fact forms the basis of standard arguments
against contextualism.

3   Assessing the Standard Views

Let's assemble the upshots of these observations.
The apparent *variability of standards* suggests that
the truth of sentences containing "know" depends
somehow on varying epistemic standards. That
would rule out strict invariantism. The facts
about *embedded occurrences* suggest that the
semantics of "know" is circumstance-invariant.
That would rule out sensitive invariantism. And
the facts about *truth ascriptions and retraction*
suggest that the semantics of "know" is use-
invariant. That would rule out contextualism.
Taken at face value, then, our three facts about use
seem to rule out all three standard views about
the semantics of "know."

What should we conclude? I think we have
three basic options:

1. We can argue that one of our three facts about
    use is a misleading guide to the semantics of
    "know," either

    (a) because it can be explained pragmati-
         cally, in terms of our broader communi-
         cative purposes, or

(b) because it can be attributed to systematic and widespread error on the part of ordinary speakers.

2. We can argue that our practice in using "know" is so confused and incoherent that knowledge-attributing sentences cannot be assigned definite truth conditions. Instead of doing semantics, we can advocate reform, perhaps through the introduction of new, unconfused terms of epistemic assessment.
3. We can try to make conceptual space for a semantics for "know" that is use-invariant and circumstance-invariant, but still somehow sensitive to changing epistemic standards.

My aim in this paper is to explore the last of these options, which I will take up in §4, below. But first I want to say a bit about why I find the other options unpromising.

3.1 Pragmatic explanations of the data

One of the most important lessons of philosophy of language in the 1960s was that the connection between meaning and use is indirect.[8] Even if we restrict ourselves to sincere, knowledgeable informants, the most we can discern directly from their use of sentences are the conditions in which they find it reasonable to use these sentences to make assertions. And these are not the same as the truth conditions. It is often reasonable to make assertions using sentences one knows to be literally false – not just because it is sometimes reasonable to lie, but because it is often reasonable to engage in hyperbole, harmless simplification, irony, and metaphor. Conversely, it is often reasonable to *refrain* from asserting something that is true, germane to the topic, and potentially informative. For example, one might refrain from asserting that Harvard has one of the fifty largest university libraries in the world – though this is true – because doing so would encourage certain audiences to infer that Harvard is closer to number fifty than to number one.

Thus the facts about use catalogued in the previous section do not *by themselves* rule out any proposal about the semantics of "know." These facts may tell us something about when people find it reasonable to use certain sentences containing "know" to make assertions, but they do not directly tell us anything about the truth-conditions of these sentences. To get from use to truth-conditions, we must rule out the possibility that it is reasonable to use these sentences *despite* their falsity, or to refrain from using them *despite* their truth. I know of no fully general way of doing this: all we can do is examine putative explanations one by one and show how they fail. Because we will consider the possibility of speaker error in §3.2, we will assume in this section that speakers are under no relevant substantive or semantic misapprehensions: when they utter false sentences, they know that they are false, and when they refrain from uttering true sentences, they know that they are true.

3.1.1 Variability of standards

The variability data is primarily a problem for strict invariantists. Strict invariantists come in two varieties. *Sceptical* invariantists hold that the fixed epistemic standards are very stringent, perhaps so stringent that human beings never meet them (at least with respect to empirical facts). *Moderate* invariantists hold that the standards are meetably lax. The two kinds of invariantists face different challenges in giving a pragmatic explanation of the variability data, so I will consider them separately.

(A) Fixed high standards

If standards are fixed and high, we need to explain why speakers should so frequently find it reasonable to claim to know things they are fully aware they don't know. (Remember, we are saving the possibility that speakers are unaware of their own ignorance for later.) One possible explanation is that they are trying not to mislead others who do not realize that the standards for knowledge are very high, and who would conclude from a denial of knowledge that the speaker was in a much poorer epistemic position than is actually the case. But this explanation applies only to the discourse of an enlightened sceptic talking to the unenlightened masses – surely a very special case. To explain the masses' own low-standards attributions of knowledge, an error theory would be needed.

Another possibility is that speakers are prone to hyperbole. Just as I might say "I could eat a horse!" instead of saying, more accurately, "I could eat ten pancakes and a four-egg omelette," so I might say that I *know* my car is in my driveway instead of saying merely that I have pretty good reason to believe this. If this kind of hyperbole were systematic and widespread, it might explain why we often claim to know things even when our grounds fall short of being conclusive.[9] But I find the prospects of such an explanation dim. Hyperbole must be deliberate: if I really believed that I could eat a horse, I would not be exaggerating in saying that I could. However, ordinary speakers don't seem to regard their ordinary knowledge claims as exaggerations. Nor do they mark any distinction between what they literally know and what they only hyperbolically "know." When their knowledge claims are challenged, they don't say "I was speaking hyperbolically," the way I would if you replied to my horse-eating boast by saying, "Not even a grizzly bear can consume an entire horse in one sitting."

In defense of the hyperbole view, Jonathan Schaffer notes that hyperbole can be "non-obvious," particularly when it is highly formulaic (forthcoming, n. 3). We are so accustomed to the trope "I'm dying of thirst" that we no longer pause to consider its literal significance; instead, we jump directly to the intended meaning. Schaffer concludes that "the fact that 'I know that I have hands' is not obviously hyperbolic is no objection." But my point is not about obviousness. Even if speakers do not realize at first that in saying "I'm dying of thirst" they are speaking hyperbolically, they will immediately concede this when it is pointed out to them. "Of course I'm not literally *dying*," they will say, "and I never meant to suggest that I was." In contrast, those who say "I know that I have hands" will not, in general, concede that they were speaking hyperbolically, even when confronted with sceptical counterpossibilities. No one reacts to the sceptic by saying, "I never meant to suggest that I literally *knew* that I had hands!"

A third approach would appeal to the *inconvenience* of adding all the pedantic hedges and qualifications that would be needed to make our ordinary knowledge claims strictly true. As long as no one is likely to be misled, it may be more efficient to assert (falsely) that one knows that *p* than to assert (truly, but cumbersomely) that one knows that probably *p*, unless of course *q*; or that one has ruled out possibilities *X*, *Y*, and *Z*, but not *W*. For the same reason, one might say "My tank holds 15 gallons" when it really holds 14.5. As the potential misleadingness of unqualified and strictly false knowledge claims varies with the conversational context, so does our willingness to make them.

Like the hyperbole view, however, this approach fails to explain how we actually react when our ordinary knowledge claims are challenged. If I say "My tank holds 15 gallons" and someone calls me on it – "But the manual says it holds 14.5!" – I will say, "I was speaking loosely: what I meant was that it holds *about* 15 gallons." But if I say "I know that my car is in my driveway" and someone calls me on it – "How can you rule out the possibility that it has been stolen?" – I will *not* say, "I was speaking loosely: what I meant was that I know that my car is *most likely* in my driveway," or "What I meant was that I know that my car is in my driveway, provided it has not been stolen or moved in some other abnormal way." In this respect I believe I am representative of ordinary speakers: otherwise, sceptical arguments would be greeted with shrugs, not surprise.

(B) FIXED LOW STANDARDS

If standards are fixed and low, then what needs explaining is why we sometimes *deny* that people know, even when they clearly meet these standards. Patrick Rysiew has suggested that we sometimes deny that we know because we do not want to implicate that we can rule out certain salient but irrelevant counterpossibilities.[10] In asserting that *p*, one ordinarily represents oneself as knowing that *p*. If I make this implicit knowledge claim explicit by saying "I *know* that my car is parked in my driveway," my choice of words will be noticed. My hearers may well wonder why I did not simply say "My car is parked in my driveway," and they may assume I meant to imply that I could rule out the conversationally salient possibility that my car had been stolen. Even if I do not need to rule out this possibility in order to count as knowing, I do not want to be taken to be implying that I can rule it out. So, Rysiew argues, I have reason to disavow knowledge.

This is an ingenious explanation, but it fails on two counts. First, although worries about misleading implicatures may be good reasons to refrain from asserting something, they aren't good reasons to assert its *negation*. Before Cal has played any games, I will refrain from asserting (truly) that Cal has won all of its games so far this season, because my doing so would misleadingly imply that Cal has played at least one game already. But these considerations do not give me any reason to assert that Cal has *not* won all of its games so far this season. Similarly, even if Rysiew's story can explain why it would be rational for me to refrain from saying that I know, it cannot explain why I should say that I *don't* know.

Second, even if Rysiew's explanation worked in the first-person case, it could not be extended to third-person knowledge attributions. It is essential to Rysiew's explanation that the question arises, "Why did the speaker say that he *knows* that p rather than just that p?" The question does not arise in the same way in third-person cases. In saying that p, one does not ordinarily implicate that someone else, X, knows that p. So an assertion that X knows that p does not call attention to itself in the same way as a first-person knowledge ascription. Thus, Rysiew's explanation does not generalize to third-person knowledge attributions. But the phenomenon it seeks to explain does extend to third-person attributions. So the explanation fails.

3.1.2   Embedded "know"

There is an easy pragmatic explanation for the infelicity of asserting "I knew that p earlier, but now that standards have gone up, I don't know that p"[11] In asserting that I knew that p earlier, I represent myself as knowing that I knew that p. But in representing myself as knowing that I knew that p, I also represent myself as knowing that p, since it is common knowledge that knowledge is factive. Thus there is a clash between what I commit myself to in asserting "I don't know that p now" and what I represent myself as knowing in asserting "I knew that p earlier."

But this explanation only takes us so far. It explains why we do not assert "I don't know now that p, but I knew then that p." But it does not explain our tendency to *deny* that we knew then that p.[12] Nor does it explain why it is infelicitous to assert "If p is true, then I knew that p before standards went up, though I don't know that p now,"[13] or "Joe doesn't know now that p, but he knew then that p," or "I know now that p, but I didn't know then that p," when all that has changed are the standards. Here, it seems, a defender of circumstance-variable semantics must resort to an error theory.

3.1.3   Truth ascriptions and retraction

It might be suggested that the *inconvenience* of reformulating knowledge claims in a way that reflects their dependence on past standards sometimes makes it reasonable to treat them as if they had been made in light of current standards – even if this means saying that they were false when we know that they were true. The differences in usage between "know" and ordinary indexicals might then be attributed to the comparative ease of reformulating claims made using ordinary indexicals when the relevant contextual factors have changed. If I say "I am tired now" at 3:30 p.m. today, others can easily re-express the content of my claim tomorrow by using the sentence "he was tired at 3:30 p.m. yesterday." But when it comes to "know" – supposing that "know" is context-sensitive – things are messier. How can we re-express a knowledge claim made in one context in another, where standards are different? I might say something like this: "I asserted that I knew, by the relatively low standards for knowing in place at the time, that my car was in my driveway." Or perhaps: "I said something that is true just in case I met the standards in place at the time for knowing that my car was in my driveway." But these reformulations are cumbersome and not very informative.[14] Even if they are correct, it may seldom be worth the trouble to use them; in many cases, it may be more efficient simply to withdraw the earlier knowledge claim. In this way, a contextualist might attempt to explain away the data about truth ascriptions and retraction that suggest a use-invariant semantics for "know."

But if this is the explanation of our retraction behavior, there ought to be *some* cases in which the disadvantages of retracting outweigh the inconvenience of reformulating. Suppose Sam is in the courtroom:

JUDGE: Did you know on December 10 that your car was in your driveway?

SAM: Yes, your honor. I knew this.

JUDGE: Were you in a position to rule out the possibility that your car had been stolen?

SAM: No, I wasn't.

JUDGE: So you didn't know that your car was in the driveway, did you?

SAM: No, I suppose I didn't, your honor.

JUDGE: But you just said you did. Didn't you swear an oath to tell the whole truth, and nothing but the truth?

However inconvenient it would be for Sam to reply,

> My claim was that on December 10 I knew, by the standards for knowledge that were in play before you mentioned car thieves, that my car was in my driveway. That was true, your honor, so I did not speak falsely,

it would surely be more inconvenient for him to be charged with perjury. Nonetheless, I think that Sam, if he is like most ordinary speakers, will concede that his previous assertion was false and promise to be more careful in his future answers. This suggests that the calculus of inconvenience alone cannot explain why speakers tend to abandon their earlier knowledge claims when they are shown to be false in light of present standards.

3.2 Error theories

A sincere speaker who wants to speak the literal truth and avoid literal falsity may fail to do so if she has false beliefs, either about the facts or about the literal meanings of the words she uses.[15] If I believe (as I once did) that "gravy" is the name of a vitamin-deficiency disease, I will refrain from asserting "I like gravy," even if I do like meaty sauce. And if I believe that whales are fish, I may assert "Whales are fish," even though this is false. Before we make any inferences from facts about ordinary use to truth conditions, then, we must rule out the possibility that ordinary speakers are systematically mistaken in certain ways. As before, we'll consider our three facts about use in turn.

3.2.1 Variability of standards

To explain the variability data, moderate strict invariantists must argue that speakers often underestimate their success in meeting the standards for knowledge and as a result disavow knowledge that they actually possess. Sceptical invariantists, by contrast, must argue that speakers systematically *over*estimate their success in meeting the standards for knowledge and as a result claim to know when in fact they do not.

The sceptical version of the error theory is sometimes rejected on the grounds that it rules expressions of paradigm cases of knowledge, like "I know that I have hands," false. But the paradigm case argument is not a good argument. A supposed paradigm case of *F*-ness can turn out

not to be an *F* at all. Whales turned out not to be fish; glass turned out not to be a solid. This might even happen on a large scale. Suppose that in 1750, all the emeralds on earth had been replaced by synthetic duplicates indistinguishable by the technology of the time. Then *none* of the extant "paradigm cases" of emeralds would have been emeralds. The sceptic's claim that ordinary speakers are mistaken in nearly all of their knowledge claims cannot be rejected out of hand.

Nonetheless, it is fair to ask the sceptical invariantist for an *explanation* of the widespread and uniform error she attributes to speakers. Why do speakers so quickly revert to making everyday knowledge claims even after they have been led through sceptical arguments?[16] Human beings are educable; the fact that the lesson does not stick deserves special explanation. Moreover, the sceptic must explain how "know" comes to have the exacting meaning it has, despite the fact that looser use is the norm. (It would be difficult to argue that "decimate" still means just "to kill one in every ten of," when it is now routinely used for cases of larger-scale destruction.) Here the sceptic will have to put great weight on certain widely accepted generalizations about knowledge (such as closure principles) that can be exploited in sceptical arguments. But it is not clear why these generalizations should have a better claim to be meaning-constituting than the "paradigm cases" the sceptic rejects. At the very least, the sceptic owes us a fancy story here.

The moderate strict invariantist does not face this problem, since she takes many of our ordinary knowledge claims to be true. But she must explain why speakers find the premises exploited in sceptical arguments so compelling, despite the implausibility of the conclusions to which they lead. If these premises are false, why do speakers not come to see their falsity and stop feeling the pull of sceptical arguments? Presumably a moderate strict invariantist will say that I can sometimes know that my car is in the driveway, even though I have been gone for fifteen minutes and cannot absolutely rule out the possibility of car theft in the interim. Why, then, does the closure-exploiting argument that I cannot know this seem so compelling? These are deep and difficult questions, to be sure. My point here is that until she answers them satisfactorily, the moderate strict invariantist cannot explain away the apparent variability of standards in our knowledge attributions.

There is a further problem with both kinds of error theory, recently emphasized by Keith DeRose and John Hawthorne.[17] Ordinary speakers accept many generalizations linking knowledge with other concepts. For example, one ought not assert something unless one knows it, one ought to decide what to do by reasoning from what one knows, and so on. The sceptical invariantist will have to hold that these generalizations, too, are in error, or else take the hard line that the vast majority of our assertions are improper and our decisions and actions irresponsible. The moderate strict invariantist will have trouble here, too, though less spectacularly, because in some situations (where much is at stake) we seem to require a very high standard of evidence before we will act on or assert a proposition. She must either say that our scruples here are unwarranted or reject the generalizations linking knowledge with assertion and action.

3.2.2 Embedded "know"

According to sensitive invariantism, the fact that speakers use the same epistemic standards in evaluating embedded and non-embedded instances of "know" reflects some kind of systematic error. But what kind? There are two possibilities. First, speakers might take the standards required to count as "knowing" to be fixed, or to be determined entirely by the context of use. Alternatively, instead of being mistaken about the semantics of "know," speakers might systematically misjudge the standards in play at different circumstances of evaluation.

There is something a bit perverse about the first explanatory strategy. One of the best arguments *in favor of* a circumstance-variable, use-invariant semantics for "know" is that it promises to explain both the variability data and the data about truth ascriptions and retraction. But it cannot explain this data unless it plays some role in guiding speakers' linguistic behavior. Thus, if we explain away the data about embedded occurrences by arguing that speakers implicitly take "know" to be circumstance-invariant and use it accordingly, we undercut one of the best arguments in favor of sensitive invariantism.

Better, then, to argue that speakers systematically misjudge the standards relevant at alternative

circumstances of evaluation. Along these lines, John Hawthorne argues that we tend to "project" the standards currently in play to other putative knowers, times, and circumstances:

> … we do have some tendency to suppose that, as more and more possibilities of error become salient to us, we are reaching an ever more enlightened perspective. Thus when we consider someone who is not alive to these possibilities, we have a tendency to let our (putatively) more enlightened perspective trump his. This tendency, when left unchecked, leads to scepticism. (Hawthorne 2004, pp. 164–5)

This kind of projection is not unprecedented: it is well known that those for whom a recent disaster is salient will overestimate risks in past, future, and counterfactual situations. In much the same way, Hawthorne urges,

> Once we have gotten ourselves into the frame of mind of thinking "I do not in fact know whether or not I'll be able to afford the Safari," as we frequently do when we use parity reasoning, we are not only unwilling to say "However I used to know that;" we are positively willing to say "I never did know that." (pp. 162–3)

This strategy is worth pursuing, but we should remind ourselves how heavy an explanatory burden it must bear. It *always* seems wrong to say that Joe knew before, but doesn't know now, when the only thing that has changed are the relevant standards. Projection might explain occasional or even frequent mistakes, but I doubt it can account for our universal unwillingness to shift standards across circumstances of evaluation.

Even if the projection strategy works, it is a double-edged sword. If it succeeds in explaining why we evaluate *embedded* occurrences of "know" in light of present standards, it should also explain why we evaluate occurrences of "know" at other *contexts of use* in light of present standards. That is, it should explain the data about truth ascriptions and retraction. Indeed, Hawthorne suggests as much himself, when he adds, immediately after the second passage quoted above: "And, if pressed, we are willing, moreover, to say that 'I was mistaken in thinking that I did know that'" (p. 163). The problem is that one of the best arguments for an invariantist semantics for "know" is that it explains the data about truth ascriptions and retraction. If that data is explained instead by the story about projection, then the argument for preferring sensitive invariantism to contextualism is significantly weakened.

3.2.3   Truth ascriptions and retraction

The data about truth ascriptions and retraction is most straightforwardly explained by a use-invariant semantics for "know." A contextualist must explain this data in some other way. We have ruled out a pragmatic explanation (§3.1.3), so it seems that a contextualist must appeal to an error theory here. Many contextualists are explicit about this: for example, Stewart Cohen (2001) says that "We *mistakenly* think that knowledge ascriptions we make in everyday contexts conflict with the skeptical judgements we make in stricter contexts" (p. 89, emphasis added).[18]

As before, there are two options: the contextualist can suppose either that ordinary speakers are wrong about the semantics of "know" – treating it as use-invariant when it is not – or that they make systematic errors about what standards are in play in contexts other than their own. The problem is that both forms of error theory threaten to undermine the positive case for contextualism. This is especially clear if the error is semantic in character. If ordinary speakers have a faulty grasp of the *meaning* of "know," then we cannot confidently appeal to variability in the standards they require someone to meet in order to count as "knowing" as support for a theory about the meaning of "know." Yet this data is the primary evidence in favor of contextualism.

What about the second option? It is undeniable that speakers often misjudge features of other contexts of use than their own, but if we are to explain the data, the error we posit must be *systematic*. We must explain why speakers *never* allow their previous day's assertion of "I know that *p*" to stand as true while asserting "I did not know that *p* yesterday." I doubt that our tendencies to project features of our present situations onto other situations are nearly strong or uniform enough to explain away the uniform data about truth ascriptions and retraction.

The "double-edged sword" point applies here, too. If the projection story works with contexts of use, it ought to work with circumstances of evaluation, too. So if it explains the data about truth ascriptions and retraction, it ought to explain the data about embedded occurrences of "know" as well. This would significantly weaken the contextualist's case against sensitive invariantism.

As should now be clear, a *general* problem with positing speaker error to explain away facts about use is that such explanations tend to undermine the evidential basis for the semantic theories they are intended to support. All of these semantic theories are justified indirectly on the basis of facts about speakers' use of sentences, and the more error we attribute to speakers, the less we can conclude from these facts. We have seen that the cost of defending sensitive invariantism in this way is that the case against contextualism is severely weakened, and conversely that the cost of defending contextualism in this way is that the case against sensitive invariantism is compromised. It is possible that an error theory can be made to work – perhaps in conjunction with pragmatic explanations – but the prospects do not look good.

3.3   Eliminativism

So far we have looked at ways of showing that one of the standard views is in fact consistent with all of the facts about use we considered in §2. An alternative response would be to concede that no single account of the semantics of "know" accounts for all of these facts.[19] Perhaps our talk of "knowledge" confuses several distinct notions, in much the same way that prescientific talk of "warmer than" confused *having a higher temperature than, having more heat energy than*, and *exchanging heat at a higher rate than*.[20] In that case there may be no fully coherent way to assign truth-conditions to our knowledge-attributing sentences. The rational course of action would be to reform our thought and talk by introducing new, unconfused terms of epistemic assessment.

At the risk of use-mention confusion, we might call this approach "eliminativism about knowledge." Like other eliminativisms, it is radical and should not be accepted unless there is no other good alternative.

3.4   Expanding the field of options

Let us sum up our conclusions so far. Together, our three facts about use suggest that an adequate semantics for "know" must be sensitive to changing epistemic standards, but that it cannot be either use-variable or circumstance-variable. That rules out all three standard views: strict invariantism because it is not sensitive to changing epistemic standards at all, sensitive invariantism because it is circumstance-variable, and contextualism because it is use-variable. We might make room for one of these views by arguing that one of our three facts about use is a poor guide to truth-conditions, but attempts to do this either pragmatically or by positing systematic error on the part of ordinary speakers have so far been unpersuasive. If there is no other option, then, it seems we are left with eliminativism.

But how *could* there be another option? How could there be a semantics for "know" that was use-invariant and circumstance-invariant, but still in some way sensitive to changing epistemic standards? What we would need is another dimension of variability. In the next section, I am going to open up room for just such a thing. This will make possible a semantics for "know" that neatly explains *all three* facts about use.

4   A Relativist Semantics for "Know"

Here is my proposal. The epistemic standards relevant to determining the extension of "know" are not those in play at the context of use or those in play at the circumstance of evaluation, but those in play at the *context of assessment*.

4.1   Assessment sensitivity

The notion of a context of assessment may be unfamiliar, but it is readily intelligible. Just as a context of use is a situation in which a sentence might be *used*, so a context of assessment is a situation in which a (past, present, or future, actual or merely possible) use of a sentence might be *assessed* for truth or falsity. I do not think that there should be any worries about the very *idea* of a context of assessment; even an arch anti-relativist ought to be able to accept it.

What is controversial is the suggestion that we relativize sentence truth not just to a context of use, but to a context of assessment as well. This is certainly a departure from semantic orthodoxy, and I will defend it shortly.[21] Here I want to focus

on what we can do with it. By making sentence truth doubly context-relative, we open up a new way in which sentences can be context-sensitive. A sentence is context-sensitive in the usual way, or *use-sensitive*, if its truth value varies with the context of use (keeping the context of assessment fixed). A sentence is context-sensitive in the new way, or *assessment-sensitive*, if its truth value varies with the context of assessment (keeping the context of use fixed). Similarly, a subsentential expression is use-sensitive if it is partially responsible for the use sensitivity of (at least some) sentences containing it, and assessment-sensitive if it is partially responsible for the assessment sensitivity of (at least some) sentences containing it.

My proposal is that "know" is sensitive to the epistemic standards in play at the context of assessment. It is a kind of contextualism, then, but not at all the usual kind. To avoid confusion, I will call it "relativism," reserving the term "contextualism" for the view that "know" is sensitive to the epistemic standards in play at the context of *use* (see Figure 53.2). Call a semantics for "know" *assessment-variable* just in case it allows the epistemic standard relevant for determining the extension of "know" to vary with the context of assessment, and *assessment-invariant* otherwise. If "know" is assessment-sensitive, then its semantics can be assessment-variable while being use- and circumstance-invariant, and in this way we can neatly explain all three facts about use:

1. *Variability of standards.* Why is it that I'll happily assert "Joe knows that his car is parked in his driveway" when standards are low, and "Joe doesn't know that his car is parked in his driveway" when standards are high? The relativist semantics affords a simple explanation: the former sentence is true as used and assessed in a context where standards are low, and the latter is true as used and assessed in a context where standards are high. Because I can properly assess each sentence as true at the context in which I utter it, there is no need to appeal to pragmatic explanations or error theories to explain the variability data. (Note that in the special case where the context of use and the context of assessment coincide, the relativist semantics yields exactly the same truth-value assignments as the standard contextualist semantics. So the relativist is in just

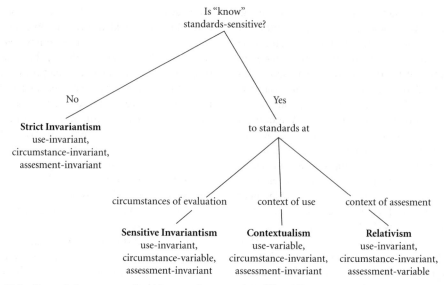

Figure 53.2   Expanded taxonomy of positions on the semantics of "know"

as good a position to explain the variability data as the contextualist. This is significant, because one of the primary selling points of the contextualist account is its ability to explain this data.)

2. *Embedded "know."* Why is it that we don't say things like "Before the standards went up, Harry knew that his car was in the driveway, but now he doesn't know this"? Or: "Harry doesn't know that his car is in the driveway, but he would know this if the possibility of car theft weren't relevant"? The relativist semantics has a straightforward explanation: the semantics of "know" is not circumstance-variable. This is the same explanation that contextualism and strict invariantism offer.

3. *Truth ascriptions and retraction.* Why is it that when standards go up, leading us to assert "Joe doesn't (and didn't) know that his car is in his driveway," we expect Joe to retract his earlier assertion of "I know that my car is in my driveway," and to concede that what he asserted was false? That is, why do we tend to use the standards appropriate to the present context in assessing past utterances? Where contextualism is forced to appeal to an error theory, the relativist semantics offers an easy, semantic explanation. Namely: the present standards *are* the appropriate standards to use in assessing past assertions, even ones that

were made when very different epistemic standards were in play. According to the relativist, knowledge claims are always properly assessed in light of the standards in play at the assessor's current context.[22]

4.2   Expressive relativism and propositional relativism

Contextualists typically hold that "know" expresses different relations at different contexts of use, and that this indexicality is the source of its use sensitivity. Must the relativist, then, hold that "know" expresses different relations relative to different contexts of assessment? This would be an odd view. It would require us to give up the idea that "knowledge" attributers are making determinate claims. Assessors at different contexts could disagree about what was said, and they could all be right! According to this *expressive relativism*, there would be no non-relative fact of the matter about what proposition was expressed by the sentence used, at its context of use.[23]

I go back and forth about the coherence of expressive relativism. It sometimes seems to me that with a bit of imagination, we can make sense of it. Even if we can make sense of it, however, it does not seem to be a very attractive view. It would require significant changes in orthodox theories of meaning. For example, we could no longer say, with Stalnaker 1978, that the effect of assertion is to add the proposition asserted to a "common ground" of presupposed propositions, for there may be no common fact of the matter about which proposition *was* asserted.[24] Moreover, although expressive relativism might help us understand *speech acts* made using "know," it would leave it rather mysterious what it is to *believe* that Joe knows that his car is in his driveway.

Fortunately, assessment sensitivity can be had without expressive relativism. Call a sentence *use-indexical* if it expresses different propositions at different contexts of use (keeping the context of assessment fixed), and *assessment-indexical* if it expresses different propositions relative to different contexts of assessment (keeping the context of use fixed). Call a subsentential expression *use-* or *assessment-indexical* if it is at least partially responsible for the use or assessment indexicality of sentences containing it. According to expressive relativism, "know" is assessment-indexical, and that is why it is assessment-sensitive. But in fact a sentence or subsentential expression can be assessment-sensitive without being assessment-indexical.

Indeed, although this is often overlooked, a sentence can be *use*-sensitive without being use-indexical. Here is an example: "The number of AIDS babies born in the United States in 2003 is greater than 1000." This sentence expresses the same proposition at every context of use, so it is not use-indexical. But it *is* use-sensitive, because its truth value varies with the world of the context of use. Uttered in a world in which there were no AIDS babies in 2003, it would express a falsehood; uttered in the actual world, it expresses a truth.[25]

To see how a sentence can be use-sensitive without being use-indexical, we need to be explicit about the relation between sentence truth at a context and proposition truth at a circumstance of evaluation. (For simplicity, let us forget for a moment about contexts of assessment.)

SENTENCE TRUTH AND PROPOSITION TRUTH I: A sentence *S* is true at a context of use *C* just in case for some proposition *p*,
1. *S* expresses *p* at *C*, and
2. *p* is true when evaluated at the circumstances determined by *C*.[26]

Notice that the context of use plays two distinct roles here: (1) it determines what proposition is

expressed by the sentence, and (2) it determines how that proposition is to be evaluated to yield a truth value for the sentence in context. Indexicality produces use sensitivity via role (1), while contingency produces use sensitivity via role (2).

The situation is much the same when we relativize sentence truth to contexts of assessment as well as contexts of use:

SENTENCE TRUTH AND PROPOSITION TRUTH II: A sentence *S* is true at a context of use C_U and context of assessment C_A just in case for some proposition *p*,
1. *S* expresses *p* at C_U and C_A, and
2. *p* is true when evaluated at the circumstances determined by C_U and C_A.

As before, there are two distinct roles for contexts to play: (1) determining which proposition is expressed and (2) determining how that proposition is to be evaluated to yield a truth value for the sentence in context. Accordingly, there are two ways in which a sentence can be assessment-sensitive: it can be assessment-indexical, or the context of assessment can play a substantive role in determining the circumstances relative to which the proposition it expresses is to be evaluated. We can state the point more simply if we define proposition truth relative to contexts in the natural way:

CONTEXTS-RELATIVE PROPOSITION TRUTH: A proposition *p* is true at a context of use C_U and context of assessment C_A just in case *p* is true when evaluated at the circumstances determined by C_U and C_A.

Call a *proposition* assessment-sensitive just in case its truth varies with the context of assessment (keeping the context of use fixed). Then a sentence can be assessment-sensitive either by being assessment-indexical or by expressing an assessment-sensitive proposition. In the former case, we have expressive relativism; in the latter case, *propositional relativism*.

It might be thought that propositional relativism would require even more radical departures from orthodox semantics than expressive relativism. But that is not so. Granted, the form of propositional relativism I am advocating does require that the circumstances of evaluation to which proposition truth is relativized include an epistemic standards parameter in addition to a world parameter. But quite a few non-relativists have countenanced parameters of circumstances of evaluation besides the world parameter, so this hardly counts as a radical departure from standard semantic assumptions. For example, Kaplan's (1989) circumstances of evaluation include a time parameter. On Kaplan's account, a tensed sentence like "Socrates is sitting" expresses the same proposition at every context of use; it nonetheless has different truth values at different contexts of use, because different contexts determine different circumstances (times and worlds) with respect to which this proposition is to be evaluated. King, forthcoming, contemplates relativizing propositional truth to both worlds and standards of precision. On the view he considers (without endorsing or rejecting it), "France is hexagonal" expresses the same proposition at every context of use; it is true at a context of use just in case this proposition is true when evaluated with respect to the world of the context of use and the standards of precision in play at the context of use. Despite their appeal to parameters of circumstances of evaluation besides worlds, neither Kaplan nor King is a propositional relativist, because neither countenances assessment-sensitive propositions.

Nor is there anything particularly novel about having an *epistemic standards* parameter in the circumstances of evaluation. The non-relativist form of contextualism about "knows" defended in Kompa 2002 requires one, too. On Kompa's view, "know" expresses the same relation at every context of use, but this relation is "unspecific," in the sense that "what counts as having the property" can vary with "the context at hand" (p. 88) – that is, the context of use. Although Kompa does not develop her view in formal detail, it is hard to see how she could do so without adding an epistemic standards parameter to the circumstances of evaluation. The intension of the relation expressed by "know" would then be a function from worlds, times, and epistemic standards to extensions. This relation would be "unspecific" in the sense that there would be no answer to the question whether a particular person and fact fall into its extension at a time and world: only when an epistemic standard was specified would it have a definite extension. Kompa could then define context-relative

sentence truth as in *Sentence Truth and Proposition Truth II*, above, taking the circumstances determined by a context of use C_U (and context of assessment C_A) to be $\langle w, t, e \rangle$, where w = the world of C_U, t = the time of C_U, and e = the epistemic standards in play at C_U. "Know" would thus turn out to be use-sensitive but not use-indexical, just like tense on Kaplan's view, vague expressions on the view explored by King, and contingent eternal sentences on just about everyone's view.

The only difference between the relativist view I am advocating and Kompa's non-relativist, non-indexicalist form of contextualism is that I take the circumstances determined by a context of use C_U and context of assessment C_A to be the ordered pair $\langle w, t, e \rangle$, where w = the world of C_U, t = the time of C_U, and e = the epistemic standards in play at C_A (not C_U).[27] In every other respect I can agree with Kompa. We can agree that proposition truth must be relativized to an epistemic standards parameter (in addition to a world and perhaps a time parameter). We can agree about which propositions are expressed by which sentences at which contexts of use. We can both accept the schematic principle *Sentence Truth and Proposition Truth II* (provided Kompa does not mind the relativization to a context of assessment, which plays no substantive role in her account but also does no harm). We will of course disagree about the extension of the relation "S is true at context of use C_U and context of assessment C_A," because we disagree about how this schematic principle is to be filled in. (That is, we disagree about which circumstances of evaluation are "determined" by which contexts of use and assessment.) But this disagreement does not concern the theory of propositions. I conclude that if propositional relativism is objectionable, it is not because it requires radical revision to our existing theories of propositions.

5   Making Sense of Relative Truth

I anticipate two objections to my proposal. First, that it is ad hoc. Good scientific practice dictates that we make central modifications to our theories only when they have great and wide-ranging explanatory value. Surely it is not a good idea to make structural changes to our semantic framework just to accommodate knowledge attributions. Second, that it is incoherent. It is one thing to talk of propositions or sentences being true with respect to one context of assessment, and not with respect to another. It is quite another thing to make sense of that talk, and there are reasons for doubting that any sense *can* be made of it.

5.1   Ad hoc?

To the first objection I have two replies. First, I believe that assessment sensitivity is not limited to knowledge-attributing sentences. I believe it is also the key to adequate semantic treatments of future contingents, epistemic modals, accommodation (in the sense of Lewis 1979 and 1980), terms like "delicious," and perhaps much else.[28] So the modification I propose is not tailor-made for a single use, but has much wider application.

Second, the structural changes that are required are less radical than one might think. As I have argued, propositional relativism requires minimal changes to existing semantic frameworks. These changes are conservative. They allow us to *describe* assessment sensitivity, but they leave open the possibility that there is no assessment sensitivity in any natural language. Existing accounts of the semantics of expressions that are not assessment-sensitive can be carried over essentially unchanged. (In these cases, the relativization to contexts of assessment will be an idle wheel, but a harmless one, because truth will not vary with the context of assessment.) Thus although one might object to the claim that "know" is assessment-sensitive, it is hard to see on what grounds one might object to the framework that makes it possible—unless one thinks that assessment-relative truth is simply incoherent.[29]

5.2   Incoherent?

What on earth can it *mean* to say that an assertion is true as assessed by me, now, but false as assessed by me, later; or true as assessed by me, but false as assessed by you? This is not the kind of question that can be answered by *defining* "true at a context of use C_U and context of assessment C_A." Indeed, we have already done that, for both sentences (p. 30) and propositions (p. 31).[30] But our definitions leave us in more or less the position of Dummett's (1959) Martian anthropologists, who know what

counts as a winning position in chess and other games, but fail to grasp the *significance* of winning. We don't know what to *do* with a claim that a sentence (or proposition) is true relative to a context of use C_U and context of assessment C_A. And until we know that, we do not really understand relative-truth talk.

The charge of incoherence arises because a standard story about the significance of "true at a context of use C_U" cannot be extended to "true at a context of use C_U and context of assessment C_A." According to this story, truth is the internal aim of assertion. Of course, people may have all kinds of goals in making assertions – influencing others, showing off, giving directions, offering reassurance – and these goals may sometimes be better served by speaking falsely than by speaking the truth. But there is a sense in which a false assertion is always incorrect *qua* assertion, even if it succeeds in promoting these other goals. It may be useful to lie, but once your assertion has been shown to be false, you must withdraw it as mistaken. Dummett argues that the concept of truth gets its significance from this normative connection to the practice of assertion: just as it is part of the concept of winning a game that a player aims to win, so "it is part of the concept of truth that we aim at making true statements" (1959, p. 143 and 1978, p. 2). But if our primary grip on the notion of truth comes from our understanding of it as the internal aim of assertion, then the idea that truth might be relativized to a context of assessment just looks incoherent.[31] It does not make *sense* to aim to assert a proposition that is true at the context of use and the context of assessment, because there is no such thing as *the* context of assessment: each assertion can be assessed from indefinitely many distinct contexts.

At this point relativists typically say that the aim of assertion is to assert something that is true relative to the context of use and the asserter's own current context of assessment (which will of course be identical with the context of use).[32] But this only gives a significance to "true at C_U, C_A" for the special case where $C_U = C_A$. The relativist has not told us what to do with "true at C_U, C_A" where C_U and C_A are distinct. As a result, the anti-relativist might justly charge that the relativist's "true at C, C" is just a notational variant of her own "true at C," and that "true at C_U, C_A" has not yet been given a sense when $C_U \neq C_A$.

In my view, the relativist should instead reject the whole idea of understanding truth as "the aim of assertion." This idea is pretty obscure anyway. Even if truth is *an* internal normative aim of assertion, it is certainly not the only such aim: it is also part of the practice of assertion that we strive to say what is relevant to the conversation at hand, and to say things that are appropriately justified (or on some accounts, known). Indeed, in his 1972 Postscript to "Truth," Dummett emphasizes that his talk of truth as the aim of assertion was intended as a placeholder for a more complex story about the role truth plays in our practice of assertion: "What has to be added to a truth-definition for the sentences of a language, if the notion of truth is to be explained, is a description of the linguistic activity of making assertions; and this is a task of enormous complexity" (Dummett 1978, p. 20).

Having given up the "aim of assertion" idea, what else might we say about the role truth plays in our practice of assertion? One plausible and widely accepted idea is that an assertion is a *commitment* to the truth of what is asserted.[33] To make an assertion – even an insincere or otherwise defective one – is, *inter alia*, to commit oneself to the truth of the proposition asserted (relative to its context of use).[34] But what is it to commit oneself to the truth of a proposition? How does one honor or violate such a commitment? Some philosophers seem to find "commitment to truth" intelligible without further analysis, but in my view, "commitment to [noun phrase]" is intelligible only when it can be glossed in terms of commitment to *do* something. For example, we can make sense of "being committed to Al Gore," but only as meaning something like "being committed to *working for* (or perhaps *supporting*) Al Gore." When no obvious agentive complement presents itself, we can't make any sense of the deontic construction at all. What would it mean, for example, to be committed to the color of the sky, or to the texture of a damp rose petal?

So, in committing myself to the truth of a proposition at a context of use, what exactly am I committing myself to *doing* (or refraining from doing)? Well, suppose I assert "Jake is in Boston." If you ask "How do you know?" or challenge my claim more directly, by giving reasons for thinking it false, then it seems to me that I have an *obligation* to respond, by giving adequate reasons for thinking that my claim was true, or perhaps by deferring to the person who told me. If I can't discharge this obligation in a way that meets the challenge, I must "uncommit myself" by retracting my assertion. If I neither withdraw the assertion nor reply to the challenge, I am shirking an obligation I incur not *qua* moral agent or friend or member of polite society, but simply *qua* asserter.

These observations suggest an answer to our question. What I have committed myself to doing, in asserting that Jake is in Boston, is vindicating my claim when it is challenged.[35] There may be no specific sanction for failing to follow through on this commitment. But if I fail too blatantly or too frequently, others may stop treating me as a being that is capable of undertaking this kind of commitment. They may still take my utterances as expressions of my beliefs, as we take a dog's excited tail wagging as an expression of its psychological state. They may even regard my utterances, if found to be reliable, as useful bits of information. But they will be treating me as a measuring instrument, not as an asserter. They will not take me to be *committing myself* to the truth of anything.

If this is right, then we should understand the "commitment to truth" incurred by an assertion as follows:

> ASSERTORIC COMMITMENT: In asserting that p at a context C_U, one commits oneself to providing adequate grounds for the truth of p (relative to C_U), in response to any appropriate challenge, or (when appropriate) to deferring this responsibility to another asserter on whose testimony one is relying. One can be released from this commitment only by withdrawing the assertion.[36]

The principle is schematic along many dimensions: to make it less schematic, one would have to say something about what kinds of challenges count as "appropriate," what grounds count as "adequate" responses to what kinds of challenges, and when it is appropriate to defer responsibility. I won't attempt to do any of this here. What is important for our purposes is that this account can be extended in a very natural way to allow for assessment-relative truth. For whenever an assertion is challenged, there are always two relevant contexts: the context in which the assertion was originally made and the context in which the challenge must be met. A natural way to give significance to doubly context-relative truth, then, would be to say that what must be established when an assertion is challenged is truth relative to the original context of use and the asserter's *current* context of assessment (at the time of the challenge):

ASSERTORIC COMMITMENT (DUAL CONTEXTS): In asserting that p at a context C_U, one commits oneself to providing adequate grounds for the truth of p (relative to C_U *and one's current context of assessment*), in response to any appropriate challenge, or (when appropriate) to deferring this responsibility to another asserter on whose testimony one is relying.[37] One can be released from this commitment only by withdrawing the assertion.[38]

Note that although this account assumes that it makes sense to talk about contexts of assessment, it does not assume that propositional truth actually *varies* with the context of assessment. So non-relativists should be able to accept it, though for them the mention of "one's current context of assessment" will be an idle wheel. What we have, then, is a plausible story about the role of truth in our practice of assertion that gives a significance to talk of truth relative to a context of assessment, without prejudging the question whether we can actually assert anything whose truth is relative in this way. Indeed, this account gives us a way to test particular semantic hypotheses that make use of relative truth, by settling the *normative* consequences of these hypotheses.

We can now get a better feel for the assessment-sensitive semantics for "know" by examining its normative consequences. Suppose that Linda asserts, in a "low standards" context C_1, that Joe knew on March 10 that his car was in his driveway. If the assertion is challenged at this point, Linda must defend it by showing that

(a) Joe's car was in his driveway on March 10, and
(b) Joe's epistemic position with respect to this fact was good enough on March 10 to meet the (low) standards in play at C_1.[39]

Suppose that a little while later, standards are raised. If Linda's assertion is challenged in this new context, C_2, she must defend it by showing that

(a) Joe's car was in his driveway on March 10, and
(b) Joe's epistemic position with respect to this fact was good enough on March 10 to meet the (higher) standards in play at C_2.

In asserting that Joe knew on March 10 that his car was in his driveway, Linda takes on an open-ended commitment to show, whenever her assertion is (appropriately) challenged at a context C, that what she asserted is true by the standards in play at C – even if these standards are different from those that were in play when she made the assertion. If she lacks the resources to reply to a challenge, or if the challenge is unanswerable, then she is obliged to withdraw her assertion.

It seems to me that there is nothing incoherent about taking on such a commitment. Indeed, the facts about our use of "know" surveyed in §2, above, suggest that we implicitly take ourselves to be bound by just such a commitment whenever we attribute knowledge.

6   Conclusion

According to the "relativist" semantics I have proposed, the epistemic standards relevant for determining whether someone can be truly said to "know" something are determined by the context of assessment, not the context of use. Consequently, in assessing knowledge claims made at different contexts for truth or falsity, one need not keep track of the standards that were in place at these contexts. The only relevant standards are the ones *now* in place.[40] This is why knowledge attributions can be reiterated and reported homophonically.

On this view, knowledge attributions are not as robustly objective as ordinary claims about the world. We must be prepared to withdraw a knowledge attribution if standards change, even if the subject's epistemic position is just as we thought it was. Relatedly, when we challenge others for having made false knowledge claims, we may be assessing them in light of standards higher than the ones they recognized when they made them. Isn't this unfair? Not unless retracting an assertion is always tantamount to admitting that the assertion was made irresponsibly: and of course it is not, even without assessment sensitivity in the picture. When standards rise, speakers withdraw their knowledge attributions and take them to have been false, but they needn't (and typically don't) take themselves to have acted irresponsibly in making them. One indication of this is that when standards fall again, they go right back to their old ways, rather than becoming more cautious in attributing knowledge. This is not so strange if we think of knowledge attributions as temporary record-keeping devices – tools for keeping track of a normative status keyed to ever-changing present circumstances – rather than straightforward statements of fact.

If I am right, then knowledge attributions made blamelessly and with full access to the relevant facts must sometimes be withdrawn as false. In my view, philosophers have been too quick to find this incoherent. Sceptics argue that we are right to withdraw our knowledge claims in the face of sceptical challenges; they conclude that these claims were not responsibly made in the first place. Dogmatists and contextualists argue that we are wrong to withdraw our knowledge claims, precisely because they were responsibly made. I say that both sides have part of the truth: we are right to withdraw our knowledge claims in the face of certain sceptical challenges, even though they were responsibly made and we haven't learned anything new. A relativist semantics for "know" allows us to understand how this can be.

Notes

1   For a kindred view, developed rather differently, see Richard 2004. I learned of Richard's work too late to take account of it in this paper. There are also some affinities between the present proposal and the "perspectival" view of knowledge attributions defended in Rosenberg 2002: ch. 5 (see esp. pp. 148–9, 163–4), though Rosenberg does not develop his proposal in a truth-conditional framework.

2   For example, it classes the view advocated in Kompa 2002 as a form of contextualism, even though on Kompa's view "know" always expresses the same, "unspecific" relation, and so would be counted a form of invariantism on some criteria. Kompa's view will be discussed later, in §4.2.

3   See DeRose 2000 and DeRose, forthcoming.

4   Noticed by Feldman 2001: 77, Rosenberg 2002, p. 164, and Hawthorne 2004, p. 163, among others.

5   See Hawthorne 2004, §2.7.

6   As Stephen Schiffer notes, "no ordinary person who utters 'I know that p,' however articulate, would dream of telling you that what he meant and was implicitly stating was that he knew that p relative to such-and-such standard." (Schiffer 1996, pp. 326–7). See also Feldman 2001: pp. 74, 78–9, Hawthorne 2004, §2.7.

7   See Stanley 2004 for a detailed discussion of differences between "know" and various kinds of context-sensitive expressions.

8   See Grice 1989, Searle 1969, ch. 6.

9   See Schaffer, forthcoming.

10   Rysiew 2001, pp. 492, 499.

11   For a slightly different version of this explanation, directed at third-person knowledge ascriptions rather than past-tensed ones, see Hawthorne 2004, p. 160.

12   See DeRose 2002, §3.

13   Hawthorne 2004, p. 166.

14   More informative reformulations would require a way of specifying epistemic standards directly, rather than as the standards in play at such-and-such a context. We do not consider speakers masters of the indexicals "here" and "now" unless they are in command of coordinate systems for specifying places and times independently of utterance events ("in Berkeley, California," "at 3:30 p.m. GMT on October 14, 2003"), which they can use to reiterate claims made using these indexicals in other contexts. Ordinary speakers possess no comparable coordinate system for specifying epistemic standards.

15   Although I doubt that a clean distinction between semantic and substantive error can be made, a rough and ready distinction will suffice for our purposes here. Note that it is ignorance about literal meaning that is at stake here, not ignorance about speaker's meaning. On many accounts of speaker's meaning, it is implausible to suppose that a speaker could be ignorant of what *she* means. Nonetheless,

she can very well be ignorant of what *her words* mean, or of what she has literally *said*. See Rysiew 2001, p. 483, commenting on §IV of Schiffer 1996.

16 Cf. Hawthorne 2004, p. 131.

17 DeRose 2002, Hawthorne 2004, pp. 132–5.

18 Cohen argues that this error theory is innocuous, on the grounds that speakers make similar mistakes with gradable adjectives like "flat" (pp. 90–1). Richard 2004 concedes Cohen's analogy and rejects his error theories, plumping for a relativist treatment of both "flat" and "know." For my part, I am not convinced of the analogy: I think that a pragmatic explanation of our retraction and reporting behavior is much more plausible for "flat" than for "know." When standards change so that the surface imperfections on pancakes count as "bumps" and "holes," a speaker might retract an earlier assertion of "pancakes are flat," but only to avoid pedantry, not because she thinks she's really contradicted herself. If enough were at stake, she would no doubt find an appropriate way to reiterate her earlier claim. (Contrast what is alleged about "know" in §3.1.3, above.)

19 See Schiffer 1996.

20 For a discussion of this example, see Churchland 1979, ch. 2.

21 The relativization of truth to a context of assessment should not be confused with the relativization of truth to a "point of evaluation" (e.g., a tuple of time, world, and variable assignment) that is standard in model-theoretic semantics. A point of evaluation is not a context, but a sequence of parameters that can be "shifted" by operators. For more on the difference, see Lewis 1980 and MacFarlane 2003, §V.

22 A full discussion of the truth ascription data would require giving a semantics (at least a naive semantics) for the monadic object-language predicate "true." I will not pause to do that here. It turns out, not surprisingly, that in a language containing assessment-sensitive expressions, object-language "true" must also be assessment sensitive.

23 Sometimes a single use of a sentence may express multiple propositions, as when a teacher says to a class of thirty: "Of the three people sitting nearest to you, only two are likely to finish this class." I take it that in this case the teacher has asserted thirty singular propositions, not a single general one. This does not amount to expressive relativism, since all parties can agree about which propositions were expressed.

24 This is pointed out by Egan, Hawthorne, and Weatherson, forthcoming, who also give other arguments against what they call "content relativism."

25 David Lewis put this point by saying that "[c]ontingency is a kind of indexicality" (Lewis 1980, p. 82 and 1998, p. 25) – using "indexicality" for what I call "use sensitivity." Other writers use "context sensitivity" for what I call "use indexicality." I think it is useful to have distinct terms for both notions.

26 This definition is a close paraphrase of Kaplan 1989, p. 522 (cf. p. 547). As it stands, it is not sufficiently general, for in some frameworks the context of use will not always determine a unique circumstance of evaluation. For example, in indeterministic frameworks allowing overlapping worlds or "histories," the context of use will not pick out a single history (see Belnap and Green 1994, MacFarlane 2003). For a more generally applicable definition, we could replace (2) with: "*p* is true when evaluated at all circumstances of evaluation compatible with *C*" (e.g., at all moment/history pairs in which the moment is the moment of *C* and the history contains the moment of *C*). We can ignore this complication for present purposes.

27 I include the time parameter for illustrative purposes only; nothing hangs on its presence. King, forthcoming, may be right that the best treatment of tense does not call for a time parameter in circumstances of evaluation, in which case I am happy to remove it.

28 I discuss future contingents in MacFarlane 2003 and the other issues in a book manuscript, in progress. For independent arguments for a relativist treatment of epistemic modals, see Egan, Hawthorne, and Weatherson, forthcoming. For a relativist treatment of accommodation (somewhat different from mine), see Richard 2004. For a relativism motivated by "delicious" and the like, see Kölbel 2002.

29 One might also worry that the extra degree of freedom I offer in constructing semantic theories does not come with sufficient counterbalancing constraints. The connections between contexts-relative truth and norms for assertion which I propose in the next section are meant to address this concern.

30 These definitions are of course schematic, but when the semantic details are filled in, they will determine an extension for "true at context of use C_U and context of assessment C_A."

31 For a development of this argument, drawing on Evans 1985, see Percival 1994, pp. 196–8.

32 See Kölbel 2002, pp. 125, Egan, Hawthorne, and Weatherson, forthcoming: 29.

33 See e.g. Searle 1979, p. 12.

34 *Inter alia*, because presumably asserting a proposition involves more than simply committing oneself to its truth. Plausibly, the commitment must be undertaken publicly, by means of an overt utterance; perhaps there are other conditions as well.

35 For this way of looking at assertoric commitment as a "conditional task responsibility" to vindicate a claim when it is challenged, see Brandom 1983 and chapter 3 of Brandom 1994. I do not develop the idea in quite the same way as Brandom, but I am much indebted to his work.

36 Several philosophers have suggested to me that this account overgeneralizes, taking the norms of the seminar room to apply to assertions in general. It may be that ordinary asserters recognize no general obligation to justify their claims in the face of reasoned challenges (though it would not follow that they are not *bound by* such a norm). But even these sceptics ought to be able to accept a weaker norm requiring withdrawal of assertions that have been shown to be untrue

(relative to the context of use). This would be enough for my purposes here.

37 In speaking of "grounds for truth," I do not mean to imply that the justification must be explicitly semantic. One can give grounds for the truth of a proposition p relative to context of use C_{U1} and context of assessment C_A simply by asserting another proposition at C_{U2} whose truth relative to C_{U2} and C_A entails, or is evidence for, the truth of p relative to C_{U1} and C_A. (The grounds one offers can themselves be challenged, of course, as can their status as grounds.)

38 Those who accept only the weaker account of assertoric commitment in note 36, above, may modify it as follows to accommodate assessment-relative truth: one who asserts that p at C_U is obliged to withdraw this assertion in context of assessment C_A if p is shown to be false relative to C_U and C_A.

39 To simplify the exposition, I am ignoring the possibility of deferring to the word of another.

40 Keith DeRose might call this view "single scoreboard semantics run amok" (see DeRose 2004). On this view, there is a "single scoreboard" not just for all parties to a single conversation, but for *all* uses of "know" as assessed from any one perspective. It seems to me that the very same arguments DeRose uses to support his view that the various parties to a conversation share a single scoreboard can be applied transtemporally to show that the semantics for "know" must be use-invariant. If we shouldn't ignore the fact that speakers in a single conversation take themselves to be contradicting and agreeing with each other in making knowledge claims, then we shouldn't ignore the fact that speakers take present knowledge claims to contradict or agree with past ones, even ones made when different standards were in play.

References

Belnap, N. and M. Green (1994). "Indeterminism and the thin red line," *Philosophical Perspectives* 8, pp. 365–88.

Brandom, R. (1983). "Asserting," *Noûs* 17, pp. 637–50.

Brandom, R. (1994). *Making It Explicit* (Cambridge: Harvard University Press).

Churchland, P. (1979). *Scientific Realism and the Plasticity of Mind* (Cambridge: Cambridge University Press).

Cohen, S. (2001). "Contextualism defended: Comments on Richard Feldman's 'Skeptical problems, contextualist solutions'" *Philosophical Studies* 103, pp. 87–98.

DeRose, K. (2000). "Now you know it, now you don't," in *Proceedings of the Twentieth World Congress of Philosophy,* Volume V: Epistemology, Bowling Green, Ohio, pp. 91–106.

—— (2002). "Assertion, knowledge, and context," *Philosophical Review* 111, pp. 167–203.

—— (2004). "Single scoreboard semantics," *Philosophical Studies* 119, pp. 1–21.

—— (2004). "The problem with subject-sensitive invariantism," *Philosophy and Phenomenological Research* 68, 2, pp. 346–50.

Dummett, M. (1959). "Truth," *Proceedings of the Aristotelian Society* n.s. 59, pp. 141–62.

—— (1978). *Truth and Other Enigmas* (Cambridge: Harvard University Press).

Egan, A., J. Hawthorne, and B. Weatherson (2005). "Epistemic modals in context," in G. Preyer and P. Peter (eds), *Contextualism in Philosophy* (Oxford: Clarendon Press), pp. 131–70.

Evans, G. (1985). "Does tense logic rest upon a mistake?" in G. Evans, *Collected Papers* (Oxford: Oxford University Press) pp. 343–63.

Feldman, R. (2001). "Skeptical problems, contextualist solutions," *Philosophical Studies* 103, pp. 61–85.

Grice, P. (1989). *Studies in the Way of Words* (Cambridge, MA: Harvard University Press).

Hawthorne, J. (2004). *Knowledge and Lotteries* (Oxford: Oxford University Press).

Kaplan, D. (1989). "Demonstratives: An essay on the semantics, logic, metaphysics, and epistemology of demonstratives and other indexicals," in J. Almog, J. Perry, and H. Wettstein (eds), *Themes from Kaplan* (Oxford: Oxford University Press) pp. 481–566.

King, J. (2003). "Tense, modality, and semantic value," in J. Hawthorne and D. Zimmerman (eds), *Philosophical Perspectives,* 17, Language and Philosophical Linguistics (Malden, MA: Blackwell), pp. 195–245.

Kölbel, M. (2002). *Truth Without Objectivity* (London: Routledge).

Kompa, N. (2002). "The context sensitivity of knowledge ascriptions," *Grazer Philosophische Studien* 64, pp. 79–96.

Lewis, D. (1979). "Scorekeeping in a language game," *Journal of Philosophical Logic* 8, pp. 339–59.

—— (1980). "Index, context, and content," in S. Kanger and S. Öhman (eds), *Philosophy and Grammar* (Dordrecht: Reidel).

—— (1998). *Papers in Philosophical Logic* (Cambridge: Cambridge University Press).

MacFarlane, J. (2003). "Future contingents and relative truth," *Philosophical Quarterly* 53(212), pp. 321–36.

Percival, P. (1994). "Absolute truth," *Proceedings of the Aristotelian Society* 94, pp. 189–213.

Richard, M. (2004). "Contextualism and relativism," *Philosophical Studies* 119, pp. 215–42.

Rosenberg, J. F. (2002). *Thinking About Knowing* (Oxford: Clarendon Press).

Rysiew, P. (2001). "The context-sensitivity of knowledge attributions," *Noûs* 35(4), pp. 477–514.

Schaffer, J. (2004). "Skepticism, contextualism, and discrimination," *Philosophy and Phenomenological Research* 69, pp. 138–55.

Schiffer, S. (1996). "Contextualist solutions to scepticism," *Proceedings of the Aristotelian Society* 96, pp. 317–33.

Searle, J. (1969). *Speech Acts* (Cambridge: Cambridge University Press).

Searle, J. R. (1979). *Expression and Meaning* (Cambridge: Cambridge University Press).

Stalnaker, R. (1978). "Assertion," in P. Cole (ed.), *Syntax and Semantics,* Vol. 9: Pragmatics (New York: Academic Press).

Stanley, J. (2004). "On the linguistic basis for contextualism," *Philosophical Studies* 119, pp. 119–46.

PART IX

Testimony, Memory, and Perception

Introduction

In this final section, we include selections on three specific ways that knowledge might be formed or transferred – through testimony, memory, and perception.

Consider, first, trust in the testimony of others (as well as, more generally, trust that others will perform as you have been led to expect). A traditional evidentialist account of the matter will require evidence for belief to be rational. Contrary to this idea, trust seems to involve beliefs which are not accepted through evidence, yet these beliefs are both tolerated and valued. For example, if our friend is accused of a crime and claims to be innocent, we are inclined to believe that our friend is innocent without evidence and sometimes despite evidence to the contrary. Baker argues that our natural conception of rationality is inadequate to account for the phenomena of trust. Nonetheless, trust is essential and desirable in that it enables communication and friendship. But Baker resists the suggestion that we view the worth of trust as a battle between its epistemic irrationality and its moral value. Instead, she explores ways of modifying the traditional conception of rationality so that trust ends up rational. We do not need to have independent evidence that our trust will not be betrayed in order to be rational to trust.

Even if Baker is right about the rationality of trust, the situation might be different when it comes to knowledge. Elizabeth Fricker asks whether we need to have independent confirmation that a speaker is trustworthy before we can know that what the speaker says is true. *Anti-reductionists* about testimony say not. We don't need independent confirmation that a speaker is trustworthy in order to know that what the speaker says is true: there is a "presumptive right" in favor of the word of others. After all, we do get knowledge through testimony even though, it seems, we lack non-circular, independent confirmation that testimony is reliable. In fact, such non-circular, independent confirmation might seem impossible to obtain. Fricker rejects this "transcendental" argument for the anti-reductionist position by rejecting the claim that we necessarily lack non-circular, independent confirmation for the trustworthiness of speakers. While we may not be able to acquire non-circular, independent confirmation that testimony in general is reliable, this does not mean that we cannot acquire utterance-specific independent confirmation – confirmation that some speaker is trustworthy on *this* occasion with regard to *this* utterance. We can do this by independently confirming that the speaker is sincere and competent with respect to the content of the utterance. And we can do *this* either by consulting the speaker's track record of utterances (often the less practical way) or by constructing, on the basis of conversational cues and evidence available to us, a psychological theory of the speaker and using it to explain the utterance (the better way). So, we can independently confirm that speakers are trustworthy with regard to specific utterances. And this is all that is needed to undercut the transcendental argument. In place of anti-reductionism, Fricker recommends *reductionism*, according to which we do need independent confirmation that a speaker is trustworthy in order for a speaker's say-so to give us knowledge.

Tyler Burge argues that in testimony and retentive memory, the epistemic status of the acquired (retained) belief is noninferentially dependent on the epistemic status of the original belief. If I accept what you say in a normal case of testimony in which the testifier lacks defeaters, my belief is warranted only if yours is as well, and in fact the warrant my belief has is the very same as the warrant yours has. The same holds for memory. My memory belief's warrant is the warrant of the original belief. In neither case is the resultant belief inferred from the previous belief. For one thing, this is psychologically unrealistic: we are not continually making inferences when we form beliefs through testimony and retain beliefs in memory. For another, if the beliefs were inferential, then warrant could not be transferred. The hearer would have to have warrants for premises (e.g., "John told me that *p*") which are irrelevant to the warrant possessed by the speaker, and same for the rememberer (the premise might be "I seem to remember that *p*."). Indeed, Burge notes that, as Chisholm recognized, the inferential view would have the consequence that very few of the beliefs we *think* are *a priori* warranted are so (in fact, for Chisholm, no beliefs that rely on sustained reasoning can be *a priori*). Burge claims that once we appreciate that warrants can be noninferentially transmitted, we can not merely accommodate the familiar idea that complex sustained reasoning can produce *a priori* warranted beliefs but arrive at the new and surprising insight that beliefs acquired through testimony can be *a priori* warranted.

The dominant view of testimonial knowledge says that in order for a hearer H to acquire knowledge that *p* from a speaker S, S must have knowledge that *p* (or for every testimonial chain of knowledge, the first speaker S1 must have had knowledge that *p*, although the chain could include speakers who do not know *p*). In contrast, Jennifer Lackey argues that H's testimonial knowledge that *p* is independent of S or S1's knowledge that *p*; statements of particular speakers can be reliably connected with the truth, though their beliefs are not. Lackey shows how H can acquire knowledge through S's testimony, even if S fails to believe that *p* (and so cannot know *p*). In addition, since *defeaters* are not necessarily transmitted via testimony, Lackey shows how a hearer can come to know that *p* even if the first speaker believed but failed to know that *p*. Statements and beliefs can come apart. Speakers can be reliable testifiers, offering truth-tracking statements, even if their beliefs are unreliable. Testimonial knowledge actually requires that if H comes to know that *p* via S's testimony, then S's statement that *p* must be appropriately connected to the fact that *p*.

Problems of accounting for the source of justification also beset beliefs formed on the basis of memory. Michael Huemer draws our attention to what he calls the problem of memory knowledge (or memory justification). At any moment, each of us has a vast store of justified memory beliefs. What makes them justified? Huemer considers three leading theories: the inferential theory (according to which memory beliefs rely for their justification on premises about seeming memory and the reliability of memory in general), foundationalism (according to which memory beliefs are justified by quasi-perceptual states of seeming memory), and preservationism (according to which memory beliefs retain the epistemic status they had originally). Huemer notes a number of problems for each theory and proposes a sort of marriage of foundationalism and preservationism, a theory he calls the *dualist* theory. For Huemer, a belief is justified if and only if it was *both* formed properly *and* maintained properly. The dualist view, like the foundationalist theory and unlike the preservationist theory, allows us to say that, as in Russell's five-minute hypothesis, if someone popped into existence with all the beliefs you now have, that person would be justified in having (most) of those beliefs, because they would be well-formed. However, like the preservationist and unlike foundationalist, the dualist need not say that one becomes justified if one forgets one's original bad reasons for one's belief.

Seemingly less controversial than testimony or memory is perception. But how can perceptual experiences justify perceptual beliefs? For it seems to be the case that our perceptual experiences could be exactly what they are even if the objects of perception were dramatically different or didn't exist at all. John McDowell argues that this assumption – common to skeptics and certain kinds of internalists – is too quick. We need not assume that there is a "highest common factor" – something in common between states of veridical perceiving and states in which we are victims of illusion. Perhaps, when we are deceived by our senses, what we experience is a mere appearance. But it does not follow from this that when we are not deceived, what we experience is a mere appearance. Rather, when we are not deceived, we directly experience the fact that makes the experience veridical. There is, of course, a sense in which both when we are deceived and when we are not, the world appears to us the same way. But, according to McDowell, this is due to the disjunctive nature of appearance. For it to appear that X is such-and-such is either for it to be a mere appearance that X is such-and-such or for the fact that X is such-and-such to be made manifest. In this sense, whether we veridically or non-veridically experience that X is such-and-such, it will appear to us that X is such-and-such. This will be so even if there is no mere appearance that is common between the two states.

McDowell takes experiences to be intentional. Can we make sense of perceptual justification if we deny this assumption, if we take experiences to be mere sensations? Stephen Reynolds argues that we can. How could a series of sensations that are not "about" anything justify a propositional belief? Reynolds suggests that perceivers develop skills connecting certain sensations with certain propositional contents. He argues that a perceptual belief is justified if and only if there are no undermining beliefs and the belief was produced as a response to a perceptual experience via an adequate exercise of properly learned recognitional skills. Such skills are accounted for by an agent's adherence to certain implicit rules governing the behavior in question, e.g., playing a piano piece. Correctly following the implicit rules governing perceptual belief production is sufficient for meriting a favorable normative judgment about epistemic justification.

Further Reading

Adler, Jonathan, "Testimony, Trust, Knowing," *Journal of Philosophy* 91 (1994), pp. 264–75.

——, *Belief's Own Ethics* (Cambridge, MA: Massachusetts Institute of Technology Press, 2002).

Brewer, Bill, *Perception and Reason* (Oxford: Oxford University Press, 2000).

Burge, Tyler, "Interlocution, Perception, and Memory," *Philosophical Studies* 86 (1997), pp. 21–47.

Chisholm, Roderick, *Perceiving: A Philosophical Study* (Ithaca, NY: Cornell University Press, 1957).

Christensen, David, and Hilary Kornblith, "Testimony, Memory and the Limits of the A Priori." *Philosophical Studies* 86 (1997), pp. 1–20.

Coady, C. A. J., *Testimony: A Philosophical Study* (Oxford: Oxford University Press, 1992).

Dancy, Jonathan (ed.), *Perceptual Knowledge* (Oxford: Oxford University Press, 1988).

Dretske, Fred, *Knowledge and the Flow of Information* (Cambridge, MA: Massachusetts Institute of Technology Press, 1981).

Foley, Richard, *Intellectual Trust in Oneself and Others* (Cambridge: Cambridge University Press, 2001).

Ginet, Carl, *Knowledge, Perception, and Memory* (Boston, MA: D. Reidel, 1975).

Goldman, Alvin, *Knowledge in a Social World* (Oxford: Oxford University Press, 1999).

Graham, Peter, "What is Testimony?" *Philosophical Quarterly* 47 (1997), pp. 227–32.

Hardwig, John, "The Role of Trust in Knowledge," *Journal of Philosophy* 88 (1991), pp. 693–708.

Harman, Gilbert, *Change in View: Principles of Reasoning* (Cambridge, MA: Massachusetts Institute of Technology Press, 1986).

Jackson, Frank, *Perception: A Representative Theory* (Cambridge: Cambridge University Press, 1977).

Lackey, Jennifer, "The Nature of Testimony," *Pacific Philosophical Quarterly* 87 (2006), pp. 177–97.

Lackey, Jennifer and Ernest Sosa (eds.), *The Epistemology of Testimony* (Oxford: Oxford University Press, 2006).

Malcolm, Norman, *Memory and Mind* (Ithaca, NY: Cornell University Press, 1977).

McDowell, John, *Mind and World* (Cambridge, MA: Harvard University Press, 1994).

McGrath, Matthew, "Memory and Epistemic Conservatism," *Synthese* (forthcoming).

Owens, David, *Reason without Freedom: The Problem of Epistemic Normativity* (London: Routledge, 2000)

Pollock, John, *Contemporary Theories of Knowledge* (Totowa, NJ: Rowman and Littlefield, 1986).

Senor, Thomas, "The Epistemological Problems of Memory," *Stanford Encyclopedia of Philosophy* (2005).

Smith, A. D., *The Problems of Perception* (Cambridge, MA: Harvard University Press, 2002).

Tye, Michael, *Consciousness, Color, and Content* (Cambridge, MA: Massachusetts Institute of Technology Press, 2000).

Webb, Gary, "Why I Know About As Much As You: A Reply to Hardwig," *Journal of Philosophy* 90 (1993), pp. 260–70.

CHAPTER 54

Trust and Rationality

Judith Baker

I want to discuss some ways in which our natural conception of rationality is inadequate to account for the phenomena of trust. Most of the paper sets out the ways in which trust, and our assessment of that trust, do not conform to this picture of rationality. A more perplexing question is what modifications of our conception would be adequate. Here I do no more than sketch the sort of program that I think might give us an understanding of the rationality of trust.

I start with the most general statement of the problem. Belief aims at the truth – that is, we want our beliefs to be true. So a very natural and compelling picture of rationality with regard to belief would be the idea that we should only accept those beliefs which are likely to be true. Hence, what may be relevant, or, strictly speaking, reasons, for believing will be those supporting facts, items, which give evidence for the truth of what is believed.

But trust seems to involve beliefs which are not accepted on the basis of evidence and beliefs which in some cases may be highly resistant to evidence that runs counter to them. One would think, in such a case, that they would be frowned on. But instead they are tolerated and, indeed, valued. The phenomena need to be sorted if the difficulties are to be assessed. Three kinds of trust

can be distinguished. In the normal run of events, we trust people because we can't check all the bases for belief. So we accept, or rather *assume*, that what they say is true. A more exact expression is that we take some things *on trust*. If the clerk says that there is no more of the item we want in the store, the gas man reads the meters, the operator gives us a telephone number, and so on, we do not double-check. There is a great range of behaviour among people regarding what will be checked, and what is suspect, and of course differences in times and cities give *reason* to check. It is not only a matter of personality. But no one can check everything. What is to be noted is that ordinarily when I accept the reading of my meter, I don't accept it on the basis of evidence. I believe, or assume, that I am being correctly informed. It is reasonable to assume that in general, because there is no other way of getting on. There may be classes of assertions *not* to be trusted – those of clerks in supermarket chains, or those of travel brochures. But to get on we must be trusting in many classes of cases, for no matter how skeptical we may be, we cannot mistrust and check every casual piece of information. Our assumptions or beliefs in these plentiful cases where we do trust are *not*, however, resistant to counter-evidence. We can find out that the gas or electrical company is robbing us.

That is not quite the end of the story, however. For we do not like people who are altogether suspicious, who do all that is humanly possible in

Originally published in *Pacific Philosophical Quarterly* 68 (1987), pp. 1–13.

these little matters to have well-confirmed belief. Such an individual, if I am correct, will have to stop somewhere. But, though forced to take matters on trust, he is only too apt to calculate the risk he takes in doing so. The individual who always calculates risks, we find lacking in spontaneity; when this trait is combined with operative distrust of others, an individual may be viewed as morally suspect.

Let me offer a composite picture of all that seems negative in such an individual. I suggest that we don't like him because we think of him as suspicious, that is, as expecting, without evidence, that each new person he encounters will behave badly. We think of him as misanthropic, as both disliking people and enjoying his bad opinion of them. He likes security and safety to an extent we don't find praiseworthy; he raises the possibility that he is overly cautious with others because he is bad himself. So, I suggest, it is not merely a matter of convenience that we take people on trust: there is a fine web of adverse judgements ready at hand against those who cannot, or will not, do so. Nonetheless, this form of trusting others does not by itself require us to modify what we regard as rational for beliefs. Someone could resist any modification by making a special case for policies, arguing that though there are a multitude of situations in which it is reasonable to adopt and act on them, that they are not fully, or genuinely, beliefs. And taking people on trust, it would be argued, is one form of policy, of deciding to act-as-if something were true in a given class of cases, but not fully believing it.

A second kind of trust involves more than our willingness to accept people or to assume things on trust. It is exemplified in cases when we do not look for references or confirmation because "the person looks honest" or "seems very decent." This differs from my first kind of trust, which was about situations and did not directly reflect the character of the agent we are believing. In my second kind of trust, we are judging an individual on the basis of an extraordinary, that is, non-ordinary, route to the truth. This presupposes an ordinary, or evidential, route. This is why we are not going on evidence insofar as we think the salesman at the door honest because he just "looks honest". But, again, such beliefs are not, nor do we think it rational that they should be, highly resistant to counter-evidence.

At this point it may be well to note that the first two classes of trust join a much larger class of ordinary beliefs about things and the world which have the common feature that they do not directly rely on evidence. Such beliefs are all over the place. But they do not, at least at a relatively superficial level of analysis, force us to revise our picture of rationality: they exhibit, rather, evidence-substitutes, accepted ways of arriving at the truth in the absence of direct evidence. Only a third kind of trust leads us to the idea of a radical form of evidence-independence.

The third kind of trust presents the greatest difficulty for our conception of rationality, for it is a case in which we think it rational to hold beliefs in the face of counter-evidence. Let me call this special trust, or friendship trust. Suppose I trust a friend who has been accused of wrong-doing, with an impressive amount of evidence brought against her. Typically, I am faced with a novel situation, where there is no prior set of tests or testing situations that she has come through with flying colours. Suppose she is accused of selling secrets to a foreign government. It is unlikely that I have ever seen her approached by foreign agents, offered vast sums of money or other inducements to betray her government, indeed, unlikely that I have witnessed any situations offering great temptations.

If I trust her in such a situation, I do not merely stand by her, acting in ways that support her, either materially or emotionally. I believe she is innocent. I do not, however, come to believe she is innocent, despite the evidence, by weighing or balancing present evidence against her past record. First, by hypothesis, there is precious little relevant past record. Second, what others regard as evidence against her isn't considered by me as evidence at all. It is not that I close my ears to what people say, or refuse to look at, or repress, the facts. I believe that there is an explanation for the alleged evidence, for the accusation, which will clear it all up.

In advance of hearing the case, I am prepared to believe that there is such an explanation. I am biased in favor of my friend, in favor of her innocence. To put it another way, I am committed to her being innocent. Moreover, as the case grows, as evidence mounts, I do not have corresponding mounting doubts. Although there may come a time when I cease to believe in my friend, there are no limits which can be set in advance, on epistemic grounds, which would determine the point at which it is irrational to continue to trust her.

I have chosen a "favored" case, the story of a friend one trusts simpliciter. There may be friends one does not trust in certain areas, or perhaps in dealings with the other sex. In the most extreme case, one might have a friend one trusted only to be honest with oneself, to do well by oneself. But even this kind of limited trust will show the features under examination here; if I ask my friend, and she proclaims her innocence, I trust her.

I believe this to be a straightforward and natural description of trust. The strongest challenge to my claims, however, comes in the form of an equally natural defense of a friend: I know my friend is innocent because I know my friend. To trust a friend accused of wrongdoing is not irrational because we *know* our friends – know their character, what motivates them, what they are likely to do in certain situations and what, psychologically, they are capable of doing. I would not wish to deny that we know our friends. What I would like to show is that such knowledge, like the particular trusting belief discussed, does not conform to our picture of rationality. To do this I will articulate two ways in which a critic might appeal to the knowledge we have of friends in order to dispute the thesis that trusting beliefs are, by conventional standards, irrational.

First, a critic might suggest that, given that we know our friends, it is not irrational to refuse to change our minds or drop our beliefs just because there are current charges and evidence against them. For we do not think a scientist irrational to continue to accept a theory when evidence is presented that runs counter to the theory, if it has been well-tested. So, the critic might say, it is not irrational to retain belief in a friend's innocence when one knows her character.

Although both the friend and the scientist may have reason to be confident, the cases are not parallel. For, typically, a friend is not someone who has come through a set of tests. Of course I will claim, of someone I trust simpliciter, that I know her character to be one which would not allow the accusation to be true. It does not follow that such knowledge is based on observation of her behaviour in similar circumstances. It is from the little things that one comes to form an impression of character: if she wouldn't pad her expense account, she wouldn't embezzle. If, however, I am challenged regarding my beliefs, I do not think I can establish that my friend is incapable of embezzling by citing her scrupulous tax returns.

It might be suggested that we were off to a false start – that it is not appropriate to try to articulate knowledge of friends in terms parallel to a scientist's acceptance of a theory. Knowledge of a friend is not sufficiently like confidence in a theory. The idea behind the criticism is, however, obvious and true: beliefs regarding a friend are not independent of observations and experience. The rationality of trust is supported by plain facts – that we come to know what people are like, that we witness a growth of understanding and knowledge of people when we do things with them, live with them, and that part of the process of becoming friends with someone is finding out who they are, when and how much we can rely on them and trust them. Even if there are no explicit tests, the conjectures or assumptions we make about a friend's character either become entrenched or are rejected as a result of our experiences.

How, then, can trust be significantly independent of evidence? I think one can acknowledge the role of experience without denying what I claim to be distinctive about trust by using the notion of *outrunning* the evidence. The resistance of trust to counter-evidence is the prime expression of this feature. The claim that trust exhibits such evidence-resistance does not rest on the idea that we have no evidence which supports beliefs about our friend but, rather, that belief runs ahead of experience and evidence. Confidence in a friend may well grow as a result of experience, with the growth of the friendship itself. But at each stage of a friendship the confidence one has in one's friend leaps ahead of what we can think of as the evidence supporting it. It is important to note that it is belief proper and not conjecture, or hypothesis, which outruns the evidence here. Popper has made both familiar and persuasive the idea that it is the business of scientific conjectures to outrun the evidence, but not to be believed. Trusting beliefs are significantly distinguished from scientific conjectures by a second feature.

The confidence one may have in a friend does not merely outrun the evidence or experiences which may have led to its formation. Let me suggest the following model: we think of a belief-forming process as rational insofar as we adjust our belief to evidence according to some rule. Then we can say that one is *committed* to a belief if one adjusts it at a slower rate than the rule provides. This is typified in the trusting beliefs regarding one's friend. Although there may come a time when I cease to trust my friend, it will take much longer and require much more evidence for me to change my mind about her than rules for the rational formation of belief allow. My claim, then, is that whether we speak of belief in a friend's innocence of a particular act of wrongdoing or of knowledge of her character, in both cases the beliefs in question will exhibit characteristics of outrunning the evidence.

I believe in my friend's innocence, I believe that she is honest with me. I cannot set in advance the point at which it would be appropriate to doubt her. But there are limits to what would be the normal expression of belief in action. These, however, are set by conflicting moral obligations or responsibilities rather than epistemic standards. On the public level, one might well have argued at the time of the Watergate investigation that some American Congressmen failed to recognize the appropriate limits which conflicting duties set. It was not justifiable, given their responsibilities to the people and to the country at large, to act on their conviction that nothing short of "the smoking gun" would cause them to doubt the President's innocence. Many of us believed those Congressmen unreasonable and irrational. But we also believed them to be irresponsible. They had responsibilities to the public which ought to have limited the ways in which they acted on their belief or trust in the President. One explanation of their irrationality relies on distinguishing the Congressmen's trust from friendship trust: it does not correspond to the model offered by friendship, but to a kind of loyalty to the office or the officer who holds authority *qua* office holder, rather than trust in the person himself. Whatever this loyalty is, it is neither trust of a friend, nor is it reasoned belief in innocence, and so we regard it as unreasonable or irrational.

I think that on a personal level, within friendship trust, we may find a similar limit set by a person's responsibilities to others. If I trust my friend, I do not lock up *my* silver, but there may be a situation in which I exercise caution with respect to others' belongings. It is not because I am willing to risk my possessions but not yours, for I do not perceive us at risk. But I cannot take responsibility for the safety of your goods on the basis of facts you would dispute. There are certain standards for the formation of rational belief which everyone accepts; although I have claimed that there are situations in which it is rational for an individual to form beliefs which do not comply with these standards, the individual can do it for herself only. People may disagree with my claim that within the personal domain responsibilities to others may limit acting on trusting beliefs, at least when those others would perceive themselves at risk. Given that I envisage conflicting responsibilities here, I cannot even appeal to one rule which would govern all situations. But the opposition, which would find trust unlimited – that claims that insofar as a person is confident she acts on the basis of that belief – can only strengthen the case for new standards of rationality.

I have argued that trust is robustly resistant to evidence which is counter to trusting belief, and that belief in a friend's innocence comes *before* hearing reasons for and against. The formation of belief discussed in the favored example runs counter to our general picture of what it is to be rational, but we not only tolerate it, we demand it of our friends, and we think well of people in general who manifest such trust. I also want to claim, and this may be more open to disagreement, that it is *rational* of me to trust my friend. I do not think the example sketched presents a conflict between morality and rationality, between *decent* belief as opposed to *rational* belief. My aim is to find ways of understanding what makes the beliefs of the trusting individual rational. But there are alternative responses to the puzzles I have presented, and I shall first attempt to say what I find inadequate about them.

Someone might try to distinguish trust from genuine or full belief. Trust, on such a view, would be a watered-down variant of belief, something more like pretence or acting-as-if something were true. But this is to view trust as a non-serious form of belief. Whereas what one demands from one's friend is belief, not pretence, that one is innocent. And what some outsiders find amazing is just the fact that serious belief continues in the face of rising evidence against it. As strategy, then, this response amounts to an arbitrary denial of the phenomena which raise the problem in the first place.

Could one recognize the phenomena, but deny that there is a serious problem?

> We would like to think our trust in friends rational if challenged to defend our beliefs as either rational or not. But we have no way to establish this, to show by epistemic standards that trust really is respectable. This needn't, however, change our trust in friends and intimates. We shall live the same, we shall only withdraw our claims to objectivity or rationality for those beliefs.

This looks, at least at first sight, to be a viable alternative. But is it? Suppose we take away the claim to rationality. This would be to view as one the beliefs we have about friends or intimates, and what I want to call pre-rational beliefs, the phenomena we observe in pet animals or young children, of trust in the adults that care for them. But, most important, although this view has the pleasant matter-of-fact tone of common sense, it cannot be made part of one's life. For we cannot stop with an observer's external description of trust. We are participants and agents as well as observers. And it does not seem possible to maintain two attitudes: the observer's belief that the trust in friends is no more than an attitude which is useful and the participant's conviction that her friend is really trustworthy. But to adopt only the epistemically respectable attitude of the observer as one's own in the midst of practical life would be to dissolve one's trust.

What may be a common sense position can be replaced, however, by a philosopher's skepticism. And the skeptic has a response to my claim that we cannot maintain the two attitudes. He recognizes that the attitudes in question drive one another off; as a participant in life he cannot trust his friend but also regard that trust as no more than a useful attitude. Nor can he, in the detachment of his study, thinking of trust as a less than reputable epistemic state, sustain conviction in his friend's trustworthiness despite the evidence. What he maintains, however, is that he needn't strive for consistency. It is just the way humans are, that they trust their friends and are "really"

convinced of their trustworthiness, in ordinary situations, in the thick of things. But a human being, or at least the skeptic, is also able to detach himself from life, to remove himself to his study and applying standards of "pure" rationality find the attitudes embodied in his daily behaviour failing with respect to rationality. If he were to try to apply those standards when he leaves the study, trust would be dissolved, or his skepticism would founder. But the skeptic can deny that any such attempt is rationally required: were we purely rational creatures, he could maintain, it would be appropriate, indeed required, always to act in accord with the principle accepted in the cool hour. But as composite creatures, true belief is only one of a variety of needs. Hence, he may believe it is not necessary in certain situations to aim for rationality.

I do not believe one can convict such a skeptic of a logical fault. His position is, nonetheless, one we may find uncomfortable. Such a life displays an alarming lack of integration: for we are to imagine him fully trusting his friend but – at moments of detachment – prying off such belief. If a competing account of rationality can be made out, it would, then, be preferable.

One might attempt, however, to cut the knot and do without trust. Although we now welcome the capacity to trust others, and judge it desirable, it might be claimed that we should take the more respectable line of dispensing with trust and therefore discouraging any disposition to trust. What I will maintain, in response, is that we cannot do without trust, that we both need it for morality and for interpersonal relationships.

So far, I have merely claimed that we cannot do without trust. I cannot do more than to suggest here some very general lines on which one might argue for such a thesis. There are three different ways in which I imagine morality might be undermined. First, as many writers have noted, many of our moral judgements about what it is right to do depend upon what may be expected of others. If I do not think anyone else will participate, I will not have the practical attitudes expressed by such thoughts as "I must do my part", or "pull my oar". If no one may be expected to keep to the rules of a game or an activity, "fair play" does not take hold. The production of certain goods depends upon what others do, and what I think they may do. A minimum of trust in others thus seems indispensable in these areas for moral principles to take hold. A quite different line might be thought of as Kantian. Respect is said to be essential to morality. But it would seem that, again, some minimum of trust in others, in their good will or in their own desire for recognition or respect, is required for there to be respect.

It might be replied that the trust which morality can be seen to require is not of a sort which our picture of rationality would find it hard to accommodate. For what is needed is not a serious belief or conviction, but acting as if others were going to do their share, acting as if, or assuming that, others have good will and a similar serious desire for respect. This we can accommodate as a reasonable procedure, and one which is obviously alterable if not successful.

I think that substitutes for belief will not do the job, but I have no adequate argument that full belief is required by morality. It may be suggested that, even if I did, the case would not yet be made that the trust required by morality presents problems for the standard picture of rationality. I claimed that only a third kind of trust, friendship trust, presented a radical challenge to our standard conception of rationality, for only beliefs of this sort were, approvably, resistant to evidence. But morality does not require that our trust in people be evidence-resistant.

The two kinds of trust discussed earlier were, first, acting or taking something *on trust*, and what I called the impression or intuitive judgement that someone was trustworthy. The first class are best understood as policies, primarily ways of acting, and therefore not full-fledged belief. On my hypothesis, the trust required by morality must be more than acting-as-if.

The required beliefs might, however, be thought similar to the second kind of trust. I acknowledged that our impressions about people joined a very large class of beliefs about the world which exhibit accepted ways of arriving at the truth in the absence of direct evidence. Members of this second class may, thus, be called evidence-substitutes. I stressed that one's impression of the individual as honest is not thought of as evidence, because it is an extraordinary route to the truth and one which, as rational people, we desire to supplant with evidence if possible. But it is clear that it is the object itself, something in the presentation of the individual, which one thinks of as justifying one's judgement that he is honest. Now, I think that what Kantian morality, for example, requires is that, independent of such presentation, we respect the individual we meet. Indeed, it is arguable that it is just because of the biases we have that the requirement would have us ignore such impressions. So there is a more radical separation of the belief from *experience* than in cases which might be considered as evidence-substitutes. Although morality does not demand that our trust in people be evidence-resistant, the independence from experience as well as evidence makes them problematic. Our picture of the rational formation of belief, even enlarged by evidence-substitutes, does not seem to have room for them.

Since I am not sure how to directly counter the proposal that substitutes for belief will do the job, I take a third approach. Both the statements of the desirability of trust for morality and the response have simply assumed the existence of rational beings capable, given certain conditions, of moral judgements and acts. But many philosophers have insisted that the possibility of there being moral agents depends upon the kind of development of children in which certain trusting relationships are indispensable, in particular, the trust children have first in their parents, and next in their peers. It is clear that trust does not take the form of pretence in these relationships. What is now to be emphasized is that we cannot expect people themselves incapable of trusting others to engender trust on the part of their children, either toward themselves or other children. Nor can we expect to develop individuals capable of trust in their formative years only. If such philosophical speculation is correct, then even if the practice of morality itself did not demand the exhibition of trusting others, the institution of morality would nonetheless require it for creatures such as ourselves in a culture such as ours.

I have claimed that we want our friends to stand by us, indeed to trust us. But this is a misleading form of expression. For to think of someone as a friend is to expect her to have one's interest at heart, to act on one's behalf, to take one's part, and to take one at one's word. To be a friend is, reciprocally, to be trustworthy oneself. If one thinks one cannot, as a reasonable or rational person, form such expectations, and manages to behave accordingly, it is hard to believe that intimacy of friendships could be preserved.

If I am correct, the advantages of trusting others, of the capacity to trust others, are apparent. For they will include the advantages of morality and friendships. If trusting others were an activity in which we could chose to engage, we would have, then, a way to understand our choice as rational. One could imagine a version of Pascal's wager: despite our inability to establish the likelihood of our friend's decency, the belief itself is an outcome which has enormous value. But in most cases we do not decide to trust others, certainly in the example I have described, one does not decide to believe one's friend innocent of wrongdoing. Indeed, to suppose we do regularly make such decisions would saddle us with the view that beliefs are subject to our control in an objectionable way.

Despite the announced difficulties, it seems promising to me to look to the standards of rationality which apply to decisions in order to understand the rationality of trust. The success of such a program would seem to me to depend upon the following ideas. First, we should take seriously the natural forms of description which emerge in the story of trust. I said I was prepared to find an explanation for the apparent evidence against my friend, that I was committed to her innocence. We should look at trust as a kind of commitment, a state of conviction which is also an inclination of will. This invites us to be skeptical about the classification of an item as either a belief or a matter of will. Second, we should hope, in understanding commitments, to be able to give a plausible and unobjectionable account of the way in which trust is subject to our control. Finally, we should insist that the rationality of trust is genuine rationality; it is not simply the propriety of pursuing means to ends we accept. To establish such an idea will require a separate program, which I only mention. We must look at the nature of moral facts. Just as trust is part of friendship, it may be that trust is both causally and logically a condition of there being truths of the sort we call moral. I will put to one side this last, most speculative idea. I will take the remaining space to discuss the first two points. I would like to make some case for considering trust in the nature of a commitment.

First, if it is a commitment, it is usually an implicit, rather than an explicit one. One makes friends with someone but realizes only when the situation prompts reflection that one has come to count on her. There is typically no moment of choice, no act of undertaking to trust or to count on another (although such things happen). Now, how would one argue that there is an implicit commitment in a friendship? I suggest that, in general, one may attribute to an agent an implicit commitment if that is required in order to make sense of his activity, to show that it has a point, or is rational. Take the example of Grice's theory of meaning. It does not look plausible to assume that the speaker is aware of or could intend the nested assumptions required for meaning p. But (as Grice himself has suggested) he might be implicitly committed to them insofar as the only way to attribute rationality to his activity would be to make the assumption that he had those intentions. I do not strictly intend to believe my friend innocent, should she be accused. I do not intend to take her word. It might, however, be suggested that we need to assume that I have such intentions, as least implicitly, in order to understand the ways in which I make myself vulnerable to my friend, as well as understand my behaviour should accusations arise.

An example that seems to be helpful in understanding trust as a form of commitment to friends comes from our own profession. As a teacher, I do not decide, in typical cases, that my students are teachable. But if I didn't make such an assumption, I couldn't teach, and it is quite likely that not only I couldn't take my profession seriously, but also students would not get taught. Here, too, I am inclined to say that we should attribute to me, as teacher, an implicit commitment to my students, to the idea that they can be taught. Now, what is interesting is that we can speak of a payoff in such cases; I shall communicate, I will have and be a friend, I will teach. But the payoff is not something independent of the activity in which I engage. The implicit commitment, or assumed intention, constitutes in some way what it is to conduct or participate in the activity in question.

If we think of trust as one kind of implicit commitment, must we think the beliefs of the trusting individual are voluntary, under her control in some objectionable way? As I have just noted, there are typically no datable events, whether of deciding, accepting, or coming to believe in the trustworthiness of a friend. Implicit commitments seem to be buried in the acts or activities they to some extent constitute. But there are many and varied acts which, for example, together comprise making a friend. These can be thought of as voluntary. If I am right, they also involve the cognitive attitudes in question. Is this formation of belief, then, objectionable?

First, I would want to distinguish between something being under one's control at the drop of a hat and only being under one's control after a period of training, or through some process. One may think it is within one's control to become a nicer person, but one would be suspicious of someone who decided to be a nicer person and could bring it about on the spot. Second, even if one could become nicer in a slow way, one couldn't become nicer in just any way or for just any reasons. It may be that with regard to belief, as with character change, we would not object if the change were slow, as a result of some process, and for the right reasons.

This format, at least, would be satisfied by the interchanges and growth of a friendship. The commitment to the friend or to the friend's decency would not be produced on the spot. But it may be that the requirements for the formation of belief are still stiffer than those for change of character just mentioned. One has no objection to someone doing what she can to alter her prejudices. It may be important that prejudices are thought of as obstacles that stand in the way of truth. Our objection to thinking belief is voluntary arises from the demand that belief should arise from the facts, the truth, the way the world is rather than how we would like it to be. So it is all right if we can remove obstacles to taking in the truth, but we should not like it to be the case that we could induce belief at will. Truth would not be served.

This distinction has a ready home in the examples discussed. For I think it part of what is offered as our commendation of friendship that on becoming friends one removes the obstacles to openness, to honesty, to the direct display of feelings, attitudes, and concerns. Moreover, if this is correct, then not only would we counter what some have found objectionable in thinking of belief as in some way voluntary, but we would have the beginning of a reply to the worry that one can account for the rationality of trust only by appealing to standards of an inferior brand of rationality. For it might be charged that, in the area of belief, end-directed rationality is second-rate. The standard form of rationality for action is that our means be adequate to our ends, but only truth-directed rationality is adequate in the area of belief. But if a result of becoming someone's friend, of one's trust, is that barriers to honesty are removed and the other person is open with us, then trust in their veracity will be merited and end-directed rationality will not be opposed to truth-directed rationality.

A more immediate source of skepticism, however, is that, barriers removed, what one sees in the other party may not be someone who is very decent or trustworthy. But of course there is trust and there is trust. Isn't it possible to trust a friend in this relative way that I think she will do well by *me*, be honest with me? I do not trust her simpliciter, without qualification. I may even think that in some areas she is not so honourable, or that with other people she is not honest. And of course I may make mistakes, trust someone and be wrong. I think I am removing those obstacles to being open and honest, but that is not what happens. I think we are friends, but we are not. These all too familiar problems should not make us deny that trust is what enables people to be friends, to be open with one another, and that it thus removes the barriers between people.

CHAPTER 55

Against Gullibility

Elizabeth Fricker

1.

One main school in the Indian classical tradition of philosophy insists that testimony – 'learning from words' – is a source or type of knowledge *sui generis*, one which cannot be reduced to any other type – not to perception, memory, or inference nor, we may add, to combinations of these. Such an irreducibility thesis could take diverse specific forms. One form it may take is as the thesis that a hearer has a presumptive epistemic right to trust an arbitrary speaker. We may essay an initial formulation of this thesis thus:

> *PR thesis*: On any occasion of testimony, the hearer has the epistemic right to assume, without evidence, that the speaker is trustworthy, i.e. that what she says will be true, unless there are special circumstances which defeat this presumption. (Thus she has the epistemic right to believe the speaker's assertion, unless such defeating conditions obtain.)

The claim that there is such a special presumptive right (PR) to trust associated with testimony constitutes a kind of irreducibility thesis, since the hearer's right to believe what she is told, on this view, stems from a special normative epistemic

Originally published in B. K. Matilal and A. Chakrabarti (eds), *Knowing from Words* (Dordrecht: Kluwer Academic Publishers, 1994), pp. 125–61.

principle pertaining to testimony, and is not a piece of common-or-garden inductively based empirical inference.

Testimony's alleged status as a special source of knowledge is underlined if this PR thesis is conjoined with a negative claim, which we may formulate initially thus:

> *NC*: It is not, generally speaking, possible for a hearer to obtain independent confirmation that a given speaker is trustworthy – that what she says will be true.

If this Negative Claim is true, then knowledge can regularly be gained through testimony only if there is no need for independent confirmation of the trustworthiness of speakers; that is, if the PR thesis holds. So the existence of this special normative epistemic principle is then essential to the gaining of knowledge through testimony. This pair of claims together is one apt explication of the irreducibility thesis of the Nyaya school of Indian philosophy.[1]

In this paper I shall give one half of a refutation of the PR thesis, by arguing against the Negative Claim, which features as a premise in one central argument for it. My discussion also shows the prima facie case against a PR. A fuller treatment would also consider, and reject, various positive arguments for a PR which may be made, which appeal to the essential nature of language, and of understanding, arguing that these imply that a general disposition to trust is essential to language, and thence to its epistemic legitimacy. Here I can only record my view that no such argument succeeds.

The Negative Claim that there can, generally speaking, be no non-circular confirmation that a given speaker is trustworthy, is false. And any fully competent participant in the social institution of a natural language simply knows too much about the characteristic role of the speaker, and the possible gaps which may open up between a speaker's making an assertion, and what she asserts being so, to want to form beliefs in accordance with the policy a PR allows. The PR thesis is an epistemic charter for the gullible and undiscriminating. This paper argues against gullibility.

2.

To say that testimony is a special source, or yields a special kind, of knowledge, could mean many things. I shall not here take it to mean that testimony constitutes an exception to an otherwise fully general, over-arching conception of knowledge. I take it that its showing knowledge to be, at some level of description, one kind of thing, albeit acquired in different ways, is an adequacy condition on an account of the concept. Such an overarching conception might be causalist or reliabilist. But I favour a justificationist conception, on which a subject's being able to defend her belief appropriately is a necessary condition for it to be knowledge.[2] The claim that testimony is an irreducible source of knowledge will not then emerge as a counter-example to the thesis that knowledge requires appropriate justification, but as a claim about what kind of justification is required for a testimony belief.[3]

The PR thesis is such a claim. It is a normative epistemic principle, amounting to the thesis that a hearer has the epistemic right to believe what she observes an arbitrary speaker to assert, just on the ground that it has been asserted: she need not attempt any assessment of the likelihood that this speaker's assertions about their subject matter will be true, nor modify her disposition to believe according to such an assessment. A corollary of the PR thesis is thus that a hearer gives a fully adequate justification of her belief just by citing the fact that "Someone told me so". This simple defence does not need supplementation with evidence for the trustworthiness of her informant. Nor, on this view, does an ordinary hearer need to supplement the simple defence by invoking the PR thesis itself. That thesis is formulated by the philosopher, as a theoretical registering of the fact that the simple defence is all that is needed.

The PR thesis is not to be confused with a descriptive premise that "speakers mainly tell the truth." The view that belief in what is asserted is justified by reference to such a descriptive premiss, cited as part of the first-level justification of the belief, is a quite different view, one which would constitute a reduction of knowledge from testimony to an ordinary case of inductively based inferential knowledge. The alleged descriptive premiss (whether claimed to be empirically confirmed fact, or a priori conceptual truth about language) might be invoked in an attempted philosophical argument for the PR thesis. But this is entirely different from its featuring among the premises which an ordinary hearer must know and be able to cite, to justify her belief.

Our target is the PR thesis. Arguments for it fall into two kinds: the positive arguments from the essential nature of language already mentioned, and a negative argument. This last is a transcendental argument which runs thus:

(1) Knowledge can be and frequently is gained by means of testimony;

(2) [NC] It is not, generally speaking, possible for a hearer to obtain independent confirmation that a given speaker is trustworthy; therefore

(3) There is knowledge gained by testimony only if there is a presumptive right on the part of any hearer to trust an arbitrary speaker; therefore

(4) There is such a presumptive right to trust.[4]

One might reject this argument by rejecting its initial premise. This is not my strategy. I agree with the proponent of the argument that it is a constraint on any epistemology of testimony, that it preserve our commonsense view that knowledge can be gained through testimony. This paper is devoted to stopping the transcendental argument by showing its second premise, the Negative Claim, to be false.

3.

The epistemological "problem of justifying belief through testimony" is the problem of showing how it can be the case that a hearer on a particular occasion has the epistemic right to believe what she is told – to believe a particular speaker's assertion. If an account showing that and how this is possible is given, then the epistemological problem of testimony has been solved.

The solution can take either of two routes. It may be shown that the required step – from "S asserted that P"[5] to "P" – can be made as a piece of inference involving only familiar deductive and inductive principles, applied to empirically established premises. Alternatively, it may be argued that the step is legitimised as the exercise of a special presumptive epistemic right to trust, not dependent on evidence.

The Negative Claim, when appropriately glossed, is equivalent to the thesis that the first, *reductionist*, route to justifying testimony is closed. The gloss in question is to fix the notion of a speaker's "trustworthiness" programmatically, as precisely that property of a speaker which would, if empirically established, allow the inference (using only standard principles) to the truth of what she has asserted. As we saw above, the *anti-reductionist* about testimony argues from the alleged closedness of the first route, to the conclusion that the second route *must* be open: to the existence of a special presumptive epistemic right to trust.

It is important to be clear that the only genuine epistemological problem is the one stated above. There is no "problem of justifying belief through testimony" over and above the task of showing that particular instances of testimony can be such as to be justifiedly believed.[6] The anti-reductionist's case, I shall show, gains most of its plausibility from confusion over just what the problem to be solved is.

Before we can consider whether the "trustworthiness" of particular speakers can be non-circularly confirmed, and so whether the reductive route to justifying testimony is open, we need to determine just what this property is best taken to be. The first requirement on an explication of this notion is that it serve the purpose in hand: it must be a property of the speaker S knowledge of which suffices, for a hearer H on an occasion O, to bridge the logical and epistemic gap between "S asserted that P", and "P".[7] That is to say, if H knows that S asserted that P on O, and she also knows that S is "trustworthy" on O, then she has a basis justifiedly to believe that P. Equally (subject to a desideratum explained below), "trustworthiness" should be no stronger than whatever property of S it takes to bridge this gap, on particular occasions. If H can know that S possesses this weakest gap-bridging property on an occasion O, this is enough to justify her in believing that S asserts on O; thus it is only this weakest gap-bridging property which must admit of non-circular confirmation, to provide a reductive solution to the problem of justifying testimony, as we have conceived it. We may also hope that our explication will answer to the intuitive notion of "trustworthiness" of a speaker. It should do so, since the intuitive notion has to it precisely this flavour of "that which warrants belief in the speaker's testimony on an occasion".

Precisely what trustworthiness, thus programmatically identified, is best taken to be, is spelled out in §7. But we may note here a second theoretical desideratum on our explication.

We may aspire to give a systematic general account of how knowledge (justified true belief) is gained through testimony; or more strictly: of how a subject's belief may be justified in virtue of its support from testimony. And this account may be conceived as having the following form: A specification of a set $\mathcal{T}$ of sentence-schemata which *characterise* cases of knowledge through testimony in the sense: A hearer H has an adequate basis for a true belief of hers to count as justified, in virtue of its support from a certain speaker's testimony, just when she has knowledge whose content is given by instances, appropriate to the content of her belief, and her situation, of each member of the set $\mathcal{T}$.[8]

Clearly, a first component of $\mathcal{T}$ will be:

T_1: "S asserted that P on O".

That T_1 is a necessary component of the set $\mathcal{T}$ (whose members represent a jointly sufficient condition for justified belief) is the hallmark of $\mathcal{T}$'s representing what it is for a subject's belief to be justified by, inter alia, evidence from testimony.

And surely it is the notion of trustworthiness, explicated in accordance with the constraints suggested above, that will furnish the second premise of the desired characteristic set $\mathcal{T}$? This is indeed so, if we gloss what it is for trustworthiness to "bridge the gap" between T_1 and "P" appropriately. But we need to be careful about just what this amounts to.

An account which renders perspicuous what is going on in the acquisition of knowledge through testimony must separate out, in H's total evidence for "P", two different strands: The independent evidence for "P" which H already has; and the evidence for "P" which H gets, given what she knows about S, from the fact that S has asserted it. Effecting this separation is essential, if we are to be able to model what goes on in a "Humean collision" – that is, a situation where the prima facie evidence for "P" from a trustworthy speaker's testimony clashes with strong evidence from other sources against "P".[9] Now specifying a truly characteristic set $\mathcal{T}$ will indeed achieve this separation. But specifying one is not so easy, because for $\mathcal{T}$ = (T_1, T_2) to be characteristic, it is not sufficient, although we may take it as necessary, that the T_1 we choose be such that T_1 and T_2 together entail "P".[10]

We want our account to separate the two strands in H's evidence for "P". And this implies a further desideratum on $\mathcal{T}$: its elements should be *epistemically independent of* "P", a notion I define thus: No element T of $\mathcal{T}$ must be such that H can know T to be true in virtue of knowing that P and knowing true the other elements of $\mathcal{T}$. This means that "P"-plus-the-rest-of-$\mathcal{T}$ must not together entail T, nor constitute strong evidence for it.

If $\mathcal{T}$ contains a T which is not epistemically independent of "P", then a situation is possible in which H knows that P, and knows that which is specified by all the elements of $\mathcal{T}$, which is not a situation in which she has knowledge that P through S's testimony; rather, it is one in which the direction of epistemic dependence is the reverse: not: H knows that P, in virtue of knowing all the elements of $\mathcal{T}$, but: H knows T in virtue of independently knowing that P, and knowing the rest of $\mathcal{T}$. Such a $\mathcal{T}$ fails to *characterise* cases of knowledge through testimony.

This desideratum that the elements of $\mathcal{T}$ all be epistemically independent of P further constrains the choice of T_2.[11] It rules out choosing the material conditional "If S asserts that P on O, then P". This looks like the right choice if we consider only our first requirement, for it is the weakest premise which one can add to "S asserted that P on O", to get a pair which together entail "P". But it is ruled out by our second desideratum, because it is itself entailed by "P", and so H is in a position to know it whenever she knows that P.[12] If she also knows that S has asserted that P, then she knows the set $\mathcal{T}$, on this choice of its elements. But she may have no grounds whatsoever for thinking that the material conditional holds of S, other than her knowledge that "P" is true. This is not a situation in which she has a basis to know that P *on the strength of S's testimony*. On the contrary, it is one exhibiting the reverse epistemic direction. Of course, a situation is *also* possible in which H knows that the material conditional holds of S *not* through knowing that P, but in virtue of knowing something genuinely about S, the intuitive property of "trustworthiness". In such a case, she does have knowledge which is based on S's testimony. The trouble with choosing the material conditional as T_2, is that the mere fact that S knows the resulting $\mathcal{T}$ does not reveal which of these situations obtains.

The same is true of "S asserted truly that P": it too fails the test of epistemic independence of "P". The epistemic direction of knowledge through testimony obtains, when H knows that "S asserted truly that P" in virtue of knowing that S asserted that P, and knowing something genuinely *about* S – namely, that S is "trustworthy". Here, H has knowledge that P in virtue of S's testimony to it. The reverse epistemic direction obtains, when she knows that S's assertion that P was true only because she already knows that P. Here S's testimony adds no further support to "P" for H. In requiring that the elements of $\mathcal{T}$ be epistemically independent of "P", our idea is precisely to find a $\mathcal{T}$ such that its identity is in itself enough to ensure that the direction of epistemic dependence is always the first, and not the second – i.e. that $\mathcal{T}$ is a characteristic set.

("S asserted truly that P" is not a suitable choice for T_2 for other reasons too: it entails "P" by itself, while we want a premise which does so only together with T_1; and in fact, predicating truth of *S*'s assertion is an inessential intermediate step, which we can skip, in identifying *H*'s shortest inferential route from "*S* asserted that *P*" to "*P*" – cf. the proposal eventually adopted below).

In describing the direction of epistemic dependence that we want to isolate, I have just employed as a primitive the intuitive notion of *S*'s "trustworthiness" which we are supposed to be explicating. But the notion we are groping towards is not doomed to remain an indispensable primitive. We can draw a useful moral from what is wrong with the material conditional. The trouble, in the first instance, is that it is not epistemically independent of "*P*". But this is a symptom of the fact that any instance of the predicate-schema "If _ asserts that *P* on *O*, then *P*", while it is grammatically predicable of *S*, does not represent a genuine property of *S*. This last is an intuitive notion we need not attempt to define here; we need only note that a genuine property of *S*, unlike the material conditional, will not be something which holds of *S* in a world, merely in virtue of the fact that "*P*" is true in that world. A hallmark of a genuine property of *S*, in short, is that (special cases apart) it will be epistemically independent of "*P*". To effect the desired separation of the two strands in *H*'s evidence for "*P*", we must find, as our explication of "trustworthiness", such a genuine property of *S*, one such that whether *S* possesses the property in a world is a matter of what *S* herself is like. Special cases apart, when "trustworthiness" is so explicated, situations in which *H* knows that *P*, and knows that *S* asserted that *P*, and that *S* is trustworthy, will be precisely those in which, intuitively, we would judge that *H* has support for "*P*" from *S*'s testimony; and, flukes apart, *H*'s evidence confirming *S*'s trustworthiness will be disjoint from her evidence confirming "*P*".

To find such a notion: which just suffices, together with "*S* asserted that *P* on *O*", to entail "*P*"; which constitutes a genuine property of *S*, hence, flukes and special cases apart, is epistemically independent of "*P*"; and which constitutes an explication of the intuitive notion of *S*'s being trustworthy on an occasion of testimony, is our aspiration. A first approximation is the property of *S* specified by the subjunctive conditional:

Trus1: "If *S* were to assert that *P* on *O*, then it would be the case that *P*."

This bridges the gap and is, special subject matters apart, epistemically independent of "*P*".[13] Knowing it to hold of *S* will, generally speaking, require having knowledge about *S* herself – her character, circumstances, etc. In fact, as we shall see in §7, the property of *S* specified by this subjunctive conditional is slightly stronger than the choice for T_2 which best fulfils our requirements. We will see there also that the best explication of *S*'s trustworthiness makes it relative not just to an occasion and an assertion-content, but to a particular utterance *U* by *S*. I shall adopt this relativisation from now on, although it is only in our final explication that it is not idle. It is in any case apt, since it is only with respect to her actual utterance that *H* *needs* to know that *S* is trustworthy.

4.

Our final explication of "trustworthiness", and detailed account of how it can be empirically confirmed by a hearer, occupies §§7, 8. But we have enough, armed with the provisional suggestion Trus1, to make some initial points regarding our central concern: the question whether the trustworthiness of a speaker can sometimes be empirically confirmed, so that the reductionist route from "*S* asserted that *P*" to "*P*" is open. The reductionist must make good the following claim (of which, accordingly, the anti-reductionist's Negative Claim is to be construed as the denial):

> *Local Reductionist Claim:* It can be the case that,[14] on a particular occasion *O* when a speaker *S* makes an utterance *U* and in doing so asserts that *P* to a hearer *H*, *H* has, or can gain, independent evidence sufficient to warrant her in taking *S* to be trustworthy with respect to *U*.

(Notice that to appeal to one's independent knowledge of the truth of what is asserted by a speaker's utterance, as evidence for her trustworthiness with respect to it, is not circular; but neither is it a case of possible knowledge through testimony. As we saw above, for just this reason our preferred explication of *S*'s trustworthiness with respect to *U* will not be such that merely knowing the truth of what is asserted by means of *U* is sufficient to establish it. Nonetheless, many instances of independent confirmation of the truth of what a certain speaker asserts provide inductive grounds to attribute a more general trustworthiness to her, as she builds up a track record of independently confirmed accuracy – see below.)

The reduction here claimed is only "local". That is to say, the claim is only that there can be occasions when a hearer has evidence that the *particular* speaker in question is to be trusted with respect to her *current* utterance, without assuming this very fact. I shall call the question whether this local reductionist claim is true the "local question" about testimony. The conception of the epistemological problem of justifying testimony adopted in §3 implies that a local reduction is all we need aspire to, or hope for. A "reductionist" account of knowledge through testimony, in the context of this approach, means such a local reduction of each instance of knowledge through testimony to broader categories of knowledge, and patterns of inference.

Thus on our conception of the problem, justifying testimony by the reductionist route does not, at least in the first instance, require showing that the blanket generalisation, "Testimony is generally reliable", (or, more simply, "Most assertions are true") can be non-circularly empirically established. Such globally independent confirmation of the veracity of testimony would require that a hearer have evidence that *most of what she has ever learned through testimony is true*, where this evidence does not in any way rest on knowledge acquired by her through testimony. The fact that such a *global reduction* is not required for it, is crucial to the local reductionist position I argue for in this paper. For, as I readily agree with the anti-reductionist, there are general reasons, stemming from the essential role of simply-trusted testimony in the causal process by which an infant develops into the possessor of a shared language and conception of the world, why the prospects for a global reduction seem hopeless. So *this* negative claim is correct; but beside the present point. Notice therefore how the plausibility of the transcendental argument evaporates, once we identify just what the relevant Negative Claim is. For then we see how modest are the possibilities of non-circular confirmation which it denies, but which are all that is required, for knowledge through testimony to be possible in the absence of a presumptive right to trust.

True, the local reductionist question would transform itself into the global one, if it were the case that the only way of showing that a given speaker was trustworthy with respect to an utterance, was via appeal to the blanket generalisation. But, I suggest, this is not so. The blanket generalisation is actually neither sufficient nor necessary evidence to justify belief, on a particular occasion, that *this* speaker is trustworthy with respect to *this* utterance of hers, which is what it takes to justify belief in what she has thereby asserted.[15] Even if the generalisation were true, there could be circumstances surrounding particular utterances which rendered the speaker's trustworthiness with respect to them doubtful in spite of it. And typically the grounds, when there are such, for expecting a speaker to be trustworthy with respect to a particular utterance of hers, relate to the circumstances and character of the speaker, and the nature of her subject matter; they do not concern the generality of assertoric utterances at all.

More prima facie plausible is the claim that the only ground a hearer could ever have for believing a speaker to be trustworthy with respect to a particular utterance, would be knowledge on her part that that particular speaker is *generally* trustworthy, at least about that kind of thing. Certainly we very often do, quite reasonably, rely on, or distrust, particular individual's testimony on precisely such grounds. But such generalisations about a particular speaker very often *can* be established non-circularly (which amounts to: without reliance on any testimony from that speaker). One means (though not the only, nor the central one, as we shall see in §8) is the approved Humean fashion, induction from observed constant conjunction – we trust one person's report, because she has built up a track record of accuracy; we distrust another because she has accumulated the opposite. And anyway, knowledge of a speaker's general trustworthiness is not the only possible ground for believing her trustworthy with respect to a particular utterance, nor is it always sufficient: someone may be notoriously inaccurate about many things, but one can still reasonably expect her to be right about such elementary matters as what she had for breakfast, or whether she has a headache, or whether a familiar object is on a table in front of her. Conversely, certain circumstances and subject matters provide grounds to expect a generally trustworthy person to be less than reliable – a matter in which she is emotionally involved; something notoriously tricky; when she has been in deceptive or inadequately informing circumstances.

(Note, however, that the prima facie incredibility of what a speaker asserts by an utterance is *not* best treated as evidence against her trustworthiness with respect to it. As explained earlier, we need to separate the evidence for "*P*" stemming from the fact that it has been asserted by a trustworthy speaker, from other evidence for or against "*P*". Where these conflict, there will ensure a Humean battle between them in the belief-updating processes of a rational hearer. To represent this battle most perspicuously, it is the *ex ante* estimate of the trustworthiness of a speaker that we should take; not one revised downwards in the light of her prima facie incredible utterance.)

Anti-reductionism about testimony looks plausible if reductionism is so construed as to involve commitment to the claim that the blanket generalisation can be non-circularly established.[16] But my "local" reductionist can happily grant that this is impossible. There is no need to show that the blanket generalisation can be non-circularly established, in order to show that a hearer can earn herself the right to trust a speaker on an occasion, without needing the gift of a PR; thereby providing a reductionist solution to the only epistemological problem of testimony which needs to be solved, viz. the local problem.

There is no space in the present paper to consider the reasons why the project of non-circularly confirming the global generalisation is hopeless, nor to defend my view that this does not undermine the rationale for insisting on justification severally for beliefs acquired through testimony. So I shall simply state my views. My view of the global "problem" about testimony is that it is not a problem. The project of trying simultaneously to justify all of our beliefs which rest in any way on testimony (or equally, to justify a single testimony-belief, but without appealing to any beliefs based on testimony) is not one that is properly embarked on, and we certainly do not need to seek to found these beliefs as a totality in something else. The desire to show that the blanket generalisation can be non-circularly established is an instance of the foundationalist

yearning to provide credentials for our system of beliefs from outside that system, or from a privileged subset of it. In this instance this task would be to hive off the part of our belief-system which rests, inter alia, on testimony, and show that it can be "founded" in the remainder which is not. My insistence that the local question is the only legitimate question about testimony is of a piece with a more general coherentist approach in epistemology. Insofar as the anti-reductionist about testimony is expressing an adherence to coherentism, in opposition to foundationalism, I am with her. But this issue of global reductionism, or foundationalism about testimony, comes apart from the issue I am concerned to address. My issue is the local reductionist question: whether, *within* a subject's coherent system of beliefs and inferential practices (in the gradual dawning of light over which testimony will have played an essential part), beliefs from testimony can be exhibited as justified in virtue of very general patterns of inference and justification; or if a normative epistemic principle special to testimony must be invoked to vindicate them and explain their status as knowledge. The issue whether there is a presumptive right to trust not based on evidence is this internal, coherentist issue.

5.

Is knowledge through testimony a distinctive category of knowledge at all? First note that we may define as our epistemic category, and topic of investigation: coming to know that something is so, through knowing that a certain speaker has asserted it to be so. This definition is restrictive in two respects. First, as to what comes to be known. This restriction is theoretically apt, since there is clearly nothing systematic and general to be said about the unrestricted topic of "whatever one may be able to infer, on an occasion, from the fact that someone has made an assertoric utterance with a certain content of that occasion"; while we may, as in the present paper, hope to say something general about the inferential path via which a hearer may come to know that which is the content of an assertion, from the fact that it has been asserted. Second, the definition restricts the means by which knowledge of that which is asserted is gained, to being via knowledge of the content and force of the speech act (which will, normally, be obtained through understanding it). This definition excludes, from counting as knowledge gained through testimony, any knowledge gained by one who takes a "barometer" approach to a group of creatures: that is, who tries to obtain information about the world, from discovering correlations between the sounds the creatures make, and how things objectively are – but who does not regard the creatures as agents nor categorise their utterances as intelligent speech acts. This exclusion is again theoretically apt, since the mechanism involved in gaining any such knowledge is quite different; but in any case, the possibilities for finding such brute phonetic type/ environmental-state correlations are very limited, with regard to a fully sophisticated human language-using practice.

But in one respect our definition is permissive: there is no restriction on the subject matter of the speaker's assertion. The domain of potential knowledge through testimony is, on this conception, that of serious assertions aimed at communication, whatever their subject matter. This is at odds with the ordinary language use of "testimony", which tends to confine it to eye-witness reports of observable events.

Testimony, defined as just suggested, does indeed constitute a distinctive kind of *epistemic link*. There is a distinctive type of connection, characteristic of testimony, between a state of affairs, and a hearer's coming to believe in its obtaining. This connection runs through another *person*, a speaker – her own original acquisition of the same belief, her other mental states, her subsequent linguistic act, which transmits that belief to the hearer.[17] There being this distinctive type of link between a hearer, and what she comes to believe, in testimony, means that there is a distinctive type of justification associated with testimony, in the sense suggested earlier: we can identify a characteristic justificatory schema $\mathcal{T}$. A hearer has knowledge through testimony just when she has knowledge whose content is given by appropriate instances of the elements of $\mathcal{T}$, and can cite such knowledge, or evidence for it, in defence of her belief. But what there is not, this paper argues, is any new *principle of inference* or other normative epistemic principle involved, which is special to testimony.

This makes the "problem of justifying testimony" unlike the "problem of induction". In the latter, the task is to show the legitimacy of a general *principle* of inference, one which is broadly comparable to the principles of deductive inference in the way in which it validates particular inferences of the form in question. It is therefore appropriate to approach the "problem of induction" at a completely general level. The task is to show that an arbitrary inductive inference is valid, by showing that the principle of inference involved in any such inference is a valid one.[18]

Now the anti-reductionist may mistakenly suppose that the task of justifying testimony must be approached by looking for some highly general premise or principle which would serve to justify an *arbitrary* testimony belief. Her error stems from a mistaken assimilation of the form of the problem of justifying testimony to that of justifying induction. An anti-reductionist who makes this mistake will start by investigating whether the blanket generalisation "Testimony is generally reliable" can be non-circularly empirically established, with the idea that this general premise, if established, would suffice to justify an arbitrary testimony belief. Finding that such global independent confirmation of testimony is unattainable, she concludes that testimony-beliefs must instead be justified by a special non-empirical normative epistemic principle.

My local-reductionist approach avoids the initial mistake, and so short-circuits the anti-reductionist's argument. If what were in question *were* a special normative epistemic principle, concerning testimony as a distinctive and unitary category of knowledge, then it would indeed apply indifferently to an arbitrary piece of testimony, and the task of justifying it would need to be conducted at an abstract general level. (Thus positive arguments *for* a blanket PR must indeed be conducted at that level.) But if there is no special epistemic principle in question, and what is common to all and only instances of knowledge through testimony is just a characteristic kind of belief-producing causal process, then there is no reason why what justifies belief in particular instances of testimony must be some proposition or principle applying to testimony in general. Instead, what justifies a particular hearer's belief in a particular assertion may be her knowledge of relevant facts about that situation and speaker, which warrant her in trusting him. (These will be, as it were, the *foreground* justifying facts – the ones in virtue of her knowledge of which she has gained *this* piece of knowledge through testimony. And which, as a minimum, we may require her to be able to articulate in its defence, for her belief to qualify as knowledge. Of course these facts can bestow knowledge of trustworthiness, and hence of what is asserted, only on a hearer who is equipped with a suitable background of more general knowledge. The account of §§7, 8 will spell out what this is.)

I suggested above that it was hopeless, but fortunately unnecessary for any legitimate enquiry, for an individual to try for *wholly independent* confirmation of the blanket generalisation that "Testimony is generally reliable". But it is only on this foundationalist conception of the project of confirmation that it is impossible. A more limited, non-foundationalist version (in which the enquirer makes no attempt to abrogate all of her existing knowledge which depends on testimony) is a perfectly feasible research project. But I think that looking for generalisations about the reliability or otherwise of testimony, in the inclusive sense of *serious assertions aimed at communication of belief*, as a homogeneous whole, will not be an enlightening project. Illuminating generalisations, if there are any, will be about particular types of testimony, differentiated according to subject matter, or type of speaker, or both. True, there is a belief-producing process characteristic of testimony, and consequently a generic type of justification, as captured in $\mathcal{T}$. This gives one sense in which it is a distinctive and unitary category of knowledge. But when it comes to the probability of accuracy of speakers' assertions, and what sorts of factors warrant a hearer in trusting a speaker, testimony is not a unitary category. The account of how trustworthiness may be empirically established given in §8 below draws on and develops this idea. One aspect of the disunity is, I shall argue, that while there are certain limited epistemic rights to trust involved in particular types of testimony, there is no *blanket* PR to believe what is asserted without needing evidence of trustworthiness, applicable to serious assertions aimed at communication as a whole, regardless of subject matter and circumstances.

6.

In §8 I shall sketch an account of how the trustworthiness with respect to an utterance of a speaker may be confirmed. The kind of confirmation described is, I maintain, often available, and is sought by a discriminating, justifiedly-believing, hearer. The account adopts the standpoint of our commonsense theory of persons and of the nature of speech acts, according to which it is a contingent matter whether a particular assertoric utterance is true, and the speaker trustworthy; and vindicates, within this framework of commonsense theory, the view that a speaker's trustworthiness with respect to an utterance is an empirically ascertainable matter.

But we need first to clarify further the PR thesis which I am opposing. It has several dimensions of possible variation in strength, which must be spelt out, if we are to see just what is the contrast between it, and the view I shall propose.

The "presumptive epistemic right" in question is a right to form belief in a certain proposition in a certain situation, without needing to have further evidence, or to make further investigations. But we get a weaker, or a stronger thesis, according to what this proposition is. The strongest PR thesis (that is, the one which demands the least of the hearer!) is one which legitimises *simple trust* as capable of yielding knowledge. A hearer has this attitude to a speaker if and only if she is disposed to form belief in any proposition which the speaker seriously asserts in an utterance whose content she grasps; and she lacks the conceptual capacity even to appreciate the possibility that what the speaker says may be false; that is, she lacks a full grasp of our *common-sense linguistics* (CSL), which contains a conception of the nature of language as a social institution, and of the epistemic link which testimony constitutes, including the nature of the speaker's action, and her typical role. (Simple trust is, plausibly, the condition of children at a certain stage in their development.) A simple truster does not have the conception of the speaker's trustworthiness or lack of it, nor appreciate the need for it, so there is no question of her believing in it. A PR thesis endorsing simple trust thus posits an epistemic right on the part of a hearer to believe what is asserted in an utterance, without further conditions, when she has perceived and grasped the content of that utterance;

thus in particular without requiring of the hearer-knower the capacity to conceive the trustworthiness of the speaker. (This cagey formulation is required, since it is doubtful whether one who lacks a full grasp of CSL, though she may respond to an utterance by forming a belief in what is asserted, can be said to conceive the utterance as an assertion in the full richness of that concept.)

A weaker PR thesis, which requires that the hearer be a master of CSL, and appreciate the need for trustworthiness, posits an epistemic right on the part of a hearer to presume an arbitrary speaker to be trustworthy, without needing to have any evidence for this, or to engage in any assessment of the speaker. This thesis is, in the first instance, a licence to believe in the trustworthiness of the speaker; and only derivatively, in the proposition she asserts.

The first, strongest PR thesis makes sense as a thesis about the conditions under which a subject may acquire knowledge from others' assertions (although of course other, "external" conditions must be added – at the very least truth of what is asserted); but only as part of a reliabilist account of that concept. It cannot be part of any plausible justificationist account, since a subject cannot defend her belief unless she understands the defence; and, as remarked, even the concept of assertion is not available to one who lacks the rest of CSL – lacks understanding that an assertion is, by the nature of the act, not necessarily true, hence the speaker needs to be trustworthy, etc. A simple truster is not in a position to say, with full understanding, even 'Someone told me so'.

We can therefore leave behind this strongest PR thesis, and consider further only the PR to assume trustworthiness; which restricts the domain of knowledge through testimony to masters of CSL, full participants in the social institution of language, conceptually equipped to play the speaker's, as well as the hearer's role.[19] The point of this PR being the consequent entitlement to believe what is asserted, it is, of course, the minimal gap-bridging property of trustworthiness of the speaker with respect to her current utterance, which is its immediate object. No epistemic right to assume any generalisation about speakers' trustworthiness is needed. Cf. the local/global distinction drawn earlier. Of course the sense in which a hearer is required by our PR to

assume, or believe, the speaker to be trustworthy, is not that she is required consciously to form that belief, or consider the question, whenever she forms a belief in what a speaker asserts; but merely that she appreciates the need for trustworthiness, and is disposed to judge the speaker to be trustworthy (or else to abandon her original belief in what was asserted), when challenged. Implicit belief in trustworthiness will always be attributable to such a hearer, when she believes an assertion.

Our epistemic right to believe (whether in trustworthiness, or in what is asserted), to be at all plausible, must be only "presumptive" – that is, it must be defeasible in appropriate circumstances. Several dimensions of variation enter here: as to what these "defeating conditions" (d.c.s) are, and what the hearer's relation to them must be. How strong an epistemic charter our PR thesis is will depend very much on these details of its specification.

A d.c. is, certainly, a condition which cancels the hearer's epistemic right to believe – in the speaker's trustworthiness or, for the strong PR, in what is asserted. That is to say, when the hearer knows one to obtain, she should not form, at any rate not without further evidence, the "defeated" belief. This gives us a first aspect of the hearer's required relation to a d.c. On a reliabilist approach, it could be enough that her disposition to believe is thus cancelled, when she is aware of a d.c. But within a justificationist approach, it must be that this disposition of the hearer stems from her appreciation of how the d.c. "defeats" this belief. Here, there is again a weaker and a stronger option. A d.c. may defeat a proposition, in the sense that it constitutes strong evidence for the falsity of that proposition. Call these *proposition-defeating* d.c.s. Alternatively, it may merely defeat, i.e. cancel, the right to presume that proposition to be true – being a circumstance which indicates that the proposition *may* not be, or cannot be assumed to be true, rather than being definite evidence for its falsity. Call these *presumption-defeating* d.c.s. Clearly, the proposition-defeating d.c.s with respect to any presumptive belief are a subset of the presumption-defeating d.c.s. So a presumptive right to believe in the trustworthiness of a speaker which is cancelled by anything which throws in doubt the presumption that a speaker is trustworthy, will be much weaker – since much more often defeated – than one which is cancelled only by definite evidence of untrustworthiness.

Similarly, a defeasible right to believe in trustworthiness is a weaker epistemic charter for hearers, than a defeasible right to believe what is asserted – since anything which defeats "*P*" will, ex post, defeat the speaker's trustworthiness with respect to any utterance she makes in which she asserts that *P*; while the converse does not hold. The strongest possible PR – to believe that *P*, just on the ground that it has been asserted that *P*, whenever one does not already possess evidence showing "*P*" to be false, is indeed an epistemic charter for gullibility! But the weakest one: Where the presumptive right is to assume trustworthiness, and a d.c. is any condition which defeats the presumption, by merely raising a question as to the speaker's likely trustworthiness, is a much more limited affair.

There remains a further dimension of variation in the hearer's required relation to the d.c.s, in whichever sense these are taken. The nub of their being d.c.s, is that when the hearer is aware of one, she should not form the "defeated" belief. When the d.c.s defeat the proposition that the speaker is trustworthy, she should not form belief in it at all; when they defeat the presumption in favour of trustworthiness, she should not believe in it without further investigation: without first engaging in some assessment of the speaker for trustworthiness. The further dimension of variation which remains is: Is the hearer required to look for, be on the alert for, the presence of such d.c.s (of whichever kind)? We know that, when aware of one, she should withhold belief: but is she in addition required to ensure that whenever a d.c. obtains, she will be aware of it, if it is within her epistemic grasp to be so? Or, if not this first, which is a very onerous requirement, then is she at least required to engage in some search for d.c.s, or to be on the alert for the presence or d.c.s?

In fact, the grid of differences set up by our dimensions of variation exhibits some collapse here. Conditions which defeat the *presumption* in favour of trustworthiness are conditions which switch on a requirement to assess the speaker for trustworthiness, i.e. they switch off the right just to assume this without checking on it, the dispensation from epistemic activity which the right to presume trustworthiness constitutes. But to be obliged to keep a constant look-out for any

conditions which would suggest that the speaker may not be trustworthy, is not very different from being obliged to assess the speaker for trustworthiness, simpliciter! Such an attenuated PR is not a PR at all: it is not a dispensation from epistemic activity. If the d.c.s defeat the *proposition* that the speaker is trustworthy, the requirement always to be on the look out for such conditions is somewhat less onerous, but still seems not to be very much weaker than a straightforward requirement to assess the speaker for trustworthiness. The notion of a PR, we may conclude, seems only to make sense when it is interpreted as giving the hearer the right to believe without engaging in epistemic activity; when there is no requirement to be on the alert for d.c.s, of either kind.

These considerations reveal the possibility of an interestingly different kind of thesis, which is not a PR, that is, a dispensation from the requirement to assess the speaker; but is rather a thesis applying within the project of assessment, about how it is properly done. I shall call it a *default-position* thesis. To say that a hearer must withhold belief in a speaker's trustworthiness whenever she is aware of signs revealing untrustworthiness, and that moreover she is obliged to be on the alert for such signs, is tantamount to saying the following: the hearer is obliged, always, to assess the speaker for trustworthiness; but within this exercise, the hypothesis of trustworthiness has special status in that it is the default position – it is to be ascribed, in the absence of positive signs of its opposite. The account given in the §8 of how a speaker's trustworthiness may be assessed by a hearer will posit limited default position precepts in favour of what we will shortly identify as the components of trustworthiness.

Our discussion has shown that a PR thesis which is strong enough to be worthy of the name, while fitting into a justificationist framework, is best formulated thus:

PR: An arbitrary hearer *H* has the epistemic right, on any occasion of testimony *O*, to assume, without any investigation or assessment, of the speaker *S* who on *O* asserts that *P* by making an utterance *U*, that *S* is trustworthy with respect to *U*, unless *H* is aware of a condition *C* which defeats this assumption of trustworthiness – that is, *C* constitutes strong evidence that *S* is not trustworthy with respect to *U*; in which case,

H should not form belief that *P* on the strength of *S*'s assertion that *P*, and should believe, at least implicitly, that *S* is not trustworthy with respect to *U*.

This PR is still programmatic, in that it does not specify just what circumstances would constitute strong evidence against trustworthiness, and there is scope for broader and narrower interpretation here. But it clearly involves what we have identified as the key element of a PR: the dispensation from the requirement to monitor or assess the speaker for trustworthiness, before believing in it. Thus it may be called a PR to believe *blindly*, or uncritically, since the hearer's critical faculties are not required to be engaged. Notice also that it is a *blanket* PR, entitling the hearer to believe in trustworthiness, hence in what is asserted, on any occasion of testimony, whatever the subject matter may be. (Assuming only that the nature of the subject matter can never in itself constitute strong *ex ante* evidence against trustworthiness.)

It is such a blanket PR to believe blindly that constitutes an epistemic charter for the gullible, and to which I am opposed. The account of how empirical confirmation of trustworthiness is possible set out in §8 involves a limited presumption in favour of trustworthiness, in the very different sense we have identified: it is, in some circumstances, the default hypothesis *within* the critical task of assessing the speaker for trustworthiness.

7.

The thesis I advocate in opposition to a PR thesis, is that a hearer should always engage in some assessment of the speaker for trustworthiness. To believe what is asserted without doing so is to believe blindly, uncritically. This is gullibility. (Though not the only kind. Believing in trustworthiness too easily, i.e. attempting assessment, but doing it badly, is also being gulled!)

So – to return to our central question – if indeed a properly discriminating hearer always assesses a speaker for trustworthiness, what precisely is this property, and how is an empirically-based estimate of it obtainable?

Our method is to develop an epistemology of testimony, including an account of what a speaker's trustworthiness with respect to an utterance consists in, by appeal to the relevant parts of our commonsense theory of the world. This stance is part of a coherentist approach in epistemology: we criticise our belief-forming methods, and standards of justification, from *within* our existing conceptual scheme, rather than attempting to find some mythical point outside it from which to do so.

Now, CSL tells us that, in the normal case,[20] a serious assertoric utterance by a speaker *S* is true just if *S* is sincere, i.e. believes what she knowingly[21] asserts, and the belief she thereby expresses is true. This breakdown is entailed by the commonsense conception of the nature of a speech act of assertion, and of the link between its occurrence, and the obtaining of the state of affairs asserted to obtain. And commonsense person-theory tells us that it is moreover contingent whether any particular utterance is both sincere, and expresses a true belief: it is inherent in the nature of the link, and the psychology of the human subjects who are speakers, that insincerity and honest error are both perfectly possible. Indeed, commonsense person theory tells us that false utterances are quite common, especially for some subject matters. (This, we may note, constitutes the prima facie case against a blanket PR to assume any assertoric utterance to be true, a fortiori against one to assume that the speaker is trustworthy. The case is an application of the epistemic precept: "If a significant percentage of *F*s are not *G*, one should not infer that *X* is *G*, merely from the fact that it is *F*." A belief so formed is not epistemically rational, which is to say it is not justified.)

In §3 we gave Trus1 as a rough initial explication of a speaker's trustworthiness with respect to an utterance *U* made on an occasion *O*, by which she asserts that *P*. Trus1 is logically equivalent to the claim: "If *S* were to assert that *P* on *O*, then her assertion would be true". We have now seen that the truth of *S*'s utterance breaks down (in the normal case to which we confine ourselves) into the utterance's being sincere, and *S*'s expressed belief being true. This suggests that we may frame a more illuminating definition of a speaker *S*'s trustworthiness with respect to an utterance *U* made on an occasion *O*, by which she asserts that *P*, thus:

Trus 2: "If *S* were to assert that *P* on *O*, then it would be the case that *S*'s assertion is sincere, and that the belief she thereby expresses is true."

Turs2 fulfils our basic requirement on T_2, that of entailing "*P*" when combined with T_1. It is more illuminating than Trus1, since *S*'s sincerity, and whether it is likely that if *S* on *O* believes that *P*, then her belief will be true, are what a hearer may, in the first instance, make an empirically-based assessment of. (It is not equivalent to Trus1, since it does not cover the fluke case of a would-be liar who unknowingly utters a truth.)

But the illumination this breakdown provides also shows that Trus2 (and so also Trus1) gives a definition of trustworthiness which is needlessly strong. To be justified in believing what is asserted by an utterance *U* of a speaker *S* on an occasion *O*, a hearer need not know that *any* utterance with that content by *S* on *O* would be sincere; it is enough that she is able to tell that *S*'s *actual* utterance *U* is so. And this difference of strength is empirically significant. We may take sincerity to be a predicate of utterances, and it is very often precisely a particular utterance that a hearer *H* is able to tell to be sincere, through sensitivity to such features of its delivery as tone of voice, and manner of the speaker. *H* may be able to tell this about an utterance of a speaker who in fact, and perhaps to *H*'s knowledge, is very often insincere – one of whom the stronger sincerity condition contained in Trus2 is false.

Thus, I suggest, our best and final definition of a speaker's trustworthiness with respect to an utterance *U* is as follows:

Trus(S, U): A speaker *S* is trustworthy with respect to an assertoric utterance by her *U*, which is made on an occasion *O*, and by which she asserts that *P*, if and only if

(i) *U* is sincere, and
(ii) *S* is *competent with respect to "P" on O*, where this notion is defined as follows:

If *S* were sincerely to assert that *P* on *O*, then it would be the case that *P*.

In this definition the relativisation to a particular utterance *U* by *S* is not idle.

Trus(S, U) fulfils, as best we can,[22] the requirements explained in §3. It combines with *T* to entail "*P*", and there is no weaker alternative which does so, and which is epistemically independent of "*P*". *S*'s "competence with respect to *P*" is defined as in (ii), rather than by a strictly weaker material conditional, in order to fulfil the desideratum of epistemic independence of "*P*", which we saw in §3 that a material conditional fails (equally when the requirement of sincerity is inserted in the antecedent).[23] Notice also that it is right to take the antecedent as in (ii), rather than "If *S* were to believe that *P* on *O* ...". The latter would give a condition which is again unnecessarily strong: perhaps it is only the worlds in which *S* believes that *P* sufficiently confidently to *assert* her belief, that are all *P*-worlds.

Trus(S, U) is weaker than the everyday notion of someone's being a trustworthy or reliable informant, since the latter usually refers to a speaker's assertions more generally, implying that she is generally sincere, and is competent with respect to most of the things she makes claims about. But a person *S* who is untrustworthy, in this generalised sense, can still be *Trus(S, U)*, and known by a hearer *H* to be so, with respect to a particular utterance *U*; in which case, *H* has grounds to believe what is asserted by that utterance. *Trus (S, U)* is the minimal gap-bridging property which we set out to find. As such, it captures the idea that *that utterance* of the speaker is to be trusted.

8.

We have identified the question how a speaker *S*'s trustworthiness regarding an utterance *U* may be empirically confirmed as the question how *Trus(S, U)* may be confirmed, that is to say, how the sincerity of *U*, and *S*'s competence with respect to the content of *U*, may be confirmed. Notice that these claims are not esoteric, nor technical, but are mere spellings out of what sheer common sense about language, and speakers, tells us.[24] Thus in requiring that hearers appreciate the need for trustworthiness, and assess the speaker for it, we are requiring nothing more than what any full participant in the institution of human language is well equipped to appreciate the need for; and, as I shall now argue, can very often achieve.

In recognising an utterance by a speaker as a speech act of serious assertion, with a certain content, a hearer is ipso facto engaging in a minimal piece of *interpretation* of the speaker – ascribing to her an intentional action of a certain kind, and hence at the very least supposing the existence of some configuration of beliefs and desires which explain that action. The theme of my account is: the epistemically responsible hearer will do a bit more of the same. She will assess the speaker for sincerity and competence, by engaging in at least a little more interpretation of her.

A speaker's sincerity and competence, or lack of them, are aspects of her psychology – in the case of competence, in a suitably "broad" sense, which takes in relevant parts of her environment. Assessment of them is part of, or a prediction from, a more extended psychological theory of her. So, in order to assess a speaker's trustworthiness, a hearer needs to piece together at least a fragment of such a theory of the speaker – an ascription of beliefs, desires, and other mental states and character traits to her. Thus it is commonsense psychology or person-theory, and the related epistemic norms for attribution of these states, that we must look to, to see how trustworthiness can be evaluated.

Notice therefore that while, as we saw in §4, one way of estimating a speaker's trustworthiness is by induction from past assertions of hers independently confirmed as accurate, this is not the best way. As always, predictions from a *theory* of the subject matter in question – in this case, the psychology of the speaker – will do better, and where there is conflict should override mere extrapolation of observed correlations with no underlying explanation of why they obtain.[25]

Indeed the primary task for the hearer is to construct enough of a theory of the speaker, and relevant portions of her past and present environment, to *explain* her utterance: to render it comprehensible why she made that assertion, on that occasion. Whether the speaker's assertion is to be trusted will, generally speaking, be fall-out from this theory which explains why she made it; and it is difficult to see how sincerity and competence could be evaluated other than through the construction of such an explanation.

(The need to explain the utterance is sharply felt, when a hitherto reliable informant makes a wildly unlikely claim. – Has she gone crazy? Or

been elaborately tricked? Is she kidding? – Or is the best explanation that her outrageous claim to have seen flying saucers is really *true*? We feel at a loss; but it is these alternative explanatory hypotheses that we dither between.)

A psychological interpretation of an individual being an explanatory theory of her, psychological concepts are theoretical in character at least in the respect that their meanings are fixed by their mutual interconnections, and their application to a subject is only holistically constrained by the "data" to be explained, the subject's actions. Thus the norms which govern ascription of sincerity and competence will be part and parcel of the norms governing the ascription of psychological states more comprehensively. Notice however that norms of ascription – call them *Norms of Interpretation* – whose existence and correctness might be explained by the thesis that they have constitutive status in defining the so-applied psychological concepts, are ones which, at least in the first instance, apply to the highly idealised enterprise of constructing an extensive interpreting description of a person, with "all" the data to hand; not to the construction of a small fragment of one, on very limited evidence. We shall return to this point below.

I shall first state what I think are the epistemic norms regarding how a speaker's sincerity with respect to an utterance, and competence regarding its content, may properly be estimated by a hearer; and then address the question of why they hold.

In claiming that a hearer is required to assess a speaker for trustworthiness, I do not mean to insist, absurdly, that she is required to conduct an extensive piece of M15-type "vetting" of any speaker before she may accept anything he says as true (cf. the implausibly onerous requirement dismissed earlier). My insistence is much weaker: that the hearer should be discriminating in her attitude to the speaker, in that she should be continually evaluating him for trustworthiness throughout their exchange, in the light of the evidence, or cues, available to her. This will be partly a matter of her being disposed to deploy background knowledge which is relevant, partly a matter of her monitoring the speaker for any tell-tale signs revealing likely untrustworthiness. This latter consists in it being true throughout of the hearer that if there were signs of untrustworthiness, she would register them, and respond appropriately.

Such monitoring of speakers, and appropriate doxastic responses formed on its basis are, I suggest, usually found in ordinary hearers, at least to some extent. However, this sort of monitoring for signs of untrustworthiness in a speaker is typically conducted at a non-conscious level. And while its results can generally be fished up into consciousness and expressed, albeit roughly, in words ("I didn't like the look of him"; "Well, she seemed perfectly normal"), no doubt the specific cues in a speaker's behaviour which constitute the informational basis for this judgement will often be registered and processed at an irretrievably sub-personal level. Can a justificationist account of knowledge allow that this kind of process may be knowledge-yielding? Yes, it can: insisting that subjects be able to retail the details of the cues they have responded to is demanding the impossible; but we may insist, compatibly with the sub-personal character of these perceptual or quasi-perceptual capacities, that the subject's beliefs must not be opaque to her, in that she must be able to defend the judgement which is the upshot of this capacity with the knowledge precisely that she indeed has such a capacity – that "she can tell" about that kind of thing; though she does not know how she does it.

Expert dissimulators amongst us being few, the insincerity of an utterance is very frequently betrayed in the speaker's manner, and so is susceptible of detection by such a quasi-perceptual capacity. But honestly expressed false belief is not so readily detectable, and an informed assessment of a speaker's competence about some subject will typically require that the hearer already know something of the speaker's cognitive talents and failings. How then is knowledge of the latter attainable by a hearer, without, if not an M15-style vetting, then at least a lot more research than is feasible, when you just want to know the time and have forgotten your watch? As regards sincerity, I suggested that it was tell-tale signs of its absence that a hearer must be disposed to pick up. The flip-side of this coin is that, while there is no right to assume sincerity without monitoring the speaker for it, sincerity is the default position, in assessing a speaker, in the sense we identified earlier; one is justified in taking a speaker to be sincere, unless one observes (and one must be alert for them) symptoms of duplicity.

And, I suggest, the same is true regarding a speaker's competence, *with respect to a certain range of subject matters* – namely, all those for which commonsense person theory tells us that people are nearly always right about such things. Just which topics come within this range is a further question; but it certainly includes such matters as: everyday perceptions of familiar types of item in one's current environment; memories, not too finely specified, of very recent events in one's personal history – such as what one had for breakfast; and a whole range of basic facts about oneself and one's life – one's name, where one works, one's tastes, etc. On such matters, I suggest, competence is the default position – that is to say, one may justifiedly assume a sincere assertion by a person of whom one has no previous knowledge to be true, when its subject matter comes within this range, just so long as one remains alert for any sign in their circumstances, or manner, to suggest otherwise, and there are no such signs.

But there are many other possible topics of assertion about which commonsense person theory tells us that people are often, even in some cases usually, wrong. For these subject matters there is no default presumption in favour of competence, and one is not justified in believing what someone says about such things unless one has specific knowledge of their relevant cognitive talents and circumstances.

9.

In virtue of what do these "default position" norms of attribution in favour of sincerity and, for certain everyday subject matters, competence, obtain? We can identify two opposed views about this. The first view, which is my own, runs as follows: These practical epistemic norms for *ascribing* the psychological attributes of sincerity, and competence, are justified because, and just insofar as, it is fact, and is part of commonsense person theory, that (i) nearly all utterances which seem sincere indeed are so; and (ii) About these everyday subject matters, where there are no special circumstances, normal people are nearly always right. (Correspondingly, there is no default position in favour of competence for non-everyday subject matters, just because it is not part of commonsense wisdom about persons that they are usually right about these things.)

The opposed view objects to mine as follows: "This explanation gets things the wrong way round. These facts of commonsense person-theory are themselves so as a consequence of the fact that the default positions are epistemic norms governing the ascription of psychological concepts; so they cannot be appealed to to explain or justify these norms. More fully: (i) The obtaining of these norms of ascription guarantees that these 'commonsense' facts will be so – so that they are not, as they might seem, contingent, but are features of individuals' psychology which are guaranteed to be so in virtue of the way psychological concepts are correctly applied. And (ii) the direction of explanation, and justification, is from the existence of the norms of ascription, to the commonsense facts, not vice versa: These norms of ascription are primitive features of psychological concepts, which serve to fix their content; not rules of application which stand in need of justification by appeal to a supposed independently fixed content."

This opposed view is mistaken, as I shall now show. I think it is plausible that there exist Norms of Interpretation (NIs), in the sense explained earlier: norms for applying psychological concepts[26] which have constitutive a priori status, fixing the content of these concepts; so that the truth of an *interpreting description*, as we may call it, of an individual reduces to its fitting the individual in accordance with the correct set of such NIs. But, as mentioned earlier, such a reduction of truth conditions to conditions of ascription will hold, if at all, only with respect to a highly idealised, fancied all-data-in interpretation exercise. And the NIs which apply in such an exercise are by no means the same thing as practical epistemic precepts, applicable in the task of estimating a speaker's trustworthiness on a very limited basis of evidence about her. Whether they transfer to this limited-evidence (and limited aspiration) case is a further question.

And, I suggest, they do not transfer. It is plausible that "Make no unforced attributions of insincerity", and the parallel principle for false beliefs, are among the correct NIs. But their being so does not ensure that the best interpreting description of an individual will show her as being mainly sincere, or as having mainly true beliefs; that depends on what departures from the default setting are forced by other NIs. Perhaps there are *also* NIs setting a lower bound on how much insincerity, or false belief, an individual may turn out to have, *salva* the hypothesis that she is indeed a subject of attitudes. But these are further, entirely distinct, constraints. And, I suggest, any such bounds, while being essentially vague, are nonetheless clearly quite low – both for truth of beliefs, and for sincerity of utterances.

If this is right, then it is indeed a contingent empirical fact, not guaranteed by any concept-constituting norms of application of psychological concepts, that, in some given linguistic community, nearly all apparently-sincere utterances are so; and that the speakers in the community nearly always have true beliefs – if not on all subjects (this being palpably false), then at least over a certain quite broad range of subject matters.

There is of course an essentially vague lower bound on the possible incidence of insincerity in a community: beyond a certain point, hearers would cease ever to have the typical responses which are partly constitutive of what it is for a sentence to have a given meaning in a community, and the language would wither away, or change its meaning. But – to reiterate the claim – this lower bound is quite low. In any case, this argument establishes no lower bound on how often any *single* member of a community may lie, *salva* the persistence of language in that community. As regards false belief, I do think it is a priori that for any individual there must be some core range of observable conditions in her immediate environment, such that she is at least disposed to have mainly true beliefs about such matters. If this is not so, she cannot be seen as having the capacity for states of informedness about her environment (which beliefs essentially are) at all. But, once more, this conceptually necessary condition is too weak to affect the current argument.

The "default position" precepts of attribution we have canvassed, applicable in the limited interpretation exercise typically engaged in by a hearer, clearly would not be justified if the commonsense facts which I have suggested to justify them were *not* so; the issue is only as to the direction of explanation between norm of attribution, and commonsense fact. If, as I have claimed, these commonsense facts are not guaranteed to hold by any constitutive attribution-norms for psychological concepts, then their contingent obtaining plays an essential part in the justifying explanation of these default position precepts, and the direction of explanation is as I have suggested: even if there are Norms of Interpretation, and amongst them default settings in favour of sincerity, and true belief, these do not transfer automatically to the limited-evidence setting, and such limited-evidence default position precepts are justified only by contingent facts of commonsense person theory, and hold only in a community in which these indeed obtain.[27]

A corollary of my account is that in a community in which these facts which justify the default position precepts were not so, knowledge (though not necessarily belief!) gained from what other people tell one would be much less easily come by, and less widespread. But a language might thrive there nevertheless. Transmission of accurate information is not the only social role and function of the social institution of human language; from many perspectives on human life it is not even the primary one.[28]

10.

The skeptical reader may want to ask at this point: – Just how different is the proposed account from a PR thesis? And can knowledge of trustworthiness obtained in the manner described really be called empirically based?

For assertions whose subject matter is outside the range for which there is a default position in favour of competence, the contrast between my account and a PR thesis is obvious. But a clear difference remains too in cases in which there is a default position in favour of both components of trustworthiness. My account requires a hearer always to take a critical stance to the speaker, to assess her for trustworthiness; while a true PR thesis, as we have seen, does not. The nub of this distinction is a clear and sharp difference: on my account, but not on a PR thesis, the hearer must always be monitoring the speaker critically. This is a matter of the actual engagement of a counterfactual sensitivity: it is true throughout of the hearer that if there were any signs of untrustworthiness, she would pick them up.

Moreover, as we have seen, the limited default positions in favour of the components of trustworthiness which my account posits, are precepts within the task of constructing a psychological theory of the speaker, not a dispensation from engaging in this task. There is no recognising their defeating conditions except through a general grasp of commonsense psychological concepts, and so the precepts can be conformed to (a fortiori appropriate defence of belief can be given), only by one who is a master of the latter. Thus, on my account, a person may gain knowledge from others only when she has the needed conceptual framework to conceive and understand them as persons and agents; and moreover engages, at least to some extent, in that interpretative task. The strongest PR thesis we identified earlier does not require this at all; our best formulation, while it required that the utterance is conceived as the speech act it is, did not require any interpretation of the speaker beyond what this itself involves.

Ascribing trustworthiness to a speaker is positing part of a larger psychological theory of her. Such a theory is empirically constrained by, and explanatory of, the speaker's behaviour. The fact that there are certain default settings regarding its construction does not detract from this. In any case the default position precepts do not allow ascription of trustworthiness on no evidence at all: even when trustworthiness is ascribed just on the strength of them, empirical warrant for this is needed, in the sense that the absence of defeaters must have been checked for – as, I have suggested, the hearer will show with such defence as "Well, she seemed perfectly normal".

But it is important to remember that, as we saw above, while our default position precepts represent what is, given the facts of commonsense psychology, sufficient ground for ascribing trustworthiness to an unknown person, what that person's indeed being trustworthy with respect to her assertion consists in is far from reducing to the obtaining of these limited-evidence ascription conditions. Consequently, while undefeated presumption gives a reasonable basis to believe a speaker to be right about, say, where she lives, one gains stronger confirmation (or disconfirmation!) of her trustworthiness about this and other matters, as one gets to know more about her – acquires more specific knowledge of her relevant cognitive talents and circumstances. A fuller treatment would refine the account offered here by introducing degrees of confirmation, and would introduce into the account of when it is rational (justified) to believe the costs of error: When it matters very much whether what someone says is true, we are less ready to accept what she says without checking her credentials.

11.

We set out to examine whether knowledge from testimony is a special, irreducible type of knowledge. In reviewing what we have discovered, we may broaden our question to ask not only whether testimony is a special epistemic category, but also whether it is a unitary one. We have found that testimony, appropriately defined, is a distinctive *epistemic link*. That is to say, it is a distinctive type of belief-producing process, and there is consequently a distinctive set of premise-schemata $\mathcal{T}$ recapitulating that process. Appropriate instances of the elements of $\mathcal{T}$, or evidence for them, when known by a hearer, may be offered by her in defence of a belief acquired through that process, and a belief of hers is known through testimony (*pace* certain qualifications made earlier) just when she is in a position so to defend it.

On the other hand, as regards the likelihood of truth of what is asserted by a speaker, and, consequently, whether a hearer is entitled to presume that she is trustworthy, we have seen that testimony, in the broad sense of serious assertions aimed at communication, is a rag-bag category. This is unsurprising, being a simple consequence of the fact, registered in commonsense person theory, that how likely people are to have true beliefs about a given subject matter depends entirely on what kind of thing it is, and how they are epistemically placed in regard to it. The epistemology of testimony can be no more homogeneous than is the psychology of belief, in this respect.

We have rejected the thesis that there is a blanket presumptive right to trust, applicable to all cases of testimony. Moreover the rag-bag nature of the category in regard of likely truth of what is asserted means that it is a mistake to expect to find *any* epistemic principles as to when one may believe testimony, which apply to all instances of

it. Our default position in favour of competence was more selective.

Our account has explained how knowledge may be gained through testimony without recourse to any mysterious epistemic primitives pertaining just to testimony. The limited default positions in favour of sincerity and competence which we have discovered, are epistemic norms within the enterprise of ascribing psychological states to others. Their existence is derived from and explained by the nature of commonsense psychological concepts, whose significance and domain of answerability is much broader than just the explanation of people's assertoric utterances. Thus the conditions under which one may believe another's assertions have been exhibited as fall-out from the nature of commonsense psychological concepts. The epistemology of testimony in this respect is but one part of the broader domain of our knowledge of other minds, and is to be subsumed under that category, not treated as a separate epistemic domain with its own, irreducible, normative epistemic principles.[29]

There is another central and fundamental respect in which testimony is a special, and unitary, epistemic category. This paper has taken for granted a hearer's knowledge that a speaker has made a speech act with a certain content and force, and has focussed on the question how she may get from there to knowledge of that which has been asserted. But the epistemology of a hearer's understanding of utterances, and appreciation of them as speech acts, will be at the heart of a full account of how knowledge is gained through testimony. Understanding, whether of one's own or others' utterances, involves special perceptual capacities and kinds of informational states, distinctive of language and of language-using creatures. The epistemology of understanding is intimately bound up with its phenomenology, and with the nature of these special states. Whether or not the best account of how a hearer may know what a speaker has said postulates any normative epistemic principles special to understanding, understanding remains a separate epistemic category in that it involves these special informational states.

The strategy of this paper – to take knowledge of what is asserted as given, and consider the next step – is valid only if the nature of understanding does not itself have implications for that next step.

This means, at the very least, that it is not intrinsic to the state of understanding an utterance that it compels the hearer towards belief in what she grasps as being asserted. It is my view that there is nothing in the nature of what it is to understand an utterance which is in tension with the view of knowledge through testimony as inferential knowledge (in the sense that it must be backed by a substantial justification) sketched in this paper, or which provides the materials to defend the presumptive right thesis. But my defence of this claim, and my rejection of other positive arguments for PR, must wait till another day.[30]

So too must wait further defence of the coherentist epistemic stance within which my account has been developed, from which comes the thesis, essential to my "local" reductionist approach, that only the local question about testimony needs to be answered, and that it should be answered, as we have done, from *within* the world picture constituted by the "commonsense" framework of beliefs which we all share; thus that it does not matter, nor does it undermine the rationale of insisting on "local" reduction and justification, if the global generalisation cannot be independently confirmed by an individual language-user; who will have made her way into her shared language, and conceptual scheme, through a process in which she was necessarily, at an earlier stage, a simple truster. In this paper I have sought only to block the transcendental argument for a presumptive right thesis, by showing how empirical confirmation of the trustworthiness of a particular speaker is possible.[31]

Notes

1 I am grateful here to accounts, both written and spoken, of the doctrines of the school. from Arindam Chakrabarti and Bimal Matilal. This pair of theses seems also to be implicit in the anti-reductionist stance of C. A. J. Coady "Testimony and Observation". *Amer. Phil. Quart.* 10, No. 2, April 1973, pp. 149–55.

2 Thus for me, the issue of what it takes for a testimony belief to be justified is one with the issue what it takes for it to be knowledge. Those for whom those issues are not the same – since they favour some other conception of knowledge – may read my account as being simply about justification.

3 I.e. a belief originally acquired through testimony, and whose status as knowledge still rests on that pedigree. In Fricker "The Epistemology of Testimony", *Proc. Aris. Soc. Suppl.* vol. for 1987, pp. 57–83, I set out a framework which exhibits the complicated interrelations involved here, between original causation, sustaining, and available justifying support of a belief.

4 This argument seems to be implicit in Coady "Testimony and Observation".

5 In this paper I am assuming that knowledge that such-and-such has been asserted is often had by hearers, and am focusing on the epistemology of the step from there, to knowledge of its truth. See §11.

6 If this is shown, then it has been shown that testimony is not just a way of acquiring beliefs, but is moreover one which is capable of yielding knowledge, what we may call an *epistemic link*. Cf. Fricker "The Epistemology of Testimony".

7 Throughout my discussion, "H", "S", and "O" are to be regarded as names for an arbitrary hearer, speaker, and occasion respectively. "P" in contrast must be considered merely a schematic letter holding a place to be occupied by an indicative sentence. Whether outside or inside quotes, "S", "H", and "O", and the possible substitution-instances for which "P" is schematic, are to be considered expressions of the metalanguage we are using to describe testimony situations. Thus schematic sentences enclosed in quotes, such as "S asserted that P", constitute (schematic) specifications by us, in our terms, of the content of a hearer's knowledge.

8 Instances of $\mathcal{T}$ are sentences of a metalanguage which *we* use to describe what H knows. There is of course no guarantee a priori that we can thus identify a *single* justificatory schema which covers all and only cases of knowledge through testimony. But it turns out that we can do pretty well. See §5 for how we should define the epistemic link of "testimony" to this end.

9 Cf. David Hume, *An Enquiry Concerning Human Understanding*, Ch. 10. An adequate treatment of such collisions of contrary evidence would introduce probabilities, as a more detailed model of knowledge through testimony would do throughout.

10 Of course the grounds justifying a belief need not be so strong as to entail it. The reason for insisting nonetheless that the elements of $\mathcal{T}$ be chosen so as to together entail P, is pragmatic and ad hoc: this represents the best strategy for finding a single characteristic justificatory schema, and the resulting account is illuminating. The possibility of grounds for belief weaker than entailment is allowed for, in this set-up, in the fact that H need only have, and cite, evidence, which may be less than conclusive, that the relevant instances of $\mathcal{T}$ obtain. What may afford this last is endlessly variable, and we cannot hope for a general description circumscribing the possibilities.

11 Note however that it is a desideratum, rather than an absolute constraint, that we thus succeed in characterising knowledge through testimony just by means of our choice of a set $\mathcal{T}$. Clearly, one cannot find a $\mathcal{T}$ which is epistemically independent of the content of S's assertion *whatever* the latter may be: cf., when it is T_2 itself, or evidence for T_2. But these are special cases, and we may hope to find a $\mathcal{T}$ which is epistemically independent of the content of S's assertion apart from such cases. As we shall see in §7, it proves difficult to achieve even this perfectly.

12 Equally, of course, when she knows that S has not asserted that P on O! But this case need not concern us, since there is no question of H gaining knowledge through S's testimony, nor of all the elements of $\mathcal{T}$ obtaining.

13 An appropriate semantics for this conditional will make it strictly stronger than the material conditional, and with no supposition of falsity of the antecedent. Roughly, it will be true just if all the *nearest S-asserts-that-P* worlds are P-worlds, where the nearness relation is reflexive. It would be nice if a case could be made for a nearness metric which does not have the consequence that

the conditional is ensured true whenever "P" is a nomological truth. I think the ordinary language locution is rightly heard thus; but finding a regimented semantics with this consequence is another matter. It would, very likely, involve relativising the standard of nearness to the identity of the antecedent.

14 It is no part of the reductionist position I am arguing for, to claim that empirical warrant for trusting the speaker is available on *every* occasion of testimony. This is clearly false. In cases where it is not, the anti-reductionist and reductionist will disagree over whether the hearer is entitled to trust the speaker, and, in the event she does believe what is asserted, can be said to gain knowledge.

15 A really strong general claim, to the effect that all, or virtually all assertions are true, *would* suffice to justify belief in an arbitrary assertion, in the absence of further "defeaters": and might indeed be employed in a meta-level argument to show the existence of a PR at object level. But a generalisation of this strength is obviously false. (A fortiori is not a conceptual truth about language, as one attempted argument for a PR would claim.)

16 As I understand it, this is an element in the Indian anti-reductionist case. And Coady "Testimony and Observation" assumes the anti-reductionist must establish generalisations about the reliability of testimony.

17 Is this connection causal? Its latter stages which are our primary concern always are, but whether the speaker's initial acquisition of her belief can be thought of as caused by its subject matter depends on what kind of thing that is, and how her belief arose.

18 If the reader is unhappy with this view of the problem of induction, she may consider the justification of deduction instead, which surely takes this form.

19 Is this unkind to children? The upshot of my casual discussions with developmental psychologists is that they (children) acquire the ability to lie, and so maybe the grasp of CSL which shows this possibility, remarkably early. But a feeling that my theory is too demanding on hearers may anyway be an intuition against the requirement that

knowledge requires justification, rather than against my account of what it takes for a testimony-belief to be justified.

20 Freak cases are possible – where a would-be deceiver happens to have a compensatingly false belief. But for our project, of giving a systematic general account of how knowledge is gained through testimony, we may set these aside, taking the normal case as our domain.

21 That S understands her own utterance we may consider to be packed into the fact that it is a serious assertion. The epistemology of such knowledge is outside the scope of this paper.

22 Note that the definition of competence given does not allow any inference "backwards" to sincerity, from knowledge of competence and the truth of what is asserted; but a stronger definition – "If S were to believe that P, then it would be the case that P", would do so. Intuitively, this kind of "backwards" knowledge of sincerity can occur. There is another difficulty, viz. that one may also know competence backwards, when "P" expresses a necessary truth and one knows this fact; and equally, in the absence of a semantics which avoids this, when one knows it to express a nomological truth (see footnote in §3 above). But there is no alternative which meets our requirements better than the $\mathcal{T}$ consisting of T_1 and $\mathrm{Trus}(S, U)$; so we must perforce complete our characterisation of knowledge through testimony by putting restrictions on how sincerity and competence are known by H, which rule out these cases of "backward" confirmation.

23 The present account thus differs from the one I offered in Fricker *op. cit.* There I opted for a material conditional expressing "competence with respect to P", for the prima facie reason in its favour, that it is the weakest further premise which validates the inference to "P". I now hold that earlier choice to be wrong because it fails the test of epistemic independence.

24 That it takes some care to arrive at a correct theoretical definition of trustworthiness in

no way undermines this claim. The difficulty of formulating explicitly conditions of which we all have a sure implicit grasp, is the general experience with analyses of ordinary concepts.

25 If Russell's chicken had only interpreted its feeder, her murderous intent on that last day would not have come as such a surprise!

26 And with them, simultaneously, semantic concepts, of course. My discussion here is too brief to bring in explicitly the fact that, in any ascription of psychological states to an individual, the meaning of the sentences she utters are always, at least in principle, also in the melting pot. But nothing I say here is in neglect of this fact, which does not invalidate the argument of this section, in particular the claims that any conceptually-ensured lower bounds on false belief, and false utterance, are quite low.

27 If considerations about interpretation do not suffice on their own to justify a default position in favour of trustworthiness, then a fortiori they do not serve to justify a PR thesis. This is one of the attempted "positive arguments" which, in my view, does not work.

28 My views here have been influenced by discussions with Prof. Mike Gilsenan, about his experiences as an anthropologist studying Middle Eastern societies. There is of course *much* more to be said on these matters.

29 It is itself part of that broader domain, rather than reducing to it, in that, as already noted, semantic and psychological concepts hang together, fitting simultaneously onto a subject.

30 See Fricker "The Epistemology of Testimony", pp. 74–5.

31 I am grateful for comments from Michael Bacharach, John Campbell, Bill Child, Dale Jamieson, Philip Pettit, and Tim Williamson. I am also particularly indebted to Arindam Chakrabarti, whose vigorous defence of the Indian view provoked this paper.

CHAPTER 56

Content Preservation

Tyler Burge

Near the beginning of *Rules for the Direction of the Mind* Descartes holds that some things known "with certainty" and "by deduction" are not evident. He notes that in long deductions, we may know that "the last link is connected with the first, even though we do not take in by means of one and the same act of vision all the intermediate links on which that connection depends, but only remember that we have taken them successively under review. ...."[1] Though he acknowledges that such knowledge is not evident or purely intuitive, and that long deductions are more subject to error than is intuitive knowledge, Descartes thinks that if the knowledge is deduced from evident mathematical premises, it is certain and demonstrative. Presumably he would not doubt that it is apriori. I lay aside certainty. But the view that the knowledge is demonstrative and apriori seems to me true.

Roderick Chisholm sees matters differently. He defines "apriori" in such a way that a proposition is apriori (and known apriori) only if it is either evident or follows directly by evident entailment from something that is evident. He explicitly rules out the results of multi-stepped deductions:

What if S derives a proposition from a set of axioms, not by means of one or two simple steps, but as a result of a complex proof, involving a

series of interrelated steps? If the proof is formally valid, then shouldn't we say that S knows the proposition a priori? I think that the answer is no.

He adds:

[I]f, in the course of a demonstration, we must rely upon memory at various stages, thus using as premisses contingent propositions about what we happen to remember, then, although we might be said to have "demonstrative knowledge" of our conclusion, in a somewhat broad sense of the expression "demonstrative knowledge," we cannot be said to have an a priori demonstration of the conclusion.[2]

Some of the difference between us derives from different conceptions of apriority. There are many such conceptions. I will be explicit about mine. I understand "*apriori*" to apply to a person's knowledge when that knowledge is underwritten by an apriori justification or entitlement that needs no further justification or entitlement to make it knowledge. A justification or entitlement is *apriori* if its justificational force is in no way constituted or enhanced by reference to or reliance on the specifics of some range of sense experiences or perceptual beliefs.

I take "apriori" to apply primarily to justifications or entitlements, rather than to truths. There are, of course, conceptual relations between these

Originally published in *The Philosophical Review* 102, 4 (Oct. 1993), pp. 457–88.

notions. Justification or entitlement aims at truth since it rationally supports belief. Moreover, the notion of apriori truth is important, though it should probably be explicated in terms of possible apriori knowledge. But in this account, justification and entitlement are fundamental.

The distinction between justification and entitlement is this: Although both have positive force in rationally supporting a propositional attitude or cognitive practice, and in constituting an epistemic right to it, entitlements are epistemic rights or warrants that need not be understood by or even accessible to the subject. We are entitled to rely, other things equal, on perception, memory, deductive and inductive reasoning, and on – I will claim – the word of others. The unsophisticated are entitled to rely on their perceptual beliefs. Philosophers may articulate these entitlements. But being entitled does not require being able to justify reliance on these resources, or even to conceive such a justification. Justifications, in the narrow sense, involve reasons that people have and have access to. These may include self-sufficient premises or more discursive justifications. But they must be available in the cognitive repertoire of the subject. The border between the notions of entitlement and justification may be fuzzy. I shall sometimes use "justified" and "justification" broadly, to cover both cases.

A person's knowledge of a proposition might be adequately supported both by an apriori body and by an empirical body of justification or entitlement. Then the person's knowledge would be heterogeneously overdetermined. The person would have both apriori and empirical knowledge of the proposition. To be apriori, the knowledge must be underwritten by an apriori justification or entitlement that needs no further justificatory help, in order for the person to have that knowledge. To be apriori, a person's justification or entitlement must retain its justificational force even if whatever empirical justifications or entitlements the person also has to believe the relevant proposition are ignored.

In holding that the justificational force of an apriori justification or entitlement is in no way constituted or enhanced by reliance on the specifics of some range of sense experiences or perceptual beliefs, I do not require that an apriori justification rely on reason or understanding alone – as pre-Kantian rationalists required.

A justification or entitlement would count as apriori if it did not rely for its justificational force on sense experience or perceptual belief at all. But it might also count if it depended on entirely general aspects of sense experience or perceptual belief, or on aspects of the structure of the subject's sense capacities and on their function in yielding categories of information.[3]

An individual need not make reference to sense experiences for his justification or entitlement to be empirical. My term "reliance on", in the explication of apriority, is meant to acknowledge that most perceptual beliefs about physical objects or properties do not refer to sense experiences or their perceptual content. Such beliefs make reference only to physical objects or properties. But the individual is empirically entitled to these perceptual beliefs. The justificational force of the entitlement backing such beliefs partly consists in the individual's having certain sense experiences, or at any rate in the individual's perceptual beliefs' being perceptual.

An apriori justification (entitlement) cannot rely on the specifics of sense experiences or perceptual beliefs for its *justificational force*. An apriori justification will usually depend on sense experiences or perceptual beliefs in some way. They are typically necessary for the acquisition of understanding or belief. But such dependence is not relevant to apriority unless it is essential to justificational force. Distinguishing the genesis of understanding and belief from the rational or normative force behind beliefs is fundamental to any view that takes apriori justification seriously.[4]

No serious conception of apriority has held that all justifications held to be apriori are unrevisable or infallible. Traditionally, the deepest apriori justifications were seen to be hard to come by. Putative apriori justifications were traditionally held to be revisable because one could fail to understand in sufficient depth the relevant propositions, or make errors of reasoning or analysis.

Traditional views did tend to overrate the tightness of connection between genuine (as opposed to putative) apriori justifications and truth. First, apriori justification (entitlement) can be nondemonstrative: an apriori justification can be outweighed without being shown to be rationally deficient or based on misunderstanding – without being shown not to have justificational force (not to be a justification). Some mathematical arguments are nondemonstrative, even broadly inductive, yet apriori in my sense. If a principle is accepted because its truth would explain or derive a variety of other accepted mathematical principles, the justification for accepting the principle is nondemonstrative; but it may not derive any of its force from perceptual beliefs. Second, although some apriori justifications or entitlements may be invulnerable to empirical counterconsiderations, such invulnerability does not follow from the notion of apriority. As will emerge, I think that some beliefs with genuine apriori justifications or entitlements are vulnerable to empirical overthrow.

In both ways, a belief's being apriori justified, for a person at a time, does not entail that it is true. There are, I think, some apriori justifications or entitlements that are demonstrative and do entail truth. But they do not do so purely by being apriori. The present conception of apriority fixes on the nature of the positive rational support for a belief. It says nothing about ways in which a belief may be vulnerable to counterconsiderations.

Thus apriori justification may be unevident, fallible, nondemonstrative, and not "certain." Beliefs thought to be apriori, and even actually justified apriori, are subject to revision. In these ways, my conception of apriority differs from Chisholm's.

Our differences are not primarily verbal, however. Chisholm regards long deductions as importing memory of particular past mental events into the justification of the deduction.[5] If such memories are a necessary part of the justification of the deduction, then – at least where they include memories of empirical beliefs or experiences (memories of reading symbols carefully, for example) – such deductions are not apriori, even on my conception of apriority.

But Chisholm's conception of the *role* of memory in demonstrative reasoning seems to me off the mark. If memory supplied, as part of the demonstration, "contingent propositions about what we happen to remember," the demonstration could not be purely logical or mathematical. But the normal role of memory in demonstrative reasoning is, I think, different. Memory does not supply for the demonstration propositions about memory, the reasoner, or past events.[6] It supplies

the propositions that serve as links in the demonstration itself. Or rather, it *preserves* them, together with their judgmental force, and makes them available for use at later times. Normally, the content of the knowledge of a longer demonstration is no more about memory, the reasoner, or contingent events than that of a shorter demonstration. One does not justify the demonstration by appeals to memory. One justifies it by appeals to the steps and the inferential transitions of the demonstration.

Why did Chisholm think otherwise? Long demonstrations are more fallible, and fallible in different ways, than short ones are. As he notes, people make mistakes of haste or incomplete understanding in judgments about relatively obvious propositions. But in longer demonstrations there are not only more opportunities to make these mistakes. One may suffer memory slips, even if one is careful and fully understands each proposition in the deduction. Traditionally, belief that appealed to apriori justification was held to be subject to error. But the sources of error were sometimes limited to failures of understanding and reason. It may seem that failure of memory is a source of error not easily accommodated by the traditional conception.

But relevant differences between short and long demonstrations are at most those between short-term and longer-term memory. Even one-step demonstrations could go bad if the reasoner's short-term memory were defective enough. So if we take vulnerability to memory failure as a sign that a justification of reasoning must *make reference to* memory, no reasoning at all will be independent of premises about memory. This is unacceptable. It is one thing to rely on memory in a demonstration, and another to use premises about memory. Any reasoning in time must rely on memory. But not all reasoning must use premises about memory or the past.

Here as elsewhere, to be justified in a cognitive process, one need not include premises in the justification that rule out all possible sources of error. This is a widely accepted point about perceptual justification. To be entitled to a perceptual belief that there is a bird there, one need not rule out all ways that one could be fooled. The same point applies to reasoning. To be justified in deductive reasoning, one need not include in one's justification propositions that guard against memory lapses, short or long term. Reliance on memory does not even add to the justificational force of the deductive justification.

If a justification depends on valid deductive reasoning from (let us presume) premises that are known apriori, then one's being justified by the justification depends only on one's *actually* understanding the reasoning sufficiently, and on one's reasoning processes' *actually* working properly. The justification does not depend on a premise that says that these conditions obtain, a premise that would itself require further justification. (I think that such dependence would involve a vicious regress.) One can presume that they obtain, without needing justification for the presumption, except in special situations in which these presumptions are called reasonably – and perhaps even correctly – into question.

In a deduction, reasoning processes' working properly depends on memory's preserving the results of previous reasoning. But memory's preserving such results does not add to the justificational force of the reasoning. It is rather a background condition for the reasoning's success. Memory is no more intrinsically an empirical faculty than it is a rational faculty. Its function in deductive reasoning is preservative. Its role in justification derives from what it preserves. Our entitlement to rely on memory in long deductions derives from our entitlement to rely on reasoning to carry out its functions. Memory failures that cause demonstrations to fail are failures of background conditions necessary to the proper function of reasoning. Hence the fallibility of memory in deductive reasoning is a source of error that can be countenanced by the traditional conception of apriority – and our conception as well.

Even in empirical reasoning, memory has a purely preservative function that does not contribute to the force of the justification, but simply helps assure the proper working of other cognitive capacities over time. When we perceive events and infer an explanation, memory preserves the perceptual beliefs as we carry out the explanation. But this preservation is not part of the justification of the explanation, nor does it add to it – even though if it were to fail, the explanation would be jeopardized. Rather, memory just holds the results of the perception intact long enough for explanation to be carried through.

Of course, memory sometimes is not purely preservative, but is an independent element in justification. Memory of events, objects, experiences, or attitudes may form a premise in a justification of an empirical belief. The beliefs that such memories support are justified partly *by reference to* the memory. Or else they may partly rely for their entitlement on memory.

Substantive memories of specific events, objects, experiences, or attitudes may play a role in deductive reasoning. They may aid reasoning without being elements in the justification they aid. So, for example, we may draw pictures in a proof, or make use of mnemonic devices to aid understanding and facilitate reasoning, without relying on them to enhance the mathematical justification. Alternatively, substantive memories may be part of an auxiliary, double-checking justification. In such cases, they may play a justificational role, yet be justificationally dispensable.

Substantive memory can even be needed to shore up gaps in a person's deductive reasoning. When a purely preservative instance is reasonably challenged, because memory has proved unreliable, one may have to rely on substantive memory. For example, if one knows one's memory has been slipping, one might have to resort to remembering counting the number of implication signs in a pair of formulas to support one's presumption that one's inference was based on correct memory. In such a case, reliance on the mnemonic devices may be indispensable to the person's justification – not merely a part of an auxiliary double-checking procedure. For the person is no longer entitled to the presumption that memory can be relied upon. I think, however, that the need to make reference to memory in deductions in order to be justified by the deductions is uncommon. In certain cases one might reasonably doubt that one is entitled to rely on one's memory, but be wrong to doubt it.

But the fact that memory can play substantive roles in justification or entitlement should not obscure the distinction between substantive and purely preservative memory. Let me summarize the distinction. Substantive memory is an element in a justification; it imports subject matter or objects into reasoning. Purely preservative memory introduces no subject matter, constitutes no element in a justification, and adds no force to a justification or entitlement. It simply maintains in justificational space a cognitive content with its judgmental force. Like inference, it makes transitions of reason possible, but contributes no propositional content. Unlike inference, it is not a transition or move – so it is not an element in a justification. Hence in deductions, neither reliance on it nor susceptibility to errors that arise from its malfunction prevents the justification associated with the deduction from being apriori.[7]

My discussion of memory is pointed toward exploring analogies between memory and acceptance of the word of others. What is the role of interlocution in the justification of our beliefs?

Relying on others is perhaps not metaphysically necessary for any possible rational being. But it is cognitively fundamental to beings at all like us. Though ontogenetically later than perception and memory, reliance on others for learning language and acquiring beliefs is deeply ingrained in our evolutionary history. Acquiring beliefs from others seems not only psychologically fundamental, but epistemically justified. We do not as individuals justify this reliance empirically, any more than we justify our use of perception empirically. But we seem entitled to such reliance. Most of the information that we have, and many of the methods we have for evaluating it, depend on interlocution. If we did not acquire a massive number of beliefs from others, our cognitive lives would be little different from the animals'.

What is the epistemic status of beliefs based on interlocution? I will state my view broadly before qualifying and supporting it. The use of perception is a background condition necessary for the acquisition of belief from others. But in many instances, perception and perceptual belief are not indispensable elements in the justification of such beliefs, or in the justificational force of entitlements underwriting such beliefs. The function of perception is often analogous to the function of purely preservative memory in reasoning. Without perception, one could not acquire beliefs from others. But perception plays a triggering and preservative role, in many cases, not a justificatory one. Sometimes, the epistemic status of beliefs acquired from others *is not empirical*. In particular, it is not empirical just by virtue of the fact that the beliefs are acquired from others.[8] Such beliefs are sometimes apriori justified in the sense that they need not rely for justificational force on the specifics of some range of sense experiences or perceptual beliefs.

Thomas Reid insightfully compares acquisition of belief from others to perception as a basic "channel to the mind," with its own functions in acquiring knowledge. Reid also claims that the tendency to rely on others for acquiring beliefs is innate:

> The wise and beneficent Author of nature, who intended that we should be social creatures, and that we should receive the greatest and most important part of our knowledge by the information of others, hath, for these purposes implanted in our natures two principles that tally with each other. The first of these principles is a propensity to speak truth … [the second] is a disposition to confide in the veracity of others, and to believe what they tell us.[9]

Reid notes that credulity, unlike reasoning and experience, is "strongest in childhood, and limited and restrained by experience." We restrain credulity by weighing the character and disinterestedness of witnesses, the possibility of collusion, the antecedent likelihood of information. Moreover, our reliance on others is more fallible than our reliance on perception – as Reid also notes. We make perceptual errors, but the errors derive from illusions that often can be explained by reference to natural law. We are led into mistakes by others through lies and emotional interferences that are capricious in comparison to the patterns of nature. Why do these considerations not show that acquisition of beliefs from others is not only necessarily empirical but far more in need of empirical expertise than ordinary perception for its justification?

Justification in acquiring beliefs from others may be glossed, to a first approximation, by this principle: *A person is entitled to accept as true something that is presented as true and that is intelligible to him, unless there are stronger reasons not to do so.* Call this the *Acceptance Principle*. As children and often as adults, we lack reasons not to accept what we are told. We are entitled to acquire information according to the principle – without *using* it as justification – accepting the information instinctively. The justification I develop below is a reflective philosophical account of an epistemic entitlement that comes with being a rational agent.

Justified (entitled) acceptance is the epistemic "default" position. We can strengthen this position with empirical reasons: "she is a famous mathematician." We can acquire empirical reasons *not* to accept what we are told: "he has every reason to lie." But to be entitled, we do not have to have reasons that support the default position, if there is no reasonable ground for doubt. Truth telling is a norm that can be reasonably presumed in the absence of reasons to attribute violations.

It is usually said that to be justified in accepting information from someone else, one must be justified in believing that the source believes the information and is justified in believing it. I think this misleading. A presupposition of the Acceptance Principle is that one is entitled not to bring one's source's sincerity or justification into question, in the absence of reasons to the contrary. This too is an epistemic default position.

The Acceptance Principle is not a statistical point about people's tending to tell the truth more often than not. Falsehoods might conceivably outnumber truths in a society. The principle is also not a point about innateness, though Reid's claim that a disposition to acceptance is innate seems to me correct. The principle is about entitlement, not psychological origin.

The epistemic default position articulated by the Acceptance Principle applies at an extremely high level of idealization in most actual communication, especially between sophisticated interlocutors. Social, political, or intellectual context often provides "stronger reasons" that counsel against immediately accepting what one is told. Given life's complexities, this default position is often left far behind in reasoning about whether to rely on a source. One might wonder, with some hyperbole, whether it can ever be the last word in the epistemology of acceptance for anyone over the age of eleven. The primary point – that it is a starting point for reason – would not be undermined if its purest applications were relatively rare. But I think that it has broader application than the hyperbolic conjecture suggests.

Acceptance underlies language acquisition. Lacking language, one could not engage in rational, deliberative activity, much less the primary forms of human social cooperation. (Indeed, this point suggests the line of justification for the principle that I shall begin to develop below.) But unquestioned reliance is also common in adult life. When we ask someone on the street the time, or the direction of some landmark, or when we ask someone to do a simple sum, we rely on the answer. We make use of a presumption of credibility when we read books, signs, or newspapers, or talk to strangers on unloaded topics. We need not engage in reasoning about the person's qualifications to be rational in accepting what he or she says, in the absence of grounds for doubt. Grounds for doubt are absent a lot of the time.

The primary default position, the Acceptance Principle, is not an empirical principle. The general form of justification associated with the principle is: *A person is apriori entitled to accept a proposition that is presented as true and that is intelligible to him, unless there are stronger reasons not to do so, because it is prima facie preserved (received) from a rational source, or resource for reason; reliance on rational sources – or resources for reason – is, other things equal, necessary to the function of reason.* The justificational force of the entitlement described by this justification is not constituted or enhanced by sense experiences or perceptual beliefs.[10] Before filling in this form of justification, I want to make some preliminary points.

I think that I need not show that other rational beings are necessary to the function of one's reason in order for one to have these entitlements. One has a general entitlement to rely on the rationality of rational beings. The Acceptance Principle can be apriori instantiated where one has apriori, undefeated, prima facie entitlement to construe something prima facie intelligible as having a rational source. So I think that to maintain that one is apriori entitled to rely upon rational interlocutors, I need not show that a solitary reasoner is impossible.

Our account distinguishes rational sources and resources for reason. Resources for reason – memory and perception, for example – need not themselves be rational beings or capacities to reason. In these senses they need not themselves be rational. Yet they may provide material and services that a rational being is apriori entitled to rely upon. Rational sources are sources that themselves are a capacity to reason or are rational beings.

As with rational sources, I think that to show that we are apriori entitled to rely upon a given resource for reason, I need not show that such a resource is necessary to any possible reasoning. One is entitled to rely upon resources for reason in general – other things equal – even if some particular resource for reason is not indispensable to the function of reason. Such resources may enrich reason without being necessary to every rational activity. This view puts pressure on explicating the notion of a resource for reason. This matter can be postponed, for it is relevant to interlocution only in special cases.

There are deeper questions about rational entitlement that I cannot pursue in depth here. One can ask why one is entitled to rely on rational sources (or resources for reason), in view of the fact that they can be mistaken or misleading. This is tantamount to a traditional skeptical question about how putative rationality or justification is associated with truth. One can apparently imagine systematic misconnections between being justified (entitled), according to ordinary canons, and having true belief. Why then should one ever think that ordinary canons provide ground for belief? I will not take on skepticism here. I will assume that we are rationally entitled to rely on reason, memory, and perception. The Acceptance Principle is an extension of this assumption: we are rationally entitled to rely on interlocution because we may presume that it has a rational source.

Now I turn to filling in the justification for the Acceptance Principle. First, if something is a rational source, it is a prima facie source of truth. For a condition on reasons, rationality, and reason is that they be guides to truth. Explicating this idea is notoriously difficult; but I do not apologize for it. An epistemic reason for believing something would not count as such if it did not provide some reasonable support for accepting it as *true*. The same point applies to rational entitlements for belief. The entitlements that I am discussing are epistemic, not matters of politesse. If one has a reason or entitlement to accept something because it is, prima facie, rationally supported, one has a reason or entitlement to accept it as true. A source is a guide to truth *in* being rational. Rational mistakes are possible. But if there is no reason to think that they are occurring, it is rational to accept the affirmed deliverances of a rational source. For other things equal, reason can be reasonably followed in seeking truth.

It is not just the rationality of a source that marks an apriori prima facie connection to truth. The very content of an intelligible message presented as true does so as well. For content is constitutively dependent, in the first instance, on patterned connections to a subject matter, connections that insure in normal circumstances a baseline of true thought presentations. So presentations' having content must have an origin in getting things right. The prima facie rationality of the source intensifies a prima facie connection to truth already present in the prima facie existence of presented content.

The remaining main step in justifying the Acceptance Principle lies in the presumption that the source of a message is a rational source, or a resource for reason. I think that one is apriori prima facie entitled to presume that the interlocutor is a rational source or resource for reason – simply by virtue of the prima facie intelligibility of the message conveyed. That is enough to presume that the interlocutor is rational, or at least a source of information that is rationally underwritten.

The idea is not that we reason thus: "If it looks like a human and makes sounds like a language, it is rational; on inspection it looks human and sounds linguistic; so it is rational." Rather, in understanding language we are entitled to presume what we instinctively do presume about our source's being a source of rationality or reason. We are so entitled because intelligibility is an apriori prima facie sign of rationality.

If something is prima facie intelligible, one is prima facie entitled to rely on one's understanding of it as intelligible. One is entitled to begin with what putative understanding one has. But anything that can intelligibly present something as true can be presumed, prima facie, to be either rational or made according to a rational plan to mimic aspects of rationality. Presentation of propositional content presupposes at least a derivative connection to a system of perceptual, cognitive, and practical interactions with a world, involving beliefs and intentional activity.[11] Belief and intention in turn presuppose operation under norms of reason or rationality – norms governing information acquisition, inference, and practical activity. For propositional attitudes, especially those complex enough to yield articulated presentations of content, are necessarily associated with certain cognitive and practical practices. To be what they are, such practices must – with allowances for some failures – accord with norms of reason or rationality.

To summarize: We are apriori prima facie entitled to accept something that is prima facie intelligible and presented as true. For prima facie intelligible propositional contents prima facie presented as true bear an apriori prima facie conceptual relation to a rational source of true presentations-as-true: Intelligible propositional expressions presuppose rational abilities and entitlements; so intelligible presentations-as-true come prima facie backed by a rational source or resource for reason; and both the content of intelligible propositional presentations-as-true and the prima facie rationality of their source indicate a prima facie source of truth.[12] Intelligible affirmation is the face of reason; reason is a guide to truth. We are apriori prima facie entitled to take intelligible affirmation at face value.

We could be apriori entitled to false beliefs. Sounds or shapes could have no source in rationality but seem intelligible. A quantum accidental sequence of sounds could correspond to those of Hamlet's most famous speech.[13] But the fact that we could be mistaken in thinking that something is a message, or in understanding a message conveyed, is compatible with our having an apriori prima facie rational right to rely on our construal of an event as having a certain meaning or intentional content. And where a message has meaning or intentional content, we are entitled to presume apriori that it has a rational source, or is a resource for reason.

Just as the Acceptance Principle does not assume that truth is in a statistical majority, the justification of the Principle does not assume that most people are rational. We could learn empirically that most people are crazy or that all people have deeply irrational tendencies – not just in their performance but in their basic capacities. Human beings clearly do have some rational entitlements and competencies, even though we have found that they are surprisingly irrational in certain tasks. The justification presupposes that there is a conceptual relation between intelligibility and rational entitlement or justification, between having and articulating propositional attitudes and having rational competencies.

Rational backing is, other things equal, a ground for acceptance of something as true. But in dealing with others, one must often take account of their lies. Why is one *apriori* entitled, except when reasonable doubt arises, to abstract from the possibility that it may be in the interlocutor's rational interest to lie?

This issue is more complex than I can see through now. I will make some general observations, and then sketch one line of reply. (I think there are others.) The Acceptance Principle and its justification are formulated so as to be neutral on whether what is "presented as true" comes from another person. Its application does not depend on an assumption that the source is outside oneself (although further articulation will, I think, give this source a place in the account). Many of the differences between content passing between minds and content processed by a single mind derive from differences in modes of acquisition and in necessary background conditions, that do not enter into the justificational force underwriting an entitlement.

An account of an entitlement that includes, as a special case, relying on the word of others must, however, acknowledge the following issue: The straight-line route from the prima facie intelligibility of a presentation-as-true to prima facie rational characteristics of the source to prima facie acceptability (truth) of the presentation, is threatened by the fact that certain aspects of *rationality* (rational lying) may go *counter* to true presentations. So why should rationality, especially in another person, be a sign of truth? One can have empirical reasons to think someone is not lying. One could have nonrational tendencies to believe, which with luck might get one by. But can one have apriori prima facie rational entitlement to accept what one is told, without considering whether the interlocutor is lying – lacking special reasons to think he is?

Apart from special information about the context or one's interlocutor, neutrality (as well as doubt) is, I think, a rationally unnatural attitude toward an interlocutor's presentation of something as true. (Compare: lying for the fun of it is a form of craziness.) Explaining why, in depth, would involve wrestling with some of the most difficult issues about the relation between "practical" reason and reason. I will broach one line of explanation.

Reason necessarily has a teleological aspect, which can be understood through reflection on rational practice. Understanding the notion of reason in sufficient depth requires understanding its primary functions. One of reason's primary functions is that of presenting truth, independently of special personal interests. Lying is sometimes rational in the sense that it is in the liar's best interests. But lying occasions a disunity among functions of reason. It conflicts with one's reason's transpersonal function of presenting the truth, independently of special personal interests.[14]

The Humean reply that reason functions *only* to serve individual passions or interests is unconvincing. Reason has a function in providing guidance to truth, in presenting and promoting truth without regard to individual interest. This is why epistemic reasons are not relativized to a person or to a desire. It is why someone whose reasoning is distorted by self-deception is in a significant way irrational – even when the self-deception serves the individual's interests. It is why one is rationally entitled to rely on deductive reasoning or memory, in the absence of counter-reasons, even if it conflicts with one's interests. One can presume that a presentation of something as true by a rational being – whether in oneself or by another – has, prima facie, something rationally to be said for it. Unless there is reason to think that a rational source is rationally disunified – in the sense that individual interest is occasioning conflict with the transpersonal function of reason – one is rationally entitled to abstract from individual interest in receiving something presented as true by such a source.

Another consideration pointing in the same direction is this. A condition on an individual's having propositional attitudes is that the content of those attitudes by systematically associated with veridical perceptions and true beliefs:[15] true contents must be presented and accepted as true within some individual; indeed, the very practice of communication depends on preservation of truth. If a rational interlocutor presents intelligible contents as true, one can rationally presume that the contents are associated with a practice of successfully aiming at and presenting truth. Now an inertial principle appears applicable: since the intelligibility of a presentation-as-true indicates a source of both rational and true content

presentations, one needs special reason to think there has been deviation from rationally based, true truth-presentation. Other things equal, one can rationally abstract from issues of sincerity or insincerity.

The apriori entitlement described by the Acceptance Principle is, of course, no guarantee of truth. It is often a much weaker sign of truth, from the point of view of certainty, than empirically justified beliefs about the interlocutor. The lines of reasoning I have proposed justify a prima facie rational presumption, a position of non-neutrality – not some source of certainty.

Even if the Acceptance Principle is not an empirical principle, it may seem that particular entitlements sanctioned by it, "applications," must inevitably be empirical. To know what one is being told, one must use perception. One must perceive words as expressing content presented as true. In interlocution, perception does inevitably figure in acquisition of understanding and belief. Perception is necessary to minimal understanding; and minimal understanding is essential to belief and justification. But our question concerns perception's role in justification or entitlement. I will first consider its role in justification in our narrow sense, and then turn to its role in entitlement.

One might reason that since the Acceptance Principle counts it rational for a person to accept what is presented as true, and since one can know what is presented as true by another person only through perceiving an event in time, a person must rely for justificational force on perception of particular events to apply the principle.

This reasoning rests on a confusion about the status of the Acceptance Principle and its justification. The Acceptance Principle is not a premise in an argument applied by recipients of information. It is a description of a norm that indicates that recipients are sometimes entitled to accept information from others *immediately* without argument. The justification of the principle is not an argument that need be used by interlocutors, but an account of why the practice of acquiring information from others is rationally justified.[16] It is well known that we do not store the physical properties of sentences we hear or read.[17] The content of the linguistic forms is what is important. We seem normally to understand content in a way whose unconscious details (inferential or otherwise) are not accessible via ordinary reflection. To be entitled to believe what one is told, one need not understand or be able to justify any transition from perceptual beliefs about words to understanding of and belief in the words' content. One can, of course, come to understand certain inferences from words to contents. Such empirical meta-skills do enrich communication. But they are not indispensable to it. To be justified in understanding, we have to reason empirically about what we perceive only when communication runs into trouble, or when special, contextual, nonliteral expressive devices are used (see note 21). Other things equal, we are entitled to presume that what seems intelligible is understood. Justification in the narrow sense is not basic to the epistemology of interlocution.

But the question of entitlement is more subtle. In ordinary perception of physical objects and properties we have sense experiences that are not ordinarily the objects of reference or the basis of a justifying inference to perceptual beliefs to which we are entitled. Yet having such experiences, or having perceptual beliefs, contributes to the justificational force of our empirical beliefs:[18] A perceptual belief's being perceptual is an element in its justificational power. The belief's being causally or constitutively associated with sense perception is part of the force of our entitlement to the belief.

In interlocution, we are also causally dependent on perception. Our entitlements are thus dependent on perception. But in my view, perception contributes nothing to the epistemic force of the fundamental "default" entitlement.

Perceptions or perceptual beliefs about physical objects are constitutively dependent on bearing natural lawlike causal relations to objects of perception – to their subject matter, physical objects. The contents of the beliefs and perceptions are what they are partly because of these relations to specific physical objects or properties. Our entitlement to rely on perception and perceptual beliefs is partly grounded in this causally patterned, content-giving relation which is partly constitutive of perception.

When we receive communication, the situation is different. The objects of cognitive interest – the contents and their subject matters – are not the objects of perception. We do not perceive the contents of attitudes that are conveyed to us; we understand them. We perceive and have perceptual beliefs about word occurrences. We may perceive them as having a certain content and subject matter, but the content is understood, not perceived. The subject matter, word occurrences, of our perceptual experiences and beliefs bears a nonconstitutive (quasi-conventional) relation to the content and subject matter of the beliefs to which we are entitled as a result of communication. So the accounts of our noninferential entitlements to perception and to interlocution must be different.

One might note that the relation between perceived words and their contents or subject matters must involve some sort of explanatory relation. So one might be tempted to think that although one does not typically infer the content from the words explicitly and consciously, the entitlement must somehow be based on this explanatory relation. But it would be a mistake to embrace this temptation without reflecting carefully on the special character of the relation as it occurs in interlocution. The relation between words and their subject matter and content is not an *ordinary*, natural, lawlike causal-explanatory relation. Crudely speaking, it involves a mind.

There are, of course, complex causal-explanatory relations that may be used to infer the content or subject matter of an interlocutor's speech from perceived word occurrences. One could give an account of entitlement centered on possible inferential interpretations, or on reason-giving explanatory connections between words and content. The interpretation might not be accessible to the recipient, but it could represent a reasonable route from the received message to a putative truth. Such an account – broadly familiar in current discussion – would make the entitlement empirical, because it would appeal in the account of justificational force to an inductive connection to perceived word occurrences.

I do *not* doubt that such accounts are true. I doubt that they are fundamental. I think that what is fundamental is not a metalinguistic connection between word occurrences, taken as objects of perception, and their contents or subject matters. What is fundamental is an apriori prima facie entitlement to rely upon putative understanding, and an apriori prima facie connection between putatively understood contents and rational sources of truths. Understanding is epistemically basic. Traditionally, a justification or entitlement was apriori if it could be derived from conceptual understanding – however experientially dependent the understanding might be. The issue over apriority begins with conceptual understanding and asks whether perceptual experience is needed to supplement the understanding for one to be justified or entitled to one's belief.

The epistemic status of perception in normal communication is like the status it was traditionally thought to have when a diagram is presented that triggers realization of the meaning and truth of a claim of pure geometry or logic. Perception of physical properties triggers realization of something abstract, an intentional content, expressed by the sentence, and (often) already mastered by the recipient. Its role is to call up and facilitate mobilization of conceptual resources that are already in place. It is probably *necessary* that one perceive symbolic expressions to accept logical axioms – just as it is necessary to perceive words in interlocution. But perception of expressions is not part of the justificational force for accepting the contents. In both cases, no reference to a possible meta-inference from expressions to contents is needed in an account of justificational force. The primary entitlement in interlocution derives from prima facie understanding of the messages, and from a presumption about the rational nature of their source – not from the role of perception, however necessary, in the process.[19]

In interlocution, perception of utterances makes possible the passage of propositional content from one mind to another rather as purely preservative memory makes possible the preservation of propositional content from one time to another. Memory and perception of utterances function similarly, in reasoning and communication respectively. Their correct functioning is necessary for the enterprises they serve. Their failure could undermine those enterprises. They preserve the content of events (past thoughts in proof, word utterances in interlocution) – events that *can* become objects known empirically. But the basic epistemic role of memory and perception in these enterprises is not to present objects of knowledge. They function to preserve and enable – not to justify.

In interlocution, the individual's basic default entitlement normally derives from the presump-

tive intelligibility of a message understood, not from anything specific in the words perceived. Unless reasonable doubt arises about the reliability or interpretation of the source, the specific perceptions of utterances need not be relied upon in contributing force to the receiver's entitlement to his understanding of or belief in what is communicated.

Perception might be thought part of the justificational force of our entitlement in another way. The justification of the Acceptance Principle says that one is entitled to accept intelligible contents "presented as true." We must perceive a speech act as involving a presentation-as-true to be justified under the principle. Why does it not follow that our entitlement to accept what we are told in particular cases relies for its force on perceptual beliefs?

The issues here are again very complex. But the short answer to the question is that one's intellectually grounded entitlement to one's understanding of content includes an entitlement to understand presentations-as-true. Understanding content presupposes and is interdependent with understanding the force of presentations of content. So entitlement to the former must presuppose entitlement to the latter. In many normal cases the epistemology of our entitlement to understanding assertive force has a default status that is parallel to that of our entitlement to understanding content. Perception is no more basic to understanding assertive force than it is to understanding conceptual content. The default position is that presumed understanding of both content and force is epistemically fundamental. Empirical justification for an interpretation of content or force is demanded only when elements in the context demand reconsideration or supplementation of the default understanding. I find the parallel compelling. But I will sketch in two steps a picture of how default understanding of a presentation-as-true can sometimes be derived from no more than default understanding of propositional content. This picture is not needed, but it may enrich the account.

First, entitlement to one's understanding of a message's content carries with it, indeed rests on, an entitlement to understanding intentional *events* as having specific content. Understanding speech acts or thoughts as they occur is the root of understanding content types. The necessary role of perception in enabling one to follow another's speaking or thinking is not fundamentally different from its role in enabling one to grasp the abstract content of another's sentence. All that I have argued on the latter score applies to the former. Perception's basic role is to make understanding possible and to trigger it on particular occasions. But the justificational force of one's basic default entitlement to understand something as an event with a specific content is not perceptual. It is intellectual in that it resides in one's putative understanding of conceptual content in application or use, in one's ability to think-with.

Second, understanding conceptual content – both abstractly and in contentful events or uses – involves understanding the content's mood. But for contents in the indicative (declarative) mood – as distinguished from interrogative or imperative mood – presentation-as-true is the defeasible default use. The connection between declarative mood and presentations-as-true is conceptual. The justificational force of the entitlement to rely on the connection is correspondingly conceptual, not perceptual.[20]

In the absence of overriding reasons, the default presumption stands. Nonassertive uses (jokes, irony, fiction) that drain declaratives of assertive implications must employ context to make themselves understood. The recipient must infer that the sentence is used nonassertively from empirical information about the context. Although affirmative use of declarative contents must, on occasion, also be inferred from special contextual information, taking a declarative sentence utterance as a presentation-as-true normally requires no such reasoning or empirical interpretation.[21]

Thus in many instances, one's entitlement to take something as a presentation-as-true in interlocution derives from understanding an event's content, and need not rely for its justificational force on perception of word occurrences. What one is entitled to on intellectual grounds is merely, prima facie, that a given content is presented as true. One gets nothing about the time, form, or circumstances of the assertion. All such information is epistemically grounded in perception of aspects of the context. But the fundamental entitlement to accept something as a presentation-as-true derives from understanding. It can even be derived sometimes from understanding of content (its tokening and the relation of its mood to presentations-as-true). The justificational force of the derivation does not depend on any supplementation from perception. Perception plays its role in making understanding possible and in justifying supplemental information about the form, existence, and context of the assertion.

In appreciating these points, one must distinguish between knowing about the assertion as part of a pattern for explaining the psychology and behavior of the asserter, and using the interlocutor as a source of information. In the former enterprise, perception of an assertion as an action by a particular individual is commonly taken as an element in the justification of an explanation, or an object of interpretation. But in interlocution, perception need not play this role unless some reasonable doubt arises about the informant's message or the recipient's understanding (see note 25).

One can know through memory the events that help recall the previous step in a proof, thereby making those events objects of knowledge. One can know on the basis of perception that a particular person made an assertion at a given time. One can surely construct an empirical meta-justification (or entitlement) for one's belief based on interlocution: "She asserted that p (known empirically); it is prima facie reasonable to rely on others' assertions; so I should rely on her assertion." Such meta-justifications supplement one's epistemic position in interlocution. But they are not, I think, fundamental. Just as remembering events does not enhance the primary object-level justification in deductive argument, so relying on perception does not contribute to the justificational force of one's fundamental entitlement to one's understanding of content, or to one's acceptance of what is presented as true.

Let us return from our entitlement to understanding to our entitlement to believe what we hear, given that we understand it. When we receive a message, we often know a lot about the context of the reception, the biography of the source, the antecedent empirical plausibility of the information. This knowledge is inevitably perceptually grounded. Does this fact make our entitlement to believe what we receive from others inevitably perceptual? I do not think so. Our initial entitlement does not depend on this knowledge for its justificational force.

In areas like politics, where cooperation is not the rule and truth is of little consequence, or philosophy, where questioning is as much at issue as belief, we engage in complex reasoning about whether to accept what we hear or read. Reasonable doubt becomes a norm. But these situations are not paradigmatic. They are parasitic on more ordinary situations where acceptance is a norm.

The default position is justified acceptance. Often we need empirical reasons to defeat reasonable doubts that threaten our right to acceptance. But sometimes empirical reasons simply reinforce and overdetermine the default entitlement. Our being justified does not then rest indispensably on empirical background information.[22]

I turn now from our entitlement to applications of the Acceptance Principle to the role of interlocution in the acquisition of knowledge. In the absence of countervailing considerations, application of the Acceptance Principle often seems to provide sufficient entitlement for knowledge. Most of our knowledge relies essentially on acceptance of beliefs from others – either through talk or through reading. Not only most of our scientific beliefs, but most of our beliefs about history, ourselves, and much of the macro-world, would have insufficient justification to count as knowledge if we were somehow to abstract from all elements of their justification, or entitlement, that depended on communication.

Our entitlement to ordinary perceptual belief is usually sufficient for perceptual knowledge. It is usually sufficient even though we may be unable specifically to rule out various possible defeating conditions. If there is no reason to think that the defeating conditions threaten, one has knowledge despite ignoring them. Something similar holds for acquisition of belief from others. Other things equal, ordinary interlocution suffices for knowledge.[23]

In knowing something through interlocution, the recipient has his own entitlement to accept the word of the interlocutor, together with any supplementary justification the recipient might have that bears on the plausibility of the information. Let this include all the reasons available to the recipient, together with all the entitlements deriving from his own cognitive resources. Call this body (i) the recipient's *own proprietary justification.*

If the recipient depends on interlocution for knowledge, the recipient's knowledge depends on the source's having knowledge as well. For if the source does not believe the proposition, or if the proposition is not true, or if the source is not justified, the recipient cannot know the proposition. The recipient's own proprietary entitlement to rely on interlocution is insufficient by itself to underwrite the knowledge.[24] In particular, the recipient depends on sources' proprietary justifications and entitlements (through a possible chain of sources). The recipient depends on at least some part of this body of justification and entitlement in the sense that without it, his belief would not be knowledge. The recipient's own justification is incomplete and implicitly refers back, anaphorically, to fuller justification or entitlement. Call the combination of the recipient's own proprietary justification with the proprietary justifications (including entitlements) in his sources on which the recipient's knowledge depends (ii) *the extended body of justification* that underwrites the recipient's knowledge.

At the outset, I explained apriori knowledge in terms of apriori justification or entitlement. The question arises whether apriori knowledge based on interlocution is underwritten by the individual's proprietary justification or by a justification that must include some nonproprietary part of the extended body of justification.

The extended body of justification – the one that reaches beyond the individual – is the relevant one. If I am apriori entitled to accept an interlocutor's word, but the interlocutor provides me with empirically justified information, it would be wrong to characterize my knowledge of the information as apriori. Similarly, if my source knows a proposition apriori, but I must rely on empirical knowledge to justify my acceptance of the source's word, it would be wrong to say that *I* know the proposition apriori – even though I have knowledge that is apriori known by someone. It seems most natural to think that a strand of justification that runs through the extended body into the individual's proprietary body of justification must be apriori for the recipient's knowledge to be apriori. People who depend on interlocution for knowledge of mathematical theorems but do not know the proofs can have apriori knowledge in this sense. The source mathematician knows the theorem apriori and the recipient is entitled apriori to accept the word of the source, in the absence of reasons to doubt. Most of us knew the Pythagorean theorem at some stage in this manner. When apriori knowledge is preserved through reports which the recipient is apriori justified in accepting, the receiver's knowledge is apriori.

The Acceptance Principle is clearly similar to what is widely called a "Principle of Charity" for translating or interpreting others. The most obvious difference is that the former applies to situations in which one is not taking another as an object of interpretation, but rather as a source of information presumed to be understood without interpretation. This situation is basic for communication.[25] Radical interpretation is not, I think, the paradigmatic situation for theorizing about linguistic interchange.

We rely on being so formed that we take in information from others without interpretation. Unlike the Principle of Charity, the Acceptance Principle presumes not only that we are like others in being rational. It presumes that we preserve content, other things equal. This presumption works because we share with others around us our cognitive tendencies and means of expressing them, and a common environment. But we do not have to *justify* a claim that these conditions for success are in place to be entitled to rely upon our understanding. (Analogously, we do not have to justify a claim that the environment is normal and we are adapted to it in order to be entitled to rely on perception.) It is enough if we learn how to understand. Once we are in a position to understand, we are entitled to the following presumption apriori, other things equal: We understand what we seem to understand. Or rather, other things equal, we need not use a distinction between understanding and seeming to understand. We need not take what we hear as an *object* of interpretation, unless grounds for doubt arise. Only then do we shift from content preservation to interpretation.

The Acceptance Principle entails a presumption that others' beliefs are justified, that others are sources of rationality or reason. The view that others' beliefs can be presumed to be true is familiar from the Principle of Charity. The presumption that others are reliable indices of truth rests on a presumption that they are rational sources. Their reliability is not some brute correlation between belief and world. We are entitled to treat others as reliable partly *because* we are entitled to presume that they are rationally justified or rationally entitled to their beliefs. We are entitled, most fundamentally, to think of others as sources of rationality or reason not because we take them as objects of interpretation and explanation, but because prima facie intelligibility is an apriori prima facie sign of rationality.

This focus on others is articulated from a first-person point of view. Each of *us* is justified in presuming that others are justified. But we are possible interlocutors too. The idea that others are prima facie justified in their beliefs makes general sense only if we presume generally: people, including each of us, are reliable rational sources of true justified beliefs. Obviously the conclusion requires qualification and elaboration. But the route to it is, I think, of interest. I arrived at it by arguing that we have intellection-grounded prima facie entitlements to applications of the Acceptance Principle, though they are empirically defeasible. I think that this approach to epistemology may help with some of the traditional problems of philosophy.

Notes

1   Descartes, *Philosophical Works*, ed. Haldane and Ross (New York: Dover, 1955), vol. 1, p. 8. Locke, in *Essay Concerning Human Understanding*, bk. 4, chap. 2, sec. 7, notes that such knowledge is "less perfect" in the sense of more subject to error than intuitive knowledge.

2   Roderick M. Chisholm, "The Truths of Reason," in *Theory of Knowledge*, 2d edn (Englewood Cliffs, NJ: Prentice Hall, 1977), reprinted in *A Priori Knowledge*, ed. Paul K. Moser (Oxford: Oxford University Press, 1987).

3   Kant thought that all synthetic apriori judgments, except those in his practical philosophy – and perhaps in the critical philosophy as a whole – rested on general ("pure") aspects of the structure of function of sense experience. In fact, he believed that the justificational force of all such judgments depended

on one's actually having had sense experiences. My conception of apriori knowledge makes room for Kant's conception. I do not, however, agree with Kant that those apriori justifications whose justificational force is not enhanced at all by sense experience are vacuous, or analytic in the sense of being true independently of any relation to a subject matter. The distinction between reliance on the specifics of a range of sense experiences, or perceptual beliefs, and reliance on the structure or function of one's sense capacities in obtaining categories of information is not sharp. I think it may remain useful.

4   This explication of apriority applies to justification of cogito-type thoughts like *I am thinking*, and of other judgments about intellection. (It does not apply to *I am having an afterimage*.) These thoughts' justification is grounded on understanding, not on sense experience or perceptual belief. I am aware that some traditional conceptions of apriority would exclude *cogito* cases. Some of these conceptions emphasize not justificational independence of sense experience, but justificational independence of any "experience" at all, including intellectual "experience." (I leave open here whether this use of "experience" is appropriate.) This is one of Leibniz's conceptions (see *New Essays* IV, ix). Of course Leibniz centered on apriori truth rather than on an individual's justification. Frege's conception features justificational independence of any relation to particular events or facts in time (see Gottlob Frege, *The Foundations of Arithmetic*, sec. 3). On his conception, only general truths and truths derivable from general truths could be known apriori.

The terminological issues here are complex; but this difference with traditional explications will not affect my argument with Chisholm, which goes through on any of these conceptions. Moreover, the broader argument of the paper does not depend on how one uses the term "apriori." I am less interested in the term than in the conception I associate with it. The argument of the paper hinges on the role of perception in justification or entitlement. I do think that there are significant substantive and historical issues regarding these different notions associated with the term "apriori" that bear on the way the issue between empiricism and rationalism has come to be understood since the work of Kant, Mill, and the positivists. For now, it is enough that the present explication signals my interest in justifications or entitlements whose force is grounded in intellection, reason, or reflection, as distinguished from perception, understood broadly to include feeling.

5   Descartes's own remark that in deductions we must remember that we have taken the links of the deduction "successively under review" may suggest this view. I find it unclear how he intended the remark.

6   Chisholm's "thus," in the quoted passage, is clearly a mistake. It does not follow from a deduction's reliance on memory that it, or any justification associated with it, uses "contingent propositions" about memory as premises.

7   The distinction between substantive memory and purely preservative memory roughly parallels a distinction in psychology between "episodic memory" and "semantic memory." There is evidence that these sorts of memory function differently in our psychologies. See E. Tulving, "Episodic and Semantic Memory," in *Organization of Memory*, ed. Tulving and Donaldson (New York: Academic Press, 1972).

Another difference between the two types of memory is that purely preservative memory necessarily plays a role in any reasoning in time. The extent to which substantive memory enters into reasoning depends on the psychology of the reasoner, the subject of the argument, and so on. One should not underestimate, however, our dependence on the use of symbols in reasoning. The role of symbols is partly that of providing perceptual objects. Explicating this sort of dependence is a difficult and important matter. Doing so may complicate or blur the distinction between the sometime dependence on substantive memory and the more general rational necessity of depending on purely preservative memory. But I think that the distinction will remain valuable.

8   Contrast Chisholm, "The Truths of Reason," sec. 5, and James F. Ross, "Testimonial Evidence," in *Analysis and Metaphysics*, ed.

Keith Lehrer (Dordrecht: D. Reidel, 1975). They assume that belief based on testimony cannot be justified apriori and, if it is knowledge at all, must be empirical.

I think that some of what I am saying here bears on the common assumption that knowledge based on the output of proofs by computers cannot be apriori. Cf. Kripke, *Naming and Necessity* (Cambridge: Harvard University Press, 1980), pp. 35; also Thomas Tymoczko, "The Four-Color Problem and its Philosophical Significance," *Journal of Philosophy* 76 (1979), pp. 57–83. Kripke says that such knowledge is based on the laws of physics. Although such knowledge depends on the functioning of a machine according to the laws of physics, it is not obvious that knowledge of the laws of physics is an indispensable part of our justification for believing in the results of such output. I discuss this issue in "Computer Proof, Apriori Knowledge, and Other Minds," *Philosophical Perspectives* 12 (1998), pp. 1–37.

9 Thomas Reid, *An Inquiry into the Human Mind* (Chicago: University of Chicago Press, 1970), chap. 6, sec. 24.

10 Principles narrower than the Acceptance Principle could with luck and context achieve the same utility: rely on the first person one comes across and no one afterward. Such principles are not rational starting points. We are entitled to something more general. In learning a language, one usually need not know the credentials of one's source – beyond the fact that the source is intelligible. Having an apriori entitlement based on the Acceptance Principle is compatible with also having empirical justifications of prima facie acceptance – or of narrower principles, such as "nonaggressive care-givers are more trustworthy than strangers who threaten one." I think that one does not have to have these empirical justifications to be entitled to accept what one is told in particular cases (even though people do have such empirical justifications).

11 The expression may be derivative in that a nonrational machine might express linguistic content. But such machines are ultimately made by beings who have propositional attitudes.

12 I think that the distinction between merely having attitudes with intentional content and being able to understand and present them is deeply significant, and marks a deeper level of rationality than that associated with merely having propositional attitudes and inferential abilities. But I need not explore this point here.

I have not here argued in depth for the connections between content, propositional attitudes, and rationality because they are a widely accepted theme in much contemporary work. The idea that language is inseparable from propositional attitudes, which are inseparable from assumptions about rationality is present, for example, in the work of Paul Grice, *Studies in the Way of Words* (Cambridge: Harvard University Press, 1989), and Donald Davidson, *Essays on Actions and Events* (Oxford: Oxford University Press, Clarendon Press, 1980) and *Inquiries into Truth and Interpretation* (Oxford: Oxford University Press, Clarendon Press, 1984). Elsewhere I have sought to show how having linguistic and propositional content is necessarily associated with individuals' having *de re* propositional attitudes to objects of reference and with their interacting practically and perceptually with such objects. See my "Belief De Re," *Journal of Philosophy* 74 (1977), pp. 338–63, and "Other Bodies," in *Thought and Object*, ed. Woodfield (Oxford: Oxford University Press, 1982). The main novelty of the above argument lies in its first step – the claim that we are apriori entitled to rely on our understanding and acceptance of something that is prima facie intelligible – and in its drawing an epistemic consequence from the constitutive, conceptual relations between content and rationality that others have long explored and elaborated.

13 In *Dialogues Concerning Natural Religion*, part 3, Hume imagines hearing an "articulate voice" from the clouds and asks whether one can avoid attributing to it some design or purpose. He never objects to this inference, though he objects to much of the theological purposes it was put to. He would, however, regard it as a non-apriori causal inference. One of the reasons that he would

invoke for thinking that the presumption of a rational source could not be based apriori on prima facie intelligibility is that one could learn empirically that the "voice" was meaningless. This reason is powerless against my conception of the presumption, for I agree that the presumption is empirically defeasible. Apriority has to do with the source of epistemic right; defeasibility is a further matter. For recent criticisms of Hume's view, see A. J. Coady, "Testimony and Observation," *American Philosophical Quarterly* 10 (1973), pp. 149–55; Frederick F. Schmitt, "Justification, Sociality, and Autonomy," *Synthese* 73 (1987), pp. 43–85. I think that empiricism cannot possibly explain all our justified acceptance of what we read or hear. The idea that we should remain neutral or skeptical of information unless we have empirical grounds for thinking it trustworthy is, I think, a wild revisionary proposal. I also think that empiricism cannot account for norms for children's relying on others in the acquisition of language or knowledge.

14 Although I think that my claim about this constitutive function of reason is apriori, I do not maintain that it is self-evident. It can be and has been coherently questioned, as I will note. But the claim has substantial initial plausibility, and I believe that this plausibility is deepened through reflection, including reflection on challenges to it.

15 These true beliefs could fail to be the individual's own, but they must occur somewhere in the development of the content – for example, in the evolution of the cognitive apparatus.

16 Here is a more sophisticated objection along the same line. Suppose that a belief acquired from others may count as knowledge, though one often lacks sufficient grounds, on one's own, to underwrite the belief as knowledge. Suppose that one knows one lacks autonomous grounds for such a belief. Then one's knowledge that the belief was acquired from others would have to be used to enable one's belief to count as knowledge, in view of the known fact that unless the belief had been acquired from others, one's lack of autonomous justification would be insufficient for knowledge. (It is assumed that knowledge

that a belief was acquired from others must be empirical. Let us grant the assumption for now.)

This reasoning again rests on a level confusion. If one has acquired one's belief from others in a normal way, and if the others know the proposition, one acquires knowledge. No further reasoning about the practice is needed for the knowledge. No reasoning that does not show that the entitlement has lapsed can undermine the entitlement (though it might mistakenly undermine one's belief that one was entitled).

17 Kenneth I. Forster, "Lexical Processing," in *An Invitation to Cognitive Psychology*, vol. 1, ed. Osherson and Lasnik (Cambridge: MIT Press, 1990).

18 Davidson and Sellars deny that having sensations plays a role in justifying perceptual beliefs. I am not convinced by their reasons as applied to entitlements to perceptual belief. See Donald Davidson, "A Coherence Theory of Truth and Knowledge," in *Truth and Interpretation*, ed. Lepore (Oxford: Basil Blackwell, 1986), p. 311; and Wilfrid Sellars, "Empiricism and the Philosophy of Mind," in *Science, Perception, and Reality* (London: Routledge and Kegan Paul, 1963), pp. 164 ff. For an alternative to their views, see Steven L. Reynolds, "Knowing How to Believe with Justification," *Philosophical Studies* 64 (1991). 273–92. My view here does not, however, rest on giving sensations (particularly seen as nonintentional) a role in perceptual entitlement. One need not think of sensations as entities, though I do. It is enough that the perceptual character of perceptual belief contribute to the force of the entitlement. Moreover, I am not convinced that there is an epistemic *transition* from perceptual experience to perceptual belief in the ordinary case. One can, of course, learn to suspend such belief. But perceptual experience seems a constituent element in perceptual belief; and perceptual belief seems to be a default position.

19 The analogy goes with certain disanalogies. Understanding a simple logical truth yields a justification; understanding a communicated message yields an entitlement. This is because in the logic case justificational force

derives from the content itself, whereas in interlocution justificational force derives from one's right to putative understanding and from the presumed status of the source of the message, not (typically) from the content itself. A corollary is that knowledge of a simple logical truth does not depend on anything further than understanding and believing it, whereas knowledge based on interlocution depends on there being knowledge in the chain of sources beyond the recipient. In neither case is correct perception of words or correct understanding of what they express necessary to the justification (or entitlement). In neither case is correct perception of words necessary even for knowledge. But in the interlocution case (because knowledge depends on inheriting knowledge from a source), correct understanding of what the interlocutor conveys by the words is necessary for knowledge based on interlocution. (Correct understanding of words or interlocutor is not necessary for knowing whatever logical truth one happens to associate with them, if one understands the logical truth sufficiently.) The important analogy between the logic and interlocution cases is that perception of words makes understanding possible, but justificational force can be derived from the individual's understanding without supplementary appeal to perception. I am abstracting, in this discussion of applications, from cases where understanding a particular content itself involves perceiving – for example, perceiving the referents of demonstratives. Such understanding is not purely conceptual; and as a consequence, the relevant entitlement to the particular belief is partly perceptual.

20 Donald Davidson has argued that there is no conventional connection between indicative sentences and assertive use. See "Moods and Performances" and "Communication and Convention" in *Inquiries into Truth and Interpretation*. His reason is that one can always use indicative utterances for nonassertive purposes. I find the argument unconvincing. A conventional connection between indicative mood and assertive use could be flouted. I believe that the connection between assertive use and indicative (declarative)

mood is deeper and firmer than merely conventional. But it is a contextually defeasible connection.

I use the term "presentation as true" to cover more than assertions and judgments. Obvious presuppositions, or conventional implicatures, are examples. When someone says to kill the shortest spy, he or she presents it as true that there is a shortest spy. In such cases, as well as the indicative cases, the entitlement to accept what is presented as true can be independent for its justificational force of perceptual connection to context (see note 21).

21 This point allies with Grice's distinction between conventional and conversational implicature. See Paul Grice, *Studies in the Way of Words*, pp. 28–31. Grice requires that to be "conversational," an implicature must be capable of being "worked out" from considerations of the conversational context. Conventional implicatures may be inferred "intuitively" from the meaning of the words. I think that understanding based on conversational implicatures *must* be justified, usually empirically, whereas understanding based on conventional implicatures can rest on apriori entitlement. Analogously, I think that a construal of a sentence or content as ironic *must* be justified, usually empirically, whereas a construal of a sentence as asserted can rest on an apriori entitlement. A parallel story needs to be told about ambiguities. Our ability to understand many ambiguous sentences as they are meant, even apart from context, indicates that certain readings are default readings.

22 The scope for intellection-based justification in interlocution is wider than these remarks may suggest. I think that in certain cases special confidence in an interlocutor can be justified on grounds that are inductive but, with subtle qualifications, intellectual. I discuss these matters further in "Computer Proof and Apriori Knowledge."

23 The fact that most of our knowledge is dependent on others and has distinctive epistemic status is increasingly widely recognized. See C. A. J. Coady, "Testimony and Observation"; John Hardwig, "Epistemic Dependence," *Journal of Philosophy* 82

(1985), pp. 335–49; Michael Welbourne, *The Community of Knowledge* (Aberdeen: Aberdeen University Press, 1986). For a wildly implausible, individualistic view of the epistemic status of testimony, see John Locke, *An Essay Concerning Human Understanding* 1.3.24.

24 Because the interlocutor must have knowledge and because of Gettier cases, the interlocutor must have more than true, justified belief if the recipient is to have knowledge. The recipient's dependence for having knowledge on the interlocutor's having knowledge is itself an instance of the Gettier point. The recipient could have true justified belief, but lack knowledge because the interlocutor lacked knowledge.

In requiring that the source have knowledge if the recipient is to have knowledge based on interlocution, I oversimplify. Some chains with more than two links seem to violate this condition. But there must be knowledge in the chain if the recipient is to have knowledge based on interlocution.

25 The principle of charity is illuminatingly used by W. V. Quine, in *Word and Object*

(Cambridge: MIT Press, 1960), chap. 2; and Donald Davidson, in "Radical Interpretation" (1973), in *Inquiries into Truth and Interpretation*. In holding that interpretation is the basic situation for understanding linguistic interchange, Davidson writes, "The problem of interpretation is domestic as well as foreign: it surfaces for speakers of the same language in the form of the question, how can it be determined that the language is the same?" (Similar passages can be found in Quine.) Davidson presupposes that determining whether we are communicating successfully when we appear to be is a question in place from the beginning. This seems to me mistaken. Such a question arises only when there is some reason to doubt that we are sharing information and preserving content. The default position is that understanding can be presumed until something goes wrong. Incidentally, I do not assume that anything as global as a communal language need be thought of as fundamental. That is a further issue.

CHAPTER 57

Testimonial Knowledge
and Transmission

Jennifer Lackey

I

We often talk about knowledge being *transferred* or *transmitted* via testimony. This suggests two things: (1) that hearers can acquire knowledge via the testimony of others; and (2) that speakers must themselves have the knowledge in question in order to pass it to their hearers. In this way the picture we have of testimonial knowledge is like a chain of people passing buckets of water to put out a fire. Each person must have a bucket of water in order to pass it to the next person, and moreover there must be at least one person who is ultimately acquiring the water from another source. Similarly, each person in the chain of transmitting knowledge that *p* must know that *p* in order to pass it to the next person, and moreover there must be at least one person in the chain who ultimately acquired knowledge that *p* from another source, e.g., sense perception, introspection, reason, and the like.

This picture is, in large part, suggested by the striking similarities which testimony bears to memory. For instance, it is often assumed that neither memory nor testimony is, strictly speaking, a generative source of knowledge: while the latter *transmits* knowledge from one speaker to another, the former *preserves* beliefs from one

time to another. In this way, just as I cannot remember that *p* unless I have something to remember, the thought underlying this picture of testimonial knowledge is that speakers cannot give knowledge that *p* unless they have something to give. So, for example, Robert Audi[1] writes that "*I* cannot (testimonially) give you knowledge that *p* without knowing that *p*. ... Testimonially based knowledge is received by transmission and so depends on the attester's knowing that *p*." In a similar spirit, James Ross lays down the following conditions for testimonial knowledge: "*S* comes to know that *h* on *W*'s testimony iff: *W* knows that *h*, tells *S*, and his telling *S* brings it about that *S* believes that *h* and *h* is evident for *S*".[2] Following this view, Michael Welbourne maintains that "I take testimony to be essentially concerned with communicating knowledge, so I hold that it is necessary, if there is to be a successful process of testimonial transmission, that the speaker knows that *p*. Thus I stipulate that the speaker knows that *p*."[3] And Tyler Burge concurs: "If the recipient depends on interlocution for knowledge, the recipient's knowledge depends on the source's having knowledge as well. For if the source does not believe the proposition, or if the proposition is not true, or if the source is not justified, the recipient cannot know the proposition."[4]

These quotations are characteristic of thesis (2) above, and it is this view of how testimonial knowledge is passed from one person to another which is the dominant one. This thesis, however, should be

Originally published in *The Philosophical Quarterly* 49, 197 (Oct. 1999), pp. 471–90.

distinguished from one that is entailed by (2) but is a much weaker view of the transmission of testimonial knowledge. We may compare with (2) above what Michael Dummett says about testimony:

> If remembering something is to count as retaining a knowledge of it, it must have been known when originally witnessed or experienced; if it was derived from a misperception or misapprehension, the memory cannot of course rank as knowledge. The same naturally applies to taking something to be so, having been told it: the original purveyor of the information – *the first link in the chain of transmission* – must himself have known it, and therefore have been in a position to know it, or it cannot be knowledge for any of those who derived it ultimately from him.[5]

The difference between this claim and the one put forth by proponents of (2) is that, on Dummett's view, *at least the first link* in the chain of testimonial transmission must know that *p* (via some non-testimonial means), whereas according to (2) *every link* in the chain must know that *p* (via either non-testimonial or testimonial means). I shall distinguish these two theses thus:

2.   For every speaker *S* and hearer *H*, if *H* comes to know that *p* via *S*'s testifying that *p*, then *S* must know that *p*

2*.   For every testimonial chain of knowledge *C*, in order for a hearer *H* in *C* to come to know that *p* via the testimony of a speaker *S* in *C*, at least the first speaker S_1 in *C* must know that *p* (in some non-testimonial way).

So proponents of (2*), unlike those who endorse (2), can countenance testimonial chains which include some speakers who know that *p* and some who do not. The crucial point of (2*) is that the original source of the knowledge that *p*, that is, the speaker who first came to know that *p* via some non-testimonial means, must know that *p*.

In this paper, however, I shall argue that both (2) and (2*) are false. Specifically, I shall claim that there are some plausible ways in which a hearer can acquire knowledge that *p* via a speaker's testimony that *p* despite the fact that even the first speaker in the chain in question fails to know that *p*. First, however, it may be helpful to make some preliminary remarks about the justification of testimonial beliefs.

II

Knowledge, it is widely agreed, is more than just true belief. There is far less agreement, however, regarding the particular nature of this additional element for knowledge. For present purposes, I shall call whatever this further element is "justification", and put forth the following schematic definition of knowledge:

> K. *S* knows that *p* iff (i) *p*; (ii) *S* believes that *p*; (iii) *S* is justified in believing that *p*.

Now, as suggested above, condition (iii) of this tripartite definition can be fleshed out in various and often competing ways. With respect to *testimonial justification* in particular, there are two main views. On the one hand, *non-reductivists*[6] maintain that testimony is just as basic a source of knowledge as sense-perception, memory, inference, and the like, and accordingly that hearers may be justified in accepting the reports of speakers, albeit defeasibly, merely on the basis of a speaker's testimony. In this way, such accounts endorse a justificatory principle like the following:

> JP. If *S* reports that *p* to *H* and *H* has no defeaters for *S*'s report that *p*, then *H* is justified in accepting that *p* on the basis of *S*'s testimony.

Reductivists, on the other hand, argue that in order to be justified in accepting the reports of speakers, hearers must have reasons for trusting certain speakers and reports, and in particular that these reasons cannot themselves be ineliminably based on the testimony of others. Instead, they are typically the result of induction: we observe a general conformity between facts and reports and, with the aid of memory and reason, we inductively infer that certain speakers are reliable sources of knowledge. In this way, the justification of testimony is *reduced* to the justification we have for sense-perception, memory and inference. Thus reductivists put forth a justificatory principle like the following:

> JP*. If *S* reports that *p* to *H*, *H* has no defeaters for *S*'s report that *p*, and *H* has positive

reasons to accept S's report that p, then H is justified in accepting that p on the basis of S's testimony.[7]

For our purposes, the crucial point to notice is that both (JP) and (JP*) include as a necessary condition for testimonial knowledge that the hearer in question must not have any defeaters for S's report that p. In this way, regardless of whether (iii) of (K) is construed non-reductively or reductively for testimonial justification, the absence of defeaters is a necessary condition for testimonial knowledge.

But what is a defeater and how does it function? With respect to these questions, there are three main responses. The first is that a defeater is a proposition D which is believed by S to be true, yet indicates that S's belief that p is either false or unreliably formed or sustained. Defeaters in this sense function by virtue of being *believed*, regardless of their truth-value.[8] For example, S may believe that Betty's dog did not trample the flowers because Betty told her that he did not. But if Polly, another neighbour, later tells S that she saw Betty's dog trample the flowers, then, given Polly's testimony and assuming that S believes her, S has evidence for the denial of the belief that Betty's dog did not trample the flowers. Or suppose that S learns and comes to believe that the textbook from which S acquired a certain belief about history was written by an incompetent scholar or a pathological liar. In that case S acquires a belief which indicates that the source of this historical belief is unreliable. Even if one's original belief was produced by a reliable belief-producing process, and even if the defeating belief in question fails to be true, the fact that S believes D is often taken to be sufficient for preventing S's belief that p from being justified.

The second response is that a defeater is a proposition D which S is justified in believing to be true, yet which indicates that S's belief that p is either false, or unreliably formed or sustained. Defeaters in this sense function by virtue of being propositions that S *should believe* given the evidence which is available to S.[9] So, for instance, Bill believes that the President is currently in Chicago, but then reads in the *New York Times* that the President is currently in China. Now if Bill continues to hold his original belief with no reason for doubting the report in the newspaper, it may

be argued that even if the President is in fact in Chicago, Bill does not know this because there is evidence available to him which defeats his justification.

The third response is that a defeater is a true proposition D such that if D were added to S's belief system, then S would no longer be justified in believing that p. Defeaters in this sense function by virtue of being *true*.[10] For instance, you may correctly believe that there is a barn in the field and yet the presence of barn façades in the vicinity may none the less prevent this belief from being an instance of knowledge. In particular, *that there are barn façades surrounding the real barn you saw* is a true proposition which, if added to your belief system, would result in your belief's being unjustified.

Thus though it is generally accepted that defeaters are indeed incompatible with knowledge, there are different views of the nature of defeat. I shall call these three conceptions of defeat *doxastic defeaters*, *normative defeaters* and *factual defeaters* respectively. For the purposes of this paper I shall focus primarily on the role that doxastic defeaters play in individual belief systems, but I shall also present cases against (2) and (2*) involving normative and factual defeaters.

The last preliminary remark is that not all cases of knowledge acquired from hearing what a speaker says are clear instances of testimonial knowledge. For instance, if I say, in a soprano voice, that I have a soprano voice, and you come to believe this, not on the basis of the content of my statement but rather on the basis of hearing my soprano voice,[11] then in this case, even though my statement may cause you to form the belief in question, the acquired knowledge is based on your perceptual experience rather than on the content of my report. Roughly, I shall say that one requirement for *testimonial knowledge* is that it must be based on the *content* of the proposition to which a speaker testifies rather than entirely on features *about* the speaker's testimony, e.g., how it was testified to, where it was testified to, and so on. So if you are unable to discriminate between soprano voices and, say, baritone voices, then the acquired knowledge in the above case would be of the testimonial sort, since it would be based on the content of the proffered statement. There are also intermediate cases in which a hearer has relevant background information and uses it to derive knowledge from the statement of a speaker. For example, suppose that you know from past experience that I report that there is no milk in the refrigerator only when there is some. Now when I report to you that there is no milk in the refrigerator you may supplement my testimony with your background information and hence derive knowledge that there is milk in the refrigerator. These types of cases, though in part based on testimony, also rely heavily on memory and inference. Thus, even though perception, memory and inference arguably play a role in the acquisition of all testimonial knowledge, I shall here focus only on cases in which the knowledge in question is clearly based on the content of a speaker's testimony.

III

With these points in mind, I shall now present two differnt kinds of counter-examples. The first type of case is where speakers fail to know that *p* because they fail to *believe* that *p*, i.e., they fail condition (ii) of (K), but a hearer can none the less come to know that *p* via their testimony. These cases will be directed specifically at (2). The second type of case is where speakers fail to know that *p* because they have a *defeater* for their belief that *p*, i.e., they fail condition (iii) of (K), but a hearer can none the less come to know that *p* via their testimony. These cases will undermine both (2) and (2*). Both types of counter-examples, I shall argue, apply to non-reductivist and reductivist accounts of testimonial justification. I shall begin with the former type of case.

Suppose that a Catholic elementary school requires that all teachers include sections on evolutionary theory in their science classes and that the teachers conceal their own personal beliefs regarding this subject-matter. Mrs Smith, a teacher at the school in question, goes to the library, researches this literature from reliable sources, and on this basis develops a set of reliable lecture notes from which she will teach the material to her students. Despite this, however, Mrs Smith is herself a devout creationist and hence does not believe that evolutionary theory is true, but she none the less follows the requirement to teach the theory to her students. Now

assuming that evolutionary theory is true, in this case it seems reasonable to assume that Mrs Smith's students can come to have knowledge via her testimony, despite the fact that she fails condition (ii) and hence does not have the knowledge in question herself. That is, it seems that she can give to her students what she does not have herself. For in spite of Mrs Smith's failure to believe and therewith to know the propositions she is reporting to her students about evolution, she is a reliable testifier for this information, and on the basis of her testimony it seems that the students in question can come to have knowledge of evolutionary theory. I take it that similar considerations apply in cases where a Kantian teaches utilitarianism, a dualist teaches physicalism, an atheist teaches Christianity, and so on. If the theory in question is true and a hearer comes to believe it by means of the teacher's testimony, then, I would say, the hearer can acquire knowledge on this basis despite the failure of condition (ii).[12]

This case can be fleshed out in certain plausible ways so that the students in question satisfy both (JP) and (JP*). For instance, we can suppose that the children have grown up in environments in which they have not acquired any reasons to favour evolutionary theory over creationism or *vice versa*. We can also assume that the students do have some positive reasons for accepting the testimony of Mrs Smith, e.g., her reports typically co-vary with their perceptual experiences, the reports of their parents and classmates, and so on. Thus according to both non-reductivist and reductivist accounts of testimonial justification, the children acquire the knowledge in question from Mrs Smith's testimony even though she does not have it herself.

There are, however, three ways in which an objector can deny that cases like that of Mrs Smith and her students provide counter-examples to thesis (2). The first is to deny that her testimony is the *source* of the children's knowledge in question, the second is to deny that the children actually do come to have *knowledge* of evolutionary theory, and the third is to deny that the teacher's statements qualify as instances of *testimony*. I shall examine these in turn.

To argue that Mrs Smith's testimony is not the source of the children's knowledge is tantamount to denying that she is a link in the testimonial chain of evolutionary knowledge. But what, we might ask, could justify such a claim? For *ex hypothesi* the children are not relying on or consulting any textbooks, but are forming their beliefs solely on the basis of the reports made by Mrs Smith. Perhaps one way to defend this position is to argue that a person who functions as a mere instrument for transmitting knowledge cannot be considered a testimonial source of knowledge. For example, one might claim that it is actually the authors of the books on evolutionary theory from which Mrs Smith derived her lecture notes who are the links in the testimonial chain leading to the students in question. Mrs Smith is merely an instrument for transmitting the knowledge of evolutionary theory from the authors of the books to the children in the elementary school, and hence such cases do not pose a problem for (2).

Now one obvious way of responding to this objection is simply to modify the counter-example so that the authors in question are merely interested in the topic of evolutionary theory but are themselves also creationists. This will, I take it, lead the objector to point to the sources from which the authors in question derived their information on evolutionary theory, so as to avoid the counter-example. And I suppose we can add further modifications and objections until ultimately we trace the chain back to Darwin himself. To my mind, however, this is an unwelcome consequence. For not only does it seem a counterintuitive picture of the way we think of testimony, it is also question-begging. Let us ask the following question: if the teacher in our envisaged case *had* had the requisite belief, would she have been the source of the children's knowledge or would it have been Darwin? I take it that proponents of (2) would respond that, in this case, Mrs Smith is the source of the knowledge in question precisely because they countenance *chains* of testimonial knowledge. That is, we need not receive the report that *p* directly from Darwin himself because testimony is a source whereby people can acquire information across times, places and persons. Given this, it seems natural to assume that proponents of (2) would countenance Mrs Smith as the source of the children's knowledge if she had had the requisite beliefs. But then to deny that she is the source in the envisaged case merely because she lacks the beliefs at issue is question-begging.

A variant of this first response is to argue that there is a difference between what we might call *direct* and *indirect* testimony and that the case of Mrs Smith is an instance of the latter. For example, I do not believe that Bill ate the last cookie but I none the less report to you that John said that Bill ate the last cookie. Here one might say that what I am testifying to is simply what John said and that it is only in an indirect way that I convey the information about Bill. Similarly one might argue that even if it is not made explicit in her reports, what Mrs Smith is testifying to is merely what the authorities on evolutionary theory accept, and hence it is only in an indirect way that she communicates information about evolutionary theory itself. In this way it may be argued that, as it stands, (2) applies only to testimonial knowledge which is acquired in a direct way, and thus the example of Mrs Smith does not pose a problem for this view.

However, it is not entirely clear what the criterion could be for distinguishing between direct and indirect testimony in such a way that Mrs Smith's reports turn out to be instances of the latter. For in the above case I report that so and so said that *p* to you, while *ex hypothesi* Mrs Smith merely reports that *p* to her students. Now the distinguishing mark between direct and indirect testimony cannot be whether the speaker in question believes or fails to believe that *p*, respectively. For instance, I may believe that Bill ate the last cookie but, because I do not want to be held accountable for divulging this information, I may none the less report that John said that Bill ate the last cookie. Here, even though I hold the belief about Bill, one might say that this is still a case of indirect testimony, since what I am testifying to is what John said. On the other hand, if the distinguishing mark of direct testimony is that the speaker did not acquire the information in question from another speaker's testimony, this has the unwelcome consequence that most of the reports we make, with the exception of, for example, reports about our perceptual experiences, are cases of indirect testimony. Given this, the way in which I would distinguish between direct and indirect testimony is by the *content* of the proffered statement. Specifically, if I report to you that *p* (whether or not I believe that *p*), then this is a case of direct testimony. On the other hand, if I report to you that so and so said that *p* (whether or not I believe that p), then this is a case of indirect testimony. In this way, Mrs Smith's reports to her students turn out to be instances of direct testimony, even though she fails the belief condition of (K).

The second strategy for responding to cases like Mrs Smith's is to deny that the children in question come to have knowledge. I must admit that this response seems quite implausible to me, but perhaps one way to support it is to argue that testimony cannot be a source of knowledge if the speaker in question is lying or falsely testifying.[13] For if one reports that p but does not believe that p, then, it might be argued, it is merely an accident if a hearer comes to believe truly that p on this basis. And since it is widely assumed that there must be some non-accidental connection between a subject's belief that p and the fact that p, in order to rule out Gettier-type cases, one cannot know that p via a speaker's false testimony. Given this, one might argue that, broadly speaking, Mrs Smith is lying to her students, since she is reporting what she herself does not believe, and hence even if her students acquire true beliefs via her testimony, this is merely an accident.

The first thing to note about this response is that *ex hypothesi* Mrs Smith consulted reliable books in the library to develop her reliable lecture notes, and hence it is unclear how there could be any unacceptable degree of accidentality in this case. For instance, if there is a secular elementary school in the area, where Mr Jones teaches evolutionary theory to his students, has the purportedly requisite beliefs, and develops reliable lecture notes which are similar to Mrs Smith's in all relevant respects, it seems fairly safe to assume that the children in the secular school acquire knowledge of evolutionary theory via Mr Jones' testimony. But then why would not the children in the Catholic school? Why should it matter that Mrs Smith is a creationist and does not believe what she is teaching to her students?

Second, it seems clear that hearers can acquire knowledge via the testimony of speakers even when the latter are pathological liars. For instance, Sally is radically yet consistently mistaken about most of her beliefs. That is, she consistently believes that objects are blue when they are in fact red, that a cat is in the room when in fact a dog is in the room, and so on for most of her beliefs. She is also a pathological yet consistent liar. For

instance, when she sees red objects and believes that they are blue, she reports that they are red with the intention to deceive her hearers. Similarly, when she sees a cat and believes it is a dog, she reports that a cat is in the room with the intention to deceive her hearers. Since Sally's reports consistently co-vary with the perceptual experiences of her hearers, not only do the hearers fail to have any defeaters for either Sally's particular reports or for her reliability as a testifier, they also have inductive evidence for believing that she is a reliable source of knowledge.[14] In a case such as this, I take it that hearers can acquire knowledge via Sally's testimony despite the fact that she consistently reports what she herself does not believe and explicitly intends to deceive her hearers. To my mind, denying that hearers can acquire knowledge via Sally's testimony conflates *reliable knowers* with *reliable testifiers*, that is, it conflates subjects reliably forming beliefs themselves with speakers reliably communicating information to others. What is crucial for hearers in order to acquire knowledge from speakers is that the proffered *statements* be reliable, that is, that they be truth-conducive in some way. One of the ways in which this link with the truth can be ensured is if the speakers in question are reliable knowers, e.g., if their beliefs are connected with the truth, they report what they believe, and hearers come to acquire beliefs via their reports. But, as I have been arguing, there is no reason to believe that this is the way it *has* to be for a hearer to acquire knowledge via testimony. So long as the statements themselves are truth-conducive, knowledge can be acquired via testimony in the absence of knowledge on the part of the speaker.

The third strategy for defending (2) from cases like Mrs Smith's is to grant that the children do come to have knowledge and that they do this via Mrs Smith's reports, but to deny that her statements qualify as instances of *testimony*. Specifically, one might argue that in order for a speaker to testify, certain conditions must be satisfied, either about the nature of the proffered statement itself or about the intentional activity of the speaker, and the satisfaction of such conditions distinguishes testimony from mere statements. In this way the children may acquire knowledge via Mrs Smith's reports, but that fails to show that they acquire knowledge via her *testimony*.

The first point which can be made on behalf of countenancing Mrs Smith's reports as testimony is that it is not uncommon for those who are interested in the epistemology of testimony to embrace a broad notion of what it is to testify, a notion under which Mrs Smith's reports clearly fall. For instance, Elizabeth Fricker argues that the domain of testimony which is of epistemological interest is that of "tellings generally" with "no restrictions either on subject matter, or on the speaker's epistemic relation to it" ("Telling and Trusting" pp. 396–7). And Robert Audi (p. 405) claims that "Testimony of the wide sort that concerns me – roughly, saying or affirming something in an apparent attempt to convey (correct) information – is what raises the question of how testimony is important for knowledge and justification". (He later adds, p. 406, that in accounting for knowledge and justification we must understand testimony as "people's telling us things".) But even for those who endorse a more restricted notion of what it is to testify, it is arguable that Mrs Smith's statements qualify as instances of testimony. For example, it has been argued that testifying requires that speakers intend to convey epistemically useful information, or that they offer statements which are evidence in some objective sense, or that there be a need for the evidence on the part of the hearer.[15] Now Mrs Smith does intend to convey information which is epistemically useful to her students; her statements are evidence in an objective sense; and her students are in need of the evidence being offered. Thus even according to many restrictive views of testimony, Mrs Smith satisfies the requisite conditions for testifying.

Moreover, it is questionable on independent grounds whether such conditions are necessary for a speaker to testify. For instance, if we require that a speaker intend to convey epistemically useful information in order to testify, then there are many situations in which we shall have to deny that certain statements are instances of testimony when they do seem to be. Posthumous publications of private journals will fail to qualify, since the authors did not intend to convey information to anybody but themselves. Or if I believe that you are already privy to the fact that p and I make a casual statement to the effect that p without intending to convey information, I fail to testify that p even if you acquire knowledge from my statement. Similarly, if one requires that the statement be some type of objective evidence, then it is arguably the case that speakers will not be able to testify about countless things, e.g., alien encounters, UFO sightings, and the like.

Even more significantly, however, if we make our definition of what it is to testify so robust that it is necessary that the speaker have certain intentions or that the statement be truth-conducive, then the work for epistemology is not to show that testimony is a reliable source of knowledge but rather to *enquire whether we have an institution of testimony*. Each time speakers report that p, we shall first have to ask "Did they *really* testify?", and, depending on the answer to this question, we might have different epistemological accounts. If testimony is, by definition, a reliable source of knowledge, e.g., if the proffered statements must be truth-conducive, then we need not give an account of the justification of testimonial beliefs. Instead, we need to show that we *do* have an institution of testimony or that when speakers are making statements, they *actually* are testifying. Similarly, if we require that a speaker have certain intentions in order to testify, then we shall have to do a bit of psychology in order to determine whether the statement is an instance of testimony. Moreover, I suppose that we shall then have an account of the justification of testimonial beliefs and a separate account of the justification of mere statements.

Since these consequences seem so unattractive, I take it that such requirements are not necessary for a speaker to testify. Surely the interesting epistemological question is how we are justified in accepting the testimony of others, rather than whether we really do have an institution of testimony. Furthermore, it seems that so far as possible we should offer a *unitary* account of the knowledge we acquire from the reports of others, which would explain how we are justified in accepting the reports of speakers like Mrs Smith. For explaining how we acquire knowledge via testimony is explaining how we acquire knowledge via the statements of others. Since the children in our case do seem to acquire knowledge via the reports of Mrs Smith, the process seems to fall under the general rubric of testimonial knowledge. Given this, such cases seem to cast serious doubt on thesis (2).

IV

In the previous section, I argued that thesis (2) is false, since a hearer can acquire knowledge that p via speakers' testimony that p even when the latter themselves fail to believe and hence fail to know that p. In this section, however, I focus on the role that defeaters play in testimonial knowledge, and I shall argue that since defeaters are not necessarily transmitted via testimony, a hearer can come to know that p via a speaker's testimony that p, despite the fact that *even the first speaker in a chain of testimonial transmission fails to know that p*. In this way I shall argue that both (2) and (2*) are false.

I shall begin with doxastic defeaters, believed propositions which defeat the justification of other beliefs. For instance, if I believe that there is coffee in the kitchen because I saw it there this afternoon, but John tells me that he has just drunk the last cup, the justification I had for believing that there is coffee in the kitchen has been defeated by my belief that John just drank the last cup. But since doxastic defeaters are themselves beliefs, they, too, are candidates for defeat. For instance, suppose I go into the kitchen to check whether John did in fact just drink the last cup of coffee, and I discover that there is still coffee in the carafe. In this case, my perceptual belief provides me with a doxastic defeater for the belief that I acquired via John's testimony, and hence it provides me with a *defeater-defeater* for my original belief that there is coffee in the kitchen. Still further, defeater-defeaters are also candidates for defeat, since they too are beliefs. Thus if I confront John and tell him that I have just seen that there is coffee in the kitchen, and he tells me that he poured tea in the carafe, his testimony provides me with a defeater for my defeater-defeater, that is, it provides me with a *defeater-defeater-defeater* for my original belief that there is coffee in the kitchen. And, as should be suspected, defeater-defeater-defeaters can also be defeated by further beliefs, which in turn can be defeated by further beliefs, and so on. Finally, when one has a defeater D for one's belief that p which is not itself defeated by another belief, one has what is called an *undefeated defeater* for one's belief that p.

With these points in place, I shall begin by considering the following case. Jane is *currently* in the grips of sceptical worries which are so strong that she can scarcely be said to know anything at all. (I here emphasize "currently" to capture the idea in contextualist views of knowledge that sceptical doubts may undermine knowledge while those doubts are being entertained, even if they need not undermine knowledge in ordinary or everyday contexts.[16]) That is, her belief that she could now be the victim of an evil demon is strong enough to defeat the justification she has for many of her ordinary beliefs and, moreover, it is currently an undefeated defeater. Jim, a passerby, approaches her, asks her where the café is, and she reports that it is around the corner, but does not report her sceptical worries to Jim. Now Jim has never considered any sceptical possibilities at all, and hence he does not have any doxastic defeaters for his ordinary beliefs. Furthermore, he does have positive reasons for accepting Jane's report, e.g., he has perceived a general conformity between facts and the reports of many speakers in these types of contexts, and he has inductively inferred that speakers are generally reliable when they are giving directions, and Jane does not exhibit any behaviour which indicates a lack of sincerity or competence with respect to her report. So Jim forms the true belief that there is a café around the corner on the basis of Jane's testimony.

Given that Jane has an undefeated defeater which Jim does not have, he has knowledge which she lacks. Yet at the same time it seems possible for Jim to come to know that the café is around the corner via Jane's testimony even though her sceptical doubts currently undermine her knowing this. In this way, Jane fails (JP) and (JP*) because she has an undefeated defeater for the belief in question, Jim satisfies (JP) and (JP*) because he does not have such a doxastic defeater, and thus it seems possible for a hearer to acquire knowledge on the basis of a speaker's testimony even when the speaker does not personally have the knowledge in question.

But the crucial thing about the above example is that Jane is the *first link in the chain of testimonial knowledge* in question. For though it is only a two-person chain, it is still a process whereby a hearer comes to have knowledge via the report of a speaker. Moreover, we can certainly imagine a much longer chain in which Jim reports that the café is around the corner to another hearer Steve, who passes it to Bill, and so on, and we can imagine that none of these speakers actually checked where the café is for himself. In this way, the chain itself finds its ultimate origin in Jane who *ex hypothesi* does not know that the café is around the corner. This shows that it is possible for a hearer to come to know that *p* via a speaker's testimony that *p* even when the first link in the testimonial chain in question fails to know that *p*. Thus even the weaker (2*) is false.

Now one may wish to deny that sceptical doubts can ever be so strong as really to do the defeating work in question. But there are other, perhaps less questionable, examples to illustrate this point. For instance, we can adapt the following example from Alvin Goldman (pp. 53–4):

> Millicent in fact possesses her normal visual powers, but has cogent reasons to believe these powers are temporarily deranged. She is a subject of a neurosurgeon's experiments, and the surgeon *falsely* tells her that current implantations are causing malfunction in her visual cortex. She is persuaded that her present visual appearances are no guide at all to reality. Yet despite this belief, she continues to place credence in her visual percepts. She ignores her well justified belief in the incapacitation of her visual faculty; she persists in believing, on the basis of visual appearances, that a chair is before her, that the neurosurgeon is wearing a yellow smock, and so on. Now these beliefs are all, in fact, true. Moreover, they are formed by the usual, quite reliable, perceptual processes. But are they specimens of knowledge? Intuitively, no. The reason is that Millicent is not *justified* in holding these beliefs; they contravene her best evidence.

So Millicent acquires an undefeated defeater for her visual powers via another person's testimony, and hence fails to have the knowledge in question. Suppose, however, that Millicent not only persists in forming perceptual beliefs, she also continues to report such experiences to her friends, though she does not report her doxastic defeater. Her friends have a sufficient amount of positive evidence to trust her reports, e.g., her reports regularly co-vary with their perceptual experiences, the reports of others, and so on. Millicent's hearers, therefore, satisfy both (JP) and (JP*), but she does not, because she has the undefeated defeater in question. Thus Millicent seems capable of giving knowledge to others which she fails to possess

herself. Indeed, like Jane, she may even be the first link in a testimonial chain, correctly reporting that she saw a groundhog in the field which no one else saw even though she is not justified in believing this herself.

What these cases point to is that doxastic defeaters *are not necessarily transmitted via testimony*. For defeaters in this sense are beliefs of the subjects in question which defeat the justification *they* have for holding another belief. In this way, doxastic defeaters do not simply "come along for the ride" when a speaker reports that *p*; instead, the defeater itself must be reported and believed by the hearer in order for it to be acquired via testimony. Doxastic defeaters can also prevent the transmission of knowledge via testimony in cases where a speaker knows and reports that *p* but a hearer fails to know that *p* on this basis because the latter has a defeater for *p*. For instance, you might truly and with justification believe that Mary stole the money because you saw her take it. But if you report this to me, I may not be justified in accepting your testimony because I have an undefeated defeater for your reliability as a testifier. Thus you know that *p*, you report that *p* to me, and yet I do not know that *p* because I have an undefeated defeater for your testimony. However, what proponents of (2) and (2*) fail to notice is that *speakers* can have doxastic defeaters which *hearers* do not have. I may report that *p* and even believe that *p*, but may not know that *p* because my justification is defeated by another belief *D*. And unless my hearers also come to believe *D*, they may know that *p* via my testimony while I do not.

However, there are two different ways in which doxastic defeaters can fail to be transmitted via testimony. The first is like the cases above where a speaker reports that *p* but fails to report an undefeated defeater *D*. The second type of case is where a speaker reports that *p* and reports a defeater *D*, but the hearer accepts only the report. Thus if Jane reports that the café is around the corner and reports her sceptical worries to Jim, but he fails to believe that he could now be the victim of an evil demon, then he can still acquire knowledge that the café is around the corner via Jane's testimony even though she fails to have it.

Moreover, there are cases in which doxastic defeaters are transmitted via testimony, but the hearer in question is in possession of a defeater-defeater, thereby enabling testimony still to impart knowledge to the hearer. So, for example, suppose that Jane does report her sceptical doubts to Jim and he comes to believe that he could be the victim of an evil demon, that is, he acquires a doxastic defeater for his ordinary beliefs. However, he later comes to believe that he has a refutation of scepticism. So he has a belief which defeats the justification for believing that he could now be the victim of an evil demon, i.e., he has a defeater-defeater for the original belief in question.

Given the role that doxastic defeaters play in individual epistemic frameworks, it is easy to imagine a chain of testifiers, some of whom have defeaters, some defeater-defeaters, some defeater-defeater-defeaters, and so on. Indeed, it is also quite easy to imagine a chain of testifiers like Jane and Millicent who have undefeated defeaters for believing that *p*, but where the very last link in the chain, Sarah, has a defeater-defeater for believing that *p*. Such a chain would include only speakers who do not have the knowledge in question, and yet Sarah, the last hearer in the chain, could none the less come to know that *p* via the testimony of other members in the chain.

Now even though I have thus far focused on the role doxastic defeaters play in individual epistemic frameworks, similar considerations can be adduced involving normative and factual defeaters. For instance, Alice is incorrectly told by an otherwise reliable optometrist that her vision is nearly completely unreliable, yet she refuses to accept his diagnosis, without having any rational basis for doing so. So, one might say, even though the optometrist's report is false, Alice should accept his diagnosis, given all of the evidence that she has available to her, and thus she has a normative defeater for her visual beliefs. Now as Alice is walking out of the doctor's office she sees a car accident, and later reports this fact to me but does not report the optometrist's diagnosis to me. In this case it seems possible for a hearer to acquire knowledge via Alice's testimony even though the presence of a normative defeater prevents her from having such knowledge. For if we assume that I have no other reasons for doubting her reliability as a testifier, and I have sufficient evidence for believing that she is reliable, then I satisfy (JP) and (JP*), while Alice does not. Moreover, we can imagine that Alice's report about the car accident is the very first link in a testimonial chain, imparting knowledge to others which she does not possess herself.

Or suppose that Farmer Brown and I are very good friends, and I have every reason to believe that he is an honest and sincere man. Several weeks ago we were having coffee and he told me that even though he does not have a real barn himself, he is vehemently opposed to a trend in his community towards making the neighbourhood appear prosperous by putting up barn façades. Today you drive past Farmer Brown's farm, notice that he has a new barn, and report this fact to me. You do not know, however, that his barn is the only real one in his community, surrounded by façades which from a distance are indistinguishable from his barn. This being so, you do not know that Farmer Brown has a new barn, because there is a factual defeater, namely, that there are barn façades surrounding the real barn, which prevents you from having knowledge. To put this another way, the barn façades are relevant alternatives which have not been eliminated or ruled out with respect to your perceptual belief. But, given my belief that Farmer Brown has vehemently spoken out against barn façades, it seems reasonable to say that such alternatives are eliminated with respect to my accepting your testimony. That is, I can come to know via your testimony that he has a new barn on his farm. For I have no reason to doubt your report and I have good reason to believe that, even if Farmer Brown's new barn were surrounded by façades, his would be a real one. Once again, your factual defeater need not be transmitted to me via your testimony.

As I have tried to show, the failure of different kinds of defeaters to be transmitted via testimony renders theses like (2) and (2*) indefensible. For once we grant, as proponents of these views do, that a hearer can have a defeater which a speaker does not, then what could justify our denying that a speaker can have a defeater which a hearer does not? That is, what could justify the claim that a speaker's defeaters are necessarily transmitted to a hearer? Given cases like the ones discussed in this section, it seems uncontentious that speakers can have various defeaters which hearers do not (and, of course, *vice versa*). This has significant epistemological consequences for the dominant picture of testimonial knowledge. Since defeaters do not necessarily come along for the ride with reports, testimonial chains can include speakers and hearers with very different epistemic status. In particular, a single chain of testimony can include speakers and hearers, some of whom have undefeated defeaters, some defeater-defeaters, some defeater-defeater-defeaters, and so on. Accordingly, such chains can include some speakers who know that p and others who fail to know that p. Indeed, as I have argued, even that first speaker in a testimonial chain need not know that p for hearers in the chain to come to know that p via that speaker's testimony. Thus the dominant picture of testimonial knowledge is false.

V

In this section, I shall offer some brief remarks regarding what *is* necessary for a hearer to acquire knowledge via the testimony of a speaker. I shall sketch an alternative thesis to (2) and (2*) which avoids the problems afflicting accounts which hold that some degree of speaker-knowledge is necessary for a hearer to acquire testimonial knowledge.

In explaining how we acquire knowledge via the testimony of others, we are interested in offering an account of how hearers can come to know that p through a speaker's statement that p. Since it is post-Gettier knowledge that is at issue, it is widely accepted that, with respect to testimonial knowledge in particular, there needs to be some non-accidental or reliable connection between a speaker's statement that p and the fact that p. Now as proponents of (2) and (2*) point out, one way in which such a connection can be secured is through the relationship between speakers' epistemic state and hearers'. If speakers' belief that p is reliably connected with the truth that p, then, assuming that speakers report what they themselves believe, hearers can reliably acquire true beliefs via this testimony. In this way, speaker-knowledge secures a non-accidental or reliable connection between the statements of speakers and the beliefs that hearers acquire via these statements. That this type of connection secures such a link with the truth seems uncontentious. But it is crucial that speaker-knowledge is only *one* of the ways in which a reliable connection between a speaker's statement that p and the fact that p can be secured. For, as I argued in §III, statements of particular speakers can be

reliably connected with the truth even if their beliefs are not. Mrs Smith's statements about evolutionary theory, for example, "track the truth" even though her specific beliefs about evolutionary theory do not. Sally, our pathological yet consistent liar who is systematically in error about her beliefs, can be a reliable testifier even though she is a radically unreliable knower. The upshot of these types of cases is that *statements and beliefs can come apart*. Speakers can be reliable testifiers who offer statements which are truth-conducive or truth-tracking even if they are radically unreliable knowers whose beliefs fail to be mostly true or truth-tracking. What is necessary for testimonial knowledge is that a speaker's *statement* be appropriately connected with the truth, where knowledge on the part of the speaker is only one such connection.

So I propose the following general thesis about the acquisition of testimonial knowledge:

2**. For every speaker S and hearer H, if H comes to know that p via S's statement that p, then S's statement that p must be appropriately connected with the fact that p.

As should be clear, (2**) does not specify what kind of connection is appropriate between S's statement that p and the fact that p. The connection can be fleshed out in terms of one's general account of epistemic justification. For instance, it may be that one's statement that p is appropriately connected with the fact that p if one's statement "tracks the truth" in Nozick's sense, i.e., if p were not true S would not state that p, and if p were true S would state that p. So, for example, Sally, our pathological yet consistent liar, states that objects are red only if they are red even though she believes that objects are red when they are not. In this way, her statements are truth-tracking even though her beliefs are not. Or it may be that one's statement that p is appropriately connected with the fact that p if one's statement that p is reliably correlated with the fact that p. Thus Mrs Smith's statements are reliably correlated with the supposed facts of evolutionary theory even though her epistemic states fail to be so correlated. But whatever one's general account of epistemic justification turns out to be, the point which is of import here is that the *relata* of the appropriate connection specified in (2**) are statements and facts. In this way, speaker-knowledge is only one means whereby a connection is secured.

Moreover, for a complete account of testimonial knowledge, (2**) needs to be combined with either (JP) or (JP*), that is, with either a reductivist or a non-reductivist account of testimonial justification. On either account, a necessary condition for knowing that p is that one must not have any defeaters for one's belief that p. Thus we may say that there are at least two necessary conditions for a hearer to acquire testimonial knowledge via the statement of a speaker, one which applies specifically to the speaker's statement, and another which applies to the epistemic states of the hearer. In particular, I propose the following minimal account of testimonial knowledge:

TK. For every speaker S and hearer H, H comes to know that p via S's statement that p only if (i) S's statement that p is appropriately connected with the fact that p; and (ii) H has no defeaters indicating the contrary.

(TK) does not specify sufficient conditions. There may be further necessary conditions which need to be added, e.g., one may endorse (JP′) and require that the hearer in question have positive reasons for accepting a speaker's statement that p. My purpose, however, is only to show that the arguments in this paper lead to the acceptance of at least (TK), though such an account can be further developed for a complete view of testimonial knowledge.

The considerations put forth in this paper suggest that, strictly speaking, knowledge is not necessarily *transmitted* via testimony, but that testimony can itself *generate* knowledge. In a testimonial chain in which each link fails to know that p because each has an undefeated defeater for the belief that p, the last hearer in such a chain can none the less come to have new knowledge via testimony, either through not having the defeater in question or through having a defeater-defeater. Thus testimony seems to differ from memory in a particularly salient respect precisely because the former can be generative while the latter is merely preservative.

Notes

1   R. Audi, "The Place of Testimony in the Fabric of Knowledge and Justification", *American Philosophical Quarterly*, 34 (1997), pp. 405–22, at p. 410.
2   J. Ross, "Testimonial Evidence", in K. Lehrer (ed.), *Analysis and Metaphysics: Essays in Honor of R.M. Chisholm* (Dordrecht: Reidel, 1975), pp. 35–55, at p. 53.
3   M. Welbourne, "Testimony, Knowledge and Belief", in B. Matilal and A. Chakrabarti (eds), *Knowing from Words* (Dordrecht: Kluwer, 1994, hereafter *KFW*), pp. 297–313, at p. 302; see also his "The Community of Knowledge", *The Philosophical Quarterly*, 31 (1981), pp. 302–14, and "The Transmission of Knowledge", *The Philosophical Quarterly*, 29 (1979), pp. 1–9.
4   T. Burge, "Content Preservation", *Philosophical Review*, 102 (1993), pp. 457–88, at p. 486. Other proponents of this view of testimonial knowledge include A. Plantinga, *Warrant and Proper Function* (Oxford University Press, 1993), ch. 4; and T. Williamson, "Knowing and Asserting", *Philosophical Review*, 105 (1996), pp. 489–523.

5   M. Dummett, "Testimony and Memory", in *KFW*, pp. 251–72, at p. 264 (my italics).
6   For different versions of non-reductivism, see Dummett; Audi; C. Coady, *Testimony: a Philosophical Study* (Oxford: Clarendon Press, 1992), and "Testimony, Observation and Autonomous Knowledge", in *KFW*, pp. 225–50; Burge, "Content Preservation", and "Interlocution, Perception, and Memory", *Philosophical Studies*, 86 (1997), pp. 21–47; R. Foley, "Egoism in Epistemology", in F. Schmitt (ed.), *Socializing Epistemology: the Social Dimensions of Knowledge* (Lanham: Rowman & Littlefield, 1994), pp. 53–73.
7   For reductivist views of testimony, see E. Fricker, "The Epistemology of Testimony", *Proceedings of the Aristotelian Society*, Supp. Vol. 61 (1987), pp. 57–83, "Against Gullibility", in *KFW*, pp. 125–61, and "Telling and Trusting: Reductionism and Anti-Reductionism in the Epistemology of Testimony", *Mind*, 104 (1995), pp. 393–411; J. Lyons, "Testimony, Induction and Folk Psychology", *Australasian Journal of Philosophy*, 75 (1997), pp. 163–78.

8   For proponents of this view, see R. Nozick, *Philosophical Explanations* (Cambridge, MA: Belknap, 1981); J. Pollock, *Contemporary Theories of Knowledge* (Totowa: Rowman & Littlefield, 1986); A. Goldman, *Epistemology and Cognition* (Harvard University Press, 1986); A. Plantinga, *Warrant and Proper Function* (Oxford University Press, 1993).

9   See, for example, Goldman; L. BonJour, "Externalist Theories of Epistemic Justification", *Midwest Studies in Philosophy*, 5 (1980), pp. 53–73, and *The Structure of Empirical Knowledge* (Harvard University Press, 1985); R. Chisholm, *Theory of Knowledge* (Englewood Cliffs: Prentice-Hall, 1989).

10   See, for example, K. Lehrer, "Knowledge, Truth, and Evidence", *Analysis*, 25 (1965), pp. 168–75, and *Knowledge* (Oxford University Press, 1974); K. Lehrer and T. Paxson, "Knowledge: Undefeated Justified True Belief", *Journal of Philosophy*, 66 (1969), pp. 225–37; P. Klein, "A Proposed Definition of Propositional Knowledge", *Journal of Philosophy*, 68 (1971), pp. 471–82, "Knowledge, Causality, and Defeasibility", *Journal of Philosophy*, 73 (1976), pp. 792–812, "Misleading 'Misleading Defeaters'", *Journal of Philosophy*, 76 (1979), pp. 382–86, and "Misleading Evidence and the Restoration of Justification", *Philosophical Studies*, 37 (1980), pp. 81–9; E. Sosa, "How Do You Know?", *American Philosophical Quarterly*, 11 (1974), pp. 113–22, and "Epistemic Presupposition", in G. Pappas (ed.), *Justification and Knowledge: New Studies in Epistemology* (Dordrecht: Reidel, 1980), pp. 79–92; M. Swain, *Reasons and Knowledge* (Cornell University Press, 1981).

11   This is a slight variation of an example found in Audi (p. 420). For a similar example, see Sosa, *Knowledge in Perspective: Selected Essays in Epistemology* (Cambridge University Press, 1991), p. 217.

12   This example undermines views of testimonial knowledge which are even weaker than (2) or (2*). For instance, John Hardwig, in "The Role of Trust in Knowledge", *Journal of Philosophy*, 88 (1991), pp. 693–708, claims that speakers must *believe* that p in order for their testimony to give hearers good reasons to believe that p. As my example shows, however, even Hardwig's weaker thesis is false.

13   See, for example, Fricker; Burge; Plantinga; Audi.

14   For a line of argument purporting to show that widespread error of this sort is incoherent, see D. Davidson, "A Coherence Theory of Truth and Knowledge", in D. Henrich (ed.), *Kant oder Hegel?* (Stuttgart: Klett-Cotta, 1983), pp. 423–38; Coady, *Testimony* ch. 9; L. Stevenson, "Why Believe What People Say?", *Synthese*, 94 (1993), pp. 429–51. For convincing replies, see R. Foley and R. Fumerton, "Davidson's Theism?", *Philosophical Studies*, 48 (1985), pp. 83–9; Plantinga ch. 4.

15   See, for example, Ross; also P. Graham, "What is Testimony?", *The Philosophical Quarterly*, 47 (1997), pp. 227–32; Coady ch. 2.

16   See, for example, K. DeRose, "Solving the Skeptical Problem", *Philosophical Review*, 104 (1995), pp. 1–52; D. Lewis, "Elusive Knowledge", *Australasian Journal of Philosophy*, 74 (1996), pp. 549–67.

CHAPTER 58

The Problem of Memory Knowledge

Michael Huemer

The sun is about 93 million miles away from the earth. How do I know that? Well, I learned it once. I don't know when or how I learned it, but I did, and I now remember it. I couldn't tell you how the distance to the sun was calculated either, but it's something that scientists have discovered. How do I know that scientists have discovered it? Well, I don't know how I learned that either, but I remember it, too.

Even granting the reliability of scientists and other experts, this does not sound like a very impressive justification. Yet arguably, *most* of our knowledge is like that. A few more examples: there is a 3-hour time difference between Los Angeles and New York; Abraham Lincoln was President of the United States during the Civil War; the word "tree" refers in English to a certain kind of plant; the square on the hypotenuse of a right triangle equals the sum of the squares on the other two sides; wood is a poor conductor of heat and electricity; China is in Asia. I don't know how I learned any of those facts, but however I learned them, I kept them in memory since then (doubtless I gained numerous confirmations of them since the first time I learned them, and I can't specifically remember any of those occasions either), and I have no serious doubt about any one of them.

Originally published in *The Pacific Philosophical Quarterly* 80, 197 (1999), pp. 346–57.

What justifies me in believing that the sun is 93 million miles from the earth? The fact that I don't remember my original reason for adopting that belief suggests that whatever that reason was, it can not be considered a reason I *now* have for my belief.[1]

In general, when S remembers that P, what kind of justification does S have for believing P? Three possible answers to this question naturally come to mind:

1. The Inferential Theory

First, perhaps my justification is inferential. And perhaps it is something like this: I now seem to remember that the earth is 93 million miles away from the sun. In the past, I have generally found that expectations formed on the basis of my seeming memories have been borne out. For example, I seemed to remember my address, and when I went to that address, I found an apartment of just the sort I was expecting. This strongly confirms that my seeming memories are highly reliable. Therefore (probably), it is true that the sun is 93 million miles away from the earth.

The most obvious problem here is one of circularity. How do I know that in the past, my seeming memories have been corroborated? Well, I seem to remember that that's generally been the case. But, on the present theory of memory knowledge,[2] I cannot trust that until I *first* prove the reliability of my memory. Therefore, I cannot use my past experiences in this way – nor, in fact, in any other way – in my argument for the reliability of memory.

Thus, if any inferential account is to work, the premises of my argument must rely solely on my present experiences and/or a priori insights. I can't use any previously-gained knowledge. It seems unlikely that I could derive the reliability of memory from premises of this kind; at any rate, I have no idea how such an inference would go. Additionally, an inferential theory would face two further constraints that increase its difficulties. First, the argument would have to be short and simple, such that one could hold it all in mind at once. Otherwise, completion of the argument would depend on one's *remembering* that the earlier stages of the argument had been correctly executed, and this would illicitly presuppose the reliability of memory.

Second, I would have to be in some sense using the argument *every time* I had a justified memory belief. It would not be enough for me to go through the argument once, and thenceforth merely remember that I had demonstrated the reliability of memory. For if merely remembering that my memory is reliable were enough for me to be justified in believing my memory is reliable, then merely remembering that the sun is 93 million miles away from the earth should be sufficient for me to be justified in believing that the sun is 93 million miles away from the earth – contrary to the present theory, but in accord with the theory to be considered in section 2.

Given that my belief that the sun is 93 million miles from the earth is continuously present (it remains as a dispositional belief even when I'm not thinking about it), I will apparently need to be employing the argument for the reliability of memory continuously, if I am to keep my justification. The defender of the inferential account may claim that I am using this argument (whatever it is) for the reliability of memory only unconsciously, but it remains implausible that I am using it all the time, even unconsciously. Indeed, there is no evidence that I have ever employed any such argument at all, so skepticism seems to be the price of the inferential account.

2. The Foundational Theory

Perhaps, then, my justification is non-inferential. Perhaps memory experiences create the same sort of foundational justification that (some epistemologists argue) sensory experiences do. Just having an experience of seeming to perceive that P makes one prima facie justified in believing that P, and similarly, having an experience of seeming to remember that P makes one prima facie justified in believing that P.[3]

This view has counter-intuitive results. Suppose I initially learn that P by means of an a priori proof of it (the proof is short, so I can hold it all in mind at once and do not need to use memory). So I have an adequate justification for believing P from the start, although the possibility of mistakes, even in short proofs, makes my justification less than completely conclusive. However, a few moments pass, and I now am able, in addition, to *recall* that P. If I entertain the proof while also remembering that P, I will now have *two* justifications for P, one inferential and one foundational. Thus, my warrant becomes more secure with the passage of time.[4]

Here's another case. Suppose that I initially adopt the unjustified belief that P (perhaps by wishful thinking or some such irrational process). The next day, however, my belief is adequately justified, because I now seem to remember that P. The passage of time has transformed my irrational belief into a rational one.

It might be argued that in this latter case, I have a defeater for P, since I can recall that I adopted P by wishful thinking.[5] Therefore, modify the case as follows: a number of years pass, and I no longer recall how I initially "learned" that P, but I still clearly "remember" that P.[6] For example, suppose that I initially accepted the existence of life after death by wishful thinking. I now no longer remember where I got that belief, but I just seem to remember that that's something I know. On the other hand, my brother Pete adopted the same belief in exactly the same way. However, his memory is better than mine, so he also remembers how he got the belief. As a result, my belief system is rational and his is not. That seems wrong.

To further confirm that this result is wrong, Thomas Senor (1993) asks us to consider an analogy to moral philosophy. Suppose there is a certain ruthless tyrant, call him "Saddam," who decides to viciously attack a neighboring country. Suppose that at the time he makes this choice, Saddam's character is such that it would be psychologically impossible for him to behave in any other way. Suppose, however, that Saddam, having begun as a normal boy, *acquired* this deplorable character as a result of a series of evil choices that he made of his own free will. In this case, we would surely not excuse Saddam's present actions on the ground that he could not do otherwise. Rather, Saddam's culpability in his past choices follows him to the present day, rendering him culpable for the present evil actions that flow from them. Similarly, argues Senor, a person's previous *epistemic* irresponsibility follows him, making him epistemically blameworthy for any present likely-to-be-false beliefs that result from his previous irrationality. A present-day belief cannot be rendered epistemically justified by the fact that, doing the best one can do *now* results in acceptance of the belief, if this situation results from previous epistemic irrationality – just as a present-day action can not be rendered morally blameless by the fact that, doing the best one can do *now* results in performance of the action, if this situation results from previous immorality.[7]

Both of the above cases – the case where memory would increase one's justification for a belief, and the case where memory would convert an unjustified belief into a justified one – point up the following general, intuitive constraint on a theory of memory justification: the justification for a belief cannot be increased by its passing into memory; it can only be lowered. The foundational theory fails to account for this.[8]

3.   The Preservation Theory

Here is a third view. When I remember that P, my justification for believing P is whatever it was to begin with. Memory just preserves the justification (or lack of it) of my beliefs.[9] So my justification for thinking that the sun is about 93 million miles away is, perhaps, that Mrs. Kim in second grade told me that it was – even if I don't know that that is my justification. On this view, the fact that I don't remember what my original justification for P was does not prevent me from still

having that justification for P. This seems more natural than the preceding two theories.

But now recall Russell's five-minute hypothesis.[10] Suppose God created someone five minutes ago in exactly the state that I was in five minutes ago, surrounded by exactly the same kinds of things. Call this person Mike2. Mike2 was created complete with false memories of his past life, identical to my memories of my past life. He thinks his name is "Mike" and is presently writing a paper about the problem of memory knowledge. His situation would be (to him) indistinguishable from my actual situation. Usually, this scenario is mentioned for the purpose of asking, How do I know I'm not actually in that situation? But here I mention it to make a positive point. What sort of things would it be *rational* for Mike2 to believe? Pretty clearly, just the same things that it is rational for me, now, to believe (modulo appropriate changes in indexical references). Most of Mike2's beliefs about his own past are *false*, but he has no way of knowing that, and no more reason for suspecting it than I have for suspecting that my beliefs about my past are false. So if I am justified in believing that I ate a bagel this morning, Mike2 is justified (though mistaken) in believing that *he* ate a bagel this morning. Furthermore, it seems that he has the same degree and kind of justification that I now have.

But of course, this contradicts the present theory of memory knowledge. According to the present view, memory merely preserves one's initial justification, if any, for a belief.[11] So I am adequately justified in believing that I ate a bagel this morning, on the basis of the sensory experiences I had then. Mike2 has no such justification, since he never had any sensory experience of eating a bagel. At minimum, he does not have the same sort of justification that I have, and it appears that he has no justification at all, since, on the preservation theory, memory experiences are not themselves a *source* of justification.[12] On this theory, then, Mike2 is highly irrational (unlike myself), even though he is intrinsically identical to me.[13]

Thus, there is an interesting problem of memory knowledge. The three most obvious theories of the justification of memory beliefs are all unacceptable. How can we find a theory that is not subject to any of the preceding objections? Our verdict on the case of Mike2 seems to demand that the justification of memory beliefs depend only on the current state of the believer, and not on his past; otherwise, Mike2 would be found to be drastically less rational than myself. But if the past history of a memory belief is thus irrelevant to its justification, won't this allow us to construct cases where memory transforms an irrational belief into a rational one (as in our objection to the foundational theory)? How, that is, can we reconcile the principle that the degree of justification of a remembered belief can never exceed the original degree of justification one had for its adoption, with the apparent lesson of the five-minute hypothesis, that the past history of a belief is irrelevant to its present justification? It seems that our intuitions are simply contradictory.

4.   A Solution: The Dualistic Theory

Not so. There is a theory that accommodates our intuitions about all of the cases, incorporating elements of both the foundational view and the preservation view. I call it the "dualistic theory" because it holds that the question, "What is my justification for believing that P?" requires a two-part answer: first, why I was justified in *adopting* the belief that P; and second, why I was justified in *retaining* it.[14] On this view, a belief is justified full stop if and only if one had an adequate justification for adopting it at some point, and thenceforward one was justified in retaining it. The normal functioning of memory, in the absence of specific reasons for revising a belief, constitutes an epistemically acceptable manner of retaining beliefs.

So far, this sounds exactly like the preservation theory. However, we will see in a moment how, having distinguished two parts of a belief's justification, the dualistic theory is in a position to make an appropriate concession to the foundationalist account that avoids the major objection to the preservation theory.

It is already clear that the present view avoids the foundationalist's main problem. The dualistic view does not allow an initially irrational belief to become rational merely by passing into memory, since a rational belief, in the full sense, requires *both* rational acquisition and rational retention.

How, then, can the dualistic theory avoid the objection from the five-minute hypothesis – how can it secure Mike2's epistemic rationality? Simply by

this posit: coming to believe something by seeming to remember it (in the absence of defeaters that one is aware of) is an epistemically rational way of acquiring the belief. This posit captures the foundationalist intuition, that I am rational in believing something I seem to remember even if on this particular occasion, unbeknownst to me, my memory is deceiving me – even if, that is to say, I never really had that belief before. From the standpoint of epistemic responsibility, this is surely correct. The unfortunate Mike2 has not committed any epistemic wrongs; he has done the best that could be expected of him. Our theory credits him this: since Mike2 acquired his belief that he ate a bagel this morning by seeming to remember it, he is rational in accepting it.[15]

But this posit does not introduce the possibility of memory's converting an irrational belief into a rational one. For the principle only applies to a case in which having a seeming memory that P was actually one's way of acquiring the belief that P. Recall the case where I believe P by wishful thinking and later seem to remember that P. Having a seeming memory in this case is not my method of acquiring the belief; wishful thinking is. Apparent memory is only my way of *retaining* the belief. Since a justified belief must have both a rational acquisition method and a rational retention method, this belief is unjustified.

It must be admitted that this view can not maintain the supervenience of epistemic justification on the current, intrinsic state of the believer. That seemingly desirable characteristic is genuinely inconsistent with the conjunction of two other principles we have been assuming: first, that memory can not convert unjustified belief to justified belief; and second, that in typical circumstances our remembered beliefs are justified. For it is possible to have two people who are in the same state presently, each having forgotten his original reason for adopting P, one of whom did and the other of whom did not originally have a good reason for accepting P. The one person must be counted justified in his present belief (else we have memory skepticism), and the other must be counted unjustified (else we have an unjustified belief converted to a justified belief by the passage of time). It follows that the justificatory status of the belief that P does not supervene on the current, intrinsic state of the believer. Of course, it may still supervene on the total history of intrinsic states of the believer.

To illustrate, return to the case of myself and Mike2. Let's suppose that, among many beliefs I have for which I do not remember my original reasons for adopting them, there are some rational beliefs and a few irrational ones. I am justified in believing P, say, but unjustified in believing Q. Mike2, likewise, will be justified in believing P. But unlike me, on the present theory, Mike2 will *also* be justified in believing Q, since he, unlike me, acquired the belief through apparent memory. So there is one way in which the victim of the five-minute hypothesis would be epistemically better off than we actually are – he has no fewer, and possibly more, justified beliefs.

On reflection, we can see that this result is correct and that the principle of current time-slice supervenience is therefore mistaken. For Mike2, there is no relevant difference between his belief that Q and his belief that P. Both are adopted in the same way, so if we grant that his belief that P is justified, we have to allow his belief that Q to be justified similarly. Recall Senor's analogy with moral philosophy. Suppose that a person (call him "Saddam2") were created and placed at the head of a country, with a compulsion to invade a neighboring country. Saddam2 is born lacking free will, his decision to invade already predetermined. In that case, Saddam2 could not be morally blamed for his action. We have already said that Saddam, who acquired a similar psychological compulsion through earlier bad choices, *can* be blamed for the same action. So the moral culpability of a decision does not supervene on the internal state of the agent at the time of decision-making; it depends, too, on the agent's past choices. Likewise, we should not be surprised that the epistemic status of a belief depends in part on the believer's past thought processes.

5. The Theory Extended: Degrees of Justification

So far, I have stated the dualistic theory as a theory of when a memory belief is *justified* or *unjustified*. But we can generalize the theory to give an account of the *degree* of justification that a belief has, and this generalization provides a further

demonstration of the superiority of the dualistic view. The natural extension of the simple dualistic view would be to say that there are two degrees of justification involved in any belief – a degree of justification associated with the adoption of the belief, and a degree of justification associated with its retention – and that the overall level of justification of a belief is the product of those two quantities. The first of these two quantities is simply a matter of the conclusiveness of the grounds one originally had (again, this holds true even if one has forgotten those grounds). We can think of it as a number between 0 and 1, with 1 representing infallible justification for believing the proposition in question, and 0 representing infallible justification for disbelieving it. The second quantity is a matter of the credibility of one's memory, and it, too, can be thought of as a number between 0 and 1. If one has a relatively faint memory, such that one is quite unsure whether one really remembers that P or not, then this number will be close to 1/2 (not 0, for even the faintest of memories would not be evidence *against* P). If one has a very firm and clear memory, the number will be close to 1. If one has special reason for doubting the reliability of one's memory (e.g., one knows that one has misremembered similar things in the past), this can lower the second number further.

One of our objections to the foundationalist account was based on the principle that the justification of a belief can be lowered through its passing into memory but can not be raised. The foundationalist could not accommodate this fact, because for him, the past justification of a belief is irrelevant to its present justification. But the generalized dualistic view easily accommodates the principle – when one multiplies the original degree of justification by a number less than or equal to 1 representing the credibility of the memory, one necessarily gets something less than or equal to the original degree of justification.

The dualistic view also surpasses the straight preservation theory in the treatment of degrees of justification. Under the straight preservation view, the justification I *now* have for P when I remember that P is the same as the justification I had for P originally. Given this, the only natural view to take as to the *degree* of justification I now have for P is that it is identical to the degree of justification I originally had, on the principle that the degree of one's justification for P is a function of what one's justification for P is. For example, suppose my original justification for P consisted in a conclusive, deductive proof of P, although I have since forgotten what my justification was. On the preservation view, I nevertheless retain my original justification for P. Therefore, my belief that P continues to be supported by a conclusive proof (the memory can hardly preserve the argument but turn it into an inconclusive one). Therefore, my degree of justification for P is the degree appropriate to having a conclusive proof, that is, conclusive justification.

But this result is wrong – one should not be as confident that P ten years after learning it as one was when it was fresh in one's mind. One should not have 100% confidence in one's memory. The passage of time introduces new possibilities of error; therefore, it lowers one's justification for believing a proposition. Here, as elsewhere, the dualistic view succeeds in accommodating our intuitions about justification, escaping the objections that tell against the two main alternatives.[16]

The preservation theorist might try arguing that as time passes, one's justification for P typically decreases, not because one's justification acquires a new, fallible component, but because one acquires new defeaters. For instance, the proposition that my memory is unreliable, or even the proposition that this particular memory experience is faint, would be defeaters for P when I seem to recall that P. In order to explain why one's justification *typically* (perhaps always) decreases with time, rather than only decreasing in certain special circumstances, the preservation theorist would have to maintain that even so weak a proposition as "my memory is not infallible" or "this memory is not *absolutely* clear" can be a defeater.

There seems to be something ad hoc about introducing a defeater that is always or nearly always present and that functions to lower one's justification for P by just the amount that one's justification would fall short of its original level *if* one's having a memory experience were part of one's justification for P. But be that as it may, there is a more serious problem. Suppose that I initially learned that P through sensory observation, and I am now, ten years later,

genuinely remembering that P. According to the preservation theory, my justification for believing P, now, consists in that same sensory experience. If this is the case, then why would a proposition about the reliability of my *memory* be a defeater for my belief? Certainly, at the time I was initially observing that P, "my memory is unreliable" would not have defeated my justification for believing P. "My memory is unreliable" is not a rebutting defeater for P (it is merely neutral with respect to the truth of P), and nor is "my memory is unreliable" an undercutting defeater for a *perceptual* justification of P – only something like "my senses are unreliable" would undercut a perceptual justification. Therefore, if my present justification for P consists in my (earlier) sensory experience, my justification should be unaffected by the discovery that my memory is unreliable.

An analogy here is instructive: suppose that I believe Q on the basis of Jones' testimony. Now suppose you come along and succeed in convincing me that *Smith* is an unreliable witness. Would this defeat my justification for believing Q? Of course not. You would have to show that *Jones* was unreliable in order to undermine my justification for Q; either that, or my justification for believing Q would have to depend at least in part on Smith's testimony (perhaps in addition to Jones'). According to the preservation theory, when I observe that P and later recall that P, my belief at the later time is based solely on the observation, not on the memory experience. Therefore, a criticism of my senses would undermine the belief, but a criticism of my memory should not. On the other hand, the dualistic view naturally explains the significance of a criticism of my memory as affecting the second factor involved in the justification of a memory belief – the factor neglected by the preservationist.

One of the two main theories of memory knowledge locates the justification of a memory belief solely in the memory impression. The other locates it solely in the original acquisition of the belief. As a result, one theory implies that memory can raise a belief's justification, while the other implies that memory cannot lower a belief's justification. The solution is to locate a belief's justification *both* in the circumstances of its initial acquisition *and* in the nature of the present memory experience.[17]

Notes

1 So argues Ginet (1975), pp. 153–6.
2 I am assuming that knowledge is a kind of justified belief, where justification is understood in terms of epistemic responsibility (see Alston's (1985) discussion of "deontological" notions of justification for more on this kind of justification). If this is not what knowledge is, then what I am looking for should be described as "a theory of the justification of memory beliefs" rather than "a theory of memory knowledge."
3 Pollock (1986), pp. 50–2 appears to defend this view. However, he has since indicated that he is addressing a different sense of "justification" than mine (personal communication).
4 Pollock (1995), pp. 101–2 points out that it need not be the case that the conjunction of two reasons for believing P provides better justification for P than either reason alone provides. As an example, he considers a case in which S_1 and S_2 are each generally reliable witnesses, but you know that S_1 tends to corroborate S_2's testimony only when the latter is a fabrication (otherwise, S_1 keeps his mouth shut). However, nothing like this is going on in my example (it isn't as if you tend to remember that P only when your argument for P was fallacious), so it's hard to see why getting a second justification for P shouldn't increase your degree of justification for P. See also the analogy below, in note 5.
5 Pollock's (1986), p. 54 remarks imply such a response, although it is not clear that the response works. Consider a similar case: suppose I initially adopt P by wishful thinking, but later I perceive that P. At this point, my belief becomes justified. The fact that I initially adopted P through wishful thinking is merely irrelevant to the truth of P – it does not count against P in the event that I discover a new justification for P. Since Pollock assimilates the epistemology of memory to that of perception, it is unclear why the same assessment would not apply when a memory experience is substituted for a perception – i.e., the memory experience provides a new justification for the initially irrational belief.
6 Annis (1980), pp. 325–6 raises this kind of counter-example to Pollock's view.

7 Senor (1993), pp. 468–9.
8 Malcolm (1963), pp. 230–1 almost says this, except he does not seem to allow the possibility of one's justification being lowered.
9 This view is defended by Malcolm (1963), pp. 229–30; Annis (1980); Naylor (1983); and Owens (1999).
10 See Russell (1971), p. 159.
11 See Malcolm (1963), p. 230: "When someone remembers that p does he have grounds for being sure that p? The answer is that he has the same grounds, if any, that he previously had."
12 Owens (1999), chapter 9 is particularly explicit about this point.
13 Pollock (1986), p. 50 poses a related objection to the preservation theory, based on ordinary cases in which your memory deceives you: He thinks that in such cases, provided you have no reason for suspecting that your memory is deceiving you, you are justified in believing what you seem to remember; yet the preservation theory implies that these beliefs are unjustified. Pollock concludes that memory must be accepted as a source of justification, and hence that the foundational theory is true.
14 Owens (1999) makes use of this distinction, but he does not take advantage of the opportunity it provides to avoid the five-minute-hypothesis objection.
15 The following objection could be pressed: Mike2 is created with a host of *dispositional* beliefs implanted in him. Having never consciously entertained the propositions that these beliefs are about, he has not had any (occurrent) experiences of seeming to remember them, so the present theory cannot account for Mike2's justification for his dispositional beliefs. An obvious response would be to say that Mike2's beliefs are justified by virtue of his *dispositional* seeming-memories (quasi-memories). But a more interesting response, and the one I favor, is that Mike2 does not (cannot) have the same dispositional beliefs that I have. A detailed discussion of this point would take us too far afield, but briefly: in order to genuinely believe that P, it is not enough that one *would*

occurrently belief P if one considered it – "dispositional belief" does not merely mean "disposition to believe." To believe P, a person must either (i) occurrently believe it, (ii) have once believed it, having never changed his mind about it, (iii) believe something else which *presupposes* it, or (iv) believe something else which obviously entails it. So there are three ways of dispositionally believing something, but each presupposes another belief or belief at an earlier time. For this reason, Mike2 cannot be created with dispositional beliefs already implanted in him; he can't have any dispositional beliefs prior to his first occurrent belief.

16 I don't count the inferential theory as one of the main alternatives, because I do not know of any philosopher who actually defends it.

17 My thanks are due to David Owens for stimulating my interest in and initial thoughts on this topic, and to both David Owens and John Pollock for discussion of various ideas in this paper. Unfortunately, I do not believe either of these philosophers would agree with more than half of what I have said here.

References

Alston, William P. (1985). "Concepts of Epistemic Justification," *The Monist* 68, pp. 57–89.

Annis, David B. (1980). "Memory and Justification," *Philosophy and Phenomenological Research* 40, pp. 324–33.

Ginet, Carl (1975). *Knowledge, Perception, and Memory*. Boston: D. Reidel.

Malcolm, Norman (1963). *Knowledge and Certainty*. Englewood Cliffs, NJ: Prentice-Hall.

Naylor, Andrew (1983). "Justification in Memory Knowledge," *Synthese* 55, pp. 269–86.

Owens, David (1999). *Reason without Freedom* (unpublished ms.), chapter 9.

Pollock, John L. (1986). *Contemporary Theories of Knowledge*. Totowa, NJ: Rowman & Littlefield.

—— (1995). *Cognitive Carpentry: A Blueprint for How to Build a Person*. Cambridge, MA: MIT Press.

Russell, Bertrand (1971). *The Analysis of Mind*. London: Allen & Unwin.

Senor, Thomas D. (1993). "Internalistic Foundationalism and the Justification of Memory Belief," *Synthese* 94, pp. 453–76.

CHAPTER 59

Criteria, Defeasibility, and Knowledge

John McDowell

It is widely believed that in his later work Wittgenstein introduced a special use of the notion of a criterion. In this proprietary use, "criteria" are supposed to be a kind of evidence.[1] Their status as evidence, unlike that of symptoms, is a matter of "convention" or "grammar" rather than empirical theory; but the support that a "criterion" yields for a claim is defeasible: that is, a state of information in which one is in possession of a "criterial" warrant for a claim can always be expanded into a state of information in which the claim would not be warranted at all.[2] This special notion is thought to afford – among much else[3] – a novel response to the traditional problem of other minds.

What follows falls into three parts. In the first, I shall express, in a preliminary way, a doubt whether the supposed novel response can work. In the second, I shall question the interpretation of Wittgenstein that yields it. I believe it issues from reading Wittgenstein in the light of tacit epistemological assumptions whose strikingly traditional character casts suspicion on their attribution to Wittgenstein himself. My concern, however, is less with exegesis than with those epistemological assumptions, and in the third part I shall begin on the project of undermining an idea that seems central to them.

Originally published in *Proceedings of the British Academy* 68 (1982), pp. 455–79.

I

It will help me to articulate my epistemological distrust if I let the "criterial" position define its stance towards our knowledge of other minds in explicit contrast with a possible alternative: namely, a position according to which, on a suitable occasion, the circumstance that someone else is in some "inner" state can itself be an object of one's experience.[4]

I once tried to capture this idea by suggesting that such a circumstance could be "available to awareness, in its own right and not merely through behavioural proxies";[5] and similarly by suggesting that

> we should not jib at, or interpret away, the commonsense thought that, on those occasions which are paradigmatically suitable for training in the assertoric use of the relevant part of a language, one can literally perceive, in another person's facial expression or his behaviour, that he is [for instance] in pain, and not just infer that he is in pain from what one perceives.[6]

In the interest of a "criterial" position, Crispin Wright has protested against this attempt to describe an alternative (which he labels "M-realism"); he writes as follows:

> But that no inference, via "proxies" or whatever, should be involved is quite consistent with what

is actually perceived being not that someone is in pain, *tout court*, but that criteria – in what I take to be the *Philosophical Investigations* sense – that he is in pain are satisfied. Criteria are not proxies, and they do not form the bases of inferences, correctly so described. But, in contrast with truth-conditions, a claim made on the basis of satisfaction of its criteria can subsequently be jettisoned, consistently with retention of the belief that criteria were indeed satisfied. So the M-realist about a particular kind of statement has to hold not just that inference via proxies is not invariably involved when the assertoric use of those statements is justified, but more: that the occasions which are "paradigmatically suitable" for training in their assertoric use involve not just satisfaction of criteria – otherwise experience of them will be experience of a situation whose obtaining is consistent with the falsity of the relevant statements – but realisation of truth-conditions, properly so regarded.[7]

For my present purposes, what is important about this passage is not the issue it raises about the formulation of M-realism, but rather its account of the "criterial" alternative. Wright's remarks bring out clearly the commitment of the "criterial" view to the thesis that, even on the occasions that seem most favourable for a claim to be able to see that someone else is in some "inner" state, the reach of one's experience falls short of that circumstance itself—not just in the sense that the person's being in the "inner" state is not itself embraced within the scope of one's consciousness, but in the sense that what is available to one's experience is something compatible with the person's not being in the "inner" state at all.

Now is this position epistemologically satisfactory?

M-realism offers a conception of what constitutes knowing that someone else is in an "inner" state, at least on certain favourable occasions: namely, experiencing that circumstance itself. Wright asks us to consider whether what is experienced on those occasions may not be something less: namely, the satisfaction of "criteria". One might incautiously assume that experiencing the satisfaction of "criteria" is meant to take over the role played in M-realism by experiencing the circumstance itself: that is, to be what, on those favourable occasions, constitutes knowing that the circumstance obtains. But since "criteria" are

defeasible, it is tempting to suppose that to experience the satisfaction of "criteria" for a claim is to be in a position in which, for all one knows, the claim may not be true. That yields this thesis: knowing that someone else is in some "inner" state can be constituted by being in a position in which, for all one knows, the person may not be in that "inner" state. And that seems straightforwardly incoherent.

This line of thought is partly vitiated by the incautious assumption. A "criterial" theorist can say: experiencing the satisfaction of "criteria" is meant to be, not what constitutes knowing that things are thus and so, but rather a "criterion" for the claim to know it. Its "criterial" support for the claim to know that things are thus and so would be defeated by anything that would defeat the original "criterial" support for the claim that that is how things are. So the "criterial" view is not required to envisage the possibility that someone may be correctly said to know something when what he supposedly knows cannot itself be correctly affirmed.[8]

Nevertheless, the "criterial" view does envisage ascribing knowledge on the strength of something compatible with the falsity of what is supposedly known. And it is a serious question whether we can understand how it can be knowledge that is properly so ascribed. Rejecting the incautious assumption leaves unchallenged the tempting thought that, since "criteria" are defeasible, someone who experiences the satisfaction of "criteria" for the ascription of an "inner" state to another person is thereby in a position in which, for all he knows, the person may not be in that "inner" state. And the question is: if that is the best one can achieve, how is there room for anything recognizable as knowledge that the person is in the "inner" state? It does not help with this difficulty to insist that being in that supposed best position is not meant to be constitutive of having the knowledge. The trouble is that if that is the best position achievable, then however being in it is supposed to relate to the claim to know that the person is in the "inner" state, it looks as if the claim can never be acceptable.

Of course my characterization of the supposed best position is tendentious. If experiencing the satisfaction of "criteria" does legitimize ("criterially") a claim to know that things are thus and so, it cannot also be legitimate to admit that the position is one in which, for all one knows, things may be otherwise. But the difficulty is to see how the fact that "criteria" are defeasible can be prevented from compelling that admission: in which case we can conclude, by contraposition, that experiencing the satisfaction of "criteria" cannot legitimize a claim of knowledge. How can an appeal to "convention" somehow drive a wedge between accepting that everything that one has is compatible with things not being so, on the one hand, and admitting that one does not know that things are so, on the other? As far as its bearing on epistemological issues is concerned, the "criterial" view looks no more impressive than any other instance of a genre of responses to scepticism to which it seems to belong: a genre in which it is conceded that the sceptic's complaints are substantially correct, but we are supposedly saved from having to draw the sceptic's conclusions by the fact that it is *not done* – in violation of a "convention" – to talk that way.[9]

This line of thought may seem to be an indiscriminate attack on the idea that knowledge can be based on an experiential intake that falls short of the fact known (in the sense I explained: namely, being compatible with there being no such fact). That would put the line of thought in doubt; but the objection fails. We can countenance cases of knowledge in which the knower's epistemic standing is owed not just to an experiential intake that falls short of the fact known, in that sense, but partly to his possession of theoretical knowledge: something we can picture as extending his cognitive reach beyond the restricted range of mere experience, so that the hostile line of thought does not get started. But that cannot be how it is in the "criterial" cases. To hold that theory contributes to the epistemic standing, with respect to a claim, of someone who experiences the satisfaction of "criteria" for it would conflict with the insistence that "criteria" and claim are related by "grammar"; it would obliterate the distinction between "criteria" and symptoms.

I have granted that experiencing the satisfaction of "criteria" had better not be conceived as constituting the associated knowledge. It is tempting to ask: when the ground for attributing knowledge is experience of the satisfaction of "criteria", what *would* constitute possessing the knowledge? Someone who admits the question

might be inclined to try this reply: the knowledge is constituted by experiencing the satisfaction of "criteria" – given that things are indeed as the person is said to know that they are. But does that specify something that we can intelligibly count as knowledge? Consider a pair of cases, in both of which someone competent in the use of some claim experiences the satisfaction of (undefeated) "criteria" for it, but in only one of which the claim is true. According to the suggestion we are considering, the subject in the latter case knows that things are as the claim would represent them as being; the subject in the former case does not. (In both cases it would be "criterially" legitimate to attribute the knowledge, but that is not to the present purpose.) However, the story is that the scope of experience is the same in each case: the fact itself is outside the reach of experience. And experience is the only mode of cognition – the only mode of acquisition of epistemic standing – that is operative; appeal to theory is excluded, as we have just seen. So why should we not conclude that the cognitive achievements of the two subjects match? How can a difference in respect of something conceived as cognitively inaccessible to both subjects, so far as the relevant mode of cognition goes, make it the case that one of them knows how things are in that inaccessible region while the other does not – rather than leaving them both, strictly speaking, ignorant on the matter?

Proponents of the "criterial" view will have been impatient with my broaching a query about the notion's epistemological status outside any semantical context. Things would look different, they will suggest, if we took note of the notion's primary role: namely, as an element in a novel, "anti-realist" conception of meaning, adumbrated in Wittgenstein's later work to replace the "realist", truth-conditional conception of Frege and the *Tractatus*.[10] In particular, it may be suggested that the question with which I have just been trying to embarrass the "criterial" view – "What would constitute possession of 'criterially' based knowledge?" – seems to need asking only in the superseded "realist" way of thinking. In the new framework, questions of the form "What would constitute its being the case that P?" lapse, to be replaced by questions of the form "What are the 'criteria' for the acceptability of the assertion that P?"

I believe that this account of the relation between the truth-conditional conception of meaning and that implicit in Wittgenstein's later work is quite misguided. Of course that is not a belief I can try to justify in this lecture.[11] But it is worth remarking that the "criterial" view seemed already to be problematic, epistemologically speaking, before I raised the contentious question what would constitute "criterially" based knowledge. If the supposed semantical context is to reveal that "criterial" epistemology is satisfactory, two conditions must be satisfied: first, it must be shown that the epistemological qualms I have aired – supposing we bracket the contentious question – arise exclusively out of adherence to the supposedly discarded "realist" framework; and, second, it must be made clear how the supposedly substituted "anti-realist" framework puts the qualms to rest. It is not obvious that either of these conditions can be met. For the first: my account of the epistemological qualms certainly made implicit play with a notion of truth-conditions, in my talk of "circumstance" and "fact". But the notion involved nothing more contentious than this: an ascription of an "inner" state to someone is true just in case that person is in that "inner" state. That is hardly a distinctively "realist" thought, or one that the later Wittgenstein could credibly be held to have rejected.[12] As for the second condition: we are told to model our conception of "anti-realist" semantics on the mathematical intuitionists' explanations of logical constants in terms of proof-conditions. But proof is precisely not defeasible, so there is nothing in the model to show us how to make ourselves comfortable with the defeasibility of "criteria".[13]

II

Understood in the way I have been considering, the notion of a criterion would be a technical notion; so commentators who attribute it to Wittgenstein ought to be embarrassed by his lack of self-consciousness on the matter. Mostly he uses "criterion" or "Kriterium" without ceremony, as if an ordinary mastery of English or German would suffice for taking his point. The striking exception (*Blue Book*,[14] pp. 24–5: the well-known passage about angina) should itself be an embarrassment, since it introduces the word, with some ceremony, in the phrase "defining criterion"; there seems to be no question of a defeasible kind of evidence here.[15] The idea that criteria are defeasible evidence has to be read into other texts, and the readings seem to me to be vitiated by reliance on non-compulsory epistemological presuppositions. I shall consider three characteristic lines of argument.[16]

The first is one that Gordon Baker formulates as follows:

> … *C*-support [criterial support] depends on circumstances. It might be thought that dependence on circumstances might be reduced or even altogether avoided by conditionalization; e.g. if *p* *C*-supports *q* under the proviso *r*, then one could claim that the conjunction of *p* and *r* *C*-supports *q* independently of the circumstance *r*, and successive steps of conditionalization would remove any dependence on circumstances, or at least any that can be explicitly stated. Wittgenstein, however, seems to dismiss this possibility with contempt. This rejection, unless groundless, must be based on the principle that *C*-support may *always* be undermined by supposing the evidence-statements embedded in a suitably enlarged context.[17]

The idea that criterial knowledge depends on circumstances is obviously faithful to Wittgenstein; but this argument rests on an interpretation of that idea that is not obviously correct. Baker's assumption is evidently this: if a condition[18] is ever a criterion for a claim, by virtue of belonging to some type of condition that can be ascertained to obtain independently of establishing the claim, then any condition of that type constitutes a criterion for that claim, or one suitably related to it. Given that such a condition obtains, further circumstances determine whether the support it affords the claim is solid; if the further circumstances are unfavourable, we still have, according to this view, a case of a criterion's being satisfied, but the support that it affords the claim is defeated. But when Wittgenstein speaks of dependence on circumstances, what he says seems to permit a different reading: not that some condition, specified in terms that are applicable independently of establishing a claim, is a criterion for the claim anyway, though whether it warrants the claim depends on further circumstances, but that whether such a condition is a criterion or not depends on the circumstances.

At *PI* §164,[19] for instance, Wittgenstein says that "in different circumstances, we apply different criteria for a person's reading". Here the point need not be that each of a range of types of condition is anyway a criterion for a person's reading, though an argument from any to that conclusion may always be undermined by embedding the condition in the wrong circumstances. The point may be, rather, that what is a criterion for a person's reading in one set of circumstances is not a criterion for a person's reading in another set of circumstances.

At *PI* §154 Wittgenstein writes:

> If there has to be anything "behind the utterance of the formula" it is *particular circumstances*, which justify me in saying I can go on – when the formula occurs to me.

I think we can take this to concern the idea that the formula's occurring to one is a criterion for the correctness of "Now I can go on", as opposed to a mere symptom, "behind" which we have to penetrate in order to find the essence of what it is to understand a series.[20] And there is no suggestion that the formula's occurring to one is a criterion anyway, independently of the circumstances. It is a criterion, rather, only in the "particular circumstances" that Wittgenstein alludes to: namely, as *PI* §179 explains, "such circumstances as that [the person in question] had learnt algebra, had used such formulae before".

In a schematic picture of a face, it may be the curve of the mouth that makes it right to say that the face is cheerful. In another picture the mouth may be represented by a perfect replica of the line that represents the mouth in the first picture, although the face is not cheerful. Do we need a relation of defeasible support in order to accommodate this possibility? Surely not. What is in question is the relation of "making it right to say"; it holds in the first case and not in the second. Since the relation does not hold in the second case, it cannot be understood in terms of entailment. But why suppose that the only alternative is defeasible support? That would require the assumption that the warranting status we are concerned with must be shared by all members of a type to which the warranting circumstance can

be ascertained to belong independently of the claim it warrants. (In this case, it would be the type of circumstance: being a picture of a face in which the mouth is represented by such-and-such a line.) That assumption looks in this case like groundless prejudice; perhaps the generalized version of it, which yields the conception of criteria that I am questioning, is similarly baseless. (I shall come shortly to the reason why commentators tend to think otherwise.)[21]

The second line of argument that I want to mention starts from the fact that criteria for a type of claim are typically multiple, and concludes that criteria may conflict. If that is so, the criterial support afforded by at least one of the conflicting criteria must be defeated.[22] This argument clearly rests on the same assumption about the generality of criterial status: that if some condition (specified in a non-question-begging way) is a criterion for a claim in some circumstances, then it is a criterion in any. Without that assumption, we are not forced to accept that the pairs of considerations that stand in some sort of confrontation, in the kind of case the commentators envisage, are both criterial. A condition that fails to warrant a claim in some circumstances – trumped, as it were, by a criterion for an incompatible claim – may not be a criterion for the claim in those circumstances, even though in other circumstances it would have been one. And its failure when it is not criterial is no ground for saying that criterial warrants are defeasible.

The third line of argument, which is the most revealing, consists in a reading of Wittgenstein's treatment of psychological concepts in the *Philosophical Investigations*. In Wittgenstein's view, clearly, there are criteria in behaviour for the ascription of "inner" states and goings-on (see *PI* §§269, 344, 580). Commentators often take it to be obvious that he must mean a defeasible kind of evidence; if it is not obvious straight off, the possibility of pretence is thought to make it so.[23] But really it is not obvious at all.

Consider a representative passage in which Wittgenstein uses the notion of a criterion for something "internal". *PI* §377 contains this:

> … What is the criterion for the redness of an image? For me, when it is someone else's image: what he says and does.

I think that amounts to this: when one knows that someone else has a red image, one can – sometimes at least – correctly answer the question "How do you know?", or "How can you tell?", by saying "By what he says and does". In order to accommodate the distinction between criteria and symptoms, we should add that inability or refusal to accept the adequacy of the answer would betray, not ignorance of a theory, but non-participation in a "convention"; but with that proviso, my paraphrase seems accurate and complete. It is an extra – something dictated, I believe, by an epistemological presupposition not expressed in the text – to suppose that "what he says and does" must advert to a condition that one might ascertain to be satisfied by someone independently of knowing that he has a red image: a condition that someone might satisfy even though he has no red image, so that it constitutes at best defeasible evidence that he has one.

Commentators often take it that the possibility of pretence shows the defeasibility of criteria.[24] That requires the assumption that in a successful deception one brings it about that criteria for something "internal" are satisfied, although the ascription for which they are criteria would be false. But is the assumption obligatory? Here is a possible alternative; in pretending, one causes it to appear that criteria for something "internal" are satisfied (that is, one causes it to appear that someone else could know, by what one says and does, that one is in, say, some "inner" state); but the criteria are not really satisfied (that is, the knowledge is not really available). The satisfaction of a criterion, we might say, constitutes a fully adequate answer to "How do you know?" – in a sense that prevents an answer to that question from counting as fully adequate if the very same answer can be really available to someone who lacks the knowledge in question. (Of course we cannot rule out its seeming to be available.)

In the traditional approach to the epistemology of other minds, the concept of pretence plays a role analogous to that played by the concept of illusion in the traditional approach to the epistemology of the "external" world. So it is not surprising to find that, just as the possibility of pretence is often thought to show the defeasibility of criteria for "inner" states of affairs, so the possibility of illusion is often thought to show the

defeasibility of criteria for "external" states of affairs. At *PI* §354 Wittgenstein writes:

> The fluctuation in grammar between criteria and symptoms makes it look as if there were nothing at all but symptoms. We say, for example: "Experience teaches that there is rain when the barometer falls, but it also teaches that there is rain when we have certain sensations of wet and cold, or such-and-such visual impressions." In defence of this one says that these sense-impressions can deceive us. But here one fails to reflect that the fact that the false appearance is precisely one of rain is founded on a definition.

Commentators often take this to imply that when our senses deceive us, criteria for rain are satisfied, although no rain is falling.[25] But what the passage says is surely just this: for things, say, to look a certain way to us is, as a matter of "definition" (or "convention", *PI* §355), for it to look to us as though it is raining; it would be a mistake to suppose that the "sense-impressions" yield the judgement that it is raining merely symptomatically – that arriving at the judgement is mediated by an empirical theory. That is quite compatible with this thought, which would be parallel to what I suggested about pretence: when our "sense-impressions" deceive us, the fact is not that criteria for rain are satisfied but that they appear to be satisfied.

An inclination to protest should have been mounting for some time. The temptation is to say: "There must be something in common between the cases you are proposing to describe as involving the *actual* satisfaction of criteria and the cases you are proposing to describe as involving the *apparent* satisfaction of criteria. That is why it is possible to mistake the latter for the former. And it must surely be this common something on which we base the judgements we make in both sorts of case. The distinction between your cases of actual satisfaction of criteria (so called) and your cases of only apparent satisfaction of criteria (so called) is not a distinction we can draw independently of the correctness or otherwise of the problematic claims themselves. So it is not a distinction by which we could guide ourselves in the practice of making or withholding such claims. What we need for that purpose is a basis for the claims that we can assure ourselves of possessing before we go on to evaluate the credentials of the claims themselves. That restricts us to what is definitely ascertainable anyway, whether the case in question is one of (in your terms) actual satisfaction of criteria or merely apparent satisfaction of criteria. In the case of judgements about the 'inner' states and goings-on of others, what conforms to the restriction is psychologically neutral information about their behaviour and bodily states.[26] So that must surely be what Wittgenstein meant by 'criteria'."

It is difficult not to sympathize with this protest, although I believe it is essential to see one's way to resisting the epistemological outlook that it expresses. I shall return to that in the last section of this lecture; the important point now is the way in which the protest exposes a background against which the reading of Wittgenstein that I am questioning seems inescapable. The protest is, in effect, an application of what has been called "the Argument from Illusion", and its upshot is to locate us in the predicament envisaged by a traditional scepticism about other minds, and by the traditional ways of trying to meet that scepticism. The predicament is as follows. Judgements about other minds are, as a class, epistemologically problematic. Judgements about "behaviour" and "bodily" characteristics are, as a class, not epistemologically problematic; or at any rate, if they are, it is because of a different epistemological problem, which can be taken for these purposes to have been separately dealt with. The challenge is to explain how our unproblematic intake of "behavioural" and "bodily" information can adequately warrant our problematic judgements about other minds.

The first two interpretative arguments that I mentioned depended on this assumption: if a state of affairs ever constitutes a criterion for some claim, by virtue of its conforming to a specification that can be ascertained to apply to it independently of establishing the claim, then any state of affairs that conforms to that specification must constitute a criterion for that claim, or one suitably related to it. What sustains that assumption is presumably the idea to which the protest gives expression: the idea that the question whether a criterion for a claim is satisfied or not must be capable of being settled with a certainty that is independent of whatever certainty can be credited to the claim itself.

With this epistemological framework in place, it is undeniable that the warrants for our judgements about other minds yield, at best, defeasible support for them. We could not establish anything more robust than that with a certainty immune to what supposedly makes psychological judgements about others, in general, epistemologically problematic. So if we take Wittgenstein to be operating within this framework, we are compelled into the interpretation of him that I am questioning. According to this view, the sceptic is right to insist that our best warrant for a psychological judgement about another person is defeasible evidence constituted by his "behaviour" and "bodily" circumstances. The sceptic complains that the adequacy of the warrant must depend on a correlation whose obtaining could only be a matter of contingent fact, although we are in no position to confirm it empirically; and Wittgenstein's distinctive contribution, on this reading, is to maintain that at least in some cases the relevant correlations are a matter of "convention", and hence stand in no need of empirical support.

To an unprejudiced view, I think it should seem quite implausible that there is anything but contingency in the correlations of whose contingency the sceptic complains.[27] And I argued in the first section of this lecture that it is quite unclear, anyway, how the appeal to "convention" could yield a response to scepticism, in the face of the avowed defeasibility of the supposedly "conventional" evidence. In fact I believe that this reading profoundly misrepresents Wittgenstein's response to scepticism about other minds. What Wittgenstein does is not to propose an alteration of detail within the sceptic's position, but to reject the assumption that generates the sceptic's problem.[28]

The sceptic's picture involves a corpus of "bodily" and "behavioural" information, unproblematically available to us in a pictured cognitive predicament in which we are holding in suspense all attributions of psychological properties to others. One way of approaching Wittgenstein's response is to remark that such a picture is attainable only by displacing the concept of a *human being* from its focal position in an account of our experience of our fellows, and replacing it with a philosophically generated concept of a *human body*.[29] Human bodies, conceived as merely material objects, form the subject-matter of the supposed unproblematically available information. The idea is that they may subsequently turn out to be, in some more or less mysterious way, points of occupancy for psychological properties as well; this would be represented as a regaining of the concept of a human being. In these terms, Wittgenstein's response to the sceptic is to restore the concept of a human being to its proper place, not as something laboriously reconstituted, out of the fragments to which the sceptic reduces it, by a subtle epistemological and metaphysical construction, but as a seamless whole of whose unity we ought not to have allowed ourselves to lose sight in the first place.[30]

Such a response might appropriately be described as urging a different view of the "conventions" or "grammar" of our thought and speech about others. But it is a misconception to suppose that the appeal to "convention" is meant to cement our concept of a human being together along the fault-line that the sceptic takes himself to detect. It is not a matter of postulating a non-contingent relation between some of what the sceptic takes to be given in our experience of others, on the one hand, and our psychological judgements about them, on the other. Rather, what Wittgenstein does is to reject the sceptic's conception of what is given.[31]

I have suggested that to say a criterion is satisfied would be simply to say that the associated knowledge is available in the relevant way: by adverting to what someone says or does, or to how things look, without having one's epistemic standing reinforced, beyond what that yields, by possession of an empirical theory. That implies an indefeasible connection between the actual, as opposed to apparent, satisfaction of a criterion and the associated knowledge. But it would be a confusion to take it that I am postulating a special, indefeasible kind of evidence, if evidence for a claim is understood – naturally enough – as something one's possession of which one can assure oneself of independently of the claim itself. It is precisely the insistence on something of this sort that dictates the idea that criteria are defeasible. Rather, I think we should understand criteria to be, in the first instance, ways of telling how things are, of the sort specified by "On the basis of what he says and does" or "By how things look"; and we should take it that knowledge that a

criterion for a claim is actually satisfied – if we allow ourselves to speak in those terms as well – would be an exercise of the very capacity that we speak of when we say that one can tell, on the basis of such-and-such criteria, whether things are as the claim would represent them as being. This flouts an idea that we are prone to find natural, that a basis for a judgement must be something on which we have a firmer cognitive purchase than we do on the judgement itself; but although the idea can seem natural, it is an illusion to suppose that it is compulsory.

III

The possibility of such a position is liable to be obscured from us by a certain tempting line of argument. On any question about the world independent of oneself to which one can ascertain the answer by, say, looking, the way things look can be deceptive: it can look to one exactly as if things were a certain way when they are not. (This can be so even if, for whatever reason, one is not inclined to believe that things are that way.[32] I shall speak of cases as deceptive when, if one were to believe that things are as they appear, one would be misled, without implying that one is actually misled.) It follows that any capacity to tell by looking how things are in the world independent of oneself can at best be fallible. According to the tempting argument, something else follows as well: the argument is that since there can be deceptive cases experientially indistinguishable from non-deceptive cases, one's experiential intake – what one embraces within the scope of one's consciousness – must be the same in both kinds of case. In a deceptive case, one's experiential intake must *ex hypothesi* fall short of the fact itself, in the sense of being consistent with there being no such fact. So that must be true, according to the argument, in a non-deceptive case too. One's capacity is a capacity to tell by looking: that is, on the basis of experiential intake. And even when this capacity does yield knowledge, we have to conceive the basis as a *highest common factor* of what is available to experience in the deceptive and the non-deceptive cases alike, and hence as something that is at best a defeasible ground for the knowledge, though available with a certainty independent of whatever might put the knowledge in doubt.

This is the line of thought that I described as an application of the Argument from Illusion. I want now to describe and comment on a way of resisting it.

We might formulate the temptation that is to be resisted as follows. Let the fallible capacity in question be a capacity to tell by experience whether such-and-such is the case. In a deceptive case, what is embraced within the scope of experience is an appearance that such-and-such is the case, falling short of the fact: a *mere* appearance. So what is experienced in a non-deceptive case is a mere appearance too. The upshot is that even in the non-deceptive cases we have to picture something that falls short of the fact ascertained, at best defeasibly connected with it, as interposing itself between the experiencing subject and the fact itself.[33]

But suppose we say – not at all unnaturally – that an appearance that such-and-such is the case can be *either* a mere appearance *or* the fact that such-and-such is the case making itself perceptually manifest to someone.[34] As before, the object of experience in the deceptive cases is a mere appearance. But we are not to accept that in the non-deceptive cases too the object of experience is a mere appearance, and hence something that falls short of the fact itself. On the contrary, we are to insist that the appearance that is presented to one in those cases is a matter of the fact itself being disclosed to the experiencer. So appearances are no longer conceived as in general intervening between the experiencing subject and the world.[35]

This may sound like an affirmation of M-realism, but I intend something more general. The idea of a fact being disclosed to experience is in itself purely negative: a rejection of the thesis that what is accessible to experience falls short of the fact in the sense I explained, namely that of being consistent with there being no such fact. In the most straightforward application of the idea, the thought would indeed be – as in M-realism – that the fact itself is directly presented to view, so that it is true in a stronger sense that the object of experience does not fall short of the fact. But a less straightforward application of the idea is possible also, and seems appropriate in at least some cases of knowledge that someone else is in an "inner" state, on the basis of experience of what he says and does. Here we might think of what is

directly available to experience in some such terms as "his giving expression to his being in that 'inner' state": this is something that, while not itself actually being the "inner" state of affairs in question, nevertheless does not fall short of it in the sense I explained.[36]

In *PI* §344 – which I quoted earlier – Wittgenstein seems concerned to insist that the appearances to which he draws attention, in order to discourage the thought that there is "nothing at all but symptoms" for rain, are appearances that it is raining. If there is a general thesis about criteria applied here, it will be on these lines: one acquires criterial knowledge by confrontation with appearances whose content is, or includes, the content of the knowledge acquired. (This would fit both the sorts of case I have just distinguished: obviously so in the straightforward sort, and in the less straightforward sort we can say that an appearance that someone is giving expression to an "inner" state is an appearance that he is in that "inner" state.)

This thesis about match in content might promise a neat justification for denying that criterial knowledge is inferential. The content of inferential knowledge, one might suggest, is generated by a transformation of the content of some data, whereas here the content of the knowledge is simply presented in the data.[37] But this does not establish the coherence of a position in which criteria are conceived as objects of experience on the "highest common factor" model, but the accusation that criteria function as *proxies* can be rejected. If the object of experience is in general a mere appearance, as the "highest common factor" model makes it, then it is not clear how, by appealing to the idea that it has the content of the knowledge that one acquires by confrontation with it, we could save ourselves from having to picture it as getting in the way between the subject and the world. Indeed, it is arguable that the "highest common factor" model undermines the very idea of an appearance having as its content that things are thus and so in the world "beyond" appearances (as we would have to put it).

This has a bearing on my query, in the first section of this lecture, as to whether the blankly external obtaining of a fact can make sense of the idea that someone experiencing a "criterion" might know that things were thus and so. Suppose someone is presented with an appearance that it is raining. It seems unproblematic that if his experience is in a suitable way the upshot of the fact that it is raining, then the fact itself can make it the case that he knows that it is raining. But that seems unproblematic precisely because the content of the appearance is the content of the knowledge. And it is arguable that we find that match in content intelligible only because we do not conceive the objects of such experiences as in general falling short of the meteorological facts. That is: such experiences can present us with the appearance that it is raining only because when we have them as the upshot (in a suitable way) of the fact that it is raining, the fact itself is their object; so that its obtaining is not, after all, blankly external.[38] If that is right, the "highest common factor" conception of experience is not entitled to the idea that makes the case unproblematic. It would be wrong to suppose that the "highest common factor" conception can capture, in its own terms, the intuition that I express when I say that the fact itself can be manifest to experience: doing so by saying that that is how it is when, for instance, experiences as of its raining are in a suitable way the upshot of the fact that it is raining. That captures the intuition all right; but – with "experiences as of its raining" – not in terms available to someone who starts by insisting that the object of experience is the highest common factor, and so falls short of the fact itself.

The "highest common factor" conception has attractions for us that cannot be undone just by describing an alternative, even with the recommendation that the alternative can cause a sea of philosophy to subside. The most obvious attraction is the phenomenological argument: the occurrence of deceptive cases experientially indistinguishable from non-deceptive cases. But this is easily accommodated by the essentially disjunctive conception of appearances that constitutes the alternative. The alternative conception can allow what is given to experience in the two sorts of case to be the same *in so far as* it is an appearance that things are thus and so; that leaves it open that whereas in one kind of case what is given to experience is a mere appearance, in the other it is the fact itself made manifest. So the phenomenological argument is inconclusive.

A more deep-seated temptation towards the "highest common factor" conception might find expression like this: "*Ex hypothesi* a mere appearance

can be indistinguishable from what you describe as a fact made manifest. So in a given case one cannot tell for certain whether what confronts one is one or the other of those. How, then, can there be a difference in what is given to experience, in any sense that could matter to epistemology?" One could hardly countenance the idea of having a fact made manifest within the reach of one's experience, without supposing that that would make knowledge of the fact available to one.[39] This protest might reflect the conviction that such epistemic entitlement ought to be something one could display for oneself, as it were from within; the idea being that that would require a non-question-begging demonstration from a neutrally available starting-point, such as would be constituted by the highest common factor.[40]

There is something gripping about the "internalism" that is expressed here. The root idea is that one's epistemic standing on some question cannot intelligibly be constituted, even in part, by matters blankly external to how it is with one subjectively. For how could such matters be other than beyond one's ken? And how could matters beyond one's ken make any difference to one's epistemic standing?[41] (This is obviously a form of the thought that is at work in the argument from my first section which I have recently reconsidered.) But the disjunctive conception of appearances shows a way to detach this "internalist" intuition from the requirement of non-question-begging demonstration. When someone has a fact made manifest to him, the obtaining of the fact contributes to his epistemic standing on the question. But the obtaining of the fact is precisely not blankly external to his subjectivity, as it would be if the truth about that were exhausted by the highest common factor.[42]

However, if that reflection disarms one epistemological foundation for the "highest common factor" conception, there are other forces that tend to hold it in place.[43]

Suppose we assume that one can come to know that someone else is in some "inner" state by adverting to what he says and does. Empirical investigation of the cues that impinge on one's sense-organs on such an occasion would yield a specification of the information received by them; the same information could be available in a deceptive case as well. That limited informational intake must be processed, in the nervous system, into the information about the person's "inner" state that comes to be at one's disposal; and a description of the information-processing would look like a description of an inference from a highest common factor. Now there is a familiar temptation, here and at the analogous point in reflection about perceptual knowledge of the environment in general, to suppose that one's epistemic standing with respect to the upshot of the process is constituted by the availability to one's senses of the highest common factor, together with the cogency of the supposed inference.

When one succumbs to this temptation, one's first thought is typically to ground the cogency of the inference on a theory. But the conception of theory as extending one's cognitive reach beyond the confines of experience requires that the theory in question be attainable on the basis of the experience in question. It is not enough that the experience would confirm the theory: the theory must involve no concept the formation of which could not intelligibly be attributed to a creature whose experiential intake was limited in the way envisaged. And when we try to conceive knowledge of the "inner" states of others on the basis of what they do and say, or perceptual knowledge of the environment in general, on this model, that condition seems not to be met.[44]

Keeping the highest common factor in the picture, we might try to register that thought by grounding the cogency of the inferences on "grammar" rather than theory; this would yield something like the conception of criteria that I have questioned. But that this would be a distortion is suggested by the fact that we have been given no idea of how to arrive at specifications of the content of the supposed "grammatically" certified warrants, other than by straightforward empirical investigation of what impinges on someone's senses on occasions when we are independently prepared to believe that he has the knowledge in question. The truth is that, for all their similarity to inferences, those processings of information are not transitions within what Wilfrid Sellars has called "the logical space of reasons",[45] as they would need to be in order to be capable of being constitutive of one's title to knowledge. Acquiring mastery of the relevant tracts of language is not, as acquiring a theory can

be, learning to extend one's cognitive reach beyond some previous limits by traversing pathways in a newly mastered region of the "space of reasons". It is better conceived as part of being initiated into the "space of reasons" itself.[46]

I want to end by mentioning a source for the attraction of the "highest common factor" conception that lies, I think, as deep as any. If we adopt the disjunctive conception of appearances, we have to take seriously the idea of an unmediated openness of the experiencing subject to "external" reality, whereas the "highest common factor" conception allows us to picture an interface between them. Taking the epistemology of other minds on its own, we can locate the highest common factor at the facing surfaces of other human bodies. But when we come to consider perceptual knowledge about bodies in general, the "highest common factor" conception drives what is given to experience inward, until it can be aligned with goings-on at our own sensory surfaces. This promises to permit us a satisfying conception of an interface at which the "inner" and the "outer" make contact. The idea that there is an interface can seem compulsory; and the disjunctive conception of appearances flouts that intuition – twice over, in its view of knowledge of others' "inner" states.[47]

No doubt there are many influences that conspire to give this picture of the "inner" and the "outer" its hold on us. The one I want to mention is our proneness to try to extend an objectifying mode of conceiving reality to human beings. In an objectifying view of reality, behaviour considered in itself cannot be expressive or significant: not human behaviour any more than, say, the behaviour of the planets.[48] If human behaviour is expressive, that fact resides not in the nature of the behaviour, as it were on the surface, but in its being the outwardly observable effect of mental states and goings-on. So the mind retreats behind the surface, and the idea that the mental is "internal" acquires a quasi-literal construction, as in Descartes, or even a literal one, as in the idea that mental states are "in the head"[49]

Modern adherents of this picture do not usually take themselves to be enmeshed in the problems of traditional epistemology. But the objectification of human behaviour leads inexorably to the traditional problem of other minds. And it is hard to see how the pictured interface can fail to be epistemologically problematic in the outward direction too: the inward retreat of the mind undermines the idea of a direct openness to the world, and thereby poses the traditional problems of knowledge about "external" reality in general. Without the "highest common factor" conception of experience, the interface can be left out of the picture, and the traditional problems lapse. Traditional epistemology is widely felt to be unsatisfying; I think this is a symptom of the error in the "highest common factor" conception, and, more generally, of the misguidedness of an objectifying conception of the human.

Notes

1   I shall put "criterion" or "criteria" in quotation marks to signal the supposed Wittgensteinian use that I am about to describe.

2   A view of Wittgenstein on these lines is unquestioned in W. Gregory Lycan's survey article, "Non-inductive evidence: recent work on Wittgenstein's 'criteria'", *American Philosophical Quarterly* viii (1971), pp. 109–25. Its outlines seem to date from Sydney Shoemaker's *Self-Knowledge and Self-Identity* (Cornell University Press: Ithaca, 1963); see P. M. S. Hacker, *Insight and Illusion* (Clarendon Press: Oxford, 1972), p. 293. My aim is to capture the common spirit of several readings that diverge in detail; so I shall try to preserve neutrality on nice questions about, for instance, what exactly the terms of the criterial relation are: see Hacker, *Insight and Illusion*, pp. 285–8, and Gordon Baker, "Criteria: a new foundation for semantics", *Ratio* xvi (1974), pp. 156–89, at p. 160; and, for a contrasting view, Crispin Wright, "Anti-realist semantics: the role of *criteria*", in Godfrey Vesey (ed.), *Idealism: Past and Present* (Cambridge University Press: Cambridge, 1982), pp. 225–48, at pp. 233–8.

3   See Baker, "Criteria".

4   I introduce this position here not in order to defend it (see §III below, especially n. 36), but purely with the aim of exploiting the contrast in order to clarify the "criterial" view.

5   "On 'The reality of the past'", in Christopher Hookway and Philip Pettit (eds), *Action and Interpretation* (Cambridge University Press: Cambridge, 1978), pp. 127–44, at p. 135.

6   Ibid., p. 136.

7   "Realism, truth-value links, other minds and the past", *Ratio* xxii (1980), pp. 112–32, at p. 123. (Clearly the last sentence should really read "… involve the availability to perception not just of the satisfaction of criteria … but of the realisation of truth-conditions …".)

8   This partly undermines n. 29 (pp. 242–3) of my "Anti-realism and the epistemology of understanding", in Herman Parret and Jacques Bouveresse (eds), *Meaning and Understanding* (De Gruyter: Berlin and New York, 1981), pp. 225–48. But, as will emerge, I stand by the spirit of what I wrote then.

9   Such responses to scepticism are quite unsatisfying. Without showing that the "conventions" are well founded, we have no ground for denying that the concession to the sceptic is an admission that we have reason to change the way we talk; and it is hard to see how we could show that the "conventions" are well founded without finding a way to withdraw the concession.

10 See Hacker, *Insight and Illusion*, ch. X; Baker, "criteria"; Wright, "Anti-realist semantics: the role of *criteria*". The general outlines of this conception of Wittgenstein's development, and of the issue between "realism" and "anti-realism" in the philosophy of language, are due to Michael Dummett: see *Truth and Other Enigmas* (Duckworth: London, 1978), especially essay 11.

11 I think what I shall say will contribute indirectly to its justification, by casting doubt on a conception of our knowledge of others that is implicit in the standard arguments for "anti-realism", and on the attribution of that conception to Wittgenstein. There is more in this vein in my "Anti-realism and the epistemology of understanding", and in my "Wittgenstein on following a rule", *Synthese* 58 (1986), pp. 325–63.

12 See, e.g., Dummett, *Truth and Other Enigmas*, pp. xxxiv–v. Baker, "Criteria", pp. 177–8, finds, behind the thought that "criteria" are

epistemologically insufficient, a baroque
argumentative structure involving the notion
(supposedly characteristic of "Classical
Semantics") of maximally consistent sets of
possible states of affairs; but I cannot find
that notion implicit in what I have said. (I
believe the idea that truth-conditions are a
matter of "language-independent possible
states-of-affairs" – Baker, p. 178, cf. p. 171 – is
a fundamental misconception of the intuition about meaning that Wittgenstein
adopted from Frege in the *Tractatus*; and
that this is in large part responsible for a distortion in the Dummettian conception of the
issue between "realism" and "anti-realism",
and of the relation between Wittgenstein's
earlier and later philosophies. There is more
in this vein in my "In defence of modesty", in
preparation for a collection of essays on
Dummett's work edited by Barry Taylor.)

13 In "Strict finitism", *Synthese* li (1982),
pp. 203–82, Wright formulates a position in
which defeasibility extends even to proof-
based knowledge; see also "Anti-realist
semantics: the role of *criteria*", p. 244. I do
not believe that this yields an adequate epistemology of proof, on the model of which
we might construct an acceptable account of
defeasible "criterial" knowledge; rather, it
saddles the epistemology of proof with problems parallel to those I have been urging
against"criterial"epistemology.(Wittgenstein,
On Certainty (Blackwell: Oxford, 1969),
§651 – cited by Wright at p. 244 of "Anti-
realist semantics: the role of *criteria*" – makes
a point about *fallibility*. Reliance on a *defeasible basis* is quite another matter: see §III
below.)

14 *The Blue and Brown Books* (Blackwell:
Oxford, 1958).

15 Baker, "Criteria", pp. 184–5, seems to deny
this, but I cannot see how he would explain
the presence of the word "defining". Most
commentators in the tradition I am concerned with deplore the passage as uncharacteristic; see, e.g., Hacker, *Insight and
Illusion*, p. 288; Wright, "Anti-realist semantics: the role of *criteria*", p. 227. There is a
satisfying explanation of its point at pp. 133–6
of John W. Cook, "Human beings", in Peter
Winch (ed.), *Studies in the Philosophy of*

Wittgenstein (Routledge and Kegan Paul:
London, 1969), pp. 117–51.

16 There may be others; but I think the ones I
shall consider illustrate the characteristic
assumptions of the reading of Wittgenstein
that I want to question. (Baker, "Criteria", pp.
159–60, 162, mentions also the ancestry of
the criterial relation in Wittgenstein's thought.
But he would presumably not suggest that its
descent, from a relation of *a priori* probabili-
fication, carries much independent weight.)

17 Ibid., pp. 161–2.

18 Or whatever is the right kind of item to be a
criterion: see n. 2 above.

19 I shall refer in this way to sections of
Philosophical Investigations (Blackwell: Oxford,
1953).

20 The word "criterion" is not used, but the
subject is the tendency to think that in
reviewing the phenomena we find nothing
but symptoms, which we have to peel away
(like leaves from an artichoke: *PI* §164) in
order to find the thing itself. On the connection with *PI* §354 ("the fluctuation in grammar between criteria and symptoms"), see
Cook, "Human beings", pp. 135–6.

21 This paragraph was suggested by pp. 138–40
of Norman Malcolm's "Wittgenstein on the
nature of mind", in his *Thought and Knowledge*
(Cornell University Press: Ithaca and London,
1977), pp. 133–58.

22 See Anthony Kenny, "Criterion", in Paul
Edwards (ed.), *The Encyclopaedia of Philosophy*,
vol. ii (Macmillan and Free Press: New York,
1967), pp. 258–61 (at p. 260); and Baker,
"Criteria", p. 162.

23 For versions of this line of interpretation, see
Kenny, "Criterion", p. 260; Hacker, *Insight
and Illusion*, pp. 289–90; John T. E. Richardson,
The Grammar of Justification (Sussex University
Press, 1976), pp. 114, 116–17. Baker, "Criteria",
p. 162, goes so far as to claim: "This principle, that *C*-support is defeasible, is explicitly
advanced in the particular case of psychological concepts."

24 The supposed obviousness of this connection allows commentators to cite as evidence
for the defeasibility of criteria passages which
show at most that Wittgenstein is not unaware
that pretence occurs. Note, e.g., Hacker's
citation (*Insight and Illusion*, p. 289) of

PI§§249–50 as showing that criteria for pain may be satisfied in the absence of pain. In fact the point of those passages is not the vulnerability to pretence, in general, of our judgements that others are in pain, but the *invulnerability* to pretence, in particular, of judgements "connected with the primitive, the natural, expressions of the sensation" and made about someone who has not yet learned "the names of sensations" (*PI* §244).

25   So Hacker, *Insight and Illusion*, pp. 289–90; Kenny, "Criterion", p. 260; Wright, "Antirealist semantics: the role of *criteria*", p. 227; James Bogen, "Wittgenstein and skepticism", *Philosophical Review* lxxxiii (1974), pp. 364–73, at p. 370.

26   Psychologically neutral information: once the appeal to pretence has done its work – that of introducing the idea of cases that are experientially indistinguishable from cases in which one can tell by what someone says and does that he is in some specified "inner" state, though he is not – it is quietly dropped. We are not meant to arrive at the idea of behavioural and bodily evidence that would *indefeasibly* warrant the judgement that someone is, so to speak, at least feigning the "inner" state. It is a nice question, on which I shall not pause, how the epistemological motivation for passing over this position should best be characterized. In the case of the "criterial" view, there is a semantical motivation as well; it is plausible that such evidence could not be specified except in terms of the concept of the "inner" state itself, and this conflicts with the idea that criteria should figure in the explanation of the associated concepts: see Wright, "Antirealist semantics: the role of *criteria*", p. 231.

27   See the splendid recanting "Postscript" to Rogers Albritton, "On Wittgenstein's use of the term 'criterion'", in George Pitcher (ed.), *Wittgenstein: The Philosophical Investigations* (Macmillan: London, 1968), pp. 231–50. (Such regularities are not "conventions" but the "very general facts of nature" on which "conventions" rest: *PI* II xi; cf. §142.)

28   Without going into even as much detail as I shall about the case of other minds in particular, there is already ground for suspicion of this reading of Wittgenstein in the way it attracts the label "foundationalist": something that is surely quite uncharacteristic of Wittgenstein's approach to epistemological questions.

29   This is the key thought of Cook's admirable "Human beings", to which I am heavily indebted in this section. (One tempting route to the substituted notion is the idea that we can cleanly abstract, from the prephilosophical conception of a human being, the mental aspect, conceived as something each of us can focus his thoughts on for himself in introspection, independently of locating it in the context of our embodied life. This putatively self-standing conception of the mental is the target of the complex Wittgensteinian polemic known as the Private Language Argument. If this were the only route to the sceptic's conception of what is given in our experience of others, the wrongness of attributing that conception to Wittgenstein would be very straightforwardly obvious: see Cook, "Human beings". But I think the situation is more complex; see §III below.)

30   I intend this to echo P. F. Strawson's thesis (*Individuals* (Methuen: London, 1959), ch. 3) that the concept of a person is primitive. Strawson's use of the notion of "logically adequate criteria" for ascriptions of psychological properties to others has often been subjected to what I believe to be a misunderstanding analogous to the misreading (as I believe) of Wittgenstein that I am considering.

31   Note that seeing behaviour as a possibly feigned expression of an "inner" state, or as a human act or response that one does not understand, is not seeing it in the way that the sceptic requires. See *PI* §420: and cf. n. 26 above.

32   On the "belief-independence" of the content of perception, see Gareth Evans, *The Varieties of Reference* (Clarendon Press: Oxford, 1982), p. 123.

33   The argument effects a transition from sheer fallibility (which might be registered in a "Pyrrhonian" scepticism) to a "veil of ideas" scepticism: for the distinction, see Richard Rorty, *Philosophy and the Mirror of Nature* (Blackwell: Oxford, 1980), p. 94 n. 8 and pp. 139 ff.

34   In classical Greek, "… φαίνεται σοφὸς ὤν [word for word: he appears wise being] generally means *he is manifestly wise*, and φαίνεται σοφὸς εἶναι [word for word: he appears wise to be], *he seems to be wise …*": William W. Goodwin, *A Greek Grammar* (Macmillan: London, 1894), p. 342.

35   See the discussion of a "disjunctive" account of "looks" statements in Paul Snowdon, "Perception, vision and causation", *Proceedings of the Aristotelian Society* lxxxi (1980/1), pp. 175–92; and, more generally, J. M. Hinton's *Experiences* (Clarendon Press: Oxford, 1973) – a work which I regret that I did not know until this lecture was virtually completed, although I expect that this section grew out of an unconscious recollection of Hinton's articles "Experiences", *Philosophical Quarterly* xvii (1967), pp. 1–13, and "Visual experiences", *Mind* lxxvi (1967), pp. 217–27.

36   M-realism might be accused of proposing a general assimilation of the second sort of case to the first. The plausibility of the assimilation in a particular case depends on the extent to which it is plausible to think of the particular mode of expression as, so to speak, transparent. (This is quite plausible for facial expressions of emotional states: see Wittgenstein, *Zettel* (Blackwell: Oxford, 1967), §§220–5. But it is not very plausible for "avowals", except perhaps in the special case of the verbal expression of thoughts.) The motivation for M-realism was the wish to deny that our experiential intake, when we know one another's "inner" states by experience, must fall short of the fact ascertained in the sense I have introduced; it was a mistake to suppose that this required an appeal, across the board, to a model of direct observation.

37   But this idea is not available to Wright, in view of his insistence that grasp of criteria should not presuppose possession of the associated concepts: see "Anti-realist semantics: the role of *criteria*", p. 231.

38   This fits the first of the two sorts of case distinguished above; something similar, though more complex, could be said about a case of the second sort.

39   This is to be distinguished from actually conferring the knowledge on one. Suppose someone has been misled into thinking his senses are out of order; we might then hesitate to say that he possesses the knowledge that his senses (in fact functioning perfectly) make available to him. But for some purposes the notion of being in a position to know something is more interesting than the notion of actually knowing it. (It is a different matter if one's senses are actually out of order, though their operations are sometimes unaffected: in such a case, an experience subjectively indistinguishable from that of being confronted with a tomato, even if it results from confrontation with a tomato, need not count as experiencing the presence of a tomato. Another case in which it may not count as that is a case in which there are a lot of tomato façades about, indistinguishable from tomatoes when viewed from the front: cf. Alvin Goldman, "Discrimination and perceptual knowledge", *Journal of Philosophy* lxxiii (1976), pp. 771–91. One counts as experiencing the fact making itself manifest only in the exercise of a (fallible) capacity to *tell* how things are.)

40   The hankering for independently ascertainable foundations is familiar in epistemology. Its implications converge with those of a Dummett-inspired thesis in the philosophy of language: namely that the states of affairs at which linguistic competence primarily engages with extra-linguistic reality, so to speak, must be effectively decidable (or fall under some suitable generalization of that concept). See Baker, "Defeasibility and meaning", in P. M. S. Hacker and J. Raz (eds), *Law, Morality, and Society* (Clarendon Press: Oxford, 1977), pp. 26–57, at pp. 50–1. For criteria as decidable, see, e.g., Wright, "Anti-realist semantics: the role of *criteria*", p. 230.

41   See, e.g., Laurence BonJour, "Externalist theories of empirical knowledge", *Midwest Studies in Philosophy* v (1980), pp. 53–74.

42   The disjunctive conception of appearances makes room for a conception of experiential knowledge that conforms to Robert Nozick's account of "internalism", at p. 281 of *Philosophical Explanations* (Clarendon Press: Oxford, 1981); without requiring, as he implies that any "internalist" position must (pp. 281–2), a reduction of "external" facts to mental facts.

43 Nozick must be a case in point. His drawing of the boundary between "internal" and "external" (see n. 2 above) must reflect something like the "highest common factor" conception; and in his case that conception cannot be sustained by the "internalist" intuition that I have just tried to disarm.

44 To the point here is Wittgenstein's polemic against the idea that "from one's own case" one can so much as form the idea of someone else having, say, feelings. On the case of perception in general, see, e.g., P. F. Strawson, "Perception and its objects", in G. F. Macdonald (ed.), *Perception and Identity* (Macmillan: London and Basingstoke, 1979), pp. 41–60.

45 "Empiricism and the philosophy of mind", in Herbert Feigl and Michael Scriven (eds), *The Foundations of Science and the Concepts of Psychology and Psychoanalysis* (Minnesota Studies in the Philosophy of Science I, University of Minnesota Press: Minneapolis, 1956), pp. 253–329, at p. 299.

46 Two supplementations to these extremely sketchy remarks. First: when we allow theory to extend someone's cognitive reach, we do not need to find him infallible in the region of logical space that the theory opens up to him; so we do not need to commit ourselves to the idea that the theory, together with the content of experience, must *entail* the content of the putative knowledge. Second: the rejection of the inferential model that I am urging does not turn on mere phenomenology (the absence of conscious inferences). Theory can partly ground a claim to knowledge even in cases in which it is not consciously brought to bear; as with a scientist who (as we naturally say) learns to see the movements of imperceptible particles in some apparatus.

47 Am I suggesting that the disjunctive conception of appearances precludes the idea that experience mediates between subject and world? It depends on what you mean by "mediate". If experience is conceived in terms of openness to the world, it will not be appropriate to picture it as an interface. (I am sceptical whether such a conception of experience is available within the dominant contemporary philosophy of mind.)

48 See Charles Taylor, *Hegel* (Cambridge University Press: Cambridge, 1975), pp. 3–11.

49 This movement of thought can find support in the idea that the mental is conceptually captured by introspective ostensive definition. (That idea is perhaps naturally understood as a response to the obliteration of the notion of intrinsically expressive behaviour). But some versions of the position are not notably introspectionist. (See n. 29 above.)

CHAPTER 60

Knowing How to Believe With Justification

Steven L. Reynolds

I will defend the unfashionable view that justified perceptual beliefs are justified in part by a relation to the appropriate sorts of perceptual experiences, where experiences are conceived as non-propositional and indeed non-intentional in character. Experiences are like itches and tickles, and unlike beliefs, in not "saying" anything or even being *about* anything. They are complex ordered masses of sensations produced in perception. There are reasons to doubt that we have such experiences, but I will not address them here. Instead I will show that, if we have such non-intentional experiences, they can help justify our perceptual beliefs.

It has been recently maintained (by, for example, Donald Davidson and Laurence BonJour) that no relation of a belief to a non-propositional experience could be epistemically justifying.[1] Those who hold this view usually concede to the experience a role in producing the belief (if they allow the existence of experiences at all), but they deny that a mental state or process which consists of sensations, and which is, consequently, not about any of the things the belief is about, could play any role in justifying that belief. In this paper I will argue against this claim, by describing a relation

of belief to experience which plausibly could be justifying.

The only recent attempt to respond directly to the Davidson–BonJour objection presents the transition from experience to belief as a kind of argument, in which the experience plays something like the role of a premise. I will argue that this response won't work. I argue instead for a view which can be expressed in the following thesis:

> A perceptual belief is justified if and only if there are no undermining beliefs, and it was arrived at in response to an experience through an adequate exercise of properly learned recognitional skills.

I shall leave the notion of undermining beliefs vague, though I recognize that a full defense of the thesis would require clarification of it. I will attempt to give non-circular explications of the normative terms "adequate exercise" and "properly learned", though we will not be prepared for that until toward the end of the paper. In addition to citing evidence for the thesis of a more or less ordinary language sort, I will also try to answer several natural objections to regarding ordinary perceptual processes as exercises of skills.

Although the view I develop in defending this thesis has points of contact with recent work by John Pollock, it is, I believe, a substantially new account of perceptual justification.

Originally published in *Philosophical Studies* 64, 3 (Dec. 1991), pp. 273–92.

I

First some remarks about epistemic justification: Justification evidently has some close relation to knowledge. Thus many recent theories make justified true belief necessary for knowledge. It is also apparently uncontroversial that some beliefs are justified, at least in part, by inferential relations to other beliefs.

Two further assumptions about justification help generate the problems about the experiential justification of beliefs. These assumptions are somewhat more controversial, but they are plausible and widely accepted, and I won't challenge them. I will try to show that they are compatible with experiential justification.

The first is that justification is a normative notion. Justified beliefs are epistemically acceptable, and may thus be retained, while unjustified beliefs should be changed. Or at least the existence of an unjustified belief indicates some sort of epistemic fault on the part of the believer – at some point he should have done, or believed, otherwise than he did.

The second is that justification has a pronounced "internalist" character. One must be able to tell whether one's beliefs are justified, or at least be able (in some sense) to recognize, and so to attempt to avoid, the things that lead to having or to retaining unjustified beliefs. That justification has this internalist character may be argued for from a deontological conception of epistemic acceptability, on the ground that the right sort of ignorance obviates obligation. Or it might be stipulated, more or less, by picking out justified belief as the subjectively accessible aspect of knowledge (understanding that a mental state may wear the aspect of knowledge without actually being knowledge). In any case, whether or not one's belief is justified is commonly thought to depend only on subjectively accessible matters, such as one's own beliefs and experiences.

So much for the assumptions about justification. Now for a few taxonomic stipulations. Coherentists hold that all justified beliefs are in effect justified by inferential relations to other beliefs. (This requires a broad conception of inferential support to be plausible.) Foundationalists hold on the contrary that some beliefs would be justified even if they had no such inferential supporting connections to other

beliefs. The view that I will defend is foundationalist in this sense. It holds that some beliefs are or could be justified, not by the existence of any supporting beliefs, but by a certain sort of relation to non-propositional experiences, together with the absence of undermining beliefs. Foundationalism proper also requires that all inferential support ultimately depends upon such basic beliefs, but I will not be discussing this further thesis. So much for taxonomy.

A foundationalist view doesn't have to say that beliefs are justified by relations to experiences. There are views that are foundational in the sense just described but which do not assign any justifying role to experiences. One such view is that all beliefs that have a certain kind of content are justified (e.g., those that are about one's own subjective perceptual states). Another is that all beliefs for which one has no countervailing reasons are justified. Still another view holds that there is something about the process of acquiring the belief apart from its relationship to experience that confers justification on it. One popular version of this last view says, roughly, that a belief is justified if and only if it was acquired by a process that reliably produces true beliefs.

But it is natural to think that a relationship to perceptual experience justifies at least some of our basic beliefs. On any plausible foundationalist view, many of the basic beliefs will be perceptual beliefs. That is, they will be beliefs caused by ordinary perceptual processes, such as seeing, hearing, smelling, tasting, and touching. In those processes, complex arrays of sensations are produced (we are assuming). It seems that these complex arrays of sensations, which I am calling "experiences", should have some role to play in justifying the resulting beliefs. If similar processes produced the same beliefs, but without producing any visual, auditory, etc., sensations, as perhaps happens in the phenomenon of "blind-sight", we would not want to regard the resulting beliefs as justified. (And indeed patients who exhibit blind-sight abilities apparently do typically regard themselves as "just guessing".[2])

Some argue on the contrary that the sensational component of perception is just window dressing, and that the (reliable) causation of appropriate sorts of beliefs is the only epistemically relevant aspect of the perceptual process.[3] But there is a strong temptation to think of the sensational aspect of perception as epistemically relevant. Before we arm ourselves with philosophical arguments to resist this temptation, perhaps we should consider whether we can respectably embrace it.

What sort of justifying relation could a non-doxastic experience have to a belief? A first step toward answering this question would be to claim that justification requires an appropriate causal connection between the experience and the belief. For example, if, while at a party, I look absentmindedly across the room, and just guess that Sam is present, not noticing that he is in fact in view, then my belief is not justified. It doesn't have the appropriate causal connection to my visual experience.

But the requirement of an appropriate causal connection is not specific enough to soothe doubts about the possibility of experiences justifying beliefs. Why should we think that that a causal connection can be justifying? Causal connections are naturalistically described, and justification is normative. We need to describe the experience-belief relation in enough detail to see how it captures the normative aspect of justification.

II

Alan Millar has attempted to show how non-propositional experiences can help justify beliefs, by comparing the transition from experience to belief to the transition from beliefs to belief in inference. (John Pollock had earlier sketched a similar view of the relation of experience to justified belief, but not while trying to answer (at least explicitly) the worries that concern us.)[4] On Millar's view, an experience of a certain type, and a belief that there are no undermining beliefs, play the role of premises in an argument-like structure whose conclusion is the justified belief. Millar classifies experiences according to the situations and objects that in fact typically produce them. An experience that could have been produced by a normal person's looking at a square yellow piece of paper in appropriate conditions is a square-yellow-piece-of-paper type experience. (This description of types of experience should not mislead us into thinking that, for Millar, the experience is *about* square yellow pieces of paper.

The description just picks out a phenomenal type by its normal causal antecedents.) According to Millar, people who have such experiences, and have mastered the appropriate concepts, will tend to arrive at beliefs about square yellow pieces of paper in response to them. If such a person also believes that there are no facts that should undermine his belief, and this belief about the absence of undermining facts appropriately affects the transition from the experience to the perceptual belief, then the resulting perceptual belief is justified. The transition from experience and belief to belief is called a "quasi-inference". We learn to make appropriate quasi-inferences from experiences to beliefs, Millar says, as a necessary part of mastering the concepts.

Millar's claim that the recognitional abilities involved are required for the mastery of the concepts seems dubious, for, as everyone now says, it seems that I might have beliefs about, say, elms, without being able to recognize elms. Perhaps however Millar intends to claim a connection between recognition and concepts, not for elms and other natural kinds, but only for concepts such as those of colors. But then what is the justificational status of recognizing elms? Does the lack of a recognition-concept connection imply that the quasi-inferences one makes in recognizing elms won't justify beliefs about elms? Or is the recognition-concept connection not really necessary for experiential justification? (Although he doesn't say so, it may be that he wants that connection because concepts are naturally connected to truth, and he wants to connect justification and truth.)

John L. Pollock also claims that the epistemic norms relevant to the justification of a belief are determined by the concepts involved (where the norms could be expressed as rules for arriving at beliefs, apparently including perceptual recognitional beliefs). He motivates this claim in part by arguing that it rules out a kind of epistemic relativism that he dislikes.[5] According to this sort of epistemic relativism, it is possible for there to be two people who hold the same belief, on the same grounds (such as being in the same non-doxastic perceptual state), but one is justified and the other is not. Their justification in holding the belief differs because they differ in the epistemic norms to which they happen to be committed. This sort of relativism is ruled out by Pollock's thesis (and presumably also by Millar's), for if the relevant epistemic norms for a belief are determined by the concepts involved in that belief, everyone who holds a particular belief is thereby committed to the same epistemic norms for it. So this sort of relativism is false.

Pollock handles the difficulty about elms by holding that two people may both have the same belief about elms, in one sense of "same belief", without having the same concept of elms.[6] There are different ways of thinking of the attribute of being an elm, that is to say, different concepts of being an elm, and people who have different concepts in this sense may nevertheless have the same belief. The relativism he rules out then applies only to beliefs individuated very narrowly – it will still be possible for two people to have exactly similar experiences, and the same belief in response (in the coarser, but much more usual sense of "same belief"), and yet one is justified and the other is not. So there may be ways to successfully finesse the apparent counterexamples to theses connecting recognitional abilities and concept possession.

The other problem with Millar's (and Pollock's) account seems to run much deeper. Millar wants us to think of the transition from experience to belief as somehow like an inference. He calls it a "quasi-inference", and he even presents it in an argument-like format. It is fairly clear why he does. He wants us to accept the transition from an experience to a belief as justifying that belief. Appropriate inferential transitions are uncontroversially justifying, so, naturally, he wants to present the experience-belief transition as analogous, in its normative aspects, to such inferences. But how is the experience-belief transition like an inference?

Inferences are typically transitions from old beliefs to new. (The exceptions are cases where an already existing belief acquires new support, but they don't pose any special problems here.) One starts off, for example, with the beliefs that business executives tend to be impatient, and that Sam is a business executive, and one moves from these pre-existing beliefs to the new belief that Sam is likely to be impatient. But not just any transition from old beliefs to new beliefs counts as an inference. The old beliefs must be regarded (in some sense) by the believer as having a relevant logical or evidential relation to the new belief.[7]

The norms for inferential transitions among beliefs are apparently analogous to the norms by which we evaluate arguments (although there are important differences between the norms of argument and the norms for inferential transitions among beliefs[8]). Thus in order to apply the norms of inference to determine the quality of a particular inference, one needs to know (at least) what relevant logical or evidential relations there are between the old and new beliefs, just as one needs to know the logical or evidential relations among premises and conclusion in order to determine the quality of an argument.

But the analogy to arguments, which seems fairly strong in the case of genuine inferences, completely breaks down for Millar's quasi-inferences from experiences and beliefs to beliefs. For experiences just aren't like the premises of arguments. They don't, and can't, have evidential or logical relations to the resulting beliefs, because they can't be true. So the truth-preserving norms that we apply to arguments evidently cannot be applied, even with modifications, to the experience-belief transition. But if those kinds of norms can't be applied, then it is not clear yet whether any other sort can be. Thus Millar's attempt to present the experience-belief transition as normative, by analogizing it to the undoubtedly normative inferential transition, fails.

III

But Millar's general strategy for answering doubts about whether experiences can justify beliefs seems to me to be very promising. The idea is to find a process which everyone accepts, or can be brought to accept, as normative in the right way, and then show it to be relevantly analogous to the transition from experience to belief. The comparison with inference doesn't work. But perhaps we can find a more appropriate comparison.

We might compare epistemic evaluation to the moral evaluation of actions. It has been held, for example, that one has epistemic duties to believe, or to refrain from believing, certain things in certain circumstances.[9] This suggests that the processes that lead to unjustified belief can be understood as analogous to actions in violation of moral duties.

But it is difficult to see how to develop this analogy in order to make it plausible that the transition from experience to belief has a similar normative aspect, perhaps because we are not very clear about the details of the normative structure of our moral evaluations. Are moral norms expressible in rules? If so, what kinds of rules? What are the relevant underlying properties of actions in terms of which such rules should be framed? We don't have uncontroversial answers to these questions, and the attempted answers we do have (utilitarianism, rights theories, virtue theories etc.) don't initially seem very promising as analogies to perceptual justification.

So I don't think that either of these paradigms, the logical evaluation of arguments, or the moral evaluation of actions, is likely to help us understand, by analogy, the normative aspect of perceptual believing.

But there is another normative paradigm worth considering seriously for this sort of project. If is our evaluations of the correctness of particular exercises of learned skills.[10]

Think of a student playing a piece at the piano from sheet music. We can talk about whether he is playing the piece correctly – whether he gets all of the indicated notes, in the right order, with the appropriate rhythm, dynamics, accents and phrasing. This sort of evaluation does not involve the difficulties and vaguenesses of true aesthetic evaluation – we're not asking whether his performance counts as *music*, but just whether it's correctly played, according to the generally accepted standards of proper piano technique.

Or think of someone speaking a natural language such as English. We can evaluate the sentences he produces for phonetic and grammatical correctness. There is clearly a normative dimension to the exercises of these skills. The performances are reliably evaluated as acceptable or unacceptable according to publicly known standards.

The standards for correctness in the exercises of these skills are taught to new performers and critics primarily by bringing to their attention examples of good performance and secondarily by expressing disapproval of performances that don't meet the standards. Rules for correct performance are rarely stated. But if we were to try to articulate in words the standards involved, we would presumably have to express them in rules.

Thus books on piano technique usually include lots of advice phrased as rules, and attempted grammars for natural languages take the form of systems of rules for forming acceptable sentences. Of course it is understood that the performers usually cannot state such rules in anything like sufficient detail, and they certainly don't explicitly consider such rules in the course of exercising their skills. Nevertheless, if we had a complete system of rules, one that really articulated all of the standards of correct performance at the piano, say, we could characterize any particular mistake (that a fully competent performer or critic would recognize as such) as a violation of the rules. And we could see the performer's attempts to meet the standards of acceptable performance as a matter of trying to follow the rules.

There is a bit of metaphor involved in calling this "rule following", but only a bit. If we are going to talk about skills in any detail, it seems that characterizing them in terms of rules is unavoidable. So the relation to these rules of the person who intentionally performs correctly may as well be called "following" them, provided we keep in mind that he doesn't (and often can't) state or consult them.

Another very important point for our purposes is that the exercise of these skills does not itself require one to have beliefs, either about the rules, or about the circumstances of the antecedent clauses of those rules. "Whenever you are in such and such circumstances, do so and so" says the rule. But to "follow" it, in the sense we have in mind, a performer need not *believe* that he is in such and such circumstances, at least not in any ordinary sense of "believe", such as concerns us while we are doing epistemology.[11] His ability to perform correctly is a matter of knowing how, which is not to be reduced to any kind of knowing, or even believing, that. The possession of a skill for speaking a language or performing music is not plausibly regarded as a matter of possessing great heaps of wonderfully detailed and instantly accessible propositional knowledge. (This point is obviously important for an account of perceptual justification that makes it analogous to correctness in exercising a skill, because denying that such exercises involve beliefs will avert otherwise threatening regresses of justification.)

Although he doesn't have beliefs that would enable him to usefully consult a rule book of the sort we have been imagining, the performer is nevertheless constantly aware of whether he is performing correctly. He monitors the process of performing, in some sort of non-doxastic way, avoiding or correcting mistakes. So correctness in exercising a skill seems to be "internal" in the way that we expect justification to be.

I claim that the normative aspect of perceptual justification is best understood by analogy with the correctness of such exercises of skills. We have *learned how* to respond to particular sorts of experiences by acquiring the appropriate sorts of beliefs. To put it more in the language of the thesis stated above: We have recognitional *skills*, which we exercise in arriving at our perceptual beliefs. If the skill has been properly learned, and the particular exercise of it is up to certain public standards, and the believer does not have other undermining beliefs, then the resulting perceptual belief counts as justified.

IV

I doubt that anyone is going to object to *calling* our perceptual recognitional abilities "skills". It is, after all, only ordinary language, or something pretty close. Ordinary language admits the existence of skilled judges of music or horses or wines or paintings. Part of what makes them skilled judges is that they are more capable of arriving at justified perceptual beliefs about their subject matter than are others who lack their talent and training. They are more sensitive to the relevant perceptual differences than are people who haven't had similar instruction and practice. But the differences to which they are sensitive are relevantly similar to the features that we become sensitive to in learning to recognize people and objects. So no one could reasonably refuse to call our recognitional abilities "skills", though some may want to claim that there are important differences between these recognitional skills and such skills as skill in playing the piano.

As in the cases of playing piano or speaking a natural language, there are public standards for correctly arriving at one's perceptual beliefs. Think of a defense attorney cross-examining a witness to a crime. She may ask questions designed to show that he lacks the relevant recognitional skills (the ability to recognize a particular person,

or a certain kind of gun, for example), or that circumstances were such that he could not, or at least did not, effectively exercise those skills (distractions, obstructions of his view, etc.). If the questions succeed, they will show that the witness's beliefs were not justified, for they will show that, in the circumstances, he should not have acquired the perceptual beliefs he has expressed. Very likely he will then feel some embarrassment about having held those beliefs. The jury can tell from the appropriate answers to the questions whether or not the standards for the acquisition of perceptual beliefs are likely to have been violated. So there must be public standards, public not in the sense that others can follow the rules by responding to the same experiences the performer does, but in the sense that others have ways of telling whether the recognitional standards the witness has have been properly learned and adequately complied with.

The witness's capacity to respond to the questions in a revealing way also seems to indicate that these standards are internally applicable, at least at the time of acquiring the beliefs. ("The shape of his chin did seem a little odd at the time, I must admit.") Memory may fail to reveal the incorrectness later, but the believer was able to tell, at the time, whether he was arriving at his perceptual beliefs correctly.

Some people may still doubt however whether these so-called perceptual skills are relevantly similar to the skills of piano playing and speaking a natural language.

There are three apparent disanalogies: 1) The normative aspect of exercises of skills such as playing the piano or speaking English can be seen as a matter of "following rules". But how can we ever hope to see perceptual judgments as a matter of following rules? How could one hope to write rules for perceptual judgment? 2) Arriving at perceptual beliefs on having experiences doesn't seem to be something that one *does*, in the way that one speaks or plays the piano. It seems to be something that just happens, like digestion. But if so, then, again, how could it be a matter of "following" prescriptive rules? 3) Correctness in exercises of the skills of piano playing and speaking English seems to be largely a matter of arbitrary cultural history. But epistemic justification is not a matter of arbitrary cultural history; cultural variation in standards of justification seems to be constrained by a close relationship between justification and truth. But how could there be such a relationship on the skills account?

V

Let us take these apparent disanalogies in order. For the first question, as to whether any system of rules could describe our transitions from the patterns of experience to beliefs, we have a model at hand in the attempts to write visual recognition programs for computer driven robots. Presumably those programs are roughly akin to the sets of rules that would (if we could only write them) capture the recognitional skills of a human being. The rules for the experience-belief transition would collectively prescribe beliefs of certain types as responses to appropriate patterns in sensory input, or in experience, where the patterns might be described, perhaps, in terms of sensory qualities occupying regions of a sensory field.

We can now try to explain the term "adequate exercise". An adequate exercise of a recognitional skill conforms to the rules that would capture that skill.

Most of the complications found in describing the patterns of experience to which one responds in recognition presumably have no particular philosophical interest, and are best left to experimentally oriented cognitive scientists. One of the advantages of giving up the claim that having recognitional abilities is somehow constitutive of having the concepts, or of understanding the meanings of the corresponding words, is that we aren't tempted to suppose, as perhaps some of the sense-data theorists did, that describing our recognitional abilities is equivalent to providing definitions, or elucidating ideas, and should therefore be capable of being done a priori.

I don't think recognitional skills can be described a priori. But I do have some speculations to offer about the structure of our recognitional abilities.

Experience is amorphous stuff, not easy to divide up into separate experiences. But suppose we agree to think of a person's total visual sensations over a period of a few seconds, as organized, as a single visual experience. We will distinguish types of such experiences by phenomenal quality – say, if it's phenomenally indistinguishable in

(accurate) memory, then it's the same type of experience. Note that Millar's classification of experiences is much coarser than this – on my classification scheme square-yellow-piece-of-paper Millar-type experiences are broken down into a vast number of phenomenally distinguishable experiences that might be caused, in part, by visual contact with a square yellow piece of paper. The finer individuation is desirable for talking about learning recognitional skills.

It seems that I am constantly having experiences of phenomenal types I have not had before, in response to which I arrive at beliefs of types that I have not had before. And it seems that the number of types of experiences that I can have, and the number of resulting types of beliefs, are practically unlimited. But how can any finite and learnable skill have this sort of protean creativity?

This question echoes the familiar question about how we can understand an indefinitely large number of sentences that we haven't heard before. The natural answer to it is similar – we must understand our skills for arriving at perceptually justified beliefs as being compounded of lesser skills which can be combined and re-combined in a practically unlimited number of ways. My ability to be perceptually justified in believing that Sam is standing in the doorway will somehow be composed of my several abilities to recognize Sam, the posture of standing, the doorway, and instances of the relation of being in. Each of these abilities can also be used in responding to many other experiences of types that I have never had before – such as when I come to believe that Irving, whom I have previously only seen in a seated posture, is standing.

So it seems that our perceptual skills for appropriately arriving at beliefs must be composed of re-combinable sub-skills, which, apparently, roughly correspond to *some* of the nouns and predicates of our language. Arriving at the justified perceptual belief that Sam is standing requires recognizing the referent of "Sam", by, for example, a pattern of visual qualities produced by light reflected from his face; it requires recognizing an instantiation of the predicate "is standing", by another pattern of visual qualities; and (to justify the combination) it requires recognizing the appropriate arrangement in the experience of the (facial) pattern for "Sam" and the (bodily) pattern for "is standing". Since the ability to recognize a pattern is presumably also the ability to tell when it is absent, justifiedly coming to believe that Sam is *not* standing also requires an exercise of the same abilities. One will be responding to the facial pattern for "Sam", and the absence, in any appropriate relation to the pattern for "Sam", of the pattern for "is standing". Perhaps for the perceptual belief that someone is standing one would only need to exercise the ability to recognize the (humani-form) visual pattern for "is standing".

These analogies between the structure of our recognitional abilities and the linguistic structures in which we express the resulting beliefs may help explain why we are tempted to say that we see what makes a certain sentence true, or that we perceive the fact that corresponds to the sentence. It also suggests some tenuous connection between truth and justification by recognitional skills, although I won't be relying on this sort of connection in reply to that objection.

This account may appear to be at odds with Quine's epistemology. He connects observation sentences, not terms, with experiences.[12] But the provision for undermining perceptual justification retains the most considerable part of Quine's holism; on this view empirical justification is not independent of systematic considerations. And Quine himself has taken a small step in the direction of connecting terms with sensory stimulations in his suggestion that some predications, such as "This pebble is blue", are compoundings of observation sentences.[13]

VI

The second objection holds that, unlike playing the piano or speaking a language, perceptually coming to believe is not something that one *does*.[14] It just happens, like digestion, so it doesn't make sense to call it a skill in the full sense of the word "skill". Of course we can evaluate it as working well or ill, as we could evaluate the workings of someone's digestive system, but we cannot evaluate it as a performance, and so regard it as correct or incorrect. On this view the rules that might be stated by cognitive scientists studying our recognitional processes should not be regarded as rules in the sense of prescriptions; instead they are generalizations about the process.

They are more like scientific laws for normal biological systems than they are like the laws of a nation. We follow such rules only in the sense in which we might be said to follow rules that describe the process of (normal) digestion. But then the normative aspect of the transition from experience to belief disappears, since the prescriptive rules in which we had hoped to represent it now appear to be instead only idealized factual generalizations.

Presumably the reason for holding that perceptual processes just happen is that they seem to be quite automatic, and not under our conscious control. But a process can be quite automatic, and even out of one's conscious control, and yet still be an instance of the exercise of a skill in the full, normatively governed sense. Indeed, the transition from deliberate, controlled, "doing" of constituent actions to their "automatic" performance is typically required for mastery of a skill. Compare a beginning piano player's laborious and deliberate search for the correct keys with the expert player's automatic reaching for them, or the novice fencer's slow, deliberate actions with the expert's "reflexive" responses. Or compare a chess novice's deliberate assessment of the material advantage by tabulating the pieces on each side with the expert's instantaneous and practically involuntary assessment.

The process of acquiring new perceptual skills evinces a similar distinction between novice and expert. A novice first identifies elms slowly and deliberately, looking for particular distinguishing features. With practice, this process becomes quicker, until at last she can't help but recognize an elm at a glance.

The objection thus seems to be claiming, absurdly, that we should stop regarding recognition as normatively governed just at the point where full proficiency is reached.

But it may be replied that control is necessary for normative evaluation to be appropriate. If the unjustified believer lacks control, he could not be at fault. In answer we may say that sufficient control is exercised in acquiring, or failing to acquire, appropriate instruction and practice, and in controlling the circumstances – e.g. making sure one gets a good look.

So I don't think it is plausible to hold that perceptual processes fail to be performances in any way that threatens our normative characterization of them as exercises of skills.

VII

The final objection holds that the skills account cannot or will not include a close relation of justification to truth, and that it consequently threatens to leave justification too dependent on the vagaries of cultural and individual development of epistemic norms.

A more or less standard account of the relation of truth and justification sees truth as a goal, and justification as an evaluation relative to that goal. One is justified if and only if one believes as one ought. This "ought" is understood on the model of the "ought" that occurs in "If you want go to the market, you ought to turn right at the second stop sign". It indicates advice about how to achieve a goal. Roughly speaking, the epistemic goal is to acquire true beliefs and avoid false beliefs. This goal is not often explicitly stated, since it is assumed that everyone has it, or, perhaps, more cautiously, that striving to realize this goal is a defining characteristic of the epistemic enterprise, so that advice in epistemic contexts always presupposes it.[15]

One might try to depict exercises of recognitional skills as always being focused, somehow, on a goal of truth, as one might try to depict exercises of piano playing skills as always aiming at a goal of beauty. But that seems most implausible. I doubt that most perceptual believers have a goal of truth, in any straightforward sense of "have a goal", and I know for a fact that not all piano students have beauty as their goal. Often they're only seeking to avoid embarrassing mistakes. They just want to play it correctly, as they were taught.

It seems more plausible to regard "epistemically justified", not as an evaluation relative to a goal of achieving true and avoiding false beliefs, but instead as an evaluation indicating an acceptable degree of conformity to epistemic norms. In the case of perceptual beliefs, it indicates an acceptable degree of conformity to the rules that would describe the appropriate recognitional skill.

What relation does justification then have to truth? I think that a tendency to produce true beliefs causally explains why we are committed to certain epistemic norms. It is true, on my view, that certain practices of belief acquisition are justifying *because* they tend to produce true beliefs. But the "because" indicates, not a goal, but the salient aspect of a causal explanation of our adoption of the epistemic norms that permit such belief acquisition.

First, notice that recognitional skills, if they are to be justifying, have to be properly learned. For example, ordinarily I would learn to recognize a particular person, Sam Smith, when he is pointed out to me, or introduced to me. Let us suppose instead that I know him by reputation, but not by sight. I acquire a recognitional skill associated with his name in the following way. At a large meeting where I expect him to be present I notice, among many people whom I do not know, someone whom I think may be Sam Smith. I look at this person several times, fixing his appearance in my memory.

Later, not recollecting these events, I see this same man coming out of Mae's restaurant, and, in response to the visual experience thus produced, I come to believe that Sam Smith is coming out of Mae's. I have a recognitional skill which I use on this occasion, yet my belief that Sam Smith is coming out of Mae's is not justified. The reason seems to be that I haven't properly learned how to recognize Sam Smith (even if this man *is* Sam Smith).

Similar stories could be told about my abilities to recognize instantiations of various predicates. It thus seems that recognitional skills have to be properly learned to be capable of helping justify the perceptual beliefs they give rise to.

Now think of our earliest acquisitions of recognitional skills, when, as children, we learned to distinguish and name such things as colors, shapes, common objects, and a few people. It is most implausible that a small child has any goal of truth in learning these skills. He has various other goals: finding Mama, taking food, seeing a certain color, avoiding falling, chewing on something soft but resistant, gaining parental approval.

He responds to a particular sort of experience, when he is hungry, by reaching and grabbing. If the experience is of a certain kind, by so doing he successfully satisfies his hunger. As this is repeated he learns to believe that there is food in front of him in response to this sort of experience. If such beliefs are likely to be true when he is having that sort of experience, the actions guided by the beliefs thus arrived at will frequently be successful. The successes encourage similar beliefs in response to similar experiences in the future. The behavior guided by these beliefs also brings approval or correction from others. (I mention the role of other people because I think there is something to the Kripke–Wittgenstein claim that prescriptive rules are possible only in a community.[16]) He thus gradually adopts as a perceptual norm this pattern of believing in response to that sort of experience.

The likelihood of developing true beliefs when responding to experiences as a norm requires is thus typically a part of the causal explanation of someone's adopting that perceptual norm.

Being likely to produce true beliefs is not essential to a properly learned recognitional skill however. If someone fraudulently introduces himself to me as Sam Smith, then I will acquire a recognitional skill that will typically lead me to have false beliefs about Sam Smith. But so long as I exercise this skill properly, and do not acquire any new reason to doubt it, the resulting beliefs will be justified. A properly learned recognitional skill is just a skill confirmed by successful actions and (a certain kind of) approval from other members of the community.

Should this soothe fears that the skills approach is prone to a bad sort of cultural or individual relativism? If my conjectures are roughly correct (and no doubt they need refinement), then, presumably, accepted epistemic practices which seem to us not to justify the resulting beliefs, fail to do so, in our opinion, because we think that some other pressures guided their adoption. They were adopted for some reason other than success in the resulting actions and the appropriate approval from the community. The dubious epistemic practices of primitive societies are seldom purely recognitional in character. But perhaps the following case sufficiently illustrates this point. A man has a powerful desire to find rare minerals easily. After finishing a good mineral identification course involving frequent correction by experts, this man, although he has normal visual acuity and color vision, confidently identifies various worthless stones as rare minerals. Evidently he has failed to benefit from correction while he was learning. The norms he has in fact

adopted were shaped not by success in his actions or by the approval or disapproval of his instructors, but by his desire to see himself as easily finding rare minerals. So his recognitional skills have not been properly learned, and, consequently, exercises of them are not justifying. Other societies' adoption of epistemic norms which seem to us not to be justifying will also, on examination, be found to have been wrongly influenced, perhaps by religion or politics, and so to have been improperly learned. The skills approach will thus rule that these practices are not epistemically justifying.

Now we are in a position to answer a final question about the relation between experience and truth. We assumed that an experience isn't propositional and isn't about anything. But by way of it, it seems, we can learn the truth. How is that possible?

I think that the experience conveys information of the truth in question, in somewhat the way that a dinosaur footprint in rock conveys information about the dinosaur. The rock isn't *about* the dinosaur, but by looking at it we can learn about the dinosaur.

Experiences differ from fossils in that experiences are typically not objects of thought for the person who obtains beliefs in response to them. He doesn't have beliefs about the experience as the paleontologist has beliefs about the fossil. So perhaps in some ways my experience is typically more like the electronic signal in a telephone line – although it brings me information, I don't think about that signal when receiving the telephone messages. Likewise, although the experience brings me information, I don't usually think about the experience itself. I just process the information from the experience into a belief that really is about the objects the information comes from.

This distinction between merely carrying information and being genuinely about something is a slippery one, but I think that the examples strongly suggest that it is genuine. The visual experience I have carries the information that Bernie is standing in the door, but I don't have any mental state that is about Bernie just in virtue of having that experience. Even if I do acquire a belief about Bernie in response to it, it will still be true that that very same complex mass of sensations was carrying lots of other information about things that I probably didn't acquire any beliefs, or other propositional mental states, about – lighting patterns, shapes etc. There is a mass of detailed information in that array of sensations, only some of which was processed into propositional mental states.[17]

The information contained in the experience has to be processed to result in a perceptual belief. I have argued that this processing is normatively governed in such a way that it is appropriate to think of it, and so of the experience, as capable of helping to justify the resulting belief.

Notes

1   Donald Davidson, "A Coherence Theory of Truth and Knowledge" in *Kant Oder Hegel*: Stuttgart: Klett-Cotta 1983, p. 428, reprinted in E. LePore (ed.) *Truth and Interpretation* (Oxford, 1986) p. 311. Laurence BonJour, *The Structure of Empirical Knowledge* (Cambridge, MA: Harvard University Press, 1985), pp. 69, 75.

2   L. Weiskrantz, "Varieties of Residual Experience" *Quarterly Journal of Experimental Psychology*, XXXIII, 3 (1980), pp. 365–86. See especially pp. 371, 374, 378.

3   Donald Davidson, "A Coherence Theory" p. 428, Laurence BonJour, *The Structure of Empirical Knowledge*, pp. 111–38.

4   Alan Millar, "Experience and the Justification of Belief", *Ratio (New Series)* II, 2 December 1989, pp. 138–52. John L. Pollock, *Contemporary Theories of Knowledge* (Savage, MD: Rowman & Littlefield, 1986), pp. 175–7.

5   John L. Pollock, *Contemporary Theories of Knowledge*, pp. 148, 175–7. It is also supposed to be useful in replying to skepticism. John L. Pollock, *Knowledge and Justification*, (Princeton: Princeton University Press, 1974), pp. 20–2.

6   John L. Pollock, *The Foundations of Philosophical Semantics* (Princeton: Princeton University Press, 1984), Chapter 2.

7   Millar, "Experience", p. 140.

8   Gilbert Harman, *Change in View*: Principles of Reasoning (Cambridge, MA: MIT Press, 1986), pp. 1–20.

9   Laurence BonJour, *The Structure of Empirical Knowledge*, chapter 1, John L. Pollock, *Contemporary Theories of Knowledge*, pp. 7–8, Roderick M. Chisholm, *Theory of Knowledge* (Englewood Cliffs, NJ: Prentice Hall, 1989), pp. 58–60. For argument against, see William P. Alston "The Deontological Conception of Epistemic Justification" in his *Epistemic Justification*: Essays in the Theory of Knowledge (Ithaca: Cornell University Press, 1989), pp. 115–52.

10 The analogy has been used for other purposes. John L. Pollock, *Knowledge and Justification* 15, and *Contemporary Theories of Knowledge*, pp. 126–32.

11 For senses that are not ordinary, see Daniel C. Dennett, *The International Stance* (Cambridge MA: MIT Press 1987).

12 Willard Van Orman Quine, *Word and Object* (Cambridge MA: The MIT Press 1960).

13 W. V. Quine, *Pursuit of Truth*, (Cambridge, MA: Harvard University Press, 1990), p. 4.

14 For discussion of the related issue of doxastic voluntarism, see William P. Alston, "The Deontological Conception of Epistemic Justification" pp. 119–33, Richard Feldman "Epistemic Obligation" in James E. Tomberlin ed. *Philosophical Perspectives*, 2 (Atascadero: Ridgeview, 1988), p. 239, Alvin I. Goldman, *Epistemology and Cognition* (Cambridge, MA: Harvard, 1986), pp. 26, 384 n. 6.

15 One statement of this standard account is in BonJour, *The Structure of Empirical Knowledge* pp. 7–8.

16 Saul A. Kripke, *Wittgenstein on Rules and Private Language* (Cambridge, MA: Harvard University Press, 1982), pp. 88–93.

17 Fred Dretske, *Knowledge and the Flow of Information* (Cambridge MA: MIT Press), 1981, chapter 6.

Index